Coopers
&Lybrand

The
Coopers
& Lybrand
SEC Manual

Sixth Edition

RONALD J. MURRAY
WILLIAM E. DECKER, JR.
NELSON W. DITTMAR, JR.

NOT JUST KNOWLEDGE. KNOW HOW.™

PRENTICE HALL
Englewood Cliffs, New Jersey 07632

Prentice-Hall International (UK) Limited, *London*
Prentice-Hall of Australia Pty. Limited, *Sydney*
Prentice-Hall Canada, Inc., *Toronto*
Prentice-Hall Hispanoamericana, S.A., *Mexico*
Prentice-Hall of India Private Limited, *New Delhi*
Prentice-Hall of Japan, Inc., *Tokyo*
Simon & Schuster Asia Pte. Ltd., *Singapore*
Editora Prentice-Hall do Brasil, Ltda., *Rio de Janeiro*

© 1993 by
Coopers & Lybrand

10   9   8   7   6   5   4   3   2   1

Library of Congress Cataloging-in-Publication Data

The Coopers & Lybrand SEC Manual / Ronald J. Murray . . . [et al.].—
   6th ed.
     p.   cm.
   Includes index.
   ISBN 0-13-300427-9
   1. United States.   Securities and Exchange Commission.
2. Securities—United States.   I. Ronald J. Murray.   II. Coopers
& Lybrand.   III. Title: Coopers and Lybrand SEC Manual.
KF1444.C66   1993
346.73'0666—dc20
[347.306666]   93-23569
ISBN 0-13-300427-9   CIP

PRENTICE HALL
Career and Personal Development
Englewood Cliffs, NJ 07632

Simon & Schuster, A Paramount Communications Company

Printed in the United States of America

ABOUT THE AUTHORS

Ronald J. Murray, CPA, is National Director, Accounting & SEC Services in the National Business Assurance Directorate of Coopers & Lybrand. He is the AICPA representative to the Board of the International Accounting Standards Committee (IASC) and Chairman of IASC's Financial Instruments Steering Committee. Mr. Murray is also a member of the Financial Accounting Standards Board's (FASB) Emerging Issues Task Force; the FASB Task Force on Accounting for the Reporting Entity, including Consolidations, the Equity Method, and related matters; and past member of the AICPA Accounting Standards Executive Committee and Chairman of its Task Force on Accounting for Pension Plans and Pension Costs.

William E. Decker, Jr., CPA, is the lead SEC partner in the National Business Assurance Directorate of Coopers & Lybrand and is Chairman of the Firm's International Capital Markets Task Force. Mr. Decker is a member of the AICPA and has served on a number of its technical committees and task forces. He is currently the Firm's representative to the AICPA's SEC Regulations Committee. He has also served on the adjunct faculty at the New York University Graduate School of Business and is a frequent speaker on U.S. accounting, SEC, and international matters.

Nelson W. Dittmar, Jr., CPA, is an SEC consulting partner in the National Business Assurance Directorate of Coopers & Lybrand and a member of the Firm's International Capital Markets Services network. Previously, Mr. Dittmar was a Business Assurance partner in the Firm's New York office and served numerous publicly held multinational companies. He is a member of the Financial Accounting Standards Board Task Force on Impairment of Long-Lived Assets.

PREFACE

This is the sixth edition of *The Coopers & Lybrand SEC Manual*. Like its predecessors, it is intended primarily as a reference source that summarizes and annotates the financial reporting and disclosure requirements and related rules and regulations of the Securities and Exchange Commission. The objective of the manual is to set forth the requirements of the SEC—both formal and informal—that are most frequently encountered in SEC practice and to supplement them with guidance on how these requirements are complied with in practice based on our experience and observations.

This manual is designed to be a reference source for public accountants, corporate officials, investment bankers, securities analysts, lawyers, and academicians, and is intended to:

- provide users with a general understanding of SEC accounting practices and procedures and an overview of the financial disclosures required in the most frequently encountered filing forms;

- facilitate an understanding of the various SEC disclosure requirements; and

- enable users to identify more easily the official sources of SEC rules and regulations.

The manual is also intended as a training aid to familiarize its users with the basic requirements and considerations involved in an SEC engagement. It is important to note, however, that this manual is not a substitute for the official instructions to the various forms or for any of the published rules and regulations of the Commission, such as Regulations S-X and S-K.

In dealing with SEC matters, the availability of up-to-date information is essential. While every effort has been made to ensure that this manual takes into account the most recent pronouncements and SEC staff positions relevant to the subject matter discussed, SEC rules and regulations are subject to periodic changes. Accordingly, when preparing or examining financial statements to be filed with the SEC, this manual should be supplemented by an up-to-date text of the published SEC rules and regulations.

Using the Manual

The manual's structure has been designed to reflect the manner in which information on SEC matters is most frequently sought and the types of questions most frequently encountered. Users should become familiar with the manual's structure and content in order to facilitate its use. The manual's detailed table of contents, index, and extensive cross-referencing between sections should enable users to readily locate all material that might be relevant to the matter in question. The manual is divided into the following eight principal sections and an appendix.

Introduction to SEC Practice

The principal objective of this section is to provide background information. It briefly discusses the federal securities laws and the organization and functions of the SEC and directs readers to the principal sources of published SEC rules and regulations. It also includes a general discussion of considerations and events involved in registering securities under the 1933 Act. While the discussion is intended to familiarize the reader with the various elements of the registration process, it contemplates an initial public offering situation and should be considered in this context. Subsequent offerings are generally processed in a more expeditious manner.

Accountants' Reports and Related Matters

The purpose of this section is to provide illustrative guidance with respect to accountants' reports, consents, and other representations required in connection with documents filed with the SEC. The examples are not intended to be all-inclusive, but should provide helpful guidance in many instances. This section also contains a discussion of the SEC's views on departures from the standard accountants' report and a discussion of letters to underwriters (comfort letters).

Shareholder Communications

Since the financial statements and other information required in a proxy statement prepared in connection with a proposed business combination differ from those required in a proxy statement prepared in connection with the annual shareholders' meeting, a discussion of the requirements for both types of documents is included in this section. This section also deals with the financial information required to be included in the annual report to shareholders and in a tender offer statement.

The SEC Forms

This section provides an overview of the principal forms used for reports and registration statements filed with the SEC under the 1933 and 1934 Acts and the information required by certain of the forms most frequently encountered in practice. When general information on the principal requirements of a particular form is sought, reference to this section of the manual should permit an overall understanding of the information that needs to be generated. This section is cross-referenced extensively to direct the user to sections of the manual where the financial information to be provided is discussed in more detail.

Complete texts of Forms 10-K, 10-KSB, 10-Q, and 10-QSB are included in this edition of the manual since they are encountered more frequently than any other form.

This section also discusses the reporting requirements under the 1934 Act when a registrant changes its fiscal year.

Foreign Registrants

This section provides an overview of the principal forms used for reports and registration statements filed with the SEC by foreign private issuers. Particular emphasis is given to the applicable financial statement requirements. Registration considerations for Canadian companies under the Multijurisdictional Disclosure System are also discussed in this section.

Regulation S-X

This section contains the full text of Regulation S-X, together with supplementary SEC pronouncements that amplify the rules, and commentary on the application of the rules, where appropriate. The full text of the Regulation is included because of the frequency with which the user of this manual may need to refer to specific rules, and to provide a basis for the commentary. However, as previously noted, SEC rules and regulations, including Regulation S-X, undergo continuous change. Consequently, any changes to Regulation S-X adopted subsequent to September 1, 1993 (FRR No. 40A) are not reflected in this manual.

Regulation S-K

Most of the instructions regarding the nature of information required in reports and registration statements filed with the SEC, other than those relating to the financial statements, are covered by Regulation S-K. This section addresses the disclosure requirements that are of particular interest to the independent accountant, such as the requirements for Selected Financial Data, Management's Discussion and Analysis of Financial Condition and Results of Operations (MD&A), and Supplementary Financial Information.

Regulation S-B

During 1992, the SEC adopted an integrated registration, reporting and qualification system for small business issuers. The system consists of specialized forms that reference disclosure requirements located in Regulation S-B. The disclosure requirements generally parallel those of Regulation S-K; however, the requirements are simplified in various respects, as discussed in this section. This section also addresses the financial statement requirements for small business issuers that are contained in Item 310 of Regulation S-B.

Appendix

Staff Accounting Bulletins that relate to or amplify the subject matter have been integrated into the applicable sections of the manual. The appendix includes the text of relevant Staff Accounting Bulletins that have not been so integrated, and topical and chronological listings of all Staff Accounting Bulletins in effect through SAB No. 92. The topical listing is cross-referenced to the section of the manual where each topic is located or discussed. The appendix also includes a chronological listing of Financial Reporting Releases and of the Accounting Series Releases that were codified by FRR No. 1.

ACKNOWLEDGMENTS

We wish to acknowledge the tremendous debt of gratitude that we owe to three of our retired partners, Louis H. Rappaport, James J. Quinn, and Fred S. Spindel. Lou established the Firm's reputation in SEC matters and led the Firm's SEC practice for over three decades. Lou was the author of *SEC Accounting Practice and Procedures*, published by The Ronald Press Co., which was the original and authoritative work on SEC matters for many years. It is not possible to overstate the importance of Lou's contributions in this regard.

Jim Quinn, a very special person, served as a mentor to the three of us. A former Vice Chairman of the Firm, Jim was responsible for the first edition of this manual and has provided inspiration and guidance for the succeeding editions. The influence of Jim's leadership in our SEC practice and on this manual will continue to be felt for many years.

We would be remiss in not expressing our thanks to Fred Spindel, who was a co-author of several editions of this manual and also played an important leadership role in our SEC practice.

We would also like to acknowledge the contributions of our partner, J. Donald Warren, Jr., who served as co-author of the fifth edition.

We acknowledge with thanks the permission granted to us by the American Institute of Certified Public Accountants, Inc., the Financial Accounting Standards Board, and the Securities and Exchange Commission to quote or paraphrase passages from their publications. Copies of the complete documents referred to in this manual can be obtained from those organizations.

We owe a special acknowledgment to William S. Bradley, a manager in the National Business Assurance Directorate of Coopers & Lybrand, for his assistance in drafting, reviewing, and revising sections of this manual as well as overseeing all aspects of the process of preparing the manuscript for publication. His dedication and efforts are greatly appreciated by the authors.

A book of this nature represents the efforts and ideas of many people. The following individuals, presently or formerly associated with Coopers & Lybrand, contributed to various portions of the book: John T. Baily, Kelley J. Brennan, Clark Chandler, Raymond L. Dever, John M. Hollenbeck, Margaret R. Horvath, Stephen J. Lis, William J. Lucchesi, Ingrid Mohapp, Dennis E. Peavey, Walter G. Ricciardi, Kirk E. Romero, and Stuart K. Webster. We also thank Nicolas Grabar, a partner with Cleary Gottlieb Steen & Hamilton, for his helpful guidance.

Our thanks also goes to the SEC staff. Over the years we have had a continuing dialogue with the staff concerning accounting, auditing, SEC disclosure and other issues, and these discussions have invariably been handled professionally and courteously. We are especially grateful for the guidance the staff has provided on a number of specific matters addressed in this manual.

We also thank Auldith Leighton, Nick Punto, and Judith Levinton for their assistance in processing and editing the manuscript throughout the entire project. To all those individuals, and any who we inadvertently omitted, go not only our thanks, but also the usual absolution from blame for errors and omissions.

Ronald J. Murray
William E. Decker, Jr.
Nelson W. Dittmar, Jr.

SUMMARY TABLE OF CONTENTS

SHAREHOLDER COMMUNICATIONS

THE SEC FORMS

REGULATION S-X

DETAILED TABLE OF CONTENTS

SHAREHOLDER COMMUNICATIONS

FOREIGN REGISTRANTS

[Rules 12-12 through 12-29 relating to management investment companies, insurance companies, face-amount certificate investment companies, and certain real estate companies are included in sections 51212
through 51229.]

REGULATION S-K

MANAGEMENT AND CERTAIN SECURITY HOLDERS 64000

REGISTRATION STATEMENT AND PROSPECTUS PROVISIONS . . . 65000

EXHIBITS 66000

REGULATION S-B

INDEX

ABOUT COOPERS & LYBRAND

Coopers & Lybrand is one of the world's leading professional services organizations. Through our Member Firms we deploy over 67,000 people providing accounting and auditing, tax and consulting services on a globally integrated basis in more than 120 countries.

Our strategic intent is to create value for our clients and to bring competitive advantage to their activities. We meet their needs by combining our international capabilities and local market knowledge with our extensive range of skills and industry experience.

ABBREVIATIONS USED IN MANUAL

The following abbreviations are used throughout this manual:

Abbreviation	Explanation
AAER	SEC Accounting and Auditing Enforcement Release
AcSEC	Accounting Standards Executive Committee
AICPA	American Institute of Certified Public Accountants
APB	Accounting Principles Board
ARB	AICPA Accounting Research Bulletin
ASB	AICPA Auditing Standards Board
ASR	SEC Accounting Series Release
AT	Attestation section of AICPA Professional Standards
AU	Auditing section of AICPA Professional Standards
EITF	FASB Emerging Issues Task Force
FASB	Financial Accounting Standards Board
FIN	Financial Accounting Standards Board Interpretation
FRP	SEC Codification of Financial Reporting Policies
FRR	SEC Financial Reporting Release
GAAP	Generally accepted accounting principles
GAAS	Generally accepted auditing standards
MD&A	Management's Discussion and Analysis of Financial Condition and Results of Operation
SAB	SEC Staff Accounting Bulletin
SAS	AICPA Statement on Auditing Standards
SEC	Securities and Exchange Commission
SFAS	Statement of Financial Accounting Standards
SOP	AICPA Statement of Position

Parenthetical references that follow the citations for the original authoritative pronouncements are to the current texts of the FASB Accounting Standards and AICPA Professional Standards.

REFERENCES

References in this edition of the manual have been updated to include changes through the issuance of Financial Reporting Release No. 40 and 40A, Staff Accounting Bulletin No. 92 and significant final SEC releases issued prior to September 1, 1993. References to AICPA and FASB pronouncements are current as of September 1, 1993.

INTRODUCTION TO SEC PRACTICE

11000. LEGISLATION GOVERNING SEC PRACTICE

11010. Introduction

The Securities and Exchange Commission (SEC) is the principal securities regulatory authority in the United States. It was created by an act of Congress in 1934 and, functioning as an independent agency, exercises a vital, quasi-judicial role in regulating the business of distributing and trading securities. The Securities Act of 1933 was originally administered by the Federal Trade Commission. The Securities Exchange Act of 1934, however, created the SEC, and in September 1934 the duty of administering the Securities Act of 1933 was transferred to the SEC.

The SEC consists of five members (commissioners) appointed by the President with the consent of the Senate. One member is designated by the President to serve as chairman. Not more than three of the commissioners may be members of the same political party. Commissioners are generally appointed for a term of five years. The SEC administers the following statutes:

- Securities Act of 1933.

- Securities Exchange Act of 1934.

- Public Utility Holding Company Act of 1935.

- Trust Indenture Act of 1939.

- Investment Company Act of 1940.

- Investment Advisers Act of 1940.

The duties and responsibilities of the SEC are set forth in the laws that it administers. It also has important functions under the Securities Investor Protection Act of 1970, which amended the Securities Exchange Act of 1934.

The SEC also serves in an advisory capacity to the federal courts in reorganization proceedings under Chapter X of the National Bankruptcy Act and has certain duties under other federal statutes.

11020. The Securities Act of 1933

The Securities Act of 1933 (the 1933 Act) was one of the earliest of the New Deal laws enacted following the stock market crash of 1929. The 1933 Act was the first in a series of laws designed to protect the public from misrepresentation, manipulation, and other fraudulent practices in connection with the purchase and sale of securities. The 1933 Act provides for the registration of securities with the SEC before their sale to the public. The 1933 Act also empowers the SEC to exempt securities from registration when offered in small amounts or when the offer is limited. Under this provision, the SEC has adopted Regulations A and E, relating to offerings of less than $5,000,000. (Regulation A is discussed in section 42800.) The SEC also adopted Regulation D, which governs the limited offer and sale of securities without registration (discussed in section 42900). Also exempt from the registration requirements are the securities of the United States government, states, municipalities, and other governmental units, and the securities of certain common carriers.

The law exempts from the registration provisions transactions not involving a public offering. For example, if an entire issue of securities is sold to an insurance company that acquires the securities for investment purposes and not with a view to distributing them, the transaction may be private and not involve an offering to the public. The determination of what constitutes a public offering is a legal question, not an accounting issue. The SEC has indicated that this determination is a question of fact and necessitates a consideration of all the surrounding circumstances, including such factors as the relationship between the offerees and the issuer, as well as the nature, scope, size, type, and manner of the offering. As in all matters involving legal interpretations, an independent public accountant is not qualified to give advice or decide whether or not registration under the 1933 Act is required. Questions of this nature should be directed by the company to its counsel.

The 1933 Act is a *disclosure* statute. Among the objectives of the 1933 Act are to provide a form of protection to prospective investors and to prevent fraud in the initial public distribution of securities by mandating disclosure of financial and other information with respect to the securities offered for sale and their issuer. The disclosure is provided by means of a registration statement. A copy of a prospectus, which is part of the registration statement, must be furnished to each buyer of the securities and is generally distributed to each offeree. A 1933 Act registration statement is a public document available for inspection by any person, and copies of any portion of the document may be obtained from the SEC at nominal cost. In certain situations, however, portions of the document may be accorded nonpublic treatment. Subject to certain exceptions, an issuer who has registered securities under the 1933 Act becomes subject to the periodic and annual reporting requirements of the 1934 Act (as discussed in section 19500).

11030. The Securities Exchange Act of 1934

The Securities Exchange Act of 1934 (the 1934 Act), also a New Deal measure, created the SEC. The overall responsibility of the SEC under both the 1933 and 1934 Acts is to protect the public—not the issuer of securities or the brokers or dealers. In contrast to the 1933 Act, which is primarily concerned with the initial distribution of securities, the 1934 Act is concerned largely with trading in outstanding securities. Among the principal objectives of the 1934 Act are:

- The dissemination of significant financial and other information relating to securities traded on national securities exchanges or in the over-the- counter market through a regulated system of reporting.

- The regulation of the securities markets, including control of the amount of credit used in these markets.

Companies whose securities are to be listed on a national securities exchange must register the securities under the 1934 Act. As a result of the Securities Acts amendments of 1964, unlisted companies are also required to register with the SEC if they meet certain size and shareholder requirements. This provision (Section 12(g) of the 1934 Act) requires a company to register with the SEC when its total assets exceed $5 million and it has a class of equity securities (other than exempted securities) held of record by 500 or more persons. The determination of what is or is not an exempt security and the number of holders of record are legal matters, and an attorney experienced in securities laws should be consulted for the determination of whether registration under the 1934 Act is required in a particular situation. Rules 12g5-1 and 12g5-2 contain definitions of the terms "held of record" and "total assets" as used in Section 12(g) of the 1934 Act.

A registration statement under the 1934 Act contains much of the same information regarding the company and its business as is contained in an initial registration statement under the 1933 Act. This information is updated by means of annual, quarterly, and certain other periodic reports.

Registration statements and reports filed under the 1934 Act are public information and are available for inspection at the SEC and at the securities exchanges on which the company's securities are listed. Copies of such information may be obtained from the SEC at nominal cost. Generally speaking, the 1934 Act registration statements and reports are intended to assist a person in reaching an informed opinion with respect to a company's securities.

Certain brokers and dealers are required under the 1934 Act to file annual reports of their financial condition and their income and expenses. The 1934 Act prohibits insider trading, market manipulations by means of wash sales or matched orders (effected to give a false or misleading appearance of active trading) or by any other deceptive device or fraudulent practice, and it restricts certain manipulative activities, such as the stabilizing of prices and short sales. The 1934 Act provides for margin requirements in the initial extension of credit for the purchase of securities and limits borrowing by brokers and dealers. The Federal Reserve Board has the power to regulate the use of credit for purchasing or carrying securities and the SEC has the power to enforce the rules. The 1934 Act also empowers the SEC to regulate the hypothecation (pledging) of customers' securities by dealers and the solicitation of proxies from the stockholders of registered companies.

The 1934 Act requires corporate insiders (directors and officers of registered corporations and principal owners of their equity securities) to file statements of their holdings of the equity securities of their company and also to file monthly reports of changes in such holdings. Certain beneficial owners of equity securities are also subject to the reporting requirements of the 1934 Act.

11040. Other Statutes Administered by the SEC

In addition to its responsibilities under the 1933 and 1934 Acts, the SEC administers other statutes relating to investment advisors, public utility holding companies, investment companies, and brokers and dealers. The principal requirements of these statutes are briefly described below, but, because of their specialized nature, the registration and reporting requirements under these statutes are not included in this manual.

11041. The Public Utility Holding Company Act of 1935. The Public Utility Holding Company Act of 1935 requires all companies holding 10 percent or more of the voting control of electric utility or retail gas companies to register with and report annually to the SEC. This Act makes it the duty of the SEC to require such companies to simplify their capital structures and to integrate their properties geographically, with the objective of restricting each holding company to a single system with a simple capitalization.

11042. The Trust Indenture Act of 1939. The Trust Indenture Act of 1939 provides that bonds, debentures, notes, and similar debt securities may not be sold to the public, subject to certain exemption limits set by the SEC, unless the securities are issued pursuant to a trust indenture that has been qualified by the SEC. The appointment of an independent trustee to protect the rights of the investors in the event of default by the issuer is an important element in the qualification process.

11043. Investment Company Act of 1940. The Investment Company Act of 1940 regulates the activities of investment companies. (The definition of an investment company generally includes any company that owns or proposes to acquire investment securities exceeding 40 percent of the value of its total assets, exclusive of government securities and cash items.) Among other things, this Act regulates the composition of an investment company's board of directors, requires shareholder approval of the independent accountants and management contracts, and restricts dividend payments.

Registration statements are required to be filed by each company subject to this Act. These documents contain financial information similar to that required in a registration statement filed under the 1933 or 1934 Acts and (among other things) textual disclosure of the company's trading and investment policies. This information is kept reasonably current by means of annual and other reports.

11044. The Investment Advisers Act of 1940. The Investment Advisers Act of 1940 requires certain persons who are engaged in the business of providing investment advice to register with the SEC. Among other provisions, the law prohibits advisors from entering into contracts with clients that provide for compensation based on a profit-sharing arrangement.

11045. Securities Investor Protection Act of 1970. The Securities Investor Protection Act of 1970 resulted from the failures and financial difficulties of securities brokers and dealers in the late 1960s. This Act created the Securities Investor Protection Corporation (SIPC) under which members are periodically assessed to ensure that a fund is maintained to protect the customers in case of financial failure by brokers and dealers. The amount of such protection is limited to $500,000 for each account, which includes a maximum of $100,000 for cash claims in each account.

11050. State Securities (Blue Sky) Requirements

Prior to the enactment of the federal securities laws, most states developed legislation governing the sale of securities within their state, the enactment of which sometimes followed major losses to uninformed investors. These laws, which vary considerably among the states, became known as blue sky laws. In some states, the prospectus and registration statement filed with the SEC fulfills the state registration requirements; in other states, additional information is required.

The independent accountant generally has little or no additional work to perform in connection with a registration statement in order to comply with state requirements. During the process of preparing a registration statement or an offering exempt from registration (e.g., under Regulation D [see section 42900]), however, inquiries should be made of counsel for the company and the underwriters to determine whether compliance with blue sky laws will require any involvement on the part of the independent accountant.

Where applicable, independent accountants should refer to the regulations covering blue sky laws when they are involved with the registration of securities in a particular state. However, legal advice should be sought when questions arise with respect to the specific provisions of the laws.

12000. LIABILITIES OF INDEPENDENT ACCOUNTANTS

12010. General

The exposure of accountants to litigation under the federal securities laws is evidenced by the number of lawsuits in which independent accounting firms have been named as defendants. Unfortunately, even with a successful defense, the professional standing of an accounting firm can be seriously affected by the adverse publicity in a lawsuit of this nature. The substantial legal expenses often incurred in the defense of such a lawsuit are also of concern to public accounting firms.

The legal responsibilities of independent accountants are complex, and the following narrative is not intended to be an exhaustive discussion.

12020. Liabilities Under the 1933 Act

Substantial liabilities under Section 11(a) of the 1933 Act can be imposed on a registrant's management personnel, underwriters, legal counsel, independent accountants, and all other parties involved if the 1933 Act registration statement they have prepared is found to contain untrue statements or material omissions. The section provides for the liabilities of persons who have signed the registration statement, directors of the issuer, underwriters, and experts (including independent accountants). Damages are generally limited to the excess of the purchase price (not exceeding the public offering price) over the later value of the security. The responsibility of accountants extends primarily to the financial statements covered by the audit report. Insofar as it relates to accountants, Section 11(a) provides, in part:

> In case any part of the registration statement, when such part became effective, contained an untrue statement of a material fact or omitted to state a material fact required to be stated therein or necessary to make the statements therein not misleading, any person acquiring such security . . . may . . . sue . . . every accountant . . . who has with his consent been named as having . . . certified any part of the registration statement . . . with respect to the statement in such registration statement . . . which purports to have been . . . certified by him.

The principal defense provided to the independent accountant by the 1933 Act is the provision in Section 11(b) that no person, other than the issuer, shall be liable who can sustain the burden of proof that:

> . . . as regards any part of the registration statement purporting to be made upon his authority as an expert . . . he had, after reasonable investigation, reasonable ground to believe and did believe, at the time such part of the registration statement became effective, that the statements therein were true and that there was no omission to state a material fact required to be stated therein or necessary to make the statements therein not misleading. . .

In other words, in order to assert a defense under the 1933 Act, independent accountants must be able to demonstrate that they have made a "reasonable investigation" (as defined in Section 11(c)) and must believe and have grounds for believing that the statements made on their authority as experts are true and that there are no omissions of material facts required to make the statement not misleading. A critical consideration in a 1933 Act filing is that the responsibility of independent accountants with respect to material events that affect the financial statements extends to the *effective date* of the registration statement and does not terminate at the date of the accountants' report (refer to section 19050 of this manual for a discussion of "keeping current" requirements).

According to Section 11, buyers of securities registered under the 1933 Act are not required to prove that the omission of a material fact or a misrepresentation in a registration statement was the cause of their loss. The individual must prove only that the defect exists. Any person acquiring a security registered under the 1933 Act may sue the certifying accountant, irrespective of the fact that the person is not the client of the accountant. There need be no legal relationship (privity) between the investor and the accountant. As a result, in cases involving assertions of defects in financial statements independent accountants must bear the burden of proving that their work met relevant professional standards. (Normally the plaintiff would have to prove *both* that the defect existed *and* that the independent accountant was negligent.) Defending these cases is often a long, difficult, and expensive proposition. Consequently, while the responsibility of independent auditors resulting from the inclusion of their report in a 1933 Act registration statement is in substance no different from that involved in other types of reporting, the sensitivity to litigation as a result of Section 11 dictates particular caution in such instances.

Financial Reporting Policy (FRP) Section 605 (formerly Accounting Series Release (ASR) No. 274) specifies that the provisions of Section 11 do not extend to accountants' review reports relating to unaudited interim financial information (American Institute of Certified Public Accountants (AICPA) Statement on Auditing Standards (SAS) No. 36 reports, as amended by SAS No. 71), even when such review reports are included or incorporated by reference in a 1933 Act registration statement (see section 20350 of this manual for a discussion of reports on unaudited interim financial information). The exclusion of SAS No. 71 reports from Section 11 liability does not extend to the provisions of Section 17(a) of the 1933 Act dealing with fraudulent acts and transactions; however, the exclusion does mean that such reports are not considered to be "expertized" (see section 17100) in the same manner as an audit report and that the "keeping current" requirements discussed in section 19050 do not apply to such reports.

In addition to the civil liabilities provided by Section 11, Section 24 of the 1933 Act imposes criminal penalties for willful violations of the 1933 Act or for willful misstatements or omissions in registration statements filed under the Act.

12021. Section 11(a) Earnings Statements. Questions are sometimes raised as to the purpose of a Section 11(a) earnings statement. The 1933 Act contains a provision designed to limit liability when a registrant has made available to its shareholders an earnings statement covering a period of 12 months beginning after the effective date of the registration statement. The applicable portion of Section 11(a) follows:

> If such person acquired the security after the issuer has made generally available to its security holders an earnings statement covering a period of at least twelve months beginning after the effective date of the registration statement, then the right of recovery under this subsection shall be conditioned on proof that such person acquired the securities relying on such untrue statement in the registration statement or relying upon the registration statement and not knowing of such omission, but such reliance may be established without proof of the reading of the registration statement by such person.

The effect of this provision is that an investor who has acquired a security *after* the issuer has made such an earnings statement generally available must, in order to recover damages, prove that he or she acquired the security *in reliance* upon an untrue statement in the registration statement or *in reliance* upon the registration statement and not knowing of a material omission. This provision has no effect on persons who acquired the security during the period when such reliance need not be proved (i.e., prior to the general availability of the aforementioned earnings statement).

Prior to the adoption of Rule 158, no clear guidelines existed for determining the meaning of and standards for satisfying the terms and conditions of this provision of Section 11(a). The SEC adopted Rule 158 to provide guidance on how to meet the earnings statement provisions of Section 11(a).

Rule 158 indicates that an earnings statement is deemed sufficient if it includes the information required for statements of income contained in one or any combination of reports required to be filed under the 1934 Act. Earnings statements filed pursuant to periodic reporting obligations under the 1934 Act are also considered to have been "made generally available." The "effective date of the registration statement" is considered to be the date on which certain post-effective amendments are filed or the date on which 1934 Act reports are incorporated by reference. Note that the financial information included in an earnings statement need not be audited to be deemed sufficient under Section 11(a).

The provisions of Rule 158 are nonexclusive, and a registrant may meet the standards and conditions of an earnings statement under Section 11(a) in other ways. When questions relating to earnings statements arise, it is suggested that the advice of legal counsel be sought.

12030. Liabilities Under the 1934 Act

The 1934 Act also provides for certain civil liabilities. Section 18(a) of the 1934 Act provides the following regarding damage suits:

> Any person who shall make or cause to be made any statement in any application, report, or document filed pursuant to this title or any rule or regulation thereunder or any undertaking contained in a registration statement as provided in subsection (d) of Section 15 of this title, which statement was at the time and in the light of the circumstances under which it was made false or misleading with respect to any material fact, shall be liable to any person (not knowing that such statement was false or misleading) who, in reliance upon such statement, shall have purchased or sold a security at a price which was affected by such statement, for damages caused by such reliance, unless the person sued shall prove that he acted in good faith and had no knowledge that such statement was false or misleading. . . .

In essence, while Section 18 establishes liability to both *buyers* and *sellers* of securities arising from a 1934 Act filing that is false or misleading, in the case of financial statements deemed to be "false and misleading," it requires the plaintiff to prove that:

- Reliance was placed on the financial statements.

- The price of the purchase or sale was affected by the financial statements.

- The damages sought were caused by reliance on the financial statements.

In response to such a suit, the independent accountant is entitled to the statutory defense that "he [or she] acted in good faith and had no knowledge that such [financial] statement was false or misleading."

The requirement to prove fraud and actual reliance has resulted in relatively few lawsuits having been brought against independent accountants under Section 18. On the other hand, the antifraud provisions in Section 10(b) and Rule 10b-5 of the 1934 Act have been the basis for a considerable amount of litigation against accountants. That section and rule follow:

Section 10(b) of the 1934 Act

It shall be unlawful for any person, directly or indirectly, by the use of any means or instrumentality of interstate commerce or of the mails, or of any facility of any national securities exchange to use or employ, in connection with the purchase or sale of any security registered on a national securities exchange or any security not so registered, any manipulative or deceptive device or contrivance in contravention of such rules and regulations as the Commission may prescribe as necessary or appropriate in the public interest or for the protection of investors.

Rule 10b-5 Under the 1934 Act

It shall be unlawful for any person, directly or indirectly, by the use of any means or instrumentality of interstate commerce, or of the mails, or of any facility of any national securities exchange,

(a) To employ any device, scheme, or artifice to defraud,

(b) To make any untrue statement of a material fact or to omit to state a material fact necessary in order to make the statements made, in the light of the circumstances under which they were made, not misleading, or

(c) To engage in any act, practice, or course of business which operates or would operate as a fraud or deceit upon any person, in connection with the purchase or sale of any security.

These provisions do not specifically provide for recovery by an injured person, but courts have found them a basis for civil remedies. (It should be noted that Section 10 and Rule 10b-5 also apply to the purchase and sale of securities of private entities that are not registered with the SEC.)

A 1976 ruling by the United States Supreme Court in the *Hochfelder* case theoretically limited the scope of the accountant's liability under Section 10(b) and Rule 10b-5 of the 1934 Act. In this case the court ruled that in order to claim damages under the antifraud provisions, a plaintiff must prove that independent accountants in their actions intended to deceive, manipulate, or defraud. Effectively, the court held that in contrast to the provisions of the 1933 Act, negligent conduct alone is *not* a basis for civil action against the independent accountant. However, developments in case law following *Hochfelder* have established that reckless disregard for the facts will be treated as the legal equivalent of an intent to deceive, manipulate, or defraud, and thus as a basis for the imposition of liability.

Section 32 of the 1934 Act imposes criminal penalties for willful violation of the Act and for willful false or misleading statements in documents filed pursuant to the Act.

In summary, independent accountants are often named as defendants under the federal securities laws, and although the exposure is technically less severe under the

1934 Act than under the 1933 Act, professional standards should not be relaxed with respect to a 1934 Act filing.

Perhaps the most significant practical impact that differences in legal liability between the two acts have on audit procedures performed by the independent accountant is with respect to requirements for "keeping current." In a registration under the 1933 Act the accountant's responsibility for the adequacy of the disclosures in the financial statements on which they reported extends through the *effective date* of the registration statement. Refer to subsection 19050 of this manual and Auditing section of AICPA Professional Standards (AU) Section 711 for required "keeping current" procedures and documentation. Under the 1934 Act, the independent accountant is responsible for events only to the date of his or her report (see AU Section 530.06). However, as discussed in AU Section 561, independent accountants have certain responsibilities in connection with the discovery of facts that existed at the date of the report but which come to their attention subsequent to the issuance of their report.

Notwithstanding the differences in the legal liability between the two acts, financial statements filed under the 1934 Act are frequently incorporated by reference into 1933 Act documents (see section 20521) and therefore become subject to the liability provisions of that Act.

13000. ORGANIZATION OF THE SEC

13010. Introduction

The principal office of the SEC is at 450 Fifth Street, N.W., Washington, D.C. 20549. The field activities of the SEC are conducted through regional offices and their respective regional branch offices in various cities across the country.

The regional offices (in conjunction with the regional branch offices) assist the SEC in its investigative and enforcement activities. Notifications and offering circulars under Regulation A (see section 42800) are processed by the regional offices. Certain offerings by small business issuers filed on Forms SB-1 and SB-2 (see sections 42600 and 42700, respectively) may also be reviewed by the regional offices.

13020. Organizational Diagram

The staff of the SEC is organized into divisions and offices as follows:

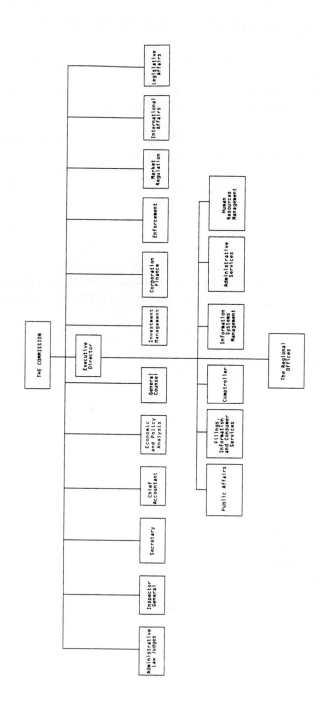

13030. Description of Functions

The organization of the SEC includes several operating divisions (section 13031), staff service offices (section 13032), the regional offices, the Administrative Law Judges, and several internal administrative offices. Independent accountants deal primarily with the Office of the Chief Accountant and the Division of Corporation Finance.

The Commission consists of five commissioners, one of whom serves as the Chairman. The commissioners are appointed by the President with the consent of the Senate, generally for a term of five years. The President designates the Chairman.

Described below are some of the operating divisions and staff offices with which independent accountants may have dealings.

13031. Operating Divisions

Division of Corporation Finance. Registration statements, as well as annual and periodic reports and proxy statements, are reviewed by the Division of Corporation Finance. The other principal responsibilities of this Division include the following:

- Establishment of standards for economic and financial disclosure information required in registration statements, reports, and other documents filed with the SEC.

- Determination of the nature of information to be included in proxy solicitations and the review of proxy-related documents submitted to the SEC.

- Enforcement of such provisions with respect to securities offered for sale to the public, listed for trading on securities exchanges, or traded in the over-the-counter market.

This Division is headed by a Director who is assisted by a Deputy Director and several associate and assistant directors. The Director's legal counsel is responsible for legal interpretations of securities laws. The Chief Accountant of the Division of Corporation Finance advises the Director on accounting matters and is responsible for the accounting activities of the Division. The Chief Accountant of the Division consults with the Chief Accountant of the SEC regarding new or important accounting and auditing problems.

The Division is presently organized into 12 branches of "corporate analysis and examination," with each branch headed by a branch chief who reports to one of six assistant directors of the Division. The Division is further subdivided into approximately 40 industry groups, with each assistant director responsible for several industry groups. Each registrant is assigned to an industry group (and thus to an assistant director and to an examining branch) based on its Standard Industrial Classification (SIC) Code. The branch is responsible for reviewing registration statements and other documents filed with the SEC by each assigned registrant. Since branch personnel are assigned by industry groups, the review process follows industry lines, and any documents filed with the SEC by a company under the various acts administered by the SEC would generally be reviewed by the same branch and industry group to which the company was assigned at the time of its initial filing.

The following diagram illustrates the line organization of the Division of Corporation Finance as it presently exists. Certain organizational changes may occur from time to time in an attempt to improve the processing system.

17

Division of Corporation Finance

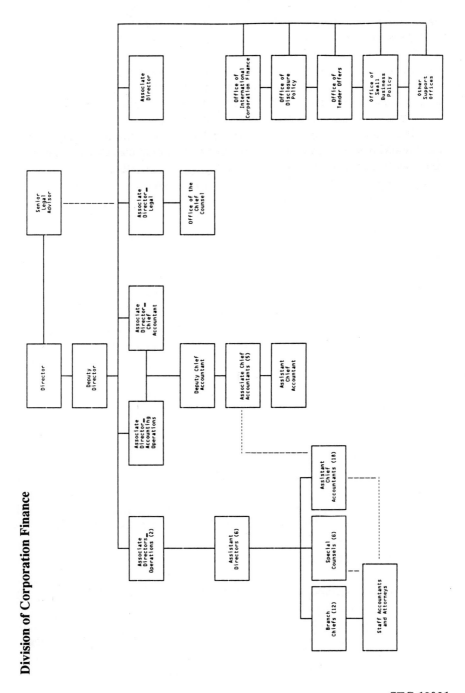

SEC 13031

The Division of Corporation Finance examines on a selective basis registration statements, prospectuses, annual and periodic reports, appraisals, engineering reports, certificates of incorporation and related documents, and amendments to all of the foregoing that are filed with the SEC with respect to securities offered for sale to the public or registered under the 1934 Act. The Division also examines proxy statements and other proxy-soliciting material required to be filed with it. Upon completion of these examinations, comments may be provided via telephone or formal letters may be prepared for issuance to registrants. A discussion of letters of comment and the SEC review process is included in section 18000. The Division also reviews the reports of trading in equity securities by officers and directors of registered corporations and principal holders of such securities ("Insider Reports").

As a general rule, accounting issues arising from a specific filing are initially addressed by the accounting staff of the Division of Corporation Finance in the branch to which the company is assigned. The branch accountants consult with the Chief Accountant of the Division in connection with new, complex, or disputed accounting issues. Accounting questions relating to basic policies of the SEC and new or controversial issues may also involve the Office of the Chief Accountant of the Commission, which also handles all questions relating to the qualifications or the independence of accountants. The Division of Corporation Finance, together with the Office of the Chief Accountant of the Commission, prepares and issues Staff Accounting Bulletins. (Refer to section 15050 for a discussion of SABs.)

The Division of Corporation Finance also has certain offices that have both operating and staff duties, such as the Office of the Chief Counsel; the Office of International Corporate Finance; the Office of Disclosure Policy; the Office of Tender Offers; the Office of Small Business Policy; and other support offices (such as the Office of the Chief Financial Analyst and the Office of Engineering). The Office of Small Business Policy is responsible for rule-making initiatives affecting small businesses.

Division of Market Regulation. This Division is responsible for the regulation of securities exchanges, national securities associations, and brokers and dealers. The Division also performs various statistical accumulation functions and is generally responsible for policing the securities markets. The Division attempts to prevent fraudulent trading practices and market manipulations and investigates unusual trading activities and unlawful practices.

Division of Enforcement. This Division is responsible for the supervision and conduct of enforcement activities under the statutes administered by the SEC, including the institution of administrative and injunctive actions and the evaluation of evidence supporting such actions. The Division has its own Chief Accountant. If criminal prosecution is deemed appropriate, the Division refers such cases to the Justice Department in collaboration with the Office of the General Counsel.

SEC 13031

Division of Investment Management. This Division administers the Investment Company Act and the Investment Advisers Act. It concentrates on all matters concerning investment companies and reviews various reports filed by such companies and/or transmitted to their shareholders. In addition, the Division administers the Public Utility Holding Company Act of 1935.

13032. Staff Service Offices. The staff offices of the SEC include the Office of the General Counsel; the Office of the Chief Accountant; and the Directorate of Economic and Policy Analysis.

Office of the General Counsel. The General Counsel is the chief legal officer of the SEC. The Office represents the Commission in judicial proceedings and provides advice and assistance to the SEC, its operating divisions, and regional offices with respect to statutory interpretations, rule making, legislative matters and other legal problems, public or private investigations, and congressional hearings and investigations. The Office reviews all cases in which criminal prosecution is recommended (see Division of Enforcement) and advises the commissioners with respect thereto. The General Counsel directs and supervises certain civil litigation matters and represents the Commission in all cases in the appellate courts.

Office of the Chief Accountant. The Chief Accountant is the principal accounting advisor to the Commission. He or she advises the commissioners with respect to difficult or controversial accounting issues and is responsible for the establishment, coordination, and expression of SEC policy regarding auditing standards and accounting principles or practices.

The Chief Accountant initiates and supervises studies relating to accounting and auditing. In connection with drafting and interpreting accounting and auditing rules and regulations, the Chief Accountant confers with accounting authorities such as professional organizations, public accountants, and officials of the federal and state governments. The Office of the Chief Accountant responds to questions received from registrants or their independent accountants dealing with accounting and auditing issues. The Office of the Chief Accountant is frequently the originator of Staff Accounting Bulletins, which are issued jointly with the Division of Corporation Finance. As discussed in section 15050, Staff Accounting Bulletins are not rules or interpretations of the Commission. They represent interpretations and practices followed by the Division of Corporation Finance and the Office of the Chief Accountant in administering the disclosure requirements of the Federal securities laws. The Office is also responsible for the preparation of official interpretations and other releases relating to accounting matters that are approved by the Commission and published as Financial Reporting Releases (formerly Accounting Series Releases—refer to section 15030 for discussion of FRRs). The Administrative Procedure Act requires that most proposed rule changes be published for comment.

The Chief Accountant is responsible for the consideration of all cases dealing with the independence and qualifications of public accountants who practice before the Commission. He supervises and makes recommendations concerning disciplinary proceedings involving public accountants under Rule 2(e) of the Commission's Rules of Practice, generally based on actions initiated by the operating divisions and regional offices.

The Chief Accountant functions as a liaison between the accounting profession and the Commission. Independent accountants may consult with the Chief Accountant with respect to any question concerning accounting or auditing that is new, complex, or controversial. In practice, however, unless an independence question is involved or the question clearly deals with a subject that the independent accountant recognizes can only be resolved by the Chief Accountant, it is generally preferable to initiate all accounting and auditing inquiries with the Office of the Chief Accountant of the Division of Corporation Finance. The decisions reached by the Office of the Chief Accountant of the Division may be appealed to the Chief Accountant of the SEC.

Directorate of Economic and Policy Analysis. The primary functions of the Directorate of Economic and Policy Analysis are to assist the Commission in the formulation of regulatory policy and to prepare statistical information relating to the capital markets.

14000. THE ROLE OF THE SEC

14010. The Function of the SEC in the Registration Process

One of the primary functions of the SEC is the review of registration statements to determine that full and accurate disclosure is made of all pertinent information relating to (among other things) the company's business, its securities, its financial position and earnings, its officers and directors, and the underwriting arrangements of the offering in order that the prospective investor may have the information necessary to make a decision whether to acquire the securities being registered. It is important to note that the responsibility of the SEC is to protect the public—not the issuer or the underwriters of the securities.

The SEC does not prohibit the sale of low-grade or speculative securities. However, a prospectus relating to an offering of any securities must include a detailed description of any risk factors involved and any other negative aspects of the offering that an investor should consider in evaluating the investment.

The fact that a registration statement is in effect with respect to a particular security does not imply that the SEC has reviewed and approved the registration statement. The outside front cover of every prospectus contains the following legend in bold face type:

THESE SECURITIES HAVE NOT BEEN APPROVED OR DISAPPROVED BY THE SECURITIES AND EXCHANGE COMMISSION NOR HAS THE COMMISSION PASSED UPON THE ACCURACY OR ADEQUACY OF THIS PROSPECTUS. ANY REPRESENTATION TO THE CONTRARY IS A CRIMINAL OFFENSE.

This mandatory statement is intended to make it clear that the SEC is not responsible for evaluating the merits of a security being registered. In practice, however, the staff will frequently scrutinize a speculative offering much more intensely than a nonspeculative offering. If the document contains significant deficiencies, the staff may request that the registration statement be withdrawn or refuse to allow the document to become effective.

While it is the issuer's responsibility to ensure that there is full and fair disclosure in the registration statement, when the filing is subject to the normal review process (see section 18000) the staff of the SEC attempts to determine that all material facts with respect to a security and its issuer are adequately disclosed in the document being filed and that no material information has been omitted. The SEC strives to prevent fraudulent practices in the offering and sale of securities but does not guarantee the investor against loss.

If all material facts regarding a security are not adequately disclosed in the registration statement, or if important information is omitted, the SEC will require that the registration statement be corrected or expanded, as required, by means of an appropriate amendment. (The SEC review procedures and the process of amending registration statements are discussed further in sections 18000 and 19000.) If the amendment does not resolve the deficiencies, the SEC may exercise its "stop-order" or "refusal-order" powers to prevent the registration statement from becoming effective and the securities from being sold until the deficiencies are corrected. Sometimes the stop-order is issued after the registration statement has become effective and the securities have been sold, in which event the order prevents further sales of the securities by the issuer or the underwriter.

The staff of the SEC frequently furnishes informal advice and assistance to registrants, prospective issuers, lawyers, and others. The staff also issues no-action and interpretive letters. These letters often deal with legal matters. However, they sometimes pertain to the requirements of the filing forms, including matters relating to the financial statements and independence of accountants. Such letters are written by members of the staff in response to inquiries citing a given set of circumstances. The inquiries, for example, frequently involve requests for concurrence that a proposed issuance of securities is exempt from registration requirements. In a no-action letter the SEC staff advises the person soliciting its views that under a described set of facts the staff would not recommend that the SEC take any action, such as enjoining the proposed transaction, if the transaction described were carried out—hence, the term *no-action letter*. If the staff member was of the opinion that the securities had to be registered in the circumstances presented, the individual would advise the interested person to that effect. No-action and interpretive letters are public documents, available for inspection by anyone.

Except for information and documents that the Commission has granted confidential treatment, all information in registration statements and reports filed with the SEC is available for public inspection. At its main office in Washington, D.C., the Commission maintains a public reference room where all such documents and information may be inspected by any interested person. Copying machines are also available in the event that a photocopy of material in the Commission's files is desired.

The Commission also furnishes (for a charge) photocopies of information on file, which may be ordered from the Public Reference Section, Securities and Exchange Commission, Washington, D.C. 20549. The availability of microfiche has also made access to such documents possible by subscribing to disclosure services.

SEC 14010

14020. The SEC and Auditing Standards

As a general rule, the SEC does not prescribe the procedures to be followed by independent public accountants in their audit of the financial statements. However, under the various acts that it administers, the SEC has broad powers that may extend to prescribing the detailed steps to be followed by accountants in "certifying" statements for filing with the SEC. The SEC is well aware of this authority and responsibility, and in its report on the investigation of McKesson & Robbins, Inc. (1940) the SEC stated that one of the purposes of the investigation was to inquire into generally accepted auditing procedures with a view toward determining their adequacy in assuring accurate and reliable financial statements. As a result of the action taken by the accounting profession to develop auditing standards, the SEC has generally relied on the public accounting profession to establish auditing standards. In ASR No. 19, which discussed the McKesson & Robbins case, the SEC described its position with respect to auditing procedures:

> We have carefully considered the desirability of specific rules and regulations governing the auditing steps to be performed by accountants in certifying financial statements to be filed with us. Action has already been taken by the accounting profession adopting certain of the auditing procedures considered in this case. We have no reason to believe at this time that these extensions will not be maintained or that further extensions of auditing procedures along the lines suggested in this report will not be made. Further, the adoption of the specific recommendations made in this report as to the type of disclosure to be made in the accountant's certificate and as to the election of accountants by stockholders should insure that acceptable standards of auditing procedures will be observed, that specific deviations therefrom may be considered in the particular instances in which they arise, and that accountants will be more independent of management. Until experience should prove the contrary, we feel that this program is preferable to its alternative—the detailed prescription of the scope and procedures to be followed in the audit for the various types of issuers of securities who file statements with us—and will allow for further consideration of varying audit procedures and for the development of different treatment for specific types of issuers.

This position has remained unchanged since 1940 when ASR No. 19 was issued. The SEC has, however, commented extensively in ASRs (now Accounting and Auditing Enforcement Releases [AAERs]—see section 15040) on audits that were, in its view, deficient.

In an accountant's report filed pursuant to Rule 2-02 of Regulation S-X, the SEC requires the "certifying" accountant to make certain representations regarding an audit. The rule requires the accountant to:

> (1) . . . state whether the audit was made in accordance with generally accepted auditing standards; and

(2) . . . designate any auditing procedures deemed necessary by the accountant under the circumstances of the particular case which have been omitted, and the reasons for their omission.

Rule 2-02 further states that nothing in the rule shall be construed to imply authority for the omission of any procedure that independent accountants would ordinarily employ in the course of an audit made for the purpose of expressing the opinions required to be expressed by the rule. Paragraph (c) of Rule 2-02 requires accountants to state clearly in their report their opinion as to:

(1) . . . the financial statements covered by the report and the accounting principles and practices reflected therein; and

(2) . . . the consistency of the application of the accounting principles, or as to any changes in such principles which have a material effect on the financial statements. [See section 50202 regarding the impact of SAS No. 58 on this requirement.]

There are exceptions to the general rule that the SEC does not prescribe audit procedures, such as in the case of certain investment companies and reports filed by certain members of national securities exchanges and brokers and dealers in securities. The SEC has set forth specific procedures to be followed in connection with such audits. In view of the specialized nature of these requirements, they are not discussed in this manual.

In summary, the SEC has generally been satisfied to allow the public accounting profession to develop auditing standards. However, the SEC has criticized inadequacies in auditing practices in a number of cases, many of which have been the subject of ASRs and AAERs, and thereby has been influential in the development or modification of auditing standards.

14030. The Influence of the SEC in the Development of Accounting Principles

The SEC has the statutory authority to prescribe the accounting principles to be followed in financial statements filed under the 1933 and 1934 Acts.

Under the 1933 Act, the SEC has broad statutory powers to make, amend, and rescind any rules and regulations that may be necessary to carry out the provisions of the law. The SEC is authorized to define accounting, technical, and trade terms used in the law and has the power to prescribe the form in which required information shall be set forth and the items or details to be presented in the financial statements. The SEC may prescribe the methods to be followed in the preparation of accounts, in the appraisal or valuation of the assets and liabilities, in the determination of depreciation and depletion, in the differentiation of recurring and nonrecurring income, in the differentiation of investment and operating income, and in the preparation of consolidated financial statements of companies controlling or controlled by the issuer or under common control with the issuer (see Section 19(a) of the 1933 Act).

Under the 1934 Act, the SEC has broad statutory powers to prescribe the form in which the information required by the law shall be set forth and the items or details to be shown in the financial statements. The SEC has the authority to prescribe the methods to be followed in the preparation of reports, in the appraisal or valuation of assets and liabilities, in the determination of depreciation and depletion, in the differentiation of investment and operating income, and in the preparation (when the SEC deems it necessary or desirable) of separate and/or consolidated financial statements of any entity controlling or controlled by the issuer or any entity under common control with the issuer. In the case, however, of reports of any company whose methods of accounting are prescribed under the provisions of any federal law or regulation, the rules of the SEC with respect to reports may not be inconsistent with the requirements imposed by such law or regulation with respect to the same subject matter (see Section 13(b) of the 1934 Act).

The SEC has invoked its authority to specify the detailed information that financial statements should contain through Regulation S-X, which sets forth its rules as to the form and content of and requirements for most financial statements filed under the several laws it administers. It has specified the books, records, and other information that must be maintained by investment advisers under the Investment Advisers Act and broker-dealers under the 1934 Act. While the SEC has expressed its views on numerous issues relating to accounting principles and practices, primarily through ASRs and now Financial Reporting Releases (FRRs), it nevertheless has principally relied on the private sector to establish the main body of such principles and practices. The SEC described its reliance on the private sector in ASR 150 (FRP 101) which states "... the Commission intends to continue its policy of looking to the private sector for leadership in establishing and improving accounting principles and standards through the FASB [Financial Accounting Standards Board] with the expectation that the body's conclusions will promote the interests of investors."

The preference of the SEC for the private sector to develop and establish accounting principles does not necessarily reflect a completely hands-off policy on the part of the SEC. The staff of the SEC is frequently involved in these developments. The professional groups responsible for developing accounting principles (and statements on auditing standards) typically consult with the staff before issuing pronouncements.

The SEC staff has periodically considered it desirable to suggest issues that should be addressed by the FASB. Suggestions have occasionally taken the form of an ASR, FRR, or Staff Accounting Bulletin (SAB) that highlights the problem, requires additional disclosure, or defines the accounting to be followed until the issue is dealt with by the FASB. The following are examples of ASRs and FRRs in which the SEC has taken initiative in expressing its views on the accounting to be followed or the disclosures to be made:

SEC 14030

Number	Description
ASR 130 and 135	Pooling of Interests Accounting
ASR 146 and 146A	Effect of Treasury Stock Transactions on Accounting for Business Combinations
ASR 268	Presentation in Financial Statements of "Redeemable Preferred Stock"
ASR 293	The Last-In, First-Out Method of Accounting for Inventories
FRR 24	Disclosure Regarding Repurchase and Reverse Repurchase Agreements
FRR 28	Accounting for Loan Losses

In some cases SEC staff policy on accounting for particular transactions is established by the issuance of Staff Accounting Bulletins. Examples of accounting issues dealt with in SABs are:

Number	Description
SAB 42 and 42A	Acquisitions Involving Financial Institutions
SAB 55	Allocation of Expenses and Related Disclosure in Subsidiaries' Financial Statements
SAB 57	Contingent Warrants
SAB 67	Income Statement Presentation of Restructuring Charges
SAB 73	Push Down Basis of Accounting
SAB 76	Risk Sharing in Pooling of Interests
SAB 79	Accounting for Expenses or Liabilities Paid by Principal Stockholder(s)
SAB 84	Accounting for Sales of Stock by a Subsidiary
SAB 86	Quasi Reorganization
SAB 91	Accounting for Income Tax Benefits Associated with Bad Debts of Thrifts
SAB 92	Accounting and Disclosures Relating to Loss Contingencies

The following are examples of accounting issues dealt with by the FASB at the request of the SEC that have resulted in the issuance of a Statement of Financial Accounting Standards (SFAS):

SFAS Number	Description
4	Reporting Gains and Losses from Extinguishment of Debt
6	Classification of Short-Term Obligations Expected To Be Refinanced
13	Accounting for Leases
16	Prior Period Adjustments
34	Capitalization of Interest Cost
68	Research and Development Arrangements
74	Accounting for Special Termination Benefits Paid to Employees
76	Extinguishment of Debt
86	Accounting for the Cost of Computer Software To Be Sold, Leased or Otherwise Marketed
94	Consolidation of All Majority-Owned Subsidiaries

The Emerging Issues Task Force (EITF) was established by the FASB in July 1984. The objective of the EITF is to assist the FASB and its staff in the identification of accounting issues and implementation problems on a timely basis. While the EITF does not have the authority to issue authoritative accounting standards, the Chief Accountant of the SEC attends EITF meetings and takes the position that since an EITF consensus sets the tone for future accounting, a registrant's accounting practice that differs from a consensus position of the EITF is open to challenge.

Furthermore, on occasion the official minutes of an EITF meeting will indicate the view of the Chief Accountant (officially referred to as the SEC observer) on a particular issue, which typically becomes SEC staff policy, until a FASB statement is issued.

The accounting principles set forth by the SEC in ASRs, and now FRRs, have frequently dealt with matters not specifically addressed in accounting literature and therefore often differ from general practice at the time of their issuance. When a new accounting pronouncement dealing with the subject matter is issued, the applicable SEC pronouncement is usually withdrawn.

As a result of amendments adopted in ASR No. 281 (now FRP Section 102.03), financial statements included in annual reports to shareholders prepared by public companies in the U.S. are required (with certain exceptions) to conform with the disclosure requirements of Regulation S-X. Accordingly, in the preparation of financial statements public companies in the U.S. must consider not only the relevant pronouncements of the professional literature establishing generally accepted accounting principles, but also the applicable published rules and regulations of the SEC.

15000. SOURCES OF SEC TECHNICAL REQUIREMENTS

15010. Introduction

The purpose of this section is to identify the sources of SEC rules, regulations, interpretations, and practices that are significant to independent accountants in connection with the preparation and review of an SEC report or registration statement.

The principal rules and regulations and guidance applicable to the form and content of and requirements for most financial statements and other financial information to be included in documents filed with the SEC are contained in:

- Instructions to the form to be filed.

- Regulation S-X.

- Financial Reporting Releases.

- Accounting and Auditing Enforcement Releases.

- Staff Accounting Bulletins.

- Regulation S-K.

- Industry Guides under the 1933 and 1934 Acts.

- Regulation S-B.

The complete and current texts of the foregoing materials should be available to independent accountants engaged in the preparation or review of a registration statement or report to be filed with the SEC. Certain Financial Reporting Releases (formerly ASRs) concurrently amend Regulation S-X, Regulation S-K, Regula-

SEC 15010

tion S-B, and the instructions to various forms; however, there is generally a time lag before such amendments are incorporated into the various published services. Consequently, when using such services consideration must be given to any amendments issued since the text was last updated. This caution also applies to material contained in this manual. The SEC also publishes General Rules and Regulations under both the 1933 and 1934 Acts. Certain of these rules and regulations are of importance to accountants because they define the terms used, prescribe the number of copies of documents required to be filed, and contain other instructions and requirements.

As previously noted, although no action and interpretive letters issued by the SEC staff often deal with legal matters, in some instances they pertain to the requirements for filing forms, including requirements for financial statements and accountants' independence.

15020. Regulation S-X

Regulation S-X is the principal accounting regulation of the SEC. The Regulation was originally adopted in 1940 and has been amended many times since then. It now contains substantially all the requirements for financial statements, related footnotes, and supplemental financial schedules required to be included in documents filed with the SEC under various acts, and its provisions (with certain exceptions) now also extend to the financial statements included in annual reports to shareholders of U.S. registrants (see discussion in section 31300). Regulation S-X specifies the persons (entities) for which financial statements are to be included, the dates and periods for which such statements must be furnished, and the information that they must contain. Although the basic disclosures and presentations are substantially those required by generally accepted accounting principles in the U.S., compliance with Regulation S-X may necessitate additional captions on the face of the financial statements, additional footnote disclosures, supplemental schedules, and other information. Regulation S-X is included in this manual beginning in section 50050.

It is important to recognize that Regulation S-X should be considered a *minimum* standard. Rule 4-01(a) of the Regulation states: "The information required with respect to any statement shall be furnished as a minimum requirement to which shall be added such further *material* information as is necessary to make the required statements, in the light of the circumstances under which they are made, not misleading." However, it should also be noted that Regulation S-X, Rule 4-02, permits the omission of items that are not *material*.

15030. Financial Reporting Releases

In 1982 the SEC replaced the Accounting Series Releases (ASRs) with two series of releases—Financial Reporting Releases (FRRs) and Accounting and Auditing Enforcement Releases (AAERs). The FRRs are designed to communicate the

SEC's positions on accounting and auditing principles and practices. They are used to adopt, amend, or interpret rules and regulations relating to accounting and auditing issues or financial statement disclosures. FRR No. 1 codified those accounting and auditing subjects of previously issued ASRs that are still relevant and the material included in the codification is referenced to the ASR from which it was extracted. FRR No. 1 did *not* establish any new interpretations or policies. Subsequent FRRs have updated the codification for new matters and future FRRs will modify or rescind sections that become obsolete. The codification of the FRRs is contained in the Financial Reporting Policies (FRP), which are organized in topical sections numbered 101 to 607.

Independent accountants need to be familiar with the FRRs since the policies stated in these releases must be followed by all SEC registrants. Pertinent sections of releases that are issued to adopt changes to Regulation S-X or to amend filing requirements are included in the text of the Regulation or the instructions to the applicable form. The complete text of the FRR, however, frequently contains additional guidelines, interpretations, examples, and other information that may be helpful in the implementation of the rules, regulations, and instructions to SEC forms and should also be referred to in order to gain a more complete understanding of the intent of the particular requirements.

Among the ASRs issued, ASR Nos. 4 and 150 (both of which are now located in Financial Reporting Policy (FRP) Section No. 101) are of particular significance. ASR No. 4 (issued in March 1938) first expressed the SEC's position that generally accepted accounting principles for which there is "substantial authoritative support" constitute the SEC standard of reporting and that disclosure is not a substitute for proper accounting in filings with the SEC. This release places responsibility on registrants and their independent accountants for having full knowledge of the rules and regulations of the SEC as well as the accounting opinions contained in FRRs (ASRs) and in official decisions and reports. Pursuant to the position expressed in ASR No. 4, a company filing financial statements reflecting an accounting principle that has been formally disapproved of by the SEC, or for which there is no substantial authoritative support, will be presumed to be filing misleading financial statements even though there is full disclosure of the accounting principle applied. The following are pertinent excerpts from ASR No. 4 as codified in FRP Section 101:

> In cases where financial statements filed with the Commission pursuant to its rules and regulations under the Securities Act or the Exchange Act are prepared in accordance with accounting principles for which there is no substantial authoritative support, such financial statements will be presumed to be misleading or inaccurate despite disclosures contained in the certificate of the accountant or in footnotes to the statements provided the matters involved are material. In cases where there is a difference of opinion between the Commission and the registrant as to the proper principles of accounting to be followed, disclosure will be accepted in lieu of correction of the financial statements themselves only if the points involved are such that there is substantial authoritative support for the practices

followed by the registrant and the position of the Commission has not previously been expressed in rules, regulations, or other official releases of the Commission, including the published opinions of its Chief Accountant.

ASR No. 150 (issued in 1973) reaffirms the policy expressed in ASR No. 4 and formally acknowledges that the pronouncements of the FASB in its statements and interpretations are considered by the SEC as having substantial authoritative support and that those contrary to such FASB pronouncements are considered not to have such support. ASR No. 150 also specifies that Accounting Research Bulletins of the Committee on Accounting Procedure of the AICPA and effective opinions of the Accounting Principles Board of the Institute should be considered as continuing in force with the same degree of authoritative support except to the extent that they are altered, amended, supplemented, revoked, or superseded by one or more Statements of Financial Accounting Standards issued by the FASB.

The ASRs covered a wide range of topics, some of which subsequently became outdated or superseded by other pronouncements. Accordingly, over the years the SEC rescinded a number of ASRs. A chronological listing of ASRs that were codified by FRR No. 1 is included in the appendix (section 83000) to this manual.

15040. Accounting and Auditing Enforcement Releases

The Accounting and Auditing Enforcement Releases (AAERs) are designed to communicate SEC enforcement actions involving accountants. Many of them discuss what the SEC concluded were violations of generally accepted auditing standards or nonconformity with generally accepted accounting principles. Consequently, AAER No. 1 contains a topical index to those ASRs that previously disclosed enforcement-related actions involving accounting, auditing, and related matters by subject matter. It also contains a complete chronological listing of the enforcement-related ASRs.

15050. Staff Accounting Bulletins

Until 1976, when the SEC issued ASR No. 180 (now FRP Section 103) announcing its intention to issue a series of Staff Accounting Bulletins, there was no effective method for advising the public of informal interpretations of accounting issues and positions taken by its staff when faced with a new or unusual problem on a particular filing. As stated in ASR No. 180, SABs are also intended as "a means by which new or revised interpretations and practices can be quickly and easily communicated to registrants and their advisors."

In 1981 the SABs were codified by topic (SAB No. 40). A topical index of SABs issued (through No. 86) is included in the appendix (section 81000) to this manual and is cross-referenced, where applicable, to the section of the manual in which the SAB topic is discussed. A numerical index is also included in the appendix (section 81500).

Staff Accounting Bulletins represent interpretations and practices followed by the Division of Corporation Finance and the Office of the Chief Accountant in connection with the administration of the disclosure requirements of the federal securities laws. SABs are published on a joint basis by the Division of Corporation Finance and the Office of the Chief Accountant. They are not an official part of Regulation S-X and, as stated in the introduction to each SAB, they are not rules or interpretations of the Commission. The SABs serve an important function, however, in that they provide the SEC with a mechanism for apprising the public of current staff practices and interpretations.

Staff Accounting Bulletins must be considered when preparing financial statements to be included in a filing with the SEC to the extent that the facts and circumstances involved in a particular situation are similar to the facts and circumstances outlined in the SAB. In SAB No. 27, the SEC emphasized that the facts and circumstances of a particular SAB should also be considered for guidance in other situations in which events and transactions have similar accounting implications. This point was also made in SAB No. 64 (codified as Topic 6-C) which states:

> The staff's purpose in issuing SABs is to disseminate guidance for application not only in the narrowly described circumstances, but also, unless authoritative accounting literature calls for different treatment, in other circumstances where events and transactions have similar accounting and/or disclosure implications.

Notwithstanding their identification as informal interpretations, in practice the SEC generally does not permit a registration statement to become effective if it considers the accounting treatment in a particular set of circumstances to be in conflict with an interpretation or position expressed in a Staff Accounting Bulletin. However, SAB No. 64 goes on to say:

> Registrants and independent accountants are encouraged to consult with the staff if they believe that particular circumstances call for accounting and/or disclosure different from that which would result from application of a SAB addressing those same or analogous circumstances.

In addition, footnote 4 of SAB Topic 5-K (see section 50503-1) states:

> ...the staff encourages registrants and their accountants to discuss with it proposed accounting treatments for transactions and events which are not specifically covered by existing accounting literature.

15060. Regulation S-K

The objective of Regulation S-K, which was adopted by the SEC in 1977 and restructured in 1982, is to standardize the nonfinancial statement disclosure requirements for documents filed with the SEC and to eliminate the need to include similar disclosure requirements in each of the registration and reporting documents. Most of the registrant-related requirements as to information to be disclosed in documents filed with the SEC by U.S. registrants is now included in Regulation S-K. The disclosure requirements for foreign registrants filing on Forms F-1, F-2, F-3, F-4, and portions of Form 20-F also refer to Regulation S-K. Certain of the detailed Regulation S-K disclosure requirements are discussed in this manual beginning in section 60000.

15070. SEC Forms

Various SEC forms are used by issuers filing reports and registration statements under the 1933 and 1934 Acts. The forms generally identify the items for which information is to be provided. In certain cases, particularly with respect to transaction-related disclosures, the forms contain the detailed instructions as to the information to be furnished. However, as described in sections 15020 and 15060, a substantial portion of the instructions as to registrant-related disclosures are included in Regulation S-K, and the financial statement requirements are set forth in Regulation S-X. Consequently, many of the items in the various forms merely refer to the provisions of these Regulations for the detailed information to be furnished. Certain of the 1933 and 1934 Act forms are discussed in more detail beginning with section 40100 of this manual.

The selection of the form to be used for a particular filing is made by the company in consultation with its legal counsel, since the determination involves interpreting the provisions of the Securities Acts and considering other factors such as the nature of the registrant and the securities to which the form applies. Independent accountants do not function as legal advisors to their clients and are therefore not in a position to make this determination.

15080. Industry Guides

In 1968 the SEC published the first of a series of Guides intended to outline policies and practices followed by the Division of Corporation Finance in the administration of the 1933 Act. A separate series of Guides under the 1934 Act was initiated in 1974. The Guides are not rules of the SEC and do not bear the Commission's official approval; however, they are intended to assist registrants in the preparation of registration statements and periodic reports. Registrants would be well-advised to consider discussing specific deviations from these Guides with the SEC staff on a prefiling basis.

In ASR 306 the SEC substantially modified the Guides by (1) eliminating those with outdated or duplicative disclosure requirements and (2) relocating requirements in certain other Guides to Regulation S-K and to other rules and regulations under the 1933 and 1934 Acts. Only those Guides pertaining to specific industries have been retained as such, including Guide 3, which contains fairly extensive disclosure requirements pertaining to bank holding companies. A listing of the remaining Guides is provided in Section 800 of Regulation S-K. A copy of that listing is included in section 68000 of this manual.

15090. Regulation S-B

In August 1992 the SEC adopted an integrated registration, reporting and qualification system for small business issuers under the 1933 Act, the 1934 Act, and the Trust Indenture Act of 1939, generally referred to as "the small business initiatives." The system consists of specialized forms that reference disclosure requirements located in one central depository—Regulation S-B. The system is designed to facilitate capital raising by small business issuers and to lower the costs of compliance with the federal securities laws. The new rules define a small business issuer as a U.S. or Canadian entity with revenues of less than $25 million unless the issuer's public float (the aggregate market value of voting stock held by nonaffiliates) is $25 million or more. Investment companies are excluded from the definition. Further, if the small business issuer is a majority owned subsidiary of another company, its parent must also meet the definition of a small business issuer.

The disclosure requirements in Regulation S-B generally parallel those of Regulation S-K; however, the requirements are simplified in various respects. The Regulation S-B disclosure requirements are discussed in this manual beginning in section 70000.

15100. EDGAR

In March 1993, the SEC adopted rules to implement its Electronic Data, Gathering, Analysis, and Retrieval (EDGAR) system. One of the principal objectives of the SEC's EDGAR Project has been to ensure that the massive volume of paperwork involved in the filings presently submitted by the more than 14,600 public companies does not adversely affect the SEC's ability to protect investors and maintain fair and orderly securities markets. The EDGAR rules and regulations are contained in new Regulation S-T, which is not presented in this manual. A general heading precedes other SEC regulations that relate to reporting as follows:

ATTENTION ELECTRONIC FILERS

THIS REGULATION SHOULD BE READ IN CONJUNCTION WITH REGULATION S-T (PART 232), WHICH GOVERNS THE PREPARATION AND SUBMISSION OF DOCUMENTS IN ELECTRONIC FORMAT. MANY PROVISIONS RELATING TO THE PREPARATION AND SUBMISSION OF DOCUMENTS IN PAPER FORMAT CONTAINED IN THIS REGULATION ARE SUPERSEDED BY THE PROVISIONS OF REGULATION S-T FOR DOCUMENTS REQUIRED TO BE FILED IN ELECTRONIC FORMAT.

Background. During 1984, the SEC started receiving registration statements and periodic reports electronically from a variety of volunteer filers as part of its EDGAR pilot program. That program, which processed over 116,000 electronic filings from more than 1,800 registrants, was closed in July 1992 and, at the same time, the new EDGAR system began receiving filings submitted by pilot program participants. When the system is fully operational, virtually all documents processed by the SEC, including correspondence and supplemental information, will be required to be submitted electronically by either direct transmission, magnetic tape, or diskette.

Mandated electronic filing by pilot program participants commenced in April 1993. All other registrants are scheduled to be brought onto the EDGAR system in a series of discrete groups pursuant to a schedule issued by the SEC. During this phase-in, it is important that each registrant determine their expected electronic filing date and consider preparing test filings. The entire phase-in is currently scheduled to be completed by May 1996.

Benefits. A number of benefits are expected for all filers:

- Time savings in delivery via direct transmission will provide filers with a greater opportunity to meet market windows and eliminate the uncertainties and delays of mail or messenger deliveries.

- The improved dissemination of information will increase public information about companies in general. In addition, the public will have faster access to EDGAR filings through a variety of sources, including subscriptions to SEC and/or private-sector data bases.

- Direct transmission filings will be accepted by the SEC up to 10 p.m. (EST); however, transmissions received after 5:30 p.m. will be considered filed on the next business day.

- Modular and segmented filings (explained below) will save time and eliminate duplicate effort on the part of filers.

- The EDGAR electronic mail/bulletin board will provide prompt filer notification of acceptance or suspension of filings and other SEC communications via the CompuServe network. Registrants that do not subscribe to this network will continue to be notified via first-class U.S. mail, which can impose time constraints on those with suspended filings. (The SEC encourages all registrants to subscribe to this service.)

- EDGAR will facilitate the SEC review process.

SEC 15100

- The system will provide a framework for future development of one-stop filing for compatible state and self-regulatory organization filings.

Structure of the System. All filers are encouraged to submit the required Form ID, the uniform application for access codes to file on EDGAR, three to six months prior to their mandated filing date so that they can become familiar with the system and prepare EDGAR test filings. Once the SEC receives a Form ID, it will provide the filer the EDGAR Filer Manual, filer assistance software (EDGARLink), and EDGAR identification codes. The procedures for preparing test filings are explained in the EDGAR Filer Manual.

Safe Harbor Rules. In response to previous concerns, the rules provide for a safe harbor, which protects electronic filers from the liability and anti-fraud provisions of the federal securities laws for an error or omission in a document that resulted solely from a good faith transmission of the document via EDGAR. The safe harbor would be conditional on correction of the error or omission as soon as reasonably practicable after the filer becomes aware of the error or omission.

Signatures. Under EDGAR, all signatures are required to be submitted in typed form. This approach eliminates the practical problems associated with personal identification numbers (PINs) used in the EDGAR pilot. Accordingly, PINs are no longer permitted to be used. Signature requirements for electronic filings remain the same as for paper format documents in all other respects.

Filers are required, however, to retain a manually signed signature page or other document authenticating, acknowledging or otherwise adopting the signatures that appear in typed form within an electronic filing, to be made available to the Commission or its staff upon request for a period of five years. Further, the signature authorization must be executed before or at the time the electronic filing is made. These rules apply equally to powers of attorney and consents.

Modular Submissions and Segmented Filings. Two useful features of the EDGAR system include modular and segmented submissions. Modular submission allows EDGAR electronic mail/bulletin board subscribers to submit information intended to be used in more than one document into a nonpublic data storage area and then transfer the information into an official filing as desired. A segmented filing allows a filer to submit different segments of material from several geographic locations (using different transmission media, if desired). The filer then designates the order of presentation of the segments by submitting a "master segment" list. A segment may be used in only one EDGAR filing.

SEC 15100

Annual and Quarterly Reports to Security Holders. Registrants subject to proxy rules are currently required to provide the SEC with copies of annual reports to security holders. The EDGAR rules allow registrants to continue providing the SEC with paper copies of such reports. Alternatively, registrants may file this information electronically. Registrants may continue to incorporate by reference (in their Form 10-K filings) certain information included in their annual reports to shareholders. Only those portions of the annual report that are incorporated by reference need to be filed electronically.

Financial Data Schedules and Data Tagging. Financial data schedules required to be filed under the rules provide a valuable tool by which the SEC as well as the general public can analyze information. Data tagging, a feature of EDGAR that identifies specific information within a financial data schedule, allows the information to be extracted and used in various financial analyses, including financial ratios and comparisons with industry data. The financial data schedules are filed as an exhibit to the filing.

Graphic Material. Initially EDGAR cannot accommodate the electronic submission of graphic material. Under the rules, however, filers must list in an appendix any omitted graphic material and provide a fair and accurate description of the information presented.

Costs of Converting to and Maintaining EDGAR. As in implementing any new system, converting from the paper-based system to EDGAR entails some additional costs. For example:

- Registrants without the necessary equipment to file electronically have to either purchase such equipment or hire outside agents to submit filings on their behalf.

- Subscribers to the EDGAR electronic mail/bulletin board service, which allows for rapid electronic communications from the SEC, have to pay subscription fees.

- Those wishing to access the EDGAR data base for investment research or other purposes may choose to subscribe to services that supply this information. (Alternatively, they may use the free public reference rooms where EDGAR terminals are located.)

All users of the system will require technical and procedural training in its use. They may also need to consider the need for changes to company policies regarding security and other control matters.

SEC 15100

16000. "GOING PUBLIC"

16010. Introduction

The phrase "going public" denotes the process by which the securities of a privately owned company are sold to the public, as a result of which the company becomes publicly owned. The securities sold may be those belonging to the owners of the company, in which event the owners receive the proceeds (a "secondary offering"). On the other hand, the company may sell unissued shares to raise additional capital, in which case the company will receive the proceeds (a "primary offering"). Sometimes the offering may be a combination, partly for the account of shareholders and partly for the account of the company.

16020. Reasons for "Going Public"

Companies decide to "go public" for many different reasons. Some of these reasons follow:

Diversification by Owner. If the owner of a business has all or most of their wealth invested in the business, "going public" is one means by which he or she can sell part of their holdings and diversify. Often the owner will sell only a portion of their holdings and retain enough to keep control of the business.

Tax Planning. The owner of a business may be facing estate-planning problems. In the event of death, shares in the company may have to be disposed of by executors in order to provide funds for estate taxes; or the owner may want to dispose of a portion of their holdings during their lifetime in order to be in a more liquid position. Such a disposition is easier when there is an established market for the securities of the company. Also, when a company's shares are widely owned by the public, the problem of setting a value for estate tax purposes is minimized.

Liquidity. It is easier for the owner of the business or any other shareholder to borrow money with collateral consisting of securities that have an established market than with securities having no market.

Access to Long-Term Capital. While it is privately owned, a company may be severely restricted in its sources of capital. For the most part, the company expands by reinvesting its undistributed earnings or by looking to its owners for

SEC 16010

additional capital funds. The company can also look to banks and institutional lenders. For long-term or permanent capital, however, the company may decide its interests are best served by the sale of its securities to the public through underwriters. Furthermore, once the company and its securities are known to the investing public, succeeding issues of the company—assuming no adverse change in its affairs—become easier to market. Lending institutions often prefer borrowers that are publicly owned, since the market represents a potential source of additional equity capital. In the long run, this may have a beneficial effect on the company's credit position.

Subsequent Capital Needs. If a substantial block of securities is to be sold to the public by the owner of a business, the securities generally must be registered under the 1933 Act before they may be offered to the public. Once the company and its securities have gone through the SEC's registration process, succeeding issues will ordinarily be processed by the same group in the SEC. This procedure usually results in a reduction of the time required before the securities actually reach the market. Registered companies may also avail themselves of simplified filing forms when offering additional securities.

Expansion Through Business Combinations. When the company's securities have an established market, it is easier to negotiate mergers or acquisitions with other companies without using the company's cash resources. When privately owned or closely held companies want to merge, there is little they can do to demonstrate the value of the company except to exhibit their financial statements. With publicly held shares, there is less room for argument about the value of those shares, since the newspaper listings of quotations show the value that the investing public places on the shares. All other things being equal, the owners of a private company are often more interested in merging with a public company than with another private company because the shareholders may prefer to exchange their holdings for a marketable security.

Employee Benefit Plans and Incentives. When a company is publicly owned, it is possible to establish stock compensation arrangements that will serve as an inducement to attract and keep personnel. Stock option plans, for example, may be more attractive to officers and other key personnel than generous salary arrangements.

16030. Disadvantages of "Going Public"

There are some significant disadvantages associated with "going public," and the owner of a business should consider them before making a decision:

SEC 16030

Lack of Operating Confidentiality. The registration statement and subsequent reports to shareholders will require disclosure of many facets of the company's business, operations, and finances that may never before have been known outside the company. Some particularly sensitive areas of disclosure will be the compensation of executive officers and directors; the interests of insiders in certain transactions; the security holdings of officers, directors, and controlling stockholders; details regarding option plans and deferred compensation plans; and complete financial information, including sales, costs of sales, gross profit, net income, and cash flows.

Lack of Business Flexibility. Prior to "going public," the owner of the business can operate it independently. He or she can take whatever risks they wish to take, secure in the knowledge that it is only their own money that is at stake. Once the company becomes publicly owned, the owner acquires as many partners as he or she has shareholders, and the owner will be accountable to them. This may have a bearing on the risks that the business is able to take. An individual is often willing to risk their own capital—but not their partners'—in a new venture. Furthermore, the ability to act quickly may be lost if the venture is one that requires a vote of shareholders.

Initial Costs of Offering. The process of "going public" is expensive and time-consuming. The preparation of the registration document is a complicated process that occupies the time of many important people within the organization and several outside experts. Ordinarily, the documents must pass critical review by two sets of lawyers, and some of the financial statements must be audited by an independent public accountant. The printing bill alone in an undertaking of this kind is often quite substantial.

Cost of Public Reporting. After "going public," most companies become subject to the SEC's periodic reporting requirements, which are designed to keep the information in the registration statement up to date. These periodic reporting requirements are discussed in section 19500 of this manual.

SEC Regulation 14A deals with the solicitation of proxies. If proxies are solicited, shareholders must be furnished certain information in the form of a "proxy statement." The proxy and the proxy statement must be filed with the SEC before they can be used. Even if proxies are not solicited, the SEC requires companies to furnish to shareholders information substantially equivalent to what would be required if proxies were solicited. (Proxies and proxy statements are discussed in section 31000.) Significant additional costs will also be incurred in the amount of executive time devoted to shareholder relations and the preparation and filing with the SEC of other reports under the 1934 Act, such as Forms 10-K, 10-Q, and 8-K.

Demand for Dividends. The owner of a private company may have declared dividends sporadically, depending on their needs and in consideration of the sections of the Internal Revenue Code dealing with unreasonable accumulations of earnings. As a publicly owned company, however, the company may have to adopt a more regular dividend policy.

As investors in the enterprise, the public is entitled to look for a return on its investment. A dividend omission is apt to have a significant effect, not only on that return, but also on the market value of the investment itself. Thus, there is pressure on the directors of publicly owned companies to declare dividends. This type of pressure may not occur in a privately owned company.

Restrictions on Management. After the public offering, the officers, directors, and principal holders of the company's equity securities will, in all probability, become subject to the insider trading provisions in Section 16 of the 1934 Act. Such persons (officers, directors, and principal shareholders) must exercise caution in trading in the company's equity securities. Gains realized by them in closed transactions (purchase and sale or sale and purchase) within a six-month period may be recoverable by the company.

Possible Loss of Management Control. If a sufficiently large proportion of the shares are sold to the public, insiders may eventually lose control of the company. While the shares initially may be widely enough held to permit control with less than a majority of the voting stock, transfer of ownership of such shares to third parties would result in significant dilution of management control.

17000. PREPARATION AND FILING OF A REGISTRATION STATEMENT

17010. Introduction

The preparation and filing of a registration statement is a relatively complicated, time-consuming, technical process requiring substantial planning and coordination in order to provide the information specified by the SEC form being used and to comply with the applicable SEC rules in the most efficient manner possible. The following sections discuss those aspects of the process that are most germane to the independent accountant. The discussion presupposes the registration of securities by a company offering stock to the public for the first time, i.e., an initial public offering (IPO). While many of the considerations are applicable to the preparation of registration statements regardless of the nature of the offering, the procedures do vary with the form being

SEC 17010

used. The SEC has adopted a number of forms that, if applicable, simplify the registration process considerably. For example, as more fully discussed in sections 42250 and 42400, respectively, a registration of securities on Form S-3 or S-8 would generally involve only certain of the steps cited in the following sections.

17020. Preliminary Considerations

While all problems cannot be anticipated, two factors essential to the successful consummation of the registration must be considered by the independent accountant immediately on learning of his involvement in the process. Independent accountants must determine whether their relationship with the registrant will qualify them as independent under the rules of the SEC and whether at the conclusion of their audit their report is likely to be acceptable to the SEC.

17030. Qualifications of Accountants—Independence

17031. General. The subject of independence is fundamental to the accountant's involvement in an SEC filing. The SEC will not accept the report of an accountant who is not independent. The basic guidelines established by the SEC as to the independence of accountants are contained in Rule 2-01 of Regulation S-X. The rule provides that accountants will not be considered independent with respect to any company ("any person or any of its parents, its subsidiaries, or other affiliates") in which they or their firm or a member thereof has or had, during the period of their professional engagement to audit the financial statements or at the date of their report, (1) any direct or material indirect financial interest or (2) any connection as a promoter, underwriter, voting trustee, director, officer, or employee. The independence requirements with respect to any activity cited under (2) also extend to the period covered by the financial statements. The rule provides, however, that former employment by a client may not impair independence if certain conditions are met. Refer to section 50201 for the specific provisions of this rule.

Rule 2-01(b) indicates that the independence requirements apply not only to the accountant but also to the accountant's firm and any member thereof. The rule defines member as "(i) all partners, shareholders, and other principals in the firm, (ii) any professional employee involved in providing any professional service to the person, its parents, subsidiaries, or other affiliates, and (iii) any professional employee having managerial responsibilities and located in the engagement office or other office of the firm which participates in a significant portion of the audit."

17032. Financial Reporting Policies Relating to Independence Matters. Rule 2-01(c) of Regulation S-X states that "in determining whether an accountant may in fact be not independent with respect to a particular person, the Commission will give appropriate consideration to all relevant circumstances . . ." Accordingly, the SEC issued a number of ASRs that provide guidance as to its rulings and administrative determinations relating to the interpretation of Rule 2-01. FRP Section 602.02 was compiled from ASR Nos. 22, 47, 81, 112, 126, 234, 251, and 291 and was subsequently amended by FRR No. 10 to conform to the more limited application of Rule 2-01(b) resulting from a revised definition of the term "member." It outlines the general philosophy of the Commission regarding the definition of independence and includes examples based on specific cases to assist in the application of that definition.

As announced in FRR Nos. 4 and 33, letters requesting the staff's views on accountants' independence and staff's responses thereto are available to the public.

The Commission's concern regarding the independence of the "certifying" accountant stems from its overall objective to provide for the adequate and accurate disclosure to the public of all material facts. The concept of independence is fundamental to accomplishing that end, since it implies an objective analysis of the situation by a disinterested third party. In that connection, the Commission has set the following guidelines (originally included in ASR Nos. 47 and 126):

- The question of independence is one of fact to be determined in the light of all the pertinent circumstances in a particular case. The existence of certain types of relationships between a registrant and the accountant might impair the accountant's objectivity and bias his judgment on accounting and auditing matters.

- Independence is a matter of appearance, in addition to being a question of fact. The appearance of independence requires that the perception of the relationship between the accountant and his or her client must be free of any interest that, whatever its actual effect, might be considered incompatible with the objectivity needed to perform professional responsibilities with impartial judgment, so that the public could not assume a lack of independence.

In addition to setting general definitions and basic guidelines to be used when dealing with the issue of independence, the Commission has published a compilation of situations that are based on specific cases and rulings regarding this issue. Certain of the more significant conditions found by the Commission to be indicative of a lack of independence, as discussed in FRP Section 602.02, include:

- Direct and material indirect financial interests in the registrant by the accountant, their spouse, or any other person under their supervision and control.

- Direct and material indirect business relationships, other than as a customer in the regular course of business.

SEC 17032

- Certain family relationships between the accountant or a member of their firm and the registrant.

- Accounting services rendered by the accountant by maintaining the records of the registrant either manually or through electronic data processing equipment.

- Funds due from the registrant to the accountant (an accountant may lack independence as a result of unpaid prior professional fees).

- Concurrent occupations of the accountant that conflict with the interests of the registrant (e.g., acting as a counselor or broker-dealer or being in direct competition with the registrant).

- Litigation creating an adversary position between a registrant and the accountant.

The SEC has stated (FRP Section 602.02.c.iii) that under certain circumstances it would not object if a domestic accounting firm or an associated foreign firm performed limited, routine, or ministerial bookkeeping services for a foreign division, subsidiary, or investee of a domestic registrant that is a client of that firm. However, there are certain conditions that must be met before these services can be performed and there is a materiality limit on the extent of such services.

The SEC has also adopted a number of disclosure requirements with respect to the relationship between registrants and their independent accountants. Such requirements (FRP Section 603) are now part of the instructions to Regulation S-X, Form 8-K, and the proxy rules. The disclosures required to be included in Form 8-K and in proxy and information statements are discussed in sections 41600 and 31200 of this manual, respectively.

17033. Comparison with AICPA and State Independence Rules. Other rules regarding independence include those developed by the AICPA (Rule 101 of the Code of Professional Conduct and related interpretations and rulings) and by state accounting statutes. The SEC rules are more restrictive than those established by the AICPA; the most significant differences are the SEC's prohibition against performing record-keeping services for clients, certain matters regarding litigation, and additional limitations on business relationships.

17034. Independence and Prospective Financial Information. It is the staff's informal position that when an accountant has assisted in the preparation of prospective financial information for a privately held company that subsequently becomes a registrant, the accountant's independence is impaired for the period during which the forecast or projection is being relied on. In the staff's view, this period would normally not be less than the first 12-month period included in the prospective financial information. The staff may grant relief in a situation of this nature when changes in the registrant's business environment or the general economy support a conclusion that the forecast or projection is no longer being relied on. If the accountant has examined the prospective financial information and does not assist in its preparation, independence is not considered to be impaired.

17040. The Accountants' Report

Rule 2-02 of Regulation S-X (included in section 20210) contains the requirements of the SEC with respect to the accountants' report. Early in the planning period of the registration process a preliminary evaluation must be made as to whether the independent accountants' report will follow the standard format prescribed in AU Section 508.08 or whether a departure from the standard format (AU Section 508.11 and 508.38) will be necessary when reporting on the financial statements to be included in a 1933 Act registration statement. This determination, which invariably must be reexamined during the registration process, is of utmost importance, since the report ultimately issued may be unacceptable to the SEC. The SEC, for example, will generally not accept an accountants' report that is qualified as a result of limitations on the scope of the audit, departures from generally accepted accounting principles, or inadequacy of disclosures. Adverse opinions and disclaimers of opinion are also unacceptable to the SEC. Section 20200 of this manual discusses more fully the various considerations that must be given to the accountants' report.

17050. Organizational Conference

As soon as it has been determined that a public offering of securities will take place, a meeting with the following persons is generally arranged:

- A financial officer of the company (registrant).

- Counsel for the company.

- A representative of the underwriters.

- Counsel for the underwriters.

- The independent accountant.

This group generally constitutes the registration team. The responsibilities of each member of the team are described in section 17080. Matters that may be discussed at the organizational conference include the nature of the offering, the SEC registration form to use (section 17060), the anticipated filing date (section 17130), and a detailed timetable for the registration process that identifies the duties to be performed by each member of the team during the registration process. An illustrative timetable is included in section 17070. Should a conference with the SEC be necessary prior to filing the registration statement, this might also be discussed at the organizational meeting. For a discussion of prefiling conferences with the SEC, refer to section 17120.

The individual in the company with the primary responsibility for the registration process normally arranges the organizational meeting.

17060. Decision as to Registration Form Required

The determination of the SEC form to be used for registration purposes must be made before preparation of the registration statement commences. (Descriptions of the principal 1933 and 1934 Act forms presently in effect are included in this manual in section 40100.) This is a legal determination and is made by the company in consultation with its counsel. The independent accountant should not make the decision.

17070. The Timetable

A timetable is generally prepared before preparation of the registration statement commences. The timetable outlines the detailed steps required to complete the proposed offering and indicates the dates on which they are to be completed. The independent public accountants play an important part in the registration process and should therefore actively participate in the development of the timetable particularly with respect to dates that are of significance to them, such as:

- The date on which the information will be submitted to the printer.

- The date on which it is proposed that the registration statement will initially be filed.

- The date on which the SEC's comments are expected to be received.

- The date on which it is expected that the registration statement will become effective.

- The closing date.

The timetable is generally prepared by company counsel after obtaining the necessary input from the independent accountants and other members of the registration team. If the accountants are not consulted in connection with the preparation of the timetable, they should determine early in the registration process whether the target dates for which they are responsible are attainable.

An example of a timetable for an initial registration of common stock under the 1933 Act is included in this section. It does not include all of the steps in the registration process; e.g., proxy solicitation and blue sky matters have been excluded. A time schedule is, of course, an estimate, and the actual dates of completion may vary from the original estimate. The time required for a seasoned public company to complete the registration process is considerably shorter and more readily estimable than that for a company registering securities for the first time. In addition to the registration time schedule, the presentation below identifies the general responsibilities for the completion of the various steps in the registration process. While the responsibility for many of the steps is noted as that of registrant's counsel, a prospective registrant may be able to perform certain of these functions using its internal legal department. This timetable is primarily intended to demonstrate the general sequence of events. It should not be viewed as necessarily indicative of other situations, since timetables vary, as do individual registrants and offerings.

Date	Description of Procedure	General Responsibility
April 20	Hold board of directors meeting to authorize:	Registrant
	Issuance of additional amount of stock to be offered.	
	Preparation of registration statement for filing with SEC.	
	Negotiation of underwriting agreement.	
April 25	Hold organizational meeting to discuss preparation of registration statement.	All parties
April 26	Begin drafting registration statement.	Registrant and counsel
April 30	Complete and distribute timetable for registration process.	Registrant's counsel
May 10	Distribute first draft of underwriting agreement for review.	Underwriters' counsel
May 15	Distribute questionnaires to directors and officers covering matters relating to registration requirements.	Registrant's counsel
May 20	Distribute first draft of textual portion of registration statement for review.	Registrant and counsel

Date	Description of Procedure	General Responsibility
May 25	Submit draft of financial statements to be included in registration statement.	Registrant and independent accountant
May 27	Review draft of registration statement.	All parties
June 1	Send complete draft of registration statement to printer.	Registrant or counsel
June 10	Approve and submit final audited financial statements and related report for inclusion in registration statement.	Independent accountant
June 12-22	Receive and correct first printed proofs of registration statement.	All parties
	Distribute proof of registration statement to directors and officers.	Registrant or counsel
	Send revised draft of registration statement to printer.	Registrant or counsel
June 23	Hold board of directors meeting to approve and sign registration statement.	Registrant
June 24	File registration statement with SEC.	Registrant's counsel
	File listing application with stock exchange for common stock to be offered.	Registrant and counsel
	Distribute preliminary ("red herring") prospectus.	Underwriters
July 15	Receive letter of comment from SEC regarding registration statement.	Registrant and counsel
July 16	Hold meeting to discuss letter of comment.	All parties
July 19	Complete draft of first amendment of registration statement and send to printer.	Registrant and counsel
July 20-21	Review printer's proof of amendment to registration statement.	All parties
	Send corrected proof to printer.	Registrant's counsel

SEC 17070

Date	Description of Procedure	General Responsibility
July 22	File amendment to registration statement to cover SEC comments and to reflect any material developments since initial filing on June 24.	Registrant and counsel
	Notify SEC in writing that a final (price) amendment will be filed on August 2 and that the company requests "acceleration" in order that the registration statement may become effective as of the close of business on that date.	Registrant or counsel
	Receive approval from stock exchange of listing application subject to official notice of issuance and subject to effectiveness of registration statement.	Registrant and counsel
July 27	Resolve any final comments and changes with SEC by telephone.	Registrant and counsel
July 29	Hold due diligence meeting.	All parties
August 1	Finalize offering price.	Registrant and underwriters
August 2	Deliver first comfort letter to underwriters.	Independent accountant
	Sign underwriting agreement.	Registrant and underwriters
	File amendment to registration statement identifying price.	Registrant and counsel
	Receive notification that registration statement has become effective.	Registrant and counsel
	Notify stock exchange of effectiveness.	Registrant or counsel
August 7	Deliver second comfort letter to underwriters.	Independent accountant
	Complete settlement with underwriters — closing date.	Registrant, registrant's counsel, underwriters and underwriters' counsel

17080. The Registration Team

The preparation of the information to be included in a registration statement is a combined effort by the company (registrant), company counsel, the underwriters, counsel for the underwriters, and the independent accountants. Company counsel generally functions as the coordinator of the registration team.

17081. The Company. The company's participation in the process of preparing the textual portion of a registration statement frequently depends on the expertise of its personnel. Some companies have personnel who are able to prepare substantially all of the first draft of the registration statement. More typically, however, company personnel rely heavily upon outside counsel to direct the preparation of the narrative portion of the document. Company personnel should, however, be prepared to promptly provide the underlying information to the persons involved in the preparation of the registration statement and to be *actively* involved in all aspects of the registration process. Independent accountants are also frequently asked to assist company personnel in the process of assembling the required financial information. In all instances, however, the preparation of the original material must be the responsibility of company personnel. When meetings are held by members of the registration team during the process of preparing the registration statement, a representative of the company should always be present.

17082. Counsel for the Company. Counsel for the company is the key member of the registration team. Their competence and familiarity with the registration process are critical to the timely and effective coordination of the engagement. They advise the company with respect to compliance with the provisions of the securities acts and the various state and other federal laws to which the company and the offering will become subject. They coordinate the progress of the various members of the registration team and ensure the timeliness and completeness of the document. Counsel also coordinates the resolution of any questions arising from the SEC review (as discussed in section 19010) and the filing of the necessary amendments (as discussed in section 19020). Should any conferences with the staff of the SEC be necessary with respect to matters unrelated to the financial statements, they usually accompany the company's representatives.

17083. The Underwriter. The principal role of the underwriter is to sell the securities to the public. However, prior to that time the underwriter plays a significant role in advising the company on the opportunities for financing and in structuring the transaction. In agreeing to underwrite the offering, the underwriter will propose one of the following types of agreements:

- *Best efforts.* The underwriter agrees to use its best effort to sell the issue but is not obligated to purchase unsold securities.

- *Best efforts, all or none.* The offering is canceled if the underwriter is unable to sell the entire issue.

- *Firm commitment.* The underwriter agrees to buy all of the issue and thereby assumes the risk for any unsold securities.

A draft of the underwriting agreement is frequently prepared early in the registration process, even though the document is generally not signed until the morning on which the offering becomes effective. The independent accountant should request a copy of this draft, as well as the letter of intent, as soon as it becomes available.

The letter of intent, which outlines the proposed terms of the offering, is generally prepared by the managing underwriter. It is so called because it acknowledges the intent of the underwriter to execute an underwriting agreement when the registration process is complete. The letter of intent permits either party to reassess the potential of the offering prior to executing the underwriting agreement. Consequently, it is not a binding agreement to underwrite the offering but rather a preliminary understanding as to the terms of the offering, the underwriter's compensation, and any reimbursement of expenses that will be incurred by the underwriter. The draft of the underwriting agreement will generally outline the accountant's responsibility in connection with the closing of the transaction. The underwriting agreement will invariably provide for the accountant to furnish a comfort letter to the underwriter on or before the effective date and the closing date, and it is important that the accountant determine early in the process the type of letter expected and the specific matters on which the accountant is expected to comment. (For further discussion of comfort letters, see section 17095.) The underwriter and the company negotiate the offering price of the securities when the underwriting agreement is signed. The offering price is based on the prevailing market conditions at the time of the offering and certain other factors, such as the company's earnings history and its earnings potential. If the company has a similar class of securities that is traded, the market price of these securities on the date the underwriting agreement is signed will be a factor in determining the offering price of the new issue.

Subsequent to the closing date and the sale of the securities, the underwriter will generally provide support for the company's securities in the market after the offering takes place. However, there are strict rules governing the extent to which the underwriter may provide this support.

17084. Counsel for the Underwriter. Counsel for the underwriter is generally responsible for drafting the underwriting agreement. They also review the entire registration statement and any related agreements and contracts that are filed as exhibits thereto. Their principal objective in reviewing the registration statement is to ascertain on behalf of the underwriter that the registration statement is complete and not misleading. (See also section 19040 for a discussion of the due diligence meeting.)

17090. The Role of the Independent Accountant in the Registration Process

17091. General. The independent accountant's principal responsibilities in connection with the preparation of a registration statement are:

- Expressing an opinion on the various financial statements that they have audited and that will be included in the document.

- Reading in depth the textual portion of the registration statement and related financial information included in the text to the financial statements and comparing it to information gathered in the course of the audit in order to ascertain any inconsistencies that may necessitate changes to the financial statements. The reading may also reveal inconsistencies and give rise to other issues that necessitate changes to the nonfinancial statement portions of the registration statement.

- Issuing a comfort letter to underwriters.

- Organizing and participating in any prefiling meetings with the SEC involving the financial statements or related financial disclosures.

- Assisting in the resolution of comments raised by the SEC staff in its review of the financial information included in the document (see section 17092).

If the registration relates to a new issue of funded debt or preferred stock, the independent accountant will also read the underlying indenture or charter provisions before the documents are finalized. This reading is performed in order to determine whether the accountant will be required to issue an opinion letter or other special report based on the provisions of the documents and what the required language of such opinion letter or other special report will be. The sections that follow discuss the foregoing responsibilities in more detail.

17092. Reporting on the Financial Statements. The principal function of the independent accountant in the registration process is to audit the financial statements and supporting schedules that are included in the document to ascertain whether they conform to generally accepted accounting principles and to furnish a report thereon. Accountants must also extend their audit to ascertain that the financial statements and

54

schedules included in the registration statement are in compliance with Regulation S-X and the instructions to the form being filed. As is further discussed in section 19050, their responsibilities with respect to the financial statements in a 1933 Act filing do not end on the date of their report, but extend to the effective date of the registration statement.

In addition to signing the report, independent accountants must also consent in writing to the use of their report and to any references in the registration statement to their firm. See sections 17110 and 20500 for further discussion of the accountants' consent.

17093. Reading the Text and Cross-Referencing the Textual Disclosures. Although independent accountants participating in the preparation of a registration statement are concerned primarily with the financial statements to which their report relates, it is essential that they carefully read the entire registration statement, not merely the financial data.

It is important to note that the textual portions of the registration statement are the responsibility of the registrant and its general counsel, not the independent accountant. However, the independent accountant may be requested by the underwriter to provide a "comfort letter" including procedures performed on the textual portions of the registration statement (see section 20605).

Another principal reason for reading the text is to determine that the representations in the text or narrative portion of the registration statement do not conflict with the financial statement disclosures or other financial sections. If conflicts exist, they must be resolved. There are a number of sections of the text that may have a direct bearing on the financial statements, and the representations in the document should confirm the results of the accountant's independent inquiry in the course of his audit. Such sections may include those dealing with material pending legal proceedings, the securities being registered, the capital structure of the registrant, the description of affiliated relationships, and any other matters that the accountants have dealt with in the course of their audit.

A further reason for reading the text is the contribution that the accountants can make to the registration statement. There are few persons connected with the registration process that are as familiar with the company and its business as the independent public accountant. During the course of an audit, the accountant acquires a substantial amount of information about the company, its plants, products, manufacturing processes and problems, labor situation, distribution problems, capital needs, and similar matters. Since this type of information makes up a substantial portion of the registration statement, the independent accountant is often in a position to make meaningful, constructive, and objective suggestions. Counsel is generally very receptive to suggestions made by accountants to improve the content of the document or the representations made. In the interest of reducing repetition within the prospectus, disclosures required in the footnotes to the financial statements may be complied with by incorporating that section of the text in which the same subject matter is discussed. Similarly, repetition in the text may be avoided by cross-referencing to disclosures in the financial statements. This is emphasized in the general instructions to the respective registration forms. The following quotation is representative of the wording in several registration forms:

> Unless clearly indicated otherwise, information set forth in any part of the prospectus need not be duplicated elsewhere in the prospectus. Where it is deemed necessary or desirable to call attention to such information in more than one part of the prospectus, this may be accomplished by appropriate cross-reference. In lieu of restating information in the form of notes to the financial statements, references should be made to other parts of the prospectus where such information is set forth.

Cross-referencing is frequently used in the disclosure of contingencies such as pending litigation. Since the text is required to include a detailed recitation of material legal proceedings, the disclosure of legal proceedings against the company in the notes to the financial statements may be cross-referenced to the applicable section of the text.

Textual material incorporated into the footnotes to the financial statements should be identified by a separate heading or subheading, or presented in a separate paragraph. When considered a part of the audited financial statements, textual information is also covered by the accountants' report. Consequently, care must be taken to ensure that the matters discussed in the text to which appropriate auditing procedures have been applied contain no ambiguities and that the portion of the text covered by the auditors' report is clearly identifiable.

17094. Reading the Indenture. If a registration statement relates to a new issue of funded debt, a new indenture is generally in the drafting process at the same time that the registration statement is being prepared. This indenture will recite the details of certain agreements (called covenants) that the borrowing company enters into as a condition for borrowing the money. In other situations, the financing may relate to a new issue of stock, the terms of which may be governed by an amendment to the company's certificate of incorporation.

If the accountants continue to serve the company, the provisions of these instruments may require their future involvement. Indentures and charters frequently contain provisions relating to the payment of dividends on preferred and common stocks and may limit payment based on earnings or working capital. Indentures sometimes provide for independent accountants to report on certain calculations, such as the amount of retained earnings available for dividends based (for example) on earnings, distributions, and working capital. Indentures sometimes contain a requirement for a letter from independent accountants concerning their knowledge of defaults by the company with respect to the indenture provisions. If the provisions of an indenture or charter amendment will require the accountants to provide an opinion letter or other special report in the future, they would be particularly well advised to review the required language of such opinion letters or reports before the requirements are finalized.

17095. Comfort Letters. Independent accountants should obtain and review a draft of the underwriting agreement as soon as it becomes available. At the time of the initial filing of the registration statement, the agreement is generally tentative and unsigned. It is ordinarily finalized and executed shortly before the public offering date of the securities to which the registration statement relates. Accountants, however, should not wait until the underwriting agreement is signed before reviewing its provisions. When the draft is prepared, there is usually agreement in principle as to what is expected of all parties to the agreement, and accountants can generally work with this draft. The principal omissions in the draft relate to price, interest or dividend rate, redemption prices, and matters that have no direct impact on independent accountants. The major reason for reading the draft of the underwriting agreement is to become familiar with the comfort letter provisions of the agreement, which generally specify the type of comfort letter to be furnished to the underwriter by the independent accountants.

Underwriters and their counsel typically request comfort from independent accountants who audit the financial statements on information that appears in the registration statement outside of the financial statements. As a result, the draft underwriting agreement may require the accountants to review and report on matters that are beyond the scope of their annual audit or beyond the area of their expertise. It is therefore important that independent accountants and the underwriter reach agreement as to the specific items to be included in the comfort letter as early as possible in the registration process, so the draft underwriting agreement can be revised accordingly and the accountants can plan their work. The necessary revisions in the provisions of this agreement that affect the accountants can usually be accomplished when it is in draft form; however, it is awkward to effect such changes after the agreement is finalized and signed. Letters for underwriters (or comfort letters) are discussed in section 20605 of this manual.

17100. Reference to Independent Accountants as Experts

As discussed in section 12020, the 1933 Act imposes liabilities for false or misleading statements in a registration statement filed under the Act. However, the Act provides that this liability may not exist, except as to the issuer, with respect to information included in any part of the registration statement that is purported to be included "on the authority of an expert" (Section 11(b)(3)(B)). Although there is no SEC requirement calling for the inclusion of an expert's section, because of the protection afforded to officers, directors, and underwriters by this provision, lawyers for the company and the underwriters usually request the insertion of language in the prospectus and the registration statement to specify that the audited financial statements and supporting schedules are included in reliance on the report of the independent accountants as "experts."

The wording used in a registration statement to refer to the independent accountants as experts needs to be reviewed to ensure that the language used does not impute to the independent accountants responsibility for financial data that they do not intend to assume. See section 20400 for further discussion of the reference to independent accountants as experts.

17110. The Consent

At least one copy of each document filed with the SEC must contain manual signatures, and, consequently, the independent accountants will be asked to manually sign their report prior to the filing. (Copies not containing manual signatures identify the signer in print and are referred to as conformed copies.) In addition, the accountants must also consent to any references to their firm as experts. The consent must be dated and signed manually and included in Part II of the registration statement. Any changes to the financial data covered by the accountants' report that occur between the initial 1933 Act filing and the filing of an amendment will require the inclusion in the amendment of a new manually signed consent under a new and more current date.

Consents are required pursuant to Section 7 of the 1933 Act, which reads as follows:

> ... If any accountant, engineer, or appraiser, or any person whose profession gives authority to a statement made by him, is named as having prepared or certified any part of the registration statement, or is named as having prepared or certified a report or valuation for use in connection with the registration statement, the written consent of such person shall be filed with the registration statement.

The SEC will consider an application to dispense with the consent requirement in certain limited circumstances in which obtaining the consent would be impractical or would result in undue hardship on the part of the registrant (see Rule 437 under the 1933 Act). However, these situations are unusual, and the application establishing the grounds for the waiver must be submitted to the SEC prior to the effective date of the registration statement.

Consents are generally not required in connection with 1934 Act filings unless:

- The accountants' report in the document is being incorporated by reference into a currently effective 1933 Act registration statement (e.g., Forms S-3 and S-8).

- The accountants' report included in a document filed under another of the acts administered by the SEC is being incorporated by reference. For example, if a company filing a Form 10-K were to incorporate by reference the accountants' report and financial statements contained in a Form S-1.

- Audited financial information previously included in a 1934 Act filing is being amended.

A consent is not required in a document filed under the 1934 Act when financial information is being incorporated by reference from another 1934 Act filing or when financial statements are incorporated by reference in Form 10-K from the annual report to shareholders (see section 41171).

Refer to section 20500 for further discussion and examples of consents.

17120. Prefiling Conferences with the SEC

A prefiling conference is recommended whenever important accounting or auditing problems need to be resolved in advance of the filing. The prefiling conference enables the issuer and their accountants to obtain the views of the staff of the SEC on a particular problem at an early date, and in that connection also affords the staff an opportunity to become familiar with the issue. The staff may, for example, ask questions and thereby elicit more background information than is usually available from the financial statements or the accountants' report. Reviewing unique issues in advance should normally speed up the review process and avoid any last-minute delays. The staff of the SEC has indicated that as a general rule prefiling conferences should be limited to novel and unique accounting and reporting issues.

Arrangements for a conference on accounting or auditing matters are generally made by the registrant with the Chief Accountant of the Division of Corporation Finance. However, if a new or controversial issue is involved that requires the views of the Chief Accountant of the Commission, it may be suggested that conference arrangements be made directly with the Office of the Chief Accountant of the Commission. Sometimes requests for a review of interpretations made at the Division level may be directed to the Chief Accountant of the Commission. If the positions taken by the staff in conference at the Division level or at the Office of the Chief Accountant are in conflict with those expressed by the registrant, the company may appeal the issue directly to the Commission. Appeals to the Commission with respect to accounting or auditing issues are extremely unusual. Such appeals have been made, however, in those situations where a registrant wished to pursue the matter in view of its significance.

Guidance as to the organization and conduct of prefiling as well as other meetings with the SEC staff is discussed in the section that follows.

17121. How to Organize and Conduct a Meeting with the SEC Staff

For a variety of reasons, a registrant or a prospective registrant and/or its outside counsel may decide that a meeting with the SEC staff to address particular accounting or reporting issues is desirable. Before agreeing to participate in (or arrange) such a meeting, it is advisable for the independent accountant to carefully consider whether:

- Instead of a meeting, a written submission, possibly followed up by a phone call, might be a more efficient approach to resolving the issue in question.

- The issue is of sufficient magnitude to merit a meeting with the SEC staff.

- Their firm has taken a prior position on the issue in other registrant situations.

- All information available concerning the SEC staff's formal *and informal* positions previously taken on the issue in question has been identified and appropriately considered.

- The issue should be directed primarily to the Office of the Chief Accountant or the Division of Corporation Finance (see section 17120).

Arranging the Meeting

If, after considering the factors described above, it is determined that a meeting with the SEC staff should be arranged, a formal appointment should be made for such purpose. The person to be contacted at the SEC depends on the assessment as to whether the issue involved should be directed primarily to the Office of the Chief Accountant or the Division of Corporation Finance. If in doubt, the Chief Accountant of the Division of Corporation Finance is generally an acceptable starting point. The call to the SEC to arrange the meeting may be made by the registrant, outside counsel, or a representative of the independent accounting firm.

The decision as to who will attend the meeting on behalf of the registrant is important, and depends entirely on the nature of the issue involved. In virtually all cases, the principal financial officer of the company or their designee should be present, together with the engagement partner from the company's independent accounting firm. Others who may be present include a technical consulting partner from the accounting firm's national office and, particularly in the case of an IPO, a representative of the company's outside law firm. It is important that the group include all persons who can effectively contribute to the presentation and resolution of the issue involved. However, a group of no more than six persons generally tends to be most efficient. If all of the issues to be discussed are accounting or reporting related, the SEC staff generally expects that the key participants in the meeting will be the company's internal and external accountants. As more fully discussed below, it is important that all parties clearly understand prior to the meeting that it is generally advisable for the registrant rather than the independent accountant to lead the discussion with the SEC staff.

The next step in the process is to prepare a letter to the SEC staff outlining the issue to be discussed at the meeting.

Written Submission Prior to Meeting

As a general rule, the SEC staff will require that a written submission be furnished in advance of the meeting. This submission will enable the staff to consider, and possibly discuss among themselves, the principal issue(s) in advance of the meeting and to determine which staff members should attend the meeting. In general, a comprehensive written submission will enhance the likelihood that the staff will be sufficiently prepared to meaningfully address, and possibly provide a final resolution of the issue in question during the course of the meeting.

While the written summary should generally be developed by the registrant, it is advisable that the independent accountant review it prior to its submission to the SEC to ensure that:

- The issue to be discussed is clearly explained, and supported by sufficient background information.

- Reference is made to all relevant sources of guidance material on the issue in the professional literature. The most effective type of presentation for this purpose is one that cites literature supporting arguments on both sides of a particular issue, with a clear explanation as to why the registrant believes that their preferred position gives rise to the preferable answer.

- To the extent the views of the independent accountant are set forth, they are properly characterized.

- The overall tone of the letter is appropriate.

Role of Independent Accountant at Meeting

The role played by the independent accountant at a meeting with the SEC staff will vary considerably, depending on the nature of the issue in question. As a general rule, especially when the issue involves a registrant-specific transaction, it is preferable for the registrant to lead the discussion with the independent accountant functioning in a support capacity reinforcing and, where necessary, clarifying the technical points made by the registrant. However, if the issue is a general accounting question (e.g., tainted treasury shares in a proposed pooling transaction), then it may be appropriate for the independent accountant to lead the discussion.

In any event, the SEC staff will generally be interested in obtaining a clear understanding of the independent accountant's position on the issue in question during the course of the meeting. In general, it is difficult for a registrant to prevail on a particular accounting issue if the SEC staff is not satisfied that its independent accountants are supportive of the position being taken.

Organizational Session Prior to Meeting

It is essential that the entire group of individuals that will participate in a meeting with the SEC staff participate in a preparatory meeting for organizational purposes. In an IPO situation, organizational meetings of this nature may take place at the offices of the registrant's outside counsel. In other situations, such meetings are frequently held at the Washington, D.C. office of the independent accountants. Among the objectives of such organizational meetings are to:

- Develop a detailed agenda for the meeting.

- Ensure that all parties are aware of the protocol for the meeting and who the participating SEC staff members are likely to be.

- Ensure that all parties to the discussion are fully informed as to the issue to be covered and the overall objectives of the meeting.

- Arrange who will lead the discussion and who will make any necessary introductions.

- Arrange who will be the principal speaker on each agenda point.

- Attempt to anticipate potential staff inquiries, and to develop appropriate responses thereto.

- Develop potential alternatives, or "fall back" positions, on key issues, where applicable.

In summary, the purpose of the organizational session is to ensure that the meeting with the SEC staff is conducted in the most organized and efficient manner possible.

SEC 17121

Other Points to Consider in Preparing for Meeting

In preparing for a meeting with the SEC staff, the following additional points are particularly worthy of consideration:

- The SEC staff is concerned about creating precedent for a particular accounting treatment or disclosure approach. The SEC staff may be more inclined to accept a position on a particular issue that departs from what may be viewed as a literal interpretation of the rules if the registrant can demonstrate that very few, if any, other registrants are likely to have the same unique fact pattern.

- If a disclosure issue is involved, a registrant will often find the SEC staff receptive to considering the inclusion of information other than that which is technically called for by the SEC rules if it can be demonstrated that this information:

  - Is more meaningful to users of the financial statements.

  - Complies with the spirit and/or intent of the technical requirements.

- Where possible, offering alternatives tends to be far more effective in dealing with the SEC staff than merely indicating that compliance with a particular disclosure requirement is impossible.

- The SEC staff may not be prepared to provide a final answer to the issue raised at the meeting. Often the SEC staff will need more time to discuss the issue further among themselves before conveying their position. In such cases, the SEC staff needs to have a clear understanding as to where inquiries may be directed for further information on any of the issues discussed at the meeting.

Confirming Letter Subsequent to Meeting

Subsequent to a meeting with the SEC staff, it is essential that a letter be prepared immediately, outlining the matters discussed and the decisions reached. It is advisable that the independent accountant review this letter prior to its submission by the registrant. The letter should be sent to the appropriate member of the SEC staff with a request that he or she confirm that his/her understanding of the facts and decisions reached is consistent with that of the registrant as set forth in the letter.

The transmittal letter accompanying any registration statement filed subsequent to a meeting with the SEC should make reference to any issue addressed at the prefiling meeting and copies of relevant correspondence relating thereto should be furnished.

SEC 17121

Summary

In summary, the principal factors to be considered in organizing and conducting a successful meeting with the SEC staff are:

- Assembling the appropriate team of professionals to participate in the meeting.

- Developing a comprehensive written submission to the staff prior to the meeting.

- Careful planning and coordination in advance of the meeting.

- Clearly articulating at the meeting the support for all positions taken and responding in an informed manner to any staff inquiries.

17130. The Filing Date

When the registration statement has been completed, an executed copy of the document, together with the specified number of conformed copies and exhibits, is mailed or delivered to the principal office of the SEC in Washington, D.C. The date on which the complete registration statement is received by the SEC is considered to be the filing date. Each amendment creates a new filing date.

18000. THE SEC REVIEW PROCESS

18010. General

Registration statements and reports filed under the 1933 and 1934 Acts are processed by the Division of Corporation Finance. Each filing is assigned to a branch headed by a branch chief. If the issuer is a registrant who has previously filed with the SEC, the filing will be assigned to the branch of the Division of Corporation Finance responsible for handling the company's filings. If the company has not previously filed with the SEC, the filing is assigned to the branch of the Division that reviews filings of companies in the same industry group. (See section 13031 for a discussion of the Division of Corporation Finance.)

18020. Selective Review System

The Division of Corporation Finance uses a selective review system to reduce delays in processing registration statements and periodic reports and to employ available staff resources more efficiently. Under this selective review system, each filed document is either subjected to a review, or not reviewed at all. The review can either be thorough or financial in nature. A financial review involves the financial statements and the other nonlegal portions of the filed document. As a general rule, registration statements filed by all issuers offering securities to the public for the first time are subjected to a thorough review. Subsequent registration statements and periodic reporting documents filed by public companies are reviewed on a selective basis.

The decision as to whether to review a registration statement or report and the type of review to be performed is made by the SEC staff after the document is filed and cannot be predetermined by the registrant. While the backlog of unprocessed filings may influence the review decision, other factors, such as the size and nature of the company, the industry in which it operates, the frequency of its security offerings, trends in the company's key financial ratios, and the nature of the filing, may also be considerations. The review decision expected to be made by the SEC staff in connection with a particular filing should, therefore, have no bearing on the procedures followed in preparing and reviewing the document to be filed.

If the SEC staff determines that no review of a registration statement will be performed, the registrant will be notified of that fact promptly after the filing date.

The representation letters from accountants acknowledging awareness of their statutory responsibilities that were formerly requested by the SEC staff in connection with the performance of what were formerly known as cursory and summary reviews are no longer required.

18030. Review Procedures and Letters of Comment

Registration statements filed by first-time issuers invariably are subjected to review by branch personnel. The staff specialists assigned to review the document generally include an accountant and an examiner (a lawyer, typically, or a financial analyst). The group may also consult with other SEC staff experts (such as mining engineers or petroleum engineers) within the Division or with other departments of the government. The SEC staff reviews the documents filed to determine whether there has been full and fair disclosure, particularly whether the document contains any untrue or misleading statements of material facts or whether there are omissions of material facts. However, the SEC review cannot be relied on for assurance as to the accuracy of the filing, and no comfort should be derived from the fact that such a review has been performed.

As a general rule, review of the financial data in a document filed with the SEC is performed by a branch accountant, who will typically read the entire prospectus and the remainder of the registration statement to become familiar with the company and its business. The accountant may also refer to published annual and interim reports and newspaper articles for information regarding the company and its industry. The accountant's review is primarily directed toward the financial statements and other financial data and the independent accountants' report, to determine whether they comply with the requirements of Regulation S-X, the Financial Reporting Policies, and the applicable pronouncements of the AICPA and the FASB, as well as with the various SEC staff interpretations (including SABs) and policies dealing with accounting and auditing issues.

Although Section 8(b) of the 1933 Act contemplates a review of registration statements filed with the SEC, the Act does not specify the review procedures to be followed by the SEC in connection with the processing of these documents. The "informal" procedures followed have been developed by the SEC to make the comments resulting from the review available to registrants and to permit necessary revisions of a registration statement without formal proceedings. The informal comment technique has proven to be an effective method of communicating and resolving issues before permitting a registration statement to become effective.

In connection with the review of a registration statement filed by a first-time issuer, the assigned branch chief of the Division of Corporation Finance, in collaboration with their group, generally drafts a letter of comment to be sent to the registrant. The letter sets forth the points noted in the review. It is signed by the branch chief and mailed to the person (usually company counsel) designated in the registration statement to receive notices from the SEC. The letter contains all of the comments, criticisms, and suggestions resulting from the review by the staff. Such letters were formerly known as deficiency letters, but because of the unintended stigma attached to this term, they came to be referred to as letters of comment, which is more descriptive of their character.

To conserve time in the registration process, company counsel generally maintains close contact with the staff of the SEC during the period that the registration statement is being reviewed. Counsel often arranges to receive SEC staff comments by telephone or fax to expedite preparation of the required amendment and/or responses. While not unprecedented, it is rare that a formal letter of comment is not issued.

As a general rule, the staff expects registrants to prepare a written response to a letter of comment detailing the proposed action to be taken on each point and providing the supplemental information requested. Between the time that comments are received and the written response and amended filing are submitted, communication with the SEC staff should generally be limited to requests for clarification of comments raised.

In the case of a carefully prepared document, the comments of the SEC staff are usually relatively few in number and minor in character. Whether the comments are few or many, however, each must be addressed and resolved before the registration statement can become effective. For comments that are well-founded and material, the registration statement must be appropriately amended. (The process of amending registration statements is discussed in section 19020.) While differences of opinion sometimes exist as to the propriety of a particular comment or request, most of the comments and suggestions made by the SEC staff prove to be constructive and appropriate. The comments result from the combined expertise of a group of lawyers, accountants, analysts, and engineers.

To ensure that each comment on the financial statements is considered before a document is refiled and to familiarize themselves with the nature of the other comments, the independent accountants should obtain a complete copy of each letter of comment received from the SEC. It is not sufficient to obtain copies of only those sections of the comment letter that deal with the financial statements, because other comments of a nonfinancial nature may have a direct impact on matters that concern the independent accountants.

18040. Review Process for Documents Filed Under the 1934 Act

In view of the increasing reliance being placed on Form 10-K and other periodic reports filed under the 1934 Act, the SEC staff has indicated that the review of these reports is being given increased emphasis. The SEC staff has indicated that two specific areas of increased attention will be the methodology used in adopting newly issued FASB pronouncements and the content of information provided by companies in Management's Discussion and Analysis of Financial Condition and Results of Operations (see section 63030).

The review process of a periodic report filed under the 1934 Act is essentially the same as that used for 1933 Act filings. However, comments resulting from the review of the document may not be received as promptly. In addition, SEC comments on annual reports on Form 10-K or quarterly reports on Form 10-Q are frequently in the form of suggestions for future reports and do not require amendment of material previously filed. If, however, the SEC concludes that the information as filed is deficient, the comment letter will request that an amendment be filed. Amendments to documents filed under the 1934 Act are filed under cover of the form amended, with amendments designated by adding the letter "A" after the form title, e.g., "Form 10-K/A" (discussed in section 41700). In extreme cases, the SEC staff may insist on the recirculation of the registrant's annual report to shareholders.

A registrant that has received a comment from the SEC staff with a suggestion that it implement the change in future filings and then ignores the suggested change in a subsequent filing will generally find that the subsequent filing will be identified as being deficient. For this reason, if a suggestion raised by the SEC staff is not expected to be followed in future reports, the registrant should communicate this fact to the SEC together with the reasons therefor.

The fact that no comment has been made on a particular issue in past filings does not preclude the SEC staff from challenging an accounting principle or disclosure in a future 1933 or 1934 Act filing. The past filing may not have been selected for review by the SEC staff. However, even if the filing had been reviewed, it is inappropriate to assume that the SEC has accepted the application of a particular accounting principle or method of disclosure simply because the SEC staff has not previously commented on it.

18050. Suggestions for Expediting the Review Process

SEC Release No. 33-5231 (issued in 1972) itemized a number of steps that should be taken by registrants, attorneys, underwriters, and accountants to help reduce the time involved in the registration process. Since the release was issued, there have been a number of changes in the SEC review process, but the following guidance in the release is still pertinent:

1. Readability

Prepare prospectuses with an emphasis on "readability" and "understandability." The function of a prospectus is to communicate through effective disclosure to the investor. Disclosure contained in a registration statement falls far short of its statutory purpose if organized and expressed in such a way as not to convey the required information to the investor in an understandable fashion. The following are some but by no means an all-inclusive list of suggestions to achieve this:

a. Write short and simple sentences rather than complex ones.

b. Do not clutter up the cover page.

c. Use visual aids, such as tables and charts.

d. Where appropriate, include an introductory statement in the forepart of the prospectus which would enumerate in a clear, concise manner the specific factors which make the purchase of the securities one of high risk. The different risk factors should be broken out into separate paragraphs with a caption in bold face type which concisely identifies the risk described therein.

e. In the case of lengthy or complex prospectuses, include a relatively short, readable summary in the forepart of the prospectus.

2. "Getting in Line"

Do not file a registration statement with the Commission which fails to meet the statutory standards in order to "get in line," in the expectation that the staff's comments will provide the requisite compliance with these standards.

3. Transmittal Letters

Submit a letter of transmittal with the registration statement, covering, among other matters, the following:

a. Particular disclosure and accounting problems;

b. A realistic desired time schedule for effectiveness of the registration statement. While the staff will endeavor to meet such time schedules, there is no assurance that this will occur; accordingly, issuers should initially recognize this in terms of their planning;

c. A representation by registrants using particular forms . . . that they have reviewed the various criteria for eligibility for a particular form and that such criteria have been satisfied;

d. [Principally deals with updating considerations that have subsequently been changed and are now in Regulation S-X. See section 50304 of this manual.]

e. A statement, where applicable, that a repeat filing is modeled after a recent effective filing of the same issuer, together with an indication of the prior registration statement number and how the present filing differs from the previous one;

f. A statement, where applicable, that the registrant is awaiting a legal opinion from counsel or a ruling from a federal or local agency at the time of filing which is relevant to the contents of the registration statement. In this connection, reference should be made to the status of that opinion or ruling and the time of its anticipated receipt; and

SEC 18050

g. A statement, if applicable, pursuant to Securities Act Release No. 5196 as to whether all 1934 Act reports required to be filed have been filed and are complete.

4. Covering Letter Accompanying Amendments

Submit a letter with each amendment including, among other matters, the following:

a. A response to each staff comment. Should a particular comment not be dealt with either in part or whole, the registrant should indicate the reasons therefor;

b. A reproduced copy of the staff's letter of comment with the appropriate indication in the margin of that letter as to the page and paragraph in the registration statement in which the response to the comment is reflected;

c. A description of what steps have been taken to comply with the provisions of Rule 15c2-8 under the Securities Exchange Act and Securities Act Release No. 4968 concerning distribution and redistribution of prospectuses; and

d. A statement as to the status of any review of the underwriting arrangements by the NASD.

5. Redlining Amendments

The redlining of the amendment should be specific so as to highlight only the particular change made, as opposed to running a red mark down the margin of the entire page or lengthy paragraph in which a more narrow revision is contained.

6. Communication with the Staff

Exercise restraint in considering whether to communicate with members of the staff, in person or by telephone. While the communication of a material development which might have an impact on the filing is encouraged, inquiries as to the status of a filing tend to contribute to the delay of the processing of all filings. Persons calling should also identify immediately the registrant involved.

The transmittal letter discussed in Item 3 above is usually prepared by counsel for the company. A draft of the letter should be obtained and reviewed by the independent accountant prior to its submission to the SEC. Item 3(a) requests that the transmittal letter cover "particular disclosure and accounting problems." The transmittal letter normally summarizes unusual accounting problems encountered and their resolution in order to facilitate the review of the registration statement by the staff of the SEC. If a prefiling conference has been held, that fact should be noted and a copy of the relevant correspondence between the registrant and the SEC staff should be provided.

19000. AMENDING THE REGISTRATION STATEMENT AND COMPLETING THE REGISTRATION PROCESS

19010. Resolution of SEC Comments

After the letter of comment from the SEC is received, the content of the letter is carefully considered by all persons associated with the registration statement. A meeting of the registration team is often held within a few days of receiving the comment letter, at which time the suggestions and comments raised by the SEC staff are discussed and the responsibilities for correcting deficiencies in the registration statement are identified. Comments that relate to the nonfinancial sections of the registration statement are usually assigned to company counsel for resolution. Comments applicable to financial statements, financial statement schedules, and the related financial data are usually delegated to the registrant's financial and accounting personnel and the independent accountants.

Most of the comments made by the staff of the SEC are valid and constructive and are complied with. At times, however, a comment is considered inappropriate or a suggestion is deemed impractical. Because time is often critical in connection with a public offering under the 1933 Act, the issuer and the underwriters are often not inclined to extend the processing period by challenging suggestions relating to matters that, in their view, are not vital. As a result, issuers sometimes comply with suggestions that they consider immaterial or without merit for the sole purpose of expediting the registration process in order that the securities can be sold.

SEC 19010

Sometimes a comment made by the staff of the SEC may result from a misunderstanding of the facts because of incomplete background information. When this situation occurs, it is appropriate to inform the SEC staff why a particular comment is inapplicable or in what respect the proposed revision is impractical. If the matter in question relates to the financial statements or financial information included in the registration statement, it may be advisable for company personnel to contact the branch accountant to discuss and resolve the matter. Once the original written submission is made (see section 17121), in certain situations, the independent accountant may be requested to participate in the discussion with the branch accountant. Discussions that relate to the textual portion of the registration statement are generally handled by company counsel.

Problems that arise in connection with an SEC letter of comment may frequently be resolved by telephone. This approach permits the presentation of facts and explanations that may not have been known to the SEC staff when the comment letter was drafted. It also affords the SEC staff an opportunity to raise questions and to explore the problem more fully. If an issue cannot be resolved by telephone, it may be appropriate for the registrant to arrange for a conference with the staff of the SEC. If an unresolved accounting issue is to be discussed, the SEC staff will generally request that a position paper concerning the matter be submitted before the conference and that the independent accountant be present at the conference. (Refer to section 17120 for a discussion of prefiling conferences.)

19020. Amending the Registration Statement

After the necessary revisions to the registration statement resulting from the comments raised by the staff of the SEC have been identified, the preparation of an amendment commences. The amendment generally results in reprinting the registration statement. Amendments to the initial registration statement may also be necessary as a result of significant developments that occur subsequent to the filing date. Examples might be a material change in the business or financial condition of the registrant or a major change in the underwriting arrangements pertaining to the offering.

The amendment reflecting the SEC staff's comments and including any required updated financial information is generally filed with the SEC as soon as possible after receiving the letter of comment. Each amendment to the registration statement is subjected to an examination that is similar to the review of the original registration statement. If the amended registration statement requires further revisions, another letter of comment may be received by the registrant. Frequently, however, any additional comments pertaining to the amendment are resolved orally with the registrant or their counsel. Further amendments are filed until the registration statement is acceptable to the SEC and to all other parties concerned.

SEC 19020

19021. Distribution of the Preliminary ("Red Herring") Prospectus. A preliminary prospectus may be sent to interested persons prior to the effective date of the registration statement. Circulation of the preliminary prospectus is important in connection with the formation of an underwriting group and establishment of the channels through which an issue is to be distributed. Rule 430 of the 1933 Act requires that the preliminary prospectus substantially conform with the requirements of Section 10 of the 1933 Act except for the omission of information with respect to the offering price, underwriting discounts or commissions, discounts or commissions to dealers, amount of proceeds, conversion rates, call prices, or other matters dependent on the offering price. Regulation S-K Item 501(c)(8) requires that the outside front cover page of the prospectus must contain, in red ink, the caption "Preliminary Prospectus," the date of its issuance, and the following statement printed in type as large as that generally used in the body of the prospectus:

> A registration statement relating to these securities has been filed with the Securities and Exchange Commission. These securities may not be sold nor may offers to buy be accepted prior to the time the registration statement becomes effective. This prospectus shall not constitute an offer to sell or the solicitation of an offer to buy nor shall there be any sale of these securities in any State in which such offer, solicitation or sale would be unlawful prior to registration or qualification under the securities laws of any such state.

Because the foregoing legend must appear in red ink, a prospectus containing this legend is referred to as a "red herring."

19022. "Tombstone" Advertisements. The 1933 Act (Section 2(10)) provides that:

> . . . a notice, circular, advertisement, letter, or communication in respect of a security shall not be deemed to be a prospectus if it states from whom a written prospectus meeting the requirements of Section 10 may be obtained and, in addition, does no more than identify the security, state the price thereof, state by whom orders will be executed, and contain such other information as the Commission . . . may permit.

Because of the form that advertisements take when prepared in accordance with this clause, they are usually referred to as "tombstone" advertisements. The "tombstone" advertisement is not intended to be a selling document. Its purpose is to assist in locating potential buyers who are sufficiently interested in the security being advertised to obtain a statutory prospectus. "Tombstone" advertisements may be used during the waiting period or after the effective date.

19023. The Waiting Period. Section 8(a) of the 1933 Act provides that a registration statement shall become effective 20 days after it has been filed, or at such earlier date as the SEC may determine. Consequently, unless the SEC institutes an administrative proceeding to prevent or suspend the effectiveness of a registration statement or, as is typically the case in an initial public offering, a delaying technique is used (as discussed in section 19024), a registration could become effective automatically after the 20-day waiting period. Each amendment to the initial filing starts a new 20-day waiting period. However, as described in section 19030, this period may be shortened if acceleration of the effective date is granted.

19024. Delaying Amendments. If a registrant has not disposed of the comments of the SEC within the initial statutory period (20 days from the filing date), technically the registration statement may become effective in deficient form. Such a situation would be undesirable to all parties involved, because if the document were allowed to become effective in deficient form, the company, its counsel, independent accountants, and the underwriters could be held liable under the 1933 Act for material misstatements or omissions (as discussed in section 12020). Prior to the adoption of Rule 473, an amendment delaying the proposed offering had to be filed on or before a specific date in order to prevent the registration statement from becoming effective in deficient form. The filing in such instances involved a brief document that postponed the proposed public offering date and was referred to as a delaying amendment.

To avoid the necessity of filing such delaying amendments, the SEC adopted 1933 Act Rule 473, pursuant to which the following legend appears on most, if not all, registration statements:

> The registrant hereby amends this registration statement on such date or dates as may be necessary to delay its effective date until the registrant shall file a further amendment which specifically states that this registration statement shall thereafter become effective in accordance with Section 8(a) of the Securities Act of 1933 or until the registration statement shall become effective on such date as the Commission acting pursuant to said Section 8(a), may determine.

As a result of Rule 473, delaying amendments are seldom filed.

19030. Acceleration

Each time an amendment to a registration statement is filed, it has the effect of starting the 20-day waiting period all over again, unless the SEC consents to the registrant's request to consider that the amendment is filed "now as of then." Consenting to such a request is referred to as granting acceleration to an amendment.

Acceleration of the effective date may be critical to the successful financing of a proposed offering. In a rapidly changing securities market, any delay in completing the registration process could interfere with the financing of the offering.

Acceleration of the effective date is not automatic. A request for acceleration must be made in writing by the issuer, the managing underwriter, and the selling security holders (if any) and must specify the date on which effectiveness is desired. The granting of acceleration is discretionary and provides the SEC with an important degree of leverage in certain situations.

The formal policy of the SEC with respect to granting acceleration is set forth in Rule 461 of the 1933 Act. That rule also identifies situations in which the SEC may refuse to accelerate the effective date of the registration statement. In practice, however, the SEC is generally cooperative with registrants in granting acceleration.

19040. The Due Diligence Meeting

As described in section 12020, the civil liabilities that can be imposed on a registrant's management personnel, the underwriter, legal counsel, and independent accountants for untrue statements or material omissions in 1933 Act registration statements are substantial. The principal defense, which is available to all persons other than the issuer, is the provision in Section 11(b) of the 1933 Act that no person shall be liable who can sustain the burden of proof that:

> . . . he had, after reasonable investigation, reasonable ground to believe and did believe, at the time such part of the registration statement became effective, that the statements therein were true and that there was no omission to state a material fact required to be stated therein or necessary to make the statements therein not misleading. . .

After a registration statement is filed, but before it becomes effective, a meeting known as the due diligence meeting is generally arranged by the principal underwriter as an important procedure in their "reasonable investigation" program. The due-diligence meeting is usually open to all persons who may be held liable under the 1933 Act with respect to the proposed offering, but is held primarily for the benefit of the underwriting group. Among those attending are principal officers of the company whose securities are proposed to be offered, counsel for the company, the underwriter and his counsel, and the independent public accountant. At this meeting, the members of the underwriting group are afforded an opportunity to exercise due diligence as to the proposed offering of securities in that they may ask any questions concerning the company and its business, products, competitive position, recent financial and other developments, and prospects. If questions are asked concerning any matter as to which the independent accountant may be expected to know the answer, the accountant is sometimes requested by company personnel to respond to the question.

The duration of due-diligence meetings varies depending on the circumstances of the filing. If the company has previously registered and sold securities, the meeting may be somewhat perfunctory, since the company and its earnings, products, and prospects are reasonably well known, and the members of the underwriting group may have all the background information that they require. If the company's securities are being offered to the public for the first time, it may be expected that the members of the underwriting group will have a large number of varied and probing questions. The independent accountant needs to consider whether the information learned at the due-diligence meeting has a bearing on the financial data included in the registration statement.

As a general rule, due-diligence meetings need to be attended by the partner responsible for the engagement. If the partner has no experience in such meetings, he or she is often accompanied by a partner who has such experience.

19050. Importance of "Keeping Current"

As discussed in section 12000, which deals with the liabilities of accountants, the financial statements in a 1933 Act registration statement must be complete and not misleading as of the *effective date* of the registration statement. As stated therein, Section 11(a) of the 1933 Act provides, in part:

> In case any part of the registration statement, when such part became effective, contained an untrue statement of a material fact or omitted to state a material fact required to be stated therein or necessary to make the statements therein not misleading, any person acquiring such security ... may ... sue ... every accountant ... who has with his consent been named as having ... certified any part of the registration statement . . . with respect to the statement in such registration statement ... which purports to have been ... certified by him.

The law further provides, however, that accountants may avoid liability if they can prove that, after *reasonable investigation*, they had reasonable grounds to believe and did believe in the truth and completeness of the statements made on their authority. The judge's decision in the case of *Escott v. Bar Chris Construction Company* (the *Bar Chris* case) in 1968 emphasized that the responsibilities of all persons concerned will be viewed in the light of the situation existing on the effective date of the registration statement. In the *Bar Chris* case, the accountants' report covered a balance sheet at December 31, 1960, and the related statements of earnings and retained earnings for the five years then ended. The accountants' report, dated February 23, 1961, was included in a 1933 Act registration statement that became effective on May 16, 1961.

The judge's opinion observed that the part of the registration statement made on the authority of the accountants as experts included the 1960 financial statements. But because the statute requires the court to determine the accountants' "belief" and the grounds thereof "at the time such part of the registration statement became effective," the judge said:

> For the purpose of this affirmative defense the matter must be viewed as of May 16, 1961, and the question is whether at that time [the independent accountants], after reasonable investigation, had reasonable ground to believe and did believe

that the 1960 figures were true and that no material fact had been omitted from the registration statement which should have been included in order to make the 1960 figures not misleading.

The *Bar Chris* case reaffirmed the fact that the responsibilities of independent accountants do not end when they have signed their report covering the financial statements and their consent (discussed in section 17110) to the inclusion of their report in the registration statement. After the filing date and up to the effective date, the accountant must take reasonable steps to ascertain whether anything has occurred in the interim with respect to the company's financial position or operations that would have a material effect on the audited financial statements. Assume, for example, that an important lawsuit was pending on the date of the financial statements and on the filing date and that prior to the effective date a decision is handed down against the registrant. If this information is not included in the registration statement, it might be construed as an omission of a material fact that would subject those participating in the registration to the liabilities provided under the 1933 Act.

Independent accountants normally cannot be expected to extend all of their auditing procedures to the effective date. The scope of a "keeping current" review is, therefore, limited. AU Section 560.12 specifies procedures that should be followed in audits of all companies, whether public or private, with respect to events occurring subsequent to the date of the audited balance sheet up to the date of the accountants' report. AU Section 711.10 relates to filings under federal securities statutes and states that the subsequent-events procedures should be repeated at or near the effective date of the registration statement and provides for certain additional procedures to be performed.

The following are the procedures specified in AU Sections 560.12 and 711.10, which may be viewed as a basic audit program for "keeping current":

1. Read the latest available interim financial statements; compare them with the financial statements being reported upon; and make any other comparisons considered appropriate in the circumstances. In order to make these procedures as meaningful as possible for the purpose expressed above, the auditor should inquire of officers and other executives having responsibility for financial and accounting matters as to whether the interim statements have been prepared on the same basis as that used for the statements under audit.

2. Inquire of and discuss with officers and other executives having responsibility for financial and accounting matters (limited where appropriate to major locations) as to:

a. Whether any substantial contingent liabilities or commitments existed at the date of the balance sheet being reported on or at the date of inquiry.

b. Whether there was any significant change in the capital stock, long-term debt, or working capital to the date of inquiry.

SEC 19050

c. The current status of items, in the financial statements being reported on, that were accounted for on the basis of tentative, preliminary, or inconclusive data.

d. Whether any unusual adjustments had been made during the period from the balance-sheet date to the date of inquiry.

3. Read the available minutes of meetings of stockholders, directors, and appropriate committees; as to meetings for which minutes are not available, inquire about matters dealt with at such meetings.

4. Inquire of client's legal counsel concerning litigation, claims, and assessments.

5. Obtain a letter of representations, dated as of the date of the auditor's report, from appropriate officials, generally the chief executive officer and chief financial officer, as to whether any events occurred subsequent to the date of the financial statements being reported on by the independent auditor that in the officer's opinion would require adjustment or disclosure in these statements. The auditor may elect to have the client include representations as to significant matters disclosed to the auditor in his performance of the procedures in subparagraphs 1. to 4. above and 6. below.

6. Make such additional inquiries or perform such procedures as he considers necessary and appropriate to dispose of questions that arise in carrying out the foregoing procedures, inquiries, and discussions.

. . .

7. Read the entire prospectus and other pertinent portions of the registration statement.

8. Inquire of and obtain written representations from officers and other executives responsible for financial and accounting matters (limited where appropriate to major locations) about whether any events have occurred, other than those reflected or disclosed in the registration statement, that, in the officers' or other executives' opinion, have a material effect on the audited financial statements included therein or that should be disclosed in order to keep those statements from being misleading.

AU Section 711.11 also discusses the procedures to be followed when the independent accountants' report is included in a registration statement but does not cover the latest year because they have been succeeded by another accountant. In such cases, the accountants generally should:

a. Read pertinent portions of the prospectus and of the registration statement.

b. Obtain a letter of representations from the successor independent auditor regarding whether his audit (including his procedures with respect to subsequent events) revealed any matters that, in his opinion, might have a material effect on the financial statements reported on by the predecessor auditor or would require disclosure in the notes thereto. [See section 20382 for a discussion and an example of such a letter.]

The purpose of the "keeping current" review is to enable independent accountants to sustain the burden of proof that they have made a "reasonable investigation" as required under the 1933 Act. The procedures for "keeping current" are separate and distinct from any procedures that may be required as a result of a request by underwriters for a comfort letter, even though they may frequently be performed at the same time.

19060. The Price Amendment (Signing of Underwriting Agreement)

When a registration statement has been filed, the issuer and the underwriter have generally reached agreement as to securities to be sold. In almost all cases, however, the issuer and the underwriter have not yet determined the price at which the securities are to be offered to the public (or the interest or dividend rate), the underwriter's discount or commission, and the net proceeds to the issuer. The negotiation and final determination of these amounts depends on a number of factors, including past and present performance of the company and conditions in the securities markets, the prices of other similar issues of the registrant's securities, and the prices of securities of companies in similar industries at the time the registration statement becomes effective.

While the amendment reflecting changes made as a result of the SEC's comments on the initial filing is being prepared, negotiations are conducted to finalize the underwriting agreement. Upon completion of negotiations (usually about the time the registration statement is ready to become effective), the agreement is signed by authorized representatives of the registrant and the underwriter. At this time, the final amendment to the registration statement is prepared including (as applicable) the agreed-on interest or dividend rate, public offering price, underwriter's discount or commission, and the net proceeds to the company. This amendment is called the price amendment, and when it is filed the registrant and underwriter customarily request acceleration (discussed in section 19030) in order that the proposed offering to the public may be made promptly. The price amendment is usually filed on the morning of the expected effective date. It is intended to be the last amendment prior to the actual offering.

In an effort to simplify filing requirements applicable to a registration statement at the time of effectiveness, the SEC issued Rule 430A to the 1933 Act. Rule 430A permits a registrant under certain conditions, to omit information concerning the public offering price, price-related information, and the underwriting syndicate from a registration statement that is declared effective. In such cases the information omitted would either be included in the final prospectus and incorporated by reference into the registration statement or included in a post-effective amendment to the registration statement. Rule 430A is limited to offerings of securities for cash and to registration statements that are declared effective. As a result, Rule 430A would not be available, for example, to a registration statement filed in connection with a business combination.

19070. Effective Date

When the staff of the Division of Corporation Finance has no important reservations with respect to the registration statement and any comments raised have been properly disposed of, the registration statement is declared effective on the basis of the final amendment. The registrant and the underwriter may then proceed with the proposed sale of securities to the public.

Technically, the SEC may permit the registration statement to become effective in deficient form if the deficiencies involved are not material. If the deficiencies are material, the SEC has the legal authority to institute proceedings to prevent the registration statement from becoming effective. However, in practice, companies and their professional advisers will not knowingly permit a registration statement to become effective in deficient form, because of the severity of the liabilities involved under the 1933 Act, as discussed in section 12020.

19080. Closing Date

The closing date, which is generally specified in the underwriting agreement, is usually a date within 10 days to two weeks after the effective date of the registration statement. At the closing, the registrant delivers the registered securities to the underwriter and receives payment for the issue. Various legal documents are also exchanged at the closing. The only function that the independent accountant is normally required to perform in connection with the closing is to deliver a second, updated comfort letter to the underwriter as of a date within five days of the closing. See section 17095 for a discussion of comfort letters.

19090. Use of Proceeds and Form SR

Form S-1 and other registration forms require disclosure in the textual portion of the prospectus of the use to which the registrant intends to apply the proceeds of the public offering. Rule 463 of the 1933 Act requires issuers filing registration statements for the first time to file Form SR. The text of the rule follows:

Report of Offering of Securities
and Use of Proceeds Therefrom

(a) Except as hereinafter provided in this section, within 10 days after the end of the first 3-month period following the effective date of the first registration statement filed under the Act by an issuer, and within 10 days after the end of each 6-month period following such 3-month period, the issuer or successor issuer shall file with the Commission four copies of a report on Form SR containing the information required by that form. A final report shall be filed within 10 days after the later of (1) the application of the offering proceeds or (2) the termination of the offering. A report on Form SR shall be filed at the same office of the Commission where the registration statement to which it relates was filed.

(b) A successor issuer shall comply with paragraph (a) of this section only to the extent that filings on Form SR are required with respect to the first effective registration statement of the predecessor issuer.

(c) For purposes of this section:

(1) The term "offering proceeds" shall not include any amount(s) received for the account(s) of any selling security holder(s).

(2) The term "application" shall not include the temporary investment of proceeds by the issuer pending final application.

(d) This section shall not apply to any effective registration statement for securities to be issued:

(1) In a business combination described in Rule 145(a);

(2) By an issuer which pursuant to a business combination described in Rule 145(a) has succeeded to another issuer that prior to such business combination had a registration statement become effective under the Act and on the date of such business combination was not subject to paragraph (a) of this section;

(3) Pursuant to an employee benefit plan;

(4) Pursuant to a dividend or interest reinvestment plan;

(5) As American depository receipts for foreign securities;

(6) By any investment company registered under the Investment Company Act of 1940 and any issuer that has elected to be regulated as a business development company under sections 54 through 64 of the Investment Company Act of 1940;

(7) By any public utility company or public utility holding company required to file reports with any State or Federal authority.

(8) In a merger in which a vote or consent of the security holders of the company being acquired is not required pursuant to applicable state law; or

(9) In an exchange offer for the securities of the issuer or another entity.

SEC 19090

A report on Form SR is required to include information as to the net proceeds from the sale of securities from the commencement of the offering to the date of the report and an itemized statement of the use made of such proceeds. If any of the proceeds were used for a purpose not described in the prospectus, that fact and the reasons for such deviation must be disclosed. The independent accountant is normally not involved in the preparation or filing of Form SR.

19100. Post-Effective Amendments

19101. General. An amendment to a registration statement filed after the effective date of that registration statement is known as a "post-effective amendment." Such an amendment would be required as a result of a major change in the underwriting arrangement or the occurrence of a materially important development subsequent to the effective date that the issuer or the underwriter considers important to the investor, and that by its omission could make the prospectus misleading. A post-effective amendment would also be necessary when pricing information was omitted from the final registration statement pursuant to Rule 430A (discussed in section 19060) and was not filed with the Commission in the final prospectus within five business days after the effective date of the registration statement. These amendments are filed with the SEC in the same manner as the original filing and other amendments to that filing.

19102. Outdated Prospectus. Section 10(a)(3) of the 1933 Act and Rule 427 under the 1933 Act contain provisions relating to prospectuses used more than nine months after the effective date of the registration statement. Section 10(a)(3) provides that:

> . . . when a prospectus is used more than nine months after the effective date of the registration statement, the information contained therein shall be as of a date not more than sixteen months prior to such use, so far as such information is known to the user of such prospectus or can be furnished to such user without unreasonable effort or expense.

Rule 427 provides:

Contents of Prospectus
Used After Nine Months

There may be omitted from any prospectus used more than 9 months after the effective date of the registration statement any information previously required to be contained in the prospectus insofar as later information covering the same subjects, including the latest available certified financial statement, as of a date not more than 16 months prior to the use of the prospectus is contained therein.

SEC 19102

The result of these provisions is that financial statements become outdated ("stale") 16 months after the date of the latest audited statements included in the prospectus. In order to avoid this problem, a Section 10(a)(3) prospectus, often referred to as a "bring-up" prospectus, may be filed as a post-effective amendment to the registration statement.

19110. Withdrawal of Registration Statement

After a registration statement is filed with the SEC, the issuer may elect to withdraw the registration statement. There may be changes in the securities market that make the proposed offering inadvisable, or the issuer may not have been able to conclude a satisfactory agreement with the underwriter. On the other hand, the company may have successfully concluded private financing arrangements while the registration statement was in the process of being reviewed by the SEC, and consequently the need for public financing no longer exists. In these and other circumstances, the registrant may wish to withdraw the registration statement.

The rules of the SEC provide that a registration statement or amendment may be withdrawn upon application to the Commission if the Commission finds such withdrawal consistent with the public interest and the protection of investors and consents to the withdrawal. In accordance with Rule 477 under the 1933 Act, the withdrawal application must be signed and must fully state the grounds on which it is made. If the Commission consents to the withdrawal, the fee paid to the SEC upon the original filing will not be refunded and the papers constituting the registration or amendment will not be removed from the SEC files but an order stating "Withdrawn upon the request of the registrant, the Commission consenting thereto" will be included in the file for the registration statement.

19200. SHELF REGISTRATION

19210. General

In 1983 the SEC adopted revised Rule 415 of Regulation C, which covers the registration of securities offered and sold on a delayed or continuous basis. Under this rule, commonly called the shelf-registration rule, certain registrants may register the debt and equity securities they reasonably expect to sell during the next two years by filing a registration statement covering a specific class of securities. The registration statement becomes effective and available for future offerings, and the securities can then be priced and offered for sale when market conditions are favorable.

Rule 415 is also applicable to the traditional shelf offerings, such as securities to be offered and sold pursuant to reinvestment plans and upon the exercise of outstanding options, warrants, or rights (e.g., filings on Form S-8). In primary offerings of equity securities, however, the benefits of Rule 415, which permit an at-the-market offering, are limited to domestic registrants eligible to use the short form registration statement of Form S-3 (see section 42250) or foreign registrants eligible to use Form F-3. This is primarily because a Form S-3 is automatically updated by the filing of the required 1934 Act reports, such as Forms 10-Q, 10-K, and 8-K. Likewise, a Form F-3 filing is automatically updated by the filing of Forms 6-K and 20-F. Consequently, post-effective amendments to update financial statements are not necessary, a method not available, for example, to registrants filing on Form S-1.

For offerings eligible for registration on Form S-3 or F-3, the rule allows registrants that are more widely followed in the market to depart significantly from the conventional registration process described in the preceding sections of this manual. Advantages of a shelf registration include reduced issuance costs and the flexibility to be able to take securities "off the shelf" whenever market conditions are favorable, generally without the filing of a post-effective amendment.

19220. Text of Rule 415

The text of Rule 415 follows:

Rule 415. Delayed or Continuous
Offering of Securities

(a) Securities may be registered for an offering to be made on a continuous or delayed basis in the future. Provided, That—

(1) The registration statement pertains only to:

    (i) Securities which are to be offered or sold solely by or on behalf of a person or persons other than the registrant, a subsidiary of the registrant or a person of which the registrant is a subsidiary;

    (ii) Securities which are to be offered and sold pursuant to a dividend or interest reinvestment plan or an employee benefit plan of the registrant;

    (iii) Securities which are to be issued upon the exercise of outstanding options, warrants or rights;

    (iv) Securities which are to be issued upon conversion of other outstanding securities;

    (v) Securities which are pledged as collateral;

    (vi) Securities which are registered on Form F-6;

    (vii) Mortgage-related securities, including such securities as mortgage-backed debt and mortgage participation or pass-through certificates;

    (viii) Securities which are to be issued in connection with business combination transactions;

    (ix) Securities the offering of which will be commenced promptly, will be made on a continuous basis and may continue for a period in excess of 30 days from the date of initial effectiveness; or

    (x) Securities registered (or qualified to be registered) on Form S-3 or Form F-3 which are to be offered and sold on a continuous or delayed basis by or on behalf of the registrant, a subsidiary of the registrant or a person of which the registrant is a subsidiary.

(2) Securities in paragraphs (a)(1)(viii) through (x) may only be registered in an amount which, at the time the registration statement becomes effective, is reasonably expected to be offered and sold within two years from the initial effective date of the registration.

(3) The registrant furnishes the undertakings required by Item 512(a) of Regulation S-K.

(4) In the case of a registration statement pertaining to an at-the-market offering of equity securities by or on behalf of the registrant:

    (i) The offering comes within paragraph (a)(1)(x);

    (ii) where voting stock is registered, the amount of securities registered for such purposes must not exceed 10% of the aggregate market value of the registrant's outstanding voting stock held by non-affiliates of the

SEC 19220

registrant (calculated as of a date within 60 days prior to the date of filing);

(iii) the securities must be sold through an underwriter or underwriters, acting as principal(s) or as agent(s) for the registrant; and

(iv) the underwriter or underwriters must be named in the prospectus which is part of the registration statement.

As used in this paragraph, the term "at the market offering" means an offering of securities into an existing trading market for outstanding shares of the same class at other than a fixed price on or through the facilities of a national securities exchange or to or though a market maker otherwise than on an exchange.

(b) This section shall not apply to any registration statement pertaining to securities issued by a face-amount certificate company or redeemable securities issued by an open-end management company or unit investment trust under the Investment Company Act of 1940 or any registration statement filed by any foreign government or political subdivision thereof.

19230. Amending the Registration Statement

As indicated in paragraph (a)(3) of Rule 415, a registrant filing a shelf-registration statement must furnish the following undertakings as set forth in Item 512(a) of Regulation S-K:

(1) To file, during any period in which offers or sales are being made, a post-effective amendment to this registration statement:

(i) To include any prospectus required by Section 10(a)(3) of the Securities Act of 1933;

(ii) To reflect in the prospectus any facts or events arising after the effective date of the registration statement (or the most recent post-effective amendment thereof) which, individually or in the aggregate, represent a fundamental change in the information set forth in the registration statement;

(iii) To include any material information with respect to the plan of distribution not previously disclosed in the registration statement or any material change to such information in the registration statement.

Provided, however, that paragraphs (a)(1)(i) and (a)(1)(ii) do not apply if the registration statement is on Form S-3 or Form S-8, and the information required to be included in a post-effective amendment by those paragraphs is contained in periodic reports filed by the registrant pursuant to section 13 or section 15(d) of the Securities Exchange Act of 1934 that are incorporated by reference in the registration statement.

(2) That, for the purpose of determining any liability under the Securities Act of 1933, each such post-effective amendment shall be deemed to be a new registration statement relating to the securities offered therein, and the offering of such securities at that time shall be deemed to be the initial bona fide offering thereof.

(3) To remove from registration by means of a post-effective amendment any of the securities being registered which remain unsold at the termination of the offering.

(4) If the registrant is a foreign private issuer, to file a post-effective amendment to the registration statement to include any financial statements required by [Rule] 3-19 of Regulation S-X at the start of any delayed offering or throughout a continuous offering.

Registration under Rule 415 is significantly different from the conventional registration process inasmuch as the offer and sale of securities need not begin when the registration statement becomes effective. For example, for securities eligible for registration on Form S-3 or F-3, there is no requirement to select the managing underwriter or fix the price of the offering at the time the shelf-registration statement is filed. Instead, the registrant may invite one or more underwriters to bid on the offering at any time after the shelf registration becomes effective.

A post-effective amendment, which creates a new effective date for the shelf-registration statement, is required if, during any period in which offers or sales are being made, there has been a "fundamental change" in the information included in the filing. Significant business acquisitions or dispositions, for example, would be considered fundamental changes and, therefore, require post-effective amendments. However, Regulation S-K Item 512(a) indicates that the filing of a post-effective amendment for a fundamental change is not necessary if the required information is included in a 1934 Act periodic report (Form 8-K, 10-Q, or 10-K) that is automatically incorporated into a Form S-3 or S-8 shelf-registration statement.

A situation sometimes arises involving registrants with currently effective shelf-registration filings, with respect to which the rules are not entirely clear. If a registrant (or prospective registrant) enters into a significant business acquisition, the consummation of which is "probable," S-X Rule 3-05 requires the inclusion of target company financial statements in a 1933 Act registration statement (see section 50314). The SEC staff has informally indicated that a registrant with a currently effective shelf filing on Form S-3 would be expected to file a Form 8-K containing the necessary target company statement when consummation of a significant business combination becomes "probable." However, it would appear that the filing of a Form 8-K in this type of situation would be relevant only if there is the possibility of a takedown of the shelf before the S-3 registration statement is updated by a filing on Form 8-K upon consummation of the acquisition.

Updating for matters that are not considered fundamental changes can be accomplished by means of a "sticker," which simply involves the addition of several pages—identified as the "Prospectus Supplement"—to the original prospectus. Prospectus supplements are used, for example, to price the offering and to indicate which underwriter(s) have been selected. Adding a "sticker" to a shelf registration does *not* extend the effective date of the registration statement.

19240. Special Considerations for Independent Accountants

The procedural differences between a shelf registration and a conventional filing give rise to certain considerations on the part of the independent accountant. As discussed in section 19050, the responsibilities of the independent accountant do not end at the filing date of the registration statement but extend through its effective date. Because a post-effective amendment technically creates a new effective date, the independent accountant must "keep current" through the effective date of the latest post-effective amendment. An updated accountants' consent is also generally required. Refer to the discussions in sections 42274 and 42280 for the requirements with respect to "keeping current" and accountants' consents in shelf-registration situations. "Keeping current" procedures for shelf-registration statements updated after the original effective date are also addressed in AU Section 9711.

When the shelf registration rule is applied, independent accountants must also consider the impact of the procedural differences in the registration process on their issuance of the required comfort letter. For a discussion of these matters, refer to section 20605, which deals with letters for underwriters, and section 20606, which deals specifically with considerations in "shelf" registration statements.

19500. PERIODIC REPORTING OBLIGATIONS

As indicated throughout this manual, the question of when an issuer is obligated to file a particular report with the SEC and the type of report to be filed is a legal one on which securities counsel should be consulted. However, accountants should also be familiar with the general requirements in order to serve their clients more effectively. The following discussion is included to serve as background material and to familiarize the reader with this subject in general terms.

The periodic reporting obligations become effective when issuers of securities meet certain conditions and thereby become subject to the 1934 Act. Section 15(d) of the 1934 Act imposes periodic reporting obligations (pursuant to Section 13) on issuers *for the year in which a 1933 Act registration statement becomes effective*. These obligations continue until the issuer meets certain conditions permitting suspension. Section 15(d) also provides that the reporting obligations under its provisions are automatically suspended if the issuer is registered under Section 12 of the 1934 Act, since periodic reporting obligations are also imposed on issuers who have securities registered under that section. Section 12 requires the registration of:

- *Any securities* listed on a national securities exchange (Section 12(b)).

- *A class of equity securities* traded over the counter and as of the last day of the fiscal year the issuer's assets exceed $5,000,000 and the class of equity securities is held of record by 500 or more persons (Section 12(g)).

The specific obligation to file reports is contained in Section 13 of the Act.

In the absence of a public offering of shares in the U.S., foreign private issuers have different requirements from domestic companies pursuant to Rule 12(g) 3-2 of the 1934 Act. Under paragraph (a) of Rule 12(g) 3-2, a foreign private issuer is exempt from Section 12(g) of the 1934 Act provided it has less than 300 holders of any class of securities resident in the U.S. When the threshold of 300 U.S. investors is reached, exemption from SEC registration may *still* be obtained under Rule 12g3-2(b) if there has been no public offering and the company's securities are not quoted on a U.S. stock exchange or on NASDAQ. In cases where this exemption is obtained, a foreign company must provide the SEC with limited information, including that which it has made public under the laws of its home country, information that it has filed with a stock exchange which was made public by that exchange, and information that it has distributed to its security holders. If these conditions are not met, a full registration with the SEC would normally be required.

Rule 12h-3 of the 1934 Act permits Section 12(g) and 15(d) issuers to obtain an immediate suspension of their periodic reporting obligations if the number of holders of securities is reduced to (1) *less than 300* persons or (2) *less than 500* persons and the total assets of the issuer have *not exceeded $5 million* on the last day of each of the issuer's *three* most recent fiscal years. Immediate suspension is not available, however, for a fiscal year in which a 1933 Act registration statement becomes effective. Section 15(d) of the 1934 Act also provides for automatic suspension of the periodic reporting obligations of Section 15(d) issuers for any year other than the year in which a 1933 Act registration statement becomes effective if *at the beginning of such fiscal year* the securities are held of record *by less than 300 persons.* In all cases Form 15 (a certification that the issuer qualifies for the suspension) must be filed to obtain the suspension.

As indicated in the foregoing summary, Section 15(d) or Section 12 of the 1934 Act imposes periodic reporting obligations upon the registrant after the 1933 Act registration statement becomes effective. Such obligations include the requirement to file current reports on Form 8-K (discussed in section 41600) or for foreign private issuers on Form 6-K (discussed in section 44200), quarterly reports (not required for foreign private issuers) on Form 10-Q (discussed in section 41400), and annual reports on Form 10-K (discussed in section 41100) or on Form 20-F (discussed in section 44100) for foreign private issuers. These obligations may or may not continue, depending on whether the issuer meets the conditions permitting suspension.

Note that conditions permitting suspension of the reporting obligations under Rule 12h-3 and Section 15(d) are based on the holders of record of securities declining to less than 300 persons. The date on which such determination is made, however, differs. Section 15(d) provides for this determination as of the beginning of the fiscal year and, accordingly, applies to that fiscal year and thereafter, whereas Rule 12h-3, on the other hand, provides for this determination at any time during the fiscal year and allows immediate suspension.

The following table provides an overview of the major reporting obligations under the 1934 Act.

OVERVIEW OF MAJOR PERIODIC REPORTING
OBLIGATIONS UNDER THE 1934 ACT
FOR DOMESTIC COMPANIES

	Section 12(b) (Any listed securities)	Section 12(g) (Equity securities traded OTC)	Section 15(d) (Any class of securities registered under the 1933 Act)
Reporting Obligations: Periodic reports on Forms 8-K, 10-Q, and 10-K	Yes	Yes	Yes
Proxy or information statements (Schedules 14A and 14C)	Yes	Yes	No
Annual report to shareholders (Rule 14a-3 or 14c-3)	Yes	Yes	No
Situations That Trigger Periodic Reporting Obligations	Listing on a national stock exchange	500 stockholders and $5 million of assets	When a 1933 Act registration statement becomes effective
Termination or Suspension of Reporting Obligations	(1)	(2)	(3)

(1) When delisting has been approved by the stock exchange and application has been made to the Commission, provided criteria in (2) or (3) are met.

(2) When (a) the issuer has (i) less than 300 security holders at any time or (ii) less than 500 security holders and the issuer's total assets were less than $5 million at the end of each of its last 3 fiscal years and (b) the issuer certifies either of these conditions to the Commission on Form 15. Although the duty to file is suspended with the submission of Form 15, all other obligations remain in effect until registration is terminated by the Commission.

(3) When (a) the issuer has (i) less than 300 security holders at any time or (ii) less than 500 security holders and the issuer's total assets were less than $5 million at the end of each of its last 3 fiscal years or (iii) less than 300 security holders at the beginning of a fiscal year and (b) the issuer certifies any of these conditions to the Commission on Form 15. Suspension is not available, however, for a fiscal year in which a 1933 Act registration statement became effective.

SEC 19500

The following chart sets forth the criteria for termination or suspension of 1934 Act reporting. The chart was originally published as an appendix to Release No. 34-18647 and has been updated for changes adopted in Release No. 34-20784.

Termination or Suspension of 1934 Act Reporting: An Algorithm

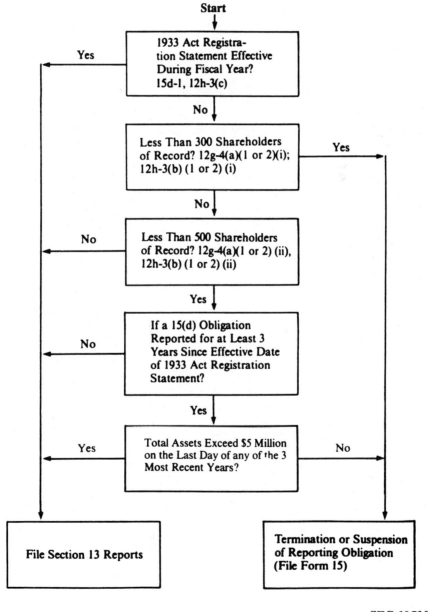

SEC 19500

19600.   LISTING SECURITIES

Companies sometimes enter the securities trading markets by listing their existing securities rather than through a public offering involving new capital. This is commonly done to increase investor interest in and access to a company's stock. Some investors are required to and/or prefer to invest only in listed securities. In some instances, listings of existing securities are preceded by a private issuance of securities (i.e., a private placement) under Regulation D (see section 42900) or Rule 144A (see section 42940). In addition, a listing of securities is often a prelude to a public offering of new capital.

To become listed, a company is typically required to meet the 1934 Act registration requirements (usually by filing a Form 10 for U.S. registrants—see section 41800—or a Form 20-F for foreign registrants—see section 44100) as well as the requirements of the particular exchange on which the securities are to be listed. Companies have the choice of listing their securities on one of the stock exchanges (e.g., the New York Stock Exchange or the American Stock Exchange) or having the securities quoted in the over-the-counter marketplace (e.g., the National Association of Securities Dealers Automated Quotation System–NASDAQ). Each securities exchange has its own listing requirements and procedures that begin with the filing of an application.

A major advantage of having securities listed and reports filed with the SEC is in the ability to raise additional capital in the future. Much of the same information required with a filing on Form 10 or Form 20-F is also required in connection with a 1933 Act registration on Form S-1 or Form F-1. In addition, the filings made for listing purposes allow the SEC staff to become familiar with the company and its operations. The same group of staff at the SEC that reviewed the earlier filing(s) is likely to also review all of a particular company's future filings, thus expediting the public offering process.

ACCOUNTANTS' REPORTS
AND RELATED MATTERS

20100. INTRODUCTION

Independent accountants' responsibilities in connection with a registration statement or periodic report filed with the SEC are based generally on the extent of their association with financial statements and financial statement schedules included in the document. The SEC's requirements with respect to accountants' reports are included in Rule 2-02 of Regulation S-X, and it is important to recognize that certain departures from a standard (unqualified) report are unacceptable to the SEC.

Independent accountants may also be associated with interim financial statements and other information (such as Selected Financial Data) included or incorporated by reference in a document filed with the SEC. Pursuant to FRP Section 605, the accountants' report on a limited review of interim financial statements may be included or incorporated by reference in a document filed with the SEC.

The degree of an accountant's association with the financial information in a registration statement filed under the 1933 Act is generally described in a portion of the prospectus referred to as the experts section. Accountants are required to acknowledge the association by furnishing a written consent to the use of their report in this context.

Normally, when an auditor is associated with unaudited financial statements, he or she is required to include a disclaimer on those financial statements in the audit report. However, the SEC will not accept a disclaimer in these circumstances. The AICPA has made a special exemption to cater to the SEC's objections. Thus, paragraph 14 of AU 504, *Association with Financial Statements*, states that "when unaudited financial statements are presented in comparative form with audited financial statements in documents filed with the Securities and Exchange Commission, such statements should be clearly marked as "unaudited" but should not be referred to in the auditors' report."

This section of the manual discusses these matters and, where applicable, includes illustrative wording for certain reports, references, and representations that may be required in SEC filings.

20200. SEC REPORTING REQUIREMENTS

20210. General

Rule 2-02 of Regulation S-X contains the requirements of the SEC with respect to the accountants' report. The text of the rule follows:

Rule 2-02. *Accountants' Reports*

(a) *Technical requirements.* The accountant's report:

   (1) shall be dated;

   (2) shall be signed manually;

   (3) shall indicate the city and state where issued; and

   (4) shall identify without detailed enumeration the financial statements covered by the report.

(b) *Representations as to the audit.* The accountant's report:

   (1) shall state whether the audit was made in accordance with generally accepted auditing standards; and

   (2) shall designate any auditing procedures deemed necessary by the accountant under the circumstances of the particular case, which have been omitted, and the reasons for their omission.

   Nothing in this rule shall be construed to imply authority for the omission of any procedure which independent accountants would ordinarily employ in the course of an audit made for the purpose of expressing the opinions required by paragraph (c) of this Rule.

(c) *Opinion to be expressed.* The accountant's report shall state clearly:

   (1) The opinion of the accountant in respect of the financial statements covered by the report and the accounting principles and practices reflected therein; and

   (2) the opinion of the accountant as to the consistency of the application of the accounting principles, or as to any changes in such principles which have a material effect on the financial statements. [See section 50202 for a discussion of the impact of SAS No. 58 on this requirement.]

(d) *Exceptions.* Any matters to which the accountant takes exception shall be clearly identified, the exception thereto specifically and clearly stated, and, to the extent practicable, the effect of each such exception on the related financial statements given. (See ASR No. 4 [FRP Section 101].)

The professional standards as to reporting on audited financial statements are set forth in AU Sections 400 and 500. Reports included in documents filed with the SEC must adhere to these requirements, and auditors examining the financial statements covered by such reports must comply with auditing standards as generally accepted in the United States.

The only provisions of Rule 2-02 that exceed professional reporting standards are the requirements that the report be signed manually and that the city and state of issuance be indicated.

20220. Statutory Certification Requirements

The federal securities laws require that certain financial statements included in documents filed with the SEC be "certified" by independent public accountants. The laws give the SEC broad authority to add and omit information required in filings and to designate which financial statements must be "certified."

The Commission has interpreted the statutory certification requirements generally as meaning an audit made in accordance with generally accepted auditing standards resulting in the expression of an unqualified opinion (i.e., a standard report; see AU Section 508.07-.09). More recently, the SEC has used the term "audited" in amendments to various forms, and explained in SAB Topic 1-E1 that its use was intended to conform terminology to that currently applied by the accounting profession, not to modify the statutory requirement.

20230. Departures from the Accountants' Standard Report

Certain qualified opinions are not acceptable in a filing under the 1933 Act. For example, the SEC will not accept an accountant's report that is qualified as a result of a departure from GAAP or limitations on the scope of the audit. This position is extensively discussed in FRP Section 607.01, which expresses the SEC's view that qualifications with respect to opening inventories are not acceptable. More recently, SAB Topic 1-E2 reiterates the staff's view that qualifications resulting from scope limitations and departures from GAAP (including adequacy of disclosures) are unacceptable. The pertinent excerpts from that SAB are:

Requirements for Audited or Certified Financial Statements—
Qualified Auditors' Opinions

Facts: The accountants' report is qualified as to scope of audit, or the accounting principles used.

Question: Does the staff consider the requirements for audited or certified financial statements met when the auditors' opinion is so qualified?

Interpretive Response: No. The staff does not accept as consistent with the requirements of Rule 2-02(b) of Regulation S-X financial statements on which the auditors' opinions are qualified because of a limitation on the scope of the audit, since in these situations the auditor was unable to perform all the procedures required by professional standards to support the expression of an opinion. This position was discussed in ASR No. 90 [FRP Section 607.01] in connection with representations concerning the verification of prior years' inventories in first audits.

Financial statements for which the auditors' opinions contain qualifications relating to the acceptability of accounting principles used or the completeness of disclosures made are also unacceptable. (See ASR No. 4 [FRP Section 101], and with respect to a "going-concern" qualification [modification], see ASR No. 115 [rescinded by FRR No. 16 as discussed below].)

A registration statement that contains a qualified report will probably give rise to a request that either the auditing procedures be extended or the financial statements corrected to permit the accountant to remove the qualification.

Adverse opinions are unacceptable to the SEC. It is unlikely that a registration statement containing an adverse opinion would be accepted for review. In any event, the cause of the adverse opinion would need to be corrected before the registration statement would be permitted to become effective.

Since a disclaimer of opinion states that the accountant does not express an opinion, this form of report does not constitute "certification" under Rule 2-02 of Regulation S-X. A registration statement containing a disclaimer of opinion would not be acceptable to the SEC and would not be permitted to become effective. However, in some cases, the staff has not objected to the inclusion of a disclaimer in a 1934 Act filing because of a material uncertainty. The staff has not provided any specific guidelines in this respect, however, and has indicated that its course of action in these types of situations is based upon the facts and circumstances of each case. It is important to note that disclaimers, as well as scope limitations, continue to be unacceptable in connection with 1933 Act filings.

As a general rule, independent accountants should not consent to the inclusion of a report that they know will be unacceptable to the SEC.

The form and content of the accountants' standard report was changed as a result of the issuance of Statement on Auditing Standards (SAS) No. 58. In addition, certain conditions that gave rise to the issuance of a qualified report prior to SAS No. 58 now result in the inclusion of an explanatory paragraph following the opinion paragraph. Among the situations specified in paragraph 11 that give rise to an explanatory paragraph are the following:

- "Uncertainties concerning future events, the outcome of which is not susceptible of reasonable estimation."

- "A material change between periods in accounting principles or in the method of their application."

- Existence of "substantial doubt about the entity's ability to continue as a going concern."

Paragraph 37 of SAS 58 provides guidance for the independent accountant who may wish to emphasize a matter but, notwithstanding the emphasis paragraph, is expressing an unqualified opinion. The SEC staff encourages independent accountants to highlight significant issues that they believe should be brought to the investor's attention.

However, the SEC staff has informally indicated that an accountants' report that contains an emphasis-of-a-matter paragraph that it believes is being inappropriately used to discuss an uncertainty or going-concern issue will be considered unacceptable for inclusion in an SEC filing. The staff has further indicated that it considers it inappropriate to use terms in an emphasis-of-a-matter paragraph that would normally be used in an uncertainty explanatory paragraph. For example, language such as, "...ultimate outcome cannot presently be determined" or "...subject to the realization of assets of $XX," is generally considered inappropriate by the staff in this context.

Historically the SEC had been reluctant to accept an accountants' report that was qualified with respect to the registrant's ability to continue as a going concern. ASR No. 115, which was rescinded by FRR No. 16, concluded that in the Commission's view an accountants' report in a 1933 Act registration statement that was qualified with respect to the registrant's ability to continue as a going concern would not meet the "certification" requirements of Regulation S-X Rule 2-02 unless a registrant could arrange its financial affairs to remove the immediate threat to its continuation as a going business.

The rescission of ASR 115 enables registrants to offer securities even though the accountants' report is modified because of uncertainties about an entity's continued existence. FRR No. 16, however, emphasizes that a filing containing a going-concern modification needs to contain appropriate and prominent disclosure of the registrant's financial difficulties and indications of a "viable plan" to overcome these difficulties. This point is discussed in FRP Section 607.02, the text of which follows:

Uncertainty About an Entity's Continued Existence

Financial statements will be considered false and misleading if those statements are prepared on the assumption of a going concern but should more appropriately be based on the assumption of liquidation or if the classification and amounts of assets and liabilities should be otherwise adjusted. Moreover, filings containing accountant's reports that are qualified as a result of questions about the entity's continued existence must contain appropriate and prominent disclosure of the registrant's financial difficulties and viable plans to overcome these difficulties. Such disclosure is required by existing rules and by the antifraud provisions of the federal securities laws.[*]

---

[*]See, e.g., Items 101, 303, 503, and 504 of Regulation S-K, Description of Business, Management's Discussion and Analysis, Summary Information and Risk Factors, and Use of Proceeds, respectively, and Rule 408 [under the 1933 Act], Additional Information.

FRP Section 607.02 cites the provisions of Regulation S-K Item 303, Management's Discussion and Analysis, as a principal source of the requirements for such disclosure, but the adoptive release goes beyond those provisions by specifying that:

. . . any registrant with such pressing financial problems should include a reasonably detailed discussion of its ability or inability to generate sufficient cash to support its operations during the twelve-month period following the date of the financial statements being reported upon. Thereafter, this discussion would be updated as necessary on a quarterly basis.

As to the auditor's responsibility in such cases, the adoptive release cites the provisions of paragraph 10 of No. 34 (AU Section 340.10) as the basis for requiring such disclosure:

The auditor should *consider* the need for, and the adequacy of, disclosure of the principal conditions that raise a question about an entity's ability to continue in existence, the possible effects of such conditions, and management's evaluation of the significance of those conditions and any mitigating factors. *If disclosure is necessary* and a satisfactory resolution of the question depends primarily on the realization of particular plans of management, the disclosure should deal with that fact and such plans. [Emphasis added]

SAS 34 was superseded by SAS 59 (AU Section 341). In addition to incorporating the disclosure requirements described above, SAS 59 added the following items:

- Possible discontinuance of operations.

- Information about the recoverability or classification of recorded asset amounts or the amounts or classification of liabilities.

SAS 59 goes on to say that if the auditor concludes that the entity's disclosures regarding its ability to continue as a going concern are inadequate, a departure from generally accepted accounting principles exists. This could result in either a qualified (except for) or an adverse opinion.

FRR 16 specifies that:

- An auditor would be required to include in their report the disclosures set forth in paragraph 10 of SAS 34 (superseded by paragraphs 10 and 11 of SAS 59) if the information is not otherwise disclosed in the financial statements.

- Paragraph 10 of SAS 34 (superseded by paragraphs 10 and 11 of SAS 59) requires the auditor to ensure the adequacy of disclosure about plans to resolve the doubts about the entity's continued existence.

FRP Section 607.02 also cautions that the SEC will consider financial statements that are prepared on a going-concern basis false and misleading if circumstances dictate the use of the liquidation basis or if the classification of assets and liabilities should otherwise have been adjusted. The adoptive release provides no specific guidance as to when the SEC considers the presentation of liquidation-basis statements to be necessary. The SEC staff, however, has indicated that the release is not intended to imply a change in the SEC's position regarding the presentation of such statements or to impose a requirement beyond current GAAP.

In addressing the issuance of audit reports in situations where it has not yet been determined that there is substantial doubt about an entity's ability to continue as a going concern, yet there remains doubt or uncertainty, the SEC staff has indicated that it would not object to an emphasis-of-a-matter paragraph that refers to the appropriate footnote where the uncertainty is discussed.

The staff also believes that in a situation where an audit report was issued with an explanatory paragraph describing an uncertainty about the entity's ability to continue as a going concern (AU 341.13) at fiscal year-end and where the uncertainty involving the substantial doubt was subsequently removed, then if the registrant were to reissue its financial statements with the audit report containing an "unqualified" opinion, the audit report should describe the event or transaction that gave rise to the removal of the explanatory paragraph.

Certain other modifications to the auditors' standard report cited in AU Section 508.11 are acceptable in SEC filings and should not prevent a company from concluding a 1933 Act offering. Among the acceptable modifications are those relating to uncertainties concerning future events the outcome of which is not currently susceptible of reasonable estimation, and those resulting from accounting changes with which the auditor concurs.

In the past, the SEC has allowed the use of legended auditors' reports in limited circumstances provided that the reason for the legend is resolved as of the effective date (i.e., a legended report is not appropriate in circumstances in which the reason for the legend is not resolved until the closing date). However, the staff has taken the position that a legended report cannot be used to avoid the issuance of a qualified report due to doubt regarding a registrant's continued existence, even if the qualification would be removed as a result of the offering (i.e., the proceeds cure the doubt). In situations where the legended approach is used in the initial filing(s), it is important to note that an auditors' report without the legend wording is required to be included in the registration statement as of the effective date or in proxy materials prior to mailing.

20240. Communication of Reporting Problems

Since the inability to express an unqualified opinion may affect a registrant's ability to register securities under the 1933 Act, the registrant and their counsel should be advised immediately if at any time during the registration process it appears that a qualified opinion, an adverse opinion, or a disclaimer of opinion may be issued.

20300. ACCOUNTANTS' REPORTS

20310. Standard Report on Financial Statements

Accountants' reports included in annual reports to shareholders of public companies and in most documents filed with the SEC are required to cover balance sheets as of the end of the registrant's two most recent fiscal years and other financial statements for the three most recent fiscal years. The following is an illustration of a suggested report on financial statements of public entities that is consistent with the wording of the standard report prescribed by paragraph 8 of SAS No. 58, *Reports on Audited Financial Statements* (AU Section 508.08):

Report of Independent Accountants

We have audited the accompanying consolidated balance sheets of XYZ Company and Subsidiaries as of December 31, 19X2 and 19X1, and the related consolidated statements of income, retained earnings, and cash flows for each of the three years in the period ended December 31, 19X2.These financial statements are the responsibility of the Company's management. Our responsibility is to express an opinion on these financial statements based on our audits.

We conducted our audits in accordance with generally accepted auditing standards. Those standards require that we plan and perform the audit to obtain reasonable assurance about whether the financial statements are free of material misstatement. An audit includes examining, on a test basis, evidence supporting the amounts and disclosures in the financial statements. An audit also includes assessing the accounting principles used and significant estimates made by management, as well as evaluating the overall financial statement presentation. We believe that our audits provide a reasonable basis for our opinion.

In our opinion, the financial statements referred to above present fairly, in all material respects, the consolidated financial position of XYZ Company and Subsidiaries as of December 31, 19X2 and 19X1, and the consolidated results of their operations and their cash flows for each of the three years in the period ended December 31, 19X2 in conformity with generally accepted accounting principles.

(Name of Firm)

City, State
Date

20320. Report on Financial Statement Schedules

When financial statement schedules are included in a document filed with the SEC, they must be covered by the accountants' report. This may be accomplished by furnishing a separate report that expands the application of the accountants' report on the financial statements to the information included in the schedules or by issuing one combined report (see section 20330). In most instances, two reports are appropriate since the primary financial statements typically are incorporated by reference from or taken directly from the annual report to shareholders.

In a Form 10-K

When two separate reports are furnished in Form 10-K, the report covering the primary financial statements would be included as part of Item 8 and the other report would be included under Item 14 with the financial statement schedules. The report in Item 8 would be identical to the standard report in section 20310. An example of the separate report on the financial statement schedules follows:

> Our report on the consolidated financial statements of XYZ Company is included on page 36 of this Form 10-K (*or* has been incorporated by reference in this Form 10-K from page 25 of the 19X3 Annual Report to Shareholders of XYZ Company). In connection with our audits of such financial statements, we have also audited the related financial statement schedules listed in the index on page 48 of this Form 10-K.
>
> In our opinion, the financial statement schedules referred to above, when considered in relation to the basic financial statements taken as a whole, present fairly, in all material respects, the information required to be included therein.
>
> (Name of Firm)
>
> City, State
> Date

In Part II of a registration statement

When two separate reports are furnished in a registration statement, the report on the primary financial statements is generally identical to the standard report in section 20310. An example of the separate report on the financial statement schedules in Part II of a registration statement follows:

> In connection with our audits of the consolidated financial statements of XYZ Company and Subsidiaries as of December 31, 19X3 and 19X2, and for each of the three years in the period ended December 31, 19X3, which financial statements are included in the Prospectus, we have also audited the financial statement schedules listed in Item XX herein.
>
> In our opinion, these financial statement schedules, when considered in relation to the basic financial statements taken as a whole, present fairly, in all material respects, the information required to be included therein.
>
> (Name of Firm)
>
> City, State
> Date

The date of the report on the financial statement schedules should be the same as the date of the report on the consolidated financial statements.

SEC 20320

As discussed in section 41173, auditors are required to manually sign one copy of their separate report on the financial statement schedules and their report on the basic financial statements included in the annual report to stockholders if the latter report is incorporated by reference in Form 10-K.

The suggested wording in the foregoing examples is based on the language used in SAS No. 29 (AU Section 551). When condensed financial information of the parent company is included in a financial statement schedule (see sections 50504 and 51204 for detailed requirements), footnote 3 of SAS 42 specifies that auditors should report on such information in the same manner as they report on other financial statement schedules.

20330. Combined Report on Financial Statements and Financial Statement Schedules

The following example of an accountants' report covering both the financial statements and the financial statement schedules makes reference to the index to financial statements described and illustrated in section 41172:

Report of Independent Accountants

We have audited the consolidated financial statements and the financial statement schedules of XYZ Company and Subsidiaries listed in the index on page 48 [*or* listed in Item 14(a)] of this Form 10-K. These financial statements and financial statement schedules are the responsibility of the Company's management. Our responsibility is to express an opinion on these financial statements and financial statement schedules based on our audits.

We conducted our audits in accordance with generally accepted auditing standards. Those standards require that we plan and perform the audit to obtain reasonable assurance about whether the financial statements are free of material misstatement. An audit includes examining, on a test basis, evidence supporting the amounts and disclosures in the financial statements. An audit also includes assessing the accounting principles used and significant estimates made by management, as well as evaluating the overall financial statement presentation. We believe that our audits provide a reasonable basis for our opinion.

In our opinion, the financial statements referred to above present fairly, in all material respects, the consolidated financial position of XYZ Company and Subsidiaries as of December 31, 19X2 and 19X1, and the consolidated results of their operations and their cash flows for each of the three years in the period ended December 31, 19X2 in conformity with generally accepted accounting principles. In addition, in our opinion, the financial statement schedules referred to above, when considered in relation to the basic financial statements taken as a whole, present fairly, in all material respects, the information required to be included therein.

(Name of Firm)

City, State
Date

When the annual report is incorporated by reference and a combined report on the financial statements and schedules is issued, the introductory paragraph would be modified as follows:

We have audited the consolidated financial statements of XYZ Company and Subsidiaries as of December 31, 19X2 and 19X1, and for each of the three years in the period ended December 31, 19X2, which financial statements are included on pages 23 through 30 of the 19X2 Annual Report to Shareholders of XYZ Company and incorporated by reference herein. We have also audited the financial statement schedules listed in the index on page 48 of this Form 10-K. These financial statements and financial statement schedules are the responsibility of the Company's management. Our responsibility is to express an opinion on these financial statements and financial statement schedules based on our audits.

The last two paragraphs of the auditors' report would be the same as shown above.

20340. Reporting on Separate Financial Statements

Under certain specified conditions, Article 3 of Regulation S-X (section 50300) requires the inclusion of separate audited financial statements for certain entities in registration statements and reports filed with the SEC.

In ASR No. 302 (now FRP Section 213) the SEC modified the Regulation S-X requirements for the presentation of separate financial statements (see section 50050). Under these rules certain registrants are required to include, as supplemental information to the consolidated financial statements, condensed financial statements of the parent company (see section 50520). In SAS No. 42 (AU Section 552), the ASB concludes that auditors should report on such condensed financial information in the same manner as they report on other supplementary schedules. See sections 20320 and 20330 for a discussion regarding reporting on financial statement schedules.

In certain instances *complete* separate financial statements are included in a footnote to the consolidated financial statements. Situations that may require complete separate financial statements include those required pursuant to Rule 3-09 relating to separate financial statements of subsidiaries not consolidated and 50 percent or less owned persons (see section 50339) and Rule 3-10 relating to financial statements of guarantors and affiliates whose securities collateralized an issue registered or being registered (see section 50344). In such cases the accountants' report may be modified as follows:

Report of Independent Accountants

We have audited the consolidated financial statements of XYZ Company and Subsidiaries listed in the accompanying index and the separate financial statements of XYZ Company, which are included in Note 12 to the consolidated financial statements. These financial statements are the responsibility of the Company's management. Our responsibility is to express an opinion on these financial statements based on our audits.

We conducted our audits in accordance with generally accepted auditing standards. Those standards require that we plan and perform the audit to obtain reasonable assurance about whether the financial statements are free of material misstatement. An audit includes examining, on a test basis, evidence supporting the amounts and disclosures in the financial statements. An audit also includes assessing the accounting principles used and significant estimates made by management, as well as evaluating the overall financial statement presentation. We believe that our audits provide a reasonable basis for our opinion.

In our opinion, the financial statements referred to above present fairly, in all material respects, the financial positions of XYZ Company and Subsidiaries and XYZ Company as of December 31, 19X2 and 19X1, and the results of their respective operations and their respective cash flows for each of the three years in the period ended December 31, 19X2 in conformity with generally accepted accounting principles.

(Name of Firm)

City, State
Date

When a company has subsidiaries, financial statements of the parent company alone are not in conformity with generally accepted accounting principles, and are not appropriate for issuance to shareholders as the financial statements of the primary reporting entity.

Occasionally, the existence of preferred stockholders, loan or other agreements, or other special requirements will necessitate the preparation of financial statements for the parent company alone. When the registrant is required to prepare such statements, it is generally considered appropriate to report on them without expressing a qualification because of the departure from generally accepted accounting principles, provided the following requirements are met:

- The consolidated financial statements (i.e., the primary financial statements) are included in the same document as parent company financial statements. The statements may be side by side or in separate sections of the document.

- The parent company statement headings indicate that the statements are those of the parent company only.

- The parent company statements disclose that the company publishes consolidated financial statements that are its primary financial statements and that the parent company statements are therefore not intended to be the primary financial statements.

- The financial statements include disclosures of (a) related-party transactions and (b) the basis on which the subsidiaries are carried in the parent company statements (cost or equity method).

If these requirements are met, the auditors' report should contain language that:

- Indicates the carrying basis of the investments in subsidiaries.

- States the intended purpose of the parent company statements.

- Cautions the reader to read the parent company statements in conjunction with the consolidated financial statements.

An illustrative auditors' report for this type of situation is as follows:

(Introductory paragraph)

We have audited the accompanying balance sheet of XYZ Company (parent company alone) as of December 31, 19XX, and the related statements of income, retained earnings, and cash flows for the year then ended (pages ____ to ____). These financial statements are the responsibility of the Company's management. Our responsibility is to express an opinion on these financial statements based on our audit.

(Scope paragraph)

We conducted our audit in accordance with generally accepted auditing standards....

(Explanatory paragraph)

The Company publishes consolidated financial statements that are its primary financial statements. The financial statements of XYZ Company (parent company alone), with investments in subsidiaries stated at cost, have been prepared solely for inclusion in the consolidated financial statements of XYZ Company and Subsidiaries. The financial statements of XYZ Company should be read in conjunction with the consolidated financial statements (pages _____ to _____) of XYZ Company and Subsidiaries.

(Opinion paragraph)

In our opinion, the financial statements referred to above present fairly, in all material respects, the financial position of XYZ Company (parent company alone) as of [at] December 31, 19XX, and the results of its operations and its cash flows for the year then ended, in conformity with generally accepted accounting principles.

If parent company financial statements required by a regulatory agency or an agreement (e.g., a loan agreement) are to be issued without the consolidated financial statements, the guidance in AU 623 should be followed.

20350. Reporting on Interim Financial Information

SAS 71 (AU Section 722) provides guidance as to the nature, timing, and extent of procedures to be applied by independent accountants in conducting reviews of interim financial information and as to the reporting applicable to such engagements. Paragraphs 36 through 39 of that section describe the auditor's responsibilities with respect to the quarterly financial information required to be included in annual reports to shareholders and in documents filed with the SEC pursuant to Regulation S-K (see section 63023).

Accountants may permit the use of their name and the inclusion or incorporation by reference of their report on a review of interim financial information in a document filed with the SEC if they have made a review of such information as specified in SAS

71. Paragraph 28 of that SAS provides the following example of the wording for such a report:

Report of Independent Accountants

We have reviewed the accompanying [*describe the statements or information reviewed*] of ABC Company and consolidated subsidiaries as of September 30, 19X1, and for the three-month and nine-month periods then ended. These financial statements (information) are (is) the responsibility of the company's management.

We conducted our review in accordance with standards established by the American Institute of Certified Public Accountants. A review of interim financial information consists principally of applying analytical procedures to financial data and making inquiries of persons responsible for financial and accounting matters. It is substantially less in scope than an audit conducted in accordance with generally accepted auditing standards, the objective of which is the expression of an opinion regarding the financial statements taken as a whole. Accordingly, we do not express such an opinion.

Based on our review, we are not aware of any material modifications that should be made to the accompanying financial statements (information) for them (it) to be in conformity with generally accepted accounting principles.

                                                        (Name of Firm)

City, State
Date

    Reference should be made to the full text of SAS 71 in connection with a review of interim financial information presented alone or that accompanies, or is included in a note to, audited financial statements.

    Reference should be made to section 20430 of this manual for a discussion of the manner in which an interim review report should be referred to in the experts section of 1933 Act registration statements and to section 20432 for a discussion of the awareness letter required of the independent accountant when such a report is included or incorporated by reference in a registration statement filed under the 1933 Act.

20360. Reporting on Condensed Financial Statements

As discussed in section 51000, interim financial statements included in documents filed with the SEC may be presented in the condensed format prescribed in Article 10 of Regulation S-X. Although interim financial statements are generally not required to be audited, in certain situations they may be presented in 1933 Act filings on an audited basis.

SAS No. 42, *Reporting on Condensed Financial Statements and Selected Financial Data* (AU Section 552.05), provides the following guidelines with respect to reporting in a client-prepared document on condensed financial statements:

> . . . the auditor's report on condensed financial statements that are derived from financial statements that he has audited should indicate (a) that the auditor has audited and expressed an opinion on the complete financial statements, (b) the date of the auditor's report on the complete financial statements, (c) the type of opinion expressed, and (d) whether, in the auditor's opinion, the information set forth in the condensed financial statements is fairly stated in all material respects in relation to the complete financial statements from which it has been derived.

The following is the wording of an auditors' report on condensed financial statements as provided in paragraph 6 of SAS No. 42 (as modified due to the issuance of SAS No. 58 and SFAS No. 95) (AU Section 552.06):

Report of Independent Accountants

We have audited, in accordance with generally accepted auditing standards, the consolidated balance sheet of X Company and Subsidiaries as of December 31, 19X0, and the related consolidated statements of income, retained earnings, and cash flows for the year then ended (not presented herein); and in our report dated February 15, 19X1, we expressed an unqualified opinion on those consolidated financial statements.

In our opinion, the information set forth in the accompanying condensed consolidated financial statements is fairly stated, in all material respects, in relation to the consolidated financial statements from which it has been derived.

[Note: The auditor may also specifically identify the condensed consolidated financial statements to which they are referring.]

If a statement is made in a client-prepared document that the condensed financial statements were derived from audited financial statements and the auditor is named, SAS No. 42 (AU Section 552.07) points out that "such a statement does not, in itself, require the auditor to report on the condensed statements, provided that they are included in a document that contains audited financial statements (or that incorporates such statements by reference to information filed with a regulatory agency)." However, if the client-prepared document in which the statement is made does not include audited financial statements (or does not incorporate such statements by reference to information filed with a regulatory agency), the auditor should request that either their name not be included in the document or that the client include the auditors' report on the condensed financial statements.

In certain situations, condensed financial statements derived from audited statements are presented on a comparative basis with interim financial information as of a subsequent date that is accompanied by an accountants' review report (discussed in section 20350). SAS No. 42 (as modified due to the issuance of SAS Nos. 56 and 58 and SFAS No. 95, and as amended by SAS No. 71) (AU Section 552.08) provides the following example of an accountants' review report to be issued in such situations. The example could apply, for instance, in a quarterly shareholders' report when the auditor is associated with the condensed balance sheet derived from the audited year-end financial statements:

Report of Independent Accountants

We have reviewed the condensed consolidated balance sheet of XYZ Company and Subsidiaries as of March 31, 19X1, and the related condensed consolidated statements of income and cash flows for the three-month periods ended March 31, 19X1 and 19X0. These financial statements are the responsibility of the company's management.

We conducted our review in accordance with standards established by the American Institute of Certified Public Accountants. A review of interim financial information consists principally of applying analytical procedures to financial data, and making inquiries of persons responsible for financial and accounting matters. It is substantially less in scope than an audit conducted in accordance with generally accepted auditing standards, the objective of which is the expression of an opinion regarding the financial statements taken as a whole. Accordingly, we do not express such an opinion.

Based on our review, we are not aware of any material modifications that should be made to the condensed consolidated financial statements referred to above for them to be in conformity with generally accepted accounting principles.

We have previously audited, in accordance with generally accepted auditing standards, the consolidated balance sheet as of December 31, 19X0, and the related consolidated statements of income, retained earnings, and cash flows for the year then ended (not presented herein); and in our report dated February 15, 19X1, we expressed an unqualified opinion on those consolidated financial statements. In our opinion, the information set forth in the accompanying condensed consolidated balance sheet as of December 31, 19X0, is fairly stated, in all material respects, in relation to the consolidated balance sheet from which it has been derived.

20370. Reporting on Selected Financial Data

Certain Selected Financial Data are required to be included in annual reports to shareholders and in certain registration statements and periodic reports filed with the SEC, as more fully discussed in section 63010. Independent accountants are sometimes requested by clients and underwriters to report on these data, and different approaches have been followed to comply with such requests. SAS No. 42 (AU Section 552) addresses this issue.

20371. Headnote. The inclusion of a headnote preceding the Selected Financial Data is optional; however, if presented, wording similar to the following may be used (the example assumes that all of the information included under Selected Financial Data has been derived from audited financial statements):

The financial data included in this table have been selected by the Company and have been derived from the consolidated financial statements for those years, which have been audited by (Name of Firm).

The SAS points out that a headnote reference to the auditor or to the fact that the data have been derived from audited financial statements does not, in itself, require the auditor to report on such data provided that the Selected Financial Data are presented in a document that contains audited financial statements (or, with respect to a public entity, that incorporates such statements by reference to information filed with a regulatory agency). If the document does not include (or incorporate by reference) audited financial statements, SAS No. 42 (AU Section 552.11) states that "the auditor should request that neither his name nor reference to him be associated with the information, or he should disclaim an opinion on the Selected Financial Data and request that the disclaimer be included in the document. If the client does not comply, the auditor should advise the client that he does not consent to either the use of his name or the reference to him, and he should consider what other actions might be appropriate."

SEC 20360

20372. Form of Report. When accountants are requested to make reference to the Selected Financial Data in their report, the following wording would be appropriate (AU Section 552.10):

Report of Independent Accountants

We have audited the consolidated balance sheets of XYZ Company and Subsidiaries as of December 31, 19X5 and 19X4, and the related consolidated statements of income, retained earnings, and cash flows for each of the three years in the period ended December 31, 19X5. These financial statements are the responsibility of the Company's management. Our responsibility is to express an opinion on these financial statements based on our audits.

We conducted our audits in accordance with generally accepted auditing standards. Those standards require that we plan and perform the audit to obtain reasonable assurance about whether the financial statements are free of material misstatement. An audit includes examining, on a test basis, evidence supporting the amounts and disclosures in the financial statements. An audit also includes assessing the accounting principles used and significant estimates made by management, as well as evaluating the overall financial statement presentation. We believe that our audits provided a reasonable basis for our opinion.

In our opinion, the consolidated financial statements referred to above present fairly, in all material respects, the financial position of XYZ Company and Subsidiaries as of December 31, 19X5 and 19X4, and the results of their operations and their cash flows for each of the three years in the period ended December 31, 19X5, in conformity with generally accepted accounting principles.

We have also previously audited, in accordance with generally accepted auditing standards, the consolidated balance sheets as of December 31, 19X3, 19X2, and 19X1, and the related statements of income, retained earnings, and cash flows for the years ended December 31, 19X2, and 19X1 (none of which are presented herein); and we expressed unqualified opinions on those consolidated financial statements.

In our opinion, the information set forth in the selected financial data for each of the five years in the period ended December 31, 19X5, appearing on page xx, is fairly stated, in all material respects, in relation to the consolidated financial statements from which it has been derived.

SEC 20372

20380. Reports of Other Independent Accountants

20381. General. In accordance with Regulation S-X Rule 2-05 (see section 50205), when the principal accountant has relied on the report of another independent accountant (AU Sections 543 and 722.19) or when the prior years' financial statements were audited by a predecessor accountant (AU Section 508), the report of the other accountant must be included as part of the registration statement or report being filed. However, when the primary accountant has assumed responsibility for the work performed by the other accountant, the report of the other accountant need not be included.

Reports of other independent accountants on which the primary accountant has relied and reports of predecessor accountants need not be included in the annual report to shareholders. However, these other reports must be included in Part II or Part IV of Form 10-K.

20382. Reliance on Other Auditors. When a significant part of the audit of the consolidated financial statements is performed by auditors other than the reporting auditors, a determination needs to be made as to whether the reporting auditors can in fact be considered the principal auditors. AU Section 543 provides guidance on the professional judgments auditors are required to make in deciding whether they may serve as principal auditors when they rely on other auditors for part of their audit; however, the literature does not specify any minimum percentages or other measurements.

20383. Predecessor Reports in 1933 Act Filings. Occasionally a company that is no longer a client files a registration statement containing financial statements for the period when accountants had served the client, and the accountants are asked to reissue their report. Because of the passage of time, the predecessor accountants need to satisfy themselves that their report can be reissued. In this regard accountants should follow the procedures described in AU Sections 711.11 and 530.06-.08.

Obtaining a letter of representation from the successor accountant is one of the required procedures. The following is an example of such a letter:

(Date)

Predecessor Firm
City and State

This letter is furnished in connection with the report you have been requested to provide with respect to the statements of income, retained earnings, and cash flows of XYZ Company for the year ended December 31, 19X1, which statements are to be included by the Company in its proposed registration statement to register under the Securities Act of 1933 an issue of (description of securities).

We have audited the balance sheets of (name of company) as of December 31, 19X3 and 19X2, and the related statements of income, retained earnings, and cash flows for the years then ended, all as included in the aforementioned registration statement. Our audits of such financial statements did not disclose any events or transactions subsequent to December 31, 19X1 that, in our opinion, would have a material effect upon the financial statements of XYZ Company for the year ended December 31, 19X1, or (except as stated in the notes to the financial statements included in the proof of [date] of the registration statement that has been furnished to you) would require disclosure in notes to the financial statements for the year ended 19X1.

Successor Firm

When the predecessor auditors are satisfied regarding the appropriateness of the financial statements covered by their report, they may reissue their report. An example of such a report follows:

We have audited the accompanying balance sheet of XYZ Company as of December 31, 19X1, and the related statements of income, retained earnings, and cash flows for the year then ended that appear in this prospectus. These financial statements are the responsibility of the Company's management. Our responsibility is to express an opinion on these financial statements based on our audit.

We conducted our audit in accordance with generally accepted auditing standards. Those standards require that we plan and perform the audit to obtain reasonable assurance about whether the financial statements are free of material misstatement. An audit includes examining, on a test basis, evidence supporting the amounts and disclosures in the financial statements. An audit also includes assessing the accounting principles used and significant estimates made by management, as well as evaluating the overall financial statement presentation. We believe that our audit provides a reasonable basis for our opinion.:

In our opinion, the financial statements referred to above present fairly, in all material respects, the financial position of XYZ Company as of December 31, 19X1, and the results of its operations and its cash flows for the year then ended in conformity with generally accepted accounting principles.

Predecessor Firm

City, State
Date (same as original report)

The predecessor auditors may become aware of events or transactions occurring subsequent to the date of their previous report on the financial statements of a prior period or may become aware of adjustments required in the prior period financial statements. In such cases, the predecessor auditors must evaluate the impact these items may have on their report. (Refer to AU Sections 711.10-.13 and 530.06-.08.)

20384. Jointly-Signed Accountants' Reports. It is not uncommon, particularly with respect to foreign registrants, for two independent auditors to sign the accountants' report included in an SEC filing by a particular company. In such situations the SEC staff has indicated that if the joint auditor approach is followed, it will be presumed that each firm has performed a sufficient level of work to qualify as the principal auditor.

20390. Reporting on Pro Forma Financial Information

20391. General. The AICPA's Statement of Standards for Attestation Engagements, *Reporting on Pro Forma Financial Information*, provides guidelines with respect to the examination and review of pro forma financial information. The AICPA's standard (AT 300) points out that the purpose of pro forma financial information is to reflect what the significant effects on historical financial information might have been had a consummated or probable transaction (or event) occurred at an earlier date. It indicates that pro forma financial information is commonly used to indicate the effects of transactions such as business combinations, changes in capitalization, dispositions of a significant portion of a business, changes in the form of a business or proposed sales of securities and application of proceeds. AT 300 further notes that the pro forma adjustments to historical financial information should be based on management assumptions and should give effect to all significant results *directly attributable* to the transaction or event. Refer to section 51100 for a discussion of the SEC's requirements regarding the form and content of pro forma financial information. See section 20525 for a discussion regarding accountants' consents issued in connection with pro forma financial information.

20392. Conditions for Reporting. According to the AICPA's attestation standard (AT 300.07) the independent accountant may agree to report on an examination or a review of pro forma financial information if the following conditions are met:

- The document containing the pro forma financial information includes (or incorporates by reference) complete historical financial statements of the entity for the most recent year (or for the preceding year if financial statements for the most recent year are not yet available). In addition, if pro forma financial information is presented for an interim period, the document should include historical interim financial information for that period. With respect to business combinations, the document should include the historical financial information for the significant constituent parts of the combined entity.

- The historical financial statements on which the pro forma financial information is based have been audited or reviewed, and the accountants' audit or review reports is included or incorporated by reference. The level of assurance given by the accountant on the pro forma financial information should be limited to the lowest level of assurance provided on the historical financial statements of any significant constituent part of the combined entity. For example, if the underlying historical financial statements of each significant constituent part of the combined entity have been audited as of year-end and reviewed as of an interim date, the accountant may perform an examination of the pro forma financial information as of year-end but is limited to performing a review as of the interim date.

- The accountant should have an appropriate level of knowledge of the accounting and financial reporting practices of each significant constituent part of the combined entity. The standard indicates that this knowledge would ordinarily have been obtained by the accountant auditing or reviewing historical financial statements of each entity for the most recent annual or interim period on which the pro forma financial information is presented. It stresses, however, that if another accountant has performed such an audit or a review, the need for the accountant reporting on the pro forma financial information to gain an understanding of the entity's accounting and financial reporting practices is not diminished, and that accountant should consider whether, under the particular circumstances, he or she can acquire sufficient knowledge of these matters to perform the procedures necessary to report on the pro forma financial information.

20393. Accountants' Objectives in an Examination of Pro Forma Financial Information. AT 300.08 indicates that the objective of the accountants' examination procedures applied to pro forma financial information is to provide reasonable assurance as to whether:

- Management's assumptions provide a reasonable basis for presenting the significant effects directly attributable to the underlying transaction (or event).

- The related pro forma adjustments give appropriate effect to those assumptions.

- The pro forma column reflects the proper application of those adjustments to the historical financial statements.

20394. Accountants' Objectives in a Review of Pro Forma Financial Information. AT 300.09 indicates that the objective of accountants' review procedures applied to pro forma financial information is to provide negative assurance as to whether any information came to their attention to cause them to believe that:

- Management's assumptions do not provide a reasonable basis for presenting the significant effects directly attributable to the transaction (or event).

- The related pro forma adjustments do not give appropriate effect to those assumptions.

- The pro forma column does not reflect the proper application of those adjustments to the historical financial statements.

20395. Reporting. According to AT 300.11, the independent accountants' report on pro forma financial information should be dated upon the completion of the appropriate procedures. This report may be combined with the accountants' report on historical financial information or, as is more typically done, may appear as a separate report. If the reports are presented together and the examination or review of pro forma information is completed after the date of completion of the audit or review of historical financial information, the report would need to be dual dated; for example, "October 15, 19X8, except for the paragraphs regarding pro forma financial information as to which the date is November 20, 19X8."

AT 300.12 indicates that the independent accountants' report on pro forma financial information should include:

- An identification of the pro forma financial information involved.

- A reference to the financial statements from which the historical financial information is derived and a statement as to whether such financial statements were audited or reviewed. The report on pro forma financial information should refer to any modification in the accountants' report on the historical financial statements.

- A statement that the examination or review of the pro forma financial information was made in accordance with standards established by the American Institute of Certified Public Accountants. If a review is performed, the report should include the following statement: "A review is substantially less in scope than an examination, the objective of which is the expression of an opinion on the pro forma financial information. Accordingly, we do not express such an opinion."

- A separate paragraph explaining the objective of pro forma financial information and its limitations.

- (1) If an examination of pro forma financial information has been performed, the accountants' opinion as to whether management's assumptions provide a reasonable basis for presenting the significant effects directly attributable to the transaction (or event), whether the related pro forma adjustments give appropriate effect to those assumptions, and whether the pro forma column reflects the proper application of those adjustments to the historical financial statements (see sections 20396 and 20397 for examples). (2) If a review of pro forma financial information has been performed, the accountants' conclusion as to whether any information came to their attention to cause them to believe that management's assumptions do not provide a reasonable basis for presenting the significant effects directly attributable to the transaction (or event), or that the related pro forma adjustments do not give appropriate effect to those assumptions, or that the pro forma column does not reflect the proper application of those adjustments to the historical financial statements.

20396. Report on Examination of Pro Forma Financial Information. The following is an example of an unqualified report on the examination of pro forma financial information (AT 300.16, Appendix A).

Independent Accountants' Report on
Pro Forma Financial Information

We have examined the pro forma adjustments reflecting the transaction *[or event]* described in Note 1 and the application of those adjustments to the historical amounts in *[the assembly of]*[1] the accompanying pro forma condensed balance sheet of X Company as of December 31, 19X1, and the pro forma condensed statement of income for the year then ended. The historical condensed financial statements are derived from the historical financial statements of X Company, which were audited by us, and of Y Company, which were audited by other accountants[2], appearing elsewhere herein *[or incorporated by reference]*. Such pro forma adjustments are based upon management's assumptions described in Note 2. Our examination was made in accordance with standards established by the American Institute of Certified Public Accountants and, accordingly, included such procedures as we considered necessary in the circumstances.

The objective of this pro forma financial information is to show what the significant effects on the historical financial information might have been had the transaction *[or event]* occurred at an earlier date. However, the pro forma condensed financial statements are not necessarily indicative of the results of operations or related effects on financial position that would have been attained had the above-mentioned transaction *[or event]* actually occurred earlier.

[Additional paragraph(s) may be added to emphasize certain matters relating to the attest engagement.]

In our opinion, management's assumptions provide a reasonable basis for presenting the significant effects directly attributable to the above-mentioned transaction *[or event]* described in Note 1, the related pro forma adjustments give appropriate effect to those assumptions, and the pro forma column reflects the proper application of those adjustments to the

---

[1]This wording is appropriate when one column of pro forma financial information is presented without separate columns of historical financial information and pro forma adjustments.

[2]If either accountants' report includes an explanatory paragraph or is other than unqualified, that fact should be referred to within this report.

historical financial statement amounts in the pro forma condensed balance sheet as of December 31, 19X1, and the pro forma condensed statement of income for the year then ended.

(Name of Firm)

City, State
Date

20397. Pro Forma Pooling-of-Interests Report. Pro forma adjustments relating to a proposed business combination to be accounted for as a pooling of interests generally affect only the equity section of the pro forma balance sheet since a pooling is accounted for by combining historical amounts retroactively. In such situations, management's assumptions need not be considered unless the pro forma financial statements include adjustments to conform the accounting principles of the combining entities. Accordingly, the accountants' report on a proposed pooling transaction need not address management's assumptions. An example of a report that does not address management's assumptions follows (AT 300.19, Appendix D):

Independent Accountants' Report on Pro Forma Financial Information Giving Effect to a Business Combination To Be Accounted for as a Pooling of Interests

We have examined the pro forma adjustments reflecting the proposed business combination to be accounted for as a pooling of interests described in Note 1 and the application of those adjustments to the historical amounts in the accompanying pro forma condensed balance sheet of X Company as of December 31, 19X1, and the pro forma condensed statements of income for each of the three years in the period then ended. These historical condensed financial statements are derived from the historical financial statements of X Company, which were audited by us[1], and of Y Company, which were audited by other accountants, appearing elsewhere herein *[or incorporated by reference]*. Our examination was made in accordance with standards established by the American Institute of Certified Public Accountants and, accordingly, included such procedures as we considered necessary in the circumstances.

---

[1] If either accountants' report includes an explanatory paragraph or is other than unqualified, the fact should be referred to within this report.

The objectives of this pro forma financial information is to show what the significant effects on the historical information might have been had the proposed transaction occurred at an earlier date.

[Additional paragraph(s) may be added to emphasize certain matters relating to the attest engagement.]

In our opinion, the accompanying condensed pro forma financial statements of X Company as of December 31, 19X1, and for each of the three years in the period then ended give appropriate effect to the pro forma adjustments necessary to reflect the proposed business combination on a pooling-of-interests basis as described in Note 1 and the pro forma column reflects the proper application of those adjustments to the historical financial statements.

(Name of Firm)

City, State
Date

20400. REFERENCES TO INDEPENDENT ACCOUNTANTS IN SEC FILINGS

20410. Expertizing 1933 Act Filings

The 1933 Act imposes liabilities for false or misleading statements in a registration statement, as discussed in section 12020. However, the Act provides that this liability may not exist, except as to the issuer of the securities, with respect to information included in any part of the registration statement that is purported to be included "on the authority of an expert" (Section 11(b)(3)(B)). Because of the protection afforded to officers, directors, and underwriters by this provision, lawyers for the registrant and the underwriters usually request the insertion of language in the prospectus to specify that the audited financial statements and supporting schedules are included in reliance on the report of the independent accountants as "experts." There is no regulatory requirement for the inclusion of an experts section; however, if the independent accountants are referred to as experts, their written consent to such reference is required.

The wording used to refer to the independent accountants as experts needs to be reviewed to ensure that it does not impute responsibility for financial data that the accountant does not intend to, or should not, assume. This expertizing declaration should be limited to financial statements and financial statement schedules covered by the accountants' report. If the accountants' report departs in any manner from a standard report, it is advisable to make reference to that fact.

20415. Use of Expertizing Language in Non-SEC Documents

Independent accountants are sometimes requested to furnish a consent in connection with expertizing language proposed to be included in a document that is not being filed with the SEC. An example of a situation in which such a request may be made is in connection with an official statement for a bond offering being filed with a state agency.

Since, as described above, the use of expertizing language is only relevant in the context of the liability provisions of the Federal Securities Acts, its inclusion in other documents is inappropriate.

During 1992, the Auditing Standards Board (ASB) issued two interpretations of AU 711 (refer to AU 9711.2 and .3) relating to consents (see section 20530) and expertizing in connection with non-SEC filings (i.e., securities offerings other than those registered under the 1933 Act). The ASB's interpretation related to expertizing states, in part, that the auditor should not consent to be named, or referred to, as an expert in an offering document in connection with securities offerings other than those registered under the 1933 Act. This is because the term "expert" is typically undefined outside of the context of the 1933 Act, and the auditor's responsibility, as a result of the use of that term, would also be undefined.

When a client wishes to refer to the auditor's role in a non-1933 Act offering document, the caption "Independent Auditors" should be used in the title of that section of the document instead of the caption "Experts," and the auditors should not be referred to as experts anywhere in the document. The following language, based on AU 9711.15, should be used to describe the auditor's role:

INDEPENDENT AUDITORS

> The financial statements as of December 31, 19XX and for the year then ended, included in this offering circular, have been audited by (Name of Firm), independent accountants, as stated in their report(s) appearing herein.

If the independent accountants' report departs in any manner from a standard report, it is advisable to make reference to that fact, using language such as the following:

> [...as stated in their report], which includes a (state manner in which report departs from standard report, e.g., explanatory paragraph, qualification, disclaimer, or adverse opinion).

20420. Standard Reference in 1933 Act Filings

As previously described (refer also to section 20500), independent accountants are required to consent in writing to any representations in the registration statement that they have audited or "certified" the financial statements and to any references to them as "experts" in accounting and auditing. Accordingly, if the expertizing language proposed by the attorneys for inclusion in the registration statement contains representations that are unacceptable, it must be corrected before the consent is signed. The expertizing language is generally similar to the following:

EXPERTS

The consolidated balance sheets as of December 31, 19X4 and 19X3 and the consolidated statements of income, retained earnings, and cash flows for each of the three years in the period ended December 31, 19X4, included [or incorporated by reference] in this prospectus, have been included [or incorporated] herein in reliance on the report of (Name of Firm), independent accountants, given on the authority of that firm as experts in accounting and auditing.

20430. Review of Interim Financial Information

20431. Reference to Accountants' Report. FRP Section 605.04 provides that when a report on a review of interim financial information in accordance with AU Section 722 (see section 20350) is included or incorporated in a registration statement, any discussions about the accountants' involvement should:

- Clarify the fact that the accountants' review report included in such registration statements is not a "report" or "part" of the registration statement within the meaning of Sections 7 and 11 of the 1933 Act.

- Specifically state that the independent accountants' Section 11 liability (see section 12020) does not extend to such report.

- Be supported by a letter from the independent accountants acknowledging their awareness that their review report is being included in the registration statement.

AU Section 711.09 provides suggested language concerning the involvement of independent accountants to be included in the experts section when a review report is incorporated by reference in a registration statement filed under the 1933 Act. Since the Independent Accountants' Section 11 liability does not extend to such a review report (discussed above), it is preferable to use the caption "Independent Public Accountants" rather than "Experts" as the title to the section. Suggested report language, consistent with the report provided in AU Section 711.09, follows:

INDEPENDENT PUBLIC ACCOUNTANTS

The consolidated balance sheets as of December 31, 19X4 and 19X3, and the consolidated statements of income, retained earnings, and cash flows for each of the three years in the period ended December 31, 19X4, incorporated by reference in this prospectus, have been included herein

SEC 20431

in reliance on the report of (Name of Firm), independent accountants, given on the authority of that firm as experts in auditing and accounting. With respect to the unaudited interim financial information for the periods ended March 31, 19X5 and 19X4, incorporated by reference in this prospectus, the independent accountants have reported that they have applied limited procedures in accordance with professional standards for a review of such information. However, their separate report included in the Company's quarterly report on Form 10-Q for the quarter ended March 31, 19X5, and incorporated by reference herein, states that they did not audit and they do not express an opinion on that interim financial information. Accordingly, the degree of reliance on their report on such information should be restricted in light of the limited nature of the review procedures applied. The accountants are not subject to the liability provisions of Section 11 of the Securities Act of 1933 for their report on the unaudited interim financial information because that report is not a "report" or a "part" of the registration statement prepared or certified by the accountants within the meaning of Sections 7 and 11 of the Act.

A similar description of the status of the accountants' review report would ordinarily be satisfactory when such report is presented in the registration statement rather than incorporated by reference. In that case, the description in the prospectus would specifically refer to the review report in the registration statement (see footnote 3 to AU Section 711).

20432. Awareness Letter. If the accountants' report on a review of interim financial information is included or incorporated by reference into a 1933 Act filing, Regulation S-K Exhibit requirements (see section 66000) specify that a letter from the accountants acknowledging the inclusion or incorporation of their report must generally be furnished as an exhibit to the registration statement.

An accountants' "awareness letter" would be required, for example, when a quarterly filing on Form 10-Q containing an accountants' report on a review of interim financial information is incorporated by reference into Form S-3 or S-8.

As discussed in sections 42274 and 42431, post-effective amendments for registration statements filed on Forms S-3 and S-8 are generally no longer required; however, periodic reports filed on Forms 10-K and 10-Q are automatically incorporated by reference into these 1933 Act filings. In such situations, if the accountants' review report is included in Form 10-Q, the required accountants' awareness letter concerning the incorporation by reference of the report in Form S-3 or S-8 should be included as an attachment to Form 10-Q. The review report should *not* be expanded to include the required awareness language.

SEC 20431

Although the awareness letter need not follow any particular format, the following example would be appropriate when the letter is furnished as an exhibit to a 1933 Act registration statement:

Securities and Exchange Commission
450 Fifth Street, N.W.
Washington, D.C. 20549

> Re: (name of registrant)
> Registration on Form

We are aware that our report dated (date of report) on our review of interim financial information of (name of registrant) for the period ended (state period) and included in the Company's quarterly report on Form 10-Q for the quarter then ended is incorporated by reference in this registration statement. Pursuant to Rule 436(c) under the Securities Act of 1933, this report should not be considered a part of the registration statement prepared or certified by us within the meaning of Sections 7 and 11 of that Act.

> (Name of Firm)

When the awareness letter is included as an attachment to Form 10-Q, the foregoing example would be modified accordingly.

20500. ACCOUNTANTS' CONSENTS

20510. Consents in 1933 Act Filings

Independent accountants are required to consent in writing to any representation in a 1933 Act registration statement that they have audited or "certified" the financial statements and that their report may be relied on as being rendered by experts in accounting and auditing. Such consents are required pursuant to Section 7 of the 1933 Act, the pertinent portion of which follows:

> If any accountant, engineer, or appraiser, or any person whose profession gives authority to a statement made by him is named as having prepared or certified . . . a report or valuation for use in connection with the registration statement, the written consent of such person shall be filed with the registration statement.

Rule 436 under the 1933 Act excludes accountants' review reports on unaudited interim financial information from the definition of a "report" within the meaning of Section 7 of the 1933 Act. Accordingly, consents are not required in connection with these reports. (Refer to section 20350 of the manual for further discussion of accountants' review reports.)

Underwriters usually request the inclusion of expertizing language in a 1933 Act prospectus to specifically define the independent accountants' responsibilities with respect to the audited financial statements and financial statement schedules, as discussed in section 20410 of this manual. The accountants' consent is required to make reference to this experts section of the registration statement.

Consents included in 1933 Act filings are typically worded as follows:

CONSENT OF INDEPENDENT ACCOUNTANTS

We consent to the inclusion in this registration statement on Form S-1 (File No. 2-0000) of our report dated February 7, 19X4, on our audits of the financial statements and financial statement schedules of XYZ Company. We also consent to the reference to our firm under the caption "Experts."

(Name of Firm)

City, State
March 17, 19X4

The accountants' consent is required to be dated, signed manually, and included in Part II of the 1933 Act registration statement. The consent is usually dated as of, or a few days prior to, the filing date of the registration statement. Any changes to the financial data covered by the accountants' report that occur between the initial 1933 Act filing and the filing of an amendment will require the inclusion in the amendment of a new manually signed consent as of a more current date. While technically not required, it is not uncommon for a registrant's counsel to request that the auditor manually sign a new consent every time an amendment is filed regardless of whether the financial data has changed.

Signing and dating a consent as of a date later than the date of the auditors' report does not update that report. Nor does the dating of a consent change in any way the auditor's responsibility to "keep current" through the effective date of the registration statement. The "keep current" review is performed to sustain the burden of proof that the auditor has made a "reasonable investigation" under Section 11 of the 1933 Act of the parts of the registration statement on which the auditor has reported. This gives the auditor "...reasonable grounds to believe....at the time such part of the registration statement became effective....there was no omission of a material fact..." (see AU Section 711).

The SEC will consider an application to dispense with the consent requirement in certain limited circumstances in which obtaining the consent would be impractical or would result in undue hardship on the part of the registrant (see Rule 437 under the 1933 Act). However, these situations are unusual, and the application establishing the grounds for the waiver needs to be submitted to the SEC prior to the effective date of the registration statement.

20520. Consents in 1934 Act Filings

A manually signed accountants' consent is required to be included in a document filed under the 1934 Act in certain situations, including the following:

- The accountants' report in the document is being incorporated by reference into a currently effective 1933 Act registration statement.

- The accountants' report included in a document filed under another of the acts administered by the SEC is being incorporated by reference.

- Audited financial information previously included in a 1934 Act filing is being amended.

A consent is not required in a document filed under the 1934 Act when financial information is being incorporated by reference from another 1934 Act filing or when financial statements are incorporated by reference in Form 10-K from the annual report to shareholders (see section 41171). However, in all such instances the auditor must manually sign at least one copy of the report when it is filed with the SEC.

20521. Incorporation of 1934 Act Report into a 1933 Act Filing. An accountants' consent is required to be included in a document filed under the 1934 Act when both of the following conditions exist: (1) the 1934 Act form is filed after a 1933 Act registration statement has become effective but before the offering involved has terminated *and* (2) the 1934 Act form is automatically incorporated into the 1933 Act registration statement. These circumstances exist, for example, when a Form 10-K is filed subsequent to the effective date of a Form S-3 (see section 42250) but prior to termination of the offering. To avoid filing an amendment to Form S-3 that would include only the accountants' consent, a consent is included in Form 10-K. An example of the wording of such a consent follows:

CONSENT OF INDEPENDENT ACCOUNTANTS

We consent to the incorporation by reference in the registration statement of XYZ, Inc. on Form S-3 (File No. 2-0000) of our report dated February 7, 19X4, on our audits of the consolidated financial statements and financial statement schedules of XYZ, Inc. as of December 31, 19X3 and 19X2, and for the years ended December 31, 19X3, 19X2, and 19X1, which report is included (or incorporated by reference) in this Annual Report on Form 10-K.

(Name of Firm)

City, State
March 28, 19X4

The date of the consent has no particular relevance, since auditors must "keep current" with respect to the financial statements on which they have reported through the *filing date* of the Form 10-K. The consent may be dated as of, or a few days prior to, the filing date of the annual report on Form 10-K. The Form S-3 registration statement is automatically amended and updated when the Form 10-K is filed. (See discussion of "keeping current" in section 19050.)

An accountants' consent covering future material incorporated by reference would constitute an "open-ended" consent and, therefore, should *not* be given.

A consent to the incorporation by reference in Form S-8 of the accountants' report included (or incorporated by reference) in Form 10-K should follow the foregoing example. (Refer also to section 42432.)

20522. Incorporation of 1933 Act Report into a 1934 Act Filing. As discussed in section 41171, Rule 12b-23 permits the incorporation by reference in a 1934 Act filing of financial statements included in a 1933 Act registration statement that has been filed with the SEC, even if the 1933 Act document is not yet effective. If the financial statements filed elsewhere with the Commission, provided they meet certain criteria, including those included in the 1933 Act registration statement, are subsequently amended, the 1934 Act filing that incorporated the financial statements by reference is also required to be amended.

Pursuant to Rule 12b-36, independent accountants must provide a written consent to the incorporation by reference in a 1934 Act filing of their report included in a filing under another act. The text of this rule follows:

Rule 12b-36. Use of Financial Statements
Filed Under Other Acts

Where copies of certified financial statements filed under other acts administered by the Commission are filed with a statement or report, the accountant's certificate shall be manually signed or manually signed copies of the certificate shall be filed with the financial statements. Where such financial statements are incorporated by reference in a statement or report, the written consent of the accountant to such incorporation by reference shall be filed with the statement or report. Such consent shall be dated and signed manually.

An example of the wording for such a consent follows:

We consent to the incorporation by reference in this annual report on Form 10-K of our report dated March 17, 19X4, on our audit of the consolidated financial statements of XYZ Company as of December 31, 19X3 and 19X2, and for the three years in the period ended December 31, 19X3, appearing in the registration statement on Form S-1 (SEC File No. 2-0000) of XYZ Co. filed with the Securities and Exchange Commission pursuant to the Securities Act of 1933.

(Name of Firm)

City, State
March 17, 19X4

Note that the date of the consent coincides with the date of the accountants' report referred to in the consent. However, this date does not change in any way the auditor's responsibility to "keep current" through the effective date of the 1933 Act registration statement (see section 20510).

20523. Amending Audited Financial Information Included in a 1934 Act Filing. Amendments to 1934 Act registration statements and reports are filed under cover of the form amended, designated by adding the letter "A" after the form title, e.g., "Form 10-K/A," as discussed in section 41700 of this manual. If an amendment to a document filed under the 1934 Act involves changes in a financial statement or financial statement schedule covered by the accountants' report, the accountant must provide a consent to be included in the amended form to acknowledge the substitution. The consent acknowledges that the report included in the original filing covers the revised information.

An example of a consent to an amendment of a balance sheet and supporting schedule follows:

We consent to the application of our report dated February 17, 19X4, included in the annual report on Form 10-K of XYZ Co. for the year ended December 31, 19X3, to the amended balance sheet as of December 31, 19X3, and amended Schedule V for the year ended December 31, 19X3, which are included in this amendment on Form 10-K/A.

(Name of Firm)

City, State
Date of Filing

20524. Impact of a SAS No. 58 Explanatory Paragraph. SAS No. 58, *Reports on Audited Financial Statements*, states that certain circumstances, while not affecting the independent accountants' unqualified opinion, may require accountants to add an explanatory paragraph to their standard report. The following are examples of situations that may require the inclusion of an explanatory paragraph:

- At the date of the accountants' report there are uncertain events that may affect the financial statements that cannot be reasonably estimated.

SEC 20522

- There is substantial doubt about the entity's ability to continue as a going concern.

- There has been a material change between periods in accounting principles or in the method of their application.

If the independent accountants' report includes an explanatory paragraph it is advisable to make reference to that fact in the expertizing statement to ensure that the financial statement reader is aware of its existence. The following is suggested wording for such a statement:

EXPERTS

The consolidated balance sheet as of December 31, 19X8 and 19X7 and the consolidated statements of income, retained earnings, and cash flows for each of the three years in the period ended December 31, 19X8, incorporated by reference in this prospectus, have been incorporated herein in reliance on the report, which includes an explanatory paragraph ... (state the subject of the paragraph), of (Name of Firm), independent accountants, given on the authority of that firm as experts in accounting and auditing.

The SEC's rules and regulations do not require that reference be made in an independent accountants' consent to an explanatory paragraph in the accountants' report. However, if the independent accountant believes it is prudent to modify the consent, a reference may be made in the consent to the explanatory paragraph. The following is an example of how the consent might be worded in this type of situation:

CONSENT OF INDEPENDENT ACCOUNTANTS

We consent to the inclusion in this registration statement on Form S-1 (File No. 2-0000) of our report, which includes an explanatory paragraph...(state the subject of the paragraph), dated February 7, 19X9 on our audit(s) of the financial statements and the financial statement schedules of XYZ Company. We also consent to the reference to our firm under the caption "Experts."

(Name of Firm)

City, State
March 17, 19X9

SEC 20524

20525. Accountants' Consents on Pro Forma Financial Statements. The SEC staff has informally expressed the following views regarding accountants' consents relating to reports issued on pro forma financial statements:

- An accountants' consent would not be required for a review report covering pro forma financial statements based on historical statements that have been reviewed, but not audited (e.g., pro formas based on interim financial statements that were subjected to a SAS 71 review).

- An accountants' consent is required if there is an examination of pro forma financial statements.

- An accountants' consent is required if a review of pro forma financial statements is performed based upon historical financial statements that have been audited.

It is important to note, however, that the issue of whether a consent is required in a particular situation is a legal determination outside the realm of expertise of the independent accountant.

20530. Consents in Non-SEC Filings

During 1992, the ASB issued two interpretations of AU 711 (refer to AU 9711.2 and .3) relating to consents and expertizing (see section 20415) in connection with non-SEC filings (i.e., securities offerings other than those registered under the 1933 Act). The interpretation states that it is not usually necessary for the accountant to provide a consent in a non-1933 Act offering document. A consent may be provided, however, if one is requested, and the following example language is presented in the interpretation:

CONSENT OF INDEPENDENT AUDITOR

We agree to the inclusion in this offering circular of our report, dated February 5, 19XX, on our audit of the financial statements of XYZ Company.

If the independent auditor's report departs in any manner from a standard report, it is advisable to make reference to that fact. The following would be appropriate to add:

[...of our report] which includes a (state manner in which the report departs from a standard report, e.g., explanatory paragraph, qualification, disclaimer, or adverse opinion.)

20600. ACCOUNTANTS' LETTERS

20605. Letters for Underwriters and Certain Other Requesting Parties

As part of their "due-diligence" activities, underwriters commonly seek "comfort" from the independent accountant, formally expressed in a "comfort letter," on financial information in registration statements that is not covered by the accountants' report and on events subsequent to the report date. The comfort letter, which is neither required by nor filed with the SEC, supplements the investigation made by an underwriter before it offers securities of an issuer to the public.

SAS No. 72 permits accountants to provide a comfort letter only to underwriters with a statutory due diligence defense under section 11 of the 1933 Act. A comfort letter may be addressed to other parties with a statutory due diligence defense under section 11 of the 1933 Act only when an attorney for the requesting party issues a written opinion to the accountant that states that such party has a due diligence defense. If the requesting party cannot provide such a letter, they must provide a representation letter addressed to the accountant and signed by the requesting party containing the following wording as prescribed by paragraph 6 of SAS No. 72:

> "This review process, applied to the information relating to the issuer, is (will be) substantially consistent with the due diligence review process that we would perform if this placement of securities (or issuance of securities in an acquisition transaction) were being registered pursuant to the Securities Act of 1933 (the Act). We are knowledgeable with respect

to the due diligence review process that would be performed if this placement of securities were being registered pursuant to the Act."

As indicated in footnote 5 to paragraph 6, the wording should be revised if the requesting party is not an underwriter as follows:

"This review process...is substantially consistent with the due diligence review process that an underwriter would perform in connection with this placement of securities. We are knowledgeable with respect to the due diligence review process that an underwriter would perform in connection with the placement of securities registered pursuant to the Securities Act of 1933."

SAS No. 72 also permits accountants to issue a comfort letter to a broker-dealer or other financial intermediary, acting as a principal or agent in an offering or a placement of securities, in connection with the following types of securities offerings, provided that the requesting party provides to the independent accountant the representation letter referred to above:

- Foreign offerings, including Regulation S, Eurodollar, and other offshore offerings.

- Transactions that are exempt from the registration requirements of section 5 of the 1933 Act, including those pursuant to Regulation A, Regulation D, and Rule 144A.

- Offerings of securities issued or backed by governmental, municipal, banking, tax-exempt, or other entities that are exempt from registration under the 1933 Act.

In addition, accountants may also issue a comfort letter pursuant to SAS No. 72 in connection with acquisitions (e.g., cross-comfort letters in a typical Form S-4 or Merger proxy situation) involving an exchange of stock when the letters are requested by the buyer and/or seller, provided that the requesting party provides to the independent accountant the representation letter referred to above.

The content of the comfort letter may vary, depending on the information included in the filing and on the information requested by the underwriter or other requesting party. SAS No. 72 provides examples of letters that may be used under various circumstances. In general, the letter may include:

- Certain representations with respect to the accountant's independence.

- An opinion on whether the audited financial statements and financial statement schedules comply as to form in all material respects with the applicable accounting requirements of the 1933 Act and the related published rules and regulations thereunder.

- Certain negative assurances or, in some cases (discussed below), reporting procedures performed and findings obtained, with respect to unaudited financial statements, condensed interim financial information, capsule financial information, pro forma financial information, financial forecasts, and changes in selected financial statement items subsequent to the date and period of the latest financial statements included (or incorporated by reference) in the registration statement.

- Comments on tables, statistics, and other financial information appearing in the registration statement.

- Negative assurance as to whether certain non-financial statement information in the registration statement complies as to form in all material respects with Regulation S-K.

As noted above, certain comments should be limited to negative assurance because the independent accountant has not performed an audit of that information in accordance with generally accepted auditing standards. Negative assurance consists of a statement by the accountant that, as a result of performing specified procedures, nothing came to their attention that caused them to believe that specified matters do not meet a specified standard (e.g., that any material modifications should be made to the unaudited financial statements for them to be in conformity with generally accepted accounting principles).

It is important to note that accountants may give negative assurance on unaudited condensed interim financial information, capsule financial information, and pro forma financial information *only* when they have, among other requirements, conducted an audit of the annual financial statements or a review of the interim financial statements in accordance with SAS No. 71 (interim financial information). Otherwise, the accountant is limited to reporting on the procedures performed and the findings obtained.

It is also important to note that the accountant may provide negative assurance *only* as to subsequent changes in specified financial statement items as of a date less than 135 days from the end of the most recent period for which the accountant has performed an audit or a review. For subsequent changes as of a date 135 days or more from the end of the most recent period for which the accountant has performed an audit or a review, the accountant is limited to reporting procedures performed and findings obtained.

Regarding financial forecasts, in order for the accountant to perform agreed-upon procedures and report the findings in a comfort letter, the accountant needs to acquire sufficient knowledge of the entity's internal control structure, and to perform procedures and follow the guidance pursuant to the Statement on Standards for Accountants' Services on Prospective Financial Information—*Financial Forecasts and Projections*. Negative assurance cannot be provided on the results of procedures performed. In addition, the accountant cannot provide negative assurance with respect to the forecast complying with Rule 11-03 of Regulation S-X (see section 51103) unless the accountant has performed an examination of the forecast in accordance with *Financial Forecasts and Projections*.

Comments on tables, statistics, and other financial information included in the textual portion of the registration statement should be identified by reference to specific captions, tables, etc. Description of the procedures followed and a statement of the findings (generally expressed in terms of agreement between items compared) may be stated individually for each item of specific information commented on; or, among other alternatives, the procedures performed may be identified with specified symbols and referenced to the items to which those procedures have been applied on a copy of the prospectus which is attached to the comfort letter. However, the independent accountant should comment only on information expressed in dollars (or in percentages derived from dollar amounts) and on quantitative information obtained from accounting records that are subject to the entity's internal control structure or that have been derived directly from such accounting records by analysis or computation. Comments on information included in the textual portion of the registration statement should be followed by a disclaimer of responsibility with respect to legal interpretations of the textual requirements and responses as well as the sufficiency of the procedures for the underwriter's intended purpose. The letter should also point out that such procedures would not necessarily disclose material misstatements or omissions in the information to which the comments relate.

The following additional points relating to comfort letters are worthy of particular note:

- Accountants should not comment on matters merely because they happen to be present and are capable of reading, counting, measuring, or performing other functions that might be applicable. Examples include square footage of facilities, number of employees (except as related to a given payroll period) and backlog information, unless such information is subject to the entity's internal control structure (which is ordinarily not the case).

- The accountant should not comment on matters that are primarily subjective in nature or that involve exercising the business judgment of management, such as the appropriateness of disclosed explanations regarding changes in financial elements contained within Management's Discussion and Analysis.

SEC 20605

- Accountants may comment on compliance with published SEC rules and regulations applicable to the form and content of financial statements and financial statement schedules, including pro forma financial statements and unaudited condensed interim financial statements; however, they should not comment on compliance with SEC rules and regulations regarding the form of other information included in the registration statement unless:

  - •• The information is derived from the accounting records subject to the internal control structure policies and procedures of the entity's accounting system, or has been derived from such accounting records by analysis or computation; and

  - •• This information is capable of evaluation against reasonable criteria that have been established by the SEC.

  Disclosure requirements that generally meet these conditions include Item 301, "Selected Financial Data," Item 302, "Supplementary Financial Information," Item 402, "Executive Compensation," and Item 503(d) "Ratio of Earnings to Fixed Charges." However, SAS No. 72 acknowledges that even with respect to these items, it may be inappropriate to provide negative assurance regarding conformity with Regulation S-K because the above conditions may not be met.

- Accountants should not give negative assurance on their report on the client's financial statements.

- Accountants should not repeat their opinion on the financial statements in the comfort letter.

- Accountants should not give negative assurance on financial statements and financial statement schedules that have been audited and are reported on in the registration statement by other accountants.

- SAS No. 72 amended various other standards to preclude their use to give comfort on items for which comfort is precluded under SAS No. 72.

Accountants should also not comment on unaudited condensed interim financial information, capsule financial information, a financial forecast when historical financial statements provide a basis for one or more significant assumptions for the forecast, or changes in capital stock, increases in long-term debt and decreases in selected financial statement items, unless they have obtained sufficient knowledge of a client's internal control structure as it relates to both annual and interim financial information.

This knowledge is ordinarily obtained through the completion of an audit for one or more periods. When the accountants have not audited the most recent annual financial statements, and therefore have not acquired sufficient knowledge of the entity's internal control structure, the accountants should perform procedures to obtain that knowledge before issuing a comfort letter.

It is important to note that it may be inappropriate to comment on information related to prior years for which the accountant has not performed an audit or otherwise became knowledgeable with respect to a client's internal control structure.

Reference should be made to the guidance and examples provided by SAS No. 72 when preparing a letter for underwriters and other requesting parties. It should be noted that if the requirements for issuing a comfort letter in accordance with SAS No. 72 are not met, accountants requested to issue letters relating to securities offerings should follow the guidance in SAS No. 35 (special reports) or AT sec. 100 (attestation standards) as applicable.

20606. Considerations in Shelf-Registration Statements. When an offering pursuant to Rule 415 (see section 19200) is made, independent accountants must consider the impact of the procedural differences in the registration process on their issuance of the comfort letter. If the managing underwriter has not been selected at the time the shelf registration initially becomes effective, a final comfort letter cannot be issued. The registrant (or legal counsel designated to represent the underwriting group) may, however, request the independent accountant to issue a comfort letter at the effective date to expedite the due-diligence activities of the managing underwriter when he or she is subsequently designated. In such a situation, a draft "standard" comfort letter describing procedures that the independent accountant would perform and comments that he or she would be willing to express as a result of those procedures may be furnished to the registrant or legal counsel for the underwriting group. The independent accountant may also perform these various steps if agreed to by the parties. The draft could then be updated to include any additional procedures considered necessary by the managing underwriter selected for the portion of the issue taken "off the shelf," and a signed comfort letter may then be issued when an underwriting agreement for an offering is signed and at each closing date.

Since shelf-registration statements may have several closing dates and different managing underwriters, descriptions of procedures and findings regarding information incorporated by reference from previous 1934 Act filings may have to be repeated in several comfort letters. To avoid restating these descriptions in each comfort letter, the comments are often issued in an appendix that can be referred to in, and attached to, subsequently issued comfort letters.

Although the independent accountant does not have to "keep current" through the date of each offering unless a post-effective amendment is involved, he or she may (depending on the circumstances) arrange with the registrant to continue to perform procedures during the shelf period that will enable him or her to issue a comfort letter on short notice.

20610. Pooling-of-Interests Letter to New York Stock Exchange

Since the adoption of APB Opinion No. 16, *Business Combinations*, the New York Stock Exchange (NYSE) had required each company applying to list additional shares in a pooling transaction to furnish the NYSE with a letter setting forth the requirements for pooling-of-interests accounting, together with an indication that the contemplated transaction meets each of those requirements. The NYSE had also required a letter from the issuer's independent accountants approving the applicability of pooling accounting in relation to the proposed transaction. The NYSE deleted both of these requirements as part of its rule changes approved in 1992.

20620. Preferability Letter to the SEC on Accounting Changes

Accounting changes are required to be reported in the financial statements in the period in which the change is made, in accordance with the provisions of APB Opinion No. 20 (as amended). Changes made during an interim period must meet the reporting requirements specified in APB Opinion No. 28 (as amended).

When an accounting change is made by a public company, the Regulation S-K Exhibit requirements (see section 66000) specify that a letter from the independent accountants commenting on the preferability of the new accounting principle must be furnished. If the change occurs during one of the first three quarters of the fiscal year, the "preferability letter" is required to be included as an exhibit to the Form 10-Q filed for the quarter in which the change is made. In such cases the letter does not have to be furnished again in Form 10-K. If a change is made in the fourth quarter of a fiscal year, the letter must be included as an exhibit to the Form 10-K. A preferability letter is not required if an accounting change is made in response to a standard adopted by the FASB that requires the change. Accordingly, the requirement for such letters is limited to discretionary accounting changes.

Paragraph 29 of APB Opinion No. 20 provides for a one-time exemption for accounting changes when a company "first issues its financial statements for any one of the following purposes: (a) obtaining additional equity capital from investors, (b) effecting a business combination, or (c) registering securities." This exemption is not available to companies whose securities currently are widely held. In circumstances under which the one-time exemption is deemed applicable, the financial statements for all prior periods presented need to be retroactively restated and disclosure provided in the financial statements of the nature of the change in accounting principle and the justification for such change. Likewise, it is the SEC's policy that these registrants may change their accounting methods without filing a preferability letter.

SEC 20620

The staff of the SEC has informally indicated that a preferability letter is required if a change in accounting is described in a document, even if the effect of the change is not material in the current period. For example, a preferability letter would be required if a change in accounting is described in MD&A but, because of immateriality, is not disclosed in the financial statements.

The staff does not require the issuance of a preferability letter upon the initial adoption of what is now referred to as category "B" GAAP (i.e., FASB Technical Bulletins and AcSEC Statements of Position and Accounting and Auditing Guides that have been cleared by the FASB).

The following is an example of an accountants' preferability letter:

ABC Corp.
(Address)

We are providing this letter to you for inclusion as an exhibit to your Form 10-Q filing pursuant to Item 601 of Regulation S-K.

We have read management's justification for the change in accounting from the _____ method to the _____ method contained in the Company's Form 10-Q for the quarter ended _____. Based on our reading of the data and discussions with Company officials of the business judgment and business planning factors relating to the change, we believe management's justification to be reasonable. Accordingly (in reliance on management's determination as regards elements of business judgment and business planning), we concur that the newly adopted accounting principle described above is preferable in the Company's circumstances to the method previously applied. [Note: the phrase in parentheses should be deleted if the accountant is not relying on management's determination in that regard in deciding whether he or she concurs with the preferability of the accounting change.]

We have not audited any financial statements of ABC Corp. as of any date or for any period subsequent to _____, nor have we audited the application of the change in accounting principle disclosed in Form 10-Q of ABC Corp. for the three months ended _____; accordingly, our comments are subject to revision on completion of an audit of the financial statements that include the accounting change.

(Name of Firm)

SEC 20620

If the letter is to be filed with Form 10-K, the form references should be changed and the third paragraph omitted.

SAB Topic 6-G2.b discusses the reporting requirements with respect to accounting changes:

Reporting Requirements for Accounting Changes
1. Preferability

Facts: Rule 10-01(b)(6) of Regulation S-X requires that a registrant who makes a material change in its method of accounting shall indicate the date of and the reason for the change. The registrant also must include as an exhibit in the first Form 10-Q filed subsequent to the date of an accounting change, a letter from the registrant's independent accountants indicating whether or not the change is to an alternative principle which in his judgment is preferable under the circumstances. A letter from the independent accountant is not required when the change is made in response to a standard adopted by the Financial Accounting Standards Board which requires such a change.

Question 1: For some alternative accounting principles, authoritative bodies have specified when one alternative is preferable to another. However, for other alternative accounting principles, no authoritative body has specified criteria for determining the preferability of one alternative over another. In such situations, how should preferability be determined?

Interpretive Response: In such cases, where objective criteria for determining the preferability among alternative accounting principles have not been established by authoritative bodies, the determination of preferability should be based on the particular circumstances described by and discussed with the registrant. In addition, the independent accountant should consider other significant information of which he is aware.

Question 2: Management may offer, as justification for a change in accounting principle, circumstances such as: their expectation as to the effect of general economic trends on their business (e.g., the impact of inflation), their expectation regarding expanding consumer demand for the company's products, or plans for change in marketing methods. Are these circumstances which enter into the determination of preferability?

Interpretive Response: Yes. Those circumstances are examples of business judgment and planning and should be evaluated in determining preferability. In the case of changes for which objective criteria for determining preferability have not been established by authoritative bodies, business judgment and business planning often are major considerations in determining that the change is to a preferable method because the change results in improved financial reporting.

SEC 20620

Question 3: What responsibility does the independent accountant have for evaluating the business judgment and business planning of the registrant?

Interpretive Response: Business judgment and business planning are within the province of the registrant. Thus, the independent accountant may accept the registrant's business judgment and business planning and express reliance thereon in his letter. However, if either the plans or judgment appear to be unreasonable to the independent accountant, he should not accept them as justification. For example, an independent accountant should not accept a registrant's plans for a major expansion if he believes the registrant does not have the means of obtaining the funds necessary for the expansion program.

Question 4: If a registrant, who has changed to an accounting method which was preferable under the circumstances, later finds that it must abandon its business plans or change its business judgment because of economic or other factors, is the registrant's justification nullified?

Interpretive Response: No. A registrant must, in good faith, justify a change in its method of accounting under the circumstances which exist at the time of the change. The existence of different circumstances at a later time does not nullify the previous justification for the change.

Question 5: If a registrant justified a change in accounting method as preferable under the circumstances, and the circumstances change, may the registrant revert to the method of accounting used before the change?

Interpretive Response: Any time a registrant makes a change in accounting method, the change must be justified as preferable under the circumstances. Thus, a registrant may not change back to a principle previously used unless it can justify that the previously used principle is preferable in the circumstances as they currently exist.

Question 6: If one client of an independent accounting firm changes its method of accounting and the accountant submits the required letter stating his view of the preferability of the principle in the circumstances, does this mean that all clients of that firm are constrained from making the converse change in accounting (e.g., if one client changes from FIFO to LIFO, can no other client change from LIFO to FIFO)?

Interpretive Response: No. Each registrant must justify a change in accounting method on the basis that the method is preferable under the circumstances of that registrant. In addition, a registrant must furnish a letter from its independent accountant stating that in the judgment of the independent accountant the change in method is preferable under the circumstances of that registrant. If registrants in apparently similar circumstances make changes in opposite directions, the staff has a responsibility to inquire as to the factors which were considered in arriving at the determination by each registrant and its independent accountant that the change was preferable under the circumstances because it resulted in improved financial reporting. The staff recognizes the importance, in many circumstances, of the judgments and plans of management and recognizes that such management judgments may, in good faith, differ. As indicated above, the concern relates to registrants in apparently similar circumstances, no matter who their independent accountants may be.

Question 7: If a registrant changes its accounting to one of two methods specifically approved by the FASB in a Statement of Financial Accounting Standards, need the independent accountant express his view as to the preferability of the method selected?

Interpretive Response: If a registrant was formerly using a method of accounting no longer deemed acceptable, a change to either method approved by the FASB may be presumed to be a change to a preferable method and no letter will be required from the independent accountant. If, however, the registrant was formerly using one of the methods approved by the FASB for current use and wishes to change to an alternative approved method, then the registrant must justify its change as being one to a preferable method in the circumstances and the independent accountant must submit a letter stating that in his view the change is to a principle that is preferable in the circumstances.

2. Filing of a Letter from the Accountants

Facts: The registrant makes an accounting change in the fourth quarter of its fiscal year. Rule 10-01(b)(6) of Regulation S-X requires that the registrant file a letter from its independent accountants stating whether or not the change is preferable in the circumstances in the next Form 10-Q. Item 601(b)(18) of Regulation S-K provides that the independent accountant's preferability letter be filed as an exhibit to reports on Forms 10-K or 10-Q.

Question 1: When the independent accountant's letter is filed with the Form 10-K, must another letter also be filed with the first quarter's Form 10-Q in the following year?

Interpretive Response: No. A letter is not required to be filed with Form 10-Q if it has been previously filed as an exhibit to the Form 10-K.

In SAB Topic 5-F the staff provides guidelines with respect to accounting changes not retroactively applied due to immateriality. The SAB states that the cumulative effect of such changes should be included in the determination of income (loss) for the period in which the change is made but *not* as a cumulative effect of a change in accounting principle pursuant to APB Opinion No. 20. The text of the SAB follows:

Accounting Changes Not Retroactively Applied
Due to Immateriality

Facts: A registrant is required to adopt an accounting principle by means of restatement of prior periods' financial statements. However, the registrant determines that the accounting change does not have a material effect on prior periods' financial statements and, accordingly, decides not to restate such financial statements.

Question: In these circumstances, is it acceptable to adjust the beginning balance of retained earnings of the period in which the change is made for the cumulative effect of the change on the financial statements of prior periods?

Interpretive Response: No. If prior periods are not restated, the cumulative effect of the change should be included in the statement of income for the period in which the change is made (not to be reported as a cumulative effect adjustment in the manner of APB Opinion No. 20). Even in cases where the total cumulative effect is not significant, the staff believes that the amount should be reflected in the results of operations for the period in which the change is made. However, if the cumulative effect is material to current operations or to the trend of the reported results of operations, then the individual income statements of the earlier years should be retroactively adjusted.

This position is consistent with the requirements of Statement of Financial Accounting Standards ("SFAS") No. 5, "Accounting for Contingencies," SFAS No. 8, "Accounting for the Translations of Foreign Currency Transactions and Foreign Currency Financial Statements" [superseded by SFAS No. 52], and SFAS No. 13, "Accounting for Leases," which indicate that "the cumulative effect [of the change] on retained earnings at the beginning of the earliest period restated shall be included in determining net income of that period."

20630. Reporting Disagreements to the SEC

As discussed in section 41640, a Form 8-K must be filed when a registrant changes its independent accountants. In such cases, Form 8-K must include disclosure of information as to disagreements, if any, between the company and its former accountant. Also required is a letter from the former accountants given to the registrant and addressed to the Commission stating whether they agree with the statements made by the company (see sample letter included in section 20631) and, if not, identifying statements with which they do not agree (see sample letters included in sections 20632-20635). The rules permit the former accountant to provide the registrant with an interim letter highlighting specific areas of concern and indicating that a more detailed letter will be forthcoming (see sample interim letter in section 20636).

SEC 20620

The registrant's letter must be filed with the SEC, and a copy sent to the accountant within five business days of the event. The accountant's final letter must be given to the registrant within ten business days, after receiving notice from the registrant.

The SEC Practice Section (SECPS) Executive Committee of the AICPA requires the auditor to notify a public client in writing within five business days when its relationship with the client has ended. The rule, which is set forth in paragraph 1000.08(m) of the AICPA's SEC Practice Section Reference Manual, applies when the auditor resigns, decides not to stand for re-election, or is dismissed. A copy of the notification is required to be sent concurrently to the Chief Accountant of the SEC (see sample letter included in section 20637). Compliance with this procedure is closely monitored by the Office of the Chief Accountant.

These notification requirements may be satisfied by faxing a copy of the SECPS letter to the SEC (202-504-2724); ATTN: SECPS/Mail Stop 9-5. A copy of the fax log should be retained by the sender as evidence of timely filing and a hard copy of the letter should be sent by regular mail to the SEC. If a fax transmission is not available, the SECPS letter may be sent to the SEC by: (1) overnight delivery, (2) courier, or (3) registered mail, "return receipt requested."

To improve compliance with the SECPS notification requirements, the exact name of the registrant, the Commission File Number as it appears on the cover page of the Form 10-K, and the complete SEC address, should be set forth in the letter. If the cessation of the client-auditor relationship affects multiple SEC registrants (e.g., a parent with publicly-registered subsidiaries, series of mutual funds), the exact name of each registrant, and each Commission File Number needs to be set forth in the SECPS letter.

20631. Letter Agreeing with the Statements in Form 8-K.

Securities and Exchange Commission
450 Fifth Street, N.W.
Washington, D.C. 20549   (Date)

Gentlemen:

We have read the statements made by (former client) (copy attached), which we understand will be filed with the Commission, pursuant to Item 4 of Form 8-K, as part of the Company's Form 8-K report for the month of _____, 19__. We agree with the statements concerning our Firm in such Form 8-K.

Very truly yours,

(Name of Firm)

SEC 20631

20632. Letter Reporting Disagreements When the Former Client Reported None.

Securities and Exchange Commission
450 Fifth Street, N.W.
Washington, D.C. 20549   (Date)

Gentlemen:

We have read the statements made by (former client) (copy attached), which we understand will be filed with the Commission, pursuant to Item 4 of Form 8-K, as part of the Company's Form 8-K report for the month of ____, 19__. We do not agree with the statements concerning our Firm contained in such Form 8-K. Disagreements with the Company relating to matters that would have led to reference thereto in our report if such matters had not been resolved to our satisfaction [that led to reference thereto in our report] follow:

(List and describe all such disagreements.)

           Very truly yours,

           (Name of Firm)

20633. Letter Reporting Additional Disagreements.

Securities and Exchange Commission
450 Fifth Street, N.W.
Washington, D.C. 20549   (Date)

Gentlemen:

We have read the statements made by (former client) (copy attached), which we understand will be filed with the Commission, pursuant to Item 4 of Form 8-K, as part of the Company's Form 8-K report for the month of ____, 19__. In addition to the disagreements reported in such Form 8-K, with which we agree, additional disagreements with the Company relating to matters that would have led to reference thereto in our report if such matters had not been resolved to our satisfaction [that led to reference thereto in our report] follow:

(List and describe all such disagreements.)

           Very truly yours,

           (Name of Firm)

SEC 20632

20634. Letter Reporting Events Other Than Disagreements When the Former Client Reported None.

Securities and Exchange Commission
450 Fifth Street, N.W.
Washington, D.C. 20549   (Date)

Gentlemen:

We have read the statements made by (former client) (copy attached), which we understand will be filed with the Commission, pursuant to Item 4 of Form 8-K, as part of the Company's Form 8-K report for the month of _____, 19__. We do not agree with the statements concerning our Firm contained in such Form 8-K. Events that should have been reported by the Company follow:

(List and describe all such reportable events.)

                              Very truly yours,

                              (Name of Firm)

20635. Letter Reporting Additional Events Other Than Disagreements.

Securities and Exchange Commission
450 Fifth Street, N.W.
Washington, D.C. 20549   (Date)

Gentlemen:

We have read the statements made by (former client) (copy attached), which we understand will be filed with the Commission, pursuant to Item 4 of Form 8-K, as part of the Company's Form 8-K report for the month of _____, 19__. In addition to the events reported in such Form 8-K, with which we agree, additional events that should have been reported by the Company follow:

(List and describe all such reportable events.)

                              Very truly yours,

                              (Name of Firm)

SEC 20635

20636. Interim Letter Reporting Lack of Agreement with Company's Form 8-K.

Securities and Exchange Commission
450 Fifth Street, N.W.
Washington, D.C. 20549   (Date)

Gentlemen:

This is our interim letter pursuant to Regulation S-K Item 304 (a) (3).

We have read the statements made by (former client) (copy attached), which we understand have been filed with the Commission, pursuant to Item 4 of Form 8-K, as part of the Company's Form 8-K report for the month of _____, 19__. While we have not completed our review of the statements concerning our Firm contained in such Form 8-K, preliminarily we do not agree with such statements as they relate to [highlight specific areas of concern].

A more detailed letter will be forthcoming shortly.

Very truly yours,

(Name of Firm)

SEC 20636

20637. Letter Confirming the Cessation of the Auditor Relationship.

Mr. John Doe
Chief Financial Officer
XYZ Corporation
Anytown, U.S.A   (Date)

Dear Mr. Doe:

This is to confirm that the client-auditor relationship between XYZ Corporation (Commission File Number X-XXXX) and (Name of Firm) has ceased.

                                        Sincerely,

                                        (Name of Firm)

cc: Office of the Chief Accountant
     SECPS Letter File
     Securities and Exchange Commission
     Mail Stop 9-5
     450 Fifth Street, N.W.
     Washington, D.C. 20549

20640. Preliminary Proxy Material—Letter as to Use of Accountants' Report

The 1934 Act does not provide for an accountants' consent to the use of their report on the audited financial statements included in preliminary proxy material filed with the Commission. Further, since preliminary proxy materials are for the information of the Commission only and are not available for public inspection before definitive material has been filed, auditors' reports in preliminary materials frequently have not been manually signed. As a result, the Commission has indicated that there have been cases in which accountants were unaware that preliminary proxy filings containing their reports had been made.

To resolve this problem, the SEC issued Release No. 34-8881 which states that preliminary proxy material should "be accompanied by a letter advising the staff whether such material has been considered by the accountants and whether the accountants are prepared to permit the use of their opinion with regard to the financial statements."

SHAREHOLDER COMMUNICATIONS

31000. INTRODUCTION

The SEC exercises considerable control over the nature of information that is required to be furnished to shareholders of companies that are registered under Section 12 of the 1934 Act, including those companies with securities traded on exchanges registered pursuant to Section 12(b) and those with securities traded over the counter registered pursuant to Section 12(g). This authority is derived from Section 14(a) of the 1934 Act, which gives the SEC broad powers over the manner in which proxies are solicited. The text of Section 14(a) follows:

> It shall be unlawful for any person, by the use of the mails or by any means or instrumentality of interstate commerce or of any facility of a national securities exchange or otherwise, in contravention of such rules and regulations as the Commission may prescribe as necessary or appropriate in the public interest or for the protection of investors, to solicit or to permit the use of his name to solicit any proxy or consent or authorization in respect of any security (other than an exempted security) registered pursuant to Section 12 of this title.

A proxy is a document prepared for a shareholder to authorize another person or group of persons to act on his or her behalf at a stockholders' meeting. The use of proxies is particularly important to large corporations that would have difficulty assembling a quorum at such a meeting if the shareholders were not able to authorize other persons to vote their shares.

If the only business to be transacted at a meeting is the election of directors, a typical proxy would read somewhat as follows:

PROXY

Annual Meeting of Stockholders of (name of company)

> The undersigned, revoking all prior proxies, hereby appoints (names of persons), or any one of them, proxies with full power of substitution to vote all of the shares the undersigned is entitled to vote at the annual meeting of stockholders to be held

at (location of meeting) on (date) at (time), and all adjournments thereof, and to vote upon the following matters:

(1)   The election of directors;

(2)   Upon such other business as may properly come before the meeting or any adjournments thereof; all as more fully set forth in the Notice of Meeting and Proxy Statement, receipt of which is hereby acknowledged.

This proxy is solicited on behalf of the management.

Dated _____   _____
                                                          (Signature(s))

As indicated in the example, the request for the proxy is accompanied by a proxy statement, the content of which is discussed in section 31200.

In accordance with Rule 14a-4(b)(2) of Regulation 14A, a proxy form related to the election of directors is required to include the names of nominees for election as directors, and clearly provide a means for security holders to withhold authority to vote for each nominee (e.g., by lining through or otherwise striking out the name of any nominee).

If the meeting involves action on certain proposals by management in addition to the election of directors, the proxy may read as follows:

(Name of Company)

PROXY—ANNUAL MEETING—(Date)

The undersigned hereby appoints (name of persons), and each of them, with power of substitution, to vote for the undersigned at the Annual Meeting of Stockholders of (name of company) to be held at (city) on (date), or any adjournments thereof, with all the power the undersigned would possess if personally present:

(1)   For the election of a Board of (number) Directors to serve until the next Annual Meeting, and until their successors are elected and shall qualify; or check here _____ if authority is to be withheld.

(2)   FOR _____ or AGAINST _____ approval of a Reorganization Agreement providing for the acquisition of substantially all of the assets of (company) by (company), as described in the accompanying Proxy Statement.

(3)   FOR _____ or AGAINST _____ a proposed increase in (company's) authorized Common Stock from (number) to (number) shares, as described in the accompanying Proxy Statement.

(4)   FOR _____ or AGAINST _____ a proposed Stock Option Plan for the benefit of selected (company) employees (including Officers and Directors), as described in the accompanying Proxy Statement.

SEC 31000

(5)   Upon all matters which may properly come before the meeting.

This proxy is solicited by the management and will be voted FOR the Election of Directors and FOR Proposals 2, 3 and 4 unless otherwise specified. The undersigned acknowledges receipt of the accompanying Notice of the Meeting and Proxy Statement.

Dated _____   _____
                                          (Signature of Stockholder)

Pursuant to the authority contained in Section 14(a) of the 1934 Act, the SEC developed Regulation 14A (see section 31100) relating to the solicitation of proxies. This regulation specifies, among other requirements, that a proxy statement prepared in accordance with Schedule 14A (see section 31200) must be furnished to each person solicited for a proxy. If the solicitation relates to an annual meeting of security holders at which directors are to be elected, then each proxy statement is to be accompanied (or preceded) by an annual report to shareholders prepared in accordance with Rule 14a-3 (see section 31300).

The information required to be set forth in a proxy statement is required to be furnished to security holders *even if proxies are not solicited*. Such disclosures need to be included in an "information statement" pursuant to Section 14(c) of the 1934 Act:

> Unless proxies, consents, or authorizations in respect of a security registered pursuant to Section 12 of this title, or a security issued by an investment company registered under the Investment Company Act of 1940, are solicited by or on behalf of the management of the issuer from the holders of record of such security in accordance with the rules and regulations prescribed under subsection (a) of this section, prior to any annual or other meeting of the holders of such security, such issuer shall, in accordance with rules and regulations prescribed by the Commission, file with the Commission and transmit to all holders of record of such security information substantially equivalent to the information which would be required to be transmitted if a solicitation were made. . . .

Regulation 14C requires the distribution to shareholders of an information statement with respect to annual and other meetings when proxies are not solicited on behalf of the management. The regulation is applicable to issuers of securities listed for trading on an exchange (registered pursuant to Section 12(b) of the 1934 Act) as well as to companies whose securities are traded over the counter but are registered pursuant to Section 12(g) of the Act.

The information statement is required to contain substantially the same information as that which would be required in a proxy statement. Accordingly, the discussion of the requirements for proxy statements is generally also applicable to information statements.

SEC 31000

The information statement is required to be sent or given to eligible shareholders at least 20 days before the meeting date (or, if no meeting is to be held, at least 20 days before corporate action is to be taken on the matters discussed in the information statement). The procedures for filing the information statement with the SEC as to number of copies, timing, and other requirements are the same as those specified in Rule 14a-6 for proxy statements (as discussed in section 31130).

The proxy rules also apply when a person or group of persons oppose a solicitation with respect to the election of directors at a meeting of security holders. The provisions applicable to election contests are set forth in Rule 14a-11 of Regulation 14A.

31100. REGULATION 14A—SOLICITATION OF PROXIES

31110. General

Regulation 14A governs the solicitation of proxies by companies with securities registered under Section 12 of the 1934 Act. The regulation does not apply to certain situations specified in Rule 14a-2.

Regulation 14A consists of a number of rules, the scope of which is indicated by the following listing:

Rule	Subject
14a-1	Definitions
14a-2	Solicitations to which Rules 14a-3 to 14a-14 apply
14a-3	Information to be furnished to security holders
14a-4	Requirements as to proxy
14a-5	Presentation of information in proxy statement
14a-6	Filing requirements
14a-7	Obligations of registrants to provide a list of, or mail soliciting material to, security holders
14a-8	Proposals of security holders
14a-9	False or misleading statements
14a-10	Prohibition of certain solicitations
14a-11	Special provisions applicable to election contests
14a-12	Solicitation prior to furnishing required proxy statement
14a-13	Obligation of registrants in communicating with beneficial owners
14a-14	Modified or superseded documents

31120. Information To Be Furnished to Security Holders (Rule 14a-3)

Rule 14a-3 of Regulation 14A describes the information required to be furnished to shareholders concurrent with or prior to the solicitation of proxies. The rule states that a proxy that is subject to Regulation 14A may not be solicited unless each person solicited receives concurrently (or has previously been furnished) a proxy statement containing the information specified in Schedule 14A (see section 31200 for a discussion of these requirements) or is furnished a written proxy statement as included and filed on Forms S-4 or F-4. (Forms S-4 and F-4 are discussed in sections 42300 and 45400, respectively.) The proxy statement is intended to provide shareholders with the information they need to decide how to assign their proxies.

Rule 14a-3 further states that if management is soliciting proxies relating to an annual meeting of shareholders at which directors are to be elected, each proxy statement needs to be accompanied (or preceded) by an annual report to shareholders that complies with certain specified requirements. A discussion of the annual report to shareholders begins with section 31300, and the text of Rule 14a-3 is included in section 31320. Small business issuers should pay particular attention to paragraph (b) of Rule 14a-3 regarding their reporting requirements.

As indicated in paragraph (c) of Rule 14a-3, seven copies of each annual report sent to shareholders is required to be mailed to the SEC, solely for its information, not later than (1) the date on which the report is first sent to or given to shareholders or (2) the date on which preliminary copies (or definitive copies if preliminary filing is not required) of the proxy material are filed with the SEC, whichever is later.

The annual report is not considered to be "soliciting material" or to be "filed" or subject to liabilities under Section 18 of the 1934 Act (see section 12030), except to the extent that the registrant specifically requests that the annual report be treated as part of the proxy soliciting material *or incorporates it by reference* in the proxy statement or other filed report in its entirety. Sections of the annual report that are intended to be incorporated by reference are generally so designated to distinguish them from the parts of the report that are not considered "filed" and therefore not subject to liabilities under Section 18. See Note D to Schedule 14A for guidance with respect to incorporation by reference in a proxy statement. Accountants' liabilities for documents filed under the 1934 Act are discussed in section 12030.

31130. Filing Requirements (Rule 14a-6)

Rule 14a-6 of Regulation 14A prescribes the number of copies of proxy statements, proxy forms, and other proxy solicitation material to be filed with the SEC and the required timing of such filings.

Paragraph (a) states that when preliminary proxy materials are required, five *preliminary* copies of the proxy statement and form of proxy and any other soliciting material to be concurrently furnished to shareholders need to be filed with the SEC at least ten calendar days before the date definitive (final) copies of such material are first sent (or given) to shareholders, or such shorter period before that date as the SEC may authorize. Preliminary proxy statements and the other required information are not required to be filed if:

- the solicitation relates to an annual (or special meeting in lieu of the annual) meeting, or

- the solicitation relates to any meeting of security holders for an investment company or business development company, at which the only matters to be acted upon are:

•• the election of directors;

•• the election, approval or ratification of accountant(s);

•• a security holder proposal (pursuant to Rule 14a-8);

•• with respect to an investment company or a business development company, a proposal to continue, with no change, any advisory or other contract or agreement that was previously the subject of a proxy solicitation and the required information was filed with the SEC; and/or

•• with respect to an open-end investment company, a proposal to increase the number of shares authorized to be issued, unless the registrant comments on or refers to an opposing solicitation in connection with the meeting in the proxy material.

Paragraph (b) requires that eight *definitive* (final) copies of the proxy statement, form of proxy, and all other soliciting material, in the form in which such material is furnished to shareholders, need to be filed with, or mailed to, the SEC not later than the date such material is first sent (or given) to shareholders. Three copies of such material must at the same time be filed with each national securities exchange on which any security of the issuer is listed and registered.

The definitive material filed with the SEC should be accompanied by a letter indicating any material changes from the preliminary material filed (if applicable) other than changes made in response to the staff's comments. Two copies of the definitive material should be marked to indicate all the changes made. Rule 14a-6 describes these requirements in more detail.

Other paragraphs of Rule 14a-6 provide additional guidance and require the filing of other material under certain circumstances. The full text of Rule 14a-6 follows:

Rule 14a-6. Filing requirements

(a) **Preliminary proxy statements.** Five preliminary copies of the proxy statement and form of proxy shall be filed with the Commission at least 10 calendar days prior to the date definitive copies of such material are first sent or given to security holders, or such shorter period prior to that date as the Commission may authorize upon a showing of good cause thereunder. A registrant, however, shall not file with the Commission a preliminary proxy statement, form of proxy or other soliciting material to be furnished to security holders concurrently therewith if the solicitation relates to an annual (or special meeting in lieu of the annual) meeting, or for an investment company registered under the Investment Company Act of 1940 or a business development company, if the solicitation relates to any meeting of security holders at which the only matters to be acted upon are:

(1) the election of directors.

(2) the election, approval or ratification of accountant(s);

(3) a security holder proposal included pursuant to Rule 14a-8;

(4) with respect to an investment company registered under the Investment Company Act of 1940 or a business development company, a proposal to continue, without change, any advisory or other contract or agreement that previously has been the subject of a proxy solicitation for which proxy material was filed with the Commission pursuant to this rule; and/or

(5) with respect to an open-end investment company registered under the Investment Company Act of 1940, a proposal to increase the number of shares authorized to be issued. This exclusion from filing preliminary proxy material does not apply if the registrant comments upon or refers to a solicitation in opposition in connection with the meeting in its proxy material.

Note 1. The filing of revised material does not recommence the ten day time period unless the revised material contains material revisions or material new proposal(s) that constitutes a fundamental change in the proxy material.

Note 2. The official responsible for the preparation of the proxy material should make every effort to verify the accuracy and completeness of the information required by the applicable rules. The preliminary material should be filed with the Commission at the earliest practicable date.

Note 3. Solicitation in opposition. For purposes of the exclusion from filing preliminary proxy material, a "solicitation in opposition" includes: (a) any solicitation opposing a proposal supported by the registrant; and (b) any solicitation supporting a proposal that the registrant does not expressly support, other than a security holder proposal included in the registrant's proxy material pursuant to Rule 14a-8. The inclusion of a security holder proposal in the registrant's proxy material pursuant to Rule 14a-8 does not constitute a "solicitation in opposition," even if the registrant opposes the proposal and/or includes a statement in opposition to the proposal.

Note 4. A registrant that is filing proxy material in preliminary form only because the registrant has commented on or referred to a solicitation in opposition should indicate that fact in a transmittal letter when filing the preliminary material with the Commission.

(b) **Definitive proxy statement and other soliciting materials.** Eight definitive copies of the proxy statement, form of proxy and all other soliciting material, in the form in which such material is furnished to security holders, shall be filed with, or mailed for filing to, the Commission not later than the date such material is first sent or given to any security holders. Three copies of such material shall at the same time be filed with, or mailed for filing to, each national securities exchange upon which any class of securities of the registrant is listed and registered.

Note: A registrant that is filing definitive proxy material without payment of a fee should state in the first paragraph of the transmittal letter that no fee is being paid because a fee was paid upon filing of preliminary proxy material.

(c) **Personal solicitation materials.** If the solicitation is to be made in whole or in part by personal solicitation, eight copies of all written instructions or other material which discusses or reviews, or comments upon the merits of, any matter to be acted upon and which is furnished to the persons making the actual solicitation for their use directly or indirectly in connection with the solicitation shall be filed with, or mailed for filing to, the Commission by the person on whose behalf the solicitation is made not later than the date any such material is first sent or given to such individuals.

(d) **Release dates.** All preliminary proxy statements and forms of proxy filed pursuant to paragraph (a) of this section shall be accompanied by a statement of the date on which definitive copies thereof filed pursuant to paragraph (b) of this section are intended to be released to security holders. All definitive material filed pursuant to paragraph (b) of this section shall be accompanied by a statement of the date on which copies of such material were released to security holders, or, if not released, the date on which copies thereof are intended to be released. All material filed pursuant to paragraph (c) of this section shall be accompanied by a statement of the date on which copies thereof were released to the individual who will make the actual solicitation or if not released, the date on which copies thereof are intended to be released.

(e) (1) **Public Availability of Information.** All copies of preliminary proxy statements and forms of proxy filed pursuant to paragraph (a) of this section shall be clearly marked "Preliminary Copies," and shall be deemed immediately available for public inspection unless confidential treatment is obtained pursuant to paragraph (e)(2) of this section.

(2) **Confidential Treatment.** If action is to be taken with respect to any matter specified in Item 14 of Schedule 14A, all copies of the preliminary proxy statement and form of proxy filed pursuant to paragraph (a) of this section shall be for the information of the Commission only and shall not be deemed available for public inspection until filed with the Commission in definitive form, provided that:

(i) the proxy statement does not relate to a matter or proposal subject to 1934 Act Rule 13e-3 or a roll-up transaction as defined in Item 901(c) of Regulation S-K of this chapter; and

(ii) the filed material is marked "Confidential. For Use of the Commission Only." In any and all cases, such material may be disclosed to any department or agency of the United States Government and to the Congress, and the Commission may make such inquiries or investigation in regard to the material as may be necessary for an adequate review thereof by the Commission.

(f) **Communications not required to be filed.** Copies of replies to inquiries from security holders requesting further information and copies of communications which do no more than request that forms of proxy theretofore solicited be signed and returned need not be filed pursuant to this rule.

(g) **Solicitation subject to Rule 14a-2(b)(1).**

(1) Any person who:

(i)   engages in a solicitation pursuant to Rule 14a-2(b)(1), and

(ii) at the commencement of that solicitation owns beneficially securities of the class which is the subject of the solicitation with a market value of over $5 million, shall furnish or mail to the Commission, not later than three days after the date the written solicitation is first sent or given to any security holder, five copies of a statement containing the information specified in the Notice of Exempt Solicitation [Rule 14a-103] which statement shall attach as an exhibit all written soliciting materials. Five copies of an amendment to such statement shall be furnished or mailed to the Commission, in connection with dissemination of any additional communications, not later than three days after the date the additional material is first sent or given to any security holder. Three copies of the Notice of Exempt Solicitation and amendments thereto shall, at the same time the materials are furnished or mailed to the Commission, be furnished or mailed to each national securities exchange upon which any class of securities of the registrant is listed and registered.

(2) Notwithstanding paragraph (g)(1) of this section, no such submission need be made with respect to oral solicitations (other than with respect to scripts used in connection with such oral solicitations), speeches delivered in a public forum, press releases, published or broadcast opinions, statements, and advertisements appearing in a broadcast media, or a newspaper, magazine or other bona fide publication disseminated on a regular basis.

(h) **Revised material.** Where any proxy statement, form of proxy or other material filed pursuant to this section is amended or revised, two of the copies of such amended or revised material filed pursuant to this rule (or in the case of investment companies registered under the Investment Company Act of 1940, three of such copies) shall be marked to indicate clearly and precisely the changes effected therein. If the amendment or revision alters the text of the material, the changes in such text shall be indicated by means of underscoring or in some other appropriate manner.

SEC 31130

(i) **Fees.** At the time of filing the proxy solicitation material, the persons upon whose behalf the solicitation is made, other than companies registered under the Investment Company Act of 1940, shall pay to the Commission the following applicable fee: (1) For definitive proxy material relating to a solicitation for which the registrant does not file preliminary proxy material, a fee of $125; (2) for preliminary proxy material that solicits proxies for business for which a stockholder vote is necessary, but apparently no controversy is involved, a fee of $125; (3) for preliminary proxy material where a contest as set forth in Rule 14a-11 is involved, a fee of $500 from each party to the controversy; (4) for preliminary proxy material involving acquisitions, mergers, spinoffs, consolidations or proposed sales or other dispositions of substantially all the assets of the company, a fee established in accordance with Rule 0-11 shall be paid, and (5) for submissions made pursuant to Rule 14a-6(g), no fee shall be required. No refund shall be given.

(j) **Merger proxies.** Notwithstanding the foregoing provisions of this section, any proxy statement, form of proxy or other soliciting material included in a registration statement filed under the Securities Act of 1933 on Form N-14, S-4, or F-4 shall be deemed filed both for the purposes of that Act and for the purposes of this section, but separate copies of such material need not be furnished pursuant to this section nor shall any fee be required under paragraph (i) of this section. However, any additional soliciting material used after the effective date of the registration statement on Form N-14, S-4 or F-4 shall be filed in accordance with this section, unless separate copies of such material are required to be filed as an amendment of such registration statement.

(k) **Computing time periods.** In computing time periods beginning with the filing date specified in Regulation 14A (Rules 14a-1 to 14b-1), the filing date shall be counted as the first day of the time period and midnight of the last day shall constitute the end of the specified time period.

(l) **Roll-up transactions.** If a transaction is a roll-up transaction as defined in Item 901(c) of Regulation S-K and is registered (or authorized to be registered) on Form S-4 or Form F-4, the proxy statement of the sponsor or the general partner as defined in Item 901(d) and Item 901(a), respectively, of Regulation S-K must be distributed to security holders no later than the lesser of 60 calendar days prior to the date on which the meeting of security holders is held or action is taken, or the maximum number of days permitted for giving notice under applicable state law.

(m) **Cover page.** Proxy materials filed with the Commission shall include a cover page in the form set forth in Schedule 14A.

31200. SCHEDULE 14A—INFORMATION REQUIRED IN PROXY STATEMENTS

31210. General

As previously indicated, Rule 14a-3 of Regulation 14A requires that, except for communications made pursuant to paragraph (f) of Rule 14a-3 (see section 31320), no solicitation subject to the proxy regulations may be made unless each person solicited is concurrently furnished, or has previously been furnished, a proxy statement containing the information specified in Schedule 14A or a prospectus on Form S-4, F-4, or Form N-14. (Forms S-4 and F-4 are discussed in sections 42300 and 45400, respectively. As described in section 40120, Form N-14 is the form used for the registration of securities issued by registered investment companies in connection with business combinations; however, this form is not discussed in this manual.) Schedule 14A sets forth the requirements as to the contents of proxy statements. The items of information and related instructions in the schedule are applicable to specified situations, depending on the matters to be acted on at the shareholders' meeting. While solicitations may pertain to a variety of matters, their general purpose is to obtain proxies either in connection with the annual meeting at which directors are to be elected or for a special meeting. Special meetings are most frequently held in order to vote on matters covered by the subjects addressed in Items 11 (Authorization or issuance of securities otherwise than for exchange), 12 (Modification or exchange of securities), and 14 (Mergers, consolidations, acquisitions, and similar matters) of Schedule 14A.

Registrants eligible to use Forms S-2 (see section 42200) and S-3 (see section 42250) are permitted to incorporate by reference financial and other information contained within documents previously filed with the SEC and documents, such as the annual report to shareholders, delivered with the proxy.

The scope of the information that may have to be furnished pursuant to Schedule 14A is indicated by the following listing of subjects:

Item	Subject
1	Date, time, and place information
2	Revocability of proxy
3	Dissenters' right of appraisal
4	Persons making the solicitation
5	Interest of certain persons in matters to be acted upon
6	Voting securities and principal holders thereof
7	Directors and executive officers
8	Compensation of directors and executive officers
9	Independent public accountants
10	Compensation plans
11	Authorization or issuance of securities otherwise than for exchange
12	Modification or exchange of securities
13	Financial and other information
14	Mergers, consolidations, acquisitions and similar matters
15	Acquisition or disposition of property
16	Restatement of accounts
17	Action with respect to reports
18	Matters not required to be submitted
19	Amendment of charter, bylaws, or other documents
20	Other proposed action
21	Voting procedures

Note G to Schedule 14A is a special note for small business issuers (see section 70100) and sets forth alternative information requirements for such companies that have filed their latest annual report pursuant to "Information Required in Annual Report of Transitional Small Business Issuers" in Form 10-KSB (see section 41200). Among other instructions, Note G specifies that small business issuers that meet the above criteria may provide the information required by Part F/S of Form 10-SB (see section 41850) rather than the requirements of Items 13 and 14. Small business issuers should refer to the complete text of Note G when filing proxy information.

In October 1992 the SEC amended its rules regarding the disclosure of director and executive compensation required by Item 8. The SEC's stated objective in making these changes was to ensure that the marketplace receives information about executive and director compensation that is easier to understand and more relevant to proxy voting and investment decisions. Item 8 references the disclosure requirements of Item 402 of Regulation S-K (see section 64020). These rules require that disclosures be made in a series of tables clearly setting forth each element of compensation paid, earned, or awarded in a given year. Item 8 states that the registrant needs to furnish the information required by Item 402 of Regulation S-K if action is to be taken with regard to:

(a) the election of directors;

(b) any bonus, profit sharing or other compensation plan, contract or arrangement in which any director, nominee for election as a director, or executive officer of the registrant will participate;

(c) any pension or retirement plan in which any such person will participate; or

(d) the granting or extension to any such person of any options, warrants or rights to purchase any securities, other than warrants or rights issued to security holders as such, on a pro rata basis. However, if the solicitation is made on behalf of persons other than the registrant, the information required need be furnished only as to nominees of the persons making the solicitation and associates of such nominees. In the case of investment companies registered under the Investment Company Act of 1940, furnish the information in Item 402(g) of Regulation S-K and the information concerning compensation of directors and officers that is required to be included in the company's registration statement form under the Investment Company Act in lieu of other compensation information required by Item 402.

Instruction. If an otherwise reportable compensation plan became subject to such requirements because of an acquisition or merger and, within one year of the acquisition or merger, such plan was terminated for purposes of prospective eligibility, the registrant may furnish a description of its obligation to the designated individuals pursuant to the compensation plan. Such description may be furnished in lieu of a description of the compensation plan in the proxy statement.

31220. Independent Public Accountants

The following information set forth in Item 9 of Schedule 14A is required to be included in proxy statements prepared in connection with an annual meeting of shareholders relating to the election of directors (or a solicitation of consents or authorizations in lieu of such meeting) or the election, approval, or ratification of the registrant's accountant:

(a) The name of the principal accountant selected or being recommended to security holders for election, approval or ratification for the current year. If no accountant has been selected or recommended, so state and briefly describe the reasons therefor.

(b) The name of the principal accountant for the fiscal year most recently completed if different from the accountant selected or recommended for the current year or if no accountant has yet been selected or recommended for the current year.

(c) The proxy statement shall indicate (1) whether or not representatives of the principal accountant for the current year and for the most recently completed fiscal year are expected to be present at the security holders' meeting, (2) whether or not they will have the opportunity to make a statement if they desire to do so and (3) whether or not such representatives are expected to be available to respond to appropriate questions.

(d) If during the registrant's two most recent fiscal years or any subsequent interim period, (1) an independent accountant who was previously engaged as the principal accountant to audit the registrant's financial statements, or an independent accountant on whom the principal accountant expressed reliance in its report regarding a significant subsidiary, has resigned (or indicated it has declined to stand for reelection after the completion of the current audit) or was dismissed, or (2) a new independent accountant has been engaged as either the principal accountant to audit the registrant's financial statements or as an independent accountant on whom the principal accountant has expressed or is expected to express reliance in its report regarding a significant subsidiary, then, notwithstanding any previous disclosure, provide the information required by Item 304(a) of Regulation S-K [see section 63040].

Note that disclosure regarding changes in accountants and any related disagreements is required even if the registrant was not subject to the 1934 Act reporting requirements when the change occurred.

Firms that are members of the SEC Practice Section (SECPS) of the AICPA Division for Accounting Firms are required to report certain information to the audit committee or board of directors of each SEC client (see section 20630). Furnishing the information set forth in SAS No. 61, *Communications with Audit Committees*, along with certain communications regarding management advisory services provided, is deemed to constitute compliance with this membership requirement. The information required to be communicated is as follows:

- The level of responsibility assumed by the auditor under generally accepted auditing standards in relation to the nature of assurance provided by an audit.

- The initial selection of and changes in significant accounting policies and the methods used to account for significant unusual transactions in controversial or emerging areas for which there is a lack of authoritative guidance.

- The process used by management in formulating particularly sensitive accounting estimates and the basis for the auditors' conclusions regarding the reasonableness of those estimates.

- Adjustments arising from the audit that could, either individually or in the aggregate, have a significant effect on the entity's financial reporting process.

- The level of responsibility taken for other information in documents containing audited financial statements, any procedures performed, and the results.

- The nature of any disagreements with management, whether or not satisfactorily resolved, about matters that individually or in the aggregate could be significant to the entity's financial statements or the auditors' report.

- The nature of consultations between management and other accountants about auditing and accounting matters and the auditors' views of these matters.

- Any major issues that were discussed with management in connection with the retention of the auditor.

- Any serious difficulties encountered in dealing with management related to the performance of the audit.

- The total fees received from the client for management advisory services during the year under audit and a description of the types of such services rendered.

31230. Financial Disclosure Requirements for Proxies Involving Item 11 and 12 Situations

If the action to be taken for which proxies are being solicited involves the type of situation covered by Item 11 (Authorization or Issuance of Securities Otherwise Than for Exchange) or Item 12 (Modification or Exchange of Securities), the financial statements and related information set forth in Item 13 (Financial and Other Information) need to be provided. The required information includes:

- Financial statements prepared in accordance with Regulation S-X, including the financial information required by Rule 3-05 and Article 11, as applicable.

- Supplementary financial information (section 63020), management's discussion and analysis of financial condition and results of operations (section 63030), and changes in and disagreements with accountants on accounting and financial disclosure (section 63040), all in accordance with the applicable provisions of Regulation S-K.

- A statement indicating whether or not representatives of the principal accountants for the current and most recently completed year:

  •• Are expected to be present at the security holders' meeting.

•• Will have the opportunity to make a statement if they so desire.

•• Are expected to be available to respond to appropriate questions.

Small business issuers, however, should refer to Note G to Schedule 14A (discussed in section 31210) for alternative information requirements if they filed their latest annual report pursuant to "Information Required in Annual Report of Transitional Small Business Issuers" in Form 10-KSB (see section 41200).

The text of Item 13, which should be referred to when evaluating the disclosure requirements of each situation, is as follows:

Item 13. Financial and Other Information

(a) Information required.

If action is to be taken with respect to any matter specified in Item 11 or 12, furnish the following information:

(1) Financial statements meeting the requirements of Regulation S-X, including financial information required by Rule 3-05 and Article 11 of Regulation S-X with respect to transactions other than that pursuant to which action is to be taken as described in this proxy statement;

(2) Item 302 of Regulation S-K, supplementary financial information;

(3) Item 303 of Regulation S-K, management's discussion and analysis of financial condition and results of operations;

(4) Item 304 of Regulation S-K, changes in and disagreements with accountants on accounting and financial disclosure; and

(5) A statement as to whether or not representatives of the principal accountants for the current year and for the most recently completed fiscal year:

(i) are expected to be present at the security holders' meeting;

(ii) will have the opportunity to make a statement if they desire to do so; and

(iii) are expected to be available to respond to appropriate questions.

(b) Incorporation by reference.

The information required pursuant to paragraph (a) of this Item may be incorporated by reference into the proxy statement as follows:

(1) S-3 registrants. If the registrant meets the requirements of Form S-3 (see Note E to this Schedule), it may incorporate by reference to previously filed documents any of the information required by paragraph (a) of this Item, provided that the requirements of paragraph (c) are met. Where the registrant

SEC 31230

meets the requirements of Form S-3 and has elected to furnish the required information by incorporation by reference, the registrant may elect to update the information so incorporated by reference to information in subsequently filed documents.

(2) All registrants. The registrants may incorporate by reference any of the information required by paragraph (a) of this Item, provided that the information is contained in an annual report to security holders or a previously filed statement or report, such report or statement is delivered to security holders with the proxy statement and the requirements of paragraph (c) are met.

(c) Certain conditions applicable to incorporation by reference.

Registrants eligible to incorporate by reference into the proxy statement the information required by paragraph (a) of this Item in the manner specified by paragraphs (b)(1) and (b)(2) may do so only if:

(1) the information is not required to be included in the proxy statement pursuant to the requirement of another Item;

(2) the proxy statement identifies on the last page(s) the information incorporated by reference; and

(3) the material incorporated by reference substantially meets the requirements of this Item or the appropriate portions of this Item.

Instructions to Item 13:

1. Notwithstanding the provisions of this Item, any or all of the information required by paragraph (a) of this Item, not material for the exercise of prudent judgment in regard to the matter to be acted upon may be omitted. In the usual case the information is deemed material to the exercise of prudent judgment where the matter to be acted upon is the authorization or issuance of a material amount of senior securities, but the information is not deemed material where the matter to be acted upon is the authorization or issuance of common stock, otherwise than in an exchange, merger, consolidation, acquisition or similar transaction, the authorization of preferred stock without present intent to issue or the authorization of preferred stock for issuance for cash in an amount constituting fair value.

2. In order to facilitate compliance with Rule 2-02(a) of Regulation S-X, one copy of the definitive proxy statement filed with the Commission shall include a manually signed copy of the accountant's report. If the financial statements are incorporated by reference, a manually signed copy of the accountant's report shall be filed with the definitive proxy statement.

SEC 31230

3. Notwithstanding the provisions of Regulation S-X, no schedules other than those prepared in accordance with Rules 12-15, 12-28, and 12-29 (or, for management investment companies, Rules 12-12 through 12-14) of that regulation need be furnished in the proxy statement.

4. Unless registered on a national securities exchange or otherwise required to furnish such information, registered investment companies need not furnish the information required by paragraphs (a)(2) or (3) of this Item.

5. If the registrant submits preliminary proxy material incorporating by reference financial statements required by this Item, the registrant should furnish a draft of the financial statements if the document from which they are incorporated has not been filed with or furnished to the Commission.

31240. Financial Disclosure Requirements for Proxies Involving Mergers, Consolidations, Acquisitions and Similar Matters

If the action to be taken at the shareholders' meeting involves a merger, consolidation or acquisition, the information set forth in Item 14 is required to be included in the proxy statement for the issuer and for each other company (person) involved in the transaction. The information required by Item 14 is separated into the following two categories: (a) information about the transaction and (b) information about the registrant and the other parties to the transaction. If the transaction involves the issuance of shares, it is probable that a Form S-4 will need to be filed. As noted in the discussion of Form S-4 (section 42300), most of the information required by Item 14 is similar to that required by Form S-4. Accordingly, the information generated in connection with the preparation of Form S-4 generally will meet the requirements of Item 14.

31241. Information About the Transaction. Much of the information about the transaction is generally presented in narrative form, and includes a brief statement as to the accounting treatment of the transaction and the federal income tax consequences. Certain financial information also needs to be furnished.

Item 14 requires the presentation of selected financial information for the registrant and each entity involved in the transaction (see section 31245). In addition, selected financial information giving pro forma effect to the transaction needs to be furnished. The proxy statement must also include, in comparative columnar form, a table containing historical and pro forma per share data for the registrant and equivalent historical and pro forma per share data for each of the entities as of the same date or the same periods for which selected financial data is furnished. For a business combination accounted for as a purchase, the pro forma financial information required is limited to the most recent fiscal year and interim period. For a business combination accounted for as a pooling of interests, pro forma financial information is required for the most recent three fiscal years and interim period, except for information as to book value, which is only required for the most recent fiscal year and interim period. The table must include income (loss) per share from continuing operations, cash dividends declared per share, and book value per share.

The instructions to the table of historical and pro forma information point out that equivalent pro forma per share amounts are to be calculated by multiplying the pro forma information by the exchange ratio so that per share amounts for each entity for which equivalent pro forma data is required to be presented are equated to the respective values for one share of the other entity. For example, if the proposed transaction provides for the registrant to issue two shares of its stock for each share of outstanding stock of the other entity, the equivalent pro forma information would be the pro forma per share data multiplied by two. Similarly, if the registrant proposes to issue one share of its outstanding stock for two shares of the stock of the other entity, in order to arrive at the pro forma information equated to the respective values for one share of the other entity, the pro forma per share data would need to be divided by two.

A full pro forma balance sheet and income statement giving effect to the transaction is also required by Article 11 of Regulation S-X. For a business combination accounted for as a purchase, the pro forma financial information required is limited to the most recent fiscal year and interim period. For a business combination accounted for as a pooling of interests, the pro forma financial information is required for the most recent three fiscal years and interim period.

31242. Information About the Registrant and the Other Entities Involved in the Transaction. The manner in which the financial statements of the registrant and the other parties to the transaction are to be furnished depends on whether the respective entities are SEC registrants. Entities meeting the criteria to file Form S-2 or S-3 may be able to incorporate by reference and deliver the information with the proxy statement similar to the manner in which such information would be furnished in a registration statement on such forms (see sections 42200 and 42250). It should be noted that, similar to the requirements for Forms S-1, S-2, and S-3, the information required by Rule 3-05 (see section 50314) and Article 11 (see section 51100) also must be furnished, if applicable.

31243. Use of Annual Report to Shareholders. Item 14(c) provides that if the meeting in which the transaction is being voted on is the annual meeting of shareholders in which the directors are being elected, much of the information may be incorporated by reference to the annual report to shareholders.

It is customary to manually sign the accountants' report in one copy of the preliminary proxy material filed with the SEC.

31244. Omission of Financial Information. The instructions to Items 13 and 14 contain language to the effect that financial information may be omitted if it is "not material for the exercise of prudent judgment in regard to the matter to be acted upon" in the proxy. Generally, the circumstances that would permit the omission of financial statements, particularly under Item 14, are rare. When registrants and their attorneys and advisers believe that financial statements are not necessary, it is generally advisable to discuss the reasons for omitting the financial statements with the staff of the SEC prior to filing the preliminary proxy material. (Reference should be made to section 17120 of this manual for a discussion of prefiling conferences with the SEC.)

31245. Text of Item 14. It is essential that a complete up-to-date text of Item 14 be referred to when evaluating the disclosure requirements of a proxy statement involving a merger, consolidation, acquisition or similar matters. The text of Item 14 is as follows:

Item 14. Mergers, Consolidations, Acquisitions and Similar Matters

If action is to be taken with respect to any transaction involving (i) the merger or consolidation of the registrant into or with any other person or of any other person into or with the registrant, (ii) the acquisition by the registrant or any of its security holders of securities of another person, (iii) the acquisition by the registrant of any other going business or of the assets thereof, (iv) the sale or other transfer of all or any substantial part of the assets of the registrant, or (v) the liquidation or dissolution of the registrant, furnish the following information:

(a) Information about the transaction.

Furnish the following information concerning the registrant and (unless otherwise indicated) each other person: which is to be merged into the registrant or into or with which the registrant is to be merged or consolidated; the business or assets of which are to be acquired; which is the issuer of securities to be acquired by the registrant in exchange for all or a substantial part of the registrant's assets; or which is the issuer of securities to be acquired by the registrant or its security holders:

(1) The name, complete mailing address (including the ZIP code) and telephone number (including the area code) of the principal executive offices.

(2) A brief description of the general nature of the business conducted by the other person.

(3) A summary of the material features of the proposed transaction. If the transaction is set forth in a written document, file three copies thereof with the Commission at the time preliminary copies of the proxy statement and form of proxy are filed pursuant to Rule 14a-6(a). The summary shall include, where applicable:

(i) a brief summary of the terms of the transaction agreement;

(ii) the reasons for engaging in the transaction;

(iii) an explanation of any material differences in the rights of security holders of the registrant as a result of this transaction;

(iv) a brief statement as to the accounting treatment of the transaction;

(v) the federal income tax consequences of the transaction; and

(vi) the information required by Item 202 of Regulation S-K, description of registrant's securities, for any securities that are exempt from registration and are being issued in connection with the transaction if the security holders entitled to vote or give an authorization or consent with regard to the transaction will receive such securities, unless: (i) the issuer of the securities would meet the requirements for use of Form S-3 and elects to furnish information in accordance with the provisions of paragraph(b)(1), (ii) capital stock is to be issued, and (iii) securities of the same class are registered under Section 12 of the Exchange Act and either (a) are listed for trading or admitted to unlisted trading privileges on a national securities exchange or (b) are securities for which bid and offer quotations are reported in an automated quotations system operated by a national securities association.

(4) A brief statement as to dividends in arrears or defaults in principal or interest in respect of any securities of the registrant or of such other person and as to the effect of the transaction thereon and such other information as may be appropriate in the particular case to disclose adequately the nature and effect of the proposed action.

(5) The information required by Item 301 of Regulation S-K, selected financial data, for the registrant and the other person.

(6) If material, the information required by Item 301 of Regulation S-K for the registrant or the other person on a pro forma basis, giving effect to the transaction.

(7) In comparative columnar form, historical and pro forma per share data of the registrant and historical and equivalent pro forma per share data of the other person for the following items:

(i) book value per share as of the date financial data is presented pursuant to Item 301 of Regulation S-K (selected financial data);

(ii) cash dividends declared per share for the periods for which financial data is presented pursuant to Item 301 of Regulation S-K (selected financial data); and

(iii) income (loss) per share from continuing operations for the periods for which financial data is presented pursuant to Item 301 of Regulation S-K (selected financial data).

Instructions to paragraphs (a)(6) and (a)(7).

For a business combination accounted for as a purchase, the financial information required by paragraphs (a)(6) and (a)(7) shall be presented only for the most recent fiscal year and interim period. For a business combination accounted for as a pooling, the financial information required by paragraphs (a)(6) and (a)(7) (except for information with regard to book value) shall be presented for the most recent three fiscal years and interim period. For a business combination accounted for as a pooling, information with regard to book value shall be presented as of the end of the most recent fiscal year and interim period. Equivalent pro forma per share amounts shall be calculated by multiplying the pro forma income (loss) per share before nonrecurring charges or credits directly attributable to the transaction, pro forma book value per share, and the pro forma dividends per share of the registrant by the exchange ratio so that the per share amounts are equated to the respective values for one share of the other person.

(8) Financial information required by Article 11 of Regulation S-X with respect to this transaction.

Instructions to paragraph (a)(8).

1. Any other Article 11 information that is presented (rather than incorporated by reference) pursuant to other Items of this schedule shall be presented together with the information provided pursuant to paragraph (a)(8), but the presentation shall clearly distinguish between this transaction and any other.

2. If pro forma financial information with respect to all other transactions is incorporated by reference pursuant to paragraph (b) of this Item, only the pro forma results need be presented as part of the pro forma financial information required by this Item.

(9) A statement as to whether any federal or state regulatory requirements must be complied with or approval must be obtained in connection with the transaction and, if so, the status of such compliance or approval.

(10) If a report, opinion or appraisal materially relating to the transaction has been received from an outside party, and such report, opinion, or appraisal is referred to in the proxy statement, furnish the same information as would be required by Item 9(b)(1) through (6) of Schedule 13E-3.

(11) A description of any past, present, or proposed material contracts, arrangements, understandings, relationships, negotiations or transactions during the periods for which financial statements are presented or incorporated by refer-

ence pursuant to this Item between the other person or its affiliates and the registrant or its affiliates such as those concerning a merger, consolidation, or acquisition; a tender offer or other acquisition of securities; an election of directors; or a sale or other transfer of a material amount of assets.

(12) As to each class of securities of the registrant or of the other person which is admitted to trading on a national securities exchange or with respect to which a market otherwise exists, and which will be materially affected by the transaction, state the high and low sale prices (or in the absence of trading in a particular period, the range of the bid and asked prices) as of the date preceding public announcement of the proposed transaction, or if no such public announcement was made, as of the day preceding the day the agreement or resolution with respect to the action was made.

(13) A statement as to whether or not representatives of the principal accountants for the current year and for the most recently completed fiscal year:

(i) are expected to be present at the security holders' meeting;

(ii) will have the opportunity to make a statement if they desire to do so; and

(iii) are expected to be available to respond to appropriate questions.

(b) Information about the registrant and the other person.

Furnish the information specified below for the registrant and for the other person designated in paragraph (a) of this Item, if applicable (hereinafter all references to the registrant should be read to include a reference to such other person unless the context otherwise indicates):

(1) Information with respect to S-3 registrants. If the registrant meets the requirements of Form S-3 (See Note E to this Schedule) and elects to furnish information in accordance with the provisions of this paragraph, furnish information as required below.

(i) Describe any and all material changes in the registrant's affairs that have occurred since the end of the latest fiscal year for which audited financial statements were included in the latest annual report to security holders and that have not been described in a report on Form 10-Q, Form 10-QSB or Form 8-K filed under the Exchange Act;

(ii) Include in the proxy statement, if not incorporated by reference from the reports filed under the Exchange Act specified in paragraph (b)(1)(iii) of this Item, from a proxy or information statement filed pursuant to section 14 of the Exchange Act, from a prospectus previously filed pursuant to Rule 424 under the Securities Act or, where no prospectus was required to be filed pursuant to Rule 424(b), the prospectus included in the registration statement at effectiveness, or from a Form 8-K filed during either of the two preceding fiscal years:

(A) Financial information required by Rule 3-05 and Article 11 of Regulation S-X with respect to transactions other than that pursuant to which action is to be taken as described in this proxy statement.

(B) Restated financial statements prepared in accordance with Regulation S-X, if there has been a change in accounting principles or a correction of an error where such change or correction requires a material retroactive restatement of financial statements;

(C) Restated financial statements prepared in accordance with Regulation S-X where one or more business combinations accounted for by the pooling of interests method of accounting have been consummated subsequent to the most recent fiscal year and the acquired businesses, considered in the aggregate, are significant pursuant to Rule 11-01(b) of Regulation S-X; or

(D) Any financial information required because of a material disposition of assets outside the normal course of business.

(iii) Incorporate by reference into the proxy statement the documents listed in paragraphs (A), (B), and, if applicable, (C) below:

(A) The registrant's latest annual report on Form 10-K or Form 10-KSB filed pursuant to section 13(a) or 15(d) of the Exchange Act which contains financial statements for the registrant's latest fiscal year for which a Form 10-K or Form 10-KSB was required to be filed;

(B) All other reports filed pursuant to section 13(a) or 15(d) of the Exchange Act since the end of the fiscal year covered by the annual report referred to in paragraph (b)(1)(iii)(A) of this Item;

(C) If capital stock is to be issued to security holders entitled to vote or give an authorization or consent and securities of the same class are registered under Section 12 of the Exchange Act and: (i) are listed for trading or admitted to unlisted trading privileges on a national securities exchange; or (ii) are securities for which bid and offer quotations are reported on an automated quotations system operated by a national securities association, the description of such class of securities which is contained in a registration statement filed under the Exchange Act, including any amendment or reports filed for the purpose of updating such description.

(iv) The proxy statement also shall state on the last page(s) that all documents subsequently filed by the registrant pursuant to sections 13(a), 13(c), 14 or 15(d) of the Exchange Act, prior to one of the following dates, whichever is applicable, shall be deemed to be incorporated by reference into the proxy statement:

(A) If a meeting of security holders is to be held, the date on which such meeting is held;

SEC 31245

178

(B) If a meeting of security holders is not to be held, the date on which the consents or authorizations are used to effect the proposed action.

(2) Information with respect to S-2 or S-3 registrants.

(i) Information required to be furnished. If the registrant meets the requirements of Form S-2 or Form S-3 (See Note E of this Schedule) and elects to comply with this paragraph, furnish the information required by either paragraph (A) or (B) of this paragraph. However, the registrant shall not provide information in the manner allowed by paragraph (A) of this paragraph, if the financial statements in the registrant's latest annual report to security holders do not reflect: restated financial statements prepared in accordance with Regulation S-X if there has been a change in accounting principles or a correction of an error where such change or correction requires a material retroactive restatement of financial statements; restated financial statements prepared in accordance with Regulation S-X where one or more business combinations accounted for by the pooling of interests method of accounting have been consummated subsequent to the most recent fiscal year and the acquired businesses, considered in the aggregate, are significant pursuant to Rule 11-01(b) of Regulation S-X; or any financial information required because of a material disposition of assets outside of the normal course of business.

(A) If the registrant elects to furnish information pursuant to this paragraph (b)(2)(i)(A) and delivers the proxy statement together with a copy of either its latest Form 10-K or Form 10-KSB filed pursuant to sections 13(a) or 15(d) of the Exchange Act or its latest annual report to security holders which, at the time of original preparation met the requirements of either Rule 14a-3 (Rule 14a-3 or 14c-3):

(1) Indicate that the proxy statement is accompanied by either a copy of the registrant's latest Form 10-K or Form 10-KSB or a copy of its latest annual report to security holders.

(2) Provide financial and other information with respect to the registrant in the form required by Part I of Form 10-Q as of the end of the most recent fiscal quarter which ended after the end of the latest fiscal year for which audited financial statements were included in the latest report to security holders and more than 45 days prior to the date the proxy statement is filed in definitive form (or as of a more recent date) by one of the following means:

(i) Including such information in the proxy statement;

(ii) Providing without charge to each person to whom a proxy statement is delivered a copy of the registrant's latest Form 10-Q or Form 10-QSB; or

SEC 31245

(iii) Providing without charge to each person to whom a proxy statement is delivered a copy of the registrant's latest quarterly report that was delivered to its security holders and that included the required financial information.

(3) If not reflected in the registrant's latest annual report to security holders, provide information required by Rule 3-05 and Article 11 of Regulation S-X with respect to transactions other than that as to which action is to be taken as described in the proxy statement.

(4) Describe any and all material changes in the registrant's affairs that have occurred between the end of the latest fiscal year for which audited financial statements were included in the latest annual report to security holders and the date the definitive proxy statement is filed and that were not described in a Form 10-Q or Form 10-QSB or quarterly report delivered with the proxy statement in accordance with paragraph (b)(2)(i)(A)(2)(ii) or (iii).

(B) If the registrant does not elect to furnish information and deliver its latest Form 10-K or Form 10-KSB or a copy of its latest annual report to security holders pursuant to paragraph (b)(2)(i)(A):

(1) Furnish a brief description of the business done by the registrant and its subsidiaries during the most recent fiscal year as required by Rule 14a-3 to be included in an annual report to security holders. The description also should take into account changes in the registrant's business that have occurred between the end of the last fiscal year and the filing of definitive proxy materials.

(2) Include financial statements and information as required by Rule 14a- 3(b)(1) to be included in the annual report to security holders. In addition, provide:

(i) The interim financial information required by Rule 10-01 of Regulation S-X for a report on Form 10-Q or Form 10 QSB;

(ii) Financial information required by Rule 3-05 and Article 11 of Regulation S-X with respect to transactions other than that as to which action is to be taken as described in this proxy statement;

(iii) Restated financial statements prepared in accordance with Regulation S-X if there has been a change in accounting principles or a correction of an error where such change or correction requires a material retroactive restatement of financial statements;

(iv) Restated financial statements prepared in accordance with Regulation S-X where one or more business combinations accounted for by the pooling of interests method of accounting have been consummated subsequent to the most recent fiscal year and the acquired businesses, considered in the aggregate, are significant pursuant to Rule 11-01(b) of Regulation S-X; and

(v) Any financial information required because of a material disposition of assets outside of the normal course of business.

(3) Furnish the information required by the following:

(i) Item 101(b), (c)(1)(i) and (d) of Regulation S-K, industry segments, classes of similar products or services, foreign and domestic operations and import sales;

(ii) Item 102 of Regulation S-K for any property involved in the transaction, if such disclosure is material to the security holder's understanding of the transaction;

(iii) Item 201 of Regulation S-K, market price of and dividends on the registrant's common equity and related stockholder matters;

(iv) Item 301 of Regulation S-K, selected financial data;

(v) Item 302 of Regulation S-K, supplementary financial information;

(vi) Item 303 of Regulation S-K, management's discussion and analysis of financial condition and results of operations; and

(vii) Item 304 of Regulation S-K, changes in and disagreements with accountants on accounting and financial disclosure.

(ii) Incorporation of certain information by reference.

If the registrant meets the requirements of Form S-2 or S-3 (See Note E of this Schedule) and elects to furnish information in accordance with the provisions of paragraph (b)(2)(i) of this Item:

(A) Incorporate by reference into the proxy statement the document listed in paragraphs (1) and (2) below and, if applicable, the portions of the documents listed in paragraphs (3) and (4) below.

(1) The registrant's latest annual report on Form 10-K or Form 10-KSB filed pursuant to section 13(a) or 15(d) of the Exchange Act which contains audited financial statements for the

registrant's latest fiscal year for which a Form 10-K or Form 10-KSB was required to be filed.

(2) All other reports filed pursuant to section 13(a) or 15(d) of the Exchange Act since the end of the fiscal year covered by the annual report referred to in paragraph (a)(2)(i)(A)(1).

(3) If the registrant elects to deliver its latest annual report to security holders pursuant to paragraph (b)(2)(i)(A) of this Item, the information furnished in accordance with the following:

(i) Item 101(b), (c)(1)(i) and (d) of Regulation S-K, industry segments, classes of similar products or services, foreign and domestic operations and export sales;

(ii) Item 201 of Regulation S-K, market price of and dividends on the registrant's common equity and related stockholder matters;

(iii) Item 301 of Regulation S-K, selected financial data;

(iv) Item 302 of Regulation S-K, supplementary financial information;

(v) Item 303 of Regulation S-K, management's discussion and analysis of financial condition and results of operations; and

(vi) Item 304 of Regulation S-K, changes in and disagreements with accountants on accounting and financial disclosure.

(4) If the registrant elects, pursuant to paragraph (b)(2)(i)(A)(2)(iii) of this Item, to provide a copy of its latest quarterly report which was delivered to security holders, financial information equivalent to that required to be presented in Part I of Form 10-Q.

(B) The registrant also may state, if it so chooses, that specifically described portions of its annual or quarterly report to security holders, other than those portions required to be incorporated by reference pursuant to paragraphs (b)(2)(ii)(A)(3) and (4) of this Item, are not part of the proxy statement. In such case, the description of portions that are not incorporated by reference or that are excluded shall be made with clarity and in reasonable detail.

(3) Information with respect to registrants other than S-2 or S-3 registrants:

(i) If the registrant does not meet the requirements of Form S-2 or S-3 (See Note E of this Schedule), or elects to comply with this paragraph (b)(3) in lieu of (b)(1) or (b)(2), furnish the following information:

(A) Information required by Item 101 of Regulation S-K, description of business.

(B) Information required by Item 102 of Regulation S-K, description of property.

(C) Information required by Item 103 of Regulation S-K, legal proceedings.

(D) Information required by Item 201 of Regulation S-K, market price of and dividends on the registrant's common equity and related stockholder matters.

(E) Financial statements meeting the requirements of Regulation S-X, including financial information required by Rule 3-05 and Article 11 of Regulation S-X with respect to transactions other than that as to which action is to be taken as described in this proxy statement.

(F) Item 301 of Regulation S-K, selected financial data.

(G) Item 302 of Regulation S-K, supplementary financial information.

(H) Item 303 of Regulation S-K, management's discussion and analysis of financial condition and results of operations.

(I) Item 304 of Regulation S-K, changes in and disagreements with accountants on accounting and financial disclosure.

(ii) If the other person is not subject to the reporting requirements of either section 13(a) or 15(d) of the Exchange Act; or, because of section 12(i) of the Exchange Act, has not furnished an annual report to security holders pursuant to Rule 14a-3 or Rule 14c-3 for its latest fiscal year, furnish:

(A) The financial statements that would have been required to be included in an annual report to security holders pursuant to Rules 14a-3(b)(1) and (b)(2) had the company been required to furnish such a report; provided, however, that the balance sheet for the year preceding the latest full fiscal year and the income statements for the two years preceding the latest full fiscal year need not be audited if they have not previously been audited. In any case, such financial statements need be audited only to the extent practicable.

(B) The quarterly financial and other information that would have been required had the company been required to file Part I of Form 10-Q or Form 10-QSB for the most recent quarter for which such a report would have been on file at the time the proxy statement is mailed or for a period ending as of a more recent date.

(C) A brief description of the business done by the company which indicates the general nature and scope of the business.

(D) The information required by paragraphs (b)(3)(i)(D) and (F)-(H) of this Item and the information required by Item 304(b) of Regulation S-K.

(E) Schedules required by Rules 12-15, 28 and 29 of Regulation S-X.

(c) Additional method of incorporation by reference.

In lieu of the provision of information about the registrant and the other person required in paragraph (b) of this Item, the registrant may incorporate by reference into the proxy statement the information required by paragraph (b)(3) of this Item if it is contained in an annual report sent to security holders pursuant to the requirement of Rule 14a-3 with respect to the same meeting or solicitation of consents or authorizations as that to which the proxy statement relates, provided such information substantially meets the requirements of paragraph (b)(3) of this Item or the appropriate portions of paragraph (b)(3) of this Item.

Instructions to Item 14:

1. In order to facilitate compliance with Rule 2-02(a) of Regulation S-X, one copy of the definitive proxy statement filed with the Commission shall include a manually signed copy of the accountant's report. If the financial statements are incorporated by reference, a manually signed copy of the accountant's report shall be filed with the definitive proxy statement.

2. Notwithstanding the provisions of this Item, any or all of the required financial statements and related information which are not material for the exercise of prudent judgment in regard to the matter to be acted upon may be omitted.

3. If the registrant or any of its securities or assets is to be acquired by the other person, the information regarding the other person that is required by this Item, other than information required by paragraphs (a)(1)-(3) and (a)(9)-(11) of this Item, need be provided only to the extent that (1) the registrant or its security holders who are entitled to vote or give an authorization or consent with regard to the action will become or remain security holders of the other person; or (2) such information is otherwise material to an informed voting decision.

4. If the plan being voted on involves only the registrant and one or more of its totally held subsidiaries and does not involve a liquidation of the registrant or a spin-off, the information required by this Item, other than information required by paragraphs (a)(1)-(4) and (a)(9)-(12) of this Item, may be omitted.

5. Notwithstanding the provisions of Regulation S-X, no schedules other than those prepared in accordance with Rules 12-15, 12-28, and 12-29

(or, for management investment companies, Rule 12-12 through 12-14) of that regulation need be furnished in the proxy statement.

6. Unless registered on a national securities exchange or otherwise required to furnish such information, registered investment companies need not furnish the information required by paragraphs (a)(5), (a)(6), (b)(3)(i)(F), (G) or (H) of this Item.

7. If the registrant submits preliminary proxy material incorporating by reference financial statements required by this Item, the registrant should furnish a draft of the financial statements if the document from which they are incorporated has not been filed with or furnished to the Commission.

31300. ANNUAL REPORT TO SHAREHOLDERS

31310. General

The SEC's jurisdiction over the information that needs to be included in annual reports sent to shareholders by listed and unlisted companies registered under Section 12 of 1934 Act is principally as a result of the proxy rules (Regulation 14A), which are discussed in section 31100.

Rule 14a-3 of Regulation 14A requires that each person solicited by management for a proxy in connection with an annual shareholders' meeting at which directors are to be elected be furnished with an annual report to shareholders that complies with the detailed requirements set forth in that rule. Rule 14c-3 of Regulation 14C (see section 31000) contains a similar provision with respect to the information to be furnished to security holders in connection with an annual meeting at which directors are to be elected, even though proxies are not solicited. The text of Rule 14a-3 is included in the next section.

A crucial aspect of the SEC's integrated disclosure program is that the financial statements included in the annual report to shareholders comply with Regulation S-X. One objective of this requirement is to encourage registrants to incorporate their financial statements by reference into Form 10-K and into certain 1933 Act registration statements. Refer to section 41171 for further discussion of the incorporation-by-reference technique and to section 41170 for a discussion of the various methods of combining Form 10-K and the annual report to shareholders.

The SEC has not objected to an alternative method of reporting information to shareholders that includes the issuance of a summary annual report. A summary annual report has no specific requirements, but typically includes condensed financial information that is supplemented by disclosures and an expanded MD&A in an easy-to-understand format. Using this method, the full audited financial statements and other information required pursuant to Rules 14a-3 and 14c-3 are included in the proxy materials sent to shareholders and the summary annual report is provided separately. The conventional annual report need not be furnished since the information required by the SEC to be distributed to shareholders is included in the proxy materials. This method, which has been endorsed by the Financial Executives Institute and adopted by a number of registrants, provides management with greater flexibility in determining the information to be communicated to shareholders. It is important to note that, as with all other corporate communications that can reasonably be expected to affect the market for the corporation's securities, summary annual reports are subject to Section 17 of the 1933 Act (fraudulent interstate transactions) and Section 10(b) of the 1934 Act (use of manipulative and deceptive devices, including misstatements or omissions of material facts).

31320. Financial Statements and Other Information Required To Be Furnished (Rule 14a-3)

Rule 14a-3 includes the detailed specifications as to the financial statements and related financial information to be presented in the annual report to shareholders. Following is the text of Rule 14a-3 with references to other sections of this manual inserted where applicable.

Rule 14a-3. Information To Be Furnished to Security Holders:

(a) No solicitation subject to this regulation shall be made unless each person solicited is concurrently furnished or has previously been furnished with a publicly-filed preliminary or definitive written proxy statement containing the information specified in Schedule 14A [see section 31200 of this manual] or with a preliminary or definitive written proxy statement included in a registration statement filed under the Securities Act of 1933 on Form S-4 or F4 [see sections 42300 or 45400, respectively, of this manual] or Form N-14 and containing the information specified in such Form.

(b) If the solicitation is made on behalf of the registrant and relates to an annual (or special meeting in lieu of the annual) meeting of security holders, or written consent in lieu of such meeting, at which directors are to be elected, each proxy statement furnished pursuant to paragraph (a) of this section shall be accompanied or preceded by an annual report to such security holders as follows:

Note to Small Business Issuers—A "small business issuer," defined under Rule 12b-2 of the Exchange Act, shall refer to the disclosure items in Regulation S-B [see section 70000] rather than Regulation S-K. If there is no comparable disclosure item in Regulation S-B, a small business issuer need not provide the information requested. A small business issuer shall provide the information in Item 310(a) of Regulation S-B in lieu of the financial information required by Rule 14a-3(b)(1). Small business issuers using the transitional small business issuers disclosure format in the filing of their most recent annual report on Form 10-KSB need not provide the information specified below. Rather, those small business issuers shall provide only the financial statements required to be filed in their most recent Form 10-KSB. The inclusion of additional information, including information required of non-transitional small business issuers, in the annual report to security holders will not cause the issuer to be ineligible for the transitional disclosure forms.

1. The report shall include, for the registrant and its subsidiaries consolidated, audited balance sheets as of the end of each of the two most recent fiscal years and audited statements of income and cash flows for each of the three most recent fiscal years prepared in accordance with Regulation S-X, except that the provisions of Article 3 [see section 50300] (other than Rules 3-03(e), 3-04 and 3-20) and Article 11 [see section 51100] shall not apply. Any financial statement schedules or exhibits or separate financial statements which may otherwise be required in filings with the Commission may be omitted. Investment companies registered under the Investment Company Act of 1940 need include financial statements only for the last fiscal year except for statements of changes in net assets which are to be filed for the two most recent fiscal years. If the financial statements of the registrant and its subsidiaries consolidated in the annual report filed or to be filed with the Commission are not required to be audited, the financial statements required by this paragraph may be unaudited.

Note 1: If the financial statements for a period prior to the most recently completed fiscal year have been examined by a predecessor accountant, the separate report of the predecessor accountant may be omitted in the report to security holders provided the registrant has obtained from the predecessor accountant a reissued report covering the prior period presented and the successor accountant clearly indicates in the scope paragraph of his report (a) that the financial statements of the prior period were examined by other accountants, (b) the date of their report, (c) the type of opinion expressed by the predecessor accountant, and (d) the substantive reasons therefor, if it was other than unqualified. It should be noted, however, that the separate report of any predecessor accountant is required in filings with the Commission. If, for instance, the financial statements in the annual report to security holders are incorporated by reference in a Form 10-K [see section 41100] or Form 10-KSB, the separate report of a predecessor accountant shall be filed in Part II or in Part IV as a financial statement schedule.

Note 2: For purposes of complying with Rule 14a-3, if the registrant, other than a registered investment company, has changed its fiscal closing date, financial statements covering two years and one period of nine to 12 months shall be deemed to satisfy the requirements for statements of income and cash flows for the three most recent fiscal years.

2. Financial statements and notes thereto shall be presented in roman type at least as large and as legible as ten-point modern type. If necessary for convenient presentation, the financial statements may be in roman type as large and as legible as eight-point modern type. All type shall be leaded at least 2-point.

3. The report shall contain the supplementary financial information required by Item 302 of Regulation S-K [see section 63020 of this manual].

4. The report shall contain information concerning changes in and disagreements with accountants on accounting and financial disclosure required by Item 304 of Regulation S-K [see section 63040 of this manual].

5.   (i) The report shall contain the selected financial data required by Item 301 of Regulation S-K [see section 63010 of this manual].

(ii) The report shall contain management's discussion and analysis of financial condition and results of operations required by Item 303 of Regulation S-K [see section 63030 of this manual] or, if applicable, a plan of operation required by Item 303(a) of Regulation S-B [see section 73032 of this manual].

6. The report shall contain a brief description of the business done by the registrant and its subsidiaries during the most recent fiscal year which will, in the opinion of management, indicate the general nature and scope of the business of the registrant and its subsidiaries.

7. The report shall contain information relating to the registrant's industry segments, classes of similar products or services, foreign and domestic operations and export sales required by paragraphs (b), (c)(1)(i) and (d) of Item 101 of Regulation S-K [see section 61010 of this manual].

[Note: Paragraph (b)(11) of this section permits the information required by this paragraph to be set forth in any form deemed suitable by management.]

8. The report shall identify each of the registrant's directors and executive officers, and shall indicate the principal occupation or employment of each such person and the name and principal business of any organization by which such person is employed.

[Note: The term "executive officer" means the president, secretary, treasurer, any vice president in charge of a principal business function (such as sales, administration, or finance), and any other person who performs similar policy-making functions for the registrant.]

9. The report shall contain the market price of and dividends on the registrant's common equity and related security holder matters required by Item 201 of Regulation S-K [see section 62010 of this manual].

10. Registrant's proxy statement, or the report, shall contain an undertaking in bold face or otherwise reasonably prominent type to provide without charge to each person solicited upon the written request of any such person, a copy of the registrant's annual report on Form 10-K, including the financial statements and the financial statement schedules, required to be filed with the Commission pursuant to Rule 13a-1 under the Act for the registrant's most recent fiscal year, and shall indicate the name and address (including title or department) of the person to whom such a written request is to be directed. At the discretion of management, a registrant need not undertake to furnish, without charge, copies

of all exhibits to its Form 10-K provided that the copy of the annual report on Form 10-K, furnished without charge to requesting security holders is accompanied by a list briefly describing all the exhibits not contained therein and indicating that the registrant will furnish any exhibit upon the payment of a specified reasonable fee which fee shall be limited to the registrant's reasonable expenses in furnishing such exhibit. If the registrant's annual report to security holders complies with all of the disclosure requirements of Form 10-K and is filed with the Commission in satisfaction of its Form 10-K filing requirements, such registrant need not furnish a separate Form 10-K to security holders who receive a copy of such annual report.

> Note: Pursuant to the undertaking required by the above paragraph (b)(10) of this section, a registrant shall furnish a copy of its annual report on Form 10-K to a beneficial owner of its securities upon receipt of a written request from such person. Each request must set forth a good faith representation that, as of the record date for the solicitation requiring the furnishing of the annual report to security holders pursuant to paragraph (b) of this section, the person making the request was a beneficial owner of securities entitled to vote.

11. Subject to the foregoing requirements, the report may be in any form deemed suitable by management and the information required by paragraphs (b)(5) to (b)(10) of this section may be presented in an appendix or other separate section of the report, provided that the attention of security holders is called to such presentation.

> Note: Registrants are encouraged to utilize tables, schedules, charts, and graphic illustrations to present financial information in an understandable manner. Any presentation of financial information must be consistent with the data in the financial statements contained in the report and, if appropriate, should refer to relevant portions of the financial statements and notes thereto.

12. Paragraphs (b)(5) through (b)(11) of this section shall not apply to an investment company registered under the Investment Company Act of 1940. Subject to the requirements of paragraphs (b)(1) through (4) of this section, the annual report to security holders of such investment company may be in any form deemed suitable by management.

13. Paragraph (b) of this section shall not apply, however, to solicitations made on behalf of the registrant before the financial statements are available if solicitation is being made at the same time in opposition to the registrant and if the registrant's proxy statement includes an undertaking in bold face type to furnish such annual report to all persons being solicited at least 20 calendar days before the date of the meeting, or if the solicitation refers to a written consent or authorization in lieu of a meeting, at least 20 calendar days prior to the earliest date on which it may be used to effect corporate action.

SEC 31320

(c) Seven copies of the report sent to security holders pursuant to this rule shall be mailed to the Commission, solely for its information, not later than the date on which such report is first sent or given to security holders or the date on which preliminary copies, or definitive copies, if preliminary filing was not required, of solicitation material are filed with the Commission pursuant to Rule 14a-6, whichever date is later. The report is not deemed to be "soliciting material" or to be "filed" with the Commission or subject to this regulation otherwise than as provided in this Rule, or to the liabilities of Section 18 of the Act, except to the extent that the registrant specifically requests that it be treated as a part of the proxy soliciting material or incorporates it in the proxy statement or other filed report by reference.

(d) An annual report to security holders prepared on an integrated basis pursuant to General Instruction H to Form 10-K [see section 41175 of this manual] may also be submitted in satisfaction of this rule. When filed as the annual report on Form 10-K, responses to the Items of that form are subject to Section 18 of the Act notwithstanding paragraph (c).

(e) Notwithstanding paragraphs (a) and (b) of this section:

1. A registrant is not required to send an annual report to a security holder of record having the same address as another security holder of record, provided that (i) such security holders are not holding such registrant's securities in nominee name, (ii) at least one report is sent to a holder of record at that address and (iii) the holders of record to whom a report is not sent agree thereto in writing; and

2. Unless state law requires otherwise, a registrant is not required to send an annual report or proxy statement to a security holder if: (i) an annual report and proxy statement for two consecutive annual meetings; or (ii) all, and at least two, payments (if sent by first class mail) of dividends or interest on securities during a 12-month period have been mailed to such security holder's address and have been returned undeliverable. If any such security holder delivers or causes to be delivered to the registrant written notice setting forth his then current address for security holder communications purposes, the registrant's obligation to deliver an annual report or a proxy statement under this section is reinstated.

(f) The provisions of paragraph (a) of this section shall not apply to a communication made by means of speeches in public forums, press releases, published or broadcast opinions, statements, or advertisements appearing in a broadcast media, newspaper, magazine or other bona fide publication disseminated on a regular basis, provided that:

(1) no form of proxy, consent or authorization or means to execute the same is provided to a security holder in connection with the communication; and

(2) at the time the communication is made, a definitive proxy statement is on file with the Commission pursuant to Rule 14a-6(b).

Paragraph (b)1 specifies the dates and periods for which financial statements are required to be included in the annual report to shareholders. Note that statements of changes in stockholders' equity are also required to be presented for each of the three most recent fiscal years.

The rule specifies that, subject to certain exceptions, the financial statements included in the annual report to shareholders need to comply with the requirements of Regulation S-X. With the exception of Rule 3-03(e) (disclosure of business segments), Rule 3-04 (changes in other stockholders' equity), and Rule 3-20 (currency for financial statements of foreign private issuers), shareholder reports need not comply with Article 3, which deals principally with additional financial statement requirements. Accordingly, any other separate financial statements required by Article 3 may be omitted, including those of acquired businesses, unconsolidated subsidiaries, and 50 percent-or-less-owned persons, guarantors of securities registered, and affiliates whose securities are pledged as collateral. It is important to note, however, that separate financial statements (or condensed financial information) may be required by GAAP (e.g., paragraph 20(d) of APB Opinion No. 18 regarding investments in common stock of corporate joint ventures or other investments accounted for by the equity method that are material in relation to the financial position or results of operations of an investor).

Rule 3-15 contains special provisions for real estate investment trusts. The SEC staff has informally indicated that, although not stated in Rule 14a-3, compliance with Rule 3-15 is expected in the annual report to shareholders. In addition, refer to the discussion below regarding the staff's views on presenting schedules of real estate and accumulated depreciation, and mortgage loans on real estate.

Financial statements included in the annual report to shareholders also need not comply with Article 11, which deals with requirements for pro forma financial information. However, once again it is important to note that pro forma information may be required by GAAP. Examples include paragraph 96 of APB Opinion No. 16, which requires supplemental pro forma information regarding business combinations accounted for by the purchase method, and AU 560.05, which indicates that when appropriate, consideration needs to be given to the desirability of presenting pro forma information with respect to certain subsequent events.

Subject to the foregoing exceptions, the consolidated financial statements in the annual report to shareholders should be identical to those included in Form 10-K.

Financial statement schedules are also not required to be included in the annual report to shareholders. However, SAB Topic 7-C describes the views of the staff on presenting schedules of real estate and accumulated depreciation, and of mortgage loans on real estate. The text of the SAB follows:

SEC 31320

Schedules of Real Estate and Accumulated
Depreciation, and of Mortgage Loans on Real Estate

Facts: Whenever investments in real estate or mortgage loans on real estate are significant, the schedules of such items (see Rules 12-28 and 12-29 of Regulation S-X) are required in a prospectus.

Question: Is such information also required in annual reports to shareholders?

Interpretive Response: Although Rules 14a-3 and 14c-3 permit the omission of financial statement schedules from annual reports to shareholders, the staff is of the view that the information required by these schedules is of such significance within the real estate industry that the information should be included in the financial statements in the annual report to shareholders.

As indicated in paragraph (b)10, a copy of Form 10-K is required to be offered without charge, including all financial statements and financial statement schedules. A reasonable fee may be charged for exhibits. However, if the annual report to shareholders complies with all of the disclosure requirements of Form 10-K, the issuer need not provide a separate Form 10-K to shareholders who received a copy of the annual report. This provision is apparently intended to encourage preparation by registrants of a completely integrated document that serves as both the annual report to shareholders and Form 10-K. (Section 41175 discusses integrating Form 10-K with the annual report to shareholders.)

Paragraph (c) of Rule 14a-3 specifies that the annual report to shareholders is not considered soliciting material or filed with the SEC or subject to liabilities under Section 18 of the 1934 Act, except to the extent that the issuer specifically requests that the annual report be treated as part of the proxy soliciting material or incorporates it by reference in the proxy statement or other filing with the SEC. Sections of the annual report that are intended to be incorporated by reference are generally so designated to distinguish them from the parts of the report that are not considered "filed," and, therefore, not subject to liabilities under Section 18. Accountants' liabilities for documents filed under the 1934 Act are discussed in section 12030.

31330. Reports of Other Independent Accountants

Rule 2-05 of Regulation S-X (see section 50205) permits the exclusion of the report of the secondary accountants from the annual report to shareholders when the principal accountants have relied on the report of secondary accountants or when the financial statements covering the prior years were audited by predecessor accountants. Rule 14a-3(b)(1) contains similar provisions as to the report of the predecessor accountants. However, note that in each case a report or a reissued report needs to be obtained by the registrant from the secondary or predecessor accountants before the principal accountants issue their report.

31340. Stock Option Disclosure Requirements

In ASR No. 280 the SEC deleted its disclosure requirements for stock options from Regulation S-X, and now only requires disclosure of the option information specified by GAAP and by Item 402 of Regulation S-K regarding Executive Compensation (see Section 64020). However, the New York and American stock exchanges continue to require stock option disclosures beyond those required by GAAP. The exchange requirements, which are identical for both the NYSE and AMEX, call for companies to disclose in annual reports to shareholders the following information:

- The number of shares of its stock issuable under outstanding options at the beginning of the year; separate totals of changes in the number of shares of its stock under option resulting from issuance, exercise, expiration, or cancellation of options; and the number of shares issuable under outstanding options at the close of the year,

- The number of unoptioned shares available at the beginning and at the close of the year for the granting of options under an option plan, and

- Any changes in the exercise price of outstanding options, through cancellation and reissuance or otherwise, except price changes resulting from the normal operation of anti-dilution provisions of the options.

In addition to the information required to be disclosed by the stock exchanges, GAAP (ARB 43, Ch. 13B, par. 15—C47.123) requires disclosure of the number and price of shares issued upon exercise of stock options for each period presented—three years for a public company. Many companies find that combining GAAP and stock exchange disclosure requirements for all three years is the most practical and appropriate method of presentation.

31350. Cash-Flow-per-Share Disclosures

In FRP Section 202 (originally issued as ASR No. 142), the SEC emphasized that the use of terminology such as "cash-flow-per-share" in the financial highlights or the president's letter section of the annual report to shareholders should generally not be used, because this and other similar terms have no precise definition, and any such disclosures may be misleading to investors. The SEC staff has informally acknowledged that certain companies have reported cash-flow-per-share data in the president's letter or other narrative sections of the annual report to shareholders even though ASR No. 142 is still in effect. However, the staff continues to discourage such disclosures and generally objects to the inclusion of such information in the Selected Financial Data or in the financial statements.

If cash-flow-per-share disclosures are made in the narrative portion of the shareholders' report, it is suggested that companies carefully set forth the information in such a way that readers of the financial statements understand what information is being disclosed, its significance, and what it represents in the context of the company's general financial condition.

31400. QUARTERLY REPORT TO SHAREHOLDERS

The New York and American stock exchanges require listed U.S. companies to publish quarterly earnings statements for the first three quarters of each fiscal year. The exchanges merely require publication of the interim data, not that the information be sent to shareholders. However, the majority of listed public companies, as well as many unlisted companies, distribute quarterly reports to their shareholders that include interim financial data that frequently is summarized in condensed form.

APB Opinion No. 28 (as amended) sets forth the minimum financial disclosures required to be included in summarized interim financial data of publicly traded companies. The stock exchanges have no requirements dealing with the presentation of the interim data that extend beyond APB Opinion No. 28.

Although there are detailed rules covering the form and content of quarterly reports filed on Form 10-Q (see section 41400), there are no SEC requirements covering the quarterly reports to shareholders. However, the SEC encourages the integration of Form 10-Q and the quarterly report to shareholders and will permit the incorporation by reference into Form 10-Q of any information in the quarterly shareholder report that meets *some or all* of the requirements of Part I of the form (see section 41440). The information called for may be so incorporated in answer *or partial answer to any item or items* of Part I of Form 10-Q.

31500. TENDER OFFERS

31510. General

A tender offer is a general, publicized bid made by an individual or a group to purchase shares of a public company, usually at a price that is higher than the current market price.

A tender offer may be initiated with or without prior notification of the management of the target company. In most cases, tender offers are initiated through summary advertisements in the financial press. If the initiation of a tender offer is publicly announced, the offeror is required to either proceed with or abandon the offer within five business days of the public announcement. Pursuant to 1934 Act Rule 143-1(a), a tender offer must remain open for at least 20 days commencing with the date the offer was first published, sent, or provided to the target company's shareholders. Rule 14d-2 of the 1934 Act addresses the date of commencement of a tender offer.

31520. Information Required To Be Disclosed

Rule 14d-6 sets forth the general disclosure requirements for information to be furnished on the date the tender offer commences. The required disclosures are dependent upon the means by which the tender offer was originally communicated.

31530. Filing Requirements

On the day the tender offer officially commences, the offeror is required to file with the SEC a Tender Offer Statement on Schedule 14D-1, provided that subsequent to acceptance of the offer, the offeror would hold more than five percent of the equity securities of the target company. In addition, the offeror is required to hand deliver the Statement to the target company's management and to the stock exchanges on which the target's stock is traded. The following are the items of information to be included in Schedule 14D-1:

Item	Subject
1	Security and subject company
2	Identity and background information
3	Past contracts, transactions or negotiations with subject company

Item	Subject
4	Source and amount of funds or other consideration
5	Purpose of the tender offer and plans or proposals of the bidder
6	Interest in securities of the subject company
7	Contracts, arrangements, understandings or relationships with respect to the subject company's securities
8	Persons retained, employed or to be compensated
9	Financial statements of certain bidders
10	Additional information
11	Material to be filed as exhibits

If a material change occurs in the information contained in Schedule 14D-1, an amendment pursuant to Rule 14d-3(b) needs to be filed and all parties immediately notified.

31540. Financial Statement Requirements

The determination as to whether financial statements of prospective bidders (see Item 9 of Schedule 14D-1) are required to be furnished in connection with a tender offer is based on the facts and circumstances of the situation, including the terms of the tender transaction. The basic principle, however, is that if the bidder's financial condition is meaningful to a decision by the shareholder of the target company as to whether to sell, tender, or hold the securities being sought in the tender offer, adequate financial information concerning the bidder needs to be provided for the benefit of such shareholder.

A situation in which financial statements would generally be required is one in which the tender involves the offering of specific securities and cash in exchange for the securities of another company. In the case of a tender for cash, where a prospective acquirer makes an offer for a specific minimum number of shares of another company, reserving the option to accept all stock tendered over the minimum as well as a lesser number of shares, questions often arise as to whether the financial statements of the bidder are required. As a matter of general practice, the SEC staff has taken the position that financial statements of the bidder are not required when a cash tender offer has been made. The exceptions to this general rule would include cases in which there is some question as to the bidder's ability to obtain the funds necessary to complete the transaction under consideration, or where the statements of the bidder would otherwise be meaningful to the shareholders of the target company.

Item 9 of Schedule 14D-1 indicates that if the bidder is subject to the periodic reporting requirements of Section 13(a) or 15(d) of the 1934 Act, financial statements contained in periodic reports (i.e., Forms 10-K, 10-Q, and 8-K) filed with the SEC may be incorporated by reference in Schedule 14D-1.

198

If the bidder is not subject to the SEC's periodic reporting requirements under the 1934 Act, the financial statements included in Schedule 14D-1 need not be audited if such audited financial statements are not available or cannot be obtained without "unreasonable cost or expense." In such cases, disclosure needs to be provided in Schedule 14D-1 indicating the reasons for including the financial statements on an unaudited basis.

The form and content of and requirements for the financial statements and financial statement schedules to be included in this schedule and the dates and periods for which they are required to be presented are set forth in Regulation S-X. A discussion of these requirements is included beginning with section 50050 of this manual.

In situations in which it is determined that financial statements are required, Schedule 14D-1 refers to Form 10 as the basis of such requirements. For ease of reference, the dates and periods for which financial statements are required are summarized as follows:

Balance Sheets	Statements of Income, Cash Flows, and Stockholders' Equity	Financial Statement Schedules
As of the end of each of the two latest fiscal years	For each of the three latest fiscal years	Required as applicable in support of primary financial statements

Interim financial statements may also be required depending on the age of the financial statements at the filing date (see section 50304).

The term "financial statement schedules" covers financial statements required in addition to the primary financial statements prescribed by Rules 3-01, 3-02, and 3-04 (see section 50300), as well as the various supporting schedules prescribed by Rule 5-04 (see section 50520) of Regulation S-X. The dates and periods to be covered by the additional financial statements are generally the same as those prescribed for the primary financial statements. The dates and periods to be covered by the various supporting schedules, which vary depending on their nature, are specified in Rule 5-04. In the event that the tender offer involves a foreign bidder, financial statements prepared in compliance with Item 17 of Form 20-F (see sections 43210 and 44100) are required.

THE SEC FORMS

40100. INTRODUCTION

Companies filing registration statements and reports under the 1933 and 1934 Acts are required to use specific forms depending on the nature of the filing and/or the issuer.

Sections 40110 and 40120 briefly identify the principal forms used for registration statements and reports filed under the 1933 and 1934 Acts. The sections are presented as an overview of the various SEC registration and reporting forms that may be encountered in practice and are intended to provide a convenient point of reference when only a general understanding of their purpose is required.

The selection of the appropriate SEC form in a given situation requires a legal determination that should not be made by the independent public accountant. However, accountants are often consulted by registrants and their other advisers in considering whether the company meets the criteria for the use of a particular form. In such situations, reference should be made to the text of the form involved.

40110. Summary of Principal 1934 Act Forms

Listed below are certain 1934 Act reporting and registration forms. Some of these forms are rarely encountered by the independent accountant. The more commonly used forms are discussed further in the referenced sections of this manual.

Form	Annual Reports	Manual Reference (Section)
10-K	Principal form used by most registrants in the United States (and Canada) for which no other form is prescribed.	41100
10-KSB	Optional form that may be used by U.S. or Canadian entities qualifying as small businesses. (Refer to section 70000.)	41200
11-K	Employee stock purchase, savings, and similar plans.	41300
18-K	Foreign governments and political subdivisions thereof.	

Form	Annual Reports	Manual Reference (Section)
20-F	Foreign private issuers (other than governments and political subdivisions thereof). Also used for registration under the 1934 Act.	44100
40-F	Canadian multijurisdictional disclosure form. Used to satisfy annual reporting obligations and to register securities under the 1934 Act. (Refer to section 46000.)	44300

Interim Reports

Form		Manual Reference (Section)
10-Q	Quarterly report required for each of the first three quarters of the fiscal year. (Filed pursuant to Rule 13a-13 or 15d-13 of the 1934 Act.)	41400
10-QSB	Optional form that may be used for quarterly reporting by U.S. or Canadian entities qualifying as small businesses. (Refer to section 70000.)	41500
8-K	Current report required to be filed when certain significant events occur.	41600
6-K	Periodic reports required to be filed by foreign issuers at the time information is otherwise made public by the foreign issuers.	44200

Registration of Securities

Form		Manual Reference (Section)
10	Securities for which no other form is prescribed. Generally used for registration under the 1934 Act.	41800
10-SB	Optional form for the registration of securities of a small business issuer under the 1934 Act. (Refer to section 70000.)	41850
18	Securities of foreign governments and political subdivisions thereof.	
8-A	Certain classes of securities pursuant to Section 12(b) or (g) of the 1934 Act.	
8-B	Securities issued in certain cases on the registrant's succession to an issuer of previously registered securities.	

Form	Other	Manual Reference (Section)
	Amending reports filed under the 1934 Act.	41700
12b-25	Notification form used when a registrant is unable to timely file Forms 10-K and 10-KSB, 11-K, 10-Q and 10-QSB, or 20-F.	41750
15	Form used to terminate registration under Section 12(g) or suspend periodic reporting obligations under Sections 13 or 15(d) of the 1934 Act. (For a discussion of periodic reporting obligations, refer to section 19500.)	
Schedule 13D	A statement required to be filed by any person who becomes a 5 percent equity security holder of a public company. The schedule is also used to report material changes in beneficial ownership.	
Schedule 13E-3	A transaction statement required to be filed by an issuer in connection with a going-private transaction (as defined in Rule 13(e)-3).	
Schedule 13E-4	A statement required to be filed by issuers regarding tender offers for their own equity securities pursuant to Rule 13(e)-4.	
Schedule 14D-1	A tender offer filing used when an offer is made to holders of equity securities of a target company if acceptance of the offer would give the offeror more than 5 percent ownership. (For further information concerning this schedule, refer to section 31500.)	
Schedule 14D-9	A statement applicable to persons who made solicitations or recommendations for the acceptance or rejection of tender offers.	

40120. Summary of Principal 1933 Act Forms

Listed below are certain 1933 Act forms. The most frequently encountered forms are discussed further in the referenced section of this manual.

Form	Purpose	Manual Reference (Section)
S-1	The general form used for the registration of securities for which no other form is prescribed.	42100
S-2	A form available for the registration of securities by most companies that have complied with the 1934 Act reporting requirements for at least 36 months. This form combines incorporation by reference with delivery of the annual shareholder report and interim reports. Form S-2, like Form S-3, is available for registering most types of securities except those issued in exchange for securities of another company.	42200
S-3	A short form available to registrants that have complied with 1934 Act reporting requirements for at least 12 months (except for offerings of investment grade asset-backed securities (defined in section 42260) for which there is no reporting history requirement) and that meet certain market value or debt-rating tests. The form is available for registering most types of securities, except those issued in an exchange offer, and provides for incorporation by reference of 1934 Act reports filed and to be filed with the SEC. Unlike Form S-2, however, delivery of the incorporated documents is not required.	42250
S-4	A form that is used to register shares offered in connection with business combinations as, for example, exchange offers for securities of another entity. The form permits the incorporation by reference of 1934 Act reports based on the concepts introduced in Forms S-2 and S-3.	42300
S-8	A form used for the registration of securities to be offered to employees pursuant to option or other employee benefit plans.	42400
S-11	A form used for registering securities of certain real estate entities.	42500

Form	Purpose	Manual Reference (Section)
SB-1	A form available to transitional small business issuers to register up to $10 million of securities, to be sold for cash, in any continuous 12-month period. (Refer to section 70000.)	42600
SB-2	A form that may be used for the registration of securities to be sold to the public for cash by small business issuers. Replaced Form S-18, which was rescinded. (Refer to section 70000.)	42700
1-A	Form of offering statement and circular to be used in connection with the issuance of securities that are exempt from registration by the provisions of Regulation A of the 1933 Act.	42800
D	The form used to file notice of sales of securities that are exempt from registration under Regulation D of the 1933 Act.	42900
F-1	The form used for the registration of securities of foreign private issuers for which no other form is prescribed. The form is similar in concept to Form S-1.	45100
F-2	A form available to foreign private issuers that have complied with 1934 Act reporting requirements for at least 36 months and that meet certain other criteria. The form is similar in concept to Form S-2.	45200
F-3	A short form available to "world class" foreign private issuers that have complied with 1934 Act reporting requirements for at least 36 months and whose aggregate market value worldwide is $300 million or more. The form is similar in concept to Form S-3.	45300
F-4	The form used to register securities by foreign private issuers in connection with business combinations. To use Form F-4, registrants must already be subject to the reporting requirements of Form 20-F. The form is similar in concept to Form S-4.	45400

Form	Purpose	Manual Reference (Section)
F-6	The form used for the registration of depositary receipts issued by a depositary against the deposit of the securities of a foreign issuer provided certain conditions are met. (Among the conditions to be met is that the deposited securities are offered or sold in transactions registered under the 1933 Act or in transactions that would be exempt from registration if made in the U.S.)	45500
F-7	The form used by eligible Canadian Multijurisdictional Disclosure System (MJDS) issuers making a rights offering.	46121
F-8/F-80	The form used by eligible Canadian MJDS issuers making an exchange offer or registering shares in connection with a business combination.	46122
F-9	The form used by eligible Canadian MJDS issuers for offerings of investment grade debt and preferred stock.	46125
F-10	The form used by eligible Canadian MJDS issuers for offerings of any securities.	46126
N-1	The form used for the registration of securities of open-ended management investment companies that are separate accounts of insurance companies as defined in the Investment Company Act of 1940.	
N-1A	The form used for the registration of securities of open-ended management investment companies except small business investment companies licensed as such by the U.S. Small Business Administration and separate accounts of insurance companies as defined in the Investment Company Act of 1940.	
N-2	The form used for the registration of securities of close-ended management investment companies except small business investment companies licensed as such by the U.S. Small Business Administration.	

Form	Purpose	Manual Reference (Section)
N-3	The form used for the registration of securities of open-ended management investment companies that are separate accounts of insurance companies offering variable annuity contracts which are registered under the Investment Company Act of 1940.	
N-4	The form used for the registration of securities of unit-investment trusts by separate accounts of insurance companies offering variable annuity contracts registered under the Investment Company Act of 1940.	
N-5	The form used for the registration of securities issued by any small business investment company that is registered under the Investment Company Act of 1940 and that is licensed under the Small Business Investment Company Act of 1958, or that has received the preliminary approval of the Small Business Administration and has been notified that it may submit a license application.	
N-14	The form used for the registration of securities issued by registered investment companies in connection with business combination transactions.	
N-SAR	The form generally used for semiannual and annual reports by registered investment companies.	

41000.   REPORTING AND REGISTRATION FORMS UNDER THE 1934 ACT

41100.   FORM 10-K

41110.   General

Form 10-K, the principal annual report form for commercial and industrial companies, is required to be filed by companies that have registered securities under Section 12 of the 1934 Act and are required by Section 13 to file periodic reports, or that have registered securities under the 1933 Act and are required by Section 15(d) of the 1934 Act to file periodic reports. (See discussion of periodic reporting requirements in section 19500.)

The following are the items of information to be included in Form 10-K:

PART I

Item

1   Business
2   Properties
3   Legal proceedings
4   Submission of matters to a vote of security holders

PART II

5   Market for registrant's common equity and related stockholder matters
6   Selected financial data
7   Management's discussion and analysis of financial condition and results of operations
8   Financial statements and supplementary data
9   Changes in and disagreements with accountants on accounting and financial disclosure

PART III

10   Directors and executive officers of the registrant
11   Executive compensation
12   Security ownership of certain beneficial owners and management
13   Certain relationships and related transactions

PART IV

14   Exhibits, financial statement schedules, and reports on Form 8-K

The requirements as to financial statements and financial statement schedules (Items 8 and 14) are included in Regulation S-X (see discussion beginning with section 50050), and the requirements for each of the other items of information in Form 10-K are set forth in Regulation S-K (see discussion beginning with section 60000).

The information required by Parts I and II (Items 1 through 9) or any portion thereof may be incorporated by reference from the registrant's annual report to shareholders (see section 41171 for further discussion). Part III (Items 10 through 13) is required to be incorporated by reference if a definitive proxy statement pursuant to Regulation 14A (or definitive information statement pursuant to Regulation 14C) involving the election of directors will be filed not later than 120 days after the end of

SEC 41110. Form 10-K

the fiscal year. (For a discussion of proxy and information statements, refer to sections 31000 through 31240.)

Note that in a filing on Form 10-K, a ratio of earnings to fixed charges is optional and is generally not furnished. If such a ratio is included, however, an exhibit needs to be furnished setting forth in reasonable detail the computations in support of the amounts shown. (For a discussion of these requirements, see section 65030.)

41120. Financial Statement Requirements

The form and content of, and requirements for, the financial statements and financial statement schedules to be included in Form 10-K and the dates and periods for which they are required to be presented are set forth in Regulation S-X. A discussion of these requirements is included beginning with section 50050 of this manual. Note, however, that in accordance with Item 8 of Form 10-K, compliance with Rule 3-05 (Financial Statements of Businesses Acquired or to be Acquired) and Article 11 (Pro Forma Financial Information) is not required in Form 10-K.

For ease of reference, the dates and periods for which financial statements are required (Rules 3-01, 3-02, and 3-04 of Regulation S-X) are summarized as follows:

Balance Sheets	Statements of Income, Cash Flows, and Stockholders' Equity	Financial Statement Schedules
As of the end of each of the two latest fiscal years	For each of the three latest fiscal years	Required as applicable in support of primary financial statements

Note that Rule 3-06 of Regulation S-X provides that under certain specified conditions, one of the required fiscal years can consist of a period of between 9 and 12 months (see section 50338). The term "financial statement schedules" covers financial statements required in addition to the primary financial statements prescribed by Rules 3-01, 3-02, and 3-04 (such as those required by Rule 3-09), as well as the various supporting schedules prescribed by Rule 5-04 of Regulation S-X. The dates and periods to be covered by the additional financial statements are generally the same as those prescribed for the primary financial statements. The dates and periods to be covered by the various supporting schedules, which vary depending on their nature, are specified in Rule 5-04.

41121. Audit Requirements.
The balance sheets, statements of income, cash flows, and stockholders' equity, and financial statement schedules need to be audited for each date and period for which they are required unless the registrant is inactive

(as defined in Regulation S-X Rule 3-11; see section 50345), in which case the financial statements may be unaudited.,

41122. Entities (Persons) for Which Financial Statements or Other Financial Information May Be Required. The following are the various entities (persons) for which financial statements or other financial information may have to be furnished and the sections of the manual where the respective requirements are discussed:

Description	Section
Registrant and its consolidated subsidiaries	50302
Registrant alone (parent company—Schedule III)	50520
Unconsolidated subsidiaries and 50 percent-or-less-owned persons	50339
Affiliates whose securities are pledged as collateral	50334
Guarantors of securities registered	50344

The primary financial statements (usually consolidated financial statements) are presented in Part II of Form 10-K, while any other required financial statements and supplemental schedules are generally included in Part IV. If complete financial statements are to be furnished for any of these entities, they should be those that would be required by Regulation S-X if each such entity were a registrant filing on Form 10-K. However, it is important to note that in certain instances only condensed financial information is required (e.g., registrant alone (parent company—Schedule III)).

41130. Signatures

Form 10-K must be signed by a majority of the board of directors of the registrant (or persons performing similar functions) in addition to its principal executive officer, its principal financial officer, and its controller or principal accounting officer.

41140. Due Date

An annual report on Form 10-K needs to be filed within 90 days after the end of the fiscal year covered by the report. However, the financial statement schedules may, at the registrant's option, be filed as an amendment to Form 10-K under cover of Form 10-K/A (discussed in section 41700) not later than 120 days after the end of the fiscal year covered by the report. For a discussion of the procedure to be followed under Rule 12b-25 under the 1934 Act in notifying the SEC of an inability to file within the required time period, refer to section 41750.

To determine the exact due date of Form 10-K, the 90 days are counted from the fiscal year-end date, with the day after the fiscal year-end date being the first day counted. In accordance with paragraph (a) of 1934 Act Rule 0-3, if the ninetieth day is a Saturday, Sunday, or legal holiday, the due date becomes the next business day. This procedure is also applicable to other periodic reports filed under the 1934 Act. The filing needs to be *received* by the SEC in Washington, D.C., on or before the due date.

The text of paragraph (a) of 1934 Act Rule 0-3 follows:

All papers required to be filed with the Commission pursuant to the Act or the rules and regulations thereunder shall be filed at the principal office in Washington, D.C. Material may be filed by delivery to the Commission, through the mails or otherwise. The date on which papers are actually received by the Commission shall be the date of filing thereof if all of the requirements with respect to the filing have been complied with, except that if the last day on which papers can be accepted as timely filed falls on a Saturday, Sunday or holiday, such papers may be filed on the first business day following.

41141. Due Date of Special Financial Report. Section 19500 outlines the periodic reporting obligations under the 1934 Act for the year in which a registration statement under the 1933 Act becomes effective. Section 41420 indicates that the first Form 10-Q is due for the first fiscal quarter following the most recent fiscal year or full quarter for which financial statements were included in the registration statement. If that registration statement did not contain audited financial statements for the fiscal year preceding the year in which it became effective, Rule 15d-2 provides for the filing of a special financial report within 90 days of the effective date containing the audited financial statements for the latest fiscal year. The text of Rule 15d-2 is as follows:

Special Financial Report

(a) If the registration statement under the Securities Act of 1933 did not contain certified financial statements for the registrant's last full fiscal year (or for the life of the registrant if less than a full fiscal year) preceding the fiscal year in which the registration statement became effective, the registrant shall, within 90 days after the effective date of the registration statement, file a special report furnishing certified financial statements for such last full fiscal year or other period, as the case may be, meeting the requirements of the form appropriate for annual reports of the registrant.

(b) The report shall be filed under cover of the facing sheet of the form appropriate for annual reports of the registrant, shall indicate on the facing sheet that it contains

SEC 41141

only financial statements for the fiscal year in question and shall be signed in accordance with the requirements of the annual report form.

41150. Numbering of Pages and Size of Paper

Documents filed with the SEC are required to be numbered sequentially. All pages need to be numbered, starting with the facing sheet and including any exhibits or other material submitted as part of the document being filed. The sequential numbering required by the SEC is supplemental to any internal numbering system used in the document.

The text of paragraph (b) of Rule 0-3, which is applicable to documents filed under the 1934 Act, follows (a similar requirement is included in 1933 Act Rule 403):

> The manually signed original (or in the case of duplicate originals, one duplicate original) of all registrations, applications, statements, reports, or other documents filed under the Securities Exchange Act of 1934, as amended, shall be numbered sequentially (in addition to any internal numbering which otherwise may be present) by handwritten, typed, printed, or other legible form of notation from the facing page of the document through the last page of that document and any exhibits or attachments thereto. Further, the total number of pages contained in a numbered original shall be set forth on the first page of the document.

The Commission requires the use of 8-1/2 x 11 inch paper for all registration statements, applications, reports, documents, and amendments. However, to the extent that reduction of larger documents would render them illegible, the documents may be filed on larger paper.

41160. Relief for Certain Wholly Owned Subsidiaries

The instructions to Form 10-K (and Form 10-Q; see section 41470) provide relief in certain situations for wholly owned subsidiaries of companies reporting under the 1934 Act on the basis that investors in debt securities presumably have informational needs different from those of investors in equity securities. General Instruction J of Form 10-K allows wholly owned subsidiaries to omit certain specified information if the following conditions are met:

> (a) All of the registrant's equity securities are owned, either directly or indirectly, by a single person which is a reporting company under the Act and which has filed all the material required to be filed pursuant to section 13, 14, or 15(d) thereof, as applicable, and which is named in conjunction with the registrant's description of its business;
>
> (b) During the preceding thirty-six calendar months and any subsequent period of days, there has not been any material default in the payment of principal, interest,

SEC 41141. Form 10-K

a sinking or purchase fund installment, or any other material default not cured within thirty days, with respect to any indebtedness of the registrant or its subsidiaries, and there has not been any material default in the payment of rentals under material long-term leases; and

(c) There is prominently set forth, on the cover page of the Form 10-K, a statement that the registrant meets the conditions set forth in General Instruction J(1)(a) and (b) of Form 10-K and is therefore filing this form with the reduced disclosure format.

For registrants meeting the foregoing conditions, the Form 10-K disclosure requirements are modified as follows:

- Business (Item 1). Only a brief description of the business done by the registrant and its subsidiaries during the most recent fiscal year is required.

- Properties (Item 2). A brief description of the material properties of the registrant and its subsidiaries is required.

- Submission of Matters to a Vote of Security Holders (Item 4). This item may be omitted.

- Selected Financial Data (Item 6). This item may be omitted.

- Management's Discussion and Analysis of Financial Condition and Results of Operations (Item 7). Only material changes in certain revenue and expense items between the most recent year and the preceding fiscal year need to be discussed, along with an explanation of the effect of any changes in accounting principles and practices or method of application that have a material effect on net income.

- Information with respect to Directors and Executive Officers of the Registrant (Item 10), Executive Compensation (Item 11), Security Ownership of Certain Beneficial Owners & Management (Item 12), Certain Relationships and Related Transactions (Item 13), and the list-of-subsidiaries exhibit called for by Item 601 of Regulation S-K may be omitted.

41170. Alternatives for Combining Form 10-K with the Annual Report to Shareholders

Most of the financial information contained in Form 10-K is also required to be included in the annual report to shareholders, which is frequently prepared at the same time. (See section 31300 for a discussion of the requirements of the annual report to shareholders.) Some accepted practices of complying with both of these requirements are to prepare:

- Two completely separate documents, an annual report on Form 10-K and an annual report to shareholders.

- Two separate but interrelated reports wherein certain of the information included in the annual report to shareholders is incorporated by reference into Form 10-K. Many registrants follow this practice, particularly since the primary financial statements and certain other information must be identical or substantially the same in both reports. (See discussion beginning with the next section.)

- One report that serves as both a Form 10-K and a shareholders' report. In this case, the required information furnished in compliance with SEC rules is supplemented by the optional additional information generally included in the shareholders' report, and a cross-reference sheet identifies the location of the required Form 10-K information. (See section 41175 for further discussion of this method.)

The use of any of these alternatives for one fiscal year does not preclude a registrant from changing to a different approach in a subsequent year.

41171. Incorporation by Reference in Form 10-K of Annual Report to Shareholders. In accordance with Rule 12b-23 of the 1934 Act, the financial statements and certain other disclosure requirements of Form 10-K may be met by incorporating by reference the financial statements and other financial information included in the annual report to shareholders.

The provisions of Rule 12b-23 are as follows:

Rule 12b-23. Incorporation by Reference

(a) Except for information filed as an exhibit which is covered by Rule 12b-32, information may be incorporated by reference in answer, or partial answer, to any item of a registration statement or report subject to the following provisions:

(1) Financial statements incorporated by reference shall satisfy the requirements of the form or report in which they are incorporated. Financial statements or other financial data required to be given in comparative form for two or more fiscal years or periods shall not be incorporated by reference unless the material incorporated by reference includes the entire period for which the comparative data is given;

(2) Information in any part of the registration statement or report may be incorporated by reference in answer, or partial answer, to any other item of the registration statement or report; and

(3) Copies of any information or financial statement incorporated into a registration statement or report by reference, or copies of the pertinent pages of the document containing such information or statement, shall be filed as an exhibit to the statement or report, except that: (i) a proxy or information statement incorporated by reference in response to Part III of Form 10-K and Form 10-KSB; and (ii) a form of prospectus filed pursuant to [1933 Act] Rule 424(b) incorporated by reference in response to Item 1 of Form 8A need not be filed as an exhibit.

(b) Any incorporation by reference of matter pursuant to this section shall be subject to the provisions of Rule 24 of the Commission's Rules of Practice restricting incorporation by reference of documents which incorporate by reference other information. Material incorporated by reference shall be clearly identified in the reference by page, paragraph, caption or otherwise. Where only certain pages of a document are incorporated by reference and filed as an exhibit, the document from which the material is taken shall be clearly identified in the reference. An express statement that the specified matter is incorporated by reference shall be made at the particular place in the statement or report where the information is required. Matter shall not be incorporated by reference in any case where such incorporation would render the statement or report incomplete, unclear or confusing.

The annual report to shareholders is required to contain the same information set forth in Items 5 through 9 (see section 31300) of Form 10-K and the SEC encourages registrants to incorporate this information by reference in Form 10-K. Sections 41172 and 41173 discuss incorporation into Form 10-K of the audited financial statements and section 41174 discusses the incorporation into Form 10-K of financial information outside of the financial statements from the annual report to shareholders.

In addition, Form 10-K requires that the sources of material incorporated by reference be set forth on the cover page, together with an indication of the parts of the form into which the information has been so incorporated.

41172. Incorporating Audited Financial Information. Item 14(a) requires the registrant to include a comprehensive listing (index) of the following items filed as a part of Form 10-K:

- Financial statements.

- Financial statement schedules.

- Exhibits, including those incorporated by reference.

As a general rule, one index is included covering the financial statements and schedules and a separate index is furnished covering the exhibits. The index of financial statements and financial statement schedules is often used as a frame of reference for identifying the audited financial information in the annual shareholders' report being incorporated into Form 10-K and to identify the material covered by the independent accountants' report. Presented below is an illustrative index to a Form 10-K that incorporates portions of the annual report to shareholders and contains supplementary financial data. The index is presented as a guide only, and other approaches are equally acceptable. No one particular method is applicable in all circumstances.

XYZ COMPANY
INDEX TO FINANCIAL STATEMENTS AND FINANCIAL
STATEMENT SCHEDULES
(Item 14(a))

	Reference (Page)	
	Form 10-K **Annual Report**	**Annual Share-** **holders' Report**
Data incorporated by reference from the attached 19x3 Annual Report to Shareholders of XYZ Company:		
Report of Independent Accountants.	—	22
Consolidated statement of income and retained earnings for the years ended December 31, 19x3, 19x2, and 19x1.	—	23
Consolidated balance sheet at December 31, 19x3 and 19x2.	—	24
Consolidated statement of cash flows for the years ended December 31, 19x3, 19x2, and 19x1.	—	25
Consolidated statement of capital stock and additional paid-in capital for the years ended December 31, 19x3, 19x2, and 19x1.	—	26
Notes to financial statements	—	27–30

SEC 41172. Form 10-K

	Reference (Page)	
	Form 10-K Annual Report	**Annual Share- holders' Report**
Data submitted herewith:		
Reports of Independent Accountants on Financial Statements of XYZ Equity Affiliate, Inc. and Schedules.	47–48	—
Financial Statements:		
Financial Statements of XYZ Equity Affiliate, Inc.:		
Statement of income and retained earnings for the years ended December 31, 19x3, 19x2, and 19x1.	56	—
Balance sheet at December 31, 19x3 and 19x2.	57	—
Statement of cash flows for the years ended December 31, 19x3, 19x2, and 19x1.	58	—
Statement of capital stock and additional paid-in capital for the years ended December 31, 19x3, 19x2, and 19x1.	59	—
Notes to financial statements.	60-62	—
Schedules:		
V. Property, plant, and equipment.	63	—
VI. Accumulated depreciation of property, plant, and equipment.	64	—
IX. Short-term borrowings.	65	—

All other schedules are omitted since the required information is not present or is not present in amounts sufficient to require submission of the schedule, or because the information required is included in the consolidated financial statements and notes thereto.

With the exception of the consolidated financial statements and the accountants' report thereon listed in the above index, the information referred to in Items 1, 5, 6, and 7, and the supplementary quarterly financial information referred to in Item 8, all of which is included in the 19x3 Annual Report to Shareholders of XYZ Company and incorporated by reference into this Form 10-K Annual Report, the 19x3 Annual Report to Shareholders is not to be deemed "filed" as part of this report.

The index identifies the financial statements (and accountants' report) in the annual shareholders' report being incorporated by reference in Form 10-K. This identification is important because those sections of the shareholders' report incorporated by reference in Form 10-K are considered filed as part of Form 10-K and are thus subject to Section 18 liabilities under the 1934 Act (as discussed in section 12030). To clearly describe and limit the material considered filed, many companies include a statement at the conclusion of the index to financial statements similar to that included in the previous example.

Pursuant to Rule 12b-23 (section 41171), the annual report to shareholders (or a copy of the pages incorporated) is required to be attached as an exhibit to Form 10-K if all or any portion of it has been incorporated by reference in Form 10-K. However, only that portion so incorporated technically is considered "filed."

41173. Reporting Considerations. Since the financial statement schedules (including any separate financial statements presented) are part of the audited financial information in Form 10-K, the independent accountants also need to opine on this information.

This requirement is often accomplished by incorporating by reference in Form 10-K the accountants' report included in the annual report to shareholders and issuing a separate report on the financial statement schedules included in Part IV (Item 14(d)) of the document. For illustrative wording of such reports, see sections 20310 and 20320. This separate report is typically dated the same as the accountants' report in the annual report to shareholders. If this approach is used, the accountants' report in the annual report to shareholders that is filed as an exhibit is required to be manually signed to comply with the requirement that a manually signed report covering the primary financial statements be filed.

In lieu of incorporating by reference the accountants' report that appears in the annual report to shareholders, a manually signed report (or two separate reports) covering the primary financial statements and the financial statement schedules may be included in Form 10-K. When one report covers both the financial statements and

SEC 41172. Form 10-K

financial statement schedules, it may be included in Item 8 with the primary financial statements. Refer to section 20330 of this manual for illustrative wording of such a report. When two separate reports are furnished, the report covering the primary financial statements is generally included as part of Item 8 and the other report under Item 14(d) together with the financial statement schedules. The report in Item 8 would be identical to that in the annual report to shareholders (see illustrative wording included in section 20310 of this manual). The accountants' report(s) included in Form 10-K is typically dated the same as the accountants' report in the annual report to shareholders.

There is no requirement to include in Form 10-K a consent to the incorporation by reference of the accountants' report on the financial statements from the annual report to shareholders. However, if the Form 10-K financial statements are being incorporated by reference into an effective 1933 Act registration statement (see section 20521), the required consent is typically included in the Form 10-K.

41174. Incorporating Other Financial Information. Information outside the audited financial statements included in the annual report to shareholders may be incorporated by reference in Form 10-K. This is usually accomplished, in accordance with paragraph (b) of Rule 12b-23 (see section 41171), by the inclusion of a statement at the appropriate location in Form 10-K that the required information is incorporated by reference from the annual report to shareholders.

41175. Integration of Shareholder Report and Form 10-K. A registrant may elect to prepare the annual (and / or quarterly) report to shareholders in a manner that will also meet the SEC requirements for Form 10-K (and / or Form 10-Q). Subject to certain minimum conditions, a registrant is permitted flexibility as to the manner in which the required information is presented, provided that a cross-reference sheet is furnished to facilitate SEC review. Instruction H to Form 10-K provides registrants with the minimum conditions for preparing integrated reports. The text of Instruction H is set forth in section 41180. (See section 41340 for a discussion of the integration of Form 10-Q and the quarterly report to shareholders.)

41176. Incorporation by Reference in Form 10-K of Financial Statements in 1933 Act Registration Statements. Rule 12b-23 permits the incorporation by reference in Form 10-K of financial statements included in 1933 Act registration statements that have been filed with the SEC, even if the 1933 Act document is not yet effective. If the financial statements included in the 1933 Act registration statement are subsequently amended, the Form 10-K that incorporated the financial statements by reference is also required to be amended. If the registration statement is withdrawn without becoming effective, Form 10-K must be amended by filing the required information under cover of Form 10-K/A (discussed in section 41700).

The independent accountants are required to provide a written consent to the incorporation by reference in Form 10-K of their report on the financial statements included in a 1933 Act registration statement (see section 20522).

41180. Text of Form 10-K

Since Form 10-K is one of the most frequently encountered SEC filing documents, the full text of this form is included herein. However, before using this section as an official reference source, the user of this manual is cautioned to ascertain whether any amendments to the text of the form have been made after September 1, 1993.

FORM 10-K

ANNUAL REPORT PURSUANT TO SECTION 13 OR 15(d) OF THE SECURITIES EXCHANGE ACT OF 1934

GENERAL INSTRUCTIONS

A. Rule as to Use of Form 10-K

This Form shall be used for annual reports pursuant to section 13 or 15(d) of the Securities Exchange Act of 1934 (the "Act") for which no other form is prescribed. This Form also shall be used for transition reports filed pursuant to section 13 or 15(d) of the Act. Annual reports on this form shall be filed within 90 days after the end of the fiscal year covered by the report. Transition reports on this form shall be filed in accordance with the requirements set forth in Rule 13a-10 or 15d-10 applicable when the registrant changes its fiscal year end. However, all schedules required by Article 12 of Regulation S-X may, at the option of the registrant, be filed as an amendment to the annual report [i.e., the Form 10-K] not later than 120 days after the end of the fiscal year covered by the report or, in the case of a transition report, not later than 30 days after the due date of the report. Such amendment shall be filed under cover of Form 8. [Note: Form 8 has been rescinded. Amendments should be filed under cover of the form amended, designated by adding the letter "A" after the form title, e.g., "Form 10-K/A." (See section 41700.)]

B. Application of General Rules and Regulations

(1) The General Rules and Regulations under the Act contain certain general requirements which are applicable to reports on any form. These general requirements should be carefully read and observed in the preparation and filing of reports on this Form.

SEC 41176. Form 10-K

(2) Particular attention is directed to Regulation 12B which contains general requirements regarding matters such as the kind and size of paper to be used, the legibility of the report, the information to be given whenever the title of securities is required to be stated, and the filing of the report. The definitions contained in Rule 12b-2 should be especially noted. See also Regulations 13A and 15D.

C. Preparation of Report

(1) This Form is not to be used as a blank form to be filled in, but only as a guide in the preparation of the report on paper meeting the requirements of Rule 12b-12. Except as provided in General Instruction G, the answers to the items shall be prepared in the manner specified in Rule 12b-13.

(2) Except where information is required to be given for the fiscal year or as of a specified date, it shall be given as of the latest practicable date.

(3) Attention is directed to Rule 12b-20, which states: "In addition to the information expressly required to be included in a statement or report, there shall be added such further material information, if any, as may be necessary to make the required statements, in the light of the circumstances under which they are made, not misleading."

D. Signature and Filing of Report

(1) Three complete copies of the report, including financial statements, financial statement schedules, exhibits, and all other papers and documents filed as a part thereof, and five additional copies which need not include exhibits, shall be filed with the Commission. At least one complete copy of the report, including financial statements, financial statement schedules, exhibits, and all other papers and documents filed as a part thereof, shall be filed with each exchange on which any class of securities of the registrant is registered. At least one complete copy of the report filed with the Commission and one such copy filed with each exchange shall be manually signed. Copies not manually signed shall bear typed or printed signatures.

(2)(a) The report shall be signed by the registrant, and on behalf of the registrant by its principal executive officer or officers, its principal financial officer, its controller or principal accounting officer, and by at least the majority of the board of directors or persons performing similar functions. Where the registrant is a limited partnership, the report shall be signed by the majority of the board of directors of any corporate general partner who signs the report. (b) The name of each person who signs the report shall be typed or printed beneath his signature. Any person who occupies more than one of the specified positions shall indicate each capacity in which he signs the report.

SEC 41180

Attention is directed to Rule 12b-11 concerning manual signatures and signatures pursuant to powers of attorney.

(3) Registrants are requested to indicate in a transmittal letter with the Form 10-K whether the financial statements in the report reflect a change from the preceding year in any accounting principles or practices, or in the method of applying any such principles or practices.

E. Disclosure With Respect to Foreign Subsidiaries

Information required by any item or other requirement of this form with respect to any foreign subsidiary may be omitted to the extent that the required disclosure would be detrimental to the registrant. However, financial statements and financial statement schedules, otherwise required, shall not be omitted pursuant to this instruction. Where information is omitted pursuant to this instruction, a statement shall be made that such information has been omitted and the names of the subsidiaries involved shall be separately furnished to the Commission. The Commission may, in its discretion, call for justification that the required disclosure would be detrimental.

F. Information as to Employee Stock Purchase, Savings and Similar Plans

Attention is directed to Rule 15d-21 which provides that separate annual and other reports need not be filed pursuant to Section 15(d) of the Act with respect to any employee stock purchase, savings or similar plan if the issuer of the stock or other securities offered to employees pursuant to the plan furnishes to the Commission the information and documents specified in the Rule.

G. Information to be Incorporated by Reference

(1) Attention is directed to Rule 12b-23 which provides for the incorporation by reference of information contained in certain documents in answer or partial answer to any item of a report.

(2) The information called for by Parts I and II of this Form (Items 1 through 9 or any portion thereof) may, at the registrant's option, be incorporated by reference from the registrant's annual report to security holders furnished to the Commission pursuant to Rule 14a-3(b) or Rule 14c-3(a) or Rule 14c-3(b) or from the registrant's annual report to security holders, even if not furnished to the Commission pursuant to Rule 14a-3(b) or Rule 14c-3(a), provided such annual report contains the information required by Rule 14a-3.

SEC 41180. Form 10-K

Note 1: *In order to fulfill the requirements of Part I of Form 10-K, the incorporated portion of the annual report to security holders must contain the information required by Items 1 through 3 of Form 10-K, to the extent applicable.*

Note 2: *If any information required by Part I or Part II is incorporated by reference into an electronic format document from the annual report to security holders as provided in General Instruction G, any portion of the annual report to security holders incorporated by reference shall be filed as an exhibit in electronic format, as required by Item 601(b)(13) of Regulation S-K.*

(3) The information required by Part III (Items 10, 11, 12 and 13) may be incorporated by reference from the registrant's definitive proxy statement (filed or to be filed pursuant to Regulation 14A) or definitive information statement (filed or to be filed pursuant to Regulation 14C) which involves the election of directors, if such definitive proxy statement or information statement is filed with the Commission not later than 120 days after the end of the fiscal year covered by the Form 10-K. However, if such definitive proxy or information statement is not filed with the Commission in the 120-day period or is not required to be filed with the Commission by virtue of Rule 3A12-3(b) under the Exchange Act, the items comprising the Part III information must be filed as part of the Form 10-K, or as an amendment to the Form 10-K under cover of Form 8 [Note: Form 8 has been rescinded. Amendments should be filed under cover of the form amended, designated by adding the letter "A" after the form title, e.g., "Form 10-K/A" (see section 41700)], not later than the end of the 120-day period. It should be noted that the information regarding executive officers required by Item 401 of Regulation S-K may be included in Part I of Form 10-K under an appropriate caption. See Instruction 3 to Item 401(b) of Regulation S-K.

(4) No item numbers or captions of items need be contained in the material incorporated by reference into the report. However, the registrant's attention is directed to Rule 12b-23(e) regarding the specific disclosure required in the report concerning information incorporated by reference. When the registrant combines all of the information in Parts I and II of this Form (Items 1 through 9) by incorporation by reference from the registrant's annual report to security holders and all of the information in Part III of this Form (Items 10 through 13) by incorporating by reference from a definitive proxy statement or information statement involving the election of directors, then, notwithstanding General Instruction C(1), this Form shall consist of the facing or cover page, those sections incorporated from the annual report to security holders, the proxy or information statement, and the information, if any, required by Part IV of this Form, signatures, and a cross-reference sheet setting forth the item numbers and captions in Parts I, II, and III of this Form and the page and/or pages in the referenced materials where the corresponding information appears.

H. Integrated Reports to Security Holders

Annual reports to security holders may be combined with the required information of Form 10-K and will be suitable for filing with the Commission if the following conditions are satisfied:

(1) The combined report contains full and complete answers to all items required by Form 10-K. When responses to a certain item of required disclosure are separated within the combined report, an appropriate cross-reference should be made. If the information required by Part III of Form 10-K is omitted by virtue of General Instruction G, a definitive proxy or information statement shall be filed.

(2) The cover page and the required signatures are included. As appropriate, a cross-reference sheet should be filed indicating the location of information required by the items of the Form.

(3) If an electronic filer files any portion of an annual report to security holders in combination with the required information of Form 10-K, as provided in this instruction, only such portions filed in satisfaction of the Form 10-K requirements shall be filed in electronic format.

I. Registrants Filing on Form S-18

[Note: The SEC rescinded Form S-18 as part of the Small Business Initiatives released in August 1992, although filings on Form S-18 were permitted through December 31, 1992. Effective August 1992, Form SB-2 (see section 42700) was designated the Securities Act Registration Form for small business issuers.]

If the registrant is subject to the reporting requirements of Section 15(d) of the Exchange Act and such obligation arises solely because the registrant has filed a registration statement on Form S-18 which has become effective during the last fiscal year, the registrant may comply with the disclosure requirements of Form S-18 Item 16, Description of Business; Item 18, Interest of Management and Others in Certain Transactions; and Item 20, Remuneration of Directors and Officers, in lieu of complying with the disclosure requirements of Item 1, Business; Item 11, Executive Compensation; and Item 13, Certain Relationships and Related Transactions, herein. Item 6 of this Form, Selected Financial Data, may be omitted at the election of such registrant.

If a registrant remains subject to Section 15(d), or becomes subject to Section 12, after the year of its Form S-18 offering, it will then be required to comply with the general Form 10-K item requirements for its subsequent reports.

SEC 41180. Form 10-K

J. Omission of Information by Certain Wholly-Owned Subsidiaries

If, on the date of the filing of its report on Form 10-K, the registrant meets the conditions specified in paragraph (1) below, then such registrant may furnish the abbreviated narrative disclosure specified in paragraph (2) below.

(1) Conditions for availability of the relief specified in paragraph (2) below.

> *(a) All of the registrant's equity securities are owned, either directly or indirectly, by a single person which is a reporting company under the Act and which has filed all the material required to be filed pursuant to Section 13, 14, or 15(d) thereof, as applicable, and which is named in conjunction with the registrant's description of its business;*

> *(b) During the preceding thirty-six calendar months and any subsequent period of days, there has not been any material default in the payment of principal, interest, a sinking or purchase fund installment, or any other material default not cured within thirty days, with respect to any indebtedness of the registrant or its subsidiaries, and there has not been any material default in the payment of rentals under material long-term leases; and*

> *(c) There is prominently set forth, on the cover page of the Form 10-K, a statement that the registrant meets the conditions set forth in General Instruction J(1) (a) and (b) of Form 10-K and is therefore filing this Form with the reduced disclosure format.*

(2) Registrants meeting the conditions specified in paragraph (1) above are entitled to the following relief:

> *(a) Such registrants may omit the information called for by Item 6, Selected Financial Data, and Item 7, Management's Discussion and Analysis of Financial Condition and Results of Operations, provided that the registrant includes in the Form 10-K a management's narrative analysis of the results of operations explaining the reasons for material changes in the amount of revenue and expense items between the most recent fiscal year presented and the fiscal year immediately preceding it. Explanations of material changes should include, but not be limited to, changes in the various elements which determine revenue and expense levels such as unit sales volume, prices charged and paid, production levels, production cost variances, labor costs, and discretionary spending programs. In addition, the analysis should include an explanation of the effect of any changes in accounting principles and practices or method of application that have a material effect on net income as reported.*

SEC 41180

(b) Such registrants may omit the list of subsidiaries exhibit called for by Item 601 of Regulation S-K.

(c) Such registrants may omit the information called for by the following otherwise required items: Item 4, Submission of Matters to a Vote of Security Holders; Item 10, Directors and Executive Officers of the Registrant; Item 11, Executive Compensation; Item 12, Security Ownership of Certain Beneficial Owners and Management; and Item 13, Certain Relationship and Related Transactions.

(d) In response to Item 1, Business, such registrant only need furnish a brief description of the business done by the registrant and its subsidiaries during the most recent fiscal year which will, in the opinion of management, indicate the general nature and scope of the business of the registrant and its subsidiaries, and in response to Item 2, Properties, such registrant only need furnish a brief description of the material properties of the registrant and its subsidiaries to the extent, in the opinion of the management, necessary to an understanding of the business done by the registrant and its subsidiaries.

SEC 41180. Form 10-K

SECURITIES AND EXCHANGE COMMISSION
Washington, D.C. 20549

Form 10-K

(Mark One)

[ ] **ANNUAL REPORT PURSUANT TO SECTION 13 OR 15(d) OF THE SECURITIES EXCHANGE ACT OF 1934** *[FEE REQUIRED]*

For the fiscal year ended . . . .

OR

[ ] **TRANSITION REPORT PURSUANT TO SECTION 13 OR 15(d) OF THE SECURITIES EXCHANGE ACT OF 1934** *[NO FEE REQUIRED]*

For the transition period from . . . . **to** . . . .

Commission file number . . . .

. . . .

(Exact name of registrant as specified in its charter)

. . . .

(State or other jurisdiction of   (IRS Employer
incorporation or organization)   Identification No.)

. . . .

(Address of principal executive offices)   (Zip Code)

Registrant's telephone number, including area code . . . .

Securities registered pursuant to Section 12(b) of the Act:

Title of each class	Name of each exchange on which registered
. . . .	. . . .
. . . .	. . . .

Securities registered pursuant to Section 12(g) of the Act:

. . . .

(Title of class)

. . . .

(Title of class)

SEC 41180

228

Indicate by check mark whether the registrant (1) has filed all reports required to be filed by Section 13 or 15(d) of the Securities Exchange Act of 1934 during the preceding 12 months (or for such shorter period that the registrant was required to file such reports), and (2) has been subject to such filing requirements for the past 90 days. Yes. . . . . . . No. . . . . . .

Indicate by check mark if disclosure of delinquent filers pursuant to Item 405 of Regulation S-K is not contained herein, and will not be contained, to the best of registrant's knowledge, in definitive proxy or information statements incorporated by reference in Part III of this Form 10-K or any amendment to this Form 10-K.[ ]

State the aggregate market value of the voting stock held by nonaffiliates of the registrant. The aggregate market value shall be computed by reference to the price at which the stock was sold, or the average bid and asked prices of such stock, as of a specified date within 60 days prior to the date of filing. (See definition of affiliate in Rule 405.)

Note: If a determination as to whether a particular person or entity is an affiliate cannot be made without involving unreasonable effort and expense, the aggregate market value of the common stock held by nonaffiliates may be calculated on the basis of assumptions reasonable under the circumstances, provided that the assumptions are set forth in this Form.

APPLICABLE ONLY TO REGISTRANTS INVOLVED IN BANKRUPTCY PROCEEDINGS DURING THE PRECEDING FIVE YEARS:

Indicate by check mark whether the registrant has filed all documents and reports required to be filed by Section 12, 13 or 15(d) of the Securities Exchange Act of 1934 subsequent to the distribution of securities under a plan confirmed by a court. Yes. . . . . . . No. . . . . . .

(APPLICABLE ONLY TO CORPORATE REGISTRANTS)

Indicate the number of shares outstanding of each of the registrant's classes of common stock, as of the latest practicable date.

DOCUMENTS INCORPORATED BY REFERENCE

List hereunder the following documents if incorporated by reference and the part of the Form 10-K (e.g., Part I, Part II, etc.) into which the document is incorporated: (1) Any annual report to security holders; (2) Any proxy or information statement; and (3) Any prospectus filed pursuant to Rule 424(b) or (c) under the Securities Act of 1933. The listed documents should be clearly described for identification purposes (e.g., annual report to security holders for fiscal year ended December 24, 1980).

SEC 41180. Form 10-K

PART I

(See General Instruction G(2))

Item 1. Business

Furnish the information required by Item 101 of Regulation S-K except that the discussion of the development of the registrant's business need only include developments since the beginning of the fiscal year for which this report is filed.

Item 2. Properties

Furnish the information required by Item 102 of Regulation S-K.

Item 3. Legal Proceedings

(a) Furnish the information required by Item 103 of Regulation S-K.

(b) As to any proceeding that was terminated during the fourth quarter of the fiscal year covered by this report, furnish information similar to that required by Item 103 of Regulation S-K, including the date of termination and a description of the disposition thereof with respect to the registrant and its subsidiaries.

Item 4. Submission of Matters to a Vote of Security Holders

If any matter was submitted during the fourth quarter of the fiscal year covered by this report to a vote of security holders, through the solicitation of proxies or otherwise, furnish the following information:

(a) The date of the meeting and whether it was an annual or special meeting.

(b) If the meeting involved the election of directors, the name of each director elected at the meeting and the name of each other director whose term of office as a director continued after the meeting.

(c) A brief description of each matter voted upon at the meeting and state the number of votes cast for, against, or withheld, as well as the number of abstentions and broker nonvotes as to each such matter, including a separate tabulation with respect to each nominee for office.

(d) A description of the terms of any settlement between the registrant and any other participant (as defined in Rule 14a-11 of Regulation 14A under the Act) terminating any solicitation subject to Rule 14a-11, including the cost or anticipated cost to the registrant.

SEC 41180

Instructions:

1. If any matter has been submitted to a vote of security holders otherwise than at a meeting of such security holders, corresponding information with respect to such submission shall be furnished. The solicitation of any authorization or consent (other than a proxy to vote at a stockholders' meeting) with respect to any matter shall be deemed a submission of such matter to a vote of security holders within the meaning of this item.

2. Paragraph (a) need be answered only if paragraph (b) or (c) is required to be answered.

3. Paragraph (b) need not be answered if (i) proxies for the meeting were solicited pursuant to Regulation 14A under the Act, (ii) there was no solicitation in opposition to the management's nominees as listed in the proxy statement, and (iii) all of such nominees were elected. If the registrant did not solicit proxies and the board of directors as previously reported to the Commission was re-elected in its entirety, a statement to that effect in answer to paragraph (b) will suffice as an answer thereto.

4. Paragraph (c) must be answered for all matters voted upon at the meeting, including both contested and uncontested elections of directors.

5. If the registrant has furnished to its security holders proxy soliciting material containing the information called for by paragraph (d), the paragraph may be answered by reference to the information contained in such material.

6. If the registrant has published a report containing all of the information called for by this item, the item may be answered by a reference to the information contained in such report.

PART II

(See General Instruction G(2))

Item 5. Market for Registrant's Common Equity and Related Stockholder Matters

Furnish the information required by Item 201 of Regulation S-K.

Item 6. Selected Financial Data

Furnish the information required by Item 301 of Regulation S-K.

SEC 41180. Form 10-K

Item 7. Management's Discussion and Analysis of Financial Condition and Results of Operations

Furnish the information required by Item 303 of Regulation S-K.

Item 8. Financial Statements and Supplementary Data

Furnish financial statements meeting the requirements of Regulation S-X except Rule 3-05 and Article 11 thereof, and the supplementary financial information required by Item 302 of Regulation S-K. Financial statements of the registrant and its subsidiaries consolidated [as required by Rule 14a-3(b)] shall be filed under this item. Other financial statements and schedules required under Regulation S-X may be filed as "Financial Statement Schedules" pursuant to item 13, Exhibits, Financial Statement Schedules, and Reports on Form 8-K, of this form.

Notwithstanding the above, if the issuer is subject to the reporting provisions of Section 15(d) and such obligation results solely from the issuer having filed a registration statement on Form S-18 which became effective under the Securities Act of 1933 during the last fiscal year, or such obligation applies as to the first or second fiscal year after the registration statement on Form S-18 became effective solely because the issuer had on the first day of the pertinent fiscal year 300 or more record holders of any of its securities to which the Form S-18 related, audited financial statements for the issuer, or for the issuer and its predecessors, may be presented as provided below. The report of the independent accountant shall in all events comply with the requirements of Article 2 of Regulation S-X.

> *(a) A Form 10-K filed for the fiscal year during which the registrant had a registration statement on Form S-18 become effective may include the following financial statements prepared in accordance with generally accepted accounting principles:*
>
> > *(1) A balance sheet as of the end of each of the two most recent fiscal years; and*
> >
> > *(2) Consolidated statements of income, statements of cash flows, and statements of other stockholders' equity for each of the two fiscal years preceding the date of the most recent audited balance sheet being filed.*
>
> *(b) A Form 10-K filed for the first fiscal year after the registrant had a registration statement on Form S-18 become effective may include financial statements prepared as follows:*

SEC 41180

(1) Financial statements for the most recent fiscal year prepared in accordance with Regulation S-X, Form and Content of and Requirements for Financial Statements; and

(2) Financial statements previously disclosed in accordance with paragraph (a) for the prior year. These statements do not need to include the compliance items and schedules of Regulation S-X, but should be recast to show the same line items as are set forth for the most recent fiscal year.

(c) A Form 10-K filed for the second fiscal year after the registrant had a registration statement on Form S-18 become effective may include financial statements for the two most recent fiscal years prepared in accordance with Regulation S-X.

Item 9. Changes in and Disagreements with Accountants on Accounting and Financial Disclosure

Furnish the information required by Item 304 of Regulation S-K.

PART III

(See General Instruction G(3))

Item 10. Directors and Executive Officers of the Registrant

Furnish the information required by Items 401 and 405 of Regulation S-K.

Instruction

Checking the box provided on the cover page of this Form to indicate that Item 405 disclosure of delinquent Form 3, 4, or 5 filers is not contained herein is intended to facilitate Form processing and review. Failure to provide such indication will not create liability for violation of the federal securities laws. The space should be checked only if there is no disclosure in this Form of reporting person delinquencies in response to Item 405 and the registrant, at the time of filing the Form 10-K, has reviewed the information necessary to ascertain, and has determined that, Item 405 disclosure is not expected to be contained in Part III of the Form 10-K or incorporated by reference.

Item 11. Executive Compensation

Furnish the information required by Item 402 of Regulation S-K.

SEC 41180. Form 10-K

Item 12. Security Ownership of Certain Beneficial Owners and Management

Furnish the information required by Item 403 of Regulation S-K.

Item 13. Certain Relationships and Related Transactions

Furnish the information required by Item 404 of Regulation S-K.

PART IV

Item 14. Exhibits, Financial Statement Schedules, and Reports on Form 8-K

(a) List the following documents filed as a part of the report:

(1) All financial statements;

(2) Those financial statement schedules required to be filed by Item 8 of this Form, and by paragraph (d) below;

(3) Those exhibits required to be filed by Item 601 of Regulation S-K and by paragraph (c) below. Identify in the list each management contract or compensatory plan or arrangement required to be filed as an exhibit to this form pursuant to item 14(c) of this report.

(b) Reports on Form 8-K. State whether any reports on Form 8-K have been filed during the last quarter of the period covered by this report, listing the items reported, any financial statements filed, and the dates of any such reports.

(c) Registrants shall file, as exhibits to this Form, the exhibits required by Item 601 of Regulation S-K.

(d) Registrants shall file, as financial statement schedules to this Form, the financial statements required by Regulation S-X which are excluded from the annual report to shareholders by Rule 14a-3(b) including (1) separate financial statements of subsidiaries not consolidated and fifty percent or less owned persons; (2) separate financial statements of affiliates whose securities are pledged as collateral and (3) schedules.

SIGNATURES

(See General Instruction D)

Pursuant to the requirements of Section 13 or 15(d) of the Securities Exchange Act of 1934, the registrant has duly caused this report to be signed on its behalf by the undersigned, thereunto duly authorized.

....
(Registrant)

By ....
(Signature and Title)*

Date ....

Pursuant to the requirements of the Securities Exchange Act of 1934, this report has been signed below by the following persons on behalf of the registrant and in the capacities and on the dates indicated.

....
(Signature and Title)*

....
(Signature and Title)*

....
(Date)

....
(Date)

*Print the name and title of each signing officer under his signature.

Supplemental Information to be Furnished With Reports Filed Pursuant to Section 15(d) of the Act by Registrants Which Have Not Registered Securities Pursuant to Section 12 of the Act.

(a) Except to the extent that the materials enumerated in (1) and/or (2) below are specifically incorporated into this Form by reference (in which case see Rule 12b-23(d)), every registrant which files an annual report on this Form pursuant to Section 15(d) of the Act shall furnish to the Commission for its information, at the time of filing its report on this Form, four copies of the following:

(1) Any annual report to security holders covering the registrant's last fiscal year; and

(2) Every proxy statement, form of proxy or other proxy soliciting material sent to more than ten of the registrant's security holders with respect to any annual or other meeting of security holders.

SEC 41180. Form 10-K

(b) The foregoing material shall not be deemed to be "filed" with the Commission or otherwise subject to the liabilities of Section 18 of the Act, except to the extent that the registrant specifically incorporates it in its annual report on this Form by reference.

(c) If no such annual report or proxy material has been sent to security holders, a statement to that effect shall be included under this caption. If such report or proxy material is to be furnished to security holders subsequent to the filing of the annual report of this Form, the registrant shall so state under this caption and shall furnish copies of such material to the Commission when it is sent to security holders.

41200. FORM 10-KSB

41210. General

Form 10-KSB may be used as an annual report form under the 1934 Act by any registrant that qualifies as a "small business issuer." This form may be used for annual and transitional reports under Section 13 or 15(d) of the 1934 Act. Annual reports on this form are required to be filed within 90 days after the end of the fiscal year covered by the report and transition reports need to be filed after an issuer changes its fiscal year-end in accordance with Rule 13a-10 or Rule 15d-10. Item 10(a) of Regulation S-B (see section 70000) contains further information as to eligibility to use Form 10-KSB.

Form 10-KSB contains disclosure alternatives for transitional small business issuers (see section 70000). The alternatives allow for simplified disclosures by furnishing information specified in Form 1-A (see section 42800) in lieu of the disclosure requirements set forth in Parts I, II, and III below. The instructions regarding transitional small business issuers included in General Instruction H and the "Information Required in Annual Report of Transitional Small Business Issuers" are included in the text of Form 10-KSB provided in section 41250.

The following are the items of information to be included in Form 10-KSB for nontransitional small business issuers. (Detailed requirements are described in the text of the form (see section 41250), and Item numbers refer to Regulation S-B, the requirements of which are more fully included in section 70000 of this manual.)

PART I

Item

1   Description of Business (Item 101 of Reg. S-B)
2   Description of Property (Item 102)
3   Legal Proceedings (Item 103)
4   Submission of Matters to a Vote of Security Holders

PART II

5   Market for Common Equity and Related Stockholder Matters (Item 201)

SEC 41200. Form 10-KSB

The requirements for completion of Form 10-KSB are set forth in the General Instructions to the Form as detailed in the individual items found in Regulation S-B (see discussion beginning with section 70000).

The information called for in Parts I and II (Items 1 through 8) may be incorporated by reference from the issuer's annual report to shareholders. Part III (Items 9 through 12) is required to be incorporated by reference if a definitive proxy statement pursuant to Schedule 14A (or definitive information statement pursuant to Schedule 14C) involving the election of directors, if such definitive proxy (or information statement) is filed not later than 120 days after the end of the fiscal year covered by this form.

41220. Financial Statement Requirements

Small business issuers are required to file an audited balance sheet as of the end of the most recent fiscal year (or a date within 135 days if the issuer has existed for less than one year), and audited statements of income, cash flows and changes in stockholders' equity for each of the two fiscal years preceding the date of the audited balance sheet. The form and content of, and other requirements for, the financial statements to be included in Form 10-KSB are set forth in Regulation S-B (see section 73100).

SEC 41220

41230. Signatures

Form 10-KSB needs to be signed by a majority of the board of directors (or persons performing similar functions) in addition to the small business issuer's principal executive officer(s), its principal financial officer, and its controller or principal accounting officer.

41240. Due Date

An annual report on Form 10-KSB needs to be filed within 90 days after the end of the fiscal year covered by the report.

41250. Text of Form 10-KSB

Since Form 10-KSB is one of the most frequently encountered SEC filing documents for small business issuers, the full text of this form is included herein. However, before using this section as an official reference source, the user of this manual is cautioned to ascertain whether any amendments to the text of the form have been made after September 1, 1993.

FORM 10-KSB
ANNUAL REPORT PURSUANT TO SECTION 13 OR 15(d)
OF THE SECURITIES EXCHANGE ACT OF 1934

GENERAL INSTRUCTIONS

A. Use of Form 10-KSB.

This Form may be used by a "small business issuer," defined in Rule 12b-2 of the Exchange Act for its annual and transitional reports under Section 13 or 15(d) of that Act. For further information as to eligibility to use this Form see Item 10(a) of Regulation S-B. Annual reports on this Form shall be filed within 90 days after the end of the fiscal year covered by the report. Transition reports shall be filed within the time period specified in Rules 13a-10 or 15d-10 of the Exchange Act.

B. Application of General Rules and Regulations.

The General Rules and Regulations under the Exchange Act, particularly Regulation 12B contain certain general requirements for reports on any form which should be carefully read and observed in the preparation and filing of reports on this Form.

SEC 41230. Form 10-KSB

C. Signature and Filing of Report.

(1) File three "complete" copies and five "additional" copies of the registration statement with the Commission and file at least one complete copy with each exchange on which the securities will be registered. A "complete" copy includes financial statements, exhibits and all other papers and documents. An "additional" copy excludes exhibits. One of the copies filed with the Commission and each exchange should be manually signed, all other copies should have typed or printed signatures.

(2) Who must sign: the small business issuer, its principal executive officer or officers, its principal financial officer, its controller or principal accounting officer and at least the majority of the board of directors or persons performing similar functions. If the issuer is a limited partnership then the general partner and a majority of its board of directors if a corporation. Any person who occupies more than one of the specified positions shall indicate each capacity in which he signs the report. See Rule 12b-11 concerning manual signatures under powers of attorney.

(3) Small business issuers are requested to indicate in a transmittal letter with the Form 10-KSB whether the financial statements in the report reflect a change from the preceding year in any accounting principles or practices or in the methods of application of those principles or practices.

D. Information as to Employee Stock Purchase, Savings and Similar Plans.

Separate annual and other reports need not be filed under Section 15(d) of the Exchange Act, for any employee stock purchase, savings or similar plan if the issuer of the securities offered under the plan furnishes to the Commission the information and documents specified in the Rule 15d-21 of the Exchange Act.

E. Information to be Incorporated by Reference.

(1) Refer to Rule 12b-23 if information will be incorporated by reference from other documents in answer or partial answer to any item of this Form.

(2) The information called for in Parts I and II of this Form, Items 1-8, may be incorporated by reference from:

> *(a) the registrant's annual report to security holders furnished to the Commission under Rule 14a-3(b) or Rule 14c-3(a) of the Exchange Act; or*

> *(b) the registrant's annual report to shareholders if it contains the information required by Rule 14a-3.*

SEC 41250

Note to electronic filers: If any information required by Part I or Part II is incorporated by reference from the annual report to security holders as allowed in General Instruction E.2.(a), any portion of the annual report to security holders incorporated by reference shall be filed as an exhibit in electronic format, as required by Item 601(b)(13) of Regulation S-B.

(3) The information required by Part III may be incorporated by reference from the registrant's definitive proxy statement (filed or to be filed in accordance with Schedule 14A) or definitive information statement (filed or to be filed pursuant to Schedule 14C) which involves the election of directors, if such definitive proxy or information statement is filed with the Commission not later than 120 days after the end of the fiscal year covered by this Form. If the definitive proxy or information statement is not filed within the 120-day period, the information called for in Part III information must be filed as part of the Form 10-KSB, or as an amendment to the Form 10-KSB under cover of Form 8 [Note: Form 8 has been rescinded. Amendments should be filed under cover of the form amended, designated by adding the letter "A" after the title of the form, e.g., "Form 10-KSB/A" (see section 41700)], not later than the end of the 120-day period.

(4) No item numbers of captions or items need be contained in the material incorporated by reference into the report. However, the registrant's attention is directed to Rule 12b-23(b) of the Exchange Act regarding the specific disclosure required in the report concerning information incorporated by reference. When the registrant combines all of the information in Parts I and II of this Form by incorporation by reference from the registrant's annual report to security holders and all of the information in Part III of this Form by incorporating by reference from a definitive proxy statement or information statement involving the election of directors, then this Form shall consist of the facing or cover page, those sections incorporated from the annual report to security holders, the proxy or information statement, and the information, if any, required by Part IV of this Form, signatures and a cross-reference sheet setting forth the item numbers and captions in Parts I, II and III of this Form and page and/or pages in the referenced materials where the corresponding information appears.

F. Integrated Reports to Security Holders.

Annual reports to security holders may be combined with the required information of this Form and will be suitable for filing with the Commission if the following conditions are satisfied:

(1) The combined report contains complete answers to all items required by Form 10-KSB. When responses to a certain item of required disclosure are separated within the combined report, an appropriate cross-reference should be made. If the informa-

SEC 41250. Form 10-KSB

tion required by Part III of Form 10-KSB is omitted by virtue of General Instruction E, a definitive proxy or information statement shall be filed.

(2) The cover page and required signatures are included. A cross-reference sheet should be filed indicating the location of information required by items of the Form.

(3) If an electronic filer files any portion of an annual report to security holders in combination with the required information of Form 10-KSB, as provided in this instruction, only such portions filed in satisfaction of the Form 10-KSB requirements shall be filed in electronic format.

G. Omission of Information by Certain Wholly-Owned Subsidiaries.

If, on the date of the filing of its report on Form 10-KSB, the registrant meets the conditions specified in paragraph (1) below, then it may furnish the abbreviated narrative disclosure specified in paragraph (2) below.

(1) Conditions for availability of relief specified in paragraph (2) below.

    (a) All of the registrant's equity securities are owned, either directly or indirectly, by a single person which is a reporting company and which has filed all the material required to be filed under Sections 13, 14 or 15(d), as applicable, and which is named in conjunction with the registrant's description of its business;

    (b) During the past thirty-six months and any subsequent period of days, there has not been any material default in the payment of principal, interest, a sinking or purchase fund installment, or any other material default not cured within thirty days, with respect to any indebtedness of the registrant or its subsidiaries, and there has not been any material default in the payment of rental under material long-term leases; and

    (c) There is prominently set forth on the cover page of the Form 10-KSB, a statement that the registrant meets the conditions set forth in General Instruction G(1)(a) and (b) of Form 10-KSB and therefore filing this Form with the reduced disclosures format.

(2) Registrants meeting the conditions specified in paragraph I above are entitled to the following relief:

    (a) Such registrants may omit the information called for by Item 303(b), Management's Discussion and Analysis, if required by the Instruction to that Item, provided that the registrant includes in the Form 10-KSB a narrative analysis of the results of operations explaining the reasons for material changes

SEC 41250

in the amount of revenue and expense items between the most recent fiscal year presented and the fiscal year immediately preceding it. Explanations of material changes should include, but not be limited to, changes in the various elements which determine revenue and expense levels, such as unit sales volume, prices charged and paid, production levels, production cost variances, labor costs and discretionary spending programs. In addition, the analysis should include an explanation of the effect of any changes in accounting principles and practices or method of application that have a material effect on net income as reported.

(b) Such registrants may omit the list of subsidiaries exhibit required by Item 601 of Regulation S-B.

(c) Such registrants may omit the information called for by the following Items: Item 4, Submission of Matters to a Vote of Security Holders; Item 9, Directors and Executive Officers, etc.; Item 10, Executive Compensation; Item 11, Security Ownership of Certain Beneficial Owners, etc.; Item 12, Certain Relationships and Related Transactions.

H. Transitional Small Business Issuers.

(a) In lieu of the disclosure requirements set forth under Parts I, II and III, a small business issuer that has not registered more than $10,000,000 in securities offerings in any continuous 12-month period since it became subject to the reporting requirements of section 13 or 15(d) of the Exchange Act may include the information required under "Information Required in Annual Report of Transitional Small Business Issuers." In calculating the $10,000,000 ceiling, issuers should include all offerings which were registered under the Securities Act, other than any amounts registered on Form S-8.

(b) A small business issuer may provide the information set forth under "Information Required in Annual Report of Transitional Small Business Issuers" until it (1) registers more than $10 million under the Securities Act in any continuous 12-month period (other than securities registered on Form S-8), (2) elects to file on a non-transitional disclosure document (other than the proxy statement disclosure in Schedule 14A), or (3) no longer meets the definition of small business issuer. Non-transitional disclosure documents include: (1) Securities Act registration statement forms other than Forms SB-1, S-3 (if the issuer incorporates by reference transitional Exchange Act reports), S-8 and S-4 (if the issuer relies upon the transitional disclosure format in that form); (2) Exchange Act periodic reporting Forms 10-K and 10-Q; (3) Exchange Act registration statement Form 10; and (4) reports or registration statements on Forms 10-KSB, 10-QSB or 10-SB which do not use the transitional disclosure document format. A reporting company may not return to the transitional disclosure forms.

SEC 41250. Form 10-KSB

U.S. SECURITIES AND EXCHANGE COMMISSION
Washington, D.C. 20549

Form 10-KSB

(Mark One)

[ ] **ANNUAL REPORT PURSUANT TO SECTION 13 OR 15(d) OF THE SECURITIES EXCHANGE ACT OF 1934** *[FEE REQUIRED]*

For the fiscal year ended . . . .

[ ] **TRANSITION REPORT PURSUANT TO SECTION 13 OR 15(d) OF THE SECURITIES EXCHANGE ACT OF 1934** *[NO FEE REQUIRED]*

For the transition period from . . . . **to** . . . .

Commission file number . . . .

. . . .
(Name of small business issuer in its charter)

. . . .
(State or other jurisdiction of   (IRS Employer
incorporation or organization)   Identification No.)

. . . .
(Address of principal executive offices)   (Zip Code)

Issuer's telephone number (   ) . . . .

Securities registered under Section 12(b) of the Exchange Act:

Title of each class	Name of each exchange on which registered
. . . .	. . . .
. . . .	. . . .

Securities registered under Section 12(g) of the Exchange Act:

. . . .
(Title of class)

. . . .
(Title of class)

SEC 41250

244

Check whether the issuer (1) filed all reports required to be filed by Section 13 or 15(d) of the Exchange Act during the past 12 months (or for such shorter period that the registrant was required to file such reports), and (2) has been subject to such filing requirements for the past 90 days. Yes. . . . . . No. . . . . .

Check if there is no disclosure of delinquent filers in response to Item 405 of Regulation S-B contained in this form, and no disclosure will be contained, to the best of registrant's knowledge, in definitive proxy or information statements incorporated by reference in Part III of this Form 10-KSB or any amendment to this Form 10-KSB.[]

State issuer's revenues for its most recent fiscal year . . . . .

State the aggregate market value of the voting stock held by nonaffiliates of the registrant. The aggregate market value shall be computed by reference to the price at which the stock was sold, or the average bid and asked prices of such stock, as of a specified date within the past 60 days. (See definition of affiliate in Rule 12b-2 of the Exchange Act).

Note: If determining whether a person is an affiliate will involve an unreasonable effort and expense, the issuer may calculate the aggregate market value of the common equity held by non-affiliates on the basis of reasonable assumptions, if the assumptions are stated.

(ISSUERS INVOLVED IN BANKRUPTCY PROCEEDINGS DURING THE PAST FIVE YEARS)

Check whether the issuer has filed all documents and reports required to be filed by Section 12, 13 or 15(d) of the Exchange Act after the distribution of securities under a plan confirmed by a court. Yes. . . . . . No. . . . . .

(APPLICABLE ONLY TO CORPORATE REGISTRANTS)

State the number of shares outstanding of each of the issuer's classes of common equity, as of the latest practicable date . . . .

DOCUMENTS INCORPORATED BY REFERENCE

If the following documents are incorporated by reference, briefly describe them and identify the part of the Form 10-KSB (e.g., Part I, Part II, etc.) into which the document is incorporated: (1) any annual report to security holders; (2) any proxy or information statement; and (3) any prospectus filed pursuant to Rule 424(b) or (c) of the Securities Act of 1933 ("Securities Act"). The listed documents should be clearly described for identification purposes (e.g., annual report to security holders for fiscal year ended December 24, 1990).

Transitional Small Business Disclosure Format (Check one):

Yes. . . . . . No. . . . . . .

SEC 41250. Form 10-KSB

PART I

Item 1. Description of Business.
Furnish the information required by Item 101 of Regulation S-B.

Item 2. Description of Property.
Furnish the information required by Item 102 of Regulation S-B.

Item 3. Legal Proceedings.
Furnish the information required by Item 103 of Regulation S-B.

Item 4. Submission of Matters to a Vote of Security Holders.
If any matter was submitted during the fourth quarter of the fiscal year covered by this report to a vote of security holders, through the solicitation of proxies or otherwise, furnish the following information:

> *(a) The date of the meeting and whether it was an annual or special meeting.*

> *(b) If the meeting involved the election of directors, the name of each director elected at the meeting and the name of each other director whose term of office as a director continued after the meeting.*

> *(c) A brief description of each matter voted upon at the meeting and state the number of votes cast for, against or withheld, as well as the number of abstentions and broker nonvotes as to each such matter; including a separate tabulation with respect to each nominee for office.*

> *(d) A description of the terms of any settlement between the registrant and any other participant (as defined in Rule 14a-11 of Regulation A under the Act) terminating any solicitation subject to Rule 14a-11, including the cost or anticipated cost to the registrant.*

Instructions to Item 4.

1. If any matter has been submitted to a vote of security holders otherwise than at a meeting of such security holders, corresponding information with respect to such submission should be furnished. The solicitation of any authorization or consent (other than a proxy to vote at a shareholders' meeting) with respect to any matter shall be deemed a submission of such matter to a vote of security holders within the meaning of this item.

2. Paragraph (a) need be answered only if paragraph (b) or (c) is required to be answered.

SEC 41250

3. Paragraph (b) need not be answered if (i) proxies for the meeting were solicited pursuant to Regulation 14A under the Act, (ii) there was no solicitation in opposition to the management's nominees as listed in the proxy statement, and (iii) all of such nominees were elected. If the registrant did not solicit proxies and the board of directors as previously reported to the Commission was re-elected in its entirety, a statement to that effect in answer to paragraph (b) will suffice as an answer thereto.

4. Paragraph (c) must be answered for all matters voted upon at the meeting, including both contested and uncontested elections of directors.

5. If the registrant has furnished to its security holders proxy soliciting material containing the information called for by paragraph (d), the paragraph may be answered by reference to the information contained in such material.

6. If the registrant published a report containing all of the information called for by this item, the item may be answered by reference to the information in that report.

PART II

Item 5. Market for Common Equity and Related Stockholder Matters.
Furnish the information required by Item 201 of Regulation S-B.

Item 6. Management's Discussion and Analysis or Plan of Operation.
Furnish the information required by Item 303 of Regulation S-B.

Item 7. Financial Statements.
Furnish the information required by Item 310(a) of Regulation S-B.

Item 8. Changes In and Disagreements With Accountants on Accounting and Financial Disclosure.
Furnish the information required by Item 304 of Regulation S-B.

PART III

Item 9. Directors, Executive Officers, Promoters and Control Persons; Compliance With Section 16(a) of the Exchange Act.
Furnish the information required by Items 401 and 405 of Regulation S-B.

Instruction to Item 9.

Checking the box provided on the cover page of this Form to indicate that Item 405 disclosure of delinquent Form 3, 4, or 5 filers is not contained herein is intended to

SEC 41250. Form 10-KSB

facilitate Form processing and review. Failure to provide such indication will not create liability for violation of the federal securities laws. The space should be checked only if there is no disclosure in this Form of reporting person delinquencies in response to Item 405 of Regulation S-B and the registrant, at the time of filing of the Form 10-KSB, has reviewed the information necessary to ascertain, and has determined that, Item 405 disclosure is not expected to be contained in Part III of the Form 10-KSB or incorporated by reference.

Item 10. Executive Compensation.
Furnish the information required by Item 402 of Regulation S-B.

Item 11. Security Ownership of Certain Beneficial Owners and Management.
Furnish the information required by Item 403 of Regulation S-B.

Item 12. Certain Relationships and Related Transactions.
Furnish the information required by Item 404 of Regulation S-B.

PART IV

Item 13. Exhibits and Reports on Form 8-K.

(a) Furnish the exhibits required by Item 601 of Regulation S-B. Where any financial statement or exhibit is incorporated by reference, the incorporation by reference shall be set forth in the list required by this item. See Exchange Act Rule 12b-23. Identify in the list each management contract or compensatory plan or arrangement required to be filed as an exhibit to this form.

(b) Reports on Form 8-K. State whether any reports on Form 8-K were filed during the last quarter of the period covered by this report, listing the items reported, any financial statements filed and the dates of such reports.

Information Required in Annual Report of
Transitional Small Business Issuers

PART I

Note: Regardless of the disclosure model used, all registrants shall furnish the financial statements required by Part F/S.

Alternative 1

Corporate issuers may elect to furnish the information required by Questions 1, 3, 4, 11, 28-43, 45, and 47-50 of Model A of Form 1-A, as well as the information in Parts II and III, below.

SEC 41250

Alternative 2

Any issuer may elect to furnish the information required by Items 6-11 of Model B of Form 1-A, as well as the information required by Parts II and III, below.

PART II

Item 1. Market Price of and Dividends on the Registrant's Common Equity and Other Shareholder Matters.
Furnish the information required by Item 201 of Regulation S-B.

Item 2. Legal Proceedings.
If Alternative 2 is used, furnish the information required by Item 103 of Regulation S-B.

Item 3. Changes in and Disagreements With Accountants.
Furnish the information required by Item 304 of Regulation S-B, if applicable.

Item 4. Submission of Matters to a Vote of Security Holders.
If any matter was submitted during the fourth quarter of the fiscal year covered by this report to a vote of security holders, through the solicitation of proxies or otherwise, furnish the following information:

(a) The date of the meeting and whether it was an annual or special meeting.

(b) If the meeting involved the election of directors, the name of each director elected at the meeting and the name of each other director whose term of office as a director continued after the meeting.

(c) A brief description of each other matter voted upon at the meeting and the number of affirmative votes and the number of negative votes cast with respect to each such matter.

(d) A description of the terms of any settlement between the registrant and any other participant (as defined in Rule 14a-11 of Regulation A under the Act) terminating any solicitation subject to Rule 14a-11, including the cost or anticipated cost to the registrant.

Instructions to Item 4

1. If any matter has been submitted to a vote of security holders otherwise than at a meeting of such security holders, corresponding information with respect to such submission should be furnished. The solicitation of any authorization or consent (other than a proxy to vote at a shareholders' meeting) with respect to any matter shall be deemed a submission of such matter to a vote of security holders within the meaning of this item.

SEC 41250. Form 10-KSB

2. Paragraph (a) need be answered only if paragraph (b) or (c) is required to be answered.

3. Paragraph (b) need not be answered if (i) proxies for the meeting were solicited pursuant to Regulation 14A under the Act, (ii) there was no solicitation in opposition to the management's nominees as listed in the proxy statement, and (iii) all of such nominees were elected. If the registrant did not solicit proxies and the board of directors as previously reported to the Commission was re-elected in its entirety, a statement to that effect in answer to paragraph (b) will suffice as an answer thereto.

4. Paragraph (c) need not be answered as to procedural matters or as to the selection or approval of auditors.

5. If the registrant has furnished to its security holders proxy soliciting material containing the information called for by paragraph (d), the paragraph may be answered by reference to the information contained in such material.

6. If the registrant published a report containing all of the information called for by this item, the item may be answered by reference to the information in that report.

Item 5. Compliance With Section 16(a) of the Exchange Act.
Furnish the information required by Item 405 of Regulation S-B.

Item 6. Reports on Form 8-K.
State whether any reports on Form 8-K were filed during the last quarter of the period covered by this report, listing the items reported, any financial statements filed and the dates of such reports.

PART F/S

Furnish the information required by Item 310(a) of Registration S-B.

PART III

Item 1. Index to Exhibits.

(a) An index to the exhibits should be presented.

(b) Each exhibit should be listed in the exhibit index according to the number assigned to it in Part III of Form 1-A or under Item 2, below.

SEC 41250

(c) The index to exhibits should identify the location of the exhibit under the sequential page numbering system for this Form 10-KSB.

(d) Where exhibits are incorporated by reference, the reference shall be made in the index of exhibits.

Instructions:

1. Any document or part thereof filed with the Commission pursuant to any Act administered by the Commission may, subject to the limitations of Rule 24 of the Commission's Rules of Practice, be incorporated by reference as an exhibit to any registration statement.

2. If any modification has occurred in the text of any document incorporated by reference since the filing thereof, the issuer shall file with the reference a statement containing the text of such modification and the date thereof.

3. Procedurally, the techniques specified in Rule 12b-23 shall be followed.

Item 2. Description of Exhibits.
As appropriate, the issuer should file those documents required to be filed as Exhibit Number 2, 3, 5, 6, and 7 in Part III of Form 1-A. The registrant also shall file:

    (12) Additional exhibits—Any additional exhibits which the issuer may wish to file, which shall be so marked as to indicate clearly the subject matters to which they refer.

    (13) Form F-X—Canadian issuers shall file a written irrevocable consent and power of attorney on Form F-X.

SIGNATURES

In accordance with Section 13 or 15(d) of the Exchange Act, the registrant caused this report to be signed on its behalf by the undersigned, thereunto duly authorized.

         . . . .
            (Registrant)

        By. . . . .
           (Signature and Title)*

Date . . . .

SEC 41250. Form 10-KSB

In accordance with the Exchange Act, this report has been signed below by the following persons on behalf of the registrant and in the capacities and on the dates indicated.

. . . .
(Signature and Title)*

. . . .
(Signature and Title)*

. . . .
(Date)

. . . .
(Date)

Print the name and title of each signing officer under his signature.

Supplemental Information to be Furnished With Reports Filed Pursuant to Section 15(d) of the Exchange Act By Nonreporting Issuers

(a) Except to the extent that the materials enumerated in (1) and/or (2) below are specifically incorporated into this Form by reference (in which case, see Rule 12b-23(b)), every issuer which files an annual report on this Form under Section 15(d) of the Exchange Act shall furnish the Commission for its information, at the time of filing its report on this Form, four copies of the following:

(1) Any annual report to security holders covering the registrant's last fiscal year; and

(2) Every proxy statement, form of proxy or other proxy soliciting material sent to more than ten of the registrant's security holders with respect to any annual or other meeting of security holders.

(b) The Commission will not consider the material to be "filed" or subject to the liabilities of Section 18 of the Exchange Act, except if the issuer specifically incorporates it in its annual report on this Form by reference.

(c) If no such annual report or proxy material has been sent to security holders, a statement to that effect shall be included under this caption. If such report or proxy material is to be furnished to security holders subsequent to the filing of the annual report on this Form, the registrant shall so state under this caption and shall furnish copies of such material to the Commission when it is sent to security holders.

SEC 41250

41300. FORM 11-K

41310. General

The registration of securities offered to employees pursuant to an employee stock purchase, savings, option, or similar type plan (typically on Form S-8—see section 42400) triggers the requirement to file annual reports to the SEC on Form 11-K, pursuant to Section 15(d) of the 1934 Act. Form 11-K is required to be filed for the fiscal year the 1933 Act report became effective and for each fiscal year thereafter, unless the plan's reporting obligations are suspended. (See periodic reporting requirements pursuant to Section 15(d) in section 19500 of this manual.)

Companies qualifying as foreign private issuers pursuant to Rule 405 of the 1933 Act (see section 50353) are required to file Form 11-K if securities under an employee benefit or similar plan are offered to employees in the U.S.

41320. Financial Statement Requirements

41321. ERISA Plans. Plans subject to the Employee Retirement Income Security Act of 1974 (ERISA) have the option to file plan financial statements and schedules in Form 11-K that are prepared in accordance with ERISA reporting requirements in lieu of the requirements specified below (see section 41322). To the extent required by ERISA, the plan financial statements are required to be audited by independent accountants. It is important to note, however, that "limited scope" audits, or modified cash basis financial statements, which are generally acceptable under ERISA regulations, are not considered acceptable for SEC filings.

ERISA requires a statement of plan income and expenses and changes in assets (generally referred to as the "statement of changes in net assets available for benefits") *only* for the plan's last fiscal year and a statement of assets and liabilities (referred to as the "statement of net assets available for benefits") reflecting plan balances as of the beginning and end of the plan year (i.e., comparative). These requirements are less extensive than for other plan filings on Form 11-K (discussed below) and, accordingly, plans subject to ERISA generally utilize this option.

In addition, plans subject to ERISA *only* need to furnish to the SEC the schedules that are required to be filed by the applicable ERISA regulations.

As an accommodation to electronic filers, plans subject to ERISA that file their financial statements and schedules in accordance with ERISA requirements may file such information in paper format under cover of Form SE. (Form SE is the form used to submit a paper document that relates to an otherwise electronic filing.)

41322. Other Plans. All other plans are required to provide the following audited financial statements in Form 11-K:

- A statement of financial condition of the plan as of the end of its latest two fiscal years (see Rule 6A-03 of Regulation S-X).

- Statements of income and changes in plan equity of the plan for each of its latest three fiscal years (see Rule 6A-04 of Regulation S-X).

Article 6A of Regulation S-X (see section 50620) specifies the form and content of the financial statements and financial statement schedules required for plans that do not file in accordance with ERISA. It is worthy of particular note that Schedule I (Investments) needs to be filed only as of the date of the most recent statement of financial condition included in the filing.

41323. Auditors' Report. Irrespective of the financial statement requirements followed, if the financial statements are required to be audited, the auditors' report(s) in Form 11-K should cover the financial statements and the financial statement schedules. In addition, if a predecessor auditor is involved, the report of the other auditor needs to be included in Form 11-K.

When the Form 11-K financial statements are incorporated by reference into a filing on Form S-8, an accountants' consent to the incorporation by reference must be included, dated and manually signed (see section 20500). Each filing of the Form 11-K that is incorporated by reference in a 1933 Act registration statement (e.g., Form S-8) is considered a new registration statement and, therefore, creates a new effective date. Accordingly, when a Form 11-K is filed after the original effective date of the Form S-8 registration statement, the independent accountant needs to perform a "keeping current" review through the date the Form 11-K is filed.

41330. Filing Options

The information required by Form 11-K may be furnished either as a separate filing or, pursuant to Rule 15d-21 of the 1934 Act, as an exhibit to the issuer's annual report on Form 10-K, provided all of the following conditions are met:

- The issuer files annual reports on Form 10-K; and

- The issuer includes the financial statements required by Form 11-K as part of Form 10-K or as an amendment to it.

The text of Rule 15d-21 follows:

Reports for Employee Stock Purchase, Savings and Similar Plans

Rule 15d-21.

(a) Separate annual and other reports need not be filed pursuant to Section 15(d) of the Act with respect to any employee stock purchase, savings or similar plan, provided—

(1) the issuer of the stock or other securities offered to employees through their participation in the plan files annual reports on Form 10-K or U5S; and

(2) such issuer furnishes, as a part of its annual report on such form or as an amendment thereto, the financial statements required by Form 11-K with respect to the plan.

(b) If the procedure permitted by this rule is followed, the financial statements required by Form 11-K with respect to the plan shall be filed within 120 days after the end of the fiscal year of the plan, either as a part of or as an amendment to the annual report of the issuer for its last fiscal year, provided that if the fiscal year of the plan ends within 62 days prior to the end of the fiscal year of the issuer, such financial statements may be furnished as a part of the issuer's next annual report. If a plan subject to the Employee Retirement Income Security Act of 1974 uses the procedure permitted by this Rule, the financial statements required by Form 11-K shall be filed within 180 days after the plan's fiscal year-end.

Additionally, any financial statements contained in any plan annual report to employees covering the latest fiscal year of the plan may be incorporated by reference from such document in response to all or part of the Form 11-K requirements, provided that:

- Such financial statements substantially meet the requirements of Form 11-K; and

- Such document is filed as an exhibit to Form 11-K.

41340. Due Date

Reports on Form 11-K that are filed separately (i.e., not as an exhibit to Form 10-K) are due within 90 days after the end of the fiscal year of the plan; however,

SEC 41330. Form 11-K

if a plan is subject to ERISA, the Form 11-K in relation to that plan may be filed within 180 days after the plan's fiscal year. When the information required by Form 11-K is filed as an exhibit to Form 10-K, the exhibit is required to be filed within 120 days after the plan's fiscal year-end. If the plan's fiscal year ends less than 62 days prior to the company's year-end, the Form 11-K information may be included with the company's next Form 10-K (as provided in paragraph (b) of the 1934 Act Rule 15d-21).

If all or any portion of Form 11-K cannot be timely filed, notification Form 12b-25 must be filed, as discussed in section 41750.

41400. FORM 10-Q

41410. General

A quarterly report on Form 10-Q is required to be filed for each of the first three quarters of the fiscal year by issuers of securities registered pursuant to Section 12 of the 1934 Act who are required to file annual reports on Form 10-K pursuant to Section 13 of that Act and by issuers of securities registered under the 1933 Act who are required to file annual reports on Form 10-K pursuant to Section 15(d) of the 1934 Act. (See discussion of periodic reporting obligations after registration under the 1933 Act in section 19500.) Investment companies required to file quarterly reports under the Investment Company Act of 1940 and foreign private issuers are exempt from the requirement to file these quarterly reports.

Form 10-Q, which consists of two parts, is both a financial and a special-events report. The following issuers may omit Part I of Form 10-Q (pursuant to Rules 13a-13 and 15d-13 of the 1934 Act), which contains the financial information described in section 41330:

- Mutual life insurance companies.

- Mining companies not in the production stage but engaged primarily in the exploration for, or the development of, mineral deposits, other than oil, gas, or coal, if the conditions outlined in the rules are met.

The items of information required to be included in Part II of Form 10-Q indicate the nature of the special events occurring during the quarter that are reportable:

Item

1   Legal proceedings*

2   Changes in securities

3   Defaults upon senior securities

4   Submission of matters to a vote of security holders

5   Other information

6   Exhibits* and Reports on Form 8-K

---

*The detailed disclosure requirements are partially included in Regulation S-K (see section 60000).

Item 5 is a general item to permit the disclosure of any information that the company considers to be of material importance to the holders of securities and that is not specifically required by the other items in the form. This item may be used to disclose information that would otherwise be included in a filing on Form 8-K, provided that the timing and disclosure requirements of Form 8-K are met by the filing of Form 10-Q.

Pursuant to subparagraph (d) of 1934 Act Rule 13a-13 and subparagraph (d) of Rule 15(d)-13, the financial information required to be presented in Part I of Form 10-Q, whether (1) presented directly in Form 10-Q, (2) incorporated by reference from an informal report (such as a prospectus or press release), or (3) included as an exhibit to Part I, is not deemed to be filed for the purpose of Section 18 of the 1934 Act or otherwise subject to the liabilities under that section of the Act (for false or misleading facts or the omission of material facts see section 12030), but is subject to all other provisions of the Act. The information included in Part II is considered to be filed in this context.

41420. Due Date

Reports on Form 10-Q are due within 45 days after the end of each of the first three fiscal quarters of each year. As indicated in Rule 0-3 (section 41140), if the 45th day is a Saturday, Sunday, or a legal holiday, the due date becomes the next business day. A report need not be filed for the fourth quarter. If all or any portion of Form 10-Q cannot be filed on time, notification Form 12b-25 needs to be filed. Form 12b-25 is discussed in section 41750.

Questions often arise as to when the first Form 10-Q is due for a company that has just completed an initial public offering. 1934 Act Rules 13a-13 and 15d-13 specify that a new registrant is required to file its first report on Form 10-Q for the quarter following the period included in the registration statement either within 45 days after the effective date of the registration statement or by the date the Form 10-Q would otherwise be due. For example, if a calendar year company has a registration statement declared effective on July 20 that includes March 31 interim information, its initial

Form 10-Q would be due on or before September 3 for the quarter ended June 30 (i.e., 45 days after July 20).

41430. Financial Information Requirements

The financial information required in Form 10-Q consists of condensed (unaudited) financial statements and Management's Discussion and Analysis of Financial Condition and Results of Operations (MD&A). The detailed financial statement requirements for Form 10-Q are included in Rule 10-01 of Regulation S-X (see section 51001). The MD&A requirements applicable to interim financial statements are set forth in Item 303 of Regulation S-K (see section 63030).

41431. Reporting Other Information. Depending on the timing of the events involved, Item 5 of Form 10-Q (see section 41470) may be used to comply with any or all of the reporting requirements under Form 8-K. Item 5 permits registrants to reduce reporting burdens by including in a report on Form 10-Q information that would be required to be reported on Form 8-K.

41440. Combining Form 10-Q and the Quarterly Report to Shareholders

The instructions to Form 10-Q provide that if a registrant makes a quarterly shareholders' report available to its stockholders or otherwise publishes all or any part of the financial information required by Part I within the period prescribed for filing the report, the information called for may be incorporated by reference from such published information to satisfy the requirements of any item or part of any item, provided that the information incorporated by reference is filed as an exhibit to the Form 10-Q report.

General Instruction E to Form 10-Q provides for the integration of the quarterly shareholders' report and Form 10-Q as follows:

> Quarterly reports to security holders may be combined with the required information of Form 10-Q and will be suitable for filing with the Commission if the following conditions are satisfied:
>
> 1. The combined report contains full and complete answers to all items required by Part I of this form. When responses to a certain item of required disclosure are separated within the combined report, an appropriate cross-reference should be made.
>
> 2. If not included in the combined report, the cover page, appropriate responses to Part II, and the required signatures shall be included in the Form 10-Q. Additionally, as appropriate, a cross-reference sheet should be filed indicating the location of information required by the items of the form.

SEC 41420. Form 10-Q

3. If an electronic filer files any portion of a quarterly report to security holders in combination with the required information of Form 10-Q, as provided in this instruction, only such portions filed in satisfaction of the Form 10-Q requirements shall be filed in electronic format.

Rule 12b-23 (see section 41171) governs incorporation of information contained in reports to shareholders or certain other documents in answer or partial answer to any item of Form 10-Q.

41450. Omission of Information by Certain Wholly Owned Subsidiaries

The Form 10-Q requirements (General Instruction H) provide that wholly owned subsidiaries may omit certain information called for in MD&A and all of the information required by Item 2—Changes in Securities, Item 3—Defaults Upon Senior Securities, and Item 4—Submission of Matters to a Vote of Security Holders, if the registrant meets the following conditions:

a. All of the registrant's equity securities are owned, either directly or indirectly, by a single person which is a reporting company under the Act and which has filed all the material required to be filed pursuant to Section 13, 14, or 15(d) thereof, as applicable;

b. During the preceding thirty-six calendar months and any subsequent period of days, there has not been any material default in the payment of principal, interest, a sinking or purchase fund installment, or any other material default not cured within thirty days, with respect to any indebtedness of the registrant or its subsidiaries, and there has not been any material default in the payment of rentals under material long-term leases; and

c. There is prominently set forth, on the cover page of the Form 10-Q, a statement that the registrant meets the conditions set forth in General Instruction H(1)(a) and (b) of Form 10-Q and is therefore filing this Form with the reduced disclosure format.

In lieu of MD&A, registrants that are wholly owned subsidiaries meeting the specified criteria are permitted to present a narrative analysis of the results of operations, explaining reasons for material changes in income statement items between the current year-to-date period and the corresponding period in the preceding fiscal year, and a discussion of any changes in accounting principles that have a material effect on net income. Similar provisions as to the omission of certain information are also applicable to Form 10-K (see section 41160).

41460. Signatures

General Instruction G of Form 10-Q states that the report should be signed by a duly authorized officer of the registrant and by the principal financial officer or chief accounting officer of the registrant. The form may be signed by only one individual if the principal financial officer or chief accounting officer is also duly authorized to sign on behalf of the registrant and the dual responsibilities of the signatory are clearly indicated.

41470. Text of Form 10-Q

Since Form 10-Q is a frequently encountered SEC filing document, the full text of this form is included here. However, before using this section as an official reference source, the user of this manual is cautioned to ascertain whether any amendments to the text of the form have been made after September 1, 1993.

FORM 10-Q

QUARTERLY REPORT UNDER SECTION 13 OR 15(d) OF THE SECURITIES EXCHANGE ACT OF 1934

GENERAL INSTRUCTIONS

A. Rule as to Use of Form 10-Q

(1) Form 10-Q shall be used for quarterly reports under Section 13 or 15(d) of the Securities Exchange Act of 1934, filed pursuant to Rule 13a-13 or Rule 15d-13. A quarterly report on this form pursuant to Rule 13a-13 or Rule 15d-13 shall be filed within 45 days after the end of each of the first three fiscal quarters of each fiscal year. No report need be filed for the fourth quarter of any fiscal year.

(2) Form 10-Q also shall be used for transition and quarterly reports under Section 13 or 15(d) of the Securities Exchange Act of 1934, filed pursuant to Rule 13a-10 or Rule 15d-10. Such transition or quarterly reports shall be filed in accordance with the requirements set forth in Rule 13a-10 or Rule 15d-10 applicable when the registrant changes its fiscal year end.

B. Application of General Rules and Regulations

(1) The General Rules and Regulations under the Act contain certain general requirements which are applicable to reports on any form. These general requirements should be carefully read and observed in the preparation and filing of reports on this form.

(2) Particular attention is directed to Regulation 12B which contains general requirements regarding matters such as the kind and size of paper to be used, the legibility of the report, the information to be given whenever the title of securities is required

to be stated, and the filing of the report. The definitions contained in Rule 12b-2 should be especially noted. See also Regulations 13A and 15D.

C. Preparation of Report

(1) This is not a blank form to be filled in. It is a guide copy to be used in preparing the report in accordance with Rules 12b-11 and 12b-12. The Commission does not furnish blank copies of this form to be filled in for filing.

(2) These general instructions are not to be filed with the report. The instructions to the various captions of the form are also to be omitted from the report as filed.

D. Incorporation by Reference

(1) If the registrant makes available to its stockholders or otherwise publishes, within the period prescribed for filing the report, a document or statement containing information meeting some or all of the requirements of Part I of this form, the information called for may be incorporated by reference from such published document or statement, in answer or partial answer to any item or items of Part I of this form, provided copies thereof are filed as an exhibit to Part I of the report on this form.

(2) Other information may be incorporated by reference in answer or partial answer to any item or items of Part II of this form in accordance with the provisions of Rule 12b-23.

(3) If any information required by Part I or Part II is incorporated by reference into an electronic format document from the quarterly report to security holders as provided in General Instruction D, any portion of the quarterly report to security holders incorporated by reference shall be filed as an exhibit in electronic format, as required by Item 601(b)(13) of Regulation S-K.

E. Integrated Reports to Security Holders

Quarterly reports to security holders may be combined with the required information of Form 10-Q and will be suitable for filing with the Commission if the following conditions are satisfied:

(1) The combined report contains full and complete answers to all items required by Part I of this form. When responses to a certain item of required disclosure are separated within the combined report, an appropriate cross-reference should be made.

(2) If not included in the combined report, the cover page, appropriate responses to Part II, and the required signatures shall be included in the Form 10-Q. Additionally, as appropriate, a cross-reference sheet should be filed indicating the location of information required by the items of the form.

(3) If an electronic filer files any portion of a quarterly report to security holders in combination with the required information of Form 10-Q, as provided in this instruction, only such portions filed in satisfaction of the Form 10-Q requirements shall be filed in electronic format.

F. Filed Status of Information Presented

(1) Pursuant to Rule 13a-13(d) and Rule 15d-13(d), the information presented in satisfaction of the requirements of Items 1 and 2 of Part I of this form, whether included directly in a report on this form, incorporated therein by reference from a report, document or statement filed as an exhibit to Part I of this form pursuant to Instruction D(1) above, included in an integrated report pursuant to Instruction E above, or contained in a statement regarding computation of per share earnings or a letter regarding a change in accounting principles filed as an exhibit to Part I pursuant to Item 601 of Regulation S-K, except as provided by Instruction F(2) below, shall not be deemed filed for the purpose of Section 18 of the Act or otherwise subject to the liabilities of that section of the Act but shall be subject to the other provisions of the Act.

(2) Information presented in satisfaction of the requirements of this form other than those of Items (1) and (2) of Part I shall be deemed filed for the purpose of Section 18 of the Act; except that, where information presented in response to Item (1) or (2) of Part I (or as an exhibit thereto) is also used to satisfy Part II requirements through incorporation by reference, only that portion of Part I (or exhibit thereto) consisting of the information required by Part II shall be deemed so filed.

G. Signature and Filing of Report

Three complete copies of the report, including any financial statements, exhibits or other papers or documents filed as a part thereof, and five additional copies which need not include exhibits, shall be filed with the Commission. At least one complete copy of the report, including any financial statements, exhibits or other papers or documents filed as a part thereof, shall be filed with each exchange on which any class of securities of the registrant is registered. At least one complete copy of the report filed with the Commission and one such copy filed with each exchange shall be manually signed on the registrant's behalf by a duly authorized officer of the registrant and by the principal financial or chief accounting officer of the registrant. Copies not

SEC 41470. Form 10-Q

manually signed shall bear typed or printed signatures. In the case where the principal financial officer or chief accounting officer is also duly authorized to sign on behalf of the registrant, one signature is acceptable provided that the registrant clearly indicates the dual responsibilities of the signatory.

H. Omission of Information by Certain Wholly-Owned Subsidiaries

If on the date of the filing of its report on Form 10-Q, the registrant meets the conditions specified in paragraph (1) below, then such registrant may omit the information called for in the items specified in paragraph (2) below.

(1) Conditions for availability of the relief specified in paragraph (2) below:

(a) All of the registrant's equity securities are owned, either directly or indirectly, by a single person which is a reporting company under the Act and which has filed all the material required to be filed pursuant to section 13, 14 or 15(d) thereof, as applicable;

(b) During the preceding thirty-six calendar months and any subsequent period of days, there has not been any material default in the payment of principal, interest, a sinking or purchase fund installment, or any other material default not cured within thirty days, with respect to any indebtedness of the registrant or its subsidiaries, and there has not been any material default in the payment of rentals under material long-term leases; and

(c) There is prominently set forth, on the cover page of the Form 10-Q, a statement that the registrant meets the conditions set forth in General Instruction H(1)(a) and (b) of Form 10-Q and is therefore filing this Form with the reduced disclosure format.

(2) Registrants meeting the conditions specified in paragraph (1) above are entitled to the following relief:

(a) Such registrants may omit the information called for by Item 2 of Part I, Management's Discussion and Analysis of Financial Condition and Results of Operations, provided that the registrant includes in the Form 10-Q a management's narrative analysis of the results of operations explaining the reasons for material changes in the amount of revenue and expense items between the most recent fiscal year-to-date period presented and the corresponding year-to-date period in the preceding fiscal year. Explanations of material changes should include, but not be limited to, changes in the various elements which determine revenue and expense levels such as unit sales volume, prices charged and paid, production levels, production cost variances, labor costs and discretionary spending programs. In addition, the analysis should include an explanation of the effect of any changes

SEC 41470

in accounting principles and practices or method of application that have a material effect on net income as reported.

(b) Such registrants may omit the information called for in the following Part II Items: Item 2, Changes in Securities; Item 3, Defaults Upon Senior Securities; and Item 4, Submission of Matters to a Vote of Security Holders.

SECURITIES AND EXCHANGE COMMISSION
WASHINGTON, D.C. 20549

FORM 10-Q

(Mark One)

[ ] **QUARTERLY REPORT PURSUANT TO SECTION 13 OR
15(d) OF THE SECURITIES EXCHANGE ACT OF 1934**

For the quarterly period ended . . . .

OR

[ ] **TRANSITION REPORT PURSUANT TO SECTION 13 OR
15(d) OF THE SECURITIES EXCHANGE ACT OF 1934**

For the transition period from . . . . **to** . . . .

Commission File number . . . .

. . . .
(Exact name of registrant as specified in its charter)

. . . .
(State or other jurisdiction of   (I.R.S. Employer
incorporation or organization)   Identification No.)

. . . .
(Address of principal executive offices)
(Zip Code)

. . . .
(Registrant's telephone number, including area code)

. . . .
(Former name, former address and former fiscal
year, if changed since last report)

Indicate by check mark whether the registrant (1) has filed all reports required to be filed by Section 13 or 15(d) of the Securities Exchange Act of 1934 during the preceding 12 months (or for such shorter period that the registrant was required to file such reports), and (2) has been subject to such filing requirements for the past 90 days. Yes. . . . . .No. . . . .

SEC 41470. Form 10-Q

APPLICABLE ONLY TO ISSUERS INVOLVED IN BANKRUPTCY
PROCEEDINGS DURING THE PRECEDING FIVE YEARS:

Indicate by check mark whether the registrant has filed all documents and reports
required to be filed by Sections 12, 13 or 15(d) of the Securities Exchange Act of
1934 subsequent to the distribution of securities under a plan confirmed by a court.
Yes..........No..........

APPLICABLE ONLY TO CORPORATE ISSUERS:

Indicate the number of shares outstanding of each of the issuer's classes of
common stock, as of the latest practicable date.

PART I—FINANCIAL INFORMATION

Item 1. Financial Statements

Provide the information required by Rule 10-01 of Regulation S-X.

Item 2. Management's Discussion and Analysis of Financial Condition and Results of Operations

Furnish the information required by Item 303 of Regulation S-K.

PART II — OTHER INFORMATION

Instruction. *The report shall contain the item numbers and captions of all applicable
items of Part II, but the text of such items may be omitted provided the responses clearly
indicate the coverage of the item. Any item which is inapplicable or to which the
answer is negative may be omitted and no reference thereto need be made in the report.
If substantially the same information has been previously reported by the registrant,
an additional report of the information on this form need not be made. The term
"previously reported" is defined in Rule 12b-2. A separate response need not be
presented in Part II where information called for is already disclosed in the financial
information provided in Part I and is incorporated by reference into Part II of the
report by means of a statement to that effect in Part II which specifically identifies the
incorporated information.*

Item 1. Legal Proceedings

*Furnish the information required by Item 103 of Regulation S-K. As to such proceed-
ings which have been terminated during the period covered by the report, provide
similar information, including the date of termination and a description of the
disposition thereof with respect to the registrant and its subsidiaries.*

SEC 41470

Instruction. *A legal proceeding need only be reported in the 10-Q filed for the quarter in which it first became a reportable event and in subsequent quarters in which there have been material developments. Subsequent Form 10-Q filings in the same fiscal year in which a legal proceeding or a material development is reported should reference any previous reports in that year.*

Item 2. Changes in Securities

(a) If the constituent instruments defining the rights of the holders of any class of registered securities have been materially modified, give the title of the class of securities involved and state briefly the general effect of such modification upon the rights of holders of such securities.

(b) If the rights evidenced by any class of registered securities have been materially limited or qualified by the issuance or modification of any other class of securities, state briefly the general effect of the issuance or modification of such other class of securities upon the rights of the holders of the registered securities.

Instruction. *Working capital restrictions and other limitations upon the payment of dividends are to be reported hereunder.*

Item 3. Defaults Upon Senior Securities

(a) If there has been any material default in the payment of principal, interest, a sinking or purchase fund installment, or any other material default not cured within 30 days, with respect to any indebtedness of the registrant or any of its significant subsidiaries exceeding 5 percent of the total assets of the registrant and its consolidated subsidiaries, identify the indebtedness and state the nature of the default. In the case of such a default in the payment of principal, interest, or a sinking or purchase fund installment, state the amount of the default and the total arrearage on the date of filing this report.

Instruction. *This paragraph refers only to events which have become defaults under the governing instruments, i.e., after the expiration of any period of grace and compliance with any notice requirements.*

(b) If any material arrearage in the payment of dividends has occurred or if there has been any other material delinquency not cured within 30 days, with respect to any class of preferred stock of the registrant which is registered or which ranks prior to any class of registered securities, or with respect to any class of preferred stock of any significant subsidiary of the registrant, give the title of the class and state the nature of the arrearage or delinquency. In the case of an arrearage in the

payment of dividends, state the amount and the total arrearage on the date of filing this report.

Instruction. *Item 3 need not be answered as to any default or arrearage with respect to any class of securities all of which is held by, or for the account of, the registrant or its totally held subsidiaries.*

Item 4. Submission of Matters to a Vote of Security Holders

If any matter has been submitted to a vote of security holders, during the period covered by this report, through the solicitation of proxies or otherwise, furnish the following information:

(a) The date of the meeting and whether it was an annual or special meeting.

(b) If the meeting involved the election of directors, the name of each director elected at the meeting and the name of each other director whose term of office as a director continued after the meeting.

(c) A brief description of each matter voted upon at the meeting and state the number of votes cast for, against, or withheld, as well as the number of abstentions and broker non-votes, as to each such matter, including a separate tabulation with respect to each nominee for office.

(d) A description of the terms of any settlement between the registrant and any other participant (as defined in Rule 14a-11 of Regulation 14A under the Act) terminating any solicitation subject to Rule 14a-11, including the cost or anticipated cost to the registrant.

Instructions.

1. If any matter has been submitted to a vote of security holders otherwise than at a meeting of such security holders, corresponding information with respect to such submission shall be furnished. The solicitation of any authorization or consent (other than a proxy to vote at a stockholders' meeting) with respect to any matter shall be deemed a submission of such matter to a vote of security holders within the meaning of this item.

2. Paragraph (a) need be answered only if paragraph (b) or (c) is required to be answered.

3. Paragraph (b) need not be answered if (i) proxies for the meeting were solicited pursuant to Regulation 14 under the Act, (ii) there was no solicitation in opposition to the management's nominees as listed in the proxy statement, and (iii) all of such nominees were elected. If the registrant did not solicit proxies and the board of directors as previously reported to the Commission was re-elected in its entirety, a statement to that effect in answer to paragraph (b) will suffice as answer thereto.

4. Paragraph (c) must be answered for all matters voted upon at the meeting, including both contested and uncontested elections of directors.

5. If the registrant has furnished to its security holders proxy soliciting material containing the information called for by paragraph (d), the paragraph may be answered by reference to the information contained in such material.

6. If the registrant has published a report containing all of the information called for by this item, the item may be answered by reference to the information contained in such report.

Item 5. Other Information

The registrant may, at its option, report under this item any information, not previously reported in a report on Form 8-K, with respect to which information is not otherwise called for by this form. If disclosure of such information is made under this item, it need not be repeated in a report on Form 8-K which would otherwise be required to be filed with respect to such information or in a subsequent report on Form 10-Q.

Item 6. Exhibits and Reports on Form 8-K

(a) Furnish the exhibits required by Item 601 of Regulation S-K.

(b) Reports on Form 8-K. State whether any reports on Form 8-K have been filed during the quarter for which this report is filed, listing the items reported, any financial statements filed, and the dates of any such reports.

SEC 41470. Form 10-Q

SIGNATURES *

Pursuant to the requirements of the Securities Exchange Act of 1934, the registrant has duly caused this report to be signed on its behalf by the undersigned thereunto duly authorized.

....
(Registrant)

Date ....
(Signature)**

Date ....
(Signature)**

---

* See General Instruction E.
** Print name and title of the signing officer under his signature.

41500. FORM 10-QSB

41510. General

A quarterly report on Form 10-QSB needs to be filed for each of the first three quarters of each fiscal year by all companies qualifying as "small business issuers" and who are required to file annual reports on Form 10-KSB (see section 41200). This Form may be used for quarterly and transition reports under Section 13 or 15(d) of the 1934 Act and Rules 13a-13 and 15d-13. Item 10(a) of Regulation S-B (see section 70160) contains further information as to eligibility to use Form 10-QSB.

Form 10-QSB, consisting of two parts, is both a financial and a special events report. The following are the items of information to be included in Form 10-QSB (detailed requirements are described in the text of the form (see section 41560), and Item numbers refer to Regulation S-B, the requirements of which are more fully included in section 70000 of this manual):

PART I FINANCIAL INFORMATION

Item

1   Financial Statements (Item 310(b) of Reg. S-B)
2   Management's Discussion and Analysis or Plan of Operation (Item 303) (Note: Special instructions are provided for transitional small business issuers—see text of requirements in section 41560.)

PART II OTHER INFORMATION

1   Legal Proceedings (Item 103)
2   Changes in Securities
3   Defaults Upon Senior Securities
4   Submission of Matters to a Vote of Security Holders
5   Other Information

Item

6 Exhibits and Reports on Form 8-K
   (a) Exhibits required by Item 601
     (Note: Special instructions are provided for transitional small business
     issuers—see text of requirements in section 41560.)
   (b) Details pertaining to any reports filed on Form 8-K during the quarter

41520. Due Date

Reports on Form 10-QSB are due within 45 days after the end of each of the first three quarters of each fiscal year.

41530. Financial Information Requirements

The financial information required in Form 10-QSB consists of condensed (unaudited) financial statements and Management's Discussion and Analysis or Plan of Operation. The detailed financial statement requirements for Form 10-QSB are included in Item 310 of Regulation S-B (see section 73100). The requirements for Management's Discussion and Analysis or Plan of Operation are set forth in Item 303 of Regulation S-B (see section 73040); however, refer to the special instructions for transitional small business issuers provided in the text of requirements in section 41560.

41540. Combining Form 10-QSB and the Quarterly Report to Shareholders

The instructions provide that if a small business issuer makes quarterly reports to security holders, these may be combined with the required information of Form 10-QSB and are suitable for filing with the Commission when certain specified conditions are satisfied.

41550. Signatures

General instruction F of Form 10-QSB states that the report should be signed by a duly authorized officer of the registrant and by the principal financial officer or chief accounting officer of the registrant. The Form may be signed by only individual if the principal financial officer or chief accounting officer is also duly authorized to sign on behalf of the registrant and the dual responsibilities of the signatory are clearly indicated.

41560. Text of Form 10-QSB

Since Form 10-QSB is a frequently encountered SEC filing document for small business issuers, the full text of this form is included herein. However, before using this section as an official reference source, the user of this manual is cautioned to ascertain whether any amendments to the text of the form have been made after September 1, 1993.

FORM 10-QSB
QUARTERLY REPORT PURSUANT TO SECTION 13 OR 15(d)
OF THE SECURITIES EXCHANGE ACT OF 1934

GENERAL INSTRUCTIONS

A. Use of Form 10-QSB

(1) A "small business issuer," defined in Rule 12b-2, may use this Form for its transition and quarterly reports under Section 13 or 15(d) of the Exchange Act and Rules 13a-13 and 15d-13. For further information as to eligibility to use of this form see Item 10(a) of Regulation S-B. A small business issuer shall file a quarterly report on this form within 45 days after the end of each of the first three fiscal quarters of each fiscal year. No report need be filed for the fourth quarter of any fiscal year. Transition reports shall be filed in accordance with the requirements set forth in Rule 13a-10 or Rule 15d-10.

B. Application of General Rules and Regulations

(1) The General Rules and Regulations under the Exchange Act, particularly Regulation 12B contain certain general requirements for reports on any form which should be carefully read and observed in the preparation and filing of reports on this form.

C. Incorporation by Reference

(1) If the registrant makes available to its stockholders or otherwise publishes, within the period prescribed for filing the report, a document or statement containing information meeting some or all of the requirements of Part I of this form, the information may be incorporated by reference from such published document or statement, in answer or partial answer to any item or items of Part I of this form provided copies of the document or statement are filed as an exhibit to Part I of the report on this form.

(2) Other information may be incorporated by reference in answer or partial answer to any item or items of Part II of this form in accordance with the provisions of Rule 12b-23 of the Exchange Act.

SEC 41560. Form 10-QSB

(3) If any information required by Part I or Part II is incorporated by reference into an electronic format document from the quarterly report to security holders as provided in General Instruction C, any portion of the quarterly report to security holders incorporated by reference shall be filed as an exhibit in electronic format, as required by Item 601(b)(13) of Regulation S-B.

D. Integrated Reports to Security Holders

Quarterly reports to security holders may be combined with the required information of Form 10-QSB and will be suitable for filing with the Commission if the following conditions are satisfied:

(1) The combined report contains full and complete answers to all items required by Part I of this form. When responses to a certain item of required disclosure are separated within the combined report, an appropriate cross-reference should be made.

(2) If not included in the combined report, the cover page, appropriate responses to Part II and the required signatures shall be included in the Form 10-QSB. Additionally, as appropriate, a cross-reference sheet should be filed indicating the location of information required by items of the form.

(3) If an electronic filer files any portion of a quarterly report to security holders in combination with the required information of Form 10-QSB, as provided in this instruction, only such portions filed in satisfaction of the Form 10-QSB requirements shall be filed in electronic format.

E. Filed Status of Information Presented

(1) Under Rule 13a-13(d) and 15d-13(d) of the Exchange Act, the information presented in satisfaction of the requirements of Items 1 and 2 of Part I of this form, whether included directly in a report on this form, incorporated therein by reference from a report, document or statement filed as an exhibit to Part I of this form pursuant to Instruction D(1) above, included in an integrated report pursuant to Instruction D above, or contained in a statement regarding computation of per share earnings or a letter regarding a change in accounting principles filed as an exhibit to Part I under Item 601 of Regulation S-B shall not be deemed filed for the purpose of Section 18 of the Exchange Act or otherwise subject to the liabilities of that section of the Act but shall be subject to the other provisions of the Act.

(2) Information presented in satisfaction of the requirements of this form other than those of Items 1 and 2 or Part I shall be deemed filed for the purpose of Section 18 of the Exchange Act; except that, where information presented in response to Item 1 or

2 of Part I (or an exhibit thereto is also used to satisfy Part II requirements through incorporation by reference, only that portion of Part I (or exhibit thereto) consisting of the information required by Part II shall be deemed so filed.

F. Signature and Filing of Report

(1) File three "complete" copies and five "additional" copies of the registration statement with the Commission and file at least one complete copy with each exchange on which the securities will be registered. A "complete" copy includes financial statement, exhibits and all other papers and documents. An "additional" copy excludes exhibits.

(2) Manually sign at least one copy of the report filed with the Commission and each exchange; other copies should have typed or printed signatures. In the case where the principal financial or chief accounting officer is also authorized to sign on behalf of the registrant, one signature is acceptable provided that the registrant clearly indicates the dual responsibilities of the signatory.

G. Omission of Information by Certain Wholly-Owned Subsidiaries

If, on the date of the filing of its Form 10-QSB, the registrant meets the conditions in paragraph (1) below, then it may omit the information in paragraph (2) below.

(1) Conditions for availability of relief specified in paragraph (2) below:

(a) All of the registrant's equity securities are owned, either directly or indirectly, by a single person which is a reporting company and which has filed all the material required to be filed pursuant to Section 13, 14 or 15(d) of the Exchange Act.

(b) During the past thirty-six calendar months and any later period, there has not been any material default in the payment of principal, interest, a sinking or purchase fund installment, or any other material default not cured within thirty days, with respect to any indebtedness of the small business issuer, and there has not been any material default in the payment of rentals under material long-term leases, and

(c) There is prominently set forth, on the cover page of the Form 10-QSB, a statement that the registrant meets the conditions set forth in this instruction and is therefore filing this form with the reduced disclosure format.

(2) Registrants meeting the conditions in paragraph (1) above are entitled to:

(a) Omit the information called for by Item 303 of Regulation S-B, Management's Discussion and Analysis provided that the issuer includes in the

SEC 41560. Form 10-QSB

Form 10-QSB a management's narrative analysis of the results of operations explaining the reasons for material changes in the amount of revenue and expense items between the most recent fiscal year-to-date period presented and the corresponding year-to-date period in the preceding fiscal year. Explanations of material changes should include, but not be limited to, changes in the various elements which determine revenue and expense levels such as unit sales volume, prices charged and paid, production levels, production cost variances, labor costs and discretionary spending programs. In addition, the analysis should include an explanation of the effect of any changes in accounting principles and practices or method of application that have a material effect on net income as reported.

(b) Such registrants may omit the information called for by the following Items in Part II: Item 2, 3 and 4.

H. *In response to Item 6(a) of this Form 10-QSB, a small business issuer that is eligible to file the information required under "Information Required in Annual Report of Transitional Small Business Issuers" in its next required Form 10-KSB may include only those exhibits required by Part III of "Information Required in Annual Report of Transitional Small Business Issuers" of Form 10-KSB.*

U.S. SECURITIES AND EXCHANGE COMMISSION
Washington, D.C. 20549

Form 10-QSB

(Mark One)

[ ] **QUARTERLY REPORT PURSUANT TO SECTION 13 OR 15(d) OF THE SECURITIES EXCHANGE ACT OF 1934**

For the quarterly period ended . . . .

[ ] **TRANSITION REPORT PURSUANT TO SECTION 13 OR 15(d) OF THE SECURITIES EXCHANGE ACT OF 1934**

For the transition period from . . . . **to** . . . .

Commission file number . . . .

. . . .
(Exact name of small business issuer as specified in its charter)

. . . .

(State or other jurisdiction of   (I.R.S. Employer
incorporation or organization)   Identification No.)

. . . .
(Address of principal executive offices)

SEC 41560

Issuer's telephone number ( ) . . . .

. . . .
(Former name, former address and former fiscal year,
if changed since last report)

Check whether the issuer (1) filed all reports required to be filed by Section 13 or 15(d) of the Exchange Act during the past 12 months (or for such shorter period that the registrant was required to file such reports), and (2) has been subject to such filing requirements for the past 90 days. Yes..........No..........

APPLICABLE ONLY TO ISSUERS INVOLVED IN BANKRUPTCY PROCEEDINGS DURING THE PRECEDING FIVE YEARS

Check whether the registrant filed all documents and reports required to be filed by Section 12, 13 or 15(d) of the Exchange Act after the distribution of securities under a plan confirmed by a court. Yes..........No..........

APPLICABLE ONLY TO CORPORATE ISSUERS

State the number of shares outstanding of each of the issuer's classes of common equity, as of the latest practicable date: . . . .

Transitional Small Business Disclosure Format (Check one):

Yes..........No..........

PART I — FINANCIAL INFORMATION

Item 1. Financial Statements.

Furnish the information required by Item 310(b) of Regulation S-B.

Item 2. Management's Discussion and Analysis or Plan of Operation.

Furnish the information required by Item 303 of Regulation S-B.

Instructions for Transitional Small Business Issuers

(1) Those transitional small business issuers which relied upon Alternative 1 under "Information Required in Annual Report of Transitional Small Business Issuers" in their most recent Form 10-KSB may, in lieu of the disclosure required by Item 303 of Regulation S-B, update the responses to Questions 47-50 in Model A of Form 1-A. This update should provide such information as will enable the reader to assess material changes since the end of the last fiscal year and for the comparable interim period in the preceding year.

SEC 41560. Form 10-QSB

(2) Those transitional small business issuers which relied upon Alternative 2 under "Information Required in Annual Report of Transitional Small Business Issuers" in their most recent Form 10-KSB may, in lieu of the disclosure required by Item 303 of Regulation S-B, update the response to Item 6(a)(3)(i) to Model B of Form 1-A. This update should provide such information as will enable the reader to assess material changes since the end of the last fiscal year and for the comparable interim period in the preceding year.

PART II — OTHER INFORMATION

Instruction to Part II.

Any item which is inapplicable or to which the answer is negative may be omitted and no reference thereto need be made in the report. If substantially the same information has been previously reported by the registrant, an additional report of the information on this form need not be made. The term "previously reported" is defined in Rule 12b-2 of the Exchange Act. A separate response need not be presented in Part II where information called for is already disclosed in the financial information in Part I and is incorporated by reference into Part II of the report by means of a statement to that effect in Part II which specifically identifies the incorporated information.

Item 1. Legal Proceedings

Furnish the information required by Item 103 of Regulation S-B. As to proceedings that terminated during the period covered by this report, furnish information similar to that required by Item 103 of Regulation S-B.

Instruction to Item 1.

A legal proceeding need only be reported in the Form 10-QSB filed for the quarter in which it first became a reportable event and in subsequent quarters in which there have been material developments. Subsequent Form 10-QSB filings in the same fiscal year in which a legal proceeding or a material development is reported should reference any previous reports in that year.

Item 2. Changes in Securities

(a) If the instruments defining the rights of the holders of any class of registered securities have been materially modified, give the title of the class of securities involved and state briefly the general effect of such modification upon the rights of holders of such securities.

SEC 41560

(b) If the rights evidenced by any class of registered securities have been materially limited or qualified by the issuance or modification of any other class of securities, state briefly the general effect of the issuance or modification of such other class of securities upon the rights of the holders of the registered securities.

Instruction to Item 2.
1. Working capital restrictions and other limitations upon the payment of dividends are to be reported.

Item 3. Defaults Upon Senior Securities

(a) If there has been any material default in the payment of principal, interest, a sinking or purchase fund installment, or any other material default not cured within 30 days, with respect to any indebtedness of the small business issuer exceeding 5 percent of the total assets of the issuer identify the indebtedness and state the nature of the default. In the case of such a default in the payment of principal, interest, or a sinking or purchase fund installment, state the amount of the default and the total arrearage on the date of filing this report.

Instruction to Item 3(a).
1. This paragraph refers only to events which have become defaults under the governing instruments, i.e., after the expiration of any period of grace and compliance with any notice requirements.

(b) If any material arrearage in the payment of dividends has occurred or if there has been any other material delinquency not cured within 30 days, with respect to any class of preferred stock of the registrant which is registered or which ranks prior to any class of registered securities, or with respect to any class of preferred stock of any significant subsidiary of the registrant, give the title of the class and state the nature of the arrearage or delinquency. In the case of such a default in the payment of dividends, state the amount and the total arrearage on the date of filing this report.

Instruction to Item 3.
1. Item 3 need not be answered as to any default or arrearage with respect to any class of securities all of which is held by, or for the account of, the registrant or its totally held subsidiaries.

Item 4. Submission of Matters to a Vote of Security Holders

If any matter was submitted to a vote of security holders during the period covered by this report, through the solicitation of proxies or otherwise, furnish the following information:

SEC 41560. Form 10-QSB

(a) The date of the meeting and whether it was an annual or special meeting.

(b) If the meeting involved the election of directors, the name of each director elected at the meeting and the name of each other director whose term of office as a director continued after the meeting.

(c) A brief description of each matter voted upon at the meeting and state the number of votes cast for, against or withheld, as well as the number of abstentions and broker nonvotes as to each such matter, including a separate tabulation with respect to each nominee for office.

(d) A description of the terms of any settlement between the registrant and any other participant (as defined in Rule 14a-11 of Regulation A under the Exchange Act) terminating any solicitation subject to Rule 14a-11, including the cost or anticipated cost to the registrant.

Instruction to Item 4.

1. If any matter has been submitted to a vote of security holders otherwise than at a meeting of such security holders, corresponding information with respect to such submission should be furnished. The solicitation of any authorization or consent (other than a proxy to vote at a shareholders' meeting) with respect to any matter shall be deemed a submission of such matter to a vote of security holders within the meaning of this item.

2. Paragraph (a) need be answered only if paragraph (b) or (c) is required to be answered.

3. Paragraph (b) need not be answered if (i) proxies for the meeting were solicited pursuant to Regulation 14A under the Exchange Act, (ii) there was no solicitation in opposition to the management's nominees as listed in the proxy statement, and (iii) all of such nominees were elected. If the registrant did not solicit proxies and the board of directors as previously reported to the Commission was re-elected in its entirety, a statement to that effect in answer to paragraph (b) will suffice as an answer thereto.

4. Paragraph (c) must be answered for all matters voted upon at the meeting including both contested and uncontested elections of directors.

5. If the registrant has furnished to its security holders proxy soliciting material containing the information called for by paragraph (d), the paragraph may be answered by reference to the information contained in such material.

6. If the registrant has published a report containing all of the information called for by this item, the item may be answered by reference to the information in that report.

Item 5. Other Information

(a) The registrant may, at its option, report under this item any information, not previously reported in a report on Form 8-K, with respect to which information is not otherwise called for by this form. If disclosure of such other information is made under this item, it need not be repeated in a Form 8-K which would otherwise be required to be filed with respect to such information or in a subsequent report on Form 10-QSB.

Item 6. Exhibits and Reports on Form 8-K

(a) Furnish the exhibits required by Item 601 of Regulation S-B.

(b) Reports on Form 8-K. State whether any reports on Form 8-K were filed during the quarter for which this report is filed, listing the items reported, any financial statements filed and the dates of such reports.

SIGNATURES

In accordance with the requirements of the Exchange Act, the registrant caused this report to be signed on its behalf by the undersigned, thereunto duly authorized.

. . . .
(Registrant)

Date . . . .
(Signature)*

Date . . . .
(Signature)*

* Print name and title of the signing officer under his signature.

SEC 41560. Form 10-QSB

41600. FORM 8-K

41610. General

Form 8-K is required to be filed if certain significant events occur and may be filed to report any event about which a prudent investor should know. The filing requirements apply to registrants subject to Rules 13a-1 and 15d-1 of the 1934 Act. (These rules relate to requirements to file annual reports with the SEC on Form 10-K.) Rule 15d-11 exempts foreign registrants, which are required to file reports on Form 6-K (see section 44200) from the filing requirements of Form 8-K. The reportable significant events include:

<u>Item</u>

1	Changes in control of the registrant
2	Acquisition or disposition of assets
3	Bankruptcy or receivership
4	Changes in registrant's certifying accountants
5	Other events
6	Resignations of registrant's directors
8	Change in fiscal year

Item 7 of the form identifies the financial statements, pro forma financial information, and exhibits required to be filed.

Events to be reported on Form 8-K are not limited to the matters specified in Items 1, 2, 3, 4, 6, and 8. Generally, consideration needs to be given to reporting any matter that might be of significance to a prudent investor (after consulting with legal counsel). If the event to be reported is not specifically identifiable under one of the above items, it is usually reported under Item 5. The financial statements required to be filed as part of Form 8-K relate to significant acquisitions of businesses reported pursuant to Item 2.

If substantially the same information as that required by this form has been previously reported by the registrant (e.g., in filing on a Form 10-Q or 10-K), an additional report of the information on this form is not required.

SEC 41610

With regard to "small business issuers," General Instruction C3 to Form 8-K states:

> A "small business issuer," defined under Rule 12b-2 of the Exchange Act shall refer to the disclosure items in Regulation S-B and not Regulation S-K. If there is no comparable disclosure item in Regulation S-B, a small business issuer need not provide the information requested. A small business issuer shall provide the information required by Item 310(a) of Regulation S-B in lieu of the financial information required by Item 7 of this Form.

41620. Due Date

Form 8-K needs to be filed within 15 calendar days after the occurrence of any event identified by Items 1, 2, 3, or 8 unless substantially the same information has been previously reported to the SEC by the registrant. As indicated in General Instruction B, since a report on Form 8-K with respect to any other materially important event reportable under Item 5 is optional, there is no mandatory time for filing. However, registrants are encouraged to file the report promptly after the occurrence of a reportable event. A change in a registrant's certifying accountants (Item 4) necessitates the filing of Form 8-K within five business days after the former accountant resigns, is dismissed, or declines to stand for re-election, or a new accountant is engaged. The letter from the independent accountants required in this connection pursuant to Item 4 of Form 8-K (see section 41640 for further discussion) may be furnished within ten business days after the filing date if it is unavailable at the time of filing Form 8-K. The former accountant may provide the registrant with an interim letter highlighting specific areas of concern and indicating that a more detailed letter will follow. In either case, the registrant is required to file the former accountant's letter within two business days of receipt. Resignations of a registrant's directors (Item 6) need to be reported on Form 8-K within five business days of receipt of the letter from the director. The financial statements of an acquired business required pursuant to Item 2 and described under Item 7 of Form 8-K (see section 41631 for further discussion) may be furnished within 60 calendar days after the filing date if it is impractical to provide the financial statements at the time the Form 8-K is filed (also see section 41431).

41630. Financial Statement Requirements

41631. Acquisition or Disposition of Assets. Item 2 of Form 8-K requires the disclosure of certain information with respect to acquisitions or dispositions involving a "significant" amount of assets otherwise than in the ordinary course of business. Instruction 2 to Item 2 defines the term "acquisition" as including "every purchase acquisition by lease, exchange, merger, consolidation, succession, or other acquisition" except construction or development of property by or for the registrant. "The

SEC 41610. Form 8-K

term 'disposition' includes every sale, disposition by lease, exchange, merger, consolidation, mortgage, or hypothecation of assets, assignment, whether for the benefit of creditors or otherwise, abandonment, destruction, or other disposition." An acquisition or disposition is deemed to involve a significant amount of assets if any of the following tests are met:

- The registrant's (and its other subsidiaries') equity in the net book value of the assets acquired or disposed of exceeds 10 percent of the registrant's consolidated assets prior to the transaction.

- The amount paid or received in connection with the acquisition or disposition exceeds 10 percent of the registrant's consolidated assets prior to the transaction.

- The "business" acquired or disposed of meets the definition of the term "significant," as defined in Rule 11-01(b) of Regulation S-X (see section 51101).

An issue that frequently arises is whether the purchase or sale of property is considered to be "in the ordinary course of business," or whether it is a Form 8-K reportable event. The SEC staff has informally expressed the view that if a registrant is in the business of buying and selling the type of property involved, the disposition may be deemed to be in the ordinary course of business—otherwise, the transaction needs to be considered from a Form 8-K reporting standpoint (see section 50315). The oil and gas and cable television industries have been cited by the staff as illustrations of industries that it does not consider to be in the business of buying and selling properties even though in these industries such transactions may be frequent.

Further, the SEC staff considers the acquisition or disposition of a *significant* property by a real estate company to be a reportable event pursuant to Item 2 of Form 8-K.

Item 7 requires the following financial statements, pro forma information, and exhibits of businesses acquired or disposed of by the registrant or by any of its majority-owned subsidiaries and disclosed in answer to Item 2:

(a) Financial statements of businesses acquired.

(1) For any business acquisition required to be described in answer to Item 2 above, financial statements of the business acquired shall be filed for the periods specified in [Regulation S-X] Rule 3-05(b).

(2) The financial statements shall be prepared pursuant to Regulation S-X except that supporting schedules need not be filed. A manually signed accountants' report should be provided pursuant to Rule 2-02 of Regulation S-X.

SEC 41631

(3) With regard to the acquisition of one or more real estate properties, the financial statements and any additional information specified by Rule 3-14 of Regulation S-X shall be filed.

(4) If it is impracticable to provide the required financial statements for an acquired business at the time the report on Form 8-K is filed, the registrant should (i) so indicate in the Form 8-K report; (ii) file such of the required financial statements as are available; (iii) state when the required financial statements will be filed; and (iv) file the required financial statement for an acquired business under cover of Form 8 as soon as practicable, but not later than 60 days after the report on Form 8-K must be filed. In such circumstances, the registrant may, at its option, include unaudited financial statements in the initial report on Form 8-K. [Note: Form 8 has been rescinded. Amendments should be filed under cover of the form amended, designated by adding the letter "A" after the title of the form, e.g., "Form 10-K/A" (see section 41700).]

(b) Pro forma financial information.

(1) For any transaction required to be described in answer to Item 2 above, furnish any pro forma financial information that would be required pursuant to Article 11 of Regulation S-X.

(2) The provisions of (a)(4) above shall also apply to pro forma financial information relative to the acquired business.

(c) Exhibits.

The exhibits shall be furnished in accordance with the provisions of Item 601 of Regulation S-K.

Paragraph (a)(1) of Item 7 refers to Rule 3-05(b) of Regulation S-X regarding the periods that the financial statements of businesses acquired need to be presented. Refer to section 50314 for the text of Rule 3-05(b) and sections 50315—50318 and 50341 for additional guidance.

41632. Extensions of Time and Requests for Waiver of Financial Statement Requirements. The audited financial statements and pro forma financial information required as a result of acquisitions reportable under Item 2 of Form 8-K are sometimes unavailable, particularly when assets constituting a business are acquired from a privately owned company or when the acquired business was a segment of an entity that was not previously reported on separately.

Paragraph (a)(4) of Item 7 of Form 8-K presently provides for an automatic 60-day extension of time if it is impracticable to provide the required financial statements for an acquired business at the time the Form 8-K is filed if the registrant:

SEC 41631. Form 8-K

- So indicates in the Form 8-K.

- Files the required financial statements that are available.

- States when the required financial statements will be filed.

- Files such statements under cover of the form amended (see section 41700) as soon as practicable, but not later than 60 days after the due date of the Form 8-K.

In any event, the registrant may, at its option, include unaudited financial statements in the initial Form 8-K filing.

In certain instances, the SEC staff will consider requests for waiver of some or all of the required information. In determining whether to grant a waiver, the staff will consider the size of the acquisition relative to the registrant, the reasons the audited statements cannot be obtained, and the financial information that the registrant can provide. However, the more significant the acquisition is to the registrant, the more reluctant the staff is to consider a registrant's request for relief. In any event, the staff rarely grants waivers. More frequently, the registrant will receive an acknowledgment that "the staff will take no action" if the financial statements required by Form 8-K are not filed. In such instances, however, the limitations described below apply.

When an extension of time for filing the required audited financial statements has been obtained or a "no-action letter" concerning the omission of such financial statements is received, the registrant may not file a registration statement under the 1933 Act or make an offering pursuant to 1933 Act Rule 415 (shelf registration—see section 19200) until the required financial statements are filed (or until the acquired company is included in the primary financial statements for a sufficient period of time; see section 50314). In addition, affiliates of the registrant may not make resales of their securities in reliance on 1933 Act Rule 144 (see section 42940). The foregoing restrictions do not apply to:

- Offerings on Form S-8.

- Offerings pursuant to a dividend or interest reinvestment plan.

- Issuance of securities pursuant to the exercise of outstanding warrants or options or upon conversion of other outstanding securities.

- Offerings made by selling shareholders that are not underwritten.

SEC 41632

41640. Changes in Accountants

Changes in a company's independent public accountants, including both the termination of the former accountant and the engagement of a new accountant, are events that must be reported pursuant to Item 4 of Form 8-K. Because of its significance to accountants, the text of this requirement is included here:

Changes in Registrant's Certifying Accountant

(a) If an independent accountant who was previously engaged as the principal accountant to audit the registrant's financial statements, or an independent accountant upon whom the principal accountant expressed reliance in its report regarding a significant subsidiary, resigns (or indicates it declines to stand for re-election after the completion of the current audit) or is dismissed, then provide the information required by Item 304(a)(1), including compliance with Item 304(a)(3), of Regulation S-K, and the related instructions to Item 304.

(b) If a new independent accountant has been engaged as either the principal accountant to audit the registrant's financial statements or as an independent accountant on whom the principal accountant has expressed, or is expected to express, reliance in its report regarding a significant subsidiary, then provide the information required by Item 304(a)(2), of Regulation S-K.

Instruction. The resignation or dismissal of an independent accountant, or its declination to stand for re-election, is a reportable event separate from the engagement of a new independent accountant. On some occasions two reports on Form 8-K will be required for a single change in accountants, the first on the resignation (or declination to stand for re-election) or dismissal of the former accountant and the second when the new accountant is engaged. Information required in the second Form 8-K in such situations need not be provided to the extent it has been previously reported in the first such Form 8-K.

For further information relating to the requirements for reporting a change in a registrant's independent accountants (including the rules issued by the SEC Practice Section of the AICPA), refer to sections 63040 and 20360.

SEC 41640. Form 8-K

41700. AMENDING REPORTS FILED UNDER THE 1934 ACT

Amendments to reports filed pursuant to Section 12, 13, or 15(d) of the 1934 Act were previously filed under cover of Form 8. Effective April 1993, the SEC changed these rules to require that all such amendments be filed under cover of the form amended, designated by adding the letter "A" after the title of the form, e.g., "Form 10-K/A." Amendments are required to be numbered sequentially and filed separately for each statement or report amended. The information to be attached to the form's cover page need only consist of the part of the document that is to be amended. When amending 1934 Act filings, it is important to note that the complete disclosure item amended is required to be filed, rather than only revised words or lines. For example, a registrant filing an amended Form 10-K to add information to its description of business would restate Item 1 of Form 10-K in its entirety. Since the financial statements and auditors' report are filed under one item, the entire financial statements and auditors' report are required to be resubmitted. Accordingly, in the Form 10-K/A consents are no longer required for amendments to 1934 Act filings. However, a consent to incorporate a 1934 Act filing into an existing 1933 Act filing would still be required.

There may be instances in which a Form 10-Q on which a SAS No. 71 interim review report (see section 20350) has been rendered and filed is amended. Since a SAS No. 71 report does not constitute a report contemplated by the consent provisions of the 1933 Act, it is not appropriate for an accountant to consent to its substitution as might be the case in Form 10-K. In such instances it would be appropriate for the auditors to furnish a letter that would be filed with the amendment acknowledging that "they are aware" of the amendment being filed. This letter would be in lieu of the form of consent described in section 20523. See section 20432 for a discussion of awareness letters.

The SEC staff has informally indicated that previously filed interim reports on Form 10-Q that were correct when filed need not be amended for a later change in accounting principles.

41750. FORM 12b-25—
EXTENSION OF TIME FOR
FURNISHING INFORMATION

41760. General

Rule 12b-25 under the 1934 Act provides that a notification form (Form 12b-25) is required to be filed by registrants who are unable to timely file all or any portion of a periodic report due on Form 10-K, 10-KSB, 20-F, 11-K, 10-Q, 10-QSB, or N-SAR. Form 12b-25 is due no later than one day after the due date of the filing form to which it relates. If the delay in filing is caused solely by the independent accountants' inability to complete their audit and to furnish their audit report by the due date, an explanatory statement from the independent accountant needs to be attached to Form 12b-25 as an exhibit. The requirement for this explanatory statement does not apply to financial statement schedules filed by amendment in accordance with General Instruction A to Form 10-K and Form 10-KSB (see section 41180) or to financial statements for unconsolidated subsidiaries and equity persons filed by amendment to Form 10-K and Form 10-KSB in accordance with Rule 3-09 of Regulation S-X (see section 50339).

According to Rule 12b-25, the late 1934 Act report will be considered to have been "timely filed" if (1) the missing information could not have been filed by the due date prescribed in the form without unreasonable effort or expense, (2) the required notification on Form 12b-25 is made, and (3) the missing information is filed (on an amended form (see section 41700)) within the specified period (15 days for Form 10-K and other annual reports, 5 days for Form 10-Q). The significance of the timely filing provision is that the requirements for use of certain forms under the 1933 Act (including Forms S-2 or F-2 and S-3 or F-3) specify that a company must have timely filed all reports required to be filed pursuant to Section 13 or 15(d) of the 1934 Act for a specified period preceding the filing of the registration statement.

It is worthy of particular note that Form 12b-25 should not be used by electronic filers unable to file a report solely due to electronic difficulties. These types of delays are addressed in Regulation S-T which is not included in this manual.

41770. Rule 12b-25

The specific provisions of Rule 12b-25 follow:

Notification of Inability to Timely File All or Any
Required Portion of a Form 10-K, 10-KSB, 20-F, 11-K,
N-SAR, Form 10-Q or Form 10-QSB

(a) If all or any required portion of an annual or transition report on Form 10-K, 10-KSB, 20-F, or 11-K or a quarterly or transition report on Form 10-Q or Form 10-QSB required to be filed pursuant to sections 13 or 15(d) of the Act and the rules thereunder or if all or any portion of a semi-annual, annual or transition report on Form N-SAR required to be filed pursuant to section 30 of the Investment Company Act of 1940 and the rules thereunder is not filed within the time period prescribed for such report, the registrant, no later than one business day after the due date for such report, shall file Form 12b-25 with the Commission which shall contain disclosure of its inability to file the report timely and the reasons therefor in reasonable detail.

(b) With respect to any report or portion of any report described in paragraph (a) of this section which is not timely filed because the registrant is unable to do so without unreasonable effort or expense, such report shall be deemed to be filed on the prescribed due date for such report if:

(1) The registrant files the Form 12b-25 in compliance with paragraph (a) of this section and, when applicable, furnishes the exhibit required by paragraph (c) of this section;

(2) The registrant represents in the Form 12b-25 that:

(i) The reason(s) causing the inability to file timely could not be eliminated by the registrant without unreasonable effort or expense; and

(ii) Either the subject annual report, semi-annual report or transition report or Form 10-K, 10-KSB, 20-F, 11-K or N-SAR, or portion thereof will be filed no later than the fifteenth calendar day following the prescribed due date or the subject quarterly report or transition report on Form 10-Q or Form 10-QSB, or portion thereof will be filed no later than the fifth calendar day following the prescribed due date; and

(3) The report/portion thereof is actually filed within the period specified by paragraph (b)(2)(ii) of this section.

(c) If paragraph (b) of this section is applicable and the reason the subject report/portion thereof cannot be filed timely without unreasonable effort or expense relates to the inability of any person, other than the registrant, to furnish any required opinion, report or certification, the Form 12b-25 shall have attached as an exhibit a statement signed by such person stating the specific reasons why such person is unable to furnish the required opinion, report or certification on or before the date such report must be filed.

(d) Notwithstanding paragraph (b) of this section, a registrant will not be eligible to use any registration statement form under the Securities Act of 1933 the use of which is predicated on timely filed reports until the subject report is actually filed pursuant to paragraph (b)(3) of this section.

(e) If a Form 12b-25 filed pursuant to paragraph (a) of this section relates only to a portion of a subject report, the registrant shall:

(1) File the balance of such report and indicate on the cover page thereof which disclosure items are omitted; and

(2) Include, on the upper right corner of the amendment to the report (required to be filed on Form 8) which includes the previously omitted information, the following statement: [Note: Form 8 has been rescinded. Amendments should be filed under cover of the form amended, designated by adding the letter "A" after the title of the form, e.g., "Form 10-K/A" (see section 41700).]

The following items were the subject of a Form 12b-25 and are included herein: (List Item Numbers)

(f) The provisions of this section shall not apply to financial statements to be filed by amendment to a Form 10-K and Form 10-KSB as provided for by paragraph (a) Rule 3-09 of Regulation S-X or schedules to be filed by amendment in accordance with General Instruction A to Form 10-K and Form 10-KSB.

(g) Electronic filings. The provisions of this section shall not apply to reports required to be filed in electronic format if the sole reason the report is not filed within the time period prescribed is that the filer is unable to file the report in electronic format. Filers unable to submit a report in electronic format within the time period prescribed solely due to difficulties with electronic filing should comply with either Rule 201 or 202 of Regulation S-T, or apply for an adjustment of filing date pursuant to Rule 13(c) of Regulation S-T.

SEC 41770. Form 12b-25

41780. Text of Form 12b-25

The text of Form 12b-25 follows.

U.S. SECURITIES AND EXCHANGE COMMISSION
WASHINGTON, D.C. 20549

FORM 12b-25 NOTIFICATION OF LATE FILING

(Check One):

[ ] Form 10-K or Form 10-KSB [ ] Form 20-F [ ] Form 11-K [ ] Form 10-Q or Form 10-QSB [ ] Form N-SAR

For Period Ended: . . . .

[ ] Transition Report on Form 10-K or Form 10-KSB
[ ] Transition Report on Form 20-F
[ ] Transition Report on Form 11-K
[ ] Transition Report on Form 10-Q or Form 10-QSB
[ ] Transition Report on Form N-SAR

For the Transition Period Ended: . . . .

Read Attached Instruction Sheet Before Preparing Form. Please Print or Type.

Nothing in this form shall be construed to imply that the Commission has verified any information contained herein.

If the notification relates to a portion of the filing checked above, identify the Item(s) to which the notification relates: . . . .

Part I-Registrant Information

Full Name of Registrant
Former Name If Applicable
Address of Principal Executive Office *(Street and Number)*
City, State and Zip Code

Part II-Rules 12b-25(b) and (c)

If the subject report could not be filed without unreasonable effort or expense and the registrant seeks relief pursuant to Rule 12b-25(b), the following should be completed. (Check box if appropriate.)

[ ] (a)The reasons described in reasonable detail in Part III of this form could not be eliminated without unreasonable effort or expense;

[ ] (b)The subject annual report, semi-annual report, transition report on Form 10-K or Form 10-KSB, Form 20-F, 11-K or Form N-SAR, or portion thereof will be filed on or before the fifteenth calendar day following the prescribed due date; or the subject quarterly report or transition report on Form 10-Q or Form 10-QSB, or portion thereof will be filed on or before the fifth calendar day following the prescribed due date; and

[ ] (c)The accountant's statement or other exhibit required by the Rule 12b-25(c) has been attached if applicable.

Part III-Narrative

State below in reasonable detail the reasons why the Form 10-K and Form 10-KSB, 20-F, 11-K, 10-Q and Form 10-QSB, N-SAR or the transition report or portion thereof could not be filed within the prescribed time period.

(Attach Extra Sheets If Needed)

[Note: In general, statements used in the narrative to explain reasons for a delayed filing are relatively standard and brief.]

Part IV-Other Information

(1) Name and telephone number of person to contact in regard to this notification.

. . . .
   (Name)   (Area Code)   (Telephone Number)

(2) Have all other periodic reports required under Section 13 or 15(d) of the Securities Exchange Act of 1934 or Section 30 of the Investment Company Act of 1940 during the preceding 12 months or for such shorter period that the registrant was required to file such report(s) been filed? If answer is no identify report(s).   [ ] Yes [ ] No

SEC 41780. Form 12b-25

(3) Is it anticipated that any significant change in results of   [ ] Yes [ ] No
operations from the corresponding period for the last fiscal
year will be reflected by the earnings statements to be included in the subject report or portion thereof?

If so: attach an explanation of the anticipated change, both narratively and
quantitatively, and, if appropriate, state the reasons why a reasonable estimate of
the results cannot be made.

. . . .
(Name of Registrant as specified in charter)

has caused this notification to be signed on its behalf by the undersigned thereunto
duly authorized.

Date . . . .   By . . . .

*INSTRUCTION: The form may be signed by an executive officer of the registrant
or by any other duly authorized representative. The name and title of the person
signing the form shall be typed or printed beneath the signature. If the statement is
signed on behalf of the registrant by an authorized representative (other than an
executive officer), evidence of the representative's authority to sign on behalf of the
registrant shall be filed with the form.*

ATTENTION

*Intentional misstatements or omissions of fact constitute Federal Criminal
Violations (see 18 U.S. C. 1001).*

GENERAL INSTRUCTIONS

*1. This Form is required by Rule 12b-25 of the General Rules and Regulations
under the Securities Exchange Act of 1934.*

*2. One signed original and four conformed copies of this Form and amendments
thereto must be completed and filed with the Securities and Exchange Commission, Washington, D.C. 20549, in accordance with Rule 0-3 of the General Rules
and Regulations under the Act. The information contained in or filed with the
Form will be made a matter of the public record in the Commission files.*

*3. A manually signed copy of the form and amendments thereto shall be filed
with each national securities exchange on which any class of securities of the
registrant is registered.*

SEC 41780

4. *Amendments to the notifications must also be filed on Form 12b-25 but need not restate information that has been correctly furnished. The form shall be clearly identified as an amended notification.*

5. *Electronic Filers. This form shall not be used by electronic filers unable to timely file a report solely due to electronic difficulties. Filers unable to submit a report within the time period prescribed due to difficulties in electronic filing should comply with either Rule 201 or Rule 202 of Regulation S-T or apply for an adjustment in filing date pursuant to Rule 13(b) of Regulation S-T.*

SEC 41780. Form 12b-25

41800. FORM 10

41810. General

Form 10 is used by registrants for the registration under Section 12(b) or (g) of the 1934 Act (see section 11030) of a class of securities for which no other form is prescribed. It is generally used by issuers that do not have securities already registered under Section 12(b) or (g) or are not currently required to report under Section 15(d). For instance, Form 10 may be filed when a company only wants to list securities on a national stock exchange or when a company grows and is required to register pursuant to Section 12(g) (see section 19500); however, these instances are rare.

The information to be furnished in Form 10 is similar to that required in Form S-1. The following are the items of information required to be included:

Item

1	Business
2	Financial information
3	Properties
4	Security ownership of certain beneficial owners and management
5	Directors and executive officers
6	Executive compensation
7	Certain relationships and related transactions
8	Legal proceedings
9	Market price of and dividends on the registrant's common equity and related stockholder matters
10	Recent sales of unregistered securities
11	Description of registrant's securities to be registered
12	Indemnification of directors and officers
13	Financial statements and supplementary data
14	Changes in and disagreements with accountants on accounting and financial disclosure
15	Financial statements and exhibits

With the exception of the financial statements and financial statement schedules, the requirements for each of the items of information in Form 10 are set forth in Regulation S-K. (See discussion beginning with section 60000.)

41820. Financial Statement Requirements

The form and content of and requirements for the financial statements and financial statement schedules to be included in this form and the dates and periods for which they are required to be presented are set forth in Regulation S-X. A discussion of these requirements is included beginning with section 50050 of this manual.

For quick reference, the dates and periods for which financial statements are required (Rules 3-01, 3-02, and 3-04 of Regulation S-X) are summarized as follows:

Balance Sheets	Statements of Income, Cash Flows, and Stockholders' Equity	Financial Statement Schedules
As of the end of each of the two latest fiscal years.	For each of the three latest fiscal years.	Required as applicable in support of primary financial statements.

Interim financial statements may also be required in Form 10 depending on the age of the financial statements at the filing date (see section 50304).

The term "financial statement schedules" covers financial statements required in addition to the primary financial statements prescribed by Rules 3-01, 3-02, and 3-04, as well as the various supporting schedules prescribed by Rule 5-04 of Regulation S-X. The dates and periods to be covered by the additional financial statements are generally the same as those prescribed for the primary financial statements. The dates and periods to be covered by the various supporting schedules, which vary depending on their nature, are specified in Rule 5-04.

41821. Entities (Persons) for Which Financial Statements May Be Required.

The following are the various financial statements that may need to be furnished in a filing on Form 10 and the sections of the manual where the respective requirements are discussed:

Description	Section
Registrant and its consolidated subsidiaries	50302
Registrant alone (parent company — Schedule III)	50520
Unconsolidated subsidiaries and 50% or less owned persons	50339
Businesses acquired or to be acquired	50314
Affiliates whose securities are pledged as collateral	50344
Guarantors of securities registered	50344

41850. FORM 10-SB

41860. General

Form 10-SB may be used by a "small business issuer" when entering the Small Business Disclosure System to register its securities under Section 12(b) or 12(g) of the 1934 Act (see section 70000). Item 10(a) of Regulation S-B (see section 70000) contains further information as to eligibility to use Form 10-SB. Similar to Form 10 (see section 41800), Form 10-SB may be filed when a "small business issuer" only wants to list securities on a national stock exchange or when a "small business issuer" grows and is required to register pursuant to Section 12(g) (see section 19500); however, these instances are rare.

Small business issuers that were not previously subject to the reporting require-ments of Section 13 or 15(d) of the 1934 Act have the option to use any of the three alternative disclosure models of Part I of Form 10-SB. Irrespective of the disclosure model used in Part I, all registrants are required to complete Parts II and III and furnish the financial statements required in Part F/S. It is important to note, however, that Alternative 1 of Part I is not considered to be a "transitional disclosure format." Accordingly, small business issuers that elect Alternative 1 are not eligible to use the transitional disclosure formats in Forms 10-KSB (see section 41200), 10-QSB (see section 41500) and SB-1 (see section 42600).

The following are the alternative disclosure models of Part I and the other items of information required to be included in Form 10-SB (unless otherwise designated, the Item numbers refer to Regulation S-B, the requirements of which are covered in more detail in section 70000 of this manual):

PART I

Alternative 1

Corporate issuers may elect to furnish the information required by Questions 1, 3, 4, 11, 14-20, 28-43, 45, and 47-50 of Model A of Form 1-A.

Alternative 2

Any issuer may elect to furnish the information required by Items 6-12 of Model B of Form 1-A.

Alternative 3

Any issuer may elect to furnish the following information:

Item

1	Description of Business (Item 101)
2	Management's Discussion and Analysis or Plan of Operation (Item 303)
3	Description of Property (Item 102)
4	Security Ownership of Certain Beneficial Owners and Management (Item 403)
5	Directors, Executive Officers, Promoters and Control Persons (Item 401)
6	Executive Compensation (Item 402)
7	Certain Relationships and Related Transactions (Item 404)
8	Description of Securities (Item 202)

PART II

1	Market Price of and Dividends on the Registrant's Common Equity and Other Shareholder Matters (Item 201)
2	Legal Proceedings (Item 103) (Note: This item is not required for registrants using Alternative 1 of Part I.)
3	Changes in and Disagreements with Accountants (Item 304, if applicable)
4	Recent Sales of Unregistered Securities (Item 701)
5	Indemnification of Directors and Officers (Item 702)

PART F/S

The information required by Item 310 of Regulation S-B needs to be furnished. However, only the financial statements for the most recent fiscal year are required to be audited if audited financial statements of (a) the registrant and its predecessors and (b) any significant business acquired or to be acquired are not otherwise available.

PART III

Item

1	Index to Exhibits
2	Description of Exhibits

SEC 41860. Form 10-SB

41900. CHANGE IN FISCAL YEAR

41910. 1934 Act Reporting Requirements

When an issuer whose securities are registered under Section 12 of the 1934 Act changes its fiscal year, a transition period report containing financial statements may need to be filed, depending on the circumstances. Rule 13a-10 of the 1934 Act, which was revised in March 1989 by FRR No. 35, deals with the transition reporting requirements in such situations. A similar rule (Rule 15d-10) is applicable to companies registered under the 1933 Act that are required to file reports pursuant to Section 15(d) of the 1934 Act. The full text of Rule 13a-10 is provided in section 41917.

Under the SEC's change in fiscal year rules, the period from the end of the most recently concluded fiscal year to the beginning of the new fiscal year is referred to as the "transition period," and the filing covering this period is known as the "transition report." The rules specify that separate transition reports are required for all transition periods exceeding one month. It is worthy of particular note that an annual report (e.g., Form 10-K or Form 10-KSB) for fiscal years ended before the decision date to change fiscal year-ends is required to be filed, and that in no event may a transition report cover 12 or more months.

For transition periods of six or more months, an annual report, including audited financial statements and all textual disclosures, needs to be filed within 90 days after the later of the election to change the fiscal year or the close of the transition period. The annual report is also required to include either financial statements for the comparable period of the prior year (that may be unaudited) or a footnote (that may be unaudited) disclosing revenues, gross profits, income taxes, income/(loss) from continuing operations before extraordinary items, cumulative effect of a change in accounting principles, and net income/(loss) from the comparable period of the prior year. If applicable, the effects of discontinued operations and/or extraordinary items are also required to be disclosed.

For transition periods shorter than six months and greater than one month, issuers have the option to file a transition report on either an annual report (as discussed above) or Form 10-Q or Form 10-QSB (including either audited or unaudited financial statements). If Form 10-Q or Form 10-QSB is used in this type of situation and *unaudited* financial statements are included, separate audited statements of income and cash flows for the transition period are required to be included in the annual report filed covering the first 12 months of the new fiscal year. The notes to financial

300

statements for the transition period may be integrated with the notes for the full fiscal period. A separate audited balance sheet as of the end of the transition period would need to be filed in the annual report only if the audited balance sheet as of the end of the fiscal year prior to the transition period is not filed. Schedules are not required to be included in transition report filings on Form 10-Q or 10-QSB.

Transition reports on Form 10-Q or 10-QSB are due within 45 days after the close of the transition period or after the date of the determination to change the fiscal year, whichever is later.

Information for periods of one month or less may be included in either the issuer's next Form 10-Q or 10-QSB or annual report.

Issuers have the option of filing Form 10-Qs or 10-QSBs for quarters that end in the transition period on the basis of either the old or new fiscal year. However, issuers are required to file a quarterly report for any quarter of the old fiscal year that ended before the date of the issuer's determination to change its year-end. The requirement to file quarterly reports on the new basis begins with the first quarter in the new fiscal year that ends after the issuer determined to change its year-end. The change in quarterly reporting from the old to the new fiscal year may result in a period of less than three months that is not covered by a separate report on Form 10-Q or 10-QSB. Rule 13a-10 specifies that unless such a period of less than three months is or will be covered in the issuer's transition report or in the first annual report for the newly adopted fiscal year, separate financial statements covering such period need to be included in the issuer's initial report on Form 10-Q or 10-QSB for the newly adopted fiscal year.

When it is not practicable or cost justifiable to include financial statements for corresponding periods of the prior year in a transition report on Form 10-Q or 10-QSB or in a quarterly report for the new fiscal year, Rule 13a-10 provides that financial statements may be included for the most nearly comparable quarters of the earlier year. In such cases the issuer is required to furnish:

- A discussion of seasonal and other factors that could affect the comparability of information or trends reflected.

- An assessment of the comparability of the data.

- A representation as to the reason recasting has not been undertaken.

An issuer is required to report a change in fiscal year on Form 8-K, describing the Form (e.g., 10-K or 10-Q) on which the transition report will be filed and the date on which the determination was made to change its fiscal year-end. The Form 8-K is required to be filed within 15 days after the determination date.

SEC 41910

41915. Successor Issuers. A successor issuer that has a different fiscal year-end from that of its predecessor is required to file a transition report covering the predecessor for any transition period between the close of the fiscal year covered by its last annual report and the date of succession. The reporting requirements are the same as those discussed above for changes in fiscal year-end of registrants, except that the due dates of the required reports are determined based on the date of succession.

41916. Foreign Private Issuers. A foreign private issuer (see section 50353) that elects to change its fiscal year-end date would fulfill its transition reporting requirements through its filings on Form 20-F.

For transition periods exceeding six months, foreign registrants are required to file a complete Form 20-F and include therein audited financial statements covering the transition period, the same as domestic issuers. This Form 20-F is due within six months after the close of the transition period or the date the determination to change the fiscal year is made, whichever is later.

For transition periods of six months or less, the financial statements included in transition reports on Form 20-F need not be audited, and much of the textual information required by Form 20-F can be omitted. This report is due within three months after the end of the transition period or the date on which the election to change the fiscal year is made, whichever is later. In these situations the financial statements would need to be included on an audited basis in the first Form 20-F for the newly adopted fiscal year.

When the transition period is one month or less, a separate transition report is not required if the first Form 20-F for the newly adopted fiscal year covers the transition period as well as the new fiscal year.

41917. Text of Requirements.

Rule 13a-10—Transition Reports

(a) Every issuer that changes its fiscal closing date shall file a report covering the resulting transition period between the closing date of its most recent fiscal year and the opening date of its new fiscal year; Provided, however, that an issuer shall file an annual report for any fiscal year that ended before the date on which the issuer determined to change its fiscal year end. In no event shall the transition report cover a period of 12 or more months.

(b) The report pursuant to this section shall be filed for the transition period not more than 90 days after either the close of the transition period or the date of the determination to change the fiscal closing date, whichever is later. The report shall be filed on the form appropriate for annual reports of the issuer, shall cover the period from the close of the last fiscal year end and shall indicate clearly the period covered. The financial statements for the transition period filed therewith shall be audited. Financial statements, which may be unaudited, shall be filed for the comparable period of the prior year, or a footnote, which may be unaudited, shall state for the comparable period of the prior year, revenues, gross profits, income taxes, income or loss from continuing operations before extraordinary items and cumulative effect of a change in accounting principles and net income or loss. The effects of any discontinued operations and/or extraordinary items as classified under the provisions of generally accepted accounting principles also shall be shown, if applicable. Per share data based upon such income or loss and net income or loss shall be presented in conformity with applicable accounting standards. Where called for by the time span to be covered, the comparable period financial statements or footnote shall be included in subsequent filings.

(c) If the transition period covers a period of less than six months, in lieu of the report required by paragraph (b) of this section, a report may be filed for the transition period on Form 10-Q and Form 10-QSB not more than 45 days after either the close of the transition period or the date of the determination to change the fiscal closing date, whichever is later. The report on Form 10-Q and Form 10-QSB shall cover the period from the close of the last fiscal year end and shall indicate clearly the period covered. The financial statements filed therewith need not be audited but, if they are not audited, the issuer shall file with the first annual report for the newly adopted fiscal year separate audited statements of income and cash flows covering the transition period. The notes to financial statements for the transition period included in such first annual report may be integrated with the notes to financial statements for the full fiscal period. A separate audited balance sheet as of the end of the transition period shall be filed in the annual report only if the audited balance sheet as of the end of the fiscal year prior to the transition period is not filed. Schedules need not be filed in transition reports on Form 10-Q and Form 10-QSB.

(d) Notwithstanding the foregoing in paragraphs (a), (b), and (c) of this section, if the transition period covers a period of one month or less, the issuer need not file a separate transition report if either:

(1) The first report required to be filed by the issuer for the newly adopted fiscal year after the date of the determination to change the fiscal year end is an annual report, and that report covers the transition period as well as the fiscal year; or

(2) (i) the issuer files with the first annual report for the newly adopted fiscal year separate audited statements of income and cash flows covering the transition period; and

(ii) the first report required to be filed by the issuer for the newly adopted fiscal year after the date of the determination to change the fiscal year end is a quarterly report on Form 10-Q and Form 10-QSB; and

(iii) information on the transition period is included in the issuer's quarterly report on Form 10-Q and Form 10-QSB for the first quarterly period (except the fourth quarter) of the newly adopted fiscal year that ends after the date of the determination to change the fiscal year. The information covering the transition period required by Part II and Item 2 of Part I may be combined with the information regarding the quarter. However, the financial statements required by Part I, which may be unaudited, shall be furnished separately for the transition period.

(e) Every issuer required to file quarterly reports on Form 10-Q and Form 10-QSB pursuant to 1934 Act Rule 13a-13 that changes its fiscal year end shall:

(1) file a quarterly report on Form 10-Q and Form 10-QSB within the time period specified in General Instruction A.1. to that form for any quarterly period (except the fourth quarter) of the old fiscal year that ends before the date on which the issuer determined to change its fiscal year end, except that the issuer need not file such quarterly report if the date on which the quarterly period ends also is the date on which the transition period ends;

(2) file a quarterly report on Form 10-Q within the time specified in General Instruction A.1. to that form for each quarterly period of the old fiscal year within the transition period. In lieu of a quarterly report for any quarter of the old fiscal year within the transition period, the issuer may file a quarterly report on Form 10-Q and Form 10-QSB for any period of three months within the transition period that coincides with a quarter of the newly adopted fiscal year if the quarterly report is filed within 45 days after the end of such three month period, provided the issuer thereafter continues filing quarterly reports on the basis of the quarters of the newly adopted fiscal year;

(3) commence filing quarterly reports for the quarters of the new fiscal year no later than the quarterly report for the first quarter of the new fiscal year that ends after the date on which the issuer determined to change the fiscal year end; and

(4) unless such information is or will be included in the transition report, or the first annual report on Form 10-K and Form 10-KSB for the newly adopted fiscal year, include in the initial quarterly report on Form 10-Q and Form 10-QSB for the newly adopted fiscal year information on any period beginning on the first day subsequent to the period covered by the issuer's final quarterly report on Form 10-Q and Form 10-QSB or annual report on Form 10-K and Form 10-KSB for the old fiscal year. The information covering such period required by Part II and Item 2 of Part I may be combined with the information regarding the quarter. However, the financial statements required by Part I, which may be unaudited, shall be furnished separately for such period.

Note to paragraphs (c) and (e): If it is not practicable or cannot be cost-justified to furnish in a transition report on Form 10-Q or a quarterly report for the newly adopted fiscal year financial statements for corresponding periods of the prior year where required, financial statements may be furnished for the quarters of the preceding fiscal year that most nearly are comparable if the issuer furnishes an adequate discussion of seasonal and other factors that could affect the comparability of information or trends reflected, an assessment of the comparability of the data, and a representation as to the reason recasting has not been undertaken.

(f) Every successor issuer with securities registered under Section 12 of this Act that has a different fiscal year from that of its predecessor(s) shall file a transition report pursuant to this section, containing the required information about each predecessor, for the transition period, if any, between the close of the fiscal year covered by the last annual report of each predecessor and the date of succession. The report shall be filed for the transition period on the form appropriate for annual reports of the issuer not more than 90 days after the date of the succession, with financial statements in conformity with the requirements set forth in paragraph (b) of this section. If the transition period covers a period of less than six months, in lieu of a transition report on the form appropriate for the issuer's annual reports, the report may be filed for the transition period on Form 10-Q and Form 10-QSB not more than 45 days after the date of the succession, with financial statements in conformity with the requirements set forth in paragraph (c) of this section. Notwithstanding the foregoing, if the transition period covers a period of one month or less, the successor issuer need not file a separate transition report if the information is reported by the successor issuer in conformity with the requirements set forth in paragraph (d) of this section.

(g)(1) Paragraphs (a) through (f) of this section shall not apply to foreign private issuers.

(2) Every foreign private issuer that changes its fiscal closing date shall file a report covering the resulting transition period between the closing date of its most recent fiscal year and the opening date of its new fiscal year. In no event shall a transition report cover a period longer than 12 months.

(3) The report for the transition period shall be filed on Form 20-F responding to all items to which such issuer is required to respond when Form 20-F is used as an annual report. Such report shall be filed within six months after either the close of the transition period or the date on which the issuer made the determination to change the fiscal closing date, whichever is later. The financial statements for the transition period filed therewith shall be audited.

(4) If the transition period covers a period of six or fewer months, in lieu of the report required by paragraph (g)(3) of this section, a report for the transition period may be filed on Form 20-F responding to Items 3, 9, 15, 16, and 17 or 18 within three months after either the close of the transition period or the date on which the issuer made the determination to change the fiscal closing date, whichever is later. The financial statements required by either Item 17 or Item 18 shall be furnished for the transition period. Such financial statements may be unaudited and condensed as permitted in Article 10 of Regulation S-X, but if the financial statements are unaudited and condensed, the issuer shall file with the first annual report for the newly adopted fiscal year separate audited statements of income and cash flows covering the transition period.

(5) Notwithstanding the foregoing in paragraphs (g)(2), (g)(3), and (g)(4) of this section, if the transition period covers a period of one month or less, a foreign private issuer need not file a separate transition report if the first annual

report for the newly adopted fiscal year covers the transition period as well as the fiscal year.

(h) The provisions of this rule shall not apply to investment companies required to file reports pursuant to Rule 30b1-1 under the Investment Company Act of 1940.

(i) No filing fee shall be required for a transition report filed pursuant to this section.

Note: In addition to the report or reports required to be filed pursuant to this section, every issuer, except a foreign private issuer or an investment company required to file reports pursuant to Rule 30b1-1 under the Investment Company Act of 1940, that changes its fiscal closing date is required to file a report on Form 8-K responding to Item 8 thereof within the period specified in General Instruction B.1. to that form.

41920. Reports Following Change in Fiscal Year

Questions frequently arise about the appropriate manner of reporting following a change in fiscal year. The following examples illustrate how various registrants might report to the SEC after a change in fiscal year resulting in interim periods of different lengths. These examples, which have been derived from those provided in FRR No. 35, focus on the effect of the change in fiscal year on the transition reports on Forms 10-Q and 10-K filed after the decision to change has been made.

In all of these examples, it is assumed that the registrant is a domestic issuer with a December 31 year-end date that files periodic reports pursuant to Section 13 or 15(d) of the 1934 Act. Although not addressed in these examples, the requirements regarding comparative financial information also need to be considered in each of the respective filings. These requirements are discussed in section 41910 and in the text of requirements in section 41917, paragraph (b), and the note to paragraphs (c) and (e).

Example A. A decision is made early in the year to change the year-end to a date already past with a resulting transition period of one month or less.

On March 1, 1994 the issuer decides to change its year-end to January 31, 1994. The following filings are required:

- Form 8-K 15 days after March 1, 1994.

- Form 10-K covering the full year ended December 31, 1993, 90 days after December 31, 1993.

- Although a separate transition report is not required, at the option of the issuer, either Form 10-Q covering the transition period 45 days after March 1, 1994 or Form 10-K covering the transition period 90 days after March 1, 1994.

- Form 10-Q covering the first quarter of the new fiscal year 45 days after April 30, 1994; if the issuer has not opted to file a separate transition report on either Form 10-Q or 10-K, the transition period must be covered in this Form 10-Q including separate financial statements, which may be unaudited.

- Form 10-Qs covering the quarters ending July 31, 1994 and October 31, 1994, 45 days after the end of the quarter.

- Form 10-K covering the full year ending January 31, 1995; if the issuer has not opted to file a separate transition report on Form 10-K, this Form 10-K must include separate audited financial statements covering the transition period.

Example B. A decision is made early in the year to change the year-end to a date already past with a resulting transition period shorter than six months but longer than one month.

On March 1, 1994 the issuer decides to change its year-end to February 28, 1994. The following filings are required:

- Form 8-K 15 days after March 1, 1994.

- Form 10-K covering the full year ended December 31, 1993, 90 days after December 31, 1993.

- Either Form 10-Q covering the transition period 45 days after March 1, 1994, or Form 10-K covering the transition period 90 days after March 1, 1994.

- Form 10-Q covering the first quarter of the new fiscal year 45 days after May 31, 1994.

- Form 10-Qs covering the quarters ending August 31, 1994 and November 30, 1994, 45 days after the end of the quarter.

- Form 10-K covering the full year ending February 28, 1995; if the transition report was filed on Form 10-Q, this Form 10-K must include separate audited financial statements covering the transition period.

SEC 41920

Example C. A decision is made early in the year to change the year-end to a future date with a resulting transition period shorter than six months but longer than one month.

On February 1, 1994 the issuer decides to change its year-end to May 31, 1994. The following filings are required:

- Form 8-K 15 days after February 1, 1994.

- Form 10-K covering the full year ended December 31, 1993, 90 days after December 31, 1993.

- Form 10-Q covering either the quarter ending February 28, 1994 of the new fiscal year, or the quarter ending March 31, 1994 of the old fiscal year, either of which is due 45 days after the quarter end.

- Either Form 10-Q covering the transition period 45 days after May 31, 1994 or Form 10-K covering the transition period 90 days after May 31, 1994.

- Form 10-Q covering the first quarter of the new fiscal year 45 days after August 31, 1994.

- Form 10-Qs covering the quarters ending November 30, 1994 and February 28, 1995, 45 days after the end of the quarter.

- Form 10-K covering the full year ending May 31, 1995; if the transition report was filed on Form 10-Q, this Form 10-K must include separate audited financial statements covering the transition period.

Example D. A decision is made early in the year to change the year-end to a future date with a resulting transition period of six months or longer.

On February 1, 1994 the issuer decides to change its year-end to September 30, 1994. The following filings are required:

- Form 8-K 15 days after February 1, 1994.

- Form 10-K covering the full year ended December 31, 1993, 90 days after December 31, 1993.

- Form 10-Qs covering the quarters ending March 31, 1994 and June 30, 1994, 45 days after the end of the quarter.

SEC 41920

- Form 10-K covering the transition period 90 days after September 30, 1994.

- Form 10-Q covering the first quarter of the new fiscal year 45 days after December 31, 1994.

Example E. A decision is made late in the year to change the year-end to a date already past with a resulting transition period of one month or shorter.

On September 1, 1994 the issuer decides to change its year-end to January 31, 1994. The following filings are required:

- Form 8-K 15 days after September 1, 1994.

- Although a separate transition report is not required, at the option of the issuer, either Form 10-Q covering the transition period 45 days after September 1, 1994 or Form 10-K covering the transition period 90 days after September 1, 1994.

- Form 10-Q covering the first quarter of the new fiscal year 45 days after October 31, 1994; if the issuer has not opted to file a separate transition report on either Form 10-Q or 10-K, the transition period must be covered in this Form 10-Q including separate financial statements, which may be unaudited. This Form 10-Q must also cover and include separate financial statements for the period from July 1, 1994 to July 31, 1994.

- Form 10-K covering the full year ending January 31, 1995; if the issuer has not opted to file a separate transition report on Form 10-K, this Form 10-K must include separate audited financial statements covering the transition period.

Example F. A decision is made late in the year to change the year-end to a date already past with a resulting transition period shorter than six months but longer than one month.

On November 1, 1994 the issuer decides to change its year-end to February 28, 1994. The following filings are required:

- Form 8-K 15 days after November 1, 1994.

- Form 10-Q covering the quarter ending September 30, 1994 of the old fiscal year, 45 days after September 30, 1994.

SEC 41920

- Either Form 10-Q covering the transition period 45 days after November 1, 1994, or Form 10-K covering the transition period 90 days after November 1, 1994.

- Form 10-K covering the full year ended December 31, 1993 90 days after December 31, 1993.

- Form 10-Q covering the third quarter of the new fiscal year 45 days after November 30, 1994.

- Form 10-K covering the full year ending February 28, 1995; if the transition report was filed on Form 10-Q, this Form 10-K must include separate audited financial statements covering the transition period.

Example G. A decision is made late in the year to change the year-end to a date already past with a resulting transition period of six months or longer.

On November 1, 1994 the issuer decides to change its year-end to September 30, 1994. The following filings are required:

- Form 8-K 15 days after November 1, 1994.

- Form 10-K covering the transition period 90 days after November 1, 1994.

- Form 10-Q covering the first quarter of the new fiscal year 45 days after December 31, 1994.

Example H. A decision is made late in the year to change the year-end to a date already past with a resulting transition period of six months or longer where fiscal quarters of the newly adopted year do not coincide with those of the old fiscal year.

On November 20, 1994 the issuer decides to change its year-end to August 31, 1994. The following filings are required:

- Form 8-K 15 days after November 20, 1994.

- Form 10-Q covering the first quarter of the new fiscal year 45 days after November 30, 1994.

- Form 10-K covering the transition period 90 days after November 20, 1994.

SEC 41920

42000. REGISTRATION FORMS UNDER THE 1933 ACT

The SEC has adopted a revised framework for registration under the 1933 Act as part of its integrated disclosure system. An underlying concept of this system is that the form that a registrant is eligible to use should depend on its following in the marketplace, its periodic reporting history, and the nature of the transaction involved.

Form S-1, which requires the inclusion of all necessary information in the prospectus, is intended to be used primarily by first-time registrants and those that have been public companies for less than three years.

Form S-2, which is available to registrants that meet a three-year reporting requirement and certain other criteria (see section 42200), provides for the incorporation by reference of the registrant's 1934 Act reports. In addition, registrants using this form are required to furnish certain registrant-related information to investors either by including the information in the prospectus or by delivering the annual shareholder report and subsequent interim reports to offerees with the prospectus.

Form S-3 is available to registrants that have been subject to 1934 Act reporting requirements for at least 12 months (except for offerings of investment grade asset-backed securities (defined in section 42260) for which there is no reporting history requirement) and that meet certain market value or debt rating tests (see section 42250). The form relies principally on the registrant's 1934 Act reports and requires the incorporation by reference of the registrant-related information from these reports. Disclosure in the prospectus is generally limited to information relating to the offering.

Form S-4 employs the principles underlying the integrated disclosure system to securities registered in connection with business combination transactions. The form provides the same means of delivering information and eliminating duplicative disclosure by permitting incorporation by reference of information included in 1934 Act reports of the issuer and/or the target company depending on whether the issuer or the company being acquired is permitted to register securities in a primary offering on Form S-1, S-2, or S-3.

The SEC has adopted a similar disclosure framework applicable to foreign registrants using Forms F-1, F-2, F-3, and F-4 (see section 45000).

The SEC has also adopted an integrated disclosure system for "small business issuers" under Regulation S-B (see section 70000). Form SB-1 is available to any nonreporting small business issuer, or any reporting small business issuer eligible to use the transitional format in Form 10-KSB (see section 41200), provided that the small business issuer has not registered more than $10 million of securities in any continuous 12-month period. Form SB-2 (see section 42700) is available to be used by small business issuers that do not qualify to register on Form SB-1 to register securities to be sold for cash. In conjunction with the issuance of these rules former 1933 Act Form S-18 was rescinded. Small business issuers are also permitted to register securities on Forms S-2, S-3, S-4, and S-8 using the disclosure requirements of Regulation S-B if they meet the eligibility requirements for use of those forms.

42100. FORM S-1

42110. General

Form S-1 is used for the registration of securities under the 1933 Act by issuers for which no other form is authorized or prescribed. It is the form most commonly used in connection with initial public offerings.

The following are the items of information to be included in Form S-1:

PART I. INFORMATION REQUIRED IN PROSPECTUS

<u>Item</u>

1   Forepart of the registration statement and outside front cover page of prospectus
2   Inside front and outside back cover pages of prospectus
3   Summary information, risk factors and ratio of earnings to fixed charges
4   Use of proceeds
5   Determination of offering price
6   Dilution
7   Selling security holders
8   Plan of distribution
9   Description of securities to be registered
10 Interests of named experts and counsel
11 Information with respect to the registrant
   (a) Description of business
   (b) Description of property
   (c) Legal proceedings
   (d) Market price of and dividends on the registrant's common equity and related stockholder matters, if common equity securities are being offered
   (e) Financial statements
   (f) Selected financial data
   (g) Supplementary financial information
   (h) Management's discussion and analysis of financial condition and results of operations
   (i) Changes in and disagreements with accountants on accounting and financial disclosure
   (j) Directors and executive officers
   (k) Executive compensation

Item

      (l)   Security ownership of certain beneficial owners and management
      (m) Certain relationships and related transactions

12   Disclosure of Commission position on indemnification for Securities Act liabilities

PART II. INFORMATION NOT REQUIRED IN PROSPECTUS

13   Other expenses of issuance and distribution
14   Indemnification of directors and officers
15   Recent sales of unregistered securities
16   Exhibits and financial statement schedules
17   Undertakings

With the exception of the financial statements (Item 11(e)) and financial statement schedules (Item 16), the requirements for each of the items of information in Form S-1 are set forth in Regulation S-K (see discussion beginning with section 60000). An accountants' consent (see sections 17110 and 20510) is also required to be included in Part II of Form S-1 pursuant to Item 601 of Regulation S-K.

42120. Financial Statement Requirements

The form and content of and requirements for the financial statements and schedules to be included in this form and the dates and periods for which they are required to be presented are set forth in Regulation S-X. A discussion of these requirements is included beginning with section 50050 of this manual.

The entities for which financial statements may be required pursuant to Articles 3 and 11 of Regulation S-X are discussed beginning in sections 50300 and 51100, respectively, of this manual.

The supporting schedules required by applicable Regulation S-X Rules 5-04, 6-10, 6A-05, 7-05, and 9-07 (see sections 50520, 50610, 50625, 50705 and 50907, respectively) need to be furnished and included in Part II of the registration statement.

Rule 5-04(b) of Regulation S-X provides that if all of the information required to be presented in a schedule is included in the financial statements or in the notes thereto, the schedule may be omitted. The schedule prescribed by Rule 12-11 (Supplementary Income Statement Information) is not required to be included in the prospectus, but it is often presented in the notes to the financial statements and thus in the prospectus. Any schedules that support an audited balance sheet or audited statement of income are also required to be audited. See section 20300 for examples of supporting schedules that may be reported on.

SEC 42110. Form S-1

42200. FORM S-2

42210. General

Form S-2 is available to registrants that have been subject to 1934 Act reporting requirements for at least three years, but that do not meet the eligibility requirements for the use of Form S-3 (see section 42260). For example, Form S-2 is available for use by certain registrants for primary offerings that do not meet the $75 million market value criteria required by Form S-3 or for nonconvertible security offerings that do not meet the investment grade criteria (see section 42260). Form S-2 may be used for the registration of any securities except those issued in an exchange offer.

The information requirements are the same irrespective of whether an issuer is registering securities on Form S-1, S-2, or S-3. The difference in these forms relates to how and where the information is provided. All information is required to be included in Form S-1 when that form is being filed. For filings made on Form S-2, certain information is required to be included in the form, certain information is incorporated by reference from the registrant's Form 10-K, and certain information is required to either be included in the form or incorporated by reference from the registrant's annual report to shareholders. If the registrant chooses to incorporate by reference information from its annual report to shareholders, the annual report is required to be provided to investors along with the prospectus. For filings made on Form S-3, the majority of the information included in the form relates specifically to that offering and all other required information is incorporated by reference from the registrant's Form 10-K. Due to the incorporation by reference features, Forms S-2 and S-3 are often referred to as "short" forms. It should also be noted that registrants eligible to file on Form S-2 or S-3 may also file on Form S-1.

The eligibility requirements for use of Form S-2 are as follows:

A. The registrant is organized under the laws of the United States or any State or Territory or the District of Columbia and has its principal business operations in the United States or its territories.

B. The registrant has a class of securities registered pursuant to Section 12(b) of the Securities Exchange Act of 1934 ("Exchange Act") or has a class of equity securities registered pursuant to Section 12(g) of the Exchange Act or is required to file reports pursuant to Section 15(d) of the Exchange Act.

C. The registrant: (1) has been subject to the requirements of Section 12 or 15(d) of the Exchange Act and has filed all the material required to be filed pursuant to Sections 13, 14 or 15(d) for a period of at least thirty-six calendar months immediately preceding the filing of the registration statement on this Form; and (2) has filed in a timely manner all reports required to be filed during the twelve calendar months and any portion of a month immediately preceding the filing of the registration statement and, if the registrant has used (during the twelve calendar months and any portion of a month immediately preceding the filing of the registration statement) Rule 12b-25(b) under the Exchange Act with respect to a report or a portion of a report, that report or portion thereof has actually been filed within the time period prescribed by that Rule.

D. Neither the registrant nor any of its consolidated or unconsolidated subsidiaries have, since the end of their last fiscal year for which certified financial statements of the registrant and its consolidated subsidiaries were included in a report filed pursuant to Section 13(a) or 15(d) of the Exchange Act: (a) failed to pay any dividend or sinking fund installment on preferred stock; or (b) defaulted (i) on any installment or installments on indebtedness for borrowed money, or (ii) on any rental on one or more long term leases, which defaults in the aggregate are material to the financial position of the registrant and its consolidated and unconsolidated subsidiaries, taken as a whole.

E. A foreign issuer, other than a foreign government, which satisfies all of the above provisions of these registrant eligibility requirements except the provisions in A. relating to organization and principal business shall be deemed to have met these registrant eligibility requirements provided that such foreign issuer files the same reports with the Commission under Section 13(a) or 15(d) of the Exchange Act as a domestic registrant pursuant to C. above.

F. If a registrant is a successor registrant it shall be deemed to have met conditions A, B, C, and D above if: (1) its predecessor and it, taken together, do so, provided that the succession was primarily for the purpose of changing the state of incorporation of the predecessor or forming a holding company and that the assets and liabilities of the successor at the time of succession were substantially the same as those of the predecessor, or (2) all predecessors met the conditions at the time of succession and the registrant has continued to do so since the succession.

G. If a registrant is a majority-owned subsidiary which does not itself meet the conditions of these eligibility requirements, it shall nevertheless be deemed to have met such conditions if its parent meets the conditions and if the parent fully guarantees the securities being registered as to principal and interest.

Note:

In such an instance the parent-guarantor is the issuer of a separate security consisting of the guarantee which must be concurrently registered but may be registered on the same registration statement as are the guaranteed securities.

H. Electronic filings. In addition to satisfying the foregoing conditions, a registrant subject to the electronic filing requirements of Rule 101 of Regulation S-T shall have filed with the Commission:

SEC 42210. Form S-2

(1) All required electronic filings, including confirming electronic copies of documents submitted in paper pursuant to a temporary hardship exemption as provided in Rule 201 of Regulation S-T; and

(2) All Financial Data Schedules required to be submitted pursuant to Item 601(c) of Regulation S-K and Item 601(c) of Regulation S-B.

Form S-2 *requires* the incorporation by reference of the registrant's 1934 Act reports in the same manner as Form S-3. Unlike Form S-3, however, registrants using this form are also required to deliver a financial disclosure package to investors either by including the information in the prospectus or by delivering the annual shareholder report and subsequent interim reports with the prospectus.

With regard to "small business issuers," Item C under the Application of General Rules and Regulations states:

A "small business issuer," defined in Rule 405 that is eligible to use Form S-2, shall refer to the disclosure items in Regulation S-B and not Regulation S-K. For example, while Item 1 of Form S-2 requires the information required by Item 501 of Regulation S-K, a small business issuer shall provide the information in Item 501 of Regulation S-B. Where Regulation S-B does not contain a comparable Item, for example there is no Item "301" in Regulation S-B, then a small business issuer may omit the Item. A small business issuer shall provide the financial information in Item 310 of Regulation S-B in lieu of the financial information called for by Item 11 of Form S-2.

It is important to note, however, that small business issuers that provided the "Information Required in Annual Report of Transitional Small Business Issuers" in its most recent annual report of Form 10-KSB (see section 41200) are not eligible to use Form S-2.

The following are the items of information to be included in Form S-2:

PART I. INFORMATION REQUIRED IN PROSPECTUS

Item

1	Forepart of the registration statement and outside front cover page of prospectus
2	Inside front and outside back cover pages of prospectus
3	Summary information, risk factors and ratio of earnings to fixed charges
4	Use of proceeds
5	Determination of offering price
6	Dilution
7	Selling security holders
8	Plan of distribution
9	Description of securities to be registered

316

10   Interest of named experts and counsel

11   Information with respect to the registrant [The registrant has an option of either furnishing certain information in the prospectus or incorporating and delivering the registrant's latest annual report to shareholders. See section 42220 for further discussion.]

12   Incorporation of certain information by reference

13   Disclosure of Commission position on indemnification for Securities Act liabilities

PART II. INFORMATION NOT REQUIRED IN PROSPECTUS

14   Other expenses of issuance and distribution

15   Indemnification of directors and officers

16   Exhibits

17   Undertakings

The requirements for Items 1 through 10, 13 through 17, and certain portions of 11 and 12 are set forth in Regulation S-K (see discussion beginning with section 60000). An accountants' consent (see sections 17110 and 20510) is required to be included in Part II of Form S-2 pursuant to Item 601 of Regulation S-K.

42220. Information with Respect to the Registrant

Item 11 of Form S-2 allows two options with respect to furnishing certain information about the registrant. It is important to note, however, that the first option is not available if the registrant meets the conditions of paragraph (c) below. The first option involves delivery with the prospectus of a copy of either the registrant's latest Form 10-K or Form 10-KSB or its latest annual report to shareholders. The following requirements apply if this option is elected:

(a) If the registrant elects to deliver this prospectus together with a copy of either its latest Form 10-K or Form 10-KSB filed pursuant to Sections 13(a) or 15(d) of the Exchange Act or its latest annual report to security holders, which at the time of original preparation met the requirements of either Rule 14a-3 or Rule 14c-3:

(1) Indicate that the prospectus is accompanied by either a copy of the registrant's latest Form 10-K or Form 10-KSB or a copy of its latest annual report to security holders, whichever the registrant elects to deliver pursuant to paragraph (a) of this Item.

(2) Provide financial and other information with respect to the registrant in the form required by Part I of Form 10-Q or Form 10-QSB as of the end of the most recent fiscal quarter which ended after the end of the latest fiscal year for

which certified financial statements were included in the latest Form 10-K or Form 10-KSB or the latest report to security holders (whichever the registrant elects to deliver pursuant to paragraph (a) of this Item), and more than forty-five days prior to the effective date of this registration statement (or as of a more recent date) by one of the following means:

(i) Including such information in the prospectus; or

(ii) Providing without charge to each person to whom a prospectus is delivered a copy of the registrant's latest Form 10-Q or Form 10-QSB; or

(iii) Providing without charge to each person to whom a prospectus is delivered a copy of the registrant's latest quarterly report which was delivered to its shareholders and which included the required financial information.

(3) If not reflected in the registrant's latest Form 10-K or Form 10-KSB or its latest annual report to security holders (whichever the registrant elects to deliver pursuant to paragraph (a) of this Item), provide information required by Rule 3-05 and Article 11 of Regulation S-X.

(4) Describe any and all material changes in the registrant's affairs which have occurred since the end of the latest fiscal year for which certified financial statements were included in the latest Form 10-K or Form 10-KSB or the latest annual report to security holders (whichever the registrant elects to deliver pursuant to paragraph (a) of this Item) and which were not described in a Form 10-Q, Form 10-QSB or quarterly report delivered with the prospectus in accordance with paragraph (a)(2)(ii) or (iii) of this Item.

Instruction. Where the registrant elects to deliver the documents identified in paragraph (a) with a preliminary prospectus, such documents need not be redelivered with the final prospectus.

If the registrant filing Form S-2 elects not to deliver its latest Form 10-K or Form 10-KSB or its annual report to shareholders or if the registrant meets the conditions of paragraph (c) below, the following provisions apply as to information to be included in the prospectus:

(b) If the registrant does not elect to deliver its latest Form 10-K or 10-KSB or its latest annual report to security holders:

(1) Furnish a brief description of the business done by the registrant and its subsidiaries during the most recent fiscal year as required by Rule 14a-3 to be included in annual reports to security holders. The description also should take into account changes in its business which have occurred between the end of the last fiscal year and the effective date of the registration statement.

(2) Include financial statements and information as required by Rule 14a-3(b)(1) to be included in annual reports to security holders as well as: (i) the interim financial information required by Rule 10-01 of Regulation S-X for a filing on Form 10-Q or Form 10-QSB; (ii) any financial information required by Rule 3-05 and Article 11 of Regulation S-X; and (iii) any financial information required because of a material disposition of assets outside the normal course of business. The financial statements shall be restated if there has been a change in accounting principles or a correction of an error where such change or correction requires a material retroactive restatement of financial statements, or where one or more business combinations accounted for by the pooling of interest method of accounting have been consummated subsequent to the most recent fiscal year and the acquired businesses, considered in the aggregate, are significant pursuant to Rule 11-01(b).

(3) Furnish information relating to industry segments, classes of similar products or services, foreign and domestic operations, and export sales required by paragraphs (b), (c)(1)(i) and (d) of Item 101 of Regulation S-K.

(4) Where common equity securities are being offered, furnish information required by Item 201 of Regulation S-K, market price and dividends on the registrant's common stock and related stockholder matters.

(5) Furnish selected financial data required by Item 301 of Regulation S-K.

(6) Furnish supplementary financial information required by Item 302 of Regulation S-K.

(7) Furnish management's discussion and analysis of the registrant's financial condition and results of operations required by Item 303 of Regulation S-K.

(8) Furnish information concerning changes in and disagreements with accountants on accounting and financial disclosure required by Item 304 of Regulation S-K.

As noted in the following paragraph, the registrant is required to provide the information specified in paragraph (b) if it meets certain conditions.

(c) The registrant shall furnish the information required by paragraph (b) of this Item if:

(1) The registrant was required to make a material retroactive restatement of financial statements because of:

(i) A change in accounting principles; or

(ii) A correction of an error; or

(iii) A consummation of one or more business combinations accounted for by the pooling of interest method of accounting was effected subsequent to the most recent fiscal year and the acquired businesses considered in the aggregate meet the test of a significant subsidiary;

SEC 42220. Form S-2

Or

(2) The registrant engaged in a material disposition of assets outside the normal course of business; and

(3) Such restatement of financial statements or disposition of assets was not reflected in the registrant's latest annual report to security holders and/or its latest Form 10-K or Form 10-KSB filed pursuant to Sections 13(a) or 15(d) of the Exchange Act.

42230. Incorporation by Reference

Item 12 of Form S-2 *requires* the incorporation by reference of the following documents irrespective of whether the annual report is delivered or the information is included in the prospectus:

(1) The registrant's latest Form 10-K filed pursuant to Section 13(a) or 15(d) of the Exchange Act which contains certified financial statements for the registrant's latest fiscal year for which a Form 10-K was required to have been filed.

(2) All other reports filed pursuant to Section 13(a) or 15(d) of the Exchange Act since the end of the fiscal year covered by the annual report referred to in (1) above.

If the registrant elects to deliver its annual report to shareholders with the prospectus (see section 42220), the following information is also required to be incorporated by reference from that report:

(i) description of business furnished in accordance with the provisions of Rule 14a-3(b)(6) under the Exchange Act;

(ii) financial statements and information furnished in accordance with the provisions of Rule 14a-3(b)(1);

(iii) information relating to industry segments, classes of similar products or services, foreign and domestic operations, and export sales furnished as required by paragraphs (b), (c)(1)(i) and (d) of Item 101 of Regulation S-K;

(iv) where common equity securities are being offered, market price and dividends on the registrant's common equity and related stockholder matters furnished as required by Item 201 of Regulation S-K;

(v) selected financial data furnished as required by Item 301 of Regulation S-K;

(vi) supplementary financial information furnished as required by Item 302 of Regulation S-K;

(vii) management's discussion and analysis of financial condition and results of operations furnished as required by Item 303 of Regulation S-K; and

SEC 42230

(viii) information concerning changes in and disagreements with accountants on accounting and financial disclosure furnished as required by Item 304 of Regulation S-K.

If the registrant elects to provide a copy of its latest quarterly report to shareholders (see section 41400), the financial information in that document equivalent to that which is required to be presented in Part I of Form 10-Q also needs to be incorporated into Form S-2.

Electronic filers electing to deliver and incorporate by reference all, or any portion, of the quarterly or annual report to security holders are required to file such quarterly or annual report to security holders as an exhibit, or any portion of such report that is incorporated by reference, in electronic format.

SEC 42230. Form S-2

42250. FORM S-3

42260. General

Form S-3 is a short-form registration statement available to registrants that have been subject to 1934 Act reporting requirements for at least 12 months (except for offerings of investment grade asset-backed securities (defined below) for which there is no reporting history requirement) and that meet certain market value or debt-rating tests. For example, primary offerings by certain registrants require that the market value of the outstanding voting stock held by nonaffiliates of the registrant be at least $75 million. In the case of nonconvertible investment grade security offerings, the securities to be offered are required to be in one of the four highest categories of a nationally recognized statistical rating organization, such as Moody's or Standard & Poor's.

Refer to section 42210 (Form S-2) regarding the different information requirements of Forms S-1, S-2, and S-3. Form S-3 has the same eligibility requirements as Form S-2 except for the following:

- The registrant is required to have been subject to the 1934 Act reporting requirements for a period of at least 12 months rather than 36 months.

- There is no reporting history requirement for registered offerings of investment grade asset-backed securities (defined below).

- Certain transaction requirements (described below) are also required to be met.

The eligibility requirements for the use of Form S-3 are as follows.

Eligibility Requirements for Use of Form S-3

This instruction sets forth registrant requirements and transaction requirements for the use of Form S-3. Any registrant which meets the requirements of A. below ("Registrant Requirements") may use this Form for the registration of securities under the Securities Act of 1933 ("Securities Act") which are offered in any transaction specified in B. below ("Transaction Requirements") provided that the requirements applicable to the specified transaction are met. With respect to majority-owned subsidiaries, see Instruction C. below.

A. Registrant Requirements

Registrants must meet the following conditions in order to use this Form for registration under the Securities Act of securities offered in the transactions specified in B. below:

1. The registrant is organized under the laws of the United States or any State or Territory or the District of Columbia and has its principal business operations in the United States or its territories.

2. The registrant has a class of securities registered pursuant to Section 12(b) of the Securities Exchange Act of 1934 ("Exchange Act") or a class of equity securities registered pursuant to Section 12(g) of the Exchange Act or is required to file reports pursuant to Section 15(d) of the Exchange Act.

3. The registrant: (a) has been subject to the requirements of Section 12 or 15(d) of the Exchange Act and has filed all the material required to be filed pursuant to Sections 13, 14 or 15(d) for a period of at least twelve calendar months immediately preceding the filing of the registration statement on this Form; and (b) has filed in a timely manner all reports required to be filed during the twelve calendar months and any portion of a month immediately preceding the filing of the registration statement and, if the registrant has used (during the twelve calendar months and any portion of a month immediately preceding the filing of the registration statement) Rule 12b-25(b) under the Exchange Act with respect to a report or a portion of a report, that report or portion thereof has actually been filed within the time period prescribed by the Rule.

4. The provisions of paragraphs A.2 and A.3(a) above do not apply to any registered offerings of investment grade asset-backed securities as defined in B.5 below.

5. Neither the registrant nor any of its consolidated or unconsolidated subsidiaries have, since the end of the last fiscal year for which certified financial statements of the registrant and its consolidated subsidiaries were included in a report filed pursuant to Section 13(a) or 15(d) of the Exchange Act: (a) failed to pay any dividend or sinking fund installment on preferred stock; or (b) defaulted (i) on any installment or installments on indebtedness for borrowed money, or (ii) on any rental on one or more long term leases, which defaults in the aggregate are material to the financial position of the registrant and its consolidated and unconsolidated subsidiaries, taken as a whole.

6. A foreign issuer, other than a foreign government, which satisfies all of the above provisions of these registrant eligibility requirements except the

SEC 42260. Form S-3

provisions in A.1 relating to organization and principal business shall be deemed to have met these registrant eligibility requirements provided that such foreign issuer files the same reports with the Commission under Section 13(a) or 15(d) of the Exchange Act as a domestic registrant pursuant to A.3 above.

7. If the registrant is a successor registrant, it shall be deemed to have met conditions 1, 2, 3, and 5 above if: (a) its predecessor and it, taken together, do so, provided that the succession was primarily for the purpose of changing the state of incorporation of the predecessor or forming a holding company and that the assets and liabilities of the successor at the time of succession were substantially the same as those of the predecessor, or (b) if all predecessors met the conditions at the time of succession and the registrant has continued to do so since the succession.

8. Electronic filings: In addition to satisfying the foregoing conditions, a registrant subject to the electronic filing requirements of Rule 101 of Regulation S-T shall have filed with the Commission:

> (1) All required electronic filings, including confirming electronic copies of documents submitted in paper pursuant to a temporary hardship exemption as provided in Rule 201 of Regulation S-T; and

> (2) All financial Data Schedules required to be submitted pursuant to Item 601(c) of Regulation S-K and Item 601(c) of Regulation S-B.

B. Transaction Requirements

Security offerings meeting any of the following conditions and made by a registrant meeting the Registrant Requirements specified in A. above may be registered on this Form:

1. Primary Offerings by Certain Registrants

Securities to be offered for cash by or on behalf of a registrant, or outstanding securities to be offered for cash for the account of any person other than the registrant, including securities acquired by standby underwriters in connection with the call or redemption by the registrant of warrants or a class of convertible securities; provided that the aggregate market value of the voting stock held by non-affiliates of the registrant is $75 million or more.

Instructions. The aggregate market value of the registrant's outstanding voting stock shall be computed by use of the price at which the stock was last sold, or the average of the bid and asked prices of such stock, as of a date within 60 days prior to the date of filing. See the definition of "affiliate" in Securities Act Rule 405.

2. Primary Offerings of Non-convertible Investment Grade Securities

Non-convertible securities to be offered for cash by or on behalf of a registrant, provided such securities at the time of sale are "investment grade securities," as defined below. A non-convertible security is an "investment grade security" if, at the time of sale, at least one nationally recognized statistical rating organization (as that term is used in Rule 15c3-1(c)(2)(vi)(F) under the Securities Exchange Act of 1934) has rated the security in one of its generic rating categories which signifies investment grade; typically, the four highest rating categories (within which there may be sub-categories or gradations indicating relative standing) signify investment grade.

3. Transactions Involving Secondary Offerings

Outstanding securities to be offered for the account of any person other than the issuer, including securities acquired by standby underwriters in connection with the call or redemption by the issuer of warrants or a class of convertible securities, if securities of the same class are listed and registered on a national securities exchange or are quoted on the automated quotation system of a national securities association. (In addition, attention is directed to General Instruction C to Form S-8 for the registration of employee benefit plan securities for resale.)

4. Rights Offerings, Dividend or Interest Reinvestment Plans, and Conversions or Warrants

Securities to be offered (a) upon the exercise of outstanding rights granted by the issuer of the securities to be offered. If such rights are granted on a pro rata basis to all existing security holders of the class of securities to which the rights attach, or (b) pursuant to a dividend or interest reinvestment plan, or (c) upon the conversion of outstanding convertible securities or upon the exercise of outstanding transferable warrants issued by the issuer of the securities to be offered, or by an affiliate of such issuer: provided the issuer has sent to all record holders of such rights, or to all participants in such plans, or to all record holders of such convertible securities or transferable warrants, respectively, material containing the information required by Rule 14a-3(b) under the Exchange Act and Items 401, 402 and 403 of Regulation S-K within the twelve calendar months immediately preceding the filing of the registration statement, except that the information required by Items 401, 402 and 403 of Regulation S-K need only be provided to holders of rights exercisable for common stock, holders of securities convertible into common stock, participants in plans which may invest in common stock, or in securities convertible into common stock or warrants exercisable for common stock, respectively.

5. Offerings of Investment Grade Asset-Backed Securities

Asset-backed securities to be offered for cash, provided the securities are "investment grade securities," as defined in B.2. above (Primary Offerings of Non-convertible Investment Grade Securities). For purposes of this Form, the term "asset-backed security" means a security that is primarily serviced by the cash flows of a discrete pool of receivables or other financial assets, either fixed or revolving, that by their terms convert into cash within a finite time period plus any rights or other assets designed to assure the servicing or timely distribution of proceeds to the security holders.

SEC 42260. Form S-3

C. Majority-Owned Subsidiaries

If a registrant is a majority-owned subsidiary, security offerings may be registered on this Form if:

1. the registrant-subsidiary itself meets the Registrant Requirements and the applicable Transaction Requirement;

2. the parent of the registrant-subsidiary meets the Registrant Requirements and the conditions of Transaction Requirements B.2. (Primary Offerings of Non-convertible Investment Grade Securities) are met; or

3. the parent of the registrant-subsidiary meets the Registrant Requirements and the applicable Transaction Requirement, and fully and unconditionally guarantees the payment obligations on the securities being registered, and the securities being registered are non-convertible securities. Note: In such an instance, the parent-guarantor is the issuer of a separate security consisting of the guarantee which must be concurrently registered but may be registered on the same registration statement as are the guaranteed securities.

As previously noted, Form S-3 relies heavily on the registrant's 1934 Act reports and *requires* the incorporation by reference of information about the registrant from these reports (i.e., Forms 8-K, 10-Q, and 10-K). All financial statements and related financial data are typically included in the 1934 Act reports, with disclosure in the prospectus generally limited to information relating to the offering.

With regard to the use of Form S-3 by "small business issuers," Item C under the Application of General Rules and Regulations states:

A "small business issuer," defined in Rule 405 that is eligible to use Form S-3 shall refer to the disclosure items in Regulation S-B and not Regulation S-K. For example, while Item 1 of Form S-3 requires the information required by Item 501 of Regulation S-K, small business issuers shall provide the information in Item 501 of Regulation S-B. Where Regulation S-B does not contain a comparable Item, for example there is no Item "301" in Regulation S-B, then small business issuers may omit the Item. Small business issuers shall provide the financial information called for by Item 310 of Regulation S-B in lieu of the financial information called for by Item 11.

The following are the items of information to be included in Form S-3:

PART I. INFORMATION REQUIRED IN PROSPECTUS

Item

1	Forepart of the registration statement and outside front cover page of prospectus
2	Inside front and outside back cover pages of prospectus
3	Summary information, risk factors and ratio of earnings to fixed charges
4	Use of proceeds
5	Determination of offering price
6	Dilution
7	Selling security holders
8	Plan of distribution
9	Description of securities to be registered
10	Interests of named experts and counsel
11	Material changes
12	Incorporation of certain information by reference
13	Disclosure of Commission position on indemnification for Securities Act liabilities

PART II. INFORMATION NOT REQUIRED IN PROSPECTUS

14	Other expenses of issuance and distribution
15	Indemnification of directors and officers
16	Exhibits
17	Undertakings.

With the exception of Items 11 and 12, the requirements for each of the items of information are set forth in Regulation S-K (see discussion beginning with section 60000). An accountants' consent (as discussed in sections 17110 and 20510) is required to be included in Part II of Form S-3 pursuant to Item 601 of Regulation S-K.

42270. Financial Statement Requirements

Except as to material changes (see section 42272), Form S-3 has no specific requirements for financial statements; however, as noted below, certain documents filed with the SEC are *required to* be incorporated by reference.

42271. Incorporation of Documents on File. Item 12 of Form S-3 requires the following documents to be incorporated in Form S-3; however, copies of these

SEC 42260. Form S-3

documents are not required to be filed with the registration statement or delivered to investors:

- The registrant's latest Form 10-K filed pursuant to Section 13(a) or 15(d) of the 1934 Act that contains financial statements for the registrant's latest fiscal year for which such statements have been filed;

- All other reports filed pursuant to Section 13(a) or 15(d) of the 1934 Act since the end of the fiscal year covered by the Form 10-K referred to above; and

- If the capital stock is to be registered and securities of the same class are registered under Section 12 of the 1934 Act, the description of such class of securities which is contained in a registration statement filed under the 1934 Act, including any amendment or reports filed for the purpose of updating such description.

42272. Material Changes. Item 11 of Form S-3 requires the disclosure of material changes in the registrant's affairs that have occurred since the end of the latest fiscal year for which audited statements were included in the latest annual shareholders' report. Such information may be omitted, however, if it has been disclosed in a filing on Form 10-Q or Form 8-K.

Item 11 further requires inclusion of financial information in the prospectus under certain conditions, unless incorporated by reference from:

- The registrant's latest Form 10-K,

- Any periodic 1934 Act report filed subsequent to the latest Form 10-K,

- A proxy or information statement,

- A previously filed 1933 Act prospectus, or

- A Form 8-K filed during either of the preceding two years.

Subject to the foregoing, the following information needs to be included in the prospectus of Form S-3:

- Information regarding financial statements required for businesses acquired or to be acquired (Rule 3-05 of Regulation S-X, see section 50314) and pro forma financial statements (Article 11 of Regulation S-X, see section 51100);

- Restated financial statements prepared in accordance with Regulation S-X if there has been a change in accounting principles or a correction of an error where such change or correction requires ⌐ material retroactive restatement of financial statements;

- Restated financial statements prepared in accordance with Regulation S-X where one or more business combinations accounted for by the pooling-of-interest method of accounting have been consummated subsequent to the most recent fiscal year and the acquired businesses, considered in the aggregate, are significant pursuant to Rule 11-01(b); or

- Any financial information required because of a material disposition of assets outside the normal course of business.

Regarding item (1) above, it is important to note that a currently effective shelf filing on Form S-3 technically needs to be updated (generally through the use of a filing on Form 8-K) for significant *probable* business acquisitions (see section 19230).

As a practical matter, however, registrants generally satisfy any Form S-3 financial statement disclosure requirements by filing Form 8-K, which is then incorporated by reference into Form S-3.

42273. Incorporation by Reference of Future Filings. Future filings, in addition to past filings, are also required to be incorporated by reference in Form S-3. Item 12(b) of the form provides that "The prospectus shall also state that all documents subsequently filed by the registrant pursuant to Section 13 (a), 13(c), 14 or 15(d) of the Exchange Act prior to the termination of the offering, shall be deemed to be incorporated by reference into the prospectus." Incorporating future 1934 Act filings in Form S-3 requires the inclusion of the following statement (undertaking) in the prospectus pursuant to Item 512 of Regulation S-K:

> The undersigned registrant hereby undertakes that, for the purposes of determining any liability under the Securities Act of 1933, each filing of the registrant's annual report pursuant to Section 13(a) or Section 15(d) of the Securities Exchange Act of 1934 (and, where applicable, each filing of an employee benefit plan's annual report pursuant to Section 15(d) of the Securities Exchange Act of 1934) that is incorporated by reference in the registration statement shall be deemed to be a new registration statement relating to the securities offered therein, and the offering of such securities at that time shall be deemed to be the initial bona fide offering thereof.

Form S-8 includes a similar requirement, as discussed in section 42431. Refer to section 42280 concerning accountants' consents required to be furnished in subsequent filings. ·

42274. Audit Requirements—"Keeping Current." An accountants' report included in a document filed under the 1934 Act (Form 10-K, for example) that is incorporated by reference in Form S-3 becomes subject to the "keeping current" provisions of the 1933 Act. Consequently, the "keeping current" requirements discussed in section 19050 need to be observed through the effective date of Form S-3 with respect to any audited financial statements reported on and included in a previously filed document.

The requirement to "keep current" also applies to audited financial statements included in documents that are incorporated by reference after the effective date of Form S-3 but before the termination of the offering. As indicated in section 42273, each filing of the registrant's annual report (and the employee benefit plan's annual report, where applicable) that is incorporated by reference in the registration statement is technically considered a new registration statement (i.e., a post-effective amendment). Consequently, while the filing of Form 10-Q ordinarily does not establish a new effective date for the Form S-3, a subsequent filing on Form 10-K does. *Accordingly, in such situations the auditor must "keep current" to the date the Form 10-K is filed.* Subsequent reports on Form 8-K that include audited financial statements (of a company acquired or to be acquired, for example) create a "keeping current" requirement *only with respect to those financial statements* included in the Form 8-K that have been reported on by the independent accountants.

42280. Accountants' Consent

The written consent of the accountants with respect to any document incorporated by reference in Form S-3 and containing their report is required to be furnished in Part II of a registration statement on Form S-3. (See section 20500 for discussion and examples of accountants' consents.)

As previously noted, Item 12 of Form S-3 requires the issuer to incorporate by reference reports subsequently filed "prior to the termination of the offering." If a Form 10-K is filed after the filing of a Form S-3 but before the termination of the offering, a consent also needs to be filed with respect to the accountants' report in that document. In this connection, Item 12 refers to 1933 Act Rule 439, which provides that:

> Where the filing of a written consent is required with respect to material incorporated in the registration statement by reference, which is to be filed subsequent to the effective date of the registration statement, such consent [for any accountant named as having certified material incorporated by reference] shall be filed as an amendment to the registration statement no later than the

date on which such material is filed with the Commission, unless express consent to incorporation by reference is contained in the material to be incorporated by reference.

It is generally possible to avoid the filing of an amendment to Form S-3 by including in the incorporated document (generally Form 10-K) a consent with respect to the incorporation of the accountants' report. See section 20521 for an example of such a consent.

An accountants' consent is not required when Form 10-Q is incorporated by reference into Form S-3; however, see section 20432 for a discussion of the requirement to include an accountants' "awareness letter" under certain circumstances.

An accountants' consent covering future material incorporated by reference would constitute an "open-ended" consent. Since this, in effect, would prospectively consent to the use of any future reports issued, such a procedure is inappropriate. When the future financial statements are filed together with the auditors' report thereon, it is always possible to include a consent in that filing.

As indicated in section 42273, Item 12(b) of Form S-3 requires that the prospectus contain an undertaking that future filings will be incorporated by reference. Accordingly, formal post-effective amendments are not filed when a Form S-3 is updated by the filing (for example) of a Form 10-K. Underwriters and their attorneys sometimes request that the experts sections of the Form S-3 registration statement be extended to acknowledge that future 1934 Act reports incorporated by reference will contain an auditors' opinion as "experts." If such a request is made, language such as the following could be used to emphasize this point:

EXPERTS

The consolidated financial statements of XYZ, Inc. and its subsidiaries, included in the report on Form 10-K of the Company for the fiscal year ended December 31, 19X3 referred to above, have been audited by (Name of Firm), independent accountants, as set forth in their report dated January 27, 19X4, accompanying such financial statements, and are incorporated herein by reference in reliance upon the report of such firm, which report is given upon their authority as experts in accounting and auditing.

Any financial statements and schedules hereafter incorporated by reference in the registration statement of which this prospectus is a part that have been audited and are the subject of a report by independent accountants will be so incorporated by reference in reliance upon such reports and upon the authority of such firms as experts in accounting and auditing to the extent covered by consents filed with the Commission.

SEC 42280. Form S-3

While the foregoing wording is not standard, an experts section of this nature should present no difficulty for the independent accountants provided that it clearly indicates that accountants' consents will be filed covering the future accountants' reports that will be incorporated by reference in the registration statement.

42290. Shelf Registration

Form S-3 may be used to register securities to be offered on a delayed or continuous basis pursuant to Rule 415 of Regulation C. Under this rule, commonly called the shelf-registration rule, certain registrants can register the debt and equity securities they expect to sell during the next two years. When market conditions are favorable, the securities can be taken "off the shelf" and sold to the public. See section 19200 for further discussion of Rule 415.

42300. FORM S-4

42310. General

Form S-4 is a registration form under the 1933 Act that is used in connection with business combination transactions. It was adopted in 1985 in an attempt to simplify the registration process and improve disclosure in connection with transactions of this nature.

More specifically, Form S-4 may be used for the registration of securities issued in connection with:

- Transactions specified in paragraph (a) of Rule 145 such as reclassifications, mergers or consolidations, or transfers of assets.

- Mergers in which the applicable state laws would not require the solicitation of the votes or consents of all of the shareholders of the company being acquired.

- Exchange offers for the securities of the issuer or another entity.

- Public reoffers or resales of securities registered on Form S-4.

If a registrant elects to incorporate information from other filings by reference into a registration statement filed on Form S-4 (see section 42330 below), the form provides that:

> The prospectus must be sent to the security holders no later than 20 business days prior to the date on which the meeting of such security holders is held or, if no meeting is held, at least 20 business days prior to either (1) the date of the votes, consents or authorizations may be used to effect the corporate action, or (2) if votes, consents or authorizations are not used, the date the transaction is consummated.

With regard to the applicability of Form S-4 to "small business issuers," Item 3 to the Application of General Rules and Regulations states:

SEC 42300. Form S-4

A "small business issuer," defined in Rule 405, shall refer to disclosure items in Regulation S-B and not Regulation S-K except with respect to disclosure called for by subpart 900 of Regulation S-K. Small business issuers shall provide or incorporate by reference the information called for by Item 310 of Regulation S-B.

Pursuant to Item 4 to the Application of General Rules and Regulations, registrants and companies to be acquired that are eligible to use Form SB-1 (see section 42600) have alternative narrative disclosure options in Form S-4 based on the disclosures provided in their most recent Form 10-KSB (see section 41200). In addition, the financial statement requirements for such registrants and companies to be acquired are contained in Part F/S of Form SB-1 (see section 42600). Refer to the official instructions to Form S-4 regarding these alternative disclosure and reporting options.

The following are the items of information required to be included in Form S-4 for registrants and companies being acquired that are not eligible to use the alternatives pursuant to Item 4 to the Application of General Rules and Regulations:

PART I. INFORMATION REQUIRED IN THE PROSPECTUS

Information About the Transaction

Item

1	Forepart of the registration statement and outside front cover page of prospectus
2	Inside front and outside back cover pages of prospectus
3	Risk factors, ratio of earnings to fixed charges and other information
4	Terms of the transaction
5	Pro forma financial information
6	Material contacts with the company being acquired
7	Additional information required for reoffering by persons and parties deemed to be underwriters
8	Interests of named experts and counsel
9	Disclosure of Commission position on indemnification for Securities Act liabilities

Information About the Registrant

10	Information with respect to S-3 registrants
11	Incorporation of certain information by reference
12	Information with respect to S-2 or S-3 registrants
13	Incorporation of certain information by reference
14	Information with respect to registrants other than S-2 or S-3 registrants

Information About the Company Being Acquired

Voting and Management Information

PART II. INFORMATION NOT REQUIRED IN PROSPECTUS

42320. Information About the Transaction

As noted above, Form S-4 (Items 1 through 9) requires the inclusion in the forepart of the prospectus of certain specified information concerning the transaction. Item 3 specifies that, among other things, selected financial data is required to be presented for five years pursuant to Regulation S-K Item 301 (see section 63000) for the registrant and the target company, and (if material) on a pro forma basis giving effect to the transaction for other periods as specified. The text of Item 3 is as follows:

Item 3. Risk Factors, Ratio of Earnings to Fixed Charges and Other Information
Provide in the forepart of the prospectus a summary containing the information required by Item 503 of Regulation S-K and the following:

(a) The name, complete mailing address (including the Zip Code), and telephone number (including the area code) of the principal executive offices of the registrant and the company being acquired;

(b) A brief description of the general nature of the business conducted by the registrant and by the company being acquired;

(c) A brief description of the transaction in which the securities being registered are to be offered;

(d) The information required by Item 301 of Regulation S-K (selected financial data) for the registrant and the company being acquired. To the extent the information is required to be presented in the prospectus pursuant to Items 12, 14, 16 or 17, it need not be repeated pursuant to this Item.

(e) If material, the information required by Item 301 of Regulation S-K for the registrant on a pro forma basis, giving effect to the transaction. To the extent the information is required to be presented in the prospectus pursuant to Items 12 or 14, it need not be repeated pursuant to this Item.

(f) In comparative columnar form, historical and pro forma per share data of the registrant and historical and equivalent pro forma per share data of the company being acquired for the following items:

(1) Book value per share as of the date financial data is presented pursuant to Item 301 of Regulation S-K (selected financial data);

(2) Cash dividends declared per share for the periods for which financial data is presented pursuant to Item 301 of Regulation S-K (selected financial data);

(3) Income (loss) per share from continuing operations for the periods for which financial data is presented pursuant to Item 301 of Regulation S-K (selected financial data).

Instructions to paragraph (e) and (f):

For a business combination accounted for as a purchase, the financial information required by paragraphs (e) and (f) shall be presented only for the most recent fiscal year and interim period. For a business combination accounted for as a pooling, the financial information required by paragraphs (e) and (f) (except for information with regard to book value) shall be presented for the most recent three fiscal years and interim period. For a business combination accounted for as a pooling, information with regard to book value shall be presented as of the end of the most recent fiscal year and interim period. Equivalent pro forma per share amounts shall be calculated by multiplying the pro forma income (loss) per share before non-recurring charges or credits directly attributable to the transaction, pro forma book value per share, and the pro forma dividends per share of the registrant by the exchange ratio so that the per share amounts are equated to the respective values for one share of the company being acquired.

(g) In comparative columnar form, the market value of securities of the company being acquired (on an historical and equivalent per share basis) and the market value of the securities of the registrant (on an historical basis) as of the date preceding public announcement of the proposed transaction, or, if no such public announcement was made, as of the day preceding the day the agreement with respect to the transaction was entered into;

(h) With respect to the registrant and the company being acquired, a brief statement comparing the percentage of outstanding shares entitled to vote held by directors, executive officers and their affiliates and the vote required for approval of the proposed transaction;

(i) A statement as to whether any federal or state regulatory requirements must be complied with or approval must be obtained in connection with the transaction, and if so the status of such compliance or approval;

(j) A statement about whether or not dissenters' rights of appraisal exist, including a cross-reference to the information provided pursuant to Item 18 or 19 of this Form; and

(k) A brief statement about the tax consequences of the transaction, or if appropriate, consisting of a cross-reference to the information provided pursuant to Item 4 of this form.

Note that the pro forma data required by this item may be omitted from this item if it is presented elsewhere in the prospectus (or incorporated by reference therein). However, the following pro forma information needs to be included in the prospectus and cannot be incorporated by reference:

Item 5. Pro Forma Financial Information
Furnish financial information required by Article 11 of Regulation S-X with respect to this transaction.

Instruction:

1. Any other Article 11 information that is presented (rather than incorporated by reference) pursuant to other Items of this Form shall be presented together with the information provided pursuant to Item 5, but the presentation shall clearly distinguish between this transaction and any other.

2. If pro forma financial information with respect to all other transactions is incorporated by reference pursuant to Item 11 or 15 of this Form only the pro forma results need be presented as part of the pro forma financial information required by this Item.

Rule 11-02 of Article 11 requires that a pro forma condensed balance sheet be presented as of the same date as the registrant's latest required consolidated balance sheet unless the transaction is already reflected in the registrant's consolidated balance sheet.

For a purchase transaction, pro forma condensed income statements are required to be filed for the latest fiscal year and any subsequent interim period for which historical statements are furnished. Rule 11-02 specifies that pro forma income statements should not be filed when the historical income statements include the transaction for a full fiscal period.

For a business combination accounted for as a pooling of interests, the pro forma income statements (which are, in effect, a restatement of the historical income statements

SEC 42320. Form S-4

as if the combination had been consummated) are required to be filed for all periods for which historical income statements of the registrant are required.

The provisions of Article 11 are discussed in section 51100 of this manual.

42330. Information About the Registrant

A registrant subject to the reporting requirements of the 1934 Act is required to present in the S-4 prospectus the same information about itself (including financial statements) as would be required in a filing on Form S-1, S-2 or S-3 (as applicable) in an offering not involving a business combination. Registrants not subject to 1934 Act reporting requirements are required to furnish the company related information required by Form S-1. Accordingly, registrants qualifying and electing to follow the Form S-3 approach (see section 42250) would incorporate by reference into the prospectus substantially all of the financial statements and related financial information. This information would not be included or need to be furnished with the prospectus.

Those registrants eligible to file Form S-2 (see section 42200) would have the option of including the required registrant-related financial statements and other financial information in the prospectus or incorporating it by reference. Under the latter approach, the annual and quarterly reports from which this information is incorporated would need to be furnished with the prospectus. Registrants following the Form S-1 approach would include all registrant-related information in the prospectus.

The full text of Items 10 through 14, which is reproduced below, should be referred to for the specific provisions relating to the presentation of registrant-related information in registration statements filed on Form S-4.

Item 10. Information with Respect to S-3 Registrants

If the registrant meets the requirements for use of Form S-3 and elects to furnish information in accordance with the provisions of this Item, furnish information as required below:

(a) Describe any and all material changes in the registrant's affairs that have occurred since the end of the latest fiscal year for which audited financial statements were included in the latest annual report to security holders and that have not been described in a report on Form 10-Q, Form 10-QSB or Form 8-K filed under the Exchange Act.

(b) Include in the prospectus, if not incorporated by reference from the reports filed under the Exchange Act specified in Item 11 of this Form, a proxy or information statement filed pursuant to Section 14 of the Exchange Act, a prospectus previously filed pursuant to Rule 424 under the Securities Act or, where no prospectus was required to be filed pursuant to Rule 424(b), the prospectus included in the registration statement at effectiveness or a Form 8-K filed during either of the two preceding fiscal years:

(1) Financial information required by Rule 3-05 and Article 11 of Regulation S-X with respect to transactions other than that pursuant to which the securities being registered are to be issued;

(2) Restated financial statements prepared in accordance with Regulation S-X if there has been a change in accounting principles or a correction of an error where such change or correction requires a material retroactive restatement of financial statements;

(3) Restated financial statements prepared in accordance with Regulation S-X where one or more business combinations accounted for by the pooling of interest method of accounting have been consummated subsequent to the most recent fiscal year and the acquired businesses, considered in the aggregate, are significant pursuant to Rule 11-01(b) of Regulation S-X; or

(4) Any financial information required because of a material disposition of assets outside the normal course of business.

Item 11. Incorporation of Certain Information by Reference

If the registrant meets the requirements of Form S-3 and elects to furnish information in accordance with the provisions of Item 10 of this Form:

(a) Incorporate by reference into the prospectus, by means of a statement to that effect listing all documents so incorporated, the documents listed in paragraphs (1), (2) and, if applicable, (3) below.

(1) The registrant's latest annual report on Form 10-K or Form 10-KSB filed pursuant to Section 13(a) or 15(d) of the Exchange Act which contains financial statements for the registrant's latest fiscal year for which a Form 10-K was required to be filed;

(2) All other reports filed pursuant to Section 13(a) or 15(d) of the Exchange Act since the end of the fiscal year covered by the annual report referred to in Item 11(a)(1) of this Form; and

(3) If capital stock is to be registered and securities of the same class are registered under Section 12 of the Exchange Act and: (i) listed for trading or admitted to unlisted trading privileges on a national securities exchange; or (ii) are securities for which bid and offer quotations are reported in an automated quotations system operated by a national securities association, the description of such class of securities which is contained in a registration statement filed under the Exchange Act, including any amendment or reports filed for the purpose of updating such description.

SEC 42330. Form S-4

(b) The prospectus also shall state that all documents subsequently filed by the registrant pursuant to Sections 13(a), 13(c), 14 or 15(d) of the Exchange Act, prior to one of the following dates, whichever is applicable, shall be deemed to be incorporated by reference into the prospectus:

(1) If a meeting of security holders is to be held, the date on which such meeting is held;

(2) If a meeting of security holders is not to be held, the date on which the transaction is consummated;

(3) If securities of the registrant are being offered in exchange for securities of any other issuer, the date the offering is terminated; or

(4) If securities are being offered in reoffering or resale of securities acquired pursuant to this registration statement, the date the reoffering is terminated.

Instruction. Attention is directed to Rule 439 regarding consent to the use of material incorporated by reference.

Item 12. Information with Respect to S-2 or S-3 Registrants

If the registrant meets the requirements for use of Form S-2 or S-3 and elects to comply with this Item, furnish the information required by either paragraph (a) or paragraph (b) of this Item. The information required by paragraph (b) shall be furnished if the registrant satisfies the conditions of paragraph (c) of this Item.

(a) If the registrant elects to deliver this prospectus together with a copy of either its latest Form 10-K or Form 10-KSB filed pursuant to Sections 13(a) or 15(d) of the Exchange Act or its latest annual report to security holders, which at the time of original preparation met the requirements of either Rule 14a-3 or Rule 14c-3:

(1) Indicate that the prospectus is accompanied by either a copy of the registrant's latest Form 10-K or Form 10-KSB or a copy of its latest annual report to security holders, whichever the registrant elects to deliver pursuant to paragraph (a) of this Item.

(2) Provide financial and other information with respect to the registrant in the form required by Part I of Form 10-Q or 10-QSB as of the end of the most recent fiscal quarter which ended after the end of the latest fiscal year for which certified financial statements were included in the latest Form 10-K or Form 10-KSB or the latest report to security holders (whichever the registrant elects to deliver pursuant to paragraph (a) of this Item), and more than forty-five days prior to the effective date of this registration statement (or as of a more recent date) by one of the following means:

(i) Including such information in the prospectus;

(ii) Providing without charge to each person to whom a prospectus is delivered a copy of the registrant's latest Form 10-Q or Form 10-QSB; or

(iii) Providing without charge to each person to whom a prospectus is delivered a copy of the registrant's latest quarterly report that was delivered to its security holders and which included the required financial information.

(3) If not reflected in the registrant's latest Form 10-K or Form 10-KSB or its latest annual report to security holders (whichever the registrant elects to deliver pursuant to paragraph (a) of this Item) provide information required by Rule 3-05 and Article 11 of Regulation S-X.

(4) Describe any and all material changes in the registrant's affairs which have occurred since the end of the latest fiscal year for which audited financial statements were included in the latest Form 10-K or 10-KSB or the latest annual report to security holders (whichever the registrant elects to deliver pursuant to paragraph (a) of this Item) and that were not described in a Form 10-Q, Form 10-QSB or quarterly report delivered with the prospectus in accordance with paragraphs (a)(2)(ii) or (iii) of this Item.

Instruction. Where the registrant elects to deliver the documents identified in paragraph (a) with a preliminary prospectus, such documents need not be redelivered with the final prospectus.

(b) If the registrant does not elect to deliver its latest Form 10-K or Form 10-KSB or its latest annual report to security holders:

(1) Furnish a brief description of the business done by the registrant and its subsidiaries during the most recent fiscal year as required by Rule 14a-3 to be included in an annual report to security holders. The description also should take into account changes in the registrant's business that have occurred between the end of the latest fiscal year and the effective date of the registration statement.

(2) Include financial statements and information as required by Rule 14a-3(b)(1) to be included in an annual report to security holders. In addition provide:

(i) The interim financial information required by Rule 10-01 of Regulation S-X for a filing on Form 10-Q;

(ii) Financial information required by Rule 3-05 and Article 11 of Regulation S-X with respect to transactions other than that pursuant to which the securities being registered are to be issued;

(iii) Restated financial statements prepared in accordance with Regulation S-X if there has been a change in accounting principles or a

SEC 42330. Form S-4

correction of an error where such change or correction requires a material retroactive restatement of financial statements;

(iv) Restated financial statements prepared in accordance with Regulation S-X where one or more business combinations accounted for by the pooling of interest method of accounting have been consummated subsequent to the most recent fiscal year and the acquired businesses, considered in the aggregate, are significant pursuant to Rule 11-01(b) of Regulation S-X; and

(v) Any financial information required because of a material disposition of assets outside of the normal course of business.

(3) Furnish the information required by the following:

(i) Item 101(b), (c)(1)(i) and (d) of Regulation S-K, industry segments, classes of similar products or services, foreign and domestic operations and export sales;

(ii) Where common equity securities are being offered, Item 201 of Regulation S-K, market price of and dividends on the registrant's common equity and related stockholder matters;

(iii) Item 301 of Regulation S-K, selected financial data;

(iv) Item 302 of Regulation S-K, supplementary financial information;

(v) Item 303 of Regulation S-K, management's discussion and analysis of financial condition and results of operations; and

(vi) Item 304 of Regulation S-K, changes in and disagreements with accountants on accounting and financial disclosure.

(c) The registrant shall furnish the information required by paragraph (b) of this Item if:

(1) The registrant was required to make a material retroactive restatement of financial statements because of

(i) A change in accounting principles; or

(ii) A correction of an error; or

(iii) A consummation of one or more business combinations accounted for by the pooling of interest method of accounting was effected subsequent to the most recent fiscal year and the acquired businesses considered in the aggregate meet the test of a significant subsidiary; or

(2) The registrant engaged in a material disposition of assets outside the normal course of business; and

(3) Such restatement of financial statements or disposition of assets was not reflected in the registrant's latest annual report to security holders and/or its latest Form 10-K or Form 10-KSB filed pursuant to Sections 13(a) or 15(d) of the Exchange Act.

Item 13. Incorporation of Certain Information by Reference

If the registrant meets the requirements of Form S-2 or S-3 and elects to furnish information in accordance with the provisions of Item 12 of this Form:

(a) Incorporate by reference into the prospectus, by means of a statement to that effect in the prospectus listing all documents so incorporated, the documents listed in paragraphs (1) and (2) of this Item and, if applicable, the portions of the documents listed in paragraphs (3) and (4) thereof.

(1) The registrant's latest annual report on Form 10-K or Form 10-KSB filed pursuant to Section 13(a) or 15(d) of the Exchange Act which contains audited financial statements for the registrant's latest fiscal year for which a Form 10-K was required to be filed.

(2) All other reports filed pursuant to Section 13(a) or 15(d) of the Exchange Act since the end of the fiscal year covered by the annual report referred to in paragraph (a)(1) of this Item.

(3) If the registrant elects to deliver its latest annual report to security holders pursuant to Item 12 of this Form, the information furnished in accordance with the following:

(i) Item 101(b), (c)(1)(i) and (d) of Regulation S-K, segments, classes of similar products or services, foreign and domestic operations and export sales;

(ii) Where common equity securities are being issued, Item 201 of Regulation S-K, market price of and dividends on the registrant's common equity and related stockholder matters;

(iii) Item 301 of Regulation S-K, selected financial data;

(iv) Item 302 of Regulation S-K, supplementary financial information;

(v) Item 303 of Regulation S-K, management's discussion and analysis of financial condition and results of operations; and

(vi) Item 304 of Regulation S-K, changes in and disagreements with accountants on accounting and financial disclosure.

(4) If the registrant elects, pursuant to Item 12(a)(2)(iii) of this Form, to provide a copy of its latest quarterly report which was delivered to security holders, financial information equivalent to that required to be presented in Part I of Form 10-Q.

SEC 42330. Form S-4

Instruction. Attention is directed to Rule 439 regarding consent to the use of material incorporated by reference.

(b) The registrant also may state, if it so chooses, that specifically described portions of its annual or quarterly report to security holders, other than those portions required to be incorporated by reference pursuant to paragraphs (a)(3) and (4) of this Item, are not part of the registration statement. In such case, the description of portions that are not incorporated by reference or that are excluded shall be made with clarity and in reasonable detail.

(c) Electronic filings. Electronic filers electing to deliver and incorporate by reference all, or any portion, of the quarterly or annual report to security holders pursuant to this Item shall file as an exhibit such quarterly or annual report to security holders, or such portion thereof that is incorporated by reference, in electronic format.

Item 14. Information with Respect to Registrants Other Than S-3 or S-2 Registrants

If the registrant does not meet the requirements for use of Form S-2 or S-3, or otherwise elects to comply with this Item in lieu of Item 10 or 12, furnish the information required by:

(a) Item 101 of Regulation S-K, description of business;

(b) Item 102 of Regulation S-K, description of property;

(c) Item 103 of Regulation S-K, legal proceedings;

(d) Where common equity securities are being issued, Item 201 of Regulation S-K, market price of and dividends on the registrant's common equity and related stockholder matters;

(e) Financial statements meeting the requirements of Regulation S-X (schedules required by Regulation S-X shall be filed as "Financial Statement Schedules" pursuant to Item 21 of this Form), as well as financial information required by Rule 3-05 and Article 11 of Regulation S-X with respect to transactions other than that pursuant to which the securities being registered are to be issued.

(f) Item 301 of Regulation S-K, selected financial data;

(g) Item 302 of Regulation S-K, supplementary financial information;

(h) Item 303 of Regulation S-K, management's discussion and analysis of financial condition and results of operations; and

(i) Item 304 of Regulation S-K, changes in and disagreements with accountants on accounting and financial disclosure.

42340. Information About the Company Being Acquired

Under the provisions of Form S-4, if the target company is an SEC reporting company, the general rule is that the prospectus is required to include the information that would be required by Form S-1, S-2 or S-3 if such company were making an offering of securities not involving a business combination. Accordingly, Form S-4 requires the inclusion (or incorporation by reference) of information relating to the target company as if it were the registrant.

Reference should be made to the full text of Items 15 through 17, which is reproduced below, for the specific requirements applicable to target company information to be included in registration statements filed on Form S-4.

Item 15. Information with Respect to S-3 Companies

If the company being acquired meets the requirements for use of Form S-3 and compliance with this Item is elected, furnish the information that would be required by Items 10 and 11 of this Form if securities of such company were being registered.

Item 16. Information with Respect to S-2 or S-3 Companies

(a) If the company being acquired meets the requirements for use of Form S-2 or S-3 and compliance with this Item is elected, furnish the information that would be required by Items 12 and 13 of this Form if securities of such company were being registered.

(b) Electronic filings. In addition to satisfying the requirements of paragraph (a) of this Item, electronic filers that elect to deliver and incorporate by reference all, or any portion, of the quarterly or annual report to security holders of a company being acquired pursuant to this Item shall file as an exhibit such quarterly or annual report to security holders, or such portion thereof that is incorporated by reference, in electronic format.

Item 17. Information with Respect to Companies Other Than S-3 or S-2 Companies

If the company being acquired does not meet the requirements for use of Form S-2 or S-3, or compliance with this Item is otherwise elected in lieu of Item 15 or 16, furnish the information required by paragraph (a) or (b) of this Item, whichever is applicable.

(a) If the company being acquired is subject to the reporting requirements of Section 13(a) or 15(d) of the Exchange Act, or compliance with this subparagraph in lieu of subparagraph (b) of this Item is selected, furnish the information that would be required by Item 14 of this Form if the securities of such company were being registered; however, only those schedules required by Rules 12-15, 28 and 29 of Regulation S-X need be provided with respect to the company being acquired.

SEC 42340. Form S-4

(b) If the company being acquired is not subject to the reporting requirements of either Section 13(a) or 15(d) of the Exchange Act; or, because of Section 12(i) of the Exchange Act, has not furnished an annual report to security holders pursuant to Rule 14a-3 or Rule 14c-3 for its latest fiscal year; furnish the information that would be required by the following if securities of such company were being registered:

(1) A brief description of the business done by the company which indicates the general nature and scope of the business;

(2) Item 201 of Regulation S-K, market price of and dividends on the registrant's common equity and related stockholder matters;

(3) Item 301 of Regulation S-K, selected financial data;

(4) Item 302 of Regulation S-K, supplementary financial information;

(5) Item 303 of Regulation S-K, management's discussion and analysis of financial condition and results of operations;

(6) Item 304(b) of Regulation S-K, changes in and disagreements with accountants on accounting and financial disclosure;

(7) Financial statements as would have been required to be included in an annual report furnished to security holders pursuant to Rules 14a-3(b)(1) and (b)(2) or Rules 14c-3(a)(1) and (a)(2), had the company being acquired been required to prepare such a report; provided, however, that the balance sheet for the year preceding the latest full fiscal year and the income statements for the two years preceding the latest full fiscal year need not be audited if they have not previously been audited. In any case, such financial statements need only be audited to the extent practicable. If this Form is used for resales to the public by any person who with regard to the securities being reoffered is deemed to be an underwriter within the meaning of Rule 145(c), the financial statements of such companies must be audited for the periods required to be presented pursuant to Rule 3-05.

(8) The quarterly financial and other information as would have been required had the company being acquired been required to file Part I of Form 10-Q or Form 10-QSB for the most recent quarter for which such a report would have been on file at the time the registration statement becomes effective or for a period ending as of a more recent date.

(9) Schedules required by Rules 12-15, 28 and 29 of Regulation S-X.

42350. Undertakings

The undertaking provisions of Form S-4 require the registrant to provide the undertaking representations required by Item 512 of Regulation S-K (see section 65120) that are, in essence, acknowledgments by the registrant that it will keep the registration statement and prospectus current as required by the 1933 Act. In Form S-4 filings, the registrant is also required to provide two additional representations as set forth below. Although these are legal determinations, the auditor should be familiar with the provisions and compare material appearing in the text to information provided in the financial statements and related notes and schedules. The text of the rule follows:

Item 22. Undertakings

(a) Furnish the undertakings required by Item 512 of Regulation S-K.

(b) Furnish the following undertaking:

> The undersigned registrant hereby undertakes to respond to requests for information that is incorporated by reference into the prospectus pursuant to Items 4, 10(b), 11, or 13 of this Form, within one business day of receipt of such request, and to send the incorporated documents by first class mail or other equally prompt means. This includes information contained in documents filed subsequent to the effective date of the registration statement through the date of responding to the request.

(c) Furnish the following undertaking:

> The undersigned registrant hereby undertakes to supply by means of a post-effective amendment all information concerning a transaction, and the company being acquired involved therein, that was not the subject of and included in the registration statement when it became effective.

Reference should be made to section 65120 for a discussion of the Regulation S-K requirements in this regard.

42360. Accountants' Consent

The written consent of the accountants with respect to any document incorporated by reference in Form S-4 and containing their report is required to be furnished in Part II of a registration statement on Form S-4. (See section 20500 for discussion and examples of accountants' consents.)

42400. FORM S-8

42410. General

Form S-8 is used for registering the following types of securities:

- Securities of the registrant to be offered to its employees, or to employees of its subsidiaries or parents, pursuant to any employee benefit plan (which may include purchase, savings, option, bonus, appreciation, profit-sharing, thrift, incentive, pension, or similar plans).

- Interests in the above plans, if such interests constitute securities required to be registered under the 1933 Act.

The issuer using this form must have been subject to the requirement to file periodic reports with the SEC under the 1934 Act (Sections 13 or 15(d); see section 19500), and must have filed all required reports and other materials during the preceding 12 months (or for such shorter period that the registrant was required to file such reports and materials).

Registrants that elect to avail themselves of the option of incorporating by reference the plan's latest annual report in the Form S-8 must already be subject to the filing requirements of Section 15(d). If the plan was not subject to the Section 15(d) filing requirements, the plan's annual report for the most recent fiscal year is required to be filed concurrently with the registration statement on Form S-8. If the plan has not been in existence for at least 90 days prior to the filing date of Form S-8, the requirement to file an annual report for the employee plan concurrently with the Form S-8 registration statement does not apply.

A further condition for the use of Form S-8 is that the issuer has furnished or will furnish an annual report to its shareholders for the last fiscal year that substantially complies with the information required by Rule 14a-3 of the proxy rules. Rule 14a-3 is discussed in section 31320. The information included in a filing on Form S-8 is updated by annual reports on Form 11-K (see section 41300).

In addition, registrants subject to the electronic filing requirements of Rule 101 of Regulation S-T are required to have filed all required electronic filings, including confirming electronic copies of documents submitted in paper pursuant to a temporary hardship exemption (provided in Rule 201 of Regulation S-T) and all Financial Data Schedules required to be submitted pursuant to Item 601(c) of Regulation S-K and Item 601(c) of Regulation S-B.

With regard to the use of Form S-8 by "small business issuers," Item 3 under the Application of General Rules and Regulations states:

> A "small business issuer," defined in Rule 405, shall refer to the disclosure items in Regulation S-B and not Regulation S-K.

The general instructions to Form S-8 contain the provisions for the use of the form. The following are the items of information to be included in Form S-8:

PART I. INFORMATION REQUIRED IN THE SECTION 10(a) PROSPECTUS

Item

1	Plan information
2	Registrant information and employee plan annual information

PART II. INFORMATION REQUIRED IN THE REGISTRATION STATEMENT

3	Incorporation of documents by reference
4	Description of securities*
5	Interests of named experts and counsel*
6	Indemnification of directors and officers*
7	Exemption from registration claimed
8	Exhibits*
9	Undertakings*

---

*Detailed disclosure requirements are included in Regulation S-K. See discussion beginning with section 60000 for further information as to certain of these requirements.

42420. Automatic Effectiveness

Registration statements on Form S-8 and post-effective amendments thereto become effective automatically when filed. All filings made on or in connection with this form become public information immediately upon filing with the Commission.

42430. Financial Statement Requirements

Form S-8 has no specific financial statement requirements; however, to the extent that the following documents (as specified in Item 3) have been filed with the SEC, they are required to be incorporated in Form S-8 by reference:

SEC 42410. Form S-8

(a) The registrant's latest annual report, and where interests in the plan are being registered, the plan's latest annual report [Forms 10-K and 11-K, for example] filed pursuant to Section 13(a) or 15(d) of the Exchange Act, or in the case of the registrant either: (1) the latest prospectus filed pursuant to Rule 424(b) under the Act that contains audited financial statements for the registrant's latest fiscal year for which such statements have been filed, or (2) the registrant's effective registration statement on Form 10, 10-SB, or 20-F, in the case of registrants described in General Instruction A.(2) of Form 40-F, on Form 40-F filed under the Exchange Act containing audited financial statements for the registrant's latest fiscal year.

(b) All other reports filed pursuant to Section 13(a) or 15(d) of the Securities Exchange Act of 1934 since the end of the fiscal year covered by the annual reports or the prospectus referred to in (a) above [Form 10-Q or 8-K, for example].

(c) If the class of securities to be offered is registered under Section 12 of the Securities Exchange Act of 1934, the description of such class of securities which is contained in a registration statement filed under such Act, including any amendment or report filed for the purpose of updating such description.

Copies of these documents need not be filed with the registration statement; however, Item 2 of the form requires the registrant to provide a written statement to participants advising them of the availability, without charge, of documents incorporated by reference in Item 3 of Part II, and stating that those documents are incorporated by reference in the Section 10(a) prospectus. In addition, the written statement is required to indicate the availability of other documents, without charge, required to be delivered to employees pursuant to Rule 428(b) of the 1933 Act.

42431. Incorporation by Reference of Future Filings. Since the plans pursuant to which securities are registered on Form S-8 generally extend over several years and the securities are continuously offered to employees, the offering prospectus needs to be kept current. Pursuant to Item 3 of Part II, documents subsequently filed pursuant to Sections 13(a), 13(c), 14, and 15(d) of the 1934 Act are automatically deemed to be incorporated by reference. Therefore, additional copies of these documents are not required to be filed as amendments to the Form S-8 registration statement. In the past this was accomplished by the filing of post-effective amendments (see section 19100) to the original registration statement. Updating is now automatically effected by incorporating into Form S-8 future periodic reports and other documents filed under the 1934 Act, in a manner similar to Form S-3 (see section 42273).

The need for post-effective amendments was discussed by the Commission in the commentary portion of Release No. 33-6202:

Although the Commission expects that the changes in Form S-8 will permit most stock purchase and stock option plans registering issuer's shares on Form S-8 to update their registration statements through Exchange Act filings, the Commission is aware that despite the simplifications of the form and the readjustment of items many employee pension and profit sharing plans will continue to require annual post-effective amendments because of the requirement in Item 12(a) to provide data to evaluate alternative investment media. . . . The Commission believes that information as to the performance of investment media should be delivered to participants on a reasonably current basis at or within a short time prior to the time when a participant makes a choice or election to change or continue the investment of his or her account.

Item 12(a), referred to in the foregoing commentary (subsequently changed to Item I(g)), requires the disclosure of data that will enable employees having the authority to direct the investment of the plan's assets to make informed investment decisions. The text of Item I(g) follows:

If participating employees may direct all or any part of the assets under the plan to two or more investment media, furnish a brief description of the provisions of the plan with respect to the alternative investment media; and provide a tabular or other meaningful presentation of financial data for each of the past three fiscal years (or such lesser period for which the data is available with respect to each investment medium) that, in the opinion of the registrant, will apprise employees of material trends and significant changes in the performance of alternative investment media and enable them to make informed investment decisions. Financial data shall be presented for any additional fiscal years necessary to keep the information from being misleading or that registrant deems appropriate, but the total period presented need not exceed five years.

Incorporating future 1934 Act filings in Form S-8 requires the inclusion of a statement (undertaking) in the prospectus pursuant to Item 512 of Regulation S-K:

The undersigned registrant hereby undertakes that, for purposes of determining any liability under the Securities Act of 1933, each filing of the registrant's annual report pursuant to Section 13(a) or Section 15(d) of the Securities Exchange Act of 1934 (and, where applicable, each filing of an employee benefit plan's annual report pursuant to Section 15(d) of the Securities Exchange Act of 1934) that is incorporated by reference in the registration statement shall be deemed to be a new registration statement relating to the securities offered therein, and the offering of such securities at that time shall be deemed to be the initial bona fide offering thereof.

42432. Audit Requirements —"Keeping Current." An accountants' report included in a document filed under the 1934 Act (Form 10-K, for example) that is incorporated by reference in Form S-8 becomes subject to the "keeping current" provisions of the 1933 Act. Consequently, the "keeping current" requirements discussed in section 19050 need to be observed through the *effective date* of Form S-8 with respect to any audited financial statements reported on and included in a previously filed document.

SEC 42431. Form S-8

The requirement to "keep current" also applies to audited financial statements included in documents that are incorporated by reference *after* the original effective date of Form S-8 but before the termination of the offering. As indicated in section 42431, each filing of the registrant's annual report (Form 10-K) and the employee benefit plan's annual report (Form 11-K) that is incorporated by reference in the registration statement is technically considered a new registration statement (i.e., a post-effective amendment) and, therefore, creates a new effective date. *Thus, when a Form 10-K or 11-K is filed after the original effective date of the Form S-8 registration statement, the independent accountant needs to perform a "keeping current" review through the dates the Forms 10-K and 11-K are filed.* A "keeping current" review is ordinarily not required in connection with a filing on a Form 10-Q, even when the independent accountant has performed a limited review of the data and issued a report in accordance with SAS No. 71 (see section 51005).

42440. Accountants' Consent

Rule 439 of Regulation C requires the written consent of the accountants with respect to any document containing their report that was *previously* filed and is incorporated by reference in the Form S-8 "unless express consent to incorporation by reference is contained in the material to be incorporated by reference." Consequently, Part II of the Form S-8 registration statement normally contains a consent signed by the accountants with respect to the incorporation of their report in a previously filed document (e.g., Form 10-K) that is incorporated by reference in the Form S-8 (see section 20500 for illustrative wording for such a consent).

Item 3 of Form S-8 further requires the issuer to incorporate by reference reports *subsequently* filed before the termination of the offering. If a Form 10-K is filed after the filing of a Form S-8 but before the termination of the offering, a consent also needs to be filed with respect to the accountants' report in that document. In this connection, Rule 439 of Regulation C provides that:

> . . . such consent shall be filed by amendment to the registration statement no later than the date on which such material is filed with the Commission, unless express consent to incorporation by reference is contained in the material to be incorporated by reference.

It is generally possible to avoid the filing of an amendment to Form S-8 by including in the incorporated document (generally Forms 10-K and 11-K) a consent with respect to the incorporation of the accountants' report. See section 20521 for an example of such a consent. An accountants' consent is ordinarily not required when Form 10-Q is incorporated by reference into Form S-8; however, see section 20432 for a discussion of the requirement to include an accountants' "awareness letter" under certain circumstances.

An accountants' consent covering future material incorporated by reference constitutes an "open-ended" consent and is inappropriate.

42500. FORM S-11

42510. General

Form S-11 is used for the registration of:

- Securities issued by real estate investment trusts, as defined in Section 856 of the Internal Revenue Code.

- Securities issued by other issuers whose business is primarily that of acquiring and holding for investment real estate or interests in real estate, or interest in other issuers whose business is primarily that of acquiring and holding real estate or interest in real estate for investment.

This form may not be used by investment companies registered or required to register under the Investment Company Act of 1940.

The following are the items of information to be included in Form S-11:

PART I. INFORMATION REQUIRED IN PROSPECTUS

Item

1   Forepart of registration statement and outside front cover page of prospectus
2   Inside front and outside back cover pages of prospectus
3   Summary information, risk factors and ratio of earnings to fixed charges
4   Determination of offering price
5   Dilution
6   Selling security holders
7   Plan of distribution
8   Use of proceeds
9   Selected financial data
10 Management's discussion and analysis of financial condition and results of operations
11 General information as to registrant
12 Policy with respect to certain activities
13 Investment policies of registrant
14 Description of real estate
15 Operating data
16 Tax treatment of registrant and its security holders

SEC   42500. Form S-11

PART II. INFORMATION NOT REQUIRED IN PROSPECTUS

The requirements for Items 1 through 10, 17 through 23, 28 through 30, 32, 33, 35, 36, and portions of 27 are set forth in Regulation S-K (see discussion beginning with section 60000). The requirements for the remaining items are set forth in the instructions to Form S-11. An accountants' consent (see sections 17110 and 20510) is required to be included in Part II of Form S-11 pursuant to Item 601 of Regulation S-K.

42520. Financial Statement Requirements

The form and content of and requirements for the financial statements and financial statement schedules to be included in this form and the dates and periods for which they are required to be presented are set forth in Regulation S-X. A discussion of these requirements is included beginning with section 50050 of this manual.

The entities for which financial statements may be required (pursuant to Article 3 of Regulation S-X) are summarized in the table in section 50300.

Rule 3-14 of Regulation S-X (section 50348) contains special instructions for real estate operations acquired or to be acquired and Rule 3-15 of Regulation S-X (section 50349) contains special provisions for financial statements of real estate investment trusts (REITs).

The supporting schedules required by Regulation S-X are required to be furnished and included in Part II of the Form S-11 registration statement, except for the following schedules, which need to be included in the prospectus (Part I):

Regulation S-X Rule	Description
12-12	Investment in Securities of Unaffiliated Issuers
12-28	Real Estate and Accumulated Depreciation
12-29	Mortgage Loans on Real Estate

42600. FORM SB-1

42610. General

Form SB-1 is available for transitional small business issuers (see section 70000) to register up to $10 million of securities in any continuous 12-month period, including the transaction to be registered. This form is only available for the registration of securities to be sold for cash. In the calculation of the $10 million ceiling, all 1933 Act offerings need to be included except for any amounts registered on Form S-8.

Form SB-1 may continue to be used by a small business issuer until it:

- Registers more than $10 million under the 1933 Act in any continuous 12-month period (other than securities registered on Form S-8);

- Elects to file a nontransitional disclosure document (other than the proxy statement disclosure in Schedule 14A). Nontransitional disclosure documents include:

  -- 1933 Act registration forms other than Forms SB-1, S-3 (if the issuer incorporates by reference transitional 1934 Act reports), S-8 and S-4 (if the issuer relies upon the transitional disclosure format in that form);

  -- 1934 Act periodic reporting Forms 10-K and 10-Q;

  -- 1934 Act registration statement Form 10; and

  -- Reports or registration statements on Forms 10-KSB, 10-QSB or 10-SB that do not use the transitional disclosure document format; or

- No longer meets the definition of a small business issuer.

The narrative disclosure requirements of Form SB-1 generally parallel those of Form 1-A of Regulation A (see section 42800). Similar to Form 1-A, corporate issuers have the option to provide narrative disclosures in a question and answer format rather than the traditional disclosure format; however, Form SB-1 requires some additional disclosures to be provided, as detailed below.

The following are the items of information to be included in Form SB-1 (unless otherwise indicated, the items refer to Regulation S-B; see section 70000):

PART I. INFORMATION REQUIRED IN PROSPECTUS

Alternative 1

Corporate issuers may elect to furnish the information required by Model A of Form 1-A, as well as the following information.

Item

1	Inside Front and Outside Back Cover Pages of Prospectus (Item 502)
2	Significant Parties
3	Relationship with Issuer of Experts Named in Registration Statement (Item 509)
4	Selling Security Holders
5	Changes in and Disagreements with Accountants (Item 304)
6	Disclosure of Commission position on Indemnification for Securities Act Liabilities (Item 510)

Alternative 2

Any issuer may elect to furnish the information required by Model B of Part II of Form 1-A, as well as the following information.

Item

1	Inside Front and Outside Back Cover Pages of Prospectus (Item 502)
2	Significant parties
3	Relationship with Issuer of Experts Named in Registration Statement (Item 509)
4	Legal Proceedings (Item 103)
5	Changes in and Disagreements with Accountants (Item 304)
6	Disclosure of Commission position on Indemnification for Securities Act Liabilities (Item 510)

PART F/S—FINANCIAL INFORMATION REQUIRED IN PROSPECTUS

Furnish the information required by Item 310 of Regulation S-B.

SEC 42610. Form SB-1

PART II. INFORMATION NOT REQUIRED IN PROSPECTUS

Item

1   Indemnification of Directors and Officers (Item 702)
2   Other Expenses of Issuance and Distribution (Item 511)
3   Undertakings (Item 512)
4   Unregistered Securities Issued or Sold Within One Year
5   Index to Exhibits
6   Description of Exhibits

42620. Financial Statement Requirements

Small business issuers are required to file an audited balance sheet as of the end of the most recent fiscal year (or a date within 135 days of the filing date if the issuer has existed for less than one year) and audited statements of income, cash flows, and changes in stockholders' equity for each of the two fiscal years preceding the date of the audited balance sheet (or such shorter period that the issuer has been in business). The form and content of, and other requirements for, the financial statements to be included in Form SB-1 are set forth in Regulation S-B (see section 73100).

An accountants' consent (see sections 17110 and 20510) is required to be included in Part II of Form SB-2 pursuant to Item 601 of Regulation S-B.

42700. FORM SB-2

42710. General

Form SB-2 was adopted by the SEC in August 1992 as part of an integrated disclosure system for "small business issuers." It replaces Form S-18 which has been rescinded. This form is a part of the SEC's initiative to revise the rules relating to 1933 Act registration exemptions under Rule 504 and Regulation A. Forms S-2, S-3, S-8, and S-4 have been amended to reflect the new disclosure requirements of Regulation S-B, and new Forms 10-SB, 10-KSB, and 10-QSB have been created to satisfy registration, annual, and quarterly reporting obligations under the 1934 Acts.

Form SB-2 is available to be used by small business issuers that do not qualify to register on Form SB-1 (see section 42600). The form may only be used to register securities to be sold for cash. A "small business issuer" is defined as a U.S. or Canadian company with revenues of less than $25 million whose aggregate public float is less than $25 million. Investment companies are excluded from the definition, and majority owned subsidiaries may use Form SB-2 only if the parent also meets the definition of a small business issuer.

Small business issuers may file initial public offerings on Form SB-2 with the regional SEC office closest to the issuer's principal place of business or at the Commission's headquarters in Washington, D.C. All subsequent filings, however, are required to be made in Washington, D.C.

The following are the items of information to be included in Form SB-2 (the items refer to Regulation S-B; see section 70000):

PART I. INFORMATION REQUIRED IN PROSPECTUS

Item

1	Front of Registration Statement and Outside Front Cover of Prospectus (Item 501)
2	Inside Front and Outside Back Cover Pages of Prospectus (Item 502)
3	Summary Information and Risk Factors (Item 503)
4	Use of Proceeds (Item 504)
5	Determination of Offering Price (Item 505)
6	Dilution (Item 506)
7	Selling Security Holders (Item 507)
8	Plan of Distribution (Item 508)
9	Legal Proceedings (Item 103)

42720. Financial Statement Requirements

Small business issuers are required to file an audited balance sheet as of the end of the most recent fiscal year (or a date within 135 days if the issuer has existed for less than one year), and audited statements of income, cash flows and changes in stockholders' equity for each of the two fiscal years preceding the date of the audited balance sheet (or such shorter period that the issuer has been in business). The form and content of, and other requirements for, the financial statements to be included in Form SB-2 are set forth in Regulation S-B (see section 73100).

An accountants' consent (see sections 17110 and 20510) is required to be included in Part II of Form SB-2 pursuant to Item 601 of Regulation S-B.

42800. FORM 1-A (REGULATION A)

42810. General

Regulation A provides a general exemption from the registration requirements for certain securities, but requires the use of an offering circular containing financial and other data in connection with their distribution. The provisions of this regulation are included in the instructions to Form 1-A and in Rules 251 through 264 of the 1933 Act.

One of the major impediments to a Regulation A financing for a small company with no established market for its securities used to be the cost of preparing the mandated offering statement. (See section 42812.) In response to this, the SEC established rules that allow a company relying on the Regulation A exemption to "test the waters" for potential interest in the company prior to filing and delivery of the offering statement. The "testing of the waters" provision begins with a written solicitation of interest required to be submitted to the SEC at the time of first use. The written "test the waters" document is a "free writing" (a document that does not have to follow a prescribed form designated by the SEC) which includes (1) a statement that no money is being solicited, or will be accepted; that no sales can be made until delivery and qualification of the offering circular, and that indications of interest involve no obligation or commitment of any kind; and (2) a brief general identification of the company's business, products, and chief executive officer. Provided that the document contains the required information, any written "test the waters" material under the 1933 Act is not deemed to be a "prospectus" as defined in section 2(10) of the 1933 Act; however, the antifraud provisions of the federal securities laws continue to apply to such materials.

A summary of the significant provisions of this regulation follows.

42811. Limitation. The exemption is available for certain securities of domestic and Canadian issuers, the aggregate offering price of which does not exceed $5,000,000 (including no more than $1,500,000 offered by all selling security holders), less the aggregate offering price for all securities sold within the 12 months before the start of and during the offering of securities in reliance upon Regulation A.

42812. Offering Statement. When a company decides to proceed with a Regulation A offering, an offering statement is required to be filed with the appropriate

SEC 42800. Form 1-A

regional office of the SEC consisting of Part I—Notification, Part II—Offering Circular, Part F/S, and Part III—Exhibits.

Part F/S contains the financial statement requirements for Regulation A offerings and is discussed in section 42820.

Issuers may begin to offer securities to be sold in a Regulation A filing as soon as the offering statement is filed. Written offers may be made after the offering statement is filed provided that a preliminary or final offering circular is used. Advertisements and radio and television broadcasts may be used to offer the securities provided they contain information regarding the issuer and the securities being issued and provided they indicate where an offering circular may be obtained. The offering statement is required to be qualified, however, before sales are made. Similar to other registered offerings, absent a delaying notation procedure an offering statement becomes qualified twenty calendar days after it is filed with the SEC. The issuer is required to deliver a preliminary or final offering circular at least 48 hours prior to the sale being confirmed.

Regarding continuous offerings, updated financial statements are required to be included in the offering circular twelve months after the original offering statement was qualified. A revised or updated offering circular is required to be filed as an amendment to the offering statement. This begins a new qualification period.

Corporate issuers have the option of using a question and answer format rather than the traditional disclosure format for providing the information required by Part II—Offering Circular.

The following are the items of information to be included in Parts I and II of the offering statement:

Part I — Notification

Item

1	Significant parties
2	Application of Rule 262
3	Affiliate sales
4	Jurisdictions in which securities are to be offered
5	Unregistered securities issued or sold within one year
6	Other present or proposed offerings
7	Marketing arrangements
8	Relationship with issuer or experts named in offering statement
9	Use of a solicitation of interest document

Part II — Offering Circular

Model A (to be used by corporate issuers)

<u>Item</u>

1	Cover page
2	The Company
3	Risk factors
4	Business and properties
5	Offering price factors
6	Use of proceeds
7	Capitalization
8	Description of securities
9	Dividends, distributions, and redemptions
10	Officers and key personnel of the company
11	Directors of the company
12	Principal stockholders
13	Management relationships, transactions, and remuneration
14	Litigation
15	Federal tax aspects
16	Miscellaneous factors
17	Financial statements
18	Management's discussion and analysis of certain relevant factors

Model B (to be used by noncorporate issuers unless the issuer elects to provide the information required by Part I of Form SB-2 (see section 42700) except that the financial statement requirements of Part F/S should be followed)

<u>Item</u>

1	Cover page
2	Distribution spread
3	Summary information, risk factors, and dilution
4	Plan of distribution
5	Use of proceeds to issuer
6	Description of business
7	Description of property
8	Directors, executive officers, and significant employees
9	Remuneration of directors and officers
10	Security ownership of management and certain security holders
11	Interest of management and others in certain transactions
12	Securities being offered

SEC 42812. Form 1-A

Part F/S

Financial statement requirements, regardless of the applicable disclosure model, are specified in Part F/S of Form 1-A (see section 42820).

Part III—Exhibits

Part III contains an index and a description of exhibits appropriate to the offering statement.

42813. Offering Circular. After the offering statement is filed and reviewed in the appropriate SEC regional office, the offering circular may be furnished to the offerees. Note that exemption from the registration requirements of the 1933 Act does not exempt the issuer from the antifraud provisions of the Act.

42820. Financial Statement Requirements

The offering circular (Part II of the offering statement) is required to contain financial statements required by Part F/S of Form 1-A. In accordance with Part F/S, the financial statements of the issuer need to be prepared in accordance with generally accepted accounting principles and practices in the United States or, for Canadian companies, in accordance with Canadian GAAP with a reconciliation to U.S. GAAP. Unless the company is subject to the reporting requirements of the 1934 Act, the financial statements need not comply with Regulation S-X except for Article 2 (see section 50200) dealing with the qualifications and reports of the independent accountant (see section 42821).

The following financial statements are required to be included in the offering circular:

- A balance sheet as of a date within 90 days prior to the filing of the offering statement, or such longer period of time (not exceeding six months) as the SEC may permit upon written request of the issuer and subject to a showing of good cause. For filings made after 90 days subsequent to the end of the most recent fiscal year, a balance sheet as of the most recent fiscal year also needs to be furnished.

- Statements of income, cash flows, and other stockholders' equity for each of the last two fiscal years and for the period, if any, between the close of the last full fiscal year and the date of the latest balance sheet presented in the document. As to any unaudited interim period presented, a statement needs to be made that in the opinion of management all adjustments necessary for a fair statement of the results for the interim period have been included. See section 50312 for a discussion of a similar requirement.

- Statements of income (which may be unaudited) for entities constituting significant past acquisitions. These requirements are limited to acquisitions during the period for which income statements of the issuer are required and that meet the test for a significant subsidiary. If an acquisition has been effected during the most recent fiscal year or in a subsequent interim period, pro forma statements of income also need to be furnished (see section 50314 for a discussion of businesses acquired or to be acquired).

- Financial statements (which may be unaudited) of entities constituting significant future probable acquisitions, including pro forma financial statements. The financial statements would be those required if the entity to be acquired were an issuer. See section 50314 for a discussion of businesses acquired or to be acquired.

In the determination of significance: (1) if none of the conditions of the significant subsidiary exceeds 40 percent, income statements of the acquired business for only the most recent fiscal year and interim period are required, unless such statements are readily available (in which case they need to be furnished) and (2) if more than one transaction has occurred or is probable, the tests of significance are to be made using the aggregate impact of the businesses and the required financial statements may be presented on a combined basis, if appropriate.

42821. Audit Requirements. The issuer's financial statements are not required to be audited unless they are otherwise available.

If the financial statements included in a filing under Regulation A are audited, the accountants need to furnish a consent to the use of their report. See section 20510 for an example of such a consent.

42900. FORM D (REGULATION D)

42910. General

Regulation D provides an exemption from the registration requirements for limited offers and sales of securities under certain circumstances. The regulation specifies, however, that certain information may need to be furnished to investors notwithstanding the offering's exemption from the registration requirements of the 1933 Act. While no document need be filed with a federal agency before securities are sold pursuant to Regulation D, the SEC does require the filing of Form D, "Notice of Sales," after the fact. The Regulation D exemption is also available to foreign private issuers. Note that exemption from the registration requirements of the 1933 Act does not exempt the issuer from the antifraud provisions of the Act. Although Regulation D is designed to achieve federal/state exemption uniformity, it does not preempt state law; the blue sky laws in certain states may require distribution of disclosure documents for offerings that otherwise qualify for exemption under Regulation D.

The provisions of this regulation are included in Rules 501 through 508 of the 1933 Act. A summary of its significant provisions follows.

42911. Limitations. Under Rule 504, issuers not subject to the reporting requirements of the 1934 Act offering up to $1,000,000 in any 12-month period are exempt from registration, and are subject only to the antifraud prohibitions of the federal securities laws. Rule 504 is not available to investment companies or to "blank check" companies (development stage companies that either have no business plan or purpose or have indicated their business plan is to engage in a merger or acquisition with an unidentified entity).

Rule 505 exempts from registration offers and sales of securities of up to $5,000,000 during any 12-month period for any issuer other than an investment company. Rule 505 also imposes a limitation on the number of purchasers of the offering that do not qualify as an "accredited investor," as defined in Rule 501(a). There can be no more than, or the issuer must *reasonably believe* there are no more than, 35 investors not meeting the accreditation criteria; however, there can be an unlimited number of accredited investors.

Rule 506 allows for the "private placement" of securities with an unlimited number of accredited investors and up to 35 nonaccredited persons regardless of the dollar amount of the offering. However, unlike under Rule 505, each nonaccredited purchaser of a Rule 506 offering (or their representative) must be, or the issuer must *reasonably believe* that they are, "sophisticated" (i.e., have the necessary knowledge and experience in financial and business matters to evaluate the merits and risks of a prospective investment).

42920. Information Requirements

Rule 502(b) deals with the information requirements in Regulation D offerings. Pursuant to Rule 502(b), an issuer is required to furnish the required information (see sections 42921 and 42922 below) to purchasers within a reasonable time prior to sale when selling securities to nonaccredited investors under Rules 505 and 506. No specified information is required to be provided when selling securities to accredited investors or when selling securities under Rule 504. However, when information is provided to nonaccredited investors, an issuer is expected to consider providing the information to accredited investors as well, in view of the antifraud provisions of the federal securities laws. The information requirements depend on whether the issuer is subject to the 1934 Act reporting requirements and on the size of the offering as discussed below.

42921. Nonreporting Companies. Issuers that are not subject to the reporting requirements of Section 13 or 15(d) of the 1934 Act (at a reasonable time prior to the sale of securities) are required to furnish purchasers with information to the extent it is material to an understanding of the issuer, its business, and the securities being offered.
Nonfinancial statement information:

- Issuers eligible to use Regulation A (see section 42800) are required to provide the same type of information as required by Part II of Form 1-A (see section 42800).

- Issuers not eligible to use Regulation A need to furnish the same kind of information as would be required in Part I of a registration statement filed under the 1933 Act on the form that the issuer would be entitled to use.

Financial statement information:

- For offerings up to $2,000,000, issuers are required to provide the same information as required in Item 310 of Regulation S-B (see section 73000) except that only the issuer's balance sheet, which needs to be as of a date within 120 days of the commencement of the offering, is required to be audited.

SEC 42911. Form D

- For offerings up to $7,500,000, issuers are required to provide the same information as would be required in Form SB-2 (see section 42700).

- For offerings over $7,500,000, issuers need to provide the same kind of information as would be required in Part I of a registration statement filed under the 1933 Act on the form that the issuer would be entitled to use.

Irrespective of the size of the offering, if an issuer (other than a limited partnership) cannot obtain audited financial statements without unreasonable effort or expense, then only the issuer's balance sheet, as of a date within 120 days of the commencement of the offering, needs to be audited. Limited partnerships may furnish tax basis financial statements if furnishing the required GAAP-based financial statements would involve unreasonable effort or expense, provided that the statements are examined and reported on in accordance with GAAS by independent accountants.

- If the offeror is a foreign private issuer, the company needs to disclose the same type of information required to be included in a registration statement filed under the 1933 Act on the form that the issuer would be entitled to use. The financial statements would need to be audited to the same extent as required above.

42922. Reporting Companies. The information requirements for companies that are subject to 1934 Act reporting requirements do *not* vary depending on the size of the offering. These issuers, however, have an option as to the form in which these financial statements may be delivered.

A reporting company may furnish its most recent annual report to shareholders (assuming it meets the requirements of Rule 14a-3 or 14c-3—see section 31300), the definitive proxy statement filed in connection with that annual report, and, if requested in writing by the offeree, the most recent Form 10-K. Alternatively, a reporting company may elect to furnish the information contained in its most recent 1934 Act report on Form 10-K, 10-KSB, 10 or 10-SB, or 1933 Act filing on Form S-1, SB-1, SB-2 or S-11. A foreign private issuer may also choose to provide the information in its most recent Form 20-F or Form F-1 in lieu of the above.

Irrespective of which option the issuer chooses, the basic information needs to be supplemented by information contained in 1934 Act reports filed after the distribution of the annual report or registration statement.

42930. Filing of Form D

Pursuant to Rule 503, Form D, "Notice of Sales of Securities," is due at the SEC within 15 days *after* the first sale in a Regulation D offering.

42940. RULE 144A

42941. General

In 1990, the SEC adopted Rule 144A covering the purchase and resale of "restricted securities" and certain amendments to Rules 144 and 145 that address the holding period for such securities. Restricted securities are those that are exempt from SEC registration requirements and cannot, therefore, be released into the public trading markets. Typically, restricted securities are offered under Regulation D (see section 42900).

Rule 144A allows privately placed securities to be offered or sold to "qualified institutional buyers" and cites insurance companies, banks, investment companies and savings and loan associations as the types of entities that may qualify for such designation. In 1992, the SEC expanded the categories of "qualified institutional buyers" to include collective and master trusts, legal forms commonly used for the collective investment of the funds of employee benefit plans. After an initial two-year holding period has been satisfied, the securities can be sold in the public markets. Availability of the rule is conditional upon the holder and potential purchaser of the securities having the right to obtain from the issuer specified information prior to the sale.

The objective of Rule 144A is to allow large institutional investors to trade restricted securities more freely with each other without subjecting the companies issuing such securities to the SEC registration and disclosure process. It is primarily intended to increase the efficiency and liquidity of the U.S. markets for equity and debt securities issued in private placements. Companies that qualify as foreign private issuers are eligible to offer securities under Rule 144A and the issuance of the Rule has increased the activity of such companies in the U.S. market.

42942. Changes to Previous Requirements

Rule 144A sets forth several changes to previous requirements, as set forth in Rules 144 and 145, which include:

- Establishing a requirement that purchasers of restricted securities be "qualified institutional buyers."

- Modifying the two-year holding period to run continuously from the time the restricted securities are acquired from the issuer. Prior to the rule, restricted securities were required to be held for at least two years before they could be resold; however, the holding period of the former owner(s) of the securities could not be combined with the holding period of the seller for purposes of determining whether the two-year restriction period expired.

- Establishing eligibility requirements for the types of restricted securities that may be sold under the rule.

- Establishing minimum informational requirements for the resale of securities to both U.S. and foreign companies.

42943. Requirements of Rule 144A

As noted above, Rule 144A provides "qualified institutional buyers" an exemption from the 1933 Act registration requirements for the resale of restricted securities. In order to be designated a "qualified institutional buyer," the general rule is that an institution must, in the aggregate, own and invest on a discretionary basis at least $100 million in securities of issuers that are not affiliated with the institution. Exceptions to the general rule include the following:

- Banks and Savings and Loan Associations. Banks and savings and loan associations must own and invest at least $100 million in securities, and have a net worth of at least $25 million.

- Registered Broker-Dealers. Broker-dealers registered under the 1934 Act must own in the aggregate and invest at least $10 million in securities of issuers that are not affiliated with the broker-dealer.

Privately placed securities that, at the time of their issuance, are comparable to securities trading on a U.S. exchange or quoted in the NASDAQ system are not eligible for resale under Rule 144A. The rule indicates that "comparable" means securities substantially the same in class or character, the determination of which is a legal matter.

For the purpose of calculating the qualifying amount of securities held, the rule indicates that the holdings of a parent company's wholly owned and majority owned subsidiaries may be aggregated, if the investments of those subsidiaries are managed under the direction of the parent.

Rule 144A also indicates that the aggregate value of the securities owned and invested is to be determined by their cost. Where the buyer reports its securities holdings in its financial statements at market value, and no current data regarding the cost of those securities are publicly available, the securities may be valued at market for purposes of making the determination set forth in the rule.

In order to apply Rule 144A, the seller of securities must "reasonably believe that the prospective purchaser is a qualified institutional buyer." The release provides examples of sources of information that may be relied upon by the seller to confirm the eligibility of the purchaser. In addition, the rule indicates that the seller may also rely on a certification by the purchaser's chief financial officer, or another executive officer.

It is important to note that Rule 144A offerings require the involvement of a securities attorney to ensure that any securities sold in this manner meet the complex eligibility requirements and other provisions of the rule.

42944. Financial Statements and Business Information Required

As a general rule, if the issuer of the securities subject to Rule 144A is not an SEC registrant, the rule requires the issuer to provide the buyer of the restricted securities the following information:

- A brief statement concerning the nature of the business of the issuer and the products and services that it offers; and

- The issuer's most recent balance sheet, profit and loss and retained earnings statements for three fiscal years. The financial statements, which are generally prepared in accordance with statutory (home country) accounting principles, are required to be audited to the extent such audited financial statements are "reasonably available."

As a general rule, if the issuer is a U.S. company already registered with the SEC, information concerning the business of the issuer and the issuer's financial statements need not be provided to the buyer of the restricted securities.

Non-U.S. companies interested in availing themselves of Rule 144A should be aware that investment bankers involved in a Rule 144A offering may, in some cases, request that narrative disclosures be provided of the differences between U.S. and statutory GAAP. In other cases, financial statements prepared in accordance with U.S. GAAP (or reconciled to U.S. GAAP) may be requested irrespective of the fact that SEC registration is not required. In other cases, quantification (which may be unaudited) of the principal differences between U.S. and statutory GAAP may be requested.

Privately held companies that meet the eligibility requirements for the use of Rule 144A need to be aware of certain asset and shareholder criteria that may trigger the need for SEC registration under Section 12(g) of the 1934 Act. As a general rule, Section 12(g) requires a U.S. company to register with the SEC when its total assets exceed $5 million and it has a class of equity securities held of record by 500 or more persons (see section 19500). With regard to foreign private issuers, registration with the SEC is generally required if total assets exceed $5 million and the issuer has a class of equity securities held of record by 500 or more persons, of which 300 or more shareholders are U.S. residents (see section 19500).

SEC 42943. Rule 144A

FOREIGN REGISTRANTS

43100. INTRODUCTION

The 1933 and 1934 Acts were designed to regulate every "person," foreign or domestic, that issues or proposes to issue securities in the United States or its territories. Accordingly, the securities of foreign issuers that are publicly offered in the United States are required to be registered with the SEC under the 1933 Act, whether they are governments or foreign private issuers, unless exempted. Also, the trading of securities of foreign entities, like those of domestic enterprises, becomes subject to certain annual and periodic reporting provisions of the 1934 Act.

As a general rule, foreign companies intending to offer or register securities in the United States are considered "foreign private issuers." Rule 405 of Regulation C (the SEC's definition rule) defines a foreign private issuer as follows:

> The term ... means any foreign issuer other than a foreign government except an issuer meeting the following conditions: (1) more than 50 percent of the outstanding voting securities of such issuer are held of record either directly or through voting trust certificates of depositary receipts by residents of the United States; and (2) any of the following: (i) the majority of the executive officers or directors are United States citizens or residents, (ii) more than 50 percent of the assets of the issuer are located in the United States, or (iii) the business of the issuer is administered principally in the United States. For the purpose of this paragraph, the term "resident," as applied to security holders, shall mean any person whose address appears on the records of the issuer, the voting trustee, or the depositary as being located in the United States.

To summarize, a foreign company qualifies as a foreign private issuer unless more than 50 percent of the outstanding voting securities are held by residents of the U.S. In such cases, the company would still qualify unless any one of the following conditions exist:

- The majority of the executive officers or directors are U.S. citizens or residents;

- More than 50 percent of its assets are located in the U.S.; or

- The business of the issuer is administered principally in the U.S.

If a non-U.S. company does not qualify as a foreign private issuer, its registration and reporting requirements are the same as for domestic companies.

Any foreign issuer may also voluntarily elect to file the registration and reporting forms that are used by domestic registrants (e.g., Forms S-1, S-2, S-3, and 10-K), unless disqualified from using these forms by the eligibility requirements that are included in the "General Instructions" section of each form. Exceptions are Regulation S-B Forms and Form 1-A (under Regulation A), which are available only to U.S. and Canadian registrants.

43200. FINANCIAL STATEMENT REQUIREMENTS FOR FOREIGN REGISTRANTS

43210. General

As a general rule, foreign private issuers are required to follow the same measurement principles in the presentation of financial statements to be included in filings with the SEC as those followed by U.S. companies. However, Rule 4-01(a)(2) of Regulation S-X (see section 50401) permits the use of accounting principles other than U.S. GAAP in the preparation of the financial statements if they are based on a "comprehensive body of accounting principles." While the rule does not specify what would constitute a comprehensive body of accounting principles, in practice this determination generally has been dependent on the formality and status of the accounting profession in the particular country. Many countries have established bodies promulgating accounting rules or have otherwise specified accounting principles to be followed. In some countries, however, the accounting principles to be followed are not very well defined and a question may arise as to whether they constitute "a comprehensive body of accounting principles." The following is the specific wording in Rule 4-01(a)(2) permitting the use of accounting principles other than U.S. GAAP:

> In all filings of foreign private issuers, except as stated otherwise in the applicable form, the financial statements may be prepared according to a comprehensive body of accounting principles other than those generally accepted in the United States if a reconciliation to United States generally accepted accounting principles and the provisions of Regulation S-X of the type specified in Item 18 of Form 20-F is also filed as part of the financial statements. Alternatively, the financial statements may be prepared according to United States generally accepted accounting principles.

The SEC staff has indicated that the 24 countries that make up the Organization for Economic Co-operation and Development (OECD) are considered to have a comprehensive body of accounting principles pursuant to Rule 4-01(a)(2). The members of the OECD consist of the 18 countries of Western Europe, Iceland, Canada, the United States, Japan, Australia, and New Zealand. In addition, the principles followed by a number of other countries have been accepted by the SEC staff in this context.

374

As indicated above, under the 1934 Act foreign issuers whose securities are widely held and traded in the United States become subject to certain periodic reporting requirements. However, certain disclosures required by U.S. GAAP and Regulation S-X (e.g., the disclosure of segment information) sometimes present foreign issuers with a substantial compliance burden. With this in mind, the SEC has adopted two different levels of financial statement disclosure requirements in Form 20-F.

The minimum disclosure requirements are included under Item 17 of Form 20-F; however, all foreign registrants are encouraged by the SEC to provide the more comprehensive financial statements and related information specified in Item 18.

SAB No. 88 was issued in 1990 in an effort to relieve the disclosure burden for foreign registrants. SAB 88 allows the foreign issuer filing under Item 17 to include U.S. GAAP disclosures not required under its home country GAAP in Management's Discussion and Analysis (MD&A) rather than in the notes to the financial statements. It also allows the foreign issuer to exclude entirely U.S. GAAP and SEC disclosures that are not considered material to an understanding of the Form 20-F. It should be noted, however, that a reconciliation of the statutory GAAP financial statements to U.S. GAAP is required irrespective of whether a non-U.S. company files under the requirements of Item 17 or 18.

One of the principal benefits of SAB 88 for those companies that elect to avail themselves of its provisions is that it provides more flexibility as to how to present the information considered relevant in the MD&A. In addition, it clearly eases the compliance burden for foreign filers that choose to report under Item 17. The major disadvantage is that Item 18 compliance (i.e., full disclosure) covering all years for which financial statements are presented is generally required when new capital is being raised in a 1933 Act filing on Form F-1 or Form F-2. Except for offerings of certain debt securities (discussed below), Item 18 compliance is also generally required in connection with a filing on Form F-3, which provides for the incorporation by reference of filings on Form 20-F. Another potential disadvantage is that analysts and investors might react negatively to a reduction in the amount of financial information presented by existing registrants. The text of SAB No. 88 (SAB Topic 1-D (1)) follows:

Disclosures required of companies complying with Item 17 of Form 20-F

Facts: A foreign private issuer may use Form 20-F as a registration statement under section 12 or as an annual report under section 13(a) or 15(d) of the Exchange Act. The registrant must furnish the financial statements specified in Item 17 of that form. However, in certain circumstances, Forms F-3 and F-2 require that the annual report include financial statements complying with Item 18 of the form. Also, financial statements complying with Item 18 are required for registration of securities under the Securities Act in most circumstances. Item 17 permits the registrant to use its financial statements that are prepared on a comprehensive basis other than U.S. generally accepted accounting principles ("GAAP"), but requires quantification of the material differences in the principles, practices, and methods of accounting. An issuer complying with Item 18 must satisfy the requirements of Item 17 and also must provide all other information required by U.S. GAAP and Regulation S-X.

Question 1: Assuming that the registrant's financial statements include a discussion of material variances from U.S. GAAP along with quantitative reconciliations of net income and material balance sheet items, does Item 17 of Form 20-F require other disclosures in addition to those prescribed by the standards and practices which comprise the comprehensive basis on which the registrant's primary financial statements are prepared?

Interpretive Response: No. The distinction between Items 17 and 18 is premised on a classification of the requirements of U.S. GAAP and Regulation S-X into those that specify the methods of measuring the amounts shown on the face of the financial statements and those prescribing disclosures that explain, modify, or supplement the accounting measurements. Disclosures required by U.S. GAAP but not required under the foreign GAAP on which the financial statements are prepared need not be furnished pursuant to Item 17.

Notwithstanding the absence of a requirement for certain disclosures within the body of the financial statements, some matters routinely disclosed pursuant to U.S. GAAP may rise to a level of materiality such that their disclosure is required by Item 9 (Management's Discussion and Analysis) of Form 20-F. Among other things, this item calls for a discussion of any known trends, demands, commitments, events or uncertainties that are reasonably likely to affect liquidity, capital resources, or the results of operations in a material way. Also, instruction 11 to this item requires a "discussion of any aspects of the difference between foreign and United States generally accepted accounting principles, not discussed in the reconciliation, that the registrant believes is necessary for an understanding of the financial statements as a whole."

Matters that may warrant MD&A coverage in the context of SAB No. 88 include the following:

- Material uncertainties (such as reasonably possible loss contingencies), commitments (such as those arising from leases), and credit risk exposures and concentrations;

- Material unrecognized obligations (such as pension obligations);

- Material changes in estimates and accounting methods, and other factors or events affecting comparability;

- Defaults on debt and material restrictions on dividends or other legal constraints on the registrant's use of its assets;

- Material changes in the relative amounts of constituent elements comprising line items presented on the face of the financial statement;

- Significant terms of financings that would reveal material cash requirements or constraints;

- Material subsequent events, such as events that affect the recoverability of recorded assets;

- Material related-party transactions that may affect the terms under which material revenues or expenses are recorded; and

- Significant accounting policies and measurement assumptions not disclosed in the financial statements, including methods of costing inventory, recognizing revenues, and recording and amortizing assets, which may bear upon an understanding of operating trends or financial condition.

As a general rule, financial statements prepared in accordance with Item 17 of Form 20-F may be worthy of consideration under the following circumstances:

- In filings on Form 20-F when the form is used to register securities under the 1934 Act, typically for an exchange listing without raising new capital.

- In filings on Form 20-F when the form is used as an annual report under the 1934 Act and no 1933 Act registrations involving the generation of new capital are contemplated (except for those specifically exempted as discussed below).

- In filings on Forms F-1, F-2, or F-3 if the only securities being registered are to be offered: (1) upon the exercise of outstanding rights granted by the issuer of the securities to be offered, if such rights are granted on a pro rata basis to all existing security holders of the class of securities to which the rights attach; or (2) pursuant to a dividend or interest reinvestment plan; or (3) upon the conversion of outstanding convertible securities or upon the exercise of outstanding transferable warrants issued by the issuer of the securities to be offered, or by an affiliate of such issuer.

- In a filing on Form F-3 where the form is used to register non-convertible "investment grade" debt securities. Securities are considered to be investment grade if at least one nationally recognized statistical rating organization (e.g., Moody's or Standard & Poor's) has rated the security in a category signifying investment grade; typically the four highest rating categories of each rating organization signify investment grade.

- In a filing on Form 40-F; however, no reconciliation is required if the securities would be eligible to be registered on 1933 Act Form F-9 (see section 46125) or Form 40-F is being filed to satisfy the reporting obligations pursuant to Section 15(d) of the 1934 Act solely due to a 1933 Act filing made on Forms F-7, F-8, F-9 or F-80.

Financial statements that comply with Item 18 (i.e., full U.S. GAAP disclosure) are required to be presented in all other cases.

As a practical matter, the Item 17 option is rarely used except in situations where a particular U.S. GAAP disclosure is very sensitive (e.g., segment data) or where certain information is simply not available.

If the financial statements of a foreign registrant are prepared in accordance with accounting principles other than those generally accepted in the U.S., Rule 4-01(a)(2) and the respective forms used by foreign issuers require a reconciliation that identifies and quantifies each material difference between the accounting principles followed in the preparation of the financial statements and U.S. GAAP. Such a reconciliation, which is required under both Items 17 and 18, is typically included in the footnotes to the financial statements.

Following is the text of Item 18 of Form 20-F, referred to in Rule 4-01(a)(2), which deals with disclosure requirements when financial statements and schedules are not prepared in accordance with U.S. GAAP:

(a) The registrant shall furnish financial statements for the same fiscal years, schedules, and accountants' certificates that would be required to be furnished if the registration statement were on Form 10 or the annual report on Form 10-K, except [compliance with Regulation S-X] Rules 12-03 and 12-05 are required only to the extent a response to Item 13 is made.

(b) The financial statements shall disclose an informational content substantially similar to financial statements that comply with United States generally accepted accounting principles and Regulation S-X.

(c) The financial statements and schedules required by paragraph (a) above may be prepared according to United States generally accepted accounting principles. Alternatively, such financial statements may be prepared according to a comprehensive body of accounting principles other than those generally accepted in the United States if the following are disclosed:

(1) An indication, in the accountants' report or in a reasonably prominent headnote before the financial statements, of the comprehensive body of accounting principles used to prepare the financial statements.

(2) If financial statements are prepared under a comprehensive body of accounting principles that does not include a requirement for a statement of changes in financial position or a statement of cash or funds flow, the basic financial statements shall include a statement of cash flows which meets the requirements of U.S. generally accepted accounting principles. If the financial statements are prepared under a comprehensive body of accounting principles that includes a requirement for a statement of cash or funds flow that differs from the requirements under U.S. generally accepted accounting principles, cash flow information that is substantially similar to the requirements under U.S. generally accepted accounting principles may be presented in a separate statement of cash flows or in a footnote.

(3) A discussion of the material variations in the accounting principles, practices, and methods used in preparing the financial statements from the principles, practices and methods generally accepted in the United States and in Regulation S-X. Such material variations shall be quantified in the following format.

(i) For each year and any interim periods for which an income statement is presented, net income shall be reconciled in a tabular format, substantially similar to the one shown below, on the face of the income statement or in a note thereto. Each material variation shall be described and quantified as a separate reconciling item, but material variations may be combined on the face of the income statement if shown separately in a note.

Net income as shown in the financial statements XXX

Description of items having the effect of increasing reported income
Item 1 XXX
Item 2, etc. XXX

Description of items having the effect of decreasing reported income
Item 1 . . . . (XXX)
Item 2, etc. . . . . (XXX)

Net income according to generally accepted accounting principles in the United States XXX

(ii) For each balance sheet presented, indicate the amount of each material variation between an amount of a line item appearing in a balance sheet and the amount determined using United States generally accepted accounting principles and Regulation S-X. Such amounts may be shown in parentheses, in columns, as a reconciliation of the equity section, as a restated balance sheet, or in any similar format that clearly presents the differences in the amounts.

(iii) For an issuer in a hyperinflationary economy that comprehensively includes the effects of price level changes in its primary financial statements, the quantification of variations required by this paragraph shall not include such effects. A reasonably prominent headnote to the financial statements shall describe the basis used to prepare the financial statements. The reconciliation shall state that such effects have not been included in the reconciliation.

(4) All other information required by United States generally accepted accounting principles and Regulation S-X unless such requirements specifically do not apply to the registrant as a foreign issuer.

Instructions:

1. If the variations quantified pursuant to paragraph (c) above are significant, the registrant should consider presenting them on the face of the financial statements.

2. Earnings per share computed according to generally accepted accounting principles in the United States shall be presented if materially different from the earnings per share otherwise presented.

Item 18(a) specifies that the periods covered by the financial statements and the form of the auditors' report must be the same as those required for U.S. registrants. However, as discussed in the next section below, Regulation S-X Rule 3-19 makes certain concessions to foreign private issuers. Items 17(b) and 18(b) further require that the financial statements "substantially" disclose information required by U.S. generally accepted accounting principles and Regulation S-X. If the registrant is required to furnish financial statements in accordance with Item 18, the term "substantially" is superseded by Item 18(c)(3), which provides that information required by U.S. generally accepted accounting principles and Regulation S-X must be furnished. While Item 17 contains instructions similar to those included under Item 18, the fundamental difference is that it does not have a provision similar to Item 18(c)(3).

The SEC staff has offered the following recommendations concerning the preparation of the U.S. GAAP reconciliation:

- The reconciliation of income statement items should be in sufficient detail to allow an investor to understand the various differences in accounting standards. Presenting reconciling items in overly broad categories should usually be avoided.

- The reconciliation format should also be in sufficient detail to allow an investor to determine the differences in each balance sheet account. As above, the format is generally improved by not grouping several balance sheet accounts in the same line item and not presenting reconciling items net of tax.

- Significant income statement classification differences should be described.

- The discussion of differences in accounting standards should be sufficiently detailed to allow an investor to understand the basis for the difference and the financial statement impact.

- In the unlikely event that there are no differences between the foreign accounting standards and U.S. standards applied to the financial statements, this fact should be disclosed.

During 1992, the SEC issued technical amendments regarding the cash flow statement that modified Form 20-F Item 18(c)(2) (refer to the above text of Item 18). The SEC staff has informally indicated that it will consider foreign private issuers to be in compliance with the requirements of Form 20-F if they provide a cash or funds flow statement in accordance with their local standards and include information in the notes to the financial statements that will allow a user to reconstruct the cash or funds flow statement to a cash flow statement prepared in accordance with SFAS 95. Some of the more common items that the staff has indicated may be required to be addressed to allow an investor to reconstruct this information include the following:

- Classification differences among categories of the cash flow statement, i.e., operating, investing, and financing. For example, the new statement on cash flows in the United Kingdom allocates cash flow among five categories and classifies certain items differently. In such cases, disclosure would be required as to how these items would be classified under SFAS 95.

- All noncash investing and financing activities. For example, Canada includes noncash items in the cash flow statements.

- Effects of any differences in the definition of cash. For example, the United Kingdom standards consider overdrafts to be cash equivalents, whereas a change in this item would be considered a financing activity under SFAS 95.

- Gross activity in amounts presented on a net basis.

- Disclosure of income taxes and interest paid.

- Changes in the specific working capital accounts, such as receivables, inventory and payables.

43220. Age of Financial Statements

The most recent date and period (the age) of the financial statements of foreign private issuers to be included in registration statements is covered by Regulation S-X Rule 3-19 (see section 50353). This rule extends the date as of which financial statements are required from the 135-day maximum applicable to U.S. issuers (see Rule 3-12 in section 50346) to a six-month maximum period for the filing and effective date of registration statements filed by foreign private issuers. However, if the effective date of a registration statement filed by a foreign private issuer falls during the period between five and six months subsequent to the registrant's fiscal year-end, as a general rule the filing must include audited financial statements for the most recent fiscal year.

As discussed in Regulation S-X Rule 3-19, interim financial statements may be required, depending on the effective date of the registration statement. Irrespective of whether the interim financial statements are audited, the financial statement schedules under Regulation S-X Article 12 (see section 51200) are not required in connection with the interim periods presented.

43230. Currency of Financial Statements

Rule 3-20 requires a foreign private issuer to present its financial statements in the currency of its country of domicile unless the issuer can demonstrate, by meeting specified conditions, that another currency is more appropriate. The rule also limits the use of dollar equivalent presentations, frequently known as "convenience statements," to the latest fiscal year and interim period. The exchange rate to be used in preparing convenience statements should be the rate as of the date of the most recent balance sheet included in the filing unless the more current rate differs materially from the rate at the most recent balance sheet date. Refer to Rule 3-20 (see section 50354) for further discussion regarding the reporting currency for financial statements prepared by foreign private issuers.

43240. Separate Financial Statements

Separate financial statements of a business acquired or to be acquired or of a subsidiary that is not consolidated and 50 percent or less owned persons may be required in a registration statement filed under the 1933 or 1934 Acts by a foreign registrant pursuant to S-X Rule 3-05 and S-X Rule 3-09, respectively. The SEC rules require that such financial statements be either prepared in accordance with U.S. GAAP or reconciled thereto.

43250. Accountants' Reports

Reports of independent accountants for foreign private issuers may be prepared in accordance with requirements of the accountant's country provided that the reports:

- Comply with the requirements of Article 2 of Regulation S-X including the independence requirements (the SEC will not accept a report that contains or implies a scope limitation even if it is acceptable in the accountant's home country);

- Include a statement that the audit was conducted in accordance with U.S. generally accepted auditing standards (GAAS). A statement that an audit was conducted in accordance with foreign auditing standards which are substantially similar to U.S. GAAS is acceptable. Alternatively, the SEC will accept a letter from the independent accountants indicating that the audit was conducted in accordance with U.S. GAAS; and

- Include a statement indicating that the financial statements were prepared in accordance with a comprehensive body of accounting principles (see section 43210), e.g., accounting principles generally accepted in the United Kingdom. Alternatively, the disclosure of the accounting principles followed may be indicated in a prominent headnote before the financial statements.

43260. Canadian Issuers

The SEC staff has informally indicated that Canadian issuers may elect to file on domestic forms (e.g., Form 10-K or 10-Q) prepared in accordance with Canadian GAAP provided they furnish the financial statement disclosures required by Item 18 of Form 20-F (see section 43210). The staff noted that providing the disclosures required by Item 17 would not be acceptable when filing on domestic forms. The staff mentioned that Canadian oil and gas companies electing to file on Form 10-K would be required to provide all information required by FASB Statement No. 69. In addition, the staff has indicated that although companies are permitted to disclose cash flow per share under Canadian standards, this information should not be included in filings made with the SEC. The SEC's position on restrictions of disclosing cash flow per share is presented in FRP Section 202.

44000. REPORTING AND REGISTRATION FORMS UNDER THE 1934 ACT FOR FOREIGN PRIVATE ISSUERS

44100. FORM 20-F

44110. General

Form 20-F is the form most commonly used either as a registration statement under Section 12 of the 1934 Act or as an annual report or transition report filed under Section 13(a) or 15(d) of the 1934 Act by any non-Canadian foreign private issuer. It is also the form that contains the instructions as to the information with respect to the registrant for the 1933 registration forms. A Canadian foreign private issuer ineligible to register under the Multijurisdictional Disclosure System (see section 46000) would also use this form as a 1934 Act registration statement and as an annual report.

The following are the items of information to be included in Form 20-F:

PART I

Item

1	Description of business
2	Description of property
3	Legal proceedings
4	Control of registrant
5	Nature of trading market
6	Exchange controls and other limitations affecting security holders
7	Taxation
8	Selected financial data

Item

9	Management's discussion and analysis of financial condition and results of operations
10	Directors and officers of registrant
11	Compensation of directors and officers
12	Options to purchase securities from registrant or subsidiaries
13	Interest of management in certain transactions

PART II

14	Description of securities to be registered
	(a) Capital stock to be registered
	(b) Debt securities to be registered
	(c) American depositary receipts
	(d) Other securities to be registered

PART III

15	Defaults upon senior securities
16	Changes in securities and changes in security for registered securities

PART IV

17	Financial statements (see section 43210)
18	Financial statements (see section 43210)
19	Financial statements and exhibits

The information specified in Items 12 and 13 of Form 20-F need be furnished only to the extent that the registrant discloses to its shareholders or otherwise makes public the information for individually named directors and officers.

44120. Disclosure Requirements

The following sections address certain of the more significant disclosure requirements of Form 20-F; however, in all instances reference needs to be made to the specific instructions to the form.

44121. Description of Business. Item 1 of Form 20-F requires the following financial disclosures, in addition to various narrative descriptions of the business:

Item 1. Description of Business

(a) Describe the business done and intended to be done by the registrant and its subsidiaries...

SEC 44110. Form 20-F

(4) The breakdown of total sales and revenue during the past three fiscal years by categories of activity and into geographical markets (with sales to unaffiliated customers and sales transfers to other categories of activity of the registrant shown separately). Any relatively homogeneous activity which contributes significantly to total sales and revenue shall be considered a separate category of activity.

Instruction.
If the contribution to total operating profit (or loss) from each of the registrant's categories of activity materially differs from their respective contributions to total sales and revenue, such categories of activity shall be identified and appropriate narrative disclosure made concerning the significance of the contributions to total operating profit (or loss) from such category of activity. The actual operating profit (or loss) attributable to each category of activity is not required to be presented unless otherwise required to be disclosed by applicable foreign law or regulations or by foreign stock exchange requirements or is otherwise disclosed.

(5) The status of a product or service if the registrant has made public information about a new product or service which would require the investment of a material amount of the assets of the registrant or is otherwise material.

(6) The research and development policy including the estimated amount spent during each of the last three fiscal years on company-sponsored research and development activities.

(b) The registrant shall also describe those distinctive or special characteristics of the registrant's operations or industry which may have a material impact upon the registrant's future financial performance. The registrant shall briefly describe any material country risks which are unlikely to be known or anticipated by investors and could materially affect the registrant's operations. Examples of factors which might be discussed include dependence on one or a few major customers or suppliers (including suppliers of raw materials or financing), existing or probable governmental regulation; expiration of material labor contracts, patents, trademarks, licenses, franchises, concessions or royalty agreements; unusual competitive conditions in the industry, cyclicality of the industry and anticipated raw material or energy shortages to the extent management may not be able to secure a continuing source of supply.

Instruction.
Furnish the information specified in any industry guide listed in Part 9 of Regulation S-K applicable to the registrant except that a registrant that furnishes the information specified in Appendix A to Item 2(b) of this Form need not furnish any additional information specified in Guide 2 relating to oil and gas operations.

44122. Selected Financial Data. The disclosure requirements are similar to those prescribed by Item 301 of Regulation S-K (see section 63010), but require foreign private issuers to provide certain additional information. The text of Item 8 of Form 20-F is as follows:

Item 8. Selected Financial Data

Furnish in comparative columnar form the selected financial data for the registrant, referred to below, for

(a) Each of the last five fiscal years of the registrant (or for the life of the registrant and its predecessors, if less), and

(b) Any additional fiscal years necessary to keep the information from being misleading.

Instructions:

1. The purpose of the selected financial data shall be to supply in a convenient and readable format selected financial data which highlight certain significant trends in the registrant's financial condition and results of operations.

2. Subject to appropriate variation to conform to the nature of the registrant's business, the following items shall be included in the table of financial data: net sales or operating revenues; income (loss) from continuing operations; income (loss) from continuing operations per common share; total assets; long-term obligations and redeemable preferred stock (including long-term debt, capital leases, and redeemable preferred stock as defined in Rule 5-02.28(a) of Regulation S-X); and cash dividends declared per common share. Registrants may include additional items which they believe would enhance an understanding of and would highlight other trends in their financial condition and results of operations. Briefly describe, or cross-reference to a discussion thereof, factors such as accounting changes, business combinations or dispositions of business operations, that materially affect the comparability of the information reflected in the selected financial data. Discussion of, or reference to, any material uncertainties shall be included where such matters might cause the data reflected herein not to be indicative of the registrant's future financial condition or results of operations.

3. Those registrants that are required to provide inflation information pursuant to Rule 3-20(c) of Regulation S-X may combine such information with the selected financial data appearing pursuant to this Item.

4. All references to the registrant in the table of selected financial data and in this Item shall mean the registrant and its subsidiaries consolidated.

5. If interim period financial statements are included, or are required to be included by Rule 3-19 of Regulation S-X in a registration statement filed under

the Securities Act of 1933, registrants should consider whether any or all of the selected financial data need to be updated for such interim periods to reflect a material change in the trends indicated; where such updating information is necessary, registrants shall provide the information on a comparative basis unless not necessary to an understanding of such updating information.

6. Disclose the following information:

> (a) In the forepart of the document and as of the latest practicable date, the exchange rate into United States currency of the foreign currency in which the financial statements are denominated;

> (b) A history of exchange rates for the five most recent years and any subsequent interim period for which financial statements are presented setting forth the rates for period end, the average rates, and the range of high and low rates for each year; and

> (c) If the registration statement or report relates to a class of equity securities, a five-year summary of dividends per share stated in both the currency in which the financial statements are denominated and United States currency based on the exchange rates at each respective payment date.

7. The selected financial data shall be presented in the same currency as the financial statements. The issuer may present the selected financial data on the basis of the accounting principles used in its primary financial statements but in such case shall present this data also on the basis of any reconciliations of such data to United States generally accepted accounting principles and Regulation S-X made pursuant to Item 17 or 18 of this Form.

8. For purposes of this rule, the rate of exchange means the noon buying rate in New York City for cable transfers in foreign currencies as certified for customs purposes by the Federal Reserve Bank of New York. The average rate means the average of the exchange rates on the last day of each month during a year.

44123. Management's Discussion and Analysis of Financial Condition and Results of Operations (MD&A). The disclosure requirements of Item 9 of Form 20-F are the same as those prescribed by Item 303 of Regulation S-K (see section 63030), except that foreign private issuers are also specifically required to provide:

1. A brief discussion of any governmental economic, fiscal, monetary, or political policies or factors that have materially affected or could materially affect, directly or indirectly, their operations or investments by U.S. nationals.

2. A reference to the reconciliation to U.S. GAAP and a discussion of any aspects of the difference between foreign and U.S. GAAP not discussed in the reconcili-

ation that the registrant believes are necessary for an understanding of the financial statements as a whole.

Because Form 20-F ordinarily would not include financial statements for interim periods (unless it is used to register securities under the 1934 Act), Regulation S-K's requirements as to MD&A for interim periods are generally not applicable. However, where financial statements are presented for interim periods, the registrant's financial condition, results of operations, and cash flows are expected to be discussed for those periods following the guidelines of Regulation S-K, Item 303(b).

The discussion presented in the MD&A is generally based on the primary financial statements but the discussion is also required to address the reconciliation to U.S. GAAP, particularly to the extent that there are material changes in the nature and relative amounts of the reconciling items.

44124. Directors and Officers of Registrant. The disclosure requirements of Item 10 of Form 20-F are similar to those of Item 401 of Regulation S-K (see section 64010), except that Form 20-F does not require the discussion of the directors' and officers' business experience and backgrounds and involvement in certain legal proceedings. The following are the specific disclosures required:

Item 10. Directors and Officers of Registrant

(a) List the names of all directors and executive officers of the registrant and all persons chosen to become directors or executive officers; indicate all positions and offices with the registrant held by each such person; state his term of office as director and/or as executive officer and the period during which he has served as such; and briefly describe any arrangement or understanding between him and any other person pursuant to which he was selected as a director or executive officer.

Instructions:
1. Do not include arrangements or understandings with directors or executive officers of the registrant acting solely in their capacities as such.

2. The term "executive officer" means the president, secretary, treasurer, any vice president in charge of a principal business function (such as sales, administration or finance) or any other person who performs similar policy making functions for the registrant. Where the registrant employs persons such as production managers, sales managers, or research scientists, who are not executive officers, but who make or are expected to make significant contributions to the business of the registrant, such persons shall be identified and their background disclosed to the same extent as in the case of executive officers.

(b) State the nature of any family relationship between any director or executive officer and any other director or executive officer.

Instruction.

The term "family relationship" means any relationship by blood, marriage or adoption, not more remote than first cousin.

44125. Compensation of Directors and Officers. The disclosure requirements under Item 11 of Form 20-F are substantially less than the requirements of Item 402 of Regulation S-K (see section 64020). Among the required disclosures are:

1. The aggregate amount of compensation paid by the registrant and its subsidiaries during the registrant's last fiscal year to all directors and officers as a group, without naming them, for services in all capacities; and

2. The aggregate amount set aside or accrued by the registrant and its subsidiaries during the last fiscal year of the registrant to provide pension, retirement or similar benefits for directors and officers of the registrant, pursuant to any existing plan provided or contributed to by the registrant or its subsidiaries.

However, if the foreign registrant discloses to its security holders or otherwise makes public compensation information for individually named directors or executive officers, that information is required to be presented in Form 20-F.

44130. Due Date

When used as an annual report, Form 20-F must be filed within six months after the end of the registrant's fiscal year.

44140. Annual Report to Shareholders

The form and content of annual reports to shareholders prepared by U.S. registrants is governed by the proxy rules. Regulation 12-3(b) of the 1934 Act exempts foreign private issuers from the proxy rules under Section 14 of the 1934 Act. Accordingly, there are no specific SEC requirements regarding the information to be included by foreign registrants in their annual reports to shareholders.

44200. FORM 6-K

Foreign private issuers are not required to file quarterly reports on Form 10-Q or current reports on Form 8-K. Instead, such registrants are required to furnish reports on Form 6-K whenever relevant information is made public to non-U.S. investors pursuant to foreign laws or stock exchange regulations or distributed to security holders. This form is used by foreign private issuers that are required to furnish reports pursuant to Rule 13a-16 or 15d-16 under the 1934 Act.

Form 6-K is usually a cover form to which certain information is attached. The type of information typically attached to or provided in Form 6-K includes data such as quarterly or semi-annual earnings releases; changes in management or control; acquisitions or dispositions of assets; bankruptcy or receivership; changes in the registrant's independent accountants; the financial condition and results of operations; material legal proceedings; changes in securities or in the security for registered securities; defaults upon senior securities; material increases or decreases in the amount outstanding of securities or indebtedness; the results of the submission of matters to a vote of security holders; transactions with directors, officers, or principal security holders; the granting of options or payment of other compensation to directors or officers; and any other significant information that the registrant deems of material importance to security holders and has found appropriate to disclose in its country of domicile. The information filed on Form 6-K is not subject to SEC requirements; it merely consists of copies of information filed or made public in the foreign private issuer's country. English translations are required in connection with press releases and information provided directly to shareholders. English translations are only required for other types of information if it is prepared by the issuer.

The report on Form 6-K is required to be submitted promptly after the material contained in the report is made public. The form consists of a cover page, a copy of the document or report involved, and a signature page.

44300. FORM 40-F

44310. General

Form 40-F was adopted as part of the Multijurisdictional Disclosure System (MJDS) for Canadian companies (see section 46000). The form is available for eligible Canadian issuers to satisfy their reporting obligations pursuant to Section 15(d) of the 1934 Act, which obligations arise solely due to their filing a 1933 Act registration statement on MJDS Forms F-7, F-8, F-9, F-10, or F-80. (It is important to note that no reporting obligation arises under the 1934 Act if securities are registered on Forms F-7, F-8, or F-80 and if the issuer is exempt from the requirements of Section 12(g) at the time of filing.)

Form 40-F may also be used by eligible Canadian issuers to register securities under Section 12 of the 1934 Act and to file reports pursuant to Section 13(a) and 15(d) of the 1934 Act.

Form 40-F is used as a wraparound report for the filing of home jurisdictional information. A Canadian issuer using Form 40-F to register its securities is required to file information of the type made public, filed with a stock exchange or distributed to security holders since the beginning of its most recent full fiscal year. A Canadian issuer using Forms 40-F and 6-K (see section 44200) to satisfy its continuous reporting obligations is required to file its home jurisdictional Annual Information Form, and its home jurisdictional audited annual financial statements and accompanying MD&A (see section 63030) under cover of Form 40-F and furnish all other material home jurisdictional information under cover of Form 6-K.

Any financial statements included in Form 40-F (other than interim financial statements) are required to be reconciled to U.S. GAAP as required by Item 17 of Form 20-F (see section 43210). However, no reconciliation is required if:

- The securities would be eligible to be registered on 1933 Act Form F-9 (see section 46125); or

- Form 40-F is being filed to satisfy the reporting obligations pursuant to Section 15(d) of the 1934 Act required solely due to a 1933 Act filing made on Forms F-7, F-8, F-9, or F-80.

44320. Eligibility Requirements

To be eligible to file this form the registrant is required to:

- Be incorporated or organized under the laws of Canada, or any Canadian Province or Territory.

- Qualify as a "foreign private issuer" pursuant to Rule 405 of the 1933 Act (as defined in section 43100) or as a Canadian "crown corporation" (a corporation whose common shares or comparable equity is all owned directly or indirectly by the Government of Canada or a Province or Territory of Canada).

- Have at least a three-year history (or one year if a crown corporation) of reporting with a Canadian securities regulatory authority and be in compliance with the requirements of such regulators.

- Have an aggregate market value of its outstanding shares of:

  •• (CN) $180 million or more if the filing relates to convertible securities of a Form F-9 eligible issuer (see section 46125).

  •• (CN) $360 million or more in all other cases; however, no market threshold needs to be met in connection with nonconvertible securities eligible for registration on Form F-9 (see section 46125).

- Have an aggregate market value of its "public float" (securities held by nonaffiliates) of (CN) $75 million or more; however, no market value threshold needs to be met in connection with nonconvertible securities eligible for registration on Form F-9 (see section 46125).

The market value of equity shares and the amount of public float may be determined as of any date within 60 days prior to the filing.

SEC 44320. Form 40-F

45000. REPORTING AND REGISTRATION FORMS
UNDER THE 1933 ACT FOR FOREIGN PRIVATE ISSUERS

Foreign private issuers eligible to use Form 20-F may qualify to use Forms F-1, F-2, or F-3 for registering securities under the 1933 Act. Like Forms S-1, S-2, and S-3, which are used by U.S. companies, Forms F-1, F-2, and F-3 are designed to establish different levels of disclosure and reporting requirements for various classes of registrants. The eligibility criteria for these forms are similar in concept to those applicable to Forms S-1, S-2, and S-3, ensuring that only foreign issuers who have been in the 1934 Act reporting system for certain specified periods of time may use the more abbreviated Forms F-2 and F-3, with only large actively traded foreign issuers eligible to use the latter. Under the Multijurisdictional Disclosure System (see section 46000) Canadian foreign private issuers registering securities under the 1933 Act that meet certain criteria are eligible to use Canadian disclosure documentation rather than Forms F-1, F-2, and F-3.

Once registered under the 1933 Act, the foreign private issuer becomes subject to the 1934 Act reporting requirements unless exempt. If not exempt, the registrant will be required to file annual reports on Form 20-F (see section 44100) and current reports on Form 6-K (see section 44200). Under the Multijurisdictional Disclosure System, Canadian foreign private issuers may satisfy their 1934 Act reporting requirements by filing Form 40-F (see section 44300).

45100.   FORM F-1

45110. General

Form F-1 is used for the registration of securities of all foreign private issuers eligible to use Form 20-F under the 1933 Act for which no other form is authorized or prescribed. Similar in concept to Form S-1 (see section 42100), Form F-1 requires a traditional full prospectus and allows the incorporation by reference of information from other filings as described in Item 1b.

Items of information required by Form F-1 are as follows:

PART I. INFORMATION REQUIRED IN PROSPECTUS

Item

1	Forepart of registration statement and outside front cover page of prospectus
2	Inside front and outside back cover pages of prospectus
3	Summary information, risk factors, and ratio of earnings to fixed charges
4	Use of proceeds
5	Determination of offering price
6	Dilution
7	Selling security holders
8	Plan of distribution
9	Description of securities to be registered
10	Interests of named experts and counsel
11	Information with respect to the registrant
12	Disclosure of Commission position on indemnification for Securities Act liabilities

PART II. INFORMATION NOT REQUIRED IN PROSPECTUS

13	Other expenses of issuance and distribution
14	Indemnification of directors and officers
15	Recent sales of unregistered securities
16	Exhibits and financial statement schedules
17	Undertakings

SEC 45100. Form F-1

With the exception of information with respect to the registrant (Item 11) and the requirements for exhibits and financial statement schedules (Item 16), the requirements for each of the items of information in Form F-1 are set forth in Regulation S-K. See discussion beginning with section 60000. An accountants' consent (see sections 17110 and 20510) is also required to be included in Part II of Form F-1 pursuant to Item 601 of Regulation S-K. The exhibit table in section 66102 should be referred to for a listing of the exhibits required to be included in a filing on Form F-1.

45120. Information with Respect to the Registrant

The information required to be furnished in Form F-1 with respect to the registrant as set forth in Item 11 are as follows:

Item 11. Information with Respect to the Registrant.

Furnish the following information with respect to the Registrant:

(a) Information required by Part I of Form 20-F;

(b) Information required by Item 18 of Form 20-F (Schedules required under Regulation S-X shall be filed as "Financial Statement Schedules" pursuant to Item 16, Exhibit and Financial Statement Schedules, of this Form), as well as any information required by Rule 3-05 and Article 11 of Regulation S-X, except as permitted by (c) below:

(c) Information required by Item 17 of Form 20-F may be furnished in lieu of the information specified by Item 18 thereof if the only securities being registered are to be offered: (1) upon the exercise of outstanding rights granted by the issuer of the securities to be offered, if such rights are granted on a pro rata basis to all existing security holders of the class of securities to which the rights attach and there is no standby underwriting in the United States or similar arrangement; or (2) pursuant to a dividend or interest reinvestment plan; or (3) upon the conversion of outstanding convertible securities or upon the exercise of outstanding transferable warrants issued by the issuer of the securities to be offered, or by an affiliate of such issuer.

Instruction:
Attention is directed to Section 10(a)(3) of the Securities Act.

45130. Financial Statement Requirements

The form and content of and requirements for the financial statements and schedules to be included in this form and the dates and periods for which they are required to be presented are set forth in Regulation S-X. A discussion of these requirements is included beginning with section 50050 of this manual. However, for an overview of the SEC's financial statement requirements as they pertain to a foreign private issuer, reference should be made to section 43200.

45200. FORM F-2

45210. General

Form F-2, which permits the use of a short prospectus with the delivery of the latest annual report on Form 20-F, is available to foreign private issuers that have been subject to 1934 Act reporting requirements for at least three years, but that do not meet the transaction requirements for the use of Form F-3 described in section 45300. It is analogous in concept to Form S-2, which is discussed in section 42200 of this manual. This form may be used for the registration of any securities except those issued in an exchange offer.

The eligibility requirements for use of Form F-2 are as follows:

A. The registrant has a class of securities registered pursuant to Section 12(b) of the Securities Exchange Act of 1934 ("Exchange Act") or has a class of equity securities registered pursuant to Section 12(g) of the Exchange Act or is required to file reports pursuant to Section 15(d) of the Exchange Act and is eligible to file and has filed annual reports on Form 20-F or Form 10-K or in, the case of registrants described in General Instruction A(2) of Form 40-F, on Form 40-F under the Exchange Act.

B. 1. The registrant: (a) has been subject to the requirements of Section 12 or 15(d) of the Exchange Act and has filed all the information required to be filed pursuant to Sections 13, 14 or 15(d) for a period of at least thirty-six calendar months immediately preceding the filing of the registration statement on this form; (b) has filed in a timely manner all reports required to be filed during the twelve calendar months and any portion of a month immediately preceding the filing of the registration statement and, if the issuer has used (during the twelve calendar months and any portion of a month immediately preceding the filing of the registration statement) Rule 12b- 25(b) under the Exchange Act with respect to a report or portion of a report, that report or portion thereof has actually been filed within the time period prescribed by the Rule.

2. The provisions of this paragraph (B)(1)(a) do not apply to any registrant if: (i) the aggregate market value worldwide of the voting stock of the registrant held by non-affiliates is the equivalent of $300 million or more, or if non-convertible debt securities that are "investment grade debt securities," as defined below, are being registered and (ii) the registrant has filed at least one Form 20-F, Form 40-F or Form 10-K that is the latest required to have been filed.

SEC 45200. Form F-2

Instructions.

1. The aggregate market value of the registrant's outstanding voting stock shall be computed by use of the price at which the stock was last sold, or the average of the bid and asked prices of such stock in the principal market for such stock, as of a date within 60 days prior to the date of filing. [See the definition of "affiliate" in Securities Act Rule 405.]

2. A non-convertible debt security is an "investment grade debt security" if, at the time of effectiveness of the registration statement, at least one nationally recognized statistical rating organization (as that term is used in Rule 15c3-1(c)(2)(vi)(F) under the Exchange Act) has rated the security in one of its generic rating categories that signifies investment grade; typically, the four highest rating categories (within which there may be sub-categories or gradations indicating relative standing) signify investment grade.

C. Neither the registrant nor any of its consolidated or unconsolidated subsidiaries have, since the end of their last fiscal year for which certified financial statements of the registrant and its consolidated subsidiaries were included in a report filed pursuant to Section 13(a) or 15(d) of the Exchange Act: (1) failed to pay any dividend or sinking fund installment on preferred stock; or (2) defaulted (a) on any installment or installments on indebtedness for borrowed money, or (b) on any rental on one or more long term leases, which defaults in the aggregate are material to the financial position of the registrant and its consolidated and unconsolidated subsidiaries, taken as a whole.

D. The financial statements in the registrant's latest filing on Form 20-F, Form 40-F or Form 10-K comply with Item 18 of Form 20-F.

E. The provisions of paragraphs (B)(1)(a) and (D) do not apply if the registrant has filed at least one Form 20-F, Form 40-F or Form 10-K that is the latest required to have been filed and if the only securities being registered are to be offered: (1) upon the exercise of outstanding rights granted by the issuer of the securities to be offered, if such rights are granted pro rata to all existing security holders of the class of securities to which the rights attach; or (2) pursuant to a dividend or interest reinvestment plan; or (3) upon the conversion of outstanding convertible securities or upon the exercise of outstanding transferable warrants, issued by the issuer of the securities to be offered, or by an affiliate of such issuer. The exemptions in this paragraph (E) are unavailable if securities are to be offered or sold in a standby underwriting in the United States or similar arrangement.

F. If a registrant is a successor registrant it shall be deemed to have met conditions A, B, C, D, and E above if: (1) its predecessor and it, taken together, do so, provided that the succession was primarily for the purpose of changing the state or other jurisdiction of incorporation of the predecessor or forming a holding company and that the assets and liabilities of the successor at the time of succession were substantially the same as those of the predecessor; or (2) all predecessors met the conditions at the time of succession and the registrant has continued to do so since the succession.

398

G. If a registrant is a majority-owned subsidiary which does not meet the conditions of these eligibility requirements, it shall nevertheless be deemed to have met such conditions if its parent meets the conditions and if the parent fully guarantees the securities being registered as to principal and interest. Note: In such an instance the parent-guarantor is the issuer of a separate security consisting of the guarantee which must be concurrently registered but may be registered on the same registration statement as are the guaranteed securities. Both the parent-guarantor and the subsidiary shall each disclose the information required by this Form as if each were the only registrant except that if the subsidiary will not be eligible to file annual reports on Form 20-F or Form 40-F after the effective date of the registration statement, then it shall disclose the information specified in Form S-2. Rule 3-10 of Regulation S-X specifies the financial statements required.

H. Electronic filings: In addition to satisfying the foregoing conditions, a registrant subject to the electronic filing requirements of Rule 101 of Regulation S-T shall have filed with the Commission all required electronic filings, including confirming electronic copies of documents submitted in paper pursuant to a temporary hardship exemption as provided in Rule 201 of Regulation S-T.

It is important to note that with regard to rights offerings, dividend or interest reinvestment plans, and conversions or warrants, financial statement information required by Item 17 of Form 20-F may be furnished in lieu of the information specified by Item 18. (See section 43210.)

The following are the items of information to be included in Form F-2:

PART I. INFORMATION REQUIRED IN PROSPECTUS

Item

1   Forepart of registration statement and outside front cover page of prospectus
2   Inside front and outside back cover pages of prospectus
3   Summary information, risk factors, and ratio of earnings to fixed charges
4   Use of proceeds
5   Determination of offering price
6   Dilution
7   Selling security holders
8   Plan of distribution
9   Description of securities to be registered
10 Interests of named experts and counsel
11 Material changes
12 Information with respect to the Registrant
13 Disclosure of Commission position on indemnification for Securities Act liabilities

SEC 45210. Form F-2

PART II. INFORMATION NOT REQUIRED IN PROSPECTUS

Item

14	Other expenses of issuance and distribution
15	Indemnification of directors and officers
16	Exhibits
17	Undertakings

An accountants' consent (see sections 17110 and 20510) is also required to be included in Part II of Form F-2 pursuant to Item 601 of Regulation S-K. The Exhibit Table in section 66102 summarizes the exhibits required to be included in Form F-2.

45220. Material Changes

Item 11 of Form F-2 deals with the disclosure requirements pertaining to material changes in the registrant's affairs. The text of Item 11 is as follows:

Item 11. Material Changes.

(a) Describe any and all material changes in the registrant's affairs which have occurred since the end of the latest fiscal year for which certified financial statements were included in the latest filing on Form 20-F, Form 40-F or Form 10-K under the Exchange Act.

(b)(1) Include in the prospectus, if not included in the reports filed under the Exchange Act which are incorporated by reference into the prospectus pursuant to Item 12: (i) information required by Rule 3-05 and Article 11 of Regulation S-X; (ii) restated financial statements if there has been a change in accounting principles or a correction of an error where such change or correction requires material retroactive restatement of financial statements; (iii) restated financial statements where one or more business combinations accounted for by the pooling of interest method of accounting have been consummated subsequent to the most recent fiscal year and the acquired businesses, considered in the aggregate, are significant under Rule 11-01(b); or (iv) any financial information required because of a material disposition of assets outside the normal course of business.

(2) If the financial statements incorporated by reference from the registrant's latest Form 20-F, Form 40-F or Form 10-K in accordance with Item 12 are not sufficiently current to comply with the requirements of Rule 3-19 of Regulation S-X, financial statements necessary to comply with that rule shall be presented either in the prospectus or in an amended Form 20-F, Form 40-F or Form 10-K.

Instruction.
Financial statements or information required to be furnished by this Item shall

be reconciled pursuant to either Item 17 or 18 of Form 20-F, whichever is applicable to the primary financial statements.

45230. Information with Respect to the Registrant

Item 12 includes the following provisions concerning information that needs to be provided with respect to the registrant in a registration statement filed on Form F-2:

Item 12. Information with Respect to the Registrant.

The registrant shall incorporate by reference and deliver with the prospectus the latest Form 20-F, Form 40-F or Form 10-K filed pursuant to the Exchange Act that contains certified financial statements for the registrant's latest fiscal year for which a Form 20-F, Form 40-F, or Form 10-K was required to have been filed and any report on Form 10-Q and 8-K filed since the end of the fiscal year covered by such annual report. The registrant may incorporate by reference and deliver with the prospectus any other Form 10-Q or Form 8-K, and any Form 6-K containing information meeting the requirements of this Form.

Instructions:

1. Reference is made to General Instruction I.D. that, in some cases, requires the financial statements in the Form 20-F, Form 40-F, or Form 10-K to comply with Item 18 of Form 20-F as a condition for eligibility to use Form F-2.

2. Attention is directed to the requirements of Section 10(a)(3) of the Securities Act.

3. Attention is directed to Rule 439 regarding consent to use material incorporated by reference.

4. The Form 20-F, Form 40-F, or Form 10-K shall be delivered with the preliminary prospectus but need not be redelivered with the final prospectus to a recipient that had previously received the Form 20-F, Form 40-F, or Form 10-K with the preliminary prospectus.

45310. General

Form F-3 is a short-form registration statement available to foreign private issuers that have been subject to 1934 Act reporting requirements for at least three years and meet certain requirements. It is analogous in concept to Form S-3, which is discussed in section 42250 of this manual. Form F-3 relies heavily on the registrant's 1934 Act reports (Forms 20-F and 6-K) and requires the incorporation by reference of information about the registrant from these reports. Disclosure in the prospectus is limited to information dealing with the offering. The Form F-3 prospectus is, therefore, generally very brief, consisting primarily of a description of the offering involved.

The eligibility requirements for the use of Form F-3 are:

A. Registrant Requirements

All registrants must meet the following conditions in order to use this Form F-3 for registration under the Securities Act of securities offered in the transactions specified in B. below:

1. The registrant has a class of securities registered pursuant to Section 12(b) of the Securities Exchange Act of 1934 ("Exchange Act") or a class of equity securities registered pursuant to Section 12(g) of the Exchange Act or is required to file reports to Section 15(d) of the Exchange Act and is eligible to file and has filed annual reports on Form 20-F, on Form 10-K or, in the case of registrants described in General Instruction A(2) of Form 40-F, on Form 40-F under the Exchange Act.

2. The registrant: (a) has been subject to the requirements of Section 12 or 15(d) of the Exchange Act and has filed all the material required to be filed pursuant to Sections 13, 14, or 15(d) for a period of at least thirty six calendar months immediately preceding the filing of the registration statement on this Form; and (b) has filed in a timely manner all reports required to be filed during the twelve calendar months and any portion of a month immediately preceding the filing of the registration statement and, if the registrant has used (during the twelve calendar months and any portion of a month immediately preceding the filing of the registration statement) Rule 12b-25(b) under the Exchange Act with respect to a report or a portion of a report, that report or portion thereof has actually been filed within the time period prescribed by the Rule.

3. Neither the registrant nor any of its consolidated or unconsolidated subsidiaries have, since the end of their last fiscal year for which certified financial

statements of the registrant and its consolidated subsidiaries were included in a report filed pursuant to Section 13(a) or 15(d) of the Exchange Act: (a) failed to pay any dividend or sinking fund installment on preferred stock; or (b) defaulted (i) on any installment or installments on indebtedness for borrowed money, or (ii) on any rental on one or more long-term leases, which defaults in the aggregate are material to the financial position of the registrant and its consolidated and unconsolidated subsidiaries, taken as a whole.

4. The aggregate market value worldwide of the voting stock held by non-affiliates of the registrant is the equivalent of $300 million or more, except that the provisions of this paragraph do not apply if the only securities being registered are to be offered in a transaction of the type described in B.2. of the Transaction Requirements.

Instructions.
The aggregate market value of the registrant's outstanding voting stock shall be computed by use of the price at which the stock was last sold, or the average of the bid and asked prices of such stock, in the principal market for such stock as of a date within 60 days prior to the date of filing. [See the definition of "affiliate" in Securities Act Rule 405.]

5. If the registrant is a successor registrant, it shall be deemed to have met conditions 1, 2, 3, and 4 above if: (a) its predecessor and it, taken together, do so, provided that the succession was primarily for the purpose of changing the state or other jurisdiction of incorporation of the predecessor or forming a holding company and that the assets and liabilities of the successor at the time of succession were substantially the same as those of the predecessor; or (b) all predecessors met the conditions at the time of succession and the registrant has continued to do so since the succession.

6. Majority-Owned Subsidiaries. If a registrant is a majority-owned subsidiary, security offerings may be registered on this Form if:

> i. The registrant-subsidiary itself meets the Registrant Requirements and the applicable Transaction Requirement;

> ii. The parent of the registrant-subsidiary meets the Registrant Requirements and the conditions of Transaction Requirement B.2. (Primary Offerings of Certain Debt Securities) are met; or

> iii. The parent of the registrant-subsidiary meets the Registrant Requirements and the applicable Transaction Requirements and fully guarantees the securities being registered as to principal and interest.

Note: In the situations described in (i), (ii), and (iii) above, the parent-guarantor is the issuer of a separate security consisting of the guarantee which must be concurrently registered but may be registered on the same registration statement as are the guaranteed securities. Both the parent-guarantor and the subsidiary shall each disclose the information required by this Form as if each

SEC 45310. Form F-3

were the only registrant except that if the subsidiary will not be eligible to file annual reports on Form 20-F or Form 40-F after the effective date of the registration statement, then it shall disclose the information specified in Form S-3. Rule 3-10 of Regulation S-X specifies the financial statements required.

7. Electronic filings. In addition to satisfying the foregoing conditions, a registrant subject to the electronic filing requirements of Rule 101 of Regulation S-T shall have filed with the Commission all required electronic filings, including confirming electronic copies of documents submitted in paper pursuant to a temporary hardship exemption as provided in Rule 201 of Regulation S-T.

B. Transaction Requirements

Security offerings meeting any of the following conditions and made by registrants meeting the Registrant Requirements above may be registered on this Form:

1. Primary Offerings by Certain Registrants

Securities to be offered for cash by or on behalf of a registrant; if the financial statements in the registrant's latest filing on Form 20-F, Form 40-F, or Form 10-K comply with Item 18 of Form 20-F.

2. Offerings of Certain Debt Securities

Non-convertible debt securities to be offered for cash if such debt securities are "investment grade debt securities," as defined below. A non-convertible debt security is an "investment grade debt security" if, at the time of effectiveness of the registration statement, at least one nationally recognized statistical rating organization (as that term is used in Rule 15c3-1(c)(2)(vi)(F) under the Exchange Act) has rated the security in one of its generic rating categories that signifies investment grade; typically, the four highest rating categories (within which there may be subcategories or gradations indicating relative standing) signify investment grade.

3. Transactions Involving Secondary Offerings

Outstanding securities to be offered for the account of any person other than the issuer, including securities acquired by standby underwriters in connection with the call or redemption by the issuer of warrants or a class of convertible securities. In addition, Form F-3 may be used by affiliates to register securities for resale pursuant to the conditions specified in General Instruction C to Form S-8 if the financial statements in the registrant's latest filing on Form 20-F, Form 40-F, or Form 10-K comply with Item 18 of Form 20-F.

4. Rights Offerings, Dividend or Interest Reinvestment Plans, and Conversions or Warrants

Securities to be offered: (a) upon the exercise of outstanding rights granted by the issuer of the securities to be offered, if such rights are granted pro rata to all existing security holders of the class of securities to which the rights attach; or (b) pursuant to a dividend or interest reinvestment plan; or (c) upon the conversion of outstanding convertible securities or upon the exercise of outstanding transferable warrants issued by the issuer of the securities to be offered, or by an affiliate of such issuer. The registration of securities to be offered or sold in a standby underwriting in the United States or similar arrangement is not permitted pursuant to this paragraph. See paragraphs (1), (2), and (3) above.

It is important to note that with regard to rights offerings, dividend or interest reinvestment plans, and conversions or warrants, as well as offerings of certain investment grade debt securities, the financial statement information required by Item 17 of Form 20-F may be furnished in lieu of the information specified by Item 18 (see section 43210).

The following are the items of information required to be included in a registration statement filed on Form F-3:

PART I. INFORMATION REQUIRED IN PROSPECTUS

Item

1	Forepart of registration statement and outside front cover page of prospectus
2	Inside front and outside back cover pages of prospectus
3	Summary information, risk factors, and ratio of earnings to fixed charges
4	Use of proceeds
5	Determination of offering price
6	Dilution
7	Selling security holders
8	Plan of distribution
9	Description of securities to be registered
10	Interests of named experts and counsel
11	Material changes
12	Incorporation of certain information by reference
13	Disclosure of Commission position on indemnification for Securities Act liabilities

PART II. INFORMATION NOT REQUIRED IN PROSPECTUS

14	Other expenses of issuance and distribution
15	Indemnification of directors and officers
16	Exhibits
17	Undertakings

SEC 45310. Form F-3

An accountants' consent (see sections 17110 and 20510) is also required to be included in Part II of Form F-3 pursuant to item 601 of Regulation S-K. The Exhibit Table in section 66102 should be referred to for a summary of the exhibits required to be included in Form F-3.

45320. Material Changes

Item 11 of Form F-3 deals with the disclosure requirements pertaining to material changes in the registrant's affairs. The text of Item 11 is as follows:

Item 11. Material Changes.

(a) Describe any and all material changes in the registrant's affairs which have occurred since the end of the latest fiscal year for which certified financial statements were included in the latest filing on Form 20-F, Form 40-F, or Form 10-K under the Exchange Act.

(b) (1) Include in the prospectus, if not included in the reports filed under the Exchange Act which are incorporated by reference into the prospectus pursuant to Item 12 or a prospectus previously filed pursuant to Rule 424(b) or (c) under the Securities Act or, where no prospectus was required to be filed pursuant to Rule 424(b), the prospectus included in the registration statement at effectiveness: (i) information required by Rule 3-05 and Article 11 of Regulation S-X where the registrant has effected or is about to effect a transaction for which such information is required; (ii) restated financial statements if there has been a change in accounting principles or a correction of an error where such change or correction requires a material retroactive restatement of financial statements; (iii) restated financial statements where one or more business combinations accounted for by the pooling of interest method of accounting have been consummated subsequent to the most recent fiscal year and the acquired businesses, considered in the aggregate, are significant under Rule 11-01(b); or (iv) any financial information required because of a material disposition of assets outside the normal course of business.

(2) If the financial statements incorporated by reference from the registrant's latest Form 20-F, Form 40-F, or Form 10-K in accordance with Item 12 are not sufficiently current to comply with the requirements of Rule 3-19 of Regulation S-X, financial statements necessary to comply with that rule shall be presented either in the prospectus or in an amended Form 20-F, Form 40-F, or Form 10-K, in which case the prospectus shall disclose that the Form 20-F, Form 40-F, or Form 10-K has been so amended.

Instruction. Financial statements or information required to be furnished by this Item shall be reconciled pursuant to either Item 17 or 18 of Form 20-F, whichever is applicable to the primary financial statements.

45330. Incorporation by Reference

Item 12 contains the requirements pertaining to the incorporation by reference of information in Form F-3. The text of Item 12 is as follows:

Item 12. Incorporation of Certain Information by Reference.

(a) The registrant's latest Form 20-F, Form 40-F, or Form 10-K filed pursuant to the Exchange Act that contains certified financial statements for the registrant's latest fiscal year for which a Form 20-F, Form 40-F, or Form 10-K was required to have been filed and any report on Form 10-Q or Form 8-K filed since the end of the fiscal year covered by such annual report shall be incorporated by reference. If capital stock is to be registered and securities of the same class are registered under Section 12 of the Exchange Act, the description of such class of securities which is contained in a registration statement filed under the Exchange Act, including any amendment or reports filed for the purpose of updating such description, shall be incorporated by reference.

Instruction. If the registrant's latest filing on Form 20-F, Form 40-F, or Form 10-K is amended to include the information specified in Item 18 of Form 20-F, the prospectus shall state that the Form 20-F, Form 40-F, or Form 10-K has been so amended. Reference is made to the Transaction Requirements in General Instruction I.B. that, in some cases, require the financial statements in the Form 20-F, Form 40-F, or Form 10-K to comply with Item 18 of Form 20-F as a condition for eligibility to use Form F-3.

(b) The prospectus also shall state that all subsequent filings on Form 20-F, Form 40-F, Form 10-K, Form 10-Q, or Form 8-K filed by the registrant pursuant to the Exchange Act, prior to the termination of the offering, shall be deemed to be incorporated by reference into the prospectus.

(c) The registrant may incorporate by reference any Form 6-K meeting the requirements of this Form.

Instructions:
1. Attention is directed to the requirements Section 10(a)(3) of the Securities Act.

2. Attention is directed to Rule 439 regarding consent to use material incorporated by reference.

45400. FORM F-4

Form F-4 is used for the registration of securities under the 1933 Act issued by certain foreign private issuers in connection with the same type of business combination transactions that are available on Form S-4 for domestic registrants (see section 42300). However, since business combinations effected through an exchange of shares between foreign private issuers and U.S. companies have been rare to date, the form has had limited applicability.

The eligibility requirements for the use of Form F-4 are:

1. This Form may be used by any foreign private issuer, as defined in Rule 405, for registration under the Securities Act of 1933 ("Securities Act") of securities to be issued: (1) in a transaction of the type specified in paragraph (a) of Rule 145; (2) in a merger in which the applicable law would not require the solicitation of the votes or consents of all of the security holders of the company being acquired; (3) in an exchange offer for securities of the issuer or another entity; (4) in a public reoffering or resale of any such securities acquired pursuant to this registration statement; or (5) in more than one of the kinds of transactions listed in (1) through (4) registered on one registration statement.

2. If the registrant meets the requirements of and elects to comply with the provisions in any Item of this Form or Form S-4 that provides for incorporation by reference of information about the registrant or the company being acquired, the prospectus must be sent to the security holders no later than 20 business days prior to the date on which the meeting of such security holders is held or, if no meeting is held, the earlier of 20 business days prior to either (1) the date the votes, consents or authorizations may be used to effect the corporate action or (2) if votes, consents or authorizations are not used, the date the transaction is consummated. Attention is directed to Sections 13(e), 14(d) and 14(e) of the Securities Exchange Act of 1934 ("Exchange Act") and the rules and regulations thereunder regarding other time periods in connection with exchange offers and going private transactions.

3. This form shall not be used if the registrant is a registered investment company.

Form F-4 is analogous to Form S-4 in that the prospectus may also serve as the proxy or information statement for the offering if a proxy statement is required to be furnished. For a foreign private issuer subject to the reporting requirements of the 1934 Act, the information provided in the prospectus is the same as that required by whichever form it could use to register a primary offering (i.e., Forms F-1, F-2, or F-3).

The following are the items of information to be included in Form F-4:

PART I. INFORMATION REQUESTED IN THE PROSPECTUS

Information About the Transaction

Item

1 Forepart of registration statement and outside front cover page of prospectus
2 Inside front and outside back cover pages of prospectus
3 Risk factors, ratio of earnings to fixed charges, and other information
4 Terms of transaction
5 Pro forma financial information
6 Material contracts with the company being acquired
7 Additional information required for reoffering by persons and parties deemed to be underwriters
8 Interests of named experts and counsel
9 Disclosure of Commission position on indemnification for Securities Act liabilities

Information About the Registrant

10 Information with respect to F-3 companies
11 Incorporation of certain information by reference
12 Information with respect to F-2 or F-3 registrants
13 Incorporation of certain information by reference
14 Information with respect to foreign registrants other than F-2 or F-3 registrants

Information About the Company Being Acquired

15 Information with respect to F-3 companies
16 Information with respect to F-2 or F-3 companies
17 Information with respect to foreign companies other than F-2 or F-3 companies

Voting and Management Information

18 Information if proxies, consents, or authorizations are to be solicited
19 Information if proxies, consents, or authorizations are not to be solicited in an exchange offer

SEC 45400. Form F-4

PART II. INFORMATION NOT REQUIRED IN PROSPECTUS

Item

20   Indemnification of directors and officers
21   Exhibits and financial statement schedules
22   Undertakings

An accountants' consent (see sections 17110 and 20510) is also required to be included in Part II of Form F-4 pursuant to Item 601 of Regulation S-K. The Exhibit Table in section 66102 summarizes the exhibits required to be included in a registration statement filed on Form F-4.

45500. FORM F-6

45510. General

Foreign companies planning to enter the U.S. securities markets have the option of offering their own securities directly to potential investors or offering their securities through the establishment of an American Depositary Receipt (ADR) program. When an ADR program is utilized, Form F-6 is used for the registration under the 1933 Act of depositary shares evidenced by ADRs. An offering of ADRs generally also requires the registration of the underlying deposited securities unless they have previously been registered or have been permitted to be traded under an exemption provision. Legal counsel should always be consulted in ADR situations to ensure that the underlying shares have been registered in compliance with the federal Securities Acts.

45520. American Depositary Receipts (ADRs)

Most depositary receipts are referred to as ADRs. However, they may also be referred to as Global Depositary Receipts (GDRs), European Depositary Receipts (EDRs) or International Depositary Receipts (IDRs). Aside from these various names, depositary receipts are the same from a legal and administrative point of view. Marketing factors generally determine which designation is used.

ADRs are negotiable receipts issued to investors by an authorized depositary (normally a U.S. bank or trust company). These receipts are evidence of ownership by the depositary of the securities of a foreign company. The depositary is empowered to transfer ownership of the ADRs from investor to investor on its own books and records but continues to be the registered holder of the underlying securities. ADRs are quoted in U.S. dollars and are structured to comprise the number of the foreign company's securities that will result in a trading price for each ADR in the generally accepted range of $10 to $30. In order to achieve a trading price in this range, each ADR will represent a multiple (or fraction) of the underlying securities. Investors in ADRs have substantially the same rights and voting privileges as owners of the underlying securities. In addition, they may choose to return ADRs to the authorized depositary at any time for cancellation and take delivery of the actual securities. Furthermore, ADRs may be sponsored by the foreign issuing company, or by an entity other than the company (referred to as unsponsored). It is relevant to note, however, that the New York and American Stock Exchanges will not list unsponsored ADRs.

SEC 45500. Form F-6

ADRs are generally considered to be the preferred vehicle for non-U.S. issuers to enter the U.S. securities market. They offer advantages over an offering of the company's own securities, including:

- ADRs simplify the sale and purchase of securities. The securities of a foreign company normally could not trade directly in the U.S. without some difficulty regarding settlement and ownership registration. ADRs standardize the procedures involved in securities trading, from the form of the ADR certificate to the transfer and clearance procedures, with resultant transaction speed and cost advantages.

- Where an ADR program is not in place, U.S. investors normally would receive dividend payments in foreign currency. ADR holders, on the other hand, benefit from a depositary's collection of foreign currency dividends directly from the foreign company and prompt issuance of dividend checks in U.S. dollars.

- The depositary provides U.S. investors with a local point of communication with the issuing company, through which they receive that company's annual and interim reports, together with other company information. This convenience may not be available to direct investors in foreign company securities.

45530. Eligibility and Reporting Requirements

In order to use Form F-6, the following conditions must be met:

(1) The holder of the ADRs is entitled to withdraw the deposited securities at any time, subject only to (i) temporary delays caused by closing transfer books of the depositary or the issuer of the deposited securities or the deposit of shares in connection with voting at a shareholders' meeting, or the payment of dividends; (ii) the payment of fees, taxes, and similar charges, and (iii) compliance with any laws or governmental regulations relating to ADRs or to the withdrawal of deposited securities;

(2) The deposited securities are offered or sold in transactions registered under the Securities Act or in transactions that would be exempt therefrom if made in the United States; and

(3) As of the filing date of this registration statement, the issuer of the deposited securities is reporting pursuant to the periodic reporting requirements of Section 13(a) or 15(d) of the Securities Exchange Act of 1934 or the deposited securities are exempt therefrom by Rule 12g3-2(b) unless the issuer of the deposited securities concurrently files a registration statement on another form for the deposited securities.

Form F-6 is available only for the registration of depositary shares to be traded publicly on a national stock exchange or over-the-counter. Should a public offering through an ADR program be contemplated, a registration with the SEC of the underlying deposited shares will be required using whatever form the registrant is eligible to use (e.g., Form F-1, F-2, or F-3). Alternatively, depositary shares may be registered on the form used to register the underlying deposited securities, as long as the registration statement includes the information required to be furnished in Parts I and II of Form F-6 and either the depositary or the legal entity created by the agreement for the issuance of ADRs signs the registration statement.

Items of information required by Form F-6 are as follows:

PART I. INFORMATION REQUIRED IN PROSPECTUS

Item

1 Description of securities to be registered
2 Available information

PART II. INFORMATION NOT REQUIRED IN PROSPECTUS

3 Exhibits
4 Undertakings

Form F-6 essentially requires a description of the ADRs and the securities to be deposited. No financial statements are required to be included in a registration statement filed on Form F-6.

Once company-sponsored ADRs are registered, the foreign issuer becomes subject to the annual reporting requirements of the 1934 Act (unless exempt). Forms 20-F (section 43200) and 6-K (section 44200) are the forms generally used for this purpose.

SEC 45530. Form F-6

46000. REGISTRATION FORMS FOR CANADIAN COMPANIES UNDER THE MULTIJURISDICTIONAL DISCLOSURE SYSTEM

46100. Introduction

In July 1991, the SEC approved the Multijurisdictional Disclosure System (MJDS) as outlined in International Release No. 291. Concurrent with this release, the Canadian Securities Administrators have adopted a parallel system, which is set forth in Canadian National Policy Statement No. 45.

The purpose of the MJDS is to facilitate cross-border offerings of investment grade debt and equity securities made by eligible U.S. and Canadian companies. In addition to investment grade debt and equity securities, the MJDS is also available for rights offerings, exchange offers, and business combinations.

The new disclosure system is intended to reduce multiple registration, listing, and reporting requirements for eligible companies in both countries by incorporating disclosures based on the registrant's home country documents. Periodic reports prepared pursuant to the requirements of the issuer's home jurisdiction may also be used to satisfy continuing reporting requirements resulting from the use of the MJDS.

An exception to full reliance on Canadian disclosure, however, is the requirement for a reconciliation of the differences between U.S. and Canadian GAAP for financial statements included in new registration Form F-10 and in certain filings using Form 40-F.

Under the release, the MJDS permits cash tender and exchange offers for Canadian companies under specified circumstances to proceed in the U.S. on the basis of Canadian tender offer rules and disclosure requirements. In addition, the rule changes allow those Canadian foreign private issuers that are not eligible for the MJDS to use the integrated disclosure system used by all other foreign private issuers (i.e.,

Forms 20-F, F-1, 6-K etc.). Previously, many Canadian companies were required to conform to the rules applicable to U.S. registrants.

It is important to note that the MJDS is not available for securities issued by investment companies that are registered or are required to be registered under the Investment Company Act of 1940.

Although relatively few U.S. companies have benefitted from the MJDS, a number of Canadian issuers have used the MJDS for their cross-border offerings. A major benefit of the rules, however, has been the provision allowing Canadian foreign private issuers not eligible for the MJDS to use the integrated disclosure system used by all other foreign private issuers (i.e., Forms 20-F, F-1, 6-K, etc.) rather than the system required for U.S. registrants. Primarily based on this provision, the MJDS has been viewed positively on an overall basis by Canadian issuers.

46110. General Eligibility Requirements

The MJDS encompasses the registration of equity securities and investment grade debt or preferred securities of large Canadian issuers as well as specified exchange offers, business combinations, and rights offers of a broader class of smaller Canadian issuers. To be eligible to use the MJDS, a Canadian issuer is required to:

- Have at least a three-year history of reporting with a Canadian securities regulatory authority and be in compliance with such regulator's requirements.

- Be incorporated or organized under the laws of Canada, or any Canadian Province or Territory.

- Meet "substantial" size tests of minimum market value and/or public float (except for rights offerings and offerings of certain nonconvertible investment grade securities that have no substantial size requirements).

- Qualify as a "foreign private issuer" pursuant to Rule 405 of the 1933 Act (as defined in section 50353) or for specified offerings as a Canadian "crown corporation" (a corporation whose common shares or comparable equity is all owned directly or indirectly by the Government of Canada or a Province or Territory of Canada).

Issuers that do not meet the definition of a "foreign private issuer" are in essence U.S. issuers and are therefore required to use the same forms used by U.S. issuers.

Securities are considered to be investment grade if at least one nationally recognized statistical rating organization (e.g., Moody's, S&P, Dominion Bond Rating Service Limited, or C.B.R.S., Inc.) has rated the security in a category signifying investment grade; typically the four highest rating categories of each rating organization signify investment grade.

46111. Substantial Size Requirements

The "substantial" size requirements were designed to dictate the amount of disclosure required and, therefore, the form to be used under specific conditions. The requirements are dependent upon whether investment grade securities are involved.

- Substantial issuers in the context of convertible investment grade debt or preferred securities are those that have a total market value for their equity shares of at least (CN) $180 million and public float of at least (CN) $75 million.

- Issuers need not meet the substantial size requirement in connection with rights offerings or for the registration of nonconvertible investment grade securities.

- In considering all other securities, the term "substantial" includes those issuers with a market value for their equity shares of at least (CN) $360 million and a public float of (CN) $75 million.

The market value of equity shares and the amount of public float may be determined as of any date within 60 days prior to the filing of the MJDS form.

46120. Reporting Requirements

46121. Rights Offers (Form F-7)

Canadian issuers making a rights offering in the U.S. under the MJDS may do so on Form F-7. In addition to the general requirements set forth in section 46110:

- The issuer must have a class of securities listed on the Toronto Stock Exchange, the Montreal Exchange, or the Senior Board of the Vancouver Stock Exchange for the 12 months immediately preceding the filing of the form and be in compliance with the requirements arising from such listing.

- The rights under the offering need to be granted upon the terms and conditions that are not less favorable than those extended to any other holder of the same class of securities.

SEC 46121

- The rights issued may not be transferable except outside the U.S. pursuant to Regulation S under the 1933 Act.

The securities purchased by existing security holders upon exercise of rights, however, are transferable in the United States.

46122. Exchange Offers and Business Combinations (Forms F-8 and F-80)

It should be noted that the term "exchange offers," as used in the MJDS, does not include exchange offers made in connection with business combinations.

46123. Exchange Offer Registration. A Canadian issuer making an exchange offer under the MJDS may include home country disclosure documents in either registration Forms F-8 or F-80, depending upon the number of shares held by U.S. holders. Form F-8 is used if U.S. holders own less than 25 percent of the class of subject securities. Form F-80 is used if U.S. ownership falls between 25 and 40 percent.

In addition to meeting the general requirements set forth in section 46110, the securities being registered under either form must be all or a portion of the consideration offered and the issuer is required to:

- Have a public float for their equity shares with a market value that equals or exceeds (CN) $75 million; however, issuer exchange offers may be registered without regard to the issuer's public float.

- Have their securities listed on the Toronto Stock Exchange, the Montreal Exchange, or the Senior Board of the Vancouver Stock Exchange for the most recent 12 months prior to the filing of the form and be in compliance with such listing requirements at the time of filing.

- Offer its securities to U.S. holders upon terms and conditions not less favorable than those offered to any other holder of the same class of securities.

Exchange offer securities may also be registered on either Form F-9 or F-10 if the offeror is eligible to use such forms, without regard to the percentage of securities held by U.S. shareholders.

46124. Business Combinations. Forms F-8 and F-80 are also available to Canadian issuers registering shares in connection with a business combination. The eligibility requirements for use of these forms in connection with business combina-

tions expand on the general requirements as set forth in section 46110, and require that:

- Each company participating in the business combination be incorporated or organized in a Canadian jurisdiction and qualify as a foreign private issuer.

- Each company participating in the business combination, other than the successor registrant, have a class of its securities listed on the Montreal Exchange, the Toronto Stock Exchange, or the Senior Board of the Vancouver Stock Exchange for the 12 months immediately prior to filing, and have a three-year reporting history with a Canadian securities regulatory agency immediately prior to the filing. Each of the companies also needs to be in compliance with such listing and reporting requirements.

- Each participating company, other than the successor registrant, have a public float of at least (CN) $75 million.

- Securities registered in connection with the combination be offered to U.S. holders upon terms and conditions not less favorable than those offered to any other holder of the same class of securities of the participating company.

Form F-8 may be used by Canadian issuers in this type of situation provided that less than 25 percent of the class of securities of the successor registrant, measured upon completion of the business combination, are held by U.S. registrants. Form F-80 may be used where less than 40 percent of the securities of the successor registrant are held by U.S. shareholders.

Registrants participating in business combinations that are ineligible to use either Form F-8 or Form F-80 may register under Form F-10, if participants accounting for at least 80 percent of total assets and gross revenues from continuing operations of the successor registrant meet the Form F-10 eligibility requirements.

46125. Offerings of Investment Grade Debt and Preferred Stock (Form F-9)

Canadian companies may register investment grade debt and preferred stock on Form F-9 provided that the securities are either nonconvertible or are convertible only after one year from the date of issuance. The securities may only be convertible into another class of securities of the issuer, or, in the case of guaranteed securities, the parent. In addition to the general requirements as set forth in section 46110:

- If the issuer qualifies as a "crown corporation," it is only required to have a 12-month history of reporting with a Canadian securities regulatory authority and be in compliance with such regulator's requirements.

- At least one nationally recognized statistical rating organization needs to rate the securities as "investment grade" at the time of effectiveness of the registration statement.

- The issuer needs to have a total market value for its equity shares of at least (CN) $180 million and public float of at least (CN) $75 million. Issuers need not meet this requirement for the registration of nonconvertible investment grade securities.

46126. Offerings of Any Securities (Form F-10)

Form F-10 is available to be used by Canadian issuers for the registration of securities offered for cash or in connection with certain exchange offers or business combinations. In addition to meeting the general requirements set forth in section 46110, the Canadian issuer using this form also needs to have a total market value for its equity shares of at least (CN) $360 million and public float of at least (CN) $75 million.

Form F-10 may also be used by a Canadian-organized, majority-owned subsidiary provided that the parent meets the aforementioned eligibility requirements and guarantees the securities being offered unconditionally. Such securities or preferred stock may be convertible or exchangeable, but only for the securities of the parent company.

Any financial statements included in Form F-10 are required to be reconciled to U.S. GAAP as required by Item 18 of Form 20-F (see section 43210). A reconciliation to U.S. GAAP is also required to satisfy the periodic reporting requirements resulting from a registration on Form F-10.

47000. SEC INTERNATIONAL PROPOSALS OUTSTANDING

Several proposals are currently outstanding that are primarily intended to relieve the regulatory burden for foreign registrants:

Release No. 33-6895, *Amendments to Rule and Form Requirements Which Govern the Age of Financial Statements of Foreign Private Issuers.* The SEC has proposed amendments to Regulation S-X Rule 3-19, 1934 Act Rule 15d-2, and Forms F-2 and F-3 that relate to the age of financial statements of foreign private issuers that register securities for sale under the 1933 Act.

SEC rules currently require that the date of the latest financial statements used in a 1933 Act registration generally be within six months of the effective date of the registration. The proposal under consideration would extend this period by providing that a registration statement that is declared effective within six months of the fiscal year-end would need to include audited financial statements for the previous two years and unaudited half-year interim information. This effectively extends, in this situation, the period between registration and the date of the latest financial information to 12 months. For example, a foreign private issuer with a calendar year-end would be able to "go effective" as late as June 29, 1992, with unaudited financial statements only as recent as June 30, 1991.

In addition, for the period between six months and ten months after the year-end date, the proposed changes would make it possible for a non-U.S. company to proceed with a registration on the basis of the latest audited year-end financial information without the need to update the unaudited interim information.

Another aspect of the proposal is that interim financial information included in a registration statement by a foreign registrant would not need to be reconciled to U.S. GAAP, if adequate narrative disclosures are provided and all significant variations were previously disclosed and quantified in the annual or semi-annual financial statements.

As proposed, the amendments would revise the requirements governing the age of financial statements in registration statements to conform to the financial statement updating requirements of the home jurisdictions of a majority of foreign issuers.

Release No. 33-6897, *Proposed Rules, Forms, and Order.* In this release, the SEC has proposed changes related to:

- Tender offers

- Exchange offers

- U.K. exchange offers

Tender Offers

The SEC has proposed changes that would permit tender offers in the United States for a foreign issuer's securities to be based on the tender offer regulations of the target company's home jurisdiction provided the following conditions are met:

- Ten percent or less of the class of securities sought in the tender offer are held by U.S. holders (not counting U.S. shareholders who individually had ten percent or more of the target securities);

- An English language translation of the offering materials is furnished to the SEC;

- U.S. shareholders are permitted to participate in the offer on equal terms with other shareholders; and

- U.S. shareholders receive all offering documents made available to other shareholders.

Tender offers meeting these conditions would not be subject to the Rule 13e-4 and 14D regulations that govern the conduct of U.S. tender offers. Insider-trading prohibitions, however, would still apply.

Exchange Offers

The SEC has also proposed two changes relating to the registration of securities to be issued in the U.S. in connection with an exchange offer for a foreign private issuer's securities.

The first, proposed Rule 802, would allow an exchange offer to proceed in the U.S. without registration as long as the aggregate dollar value of the securities offered for exchange in the U.S. is $5 million or less.

Under the second proposed rule, a foreign company would be able to register the shares to be issued under the 1933 Act using disclosure documents prepared in accordance with the foreign target company's home country registration requirements. The proposal would eliminate for exchange offers of this nature the requirement that foreign financial statements be reconciled with U.S. GAAP. Exchange offers would be eligible if five percent or less of the foreign target's securities are held by U.S. shareholders prior to the exchange offer, not counting U.S. shareholders who individually hold ten percent or more of the target securities. In addition, the foreign private issuer would be required to:

- Submit information pursuant to the 1934 Act's Rule 12g3-2(b) on or before the filing; i.e., the information filed by the issuer in the issuer's home country;

- Have been listed or traded for at least 36 months on one of 19 designated non-U.S. securities markets prior to the exchange offer or have a 36-month operating history and a public float of $75 million; and

- Be in compliance with applicable listing and reporting requirements of the foreign securities market at the time of the exchange offer.

If adopted, foreign private issuers would also not be subject to the SEC's periodic reporting requirements (i.e., filing Forms 20-F and 6-K) solely as a result of registering shares in a situation of this nature.

Exchange offers that meet the requirements described above for tender offers would also be permitted to proceed with the offer on the basis of the regulatory provisions of the target company's home jurisdiction.

U.K. Tender Offers

The SEC has identified six areas relating to the conduct of a tender offer in which the U.K. tender offer rules conflict with those of the United States. The Commission is proposing changes that would codify accommodations arrived at with the U.K.'s Panel on Takeovers and Mergers. The proposal would allow tender offers for securities of a U.K. chartered company to be conducted in the U.S. pursuant to the requirements of the City Code, the U.K. equivalent of the Williams Act. This proposal would permit offering materials in these situations to be prepared in accordance with U.K. disclosure requirements.

Release No. 33-6896, *Cross-Border Rights Offers; Amendments to Form F-3*. The SEC has proposed a new rule and registration form (Form F-11) under the 1933 Act to facilitate the extension of rights offerings by foreign private issuers to their existing U.S. shareholders. The proposed exemptive Rule 801, under Section 3(b) of the 1933 Act, would provide exemption from U.S. registration for issues of rights offerings of up to $5 million. Further, proposed Form F-11 would permit registration of rights offerings of any size on the basis of home country disclosures, provided that the requirements for use of Form F-12 (as outlined in Release No. 33-6897) have been met.

If adopted, the proposal would eliminate the requirement that foreign financial statements be reconciled with U.S. GAAP in connection with a rights offering. In addition, foreign private issuers registering shares on Form F-11 would not become subject to the SEC periodic reporting requirements.

The SEC has also proposed an amendment to extend the availability of Form F-3 to foreign private issuers listed on a U.S. stock exchange that register shares in connection with a rights offering. Under the proposal, Form F-3 would be available even if the company does not meet the form's current eligibility requirements of a minimum three-year reporting history under the 1934 Act and a minimum $300 million public float. Reference should be made to section 45300 for a discussion of Form F-3.

REGULATION S-X

50050. INTRODUCTION

Regulation S-X governs the form and content of and requirements for financial statements (including the financial statement schedules) to be filed with the SEC under the various acts. The Regulation contains uniform instructions as to the financial statements to be included in most SEC filings and the entities ("persons"), dates, and periods for which statements must be furnished. It is the principal repository for these requirements, and its provisions generally apply to all documents filed with the SEC that require financial statements.

The disclosures required by Regulation S-X are considered to be a minimum standard. Rule 4-01(a) provides: "The information with respect to any statement shall be furnished as a minimum requirement to which shall be added such further material information as is necessary to make the required statements, in the light of the circumstances under which they are made, not misleading." Rule 4-02, however, permits omission of items that are not material, and Rule 4-03, items that are inapplicable.

A heading precedes Regulation S-X as follows:

ATTENTION ELECTRONIC FILERS

THIS REGULATION SHOULD BE READ IN CONJUNCTION WITH REGULATION S-T (PART 232 OF THIS CHAPTER), WHICH GOVERNS THE PREPARATION AND SUBMISSION OF DOCUMENTS IN ELECTRONIC FORMAT. MANY PROVISIONS RELATING TO THE PREPARATION AND SUBMISSION OF DOCUMENTS IN PAPER FORMAT CONTAINED IN THIS REGULATION ARE SUPERSEDED BY THE PROVISIONS OF REGULATION S-T FOR DOCUMENTS REQUIRED TO BE FILED IN ELECTRONIC FORMAT.

Refer to discussion regarding the SEC's Electronic Data Gathering, Analysis and Retrieval system (EDGAR) in section 15100.

50051. Information Unknown or Not Reasonably Available

Rule 409 under the 1933 Act deals with information (including financial information) that is unknown or not reasonably available. It is important to note that the absence of particularly important information may affect the accountants' report. For a discussion of accountants' reports and other related matters, refer to sections in this manual beginning with section 20100. The text of Rule 409 follows:

Rule 409. Information Unknown or Not Reasonably Available

Information required need be given only insofar as it is known or reasonably available to the registrant. If any required information is unknown and not reasonably available to the registrant, either because the obtaining thereof would involve unreasonable effort or expense, or because it rests peculiarly within the knowledge of another person not affiliated with the registrant, the information may be omitted, subject to the following conditions:

(a) The registrant shall give such information on the subject as it possesses or can acquire without unreasonable effort or expense, together with the sources thereof.

(b) The registrant shall include a statement either showing that unreasonable effort or expense would be involved or indicating the absence of any affiliation with the person within whose knowledge the information rests and stating the result of a request made to such person for the information.

Rule 12b-21 under the 1934 Act is similar to Rule 409.

50052. Content of Regulation S-X

Regulation S-X consists of a number of sections designated as "articles," each of which contains certain rules. The articles and the subject matter they cover are summarized as follows:

Article	Manual Section	Subject	Summary of Contents
1	50100	Application of Regulation S-X	Specifies the registration statements and reports to which Regulation S-X is applicable and defines terminology used in the Regulation.
2	50200	Qualifications and Reports of Accountants	Contains the requirements as to the qualifications (independence) of accountants and the contents of their reports.
3	50300	General Instructions for Financial Statements	Sets forth instructions for (a) the nature of financial statements required and the entities, dates, and periods they must cover and (b) the age of interim financial statements required to be included in registration and proxy statements.
3A	50370	Consolidated and Combined Financial Statements	Contains the requirements for the presentation of consolidated and combined financial statements.
4	50400	Rules of General Application	Contains the rules for form, order and terminology and for certain of the footnotes required to be furnished as part of the financial statements.
5	50500	Commercial and Industrial Companies	Sets forth the information to be included in balance sheet and statement of income captions for commercial and industrial companies. Also specifies the schedules that are to be filed.
6	50600	Registered Investment Companies	These articles set forth the information to be included in financial statements of special types of entities.
6A	50620	Employee Stock Purchase Savings and Similar Plans	
7	50700	Insurance Companies	
9	50900	Bank Holding Companies	
10	51000	Interim Financial Statements	Sets forth the form and content of interim financial statements and the periods for which such statements need to be presented in Form 10-Q.
11	51100	Pro Forma Financial Information	Specifies the form and content of pro forma financial disclosures and when such disclosures are required. Also provides guidance for the presentation of financial forecasts that may be furnished in lieu of pro forma disclosures.
12	51200	Form and Content of Schedules	Sets forth the form and content of schedules required in accordance with Rule 5-04 (and certain other rules for special types of entities).

50100. ARTICLE 1.
APPLICATION OF REGULATION S-X

50101. Rule 1-01. Application of Regulation S-X

(a) This part (together with the Financial Reporting Releases) sets forth the form and content of and requirements for financial statements required to be filed as a part of—

(1) Registration statements under the Securities Act of 1933 except as otherwise specifically provided in the forms which are to be used for registration under this Act;

(2) Registration statements under Section 12, annual or other reports under Sections 13 and 15(d), and proxy and information statements under Section 14 of the Securities Exchange Act of 1934 except as otherwise specifically provided in the forms which are to be used for registration and reporting under these sections of this Act;

(3) Registration statements and annual reports filed under the Public Utility Holding Company Act of 1935 by public utility holding companies registered under such Act; and

(4) Registration statements and shareholder reports under the Investment Company Act of 1940, except as otherwise specifically provided in the forms which are to be used for registration under this Act.

(b) The term "financial statements" as used in this part shall be deemed to include all notes to the statements and all related schedules.

(c) In addition to filings pursuant to the Federal securities laws, Rule 4-10 applies to the preparation of accounts by persons engaged, in whole or in part, in the production of crude oil or natural gas in the United States pursuant to Section 503 of the Energy Policy and Conservation Act of 1975 ("EPCA") and Section 1 (c) of the Energy Supply and Environment Coordination Act of 1974, as amended by Section 505 of EPCA.

This rule identifies the Acts to which Regulation S-X is applicable. However, the instructions to the various forms also specify when the regulation is applicable. Generally, financial statements and financial statement schedules filed with the SEC must comply with Regulation S-X unless the form specifically exempts or modifies the applicability of the regulation. For example, small business issuers eligible to file on Forms 10-KSB (see section 41200), 10-QSB (see section 41500), 10-SB (see section 41850), SB-1 (see section 42600), or SB-2 (see section 42700) are referred to the requirements of Regulation S-B (see section 70000) rather than Regulation S-X.

50102. Rule 1-02. Definitions of Terms Used in Regulation S-X

Unless the context otherwise requires, terms defined in the general rules and regulations or in the instructions to the applicable form, when used in Regulation S-X shall have the respective meanings given in such instructions or rules. In addition, the following terms shall have the meanings indicated in this rule unless the context otherwise requires.

(a) Accountants' report. *The term "accountant's report," when used in regard to financial statements, means a document in which an independent public or certified public accountant indicates the scope of the audit (or examination) which he has made and sets forth his opinion regarding the financial statements taken as a whole, or an assertion to the effect that an overall opinion cannot be expressed. When an overall opinion cannot be expressed, the reasons therefor shall be stated.*

(b) Affiliate. *An "affiliate" of, or a person "affiliated" with, a specific person is a person that directly, or indirectly through one or more intermediaries, controls, or is controlled by, or is under common control with, the person specified.*

(c) Amount. *The term "amount," when used in regard to securities, means the principal amount if relating to evidences of indebtedness, the number of shares if relating to shares, and the number of units if relating to any other kind of security.*

(d) Audit (or examination). *The term "audit" (or "examination"), when used in regard to financial statements, means an examination of the statements by an accountant in accordance with generally accepted auditing standards for the purpose of expressing an opinion thereon.*

(e) Bank holding company. *The term "bank holding company" means a person which is engaged, either directly or indirectly, primarily in the business of owning securities of one or more banks for the purpose, and with the effect, of exercising control.*

(f) Certified. *The term "certified," when used in regard to financial statements, means examined and reported upon with an opinion expressed by an independent public or certified public accountant.*

Many SEC rules and regulations use the term "certified," instead of the more preferable term "audited." SAB Topic 1-E1 states that the two terms have the same meaning.

428

Meaning of the Word "Audited"

Facts: Amendments adopted in Accounting Series Release No. 155 changed the requirement in various forms from "certified" to "audited" financial statements.

Question: Does the word "audited" have the same meaning as the word "certified"?

Interpretive Response: No difference in meaning or change in requirements was intended or effected by ASR No. 155 which was a continuation of a program to conform the terminology used in the forms to that currently applied by the accounting profession (see ASR No. 125).

(g) Control. *The term "control" (including the terms "controlling," "controlled by" and "under common control with") means the possession, direct or indirect, of the power to direct or cause the direction of the management and policies of a person, whether through the ownership of voting shares, by contract, or otherwise.*

Note that the definition of "control" does not necessarily contemplate majority ownership. Consequently, an entity may be subject to "control" and not be "majority-owned." See the separate definition of "majority-owned subsidiary" in Rule 1-02(m).

(h) Development stage company. *A company shall be considered to be in the development stage if it is devoting substantially all of its efforts to establishing a new business and either of the following conditions exists: (1) Planned principal operations have not commenced; (2) Planned principal operations have commenced, but there has been no significant revenue therefrom.*

(i) Equity security. *The term "equity security" means any stock or similar security; or any security convertible, with or without consideration, into such a security, or carrying any warrant or right to subscribe to or purchase such a security; or any such warrant or right.*

(j) Fifty-percent-owned person. *The term "50-percent-owned person," in relation to a specified person, means a person approximately 50 percent of whose outstanding voting shares is owned by the specified person either directly, or indirectly through one or more intermediaries.*

Ever since the equity method of accounting was adopted in APB Opinion No. 18, investees have been referred to as "50 percent-or-less-owned persons accounted for by the equity method" in Article 3 of Regulation S-X. See section 50339 for a discussion of the financial statement requirements for such entities.

(k) Fiscal year. *The term "fiscal year" means the annual accounting period or, if no closing date has been adopted, the calendar year ending on December 31.*

SEC 50102. Rule 1-02

(l) Insurance holding company. *The term "insurance holding company" means a person which is engaged, either directly or indirectly, primarily in the business of owning securities of one or more insurance companies for the purpose, and with the effect, of exercising control.*

(m) Majority-owned subsidiary. *The term "majority-owned subsidiary" means a subsidiary more than 50 percent of whose outstanding voting shares is owned by its parent and/or the parent's other majority-owned subsidiaries.*

(n) Material. *The term "material," when used to qualify a requirement for the furnishing of information as to any subject, limits the information required to those matters about which an average prudent investor ought reasonably to be informed.*

(o) Parent. *A "parent" of a specified person is an affiliate controlling such person directly, or indirectly through one or more intermediaries.*

(p) Person. *The term "person" means an individual, a corporation, a partnership, an association, a joint-stock company, a business trust, or an unincorporated organization. [Note: The term "person," when used in SEC rules and regulations, generally refers to an "entity."]*

(q) Principal holder of equity securities. *The term "principal holder of equity securities," used in respect of a registrant or other person named in a particular statement or report, means a holder of record or a known beneficial owner of more than 10 percent of any class of equity securities of the registrant or other person, respectively, as of the date of the related balance sheet filed.*

(r) Promoter. The term "promoter" includes:

(1) Any person who, acting alone or in conjunction with one or more other persons, directly or indirectly takes initiative in founding and organizing the business or enterprise of an issuer;

(2) Any person who, in connection with the founding and organizing of the business or enterprise of an issuer, directly or indirectly receives in consideration of services or property, or both services and property, 10 percent or more of any class of securities of the issuer or 10 percent or more of the proceeds from the sale of any class of securities. However, a person who receives such securities or proceeds either solely as underwriting commissions or solely in consideration of property shall not be deemed a promoter within the meaning of this paragraph if such person does not otherwise take part in founding and organizing the enterprise.

SEC 50102

430

(s) Registrant. *The term "registrant" means the issuer of the securities for which an application, a registration statement, or a report is filed.*

(t) Related parties. *The term "related parties" is used as that term is defined in the Glossary to Statement of Financial Accounting Standards No. 57, "Related Party Disclosures" [SFAS No. 57].*

Paragraph 24 of SFAS No. 57 defines related parties as "affiliates of the enterprise; entities for which investments are accounted for by the equity method by the enterprise; trusts for the benefit of employees, such as pension and profit-sharing trusts that are managed by or under the trusteeship of management; principal owners of the enterprise; its management; members of the immediate families of principal owners of the enterprise and its management; and other parties with which the enterprise may deal if one party controls or can significantly influence the management or operating policies of the other to an extent that one of the transacting parties might be prevented from fully pursuing its own separate interests. Another party also is a related party if it can significantly influence the management or operating policies of the transacting parties or if it has an ownership interest in one of the transacting parties and can significantly influence the other to an extent that one or more of the transacting parties might be prevented from fully pursuing its own separate interests."

(u) Share. *The term "share" means a share of stock in a corporation or unit of interest in an unincorporated person.*

(v) Significant subsidiary. *The term "significant subsidiary" means a subsidiary, including its subsidiaries, which meets any of the following conditions:*

> *(1) The registrant's and its other subsidiaries' investment in and advances to the subsidiary exceed 10 percent of the total assets of the registrant and its subsidiaries consolidated as of the end of the most recently completed fiscal year (for a proposed business combination accounted for as a pooling of interests, this condition is also met when the number of common shares exchanged or to be exchanged by the registrant exceeds 10 percent of its total common shares outstanding at the date the combination is initiated); or*

> *(2) The registrant's and its other subsidiaries' proportionate share of the total assets (after intercompany eliminations) of the subsidiary exceed 10 percent of the total assets of the registrant and its subsidiaries consolidated as of the end of the most recently completed fiscal year; or*

> *(3) The registrant's and its other subsidiaries' equity in the income from continuing operations before income taxes, extraordinary items and cumulative*

effect of a change in accounting principle of the subsidiary exceeds 10 percent of such income of the registrant and its subsidiaries consolidated for the most recently completed fiscal year.

Computational note: *For purposes of making the prescribed income test the following guidance should be applied:*

1. When a loss has been incurred by either the parent and its subsidiaries consolidated or the tested subsidiary, but not both, the equity in the income or loss of the tested subsidiary should be excluded from the income of the registrant and its subsidiaries consolidated for purposes of the computation.

2. If income of the registrant and its subsidiaries consolidated for the most recent fiscal year is at least 10 percent lower than the average of the income for the last five fiscal years, such average income should be substituted for purposes of the computation. Any loss years should be omitted for purposes of computing average income.

3. Where the test involves combined entities, as in the case of determining whether summarized financial data should be presented, entities reporting losses shall not be aggregated with entities reporting income.

The significant subsidiary criteria and their applicability are discussed in section 50341.

(w) Subsidiary. *A "subsidiary" of a specified person is an affiliate controlled by such person directly, or indirectly through one or more intermediaries.*

(x) Totally held subsidiary. *The term "totally held subsidiary" means a subsidiary:*

(1) Substantially all of whose outstanding equity securities are owned by its parent and/or the parent's other totally held subsidiaries, and

(2) Which is not indebted to any person other than its parent and/or the parent's other totally held subsidiaries, in an amount which is material in relation to the particular subsidiary, excepting indebtedness incurred in the ordinary course of business which is not overdue and which matures within one year from the date of its creation, whether evidenced by securities or not. Indebtedness of a subsidiary which is secured by its parent by guarantee, pledge, assignment or otherwise is to be excluded for purposes of (2) herein.

The definition of "totally held subsidiary" was important under a previous rule relating to the requirement for parent company financial statements. The rule has since been revised, and consequently this definition is no longer important. In practice this definition is considered to be synonymous with that of a "wholly owned subsidiary."

(y) Voting shares. *The term "voting shares" means the sum of all rights, other than as affected by events of default, to vote for election of directors and/or the sum of all interests in an unincorporated person.*

(z) Wholly owned subsidiary. *The term "wholly owned subsidiary" means a subsidiary substantially all of whose outstanding voting shares are owned by its parent and/or the parent's other wholly owned subsidiaries.*

(aa) Summarized financial information.

(1) Except as provided in paragraph (aa)(2), "summarized financial information" referred to in this regulation shall mean the presentation of summarized information as to the assets, liabilities and results of operations of the entity for which the information is required. Summarized financial information shall include the following disclosures:

> *(i) Current assets, noncurrent assets, current liabilities, noncurrent liabilities, and, when applicable, redeemable preferred stocks (see Rule 5-02-28) and minority interests (for specialized industries in which classified balance sheets are normally not presented, information shall be provided as to the nature and amount of the major components of assets and liabilities);*

> *(ii) Net sales or gross revenues, gross profit (or, alternatively, costs and expenses applicable to net sales or gross revenues), income or loss from continuing operations before extraordinary items and cumulative effect of a change in accounting principle, and net income or loss (for specialized industries, other information may be substituted for sales and related costs and expenses if necessary for a more meaningful presentation); and*

(2) Summarized financial information for unconsolidated subsidiaries and 50 percent or less owned persons referred to in and required by Rule 10-01(b) for interim periods shall include the information required by paragraph (aa)(1)(ii) of this section.

The presentation of summarized financial information is discussed in section 50343.

50200. ARTICLE 2. QUALIFICATIONS AND REPORTS OF ACCOUNTANTS

50201. Rule 2-01. Qualifications of Accountants

(a) The Commission will not recognize any person as a certified public accountant who is not duly registered and in good standing as such under the laws of the place of his residence or principal office. The Commission will not recognize any person as a public accountant who is not in good standing and entitled to practice as such under the laws of the place of his residence or principal office.

(b) The Commission will not recognize any certified public accountant or public accountant as independent who is not in fact independent. For example, an accountant will be considered not independent with respect to any person or any of its parents, its subsidiaries, or other affiliates (1) in which, during the period of his professional engagement to examine the financial statements being reported on or at the date of his report, he, his firm, or a member of his firm had, or was committed to acquire, any direct financial interest or any material indirect financial interest; (2) with which, during the period of his professional engagement to examine the financial statements being reported on, at the date of his report or during the period covered by the financial statements, he, his firm, or a member of his firm was connected as a promoter, underwriter, voting trustee, director, officer, or employee. A firm's independence will not be deemed to be affected adversely where a former officer or employee of a particular person is employed by or becomes a partner, shareholder or other principal in the firm and such individual has completely disassociated himself from the person and its affiliates and does not participate in auditing financial statements of the person or its affiliates covering any period of his employment by the person. For the purposes of Rule 2-01(b), the term "member" means [i] all partners, shareholders, and other principals in the firm, [ii] any professional employee involved in providing any professional service to the person, its parents, subsidiaries, or other affiliates, and [iii] any professional employee having managerial responsibilities and located in [the engagement office] or other office of the firm which participates in a significant portion of the audit.

(c) In determining whether an accountant may in fact be not independent with respect to a particular person, the Commission will give appropriate consideration to all

relevant circumstances, including evidence bearing on all relationships between the accountant and that person or any affiliate thereof, and will not confine itself to the relationships existing in connection with the filing of reports with the Commission.

This rule sets forth the independence requirements of accountants, which are discussed in section 17030 of this manual.

50202. Rule 2-02. Accountants' Reports

(a) Technical requirements. *The accountants' report (1) shall be dated; (2) shall be signed manually; (3) shall indicate the city and state where issued; and (4) shall identify without detailed enumeration the financial statements covered by the report.*

(b) Representations as to the audit. *The accountant's report (1) shall state whether the audit was made in accordance with generally accepted auditing standards; and (2) shall designate any auditing procedures deemed necessary by the accountant under the circumstances of the particular case, which have been omitted, and the reasons for their omission. Nothing in this rule shall be construed to imply authority for the omission of any procedure which independent accountants would ordinarily employ in the course of an audit made for the purpose of expressing the opinions required by paragraph (c) of this rule.*

(c) Opinion to be expressed. *The accountants' report shall state clearly: (1) the opinion of the accountant in respect of the financial statements covered by the report and the accounting principles and practices reflected therein; and (2) the opinion of the accountant as to the consistency of the application of the accounting principles, or as to any changes in such principles which have a material effect on the financial statements.*

(d) Exceptions. *Any matters to which the accountant takes exception shall be clearly identified, the exception thereto specifically and clearly stated, and, to the extent practicable, the effect of each such exception on the related financial statements given. (See Section 101 of the Codification of Financial Reporting Policies.)*

Statement on Auditing Standards No. 58, issued in 1988, revised the second standard of reporting as follows: "The report shall identify those circumstances in which such [accounting] principles have not been consistently observed in the current period in relation to the preceding period." (Footnote 2 to paragraph 4) Previously, the second standard required the auditors' report to specifically indicate whether accounting principles had been consistently applied. As revised, the second standard requires auditors to add an explanatory paragraph to their report only if accounting principles have not been applied consistently. Although the text of this rule has not yet been revised to incorporate this change, SAS 58 should be considered applicable for SEC reporting purposes.

SEC 50201. Rule 2-01

A discussion of accountants' reports and related matters is included in this manual beginning with section 20100.

50203. Rule 2-03. Examination of Financial Statements by Foreign Government Auditors

Notwithstanding any requirements as to examination by independent accountants, the financial statements of any foreign governmental agency may be examined by the regular and customary auditing staff of the respective government if public financial statements of such governmental agency are customarily examined by such auditing staff.

50204. Rule 2-04. Examination of Financial Statements of Persons Other Than the Registrant

If a registrant is required to file financial statements of any other person, such statements need not be examined if examination of such statements would not be required if such person were itself a registrant.

50205. Rule 2-05. Examination of Financial Statements by More Than One Accountant

If, with respect to the examination of the financial statements, part of the examination is made by an independent accountant other than the principal accountant and the principal accountant elects to place reliance on the work of the other accountant and makes reference to that effect in his report, the separate report of the other accountant shall be filed. However, notwithstanding the provisions of this section, reports of other accountants which may otherwise be required in filings need not be presented in annual reports to security holders furnished pursuant to the proxy and information statement rules under the Securities Exchange Act of 1934 (Rules 14a-3 and 14c-3).

The guidelines for reporting when part of the audit is performed by other auditors are included in AU Section 543. If the principal auditors, following those guidelines, assume responsibility for the entire audit, the report of such other auditors need not be filed. In such a case, it would be inappropriate for the principal auditors to state in their report that part of the audit was made by other auditors, because to do so may mislead a reader. However, if the principal auditors do not assume responsibility and make reference in their report to other auditors, the manually signed report of the other auditors is required to be included in the document being filed. The provisions of Rule 2-01, Qualifications of Accountants, and Rule 2-02, Accountants' Reports, also apply to other auditors and their audits. Rule 2-05 permits the annual report to shareholders to exclude reports of secondary auditors on which the primary auditors have relied.

50300. ARTICLE 3.
GENERAL INSTRUCTIONS AS TO FINANCIAL STATEMENTS

General Instructions as to Financial Statements

Note: These instructions specify the balance sheets and statements of income and cash flows to be included in disclosure documents prepared in accordance with Regulation S-X. Other portions of Regulation S-X govern the examination, form and content of such financial statements, including the basis of consolidation and the schedules to be filed. The financial statements described below shall be audited unless otherwise indicated.

For filings under the Securities Act of 1933, attention is directed to Rule 411(b) regarding incorporation by reference to financial statements and to Section 10(a) (3) of the Act regarding information required in the prospectus.

For filings under the Securities Exchange Act of 1934, attention is directed to Rule 12b-23 regarding incorporation by reference and Rule 12b-36 regarding use of financial statements filed under other acts.

Article 3 includes the requirements for financial statements to be included in most disclosure documents and specifies the periods to be covered by such statements. This article also specifies the interim financial information to be included in 1933 and 1934 Act registration statements and in certain proxy statements (see sections 50301 through 50311). The following table provides an overview of the entities ("persons") for which financial statements may be required. Sections 50303 through 50311 summarize the dates and periods for which financial statements are required in disclosure documents.

ENTITIES FOR WHICH FINANCIAL STATEMENTS MAY BE REQUIRED

	Manual Reference
Registrant and Its Consolidated Subsidiaries	50302
Registrant (Parent Company—Schedule III)	50520
Unconsolidated Subsidiaries and 50 Percent-or-Less-Owned Persons	
• Full Financial Statements	50339
• Summarized Financial Information	50408
Businesses Acquired or to Be Acquired	50314
Affiliates Whose Securities Are Pledged as Collateral	50344
Guarantors of Securities Registered	50344

Article 3 also specifies modifications that need to be made to the basic financial statements in certain situations and additional requirements as listed below:

	Manual Reference
Inactive Registrants	50345
Real Estate Operations Acquired or To Be Acquired	50348
Real Estate Investment Trusts (REITs)	50349
Reorganization of the Registrant	50350
Registered Management Investment Companies	50352
Foreign Private Issuers	50353

50301. Rule 3-01. Consolidated Balance Sheets

(a) There shall be filed, for the registrant and its subsidiaries consolidated, audited balance sheets as of the end of each of the two most recent fiscal years. If the registrant has been in existence for less than one fiscal year, there shall be filed an audited balance sheet as of a date within 135 days of the date of filing the registration statement.

(b) If the filing, other than a filing on Form 10-K or Form 10, is made within 45 days after the end of the registrant's fiscal year and audited financial statements for the most recent fiscal year are not available, the balance sheets may be as of the end of the two preceding fiscal years and the filing shall include an additional balance sheet

SEC 50300. Article 3

as of an interim date at least as current as the end of the registrant's third fiscal quarter of the most recently completed fiscal year.

(c) The instruction in paragraph (b) is also applicable to filings, other than on Form 10-K or Form 10, made after 45 days but within 90 days of the end of the registrant's fiscal year, provided that the following conditions are met:

(1) The registrant files annual, quarterly and other reports pursuant to section 13 or 15(d) of the Securities Exchange Act of 1934 and all reports due have been filed;

(2) For the most recent fiscal year for which audited financial statements are not yet available the registrant reasonably and in good faith expects to report income, after taxes but before extraordinary items and cumulative effect of a change in accounting principle; and

(3) For at least one of the two fiscal years immediately preceding the most recent fiscal year the registrant reported income, after taxes but before extraordinary items and cumulative effect of a change in accounting principle.

(d) For filings made after 45 days but within 90 days of the end of the registrant's fiscal year where the conditions set forth in paragraph (c) of this section are not met, the filing must include the audited balance sheets required by paragraph [(a)] of this section.

(e) For filings made after 134 days subsequent to the end of the registrant's most recent fiscal year the filing shall also include a balance sheet as of an interim date within 135 days of the date of filing.

(f) Any interim balance sheet provided in accordance with the requirements of this section may be unaudited and need not be presented in greater detail than is required by Rule 10-01. Notwithstanding the requirements of this section, the most recent interim balance sheet included in a filing shall be at least as current as the most recent balance sheet filed with the Commission on Form 10-Q.

(g) For filings by registered management investment companies, the requirements of Rule 3-18 shall apply in lieu of the requirements of this section.

(h) Any foreign private issuer, other than a registered management investment company or an employee plan, may file the financial statements required by Rule 3-19 in lieu of the financial statements specified in this rule.

SEC 50301

50302. Rule 3-02. Consolidated Statements of Income and Changes in Cash Flows

(a) There shall be filed, for the registrant and its subsidiaries consolidated and its predecessors, audited statements of income and cash flows for each of the three fiscal years preceding the date of the most recent audited balance sheet being filed or such shorter period as the registrant (including predecessors) has been in existence.

(b) In addition, for any interim period between the latest audited balance sheet and the date of the most recent interim balance sheet being filed, and for the corresponding period of the preceding fiscal year, statements of income and cash flows shall be provided. Such interim financial statements may be unaudited and need not be presented in greater detail than is required by Rule 10-01.

See also Instructions under Rule 3-06.

(c) For filings by registered management investment companies, the requirements of Rule 3-18 shall apply in lieu of the requirements of this section.

(d) Any foreign private issuer, other than a registered management investment company or an employee plan, may file the financial statements required by Rule 3-19 in lieu of the financial statements specified in this rule.

50303. Uniform Requirements for Financial Statements

Rules 3-01 and 3-02 set forth the requirements for filing consolidated balance sheets and consolidated statements of income and cash flows. When consolidated financial statements are presented, they are usually considered the primary statements in the document being filed, with generally accepted accounting principles for consolidations followed in their preparation. While Article 3A of Regulation S-X (section 50372) contains the specific SEC rules relating to the preparation of consolidated and combined statements, these rules do not differ substantially from the accounting principles outlined in SFAS No. 94, *Consolidation of All Majority-Owned Subsidiaries.* Consequently, as a general rule the consolidation principles followed by a registrant in an SEC filing do not vary from those normally followed for other reporting purposes.

When required, interim financial statements may be furnished in condensed form, as provided by Article 10 (see section 51000). Separate financial statements, such as those for unconsolidated subsidiaries and 50 percent-or-less-owned equity affiliates ("persons"), and supporting Regulation S-X schedules need not be furnished for interim periods (see section 50342).

Note that Rule 3-02(a) calls for audited consolidated statements of income for the registrant "and its predecessors" for each of the three most recent fiscal years. While the determination whether a prior activity would constitute a "predecessor" would depend on the particular circumstances, Rule 405 of Regulation C defines the term as follows:

> The term "predecessor" means a person the major portion of the business and assets of which another person acquired in a single succession, or in a series of related successions in each of which the acquiring person acquired the major portion of the business and assets of the acquired person.

The foregoing definition refers to the major portion of the business and assets as they relate to the acquiring company. In practice, however, the SEC staff is also concerned with the relationship of the acquired business to the acquiring company. For example, if ABC company was formed to acquire the business and assets of XYZ company and as a result the acquisition constituted the major portion of the business and assets of ABC company, XYZ company would probably be considered a "predecessor" of ABC company.

The requirement to provide statements of income for predecessors of the registrant is based on the premise that the absence of such information would exclude a significant part of the past operating performance of the registrant's current activity and thereby limit the ability of readers of the financial statements to evaluate the historical operating results of the registrant's present business.

Although Rule 3-01 regarding the filing of consolidated balance sheets does not contain the term "predecessors," the SEC staff's practice is generally to apply the same principle as discussed above. Accordingly, a separate audited balance sheet of the predecessor may be required to satisfy the balance sheet requirements pursuant to Rule 3-01. See section 50320 for further discussion of predecessor companies.

50304. Age of Financial Statements at Filing Date

Rules 3-01 and 3-02 specify the age of financial statements to be included in a registration statement as of the filing date. Note, however, that Rule 3-12 (see section 50346) contains similar provisions that apply to the age of the financial statements as of the anticipated effective date of the registration statement or the proposed mailing date of a proxy. Thus, although the following discussion refers to the filing date, it is equally applicable to updating financial statements as of the effective date. These rules also set forth the conditions as to when financial statements of the registrant's latest fiscal year need to be furnished in the document being filed. The following summary may help in understanding the effect of these provisions:

- When a registration statement is filed *within 90 days* after the fiscal year-end date, audited financial statements for the latest fiscal year may be omitted if the conditions specified in Rule 3-01 are met.

- When a registration statement is filed *between 90 and 134 days* after the fiscal year-end date, audited financial statements for the latest fiscal year are required but interim statements may be omitted.

- When a registration statement is filed *more than 134 days* after the fiscal year-end date, interim statements are required to be as current as those included in the most recent Form 10-Q filed by the registrant (or as of a date within 135 days of the filing date).

50305. Filings within 90 days after fiscal year-end. When financial statements for the latest fiscal year are included in a filing, interim financial statements are not required unless a registration statement is filed *more than* 134 days after year-end. Rules 3-01 and 3-02 also provide for the possible omission of the audited financial statements of the registrant for the latest fiscal year if such statements are not available *and* the registration statement is filed within 90 days after the fiscal year-end. However, Rule 3-01 separates this 90-day period into two segments: (1) filings within 45 days after year-end and (2) filings more than 45 days but within 90 days after year-end.

50306. Filings within 45 days after fiscal year-end. When a registration statement is filed within 45 days after the registrant's year-end *and* audited financial statements for the most recent fiscal year are not yet complete and available to be included in the document, the rules permit the filing of audited balance sheets as of the end of the two preceding fiscal years, along with audited statements of income and cash flows for each of the three fiscal years preceding the most recent audited balance sheet. Under these circumstances, an additional interim balance sheet (unaudited and in condensed format as specified in Article 10; see section 51000) would be required as of a date at least as current as the end of the third fiscal quarter of the registrant's most recently completed fiscal year. Comparative year-to-date unaudited statements of income and cash flows would also be required (in condensed format) for the interim period between the date of the most recent audited balance sheet presented and the date of the most recent interim balance sheet being filed. These provisions are applicable to all registrants. Note, however, that Rule 3-12 (see section 50346) requires updating of the financial statements to the anticipated effective date.

50307. Filings more than 45 days but within 90 days after fiscal year-end. Registration statements filed more than 45 days but within 90 days after the end of the registrant's fiscal year ("45-day window") may follow the same provisions applicable to filings within 45 days if the registrant meets *all* the following conditions specified in paragraph (c) of Rule 3-01:

- The registrant is required to file periodic reports under the 1934 Act (Section 13 or 15(d)) and has filed all such reports (Forms 10-K, 10-Q, and 8-K) due at the time of filing.

- The registrant reasonably expects income (as opposed to a loss), after taxes but before extraordinary items and cumulative effect of a change in accounting principle, for the most recent fiscal year for which audited financial statements are not yet available.

- The registrant has reported income (as opposed to a loss), after taxes but before extraordinary items and cumulative effect of a change in accounting principle, for at least one of the two immediately preceding fiscal years for which audited financial statements are available.

Registrants who file (or whose registration statements will become effective—see Rule 3-12 in section 50346) in the "45-day window" period but that do not meet the conditions noted above are required to provide audited financial statements for the most recently completed fiscal year in the registration statement.

The rule essentially requires audited financial statements for the most recent fiscal year when initial public offering documents are filed more than 45 days after the end of the fiscal year. Although the rule does not specifically so state, audited financial statements for the most recently completed fiscal year would also be required in registration statements filed more than 90 days but within 135 days after the end of the fiscal year.

SAB Topic 1-C describes the views of the staff with respect to including unaudited financial statements for a full fiscal year in a registration statement. The text of the SAB follows:

Unaudited Financial Statements for a Full Fiscal Year

Facts: Company A, which is a reporting company under the Securities Exchange Act of 1934, proposes to file a registration statement within 90 days of its fiscal year-end but does not have audited year-end financial statements available. The Company meets the criteria under Rule 3 01 of Regulation S-X and is therefore not required to include year-end audited financial statements in its registration statement. However, the Company does propose to include in the prospectus the unaudited results of operations for its entire fiscal year.

Question: Would the staff find this objectionable?

Interpretive Response: The staff recognizes that many registrants publish the results of their most recent year's operations prior to the availability of year-end audited financial statements. The staff will not object to the inclusion of unaudited results for a full fiscal year and indeed would expect such data in the registration statement if the registrant has published such information. When such data is included in a prospectus, it must be covered by a management's representation that all adjustments necessary for a fair statement of the results have been made. [This representation is discussed in section 50312.]

50308. Filings more than 134 days after fiscal year-end. When a registration statement is filed more than 134 days after the end of a registrant's fiscal year, unaudited interim financial statements are required as of an interim date within 135 days of the date of filing. The balance sheet is required to be as of a date at least as current as the date of the most recent quarterly data filed with the Commission on Form 10-Q and may be presented in condensed format as prescribed by Article 10 (see section 51000). Statements of income and cash flows, in comparative form, are also required for the interim period between the date of the most recent year-end audited balance sheet and the date of the most recent interim balance sheet being filed. Note that Rule 3-12 (see section 50346) requires the financial statements to be updated to the effective date.

50309. Flexibility of Interim Date Requirements

Rule 3-01 permits some flexibility as to the date for interim financial statements to be included by registrants who are not required to file quarterly reports on Form 10-Q. For example, a calendar-year company not subject to quarterly reporting requirements under the 1934 Act (and therefore not required to file Form 10-Q) may, in a filing on April 20 that is expected to become effective on May 30, include interim financial statements as of the end of January or February. Such statements may be easier to generate than statements as of the end of the first fiscal quarter (March 31) and will be considered acceptable for such registrants as long as the interim statements are within the prescribed 135-day period prior to the date of filing (and the effective date; see Rule 3-12 in section 50346).

50310. Capsule Updating

In certain circumstances, capsule data may be an appropriate form of presentation of interim data in a registration statement, e.g., when financial information has been released to the public prior to the effective date of the registration statement and prior to completion and filing of Form 10-Q. In all cases a registrant should ensure that information in the filing is no less complete and current than data available elsewhere in the public domain. The requirements for capsule data are not specified or defined in the literature; however, paragraph 30 of APB Opinion No. 28 provides that summarized interim financial data should (at a minimum) include:

Sales or gross revenues, provision for income taxes, extraordinary items (including related income tax effects), cumulative effect of a change in accounting principles or practices, . . . net income . . . [and] earnings per share data. . . .

SEC 50307. Rule 3-02

If capsule information is presented, it is normally unaudited and should be accompanied by a management representation that the amounts shown include all adjustments necessary to a fair presentation of the results of operations for the periods (as discussed in section 50312). Capsule data may be presented either in narrative or tabular form.

50311. Summary of Requirements

In summary, Rules 3-01 and 3-02 set forth the requirements as to when registration and proxy statements must include audited financial statements for the recently completed fiscal year and when, in addition, they are required to include unaudited interim financial statements. The table on the following page summarizes (1) when financial statements of a recently completed fiscal year must be furnished, and (2) the related requirements for including financial statements (based on the effective date of the document being filed). Note that while Rules 3-01 and 3-02 specify the age of financial statements as of the filing date, Rule 3-12 contains similar provisions that apply to the effective date.

Age of Financial Statements

Number of days after year-end when the registration statement becomes effective or the proxy statement is mailed	Financial Statement Requirements			
	Balance Sheets		Income Statements[1]	
	Year-End Date (Audited)	Interim Date (Unaudited)[2]	Fiscal Year (Audited)	Interim Period (Unaudited)[2]
1-45 days—audited statements for the most recent fiscal year are not required	Two fiscal years preceding the most recently completed fiscal year	At least as current as third quarter of most recently completed fiscal year	Three years preceding the most recent audited balance sheet presented	Period between latest audited and most recent interim balance sheet (comparative)
46-90 days: a) If three conditions are met (see Rule 3-01), audited statements for the most recent fiscal year are not required	Same as for 1-45 days	Same as for 1-45 days		
b) If three conditions are not met, audited year-end statements for the most recent fiscal year are required		None	Three most recent fiscal years	None
91-134 days—audited year-end statements for the most recent fiscal year are required	Two most recent fiscal year-ends	None		None
Over 134 days—audited year-end statements for the most recent fiscal year are required		As of a date within 135 days		Period between latest audited and most recent interim balance sheet (comparative)

[1] The requirements are the same for the statements of cash flows and other stockholders' equity.

[2] The interim data must be at least as current as that already filed with the SEC on Form 10-Q or otherwise available. (The term "available" is generally intended to mean complete as to form and content.)

SEC 50311. Rule 3-02

50312. Rule 3-03. Instructions to Income Statement Requirements

(a) The statements required shall be prepared in compliance with the applicable requirements of this Regulation.

(b) If the registrant is engaged primarily (1) in the generation, transmission or distribution of electricity, the manufacture, mixing, transmission or distribution of gas, the supplying or distribution of water, or the furnishing of telephone or telegraph service; or (2) in holding securities of companies engaged in such businesses, it may at its option include statements of income and cash flows (which may be unaudited) for the twelve-month period ending on the date of the most recent balance sheet being filed, in lieu of the statements of income and cash flows for the interim periods specified.

(c) If a period or periods reported on include operations of a business prior to the date of acquisition, or for other reasons differ from reports previously issued for any period, the statements shall be reconciled as to sales or revenues and net income in the statement or in a note thereto with the amounts previously reported; provided, however, that such reconciliations need not be made if (1) they have been made in filings with the Commission in prior years or (2) the financial statements which are being retroactively adjusted have not previously been filed with the Commission or otherwise made public.

(d) Any unaudited interim financial statements furnished shall reflect all adjustments which are, in the opinion of management, necessary to a fair statement of the results for the interim periods presented. A statement to that effect shall be included. Such adjustments shall include, for example, appropriate estimated provisions for bonus and profit sharing arrangements normally determined or settled at year-end. If all such adjustments are of a normal recurring nature, a statement to that effect shall be made; otherwise, there shall be furnished information describing in appropriate detail the nature and amount of any adjustments other than normal recurring adjustments entering into the determination of the results shown.

(e) Disclosures regarding business segments required by generally accepted accounting principles (Statement of Financial Accounting Standards No. 14) shall be provided for each year for which an audited statement of income is presented. To the extent that the segment information presented pursuant to this instruction complies with the provisions of Item 101 of Regulation S-K, the disclosures may be combined by cross referencing to or from the financial statements.

Paragraph (b) of this rule permits companies engaged in the electric, gas, or telephone businesses to present a 12-month income statement ending on the date of the most recent balance sheet included in the document in lieu of the comparative interim periods referred to in section 50302. For example, a calendar-year utility presenting an interim balance sheet as of March 31 may include a statement of income for the 12 months ended March 31 (in addition to statements of income for each of the three most recent calendar years) in lieu of comparative interim statements of income for the three months ended March 31.

Paragraph (c) requires that the financial statements be reconciled as to sales or revenues and net income if such data differs for any reason from reports "previously issued" for any period. Such differences may arise as a result of retroactive restatements for poolings of interests, changes in accounting principles, or other causes. The reconciliation may be presented in the statement of income or in a note thereto. As stated in the rule, a reconciliation need not be furnished if it has already been included in a document previously filed with the SEC or if financial statements for the periods being restated have not previously been included in a document filed with the SEC or otherwise made public.

Paragraph (d) of the rule requires a representation by the registrant with respect to any interim period presented that "all adjustments...necessary to a fair statement of the results for such period have been included..." The representation, which also needs to indicate whether the adjustments are of a normal and recurring nature, is typically included in a footnote to the interim statements. Note that such representation is also required when unaudited results of operations for the entire fiscal year are included in a registration statement (see SAB Topic 1-C in section 50307).

Paragraph (e) provides that business segment information in accordance with the provisions of FASB Statement No. 14, *Financial Reporting for Segments of a Business Enterprise,* is required to be presented for each year for which an audited income statement is presented. Accordingly, segment information is usually required for the three latest fiscal years. This requirement is consistent with the period for which segment information is required to be included in the textual portion of the document by Regulation S-K (Business). Paragraph (e) further provides that to the extent the segment information included in the financial statements complies with the provisions of Regulation S-K, these disclosures need not be duplicated and may be satisfied by cross-referencing *either to or from* the financial statements.

50313. Rule 3-04. Changes in Other Stockholders' Equity

An analysis of the changes in each caption of other stockholders' equity presented in the balance sheets shall be given in a note or separate statement. This analysis shall be presented in the form of a reconciliation of the beginning balance to the ending balance for each period for which an income statement is required to be filed with all significant reconciling items described by appropriate captions. State separately the adjustments to the balance at the beginning of the earliest period presented for items which were retroactively applied to periods prior to that period. With respect to any dividends, state the amount per share and in the aggregate for each class of shares.

This rule requires a summary of each account presented under Regulation S-X balance sheet caption 31, Other Stockholders' Equity (paid-in additional capital, other additional capital, and retained earnings), for each period for which an income statement is required to be filed (generally three years; see discussion of Rule 3-02 in section 50302).

Many registrants prefer to present a single statement of stockholders' equity that includes the information as to changes in capital shares as illustrated below. However, refer to comments following captions 28 and 30 of Rule 5-02 (section 50502) regarding the presentation of redeemable preferred stock and the SEC staff's preference that the number of shares outstanding be presented on the face of the balance sheet.

The following is an example of how the analysis required by Rule 3-04 might be presented, recognizing that it covers only one year instead of the required three years and that additional stockholders' equity accounts (e.g., preferred stock, translation adjustment, etc.) may be encountered.

XYZ COMPANY
CONSOLIDATED STATEMENT OF STOCKHOLDERS' EQUITY
(Thousands)

| | Common Stock | | Capital in Excess of Par Value | Retained Earnings | Total Stockholders' Equity |
	Shares	Amount			
Balance, January 1, 19X4	1,000	$2,000	$10,500	$20,500	$33,000
Net Income	—	—	—	1,700	1,700
Cash dividend of $.50 per share	—	—	—	(500)	(500)
10% common stock dividend	100	200	2,800	(3,000)	-
Exercise of common stock options	125	250	2,250	—	2,500
Balance, December 31,19X4	1,225	$2,450	$15,550	$18,700	$36,700

50314. Rule 3-05. Financial Statements of Businesses Acquired or to Be Acquired

(a) Financial statements required.

(1) Financial statements prepared and audited in accordance with this regulation should be furnished for the periods specified in (b) below if any of the following conditions exist:

(i) Consummation of a business combination accounted for as a purchase has occurred or is probable (for purposes of this rule, the term "purchase" encompasses the purchase of an interest in a business accounted for by the equity method); or

(ii) Consummation of a business combination to be accounted for as a pooling of interests is probable.

(2) For purposes of determining whether the provisions of this rule apply, the determination of whether a "business" has been acquired should be made in accordance with the guidance set forth in Rule 11-01(d).

(3) If consummation of more than one transaction has occurred or is probable, the required financial statements may be presented on a combined basis, if appropriate.

(4) This rule shall not apply to a business which is totally held by the registrant prior to consummation of the transaction.

(b) Periods to be presented.

(1) If securities are being registered to be offered to the security holders of the business to be acquired, the financial statements specified in Rules 3-01 and 3-02 shall be furnished for the business to be acquired, except as provided otherwise for filings on Form N-14, S-4 or F-4. In all other cases, financial statements of the business acquired or to be acquired shall be filed for the periods specified in this paragraph or such shorter period as the business has been in existence. The financial statements covering fiscal years shall be audited except as provided in Item 14 of Schedule 14A, with respect to certain proxy statements or in a registration statement filed on Form N-14, S-4 or F-4. The periods for which such financial statements are to be filed shall be determined using the conditions specified in the definition of significant subsidiary in Rule 1-02 (v) as follows:

(i) If none of the conditions exceeds 10 percent, financial statements are not required. However, if the aggregate impact of the individually insignificant businesses acquired since the date of the most recent audited balance sheet filed for the registrant exceeds 20 percent, financial statements covering at least the substantial majority of the businesses acquired, combined if appropriate, shall be furnished. Such financial statements shall be for at least the most recent fiscal year and any interim periods specified in Rules 3-01 and 3-02.

(ii) If any of the conditions exceeds 10 percent, but none exceed 20 percent, financial statements shall be furnished for at least the most recent fiscal year and any interim periods specified in Rules 3-01 and 3-02.

SEC 50314. Rule 3-05

(iii) If any of the conditions exceeds 20 percent, but none exceeds 40 percent, financial statements shall be furnished for at least the two most recent fiscal years and any interim periods specified in Rules 3-01 and 3-02.

(iv) If any of the conditions exceeds 40 percent, the full financial statements specified in Rules 3-01 and 3-02 shall be furnished.

The determination shall be made by comparing the most recent annual financial statements of each such business to the registrant's most recent annual consolidated financial statements filed at or prior to the date of acquisition. However, if the registrant made a significant acquisition subsequent to the latest fiscal year-end and filed a report on Form 8-K which included audited financial statements of such acquired business for the periods required by this section and the pro forma financial information required by Article 11, such determination may be made by using the pro forma amounts for the latest fiscal year in the report on Form 8-K rather than by using the historical amounts for the latest fiscal year of the registrant. The tests may not be made by "annualizing" data.

(2) *(i) Notwithstanding the requirements in (b)(1) above, separate financial statements of the acquired business need not be presented once the operating results of the acquired business have been reflected in the audited consolidated financial statements of the registrant for a complete fiscal year unless such financial statements have not been previously filed or unless the acquired business is of such significance to the registrant that omission of such financial statements would materially impair an investor's ability to understand the historical financial results of the registrant. For example, if, at the date of acquisition, the acquired business met at least one of the conditions in the definition of significant subsidiary in Rule 1-02(v) at the 80 percent level the income statements of the acquired business should normally continue to be furnished for such periods prior to the purchase as may be necessary when added to the time for which audited income statements after the purchase are filed to cover the equivalent of the period specified in Rule 3-02.*

(ii) A separate audited balance sheet of the acquired business is not required when the registrant's most recent audited balance sheet required by Rule 3-01 is for a date after the date the acquisition was consummated.

50315. General Comments

Rule 3-05 needs to be taken into consideration when a business combination accounted for as a purchase has occurred during the period for which a registrant's financial statements are included in a registration statement (or during the period between the latest balance sheet included and the anticipated effective date) and the business acquired is "significant" as defined in the rule. See section 50341 for a discussion of the significant subsidiary test. Rule 3-05 must also be considered if, at the anticipated effective date of the registration statement, a business combination (to be accounted for either as a purchase or a pooling of interests) is probable and the business to be acquired is "significant." Article 11 (see section 51100) sets forth the pro forma financial information that may be required when a business is acquired or is to be acquired. Article 11 also contains certain guidelines as to what constitutes a "business" in the context of an acquisition.

Rule 3-05 specifies the extent to which audited financial statements of the target company prior to the date of acquisition are required to be included separately in the document being filed. The considerations entering into this determination include:

- The timing of the acquisition (i.e., the time elapsed since the date of acquisition and the latest date for which audited financial statements of the registrant are presented).

- The materiality of the acquisition to the registrant at the date of acquisition (i.e., whether the acquisition is "significant" under the tests specified in the rule).

- In the case of past acquisition, the accounting treatment (i.e., whether it was accounted for as a purchase, since in the case of a pooling of interests the financial statements of the target company would already be combined with those of the registrant).

For purposes of this rule, the acquisition of an investment in a company that is accounted for under the equity method (APB Opinion No. 18) is also considered to be the acquisition of a business.

While Item 7 of Form 8-K (see section 41600) also contains requirements for the filing of audited financial statements when "significant" acquisitions have occurred (i.e., are consummated), Rule 3-05 extends this requirement to future business combinations the consummation of which is "probable," regardless of whether the transaction is to be accounted for as a purchase or a pooling of interests.

The SEC staff's view of what constitutes a "probable" acquisition may extend to circumstances in which no formal agreements have been signed. Discussions of contemplated acquisitions in a registration statement may be considered sufficiently pertinent to an understanding of the financial affairs of the registrant to require that financial statements of the business be furnished. In discussing the rule in FRR No. 2 (FRP Section 506.02), the SEC stated that:

> . . . guidance as to when consummation of a transaction is probable cannot be given because such a determination is dependent upon the facts and circumstances. In

SEC 50315. Rule 3-05

essence, however, consummation of a transaction is considered to be probable whenever the registrant's financial statements alone would not provide investors with adequate financial information with which to make an investment decision . . .

Rule 3-05 applies only to the acquisition of a "business," not to the acquisition of unrelated assets. There is a presumption that a separate entity, a subsidiary, or a division is a "business"; however, a lesser component of an entity may also constitute a "business." The determination of whether a "business" has been acquired should be made using the guidance in Rule 11-01(d)(section 51101), which, although not absolute, does provide some parameters. The SEC staff considers the continuity of the business operations to be a significant factor in determining whether a business has been acquired. For example, if a manufacturing plant is acquired and the acquiror elects to (1) produce a different product, (2) use a different sales and labor force, and (3) re-tool the plant, the SEC staff would probably conclude that this transaction involved a fixed asset acquisition since it is not a continuing business operation. Pursuant to Item 8 of Form 10-K, Rule 3-05 and Article 11 do not apply to annual reports filed on Form 10-K. Similarly, they do not apply to annual reports filed by foreign registrants on Form 20-F.

As a general rule, the SEC staff does not require financial statement schedules (see section 50520) to be furnished with Rule 3-05 statements. However, if the acquired business is effectively a predecessor of the registrant (see section 50320), the staff would require the inclusion of such schedules.

SAB Topic 1-J (SAB No. 80) sets forth the staff's views regarding the application of Rules 3-05 and 1-02(v) of Regulation S-X to certain initial public offerings involving companies that have grown significantly as a result of a series of acquisitions. Reference should be made to section 50322 of this manual for a discussion of this SAB.

50316. Decision Chart on Financial Statement Requirements

Questions frequently arise about the requirements for financial statements to be included in registration statements when business combinations have occurred or are about to occur. The following chart presents an overview of the financial statements and periods to be presented as required by Rule 3-05(b). This chart should be used in conjunction with the text of Rule 3-05 and the discussion in section 50317. Also, see Article 11 (section 51100) for pro forma financial statement requirements.

454

Overview of Rule 3-05 Provisions

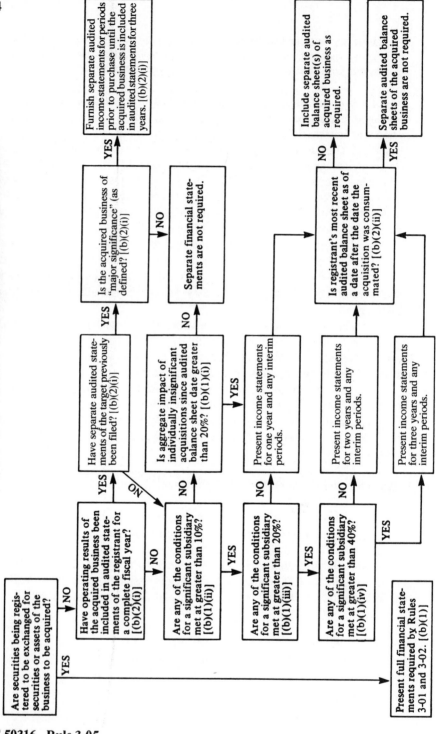

Are securities being registered to be exchanged for securities or assets of the business to be acquired?

YES → Present full financial statements required by Rules 3-01 and 3-02. [(b)(1)]

NO →

Have operating results of the acquired business been included in audited statements of the registrant for a complete fiscal year? [(b)(2)(ii)]

YES →

Have separate audited statements of the target previously been filed? [(b)(2)(i)]

YES →

Is the acquired business of "major significance" (as defined)? [(b)(2)(i)]

YES → Furnish separate audited income statements for periods prior to purchase until the acquired business is included in audited statements for three years. [(b)(2)(i)]

NO → Separate financial statements are not required.

NO (ON) →

Are any of the conditions for a significant subsidiary met at greater than 10%? [(b)(1)(ii)]

NO → Is aggregate impact of individually insignificant acquisitions since audited balance sheet date greater than 20%? [(b)(1)(i)]

NO → Separate financial statements are not required.

YES → Present income statements for one year and any interim periods.

YES →

Are any of the conditions for a significant subsidiary met at greater than 20%? [(b)(1)(iii)]

NO → Present income statements for one year and any interim periods.

YES →

Are any of the conditions for a significant subsidiary met at greater than 40%? [(b)(1)(iv)]

NO → Present income statements for two years and any interim periods.

YES → Present income statements for three years and any interim periods.

Is registrant's most recent audited balance sheet as of a date after the acquisition was consummated? [(b)(2)(ii)]

NO → Include separate audited balance sheet(s) of acquired business as required.

YES → Separate audited balance sheets of the acquired business are not required.

SEC 50316. Rule 3-05

50317. Financial Statement Requirements

The financial statement requirements set forth in this rule generally do not apply to the acquisition of a business unless such business meets the so-called "significant subsidiary" test. However, when any of the securities being registered are to be exchanged for securities or assets of the target company, full financial statements as specified in Rules 3-01 and 3-02 may be required even though the acquired business does not meet the significance test.

Separate audited historical financial statements of an acquired business are *not* required in a registration statement when the operating results of the business are included in the audited financial statements of the registrant for a complete fiscal year unless:

- The financial statements of the acquired business technically were required but were not filed (if, for example, a "no action" letter was obtained in connection with the filing of Form 8-K—see section 50318) or

- The acquired business is of "major significance" to the registrant.

The SEC staff has indicated that the historical financial statements of an acquired business are not required when financial statements have been filed previously and the acquired operations are included in the audited financial statements for at least nine months, unless the acquisition is of major significance.

Rule 3-05 indicates that an example of "major significance" might be one in which the significant subsidiary conditions were met at the 80 percent level at the date of acquisition. This is used as an example and, accordingly, should not necessarily be regarded as a minimum level in determining whether the acquisition is considered to be of major significance. The SEC staff has indicated that it presumes that an acquisition is of major significance if:

- It is included in audited results for less than 12 months and was significant at the 50 percent or greater level; or

- It is included in audited results for less than 21 months and was significant at the 70 percent or greater level.

If the business acquired is of major significance, separate audited income statements of the acquired business would normally continue to be included until postacquisition results of operations of the acquired business have been included in the audited income statements of the registrant for the period specified in Rule 3-02 (i.e., three years).

If the operating results of the acquired business have not been included in the audited financial statements of the registrant for at least a complete fiscal year, the rule contains certain percentage criteria to determine whether separate preacquisition financial statements of the acquired business are required. The determination of whether a business constitutes a "significant" acquisition to the registrant depends on whether the acquisition would, if measured by the criteria provided in Rule 1-02(v) (as discussed in section 50341), constitute a significant subsidiary at the date of acquisition. However, since the importance of an acquisition is affected by both the size of the acquisition and the passage of time, the instructions permit the application of different percentages in the calculation to determine the number of fiscal years for which the financial statements of the acquired business are required to be presented:

If any of the conditions for a significant subsidiary exceed	Periods to be presented
10% but are less than 20%	One year and any interim periods
20% but are less than 40%	Two years and any interim periods
40%	Full financial statements as required by Rules 3-01 and 3-02

For purposes of the test of significance, the target company is to be compared to the registrant *at the date of acquisition*. The registrant's consolidated statements to be used are the most recent annual consolidated financial statements prior to the acquisition. This is an important point to remember, since the test is frequently made in connection with a 1933 Act filing some time after the acquisition has occurred. The acquired company's financial statements to be used in the test are also those of the most recent annual period at or before the date of acquisition irrespective of whether the target company's fiscal year-end date is the same as that of the registrant. The "major significance" test, therefore, is based on the financial statements of both the registrant and the acquired company for the last full fiscal year before the acquisition; however, Rule 3-05(b)(1)(iv) includes a special provision for registrants who have made significant acquisitions after the latest fiscal year-end and have filed a Form 8-K that includes audited financial statements of the acquired business for the periods specified in Rule 3-05 and the pro forma financial information required by Article 11. Under such circumstances, the pro forma amounts for the latest fiscal year included in the Form 8-K filing, rather than the historical amounts for the registrant's latest fiscal year, may be used for purposes of applying the significant subsidiary tests to new acquisitions.

The determination of significance under Rule 3-05 should be made separately for each acquisition. In applying the test, if none of the conditions exceeds 10 percent, financial statements are not required. However, if several acquisitions occur during the same time period and the aggregate impact of the individually insignificant businesses acquired since the date of the most recent audited balance sheet filed exceeds 20 percent for any of the tests, financial statements covering at least the substantial majority of the businesses acquired, combined if appropriate, needs to be furnished for at least the most recent fiscal year and the latest interim periods preceding the acquisition. In determining the financial statements to be provided in these situations for at least the substantial majority of the business acquired, the SEC staff has informally indicated that audited financial statements should be furnished with respect to at least a mathematical majority of the acquirees (i.e., more than 50 percent of combined assets, pretax income and investment).

Balance sheets of an acquired business need only be furnished when the acquisition was consummated subsequent to the date of the registrant's most recent audited balance sheet. In that case, comparative balance sheets need to be presented as required by Rule 3-01 (section 50301) except when the conditions for significance exceed 10 percent but are less than 20 percent, in which case a balance sheet for only the most recent fiscal year and interim period would have to be furnished. Note that such statements must comply with Regulation S-X.

As mentioned previously, the SEC staff generally does not require financial statement schedules (see section 50520) to be furnished with Rule 3-05 statements. However, if the acquired business is effectively a predecessor of the registrant (see section 50320), the staff would expect the inclusion of supplemental schedules.

Rule 3-06 of Regulation S-X specifies that the inclusion of one period of nine to twelve months is acceptable to the SEC in the context of financial statements required pursuant to Rule 3-05 for a significant business acquisition (section 50338).

SAB No. 89, Topic 1-K sets forth the staff's views on the financial statement requirements relating to the acquisitions of troubled financial institutions. The text of this SAB is included in section 50901.

50318. Age of Financial Statements

The SEC staff's informal positions regarding the required age of Rule 3-05 financial statements are as follows:

1933 Act Filings

If the *effective* date of the filing is more than 89 days subsequent to the acquiree's fiscal year-end, the financial statements covering the acquiree's most recent fiscal year must be audited.

If the effective date of the filing is after 45 days, but within 90 days of the acquiree's fiscal year-end, the staff has interpreted the updating requirements to be dependent upon the eligibility of the registrant (not the acquiree), for relief under paragraph (c) of Regulation S-X Rule 3-01.

1934 Act Filings

For purposes of 1934 Act filings on Form 8-K, the staff generally does not require audited financial statements of the acquiree's most recently completed fiscal year unless the Form 8-K filing reporting the acquisition was filed 90 days or more after the acquired company's fiscal year-end. It is important to note that the staff believes that the age of financial statements in Form 8-K should be determined by reference to the filing date (or the required filing date) of the Form 8-K that initially reports the consummation of the business acquisition.

1933 and 1934 Act Integrated Filings

When filing on 1933 Act registration Form S-2, S-3, or S-4, the staff has indicated that a registrant should comply with the age of financial statement rules with respect to itself and all completed and probable acquirees at the date of effectiveness. Any updated financial statements required to be included or incorporated by reference in the registration statement (which were not required to be previously furnished in a specific 1934 Act report) may be furnished in a filing on Form 8-K. The following example illustrates the SEC staff's position:

> Assume an acquisition occurs on September 15, 1992 and both the registrant and the target have December 31, 1991 year-ends. In addition, assume that a Form 8-K reporting the acquisition was timely filed in October 1992, providing audited financial statements of the target as of December 31, 1991, and unaudited interim financial statements of the target through June 30, 1992.
>
> If the registrant files a Form S-3 that will go effective on January 15, 1993, the registrant would need to provide updated unaudited interim financial statements of the target as of a date within 135 days of the effective date of the Form S-3.

The staff has indicated, however, that it will consider a request to waive updating of an acquiree's financial statements if both the Form 8-K reporting the acquisition and the financial statements of the acquired business were filed on a timely basis. However, for such a request to be favorably considered the staff has indicated that a registrant would need to demonstrate that such an update would involve unreasonable expense and effort and the registration would need to include at least one completed quarter of unaudited postacquisition operating results of the registrant. The staff has further indicated, however, that it is unlikely to waive the requirements of the rule if the target was significant (i.e., over the 20 percent level).

SEC 50318. Rule 3-05

50319. Audit Requirements and Waiver Requests

As discussed in section 41600, Form 8-K also requires a registrant to file audited financial statements for significant business acquisitions that have been consummated. If such financial statements cannot be generated, the staff of the SEC may, after considering a registrant's request for a waiver, respond that "they will not take action if such financial statements are not filed with the Form 8-K" (see section 41632). Although such a response is technically not a waiver, it is generally viewed as such. However, any such response would generally be limited to Form 8-K and would not extend to 1933 Act filings. Former SEC Release No. 33-4950 contained provisions for requesting waivers from audit requirements in situations of this nature. In rescinding the release in FRR No. 2, the SEC pointed out that the revised requirements made the waiver procedures set forth in Release No. 33-4950 obsolete.

The inability of a registrant to furnish the required audited financial statements for an acquired business may create significant problems in connection with 1933 Act filings. Note that in determining the periods for which audited financial statements of an acquired business are required, the periods prior to acquisition may be added to the periods subsequent to acquisition for which results of the acquired business are reflected in the registrant's audited financial statements. For example, assume Rule 3-05(b)(1)(ii) requires a registrant to provide audited financial statements (statements) of an acquired company for the two most recent fiscal years. Additionally, assume separate statements of the acquired company are available only for fiscal 19X1 and the acquisition occurred immediately afterward. The requirement of Rule 3-05 for two years' statements may be fulfilled after the passage of time with (1) the separate statements of the acquired company for fiscal 19X1 and (2) the registrant's consolidated statements for fiscal 19X2 (which include one full year of operations of the acquired company).

SAB Topic 1-A discusses a problem encountered when a target company refuses to furnish its financial statements to the issuer. The text of the SAB follows:

Target Companies

Facts: Company X proposes to file a registration statement covering an exchange offer to stockholders of Company Y, a publicly held company. Company X asks Company Y to furnish information about its business, including current audited financial statements, for inclusion in the prospectus. Company Y declines to furnish such information.

Question 1: In filing the registration statement without the required information about Company Y, may Company X rely on Rule 409 in that the information is "unknown or not reasonably available"?

Interpretive Response: Yes, but to determine whether such reliance is justified, the staff requests the registrant to submit as supplemental information copies of correspondence between the registrant and the target company evidencing the request for and the refusal to furnish the financial statements. In addition, the prospectus must include any financial statements which are relevant and available from the Commission's public files and must contain a statement adequately describing the situation and the sources of information about the target company. Other reliable sources of financial information should also be utilized.

Question 2: Would the response change if Company Y was a closely held company?

Interpretive Response: Yes. The staff does not believe that Rule 409 is applicable to negotiated transactions of this type. . . .

Rule 409 is discussed in section 50051.

50320. Predecessor Companies

There are instances in which holding companies are formed to acquire existing entities or parts of existing entities (e.g., divisions or segments of a business). While these types of transactions may be viewed as acquisitions by the registrant (the holding company) they are technically predecessors of the registrant since the entire activity of the holding company or the registrant constitutes a "successor" to the acquired business. Rule 405 of Regulation C defines a "predecessor" as, "... a person the major portion of the business and assets of which another person acquired in a single succession, or in a series of related successions in each of which the acquiring person acquired the major portion of the business and assets of the acquired person." Although each instance is evaluated on a case-by-case basis, the SEC staff has generally taken the position that an acquired business or group of related businesses that represents more than half of the ongoing registrant constitutes a predecessor. In such instances, reference should be made to Rule 3-02 (section 50302), which addresses the financial statement requirements of the registrant and its consolidated subsidiaries "and its predecessors." Accordingly, when considering the requirements for audited statements of income and cash flows for each of the three fiscal years preceding the date of the most recent audited balance sheet being filed, the predecessor activity is required to be included, with no lapse in audited information (i.e., interim periods of the predecessor prior to being subsumed by the registrant should be audited).

In addition, although Rule 3-01 regarding the filing of consolidated balance sheets does not contain the term "predecessors," the SEC staff's practice is generally to apply the same principle as discussed above. Accordingly, a separate audited balance sheet of the predecessor may be required to satisfy the balance sheet requirements pursuant to Rule 3-01. Schedules required by Article 12 (see section 51200) are also required for predecessor entities.

SEC 50319. Rule 3-05

50321. Reporting on Post Balance Sheet Poolings of Interests

When a pooling-of-interests transaction is consummated subsequent to the most recent audited balance sheet date or unaudited interim balance sheet, paragraph 61 of APB Opinion No. 16 states that the financial statements presented should be those of the combining company and not those of the resulting combined entity. This required method of presentation sometimes presents a problem in a registration statement that is being filed during that period, since the financial information that a prospective investor would probably consider to be the most relevant are statements that give effect to the pooling of interests.

We understand that the SEC staff generally takes the position that financial statements giving retroactive effect to a pooling of interests are the most meaningful in this type of situation and, therefore, should be reported on by the auditors. Any presentation of financial statements on a combined basis in connection with a transaction of this nature would need to be considered "supplemental" information pursuant to paragraph 61 of APB Opinion No. 16.

An exception to this guidance, however, is that the staff will allow restatement of the historical financial statements in an initial filing of a pre-effective S-1 registration statement, provided that the registration will be updated with more current financial statements as of a date subsequent to the consummation of the pooling prior to going effective. This exception is only allowed by the SEC if there is no preliminary prospectus (red herring) distributed until after the financial statements subsequent to the consummation of the pooling are filed.

When independent accountants are to report on supplemental financial statements, such a report might be worded as set forth below. This approach was considered appropriate by the SEC staff in a particular registration situation. However, this should not be viewed as the only available approach since modifications in the wording of the report might be equally acceptable. Please note that the actual wording of the report originally accepted by the staff has been revised to incorporate the provisions of SAS No. 58 (AU Section 508).

Report of Independent Accountants

The Board of Directors and Shareholders of Example Co.:

We have audited the supplemental consolidated statements of financial position of Example Co. and subsidiaries as of December 31, 19X5 and 19X4, and the related supplemental consolidated statements of income, changes in shareholders' equity and cash flows for each of the years in the three-year period ended December 31, 19X5. These financial statements are the responsibility of the Company's management. Our responsibility is to express an opinion on these financial statements based on our audits.

We conducted our audits in accordance with generally accepted auditing standards. Those standards require that we plan and perform the audit to obtain reasonable assurance about whether the financial statements are free of material misstatement. An audit includes examining, on a test basis, evidence supporting the amounts and disclosures in the financial statements. An audit also includes assessing the accounting principles used and significant estimates made by management, as well as evaluating the overall financial statement presentation. We believe that our audits provide a reasonable basis for our opinion.

The supplemental financial statements give retroactive effect to the merger of Example Co. and Illustration, Inc. on October 15, 19X6, which has been accounted for as a pooling of interests as described in the notes 1 and 2 to the supplemental consolidated financial statements. Generally accepted accounting principles proscribe giving effect to a consummated business combination accounted for by the pooling of interests methods in financial statements that do not include the date of consummation. These financial statements do not extend through the date of consummation; however, they will become the historical consolidated financial statements of Example Co. and subsidiaries after financial statements covering the date of consummation of the business combination are issued.

In our opinion, the financial statements referred to above present fairly, in all material respects, the consolidated financial position of Example Co. and subsidiaries at December 31, 19X5 and 19X4, and the consolidated results of their operations and their cash flows for each of the years in the three-year period ended December 31, 19X5 in conformity with generally accepted accounting principles applicable after financial statements are issued for a period which includes the date of consummation of the business combination.

City, State
October 15, 19X6

In the footnotes to the financial statements in the foregoing example the following disclosure was suggested:

SEC 50321. Rule 3-05

EXAMPLE CO.

Notes to Supplemental Consolidated Financial Statements

December 31, 19X5, 19X4 and 19X3

(1) Summary of Accounting Policies

(a) Basis of Presentation

The supplemental consolidated financial statements of Example Co. and subsidiaries (the Company) have been prepared to give retroactive effect to the merger with Illustration, Inc. on October 15, 19X6. Generally accepted accounting principles proscribe giving effect to a consummated business combination accounted for by the pooling-of-interests methods in financial statements that do not include the date of consummation. These financial statements do not extend through the date of consummation; however, they will become the historical consolidated financial statements of Example Co. and subsidiaries after financial statements covering the date of consummation of the business combination are issued.

(2) Merger and Acquisitions

During 19X5, the Company entered into a definitive agreement to merge with Illustration, Inc. On October 15, 19X6 Illustration, Inc. and its operating subsidiary were merged with and into the Company. Under terms of the merger agreement, each share of Illustration, Inc. common stock was exchanged for one share of the Company's common stock. XXX,XXX shares of the Company's common stock were exchanged for all the outstanding stock of Illustration, Inc.

50322. Application of Rule 3-05 in Initial Public Offerings

The SEC staff believes that a literal application of Rule 3-05 in certain initial public offering situations may require a registrant to include financial statements for one or more acquired entities that may not be significant to investors at the time the registration statement is filed. The specific fact pattern covered by the SAB involves a registrant that has experienced substantial growth due to a series of acquisitions. SAB Topic 1-J (SAB 80) was issued to provide guidance with respect to the staff's views concerning this issue.

It is important to note that the guidance in this SAB applies only to first-time registrants that have experienced significant growth through acquisitions of discrete distinguishable businesses whose operations are not significantly affected as a result of the business combination. The SAB states that, in the staff's view, these situations were not contemplated when Rule 3-05 was drafted and, accordingly, under these circumstances, alternative tests of significance may be performed based on the size of the registrant at the time the registration statement is filed, rather than when the acquisition was made.

In footnote 3 to this SAB, the staff has noted that if the alternative tests in the SAB require the acquiree's preacquisition financial statements to be audited, the interim period between the acquiree's latest pre-acquisition fiscal year-end and prior to its acquisition would also generally be required to be audited.

In this SAB the staff also expresses a willingness to accept the inclusion of financial statements for periods of (not less than) 9, 21, and 33 consecutive months as being in substantial compliance with requirements to furnish financial statements for 1, 2, and 3 years, respectively.

The SEC staff has indicated that the provisions of SAB 80 may be applied to initial registrations under the 1934 Act (Form 10), as well as to significant acquisitions by companies that had themselves acquired companies (second-tier subsidiaries).

The text of SAB 80 follows:

Application of Rule 3-05 in Initial Public Offerings

Facts: Rule 3-05 of Regulation S-X establishes the financial statement requirements for businesses acquired or to be acquired. If required, financial statements must be provided for one, two or three years depending upon the relative significance of the acquired entity as determined by the application of Rule 1-02(v) of Regulation S-X. The calculations required for these tests are applied by comparison of the financial data of the registrant and acquiree(s) for the fiscal years most recently completed prior to the acquisition. The staff has recognized that these tests literally applied in some initial public offerings may require financial statements for an acquired entity which may not be significant to investors because the registrant has had substantial growth in assets and earnings in recent years.[1]

Question: How should Rules 3-05 and 1-02(v) of Regulation S-X be applied in determining the periods for which financial statements of acquirees are required to be included in registration statements for initial public offerings?

Interpretive Response: It is the staff's view that initial public offerings involving businesses that have been built by the aggregation of discrete businesses that remain substantially intact after acquisition[2] were not contemplated during the drafting of Rule 3-05 and that the significance of an acquired entity in such situations may be better measured in relation to the size of the registrant at the time the registration statement is filed, rather than its size at the time the acquisition was made. Therefore, for a first time registrant, the staff has indicated that in

SEC 50322. Rule 3-05

applying the 10%, 20% and 40% tests in Rule 3-05, the three tests in Rule 1-02(v) generally can be measured against the combined entities, including those to be acquired, which comprise the registrant at the time the registration statement is filed. The staff's policy is intended to ensure that the registration statement will include not less than three, two and one year(s) of audited financial statements for not less than 60%, 80% and 90%, respectively, of the constituent businesses that will comprise the registrant on an ongoing basis. In all circumstances, the audited financial statements of the registrant are required for three years, or since its inception if less than three years. The requirement to provide the audited financial statements of a constituent business in the registration statement is satisfied for the post-acquisition period by including the entity's results in the audited consolidated financial statements of the registrant. If additional periods are required, the entity's separate audited financial statements for the immediate pre-acquisition period(s) should be presented.[3]

In order for the pre-acquisition audited financial statements of an acquiree to be omitted from the registration statement, the following conditions must be met:

a. the combined significance of businesses acquired or to be acquired for which audited financial statements cover a period of less than 9 months[4] may not exceed 10%;

b. the combined significance of businesses acquired or to be acquired for which audited financial statements cover a period of less than 21 months may not exceed 20%; and

c. the combined significance of businesses acquired or to be acquired for which audited financial statements cover a period of less than 33 months may not exceed 40%.

Combined significance is the total, for all included companies, of each individual company's highest level of significance computed under the three tests of significance. The significance tests should be applied to pro forma financial statements of the registrant, prepared in a manner consistent with Article 11 of Regulation S-X. The pro forma balance sheet should be as of the date of the registrant's latest balance sheet included in the registration statement, and should give effect to businesses acquired subsequent to the end of the latest year or to be acquired as if they had been acquired on that date. The pro forma statement of operations should be for the registrant's most recent fiscal year included in the registration statement and should give effect to all acquisitions consummated during and subsequent to the end of the year and probable acquisitions as if they had been consummated at the beginning of that fiscal year.

The three tests specified in Rule 1-02(v) should be made in comparison to the registrant's pro forma consolidated assets and pretax income from continuing operations. The assets and pretax income of the acquired businesses which are being evaluated for significance should reflect any new cost basis arising from purchase accounting.

EXAMPLE: On February 20, 19X9 Registrant files Form S-1 containing its audited consolidated financial statements as of and for the three years ended December 31, 19X8.

Acquisitions since inception have been:

Acquiree	Fiscal Year End	Date of Acquisition	Highest Significance at Acquisition
A	3/31	1/1/X7	60%
B	7/31	4/1/X7	45%
C	9/30	9/1/X7	40%
D	12/31	2/1/X8	21%
E	3/31	11/1/X8	11%
F	12/31	to be acquired	11%

The following table reflects the application of the significance tests to the combined financial information at the time the registration statement is filed.

Component Entity	Assets	Significance of Earnings	Investment	Highest Level of Significance
A	12%	23%	12%	23%
B	10	21	10	21
C	21	3	4	21
D	10	5	13	13
E	4	9 loss	3	9
F	2	11	6	11

Year 1 (most recent fiscal year) - Entity E is the only acquiree for which pre-acquisition financial statements may be omitted for the latest year since significance for each other entity exceeds 10% under one or more test.

Year 2 (preceding fiscal year) - Financial statements for E and F may be omitted since their combined significance is 20% and no other combination can be formed with E which would not exceed 20%.

Year 3 (second preceding fiscal year) - Financial statements for D, E and F may be omitted since the combined significance of these entities is 33%[5] and no other combination can be formed with E and F which would not exceed 40%.

The financial statement requirements must be satisfied by filing separate pre-acquisition audited financial statements for each entity that was not included in the consolidated financial statements for the periods set forth above. The following table illustrates the requirements for this example.

SEC 50322. Rule 3-05

Component Entity	Date of Acquisition	Minimum Financial Statement Requirement	Separate Period in Consolidated F/S	Pre-Acquisition Audited F/S
			(months)	
Registrant	N/A	33	36	-
A	1/1/X7	33	24	9
B	4/1/X7	33	21	12[6]
C	9/1/X7	33	16	17
D	2/1/X8	21	11	10
E	11/1/X8	-	2	-
F	to be acquired	9	-	9

[1] An acquisition which was relatively significant in the earliest year for which a registrant is required to file financial statements may be insignificant to its latest fiscal year due to internal growth and/or subsequent acquisitions. Literally applied, Rules 3-05 and 1-02(v) might still require separate financial statements for the now insignificant acquisition.

[2] For example, nursing homes, hospitals or cable TV systems. This interpretation would not apply to businesses for which the relative significance of one portion of the business to the total business may be altered by post acquisition decisions as to the allocation of incoming orders between plants or locations. This bulletin does not address all possible cases in which similar relief may be appropriate but, rather, attempts to describe a general framework within which administrative policy has been established. In other distinguishable situations, registrants may request relief as appropriate to their individual facts and circumstances.

[3] If audited pre-acquisition financial statements of a business are necessary pursuant to the alternative tests described here, the interim period following that entity's latest pre-acquisition fiscal year end but prior to its acquisition by the registrant generally would be required to be audited.

[4] As a matter of policy the staff accepts financial statements for periods of not less than 9, 21 and 33 consecutive months (not more than 12 months may be included in any period reported on) as substantial compliance with requirements for financial statements for 1, 2 and 3 years, respectively.

[5] Combined significance is the sum of the significance of D's investment test (13%), E's earnings test (9%) and F's earnings test (11%).

[6] The audited pre-acquisition period need not correspond to the acquiree's pre-acquisition fiscal year. However, audited periods must not be for periods in excess of 12 months.

50333. SEC Views on Accounting for Poolings of Interests

As discussed in section 14030, the SEC has generally relied on the private sector to establish accounting principles and practices. However, on certain occasions the staff has expressed its views on particular accounting issues. One of the accounting issues in which the SEC has historically taken a particular interest is the accounting for business combinations. APB Opinion No. 16, *Business Combinations*, sets forth the accounting principles to be followed in accounting for business combinations and the criteria for determining whether a business combination is to be accounted for as a pooling of interests or a purchase. The SEC has found it necessary to interpret certain of the provisions of APB Opinion No. 16 in various Accounting Series Releases, Staff Accounting Bulletins, and informal interpretations. A number of these views are summarized below. For the most part these issues were discussed by members of the staff in the context of a specific example or particular registrant situation; therefore, it is not always clear how the staff will deal with similar cases. The following informal interpretations relating to pooling-of-interests accounting have been provided by the SEC staff:

50333.10. Alterations of Equity Interests — General

50333.11. Granting of Stock Options

50333.12. LBO—Change in Control

50333.13. Sale of Stock to an ESOP

50333.14. Effect of Unallocated Shares in an ESOP

50333.15. Acquisition of Employer Shares for/by an Employee Benefit Trust

50333.16. Distributions by Subchapter S Corporations

50333.17. Defensive Measures

50333.20. Stock Compensation Plans, Stock Options, Warrants, and Convertible Securities

50333.21. Alterations in Stock Compensation Plans

50333.22. Acceleration and Termination of Stock Options

50333.23. Stock Option Repricing

50333.24. Stock Option Pyramiding by Affiliates

50333.25. Convertible Securities That Are "Essentially the Same" as Common Stock

SEC 50333. Rule 3-05

50333.30. Dividends, Stock Dividends, and Stock Splits

50333.31. Payment of Dividends

50333.32. Stock Dividends

50333.33. Stock Splits

50333.40. Contingencies

50333.41. General Management Representations

50333.42. Environmental Contingencies

50333.50. Absence of Planned Transactions

50333.51. Sale of Assets Within Two Years

50333.52. Sales of Stock of a Subsidiary

50333.53. Costs of Initial Registration

50333.60. Other Matters

50333.61. Stock for Net Assets

50333.62. Cash Payments to Executives

50333.63. Actions of Controlling Shareholders

50333.64. 90 Percent Exchange Test

50333.65. Cash and Stock to Individual Shareholders

50333.10. Alterations of Equity Interests — General

The SEC staff's informal position is that the closer an alteration of equity interests occurs to the combination date, the more persuasive the contrary evidence needs to be in order to overcome the presumption that the alteration was made in contemplation of the business combination.

50333.11. *Granting of Stock Options.* A fact pattern considered persuasive by the staff in one registrant situation in overcoming the presumption that an alteration of equity interests was made in contemplation of a business combination was as follows:

- The registrant was contemplating an unusual grant of an abnormal amount of options for an existing plan prior to the initiation of the business combination.

- The information submitted to the staff included:

  - •• Board minutes documenting that the option grants were discussed prior to discussions concerning the business combination.

  - •• Documentation supporting the nature of the grant and how the amount of the grant was determined.

  - •• A compensation study was performed by an outside consultant.

50333.12. *LBO—Change in Control.* In the staff's view, a NEWCO arising from an LBO that involved a change in control (as defined in EITF Issue No. 88-16) generally can be pooled within the two-year "window" period prescribed in paragraph 47(c) or (d), provided the LBO transaction was not entered into in contemplation of the subsequent pooling. If there was no change in control at the date of the LBO, the SEC staff considers the LBO to have been a recapitalization, and does not believe that NEWCO is poolable until the two-year period has expired.

50333.13. *Sale of Stock to an ESOP.* Generally, the SEC staff considers the sale of common stock or convertible preferred stock to an ESOP to be a change in equity interests pursuant to paragraph 47(c) of APB Opinion No. 16, *Business Combinations,* that would preclude a pooling. However, the staff has indicated that it would consider certain factors when assessing whether the sale to an ESOP is "in contemplation of the business combination." The factors include when the ESOP was planned and designed in relation to the initiation of the business combination, and the reasonableness of the award relative to compensation considerations. The closer the date of the transaction to the business combination is, the more persuasive the staff believes the evidence must be.

50333.14. *Effect of Unallocated Shares in an ESOP.* EITF Issue No. 88-27, "Effect of Unallocated Shares in an Employee Stock Ownership Plan on Accounting for Business Combinations," and Topic D-19, "Impact on Pooling-of-Interests Accounting of Treasury Shares Acquired to Satisfy Conversions in a Leveraged Preferred

Stock ESOP," state that unallocated shares (i.e., shares of the sponsoring entity that are not allocated to participants in the plan) held by an ESOP should not be considered tainted shares for purposes of determining whether the pooling-of-interests method of accounting is appropriate unless:

- There is more than a remote possibility that such shares could revert to the sponsoring entity,

- There exists an agreement or intent, either written or implicit, whereby the sponsoring entity will repurchase or reacquire shares from the ESOP or from an employee that receives shares in a distribution (except if required by law to provide liquidity to the plan participant), or

- The shares were acquired to circumvent the requirements of APB Opinion16.

50333.15. *Acquisition of Employer Shares for/by an Employee Benefit Trust.* EITF Issue No. 93-2, "Acquisition of Employer Shares for/by an Employee Benefit Trust," discusses a situation in which an employer (Company) establishes an irrevocable grantor Trust (Trust), similar to an ESOP, to prefund certain employee benefits. The Company sells shares of its stock to the Trust in return for a note payable and, at or about the same time, acquires treasury shares. Alternatively, the Trust may acquire Company shares in the marketplace using funds borrowed from the Company. The shares will be released from the Trust in future periods as debt is repaid or forgiven and will be used to meet obligations of the Company to various employee benefit plans.

The discussion of this issue refers to the proposed AICPA Statement of Position, *Employers' Accounting for Employee Stock Ownership Plans,* which defines Type I and Type II ESOPs as follows:

- Type I — shares are released to compensate employees directly. Such ESOPs are not used to fund other employee benefits and the fair value of the shares at the time of release is not a factor at the time of release. These ESOPs are the typical ESOPs that existed at the time SOP 76-3, *Accounting Practices for Certain Employee Stock Ownership Plans,* was issued.

- Type II —shares are released to settle or fund liabilities for other specified or determinable employee benefits, such as an employer's match of a 401(k) plan. The fair value of shares released is used to determine how many shares are needed to satisfy an obligation that arose outside the ESOP.

The SEC staff believes that the application of the consensus in EITF Issue No. 88-27 (see section 50333.14) and the statements made in Topic D-19 should be limited to Type I ESOPs (as defined above). However, the staff has indicated that it will not object to the application of the consensus in EITF Issue No. 88-27 and Topic D-19 for shares held by a Type II ESOP as of January 21, 1993, provided the respective criteria set forth therein are satisfied. Shares purchased by a Type II ESOP subsequent to January 21, 1993 would be considered by the staff to be treasury stock directly acquired by the employer and presumed to be tainted shares for the purpose of applying the pooling-of-interest provisions of APB Opinion No. 16.

In relating this guidance to the situation discussed in EITF Issue No. 93-2, the SEC observer at the EITF meeting stated that in his view, the trust arrangement described in this issue is neither a Type I nor a Type II ESOP. Therefore, the SEC staff's position is that shares acquired in the past or in the future and placed in trust to fund future corporate obligations, such as the trust vehicle described in this issue, are treasury stock directly acquired by the employer and presumed to be tainted shares for the purpose of applying the pooling-of-interest provisions of APB Opinion No. 16.

50333.16. *Distributions by Subchapter S Corporations.* Paragraph 47(c) of APB Opinion No. 16 specifies that distributions to stockholders that are no greater than normal, based on earnings and past dividend policy and patterns, would not be a violation of the pooling criteria. The staff's position is that this provision is generally applicable to the evaluation of distributions to shareholders of subchapter S corporations as well. However, due to the unique tax status of subchapter S corporations, the staff has taken the position that distributions by these corporations prior to a business combination would not prevent pooling accounting when the distribution amount is only the amount required to meet the current tax obligations of its shareholders, irrespective of the past pattern of distributions. It is important to note, however, that distributions that exceed the cumulative earnings of the subchapter S corporation may preclude pooling accounting.

50333.17. *Defensive Measures.* Merger agreements often contain defensive provisions designed to deter competing offers and enhance the likelihood of consummating a combination with the offering party. In one such measure, generally referred to as a "crown jewel option," the target company gives the offering party an option to purchase a significant asset or subsidiary of the target. Another measure, often referred to as the "lock-up option," typically involves a situation in which the target company gives the offering party an option to buy the target's securities.

The staff has indicated that it generally will not take exception to such measures in a transaction structured to meet pooling-of-interests criteria provided (1) the options are granted without monetary consideration and (2) the options remain unexercised at the consummation of the merger.

Another common defensive measure is the "break-up fee" or "termination fee" arrangement in which the merger agreement calls for the target to reimburse the out-of-pocket expenses of the offering company under certain circumstances. Alternatively, the "break-up fee" may be based on some percentage of the value of the target. The "break-up fee" arrangement is sometimes structured to be payable if the merger agreement is terminated, and, in other cases, only if the target merges with another party within a specified period.

Aside from the reimbursement of out-of-pocket expenses, the staff has taken the position that a "break-up fee" may be viewed as representing compensation to the offering company (i.e., for lost opportunity costs, restricting capital and general risk). Accordingly, the staff's position is that "break-up fees" should be evaluated in a manner similar to other defensive measures, and provided that the contractual provision for a "break-up fee" expires unexercised and no monetary consideration is exchanged, the staff generally will not take exception to the existence of "termination" or "break-up" fee arrangements in a business combination that otherwise qualifies as a pooling of interests. On the other hand, when any of the defensive measures described above are triggered *in contemplation of* a subsequent business combination, the staff has indicated that it may view these to be alterations of equity interests that violate the pooling criteria (paragraph 47 (c) of APB Opinion No. 16). The triggering of a defensive measure that is *not in contemplation of* a subsequent business combination, however, would not generally preclude a pooling.

50333.20. Stock Compensation Plans, Stock Options, Warrants, and Convertible Securities

50333.21. *Alterations in Stock Compensation Plans.* The SEC staff generally considers alterations in stock compensation plans prior to a pooling to be an alteration of equity interests that defeats accounting as a pooling. Therefore, the staff believes that, as a general rule, modifications to the terms of stock options, warrants and similar awards within two years prior to a combination constitute a change in equity interests that would preclude a pooling. In some cases, the terms of a stock option plan may *require* the acceleration of the options in the event of a business combination or change in control. Provided that acceleration is automatic and the provision was not adopted in contemplation of the business combination, the staff typically will not object to pooling accounting. However, the staff has indicated that an acceleration of stock options by a Board of Directors that is made in contemplation of a business combination is a change in equity interests, even if the option plan provides such an option to the directors.

In addition, the staff believes that *any* cash-out of stock options, even one pursuant to a contractual arrangement established more than two years prior to the initiation of the business combination, would prevent pooling accounting.

The staff has indicated, however, that it would not object to pooling accounting if an amendment that resulted in a change in equity interest, such as providing for the acceleration or cash-out of options, is, shortly thereafter, rescinded, as long as (1) the rescission affects all parties that were granted the rights and (2) none of the rights pursuant to the amendment were operative or had been exercised.

50333.22. *Acceleration and Termination of Stock Options.* As discussed above, the SEC staff's informal position is that when a stock option plan specifically calls for automatic acceleration of the vesting date or exercise date of the options in the event of a business combination and the plan was initiated before the two-year period prior to the business combination, the acceleration would not be considered an alteration of equity interests. The staff has indicated that it would not object to the acceleration of vesting of outstanding stock options in a merger to be accounted for as a pooling, provided the contractual acceleration provision was not adopted in contemplation of the business combination. However, the staff has indicated that if the plan allows for general acceleration at the discretion of the board of directors, any acceleration within the two-year period prior to the business combination would be considered to have been in contemplation of the business combination and thus would preclude a pooling of interests.

In considering provisions of residual equity securities that trigger a cash redemption upon a change in control, the staff indicated that it would object to pooling accounting where the residual equity interests were redeemed for cash in the merger, other than pursuant to dissenters' rights or as fractional shares. The staff believes that a contractual provision that contemplates the intentional termination of a residual equity interest is inconsistent with the basic concept of pooling.

The staff's view is that employee stock options may be exchanged for either similar options of the issuing company or common stock of the issuing company (based on the fair value of the options).

50333.23. *Stock Option Repricing.* The staff has considered pooling treatment acceptable in a particular situation involving options repriced near the initiation date of the transaction. In the fact pattern involved, the issuing company repriced its options and there did not appear to be any imbedded premium in the repricing based upon the expected merger. In addition, the options subject to repricing (1) were held by a large employee base, (2) excluded certain senior management, (3) required the employees to hold the repriced shares for one year, and (4) were approved by independent, outside board members.

Ordinarily, the staff considers it very difficult for a target company to sustain a position that a repricing of stock options is not in contemplation of a business combination. However, in another case, the staff did not take exception to a pooling with a target with a fact pattern similar to the foregoing example, but where the target company provided evidence that the repricing of the stock options was necessary due to competitive pressures. The target's competitors in the high-tech industry involved had recently repriced their options in an attempt to entice the target's employees to seek employment with them. Thus, the target was able to demonstrate that the stock option repricing was effected to address market considerations.

50333.24. *Stock Option Pyramiding by Affiliates.* Stock option "pyramiding" and "phantom stock-for-stock exercises" of options (sometimes referred to as "cashless exercises") occur when an employee exchanges or tenders shares held (rather than cash) in connection with the exercise of stock options. In the staff's view, *an affiliate's* cashless exercise of options would *not* preclude a pooling. The basis for the staff's position is that the intrinsic value of the affiliate's holdings after a cashless exercise remains the same as immediately before exercise. Also, unlike the effect of selling stock, in an arrangement of this nature, the affiliate does not reduce its investment.

50333.25. *Convertible Securities That Are "Essentially the Same" as Common Stock.* The staff has indicated that in its view, options and warrants are essentially the same as common stock for purposes of paragraph 47(b) of APB Opinion No. 16. An important consideration applied by the staff in determining whether a convertible security is "essentially the same" as common stock is whether the security's value is driven by its common stock characteristics. The staff concluded in one particular case that convertible preferred stock is essentially the same as common stock when it is only slightly "in the money" prior to initiation, but deeply into the money after the merger announcement. The staff objected to the exchange of cash for the stock since the payment was driven solely by the value of the common stock.

50333.30. Dividends, Stock Dividends, and Stock Splits

50333.31. *Payment of Dividends.* With regard to the payment of dividends in the context of paragraph 47(c) of APB Opinion No. 16, it is the staff's view that between the initiation and consummation date of a business combination, a target company may pay either its normal dividend (normal in terms of both amount and timing) or the normal dividend of the acquiror adjusted for the exchange ratio, but not any amount in between, without violating the pooling rules.

50333.32. *Stock Dividends.* The staff has expressed the view that a stock dividend issued prior to a pooling in a situation where the market price does not completely adjust for the dividend may preclude pooling treatment due to the favorable impact on one of the shareholder groups. In assessing whether a stock dividend would preclude a pooling, the staff has indicated that it will consider the reasons for the stock dividend, the registrant's historical dividend pattern, the proximity of the dividend to the business combination, the effect on the stock price, and the potential of the dividend to affect the exchange ratio.

SEC 50333.32

In a recent case, a registrant was able to demonstrate that its stock price had responded (gone down) to the stock dividend and pooling accounting was permitted by the staff.

50333.33. *Stock Splits.* The staff has indicated that, as a general rule, it does not consider stock splits to be a violation of the pooling rules as long as the relative ownership interests are not changed.

50333.40. Contingencies

50333.41. *General Management Representations.* With regard to the resolution of "general management representations" that would result in an adjustment to the total number of shares exchanged in a pooling, the SEC staff's informal view is that the maximum time period permitted to resolve such contingencies is the lesser of one year or completion of the first audit of the financial statements that contain the combined results of the pooled entity.

50333.42. *Environmental Contingencies.* The staff believes that under certain circumstances, an environmental contingency may be considered a "specific" contingency. In such instances, however, the staff's view is that the contingency must be precisely defined. Furthermore, the staff may request that the following information be provided:

- The specific nature and type of environmental contamination involved.

- The specific locations involved.

- Any other relevant information.

However, the determination of whether an environmental contingency is considered to be a specific contingency is based on the facts and circumstances of each case.

50333.50. Absence of Planned Transactions

50333.51. *Sale of Assets Within Two Years.* With regard to the sale of assets within two years following a pooling, the staff has indicated that it would challenge pooling accounting when a sale was planned in connection with a business combination if the sale was significant. The staff considers the following factors to be relevant in determining significance:

- The net assets to be sold relative to the net assets of the combining companies measured on both book and market values,

SEC 50333.32. Rule 3-05

- The revenues of the operation sold relative to the revenues of the combining companies,

- The earnings of the operation sold relative to the earnings of the combining companies, and

- The gain or loss on the sale relative to the earnings of the combined companies.

The disposal would generally be considered by the staff to be significant if one of these measures were to exceed 10 percent. Further, the staff has indicated that it may also consider the qualitative aspects of the disposal. For example, if the parties to the transaction plan to dispose of a significant portion of nonperforming assets shortly after the transaction is completed, we understand that the staff believes that the qualitative characteristics of the assets may suggest that a threshold lower than 10 percent is likely to be appropriate for determining significance.

50333.52. *Sales of Stock of a Subsidiary.* Paragraph 48(c) of APB Opinion No. 16 prohibits certain planned dispositions at the date of a combination to be accounted for as a pooling. The staff's basic presumption is that any creation of a minority interest would violate the pooling criteria (see first example below). However, the staff has described a fact pattern in which this presumption may be overcome (see second example below). Other fact patterns also may exist to overcome the presumption and they would need to be evaluated on a case-by-case basis.

- A combined corporation planned to sell shares of a subsidiary within two years after the combination, creating a minority interest in the consolidated financial statements. In this situation, the staff's position was that if the sale of a subsidiary represents a significant disposition, the provisions of paragraph 48 (c) would be violated.

- A new subsidiary (that included the combined company) sold its own shares shortly after the combination. The business combination was not contingent upon the subsequent transaction; however, the transaction was clearly planned at the date of combination. In this example, the staff's position was that provisions of paragraph 48(c) were not violated because (1) the subsidiary retained the proceeds to finance its internal business development needs, (2) consistent with viewing the transaction as a financing transaction rather than a disposition, the combined corporation reported the increase in its interest in the net assets of the subsidiary as a capital transaction (rather than as a gain as permitted under SAB 51, *Accounting for Sales of Stock by a*

Subsidiary), and (3) the shares sold represented less than a 50 percent interest in the subsidiary.

50333.53. *Costs of Initial Registration.* Paragraph 48(b) of APB Opinion No. 16 prohibits the combined corporation from entering into financial arrangements for the benefit of the former stockholders of a combining company in a business combination to be accounted for as a pooling. However, Interpretation 21 of APB Opinion No. 16, *Pooling with Bailout*, would allow for the combined corporation to agree to pay the costs of initial registration when unregistered stock is issued. With regard to this interpretation, the staff's view is that costs of registration would include legal, accounting, printing, filing and related fees associated with a registration statement being declared effective. The staff differentiates, however, between the costs of initial registration of shares and the costs of disposing of shares. In the staff's view, an agreement by the combined corporation to bear shareholders' costs of *disposing* of shares, such as underwriting fees, broker costs, discounts, commissions, marketing and distribution fees and similar transaction costs would violate the provisions of paragraph 48(b), whether registered or unregistered stock is being issued.

50333.60. Other Matters

50333.61. *Stock for Net Assets.* The staff has expressed its position with respect to a situation in which an issuing company proposed to exchange shares for all of the net assets of the target, except for an operating facility with an environmental liability problem. In the particular case involved, the obligation for the environmental problem was to be assumed by the target shareholders along with the retention of the facility within the target's corporate structure. Although the book value of the operating asset was less than 10 percent of net assets and its fair market value was arguably less than that, the staff took the position that leaving behind an operating asset did not in this case meet the requirement in APB Opinion No. 16 that "all the net assets" be transferred, nor did it meet the exception that permits temporarily leaving certain monetary assets in a target company to settle disputed liabilities.

The staff has described a situation in which shares of the issuing company were placed in a liquidating trust to be used to settle a pending lawsuit. In this case the staff was able to overcome concerns about a potential violation of paragraph 47(f) of APB Opinion No. 16, which requires that stockholders are neither deprived of nor restricted in exercising their voting rights—even for a temporary period. In this case, the trustee voted the shares proportionately in accordance with the wishes of the beneficial owners (the target company shareholders).

50333.62. *Cash Payments to Executives.* The issue of whether cash payments to executives or shareholders of the target should be considered violations of the restrictions of paragraph 47(g) of APB Opinion No. 16 frequently arises. These payments typically include payments for employment contracts, golden parachutes, consulting arrangements, and covenants not to compete. Two examples serve to illustrate the staff's views in this area:

- The president and majority shareholder of the target (who was also the chief negotiator in the transaction) received a cash payment of $2 million for a covenant not to compete, in an exchange for shares totaling approximately $6 million. Also, the president received a multi-year employment agreement and a seat on the issuing company's Board of Directors. In this transaction, the staff considered pooling to be inappropriate. The cash payment was viewed by the staff not to be reasonable in comparison to the size of the transaction. In addition, the payment could not, in the staff's view, be reasonably separated from the recipient in his position as the majority shareholder and as the primary negotiator of the merger transaction.

- A large cash bonus plan was initiated by a target (a company in the developmental stage) in anticipation of its sale. Approximately 85 percent of the target company's shares were held by outside venture capital interests. None of the individual venturers held a majority interest. The remaining 15 percent was held by employees, with virtually all employees holding some shares. The 85 percent shareholders agreed to provide the large cash bonus payment to virtually all the employees in order to obtain the assistance of management and others in selling the company. The proposed payments were based upon the employees' positions within the company and not on their percentages of stock ownership.

   The staff objected to this arrangement from a pooling standpoint on the basis that it effectively involved a part cash–part stock transaction for the minority shareholders. The timing of the bonus plan inception and the inclusion of all minority shareholders, rather than limiting it to those who would be assisting in the merger negotiations, were considered to be other negative factors.

50333.63. *Actions of Controlling Shareholders.* The staff has taken the view that actions of controlling shareholders of the target through "side deals," which would be prohibited if entered into by the combining company, would preclude a pooling. For example, the staff has objected to a situation in which the control group shareholders of the target entered into a side agreement that would give a disproportionate interest in shares received to certain shareholders as a means of encouraging them to accept the offer.

50333.64. *90 Percent Exchange Test.* Pursuant to paragraph 47(b) of APB Opinion No. 16, the staff has indicated that it applies the 90 percent test for securities to be exchanged in the following manner:

- The issuer must meet the 90 percent test *in the aggregate* for both common stock and securities deemed to be essentially the same.

- The issuer must meet the 90 percent test solely in relation to the exchange of the common stock.

50333.65. *Cash and Stock to Individual Shareholders.* The staff's position is that an individual shareholder cannot receive both cash and stock in a pooling exchange irrespective of amount. This is based on the premise that a shareholder cannot be both a dissenter and a continuing shareholder.

50334. Risk sharing. In ASR No. 130, as amended by ASR No. 135 (now FRP Section 201.01), the SEC states its position that, notwithstanding the absence of a "continuity of ownership" criterion in APB Opinion No. 16, divestitures by shareholders considered to be "affiliates" during specified periods of time would conflict with the "risk sharing" concept of pooling-of-interests accounting. The release concludes that affiliates must stay at risk with respect to the shares received in the exchange for a specified time period in order for the business combination to be accounted for as a pooling of interests.

The release sets the appropriate time limit for risk sharing as a date when financial results covering 30 days of postmerger combined operations have been published. The release, however, does not specify the start of the period when divestitures are precluded. The staff subsequently issued SAB No. 65, which clarifies that dispositions by affiliates will not be questioned if they are made prior to 30 days before consummation of a business combination. (The complete text of SAB No. 65 appears later in this section.)

The term "affiliate" in ASR No. 130 is intended to cover any person who is deemed to be an affiliate under the 1933 or 1934 Act, and would generally include officers, directors, and holders of 10 percent or more of the shares. The following is the text of the release, as codified in FRP Section 201.01:

Risk-Sharing in Business Combinations Accounted for as Pooling-of-Interests

ASR 130:

The Commission noted an increasing number of business combinations which appear to meet the individual requirements for pooling-of-interests accounting set forth in APBO [Accounting Principles Board Opinion] No. 16 but which did not conform with the overriding thrust of that Opinion, which requires that a combination represent a sharing of rights and risks among constituent stockholder groups if it is to be a pooling of interests. Paragraphs 28, 45 and 47 of that Opinion clearly provide that such a sharing of risk is an essential element in poolings, and the specific requirements set forth in paragraphs 46, 47 and 48 should certainly not be construed as a formula which, if followed with precision, may be used to overcome an essential concept which underlies the entire Opinion. Despite the clarity of the Opinion in articulating the need for a sharing of risk, a number of registrants and their auditors proposed to account for combinations which did not meet this basic requirement as poolings.

Accordingly, the Commission concluded that any confusion regarding this matter should be laid to rest. It is the Commission's understanding that the Accounting Principles Board authorized its staff to issue an interpretation [Interpretation No. 37 of APB Opinion No. 16, issued November 1972] providing that a business combination should be accounted for as a purchase if its consummation is contingent upon the purchase by a third party of any of the common stocks to be issued. Including such a contingency in the arrangement of the combination, either explicitly or by intent, would be considered a financial arrangement which is precluded in a pooling under APBO 16. The Commission endorses this interpretation.

As a matter of policy, the Commission believes that it is unwise to set forth absolute rules in such an accounting matter which will be followed regardless of all other factual situations which may surround a particular transaction. To so do would be to encourage the application of form over substance. Nevertheless, it appears reasonable for the Commission to establish guidelines which it will use in making determinations as to disposition of various individual cases brought before it and to make these guidelines known to registrants and independent public accountants.

ASR 135:

The Commission will henceforth consider that the risk sharing required for the applicability of pooling-of-interests accounting will have occurred if no affiliate of either company in the business combination sells or in any other way reduces his risk relative to any common shares received in the business combination until such time as financial results covering at least 30 days of post-merger combined operations have been published. This would include all sales whether private or public. Publication of combined financial results can take the form of a post-effective amendment, a Form 10-Q or 8-K filing, the issuance of a quarterly earnings report, or any other public issuance which includes combined sales and net income.

482

This policy is not intended to restrict sale of stock at the option of the stockholders subsequent to the pooling as long as a sharing of risks for the period of time indicated above has taken place. An arrangement to register shares subsequent to the combination would therefore not bar pooling. However, an agreement which requires sale of shares after such a period would preclude pooling treatment as would any agreement to reduce the risk borne by the stockholders subsequent to the transaction.

SAB Topic 2-E (issued as SAB No. 65 and amended by SAB 76) discusses the staff's views on certain matters involving the application of Accounting Series Release Nos. 130 and 135 regarding risk sharing in business combinations accounted for as poolings of interests. The text of SAB Topic 2-E follows:

Risk Sharing in Pooling of Interests

Facts: The Commission established and published guidelines in Accounting Series Release Nos. 130 and 135 which are used in making determinations on whether the sharing of rights and risks among constituent stockholder groups will have occurred in order for a business combination to be accounted for as a pooling of interests. Those guidelines indicate that the requisite risk sharing will have occurred if no affiliate of either company reduces his risk relative to any common shares received in the business combination until publication of financial results covering at least 30 days of post-merger combined operations.

Question 1: Are affiliates of each combining company restricted from dispositions of their shares or do the restrictions apply only to affiliates of the "target" company actually receiving shares in the business combination?

Interpretive Response: Affiliates of each combining company may not reduce their risk relative to their common shareholder positions during the indicated time period in order to achieve the risk sharing required for the applicability of pooling of interests accounting. Any one of the combining companies may issue shares in exchange for the shares of the other combining companies. Alternatively, a new corporation may be formed to issue its shares to effect a combination of the companies. As indicated in APB Opinion 16, "the choice of issuing corporation is essentially a matter of convenience." The staff therefore believes that allowing affiliates of the issuing company to immediately sell or otherwise dispose of their shares while restricting such actions by affiliates of the "target" company would be inconsistent with the risk sharing element that is essential in poolings.

Question 2: Will a disposition of shares by an affiliate, before the exchange of shares to effect the combination occurs, cause the staff to question the application of pooling of interests accounting?

Interpretive Response: Yes, in some cases. Although continuity of ownership interests is not a condition to accounting for a business combination by the pooling of interests method under APB Opinion 16, the Opinion clearly articulates the need for a sharing of risk. To allow affiliates to sell their shares shortly before the consummation of the combination while restricting such sales immediately following the exchange would be inconsistent.

The Opinion contemplates that business combinations accounted for as poolings of interests must normally be consummated within one year after the plan of combination is initiated and the staff notes that such combinations have typically been consummated within a few months of initiation. While it can be argued that risk sharing should begin when a formal plan of combination is initiated, in some situations this may be an unreasonably long period to restrict affiliates from selling their shares or otherwise reducing their risk with respect to the combined company. This is particularly the case in combinations that require a lengthy period between initiation and consummation (such as between financial institutions that require regulatory approval) and where the affiliate transactions are relatively minor and routine. In view of these practical considerations, the staff will generally not raise a question about the applicability of pooling of interests accounting as a result of dispositions of shares by affiliates prior to 30 days before consummation of a business combination.

Additionally, the staff will generally not question the use of the pooling of interests accounting method because of sales by affiliates which occur after a date 30 days prior to the consummation of the combination and prior to the publication of financial results covering at least 30 days of post-merger combined operations, if those sales are de minimis in amount.[3] To be viewed as de minimis, (i) the sales by an affiliate must not be greater than 10 percent of the affiliate's pre-combination (or equivalent post-combination) shares, and (ii) the aggregate sales by all affiliates of a combination company must not exceed the equivalent of 1 percent of that company's pre-combination outstanding shares.[4,5] Furthermore, the staff will generally not raise a question as the result of charitable contributions or bona fide gifts;[6] however, the recipients of such gifts would have to hold the shares for the period indicated by Accounting Series Release Nos. 130 and 135.[7]

---

[3]It should be noted, however, that nothing herein should be construed as addressing any issues relating to the applicability of Section 16(b) of the Securities Exchange Act of 1934 to sales during this period.

[4]Where the consummation dates for two or more pooling of interests business combinations result in the overlapping of the periods during which sales by affiliates are restricted, these limits would apply to the aggregate sales during the combined period. Thus, for example, if the periods for two combinations overlap, an individual affiliate's aggregate sales during the combined period could not exceed 10 percent, rather than 20 percent, of the affiliate's precombination (i.e., before either of the pooling transactions, even if one has been consummated) shares.

[5]The question of whether outstanding stock options should be considered outstanding shares and shares owned by an affiliate in computing, respectively, the 1

percent and 10 percent limits, depends on an assessment of facts and circumstances such as the relation of the option price to the market value of the stock, the imminence of exercisability and/or expiration, and the number of options held by an affiliate in relation to the number of shares owned and the effect, if any, the consummation of the combination will have on the terms of the options. Thus, for example, it would clearly be inappropriate to include in calculating the limits any outstanding stock options of a combining company for which the issuer will not issue replacement options or common stock.

[6]Transfer of shares to other parties that are required or inspired by any legal duties to support dependents or that are in any sense a payment to settle a debt or other obligation would not be considered to be "bona fide" gifts.

[7]For practical reasons, the holding period restrictions would not normally attach to shares donated to charitable institutions that have traditionally been supported by contributions from the general public (as opposed to supported largely by a specific donor).

The staff believes that the above guidance should not be applied when the results would be abusive. The factors that would contribute to a sale being viewed as abusive by the staff, and, therefore, preclude a pooling are:

- The proximity of the sale to the 30-day precombination time period,

- The magnitude of the shares disposed of relative to affiliate holdings and relative to the combining entity,

- The reason for such disposal, and

- The nature of the affiliate (i.e., an officer or director would heighten the staff's concern).

50335. Effect of treasury stock transactions. In ASR No. 146, as subsequently interpreted by ASR No. 146A (FRP Section 201.02), the SEC discusses the provisions of paragraphs 47(c) and 47(d) of APB Opinion No. 16 and the impact on pooling accounting when a company reacquires voting common stock within two years of a business combination. The release concludes that under certain conditions, such acquisitions could impair the accounting for the business combination as a pooling of interests. This conclusion is based in part on AICPA Accounting Interpretation No. 20 of APB Opinion No. 16 that states, "In the absence of persuasive evidence to the contrary, however, it should be presumed that all acquisitions of treasury stock during the two years preceding the date a plan of combination is initiated. . . and between initiation and consummation were made in contemplation of effecting business combinations to be accounted for as a pooling of interests."

SEC 50334. Rule 3-05

The release points out, however, that this presumption may be overcome when the acquisition of treasury shares is for a specific purpose unrelated to the business combination. The release emphasizes that, in these situations, reference needs to be made to the actual or probable issuance of shares for the particular purpose unrelated to the business combination. Guidance is provided in ASR Nos. 146 and 146A in making these determinations.

When treasury shares are acquired within two years of a business combination, the release also establishes how a company may "cure" a condition that otherwise would preclude pooling-of-interests accounting by selling common shares prior to the consummation of the combination.

In this release, the SEC staff also concludes that the acquisition of treasury shares during the restricted period (for the purpose of stock option and compensation plans and other recurring distributions) will generally be considered "tainted" unless:

- The shares are acquired in a systematic pattern of reacquisitions established at least two years prior to initiation of the plan of combination (or coincidentally with the adoption of a new stock option or compensation plan); and

- There is reasonable expectation that shares will be issued for such purposes.

Guidance is provided in demonstrating that a systematic pattern of reacquisitions exists as well as in determining what constitutes a reasonable expectation that the shares will be issued for such purposes.

Acquisition of treasury stock subsequent to the consummation of a business combination, which is not addressed in APB Opinion No. 16, is also discussed in this release including instances that may negate pooling-of-interests accounting.

ASR Nos. 146 and 146A were codified in FRP Section 201.02, the text of which follows:

Effect of Treasury Stock Transactions

a. General

ASR 146:

Accounting Principles Board (APB) Opinion No. 16 identifies certain conditions which must be present (or in some cases absent) if a business combination is to be accounted for as a pooling of interests. Two of these conditions, which are set forth in paragraphs 47-c and 47-d, include provisions related to the reacquisition of voting common stock within two years prior to initiation and between initiation and consummation of a business combination which is planned to be accounted for by the pooling-of-interests method. The Commission observed that these provisions were subject to varying interpretations in practice, and concluded that certain of these interpretations are not compatible with concepts underlying the Opinion. Accordingly, the Commission set forth its conclusions as to certain problems relating to the effect of treasury stock transactions on accounting for business combinations.

When cash or other assets are used or liabilities are incurred to effect a business combination, APB Opinion No. 16 concludes that the combination should be accounted for as a purchase. This concept might be circumvented if cash or other assets were used or liabilities were incurred to reacquire common shares and common shares were then exchanged to consummate the combination. Therefore, for the pooling-of-interests method to apply, paragraph 47-c of the Opinion requires that "none of the combining companies changes the equity interest of the voting common stock in contemplation of effecting the combination either within two years before the plan of combination is initiated or between the dates the combination is initiated and consummated. . . ." Further, paragraph 47-d stipulates that "each of the combining companies [may reacquire] shares of voting common stock only for purposes other than business combinations. . . ."

In some cases, it is difficult to determine the purposes of treasury stock acquisitions. An AICPA Accounting Interpretation of Opinion No. 16 (No. 20 issued September 1971) states: "In the absence of persuasive evidence to the contrary, however, it should be presumed that all acquisitions of treasury stock during the two years preceding the date a plan of combination is initiated. . . . and between initiation and consummation were made in contemplation of effecting business combinations to be accounted for as a pooling of interests. Thus, lacking such evidence, this combination would be accounted for by the purchase method regardless of whether treasury stock or unissued shares or both are issued in the combination." The Commission believes that this presumption and conclusion should be followed.

In determining the purposes of treasury stock acquisitions, it is ordinarily appropriate to focus on the intended subsequent distribution of common shares rather than on the business reasons for acquiring treasury shares. For example, shares may be reacquired because management believes the company is overcapitalized or considers that "the price is right," but such reasons do not overcome the presumption that they were acquired in contemplation of effecting business combinations to be accounted for as pooling of interests. On the other hand, the presumption may be overcome when shares are acquired for a specific use unrelated to business combinations, such as stock option or purchase plans or stock dividends, are associated with a combination accounted for as a purchase, or are acquired to resolve an existing contingent share agreement. However, the mere assertion that common shares are reacquired for such purposes, even where the assertion is formalized by action of the board of directors reserving the treasury shares, does not provide persuasive evidence that they were not reacquired in contemplation of pooling-of-interests combinations. If a resolution of the board of directors or other statement of intent were sufficient to provide persuasive contrary evidence, the restrictions on treasury stock acquisitions would be totally ineffective. Accordingly, while a board resolution made prior to acquisition of treasury shares may be useful evidence as to corporate intent, reference also must be made to the actual or probable issuance of shares for purposes unrelated to pooling-of-interests business combinations.

When treasury shares are acquired during a period beginning two years prior to initiation and ending at the date of consummation of a business combination to be accounted for as a pooling of interests (hereinafter referred to as the "restricted period") the issuance of an equivalent number of shares prior to the date of consummation would generally provide persuasive evidence that the treasury shares were not acquired in contemplation of the combination. The shares issued may be treasury shares or previously unissued shares since, with regard to the equity interests of the common shareholders, there is no substantive difference between the two. Thus, a company might "cure" a condition which would preclude pooling-of-interests accounting by selling common shares prior to consummation of the combination. The "cure" could not be effected by merely retiring treasury shares.

Paragraph 47-d of APB Opinion No. 16 includes the statement that "treasury stock acquired for purposes other than business combinations includes shares for stock option and compensation plans and other recurring distributions provided a systematic pattern of reacquisitions is established at least two years before the plan of combination is initiated." Further, "a systematic pattern of reacquisitions may be established for less than two years if it coincides with the adoption of a new stock option or compensation plan." In AICPA Accounting Interpretation No. 20 of Opinion No. 16, no reference is made to a systematic pattern of reacquisition, and some accountants have asserted that this test has been effectively superseded. The Commission does not accept this assertion. Accordingly, the Commission concludes that treasury shares acquired in the restricted period for recurring distributions should be considered "tainted" unless they are acquired in a systematic pattern of reacquisitions established at least two years before the plan of combination is initiated (or coincidentally with the adoption of a new stock option or compensation plan) and there is reasonable expectation that shares will be issued for such purposes.

A systematic pattern of reacquisitions might be demonstrated by the reacquisition of a specified number of shares in successive time periods, e.g., 1,000 shares per month. A systematic pattern might also be demonstrated where, pursuant to a formal reacquisition plan, shares are acquired based on specified criteria such as the market price of the stock and cash availability. The criteria of the reacquisition plan must be sufficiently explicit so that the pattern of reacquisitions may be objectively compared to the plan. Unanticipated interruptions caused by legal constraints on a company's ability to reacquire shares would not upset an otherwise systematic pattern of reacquisitions.

The determination of whether there is reasonable expectation that shares will be issued for the stated purposes of acquiring the shares is a matter of judgment. Generally, there would appear to be such reasonable expectation where the following circumstances exist at the time a reacquisition plan is adopted or shares are reacquired:

1. As to stock option plans, warrants or convertible securities, the quoted price of the common shares is not less than 75 percent of the exercise or conversion price.

2. As to stock purchase or bonus plans or stock dividends, either (a) shares are reacquired to fulfill existing commitments or dividends declared or (b) based on a pattern of issuing shares for such purposes in the prior two years, the shares are reacquired to fulfill anticipated requirements in the succeeding year.

A systematic pattern of reacquisitions test would not apply to treasury shares acquired for issuance in a specific "purchase" business combination or to resolve an existing contingent share agreement from a prior business combination, as these issuances would not be regarded as recurring distributions. Thus, shares acquired and reserved for these purposes at the date a pooling-of-interests business combination is consummated would not be regarded as "tainted" when, based on current negotiations, presently existing earnings levels or market price of shares, etc., there is reasonable expectation that shares will be issued for the stated purposes.

APB Opinion No. 16 does not discuss treasury share acquisitions subsequent to consummation of a business combination. In specific fact situations, subsequent reacquisitions may be so closely related to the prior combination that they should be considered part of the combination plan. Thus, significant reacquisitions closely following a combination which otherwise qualifies as a pooling of interests may invalidate the applicability of that method. Conversely. significant reacquisitions following a combination accounted for as a purchase might be associated with that purchase and would not adversely affect subsequent pooling combinations.

ASR 146-A:

On October 5, 1973, in Securities Act Release No. 5429, the Commission requested comments on the substance of Accounting Series Release No. 146 and stated that until these comments were considered the Commission would accept filings from registrants using principles of accounting for business combinations in accordance with practice deemed acceptable by public accountants prior to ASR 146. Comments were received from numerous individuals, companies and groups.

After considering these comments, the Commission concluded that the statement of policy set forth in ASR 146 represents a proper interpretation of Accounting Principles Board Opinion No. 16 which deals with accounting for business combinations.

A number of comment letters indicated a need for the clarification of certain aspects of ASR 146. The following interpretive comments are designed to guide registrants and their independent public accountants.

SEC 50335. Rule 3-05

b. Purpose of Acquisition of Shares

ASR 146-A:

In determining the purposes of treasury stock acquisitions, it is ordinarily appropriate to focus on the intended subsequent distribution of shares, e.g., exercise of options, conversion of preferred stock, etc. APB Opinion No. 16, AICPA Accounting Interpretation No. 20 thereof, and ASR 146 all discuss and emphasize subsequent distribution in assessing purpose of acquisition. It must be recognized, however, that circumstances may exist where a company is obliged by contract to reacquire specific shares or must reacquire specific shares to settle outstanding claims. For example, reacquisition might be made to (1) comply with an agreement to purchase stock upon the death of a stockholder, (2) settle a claim or lawsuit involving alleged misrepresentation or other acts relating to the original issuance of stock, (3) repossess stock pledged as collateral for a receivable or other contractual obligation, and (4) repurchase stock from employees pursuant to contractual rights or obligations. Such contracts or claims provide persuasive evidence that resulting reacquisitions were not made in contemplation of a business combination to be treated as a pooling of interests. Accordingly, unless it appears that such rights or obligations are contrived to skirt the requirements of APB Opinion No. 16, resulting reacquisitions would not result in "tainted" shares.

c. Reasonable Expectation of Reissuance

ASR 146-A:

Many of those commenting on ASR 146 expressed concern that the guidelines relating to reasonable expectation of issuance of shares for stock option plans, warrants or convertible securities, i.e., the quoted price of common shares is not less than 75 percent of the exercise or conversion price, would be applied as an immutable rule. The Commission does not intend that this guideline be a rule. Reasonable expectation is a matter of judgment. Some of the other factors which may affect that judgment are the volatility of quoted prices, the remaining time period before conversion or exercise rights expire, and price and earnings trends. The Commission intends that the 75 percent guideline be viewed as a presumption which may be rebutted by relevant, probative evidence.

d. Acquisitions Subsequent to Consummation

ASR 146-A:

Several of those commenting on ASR 146 were concerned about the lack of specific guidelines for determining when there are "significant reacquisitions closely following a combination." The Commission does not intend to establish an additional criterion for determining the accounting treatment of a business combination. Rather, it intended simply to caution registrants and auditors that the substance of reacquisitions closely following consummation of a combination should not be ignored. For example, if a company wished to replace untainted shares issued in a purchase by acquiring an equivalent number of shares closely following its consummation, such shares would not be tainted. Conversely, if an enterprise were to complete a pooling and a very short time thereafter repurchase an equivalent number of shares, such a purchase could affect the status of the combination and bar pooling accounting.

e. Materiality

ASR 146-A:

AICPA Interpretation No. 20 of APB Opinion No. 16 indicates that the presence of "tainted" treasury shares will not preclude pooling-of-interests accounting if the number of shares is not material in relation to the total number of shares issued to effect the combination. In practice, "tainted" shares are apparently being considered together with other items under paragraph 47-b. This would limit "tainted" shares to a maximum of 10% of the total number of shares issued to effect the combination. ASR 146 does not address this matter because practice appears reasonable and reasonably uniform.

The following informal interpretations were published in the November 1974 issue of the Journal of Accountancy to provide guidance as to the application of ASR Nos. 146 and 146A to particular situations and the circumstances under which "reacquisitions" of a company's stock during a two-year period prior to a business combination would not invalidate pooling accounting.

Implementing SEC Rules on "Effect of Treasury Stock Transactions on Accounting for Business Combinations" —ASR Nos. 146 and 146A

This interpretation summarizes discussions held with members of the Securities and Exchange Commission's staff and AICPA representatives concerning implementation and interpretation matters relating to SEC Accounting Series Release Nos. 146 and 146A. The discussions were informal and it should be recognized that the views expressed do not constitute an official position of the Commission. (Questions 1, 2, and 3 related to implementation issues and are no longer germane.)

Systematic Pattern Test

ASR Nos. 146 and 146A include the following examples:

Purposes Which Must Meet Systematic Pattern Test

Stock option plans

Stock purchase plans

Stock compensation plans

SEC 50335. Rule 3-05

Convertible debentures

Convertible stock

Warrants

Stock dividends (paid, declared, or planned) considered to be a recurring distribution. (A paid, declared, or planned stock dividend is considered "recurring" when at least one stock dividend similar in amount was paid in each of the two preceding years.)

Purposes for Which It Is Not Necessary to Meet Systematic Pattern Test

Specific purchase business combination

Existing contingent share agreement from a prior business combination

Contractual obligations:

Comply with an agreement to purchase stock upon the death of a stockholder

Settle a claim or lawsuit involving alleged misrepresentation or other acts relating to the original issuance of stock

Repossess stock pledged as collateral for a receivable or other contractual obligation

Repurchase stock from employees pursuant to contractual rights or obligations

In respect to treasury shares reacquired pursuant to contractual obligations, an intended subsequent distribution of shares is not necessary to meet the criteria of ASR Nos. 146 and 146A.

Question 4. ASR No. 146 states that "the Commission concludes that treasury shares acquired in the restricted period for recurring distributions should be considered 'tainted' unless they are acquired in a systematic pattern of reacquisitions established at least two years before the plan of combination is initiated (or coincidentally with the adoption of a new stock option or compensation plan) and there is reasonable expectation that shares will be issued for such purposes." ASR No. 146 further states that "unanticipated interruptions caused by legal constraints on a company's ability to reacquire shares would not upset an otherwise systematic pattern of reacquisitions." What are the circumstances which would permit the interruption of an otherwise systematic pattern without tainting treasury share acquisitions?

Answer. A registrant may be required to temporarily discontinue its systematic pattern because of the constraints of SEC regulations on the aggregate number of treasury shares which may be purchased during a given period, or during the period when a registration statement is in process. A registrant may also discontinue a systematic pattern because it concludes there is no longer reasonable expectation of reissuance. (This conclusion might be required if the market price of its stock is less than the 75% of exercise or conversion price.) The terms of debt agreements may also require the discontinuance of a systematic pattern, e.g., maintenance of working capital or aggregate dollar amount permitted for dividends and treasury share acquisitions based on net income.

The foregoing examples of interruptions would not cause the otherwise untainted treasury shares acquired prior to interruption of the systematic pattern to become tainted. Similarly, a resumption of treasury share acquisitions following the removal of the constraint would be considered as a continuation of the previously established systematic pattern.

Question 5. If the acquisition of tainted treasury shares interrupts an otherwise systematic pattern of untainted treasury share acquisitions, do the otherwise previously or subsequently acquired untainted shares become tainted?

Answer. No.

Example.

Treasury Shares Acquired

	Systematic Pattern	Other (Tainted)
May 1974	5,000	
June 1974	8,000	
July 1974	6,000	
August 1974	10,000	100,000
September 1974	7,500	

Although the 100,000 shares are tainted, the shares acquired under the systematic pattern remain untainted.

Question 6. If a company starts a systematic pattern of treasury share acquisitions after April 11, 1974 and the shares acquired meet the purpose and reasonable expectation tests, are the treasury shares acquired after April 11, 1974 tainted for a two-year period?

Answer. Yes, unless the treasury shares acquired after April 11, 1974 are for a purpose qualifying as an exception, such as a new stock option plan.

Example. In June 1974 a company adopts a new qualified stock option plan and grants options to purchase 100,000 shares. In July, pursuant to a resolution by the board of directors, the company adopts a systematic pattern to purchase treasury shares to satisfy its option commitments. In October, when legal constraints on purchasing treasury stock are removed, the company begins to implement its systematic pattern. Provided the reasonable expectation test is met, the shares purchased to fulfill the option commitments for the June 1974 Option Plan are untainted when purchased (i.e., a systematic pattern does not have to be in effect for a two-year period).

In the above example it would not be necessary for the systematic pattern adopted in July 1974 to cover all of the outstanding options.

Question 7. Can a change in an existing stock plan constitute a new plan under APB Opinion No. 16, paragraph 47-d?

SEC 50335. Rule 3-05

Answer. Yes, if a stock plan is revised by significant changes in such provisions as price or terms of exercise, such a revised plan can be considered a new plan.

Question 8. If a company started a systematic pattern of treasury share acquisitions before April 12, 1974 and continues the systematic pattern after April 11, 1974, are the treasury shares acquired after April 11, 1974 tainted for a two-year period beginning on the date the systematic pattern was begun?

Answer. Yes, unless the systematic pattern was begun in conjunction with the adoption of a new stock option plan or other purpose for which the systematic pattern test must be met.

Example. In January 1974 a company adopted a systematic pattern to purchase treasury shares to satisfy its stock option commitments under a stock option plan adopted in 1972 and the systematic pattern is continued after April 11, 1974. Treasury shares acquired after April 11, 1974 are tainted for a two-year period which began in January 1974.

Question 9. Can a systematic pattern be revised at a later date to increase or decrease the number of treasury shares being acquired?

Answer. Yes, if there is a reasonable basis for the revision. For example, the number of shares acquired pursuant to a reacquisition plan might change because of changes in the criteria used (cash availability, market price, etc.) or because of changes in the anticipated timing or number of shares needed for the purpose of reacquisition.

Example. A systematic pattern of acquiring 3,000 to 5,000 shares a month could be revised at the end of 6 months to provide for the acquisition of 1,000 to 2,000 shares a month for the next 6 months because of a change in the number of shares expected to be issued for a stock option plan.

Question 10. Can a systematic pattern of treasury stock acquisitions be based on (a) a dollar amount of treasury stock purchases, or (b) a percentage of trading activity in a company's stock?

Answer. Yes for (a) and (b).

Example. A company's systematic pattern of treasury stock acquisitions could be based on (a) $ 10,000 of purchases per month, or (b) 1/4 of 1% of shares traded per month.

Question 11. If a company's board of directors adopts a resolution to purchase unsolicited blocks of treasury shares in amounts not to exceed a specified number of shares per block or a specified total number of shares per year, would shares purchased under such a plan constitute a systematic pattern?

Answer. Yes.

Question 12. If options granted under a nonqualified stock option plan adopted before or after April 11, 1974, may not be exercised for five years and a plan for systematic reacquisition is adopted coincidentally with adoption of the plan, which calls for purchases of treasury stock to begin after three years, will the first shares reacquired be untainted without an additional two-year waiting period?

Answer. Yes.

Question 13. If a company has an employment agreement which requires a one-time issuance of common shares at a later date, must treasury shares acquired for this purpose meet the systematic pattern test?

Answer. No, assuming the agreement is isolated and not substantively part of a stock compensation or other plan for recurring distributions.

Question 14. A company starts a systematic pattern of treasury stock acquisitions in May 1974 by purchasing approximately 5,000 shares per month for a pre-April 12, 1974 commitment to issue shares for a purpose which must meet a systematic pattern test. In October 1974 the company consummates a business combination in which it issues 25,000 shares. Since the business combination must be accounted for as a purchase (caused by the existence of a sufficient number of tainted treasury shares because a systematic pattern has not been followed for two years), does the two-year period start over again in October 1974?

Answer. No, the starting date of the systematic pattern remains in May 1974, and up to 25,000 treasury shares acquired between May 1974 and October 1974 would be cured as a result of issuing 25,000 shares in the October 1974 business combination. (See Question 16, Example F.)

Question 15. Subsequent to a business combination, is the systematic pattern of treasury stock reacquisitions of the combined company determined by the issuing company's pattern, the acquired company's pattern, or some combination of the two patterns?

Answer. The answer to this question will depend on the facts in each case. If the business combination is accounted for as a purchase, the acquiring company's pattern carries forward. If new purposes for which untainted treasury shares might be purchased arise from a purchase combination, a plan for systematically acquiring treasury shares could be established coincidentally and a two-year waiting period would not be required. If the combination is accounted for as a pooling of interests, the existing reacquisition plans of either or both companies can be carried forward as they relate to securities which survive the combination.

Issuance of Shares After April 11, 1974

If treasury shares have been acquired and shares are later issued (treasury or unissued), it is sometimes necessary to "apply" the subsequently issued shares to determine the status of the remaining treasury shares.

SEC 50335.   Rule 3-05

Question 16. How are shares issued* after April 11, 1974, to be applied to previously acquired treasury shares —FIFO, LIFO, tainted, untainted, etc.?

Answer. The answer depends on the status of the treasury shares acquired prior to the issuance of the shares. First, the application is only necessary for treasury shares acquired within the previous two years. Second, the application will depend on whether the treasury shares are tainted or untainted; if all treasury shares are untainted, it should not make any difference whether or how the shares issued are applied because the status of treasury shares would continue untainted. If all treasury shares are tainted, then the shares issued should generally be applied to the tainted treasury shares on a LIFO basis (Example A). If there are both tainted and untainted treasury shares, the purpose of the shares subsequently issued should be considered. Shares issued for purposes which qualified the shares acquired as untainted should be applied to the untainted shares (Examples B and C). If, however, the shares issued were for a business combination accounted for as a pooling of interests, they would be applied only to tainted treasury shares** (Examples D and E). Similarly, if the shares issued were either in a business combination accounted for as a purchase or sold for cash (a "cure"), an application would only be made to any tainted treasury shares (Example F).

---

*ASR No. 146 states: "The shares issued may be treasury shares or previously unissued shares since, with regard to the equity interests of the common shareholders, there is no substantive difference between the two."
**See discussion of Materiality test.

Example (A)	Total	Treasury Shares Acquired Within Two Years	
		Tainted	Untainted
Status of treasury shares before application:			
Acquired in May 1974	20,000	20,000	
Acquired in Sept. 1974	40,000	40,000	
	60,000	60,000	
Application of shares issued for any reason	(50,000)	(50,000)	
Status of treasury shares after application*	10,000	10,000	(May 1974)

---

*"Status of treasury shares" means only those treasury shares acquired within the prior two years which, on a memorandum basis, should be considered in deciding the appropriate accounting for a business combination. The actual number of treasury shares may differ from "status of treasury shares" because (1) actual treasury shares may have been retired, (2) an application of treasury shares may be required when previously unissued common shares are issued, or (3) an

SEC 50335

application of treasury shares may not be appropriate when there are not any tainted treasury shares.

Example (B)	Total	Treasury Shares Acquired Within Two Years	
		Tainted	Untainted
Status of treasury shares before application	120,000	20,000	100,000
Application of shares issued for purposes (e.g., options or conversions) for which:			
(a) Untainted shares were not acquired	(20,000)	(20,000)	
(b) Untainted shares were acquired	(5,000)		(5,000)
Status of treasury shares after application	95,000	-0-	95,000

Example (C)	Total	Treasury Shares Acquired Within Two Years	
		Tainted For 1972 Stock Option Plan	Untainted For 1974 Stock Option Plan
Status of treasury shares before application — shares acquired after April 11, 1974	20,000	10,000	10,000
Application of shares issued for 1972 stock option plan	(5,000)	(5,000)	
Application of shares issued for 1974 stock option plan	(5,000)		(5,000)
Status of treasury shares after application	10,000	5,000	5,000

SEC 50335. Rule 3-05

Example (D)	Total	Treasury Shares Acquired Within Two Years	
		Tainted	**Untainted**
Status of treasury shares before application	120,000	10,000	110,000
Application of 10,000 shares issued in a pooling (total shares issued is 120,000)(a)	(10,000)	(10,000)	
Status of treasury shares after application	110,000	-0-	110,000

(a) It is assumed that the 10,000 tainted treasury shares were within the 10% materiality test.

Example (E)	Total	Treasury Shares Acquired Within Two Years	
		Tainted	**Untainted**
Status of treasury shares before application	120,000		120,000
Application of shares issued in a pooling of interests	(No application appropriate)		
Status of treasury shares after application	120,000		120,000

Example (F)	Total	Treasury Shares Acquired Within Two Years	
		Tainted	**Untainted**
Status of treasury shares before application	120,000	100,000	20,000
Application of shares issued in a purchase acquisition or sold for cash	(80,000)(a)	(80,000)	
Status of treasury shares after application	40,000	20,000	20,000

(a) If more than 100,000 shares were issued, no application would be appropriate or necessary for the untainted treasury shares.

Question 17. What is the status of tainted treasury shares following the expiration of a two-year period since the date the shares were acquired?

Answer. Upon expiration of a two-year period following the purchase of tainted treasury shares, the shares are no longer tainted and the status of such shares does not have to be considered in deciding the appropriate accounting for a business combination.

Example (G)	Total	Treasury Shares Acquired Within Two Years	
		Tainted	Untainted
Status of treasury shares	120,000	10,000	110,000
Expiration of two-year period following purchase of tainted treasury shares	_____	(10,000)	10,000
Status of treasury shares	120,000	-0-	120,000

Question 18. If, after April 11, 1974, a systematic pattern of acquisitions of treasury shares is started coincident with the adoption of a stock option plan and options under that plan are exercised for a number of shares that exceeds the number of treasury shares acquired, does the excess apply to subsequent acquisitions which are part of the systematic pattern?

Answer. Yes.

Example. A stock option plan is adopted in May 1974 and a systematic pattern of treasury share acquisitions is begun. By May 1975, 40,000 treasury shares have been acquired in a systematic pattern at which time options are exercised for 70,000 shares. There are no other treasury shares. The issuance of 70,000 shares for options exercised results in a 30,000 share excess to which 30,000 treasury shares subsequently acquired in a continuation of the systematic pattern are to be applied.

Purpose Test

Question 19. Under what circumstances may treasury shares acquired for stock dividends be considered untainted?

Answer. Untainted treasury shares may be acquired in a systematic pattern to satisfy shares required for recurring* stock dividends for approximately one year in the future where there is a previous history of issuing stock dividends, and either stock dividends are declared but not yet issued, or there is a definite plan to declare a stock dividend. Untainted treasury shares** may not be acquired for stock dividends which are not recurring nor will issuance of shares for a nonrecurring stock dividend be applied against (or cure) existing tainted treasury shares.

SEC 50335. Rule 3-05

Example (A). A registrant who usually issues a 2% stock dividend annually may purchase untainted treasury shares in a systematic pattern to satisfy this requirement. Shares issued for recurring stock dividends may be applied against existing tainted treasury shares to the extent that untainted treasury shares acquired for this purpose do not exist (see Question 16, Example A).

Example (B). A registrant without a previous history of declaring stock dividends declares a 4% stock dividend payable in July 1974. Untainted treasury shares may not be acquired for this stock dividend, nor will issuance of shares for this stock dividend cure existing tainted treasury shares.

---

*A paid, declared or planned stock dividend is considered "recurring" when at least one stock dividend similar in amount was paid in each of the two preceding years.

**It should be noted that treasury shares purchased for nonrecurring stock dividends are not only tainted, but they may also result in a company being unable to satisfy paragraph 47-c of APB Opinion No. 16.

Question 20. ASR No. 146A states "repurchase [of] stock from employees pursuant to contractual rights or obligations . . . would not result in 'tainted' shares." If a company repurchases shares from an employee or other stockholder under a right of first refusal, are the shares untainted?

Answer. Yes, shares purchased from an employee or other stockholder pursuant to a contractual right are untainted.

Reasonable Expectation Test

Question 21. Is it necessary that exercise of stock options or conversions of equity or debt securities actually occur to meet the reasonable expectation test?

Answer. No, the reasonable expectation test should be determined at the time the reacquisition plan is adopted or when the shares are acquired and only at those times.

Question 22. If the reasonable expectation test is met at the time a stock option plan is adopted, do shares later acquired for the plan at a time when the quoted price of the common shares is less than 75% of the exercise price meet the reasonable expectation test?

Answer. Yes, if the circumstances are such that there continues to be reasonable expectation of reissuance.

Example. In March 1974 a company adopts a five-year stock option plan and grants options to purchase common shares at an exercise price of $10 per share (market price at date of grant). Treasury shares are acquired as follows:

	Shares	Market Price
March 1974	2,000	$10
June 1974	2,000	9
September 1974	2,000	8
December 1974	2,000	7
March 1975	1,000	6
June 1975	1,000	5

The shares acquired in December 1974 and March and June 1975 meet the reasonable expectation test because (1) the options still have approximately four years before expiration, and (2) the market decline in the company's stock is considered to be part of an overall market decline which will reverse within four years; therefore, there continues to be reasonable expectation that the shares will be reissued.

Question 23. ASR No. 146 states:

"A systematic pattern of reacquisitions test would not apply to treasury shares acquired for issuance in a specific 'purchase' business combination or to resolve an existing contingent share agreement from a prior business combination, as these issuances would not be regarded as recurring distributions. Thus, shares acquired and reserved for these purposes at the date a pooling-of-interests business combination is consummated would not be regarded as 'tainted' when, based on current negotiations, presently existing earnings levels or market price of shares, etc., there is reasonable expectation that shares will be issued for the stated purposes."

Does this statement mean that treasury shares acquired for such purposes must meet the reasonable expectation test both at the time the shares are acquired and at the date a pooling of interests is consummated?

Answer. The test of reasonable expectation would relate primarily to the date the shares were acquired; however, the purpose for which shares were acquired must continue to exist at the date a pooling of interests business combination is consummated for the shares to be regarded as untainted at that date.

Example. In January 1975 a company acquires 100,000 treasury shares for issuance in a planned purchase. In March 1975 negotiations for the planned purchase are dropped. The 100,000 shares would be regarded as untainted with respect to a pooling of interests business combination consummated in February 1975 but as tainted with respect to a pooling of interests business combination consummated in June 1975.

Treasury Share Acquisitions Subsequent to a Business Combination

ASR No. 146A states that the Commission intends "to caution registrants and auditors that the substance of reacquisitions closely following consummation of a combination should not be ignored."

SEC 50335. Rule 3-05

Example (A). 500,000 shares are issued in an August 1974 pooling of interests; 90 days following the pooling, 400,000 tainted treasury shares are acquired from sources unrelated to the shareholders of the pooled company. The acquisition of treasury shares should not affect the August pooling.

If, however, 400,000 tainted treasury shares are acquired from sources unrelated to the stockholders of the pooled company 30 days following the pooling, an invalidation of the August 1974 pooling would be presumed under ASR No. 146. This presumption could be overcome by evidence to support that the tainted treasury shares were acquired for another specific purpose unrelated to the pooling of interests.

If 100,000 tainted treasury shares are acquired from sources unrelated to the stockholders of the pooled company 30 days following the pooling, the pooling would not be affected.

(In any case, if the treasury shares subsequently acquired were untainted, there would be no effect on the August pooling of interests.)

Example (B). A company without tainted treasury shares issues 300,000 shares in an August 1974 business combination accounted for as a purchase. Up to 300,000 treasury shares could be acquired in the next several months for the stated purpose of replacing the shares issued in the August purchase and these treasury shares would be untainted.

If, however, the 300,000 shares issued in the purchase combination were tainted, then the replacement treasury shares would also be tainted.

Materiality Test

ASR No. 146A accepts the materiality test set forth in AICPA Accounting Interpretation No. 20 of APB Opinion No. 16. This means that tainted treasury shares are not material if they are within the 10% margin which is available in all poolings of interests to accommodate cash purchases and minority interests which remain outstanding.

Example

Shares to be issued in proposed business combination (assuming 100% exchange of shares)	<u>500,000</u>
10% margin for tainted treasury shares, intercorporate investments of the combining companies, dissenters' and fractional shares acquired for cash, minority interests which remain outstanding, etc.	<u>50,000</u>

As long as the tainted treasury shares and other elements covered by the 10% margin total less than the equivalent (including cash) of 50,000 shares, a pooling of interests would not be proscribed.

The SEC staff has informally indicated that it may consider systematic patterns of treasury share acquisitions during the two years preceding a pooling-of-interests business combination to be acceptable, provided that there is reasonable expectation that the shares reacquired are to be used for stock options or warrants. The staff believes that the number of treasury shares reacquired in a systematic pattern should be limited to the number of shares expected to be needed for conversions and for the exercise of options and warrants during the next two to three years. The staff has indicated that in making this determination the estimate of the number of shares expected to be converted or exercised should be based on the specific facts of the plan(s) involved and the historical experience of the registrant.

If general-purpose treasury stock acquisitions are made (e.g., under a stock repurchase program), and the number of shares acquired exceeds the number reasonably expected to be reissued (as defined above), the staff will permit the shares to be split into those permitted under ASR 146 and those that are considered tainted. However, the staff has indicated that it will require the registrant to demonstrate an advance determination that the shares were reacquired for both purposes.

50336. Staff Accounting Bulletins. In SAB Topic 2-A1, the staff concluded that certain contingencies impair pooling accounting. The text of the SAB follows:

Cash Contingencies

Facts: Registrant is to acquire Company A for common stock and Company B for common stock and cash. The cash is to be obtained from a private placement of preferred stock and a bank loan. However, the private placement is contingent upon the acquisition of Company A and the bank loan is contingent upon both the acquisition of Company A and the private placement.

Question: May the registrant account for the acquisitions of companies A and B on a pooling-of-interests basis and a purchase basis, respectively?

Interpretive Response: The staff believes that although there are no express agreements between companies A and B, the cash contingencies create what amounts to mutual contingencies necessitating purchase treatment for both acquisitions. (See Interpretation 38 of APB Opinion No. 16.)

SAB Topic 2-B affirms the staff's view that expenses incurred in connection with business combinations accounted for as poolings of interests should be charged to income. The text of the SAB follows:

Merger Expenses

Facts: A registrant that had been growing by acquisitions entered into a merger agreement which called for the issuance of shares of its common stock in exchange for all the outstanding shares of Company X; the combination is to be accounted for as a pooling of interests. A fraction of each share to be issued was to be sold by the escrow agent and the proceeds used to pay the expenses of the transaction. These expenses totaled nearly $525,000 and consisted of a finder's fee of $310,000 and various other legal, accounting and printing expenses. This total would be material to the combined income statement of the registrant and Company X. There was no prior fee arrangement between Company X and the finder.

The registrant proposes not to charge combined operations for the merger expenses, arguing that neither the spirit nor the specific provisions of APB Opinion No. 16 would be violated because (a) the arrangements were determined by "arms-length" negotiations between buyer and seller; (b) the acquisition costs were borne proportionately by all Company X stockholders; and (c) the merger agreement did not indicate that additional shares were to be issued to the stockholders for such costs.

Question: Does the staff believe that this proposed treatment is appropriate?

Interpretive Response: The staff is of the view that all expenses relating to the merger would have to be charged to the combined income statement in compliance with APB Opinion No. 16. The registrant was growing by acquisitions, and these costs would be recurring and ordinary expenses.

SAB Topic 2-C discusses the need to present pro forma financial information to show the impact, if significant, of an adjustment in officers' salaries following the consummation of a merger accounted for as a pooling of interests. The text of the SAB is included in section 51111.

50337. SEC Views on Accounting for a Purchase and "Push Down" Accounting

In SAB Topic 2-A2, the staff discussed factors that may rebut the general presumption set forth in paragraph 70 of APB Opinion No. 16 that the acquiring company in a business combination is the company receiving the larger portion of voting rights in the combined corporation. This guidance is often applied to other situations, referred to as "reverse acquisitions," in which the legal acquiror may not be the same as the accounting acquiror.

In a reverse acquisition, the determination of the cost of the acquired assets may be somewhat unusual since the accounting acquiror receives both the issuer's stock and assets. Where the issuer is a public entity, the SEC staff has indicated that the cost of the acquired assets should be based on the aggregate fair value of the issuer's outstanding stock at the date of acquisition. Following the guidance in APB Opinion No. 16, the staff believes the cost should be allocated to the *issuer's* net assets and the excess cost, if any, should be recognized as goodwill.

When the fair value of the issuer's stock cannot be determined, pursuant to the guidance provided in APB Opinion No. 16, the staff believes that the cost should be determined based on the fair value of the issuer's net assets acquired. However, the

SEC staff believes it is inappropriate to recognize goodwill when the costs of the acquired assets is based on the fair value of the issuer's net assets. In reverse acquisitions, it is important to note that pro forma information needs to be presented in accordance with APB Opinion No. 16 or Article 11 of Regulation S-X (see section 51100), as appropriate.

The financial statements after a reverse acquisition may also be somewhat unusual. While the legal acquiror's name will appear on the financial statements, the historical information should be that of the accounting acquiror. The SEC staff has indicated that the accounting acquiror's historical stockholder's equity prior to the merger should be retroactively restated (i.e., recapitalized) for the equivalent number of shares received in the transaction with any difference between the par value of the issuer's and acquiror's stock recorded with an offset to paid-in capital. In the staff's view, historical retained earnings (deficiency) of the accounting acquiror should be carried forward after the acquisition. The staff also believes that in the absence of cheap stock (see section 50503-20), earnings per share should be restated for all periods prior to the acquisition to include the number of equivalent shares received by the accounting acquiror.

The staff has provided the following example of a note to financial statements describing a reverse acquisition:

> On May 1, 19X9, Issuer Company acquired all of the outstanding common stock of Target Company. For accounting purposes, the acquisition has been treated as a recapitalization of Target Company with Target Company as the acquiror (reverse acquisition). The historical financial statements prior to May 1, 19X9 are those of Target Company. Pro forma information giving effect to the acquisition as if the acquisition took place January 1, 19X8 is as follows....

The staff has indicated that when the issuer is a public shell (typically formed for the sole purpose of seeking a nonpublic acquiror), the accounting acquiror would be expected to record the transaction as the issuance of stock for cash, with no goodwill recorded. The staff's position is based on the view that this type of transaction is essentially a capital stock transaction rather than a business combination. Therefore, the staff has indicated that pro forma information need not be presented. In such situations, the proposed footnote above would be altered accordingly to describe the transaction (including the reason for the absence of pro forma data). In addition, the staff has indicated that costs of such transactions may be either expensed or charged to stockholders' equity, but should not be capitalized.

Lastly, when a reverse acquisition includes earnouts for contingent shares to be issued, the staff believes that since such shares would be issued to the accounting

SEC 50337. Rule 3-05

acquiror, the shares should be accounted for similar to a stock dividend (i.e., included in earnings per share from the date of issuance).

The text of SAB Topic 2-A2 follows:

Determination of the Acquiring Corporation

Facts: Companies X and Y reach an agreement in principle to merge under which the former common shareholders of company X are to receive common stock representing 55 percent of the outstanding shares and the former common shareholders of company Y are to receive both common and preferred stock representing 45 percent of the outstanding voting stock in the combined corporation. The Chairman of the Board and Chief Executive Officer and the Chief Operating Officer of the combined corporation would be the individuals currently holding these positions in company Y. Substantially all the proposed directors of the combined corporation are directors of company Y. (The Board of Directors of company Y consists principally of non-management directors whereas the Board of Directors of company X consists principally of management directors.) The Chairman of the Executive Committee of the combined corporation would be the current Chairman of the Board and Chief Executive Officer of company X. That individual and his family would hold approximately 18 percent of the outstanding voting stock of the combined corporation; 8 1/2 percent would be held in a trust, and, with respect to the other 9 1/2 percent of the shares, he has agreed "not to solicit proxies or to participate in an election contest." (No other shareholder of the combined corporation would hold 5 percent or more of the outstanding common stock.) The assets, revenues, net earnings and current market value of company Y significantly exceed those of company X. In addition, the market value of the securities to be received by the former common shareholders of company Y significantly exceed those of company X. Companies X and Y propose to account for this business combination as a purchase by company X of company Y because the former shareholders of company X will hold a controlling interest (55 percent) in the outstanding voting stock of the combined corporation.

Question: Given the above facts, is there other evidence indicating that company Y is the acquiror in this business combination which rebuts the presumption that company X is the acquiror since its former common shareholders will receive the larger portion of the voting rights of the combined corporation?

Interpretive Response: Paragraph 70 of Accounting Principles Board Opinion No. 16 states:

"The Board concludes that presumptive evidence of the acquiring corporation in combinations effected by an exchange of stock is obtained by identifying the former common stockholder interests of a combining company which either retain or receive the larger portion of the voting rights in the combined corporation. That corporation should be treated as the acquiror unless other evidence clearly indicates that another corporation is the acquiror."

SEC 50337

Companies X and Y took the position that because the former common sharehold-ers of company X will receive 55 percent of the outstanding voting stock of the combined corporation, it is the acquiring corporation and the other circumstances of the business combination do not rebut that evidence.

The staff took the position that company Y is the acquiring corporation because the other circumstances of this business combination rebut the normal pre-sumption that company X is the acquiror (i.e., that company is the acquiror whose former common shareholders receive the larger portion of the voting stock of the combined corporation). The facts that: (i) there would be restric-tions on the ability of the former chairman of the board of company X to solicit proxies or to participate in an election contest; (ii) top management and the board of directors of the combined corporation would be substantially indi-viduals currently holding such positions in company Y; (iii) the assets, reve-nues, net earnings and current market value of company Y significantly exceed those of company X; and (iv) the market value of the securities to be received by the former common shareholders of company Y significantly exceeds the market value of the securities to be received by the former common sharehold-ers of company X, all taken together, provide sufficient other evidence to indicate that company Y is the acquiror and that these factors outweigh the fact that the former common shareholders of company X received the larger portion of the voting rights of the combined corporation.

SEC Views on Acquisitions
Involving Financial Institutions

In SAB Topic 2-A3, issued as SAB No. 42, the staff discussed various consid-erations that should be given to the acquisition of financial institutions in a business combination accounted for under the purchase method. The facts presented in the SAB relate to the acquisition of financial institutions in periods of high interest rates and the significant and varied effects the use of the purchase method may have on the combined companies' results of operations.

In particular, the SAB discusses considerations in determining the allocation of the purchase price to acquired tangible and intangible assets, the appropriate measure of the fair value of deposit liabilities, and the appropriate amortization periods and methods for intangible assets acquired.

The SAB indicates that the basis for the SEC staff's positions expressed therein is the guidance provided in APB Opinion No. 16, *Accounting for Business Combina-tions*, APB Opinion No. 17, *Accounting for Intangible Assets,* and by FASB Interpre-tation No. 9, *Applying APB Opinions No. 16 and 17 When a Savings and Loan Association or a Similar Institution Is Acquired in a Business Combination Accounted for by the Purchase Method.*

The text of the SAB follows:

SEC 50337. Rule 3-05

Acquisitions Involving Financial Institutions

Facts: When financial institutions are acquired in periods of high interest rates, the use of the purchase method of accounting may result in significant effects on the reported results of operations of the combined companies. In such periods, a substantial discount is applied to the historical cost of any low-yielding mortgage loans and investments to determine their fair value at the acquisition date. The amount paid by the acquiring entity can be significantly higher than the amounts allocated to the identifiable assets acquired. Therefore, the amount of the purchase price in excess of the fair value of the tangible and identifiable intangible assets acquired which is allocated to purchased goodwill is often very significant. The discount on the loans and investments is accreted to income using the interest method to report a market yield on the acquired assets over a relatively short period based on the estimated life of the loans and investments. Goodwill has been amortized over as many as 40 years on a straight-line basis. The accretion of the discount to income over a short period, which is partially offset by the amortization on a straight-line method over longer periods of the purchase price amounts allocated to goodwill, often results in substantial positive effects on the reported results of operations in the first few years subsequent to the acquisition. The effect on the reported results of operations of such business combinations varies depending on the amount of discount applied to the loan and investment portfolios to record them at their fair values, the purchase price allocated to tangible and identifiable intangible assets and to goodwill, and the related accretion and amortization periods and methods selected. In certain filings with the Commission involving banks and savings and loan institutions where this effect has been significant, the staff has questioned whether the financial statements and pro forma results of operations properly reflected the economics of the purchase transaction.

Question 1: Are there any unique considerations in the allocation of purchase price to acquired tangible and intangible assets in the acquisition of financial institutions?

Interpretive Response: The staff believes that adequate guidance is provided by Accounting Principles Board ("APB") Opinion No. 16, "Accounting for Business Combinations," APB Opinion No. 17, "Accounting for Intangible Assets," and by Financial Accounting Standards Board ("FASB") Interpretation No. 9, "Applying APB Opinions No. 16 and 17 When a Savings and Loan Association or a Similar Institution is Acquired in a Business Combination Accounted for by the Purchase Method."[1] These accounting standards generally require that all tangible and identifiable intangible assets acquired be recorded on the basis of their fair values at the acquisition date. The cost of unidentifiable intangible assets purchased (goodwill) is measured by the total cost of the purchase less the sum of the amounts assigned to the fair value of identifiable tangible and intangible assets and less the fair value of deposits and other liabilities assumed. In practice, however, some of the principles in these standards may be difficult to apply to acquisitions of financial institutions.

Determination of the fair value of loans and other investments acquired in a business combination involving financial institutions may not be difficult since

508

these values are computed based on a comparison of the historical interest yields of the acquired portfolios and market yields for comparable loans and investments. However, the staff's experience has been that the applicable accounting standards have not always been properly considered. Many factors may need to be evaluated in the selection of an interest rate which properly reflects a comparable market yield. The discount applied to loans and investments to attain a market yield should be accreted using the interest method. The accretion period for the loan discount should be the remaining contractual term to maturity of the portfolio adjusted for anticipated prepayments. Recent trends which indicate slower turnovers of mortgaged residential properties should be considered when determining expected prepayments. The impact of any estimated future tax effects of differences between the tax bases and the amounts otherwise assignable to any assets acquired must be considered in estimating their fair value (paragraph 89 of APB Opinion No. 16).

Determination of the values of identifiable intangible assets purchased is often considered impracticable because they are not easily quantified. As a result, the methods of applying this aspect of the standards have varied considerably in financial statements included in registrant filings. A discussion of purchased identifiable intangible assets is contained in paragraph 8 of FASB Interpretation No. 9:

> "The purchase price paid for a savings and loan association may include an amount for one or more factors, such as the following:
>
> (a) Capacity of existing savings accounts and loan accounts to generate future income,
>
> (b) Capacity of existing savings accounts and loan accounts to generate additional business or new business, and
>
> (c) Nature of territory served."

Application of the guidance provided in FASB Interpretation No. 9 could result in values assigned to various identifiable intangible assets in commercial bank or savings and loan association acquisitions, including:

- mortgage escrow deposits
- branch networks
- mortgage servicing rights
- customer base
- deposit relationships
- name in the marketplace
- earning capacity.

The values inherent in some of these identifiable intangibles overlap. Determination of the specific intangibles purchased, as well as the fair values thereof, has to be made based on the individual facts and circumstances. The staff recognizes that

SEC 50337. Rule 3-05

this process is often difficult and that little practical guidance exists to facilitate such valuations. However, when the purchase price is not properly allocated to all intangibles, there may be a significant effect on the reported results of operations of the consolidated entity because the amount assigned to goodwill, which has usually been amortized over long periods, could be overstated. Although the practice of allocating costs to values associated with the earnings potential of acquired deposits has gained increased acceptance, the staff believes that the allocation of purchase price to all identifiable intangible assets acquired has often not received adequate consideration in business combinations involving financial institutions.

Question 2: What is the appropriate measure of the fair value of deposit liabilities assumed in the purchase of financial institutions?

Interpretive Response: The staff believes that the standards set forth in paragraph 7 of FASB Interpretation No. 9 for valuing the deposits of a savings and loan association are appropriate for other financial institutions. The fair value of such liabilities is the present value of the amounts to be paid using prevailing interest rates for similar deposits at the acquisition date. For example, the values assigned to passbook savings accounts paying interest at the maximum allowable rate would be the historical cost of the savings deposits to the acquired association plus any accrued interest. Noninterest bearing demand deposits of an acquired commercial bank would be recorded at their carrying amount. Acquired time deposits with interest rates less than the prevailing interest rate for similar time deposits would be recorded at a discount to their carrying value on an individual or on some aggregate basis and the discount would be amortized to report the prevailing interest rate on the acquired deposits. Any discount on deposits should be amortized using the interest method.

Consideration should be given to adjusting the fair value of deposits for the estimated future tax effects of differences in the tax bases and amounts otherwise assignable to the deposits, as specified in paragraph 89 of APB Opinion No. 16.

As discussed in Question 1 above, any purchased identifiable intangible assets associated with the deposits of the acquired institution should be recorded at their estimated fair values at acquisition.

Question 3: What are the appropriate amortization periods and methods for intangible assets acquired in the acquisition of financial institutions?

Interpretive Response: APB Opinion No. 17 and FASB Interpretation No. 9 provide appropriate guidance on this matter. The amortization period should be determined separately for each identifiable intangible asset acquired and for goodwill. The amortization period for identifiable intangibles may be readily determinable. However, determination of the appropriate amortization period for goodwill is more difficult and should be carefully evaluated.

The lives of identifiable intangible assets are often closely related to other assets acquired or liabilities assumed. For example, an intangible asset whose fair value is the present value of expected earnings from mortgage escrow deposits should be amortized over the estimated life of the related mortgage investments; an amortization method should be used which reflects the decreasing escrow levels resulting from expected payoffs of the mortgage loans. An intangible asset whose fair value is the present value of expected net interest margins to be earned from other purchased deposits normally should be amortized on an accelerated basis over a period which reflects the pattern of the expected runoff of the related deposits.

When identifiable intangible assets have been purchased in the acquisition of a financial institution, but their fair values are not determinable, these costs should be assigned to goodwill. Paragraph 30 of APB Opinion No. 17 requires that goodwill be amortized on a straight-line basis unless it is demonstrated that an accelerated method is more appropriate. Paragraph 9 of FASB Interpretation No. 9 indicates that an accelerated method of amortization would be appropriate and may be used for goodwill when the amount assigned to goodwill includes costs for identifiable intangibles whose fair values are not determinable and the benefits expected to be received from these intangibles decline over the expected life of the factors which are the basis for those intangibles. The staff believes that such circumstances demonstrate that an accelerated method of amortization for goodwill is more appropriate than a straight-line method and should be used.

Paragraph 27 of APB Opinion 17 provides factors which should be considered in estimating the useful lives of intangible assets. There are many relevant matters which should be evaluated when applying these guidelines to determine the appropriate amortization period for goodwill. Regulated depository institutions, for example, are experiencing erosions of their traditional markets because of inroads made by unregulated financial segments. Competitive pressures, the potential effects of deregulatory initiatives, and rapid technology changes in the industry create an uncertain environment which must be considered when determining the period in which goodwill benefits will exist. This uncertainty may be greater for savings and loan associations and savings banks since high interest rates have adversely affected their financial positions due to the funding costs of their fixed-rate loan portfolios.

The staff believes that the automatic selection of a 40-year amortization period for goodwill purchased in a financial institution acquisition is not appropriate. The uncertainty which results from the economic, competitive and organizational changes facing these institutions suggests that it is usually not realistic to conclude that purchased goodwill benefits have indefinite lives. In some of the financial institution filings which the staff has reviewed, the staff concluded, based on the facts and circumstances, that short amortization periods were appropriate with respect to the business combinations reflected in the filings. The allocation to goodwill of significant amounts of the purchase price, which appeared to be the result of a failure to properly identify and quantify all intangible assets purchased, was often a factor which influenced these decisions. The staff recognizes that under certain circumstances, goodwill benefits may exist beyond a short-term period.

SEC 50337. Rule 3-05

For example, in a recent discussion with a savings and loan registrant, the staff agreed that an entrance into major new market areas resulting from an acquisition provided a basis for concluding that the purchased goodwill benefits could exist beyond a short-term period. In reaching this decision, the staff was influenced by the fact that the expected financial results appeared to adequately reflect the economic realities of the transaction.

---

[1]Footnote 1 to FASB Interpretation No. 9 states that the Interpretation is applicable to financial institutions other than savings and loan associations which have similar types of assets and liabilities.

SAB Topic 2-A4, issued as SAB No. 42A, expresses the staff's view that 25 years is the maximum acceptable life for amortization of goodwill arising in connection with acquisitions of financial institutions. The text of the SAB follows:

Amortization of Goodwill by Financial Institutions Upon Becoming SEC Registrants

Facts: During 1981 (a period of high interest rates and increasing merger activity involving financial institutions), the staff noted that the use of the purchase method of accounting often resulted in substantial positive effects on earnings in the first few years following an acquisition of a financial institution. Often this was so because a low-yielding mortgage portfolio was discounted to fair value and the discount was taken into income using the interest method over the estimated life of the portfolio, while the excess of cost over the fair value of net assets acquired (goodwill), which often arose primarily as a result of discounting the mortgage portfolio, was charged to income on a straight-line basis over a period up to 40 years. For example, an institution which had been incurring losses could be acquired by another entity and report a significant contribution to the combined entity's financial results due to excessively long amortization periods for the recorded goodwill compared to short periods used for accretion of the discount. Since this result did not reflect what the staff believed were the economics of the transaction (particularly when a troubled financial institution was acquired), the staff requested that goodwill be amortized over a shorter period than the 40 year maximum amortization period, provided for in Accounting Principles Board Opinion No. 17.

On December 23, 1981, the staff issued Staff Accounting Bulletin No. 42 to publicize views on acquisitions of financial institutions. Among other things, the SAB noted that:

> Regulated depository institutions are experiencing erosion of traditional markets because of inroads made by unregulated financial segments. Competitive pressure; the potential effects of deregulatory initiatives; and rapid technology changes create an uncertain environment which must be considered when

512

determining the period in which goodwill benefits will exist. This uncertainty may be greater for savings and loan associations and savings banks since high interest rates have adversely affected their financial positions due to the funding costs of their fixed rate loan portfolios.

The SAB went on to note that the automatic selection of the maximum 40-year amortization period allowed by generally accepted accounting principles is not appropriate, and that shorter amortization periods are usually called for.

During 1982, the staff continued to review filings involving acquisitions of financial institutions using the factors set forth in SAB No. 42. While SAB No. 42 did not specify a maximum acceptable goodwill life, practice evolved to the point where the maximum goodwill life that could be justified to the staff was 25 years.

Statement of Financial Accounting Standards No. 72 "Accounting for Certain Acquisitions of Banking or Thrift Institutions," effective for business combinations initiated after September 30, 1982, essentially requires that for acquisitions of certain institutions (those acquisitions in which the fair value of liabilities assumed exceeds the fair value of tangible and identified intangible assets acquired) goodwill representing the excess of liabilities over assets on a fair value basis must be written off over the life of the long-term interest-bearing assets. Statement No. 72 did not address the amortization period for any remaining goodwill.[1]

In recent years, increasing numbers of financial institutions formed holding companies which became subject to SEC reporting requirements.[2] Some of these financial institutions, prior to the formation of the holding company, entered into business combinations after the issuance of SAB No. 42 on December 23, 1981, and used goodwill amortization periods of greater than 25 years.

Question: Should financial institutions which are amortizing goodwill arising from acquisitions which occurred after December 23, 1981, over periods greater than 25 years adjust such amortization at the time the institutions become SEC registrants?

Interpretive Response: The Commission's staff believes that a new SEC registrant should reexamine its accounting policies and practices prior to its initial filing with the SEC. When a registrant files with the SEC, it is expected to follow the guidance in Staff Accounting Bulletin No. 42. With respect to selection of the appropriate amortization period for goodwill acquired in business combinations after December 23, 1981, the automatic selection of a 40 year amortization period is not appropriate; therefore, a new registrant should be prepared to justify the use of a long amortization period. For business combinations initiated after September 30, 1982, the staff believes that 25 years is the maximum goodwill life that is acceptable.

Ordinarily, a registrant which amended its accounting policy regarding goodwill amortization would be permitted to do so on a prospective basis, providing, of course, that appropriate disclosure of the impact of the prospective change is made in the initial filing.[3] For example, assume a financial institution which previously had amortized goodwill acquired in a January 1, 1983 acquisition over a 40 year period formed a holding company on January 1, 1985, and was thereafter required to file with the SEC. Further assume that the financial institution used a 20 year amortization period for goodwill in financial statements filed with the SEC. In this situation, the institution would amortize the remaining goodwill balance over the remaining 18 years of the 20 year total amortization period, beginning in 1985.

---

[1]The authoritative literature governing the amortization period of remaining goodwill is Accounting Principles Board Opinion No. 17.

[2]Section 12(i) of the Securities Exchange Act of 1934 ("Exchange Act"), provides for federally insured publicly-held banks and savings and loans to file Exchange Act reports with the appropriate bank regulatory agency and the Federal Home Loan Bank Board, respectively, in lieu of filing with the SEC. Holding companies, however, file their reports with the SEC.

[3]It should be noted, however, that if an amortization period previously used was clearly improper because it did not adequately reflect the economic realities of the combination, a registrant would be expected to retroactively restate its financial statements to reflect the selection of an appropriate amortization period. Further, the staff understands that there may have been situations where two or more failing institutions were merged and that such transactions were accounted for as purchases using 40 year goodwill lives. This bulletin does not apply to any such cases, which may require restatement if filed with the Commission.

With regard to the acquisition of banks and thrift institutions, the SEC staff's preference in situations in which value is assigned to identifiable intangibles (such as core deposits of financial institutions) is for such amounts to be amortized using an accelerated method (i.e., a method similar to the double-declining balance depreciation method) over a period that does not exceed ten years. Furthermore, the staff's informal view is that the remaining unallocated amount (goodwill) in a purchase of this nature should be amortized over a period not to exceed 25 years on a straight-line basis. In situations in which value has been allocated to the core deposits, the staff's informal position is that, as a general rule, the amortization period for goodwill should not exceed ten years using an accelerated method.

With respect to financial institution acquisitions, the staff has indicated that it will generally take exception to an amortization period for negative goodwill that is shorter than ten years on a straight-line basis. The staff has indicated that negative goodwill in other industries will be evaluated on the basis of the individual facts and circumstances.

SAB Topic 2-A5, added by SAB No. 61, expresses the staff's views regarding adjustments of allowances for loan losses in connection with business combinations accounted for by the purchase method. In issuing this SAB, the staff was apparently concerned with the potential for abuse in applying the purchase method; however, many accountants believe this SAB may conflict with certain provisions of APB Opinion No. 16. The staff has informally indicated that it may apply the provisions of SAB No. 61 to other reserves of an acquired company (e.g., inventory, bad debt, or warranty provisions) revalued by the acquiring company depending on specific facts and circumstances. The text of the SAB follows:

Adjustments to Allowances for Loan Losses in Connection With Business Combinations

Facts: Bank A acquires Bank B in a transaction to be accounted for by the purchase method in accordance with Accounting Principles Board Opinion No. 16.

Question: Are there circumstances in which it is appropriate for Bank A, in assigning acquisition cost to the loan receivables acquired from Bank B, to adjust Bank B's carrying value for those loans not only to reflect appropriate current interest rates, but also to reflect a different estimate of uncollectibility?[1]

Interpretive Response: Needed changes in allowances for loan losses are ordinarily to be made through provisions for loan losses rather than through purchase accounting adjustments. Except in the limited circumstances discussed below, where Bank A has plans for ultimate recovery of loans acquired from Bank B that are demonstrably different from plans that had served as the basis for Bank B's estimate of loan losses, purchase accounting adjustments reflecting different estimates of uncollectibility may raise questions from the staff as to: (a) the reasonableness of the preacquisition allowance for loan losses recorded by Bank B, or (b) whether the adjustments will have a distortive effect on current or future period financial statements of Bank A. Similar questions may be raised by the staff regarding significant changes in allowances for loan losses that are recorded by a bank shortly before it is acquired.

Estimation of probable loan losses involves judgment, and Bank A and B may differ in their systematic approaches to such estimation. Nevertheless, assuming that appropriate methodology (i.e., giving due consideration to all relevant facts and circumstances affecting collectibility) is followed by each bank, the staff believes that each bank's estimate of the uncollectible portion of Bank B's loan portfolio should fall within a range of acceptability. That is, the staff believes that the uncollectible portion of Bank B's loans as estimated separately by the two banks ordinarily should not be different by an amount that is material to the financial statements of Bank B and, therefore, an adjustment to the net carrying value of Bank B's loan portfolio at the acquisition date to reflect a different estimate of uncollectibility ordinarily would be unnecessary and inappropriate.

SEC 50337. Rule 3-05

However, a purchase accounting adjustment to reflect a different estimate of uncollectibility may be appropriate where Bank A has plans regarding ultimate recovery of certain acquired loans demonstrably different from the plans that had served as the basis for Bank B's estimation of losses on those loans.[2] In such circumstances, Bank B's estimate of uncollectibility for those certain loans may be largely or entirely irrelevant for purposes of determining the net carrying value at which those loans should be recorded by Bank A. For example, if Bank B had intended to hold certain loans to maturity but Bank A plans to sell them, the acquisition cost allocated to those loans should equal the value that currently could be obtained for them in a sale.[3] In that case, Bank A would report those loans as assets held for sale rather than a part of its loan portfolio, and would report them in postacquisition periods at the lower of cost or market value until sold.

The staff does not intend to suggest that an acquiring bank should record acquired loans at an amount that reflects an unreasonable estimate of un-collectibility. If Bank B's financial statements as of the acquisition date are not fairly stated in accordance with generally accepted accounting principles because of an unreasonable allowance for loan losses, that allowance for loan losses should not serve as a basis for recording the acquired loans. Rather, Bank B's preacquisition financial statements should be restated to reflect an appropriate allowance, with the resultant adjustment being applied to the restated preacquisition income statement of Bank B for the period(s) in which the events or changes in conditions that gave rise to the needed change in the allowance occurred.

---

[1]Under APB Opinion No. 16, the guideline for allocating acquisition cost to receivables is ". . . at present values of amounts to be received determined at appropriate current interest rates, less allowances for uncollectibility and collection costs, if necessary."

[2]A bank's plans for recovering the net carrying value of certain individual loans or groups of loans may differ from its plans regarding other loans. The plan for recovering the net carrying value of a loan might be, for example, (a) holding the loan to maturity, (b) selling it, or (c) foreclosing on the collateral underlying the loan. The net carrying value of loans should be based on the plan for recovery.

[3]It is not acceptable to recognize losses on loans that are due to concerns as to ultimate collectibility through a purchase accounting adjustment, nor is it acceptable to report such losses as "loss on sale." An excess of carrying value of Bank B's loans over their market value at the acquisition date that is due to concerns as to ultimate collectibility should have been recognized by Bank B through its provision for loan losses.

SAB Topic 2-A6, added by SAB No. 77, sets forth the staff's views regarding the allocation of debt issue costs in a business combination accounted for as a purchase. The staff indicates in this SAB that fees paid to an investment banker in a purchase transaction in which the investment banker is also providing interim financing or

516

underwriting services need to be allocated between direct costs of the acquisition and debt issue costs. The staff provides guidance in determining a reasonable allocation. In addition, the staff believes that debt issue costs of an interim bridge financing should be amortized over the estimated life of *only* the bridge financing.

The text of the SAB follows:

Debt Issue Costs

Facts: Company A is to acquire the net assets of Company B in a transaction to be accounted for as a business combination using the purchase method. In connection with the transaction, Company A has retained an investment banker to provide advisory services in structuring the acquisition and to provide the necessary financing. It is expected that the acquisition will be financed on an interim basis using "bridge financing" provided by the investment banker. Permanent financing will be arranged at a later date through a debt offering, which will be underwritten by the investment banker. Fees will be paid to the investment banker for the advisory services, the bridge financing and the underwriting of the permanent financing. These services may be billed separately or as a single amount.

Question 1: Are all fees paid to the investment banker a direct cost of the acquisition and, as such, accounted for as an element of the purchase price of the business acquired?

Interpretive Response: No. Fees paid to an investment banker in connection with a business combination accounted for as a purchase, when the investment banker is also providing interim financing or underwriting services, must be allocated between direct costs of the acquisition and debt issue costs.

Paragraph 76 of Accounting Principles Board Opinion No. 16[1] and the related Interpretation No. 33 provide that direct costs such as finder's fees and fees paid to outside consultants should be treated as components of the cost of the acquisition, while the costs of registering and issuing any equity securities are treated as a reduction of the otherwise determined fair value of the equity securities. However, debt issue costs are an element of the effective interest cost of the debt, and neither the source of the debt financing nor the use of the debt proceeds changes the nature of such costs. Accordingly, they should not be considered a direct cost of the acquisition.

The portions of the fees allocated to direct costs and to debt issue costs should be representative of the actual services provided. Thus, in making a reasonable allocation (or in determining that an allocation made by the investment banker is reasonable[2]) factors such as (i) the fees charged by investment bankers in connection with other recent bridge financings and (ii) fees charged for advisory services when obtained separately, should normally be considered to determine the relative fair values of the two services. Whether these or other factors are considered, the allocation should normally result in an effective debt service cost (interest and amortization of debt issue costs[3]) which is comparable to the effective cost of other recent debt issues of similar investment risk and maturity. The amount accounted for as debt issue costs should be separately disclosed, if material.[4]

Question 2: May the debt issue costs of the interim "bridge financing" be amortized over the anticipated combined life of the bridge and permanent financings?

Interpretive Response: No. Debt issue costs should be amortized by the interest method over the life of the debt to which they relate. Debt issue costs related to the bridge financing should be recognized as interest cost during the estimated interim period preceding the placement of the permanent financing with any unamortized amounts charged to expense if the bridge loan is repaid prior to the expiration of the estimated period. Where the bridge financing consists of increasing rate debt, the consensus reached by the Financial Accounting Standards Board's Emerging Issues Task Force ("EITF") on this issue[5] should be followed.

---

[1] Accounting Principles Board Opinion No. 16 establishes standards for the reporting of business combinations.

[2] This would apply irrespective of whether the fees for the services were billed as a single amount or separately, since the separate billing of the services implicitly involves an allocation by the investment banker.

[3] See Question 2 regarding the period over which the debt issue costs related to bridge financings should be amortized.

[4] See Rule 5-02-17 of Regulation S-X.

[5] The EITF in Issue 86-15 (May 1, 1986) addressed the accounting for interest expense and debt issue costs for a debt instrument which matures at a stated date, but which may be consecutively extended for specific periods at the option of the borrower until a set, final, maturity date. The interest rate on the debt increases by a specific amount at each renewal/extension ("increasing rate debt"). The EITF reached a consensus that (i) periodic interest cost should be determined using the interest method, based on the estimated outstanding term of the debt taking into consideration the borrower's plans, ability and intent to service the debt, and (ii) debt issue costs should be amortized over the same period used in determining interest cost.

SAB Topic 2-A7, added by SAB 92, discusses the SEC staff's views regarding the accounting and disclosure requirements for contingent liabilities that have been assumed in a business combination that is accounted for as a purchase. The SAB indicates that the guidance contained in FASB Statement No. 5, *Accounting for Contingencies*, and FASB Interpretation No. 14, *Reasonable Estimation of the Amount of a Loss*, should be applied when the fair value of contingencies are not determinable at the date of acquisition. In situations in which the registrant has arranged to obtain additional information during the allocation period specified by

518

FASB Statement No. 38, *Accounting for Preacquisition Contingencies of Purchased Enterprises*, the staff believes that the registrant should:

- Disclose that the purchase price allocation is preliminary;

- Describe the nature of the contingency and include other information that may be available to indicate the potential impact the contingency may have on the final purchase price allocation and the operating results of the registrant subsequent to the acquisition; and

- Include a discussion in MD&A on any unrecognized preacquisition contingency and its reasonably likely effects on operating results, liquidity, and financial condition.

Regarding the allocation period, the staff believes that the period should not exceed the minimum reasonable period required to obtain the information to measure the contingency. The SAB encourages registrants to discuss situations with the staff when the registrant will require more than a one-year allocation period. In addition, the SAB states that the allocation period should not be extended unless information to measure the contingency is known to be obtainable at the time of the initial purchase price allocation. According to the SAB, adjustments to contingent liabilities subsequent to the allocation period are to be recognized in the income statement.

The text of the SAB follows:

Loss Contingencies Assumed in a Business Combination

Facts: A registrant acquires a business enterprise in a transaction accounted for by the purchase method. In connection with the acquisition, the acquiring company assumes certain contingent liabilities of the acquired company.

Question: How should the acquiring company account for and disclose contingent liabilities that have been assumed in a business combination?

Interpretive Response: In accordance with Accounting Principles Board Opinion No. 16, "Business Combinations," the acquiring company should allocate the cost of an acquired company to the assets acquired and liabilities assumed based on their fair values at the date of acquisition. With respect to contingencies for which a fair value is not determinable at the date of acquisition, the guidance of Statement of Financial Accounting Standards No. 5, "Accounting for Contingencies" and Financial Accounting Standards Board Interpretation No. 14, "Reasonable Estimation of the Amount of a Loss" should be applied. If the registrant is awaiting additional information that it has arranged to obtain for the measurement of a contingency during the allocation period specified by Statement of Financial Accounting Standards No. 38, "Accounting for Preacquisition Contingencies of Purchased Enterprises," the staff believes that the registrant should disclose that the purchase price allocation is preliminary. In that circumstance, the registrant should describe the nature of the contingency and furnish other available information that will enable a reader to understand its potential effects on the final allocation and on post-acquisition operating results. Management's Discussion and Analysis should include appropriate disclosure regarding any unrecognized preacquisition contingency and its reasonably likely effects on operating results, liquidity, and financial condition.

The staff believes that the allocation period should not extend beyond the minimum reasonable period necessary to gather the information that the registrant has arranged to obtain for purposes of the estimate. Since an allocation period usually should not exceed one year, registrants believing that they will require a longer period are encouraged to discuss their circumstances with the staff. If it is unlikely that the liability can be estimated on the basis of information known to be obtainable at the time of the initial purchase price allocation, the allocation period should not be extended with respect to that liability. An adjustment to the contingent liability after the expiration of the allocation period would be recognized as an element of net income.

The following informal interpretations relating to purchase accounting have been provided by the SEC staff:

- EITF Issue No. 87-11, "Allocation of Purchase Price to Assets to Be Sold," discusses a purchase transaction, financed with debt, in which the acquiring company identifies one of the acquiree's subsidiaries to be sold within one year of the acquisition. The proceeds from the sale of the subsidiary are to be used to reduce the debt incurred to finance the transaction. Based on the facts and circumstances described in this issue, the EITF reached a consensus based on the premise that the net cash flows associated with:

  - the subsidiary's operations during the holding period;

  - the interest incurred during the holding period on that portion of the debt used to finance the purchase of the subsidiary; and

  - the proceeds from the ultimate sale of the subsidiary

  should be considered in the purchase price allocation of the subsidiary under APB Opinion No. 16. Accordingly, these items should not affect the consolidated income statement of the acquiror. The SEC observer indicated that the consensus differs from the previous SEC staff position that interest cost incurred during the holding period should be included in the acquiror's income statement unless the acquiror had a binding sales agreement at the date of acquisition. The SEC observer indicated, however, that the staff would accept the EITF's consensus provided that the conditions identified in EITF Issue No. 87-11 are met. The SEC staff has indicated that this guidance would also apply to purchase transactions in which selected assets are held for disposition.

- In accounting for a transaction as a combination of entities under common control, the staff has indicated that:

  -- It will require that the common shareholder has ownership of a majority of the voting shares in each of the combining entities; and

  -- Entities under common control that have been combined should be recorded on the historical cost basis, i.e., on an "as-if pooling" basis. The staff has indicated that this position applies not only to stock transactions, but also those including cash or debt. The staff believes that cash distributed or debt incurred in connection with a reorganization should be recorded currently as a nonequity transaction and not pushed back to previous periods. If a minority interest is acquired, purchase accounting should be applied. Further, the staff believes that historical EPS would be misleading and, therefore, should not be presented when a material amount of cash has been distributed or debt incurred in connection with a reorganization. Rather, pro forma financial statements, including pro forma EPS, should be presented for the latest year and any subsequent interim periods giving effect to the transaction, including any increase in the net interest expense.

- Regarding disclosures required in SEC filings involving leveraged buyouts, the staff has indicated that the footnotes of the financial statements should contain details of the cost of the acquisition and allocation of the purchase price.

- With regard to the valuation of consideration in a purchase acquisition, paragraph 74 of APB No. 16 states that "the market price for a reasonable period before and after the date of the acquisition is agreed to and announced should be considered in determining fair value of securities issued." Paragraph 94, on the other hand, states that "the cost of an acquired company and the values assigned to assets acquired and liabilities assumed should be determined as of the date of acquisition." The staff believes that the cost of the acquisition should be determined at the consummation date of the transaction. However, when valuing the consideration to be exchanged, the staff has informally indicated that it generally will accept the use of the market value of the issuer's common stock within a reasonable period of time before and after the date the combination is agreed to and announced. The exceptions to this general rule would involve situations in which there has not been a significant change in the market value of the issuer's common stock after the transaction has been announced to the public.

- Concerning the issue of when a registrant should apply the provisions of the consensus in EITF 88-16, "Basis in Leveraged Buyout Transactions," for LBO transactions, the staff has interpreted the term "highly leveraged transaction" (HLT), and has indicated that if debt financing is used for more than 50 percent (but less than 60 percent) of the cost of the purchase, it will question whether the transaction should be considered an HLT. As a general rule, the staff considers the use of debt financing for 60 percent or more of the cost to be an HLT.

- Regarding the purchase price allocation periods for business combinations, the staff has indicated that it does not believe that SFAS No. 38, *Accounting for Preacquisition Contingencies of Purchased Enterprises*, is intended to provide all companies with the option to keep the purchase price allocation period open for a year. The staff believes that, as a general rule, the allocation period should not be held open solely because the effect of an acquisition contingency cannot be estimated. Paragraph 4b of SFAS No. 38 limits the allocation period to the period while awaiting information known to be obtainable. Furthermore, if a registrant has entered into a business acquisition and there are preacquisition contingency items left open for adjustment pursuant to SFAS No. 38, the staff believes these items should be specifically identified and disclosed. This would apply to interim financial statements if this information was not previously disclosed in the annual financial instruments. Further, the staff believes that information as to the range of outcomes based on material that is currently available also should be disclosed.

The staff anticipates that management of the company will diligently gather information to resolve any uncertainties remaining in a purchase transaction, and that as soon as the appropriate information and estimates have been determined, the purchase price allocation should be adjusted and the allocation period closed.

The staff does not believe that SFAS No. 38 is intended to provide a one-year "window" available to all companies to handle general uncertainties that arise in a purchase transaction. In summary, the staff believes that SFAS No. 38 is primarily intended to assist companies that have made an acquisition in a hostile environment where they may not have had an opportunity to perform the necessary due-diligence procedures. In any case, any registrant who believes that an uncertainty will extend beyond one year would be well advised to contact the SEC staff to discuss the situation.

SEC Views on "Push Down" Accounting

SAB Topic 5-J discusses the staff's views on the application of the "push down" basis of accounting in the separate financial statements of subsidiaries acquired in purchase transactions. Under the "push down" theory, when a major change in the ownership of a company's voting stock occurs, the economic effect of that change should be reflected (pushed down) in the financial statements of the acquired company. The SEC staff believes that "push down" accounting should be used when a purchase acquisition results in an entity's becoming "substantially wholly owned" as defined in Rule 1-02(z) of Regulation S-X (see section 50102). As a general rule the staff will insist that "push down" accounting be followed any time the separate financial statements of the acquired entity are included in an SEC filing as, for example, in:

- Registration statements of a subsidiary when the subsidiary is registering either stock or debt.

- Separate financial statements of a subsidiary included in its parent's 1933 or 1934 Act filings pursuant to Rule 3-09.

- Summarized financial information on unconsolidated subsidiaries included in the footnotes of the parent's consolidated financial statements pursuant to Rule 4-08(g).

- Separate financial statements of a subsidiary included in a merger proxy statement at the time of sale by its parent.

The staff encourages but generally does not insist on the application of "push down" accounting when the subsidiary has publicly held debt or preferred stock that has been registered with the SEC. The text of the SAB follows:

Push Down Basis of Accounting Required in Certain Limited Circumstances

Facts: Company A (or Company A and related persons) acquired substantially all of the common stock of Company B in one or a series of purchase transactions.

SEC 50337. Rule 3-05

Question 1: Must Company B's financial statements presented in either its own or Company A's subsequent filings with the Commission reflect the new basis of accounting arising from Company A's acquisition of Company B when Company B's separate corporate entity is retained?

Interpretive Response: Yes. The staff believes that purchase transactions that result in an entity becoming substantially wholly owned (as defined in Rule 1-02(z) of Regulation S-X) establish a new basis of accounting for the purchased assets and liabilities. When the form of ownership is within the control of the parent the basis of accounting for purchased assets and liabilities should be the same regardless of whether the entity continues to exist or is merged into the parent's operations. Therefore, Company A's cost of acquiring Company B should be "pushed down," i.e., used to establish a new accounting basis in Company B's separate financial statements.[1]

---

[1]The Task Force on Consolidation Problems, Accounting Standards Division of the American Institute of Certified Public Accountants issued a paper entitled "Push Down" Accounting, October 30, 1979. This paper addresses the issues relating to "push down" accounting, cites authoritative literature and indicates that a substantial change in ownership justifies a new basis of accounting. The AICPA submitted the paper to the FASB with a recommendation that the Board consider the issue. The FASB has included push down accounting as an issue to be addressed in its major project on consolidation accounting. [Note: As an update to this footnote, the FASB continues to address this issue in the new basis accounting portion of its project on consolidations and related matters. In December 1991 a Discussion Memorandum, "New Basis Accounting," was issued that included the purchase transaction discussed in the AICPA's Issues Paper as well as other matters leading to questions about an entity's basis of accounting and reporting.]

Question 2: What is the staff's position if Company A acquired less than substantially all of the common stock of Company B or Company B had publicly held debt or preferred stock at the time Company B became wholly owned?

Interpretive Response: The staff recognizes that the existence of outstanding public debt, preferred stock or a significant minority interest in a subsidiary might impact the parent's ability to control the form of ownership. Although encouraging its use, the staff generally does not insist on the application of push down accounting in these circumstances.

Question 3: Company A borrows funds to acquire substantially all of the common stock of Company B. Company B subsequently files a registration statement in connection with a public offering of its stock or debt.[1] Should Company B's new basis ("push down") financial statements include Company A's debt related to its purchase of Company B?

Interpretive Response: The staff believes that Company A's debt[2], related interest expense, and allocable debt issue costs should be reflected in Company B's financial statements included in the public offering (or an initial registration under the Exchange Act) if: (1) Company B is to assume the debt of Company A, either presently or in a planned transaction in the future; (2) the proceeds of a debt or equity offering of Company B will be used to retire all or a part of Company A's debt; or (3) Company B guarantees or pledges its assets as collateral for Company A's debt.

Other relationships may exist between Company A and Company B, such as the pledge of Company B's stock as collateral for Company A's debt.[3] While in this latter situation, it may be clear that Company B's cash flows will service all or part of Company A's debt, the staff does not insist that the debt be reflected in Company B's financial statements providing there is full and prominent disclosure of the relationship between Companies A and B and the actual or potential cash flow commitment. In this regard, the staff believes that Statements of Financial Accounting Standards Nos. 5 and 57 require sufficient disclosure to allow users of Company B's financial statements to fully understand the impact of the relationship on Company B's present and future cash flows. Rule 4-08(e) of Regulation S-X also requires disclosure of restrictions which limit the payment of dividends. Therefore, the staff believes that the equity section of Company B's balance sheet and any pro forma financial information and capitalization tables should clearly disclose that this arrangement exists.[4]

Regardless of whether the debt is reflected in Company B's financial statements, the notes to Company B's financial statements should generally disclose, at a minimum: (1) the relationship between Company A and Company B; (2) a description of any arrangements that result in Company B's guarantee, pledge of assets[5] or stock, etc. that provides security for Company A's debt; (3) the extent (in the aggregate and for each of the five years subsequent to the date of the latest balance sheet presented) to which Company A is dependent on Company B's cash flows to service its debt and the method by which this will occur; and (4) the impact of such cash flows on Company B's ability to pay dividends or other amounts to holders of its securities.

Additionally, the staff believes Company B's Management's Discussion and Analysis of Financial Condition and Results of Operations should discuss any material impact of its servicing of Company A's debt on its own liquidity pursuant to Item 303(a) (1) of Regulation S-K.

---

[1]The guidance in this Staff Accounting Bulletin should also be considered for Company B's separate financial statements included in its public offering following Company B's spin-off or carve-out from Company A.

[2]The guidance in this Staff Accounting Bulletin should also be considered where Company A has financed the acquisition of Company B through the issuance of mandatorily redeemable preferred stock.

[3]The staff does not believe Company B's financial statements must reflect the debt in this situation because in the event of default on the debt by Company A, the debt holder(s) would only be entitled to B's stock held by Company A. Other

equity or debt holders of Company B would retain their priority with respect to the net assets of Company B.

[4]For example, the staff has noted that certain registrants have indicated on the face of such financial statements (as part of the stockholders' equity section) the actual or potential financing arrangement and the registrant's intent to pay dividends to satisfy its parent's debt service requirements. The staff believes such disclosures are useful to highlight the existence of arrangements that could result in the use of Company B's cash to service Company A's debt.

[5]A material asset pledge should be clearly indicated on the face of the balance sheet. For example, if all or substantially all of the assets are pledged, the "assets" and "total assets" captions should include parenthetically: "pledged for parent company debt —See Note X."

Questions often arise as to the acceptability of push down accounting in situations in which ownership changes are less than 100 percent. As a general rule the SEC staff requires push down when the ownership change is greater than 95 percent (unless the entity has outstanding public debt), permits push down if the change is between 80 and 95 percent, and objects to push down when the ownership change is less than 80 percent.

50338. Rule 3-06. Financial Statements Covering a Period of Nine to Twelve Months

Except with respect to registered investment companies, the filing of financial statements covering a period of nine to twelve months shall be deemed to satisfy a requirement for filing financial statements for a period of one year where:

(a) the issuer has changed its fiscal year;

(b) the issuer has made a significant business acquisition for which financial statements are required under Rule 3-05 of Regulation S-X [see section 50317] and the financial statements covering the interim period pertain to the business being acquired; or

(c) the Commission so permits pursuant to Rule 3-13 of Regulation S-X.

Where there is a requirement for filing financial statements for a time period exceeding one year but not exceeding three consecutive years (with not more than 12 months included in any period reported upon), the filing of financial statements covering a period of nine to 12 months shall satisfy a filing requirement of financial statements for one year of that time period only if the conditions described in either paragraph (a), (b), or (c) of this section exist and financial statements are filed that cover the full fiscal year or years for all other years in the time period.

In FRR No. 35, the Commission adopted Rule 3-06 of Regulation S-X, which provides that, under specified conditions, the filing of financial statements covering a period of (no less than) nine months will be deemed to be the equivalent of one year for SEC filing purposes. However, the effect of the rule is that if financial statements covering a multiple-year period are required, only one period of between nine and twelve months is generally permissible. No single period in excess of 12 months may be presented.

50339. Rule 3-09. Separate Financial Statements of Subsidiaries Not Consolidated and 50 Percent-or-Less-Owned Persons

(a) If any of the conditions set forth in Rule 1-02(v), substituting 20 percent for 10 percent in the tests used therein to determine a significant subsidiary, are met for a majority-owned subsidiary not consolidated by the registrant or by a subsidiary of the registrant, separate financial statements of such subsidiary shall be filed. Similarly, if any of the conditions set forth therein, substituting 20 percent for 10 percent, are met by a 50 percent-or-less-owned person accounted for by the equity method either by the registrant or a subsidiary of the registrant, separate financial statements of such 50 percent-or-less-owned person shall be filed.

(b) Insofar as practicable, the separate financial statements required by this section shall be as of the same dates and for the same periods as the audited consolidated financial statements required by Rules 3-01 and 3-02. However, these separate financial statements are required to be audited only for those fiscal years in which any of the conditions described in Rule 1-02(v), substituting 20 percent for 10 percent, are met. For purposes of a filing on Form 10-K, if the fiscal year of any majority-owned subsidiary not consolidated or any 50 percent-or-less-owned person ends within 90 days before the date of filing, or if the fiscal year ends after the date of filing, the required financial statements may be filed as an amendment to the report within 90 days after the end of such subsidiary's or person's fiscal year.

(c) Notwithstanding the requirements for separate financial statements in paragraph (a) of this section, where financial statements of two or more majority-owned subsidiaries not consolidated are required, combined or consolidated statements of such subsidiaries may be filed subject to principles of inclusion and exclusion which clearly exhibit the financial position, cash flows and results of operations of the combined or consolidated group. Similarly, where financial statements of two or more 50 percent-or-less-owned persons are required, combined or consolidated statements of such persons may be filed subject to the same principles of inclusion or exclusion referred to above.

SEC 50338. Rule 3-06

50340. General Comments on Presenting Information for Unconsolidated Subsidiaries and 50 Percent-or-Less-Owned Persons

Paragraph 20(d) of APB Opinion No. 18 states that "when investments in common stock of corporate joint ventures or other investments accounted for under the equity method are, in the aggregate, material in relation to the financial position or results of operations of an investor, it may be necessary for summarized information as to assets, liabilities, and results of operations of the investees to be presented in the notes or in separate statements, either individually or in groups, as appropriate." The Regulation S-X requirements for determining whether a material relationship with the investor exists and the manner in which financial information is to be furnished if such a relationship does exist are much more specific than those of APB Opinion No. 18.

Rule 3-09 specifies when full financial statements of the unconsolidated subsidiary and 50 percent-or-less-owned person are to be presented (see discussion in section 50342) and Rule 4-08(g) (section 50408) specifies when summarized financial information is to be presented (see discussion in section 50343). Both rules determine whether a material relationship exists using the definition of a significant subsidiary in Rule 1-02(v) of Regulation S-X (see discussion in section 50341), but Rule 3-09 substitutes a 20 percent materiality threshold for the 10 percent used in Rule 1-02(v).

In 1987, the FASB issued SFAS No. 94, *Consolidation of All Majority-Owned Subsidiaries,* that, among other matters, amended ARB No. 51, *Consolidated Financial Statements,* to require all majority-owned subsidiaries to be consolidated unless control is temporary or does not rest with the majority owner. Reference should be made to that Statement regarding the applicable reporting and disclosure requirements. Because of the requirements of this Statement, the portion of Rule 3-09 relating to unconsolidated subsidiaries has little practical impact.

SAB Topic 5-J discusses the SEC staff's views on the application of the "push down" basis of accounting in the separate financial statements of subsidiaries acquired in purchase transactions. The text of this SAB as well as other staff views on the subject are included in section 50337 of this manual.

SAB Topic 6-K4(a) discusses the disclosure of separate financial statements of third-tier subsidiaries and investees of unconsolidated subsidiaries and equity persons (Rule 3-09) when they are significant. The SAB points out that financial statements of third-tier companies may have to be furnished if they are "significant" in relation to the "registrant." The text of the SAB follows:

Separate Financial Statement Requirements

Facts: Rule 3-09 of Regulation S-X requires the presentation of separate financial statements of unconsolidated subsidiaries and of 50% or less owned persons (investee) accounted for by the equity method either by the registrant or by a subsidiary of the registrant in filings with the Commission if any of the tests of a significant subsidiary are met at a 20% level.

Question 1: Are the requirements for separate financial statements also applicable to an investee accounted for by the equity method by an investee of the registrant?

Interpretive Response: Yes. Rule 3-09 is intended to apply to all investees which are material to the financial position or results of operations of the registrant, regardless of whether the investee is held by the registrant, a subsidiary or another investee. Separate financial statements should be provided for any lower tier investee where such an entity is significant to the registrant's consolidated financial statements.

Question 2: How is the significant subsidiary test applied to the lower tier investee in the situation described in Question 1?

Interpretive Response: Since the disclosures provided by separate financial statements of an investee are considered necessary to evaluate the overall financial condition of the registrant, the significant subsidiary test is computed based on the materiality of the lower tier investee to the registrant consolidated. An example of the application of the assets test of the significant subsidiary rules to such an investee situation will illustrate the materiality measurement. A registrant with total consolidated assets of $5000 owns 50% of Investee A, whose total assets are $3800. Investee A has a 45% investment in Investee B, whose total assets are $4800. There are no intercompany eliminations. Separate financial statements are required for Investee A, and they are required for Investee B because the registrant's share of B's total assets exceeds 20% of consolidated assets [(50% x 45% x $4800)/$5000 = 22%].

50341. Significant Subsidiary Determination

The following definition of a significant subsidiary is included in Regulation S-X Rule 1-02(v):

(v) **Significant Subsidiary.** The term "significant subsidiary" means a subsidiary, including its subsidiaries, which meets any of the following conditions:

(1) The registrant's and its other subsidiaries' investments in and advances to the subsidiary exceed 10 percent of the total assets of the registrant and its subsidiaries consolidated as of the end of the most recently completed fiscal year (for a proposed business combination to be accounted for as a pooling of interests, this condition is also met when the number of common shares exchanged or to be exchanged by the registrant exceeds 10 percent of its total common shares outstanding at the date the combination is initiated); or

(2) The registrant's and its other subsidiaries' proportionate share of the total assets (after intercompany eliminations) of the subsidiary exceeds 10 percent of the total assets of the registrant and its subsidiaries consolidated as of the end of the most recently completed fiscal year; or

(3) The registrant's and its other subsidiaries' equity in the income from continuing operations before income taxes, extraordinary items and cumulative effect of a change in accounting principle of the subsidiary exceeds 10 percent of such income of the registrant and its subsidiaries consolidated for the most recently completed fiscal year.

Computational note: For purposes of making the prescribed income test the following guidance should be applied:

1. When a loss has been incurred by either the parent and its subsidiaries consolidated or the tested subsidiary, but not both, the equity in the income or loss of the tested subsidiary should be excluded from the income of the registrant and its subsidiaries consolidated for purposes of the computation.

2. If income of the registrant and its subsidiaries consolidated for the most recent fiscal year is at least 10 percent lower than the average of the income for the last five fiscal years, such average income should be substituted for purposes of the computation. Any loss years should be omitted for purposes of computing average income.

3. Where the test involves combined entities, as in the case of determining whether summarized financial data should be presented, entities reporting losses shall not be aggregated with entities reporting income.

The foregoing rule requires calculations with respect to (1) investments and advances, (2) the proportionate share of the total assets (after intercompany eliminations), and (3) income from continuing operations. An entity is deemed "significant" if it meets *any* of these tests. When used in connection with Rule 4-08(g), the calculation is required to be made on an aggregate basis and the unconsolidated subsidiaries and 50 percent-or-less-owned persons considered one group, even though they may not be combined when presenting summarized financial information.

For purposes of Rule 3-09, the test in Rule 1-02(v) is to be applied by substituting 20 percent for 10 percent. (For purposes of Rule 3-05 and for reporting on Form 8-K, an additional calculation is required. When shares are issued in a business combination accounted for as a pooling of interests, the acquired company would also constitute a significant subsidiary when the number of common shares issued by the acquiring company in connection with the acquisition exceeds 10 percent of the total common shares outstanding at the date the combination is initiated.)

The calculation of the proportionate share of the total assets (Rule 1-02(v)(2)) requires elimination of intercompany accounts. An existing interpretation (as published in the December 1974 issue of the *Journal of Accountancy*) discusses the intercompany eliminations to be considered. The interpretation points out that:

- Receivables *from members of the consolidated group* of the tested subsidiary should be eliminated before determining the consolidated group's proportionate share of total assets of the tested subsidiary.

- Receivables *from unconsolidated subsidiaries and 50 percent-or-less-owned persons* of the tested subsidiary should not be eliminated before determining the consolidated group's proportionate share of total assets of the tested subsidiary.

- No adjustments would be made to consolidated assets included in the denominator of the fraction, since all appropriate intercompany eliminations are already made in consolidation.

- Although the phrase "after intercompany eliminations" is not used in Rule 1-02(v)(3), adjustments to income from continuing operations for intercompany profits should be made to the entity being tested similar to those made in recording earnings of the entity in consolidation.

The following informal interpretations relating to the application of the significance tests have been provided by the SEC staff:

- For a business combination accounted for as a purchase, the registrant's investment in (or consideration paid for) an acquiree should be compared to the registrant's consolidated assets.

  - Contingent consideration in a business combination should be considered as part of the total investment in the acquiree when making the calculations to determine whether an acquired business is "significant" unless its payment is deemed remote.

- With regard to the aggregation of individually insignificant acquisitions, separate calculation should be performed for profitable entities and those with losses. Each group should then be measured separately against the consolidated totals.

- When applying the significance test to foreign acquisitions, the calculations should generally be based on U.S. GAAP data. If the foreign company's financial statements are prepared in accordance with the accounting principles of another country, the test should generally be applied after adjusting those financial statements to U.S. GAAP.

SEC 50341. Rule 3-09

- The calculation of the significant subsidiary test for a business combination should be performed on a stand-alone basis. That is, the target company's balances should not be added to the registrant's amounts.

- In the calculation of the income test, the staff will consider adjustment for both the registrant and subsidiary for an event or transaction not reasonably expected to recur in the foreseeable future.

- The registrant may not exclude that portion of a business acquired that it expects to dispose of in calculating the significant subsidiary test. If there is a reasonable expectation of sale within one year and the registrant meets the conditions in EITF 87-11 for the allocation of purchase price to assets to be sold for purposes of calculating the significant subsidiary test, the registrant may present the assets held for sale net of related liabilities.

- Computational note 2 to Rule 1.02(v) states that when the registrant's most recent earnings are at least 10 percent lower than its average for the most recent five years, such average may be used in evaluating a subsidiary's significance. Computational note 2 also permits exclusion of loss years from this average. The staff has indicated that in such cases, average income should be computed with loss years assigned a value of zero in computing the numerator and the denominator should be "5." In addition, the staff has indicated that the earnings of the subsidiary being tested may not be averaged.

  - If a registrant has reported a loss in its most recent year, the five-year averaging method is not permitted; the significance of a subsidiary should be evaluated relative to the absolute value of the most recent year's loss.

- If the registrant acquires 95 percent of a company, the asset and income test may be calculated based on the proportionate share, or 95 percent, of the respective amounts unless the registrant intends to acquire the remaining interest or the minority interest is held by related parties.

- Where only direct revenues and expenses of a lesser component are available, the excess of revenues over expenses may be compared to the comparable amount of the registrant; however, if the component's expenses exceed revenues, other expected costs of operations also need to be considered in the evaluation of significance.

- For a pooling or reorganization, the number of shares exchanged should be compared with the registrant's outstanding shares immediately before the combination.

- If a registrant increases its investment in a business relative to the prior year, the tests of significance should be based on the increase in the registrant's proportionate interest in assets and net income during the year, rather than the cumulative interest to date.

- Trade receivables not acquired should be included in making the tests of significance on the theory that working capital will be required for this purpose after the acquisition.

- A registrant's assets may not be increased to reflect the pro forma effect of anticipated public offering proceeds for purposes of making the significant subsidiary tests.

- If an investee was significant in an earlier year but is not significant in the latest year, the SEC staff will consider a waiver of the requirement to provide the investee's financial statements if the registrant can demonstrate that the investee is likely to remain insignificant in future years.

Additional guidance provided by the SEC staff is as follows:

- Under certain situations, the staff may agree to accept audited statements of assets and liabilities acquired and revenues and expenses directly related to the business if the registrant can clearly demonstrate that it is impracticable to prepare the full financial statements required by Regulation S-X, and the registrant includes this explanation in the filing. Unallocated items (corporate overhead, interest, taxes) may be excluded from these statements, but amounts of this nature expected after the acquisition should be reflected in the pro forma statements.

- If none of the conditions exceeds 10 percent, financial statements are not required. However, if the aggregate impact of the individually insignificant businesses acquired since the date of the most recent audited balance sheet filed for the registrant exceeds 20 percent for any of the tests, financial statements covering at least the substantial majority of the businesses acquired, combined if appropriate, should be furnished for the most recent fiscal year and the latest interim period preceding the acquisition.

SEC 50341. Rule 3-09

•• In determining the financial statements to be provided for at least the substantial majority of the businesses acquired, audited financial statements should be furnished with respect to at least a mathematical majority of the acquirees (i.e., more than 50 percent of combined assets, pre-tax income and investment.)

50342. Separate Financial Statements

Separate financial statements are required only when the entities for which the calculation is made individually meet the significant subsidiary test in Rule 1-02(v), substituting a 20 percent materiality threshold for the 10 percent used in the rule. FRP Section 213.03.a points out that when separate financial statements are required, they "should comply with all provisions of Regulation S-X, including the schedule requirements." It also indicates that separate statements "are required in [filings] with the Commission, but not in annual reports to security holders."

Paragraph (b) of Rule 3-09 states that when separate financial statements are required for unconsolidated subsidiaries or 50 percent-or-less-owned persons, they should be presented as of the same dates and for the same periods as the *audited* consolidated statements in accordance with Rules 3-01 and 3-02 (balance sheets should be as of the two latest fiscal years and all other statements should cover the three latest fiscal years). Consequently, the updating requirements for 1933 Act registration statements (as discussed in sections 50301, 50302, and 50346) are not applicable to such entities. The supplementary (narrative) information originally included in ASR No. 281 makes this clear by stating that the rules adopted by the release "eliminate the interim period requirements for separate financial statements for separate entities such as parent company only, unconsolidated subsidiaries or 50 percent-or-less-owned persons."

Paragraph (b) of Rule 3-09 also defines the extent to which the separate financial statements are required to be audited. The rule permits the presentation of prior years' financial statements on an unaudited basis for years in which an entity was not significant. Consequently, financial statements for prior years need only be presented on an audited basis if the entity would have constituted a significant subsidiary in that year using a 20 percent materiality threshold.

Paragraph (c) of Rule 3-09 allows separate financial statements of more than one unconsolidated subsidiary or 50 percent-or-less-owned person to be presented on a combined or consolidated basis. Judgment needs to be exercised in determining whether a particular grouping of companies results in a reasonable financial presentation; however, financial statements of unconsolidated subsidiaries may not be combined with those of 50 percent-or-less-owned persons.

SEC 50342

50343. Summarized Financial Information

Rule 4-08(g) (section 50408-g) requires the presentation of summarized financial information for *all* unconsolidated subsidiaries and 50 percent-or-less-owned persons when in the *aggregate* they constitute a "significant subsidiary" as defined in Rule 1-02(v). FRP Section 213.03.b emphasizes that none may be omitted by stating that "since the Commission believes that the summarized information should be complete, requests for permission to omit some entities from the summarized financial information will not be granted in a routine manner."

Summarized financial information should generally be included in the footnotes to the primary financial statements and, insofar as is practicable, should cover the same dates and periods for which audited primary financial statements are required. However, the information with respect to unconsolidated subsidiaries may not be combined with that for 50 percent-or-less-owned persons.

Rule 1-02(aa) (section 50102) specifies the detailed information covering assets, liabilities, and results of operations to be provided but permits some flexibility for specialized industries for which other information may be more meaningful. A bank, for example, could present total interest income, total interest expense, provision for loan losses, and security gains and losses in lieu of sales related costs and expenses. Similarly, an insurance company could present information as to net premiums earned, net investment income, underwriting costs and expenses, and realized gains or losses on investments. The adoptive release indicated that additional disclosures with respect to summarized financial information are not necessary unless they are deemed "material to the consolidated financial statements of the primary reporting entity."

Note that the summarized financial information is also required to include those entities for which separate financial statements have been furnished pursuant to Rule 3-09, except when separate financial statements of those entities are included in the annual report to shareholders. SAB Topic 6-K4(b) points out that if separate or condensed financial statements of significant unconsolidated subsidiaries are included in an annual report to shareholders, the summarized data pursuant to Rule 4-08(g) is not required. In addition, the SAB states that pursuant to Rule 4-08(g), summarized information must cover all entities; however, the staff indicates that the exclusion of such data is appropriate for certain entities where it is impractical to gather the information and such information is de minimis. The text of the SAB follows:

Summarized Financial Statement Requirements

Facts: Rule 4-08-g of Regulation S-X requires summarized financial information about unconsolidated subsidiaries and 50% or less owned persons (investee) to be included in the footnotes to the financial statements if, in the aggregate, they meet the tests of a significant subsidiary set forth in Rule 1-02(v).

Question 1: Must a registrant which includes separate financial statements or condensed financial statements for unconsolidated subsidiaries or investees in its annual report to shareholders also include in such report the summarized financial information for these entities pursuant to Rule 4-08(g)?

Interpretive Response: No. The purpose of the summarized information is to provide minimum standards of disclosure when the impact of such entities on the consolidated financial statements is significant. If the registrant furnishes more information in the annual report than is required by these minimum disclosure standards, such as condensed financial information or separate audited financial statements, the summarized data can be excluded. The Commission's rules are not intended to conflict with the provisions of APB Opinion No. 18, par. 20(c) and (d), which provide that either separate financial statements of investees be presented with the financial statements of the reporting entity or that summarized information be included in the reporting entity's financial statement footnotes.

Question 2: Can summarized information be omitted for individual entities as long as the aggregate information for the omitted entity(s) does not exceed 10% under any of the significance tests of Rule 1-02(v)?

Interpretive Response: The 10% measurement level of the significant subsidiary rule was not intended to establish a materiality criteria for omission, and the arbitrary exclusion of summarized information for selected entities up to a 10% level is not appropriate. Rule 4-08(g) requires that the summarized information be included for all unconsolidated subsidiaries and investees. However, the staff recognizes that exclusion of the summarized information for certain entities is appropriate in some circumstances where it is impracticable to accumulate such information and the summarized information to be excluded is de minimis.

50344. Rule 3-10. Financial Statements of Guarantors and Affiliates Whose Securities Collateralize an Issue Registered or Being Registered

(a) For each guarantor of any class of securities of a registrant and for each of the registrant's affiliates whose securities constitute a substantial portion of the collateral for any class of securities registered or being registered, there shall be filed the financial statements that would be required if the guarantor or affiliate were a registrant and required to file financial statements. However, financial statements need not be filed pursuant to this provision for any person whose statements are otherwise separately included in the filing on an individual basis or on a basis consolidated with its subsidiaries.

(b) For the purposes of this instruction, securities of a person shall be deemed to constitute a substantial portion of collateral if the aggregate principal amount, par value, or book value as carried by the registrant, or market value of such securities, whichever is the greatest, equals 20 percent or more of the principal amount of the secured class of securities.

536

The requirement for financial statements pursuant to this rule includes those of guarantors of securities registered or being registered. Such financial statements are required since they are considered necessary for an assessment of the ability of the guarantor to satisfy the commitment. The supplementary (narrative) information originally included in ASR No. 302 (FRP Section 213.05), which amended Rule 3-10 to include guarantors, points out that such statements have usually been required despite the lack of specificity in the prior rule. The adoptive release states that "to clarify the Commission's practice, the rules have been amended to specify that separate financial statements of guarantors are required in Commission filings."

If the securities of an affiliate constitute or are to constitute a "substantial" portion of the collateral of any class of securities being registered (or that are registered), this rule also specifies that the financial statements of that affiliate need to be included in the document being filed. For example, under this rule financial statements would be required when, in connection with an offering of debentures by a subsidiary, its parent pledges the stock of another subsidiary to collateralize the debt. In this case the financial statements of the subsidiary whose securities are pledged as collateral would need to be included in the registration statement or report in the same form and for the same periods as those of the subsidiary registering the debt, assuming the criteria described in the rule are met.

SAB Topic 1-G discusses the financial statement requirements in filings involving the guarantee of securities by a parent and indicates that in certain circumstances full financial statement disclosure by the issuer of the guaranteed security may be unnecessary. The text of the SAB follows:

Financial Statement Requirements in Filings
Involving the Guarantee of Securities by a Parent

Facts: Company B files a registration statement under the Securities Act of 1933 (the "Securities Act") involving the issuance of debt guaranteed by its parent, Company A. Company B is a consolidated subsidiary of Company A.

Question 1: Must Company B's registration statement always contain all of the financial statements specified by the applicable registration form?

Interpretive Response: No, provided that certain conditions are met.

The disclosure provisions of the Securities Act generally mandate full disclosure for each issuer that is registering the sale of its securities. Because the registration of a guaranteed security involves the registration of two securities[1], each by a separate issuer, the general requirement is for full financial statement disclosure by both the issuer of the guaranteed security and the guarantor of that security. The staff believes, however, that under certain circumstances full financial statement disclosure by the issuer of the guaranteed security may be unnecessary. The appropriate disclosure for the issuer of the guaranteed security will depend on the nature of that entity in relation to the guarantor and the nature of the guarantee.

SEC 50344. Rule 3-10

The staff is of the view that such factors can justify three levels of disclosure: no separate disclosure, summarized disclosure and full disclosure.

No Separate Disclosure. Where the issuer of the guaranteed security is wholly owned (as defined in Rule 1-02(z) of Regulation S-X) by the guarantor and essentially has no independent operations, and where the guarantee is full and unconditional, the staff generally will not require separate financial statements of the issuer of the guaranteed security because the consolidated financial statements of the guarantor parent are adequate for the protection of investors. Subsidiaries that typically fall into this category are foreign financing subsidiaries, export-import subsidiaries, and other entities that function essentially as special purpose divisions of the parent. In these cases, the investor's investment decision is based on the credit worthiness of the guarantor.

Summarized Disclosure. Where the issuer of the guaranteed security is wholly owned by the guarantor but has more than minimal independent operations of its own, and where the guarantee is full and unconditional, the staff generally will not require the issuer of the guaranteed security to present all the financial information specified by the applicable registration form if the registration statement contains summarized financial information regarding the subsidiary. Such information should include at least that described in the definition of "summarized financial information" in Rule 1-02(aa)(1) of Regulation S-X. The summarized financial information should be included in the footnotes to the audited consolidated financial statements of the guarantor parent, and should be as of the same dates and for the same periods as the consolidated financial statements.

Full Disclosure. Where the issuer of the guaranteed security is not wholly owned by the guarantor, or where the guarantee is not full and unconditional, the staff generally will require the issuer subsidiary to include all the financial statements required by the applicable registration form as well as the financial statements of the guarantor parent.

Question 2: What financial statements of the issuer subsidiary must be included in reports filed pursuant to the Securities Exchange Act of 1934 (the "Exchange Act")?

Interpretive Response: Generally, the staff will apply the same criteria used in determining the level of disclosure for the issuer of a guaranteed security under the Securities Act to govern questions regarding that issuer's reporting obligations under the Exchange Act. Thus, if the issuer of a guaranteed security falls into the first category above—that is, it is wholly owned, it essentially has no independent operations, and the guarantee is full and unconditional—separate financial information for the issuer will generally be unnecessary. If the issuer of the guaranteed security falls into the second category above—that is, it is wholly owned, it has more than minimal independent operations of its own, and the guarantee is full and unconditional—it generally will be sufficient to include summarized financial information about the issuer subsidiary in the notes to the parent guarantor's consolidated financial statements.[2] Finally, if the issuer of the guaranteed security is in the third category above—that is, it is not wholly owned by the guarantor or the guarantee is not full and unconditional—the issuer of the guaranteed security would have to satisfy all Exchange Act reporting obligations.

---

[1]See Section 2(1) of the Securities Act.

[2]Further, in situations where the parent guarantor of an issuer subsidiary in either the first or second category is a reporting company under the Exchange Act, upon application to the Commission such a subsidiary would be conditionally exempted pursuant to Section 12(h) of the Exchange Act from reporting obligations under such Act.

SAB Topic 1-H discusses the financial statement requirements in filings involving the guarantee of securities by a subsidiary and clarifies the relationship of the requirements of Rule 3-10 to those of Rule 3-09. The text of the SAB follows:

Financial Statement Requirements in Filings Involving the Guarantee of Securities by a Subsidiary

Facts: Company A files a registration statement involving the issuance of debt guaranteed by its subsidiary, Company B.

Question 1: Does Rule 3-10(a) of Regulation S-X require the inclusion in the registration statement of the financial statements of Company B?

Interpretive Response: In the relatively infrequent situations where a registration statement covers the issuance by a parent of a security that is guaranteed by its subsidiary, the staff has concluded that, as a general rule, financial statements for both of the issuers would be material to the investment decision.[1]

---

[1]Rule 3-10(a) of Regulation S-X recently was amended to reflect the requirement that a guarantor must provide financial statements when the guaranteed security is registered or being registered. . . . Certain registrants have misinterpreted the last sentence of Rule 3-10(a) as requiring only the consolidated financial statements of the parent in situations where a consolidated subsidiary has guaranteed the parent's securities. Under this interpretation registrants have asserted that the guarantor subsidiary's financial statements are filed by virtue of inclusion in the parent's consolidated financial statements. Rather, the last sentence of Rule 3-10(a) clarifies the relationship of the requirements of that rule to those of Rule 3-09. For example, financial statements of an unconsolidated guarantor subsidiary filed pursuant to the requirements of Rule 3-09 on an individual basis or consolidated with its subsidiaries will satisfy the requirements of Rule 3-10(a). However, financial statements of such a guarantor subsidiary filed on a combined basis with other unconsolidated subsidiaries pursuant to Rule 3-09(c) will not satisfy the requirements of Rule 3-10(a).

SEC 50344. Rule 3-10

As discussed in SAB Topic 1-H, if securities are guaranteed by one or more subsidiaries that are consolidated with the registrant, separate financial statements of the subsidiaries are usually required; however, the SEC staff has informally provided the following examples in which this requirement has been modified:

- If all of an issuer's subsidiaries guarantee the security on a full, unconditional, and joint and several basis, no separate or additional financial information about the subsidiaries is required. Also, if the guarantee is unconditional and joint and several, but less than full solely to comply with fraudulent conveyance statutes applicable to the subsidiaries and such limitation is no greater than 10 percent of the subsidiaries' net equity, no separate financial information relative to the subsidiaries is required.

  In such cases the registration statement and subsequent filings on Form 10-K filed by the issuer would need to explain that the financial statements of the guarantor subsidiaries are omitted because all of the issuer's subsidiaries guarantee the security on a full, unconditional, and joint and several basis.

- If some but not all of an issuer's subsidiaries guarantee the security, but the guarantee extended by each of such guarantor subsidiaries is full, unconditional, and joint and several, only summarized financial information of the guarantor subsidiaries is required in an audited footnote to the registrant's financial statements. This concession is only operative, however, if the total assets, net equity and net income of all the subsidiaries not guaranteeing the security on a combined basis are less than 10 percent of the respective amounts reported in the issuer's consolidated financial statements. A statement to this effect would need to be included in the registration statement and subsequent filings on Form 10-K when the guarantor financial statements are omitted and summarized information is presented.

The staff has indicated, however, that in the event that an issuer's default occurs or becomes probable, omission of the separate financial statements of the guarantor subsidiaries is unlikely to be appropriate.

In addition, the staff has indicated that in certain circumstances, in lieu of separate financial statements, it has accepted separate consolidating financial statements that reflect each of the guarantor subsidiaries in separate columns, culminating in the parent's consolidated financial statements in the final column. The staff has also noted that some condensation of financial data may be appropriate when numerous subsidiaries are guarantors, and a single set of footnotes may cover the financial statements for the combined subsidiaries provided disclosure is made of any significant matters to an individual guarantee.

50345. Rule 3-11. Financial Statements of an Inactive Registrant

If a registrant is an inactive entity as defined below, the financial statements required by this regulation for purposes of reports pursuant to the Securities Exchange Act of 1934 may be unaudited. An inactive entity is one meeting all of the following conditions:

> *(a) Gross receipts from all sources for the fiscal year are not in excess of $100,000;*
>
> *(b) The registrant has not purchased or sold any of its own stock, granted options therefor, or levied assessments upon outstanding stock;*
>
> *(c) Expenditures for all purposes for the fiscal year are not in excess of $100,000;*
>
> *(d) No material change in the business has occurred during the fiscal year, including any bankruptcy, reorganization, readjustment or succession, or any material acquisition or disposition of plants, mines, mining equipment, mine rights, or leases; and*
>
> *(e) No exchange upon which the shares are listed, or governmental authority having jurisdiction, requires the furnishing to it or the publication of audited financial statements.*

This rule is primarily applicable to annual reports filed on Form 10-K by development stage companies and dormant registrants.

50346. Rule 3-12. Age of Financial Statements at Effective Date of Registration Statement or at Mailing Date of Proxy Statement

(a) If the financial statements in a filing are as of a date 135 days or more prior to the date the filing is expected to become effective or proposed mailing date in the case of a proxy statement, the financial statements shall be updated, except as specified in the following paragraphs, with a balance sheet as of an interim date within 135 days and with statements of income and cash flows for the interim period between the end of the most recent fiscal year and the date of the interim balance sheet provided and for the corresponding period of the preceding fiscal year. Such interim financial statements may be unaudited and need not be presented in greater detail than is required by Rule 10-01. Notwithstanding the above requirements, the most recent interim financial statements shall be at least as current as the most recent financial statements filed with the Commission on Form 10-Q.

(b) Where the anticipated effective date of a filing, or in the case of a proxy statement the proposed mailing date, falls within 90 days subsequent to the end of the fiscal year,

the filing need not include financial statements more current than as of the end of the third fiscal quarter of the most recently completed fiscal year unless the audited financial statements for such fiscal year are available or unless the anticipated effective date or proposed mailing date falls after 45 days subsequent to the end of the fiscal year and the registrant does not meet the conditions prescribed under paragraph (c) of Rule 3-01. If the anticipated effective date or proposed mailing date falls after 45 days subsequent to the end of the fiscal year and the registrant does not meet the conditions prescribed under paragraph (c) of Rule 3-01, the filing must include audited financial statements for the most recently completed fiscal year.

(c) Where a filing is made near the end of a fiscal year and audited financial statements for that fiscal year are not included in the filing, the filing shall be updated with such audited financial statements if they become available prior to the anticipated effective date, or proposed mailing date in the case of a proxy statement.

(d) The age of the registrant's most recent audited financial statements included in a registration statement filed under the Securities Act of 1933 or filed on Form 10 under the Securities Exchange Act of 1934 shall not be more than one year and 45 days old at the date the registration statement becomes effective if the registration statement relates to the security of an issuer that was not subject, immediately prior to the time of filing the registration statement, to the reporting requirements of Section 13 or 15(d) of the Securities Exchange Act of 1934.

(e) For filings by registered management investment companies, the requirements of Rule 3-18 shall apply in lieu of the requirements of this section.

(f) Any foreign private issuer may file financial statements whose age is specified in Rule 3-19.

This rule requires updating the financial statements included in a filed document to ensure that they are within 135 days of the date the registration statement is expected to become effective. The requirements are similar to those in Rules 3-01 and 3-02, which contain provisions that apply to the filing date; consequently, this rule is discussed with Rules 3-01 and 3-02 (see section 50304).

This updating rule also applies to proxy statements, in which case the proposed mailing date is to be considered in lieu of the expected effective date. In a combination S-4/proxy statement, however, the updating rule is determined by the effective date of the S-4, instead of the proxy mailing date, unless the mailing is unreasonably delayed.

The updated financial statements are required to be as current as the most recent financial statements filed with the Commission on Form 10-Q and audited year-end financial statements should be included if they become available before the effective date.

SEC 50346

As an accommodation to repeat issuers that have filed timely all materials required pursuant to Sections 13 or 15(d) of the 1934 Act for a period of at least 12 months, the SEC staff has indicated that it will not decline to accelerate the effective date provided the latest interim statements in the filing are at least as current as the statements required in the registrant's latest Form 10-Q.

In addition, the SEC staff has indicated that once continuous and shelf offerings are declared effective, they are subject only to the updating requirements of Section 10(a)3. Offers registered on Form F-3, however, require compliance with S-X Rule 3-19 at the start of any delayed offering and throughout a continuous offering pursuant to the Item 512(a)(4) undertaking in Regulation S-K.

50347. Rule 3-13. Filing of Other Financial Statements in Certain Cases

The Commission may, upon the informal written request of the registrant, and where consistent with the protection of investors, permit the omission of one or more of the financial statements herein required or the filing in substitution therefor of appropriate statements of comparable character. The Commission may also by informal written notice require the filing of other financial statements in addition to, or in substitution for, the statements herein required in any case where such statements are necessary or appropriate for an adequate presentation of the financial condition of any person whose financial statements are required, or whose statements are otherwise necessary for the protection of investors.

While the financial statement instructions in Regulation S-X are specific, conditions or circumstances in a particular case may, according to this rule, permit some flexibility on the part of the registrant if exceptions are requested in writing and approved. More importantly, this rule also means that the financial statement requirements are not necessarily all-inclusive and that in a particular case the staff may add to the requirements after reviewing the document. If SEC requirements do not appear to result in the most meaningful presentation or if they present significant hardship to the registrant, the rationale for omitting the required financial statements may be presented to the staff of the SEC for its consideration, usually in advance of the filing. (Refer to section 17120 of this manual for a discussion of prefiling conferences with the SEC.)

50348. Rule 3-14. Special Instructions for Real Estate Operations [Acquired or] to Be Acquired

(a) If, during the period for which income statements are required, the registrant has acquired one or more properties which in the aggregate are significant, or since the date of the latest balance sheet required has acquired or proposes to acquire one or

more properties which in the aggregate are significant, the following shall be furnished with respect to such properties:

(1) Audited income statements (not including earnings per unit) for the three most recent fiscal years, which shall exclude items not comparable to the proposed future operations of the property such as mortgage interest, lease-hold rental, depreciation, corporate expenses and Federal and state income taxes: Provided, however, that such audited statements need be presented for only the most recent fiscal year if (i) the property is not acquired from a related party; (ii) material factors considered by the registrant in assessing the property are described with specificity in the filing with regard to the property, including sources of revenue (including, but not limited to, competition in the rental market, comparative rents, occupancy rates) and expense (including, but not limited to, utility rates, ad valorem tax rates, maintenance expenses, capital improvements anticipated); and (iii) the registrant indicates in the appropriate filing that, after reasonable inquiry, the registrant is not aware of any material factors relating to that specific property other than those discussed in response to paragraph (a)(l)(ii) of this section that would cause the reported financial information not to be necessarily indicative of future operating results.

Note. *The discussion of material factors considered should be combined with that required by Item 15 of Form S-11.*

(2) If the property is to be operated by the registrant, there shall be furnished a statement showing the estimated taxable operating results of the registrant based on the most recent 12-month period including such adjustments as can be factually supported. If the property is to be acquired subject to a net lease the estimated taxable operating results shall be based on the rent to be paid for the first year of the lease. In either case, the estimated amount of cash to be made available by operations shall be shown. There shall be stated in an introductory paragraph the principal assumptions which have been made in preparing the statements of estimated taxable operating results and cash to be made available by operations.

(3) If appropriate under the circumstances, there shall be given in tabular form for a limited number of years the estimated cash distribution per unit showing the portion thereof reportable as taxable income and the portion representing a return of capital together with an explanation of annual variations, if any. If taxable net income per unit will become greater than the cash available for distribution per unit, that fact and approximate year of occurrence shall be stated, if significant.

(b) Information required by this section is not required to be included in a filing on Form 10-K.

This rule is primarily applicable to real estate companies filing registration statements on Forms S-1 and S-11 and is not applicable to annual reports filed on Form 10-K. The SEC staff has informally indicated that financial statements of properties acquired or to be acquired are required when they are significant at the 10 percent level either individually or in the aggregate. The determination of significance is based on the significant subsidiary test discussed in section 50341 of this manual. The determination of significance in the context of this requirement is also discussed in an interpretation of ASR No. 155 (*Journal of Accountancy,* December 1974):

> In determining significance, the guides set forth in the test for significant subsidiary should be observed, except that, as to the income test, the SEC will consider income before depreciation and interest to be an indicative measure. Generally, the data may be combined for all properties.

Audited income statements with respect to the properties are required for the three most recent fiscal years unless the conditions set forth in paragraph (1) are met, in which case the audited income statement for only the most recent fiscal year need be presented. The SEC staff has indicated that the income statements should exclude items that are not comparable to the future operations of the property such as mortgage interest, depreciation, and corporate expense. In these situations, the independent accountants will typically issue a special report such as the one identified in AU Section 623. The staff generally does not require that these statements be updated pursuant to the 135-day rule (section 50308) applicable to the primary financial statements. The financial statements required by paragraph (1) evidently are not expected to reflect results of operations. Consequently, the auditors' report needs to be modified to acknowledge that the financial statements exclude certain elements of historical financial information. Such modifications of the auditors' report are generally acceptable to the SEC. The financial statements, however, need to be audited. An example of an auditors' report to be issued in a situation of this nature is included in AU Section 623.26.

SAB Topic 1-I, added by SAB Nos. 71 and 71A, discusses the staff's views with respect to financial statements of properties securing mortgage loans. In these SABs, the staff sets forth its positions regarding (1) the requirements for financial statements of properties securing mortgage loans; (2) determining the adequacy of a borrower's equity in the underlying property; (3) the financial statements to be furnished for loan arrangements reported as investments in real estate in filings under the 1933 and 1934 Acts; and (4) loans entered into prior to the issuance of these SABs. In particular, the SEC staff indicates that operating properties underlying certain mortgage loans, which in economic substance represent an investment in real estate or a joint venture rather than a loan, are included in the category of properties specified in Rule 3-14. These properties include those having characteristics such as properties securing acquisition development and construction ("ADC") arrangements, in which the lender has prac-

SEC 50348. Rule 3-14

tically the same risks and rewards of the owner or joint venturer and participates in expected residual profit. These characteristics are set forth in the AICPA's February 1986 Notice to Practitioners—ADC Arrangements (referred to as the third Notice). In EITF Issue No. 86-21, "Application of the AICPA Notice to Practitioners Regarding Acquisition, Development and Construction Arrangements to Acquisition of an Operating Property," the EITF reached a consensus that, "although the third Notice was issued to address the real estate ADC arrangements of financial institutions, preparers and auditors should consider the guidance in the third Notice in accounting for shared appreciation mortgages, loans on operating real estate, and real estate ADC arrangements entered into by enterprises other than financial institutions."

The text of SAB Topic 1-I follows:

Financial Statements of Properties Securing Mortgage Loans

Facts: A registrant files a Securities Act registration statement covering a maximum of $100 million of securities. Proceeds of the offering will be used to make mortgage loans on operating residential or commercial property. Proceeds of the offering will be placed in escrow until $1 million of securities are sold, at which point escrow may be broken, making the proceeds immediately available for lending, while the selling of securities would continue.

Question 1: Under what circumstances are the financial statements of a property on which the registrant makes or expects to make a loan required to be included in a filing?

Interpretive Response: Rule 3-14 of Regulation S-X specifies the requirements for financial statements when the registrant has acquired one or more properties which in the aggregate are significant, or since the date of the latest balance sheet required has acquired or proposes to acquire one or more properties which in the aggregate are significant.

Included in the category of properties acquired or to be acquired under Rule 3-14 are operating properties underlying certain mortgage loans which in economic substance represent an investment in real estate or a joint venture rather than a loan. Certain characteristics of a lending arrangement indicate that the "lender" has the same risks and potential rewards as an owner or joint venturer. Those characteristics are set forth in the American Institute of Certified Public Accountants' February 1986 Notice to Practitioners—ADC[1] Arrangements (the "Notice") as published in the April 1986 issue of the Journal of Accountancy. In September 1986 the Financial Accounting Standards Board's Emerging Issues Task Force[2] reached a consensus on this issue[3] to the effect that, although the Notice was issued to address the real estate ADC arrangements of financial institutions, preparers and auditors should consider the guidance contained in the Notice in accounting for shared appreciation mortgages, loans on operating real estate and real estate ADC arrangements entered into by enterprises other than financial institutions. [The AICPA Accounting Standards Executive Committee

(AcSEC) formed a task force in 1989 on ADC arrangements in order to develop implementation guidance on the Notice. This guidance has not yet been issued in final form.]

In certain cases the "lender" has virtually the same potential rewards as those of an owner or a joint venturer by virtue of participating in expected residual profit.[4] In addition, the Notice includes a number of other characteristics which, when considered individually or in combination, would suggest that the risks of an ADC arrangement are similar to those associated with an investment in real estate or a joint venture or, conversely, that they are similar to those associated with a loan. Among those other characteristics is whether the lender agrees to provide all or substantially all necessary funds to acquire the property, resulting in the borrower having title to, but little or no equity in, the underlying property. The staff believes that the borrower's equity in the property is adequate to support accounting for the transaction as a mortgage loan when the borrower's initial investment meets the criteria in paragraph 11 of Statement of Financial Accounting Standards No. 66 ("SFAS 66")[5] and the borrower's payments of principal and interest on the loan are adequate to maintain a continuing investment in the property which meets the criteria in paragraph 12 of SFAS 66.[6]

The financial statements of properties which will secure mortgage loans made or to be made from the proceeds of the offering which have the characteristics of real estate investments or joint ventures should be included as required by Rule 3-14 in the registration statement when such properties secure loans previously made, or have been identified as security for probable loans prior to effectiveness, and in filings made pursuant to the undertaking in Item 20D of Securities Act Industry Guide 5.

Rule 1-02(v) of Regulation S-X includes the conditions used in determining whether an acquisition is significant. The separate financial statements of an individual property should be provided when a property would meet the requirements for a significant subsidiary under this rule using the amount of the "loan" as a substitute for the "investment in the subsidiary" in computing the specified conditions.

Under certain circumstances, information may also be required regarding operating properties underlying mortgage loans where the terms do not result in the lender having virtually the same risks and potential rewards as those of owners or joint venturers. Generally, the staff believes that, where investment risks exist due to substantial asset concentration, financial and other information should be included regarding operating properties underlying a mortgage loan that represents a significant amount of the registrant's assets. Such presentation is consistent with Rule 3-13 of Regulation S-X and Rule 408 under the Securities Act of 1933.

Where the amount of a loan exceeds 20% of the amount in good faith expected to be raised in the offering, disclosures would be expected to consist of financial statements for the underlying operating properties for the periods contemplated by Rule 3-14. Further, where loans on related properties are made to a single person or group of affiliated persons which in the aggregate amount to more than 20% of the amount expected to be raised, the staff believes that such lending arrangements result in a sufficient concentration of assets so as to warrant the inclusion of financial and other information regarding the underlying properties.

Question 2: Will the financial statements of the mortgaged properties be required in filings made under the 1934 Act?

Interpretive Response: Rule 3-09 of Regulation S-X specifies the requirements for significant, as defined, investments in operating entities, the operations of which are not included in the registrant's consolidated financial statements.[7] Accordingly, the staff believes that the financial statements of properties securing significant loans which have the characteristics of real estate investments or joint ventures should be included in subsequent filings as required by Rule 3-09. The materiality threshold for determining whether such an investment is significant is the same as set forth in paragraph (a) of that Rule.[8]

Likewise, the staff believes that filings made under the 1934 Act should include the same financial and other information relating to properties underlying any loans which are significant as discussed in the last paragraph of Question 1, except that in the determination of significance the 20% disclosure threshold should be measured using total assets. The staff believes that this presentation would be consistent with Rule 12b-20 under the Securities Exchange Act of 1934.

Question 3: The interpretive response to question 1 indicates that the staff believes that the borrower's equity in an operating property is adequate to support accounting for the transaction as a mortgage loan when the borrower's initial investment meets the criteria in paragraph 11 of Statement of Financial Accounting Standards No. 66 ("SFAS 66") and the borrower's payments of principal and interest on the loan are adequate to maintain a continuing investment in the property which meets the criteria in paragraph 12 of SFAS 66. Is it the staff's view that meeting these criteria is the only way the borrower's equity in the property is considered adequate to support accounting for the transaction as a mortgage loan?

Interpretive Response: No. It is the staff's position that the determination of whether loan accounting is appropriate for these arrangements should be made by the registrant and its independent accountants based on the facts and circumstances of the individual arrangements, using the guidance provided in the February 10, 1986, Notice to Practitioners ("Notice"). [The AICPA Accounting Standards Executive Committee (AcSEC) formed a task force in 1989 on ADC arrangements in order to develop implementation guidance on the Notice. This guidance has not yet been issued in final form.] As stated in the Notice, loan accounting may not be appropriate when the lender participates in expected residual profit and has virtually the same risks as those of an owner, or joint venturer. In assessing the question of whether the lender has virtually the same risks as an owner, or joint venturer, the essential test that needs to be addressed is whether the borrower has and is expected to continue to have a substantial amount at risk in the project.[9] The criteria described in SFAS 66 provide a "safe harbor" for determining whether the borrower has a substantial amount at risk in the form of a substantial equity investment. The borrower may have a substantial amount at risk without meeting the criteria described in SFAS 66.

Question 4: What financial statements should be included in filings made under the Securities Act regarding investment-type arrangements that individually amount to 10% or more of total assets?

Interpretive Response: In the staff's view, separate audited financial statements should be provided for any investment-type arrangement that constitutes 10% or more of the greater of (i) the amount of minimum proceeds or (ii) the total assets of the registrant, including the amount of proceeds raised, as of the date the filing is required to be made. Of course, the narrative information required by items 14 and 15 of Form S-11 should also be included with respect to these investment-type arrangements.

Question 5: What information must be provided under the Securities Act for investment-type arrangements that individually amount to less than 10%?

Interpretive Response: No specific financial information need be presented for investment-type arrangements that amount to less than 10%. However, where such arrangements aggregate more than 20%, a narrative description of the general character of the properties and arrangements should be included that gives an investor an understanding of the risks and rewards associated with these arrangements. Such information may, for example, include a description of the terms of the arrangements, participation by the registrant in expected residual profits, and property types and locations.

Question 6: What financial statements should be included in annual reports filed under the Exchange Act with respect to investment-type arrangements that constitute 10% or more of the registrant's total assets?

Interpretive Response: In annual reports filed with the Commission, the staff has advised registrants that separate audited financial statements should be provided for each non-consolidated investment-type arrangement that is 20% or more of the registrant's total assets. While the distribution is ongoing, however, the percentage may be calculated using the greater of (i) the amount of the minimum proceeds or (ii) the total assets of the registrant, including the amount of proceeds raised, as of the date the filing is required to be made. In annual reports to shareholders registrants may either include the separate audited financial statements for 20% or more non-consolidated investment-type arrangements or, if those financial statements are not included, present summarized financial information for those arrangements in the notes to the registrant's financial statements.

The staff has also indicated that separate summarized financial information (as defined in Rule 1-02.(aa) of Regulation S-X) should be provided in the footnotes to the registrant's financial statements for each non-consolidated investment-type arrangement that is 10% or more but less than 20%. Of course, registrants should also make appropriate textual disclosure with respect to material investment-type arrangements in the "business" and "property" sections of their annual reports to the Commission.[10]

SEC 50348. Rule 3-14

Question 7: What information should be provided in annual reports filed under the Exchange Act with respect to investment-type arrangements that do not meet the 10% threshold?

Interpretive Response: The staff believes it will not be necessary to provide any financial information (full or summarized) for investment-type arrangements that do not meet the 10% threshold. However, in the staff's view, where such arrangements aggregate more than 20%, a narrative description of the general character of the properties and arrangements would be necessary. The staff believes that information should be included that would give an investor an understanding of the risks and rewards associated with these arrangements. Such information may, for example, include a description of the terms of the arrangements, participation by the registrant in expected residual profits, and property types and locations. Of course, disclosure regarding the operations of such components should be included as part of the Management's Discussion and Analysis where there is a known trend or uncertainty in the operations of such properties, either individually or in the aggregate, which would be reasonably likely to result in a material impact on the registrant's future operations, liquidity or capital resources.

Question 8: What consideration will be given by the staff to those registrants that are unable to obtain the requisite information with respect to investment-type arrangements entered into prior to SAB 71?

Interpretive Response: For transactions with unaffiliated parties closed before December 15, 1987, the staff has taken the position that the disclosures contemplated by SABs 71 and 71A should be included unless the registrant has no contractual right to such information and cannot practicably obtain such information. In that event, the filing in which the information otherwise would be included should clearly state that the information is not included because the registrant has no contractual right to the information and cannot otherwise practicably obtain the information.

For transactions with unaffiliated parties closed on or after December 15 1987, the staff believes that the information should be included in all filings. The staff believes information with respect to any transaction with an affiliate is available to the registrant and should therefore be provided regardless of the date of the transaction.

---

[1] Acquisition, development and construction.

[2] The Emerging Issues Task Force ("EITF") was formed in 1984 to assist the Financial Accounting Standards Board in the early identification and resolution of emerging accounting issues. Topics to be discussed by the EITF are publicly announced prior to its meetings and minutes of all EITF meetings are available to the public.

[3] See Issue No. 86-21 (September 4, 1986).

[4] Expected residual profit is defined in the Notice as the amount of profit, whether called interest or another name, such as equity kicker, above a reasonable amount of interest and fees expected to be earned by the "lender."

[5] SFAS 66 establishes standards for the recognition of profit on real estate sales transactions. Paragraph 11 states that the buyer's initial investment shall be

adequate to demonstrate the buyer's commitment to pay for the property and shall indicate a reasonable likelihood that the seller will collect the receivable. Guidance on minimum initial investments in various types of real estate is provided in paragraphs 53 and 54 of SFAS 66.

[6]Paragraph 12 of SFAS 66 states that the buyer's continuing investment in a real estate transaction shall not qualify unless the buyer is contractually required to pay each year on its total debt for the purchase price of the property an amount at least equal to the level annual payment that would be needed to pay that debt and interest on the unpaid balance over not more than (a) 20 years for debt for land and (b) the customary amortization term of a first mortgage loan by an independent established lending institution for other real estate.

[7]Rule 3-14 states that the financial statements of an acquired property should be furnished if the acquisition took place during the period for which the registrant's income statements are required. Paragraph (a) of the Rule states that the information required by the Rule is not required to be included in a filing on Form 10-K. That exception is consistent with Item 8 of Form 10-K, which excludes acquired company financial statements, which would otherwise be required by Rule 3-05 of Regulation S-X, from inclusion in filings on that Form. Those exceptions are based, in part, on the fact that acquired properties and acquired companies will generally be included in the registrant's consolidated financial statements from the acquisition date.

[8]Rule 3-09(a) states, in part, that if any of the conditions set forth in Rule 1-02(v), substituting 20 percent for 10 percent in the tests used therein to determine significant subsidiary, are met...separate financial statements...shall be filed.

[9]Regarding the composition of the borrower's investment, paragraph 9b of the Notice indicates that the borrower's investment may include the value of land or other assets contributed by the borrower, net of encumbrances. The staff emphasizes that such paragraph indicates, ". . . recently acquired property generally should be valued at no higher than cost. . . ." Thus, for such recently acquired property, appraisals will not be sufficient to justify the use of a value in excess of cost.

[10]Registrants are reminded that in filings on Form 8-K that are triggered in connection with an acquisition of an investment-type arrangement, separate audited financial statements are required for any such arrangement that individually constitutes 10% or more.

The SEC staff has become aware that entities have been formed to acquire operating real estate properties from the Resolution Trust Corporation (RTC). In certain circumstances, the auditor is unable to express an opinion on the financial statements as required by Rule 3-14, because the RTC will not provide the necessary letter of representations. In these instances, registrants may request relief from the Division of Corporation Finance.

The staff generally will not object if the registrant is unable to furnish audited financial statements of properties acquired during the distribution period (Item 20, Industry Guide 5), and appropriate risk disclosure is made. In such situations, the statement of operations must otherwise comply with Rule 3-14, but may be unaudited for the period of RTC ownership. Furthermore, the staff's position is that the

SEC 50348. Rule 3-14

registrant's management needs to take appropriate steps to establish the reasonableness of the information underlying the unaudited financial statements and should include other disclosures that facilitate investors' understanding of the status and prospects of the distressed property.

The SEC staff has informally indicated that it will apply the principles set forth in AAER No. 245 to the following types of real estate transactions:

- Contemporaneous purchases and sales of real estate,

- Oral agreements in real estate transactions, and

- Loans made to third parties as an accommodation to purchasers of real estate.

This enforcement release discusses an SEC action against a company that made loans to third parties to accommodate a sale of real estate, and used the full accrual method of profit recognition for a variety of real estate transactions where, in the SEC's view, the earnings process had not been completed. The company also recognized income on nonmonetary exchanges of real estate.

50349. Rule 3-15. Special Provision as to Real Estate Investment Trusts

(a)(1) The income statement prepared pursuant to Rule 5-03 shall include the following additional captions between those required by Rule 5-03.15 and 16: (i) Income or loss before gain or loss on sale of properties, extraordinary items and cumulative effects of accounting changes, and (ii) gain or loss on sale of properties, less applicable income tax. (2) The balance sheet required by Rule 5-02 shall set forth in lieu of the captions required by Rule 5-02.31(a)(3): (i) The balance of undistributed income from other than the gain or loss on sale of properties and (ii) accumulated undistributed net realized gain or loss on sale of properties. The information specified in Rule 3-04 shall be modified similarly.

(b) The trust's status as a "real estate investment trust" under applicable provisions of the Internal Revenue Code as amended shall be stated in a note referred to in the appropriate statements. Such note shall also indicate briefly the principal present assumptions on which the trust has relied in making or not making provisions for Federal income taxes.

(c) The tax status of distributions per unit shall be stated (e.g., ordinary income, capital gain, return of capital).

This rule requires real estate investment trusts (REITs) to prepare their financial statements and accounting disclosures in accordance with Regulation S-X Rules 5-02 and 5-03, with certain modifications. The purpose of these modifications is to distinguish between distributions from net investment income and distributions from

552

accumulated realized gains and to show the remaining undistributed balances in these accounts for all years presented.

This rule further requires that the trust's status as a real estate investment trust under applicable provisions of the Internal Revenue Code (as amended) be stated in a note referred to in the appropriate statements. The note must also briefly indicate the principal present assumptions on which the trust has relied in omitting or including a provision for Federal income taxes and, on a per-unit basis, the tax status of distributions.

50350. Rule 3-16. Reorganization of Registrant

(a) If, during the period for which its income statements are required, the registrant has emerged from a reorganization in which substantial changes occurred in its asset, liability, capital shares, other stockholders' equity or reserve accounts, a brief explanation of such changes shall be set forth in a note or supporting schedule to the balance sheets filed.

(b) If the registrant is about to emerge from such a reorganization, there shall be filed, in addition to the [historical] balance sheets of the registrant otherwise required, a balance sheet giving effect to the plan of reorganization. These balance sheets shall be set forth in such form, preferably columnar, as will show in related manner the balance sheet of the registrant prior to the reorganization, the changes to be effected in the reorganization and the balance sheet of the registrant after giving effect to the plan of reorganization. By a footnote or otherwise a brief explanation of the changes shall be given.

A reorganization under Chapter XI of the Federal Bankruptcy Act is an example of a situation requiring disclosure pursuant to this rule.

It is the SEC staff's position that filing for bankruptcy does not relieve a registrant from the reporting requirements of the 1934 Act. However, the staff has demonstrated a willingness to grant relief from these requirements under certain circumstances as, for example, where excessive costs are involved in completing an audit of the accounts. In such situations, the staff has accepted reports that were submitted to the bankruptcy court, in lieu of audited financial statements. The staff has emphasized, however, that as a general rule this type of accommodation will be granted only if the request is made prior to the due date of the required filing. If the filing date of the Form 10-K has passed, the staff has expressed an unwillingness to consider modifications to the reporting requirements. It should also be noted that as a matter of policy the staff will not grant a complete waiver of the reporting requirements for a bankrupt company.

A number of registrants emerging from bankruptcy have argued that the provisions of SFAS No. 15, *Accounting by Debtors and Creditors for Troubled Debt Restructurings*, should be applied rather than the guidelines set forth in SOP 90-7, *Financial Reporting by Entities in Reorganization Under the Bankruptcy Code.*

Paragraph 10 of SFAS No. 15 states that the Statement's provisions apply to debt restructurings consummated under the Federal Bankruptcy Act, but footnote 4 indicates that "this Statement does not apply if under provisions of those Federal statutes... the debtor restates its liabilities generally." The SEC staff has taken the position that a general restatement of liabilities would constitute a restatement of more than 50 percent. Therefore, the staff's position is that the provisions of SOP 90-7 would apply if more than 50 percent of the liabilities are restated and SFAS No. 15 would apply if 50 percent or less are restated.

The staff has indicated that when a range of alternative results in connection with a restructuring plan exists, the presentation of alternative pro forma financial statements may be appropriate.

SAB Topic 5-S expresses the staff's views in connection with quasi reorganizations. The SAB indicates, among other things, that the staff considers a deficit reduction of any nature to be a quasi reorganization. It goes on to state that assets and liabilities should be adjusted to fair value in connection with this type of transaction, but that such adjustments should not result in a net increase in net assets. The text of the SAB follows:

Quasi-Reorganization

Facts: As a consequence of significant operating losses and/or recent write-downs of property, plant and equipment, a company's financial statements reflect an accumulated deficit. The company desires to eliminate the deficit by reclassifying amounts from paid-in-capital. In addition, the company anticipates adopting a discretionary change in accounting principles[1] that will be recorded as a cumulative-effect type of accounting change. The recording of the cumulative effect will have the result of increasing the company's retained earnings.

Question 1: May the company reclassify its capital accounts to eliminate the accumulated deficit without satisfying all of the conditions enumerated in Section 210[2] of the Codification of Financial Reporting Policies for a quasi-reorganization?

Interpretive Response: No. The staff believes a deficit reclassification of any nature is considered to be a quasi-reorganization. As such, a company may not reclassify or eliminate a deficit in retained earnings unless all requisite conditions set forth in Section 210[3] for a quasi-reorganization are satisfied.[4]

Question 2: Must the company implement the discretionary change in accounting principle simultaneously with the quasi-reorganization or may it adopt the change after the quasi-reorganization has been effected?

Interpretive Response: The staff has taken the position that the company should adopt the anticipated accounting change prior to or as an integral part of the quasi-reorganization. Any such accounting change should be effected by following generally accepted accounting principles with respect to the change.[5]

Chapter 7A of Accounting Research Bulletin (ARB) No. 43 indicates that, following a quasi-reorganization, a "company's accounting should be substantially similar to that appropriate for a new company." The staff believes that implicit in this "fresh-start" concept is the need for the company's accounting principles in place at the time of the quasi-reorganization to be those planned to be used following the reorganization to avoid a misstatement of earnings and retained earnings after the reorganization.[6]

Chapter 7A of ARB No. 43 states, in part, "... in general, assets should be carried forward as of the date of the readjustment at fair and not unduly conservative amounts, determined with due regard for the accounting to be employed by the Company thereafter."

In addition, the staff believes that adopting a discretionary change in accounting principle that will be reflected in the financial statements within 12 months following the consummation of a quasi-reorganization leads to a presumption that the accounting change was contemplated at the time of the quasi-reorganization.[7]

Question 3: In connection with a quasi-reorganization, may there be a write-up of net assets?

Interpretive Response: No. The staff believes that increases in the recorded values of specific assets (or reductions in liabilities) to fair value are appropriate providing such adjustments are factually supportable, however, the amount of such increases are limited to offsetting adjustments to reflect decreases in other assets (or increases in liabilities) to reflect their new fair value. In other words, a quasi-reorganization should not result in a write-up of net assets of the registrant.

[Note: Question 4 has not been presented as it is no longer applicable.]

Question 5: If a company had previously recorded a quasi-reorganization that only resulted in the elimination of a deficit in retained earnings, may the company reverse such entry and "undo" its quasi-reorganization?

Interpretive Response: No. The staff believes APB Opinion No. 20 would preclude such a change in accounting. It states: "a method of accounting that was previously adopted for a type of transaction or event which is being terminated or which was a single, nonrecurring event in the past should not be changed.[13]

---

[1]Discretionary accounting changes require the filing of a preferability letter by the registrant's independent accountant pursuant to Items 601 of Regulation S-K and Rule 10-01(b)(6) of Regulation S-X, 17 CFR §§ 229.601 and 210.10-01(b)(6), respectively.

[2]Accounting Series Release No. 25 (May 29, 1941).

[3]Section 210 indicates the following conditions under which a quasi-reorganization can be effected without the creation of a new corporate entity and without the intervention of formal court proceedings:

(1) Earned surplus, as of the date selected, is exhausted;

(2) Upon consummation of the quasi-reorganization, no deficit exists in any surplus account;

(3) The entire procedure is made known to all persons entitled to vote on matters of general corporate policy and the appropriate consents to the particular transactions are obtained in advance in accordance with the applicable laws and charter provisions;

(4) The procedure accomplishes, with respect to the accounts, substantially what might be accomplished in a reorganization by legal proceedings— namely, the restatement of assets in terms of present conditions as well as appropriate modifications of capital and capital surplus, in order to obviate so far as possible the necessity of future reorganizations of like nature.

[4] In addition, Accounting Research Bulletin (ARB) No. 43, Chapter 7A, outlines procedures that must be followed in connection with and after a quasi-reorganization.

[5] Accounting Principles Board Opinion No. 20 provides accounting principles to be followed when adopting accounting changes. In addition, many newly issued accounting pronouncements provide specific guidance to be followed when adopting the accounting specified in such pronouncements.

[6] Certain newly issued accounting standards do not require adoption until some future date. The staff believes, however, that if the registrant intends or is required to adopt those standards within 12 months following the quasi-reorganization, the registrant should adopt those standards prior to or as an integral part of the quasi-reorganization. Further, registrants should consider early adoption of standards with effective dates more than 12 months subsequent to a quasi-reorganization.

[7] Certain accounting changes require restatement of prior financial statements. The staff believes that if a quasi-reorganization had been recorded in a restated period, the effects of the accounting change on quasi-reorganization adjustments should also be restated to properly reflect the quasi-reorganization in the restated financial statements.

[8] Supra Note 3.

[Note: Footnotes 9-12 have not been presented as they are no longer applicable.]

[13] Accounting Principles Board Opinion No. 20 (July 1971); paragraph 16.

Subsequent to the issuance of this SAB, the SEC staff informally expressed its views concerning debt restructurings that are coincident with quasi reorganizations. In such situations, the staff believes a debtor would be viewed as "restating its liabilities generally" and that the application of SFAS No. 15, *Accounting by Debtors and Creditors for Troubled Debt Restructurings*, would therefore be inappropriate. The staff believes that in situations of this nature, the effects of the restructuring should be recorded pursuant to APB Opinion No. 26, *Early Extinguishment of Debt*, with any gain from the extinguishment of debt recorded in the statement of operations prior to the quasi reorganization. In the past the staff has not objected to recording the gain as a direct addition to capital. The staff has reconsidered this view, and now takes the position that any gain associated with a debt restructuring should be presented as an extraordinary item in the statement of operations. The staff has stressed that its position on this matter in no way modifies its view that valuation adjustments made as part of a quasi reorganization may not result in a write-up of net assets.

The following informal interpretations relating to quasi reorganizations have been provided by the SEC staff:

- The staff has indicated that it would generally not challenge the retention of goodwill in a quasi reorganization provided the fair value of the business still justifies the amount recognized, and all other assets and liabilities are stated at fair value. However, the staff will object to the *creation* of goodwill in a quasi reorganization.

- In the revaluation process, the staff believes that all previously unrecognized pension, OPEB or postemployment obligations under SFAS Nos. 87, *Employers' Accounting for Pensions*, 106, *Employers' Accounting for Postretirement Benefits Other Than Pensions*, and 112, *Employers' Accounting for Postemployment Benefits*, need to be recognized in a quasi reorganization. To the extent that such obligations were not required to be recognized prior to the date of the quasi reorganization (i.e., they were being amortized), the staff has indicated that it will not object to the inclusion of the offsetting entry directly in equity.

- The staff's views concerning whether there is a limit as to the time period over which revaluations of amounts provided at the date of a quasi reorganization may be charged to capital surplus are best illustrated by the following two cases in which the staff raised no objection to recognizing adjustments of pre-quasi-reorganization liabilities directly to capital surplus several years after the date of the quasi reorganization:

  - A registrant was named as a "potentially responsible party" in an environmental suit 13 years after the date of the quasi reorganization. The suit stemmed from operations that were liquidated in connection with the quasi reorganization.

  - A registrant established an estimated liability for a lease commitment for operating facilities that had been abandoned just prior to the quasi reorganization. The estimated liability was recorded net of anticipated revenues under a sublease. Several years after the quasi reorganization, the tenant defaulted on the sublease.

SEC 50350. Rule 3-16

In each of the cases described above, the loss related to operations prior to the quasi reorganization; therefore, the staff did not object to the companies carrying the losses to capital surplus as provided in paragraph 5 of Chapter 7 of ARB 43.

The staff believes that unresolved pre-quasi-reorganization contingencies should be disclosed in the financial statements subsequent to the date of the reorganization as long as such contingencies remain outstanding. In addition, the staff generally requires the continued dating of retained earnings for as long as there is a reasonable possibility that adjustments to pre-quasi-reorganization items may be carried directly to capital surplus, irrespective of the fact that ARB 46, *Discontinuance of Dating Earned Surplus*, states that the dating of retained earnings following a quasi reorganization would rarely be of significance after a period of ten years.

- The staff's view regarding the adjustment of pre-quasi-reorganization liabilities set forth above should be distinguished from its position regarding the accounting for the subsequent resolution of uncertainties that existed at the date "fresh-start" reporting is adopted pursuant to SOP 90-7. In the latter instance, the staff believes that the resolution of the uncertainties would need to be reflected in net income. The staff's view is that upon adoption of fresh-start reporting, a new reporting entity is created and there is no provision in the accounting literature that would permit a newly formed entity to record changes in estimated liabilities directly in capital surplus. Furthermore, the staff has taken exception to the application of the allocation period concepts in SFAS 38, *Accounting for Preacquisition Contingencies of Purchased Enterprises (an Amendment of APB Opinion No. 16)*, to adjustments subsequent to the fresh-start reporting.

50351. Rule 3-17. Financial Statements of Natural Persons

(a) In lieu of the financial statements otherwise required, a natural person may file an unaudited balance sheet as of a date within 90 days of date of filing and unaudited statements of income for each of the three most recent fiscal years.

(b) Financial statements conforming with the instructions as to financial statements of subsidiaries not consolidated and 50 percent or less owned persons under Rule 3-09(a) shall be separately presented for: (1) each business owned as a sole proprietor, (2) each partnership, business trust, unincorporated association, or similar business organization of which the person holds a controlling interest and (3) each corporation of which the person, directly or indirectly, owns securities representing more than 50 percent of the voting power.

(c) *Separate financial statements may be omitted, however, for each corporation, business trust, unincorporated association, or similar business organization if the person's total investment in such entity does not exceed 5 percent of his total assets and the person's total income from such entity does not exceed 5 percent of his gross income, provided that the person's aggregate investment in and income from all such omitted entities shall not exceed 15 percent of his total assets and gross income, respectively.*

50352. Rule 3-18. Special Provisions as to Registered Management Investment Companies and Companies Required to be Registered as Management Investment Companies

(a) *For filings by registered management investment companies, the following financial statements shall be filed:*

(1) *An audited balance sheet or statement of assets and liabilities as of the end of the most recent fiscal year;*

(2) *An audited statement of operations for the most recent fiscal year conforming to the requirements of Rule 6-07.*

(3) *An audited statement of cash flows for the most recent fiscal year if necessary to comply with generally accepted accounting principles. (Further references in this rule to the requirement for such statement are likewise applicable only to the extent that they are consistent with the requirements of generally accepted accounting principles.)*

(4) *Audited statements of changes in net assets conforming to the requirements of Rule 6-09 for the two most recent fiscal years.*

(b) *If the filing is made within 60 days after the end of the registrant's fiscal year and audited financial statements for the most recent fiscal year are not available, the balance sheet or statement of assets and liabilities may be as of end of the preceding fiscal year and the filing shall include an additional balance sheet or statement of assets and liabilities as of an interim date within 245 days of the date of the filing. In addition, the statements of operations and cash flows (if required by generally accepted accounting principles) shall be provided for the preceding fiscal year and the statement of changes in net assets shall be provided for the two preceding fiscal years, and each of the statements shall be provided for the interim period between the end of the preceding fiscal year and the date of the most recent balance sheet or statement of assets and liabilities being filed. Financial statements for the corresponding period of the preceding fiscal year need not be provided.*

SEC 50351. Rule 3-17

(c) If the most current balance sheet or statement of assets and liabilities in a filing is as of a date 245 days or more prior to the date the filing is expected to become effective, the financial statements shall be updated with a balance sheet or statement of assets and liabilities as of an interim date within 245 days. In addition, the statements of operations, cash flows, and changes in net assets shall be provided for the interim period between the end of the most recent fiscal year for which a balance sheet or statement of assets and liabilities is presented and the date of the most recent interim balance sheet or statement of assets and liabilities filed.

(d) Interim financial statements provided in accordance with these requirements may be unaudited but shall be presented in the same detail as required by Rules 6-01 to 6-10. When unaudited financial statements are presented in a registration statement, they shall include the statement required by Rule 3-03(d).

50353. Rule 3-19. Special Provisions as to Financial Statements for Foreign Private Issuers

Foreign private issuers use Form 20-F. The specific requirements of Form 20-F are discussed in sections 43200 and 44100.

(a) A foreign private issuer, as defined in Rule 405, other than a registered management investment company or an employee plan, shall include the following financial statements for the registrant and its subsidiaries consolidated and, where appropriate, its predecessors:

(1) Audited balance sheets as of the end of each of the two most recent fiscal years.

(2) Audited statements of income and cash flows for each of the three fiscal years preceding the date of the most recent audited balance sheet being filed.

(b) If the filing, other than an annual report on Form 20-F, is made within six full months after the end of the registrant's fiscal year and if the audited balance sheet for the most recent fiscal year is not available, the audited balance sheets in the filing may be as of the end of the two preceding fiscal years; Provided, That on the effective date the filing shall include a balance sheet as of an interim date within six months of the effective date (except as permitted in paragraph (e) of this section), and Provided Further, That if the effective date falls after five months subsequent to the end of the most recent fiscal year, the filing shall include an audited balance sheet for the most recent fiscal year.

(c) If the filing is made after six full months subsequent to the end of the most recent fiscal year, the filing shall include a balance sheet, which may be unaudited, as of an

interim date within six months (except as permitted in paragraph (e) of this section) of the effective date.

(d) If an interim balance sheet is required by this rule, statements of income and cash flows for the interim period between the latest audited balance sheet and the date of the interim balance sheet being filed and for the corresponding period of the preceding fiscal year shall also be filed. Such interim financial statements may be unaudited and need not be presented in greater detail than is required by Rule 10-01.

(e) The balance sheet shall be as of the date within one year of the effective date if the only securities to be offered are (1) upon the exercise of outstanding rights granted by the issuer of the securities to be offered, if such rights are granted pro rata to all existing security holders of the class of securities to which the rights attach; or (2) pursuant to a dividend or interest reinvestment plan; or (3) upon the conversion of outstanding convertible securities or upon the exercise of outstanding transferable warrants issued by the issuer. The provisions of this paragraph (e) are not applicable if securities are to be offered or sold in a standby underwriting in the United States or similar arrangement.

(f) Notwithstanding the above provisions of this rule, if a foreign private issuer prepares and discloses to its shareholders or otherwise makes public, pursuant to applicable foreign laws or regulations or stock exchange requirements or otherwise, interim financial information relating to revenues and income that is more current than the financial statements required by this rule, such information shall be included in the filing and reconciled according to the provisions of either Item 17 or Item 18 of Form 20-F, whichever applies to the audited financial statements in the filing.

Foreign private issuer is defined in Rule 405 of Regulation C, which states:

The term . . . means any foreign issuer other than a foreign government except an issuer meeting the following conditions: (1) more than 50 percent of the outstanding voting securities of such issuer are held of record either directly or through voting trust certificates of depository receipts by residents of the United States; and (2) any of the following: (i) the majority of the executive officers or directors are United States citizens or residents, (ii) more than 50 percent of the assets of the issuer are located in the United States, or (iii) the business of the issuer is administered principally in the United States. For the purpose of this paragraph, the term "resident," as applied to security holders, shall mean any person whose address appears on the records of the issuer, the voting trustee, or the depository as being located in the United States.

Generally non-U.S. issuers are required to follow the same rules in the presentation of financial statements to be included in filings with the SEC as are appropriate for U.S. companies. Rule 4-01(a)(2), however (see section 50401), permits the use of accounting principles other than U.S. GAAP in the preparation of the financial statements if they are based on a "comprehensive body of accounting principles." While the rule does not specify what would constitute a comprehensive body of accounting principles, in practice this determination has been based on the formality and status of the accounting profession in the particular foreign country. Many countries have established bodies promulgating accounting rules or otherwise specify accounting principles to be followed. In addition, International Accounting Standards, established by the International Accounting Standards Committee, are considered to represent a "comprehensive body of accounting principles." In some countries, however, the accounting principles to be followed are less well defined and a question may arise whether they would constitute "a comprehensive body of accounting principles." The following is the specific wording in Rule 4-01(a)(2) permitting the use of other accounting principles:

> In all filings of foreign private issuers, except as stated otherwise in the applicable form, the financial statements may be prepared according to a comprehensive body of accounting principles other than those generally accepted in the United States if a reconciliation to United States generally accepted accounting principles and the provisions of Regulation S-X of the type specified in Item 18 of Form 20-F is also filed as part of the financial statements. Alternatively, the financial statements may be prepared according to United States generally accepted accounting principles.

If the financial statements are prepared in accordance with accounting principles other than those generally accepted in the U.S., the foregoing rule requires a reconciliation that identifies and quantifies each material difference between the accounting principles followed in the preparation of the financial statements and U.S. GAAP. This reconciliation is included in the footnotes to the financial statements. The text of Item 18 of Form 20-F, referred to in Rule 4-01(a)(2), deals with disclosure requirements when financial statements and schedules are not prepared in accordance with U.S. GAAP and is discussed in detail in section 43210 of this manual.

The Item 18 disclosures are mandatory when a foreign private issuer files a registration statement under the 1933 Act. For filings under the 1934 Act, the provisions of paragraph (c)(3) to furnish "all other information required by United States generally accepted accounting principles and Regulation S-X" need not be complied with. In such cases, Item 17 of Form 20-F, which excludes paragraph (c)(3), may be followed. However, if Item 17 is elected in lieu of Item 18, the Form 20-F financial statements will not be suitable for inclusion or incorporation by reference in future 1933 Act filings without modification. Refer to section 43210 for a detailed discussion of the Item 17 and Item 18 requirements.

Rule 3-19 also extends the required age of financial statements of foreign private issuers to be included in a registration statement from the 135-day limitation applicable to U.S. issuers (see Rule 3-12 in section 50346) to a six-month period. However, if the effective date of a registration statement filed by a foreign private issuer falls during the period between five and six months subsequent to the registrant's fiscal year-end, as a general rule the filing must include audited financial statements for the most recent fiscal year.

Regardless of the other provisions of Rule 3-19, paragraph (f) states that if a foreign private issuer publicly discloses interim financial information that is more current than the financial statements provided pursuant to Rule 3-19, such information is required to be included in the filing with a reconciliation pursuant to Item 17 or Item 18 of Form 20-F, whichever is applicable to the filing.

50354. Rule 3-20. Currency for Financial Statements of Foreign Private Issuers

(a) A foreign private issuer, as defined in Rule 405, shall state its primary financial statements only in the currency of the country in which the issuer is incorporated or organized, except that a different currency may be used if all the following conditions are met:

> *(1) The other currency is the currency of the primary economic environment in which the operations of such issuer and its subsidiaries are conducted; normally that is the currency of the environment in which such issuer primarily generates and expends cash. (The practice of linking or indexing transactions to a particular currency is not determinative that such currency is the reporting currency.);*

> *(2) There are no material exchange restrictions or controls relating to that currency; and*

> *(3) The issuer publishes its financial statements for all of its shareholders in the other currency.*

(b) The currency in which the financial statements are prepared shall be disclosed prominently on the face of the financial statements. Dollar-equivalent financial statements or convenience translations shall not be presented except a translation may be presented of the most recent fiscal year and any subsequent interim period presented using the exchange rate as of the most recent balance sheet included in the filing except a rate as of the most recent practicable date shall be used if materially different.

(c) If the financial statements of a foreign private issuer (1) are denominated in a currency of a country that has experienced cumulative inflationary effects exceeding a total of 100 percent over the most recent three year period, and (2) have not been recast or otherwise supplemented to include information on a constant currency or

current cost basis prescribed or permitted by appropriate authoritative standards, the issuer shall present supplementary information to quantify the effects of changing prices upon its financial condition and results of operations.

Rule 3-20 provides the *reporting* currency requirements for financial statements of foreign private issuers and should be distinguished from the *functional* currency determination required by SFAS No. 52, *Foreign Currency Translation.* Although the determination criteria are similar, Rule 3-20 only deals with the issue of *reporting* currency.

Paragraph (a) of Rule 3-20 requires a foreign private issuer to present the financial statements in the currency of the country in which it is incorporated (even if it has no operations there) or organized, except that a different currency *may* be used (i.e., optional) if the issuer can demonstrate that another currency is more appropriate by meeting all the following conditions:

- The other currency is the currency of the primary economic environment in which the issuer and its subsidiaries conduct their operations. The rule states that this is normally the currency of the economic environment in which the issuer primarily generates and expends cash;

- No material exchange restrictions or controls relating to that currency exist; and

- The issuer uses the other currency to publish its financial statements for all shareholders.

In determining the currency of the primary economic environment, the SEC staff has indicated that issuers can consider future events, in certain circumstances. For example, assume that subsequent to year-end a Canadian company acquires a business in the United States, causing the currency of the primary economic environment to change from the Canadian dollar to the U.S. dollar. In this situation the staff would not object to the issuer changing the reporting currency to the U.S. dollar for all periods presented.

If economic facts and circumstances change, such as in the previous example, the staff has indicated that the financial statements should be prepared using the same reporting currency for all periods. Prior periods should be recast into the new reporting currency using a method of translation consistent with SFAS 52. A convenience translation using the same exchange rate for all periods would not be considered appropriate.

An anomaly of Rule 3-20 is that a foreign private issuer can use a reporting currency that has nothing to do with its operations. Consequently, the SEC staff has indicated that it would not object to the use of the U.S. dollar as the reporting currency of a foreign private issuer if the currency of the country in which the issuer is incorporated is tied or fixed to the U.S. dollar. The Netherlands Antilles, Panama, the Virgin Islands, and Bermuda are examples of such countries noted by the staff. In addition, the staff has noted that the Grand Duchy of Luxembourg allows companies to be capitalized in different currencies. Once designated, the company is required by Luxembourg law to prepare its financial statements and pay dividends in that currency. Notwithstanding the fact that the currency of that country is the Luxembourg franc, the staff has indicated that it would not object to the use of the U.S. dollar as a reporting currency in this situation. In these situations, it is important to note that the issuer is required to publish its financial statements for all shareholders using the U.S. dollar.

Paragraph (b) of Rule 3-20 states that the currency in which the financial statements are prepared should be disclosed prominently on the face of the financial statements. The SEC staff has indicated that the currency in which dividends will be paid should also be disclosed if that currency is different from the reporting currency. In addition, this paragraph also limits the use of dollar-equivalent presentations, frequently referred to as "convenience statements," to the latest fiscal year and interim period.

If dollar-equivalent financial statements are presented by a foreign private issuer, the exchange rate used should be the rate in effect as of the end of the most recent balance sheet date except that the rate as of a more recent date should be applied if there has been a significant change in the rate since the balance sheet date. The same rate is required to be used in translating both the balance sheet and income statement in dollar-equivalent financial statements.

Paragraph (c) of Rule 3-20 states that registrants preparing financial statements in a currency of a hyperinflationary environment are required to either prepare price level adjusted financial statements, or provide supplemental price level adjusted information. Issuers that comprehensively include the effects of price level changes in their primary financial statements do not need to quantify its effect in their reconciliation to U.S. GAAP pursuant to Items 17 and 18 of Form 20-F. Such issuers should disclose the basis used to prepare the financial statements and the effective price level changes that have not been included in the reconciliation.

The SEC staff has indicated that foreign private issuers operating in a hyperinflationary economy that elect to prepare their primary financial statements in accordance with U.S. GAAP are required to apply the accounting principles provided in Accounting Principles Board (APB) Statement No. 3, *Financial Statements Restated for General Price Level Changes*. Although APB Statement No. 3 has been rescinded by SOP 93-3, footnote 3 to the SOP states, "AcSEC agrees with the conclusions of the APB, expressed in paragraph 26 of APB Statement No. 3, regarding general price-level financial statements of companies operating in hyperinflationary economies," and the SEC staff continues to view the guidance to be appropriate in situations of this nature.

SEC 50354. Rule 3-20

50370. ARTICLE 3A. CONSOLIDATED AND COMBINED FINANCIAL STATEMENTS

50371. Rule 3A-01. Application of Rules 3A-01 to 3A-05

Rules 3A-01 to 3A-05 shall govern the presentation of consolidated and combined financial statements.

50372. Rule 3A-02. Consolidated Financial Statements of the Registrant and Its Subsidiaries

In deciding upon consolidation policy, the registrant must consider what financial presentation is most meaningful in the circumstances and should follow in the consolidated financial statements principles of inclusion or exclusion which will clearly exhibit the financial position and results of operations of the registrant. There is a presumption that consolidated statements are more meaningful than separate statements and that they are usually necessary for a fair presentation when one entity directly or indirectly has a controlling financial interest in another entity. Other particular facts and circumstances may require combined financial statements, an equity method of accounting, or valuation allowances in order to achieve a fair presentation. In any case, the disclosures required by Rule 3A-03 should clearly explain the accounting policies followed by the registrant in this area, including the circumstances involved in any departure from the normal practice of consolidating majority owned subsidiaries and not consolidating entities that are less than majority owned. Among the factors that the registrant should consider in determining the most meaningful presentation are the following:

    (a) Majority ownership: Generally, registrants shall consolidate entities that are majority owned and shall not consolidate entities that are not majority owned. The determination of "majority ownership" requires a careful analysis of the facts and circumstances of a particular relationship among entities. In rare situations, consolidation of a majority owned subsidiary may not result in a fair presentation, because the registrant, in substance, does not have a controlling financial interest (for example, when the subsidiary is in legal

566

reorganization or in bankruptcy, or when control is likely to be temporary). In other situations, consolidation of an entity, notwithstanding the lack of technical majority ownership, is necessary to present fairly the financial position and results of operations of the registrant, because of the existence of a parent-subsidiary relationship by means other than record ownership of voting stock.

(b) Different fiscal periods: Generally, registrants shall not consolidate any entity whose financial statements are as of a date or for periods substantially different from those of the registrant. Rather, the earnings or losses of such entities should be reflected in the registrant's financial statements on the equity method of accounting. However:

(1) A difference in fiscal periods does not of itself justify the exclusion of an entity from consolidation. It ordinarily is feasible for such entity to prepare, for consolidation purposes, statements for a period which corresponds with or closely approaches the fiscal year of the registrant. Where the difference is not more than 93 days, it is usually acceptable to use, for consolidation purposes, such entity's statements for its fiscal period. Such difference, when it exists, should be disclosed as follows: the closing date of the entity should be expressly indicated, and the necessity for the use of different closing dates should be briefly explained. Furthermore, recognition should be given by disclosure or otherwise to the effect of intervening events which materially affect the financial position or results of operations.

(2) Notwithstanding the 93-day provision specified in (b)(1) above, in connection with the retroactive combination of financial statements of entities following a "pooling of interests," the financial statements of the constituents may be combined even if their respective fiscal periods do not end within 93 days, except that the financial statements for the latest fiscal year shall be recast to dates which do not differ by more than 93 days, if practicable. Disclosure shall be made of the periods combined and of the sales or revenues, net income before extraordinary items and net income of any interim periods excluded from or included more than once in results of operations as a result of such recasting.

(c) Bank Holding Company Act: Registrants shall not consolidate any subsidiary or group of subsidiaries of a registrant subject to the Bank Holding Company Act of 1956 as amended as to which (1) a decision requiring divestiture has been made, or (2) there is substantial likelihood that divestiture will be necessary in order to comply with provisions of the Bank Holding Company Act.

(d) Foreign subsidiaries: Due consideration shall be given to the propriety of consolidating with domestic corporations foreign subsidiaries which are oper-

ated under political, economic or currency restrictions. If consolidated, disclosure should be made as to the effect, insofar as this can reasonably be determined, of foreign exchange restrictions upon the consolidated financial position and operating results of the registrant and its subsidiaries.

A definition of majority-owned subsidiary is included in Rule 1-02(m). FRR No. 25 (see FRP 105), which was issued in 1986, amended Rule 3A-02. The principal purpose of the amendment was to eliminate wording in the previous rule that indicated that a registrant "shall not consolidate any subsidiary which is not majority owned." This FRR emphasizes that the substance of an affiliation as opposed to its form needs to be considered in preparing financial statements. However, it does point out that Rule 3A-02, as amended, is intended to conform to the SEC's current position on consolidation with existing literature. The FASB is currently dealing with this issue and it is possible that new accounting rules dealing with consolidation matters will emerge in the near future.

In 1987 SFAS No. 94, *Consolidation of All Majority-Owned Subsidiaries*, was issued. It amends ARB No. 51, *Consolidated Financial Statements,* to require consolidation of all majority-owned subsidiaries unless control is temporary or does not rest with the majority owner, including those that were previously unconsolidated because of "nonhomogeneous" operations, such as finance subsidiaries of manufacturing companies, a large minority interest, or a foreign location. Summarized information covering the assets, liabilities, and results of operations of previously unconsolidated majority-owned subsidiaries is required to be furnished pursuant to SFAS No. 94.

Members of the SEC staff have provided the following informal interpretations regarding the evaluation of whether a joint venture (JV) needs to be consolidated. The staff's view is that an agreement between the venturers that requires the consent of both venture parties for typical corporate actions generally indicates neither venturer has control. For example, if a majority holder cannot order the sale of assets in the ordinary course of business without the consent of its JV partner, the staff believes that the majority owner does not have control. However, if the JV agreement requires the consent of both parties only in the case of a disposition of "substantially all" assets, an action that is clearly not in the ordinary course of business, the staff has indicated that it would not conclude that this provision would negate other aspects of control. The staff has provided the following examples in this regard:

- In one situation, the majority owner did not have the unilateral ability to buy, sell, or pledge assets without the consent of its JV partner if the transaction exceeded five percent of the JV asset base. In this case, the staff took the position that control was not present.

SEC 50372

- In another situation, a 50 percent owner had (1) the tie-breaking vote with respect to operating and financial policies of the JV, (2) the ability to acquire and dispose of assets in the ordinary course of business, and (3) the right to dispose of up to 95 percent of JV assets without the consent of the JV partner. The staff took the position in this case that the 50 percent owner had control.

Paragraph (b) of Rule 3A-02 permits the combination of pooled entities notwithstanding the 93-day rule, but requires restatement of financial statements for the latest fiscal year and, if necessary, a change in fiscal year of one of the constituent entities subsequent to the combination. The manner in which the foregoing is generally accomplished is to credit retained earnings for the net income of any interim periods excluded from the results of operations or to charge retained earnings for any net income included more than once in results of operations.

The provisions in paragraph (d) as to consolidation of foreign subsidiaries are similar to those contained in Chapter 12 of ARB No. 43, which was amended by SFAS No. 94 and makes no distinction between foreign and domestic subsidiaries. Accordingly, as a general rule if the specified conditions are met, foreign subsidiaries are required to be consolidated.

Subsidiaries excluded from consolidation should be described. Rule 3A-A3(b) requires disclosure of changes in subsidiaries included or excluded from consolidation. The financial statement requirements for unconsolidated subsidiaries are set forth in Rule 3-09 (see section 50339).

50373. Rule 3A-03. Statement as to Principles of Consolidation or Combination Followed

(a) A brief description of the principles followed in consolidating or combining the separate financial statements, including the principles followed in determining the inclusion or exclusion of (1) subsidiaries in consolidated or combined financial statements and (2) companies in consolidated or combined financial statements, shall be stated in the notes to the respective financial statements.

(b) As to each consolidated financial statement and as to each combined financial statement, if there has been a change in the persons included or excluded in the corresponding statement for the preceding fiscal period filed with the Commission which has a material effect on the financial statements, the persons included and the persons excluded shall be disclosed. If there have been any changes in the respective fiscal periods of the persons included made during the periods of the report which have a material effect on the financial statements, indicate clearly such changes and the manner of treatment.

SEC 50372. Rule 3A-02

The disclosures required by paragraph (a) of this rule are similar to those required by paragraph 5 of ARB No. 51 and are generally provided for as part of the accounting policies described pursuant to APB Opinion No. 22.

The disclosure required by paragraph (b) of this rule is similar to that required by paragraphs 34 and 35 of APB Opinion No. 20. This portion of the rule requires disclosure of any changes in the composition of the consolidated or combined group between fiscal periods. If such changes have occurred, the names of the subsidiaries involved should be disclosed.

50374. Rule 3A-04. Intercompany Items and Transactions

In general, there shall be eliminated intercompany items and transactions between persons included in the (a) consolidated financial statements being filed and, as appropriate, (b) unrealized intercompany profits and losses on transactions between persons for which financial statements are being filed and persons the investment in which is presented in such statements by the equity method. If such eliminations are not made, a statement of the reasons and the methods of treatment shall be made.

The accounting for intercompany items and transactions described in this rule is similar to that prescribed by paragraph 7 of ARB No. 51. See also the disclosure required by Rule 4-08(1) and SFAS No. 57 (section 50408 in this manual).

50375. Rule 3A-05. Special Requirements as to Public Utility Holding Companies

There shall be shown in the consolidated balance sheet of a public utility holding company the difference between the amount at which the parent's investment is carried and the underlying book equity of subsidiaries as at the respective dates of acquisition.

50400. ARTICLE 4.
RULES OF GENERAL APPLICATION

50401. Rule 4-01. Form, Order, and Terminology

(a) Financial statements should be filed in such form and order, and should use such generally accepted terminology, as will best indicate their significance and character in the light of the provisions applicable thereto. The information required with respect to any statement shall be furnished as a minimum requirement to which shall be added such further material information as is necessary to make the required statements, in the light of the circumstances under which they are made, not misleading.

(1) Financial statements filed with the Commission which are not prepared in accordance with generally accepted accounting principles will be presumed to be misleading or inaccurate, despite footnote or other disclosures, unless the Commission has otherwise provided. This article and other articles of Regulation S-X provide clarification of certain disclosures which must be included in any event in financial statements filed with the Commission.

(2) In all filings of foreign private issuers (see Rule 405 of Regulation C), except as stated otherwise in the applicable form, the financial statements may be prepared according to a comprehensive body of accounting principles other than those generally accepted in the United States if a reconciliation to United States generally accepted accounting principles and the provisions of Regulation S-X of the type specified in Item 18 of Form 20-F is also filed as part of the financial statements. Alternatively, the financial statements may be prepared according to United States generally accepted accounting principles.

(b) All money amounts required to be shown in financial statements may be expressed in whole dollars or multiples thereof, as appropriate; Provided, That when stated in

other than whole dollars, an indication to that effect is inserted immediately beneath the caption of the statement or schedule, at the top of the money columns, or at an appropriate point in narrative material.

(c) Negative amounts (red figures) shall be shown in a manner which clearly distinguishes the negative attribute. When determining methods of display, consideration should be given to the limitations of reproduction and microfilming processes.

Paragraph (a) requires that financial statements be presented in such form, order, and terminology as will best indicate their significance and character. The requirement to add disclosures wherever necessary in order to make the financial information complete and not misleading is a precept of generally accepted accounting principles.

Subparagraph (a)(1) sets forth the policy of the SEC with respect to financial statements that are not prepared in accordance with generally accepted accounting principles. As discussed in section 15030, this policy was initially described in ASR No. 4. Subparagraph (a)(2) permits foreign private issuers to prepare financial statements according to foreign accounting principles (see section 43210), provided that a reconciliation with U.S. GAAP and Regulation S-X disclosure requirements of the type specified in Item 18 of Form 20-F is filed.

Although paragraph (b) presumes that the financial statements are expressed in U.S. dollars, certain foreign private issuers are required by Rule 3-20 (see section 50354) to state their primary financial statements in currencies other than U.S. dollars.

Paragraph (b) permits registrants some latitude in the manner in which financial statements are prepared. SAB Topic 11-E, however, emphasizes the importance of consistency in the manner in which data is presented:

Chronological Ordering of Data

Question: Does the staff have any preference as to what order tabular data are presented (e.g., the most current data displayed first, etc.)?

Interpretive Response: The staff has no preference as to order; however, financial statements and other data presented in tabular form should read consistently from left to right in the same chronological order throughout the filing. Similarly, numerical data included in narrative sections should also be consistently ordered.

Paragraph (c) allows flexibility as to the presentation of negative amounts. Previously, the rule has required the use of brackets or parentheses for negative amounts.

50402. Rule 4-02. Items Not Material

If the amount which would otherwise be required to be shown with respect to any item is not material, it need not be separately set forth. The combination of insignificant amounts is permitted.

Since there is no all-inclusive concept of materiality, each situation needs to be evaluated subjectively. Quantitative materiality tests are sometimes provided in connection with certain disclosure requirements. The provisions in certain of the balance sheet rules require the presentation of selected captions or the disclosure of information only if certain percentage criteria are exceeded. The provisions in Rule 5-04 permitting the omission of schedules under certain conditions are examples of such quantitative materiality tests.

The definition of materiality included in Rule 1-02(n) of Regulation S-X states: "The term 'material,' when used to qualify a requirement for the furnishing of information as to any subject, limits the information required to those matters about which an average prudent investor ought reasonably to be informed."

50403. Rule 4-03. Inapplicable Captions and Omission of Unrequired or Inapplicable Financial Statements

(a) No caption should be shown in any financial statement as to which the items and conditions are not present.

(b) Financial statements not required or inapplicable because the required matter is not present need not be filed.

(c) The reasons for the omission of any required financial statements shall be indicated.

The disclosures required by this rule are generally made as part of a statement following the listing of the financial statements and schedules filed or the index to the financial statements (see section 41172). The following is an example of wording that may be used in such instances:

> Schedules other than those listed above have been omitted since they are either not required or not applicable, or since the required information is shown in the financial statements or related notes.

> Financial statements for 50 percent-or-less-owned persons are omitted pursuant to Rule 3-09(a) of Regulation S-X.

50404. Rule 4-04. Omission of Substantially Identical Notes

If a note covering substantially the same subject matter is required with respect to two or more financial statements relating to the same or affiliated persons, for which separate sets of notes are presented, the required information may be shown in a note to only one of such statements, provided that a clear and specific reference thereto is made in each of the other statements with respect to which the note is required.

Frequently, information to be disclosed with respect to certain additional financial statements included in a document may be the same as that already provided for in the consolidated financial statements. A statement to that effect will suffice and the information need not be repeated.

50405. Rule 4-05. Current Assets and Current Liabilities

If a company's normal operating cycle is longer than one year, generally recognized trade practices should be followed with respect to the inclusion or exclusion of items in current assets or current liabilities. An appropriate explanation of the circumstances should be made and, if practicable, an estimate given of the amount not realizable or payable within one year. The amounts maturing in each year (if practicable) along with the interest rates or range of rates also shall be disclosed.

Current assets, current liabilities, and the circumstances permitting the use of an operating cycle in excess of one year are discussed in ARB No. 43, Chapter 3A, *Working Capital—Current Assets and Current Liabilities*, as amended by FASB Statement No. 6, *Classification of Short-Term Obligations Expected To Be Refinanced*. The classification of obligations callable by a creditor is discussed in FASB Statement No. 78, *Classification of Obligations That Are Callable by the Creditor.*

50406. Rule 4-06. Reacquired Evidences of Indebtedness

Reacquired evidences of indebtedness shall be deducted from the appropriate liability caption. However, reacquired evidences of indebtedness held for pension and other special funds not related to the particular issues may be shown as assets, provided that there be stated the amount of such evidences of indebtedness, the cost thereof, the amount at which stated, and the purpose for which acquired.

See the discussion following caption 22 of section 50502 for comments regarding extinguishment of debt.

50407. Rule 4-07. Discount on Shares

Discount on shares, or any unamortized balance thereof, shall be shown separately as a deduction from the applicable account(s) as circumstances require.

50408. Rule 4-08. General Notes to Financial Statements

If applicable to the person for which the financial statements are filed, the following shall be set forth on the face of the appropriate statement or in appropriately captioned notes. The information shall be provided for each statement required to be filed, except that the information required by items (b), (c), (d), (e), and (f) shall be provided as of the most recent audited balance sheet being filed and for item (j) as specified therein. When specific statements are presented separately, the pertinent notes shall accompany such statements unless cross-referencing is appropriate.

This rule sets forth certain disclosure requirements that in the Commission's view are not included in authoritative accounting pronouncements promulgated by the private sector. The balance sheet disclosures that are required for the most recent audited balance sheet need not be furnished for the audited balance sheet of the prior period.

The requirement to reference from the financial statements to the related footnotes was deleted from this rule by ASR No. 280; however, to aid in the readability of financial statements, such references are sometimes necessary. When it is concluded that references are to be included on the face of the financial statements, it is preferable to reference all applicable notes, since cross-referencing on a piecemeal basis may be misleading.

(a) Principles of consolidation or combination. *With regard to consolidated or combined financial statements, refer to Rule 3A-01 to 3A-08 for requirements for supplemental information in notes to the financial statements.*

(b) Assets subject to lien. *Assets mortgaged, pledged, or otherwise subject to lien, and the approximate amounts thereof, shall be designated and the obligations collateralized briefly identified.*

(c) Defaults. *The facts and amounts concerning any default in principal, interest, sinking fund, or redemption provisions with respect to any issue of securities or credit agreements, or any breach of covenant of a related indenture or agreement, which default or breach existed at the date of the most recent balance sheet being filed and which has not been subsequently cured, shall be stated in the notes to the financial statements. If a default or breach exists, but acceleration of the obligation has been* *waived for a stated period of time beyond the date of the most recent balance sheet being filed, state the amount of the obligation and the period of the waiver.*

Under this rule, only defaults that existed at the date of the most recent balance sheet filed and that have not been subsequently cured are required to be disclosed in the notes to the financial statements.

FASB Statement No. 78, *Classification of Obligations That Are Callable by the Creditor,* provides guidance on obligations that are callable by the creditor because of violations of a debt agreement and whether they should be classified as current or noncurrent. In addition, the standard requires disclosure of the circumstances related to debt that is currently in default but for which a grace period extending beyond the date of the financial statements is provided when that debt is not classified as current because it is probable that the violation will be cured within the grace period.

In EITF Issue No. 86-30, "Classification of Obligations When a Violation Is Waived by the Creditor," the EITF reached a consensus that, unless the facts and circumstances indicate otherwise, a borrower should generally classify an obligation as noncurrent unless the following two conditions are met:

- "A covenant violation has occurred at the balance sheet date or would have occurred absent a loan modification."

- "It is probable that the borrower will not be able to cure the default (comply with the covenant) at measurement dates that are within the next 12 months."

(d) Preferred shares.

(1) Aggregate preferences on involuntary liquidation, if other than par or stated value, shall be shown parenthetically in the equity section of the balance sheet.

(2) Disclosure shall be made of any restriction upon retained earnings that arises from the fact that upon involuntary liquidation the aggregate preferences of the preferred shares exceed the par or stated value of such shares.

This rule requires that the involuntary liquidation value of preferred stock be shown on the face of the balance sheet whenever preferred stock is recorded and carried at less than its involuntary liquidation value. This presentation is also required by APB Opinion No. 10.

SAB Topic 3-C discusses the presentation of preferred stock when it is carried at less than the involuntary liquidation value. The text of the SAB is included in section 50502-28.

(e) Restrictions which limit the payment of dividends by the registrant.

(1) Describe the most significant restrictions, other than as reported under paragraph (d) of this section, on the payment of dividends by the registrant, indicating their sources, their pertinent provisions, and the amount of retained earnings or net income restricted or free of restrictions.

(2) Disclose the amount of consolidated retained earnings which represents undistributed earnings of 50 percent or less owned persons accounted for by the equity method.

(3) The disclosures in paragraphs (3)(i) and (ii) in this section shall be provided when the restricted net assets of consolidated and unconsolidated subsidiaries and the parent's equity in the undistributed earnings of 50 percent or less owned persons accounted for by the equity method together exceed 25 percent of consolidated net assets as of the end of the most recently completed fiscal year.

For purposes of this test, restricted net assets of subsidiaries shall mean that amount of the registrant's proportionate share of net assets (after intercompany eliminations) reflected in the balance sheets of its consolidated and unconsolidated subsidiaries as of the end of the most recent fiscal year which may not be transferred to the parent company in the form of loans, advances or cash dividends by the subsidiaries without the consent of a third party (i.e., lender, regulatory agency, foreign government, etc.). Not all limitations on transferability of assets are considered to be restrictions for purposes of this test, which considers only specific third party restrictions on the ability of subsidiaries to transfer funds outside of the entity. For example, the presence of subsidiary debt which is secured by certain of the subsidiary's assets does not constitute a restriction under this rule. However, if there are any loan provisions prohibiting dividend payments, loans or advances to the parent by a subsidiary, these are considered restrictions for purposes of computing restricted net assets. When a loan agreement requires that a subsidiary maintain certain working capital, net tangible assets, or net asset levels, or where formal compensating arrangements exist, there is considered to be a restriction under the rule because the lender's intent is normally to preclude the transfer by dividend or otherwise of funds to the parent company. Similarly, a provision which requires that a subsidiary reinvest all of its earnings is a restriction, since this precludes loans, advances or dividends in the amount of such undistributed earnings by the entity. Where restrictions on the amount of funds which may be loaned or advanced differ from the amount restricted as to transfer in the form of cash dividends, the amount least restrictive to the subsidiary shall be used. Redeemable preferred stocks (Rule 5-02-28) and minority interests shall be deducted in computing net assets for purposes of this test.

(i) Describe the nature of any restrictions on the ability of consolidated subsidiaries and unconsolidated subsidiaries to transfer funds to the registrant in the form of cash dividends, loans or advances (i.e., borrowing arrangements, regulatory restraints, foreign government, etc.).

(ii) Disclose separately the amounts of such restricted net assets for unconsolidated subsidiaries and consolidated subsidiaries as of the end of the most recently completed fiscal year.

Paragraph (1) of this rule requires disclosure of restrictions on the payment of dividends by the registrant to shareholders. Any restrictions, such as debt limitations, minimum working capital requirements, and minimum levels of net income, are required to be described. However, the effect on retained earnings or net income need only be disclosed for the most significant of these provisions. Because the declaration and payment of dividends depends on factors other than the absence of restrictions, the disclosure of restrictions on dividends pursuant to this rule should not imply that dividends will necessarily be declared from retained earnings in excess of the restrictions noted.

Paragraph (2) of this rule requires registrants to disclose the amount of retained earnings of the issuer that represents undistributed earnings of 50 percent-or-less-owned persons. Disclosure of this information is not required under generally accepted accounting principles. Guidance on the computation of this information is included in SAB Topic 6-K3, the text of which immediately precedes the discussion of Rule 4-08(f).

Paragraph (3) of Rule 4-08(e) requires certain computations to determine whether the disclosures required pursuant to subparagraphs (i) and (ii) need to be made. If the calculations are performed as indicated below, they will also allow a company to determine whether completion of Schedule III, Condensed Financial Information of the Registrant, pursuant to Rule 5-04 (section 50520), is required.

Step 1— Compute the registrant's (parent's) proportionate share of the total net assets of consolidated subsidiaries that may not be transferred to it in the form of loans, advances, or cash dividends.

Step 2— Compute the registrant's (parent's) proportionate share of the total net assets of *unconsolidated subsidiaries* similarly restricted.

Step 3— Determine the registrant's (parent's) equity in the undistributed earnings of *50 percent-or-less-owned persons accounted for by the equity method.*

Step 4— Compute the consolidated net assets of the registrant as of the end of the most recent fiscal year. For this purpose, redeemable preferred stock and minority interest should be deducted in computing net assets.

Step 5— If the combined total of the amounts determined in Steps 1, 2, and 3 exceed 25 percent of the amount computed in Step 4, the disclosures required by subparagraphs (3)(i) and (ii) of Rule 4-08(e) need to be furnished.

Step 6— If the amount determined in Step 1 exceeds 25 percent of the amount computed in Step 4, the condensed financial information of the registrant required by Rule 5-04 Schedule III (section 50520) is also required to be furnished.

ASR No. 302, which amended Rule 4-08(e), points out that the disclosures required by subparagraph (3)(i) of Rule 4-08(e) include (a) a description of the restrictions on the ability of consolidated and unconsolidated subsidiaries to transfer funds to the parent in the form of loans, advances, or cash dividends; (b) an identification of the sources of the restrictions (e.g., lender, regulatory agency, or foreign government); and (c) the aggregate amount restricted relative to total consolidated net assets as of the end of the most recent fiscal year. Although this portion of ASR No. 302 was not incorporated into the Codification of Financial Reporting Policies, disclosures made pursuant to subparagraph 3(i) should include the elements described. The information disclosed pursuant to subparagraph (3)(ii) of Rule 4-08 would consist of the amounts determined in Steps 1 and 2 above.

SAB Topics 6-K2 and 3 discuss various questions that may arise in the determination of the restrictions that limit the payment of dividends (Rule 4-08(e)), such as how restricted net assets of subsidiaries are to be computed, whether a decision to permanently reinvest constitutes a restriction, and when parent company footnote or schedule disclosures are required. The text of the SAB follows:

2. Parent Company Financial Information

a. Computation of Restricted Net Assets of Subsidiaries

Facts: The revised rules for parent company disclosures adopted in Accounting Series Release No. 302 require, in certain circumstances, (1) footnote disclosure in the consolidated financial statements about the nature and amount of significant restrictions on the ability of subsidiaries to transfer funds to the parent through intercompany loans, advances or cash dividends [Rule 4-08(e)(3)], and (2) the presentation of condensed parent company financial information and other data in a schedule (Rule 12-04). To determine which disclosures, if any, are required, a registrant must compute its proportionate share of the net assets of its consolidated and unconsolidated subsidiary companies as of the end of the most recent fiscal year which are restricted as to transfer to the parent company because the consent of a third party (a lender, regulatory agency, foreign government, etc.)

SEC 50408. Rule 4-08(e)

is required. If the registrant's proportionate share of the restricted net assets of consolidated subsidiaries exceeds 25% of the registrant's consolidated net assets, both the footnote and schedule information are required. If the amount of such restrictions is less than 25%, but the sum of these restrictions plus the amount of the registrant's proportionate share of restricted net assets of unconsolidated subsidiaries plus the registrant's equity in the undistributed earnings of 50% or less owned persons (investees) accounted for by the equity method exceed 25% of consolidated net assets, the footnote disclosure is required.

Question 1: How are restricted net assets of subsidiaries computed?

Interpretive Response: The calculation of restricted net assets requires an evaluation of each subsidiary to identify any circumstances where third parties may limit the subsidiary's ability to loan, advance or dividend funds to the parent. This evaluation normally comprises a review of loan agreements, statutory and regulatory requirements, etc., to determine the dollar amount of each subsidiary's restrictions. The related amount of the subsidiary's net assets designated as restricted, however, should not exceed the amount of the subsidiary's net assets included in consolidated net assets, since parent company disclosures are triggered when a significant amount of consolidated net assets are restricted. The amount of each subsidiary's net assets included in consolidated net assets is determined by allocating (pushing down) to each subsidiary any related consolidation adjustments such as intercompany balances, intercompany profits, and differences between fair value and historical cost arising from a business combination accounted for as a purchase. This amount is referred to as the subsidiary's adjusted net assets. If the subsidiary's adjusted net assets are less than the amount of its restrictions because the push down of consolidating adjustments reduced its net assets, the subsidiary's adjusted net assets is the amount of the subsidiary's restricted net assets used in the tests.

Registrants with numerous subsidiaries and investees may wish to develop approaches to facilitate the determination of its parent company disclosure requirements. For example, if the parent company's adjusted net assets (excluding any interest in its subsidiaries) exceed 75% of consolidated net assets, or if the total of all of the registrant's consolidated and unconsolidated subsidiaries' restrictions and its equity in investees' earnings is less than 25% of consolidated net assets, then the allocation of consolidating adjustments to the subsidiaries to determine the amount of their adjusted net assets would not be necessary since no parent company disclosures would be required.

Question 2: If a registrant makes a decision that it will permanently reinvest the undistributed earnings of a subsidiary, and thus does not provide for the income taxes thereon because it meets the criteria set forth in APB Opinion No. 23, is there considered to be a restriction for purposes of the test?

Interpretive Response: No. The rules require that only third party restrictions be considered. Restrictions on subsidiary net assets imposed by management are not included.

SEC 50408

b. Application of Tests for Parent Company Disclosures

Facts: The balance sheet of the registrant's 100%-owned subsidiary at the most recent fiscal year-end is summarized as follows:

Current assets	$120	Current liabilities	$ 30
Noncurrent assets	45	Long-term debt	60
			90
		Common stock	25
		Retained earnings	50
			75
	$165		$165

Net assets of the subsidiary are $75. Assume there are no consolidating adjustments to be allocated to the subsidiary. Restrictive covenants of the subsidiary's debt agreement provide that:

—net assets, excluding intercompany loans, cannot be less than $35.

—60% of accumulated earnings must be maintained.

Question: What is the amount of the subsidiary's restricted net assets?

Interpretive Response:

Restrictions	*Computed Restrictions*
• Net assets: currently $75, cannot be less than $35; therefore—	$35
• Dividends: 60% of accumulated earnings ($50) cannot be paid out; therefore—	$30

Restricted net assets for purposes of the test are $35. The maximum amount that can be loaned or advanced to the parent without violating the net asset covenant is $40 ($75 - 35). Alternatively, the subsidiary could pay a dividend of up to $20 ($50 - 30) without violating the dividend covenant, and loan or advance up to $20, without violating the net asset provision.

Facts: The registrant has one 100%-owned subsidiary. The balance sheet of the subsidiary at the latest fiscal year-end is summarized as follows:

Current assets	$ 75	Current liabilities	$ 23
Noncurrent assets	90	Long-term debt	57
		Redeemable preferred stock	10
		Common stock	30
		Retained earnings	45
			75
	$165		$165

SEC 50408. Rule 4-08(e)

Assume that the registrant's consolidated net assets are $130 and there are no consolidating adjustments to be allocated to the subsidiary. The subsidiary's net assets are $75. The subsidiary's noncurrent assets are comprised of $40 in operating plant and equipment used in the subsidiary's business and a $50 investment in a 30% investee. The subsidiary's equity in this investee's undistributed earnings is $18. Restrictive covenants of the subsidiary's debt agreements are as follows:

1. Net assets, excluding intercompany balances, cannot be less than $20.

2. 80% of accumulated earnings must be reinvested in the subsidiary.

3. Current ratio of 2:1 must be maintained.

Question: Are parent company footnote or schedule disclosures required?

Interpretive Response: Only the parent company footnote disclosures are required. The subsidiary's restricted net assets are computed as follows:

Restrictions	Computed Restrictions
• Net assets: currently $75, cannot be less than $20; therefore—	$20
• Dividends: 80% of accumulated earnings ($45) cannot be paid; therefore—	$36
• Current ratio: must be at least 2:1 ($46 current assets must be maintained since current liabilities are $23 at fiscal year-end); therefore—	$46

Restricted net assets for purposes of the test are $20. The amount computed from the dividend restriction ($36) and the current ratio requirement ($46) are not used because net assets may be transferred by the subsidiary up to the limitation imposed by the requirement to maintain net assets of at least $20, without violating the other restrictions. For example, a transfer to the parent of up to $55 of net assets could be accomplished by a combination of dividends of current assets of $9 ($45-$36), and loans or advances of current assets of up to $20 and noncurrent assets of up to $26.

Parent company footnote disclosures are required in this example since the restricted net assets of the subsidiary and the registrant's equity in the earnings of its 100%-owned subsidiary's investee exceed 25% of consolidated net assets [($20 + 18)/$130 = 29%]. The parent company schedule information is not required since the restricted net assets of the subsidiary are only 15% of consolidated net assets ($20/$130 = 15%).

Although the subsidiary's noncurrent assets are not in a form which is readily transferable to the parent company, the illiquid nature of the assets is not relevant for purposes of the parent company tests. The objective of the tests is to require

582

parent company disclosures when the parent company does not have control of its subsidiaries' funds because it does not have unrestricted access to their net assets. The tests trigger parent company disclosures only when there are significant third party restrictions on transfers by subsidiaries of net assets and the subsidiaries' net assets comprise a significant portion of consolidated net assets. Practical limitations, other than third party restrictions on transferability at the measurement date (most recent fiscal year-end), such as subsidiary illiquidity, are not considered in computing restricted net assets. However, the potential effect of any limitations other than those imposed by third parties should be considered for inclusion in Management's Discussion and Analysis of liquidity.

Facts:

	Net assets
Subsidiary A	$(500)
Subsidiary B	$2,000
Consolidated	$3,700

Subsidiaries A and B are 100% owned by the registrant. Assume there are no consolidating adjustments to be allocated to the subsidiaries. Subsidiary A has restrictions amounting to $200. Subsidiary B's restrictions are $1,000.

Question: What parent company disclosures are required for the registrant?

Interpretive Response: Since subsidiary A has an excess of liabilities over assets, it has no restricted net assets for purposes of the test. However, both parent company footnote and schedule disclosures are required, since the restricted net assets of subsidiary B exceed 25% of consolidated net assets ($1,000/$3,700 = 27%).

Facts:

	Net assets
Subsidiary A	$850
Subsidiary B	$300
Consolidated	$3,700

The registrant owns 80% of subsidiary A. Subsidiary A owns 100% of subsidiary B. Assume there are no consolidating adjustments to be allocated to the subsidiaries. A may not pay any dividends or make any affiliate loans or advances. B has no restrictions. A's net assets of $850 do not include its investment in B.

Question: Are parent company footnote or schedule disclosures required for this registrant?

Interpretive Response: No. All of the registrant's share of subsidiary A's net assets ($680) are restricted. Although B may pay dividends and loan or advance funds to A, the parent's access to B's funds through A is restricted. However, since there are no limitations on B's ability to loan or advance funds to the parent, none of the parent's share of B's net assets are restricted. Since A's restricted net assets are

SEC 50408. Rule 4-08(e)

less than 25% of consolidated net assets ($680/$3,700 = 18%), no parent company disclosures are required.

Facts: The consolidating balance sheet of the registrant at the latest fiscal year-end is summarized as follows:

	Registrant	Subsidiary	Consolidating Adjustments	Consolidated
Current assets	$ 800	$ 700	$ —	$1,500
30% investment in affiliate	175	—	—	175
Investment in subsidiary	350	—	(350)	—
Other noncurrent assets	625	300	(100)	825
	$1,950	$1,000	$(450)	$2,500

	Registrant	Subsidiary	Consolidating Adjustments	Consolidated
Current liabilities	$ 600	$ 400	$ —	$1,000
Noncurrent liabilities	375	150	—	525
Redeemable preferred stock	275	—	—	275
Common stock	110	1	(1)	110
Paid-in capital	290	49	(49)	290
Retained earnings	300	400	(400)	300
	700	450	(450)	700
	$1,950	$1,000	$(450)	$2,500

The acquisition of the 100%-owned subsidiary was consummated on the last day of the most recent fiscal year. Immediately preceding the acquisition, the registrant had net assets of $700, which included its equity in the undistributed earnings of its 30% investee of $75. Immediately after acquiring the subsidiary's net assets, which had an historical cost of $450 and a fair value of $350, the registrant's net assets were still $700 since debt and preferred stock totaling $350 were issued in the purchase. The subsidiary has debt covenants which permit dividends, loans or advances, to the extent, if any, that net assets exceed an amount which is determined by the sum of $100 plus 75% of the subsidiary's accumulated earnings.

Question: What is the amount of the subsidiary's restricted net assets? Are parent company footnote or schedule disclosures required?

Interpretive Response: Restricted net assets for purposes of the test are $350, and both the parent company footnote and schedule disclosures are required.

The amount of the subsidiary's restrictions at year-end is $400 [$100 + (75% x $400)]. The subsidiary's adjusted net assets after the push down of the consolidation entry to the subsidiary to record the noncurrent assets acquired at their fair value is $350 ($450 - $100). Since the subsidiary's adjusted net assets ($350) are less than the amount of its restrictions ($400), restricted net assets are $350. The computed percentages applicable to each of the disclosure tests are in excess of 25%. Therefore, both parent company footnote and schedule information are required. The percentage applicable to the footnote disclosure test is 61% [($75 + $350)/$700]. The computed percentage for the schedule disclosure is 50% ($350/$700).

3. Undistributed Earnings of 50% or Less Owned Persons

Facts: Rule 4-08(e)(2) of Regulation S-X requires footnote disclosure of the amount of consolidated retained earnings which represents undistributed earnings of 50% or less owned persons (investee) accounted for by the equity method. The test adopted in ASR 302 to trigger disclosures about the registrant's restricted net assets [Rule 4-08(e)(3)] includes the parent's equity in the undistributed earnings of investees.

Question: Is the amount required for footnote disclosure the same as the amount included in the test to determine disclosures about restrictions?

Interpretive Response: Yes. The amount used in the test in Rule 4-08(e)(3) should be the same as the amount required to be disclosed by Rule 4-08(e)(2). This is the portion of the registrant's consolidated retained earnings which represents the undistributed earnings of an investee since the date(s) of acquisition. It is computed by determining the registrant's cumulative equity in the investee's earnings, adjusted by any dividends received, related goodwill amortized, and any related income taxes provided.

(f) Significant changes in bonds, mortgages, and similar debt. *Any significant changes in the authorized or issued amounts of bonds, mortgages, and similar debt since the date of the latest balance sheet being filed for a particular person or group shall be stated.*

AU Section 560 requires the disclosure of events or transactions that occur subsequent to the balance sheet date but prior to the issuance of the financial statements that have a material effect on the financial statements. The disclosure required by this rule is specifically directed to "significant" changes in bonds, mortgages, and similar debt since the date of the latest balance sheet.

(g) Summarized financial information of subsidiaries not consolidated and 50 percent or less owned persons.

(1) The summarized information as to assets, liabilities and results of operations as detailed in Rule 1-02(aa) shall be presented in notes to the financial statements on an individual or group basis for (i) subsidiaries not consolidated and (ii) for 50 percent

or less owned persons accounted for by the equity method by the registrant or by a subsidiary of the registrant, if the criteria in Rule 1-02(v) for a significant subsidiary are met (A) individually by any subsidiary not consolidated or any 50% or less owned person or (B) on an aggregate basis by any combination of such subsidiaries and persons.

(2) Summarized financial information shall be presented insofar as is practicable as of the same dates and for the same periods as the audited consolidated financial statements provided and shall include the disclosures prescribed by Rule 1-02 (aa). Summarized information of subsidiaries not consolidated shall not be combined for disclosure purposes with the summarized information of 50 percent or less owned persons.

See section 50343 for a discussion of the information required to be disclosed pursuant to this rule.

(h) Income tax expense.

(1) Disclosure shall be made in the income statement, or a note thereto, of:

(i) the components of income (loss) before income tax expense (benefit) as either domestic or foreign;

(ii) the components of income tax expense, including

(A) taxes currently payable and

(B) the net tax effects, as applicable, of timing differences (indicate separately the amount of the estimated tax effect of each of the various types of timing differences, such as depreciation, warranty costs, etc., where the amount of each such tax effect exceeds five percent of the amount computed by multiplying the income before tax by the applicable statutory Federal income tax rate; other differences may be combined).

Note: *Amounts applicable to United States Federal income taxes, to foreign income taxes and the other income taxes shall be stated separately for each major component. Amounts applicable to foreign income (loss) and amounts applicable to foreign or other income taxes which are less than five percent of the total of income before taxes or the component of tax expense, respectively, need not be separately disclosed. For purposes of this rule, foreign income (loss) is defined as income (loss) generated from a registrant's foreign operations, i.e., operations that are located outside of the registrant's home country.*

SEC 50408

586

(2) Provide a reconciliation between the amount of reported total income tax expense (benefit) and the amount computed by multiplying the income (loss) before tax by the applicable statutory Federal income tax rate, showing the estimated dollar amount of each of the underlying causes for the differences. If no individual reconciling item amounts to more than five percent of the amount computed by multiplying the income before tax by applicable statutory Federal income tax rate, and the total difference to be reconciled is less than five percent of such computed amount, no reconciliation need be provided unless it would be significant in appraising the trend of earnings. Reconciling items that are individually less than five percent of the computed amount may be aggregated in the reconciliation. The reconciliation may be presented in percentages rather than in dollar amounts. Where the reporting person is a foreign entity, the income tax rate in that person's country of domicile should normally be used in making the above computation, but different rates should not be used for subsidiaries or other segments of a reporting entity. When the rate used by a reporting person is other than the United States Federal corporate income tax rate, the rate used and the basis for using such rate shall be disclosed.

(3) Paragraphs (h)(1) and (2) of this section shall be applied in the following manner to financial statements which reflect the adoption of Statement of Financial Accounting Standards 109, Accounting for Income Taxes [SFAS No. 109].

> *(i) The disclosures required by paragraph (h)(1)(ii) of this section and by the parenthetical instruction at the end of paragraph (h)(1) of this section and by the introductory sentence of paragraph (h)(2) of this section shall not apply.*

> *(ii) The instructional note between paragraphs (h)(1) and (2) of this section and the balance of the requirements of paragraph (h)(1) and (2) of this section shall continue to apply.*

Paragraph (h)(3) of Rule 4-08 applies to companies that have adopted SFAS No. 109. The effect of this paragraph is to delete the SEC requirements that would be duplicative for registrants complying with SFAS No. 109 as follows:

- Rule 4-08(h)(1)(ii)(A) requiring the disclosure of income tax expense currently payable duplicates the components of income tax expense required by paragraph 45 of SFAS No. 109.

- Rule 4-08(h)(1)(ii)(B) regarding the disclosure of the net tax effects on income tax expense of significant timing differences duplicates the disclosure of the tax effects of principal temporary differences required by paragraph 43 of SFAS No. 109.

SEC 50408. Rule 4-08(h)

- The requirement of Rule 4-08(h)(1)(ii) to provide the amount of the estimated tax effect of each of the various types of significant timing differences has been deleted. Paragraph 43 of Statement No. 109 requires disclosure of "the approximate tax effect of each type of temporary difference and carryforward that gives rise to a significant portion of deferred tax liabilities and assets (before allocation of valuation allowances)."

- The introductory sentence to Rule 4-08(h)(2) regarding a reconciliation between the amount of reported total income tax expense (benefit) and the amount computed by multiplying the income (loss) before tax by the applicable statutory Federal income tax rate duplicates a similar reconciliation required by paragraph 47 of SFAS No. 109.

Many of the SABs that are discussed in this section refer to the Rule 4-08 provisions that have been deleted. However, since most of this information is still required by Statement No. 109, the guidance in these SABs is still useful.

Paragraph (1) of Rule 4-08(h) requires that income (loss) before income tax expense (benefit) and the components of income tax expense be separated between domestic and foreign amounts. The rule defines foreign income on the same basis as FASB Statement No. 14 (paragraph 31). However, FASB Statement No. 14 limits the required disclosure to operating profit or loss, whereas Rule 4-08(h) requires the apportionment of income before income taxes.

FRP Section 204 indicates that although disclosure of a situation where future cash outlays for income taxes is anticipated to substantially exceed income tax expense is not explicitly required in Management's Discussion and Analysis, "this is the type of information which should be provided..." If applicable, this information would probably be discussed under "liquidity" (see discussion of MD&A in section 63030).

In addition to the disclosure required by this rule, the effect of "tax holidays" also needs to be disclosed in accordance with SAB Topic 11-C (see section 50503 following caption 11 for the text of this SAB).

The manner in which the information required by Rule 4-08(h) is to be presented is discussed in SAB Topic 6-17, which concludes that when income tax expense is allocated to more than one financial statement caption, the components of income tax expense may be presented in total, with the captions to which they relate identified separately. The text of SAB Topic 6-17 follows:

Tax Expense Components v. "Overall" Presentation

Facts: Rule 4-08(h) requires that the various components of income tax expense be disclosed, e.g., currently payable domestic taxes, deferred foreign taxes, etc. Frequently income tax expense will be included in more than one caption in the financial statements. For example, income taxes may be allocated to continuing operations, discontinued operations, extraordinary items, cumulative effects of an accounting change and direct charges and credits to shareholders' equity.

Question: In instances where income tax expense is allocated to more than one caption in the financial statements, must the components of income tax expense included in each caption be disclosed or will an "overall" presentation such as the following be acceptable?

The components of income tax expense are:

Currently payable (per tax return):

Federal	$350,000
Foreign	150,000
State	50,000

Deferred:

Federal	125,000
Foreign	75,000
State	50,000
	$800,000

Income tax expense is included in the financial statements as follows:

Continuing operations	$600,000
Discontinued operations	(200,000)
Extraordinary income	300,000
Cumulative effect of change in accounting principle	100,000
	$800,000

Interpretive Response: An overall presentation of the nature described will be acceptable.

When items in the financial statements are reported on a net of tax basis, SAB Topic 6-I3 provides that the tax components also need to be disclosed:

Net of Tax Presentation

Question: What disclosure is required when an item is reported on a net of tax basis (e.g., extraordinary items, discontinuance or disposals of business segments, or cumulative adjustment related to accounting change)?

Interpretive Response: When an item is reported on a net of tax basis, additional disclosure of the nature of the tax component should be provided by reconciling the tax component associated with the item to the applicable statutory Federal income tax rate or rates.

Paragraph (2) of Rule 4-08(h) and paragraph 47 of SFAS No. 109 require a reconciliation of the amount of income tax expense reported and the amount deter-

SEC 50408. Rule 4-08(h)

mined by applying the statutory rate to pretax income. This reconciliation needs to be presented for each period for which an audited income statement is *required* to be presented if the materiality test described in the rule is met. The tax rate to be used in the reconciliation of the tax provision should be the actual statutory rate applicable to each period, as discussed in SAB Topic 6-I1. The text of the SAB follows:

Tax Rate

Question 1: In reconciling to the effective tax rate should the rate used be a combination of state and Federal income tax rates?

Interpretive Response: No, the reconciliation should be made to the Federal income tax rate only.

Question 2: What is the "applicable statutory Federal income tax rate"?

Interpretive Response: The applicable statutory Federal income tax rate is the normal rate applicable to the reporting entity. Hence, the statutory rate for a U.S. partnership is zero. If, for example, the statutory rate for U.S. corporation is 22% on the first $25,000 of taxable income and 46% on the excess over $25,000, the "normalized rate" for corporations will fluctuate in the range between 22% and 46% depending on the amount of pretax accounting income a corporation has.

A reconciliation also needs to be furnished for tax recoveries in loss years, as discussed in SAB Topic 6-I4:

Loss Years

Question: Is a reconciliation of a tax recovery in a loss year required?

Interpretive Response: Yes, in loss years the actual book tax benefit of the loss should be reconciled to expected normal book tax benefit based on the applicable statutory Federal income tax rate.

The manner in which foreign registrants are to provide the reconciliation is discussed in SAB Topic 6-I5 as follows:

Foreign Registrants

Question 1: Occasionally, reporting foreign persons may not operate under a normal tax base rate such as the current U.S. Federal corporate income tax rate. What form of disclosure is acceptable in these circumstances?

Interpretive Response: In such instances, reconciliations between year-to-year effective rates or between a weighted average effective rate and the current effective rate of total tax expense may be appropriate in meeting the requirements of Rule 4-08(h). A brief description of how such a rate was determined would be required in addition to other required disclosures. Such an approach would not be acceptable for a U.S. registrant with foreign operations. Foreign registrants with unusual tax situations may find that these guidelines are not fully responsive to their needs. In such instances, registrants should discuss the matter with the staff.

Question 2: Where there are significant reconciling items that relate in significant part to foreign operations as well as domestic operations, is it necessary to disclose the separate amounts of the tax component by geographical area (e.g., statutory depletion allowances provided for by U.S. and by other foreign jurisdictions)?

Interpretive Response: It is not practicable to give an all-encompassing answer to this question. However, in many cases such disclosure would seem appropriate.

Certain disclosures may also be required for investee companies accounted for by the equity method, as discussed in SAB Topic 6-I2:

Taxes of Investee Company

Question: If a registrant records its shares of earnings or losses of a 50% or less owned person on the equity basis, and such person has an effective tax rate which differs by more than 5% from the applicable statutory Federal income tax rate, is a reconciliation as required by Rule 4-08(h) necessary?

Interpretive Response: Whenever the tax components are known and material to the investor's (registrant's) financial position or results of operations, appropriate disclosure should be made. In some instances where 50% or less owned persons are accounted for by the equity method of accounting in the financial statements of the registrant, the registrant may not know the rate at which the various components of income are taxed and it may not be practicable to provide disclosure concerning such components.

It should also be noted that it is generally necessary to disclose the aggregate dollar and per-share effect of situations where temporary tax exemptions or "tax holidays" exist, and that such disclosures are also applicable to 50% or less owned persons. Such disclosures should include a brief description of the factual circumstances and give the date on which the special tax status will terminate. See paragraph C of Topic 11 [Tax Holidays—see caption 11 of Rule 5-03 in section 50503-11].

SAB Topic 6-I6 states that if the tax on the securities gains and losses of banks and insurance companies varies by more than five percent from the applicable Federal statutory rate, a reconciliation should be provided. The text of the SAB follows:

SEC 50408. Rule 4-08(h)

Securities Gains and Losses

Question: If the tax on the securities gains and losses of banks and insurance companies varies by more than 5% from the applicable statutory Federal income tax rate, should a reconciliation to the statutory rate be provided?

Interpretive Response: Yes.

In order to clarify the disclosure requirements of Rule 4-08(h), the SEC provided the following exhibit to FRP Section 204. Note that FRP Section 204 was originally issued as ASR No. 149 in 1973 and, accordingly, the assumptions are based on then existing tax rates and accounting practices. It should also be noted that the table in the illustrative note below that presents the timing differences that result in deferred tax expense is no longer required for companies that have adopted SFAS No. 109. However, paragraph 43 of SFAS No. 109 does require the disclosure of the tax effects of principal temporary differences. The reader should note that this example reflects the income statement approach of APB Opinion No. 11, *Accounting for Income Taxes,* while SFAS No. 109, *Accounting for Income Taxes,* has a balance sheet orientation.

The following example of the disclosure required under Rule 4-08(h) is provided to assist registrants in appraising the proposal and in complying with it.

I. Assumptions

The following facts apply to a hypothetical business corporation for the calendar year 1973 (all figures in thousands):

Book income before tax . . . . $15,000.

(1) Assets purchased at the beginning of 1973 at a cost of $10,000, eight-year life, double declining balance depreciation for tax purposes, straight line on books, eligible for 7% investment credit.

(2) Research costs of $3,000 deducted on tax return but amortized over following years for book purposes.

(3) Warranty reserve of $1,400 provided for book purposes is not deductible for tax purposes until warranty costs are incurred.

(4) Income before taxes includes $2,000 related to construction-type contracts still in process which are accounted for on the percentage of completion method for book purposes and on the completed contract method for tax purposes.

(5) Amortization of goodwill of $800 is not deductible for tax purposes.

(6) Book income before taxes includes $2,400 which represents the net income of wholly owned foreign subsidiaries that are expected to indefinitely invest their undistributed earnings. Foreign Subsidiary A is permitted under its local tax laws to deduct a provision for an inventory reserve related to increased inventory levels.

SEC 50408

The reserve would be reduced in periods of inventory decline. For consolidated financial statement purposes, no such accrual is made and the associated deferred tax expense is $420. The subsidiaries have reportable taxes in their respective foreign jurisdictions as follows:

	Foreign Subsidiary A	Foreign Subsidiary B	Total
Foreign book income before taxes	$2,100	$300	$2,400
Foreign jurisdiction tax rate	30%	50%	—
Currently taxable income	$ 700	$300	$1,000
Current tax expense	210	150	360
Deferred tax expense	420	—	420
Total foreign income tax expense	$ 630	$150	$ 780

(7) Investments sold during the year resulted in a gain of $1,000, which is taxed at capital gain rates of 30%.

(8) Included in income is $1,500 of interest on tax-exempt municipal bonds.

(9) State and local income taxes amounted to $400.

II. Illustrative Note

Note—Income tax expense (all data in thousands).

Income tax expense is made up of the following components:

	U.S. Federal	Foreign	State & Local	Total
Current tax expense	$2,312	$360	$400	$3,072
Deferred tax expense	2,328	420	—	2,748
	$4,640	$780	$400	$5,820

Deferred tax expense results from timing differences in the recognition of revenue and expense for tax and financial statement purposes. The sources of these differences in 1973 and the tax effect of each were as follows:

Excess of tax over book depreciation	$ 600
Research and development costs expensed on tax return and deferred on books	1,440
Revenue recognized on completed contract basis on tax return and on percentage of completion basis on books	960
Tax deductible inventory reserve provided in foreign tax jurisdiction	420
Warranty cost charged to expense on books but not deductible until paid	(672)
	$2,748

SEC 50408. Rule 4-08(h)

Total tax expense amounted to $ 5,820 (an effective rate of 38.8%), a total less than the amount of $7,200 computed by applying the U.S. Federal income tax rate of 48% to income before tax. The reasons for this difference are as follows:

	Amount	% of Pretax Income
Computed "expected" tax expense	$7,200	48.0%
Increases (reductions) in taxes resulting from: Foreign income subject to foreign income tax but not expected to be subject to U.S. tax in foreseeable future ($2,400 X 48%) - $ 780 = $372	(372)	(2.5)
Tax exempt municipal bond income	(720)	(4.8)
Investment tax credit on assets purchased in 1973	(700)	(4.7)
Goodwill amortization not deductible for tax purposes	384	2.6
State and local income taxes, net of Federal income tax benefit	208	1.4
Benefit from income taxed at capital gains rate (1,000 X 48%) - (1,000 X 30%) = $180*	(180)	(1.2)
Actual tax expense	$5,820	38.8%

*Since these amounts are less than 5% of the computed "expected" tax expense, they could be combined with any other items less than $360 into an aggregate total. For example, these items could be disclosed as follows: "Miscellaneous items . . . $28 . . 0.2%."

If no single item had exceeded $360 in this case and the total net difference of all items was also less than $360, this reconciliation would not have been required.

III. Computational Guide

(Furnished only to enable interested parties to determine source of numbers shown in above illustrative note; not to be required of registrants in filings.)

Tax computations		
Book income before tax		$15,000
State income tax		(400)
Permanent differences:		
Goodwill amortization	$ 800	
Municipal bond income	(1,500)	
Foreign income, no domestic income tax	(2,400)	
Capital gain	(1,000)	(4,100)
		$10,500

Timing differences:

Excess depreciation		$(1,250)
R & D deducted on tax return		(3,000)
Warranty cost not deductible until paid		1,400
Percentage of completion income		(2,000)
Taxable income (excl. cap. gain)		$5,650

Tax to be paid

Tax on ordinary income	.48 x 5,650	$ 2,712
Plus capital gain tax	.30 x 1,000	300
Less investment credit		(700)
Actual tax paid		$2,312

Tax expense per books

Tax expense on ordinary income	.48 x 10,500	$5,040
Plus capital gain tax		300
Less investment credit		(700)
Tax expense—federal		$4,640
Foreign tax		$ 780
State and local income tax		$ 400

Computations of disclosure limits

Computed amount	$15,000 x .48 =	$7,200
5% of computed amount	.05 x $ 7,200 =	$360

Note: This example was originally published prior to adoption in ASR No. 280 of the requirement for separate disclosure of domestic and foreign pretax income. Therefore, it does not illustrate disclosures under that requirement.

When a member of a group that files a consolidated tax return issues separate financial statements, a question frequently arises as to how to allocate the consolidated tax amounts for financial reporting purposes to the individual entity. Paragraph 40 of SFAS 109 does not require a single allocation method. Two broad approaches both considered acceptable by the FASB staff are often referred to as the "top down" and the "bottom up" approaches. In the "top down" approach the consolidated total tax expense (both current and deferred calculated in accordance with Statement 109) is allocated among the members of the consolidated group in a systematic, rational, and consistent manner.

The "bottom up" approach allocates current and deferred taxes to members of the group by applying Statement 109 to each member as if it were a separate taxpayer

SEC 50408. Rule 4-08(h)

(i.e., separate return method). However, the SEC staff has taken the position in its review of a number of recent filings that the only acceptable method is to calculate the tax amounts included in the subsidiary's financial statements on a separate return basis (i.e., the "bottom up" approach). This position is narrower than the guidance included in SEC SAB Topic 1-B, which indicates that registrants may provide pro forma disclosure of tax amounts calculated on a separate return basis.

With respect to the propriety of using a tax-planning strategy that involves the sale of *certain* appreciated assets (i.e., "cherry picking"), the SEC staff's view is that if there is significant negative evidence, paragraph 24(b) of SFAS 109 would preclude use of a tax-planning strategy to sell certain appreciated assets unless there is an excess of the appreciated asset value over the tax basis of the entity's *net* assets in an amount sufficient to realize the deferred tax asset. If there is no negative evidence, the staff's view is that neither paragraph 22 nor paragraph 24 of SFAS 109 requires appreciation of the *net* assets to use a tax-planning strategy.

Under Statement 109, expectations about future taxable income are considered. A deferred tax asset is initially recognized for the estimated future tax effects of deductible temporary differences, and for operating loss and other credit carryforwards using the applicable tax rate. A deferred tax asset should be reduced by a valuation allowance if, based on the weight of evidence, it is *more likely than not* that some portion or all of the potential deferred tax asset will not be realized. The valuation allowance for deferred tax assets is adjusted to avoid recognition of tax benefits that, based on available evidence, are not expected to be realized.

Registrants that have recognized in accordance with Statement 109 material net deferred tax assets (in excess of existing deferred tax liabilities) have been required by the SEC staff to discuss in MD&A uncertainties surrounding realization of the asset and material assumptions underlying management's determination that the net asset will be realized. See section 63030 for a full discussion of MD&A requirements.

The staff expects the following disclosures to be included in MD&A by registrants in situations in which the net deferred tax asset comprises a significant portion of the registrant's total assets and/or stockholder's equity and existing levels of income do not appear to be sufficient to ensure realizability of the deferred tax asset:

- A discussion of the minimum amount of future taxable income that would need to be generated to realize the deferred tax asset and whether the existing levels of pretax earnings for financial reporting purposes are sufficient to generate that minimum amount of future taxable income;

- A description of operating improvements necessary to realize the deferred tax asset;

- A discussion of the historical relationship between pretax earnings for financial reporting purposes and taxable income for income tax purposes, including the nature and amount of material differences between such amounts. A table reconciling pretax income and taxable income for each of the years for which financial statements are presented has been used by some registrants to provide this information;

- A description of material asset sales or other nonroutine transactions (e.g., tax-planning strategies); and

- The annual amounts of net operating loss carryforwards for income tax purposes that expire by year of expiration.

(i) Warrants or rights outstanding. *Information with respect to warrants or rights outstanding at the date of the related balance sheet shall be set forth as follows:*

(1) Title of issue of securities called for by warrants or rights.

(2) Aggregate amount of securities called for by warrants or rights outstanding.

(3) Date from which warrants or rights are exercisable.

(4) Price at which warrant or right is exercisable.

(j) Reserved for future use.

(k) Related party transactions which affect the financial statements.

(1) Related party transactions should be identified and the amounts stated on the face of the balance sheet, income statement or statement of cash flows.

(2) In cases where separate financial statements are presented for the registrant, certain investees, or subsidiaries, separate disclosure shall be made in such statements of the amounts in the related consolidated financial statements which are (i) eliminated and (ii) not eliminated. Also, any intercompany profits or losses resulting from transactions with related parties and not eliminated and the effects thereof shall be disclosed.

The related-party disclosures required in accordance with generally accepted accounting principles are set forth in FASB Statement No. 57, *Related Party Disclosures*. Paragraph (1) of this rule goes beyond this standard by requiring that related-party amounts be stated separately on the face of the financial statements.

Paragraph (2) of this rule applies to separate financial statements of the registrant, certain investees, and subsidiaries. It requires disclosure in the separate statements of these entities (when such statements are required) of amounts in the related consolidated financial statements that have been eliminated and of amounts that have not been eliminated. Also, any intercompany profits or losses resulting from transactions with related parties not eliminated need to be disclosed.

The SEC staff takes a great interest in the accounting for related-party transactions and in related-party disclosures during the SEC review process. In a 1991 letter to the AICPA, the staff indicated that "auditors with clients that have complex organizational forms, such as holding companies, should consider whether they have obtained sufficient information about the structure of the entities, the control relationships and the substance of any transactions between the parties when evaluating the effect on the financial statements. The staff noted that particular attention should be given to nonmonetary exchanges that provide gains to one or more parties and to year-end transactions that aid one of the parties in reaching its earnings forecasts, meeting debt covenants, etc."

(l) Reserved for future use.

(m) Repurchase and reverse repurchase agreements.

(1) Repurchase agreements (assets sold under agreements to repurchase).

(i) If, as of the most recent balance sheet date, the carrying amount (or market value, if higher than the carrying amount or if there is no carrying amount) of the securities or other assets sold under agreements to repurchase ("repurchase agreements") exceeds 10% of total assets, disclose separately in the balance sheet the aggregate amount of liabilities incurred pursuant to repurchase agreements including accrued interest payable thereon.

(ii) (A) If, as of the most recent balance sheet date, the carrying amount (or market value, if higher than the carrying amount) of securities or other assets sold under repurchase agreements, other than securities or assets specified in (1)(ii)(B) of this section, exceeds 10% of total assets, disclose in an appropriately captioned footnote containing a tabular presentation, segregated as to type of such securities or assets sold under agreements to repurchase (e.g., U.S. Treasury obligations, U.S. Government agency obligations and loans), the following information as of the balance sheet date for each such agreement or group of agreements (other than agreements involving securities or assets specified in (1)(ii)(B) of this section) maturing (1) overnight; (2) term up to 30 days; (3) term of 30 to 90 days; (4) term over 90 days and (5) demand:

(1) The carrying amount and market value of the assets sold under agreement to repurchase, including accrued interest plus any cash or other assets on deposit under the repurchase agreements; and

(2) The repurchase liability associated with such transaction or group of transactions and the interest rate(s) thereon.

SEC 50408

(B) For purposes of (1)(ii)(A) of this section only, do not include securities or other assets for which unrealized changes in market value are reported in current income or which have been obtained under reverse repurchase agreements.

(iii) If, as of the most recent balance sheet date, the amount at risk under repurchase agreements with any individual counterparty or group of related counterparties exceeds 10% of stockholders' equity (or in the case of investment companies, net asset value), disclose the name of each such counterparty or group of related counterparties, the amount at risk with each, and the weighted average maturity of the repurchase agreements with each. The amount at risk under repurchase agreements is defined as the excess of carrying amount (or market value, if higher than the carrying amount or if there is no carrying amount) of the securities or other assets sold under agreement to repurchase including accrued interest plus any cash or other assets on deposit to secure the repurchase obligation, over the amount of the repurchase liability (adjusted for accrued interest). (Cash deposits in connection with repurchase agreements shall not be reported as unrestricted cash pursuant to rule 5-02.1.)

(2) Reverse repurchase agreements (assets purchased under agreements to resell).

(i) If, as of the most recent balance sheet date, the aggregate carrying amount of "reverse repurchase agreements" (securities or other assets purchased under agreements to resell) exceeds 10% of total assets:

(A) disclose separately such amount in the balance sheet; and

(B) disclose in an appropriately captioned footnote:

(1) the registrant's policy with regard to taking possession of securities or other assets purchased under agreements to resell; and

(2) whether or not there are any provisions to ensure that the market value of the underlying assets remains sufficient to protect the registrant in the event of default by the counterparty and, if so, the nature of those provisions.

(ii) If, as of the most recent balance sheet date, the amount at risk under reverse repurchase agreements with any individual counterparty or group of related counterparties exceeds 10% of stockholders' equity (or in the case of investment companies, net asset value), disclose the name of each such counterparty or group of related counterparties, the amount at risk with each, and the weighted average maturity of the reverse repurchase agreements with each. The amount at risk under reverse repurchase agreements is defined as the excess of the carrying amount of the reverse

SEC 50408.   Rule 4-08(m)

repurchase agreements over the market value of assets delivered pursuant to the agreements by the counterparty to the registrant (or to a third party agent that has affirmatively agreed to act on behalf of the registrant) and not returned to the counterparty, except in exchange for their approximate market value in a separate transaction.

50410. Rule 4-10. Financial Accounting and Reporting for Oil and Gas Producing Activities Pursuant to the Federal Securities Laws and the Energy Policy and Conservation Act of 1975

This section prescribes financial accounting and reporting standards for registrants of the Commission engaged in oil and gas producing activities in filings under the federal securities laws and for the preparation of accounts by persons engaged, in whole or in part, in the production of crude oil or natural gas in the United States, pursuant to Section 503 of the Energy Policy and Conservation Act of 1975 ("EPCA") and Section 11(c) of the Energy Supply and Environmental Coordination Act of 1974 ("ESECA"), as amended by Section 505 of EPCA. The application of this section to those oil and gas producing operations of companies regulated for rate-making purposes on an individual-company-cost-of-service basis may, however, give appropriate recognition to differences arising because of the effect of the rate-making process.

Exemption. *Any person exempted by the Department of Energy from any record-keeping or reporting requirements pursuant to Section 11(c) of ESECA, as amended, is similarly exempted from the related provisions of this section in the preparation of accounts pursuant to EPCA. This exemption does not affect the applicability of this section to filings pursuant to the Federal securities laws.*

It should be noted that all of the SEC staff's interpretations of matters involving oil and gas producing activities are included in SAB Topic 12. This guidance has not been included in this manual.

DEFINITIONS

(a) Definitions. *The following definitions apply to the terms listed below as they are used in this section:*

(1) Oil and gas producing activities.

(i) Such activities include:

(A) The search for crude oil, including condensate and natural gas liquids, or natural gas ("oil and gas") in their natural states and original locations.

SEC 50410

(B) The acquisition of property rights or properties for the purpose of further exploration and/or for the purpose of removing the oil and gas from existing reservoirs on those properties.

(C) The construction, drilling and production activities necessary to retrieve oil and gas from its natural reservoirs, and the acquisition, construction, installation, and maintenance of field gathering and storage systems—including lifting the oil and gas to the surface and gathering, treating, field processing (as in the case of processing gas to extract liquid hydrocarbons) and field storage. For purposes of this section, the oil and gas production function shall normally be regarded as terminating at the outlet valve on the lease or field storage tank; if unusual physical or operational circumstances exist, it may be appropriate to regard the production functions as terminating at the first point at which oil, gas, or gas liquids are delivered to a main pipeline, a common carrier, a refinery, or a marine terminal.

(ii) Oil and gas producing activities do not include:

(A) The transporting, refining and marketing of oil and gas.

(B) Activities relating to the production of natural resources other than oil and gas.

(C) The production of geothermal steam or the extraction of hydrocarbons as a by-product of the production of geothermal steam or associated geothermal resources as defined in the Geothermal Steam Act of 1970.

(D) The extraction of hydrocarbons from shale, tar sands, or coal.

(2) Proved oil and gas reserves. *Proved oil and gas reserves are the estimated quantities of crude oil, natural gas, and natural gas liquids which geological and engineering data demonstrate with reasonable certainty to be recoverable in future years from known reservoirs under existing economic and operating conditions, i.e., prices and costs as of the date the estimate is made. Prices include consideration of changes in existing prices provided only by contractual arrangements, but not on escalations based upon future conditions.*

(i) Reservoirs are considered proved if economic producibility is supported by either actual production or conclusive formation test. The area of a reservoir considered proved includes (A) that portion delineated by drilling and defined by gas-oil and/or oil-water contacts, if any, and (B) the immediately adjoining portions not yet drilled, but which can be reasonably judged as economically productive on the basis of available geological and engineering data. In the absence of information on fluid

SEC 50410. Rule 4-10(a)

contacts, the lowest known structural occurrence of hydrocarbons controls the lower proved limit of the reservoir.

(ii) Reserves which can be produced economically through application of improved recovery techniques (such as fluid injection) are included in the "proved" classification when successful testing by a pilot project, or the operation of an installed program in the reservoir, provides support for the engineering analysis on which the project or program was based.

(iii) Estimates of proved reserves do not include the following: (A) oil that may become available from known reservoirs but is classified separately as "indicated additional reserves"; (B) crude oil, natural gas, and natural gas liquids, the recovery of which is subject to reasonable doubt because of uncertainty as to geology, reservoir characteristics, or economic factors; (C) crude oil, natural gas, and natural gas liquids, that may occur in undrilled prospects; and (D) crude oil, natural gas, and natural gas liquids, that may be recovered from oil shales, coal, gilsonite and other such sources.

(3) Proved developed oil and gas reserves. *Proved developed oil and gas reserves are reserves that can be expected to be recovered through existing wells with existing equipment and operating methods. Additional oil and gas expected to be obtained through the application of fluid injection or other improved recovery techniques for supplementing the natural forces and mechanisms of primary recovery should be included as "proved developed reserves" only after testing by a pilot project or after the operation of an installed program has confirmed through production response that increased recovery will be achieved.*

(4) Proved undeveloped reserves. *Proved undeveloped oil and gas reserves are reserves that are expected to be recovered from new wells on undrilled acreage, or from existing wells where a relatively major expenditure is required for recompletion. Reserves on undrilled acreage shall be limited to those drilling units offsetting productive units that are reasonably certain of production when drilled. Proved reserves for other undrilled units can be claimed only where it can be demonstrated with certainty that there is a continuity of production from the existing productive formation. Under no circumstances should estimates for proved undeveloped reserves be attributable to any acreage for which an application of fluid injection or other improved recovery technique is contemplated, unless such techniques have been proved effective by actual tests in the area and in the same reservoir.*

(5) Proved properties. *Properties with proved reserves.*

(6) Unproved properties. *Properties with no proved reserves.*

SEC 50410

602

(7) Proved area. *The part of a property to which proved reserves have been specifically attributed.*

(8) Field. *An area consisting of a single reservoir or multiple reservoirs all grouped on or related to the same individual geological structural feature and/or stratigraphic condition. There may be two or more reservoirs in a field that are separated vertically by intervening impervious strata, or laterally by local geologic barriers, or by both. Reservoirs that are associated by being in overlapping or adjacent fields may be treated as a single or common operational field. The geological terms "structural feature" and "stratigraphic condition" are intended to identify localized geological features as opposed to the broader terms of basins, trends, provinces, plays, areas-of-interest, etc.*

(9) Reservoir. *A porous and permeable underground formation containing a natural accumulation of producible oil and/or gas that is confined by impermeable rock or water barriers and is individual and separate from other reservoirs.*

(10) Exploratory well. *A well drilled to find and produce oil or gas in an unproved area, to find a new reservoir in a field previously found to be productive of oil or gas in another reservoir, or to extend a known reservoir. Generally, an exploratory well is any well that is not a development well, a service well, or a stratigraphic test well as those items are defined below.*

(11) Development well. *A well drilled within the proved area of an oil or gas reservoir to the depth of a stratigraphic horizon known to be productive.*

(12) Service well. *A well drilled or completed for the purpose of supporting production in an existing field. Specific purposes of service wells include gas injection, water injection, steam injection, air injection, salt-water disposal, water supply for injection, observation, or injection for in-site combustion.*

(13) Stratigraphic test well. *A drilling effort, geologically directed, to obtain information pertaining to a specific geologic condition. Such wells customarily are drilled without the intention of being completed for hydrocarbon production. This classification also includes tests identified as core tests and all types of expendable holes related to hydrocarbon exploration. Stratigraphic test wells are classified as (i) "exploratory-type," if not drilled in a proved area, or (ii) "development- type," if drilled in a proved area.*

(14) Acquisition of properties. *Costs incurred to purchase, lease or otherwise acquire a property, including costs of lease bonuses and options to purchase or lease properties, the portion of costs applicable to minerals when land including mineral rights is purchased in fee, brokers' fees, recording fees, legal costs, and other costs incurred in acquiring properties.*

SEC 50410. Rule 4-10(a)

(15) Exploration costs. *Costs incurred in identifying areas that may warrant examination and in examining specific areas that are considered to have prospects of containing oil and gas reserves, including costs of drilling exploratory wells and exploratory-type stratigraphic test wells. Exploration costs may be incurred both before acquiring the related property (sometimes referred to in part as prospecting costs) and after acquiring the property. Principal types of exploration costs, which include depreciation and applicable operating costs of support equipment and facilities and other costs of exploration activities, are:*

(i) Costs of topographical, geographical and geophysical studies, rights of access to properties to conduct those studies, and salaries and other expenses of geologists, geophysical crews, and others conducting those studies. Collectively, these are sometimes referred to as geological and geophysical or "G&G" costs.

(ii) Costs of carrying and retaining undeveloped properties, such as delay rentals, ad valorem taxes on properties, legal costs for title defense, and the maintenance of land and lease records.

(iii) Dry hole contributions and bottom hole contributions.

(iv) Costs of drilling and equipping exploratory wells.

(v) Costs of drilling exploratory-type stratigraphic test wells.

(16) Development costs. *Costs incurred to obtain access to proved reserves and to provide facilities for extracting, treating, gathering and storing the oil and gas. More specifically, development costs, including depreciation and applicable operating costs of support equipment and facilities and other costs of development activities, are costs incurred to:*

(i) Gain access to and prepare well locations for drilling, including surveying well locations for the purpose of determining specific development drilling sites, clearing ground, draining, road building, and relocating public roads, gas lines, and power lines, to the extent necessary in developing the proved reserves.

(ii) Drill and equip development wells, development-type stratigraphic test wells, and service wells, including the costs of platforms and of well equipment such as casing, tubing, pumping equipment, and the wellhead assembly.

(iii) Acquire, construct, and install production facilities such as lease flow lines, separators, treaters, heaters, manifolds, measuring devices, and production storage tanks, natural gas cycling and processing plants, and central utility and waste disposal systems.

(iv) Provide improved recovery systems.

SEC 50410

(17) Production costs.

(i) Costs incurred to operate and maintain wells and related equipment and facilities, including depreciation and applicable operating costs of support equipment and facilities and other costs of operating and maintaining those wells and related equipment and facilities. They become part of the cost of oil and gas produced. Examples of production costs (sometimes called lifting costs) are:

(A) Costs of labor to operate the wells and related equipment and facilities.

(B) Repairs and maintenance.

(C) Materials, supplies, and fuel consumed and supplies utilized in operating the wells and related equipment and facilities.

(D) Property taxes and insurance applicable to proved properties and wells and related equipment and facilities.

(E) Severance taxes.

(ii) Some support equipment or facilities may serve two or more oil and gas producing activities and may also serve transportation, refining, and marketing activities. To the extent that the support equipment and facilities are used in oil and gas producing activities, their depreciation and applicable operating costs become exploration, development or production costs, as appropriate. Depreciation, depletion, and amortization of capitalized acquisition, exploration, and development costs are not production costs but also become part of the cost of oil and gas produced along with production (lifting) costs identified above.

SUCCESSFUL EFFORTS METHOD

(b) Costs to be capitalized if the successful efforts method of accounting is followed. *The costs of the following assets involved in oil and gas producing activities are to be capitalized when incurred:*

(1) Mineral interests in properties. *Including (i) fee ownership or a lease, concession, or other interest representing the right to extract oil or gas subject to such terms as may be imposed by the conveyance of that interest; (ii) royalty interests, production payments payable in oil or gas, and other nonoperating interests in properties operated by others; and (iii) those agreements with foreign governments or authorities under which a reporting entity participates in the operation of the related properties or otherwise serves as "producer" of the underlying reserves (as opposed to being an independent purchaser, broker,* *dealer, or importer). Properties do not include other supply agreements or contracts that represent the right to purchase, rather than extract, oil and gas.*

(2) Wells and related equipment and facilities. *Including: (i) costs incurred to drill and equip those exploratory wells and exploratory-type stratigraphic test wells that have found proved reserves and (ii) development costs, i.e., costs incurred to obtain access to proved reserves and provide facilities for extracting, treating, gathering, and storing the oil and gas, including the drilling and equipping of development wells and development-type stratigraphic test wells (whether those wells are successful or unsuccessful) and service wells.*

(3) Support equipment and facilities used in oil and gas producing activities. *Items such as seismic equipment, drilling equipment, construction and grading equipment, vehicles, repair shops, warehouses, supply points, camps, and division, district, or field offices.*

(4) Uncompleted wells, equipment and facilities. *Including costs incurred to: (i) drill and equip wells that are not yet completed and (ii) acquire or construct equipment and facilities that are not yet completed and installed.*

(5) Geological and geophysical studies. *G&G studies may be conducted on a property owned by another person, in exchange for an interest in the property if proved reserves are found or to be reimbursed if proved reserves are not found. In such cases, the G&G costs shall be accounted for as a receivable when incurred and, if proved reserves are found, they shall become the cost of the proved property acquired.*

(c) Assessment of unproved properties if the successful efforts method of accounting is followed. *Unproved properties shall be assessed periodically to determine whether they have been impaired. A property would likely be impaired, for example, if a dry hole has been drilled on it and the reporting entity has no firm plans to continue drilling. Also, the likelihood of partial or total impairment of a property increases as the expiration of the lease term approaches if drilling activity has not commenced on the property or on nearby properties. Information that becomes available after the end of the period covered by the financial statements but before those financial statements are issued shall be taken into account in evaluating conditions that existed at the balance sheet date.*

(1) If the results of the assessment indicate impairment, a loss shall be recognized by providing a valuation allowance. Impairment of individual unproved properties whose acquisition costs are relatively significant shall be assessed on a property-by-property basis, and an indicated loss shall be recognized by providing a valuation allowance. When a reporting entity has a relatively large number of unproved properties whose acquisition costs are not individually

significant, it may not be practical to assess impairment on a property-by-property basis, in which case the amount of loss to be recognized and the amount of the valuation allowance needed to provide for impairment of those properties shall be determined by amortizing those properties, either in the aggregate or by groups, on the basis of the experience of the entity in similar situations and other information about such factors as the primary lease terms of those properties, the average holding period of unproved properties, and the relative proportion of such properties on which proved reserves have been found in the past.

(2) A property shall be reclassified from unproved properties to proved properties when proved reserves are discovered on or otherwise attributed to the property. Occasionally, a single property such as a foreign lease or concession covers so vast an area that only the portion of the property to which the proved reserves relate—determined on the basis of geological structural features or stratigraphic conditions—should be reclassified from unproved to proved. For a property whose impairment has been assessed individually, the net carrying amount (acquisition cost minus valuation allowance) shall be reclassified to proved properties; for properties amortized by providing a valuation allowance on a group basis, the gross acquisition cost shall be reclassified..

(d) Surrender or abandonment of properties if the successful efforts method of accounting is followed. *When an unproved property is surrendered, abandoned, or otherwise deemed worthless, capitalized acquisition costs relating thereto shall be charged against the related allowance for impairment to the extent an allowance has been provided; if the allowance previously provided is inadequate, a loss shall be recognized. Normally, no gain or loss shall be recognized if only an individual well or individual item of equipment is abandoned or retired or if only a single lease or other part of a group of proved properties constituting the amortization base is abandoned or retired as long as the remainder of the property or group of properties continues to produce oil or gas. Instead, the asset being abandoned or retired shall be deemed to be fully amortized, and its costs shall be charged to accumulated depreciation, depletion, or amortization. When the last well on an individual property (if that is the amortization base) or group of properties (if amortization is determined on the basis of an aggregation of properties with a common geological structure) ceases to produce and the entire property or property group is abandoned, gain or loss shall be recognized. Occasionally, the partial abandonment or retirement of a proved property or group of proved properties or the abandonment or retirement of wells or related equipment or facilities may result from a catastrophic event or other major abnormality. In those cases, a loss shall be recognized at the time of abandonment or retirement.*

SEC 50410. Rule 4-10(c)

(e) Amortization of capitalized costs if the successful efforts method of accounting is followed.

(1) Capitalized acquisition costs of proved properties shall be amortized using the unit-of-production method on the basis of total estimated units of proved oil and gas reserves.

(2) Capitalized costs of exploratory wells and exploratory-type stratigraphic test wells that have found proved reserves and capitalized development costs shall be amortized (depreciated) using the unit-of-production method on the basis of total estimated units of proved developed reserves. However, it may be more appropriate, in some cases, to depreciate natural gas cycling and processing plants by a method other than the unit-of-production method.

(3) Amortization, using the unit-of-production method as required by paragraphs (1) and (2) of this section, may be computed either on a property-by-property basis or on the basis of some reasonable aggregation of properties with a common geological structural feature or stratigraphic condition, such as a reservoir or field. When a reporting entity has a relatively large number of royalty interests whose acquisition costs are not individually significant, they may be aggregated, for purposes of computing amortization, without regard to commonality of geological structural features or stratigraphic conditions; if information is not available to estimate reserve quantities applicable to royalty interests owned, a method other than the unit-of-production method may be used to amortize their acquisition costs. If significant development costs (such as the cost of an off-shore production platform) are incurred in connection with a planned group of development wells before all of the planned wells have been drilled, it will be necessary to exclude a portion of those development costs in determining the unit-of-production amortization rate until the additional development wells are drilled. Similarly, it will be necessary to exclude, in computing the amortization rate, those proved developed reserves that will be produced only after significant additional development costs are incurred, such as for improved recovery systems. However, in no case should future development costs be anticipated in computing the amortization rate. Estimated dismantlement, restoration, and abandonment costs and estimated residual salvage values shall be taken into account in determining amortization and depreciation rates. For those properties or groups of properties containing both oil reserves and gas reserves, the units of oil and gas used to compute amortization shall be converted to a common unit of measure on the basis of their approximate relative energy content (without considering their relative sales values). However, if the relative proportion of gas and oil extracted in the current period is expected to continue throughout the remaining productive life of the property, unit-of-production amortization may be computed on the basis of one of the two minerals

only; similarly, if either oil or gas clearly dominates both the reserves and the current production (with dominance determined on the basis of relative energy content), unit-of-production amortization may be computed on the basis of the dominant mineral only. Unit-of-production amortization rates shall be revised whenever there is an indication of the need for revision but at least once a year; those revisions shall be accounted for prospectively as changes in accounting estimates..

(f) Costs to be charged to expense if the successful efforts method of accounting is followed. *Costs incurred in oil and gas producing activities other than those described in paragraph (b) of this section shall be charged to expense. Examples include geological and geophysical costs, costs of carrying and retaining undeveloped properties, dry hole and bottom hole contributions, the costs of drilling those exploratory wells and exploratory-type stratigraphic test wells that do not find proved reserves (see paragraph (g) of this section), and the costs of oil and gas produced.*

(g) Accounting for the costs of exploratory wells and exploratory-type stratigraphic test wells if the successful efforts method of accounting is followed. *The costs of drilling exploratory wells and the cost of drilling exploratory-type stratigraphic test wells shall be capitalized as part of the reporting entity's uncompleted wells, equipment, and facilities pending determination of whether the well has found proved reserves. If the well has found proved reserves, the capitalized costs of drilling the well shall become part of the entity's wells and related equipment and facilities (even though the well may not be completed as a producing well); if, however, the well has not found proved reserves, the capitalized costs of drilling the well, net of any salvage value, shall be charged to expense. The determination of whether proved reserves are found is usually made on or shortly after completion of drilling the well, and the capitalized costs shall either be charged to expense or be reclassified as part of the costs of wells and related equipment and facilities at that time. Information that becomes available after the end of the period covered by the financial statements but before those financial statements are issued shall be taken into account in evaluating conditions that existed at the balance sheet date. Occasionally, an exploratory well or an exploratory-type stratigraphic test well may be determined to have found oil and gas reserves, but classification of those reserves as proved cannot be made when drilling is completed. In those cases, one of the three subparagraphs set forth below shall apply. Subparagraphs (g)(1) and (2) are intended to prohibit, in all cases, the deferral of the costs of exploratory wells that find some oil and gas reserves merely on the chance that some event totally beyond the entity's control will occur, e.g., on the chance that the selling prices of oil and gas will increase sufficiently to result in classification of reserves as proved that are not commercially recoverable at current prices.*

SEC 50410. Rule 4-10(e)

(1) Exploratory wells that find oil and gas reserves in an area requiring a major capital expenditure, such as a trunk pipeline, before production could begin. On completion of drilling, an exploratory well may be determined to have found oil and gas reserves, but classification of those reserves as proved depends on whether a major capital expenditure can be justified which, in turn, depends on whether additional exploratory wells find a sufficient quantity of additional reserves. In that case, the cost of drilling the exploratory well shall continue to be carried as an asset pending determination of whether proved reserves have been found only as long as both of the following conditions are met: (i) the well has found a sufficient quantity of reserves to justify its completion as a producing well if the required capital expenditure is made, and (ii) drilling of the additional exploratory wells is under way or firmly planned for the near future. Otherwise, the exploratory well shall be assumed to be impaired, and its costs shall be charged to expense.

(2) All other exploratory wells that find oil and gas reserves. In the absence of a determination as to whether the reserves that have been found can be classified as proved, the costs of drilling such an exploratory well shall not be carried as an asset for more than one year following completion of drilling. If, after that year has passed, a determination that proved reserves have been found cannot be made, the well shall be assumed to be impaired, and its costs shall be charged to expense.

(3) Exploratory-type stratigraphic test wells that find oil and gas reserves. On completion of drilling, such a well may be determined to have found oil and gas reserves, but classification of those reserves as proved depends on whether a major capital expenditure (usually a production platform) can be justified which, in turn, depends on whether additional exploratory-type stratigraphic test wells find a sufficient quantity of additional reserves. In that case, the cost of drilling the exploratory-type stratigraphic test well shall continue to be carried as an asset pending determination of whether proved reserves have been found only as long as both of the following conditions are met: (i) the well has found a quantity of reserves that would justify its completion for production had it not been simply a stratigraphic test well, and (ii) drilling of the additional exploratory-type stratigraphic test wells is under way or firmly planned for the near future. Otherwise, the exploratory-type stratigraphic test well shall be assumed to be impaired, and its costs shall be charged to expense.

(h) Mineral property conveyances and related transactions if the successful efforts method of accounting is followed.

(1) Certain transactions, sometimes referred to as conveyances, are in substance borrowings repayable in cash or its equivalent and shall be accounted for as borrowings. The following are examples of such transactions:

(i) *Entities seeking supplies of oil or gas sometimes make cash advances to operators to finance exploration in return for the right to purchase oil or gas discovered. Funds advanced for exploration that are repayable by offset against purchases of oil or gas discovered, or in cash if insufficient oil or gas is produced by a specified date, shall be accounted for as a receivable by the lender and as a payable by the operator.*

(ii) *Funds advanced to an operator that are repayable in cash out of the proceeds from a specified share of future production of a producing property, until the amount advanced plus interest at a specified or determinable rate is paid in full, shall be accounted for as borrowing. The advance is a payable for the recipient of the cash and a receivable for the party making the advance. Such transactions, as well as those described in paragraph (h)(5)(i) of this section, are commonly referred to as production payments. The two types differ in substance, however, as explained in paragraph (h)(5)(i) of this section.*

(2) In the following types of conveyances, gain or loss shall not be recognized at the time of conveyance:

(i) *A transfer of assets used in oil and gas producing activities (including both proved and unproved properties) in exchange for other assets also used in oil and gas producing activities.*

(ii) *A pooling of assets in a joint undertaking intended to find, develop, or produce oil or gas from a particular property or group of properties.*

(3) In the following types of conveyances, gain shall not be recognized at the time of the conveyance:

(i) *A part of an interest owned is sold and substantial uncertainty exists about recovery of the costs applicable to the retained interest.*

(ii) *A part of an interest owned is sold and the seller has a substantial obligation for future performance, such as an obligation to drill a well or to operate the property without proportional reimbursement for that portion of the drilling or operating costs applicable to the interest sold.*

(4) If a conveyance is not one of the types described in paragraphs (h)(2) and (3) of this section, gain or loss shall be recognized unless there are other aspects of the transaction that would prohibit such recognition under accounting principles applicable to enterprises in general.

(5) In accordance with paragraphs (h)(2) through (4) of this section, the following types of transactions shall be accounted for as indicated in each example. No attempt has been made to include the many variations of those

arrangements that occur, but paragraphs (h)(2) through (4) of this section shall, where applicable, determine the accounting for those other arrangements as well.

(i) Some production payments differ from those described in paragraph (h)(1)(ii) of this section in that the seller's obligation is not expressed in monetary terms but as an obligation to deliver, free and clear of all expenses associated with operation of the property, a specified quantity of oil or gas to the purchaser out of a specified share of future production. Such a transaction is a sale of a mineral interest for which gain shall not be recognized because the seller has a substantial obligation for future performance. The seller shall account for the funds received as unearned revenue to be recognized as the oil or gas is delivered. The purchaser of such a production payment has acquired an interest in a mineral property that shall be recorded at cost and amortized by the unit-of-production method as delivery takes place. The estimated oil or gas reserves and production data shall be reported, in accordance with paragraph (k) of this section, as those of the purchaser of the production payment and not of the seller.

(ii) An assignment of the operating interest in an unproved property with retention of a nonoperating interest in return for drilling, development and operation by the assignee is a pooling of assets in a joint undertaking for which the assignor shall not recognize gain or loss. The assignor's cost of the original interest shall become the cost of the interest retained. The assignee shall account for all costs incurred as specified by paragraphs (b) through (g) of this section and shall allocate none of those costs to the mineral interest acquired. If oil or gas is discovered, each party shall report its share of oil and gas reserves and production, in accordance with paragraph (k) of this section.

(iii) An assignment of a part of an operating interest in an unproved property in exchange for a "free well" with provision for joint ownership and operation is a pooling of assets in a joint undertaking by the parties. The assignor shall record no cost for the obligatory well; the assignee shall record no cost for the mineral interest acquired. All drilling, development, and operating costs incurred by either party shall be accounted for as provided in paragraphs (b) through (g) of this section. If the conveyance agreement requires the assignee to incur geological or geophysical expenditures instead of, or in addition to, a drilling obligation, those costs shall likewise be accounted for by the assignee as provided in paragraphs (b) through (g) of this section. If reserves are discovered, each party shall report its share of reserves and production, in accordance with paragraph (k) of this section.

SEC 50410

(iv) A part of an operating interest in an unproved property may be assigned to effect an arrangement called a "carried interest" whereby the assignee (the carrying party) agrees to defray all costs of drilling, developing, and operating the property and is entitled to all of the revenue from production from the property, excluding any third party interest, until all of the assignee's costs have been recovered, after which the assignor will share in both costs and production. Such an arrangement represents a pooling of assets in a joint undertaking by the assignor and assignee. The carried party shall make no accounting for any costs and revenue until after recoupment (payout) of the carried costs by the carrying party. Subsequent to payout the carried party shall account for its share of revenue, operating expenses, and (if the agreement provides for subsequent sharing of costs rather than a carried interest) subsequent development costs. During the payout period the carrying party shall record all costs, including those carried, as provided in paragraphs (b) through (g) of this section, and shall record all revenue from the property including that applicable to the recovery of costs carried. The carried party shall report as oil or gas reserves, in accordance with paragraph (k) of this section, only its share of proved reserves estimated to remain after payout, and unit-of-production amortization of the carried party's property costs shall not commence prior to payout. Prior to payout the carrying party's reserve estimates and production data, reported in accordance with paragraph (k) of this section, shall include the quantities applicable to recoupment of the carried costs.

(v) A part of an operating interest owned may be exchanged for a part of an operating interest owned by another party. The purpose of such an arrangement, commonly called a joint venture in the oil and gas industry, often is to avoid duplication of facilities, diversify risks, and achieve operating efficiencies. Such reciprocal conveyances represent exchanges of similar productive assets and no gain or loss shall be recognized by either party at the time of the transaction. In some joint ventures which may or may not involve an exchange of interests, the parties may share different elements of costs in different proportions. In such an arrangement, a party may acquire an interest in a property or in wells and related equipment that is disproportionate to the share of costs borne by it. As in the case of a carried interest or a free well, each party shall account for its own cost under the provisions of this section. No gain shall be recognized for the acquisition of an interest in joint assets, the cost of which may have been paid in whole or in part by another party.

(vi) In a unitization all of the operating and nonoperating participants pool their assets in a producing area (normally a field) to form a single

SEC 50410. Rule 4-10(h)

unit and in return receive an undivided interest (of the same type as previously held) in that unit. Unitizations generally are undertaken to obtain operating efficiencies and to enhance recovery of reserves, often through improved recovery operations. Participation in the unit is generally proportionate to the oil and gas reserves contributed by each. Because the properties may be in different stages of development at the time of unitization, some participants may pay cash and others may receive cash to equalize contributions of wells and related equipment and facilities with the ownership interests in reserves. In those circumstances, cash paid by a participant shall be recorded as an additional investment in wells and related equipment and facilities, and cash received by a participant shall be recorded as a recovery of cost. The cost of the assets contributed plus or minus cash paid or received is the cost of the participant's undivided interest in the assets of the unit. Each participant shall include its interest in reporting reserve estimates and production data.

(vii) If the entire interest in an unproved property is sold for cash or cash equivalent, recognition of gain or loss depends on whether, in applying paragraph (c) of this section, impairment had been assessed for that property individually, or by amortizing that property as part of a group. If impairment was assessed individually, gain or loss shall be recognized. For a property amortized by providing a valuation allowance on a group basis, neither gain nor loss shall be recognized when an unproved property is sold unless the sales price exceeds the original cost of the property, in which case gain shall be recognized in the amount of such excess.

(viii) If a part of the interest in an unproved property is sold, even though for cash or cash equivalent, substantial uncertainty usually exists as to recovery of the cost applicable to the interest retained. Consequently, the amount received shall be treated as a recovery of cost. However, if the sales price exceeds the carrying amount of a property whose impairment has been assessed individually in accordance with paragraph (c) of this section, or exceeds the original cost of a property amortized by providing a valuation allowance on a group basis, gain shall be recognized in the amount of such excess.

(ix) The sale of an entire interest in a proved property that constitutes a separate amortization base is not one of the types of conveyances described in paragraphs (h)(2) and (h)(3) of this section. The difference between the amount of sales proceeds and the unamortized cost shall be recognized as a gain or loss.

(x) The sale of a part of a proved property, or of an entire proved property constituting a part of an amortization base, shall be accounted for as the sale of an asset, and a gain or loss shall be recognized, since it is not one of the conveyances described in paragraphs (h)(2) and (h)(3) of this section. The unamortized cost of the property or group of properties a part of which was sold shall be apportioned to the interest sold and the interest retained on the basis of the fair values of those interests. However, the sale may be accounted for as a normal retirement under the provisions of paragraph (d) of this section with no gain or loss recognized if doing so does not significantly affect the unit-of-production amortization rate.

(xi) The sale of operating interest in a proved property for cash with retention of a nonoperating interest is not one of the types of conveyances described in paragraphs (h)(2) and (h)(3) of this section. Accordingly, it shall be accounted for as the sale of an asset, and any gain or loss shall be recognized. The seller shall allocate the cost of proved property to the operating interest sold and the nonoperating interest retained on the basis of the fair values of those interests.

(xii) The sale of a proved property subject to a retained production payment that is expressed as a fixed sum of money payable only from a specified share of production from that property, with the purchaser of the property obligated to incur the future costs of operating the property, shall be accounted for as follows: If satisfaction of the retained production payment is reasonably assured, the seller of the property, who retained the production payment, shall record the transaction as a sale, with recognition of any resulting gain or loss. The retained production payment shall be recorded as a receivable, at an amount reflecting appropriate considerations of imputed interest thereon. The purchaser shall record as the cost of the assets acquired the cash consideration paid plus the present value of the retained production payment, which shall be recorded as payable. The oil and gas reserve estimates and production data, including those applicable to liquidation of the retained production payment, shall be reported by the purchaser of the property. If satisfaction of the retained production payment is not reasonably assured, the transaction is in substance a sale with retention of an overriding royalty that shall be accounted for in accordance with paragraph (h)(5)(xi) of this section.

(xiii) The sale of a proved property subject to a retained production payment that is expressed as a right to a specified quantity of oil or gas out of a specified share of future production shall be accounted for in accordance with paragraph (h)(5)(xi) of this section.

SEC 50410.   Rule 4-10(h)

FULL COST METHOD

(i) Application of the full cost method of accounting. *A reporting entity that follows the full cost method shall apply that method to all of its operations and to the operations of its subsidiaries, as follows:*

(1) Determination of cost centers. *Cost centers shall be established on a country-by-country basis.*

(2) Costs to be capitalized. *All costs associated with property acquisition, exploration, and development activities (as defined in paragraph (a) of this section) shall be capitalized within the appropriate cost center. Any internal costs that are capitalized shall be limited to those costs that can be directly identified with acquisition, exploration, and development activities undertaken by the reporting entity for its own account, and shall not include any costs related to production, general corporate overhead, or similar activities.*

(3) Amortization of capitalized costs. *Capitalized costs within a cost center shall be amortized on the unit-of-production basis using proved oil and gas reserves, as follows:*

(i) Costs to be amortized shall include (A) all capitalized costs, less accumulated amortization, other than the cost of properties described in paragraph (ii) below; (B) the estimated future expenditures (based on current costs) to be incurred in developing proved reserves; and (C) estimated dismantlement and abandonment costs, net of estimated salvage values.

(ii) The cost of investments in unproved properties and major development projects may be excluded from capitalized costs to be amortized, subject to the following:

(A) All costs directly associated with the acquisition and evaluation of unproved properties may be excluded from the amortization computation until it is determined whether or not proved reserves can be assigned to the properties, subject to the following conditions:

(1) Until such a determination is made, the properties shall be assessed at least annually to ascertain whether impairment has occurred. Unevaluated properties whose costs are individually significant shall be assessed individually. Where it is not practicable to individually assess the amount of impairment of properties for which costs are not individually significant, such properties may be grouped for purposes of assessing impairment. Impairment may be estimated by applying factors based

on historical experience and other data such as primary lease terms of the properties, average holding periods of unproved properties, and geographic and geologic data to groupings of individually insignificant properties and projects. The amount of impairment assessed under either of these methods shall be added to the costs to be amortized..

(2) The costs of drilling exploratory dry holes shall be included in the amortization base immediately upon determination that the well is dry.

(3) If geological and geophysical costs cannot be directly associated with specific unevaluated properties, they shall be included in the amortization base as incurred. Upon complete evaluation of a property, the total remaining excluded cost (net of any impairment) shall be included in the full cost amortization base.

(B) Certain costs may be excluded from amortization when incurred in connection with major development projects expected to entail significant costs to ascertain the quantities of proved reserves attributable to the properties under development (e.g., the installation of an offshore drilling platform from which development wells are to be drilled, the installation of improved recovery programs, and similar major projects undertaken in the expectation of significant additions to proved reserves). The amounts which may be excluded are applicable portions of (1) the costs that relate to the major development project and have not previously been included in the amortization base, and (2) the estimated future expenditures associated with the development project. The excluded portion of any common costs associated with the development project should be based, as is most appropriate in the circumstances, on a comparison of. either (i) existing proved reserves to total proved reserves expected to be established upon completion of the project, or (ii) the number of wells to which proved reserves have been assigned and total number of wells expected to be drilled. Such costs may be excluded from costs to be amortized until the earlier determination of whether additional reserves are proved or impairment occurs.

(C) Excluded costs and the proved reserves related to such costs shall be transferred into the amortization base on an ongoing (well-by-well or property-by-property) basis as the project is evaluated and proved reserves established or impairment determined. Once proved reserves are established, there is no further justification for continued

exclusion from the full cost amortization base even if other factors prevent immediate production or marketing.

(iii) Amortization shall be computed on the basis of physical units, with oil and gas converted to a common unit of measure on the basis of their approximate relative energy content, unless economic circumstances (related to the effects of regulated prices) indicate that use of units of revenue is a more appropriate basis of computing amortization. In the latter case, amortization shall be computed on the basis of current gross revenues (excluding royalty payments and net profits disbursements) from production in relation to future gross revenues, based on current prices (including consideration of changes in existing prices provided only by contractual arrangements), from estimated production of proved oil and gas reserves. The effect of a significant price increase during the year on estimated future gross revenues shall be reflected in the amortization provision only for the period after the price increase occurs.

(iv) In some cases it may be more appropriate to depreciate natural gas cycling and processing plants by a method other than the unit-of-production method.

(v) Amortization computations shall be made on a consolidated basis, including investees accounted for on a proportionate consolidation basis. Investees accounted for on the equity method shall be treated separately.

(4) Limitation on capitalized costs:

(i) For each cost center, capitalized costs, less accumulated amortization and related deferred income taxes, shall not exceed an amount (the cost center ceiling) equal to the sum of: (A) the present value of future net revenues computed by applying current prices of oil and gas reserves (with consideration of price changes only to the extent provided by contractual arrangements) to estimated future production of proved oil and gas reserves as of the date of the latest balance sheet presented, less estimated future expenditures (based on current costs) to be incurred in developing and producing the proved reserves computed using a discount factor of ten percent and assuming continuation of existing economic conditions; plus (B) the cost of properties not being amortized pursuant to paragraph (i) (3) (ii) of this section; plus (C) the lower of cost or estimated fair value of unproved properties included in the costs being amortized; less (D) income tax effects related to differences between the book and tax basis of the properties referred to in paragraph (i)(4)(i)(B) and (C) of this section.

(ii) If unamortized costs capitalized within a cost center, less related deferred income taxes, exceed the cost center ceiling, the excess shall be

618

charged to expense and separately disclosed during the period in which the excess occurs. Amounts thus required to be written off shall not be reinstated for any subsequent increase in the cost center ceiling.

(5) Production costs. *All costs relating to production activities, including work-over costs incurred solely to maintain or increase levels of production from an existing completion interval, shall be charged to expense as incurred.*

(6) Other transactions. *The provisions of paragraph (h) of this section, "Mineral property conveyances and related transactions if the successful efforts method of accounting is followed," shall apply also to those reporting entities following the full cost method except as follows:*

(i) Sales and abandonments of oil and gas properties. Sales of oil and gas properties, whether or not being amortized currently, shall be accounted for as adjustments of capitalized costs, with no gain or loss recognized, unless such adjustments would significantly alter the relationship between capitalized costs and proved reserves of oil and gas attributable to a cost center. For instance, a significant alteration would not ordinarily be expected to occur for sales involving less than 25% of the reserve quantities of a given cost center. If gain or loss is recognized on such a sale, total capitalization costs within the cost center shall be allocated between the reserves sold and reserves retained on the same basis used to compute amortization, unless there are substantial economic differences between the properties sold and those retained, in which case capitalized costs shall be allocated on the basis of the relative fair values of the properties. Abandonments of oil and gas properties shall be accounted for as adjustments of capitalized costs; that is, the cost of abandoned properties shall be charged to the full cost center and amortized (subject to the limitation on capitalized costs in paragraph (b) of this section).

(ii) Purchases of reserves. Purchases of oil and gas reserves in place ordinarily shall be accounted for as additional capitalized costs within the applicable cost center; however, significant purchases of production payments or properties with lives substantially shorter than the composite productive life of the cost center shall be accounted for separately.

(iii) Partnerships, joint ventures and drilling arrangements.

(A) Except as provided in subparagraph (i)(6)(i) of this section, all consideration received from sales or transfers of properties in connection with partnerships, joint venture operations, or various other forms of drilling arrangements involving oil and gas exploration and development activities (e.g. carried interest, turnkey wells, manage-

ment fees, etc.) shall be credited to the full cost account, except to the extent of amounts that represent reimbursement of organization, offering, general and administrative expenses, etc., that are identifiable with the transaction, if such amounts are currently incurred and charged to expense.

(B) Where a registrant organizes and manages a limited partnership involved only in the purchase of proved developed properties and subsequent distribution of income from such properties, management fee income may be recognized provided the properties involved do not require aggregate development expenditures in connection with production of existing proved reserves in excess of 10% of the partnership's recorded cost of such properties. Any income not recognized as a result of this limitation would be credited to the full cost account and recognized through a lower amortization provision as reserves are produced.

(iv) Other services. No income shall be recognized in connection with contractual services performed (e.g. drilling, well service, or equipment supply services, etc.) in connection with properties in which the registrant or an affiliate (as defined in Rule 1-02(b)) holds an ownership or other economic interest, except as follows:

(A) Where the registrant acquires an interest in the properties in connection with the service contract, income may be recognized to the extent the cash consideration received exceeds the related contract costs plus the registrant's share of costs incurred and estimated to be incurred in connection with the properties. Ownership interests acquired within one year of the date of such a contract are considered to be acquired in connection with the service for purposes of applying this rule. The amount of any guarantees or similar arrangements undertaken as part of this contract should be considered as part of the costs related to the properties for purposes of applying this rule.

(B) Where the registrant acquired an interest in the properties at least one year before the date of the service contract through transactions unrelated to the service contract, and that interest is unaffected by the service contract, income from such contract may be recognized subject to the general provisions for elimination of intercompany profit under generally accepted accounting principles.

(C) Notwithstanding the provisions of (A) and (B) above, no income may be recognized for contractual services performed on behalf of investors in oil and gas producing activities managed by the registrant or an affiliate. Furthermore, no income may be recognized for contractual services to the extent that the consideration received for such services represents an interest in the underlying property.

(D) Any income not recognized as a result of these rules would be credited to the full cost account and recognized through a lower amortization provision as reserves are produced.

(7) Disclosures. Reporting entities that follow the full cost method of accounting shall disclose all of the information required by paragraph (k) of this section, with each cost center considered as a separate geographic area, except that reasonable groupings may be made of cost centers that are not significant in the aggregate. In addition:

(i) For each cost center, for each year that an income statement is required, disclose the total amount of amortization expense (per equivalent physical unit of production if amortization is computed on the basis of physical units or per dollar of gross revenue from production if amortization is computed on the basis of gross revenue).

(ii) State separately on the face of the balance sheet the aggregate of the capitalized costs of unproved properties and major development projects that are excluded, in accordance with paragraph (i)(3) of this section, from the capitalized costs being amortized. Provide a description in the notes to the financial statements of the current status of the significant properties or projects involved, including the anticipated timing of the inclusion of the costs in the amortization computation. Present a table that shows, by category of cost, (A) the total costs excluded as of the most recent fiscal year, and (B) the amounts of such excluded costs, incurred (1) in each of the three most recent fiscal years and (2) in the aggregate for any earlier fiscal years in which the costs were incurred. Categories of cost to be disclosed include acquisition costs, exploration costs, development costs in the case of significant development projects and capitalized interest.

INCOME TAXES

(j) Income taxes. Comprehensive interperiod income tax allocation by a method which complies with generally accepted accounting principles shall be followed for intangible drilling and development costs and other costs incurred that enter into the determination of taxable income and pretax accounting income in different periods.

SEC 50410.   Rule 4-10(i)

50500. ARTICLE 5. COMMERCIAL AND INDUSTRIAL COMPANIES

50501. Rule 5-01. Application of Article 5

(a) This Article shall be applicable to financial statements filed by all persons except—

(A) Registered investment companies (see Article 6).

(B) Employee stock purchase, savings and similar plans (see Article 6A).

(C) Insurance companies (see Article 7).

(D) Bank holding companies and banks (see Article 9).

(E) Brokers and dealers when filing Form X-17 A-5 (see Rules 17a-5 and 17a-10 under the Securities Exchange Act of 1934).

(b) Companies in the development stage. Rule 5A-02 prescribes additional information to be included in financial statements filed by companies in the development stage.

Article 5 specifies the information to be included in the financial statements of commercial and industrial companies and the related supporting schedules that may have to be furnished.

50502. Rule 5-02. Balance Sheets

The purpose of this rule is to indicate the various line items and certain additional disclosures which, if applicable, and except as otherwise permitted by the Commis-

sion, should appear on the face of the balance sheets or related notes filed for the persons to whom this article pertains (see Rule 4-01(a)).

This rule sets forth in considerable detail (by caption) the information to be shown in the balance sheet. Even though a sequence of captions is set forth in Rule 5-02, deviations in presentation are permitted. Rule 4-01 states: "Financial statements may be filed in such form and order, and should use such generally accepted terminology, as will best indicate their significance and character in light of the provisions applicable thereto." Furthermore, Rules 4-02 and 4-03 permit the omission of immaterial and inapplicable captions. Rule 5-02 sets forth materiality guidelines for certain balance sheet captions.

SAB Topic 11-D states that it is inappropriate to offset assets and liabilities on the balance sheet without the benefit of an existing legal right. The text of the SAB follows:

Offsetting Assets and Liabilities

Facts: In Company D's balance sheet, assets have been offset by liabilities which are directly related to the asset.

Question: Will the staff accept such financial statements?

Interpretive Response: It is the staff's opinion that even when items can be directly associated, it is not appropriate to offset assets and liabilities without the benefit of an existing legal right.

The following are typical situations:

1. A registrant might engage in money market transactions in which the proceeds of short-term borrowings are simultaneously invested, at higher rates, in matching deposits with major international banks. In the absence of a legal right of offset, the loan may not be offset against the deposit.

2. Carrying values of properties should not be reduced by purchase money mortgages even if the liability on such a mortgage is only a liability against the property.

3. When a registrant sells property subject to a mortgage and takes from the purchaser a wrap-around mortgage which provides that the registrant will continue the payments on the prior mortgage, the registrant's balance sheet should show the wrap-around mortgage as a receivable. The balance of the previously existing mortgage should not be offset against the receivable on the wrap-around mortgage.

The wrap-around mortgage situation should be distinguished from a subordinate lien. If a registrant lends money on property owned by another party and arranges to collect amounts from the borrower to be used to make payments against an existing mortgage (thus assuring registrant that prior lien obligations are being met), the prior lien is not an obligation of the registrant and therefore the registrant's receivable is a subordinate lien rather than a wrap-around mortgage.

SEC 50502. Rule 5-02

In this connection, paragraph 5 of FASB Interpretation No. 39, *Offsetting of Amounts Related to Certain Contracts,* specifies that "a right of setoff exists when all of the following conditions are met:

- Each of the *two* parties owes the other determinable amounts.

- The reporting party has the right to set off the amount owed with the amount owed by the other party.

- The reporting party intends to set off.

- The right of offset is enforceable at law.

A debtor having a valid right of setoff may offset the related asset and liability and report the net amount."

SAB Topic 5-G affirms the staff's longstanding position that when a company acquires assets from promoters and shareholders in exchange for stock prior to or at the time of its initial public offering, such assets should generally be recorded at the predecessor's cost. The text of the SAB follows:

Transfers of Nonmonetary Assets by Promoters or Shareholders

Facts: Nonmonetary assets are exchanged by promoters or shareholders for all or part of a company's common stock just prior to or contemporaneously with a first-time public offering.

Question: Since paragraph 4 of Accounting Principles Board Opinion No. 29, "Accounting for Nonmonetary Transactions," states that the Opinion is not applicable to transactions involving the acquisition of nonmonetary assets or services on issuance of the capital stock of an enterprise, what value should be ascribed to the acquired assets by the company?

Interpretive Response: The staff believes that transfers of nonmonetary assets to a company by its promoters or shareholders in exchange for stock prior to or at the time of the company's initial public offering normally should be recorded at the transferor's historical cost basis determined under generally accepted accounting principles.

The staff will not always require that predecessor cost be used to value nonmonetary assets received from an enterprise's promoters or shareholders. However, deviations from this policy have been rare, applying generally to situations where the fair value of either the stock issued* or assets acquired is objectively measurable and the transferor's stock ownership following the transaction was not so significant that the transferor had retained a substantial indirect interest in the assets as a result of stock ownership in the company.

---

*Estimating fair value of the common stock issued, however, is not appropriate when the stock is closely held and/or seldom or ever traded.

Note that the SAB uses the phrase "normally should be recorded at the transferor's historical cost." The SEC staff may not insist on the use of the transferor's historical cost basis if a party unrelated to the promoter or shareholder contributes cash in exchange for an equity interest of at least 50 percent concurrent with the transfer of nonmonetary assets by the promoter or shareholder. The cash contribution by an unrelated party could serve as an objective measure of the fair value of the nonmonetary assets transferred by the promoter or shareholder, thereby permitting a step-up in basis. However, for this to apply, the cash contributed would need to remain in the entity (i.e., no distributions).

SAB Topic 5-J discusses the staff's views on the application of the "push down" basis of accounting in the separate financial statements of subsidiaries acquired in purchase transactions. The text of the SAB is included in section 50337 of this manual.

ASSETS AND OTHER DEBITS

Current Assets, When Appropriate
(See Rule 4-05)

1. Cash and cash items. *Separate disclosure shall be made of the cash and cash items which are restricted as to withdrawal or usage. The provisions of any restrictions shall be described in a note to the financial statements. Restrictions may include legally restricted deposits held as compensating balances against short-term borrowing arrangements, contracts entered into with others, or company statements of intention with regard to particular deposits; however, time deposits and short-term certificates of deposit are not generally included in legally restricted deposits. In cases where compensating balance arrangements exist but are not agreements which legally restrict the use of cash amounts shown on the balance sheet, describe in the notes to the financial statements these arrangements and the amount involved, if determinable, for the most recent audited balance sheet required and for any subsequent unaudited balance sheet required in the notes to the financial statements. Compensating balances that are maintained under an agreement to assure future credit availability shall be disclosed in the notes to the financial statements along with the amount and terms of such agreement.*

Legally restricted deposits held as compensating balances against short-term borrowing arrangements need to be segregated on the balance sheet. Those that are not subject to legal agreements or those that are maintained to assure future credit availability are required to be disclosed in the notes to the financial statements.

In FRP Section 203 (formerly ASR No. 148), the SEC provides guidelines with respect to the disclosure of compensating balances and information about short-term debt and unused lines of credit. Interpretations relating to these disclosure require-

ments are provided in SAB Topics 6-H1, 6-H3, and 6-H4. The text of these requirements are not included in this manual but should be referred to in applicable situations.

2. Marketable securities. *The accounting and disclosure requirements for current*
marketable equity securities are specified by generally accepted accounting princi-
ples. With respect to all other current marketable securities, state, parenthetically or
otherwise, the basis of determining the aggregate amount shown in the balance sheet,
along with the alternatives of the aggregate cost or the aggregate market value at the
balance sheet date.

FASB Statement No. 115, *Accounting for Certain Investments in Debt and Equity*
Securities, describes the accounting and reporting requirements for investments in all debt
securities and in equity securities that have readily determinable fair values. This Statement
supersedes FASB Statement No. 12, *Accounting for Certain Marketable Securities,* and
is effective for fiscal years beginning after December 15, 1993.

FASB Statement No. 12 describes the accounting and reporting requirements
for investments in marketable securities. The Statement differentiates between marketable equity securities and other marketable securities. Pursuant to FASB Statement
No. 12, a marketable equity securities portfolio is required to be carried at the lower
of its aggregate cost or market value, determined at the balance sheet date. In the case
of a classified balance sheet, in order to compare aggregate cost and market value,
marketable equity securities are required to be grouped into two separate portfolios
based on whether the securities are classified as current or noncurrent. The net
unrealized loss (i.e., the excess of aggregate cost over market value) of the marketable
equity securities portfolio is required to be accounted for as a valuation allowance.
Changes in the valuation allowance relating to current assets are required to be
reflected in the determination of net income for the period, whereas accumulated
changes that relate to noncurrent assets are to be included as a separate line item in
the stockholders' equity section of the balance sheet. Realized gains and losses are
required to be reflected in net income in the period in which they occur. Please note
that for purposes of FASB Statement No. 12, the accounting for marketable equity
securities portfolios in nonclassified balance sheets follow the same treatment as that
of noncurrent assets.

FASB Statement No. 115 requires investments to be classified into three
categories, with each category having different accounting requirements as follows:

- Held-to-maturity securities represent investments in debt securities for which
  an entity has the positive intent and ability to hold to maturity. Such securities
  are to be reported at amortized cost and individual securities are to be
  classified as either a current or noncurrent asset pursuant to Chapter 3A of
  ARB No. 43, *Working Capital—Current Assets and Current Liabilities.*

SEC 50502

- Trading securities represent investments in debt and equity securities that are bought, held for a short period of time and then sold, generally for the purpose of profiting on short-term variation of prices. Trading typically entails active and frequent buying and selling of securities. Such securities are to be reported at fair value and classified as a current asset in the balance sheet. Unrealized holding gains and losses for trading securities are required to be reflected in the income statement. In accordance with this Statement, mortgage-backed securities held for sale in connection with mortgage banking activities, discussed in FASB Statement No. 65, *Accounting for Certain Mortgage Banking Activities*, are required to be classified as trading securities.

- Available-for-sale securities include investments in debt and equity securities that are not classified as either held-to-maturity securities or trading securities. These securities are to be reported at fair value and individual securities are required to be classified as a current or noncurrent asset pursuant to Chapter 3A of ARB No. 43. Unrealized holding gains and losses for all available-for-sale securities are required to be reported net, as a separate component of shareholders' equity, until the gains and losses are realized.

It is important to note that cash flows from purchases, sales, and maturities of securities categorized as available-for-sale and held-to-maturity are required to be reported gross for each security classification and classified as cash flows from investing activities in the statement of cash flows, whereas cash flows from securities categorized as trading are required to be classified as cash flows from operating activities. Refer to FASB Statement No. 115 for additional guidance regarding the accounting and reporting requirements for debt securities and applicable equity securities including the accounting for transfers of investments between categories.

Sections 50502-12 should be referred to for additional guidance on accounting and disclosure requirements for marketable securities.

The schedule prescribed by Rule 12-02 (Schedule I) may need to be furnished in support of this caption if (1) the materiality criteria cited in Rule 5-04 are exceeded (see section 50520—Schedule I) and (2) the information required by the schedule is not included in a footnote to the financial statements.

3. Accounts and notes receivable.

(a) State separately amounts receivable from:

(1) Customers (trade);

(2) Related parties (see Rule 4-08(k));

(3) Underwriters, promoters, and employees (other than related parties) which arose in other than the ordinary course of business; and

SEC 50502. Rule 5-02-2

(4) Others.

(b) If the aggregate amount of notes receivable exceeds 10 percent of the aggregate amount of receivables, the above information shall be set forth separately, in the balance sheet or in a note thereto, for accounts receivable and notes receivable.

(c) If receivables include amounts due under long-term contracts (see Rule 5-02. 6(d)), state separately in the balance sheet or in a note to the financial statements the following amounts:

(1) Balances billed but not paid by customers under retainage provisions in contracts.

(2) Amounts representing the recognized sales value of performance and such amounts that had not been billed and were not billable to customers at the date of the balance sheet. Include a general description of the prerequisites for billing.

(3) Billed or unbilled amounts representing claims or other similar items subject to uncertainty concerning their determination or ultimate realization. Include a description of the nature and status of the principal items comprising such amount.

(4) With respect to (1) through (3) above, also state the amounts included in each item which are expected to be collected after one year. Also state, by year, if practicable, when the amounts of retainage (see (1) above) are expected to be collected.

The SEC staff has indicated that if the amount of installment receivables that will be collected after one year is material to an understanding of liquidity, the inclusion of a schedule of annual amounts due would be appropriate in the notes to financial statements.

The schedule prescribed by Rule 12-03 is required to be furnished with respect to amounts receivable from related parties and underwriters, promoters, directors, officers, and employees other than related parties if (1) the materiality criteria cited in Rule 5-04 are exceeded and (2) the information required by the schedule is not included in a footnote to the financial statements. As indicated in the discussion following Rule 5-04, if an aggregate indebtedness of more than $100,000 or one percent of total assets (whichever is less) was owed by any of these persons at any time during the fiscal period for which an audited income statement is required to be filed, the information required by Rule 12-03 (Schedule II) needs to be furnished.

Paragraph (c) describes the disclosures required by registrants engaged in defense and long-term contract activities. ASR No. 164 (now FRP Section 206) amended this rule to require this disclosure and also amended Rule 5-02-6 (inventories). FRP Section 206.03 provides the following example to illustrate the information that might be disclosed in response to Rules 5-02-3 and 5-02-6:

SEC 50502

XYZ Company and Subsidiaries
Consolidated Balance Sheets

	December 31,	
	19X4	19X3
	(000 omitted)	

ASSETS

CURRENT ASSETS:

	19X4	19X3
Cash	$ 438	$ 627
Accounts receivable:		
Trade and other receivables, net of allowance for uncollectible accounts of $38,000 in 19X4 and $36,000 in 19X3	2,846	2,396
Long-term contracts and programs (notes 1 and 2)	18,985	19,036
Total accounts receivable	21,831	21,432
Inventories and costs relating to long-term contracts and programs in process, net of progress payments (notes 1 and 3)	6,278	6,257
Prepaid expenses	46	27
Total current assets	$28,593	$28,343

Note 1—Summary of Significant Accounting Policies

Revenue Recognition. Sales of commercial products under long-term contracts and programs are recognized in the accounts as deliveries are made. The estimated sales values of performance under Government fixed-price and fixed-price incentive contracts in process is recognized under the percentage of completion method of accounting whereunder the estimated sales value is determined on the basis of physical completion to date (the total contract amount multiplied by percent of performance to date less sales value recognized in previous periods) and costs (including general and administrative, except as described below) are expensed as incurred. Sales under cost-reimbursement contracts are recorded as costs are incurred and include estimated earned fees in the proportion that costs incurred to date bear to total estimated costs. The fees under certain Government contracts may be increased or decreased in accordance with cost or performance incentive provisions which measure actual performance against established targets or other criteria. Such incentive fee awards or penalties are included in sales at the time the amounts can be determined reasonably.

Inventories. Inventories, other than inventoried costs relating to long-term contracts and programs, are stated at the lower of cost (principally first-in, first-out) or market. Inventoried costs relating to long-term contracts and programs are stated at the actual production cost, including factory overhead, initial tooling and other related non-recurring costs, incurred to date reduced by amounts identified with revenue recognized on units delivered or progress completed. General and administrative costs applicable to cost-plus Government contracts are also included in inventories. Inventoried costs relating to long-term contracts and programs are reduced by charging any amounts in excess of estimated realizable value to cost of sales. The costs attributed to units delivered under long-term commercial contracts and programs are based on the estimated average cost of all units expected to be produced and are determined under the learning curve concept which anticipates a predictable decrease in unit costs as tasks and production techniques become more efficient through repetition.

In accordance with industry practice, inventories include amounts relating to contracts and programs having production cycles longer than one year and a portion thereof will not be realized within one year.

Note 2—Accounts Receivable

The following tabulation shows the component elements of accounts receivable from long-term contracts and programs:

	19X4	19X3
	(000 omitted)	
U.S. Government:		
Amounts billed	$7,136	$6,532
Recoverable costs and accrued profit on progress completed — not billed	4,173	3,791
Unrecovered costs and estimated profits subject to future negotiation — not billed	1,468	1,735
	12,777	12,058
Commercial Customers:		
Amounts billed	1,937	3,442
Recoverable costs and accrued profit on units delivered — not billed	1,293	364
Retainage, due upon completion of contracts	2,441	2,279
Unrecovered costs and estimated profits subject to future negotiation — not billed	537	893
	$18,985	$19,036

The balances billed but not paid by customers pursuant to retainage provisions in construction contracts will be due upon completion of the contracts and acceptance by the owner. Based on the Company's experience with similar contracts in recent years, the retention balances at December 31, 19X4 are expected to be collected as follows: $270,000 in 19X5, $845,000 in 19X6 and the balance in 19X7.

SEC 50502

Recoverable costs and accrued profit not billed comprise principally amounts of revenue recognized on contracts for which billings had not been presented to the contract owners because the amounts were not billable at balance sheet date. It is anticipated such unbilled amounts receivable from the U.S. Government at December 31, 19X4 will be billed over the next 60 days as units are delivered. The unbilled accounts receivable applicable to commercial customers are billable upon completion of performance tests which are expected to be completed in September 19X5.

Unrecovered costs and estimated profits subject to future negotiation, the principal amount of which is expected to be billed and collected within one year, consist of the following elements:

	19X4	19X3
	(000 omitted)	
U.S. Government Contracts:		
Excess of estimated or proposed over provisional price	$ 190	$ 157
Amounts claimed for incremental costs arising from customer occasioned contract delays	1,278	1,578
	1,468	1,735
Commercial Contracts:		
Unrecovered costs and estimated profit relating to work not specified in express contract provisions	537	893
	$2,005	$2,628

Note 3—Inventories

Inventories and inventoried costs relating to long-term contracts and programs are classified as follows:

	December 31,	
	19X4	19X3
	(000 omitted)	
Finished goods	$3,562	$3,435
Inventoried costs relating to long-term contracts and programs, net of amounts attributed to revenues recognized to date	2,552	2,638
Work in process	738	947
Raw materials	453	383
Supplies	112	71
	7,417	7,474
Deduct progress payments related to long-term contracts and programs	1,139	1,217
	$6,278	$6,257

SEC 50502. Rule 5-02-3

The following tabulation shows the cost elements included in inventoried costs related to long-term contracts:

	December 31,	
	19X4	19X3
	(000 omitted)	
Production costs of goods currently in process	$1,184	$ 960
Excess of production cost of delivered units over the estimated average cost of all units expected to be produced	647	893
Unrecovered costs subject to future negotiation	280	310
General and administrative costs	260	270
Initial tooling and other non-recurring costs	181	205
	$2,552	$2,638

The inventoried costs relating to long-term contracts and programs includes unrecovered costs of $280,000 and $310,000 at December 31, 19X4 and 19X3, respectively, which are subject to future determination through negotiation or other procedures not complete at balance sheet dates. Of such amounts, $260,000 and $280,000 are in respect to contracts under which all goods have been delivered at December 31, 19X4 and 19X3, respectively. The unrecovered amount at December 31, 19X3 consisted of three items, one of which was settled during 19X4. The amount remaining at December 31, 19X4 is represented principally by a claim asserted against a customer for amounts incurred as a result of faulty materials furnished by the customer which in turn caused delays in performance under the contract. In the opinion of management these costs will be recovered by contract modification or litigation. It is expected that the negotiations which are being conducted currently with the customer will be successfully concluded during the next twelve months. If this expectation is not realized, the matter will be referred to the Armed Services Board of Contract Appeals, with the consequence that settlement could be delayed for an indeterminate period.

The actual per unit production cost of the NX-4C aircraft produced during the most recent fiscal year was less than the estimated average per unit cost of all units expected to be produced under the program. Prior to 19X4, the Company's NX-4C commercial aircraft program was in the early high cost period. During the initial years of the program, the cost of units produced exceeded the sales price of the delivered units and the estimated average unit cost of all units to be produced under the program. At December 31, 19X4, inventories included costs of $647,000 representing the excess of costs incurred over estimated average costs per aircraft for the 117 aircraft delivered through the year end. The estimated average unit cost is predicated on the assumption that 250 planes will be produced and that production costs (principally labor and materials) will decrease as the project matures and efficiencies associated with increased volume, improved production techniques and the performance of repetitive tasks (the learning curve concept) are realized. (Note: The amount by which the production costs of the equivalent finished units in process at the date of the latest balance sheet exceeds the cost of such units on the basis of the estimated average unit cost of all units expected to be produced under the program should be stated. Since, as stated above, the actual per unit production cost is currently less than the estimated average per unit cost of all units expected to be produced under the program, no such excess is assumed in this example.)

Recovery of the deferred production, initial tooling and related non-recurring costs is dependent on the number of aircraft ultimately sold and actual selling prices and production costs associated with future transactions. Sales significantly under estimates or costs significantly over estimates could result in the realization of substantial losses on the program in future years. Realization of approximately $421,000 of the gross commercial aircraft inventories at December 31, 19X4 is dependent on receipt of future firm orders.

Based on studies by and on behalf of the Company, management believes there exists for this aircraft a market for over 250 units, including deliveries to date, with production and deliveries continuing at a normal rate to at least 19Y0. At December 31, 19X4, 117 aircraft had been delivered under the program, and the backlog included 64 firm unfilled orders and options for 43 units.

The aggregate amounts of general and administrative costs incurred during 19X4 and 19X3 were $2,251,000 and $2,238,000, respectively. As stated in Note 1, the Company allocates general and administrative costs to certain types of Government contracts. The amounts of general and administrative costs remaining in inventories at December 31, 19X4 and 19X3 are estimated at $260,000 and $270,000, respectively. Such estimates assume that costs have been removed from inventories on a basis proportional to the amounts of each cost element expected to be charged to cost of sales.

4. Allowances for doubtful accounts and notes receivable. *The amount is to be set forth separately in the balance sheet or in a note thereto.*

Additional information with respect to this account may be required to be furnished in the schedule prescribed by Rule 12-09 (Schedule VIII—Valuation and Qualifying Accounts) if the information required by the schedule is not included in a footnote to the financial statements.

5. Unearned income.

6. Inventories.

(a) State separately in the balance sheet or in a note thereto, if practicable, the amounts of major classes of inventory such as: (1) finished goods; (2) inventoried costs relating to long-term contracts or programs (see (d) below and Rule 4-05); (3) work in process

SEC 50502. Rule 5-02-3

(see Rule 4-05); (4) raw materials; and (5) supplies. If the method of calculating a LIFO inventory does not allow for the practical determination of amounts assigned to major classes of inventory, the amounts of those classes may be stated under cost flow assumptions other than LIFO with the excess of such total amount over the aggregate LIFO amount shown as a deduction to arrive at the amount of the LIFO inventory.

(b) The basis of determining the amounts shall be stated. If "cost" is used to determine any portion of the inventory amounts, the description of this method shall include the nature of the cost elements included in inventory. Elements of "cost" include, among other items, [1] retained costs representing the excess of manufacturing or production costs over the amounts charged to cost of sales or [to] delivered or in-process units, [2] initial tooling or other deferred start-up costs, or [3] general and administrative costs.

The method by which amounts are removed from inventory (e.g., "average cost," "first-in, first-out," "last-in, first-out," "estimated average cost per unit") shall be described. If the estimated average cost per unit is used as a basis to determine amounts removed from inventory under a total program or similar basis of accounting, the principal assumptions (including, where meaningful, the aggregate number of units expected to be delivered under the program, the number of units delivered to date and the number of units on order) shall be disclosed.

If any general and administrative costs are charged to inventory, state in a note to the financial statements the aggregate amount of the general and administrative costs incurred in each period and the actual or estimated amount remaining in inventory at the date of each balance sheet.

(c) If the LIFO inventory method is used, the excess of replacement or current cost over stated LIFO value shall, if material, be stated parenthetically or in a note to the financial statements.

(d) For purposes of Rules 5-02-3 and 5-02-6, long-term contracts or programs include (1) all contracts or programs for which gross profits are recognized on a percentage-of-completion method of accounting or any variant thereof (e.g., delivered unit, cost to cost, physical completion) and (2) any contracts or programs accounted for on a completed contract basis of accounting where, in either case, the contracts or programs have associated with them material amounts of inventories or unbilled receivables and where such contracts or programs have been or are expected to be performed over a period of more than twelve months. Contracts or programs of shorter duration may also be included, if deemed appropriate.

SEC 50502

For all long-term contracts or programs, the following information, if applicable, shall be stated in a note to the financial statements:

> *(i) The aggregate amount of manufacturing or production costs and any related deferred costs (e.g., initial tooling costs) which exceeds the aggregate estimated cost of all in-process and delivered units on the basis of the estimated average cost of all units expected to be produced under long-term contracts and programs not yet complete, as well as that portion of such amount which would not be absorbed in cost of sales based on existing firm orders at the latest balance sheet date. In addition, if practicable, disclose the amount of deferred costs by type of cost (e.g., initial tooling, deferred production, etc.).*

> *(ii) The aggregate amount representing claims or other similar items subject to uncertainty concerning their determination or ultimate realization, and include a description of the nature and status of the principal items comprising such aggregate amount.*

> *(iii) The amount of progress payments netted against inventory at the date of the balance sheet.*

In 1984 the AICPA released an Issues Paper, *Identification and Discussion of Certain Financial Accounting and Reporting Issues Concerning LIFO Inventories.* The SEC staff has indicated that in the absence of existing authoritative literature on LIFO accounting, registrants and their independent accountants should look to this Issues Paper for guidance in determining what constitutes acceptable LIFO accounting practices. SAB Topic 5-L describes the staff's views of this paper in further detail:

LIFO Inventory Practices

Question 1: What is the SEC staff's position on the recently released issues paper?

Interpretive Response: In the absence of existing authoritative literature on LIFO accounting, the staff believes that registrants and their independent accountants should look to the paper for guidance in determining what constitutes acceptable LIFO accounting practice.[1] In this connection, the staff considers the paper to be an accumulation of existing acceptable LIFO accounting practices which does not establish any new standards and does not diverge from generally accepted accounting principles.

The staff also believes that the advisory conclusions recommended in the issues paper are generally consistent with conclusions previously expressed by the Commission, such as:

> 1. Pooling—paragraph 4-6 of the paper discusses LIFO inventory pooling and concludes "establishing separate pools with the principal objective of facilitating inventory liquidations is unacceptable." In Accounting and Auditing Enforcement Release No. 35, August 13, 1984, the Commission stated that it

SEC 50502. Rule 5-02-6

believes that the Company improperly realigned its LIFO pools in such a way as to maximize the likelihood and magnitude of LIFO liquidations and thus overstated net income.

2. New Items—paragraph 4-27 of the paper discusses determination of the cost of new items and concludes "if the double extension or an index technique is used, the objective of LIFO is achieved by reconstructing the base year cost of new items added to existing pools." In Accounting Series Release No. 293, the Commission stated that when the effects of inflation on the cost of new products are measured by making a comparison with current cost as the base-year cost, rather than a reconstructed base-year cost, income is improperly increased.

Question 2: If a registrant utilizes a LIFO practice other than one recommended by an advisory conclusion in the issues paper, must the registrant change its practice to one specified in the paper?

Interpretive Response: Now that the issues paper is available, the staff believes that a registrant and its independent accountants should re-examine previously adopted LIFO practices and compare them to the recommendations in the paper. In the event that the registrant and its independent accountants conclude that the registrant's LIFO practices are preferable in the circumstances, they should be prepared to justify their position in the event that a question is raised by the staff.

[Note: Question 3 has not been presented as it is no longer applicable.]

---

[1]In Accounting Series Release No. 293 (July 2, 1981), see Financial Reporting Codification Section 205, the Commission expressed its concerns about the inappropriate use of Internal Revenue Service (IRS) LIFO practices for financial statement preparation. Because the IRS amended its regulations concerning the LIFO conformity rule on January 13, 1981, allowing companies to apply LIFO differently for financial reporting purposes than for tax purposes, the Commission strongly encouraged registrants and their independent accountants to examine their financial reporting LIFO practices. In that release, the Commission acknowledged the "task force which has been established by AcSEC to accumulate information about [LIFO] application problems" and noted that "This type of effort, in addition to self-examination [of LIFO practices] by individual registrants, is appropriate. . ."

ARB No. 43, Chapter 4, Inventory Pricing, requires a description of the method of determining cost and the method of determining market if other than current replacement cost.

Rule 4-05, which is referred to in paragraph (a) of this rule, specifies the conditions under which assets such as inventories long in process may be classified as current.

Paragraph (c) of this rule requires registrants using the LIFO inventory method to disclose the excess of replacement cost or current cost over LIFO value. FRP Section

205.02 (formerly ASR No. 141) states that in determining the replacement or current cost for the purpose of this disclosure, any inventory method that arrives at approximate current cost (such as FIFO or average cost) may be used. Note that the information required by this rule is the effect on the balance sheet of the difference in the method of calculating inventories and not the effect on net income as a result of using the LIFO method.

SAB Topic 11-F requires disclosure of the effects of significant LIFO liquidations as follows:

LIFO Liquidations

Facts: Registrant on a LIFO basis of accounting liquidates a substantial portion of its LIFO inventory and as a result includes a material amount of income in its income statement which would not have been recorded had the inventory liquidation not taken place.

Question: Is disclosure required of the amount of income realized as a result of the inventory liquidation?

Interpretive Response: Yes. Such disclosure would be required in order to make the financial statements not misleading. Disclosure may be made either in a footnote or parenthetically on the face of the income statement.

The SEC staff has informally indicated that if a reduction of prior-year LIFO inventory quantities (either of the aggregate LIFO inventory or of individual LIFO pools if the aggregate LIFO inventory increases) has a material effect on gross profit, the effect on the income statement and earnings per share should be disclosed in the notes to the financial statements. The income effect should be calculated based on what it would have cost to replace the liquidated inventory. The effect should generally be based on the total of all LIFO pools that individually decrease, rather than on the net effect of pools decreasing less pools increasing. (The SEC staff has been adamant in its position that there be no netting in this calculation.)

FRP Section 205 (formerly ASR No. 293) expresses the SEC's view on various aspects of LIFO accounting and emphasizes that it does not agree with the approach of viewing IRS LIFO regulations as if they were generally accepted accounting principles. FRP Section 205 cites a number of examples of inappropriate accounting under the LIFO method.

FRP Section 205 also discusses the SEC's view as to the manner in which non-LIFO information should be disclosed by LIFO companies and indicates that supplemental presentation of non-LIFO earnings information is acceptable if the disclosures are "properly formed and located." The disclosures should (1) state clearly that the use of LIFO results in a better matching of costs and revenues, (2) indicate why supplemental income disclosures (e.g., FIFO) are provided, and (3) present essential information about the supplemental income calculation so users can appreciate the quality of the information. If FIFO-based disclosures are provided for comparison to the operating results of non-LIFO companies, the SEC's position is that they should be contained in footnotes to the financial statements or in Management's Discussion and Analysis, not in financial highlights, president's letters, or press releases.

Regarding accounting changes, the SEC staff will typically question a registrant's justification for a change from LIFO to FIFO or another inventory method, especially if the company only recently adopted LIFO. However, SEC staff members have indicated that while such changes are not encouraged and generally not permitted, in certain limited situations the SEC staff has not objected to registrants and their auditors concluding that an accounting change from the LIFO method to the FIFO method of valuing inventory was preferable. Examples of these situations may include:

- Companies in troubled situations that lead creditors to place a greater emphasis on the balance sheet.

- Companies experiencing increased productivity gains (e.g., because of technological advances) and the unit cost of inventory items has significantly declined as a result.

- Companies experiencing *permanent* declines in inventory costs because of supply and demand forces in the marketplace (e.g., commodities).

In a registrant matter, the staff was asked to consider the following reasons for a change from the LIFO method back to the FIFO method:

- The change would provide the company additional equity and, therefore, relief under their existing debt covenants,

- The cost of performing the LIFO calculation was too great, and

- The company did not believe that inflation in the 1990s would be as great as it was in the 1970s when the company initially adopted LIFO.

The staff did *not* believe the above reasons support the preferability of this accounting change and thus rejected such proposed change. Given the specific facts and circumstances noted above, the staff believed that management's plans and judgments were not persuasive and thus a change to the FIFO method of valuing inventory was not preferable in the circumstances.

Long-term contract activities: FRP Section 206 (originally issued as ASR No. 164) specifies the information to be furnished by registrants engaged in defense and long-term contract activities. It indicates that, in the context of long-term contracts, inventory cost elements might include costs that are typically not considered inventoriable, such as initial tooling and other deferred start-up costs and general and administrative costs. An example of a footnote that might be furnished in response to these requirements is included in this section in the discussion following caption 3.

7. Prepaid expenses.

8. Other current assets. *State separately, in the balance sheet or in a note thereto, any amounts in excess of 5 percent of total current assets.*

9. Total current assets, when appropriate.

Investments

10. Securities of related parties. *(See Rule 4-08 (k).) [See section 50408(k).]*

11. Indebtedness of related parties—not current. *(See Rule 4-08 (k).) [See section 50408(k).]*

12. Other investments. *The accounting and disclosure requirements for noncurrent marketable equity securities are specified by generally accepted accounting principles. With respect to other security investments and any other investment, state, parenthetically or otherwise, the basis of determining the aggregate amounts shown in the balance sheet, along with the alternate of the aggregate cost or aggregate market value at the balance sheet date.*

The accounting and disclosure requirements for all debt securities and equity securities that have readily determinable fair values are prescribed by FASB Statement No. 115, *Accounting for Certain Investments in Debt and Equity Securities.* This Statement supersedes FASB Statement No. 12, *Accounting for Certain Marketable Securities,* and is effective for fiscal years beginning after December 15, 1993. Refer to section 50502-2 (Marketable securities) for a discussion of these requirements.

The following schedules are required to be furnished in support of the indicated investment captions if (1) the materiality criteria cited in Rule 5-04 are exceeded (see section 50520—Schedules I, IV, and XIII) *and* (2) the information required by the schedule is not included in a footnote to the financial statements:

Caption	Schedule Required by Rule
11. Indebtedness of related parties— not current	12-05 (Schedule IV)
12. Other investments	12-01 (Schedules I and XIII)

SEC 50502. Rule 5-02-6

SAB Topic 5-M discusses the SEC staff's views on accounting for noncurrent marketable equity securities when a decline in market value occurs and such a decline is considered "other than temporary." Although the SAB discusses "other than temporary" impairment in the context of FASB Statement No. 12, footnote 4 to FASB Statement No. 115 continues to refer to the guidance of this SAB along with other accounting literature. In addition, paragraph 112 of FASB Statement No. 115 states that "the Board concluded that it is important to recognize in earnings all declines in fair value below the amortized cost basis that are considered to be "other than temporary"; a loss inherent in an investment security should be recognized in earnings even if it has not been sold. This is consistent with the other-than-temporary-impairment notion that was included in Statement 12." Accordingly, the discussion that follows and the text of SAB Topic 5-M continue to be relevant.

In SAB Topic 5-M, the SEC staff states that it believes that the FASB consciously chose the phrase "other than temporary" in evaluating market-value declines because it did not intend that the test be "permanent impairment." Although numerous factors will be involved when evaluating impairment and each case will vary, the staff has provided the following factors that it believes may indicate that a decline is other than temporary and that a writedown of the carrying value is required:

- The duration and extent to which the market value has been less than cost.

- The financial condition and near-term prospects of the issuer, including events that may impact the issuer's operations and impair the earnings potential of the investment.

- The ability and intent of the holder to keep the investment for a sufficient period to allow for an anticipated recovery in market value.

The text of the SAB follows:

Noncurrent Marketable Equity Securities

Facts: Paragraph 21 of Financial Accounting Standards Board ("FASB") Statement No. 12, "Accounting for Certain Marketable Securities," specifies that "a determination must be made as to whether a decline in market value below cost as of the balance sheet date of an individual security is other than temporary. If the decline is judged to be other than temporary, the cost basis of the individual security shall be written down to a new cost basis and the amount of the write-down shall be accounted for as a realized loss." Statement No. 12 does not define the phrase "other than temporary." In applying this guidance to its own situation, Company A has interpreted "other than temporary" to mean permanent impairment. Therefore, because Company A's management has not been able to determine that its investment in Company B is permanently impaired, no realized loss has been recognized even though the market price of B's shares is currently less than one third of A's average acquisition price.

Question 1: Does the staff believe that the phrase "other than temporary" should be interpreted to mean "permanent"?

Interpretive Response: No. The staff believes that the FASB consciously chose the phrase "other than temporary" because it did not intend that the test be "permanent impairment," as has been used elsewhere in accounting practice.[1]

The value of investments in marketable securities classified as noncurrent assets may decline for various reasons. The market price may be affected by general market conditions which reflect prospects for the economy as a whole or by specific information pertaining to an industry or an individual company. Such declines require further investigation by management. Acting upon the premise that a write-down may be required, management should consider all available evidence to evaluate the realizable value of its investment.

There are numerous factors to be considered in such an evaluation and their relative significance will vary from case to case. The staff believes that the following are only a few examples of the factors which, individually or in combination, indicate that a decline is other than temporary and that a write-down of the carrying value is required:

a. The length of the time and the extent to which the market value has been less than cost;

b. The financial condition and near-term prospects of the issuer, including any specific events which may influence the operations of the issuer such as changes in technology that may impair the earnings potential of the investment or the discontinuance of a segment of the business that may affect the future earnings potential; or

c. The intent and ability of the holder to retain its investment in the issuer for a period of time sufficient to allow for any anticipated recovery in market value.

Unless evidence exists to support a realizable value equal to or greater than the carrying value of the investment, a write-down accounted for as a realized loss should be recorded. In accordance with the guidance of paragraph 11 of Statement No. 12, such loss should be recognized in the determination of net income of the period in which it occurs. The written down value of the investment in the company becomes the new cost basis of the investment.

Question 2: When management determined that a write-down, accounted for as a realized loss, is necessary, how should the amount of the write-down be determined?

Interpretive Response: The carrying value of the investment should be written down to reflect realizable value. The particular facts and circumstances dictate the amount of realized loss to be recognized on a case-by-case basis.

---

[1]Footnote 8 to Statement No. 12 refers to an Auditing Interpretation published by the staff of the Auditing Standards Divisions, AICPA, "Evidential Matter for the Carrying Amount of Marketable Securities," in The Journal of Accountancy, April

1975, for a discussion of considerations applicable to a determination as to whether a decline in market value below cost, at a particular point in time, is other than temporary. [That interpretation can be found in AU Section 9332.]

During 1991, two AAERs were issued requiring registrants to restate their quarterly and annual financial statements on the basis of the SEC's conclusion that declines in the market value of individual marketable equity securities within their investment portfolio were "other than temporary." Although FASB Statement No. 115 was issued subsequent to these AAERs, many of the same issues apply in determining whether declines are "other than temporary."

In the AAERs, the SEC identified several negative factors that served as a basis for its conclusions. These factors were identified by the SEC based on specific facts and circumstances in the enforcement cases and are not intended to be an all-inclusive list. Further, the SEC emphasized that it is not necessary for all these factors to be present to conclude a writedown is necessary and that a decline in value may be indicated by one or more of these factors.

The negative factors identified by the SEC were:

- Investees had experienced net losses or substantially reduced earnings in each of the four most recent quarters (or four of the last five quarters) and for the most recent year.

- Investees had reduced or ceased paying dividends.

- Investees have experienced deteriorating asset quality (e.g., increase in nonperforming asset-to-asset ratios, decreases in stockholders' equity-to-asset ratios, and large increases in nonperforming loans, repossessed property, and loan charge-offs).

- Investees announced other adverse changes or events such as changes in senior management, salary reductions and/or freezes, elimination of positions, sale of assets, problems with equity investments, or had become subject to federal regulatory agreements, some of which imposed operating restrictions and remedial actions.

- The level of earnings or asset quality of the investees was below those of their peer groups on a national basis.

- Investees received qualified audit opinions on their financial statements.

- Investees experienced debt-rating downgrades by rating services.

642

- The general market condition of either the geographic area or industry in which the investee operates was weak and there was no immediate prospect of recovery.

As a result of these actions, the SEC staff has provided the following guidelines in this area:

- The SEC staff expects registrants to begin with contemporaneous market prices in assessing the realizable value of noncurrent marketable equity securities. If market value is below cost, the initial presumption is that a writedown is necessary. However, this presumption can be overcome if objective evidence is available to support a realizable value in excess of market price.

- The SEC staff expects registrants to have a systematic methodology that includes documentation of the factors considered in making quarterly and year-end determinations. Such methodology should ensure that all available evidence concerning the decline in market value below cost will be identified and evaluated in a disciplined manner. The specific rationale and objective evidence supporting the realizable values of those securities that have experienced market-value declines below cost should be documented to justify the registrant's carrying costs, improve auditability, and to aid future determinations.

- The SEC staff expects that a registrant's internal accounting controls will be sufficient to provide reasonable assurances that information pertinent to the proper accounting of its investments is adequately considered in making evaluations.

- In consideration of the entity's ability and intent to retain the investments for a period of time sufficient to allow for anticipated recovery of market value, the auditor should obtain evidence supporting assumptions regarding holding periods that appear unreasonably long.

- The SEC staff will generally not accept a formula approach in establishing the amount of writedown, e.g., a 25 percent writedown for a security which is 50 percent below market.

- The use of comparison of a security's book value to its cost basis as the principal analytical tool for evaluating that security's realizable value is considered by the staff to be insufficient. While comparisons to the issuer's book value may be an element of an entity's analysis, in the staff's view, they are, by themselves, inadequate determinants of realizable value.

- Individual securities should be evaluated on a quarterly basis to determine whether a writedown is necessary for declines in market values that are "other than temporary."

Although the two enforcement releases discussed above involved actions against financial institutions and related to market-value declines of marketable *equity* securities, the SEC staff has stressed that its views regarding "other than temporary" impairment of marketable securities relate both to *debt* and *equity* securities and to industries other than financial institutions.

The SEC staff has also indicated that the issue of whether *debt* securities have experienced an "other than temporary" market-value decline continues to receive a great deal of emphasis in the review process. Auditing Interpretation 9332.10 states that market-value declines in debt securities may be considered temporary "unless the evidence indicates that such investments will be disposed of before they mature or that they may not be realizable." The staff has indicated that it interprets this provision quite literally and that it takes the view that debt securities need to be carefully evaluated to determine whether there is an ability and intent to hold to maturity *and* whether the ultimate amount will be realized.

In addition, the staff has indicated that in the review process it will routinely evaluate the amount of trading in long-term investment portfolios. If a significant amount of trading has occurred, the staff is likely to challenge the investment classification of the portfolio. In addition, prior to the issuance of FASB Statement No. 115, the Chief Accountant of the Division of Corporation Finance has stated that the staff is likely to challenge registrants "whose investment policy footnote identifies a practice that entails responding to changes in interest rates, prepayments, and similar economic factors that may be reasonably expected to result in sales of investment securities prior to maturity. In such instances, the staff typically will request a revision to the financial statements to classify securities that will be held for indefinite periods of time as available for sale and to account for such securities at the lower of cost or market value. A revision of the investment policy footnote may also be required to clarify that securities held for indefinite periods of time, including securities that management intends to use as part of its asset/liability strategy, or that may be sold in response to changes in interest rates, prepayments, regulatory capital requirements or other similar factors are classified as held for sale and carried at lower of cost or market value. Additional clarification that investment securities are carried at amortized costs because of the registrant's ability to hold such securities to maturity, and the intent of management is to hold such securities on a long-term basis or until maturity may also be required. Management's Discussion and Analysis and other textual disclosures should be revised to be consistent with the accounting policy."

SEC 50502

Property

13. Property, plant and equipment.

(a) State the basis of determining the amounts.

(b) Tangible and intangible utility plant of a public utility company shall be segregated so as to show separately the original cost, plant acquisition adjustments, and plant adjustments, as required by the system of accounts prescribed by the applicable regulatory authorities. This rule shall not be applicable in respect to companies which are not required to make such a classification.

14. Accumulated depreciation, depletion and amortization of property, plant and equipment. *The amount is to be set forth separately in the balance sheet or in a note thereto.*

The schedules prescribed by Rules 12-06 (Schedule V) and 12-07 (Schedule VI) are required to be furnished in support of these captions if (1) the materiality criteria cited in Rule 5-04 are exceeded (see section 50520—Schedules V and VI) *and* (2) the information required by the schedule is not included in a footnote to the financial statements. Disclosure of the amount of accumulated depreciation, depletion, and amortization may be included in a note to the financial statements.

Intangible Assets

15. Intangible assets. *State separately each class of such assets which is in excess of 5 percent of total assets, along with the basis of determining the respective amounts. Any significant addition or deletion shall be explained in a note.*

The SEC staff has generally indicated that intangible assets acquired in a business combination that are recognized for tax-reporting purposes should be evaluated for recognition in the financial statements.

With regard to goodwill, the staff has informally indicated that as a general rule it considers the write-off of goodwill resulting from a recent business combination to be inappropriate unless a significant event has occurred, or the environment in which the business operates has changed significantly. In the staff's view, either factor may suggest that the intangible asset has been impaired.

On the other hand, in a situation in which an acquired business has a history of operating losses and the registrant projects that the business will continue to incur operating losses in the foreseeable future, the staff believes that consideration needs to be given to the issue of whether a writedown of goodwill is necessary.

The staff has indicated that it considers the following considerations to be relevant when assessing whether a writedown of goodwill is necessary:

SEC 50502. Rule 5-02-13

- The analysis should not be made on a consolidated basis, but on the basis of the operations of the particular entity to which the goodwill relates.

- Impairment of goodwill and a change in the life of goodwill amortization are two separate issues that should be analyzed separately.

- It is generally inappropriate to lengthen the amortization period of goodwill once the period has been established at the acquisition date.

The staff has consistently taken the position that amortization of intangibles, including goodwill, should be classified in the income statement as an operating expense.

Regarding goodwill in the high-technology industries, due to competitive, technological, and economic factors, the staff believes that goodwill should ordinarily be amortized over periods significantly shorter than 40 years. The SEC staff has indicated that periods of less than ten years are generally appropriate and a period ranging from five to seven years may be necessary for a company with a single product.

16. Accumulated depreciation and amortization of intangible assets. *The amount is to be set forth separately in the balance sheet or in a note thereto.*

Other Assets and Deferred Charges

17. Other assets. *State separately, in the balance sheet or in a note thereto, any other item not properly classed in one of the preceding asset captions which is in excess of 5 percent of total assets. Any significant addition or deletion should be explained in a note. With respect to any significant deferred charge, state the policy for deferral and amortization.*

This rule requires disclosure of any "other" asset account (not includible in other captions) that exceeds five percent of total assets. The rule also requires disclosure of significant additions or deletions during the period.

With regard to tangible assets, the staff has informally indicated that it considers the following factors to be particularly relevant in determining whether the value of a company's assets may be considered impaired:

- A substantial reduction in the fair value of the assets due to technological changes.

- Historical negative cash flows from operations.

SEC 50502

- A significant change in the manner in which the assets are used. The staff has expressed the view that a writedown of the assets should be recorded when it is probable that the estimated undiscounted future cash flows will be less than the net book value of the company's tangible assets. The staff will also accept, but not require, recognition of impairments based on discounted future cash flows from operations. In addition, the staff believes that any writedown resulting from an impairment should be presented as an *operating* charge.

The staff has also indicated that disclosure of a potential writedown is required in the notes to the financial statements *and MD&A* if a registrant determines that it is reasonably possible that the undiscounted future cash flows will be less than the net book value of the tangible assets. The FASB is considering this impairment issue in its project on Impairment of Long-Lived Assets.

SAB Topic 5-A discusses the criteria for deferring expenses incurred in connection with an offering of securities:

Expenses of Offering

Facts: Prior to the effective date of an offering of equity securities, Company Y incurs certain expenses related to the offering.

Question: Should such costs be deferred?

Interpretive Response: Specific incremental costs directly attributable to a proposed or actual offering of securities may properly be deferred and charged against the gross proceeds of the offering. However, management salaries or other general and administrative expenses may not be allocated as costs of the offering and deferred costs of an aborted offering may not be deferred and charged against proceeds of a subsequent offering. A short postponement (up to 90 days) does not represent an aborted offering.

The SEC staff generally will not permit deferred compensation expense resulting from stock compensation arrangements or similar debits arising from the issuance of stock to be classified as an asset. Rather, its view is that such amounts should be reflected as a separate caption in the equity section of the balance sheet and deducted from total stockholders' equity or—if such caption is not presented—from other stockholders' equity.

The SEC staff has informally expressed concerns regarding the deferral of the following types of costs:

- Media advertising costs.

SEC 50502. Rule 5-02-17

- Marketing and promotional costs (including costs associated with direct mail campaigns such as designing, printing, shipping, and handling costs).

- Personnel and recruitment cost (relocation, training, media advertisement, commissions, training, and travel).

- Customer acquisition (such as commissions paid to third parties).

As a general rule, the staff's informal position is that costs of this nature represent recurring period costs that should be expensed as incurred. However, the staff generally has not objected to the deferral of specific, direct costs where quantifiable future benefits are probable and the amortization period is relatively short (usually less than one year). In these situations, the registrant has presented documented evidence of past history demonstrating the achievement of specific benefits corresponding with the specific outlays.

With regard to preoperating (or preopening) and start-up costs, the predominant practice appears to be to expense these costs as incurred. The SEC staff prefers this practice. The staff has acknowledged, however, that while it generally considers the deferral of start-up costs to be unacceptable, it may not object to the deferral of direct preoperating costs if the following criteria are met:

- The costs are separately identifiable and incremental to ordinary operating expenses;

- The recoverability of the costs from gross profits of the new facility is probable;

- The amortization period is relatively short (not exceeding one to two years); and

- The operating history of the registrant in the product line and geographic region supports the recoverability assessment and amortization period.

With regard to differentiating between preoperating and start-up costs, the staff appears to define preoperating costs as those costs incurred prior to the commencement of operations or production. Start-up costs, on the other hand, are considered to be those incurred after operations have begun, but before the enterprise has reached anticipated productive capacity.

In the case of restaurants, the staff generally requires that preopening costs be amortized over a period not to exceed 12 months. In addition, the staff believes that only direct incremental costs related to the facility should be deferred as preopening costs. The staff has indicated that it has taken exception to the deferral of amounts calculated by "backing into" the direct incremental costs by subtracting normal gross margins from actual gross margins. In addition, the staff has indicated that managerial salaries and other overhead expenses that would be incurred in the absence of preopening activities should not be deferred.

The staff believes that deferral of preoperating costs should cease when operations begin, *not* when predetermined capacity levels or efficiency rates are met. The staff has indicated that it generally equates the reporting of revenues with the beginning of operations. However, the staff has acknowledged that some sales may occur during the testing phase of a new facility, and has indicated that revenues from sales prior to completion of the facility should be recognized as credits to the cost of the facility. However, the staff has indicated that it will take exception to the deferral of costs and revenues until a desired capacity level is achieved based on the staff's view that deferrals should stop when the facility is substantially complete and ready for its intended use.

18. Total assets.

LIABILITIES AND STOCKHOLDERS' EQUITY

Current Liabilities, When Appropriate
(See Rule 4-05)

19. Accounts and notes payable.

(a) State separately amounts payable to:

(1) Banks for borrowings;
(2) Factors or other financial institutions for borrowing;
(3) Holders of commercial paper;
(4) Trade creditors;
(5) Related parties (see Rule 4-08(k));
(6) Underwriters, promoters, and employees (other than related parties); and
(7) Others.

Amounts applicable to (1), (2), and (3) may be stated separately in the balance sheet or in a note thereto.

(b) The amount and terms (including commitment fees and the conditions under which lines may be withdrawn) of unused lines of credit for short-term financing shall be disclosed, if significant, in the notes to the financial statements. The amount of these lines of credit which support a commercial paper borrowing arrangement or similar arrangements shall be separately identified.

FASB Statement No. 6, *Classification of Short-Term Obligations Expected To Be Refinanced,* and Interpretation No. 8, *Classification of a Short-Term Obligation Repaid Prior to Being Replaced by a Long-Term Security,* deal with the accounting for short-term debt expected to be refinanced. Refer to section 50502.22 for discussion regarding these standards.

SAB Topic 6-H1 contains interpretations dealing with the applicability of short-term borrowing disclosures to specific situations. Additional disclosures regarding short-term borrowings are required in the supplementary financial schedule described in Rule 12-10 of Regulation S-X (see section 51210).

SAB Topic 6-H2(a) presents the staff's views with respect to classification of short-term obligations related to long-term construction projects.

Debt Related to Long-Term Projects

Facts: Companies engaging in significant long-term construction programs frequently arrange for revolving cover loans which extend until the completion of long-term construction projects. Such revolving cover loans are typically arranged with substantial financial institutions and typically have the following characteristics:

1) A firm long-term mortgage commitment is obtained for each project.

2) Interest rates and terms are in line with the company's normal borrowing arrangements.

3) Amounts are equal to the expected full mortgage amount of all projects.

4) The company may draw down funds at its option up to the maximum amount of the agreement.

5) The company uses short-term interim construction financing (commercial paper, bank loans, etc.) against the revolving cover loan. Such indebtedness is rolled over or drawn down on the revolving cover loan at the company's option. The company typically has regular bank lines of credit, but these generally are not legally enforceable.

Question: Under FASB No. 6 and ASR No. 172, will the classification of loans such as described above as long-term be acceptable?

Interpretive Response: Where such conditions exist providing for a firm commitment throughout the construction program as well as a firm commitment for permanent mortgage financing, and where there are no contingencies other than the completion of construction, the guideline criteria are met and the borrowing under such a program should be classified as long-term with appropriate disclosure.

Paragraph (b) of Rule 5-02-19 requires that the amount and terms of significant unused lines of credit or commitments be disclosed in the notes to the financial statements and that amounts that support a commercial paper borrowing arrangement or similar arrangements be separately identified. FRP Section 203 contains certain guidelines with respect to these disclosures.

20. Other current liabilities. *State separately, in the balance sheet or in a note thereto, any item in excess of 5 percent of total current liabilities. Such items may include, but are not limited to, accrued payrolls, accrued interest, taxes, indicating the current portion of deferred income taxes and the current portion of long-term debt. Remaining items may be shown in one amount.*

Refer to section 50408(h) for discussion regarding income tax disclosures.

21. Total current liabilities, when appropriate.

Long-Term Debt

22. Bonds, mortgages and other long-term debt, including capitalized leases.

(a) State separately, in the balance sheet or in a note thereto, each issue or type of obligation and such information as will indicate (see Rule 4-06):

(1) The general character of each type of debt including the rate of interest;

(2) The date of maturity, or, if maturing serially, a brief indication of the serial maturities, such as "maturing serially from 1980 to 1990";

(3) If the payment of principal or interest is contingent, an appropriate indication of such contingency;

(4) A brief indication of priority; and

(5) If convertible, the basis.

For amounts owed to related parties, see Rule 4-08(k).

(b) The amount and terms (including commitment fees and the conditions under which commitments may be withdrawn) of unused commitments for long-term financing arrangements that would be disclosed under this rule if used shall be disclosed in the notes to the financial statements, if significant.

Rule 4-06, referred to in paragraph (a), specifies that debt that has been repaid but not retired (e.g., treasury bonds) should be deducted from the corresponding liability account unless the debt is held for pension or other special funds not related to the debt issue.

FASB Statement No. 76, *Extinguishment of Debt*, describes the circumstances under which a company should consider debt to be extinguished for financial reporting purposes, and provides specific criteria that must be met for debt to be considered extinguished in an in-substance defeasance transaction. In-substance defeasance transactions typically involve the placement of certain risk-free assets, such as U.S. government securities, in a trust that uses income and principal collections from the securities to service outstanding debt obligations. Although the amount of securities placed in the trust is calculated to meet all principal and interest payments required on the debt, the debtor remains primarily responsible. In FRR No. 15 (FRP Section 217), the SEC recognized the issuance of SFAS No. 76 and rescinded FRR No. 3, which had placed a moratorium on in-substance defeasance accounting. The release emphasizes the importance of the trustee's independence from the company, the risk-free nature of the assets placed in the trust, the timing of the interest and principal to be collected from those assets, and the irrevocability of the trust's rights to those assets in order to service the debt. Subsequently, the FASB issued Technical Bulletin 84-4, which clarified the application of certain provisions in SFAS No. 76.

Certain guidelines as to the information on unused commitments to be provided in accordance with paragraph (b) are included in this section in the discussion following caption 1 (cash and cash items).

The discussion following Rule 4-08(c) deals with the classification of debt when a default or breach has occurred (see section 50408).

FASB Statement No. 6, *Classification of Short-Term Obligations Expected To Be Refinanced*, describes the following conditions required to be met in order for a company to classify a short-term obligation as noncurrent:

- The company intends to refinance the obligation on a long-term basis (paragraph 10); and

- The company's intent to refinance is supported by an ability to consummate the refinancing by either:

  •• Refinancing the short-term obligation by issuance of a long-term obligation or equity securities after the balance sheet date but before the balance sheet is issued; or

  •• Entering into a financing agreement, before the balance sheet is issued, that clearly permits the company to refinance the short-term obligation on a long-term basis, provided that certain other conditions are met as addressed in FASB No. 6 (paragraph 11).

Paragraph 3 of FASB Interpretation No. 8, *Classification of a Short-Term Obligation Repaid Prior to Being Replaced by a Long-Term Security*, clarifies that in a situation in which a short-term obligation is repaid after the balance sheet date and the proceeds from a subsequent issuance of a long-term obligation or equity securities are used to replenish current assets prior to the balance sheet being issued, the short-term obligation should continue to be classified as a current liability as of the balance sheet date.

SAB Topic 4-A (included in discussion following Rule 5-02-31) states that subordinated debt may not be included in the stockholders' equity section of the balance sheet or combined with that caption.

SAB Topic 5-R discusses the staff's views with respect to the accounting and balance sheet presentation for nonrecourse debt that is collateralized by lease receivables and/or the related leased assets. In such borrowings, the SEC staff indicates that the lease receivables and nonrecourse debt cannot be removed from the balance sheet by either accounting for the transaction as a sale or assignment of the lease receivable or by offsetting the lease receivables and nonrecourse debt. The text of the SAB follows:

Accounting for Non-recourse Debt Collateralized by Lease Receivables and/or Leased Assets

Facts: A registrant borrows on a non-recourse basis and assigns to the lender a security interest in lease receivables and/or the related lease assets.

Question: Can the lease receivables and non-recourse debt be removed from the balance sheet either by (a) accounting for this transaction as a sale or assignment of the lease receivables or (b) by offsetting the lease receivables and non-recourse debt?

Answer: No. The staff believes that under existing generally accepted accounting principles this type of transaction should be accounted for as a borrowing and, as such, the resultant debt should be reflected in the registrant's balance sheet.[1] Paragraph 20 of FASB Statement No. 13, as amended by FASB Statement No. 77, indicates that the "sale or assignment of a lease or of property subject to a lease accounted for as a sales-type or direct financing shall not negate the original accounting treatment accorded the lease" and that "any profit or loss on the sale or assignment shall be recognized at the time of the transaction."[2] However, the staff understands that the FASB intended the term "assignment" as used in that Statement to represent the transfer from one party to another of a direct interest in a contractual right or property, and not a security interest in a right or property. Non-recourse borrowing arrangements that involve the assignment[3] of a security interest in a lease and/or property subject to lease, therefore, do not result in recognition "as if" a sale had occurred under the provisions of paragraph 20 of FASB Statement No. 13.[4]

Further, the accounting literature[5] generally does not allow non-recourse debt and lease receivables and/or the related leased assets to be offset in the balance sheet. This was recently reaffirmed by the staff of the FASB in Technical Bulletin No. 86-2, "Accounting for an Interest in the Residual Value of a Leased Asset."[6]

[Note: The remainder of this SAB discussed the initial application of the guidance presented and is no longer applicable. Accordingly, this text is not reproduced herein.]

SEC 50502. Rule 5-02-22

[1]The staff also has noted certain transactions in which leasing companies borrow non-recourse by collateralizing with lease receivables and/or the related leased assets and also sell a portion of the interest in the residual value of the leased assets to third party investors. These transactions may include the sale of the assets (subject to the leasing company's non-recourse borrowing and the lender's interest in the lease receivables and related lease assets) to the investor group, with the retention by the leasing company of a portion of the residual interest in the leased assets. The staff believes transactions in which the leasing company retains a future benefit in the leased assets and is not relieved of its (non-recourse) debt obligation do not alter the leasing company's status with respect to either the end user of the assets (lessee) or the lender under the non-recourse borrowing and should not result in the recognition of a sale of the lease receivables or the offsetting of the lease receivables and debt.

[2]Special provisions apply, however, if the sale or assignment is between related parties or with recourse.

[3]The term "sale" is generally used to refer to a contract or agreement by which property is transferred from a seller to a buyer in exchange for cash or a promise to pay a fixed price. "Assignment" is generally used to describe transfers of interests or rights. The legal determination of when a particular transaction represents a "sale" or an "assignment" is a matter of individual state law.

[4]In addition, the staff does not believe that non-recourse borrowing arrangements (which may be structured as sales with repurchase options) involving operating leases and/or the underlying leased assets should result in the recognition of a sale of the leased assets. Therefore, registrants involved in these transactions should continue to reflect the assets under lease on their balance sheets and should also record the resultant non-recourse debt.

[5]Paragraph 7 of Accounting Principles Board (APB) Opinion No. 10 indicates that "it is a general principle of accounting that the offsetting of assets and liabilities in the balance sheet is improper except where a right of setoff exists." Topic 11-D of the staff accounting bulletin series also indicates that "even when items can be directly associated it is not appropriate to offset assets and liabilities without the benefit of an existing legal right." The concept of legal right of offset embodied in Topic 11-D refers to the existence of a right between two parties, owing ascertainable amounts to each other, to set off their respective debts by way of mutual deduction so that in any action brought for the larger debt, only the remainder after the deduction may be recovered. The debts must, therefore, be to and from the same parties acting on their own behalf. It should be noted that "right of setoff" as embodied in APB Opinion No. 10 and the concept of legal right of offset in Topic 11-D are intended to be similar in meaning.

[6]Paragraph 21 of this Technical Bulletin indicates that "offsetting the lease receivable with non-recourse debt is appropriate only in those circumstances in which a legal right of offset exists or when, at the inception of the lease, the lease

meets all the characteristics of paragraph 42 of Statement 13 and is appropriately classified as a leveraged lease."

FASB Interpretation No. 39 specifies when a right of setoff exists as discussed in section 50502.

23. Indebtedness to related parties—noncurrent. *Include under this caption indebtedness to related parties as required under Rule 4-08(k).*

Refer to section 50408(k) for the requirements of Rule 4-08(k) and additional guidance regarding related-party transactions and disclosures.

The schedule prescribed by Rule 12-05 (Schedule IV) is required to be furnished in support of this caption if (1) the materiality criteria cited in Rule 5-04 are exceeded (see section 50520—Schedule IV) *and* (2) the information required by this schedule is not included in a footnote to the financial statements.

Other Liabilities and Deferred Credits

24. Other liabilities. *State separately, in the balance sheet or in a note thereto, any item not properly classified in one of the preceding liability captions which is in excess of 5 percent of total liabilities.*

SAB Topic 5-O addresses certain aspects of accounting for an entity's obligation to another party when the entity's research and development is being funded by the other party, as discussed in FASB No. 68, *Research and Development Arrangements*, and provides guidance on the term "significant related party relationship" as used therein. The text of SAB Topic 5-O follows:

Research and Development Arrangements

Facts: FASB Statement No. 68 paragraph 7 states that conditions other than a written agreement may exist which created a presumption that the enterprise will repay the funds provided by other parties under a research and development arrangement. Paragraph 8(c) lists as one of those conditions the existence of a "significant related party relationship" between the enterprise and the parties funding the research and development.

Question 1: What does the staff consider a "significant related party relationship" as that term is used in paragraph 8(c) of FASB Statement No. 68?

Interpretive Response: The staff believes that a significant related party relationship exists when 10 percent or more of the entity providing the funds is owned by related parties. In unusual circumstances, the staff may also question the appropriateness of treating a research and development arrangement as a contract to perform service for others at the less than 10 percent level. In reviewing these matters, the staff will consider, among other factors, the percentage of the funding entity owned by the related parties in relationship to their ownership in and degree of influence or control over the enterprise receiving the funds.

Question 2: Paragraph 7 of FASB Statement No. 68 states that the presumption of repayment "can be overcome only by substantial evidence to the contrary." Can the presumption be overcome by evidence that the funding parties were assuming the risk of the research and development activities since they could not reasonably expect the enterprise to have resources to repay the funds based on its current and projected future financial conditions?

Interpretive Response: No. Paragraph 5 of FASB Statement No. 68 specifically indicates that the enterprise "may settle the liability by paying cash, by issuing securities, or by some other means." While the enterprise may not be in a position to pay cash or issue debt, repayment could be accomplished through the issuance of stock or various other means. Therefore, an apparent or projected inability to repay the funds with cash (or debt which would later be paid with cash) does not demonstrate that the funding parties were accepting the entire risks of the activities.

The SEC staff has indicated that in some circumstances it may grant relief from the foregoing repayment presumption, but that such situations are rare and are limited to situations in which the related parties do not exert significant influence over the company receiving the funds.

25. Commitments and contingent liabilities.

Disclosures of contingent liabilities often include a description of legal proceedings, either in process or threatened, that are also described in the narrative (textual) portion of the SEC document. The discussion of such matters in the text (e.g., Item 3 of Form 10-K) needs to be read to ensure that the conclusions as to the impact of such matters on the financial statements as disclosed in the notes therein are consistent with the disclosures in the textual portion of the document. Particular consideration needs to be given to legal matters discussed in the text that are not disclosed in the notes to the financial statements from the standpoint of their potential impact on the statements and whether additional disclosure is necessary. When the text describes the contingencies to be disclosed in the financial statements, such information may be incorporated by reference in the notes to the financial statements. (See discussion of cross-referencing in section 17093.) Also refer to S-X Rule 5-02-1 (section 50502-1) and the discussions in FRP Section 104 with respect to the disclosure of oral guarantees.

SAB Topic 5-Y (SAB No. 92) discusses the SEC staff's views regarding accounting and disclosures relating to loss contingencies. While the primary focus of the SAB is environmental and product liabilities, the SEC staff has indicated that, in general, it will apply the positions outlined in SAB No. 92 to all loss contingencies.

In EITF Issue No. 93-5, "Accounting for Environmental Liabilities," the EITF reached a consensus that environmental liabilities should be evaluated independently from any potential recovery of the costs from insurance carriers or other third parties. Statement of Financial Accounting Standards No. 5, *Accounting for Contingencies,* requires an accrual to be made when a loss is probable and the amount can be reasonably estimated. Prior to EITF Issue No. 93-5, it was considered acceptable to make the probability determination on a net basis, e.g., after considering insurance recoveries. Thus, as long as full insurance recovery was "reasonably possible," there was not a "probable" loss and no accrual was necessary. As a result of EITF Issue No. 93-5, this interpretation is no longer acceptable.

The consensus on EITF Issue 93-5 indicates that a claim for recovery may only be recorded if it is "probable" (referred to in SFAS No. 5 as "likely to occur") of realization. It is important to note that there is actually a higher threshold for recording contingent assets under the provisions of SFAS No. 5. Accordingly, the consensus lowers the threshold for recording contingent assets in these instances. The SEC staff accepts the consensus reached by the EITF regarding Issue No. 93-5.

The EITF did not address the related balance sheet presentation, but noted that in practice it has been considered acceptable to net the two amounts on the balance sheet. The interpretive response to question 1 of SAB No. 92 expresses the SEC staff's view that net presentation is appropriate only in those circumstances where a right of setoff exists, as defined in FASB Interpretation No. 39, *Offsetting of Amounts Relating to Certain Contracts* (FIN No. 39) (see section 50502). Until FIN No. 39 is applied, the staff believes registrants should disclose in the notes to the financial statements the gross amount of any claims for recovery that are netted against liabilities. However, once the provisions of FIN No. 39 are required to be applied (periods beginning after December 15, 1993), the SEC staff will object to the offsetting of liabilities with probable recoveries from third parties unless the right of setoff exists.

SAB No. 92 also includes a rebuttable presumption that no asset should be recognized for a claim for recovery from a party that is contesting the claim. The staff believes that registrants who overcome the rebuttable presumption should disclose the reasons for concluding that the amounts are probable of recovery.

The interpretive response to question 2 of SAB No. 92 indicates that a registrant who is jointly and severally liable with respect to a contaminated site need not recognize a liability with respect to the costs apportioned to the other parties provided there is a reasonable basis for apportionment of costs among responsible parties. However, the SAB also indicates that if it is probable that other responsible parties will not fully pay their share of the costs, the recorded liability should include the registrant's best estimate of additional costs the registrant expects to pay.

Regarding the timing of recognition and measurement of the liability, SAB No. 92 states that (1) management may not delay the accrual of a contingent liability until

SEC 50502. Rule 5-02-25

only a single amount can be reasonably estimated, and (2) recognition of a loss equal to the lower limit of a range of losses is necessary even if the upper limit of the range is uncertain. In addition, the staff indicates that registrants may have sufficient information necessary to estimate the range of loss *prior* to the performance of any detailed remediation study, and the following factors should be considered in estimating the liability:

- Prior experience in remediation of contaminated sites.

- *Currently* enacted laws and regulations.

- *Existing* technology.

- Effects of inflation.

- Information published by EPA or other organizations.

In EITF Issue No. 93-5, the EITF specified the factors that must be present to apply discounting methodologies to an environmental liability but did not conclude on rate considerations. SAB No. 92 requires the use of the discount rate that will produce an amount at which the environmental or product liability could be settled in an arm's-length transaction with a third party. If that rate is not readily determinable, the SAB states that the discount rate used should not exceed the interest rate on monetary assets that are essentially risk-free and have maturities comparable to that of the liability.

In the interpretive response to question 5 of SAB No. 92, the staff provided the following examples of financial statement disclosures that may be necessary regarding recorded and unrecorded liabilities:

- Circumstances affecting the reliability and precision of loss estimates.

- The impact of unasserted claims on accruals.

- Impact of joint and several liabilities, including a description of any cost-sharing arrangements.

- Extent to which unrecognized contingent losses are expected to be recovered from third parties.

- Uncertainties regarding insurance recovery.

- The time frame for payment of accrued and unrecognized amounts.

SEC 50502

- Material components of accruals and significant assumptions underlying estimates.

In addition, the staff indicates that the following types of specific separate disclosures should be considered in complying with the requirements of Items 101 (Description of Business), 103 (Legal Proceedings), and 303 (Management's Discussion and Analysis) of Regulations S-K and S-B:

- Environmental liabilities:

  - •• Recurring costs associated with managing hazardous substances and pollution in ongoing operations.

  - •• Capital expenditures to limit or monitor hazardous substances or pollutants.

  - •• Mandated expenditures to remediate previously contaminated sites.

  - •• Other infrequent or nonrecurring clean-up expenditures that can be anticipated but which are not required in the present circumstances.

  - •• Disaggregated disclosure that describes accrued and reasonably likely losses with respect to individually material sites.

- Product liability:

  - •• The nature of personal injury or property damages alleged by claimants.

  - •• Aggregate settlement costs by type of claim and related costs of administering and litigating claims.

  - •• Accrued and reasonably likely losses of individual material claims.

  - •• The number of claims pending at each balance sheet date.

  - •• The number of claims filed during each period presented.

  - •• The number of claims dismissed, settled, or otherwise resolved during each period.

  - •• The average settlement amount per claim.

SEC 50502. Rule 5-02-25

Paragraph 10 of Statement No. 5 requires disclosure of reasonably possible losses in excess of the amount accrued. SAB No. 92 expresses the SEC staff's view that in determining whether such disclosures need to be made, the registrant should consider whether the additional loss would be material to a decision to buy or sell the registrant's securities.

SAB No. 92 indicates that, on the basis of accepted practice in certain industries, the SEC staff will not object to the accrual of estimated environmental exit costs (including site restoration costs and post-closure and monitoring costs) over the useful life of the asset. In addition, the SAB specifies the following disclosures for exit costs associated with assets at various stages of their useful lives:

- Potential asset dispositions—Disclose material liabilities for exit costs that may occur on the sale, disposal or abandonment of a property including: the nature of the costs involved, total anticipated costs, total costs accrued to date, balance sheet classification and range of reasonably possible additional losses.

- Planned asset disposition/development—Disclose how costs associated with remediation, which must be performed prior to or during the development or sale of an asset, are considered in the assessment of the asset's net realizable value.

- Past asset disposals—Disclose liability for remediation of environmental damage relating to assets or businesses previously disposed, unless the likelihood of material loss is remote.

The text of SAB Topic 5-Y follows:

Accounting and Disclosures Relating to Loss Contingencies

Facts: A registrant believes it may be obligated to pay material amounts as a result of product or environmental liability. These amounts may relate to, for example, damages attributed to the registrant's products or processes, clean-up of hazardous wastes, reclamation costs, fines, and litigation costs. The registrant may seek to recover a portion or all of these amounts by filing a claim against an insurance carrier or other third parties.

Paragraph 8 of Statement of Financial Accounting Standards No. 5, "Accounting for Contingencies" ("SFAS 5"), states that an estimated loss from a loss contingency shall be accrued by a charge to income if it is probable that a liability has been incurred and the amount of the loss can be reasonably estimated. The Emerging Issues Task Force ("EITF") of the Financial Accounting Standards Board reached a consensus on EITF Issue 93-5, "Accounting for Environmental

Liabilities," that an environmental liability should be evaluated independently from any potential claim for recovery. Under that consensus, any loss arising from the recognition of an environmental liability should be reduced by a potential claim for recovery only when that claim is probable[1] of realization. The EITF also reached a consensus that discounting an environmental liability for a specific clean-up site to reflect the time value of money is appropriate only if the aggregate amount of the obligation and the amount and timing of the cash payments are fixed or reliably determinable for that site. Further, any asset that is recognized relating to a claim for recovery of a liability that is recognized on a discounted basis also should be discounted to reflect the time value of money.

Because uncertainty regarding the alternative methods of presenting in the balance sheet the amounts recognized as contingent liabilities and claims for recovery from third parties was not resolved by the EITF and current disclosure practices remain diverse, the staff is publishing its interpretation of the current accounting literature and disclosure requirements to serve as guidance for public companies. The AICPA's Accounting Standards Executive Committee has appointed a task force to address environmental concerns. The staff encourages efforts by the profession to develop comprehensive guidance applicable to the accounting and financial statement disclosures relating to environmental matters.

Question 1: Does the staff believe that it is appropriate to offset in the balance sheet a claim for recovery that is probable of realization against a probable contingent liability, that is, report the two as a single net amount on the face of the balance sheet?

Interpretive Response: Not ordinarily. The staff believes that separate presentation of the gross liability and related claim for recovery in the balance sheet most fairly presents the potential consequences of the contingent claim on the company's resources and is the preferable method of display. Recent reports of litigation over insurance policies' coverage of product and environmental liabilities and financial failures in the insurance industry indicate that there are significant uncertainties regarding both the timing and the ultimate realization of claims made to recover amounts from insurance carriers and other third parties. The risks and uncertainties associated with a registrant's contingent liability are separate and distinct from those associated with its claim for recovery from third parties.

Separate presentation of the gross liability and the claim for recovery is consistent with the recent consensus of the EITF, which concluded that the amounts of the contingent liability and any claim for recovery should be estimated and evaluated independently. Furthermore, accounting guidance generally proscribes the offsetting of assets and liabilities except where a right of setoff exists.[2] This general proscription was strengthened by the recent issuance of Financial Accounting Standards Board Interpretation No. 39, "Offsetting of Amounts Relating to Certain Contracts" ("FIN 39"), which is effective for financial statements issued for periods beginning after December 15, 1993. The guidance in that interpretation

SEC 50502. Rule 5-02-25

indicates that the prohibition on setoff in the balance sheet should be applied more comprehensively than previously may have been the practice.

It is the staff's view that presentation of liabilities net of claims for recovery will not be appropriate after the provisions of FIN 39 are required to be applied in financial statements. In the interim, registrants should ensure that notes to the financial statements include information necessary to an understanding of the material uncertainties affecting both the measurement of the liability and the realization of recoveries. The staff believes these disclosures should include the gross amount of any claims for recovery that are netted against the liability.

Question 2: If a registrant is jointly and severally liable with respect to a contaminated site but there is a reasonable basis for apportionment of costs among responsible parties, must the registrant recognize a liability with respect to costs apportioned to other responsible parties?

Interpretive Response: No. However, if it is probable that other responsible parties will not fully pay costs apportioned to them, the liability that is recognized by the registrant should include the registrant's best estimate, before consideration of potential recoveries from other parties, of the additional costs that the registrant expects to pay. Discussion of uncertainties affecting the registrant's ultimate obligation may be necessary if, for example, the solvency of one or more parties is in doubt or responsibility for the site is disputed by a party. A note to the financial statements should describe any additional loss that is reasonably possible.

Question 3: Estimates and assumptions regarding the extent of environmental or product liability, methods of remedy, and amounts of related costs frequently prove to be different from the ultimate outcome. How do these uncertainties affect the recognition and measurement of the liability?

Interpretive Response: The measurement of the liability should be based on currently available facts, existing technology, and presently enacted laws and regulations, and should take into consideration the likely effects of inflation and other societal and economic factors. Notwithstanding significant uncertainties, management may not delay recognition of a contingent liability until only a single amount can be reasonably estimated. If management is able to determine that the amount of the liability is likely to fall within a range and no amount within that range can be determined to be the better estimate, the registrant should recognize the minimum amount of the range pursuant to Financial Accounting Standards Board Interpretation No. 14, "Reasonable Estimation of the Amount of a Loss" ("FIN 14"). The staff believes that recognition of a loss equal to the lower limit of the range is necessary even if the upper limit of the range is uncertain.

In measuring its environmental liability, a registrant should consider available evidence including the registrant's prior experience in remediation of contaminated sites, other companies' clean-up experience, and data released by the

Environmental Protection Agency or other organizations. Information necessary to support a reasonable estimate or range of loss may be available prior to the performance of any detailed remediation study. Even in situations in which the registrant has not determined the specific strategy for remediation, estimates of the costs associated with the various alternative remediation strategies considered for a site may be available or reasonably estimable. While the range of costs associated with the alternatives may be broad, the minimum clean-up cost is unlikely to be zero. As additional information becomes available, changes in estimates of the liability should be reported in the period that those changes occur in accordance with paragraphs 31-33 of Accounting Principles Board Opinion No. 20, "Accounting Changes."

Question 4: Assuming that the registrant's estimate of an environmental or product liability meets the conditions set forth in the consensus on EITF Issue 93-5 for recognition on a discounted basis, what discount rate should be applied?

Interpretive Response: The staff believes that the rate used to discount the cash payments should be the rate that will produce an amount at which the environmental or product liability could be settled in an arm's-length transaction with a third party. If that rate is not readily determinable, the discount rate used to discount the cash payments should not exceed the interest rate on monetary assets that are essentially risk free[3] and have maturities comparable to that of the environmental or product liability.

If the liability is recognized on a discounted basis to reflect the time value of money, the notes to the financial statements should, at a minimum, include disclosures of the discount rate used, the expected aggregate undiscounted amount, expected payments for each of the five succeeding years and the aggregate amount thereafter, and a reconciliation of the expected aggregate undiscounted amount to amounts recognized in the statements of financial position. Material changes in the expected aggregate amount since the prior balance sheet date, other than those resulting from pay-down of the obligation, should be explained.

Question 5: What financial statement disclosures should be furnished with respect to recorded and unrecorded product or environmental liabilities?

Interpretive Response: Paragraphs 9 and 10 of SFAS 5 identify disclosures regarding loss contingencies that generally are furnished in notes to financial statements. The staff believes that product and environmental liabilities typically are of such significance that detailed disclosures regarding the judgments and assumptions underlying the recognition and measurement of the liabilities are necessary to prevent the financial statements from being misleading and to inform readers fully regarding the range of reasonably possible outcomes that could have a material effect on the registrant's financial condition, results of operations, or liquidity. Examples of disclosures that may be necessary include:

- Circumstances affecting the reliability and precision of loss estimates.

SEC 50502. Rule 5-02-25

- The extent to which unasserted claims are reflected in any accrual or may affect the magnitude of the contingency.

- Uncertainties with respect to joint and several liability that may affect the magnitude of the contingency, including disclosure of the aggregate expected cost to remediate particular sites that are individually material if the likelihood of contribution by the other significant parties has not been established.

- Disclosure of the nature and terms of cost-sharing arrangements with other potentially responsible parties.

- The extent to which disclosed but unrecognized contingent losses are expected to be recoverable through insurance, indemnification arrangements, or other sources, with disclosure of any material limitations of that recovery.

- Uncertainties regarding the legal sufficiency of insurance claims or solvency of insurance carriers.[4]

- The time frame over which the accrued or presently unrecognized amounts may be paid out.

- Material components of the accruals and significant assumptions underlying estimates.

Registrants are cautioned that a statement that the contingency is not expected to be material does not satisfy the requirements of SFAS 5 if there is at least a reasonable possibility that a loss exceeding amounts already recognized may have been incurred and the amount of that additional loss would be material to a decision to buy or sell the registrant's securities. In that case, the registrant must either (a) disclose the estimated additional loss, or range of loss, that is reasonably possible, or (b) state that such an estimate cannot be made.

Question 6: What disclosures regarding loss contingencies may be necessary outside the financial statements?

Interpretive Response: Registrants should consider the requirements of Items 101 (Description of Business), 103 (Legal Proceedings), and 303 (Management's Discussion and Analysis) of Regulations S-K and S-B. The Commission has issued two interpretive releases that provide additional guidance with respect to these items.[5] In a 1989 interpretive release, the Commission noted that the availability of insurance, indemnification, or contribution may be relevant in determining whether the criteria for disclosure have been met with respect to a contingency.[6] The registrant's assessment in this regard should include consideration of facts such as the periods in which claims for recovery may be realized, the likelihood that the claims may be contested, and the financial condition of third parties from which recovery is expected.

Disclosures made pursuant to the guidance identified in the preceding paragraph should be sufficiently specific to enable a reader to understand the scope of the contingencies affecting the registrant. For example, a registrant's discussion of historical and anticipated environmental expenditures should, to the extent material, describe separately (a) recurring costs associated with managing hazardous substances and pollution in on-going operations, (b) capital expenditures to limit or monitor hazardous substances or pollutants, (c) mandated expenditures to remediate previously contaminated sites, and (d) other infrequent or non-recurring clean-up expenditures that can be anticipated but which are not required in the present circumstances. Disaggregated disclosure that describes accrued and reasonably likely losses with respect to particular environmental sites that are individually material may be necessary for a full understanding of these contingencies. Also, if management's investigation of potential liability and remediation cost is at different stages with respect to individual sites, the consequences of this with respect to amounts accrued and disclosed should be discussed.

Examples of specific disclosures typically relevant to an understanding of historical and anticipated product liability costs include the nature of personal injury or property damages alleged by claimants, aggregate settlement costs by type of claim, and related costs of administering and litigating claims. Disaggregated disclosure that describes accrued and reasonably likely losses with respect to particular claims may be necessary if they are individually material. If the contingency involves a large number of relatively small individual claims of a similar type, such as personal injury from exposure to asbestos, disclosure of the number of claims pending at each balance sheet date, the number of claims filed for each period presented, the number of claims dismissed, settled, or otherwise resolved for each period, and the average settlement amount per claim may be necessary. Disclosures should address historical and expected trends in these amounts and their reasonably likely effects on operating results and liquidity.

Question 7: What disclosures should be furnished with respect to site restoration costs or other environmental exit costs?

Interpretive Response: The staff believes that material liabilities for site restoration, post-closure, and monitoring commitments, or other exit costs that may occur on the sale, disposal, or abandonment of a property should be disclosed in the notes to the financial statements. Appropriate disclosures generally would include the nature of the costs involved, the total anticipated cost, the total costs accrued to date, the balance sheet classification of accrued amounts, and the range or amount of reasonably possible additional losses. If an asset held for sale or development will require remediation to be performed by the registrant prior to development, sale, or as a condition of sale, a note to the financial statements should describe how the necessary expenditures are considered in the assessment of the asset's net realizable value. Additionally, if the registrant may be liable for remediation of environmental damage relating to assets or businesses previously disposed, disclosure should be made in the financial statements unless the likelihood of a material unfavorable outcome of that contingency is remote. The registrant's accounting policy with respect to such costs should be disclosed in accordance with Accounting Principles Board Opinion No. 22, "Disclosure of Accounting Policies."

Question 8: A registrant expects to incur site restoration costs, post-closure and monitoring costs, or other environmental exit costs at the end of the useful life of the asset. Would the staff object to the registrant's proposal to accrue the exit costs over the useful life of the asset?

Interpretive Response: No. This is an established accounting practice in some industries. In other industries, the staff will raise no objection to that accounting provided that the criteria in paragraph 8 of SFAS 5 are met. The staff acknowledges that in some circumstances the use of the asset in operations gives rise to growing exit costs that represent a probable liability. The accrual of the liability should be recognized as an expense in accordance with the consensus on EITF Issue 90-8, "Capitalization of Costs to Treat Environmental Contamination." See interpretive responses to questions 7 and 8 for guidance on appropriate disclosures.

---

[1] Paragraph 3 of SFAS 5 defines probable as "likely to occur."

[2] Paragraph 7 of Accounting Principles Board Opinion No. 10, "Omnibus Opinion." Also, FASB Technical Bulletin 88-2, "Definition of a Right of Setoff."

[3] As described in paragraph 4(a) of Statement of Financial Accounting Standards No. 76, "Extinguishment of Debt."

[4] The staff believes there is a rebuttable presumption that no asset should be recognized for a claim for recovery from a party that is asserting that it is not liable to indemnify the registrant. Registrants that overcome that presumption should disclose the amount of recorded recoveries that are being contested and discuss the reasons for concluding that the amounts are probable of recovery.

[5] See Securities Act Release No. 6130 (September 27, 1979) and Financial Reporting Release No. 36 (May 18, 1989).

[6] See, for example, footnote 30 of Financial Reporting Release No. 36 [footnote 17 of Section 501.02 of the Codification of Financial Reporting Policies].

Topic 11-J (SAB No. 60) discusses the staff's views regarding accounting for and disclosure of certain types of financial guarantees. In the SAB, the staff takes the position that the consensus reached in EITF Issue No. 85-20, "Recognition of Fees for Guaranteeing a Loan," needs to be followed by all registrants where the aggregate amounts guaranteed are material to either consolidated equity or results of operations before income taxes and realized gains or losses on investments. The staff also indicates the disclosures that should generally cover such guarantees. The text of the SAB follows:

Financial Guarantees

Facts: Insurance companies and other financial institutions have been issuing guarantees of the debts of municipalities and other entities at an increasing rate during recent years.[1] Typically the issuer of debt pays a fee to obtain an enhancement of the credit rating attached to its debt[2] with a corresponding decrease in the interest rate it must offer. In return for the fee, guarantors promise to make payment of interest and principal, either as they become due under terms of the debt instrument or on an accelerated basis, if the issuer of the debt is unable to pay.

The fee is generally a negotiated portion of the interest savings attributed to the guarantee[3] and is not necessarily related to the risk undertaken.[4] Guarantors, of course, may attempt to underwrite only risks where potential loss is deemed to be remote. However, the confidence level in predictions of any entity's future financial condition decreases as the number of future years involved increases. Some issues of guaranteed debt have maturities that exceed thirty years.

In mid-1985, the Emerging Issues Task Force ("EITF") of the Financial Accounting Standards Board ("FASB") addressed the following two issues:

—When the guarantor should recognize the fees in income, and

—Whether the guarantor should recognize a liability for the obligation under guarantee.

On June 27, the members of the EITF reached a consensus that the guarantor should:

—Recognize fee income over the guarantee period.

—Disclose the guarantee by footnote, if material.

—Perform an ongoing assessment of the probability of loss to determine if a liability and a loss should be recognized under FASB Statement No. 5 "Accounting for Contingencies," and

—Recognize direct costs associated with the guarantee in a manner relative to the fee income.

Registrants have raised questions about the applicability of the EITF consensus to insurance companies.

Question 1: Does the staff believe that the June 1985 consensus of the EITF regarding accounting for and disclosure about loan guarantees applies to all registrants?

SEC 50502. Rule 5-02-25

Interpretive Response: The staff believes that the consensus of the EITF should be applied by all registrants where the aggregate amounts guaranteed are material to consolidated equity or where there is a material effect on results of operations before income taxes and realized gains or losses on investments.

Question 2: What kind of disclosure does the staff expect?

Interpretive Response: The staff believes that the disclosure should cover matters such as the following:

—A general description of the type of obligations guaranteed (e.g., corporate, municipal general obligation, industrial revenue, etc.), the relative amount and range of maturity dates of each, and the degree of risk involved.

—The amount of exposure with respect to the debts of others guaranteed at the date of each balance sheet presented including a discussion of how the participation by other parties and other factors that may reduce exposure are treated in determining the amount reported.

—The manner in which the registrant recognizes revenue with respect to the guarantees.

—The amount of unearned premiums as of the date of each balance sheet.

—Whether the registrant provides a reserve for losses by charges against income and, if so, the basis for the reserve and its amount at each balance sheet date.

—Any other information that may be necessary to adequately describe the nature and extent of the obligations guaranteed and the degree of risk related to the guarantees.

---

[1]". . . Outstanding guarantees [of all types] backed by banks and insurance companies have increased from $161 billion in 1980 to more than $437 billion in 1984 . . . " according to "Bests' Review—Property/Casualty Edition" in an October 1985 article entitled "Financial Guarantees: Too Hot to Handle."

[2]At times, the guarantees are purchased by persons attempting to resell large blocks of debt securities in the secondary market.

[3]"Usually, the insurer and issuer split the difference between the insured rate interest and the interest that would be paid without the insurance; the insurer's portion is its 'premium'," according to the article from Bests' Review cited above.

[4]According to an article in the October 9, 1985 edition of Forbes entitled "Spores of Disaster": "Since no actuarial table can forecast the future course of economic events, it is impossible to predict with any reliability what the long-term soundness of any investment will be. Thus, there is no possible way to price accurately the risk of the guarantee itself. As a result, pricing is based not on risk to the guarantor (the normal arrangement for insurance underwriting) but on how much in interest charges the borrower saves by floating paper with a guarantee attached to it."

In certain situations credit enhancements are provided to the issuer of a security by a third party in order to lower the issuer's cost of capital on the transaction. Such enhancements may involve insurance agreements (such as surety bonds), letters of credit, or agreements to maintain specified levels of working capital or fixed-charge coverage.

The SEC staff's view is that if the credit enhancement is material to the investor's decision to invest, in addition to the guarantor's disclosures required by SAB No. 60 (discussed above), financial information of the provider of the credit enhancement should also be included in a registration statement covering the underlying security. The staff uses 20 percent as a materiality threshold (i.e., the value of the enhancement in relation to the amount expected to be raised in the offering), generally based on the guidance included in SAB 71 (Topic 1-I, see section 50348).

Under certain conditions the staff has accepted various forms of financial information in lieu of full financial statements in situations of this nature, including: (1) capsule data, where the provider of the enhancement is a registrant, (2) references to availability or sources of the financial statements of the provider of the enhancement, where the provider is a registrant, and (3) audited foreign GAAP statements with a reconciliation to U.S. GAAP. The financial information requirements in situations of this nature are generally determined by the SEC staff on a case-by-case basis.

The schedule prescribed by Rule 12-08 (Schedule VII) may need to be furnished as to certain guarantees if the information required by this schedule is not included in a footnote to the financial statements.

Defense Contractors: As a result of its concern relating to the ongoing government investigation into potential illegal or unethical activities in connection with the procurement of defense contracts, in August 1988 the SEC issued FRR No. 32. The release reminds registrants of the disclosure obligations under the 1933 and 1934 Acts and the Investment Company Act of 1940 in connection with issues arising from this investigation.

Companies that are engaged in the defense industry and investment companies that concentrate their investments in an industry dependent upon government defense contracts would be well advised to make reference to this release in connection with any filing made with the SEC.

26. Deferred credits. *State separately in the balance sheet amounts for (a) deferred income taxes, (b) deferred tax credits, and (c) material items of deferred income.*

The current portion of deferred income taxes should be included under caption 20, Other Current Liabilities.

SEC 50502. Rule 5-02-25

Minority Interests

27. Minority interest in consolidated subsidiaries. *State separately in a note the amounts represented by preferred stock and the applicable dividend requirements if the preferred stock is material in relation to the consolidated stockholders' equity.*

Redeemable Preferred Stocks

28. Preferred stocks subject to mandatory redemption requirements or whose redemption is outside the control of the issuer.

(a) Include under this caption amounts applicable to any class of stock which has any of the following characteristics: (1) it is redeemable at a fixed or determinable price on a fixed or determinable date or dates, whether by operation of a sinking fund or otherwise; (2) it is redeemable at the option of the holder; or (3) it has conditions for redemption which are not solely within the control of the issuer, such as stocks which must be redeemed out of future earnings. Amounts attributable to preferred stock which is not redeemable or is redeemable solely at the option of the issuer shall be included under Rule 5-02-29 unless it meets one or more of the above criteria.

(b) State on the face of the balance sheet the title of each issue, the carrying amount, and redemption amount. (If there is more than one issue, these amounts may be aggregated on the face of the balance sheet and details concerning each issue may be presented in the note required by paragraph (c) below.) Show also the dollar amount of any shares subscribed but unissued, and show the deduction of subscriptions receivable therefrom. If the carrying value is different from the redemption amount, describe the accounting treatment for such difference in the note required by paragraph (c) below. Also state in this note or on the face of the balance sheet, for each issue, the number of shares authorized and the number of shares issued or outstanding, as appropriate. (See Rule 4-07.)

(c) State in a separate note captioned "Redeemable Preferred Stocks" (1) a general description of each issue, including its redemption features (e.g., sinking fund, at option of holders, out of future earnings) and the rights, if any, of holders in the event of default, including the effect, if any, on junior securities in the event a required dividend, sinking fund, or other redemption payment(s) is not made; (2) the combined aggregate amount of redemption requirements for all issues each year for the five years following the date of the latest balance sheet; and (3) the changes in each issue for each period for which an income statement is required to be filed. [See also Rule 4-08(d).]

(d) Securities reported under this caption are not to be included under a general heading "stockholders' equity" or combined in a total with items described in captions 29, 30 or 31, which follow.

SEC 50502

670

A registrant having a class of redeemable preferred stock outstanding that meets any of the criteria set forth in paragraph (a) of this rule is required to classify the preferred stock under this caption. Such registrant is precluded from including such amounts on the balance sheet under a general heading of "Stockholders' Equity." A total that includes redeemable preferred stock with nonredeemable preferred stock, common stock, and other stockholders' equity is also prohibited. However, a registrant may combine nonredeemable preferred stock, common stock, and other stockholders' equity under an appropriately designated caption. Registrants that do not have a class of preferred stock outstanding within the definition of this rule may use the heading "Stockholders' Equity" and include on the balance sheet a combined total of preferred stock, common stock, and other stockholders' equity.

FRP Section 211 (formerly ASR No. 268) emphasizes that preferred stocks that meet one or more of the criteria specified in Rule 5-02-28(a) should be considered redeemable preferred stock regardless of their other attributes, such as voting rights, dividend rights, or conversion features. Note that Rule 5-02-28(a) refers to "any class of stock" that meets the specified criteria. Therefore, the rule may apply to other equity securities with similar features.

If there is more than one issue of redeemable preferred stock, paragraph (b) of this rule permits presentation of the detailed information on each issue in a note to the financial statements, with only the aggregate amount presented on the face of the balance sheet.

The reference to Rule 4-07 at the end of paragraph (b) is to draw attention to the rule covering the balance sheet presentation of discount on capital shares.

Paragraph (c) of this rule requires disclosure of the aggregate amount of redemption requirements for all issues of redeemable preferred stock for each of the five years following the date of the latest balance sheet, a requirement similar to one that pertains to long-term debt (see Rule 5-02-22). However, FRP Section 211 emphasizes that redeemable preferred stock should not be regarded as a liability, and that the classification should not require any change in the calculation of debt/equity ratios or similar statistical calculations. FRP Section 211 does point out, however, that where significant amounts of redeemable preferred stock are combined with other equity accounts for the purpose of presenting ratios, a similar ratio that includes the redeemable preferred stock as part of debt should also be presented.

The SEC staff has informally expressed the following views concerning the accounting and reporting for redeemable preferred stock:

- The staff has addressed an issue involving a type of warrant typically issued in connection with the purchase of a company's stock. The type of warrant in question, commonly referred to as a "fair value redeemable warrant," is typically issued in connection with debt, is detachable, and may be put to the company for a cash amount equal to the fair or appraised value of the company's common stock, less the warrant exercise price. The staff views a warrant of this nature as analogous to mandatorily redeemable preferred stock requiring separate presentation outside shareholders' equity in the balance sheet. Further, the staff has indicated that it would require that the carrying amount of this type of warrant be adjusted periodically, similar to the accretion for preferred stock subject to redemption provisions, and that the provisions of SAB 64 be followed for calculating earnings per share and determining earnings available for common stock.

- The staff has indicated that a number of registrants have apparently included instruments, which it views as "substantively the same" as mandatorily redeemable securities, as a component of shareholders' equity in the balance sheet. An example that has been cited is common stock that can be put back to the company at death of the holder. Another is common stock that may be put back to the company upon the disability, retirement or termination of officers or employees. Because redemption of these instruments is outside of the registrant's control, the staff has indicated that these instruments should be classified outside of equity, as set forth in FRP Section 211.

SAB Topic 3-C describes the balance sheet presentation of preferred stock where fair value at date of issue is less than mandatory redemption value. The text of the SAB follows:

Redeemable Preferred Stock

Facts: Rule 5-02-28 of Regulation S-X states that redeemable preferred stocks are not to be included in amounts reported as stockholders' equity, and that their redemption amounts are to be shown on the face of the balance sheet. However, the Commission's rules and regulations do not address the carrying amount at which redeemable preferred stock should be reported, or how changes in its carrying amount should be treated in calculations of earnings per share and the ratio of earnings to combined fixed charges and preferred stock dividends.

Question 1: How should the carrying amount of redeemable preferred stock be determined?

Interpretive Response: The initial carrying amount of redeemable preferred stock should be its fair value at date of issue. Where fair value at date of issue is less than the mandatory redemption amount, the carrying amount shall be increased by periodic accretions, using the interest method, so that the carrying amount will equal the mandatory redemption amount at the mandatory redemption date. The carrying amount shall be further periodically increased by amounts representing dividends not currently declared or paid, but which will be payable under the mandatory redemption features, or for which ultimate payment is not solely within the control of the registrant (e.g., dividends that will be payable out of future earnings). Each type of increase in carrying amount shall be effected by charges against retained earnings or, in the absence of retained earnings, by charges against paid-in capital.

The accounting described in the preceding paragraph would apply irrespective of whether the redeemable preferred stock may be voluntarily redeemed by the issuer prior to the mandatory redemption date, or whether it may be converted into another class of securities by the holder.

Question 2: How should periodic increases in the carrying amount of redeemable preferred stock be treated in calculations of earnings per share and ratios of earnings to combined fixed charges and preferred stock dividends?

Interpretive Response: Each type of increase in carrying amount described in the Interpretive Response to Question 1 should be treated in the same manner as dividends on nonredeemable preferred stock.

Non-Redeemable Preferred Stocks

29. Preferred stocks which are not redeemable or are redeemable solely at the option of the issuer. *State on the face of the balance sheet, or if more than one issue is outstanding state in a note, the title of each issue and the dollar amount thereof. Show also the dollar amount of any shares subscribed but unissued, and show the deduction of subscriptions receivable therefrom. State on the face of the balance sheet or in a note, for each issue, the number of shares authorized and the number of shares issued or outstanding, as appropriate. (See Rule 4-07.) Show in a note or separate statement the changes in each class of preferred shares reported under this caption for each period for which an income statement is required to be filed. (See also Rule 4-08(d).)*

Paragraph (a) of Rule 5-02-28 includes a definition of preferred stock subject to mandatory redemption requirements or whose redemption is outside the control of the issuer. Rule 5-02-29 pertains to preferred stock that does not meet the criteria for this classification.

If more than one issue of nonredeemable preferred stock is outstanding, this rule allows the presentation of the title and amounts of each issue in a note rather than on the face of the balance sheet.

SAB Topic 5-Q, added by SAB No. 68, discusses the position of the staff with respect to accounting for certain nonredeemable preferred stocks referred to as "increasing rate preferred stocks." In SAB No. 68, the SEC staff indicates that increasing-rate-preferred stock should be recorded in the balance sheet at its fair value at the date of issuance, similar to the accounting for other types of securities. The staff indicates, however, that the dividend costs of increasing-rate-preferred stocks should not be recognized in accordance with their stated dividend schedules. Rather, any discount relating to the absence of dividends, or gradually increasing dividends, should be amortized by reducing retained earnings for the imputed dividend cost and increasing the carrying value of the preferred stock by the same amount. The amortization period specified by the staff is the period(s) prior to the start of a perpetual dividend. In this SAB the staff also addresses the calculation of the discount and the rationale for its views.

The text of the SAB follows:

Increasing Rate Preferred Stock

Facts: A registrant issues Class A and Class B nonredeemable preferred stock[1] on 1/1/X1. Class A, by its terms, will pay no dividends during the years 19X1 through 19X3. Class B, by its terms, will pay dividends at annual rates of $2, $4, and $6 per share in the years 19X1, 19X2, 19X3, respectively. Beginning in the year 19X4 and thereafter as long as they remain outstanding, each instrument will pay dividends at an annual rate of $8 per share. In all periods, the scheduled dividends are cumulative.

At the time of issuance, eight percent per annum was considered to be a market rate for dividend yield on Class A, given its characteristics other than scheduled cash dividend entitlements (voting rights, liquidation preference, etc.), as well as the registrant's financial condition and future economic prospects. Thus, the registrant could have expected to receive proceeds of approximately $100 per share for Class A if the dividend rate of $8 per share (the "perpetual dividend") had been in effect at date of issuance. In consideration of the dividend payment terms, however, Class A was issued for proceeds of $79-3/8 per share. The difference, $20-5/8, approximated the value of the absence of $8 per share dividends annually for three years, discounted at 8%.

The issuance price of Class B shares was determined by a similar approach, based on the terms and characteristics of the Class B shares.

Question 1: How should preferred stocks of this general type (referred to as "increasing rate preferred stocks") be reported in the balance sheet?

Interpretive Response: As is normally the case with other types of securities, increasing rate preferred stock should be recorded initially at its fair value on date of issuance. Thereafter, the carrying amount should be increased periodically as discussed in the Interpretive Response to Question 2.

Question 2: Is it acceptable to recognize the dividend costs of increasing rate preferred stocks according to their stated dividend schedules?

Interpretive Response: No. The staff believes that when consideration received for preferred stocks reflects expectations of future dividend streams, as is normally the case with cumulative preferred stocks, any discount due to an absence of dividends (as with Class A) or gradually increasing dividends (as with Class B) for an initial period represents prepaid, unstated dividend cost.[2] Recognizing the dividend cost of these instruments according to their stated dividend schedules would report Class A as being cost-free, and would report the cost of Class B at less than its effective cost, from the standpoint of common stock interests (i.e., for purposes of computing income applicable to common stock and earnings per common share) during the years 19X1 through 19X3.

Accordingly, the staff believes that discounts on increasing rate preferred stock should be amortized over the period(s) preceding commencement of the perpetual dividend, by charging imputed dividend cost against retained earnings and increasing the carrying amount of the preferred stock by a corresponding amount. The discount at time of issuance should be computed as the present value of the difference between (a) dividends that will be payable, if any, in the period(s) preceding commencement of the perpetual dividend; and (b) the perpetual dividend amount for a corresponding number of periods; discounted at a market rate for dividend yield on preferred stocks that are comparable (other than with respect to dividend payment schedules) from an investment standpoint. The amortization in each period should be the amount which, together with any stated dividend for the period (ignoring fluctuations in stated dividend amounts that might result from variable rates[3], results in a constant rate of effective cost vis-a-vis the carrying amount of the preferred stock (the market rate that was used to compute the discount).

Simplified (ignoring quarterly calculations) application of this accounting to the Class A preferred stock described in the "Facts" section of this bulletin would produce the following results on a per share basis:

	Carrying amount of preferred stock		
	Beginning of year (BOY)	Imputed dividend (8% of carrying amount at BOY)	End of year
Year 19X1	$79.38	$6.35	$ 85.73
Year 19X2	85.73	6.86	92.59
Year 19X3	92.59	7.41	100.00

During 19X4 and thereafter, the stated dividend of $8 measured against the carrying amount of $100[4] would reflect dividend cost of 8%, the market rate at time of issuance.

The staff believes that existing authoritative literature, while not explicitly addressing increasing rate preferred stocks, implicitly calls for the accounting described in this bulletin.[5]

The pervasive, fundamental principle of accrual accounting would, in the staff's view, preclude registrants from recognizing the dividend cost on the basis of whatever cash payment schedule might be arranged. Furthermore, recognition of the effective cost of unstated rights and privileges is well-established in accounting, and is specifically called for by APB Opinion No. 21 and Topic 3-C of the staff accounting bulletin series for unstated interest costs of debt capital and unstated dividend costs of redeemable preferred stock capital, respectively. The

SEC 50502. Rule 5-02-29

staff believes that the requirement to recognize the effective periodic cost of capital applies also to nonredeemable preferred stocks because, for that purpose, the distinction between debt capital and preferred equity capital (whether redeemable[6] or nonredeemable) is irrelevant from the standpoint of common stock interests.

Question 3: Would the accounting for discounts on increasing rate preferred stock be affected by variable stated dividend rates?

Interpretive Response: No. If stated dividends on an increasing rate preferred stock are variable, computations of initial discount and subsequent amortization should be based on the value of the applicable index at date of issuance and should not be affected by subsequent changes in the index.

For example, assume that a preferred stock issued 1/1/X1 is scheduled to pay dividends at annual rates, applied to the stock's par value, equal to 20% of the actual (fluctuating) market yield on a particular Treasury security in 19X1 and 19X2, and 90% of that fluctuating market yield in 19X3 and thereafter. The discount would be computed as the present value of a two-year dividend stream equal to 70% (90% less 20%) of the 1/1/X1 Treasury security yield, annually, on the stock's par value. The discount would be amortized in years 19X1 and 19X2 so that, together with 20% of the 1/1/X1 Treasury yield on the stock's par value, a constant rate of cost vis-a-vis the stock's carrying amount would result. Changes in the Treasury security yield during 19X1 and 19X2 would, of course, cause the rate of total reported preferred dividend cost (amortization of discount plus cash dividends) in those years to be more or less than the rate indicated by discount amortization plus 20% of the 1/1/X1 Treasury security yield. However, the fluctuations would be due solely to the impact of changes in the index on the stated dividends for those periods.

[Note: Question 4 has not been presented as it is no longer applicable.]

---

[1]"Nonredeemable" preferred stock, as used in this bulletin, refers to preferred stocks which are not redeemable or are redeemable only at the option of the issuer.

[2]As described in the "Facts" section of this bulletin, a registrant would receive less in proceeds for a preferred stock, if the stock were to pay less than its perpetual dividend for some initial period(s), than if it were to pay the perpetual dividend from date of issuance. The staff views the discount on increasing rate preferred stock as equivalent to a prepayment of dividends by the issuer, as though the issuer had concurrently (a) issued the stock with the perpetual dividend being payable from date of issuance, and (b) returned to the investor a portion of the proceeds representing the present value of certain future dividend entitlements which the investor agreed to forgo.

[3]See Question 3 regarding variable increasing rate preferred stocks.

[4]It should be noted that the $100 per share amount used in this bulletin is for illustrative purposes, and is not intended to imply that application of this bulletin will necessarily result in the carrying amount of a nonredeemable preferred stock

being accreted to its par value, stated value, voluntary redemption value or involuntary liquidation value.

[5]In Staff Accounting Bulletin No. 57 (July 1984), the staff stated its view that, in the absence of explicitly applicable authoritative literature, registrants and their independent accountants must determine the appropriate accounting "based on some pervasive, fundamental principle or an analogy to transactions with similar economic substance for which the accounting literature does provide specific guidance."

[6]Application of the interest method with respect to redeemable preferred stocks pursuant to Topic 3-C results in accounting consistent with the provisions of this bulletin irrespective of whether the redeemable preferred stocks have constant or increasing stated dividend rates. The interest method, as described in APB Opinion No. 12, produces a constant effective periodic rate of cost that is comprised of amortization of discount as well as the stated cost in each period.

Common Stocks

30. Common stocks. *For each class of common shares state, on the face of the balance sheet, the number of shares issued or outstanding, as appropriate [see Rule 4-07], and the dollar amount thereof. If convertible, this fact should be indicated on the face of the balance sheet. For each class of common shares state, on the face of the balance sheet or in a note, the title of the issue, the number of shares authorized, and, if convertible, the basis of conversion [see also Rule 4-08(d)]. Show also the dollar amount of any common shares subscribed but unissued, and show the deduction of subscriptions receivable therefrom. Show in a note or statement the changes in each class of common shares for each period for which an income statement is required to be filed.*

This rule specifies the information to be disclosed pertaining to common stock. The information as to changes in each class of common stock is required to be furnished for each period for which an income statement is required to be filed. This data may be presented either in a footnote or in a separate statement of stockholders' equity (see discussion in this section following caption 31). Certain of the detailed information required under this caption, such as the number of shares authorized, title of the issue and, if convertible, the basis of conversion, may be disclosed in a note to the financial statements. As a general rule, however, the SEC staff prefers that the number of shares be presented on the face of the balance sheet. Consequently, the note disclosure approach should only be used when it is impractical for this information to be presented on the face of the statement.

Other Stockholders' Equity

31. Other stockholders' equity.

(a) Separate captions shall be shown for:

    (1)   Additional paid-in capital,

    (2)   Other additional capital and

    (3)   Retained earnings

        (i) Appropriated and

        (ii) Unappropriated. [See Rule 4-08(e).]

Additional paid-in capital and other additional capital may be combined with the stock caption to which it applies, if appropriate.

(b) For a period of at least 10 years subsequent to the effective date of a quasi-reorganization, any description of retained earnings shall indicate the point in time from which the new retained earnings dates and for a period of at least three years shall indicate, on the face of the balance sheet, the total amount of the deficit eliminated.

Rule 3-04 requires an analysis of the changes in each caption of other stockholders' equity presented in the balance sheets to be included in a note or separate statement. Registrants are further required by APB Opinion No. 12 (paragraph 10) to disclose changes in the separate accounts making up stockholders' equity when both financial position and results of operations are presented. The Staff Accounting Bulletin topics discussed below deal with issues that are directly or indirectly related to the presentation of stockholders' equity.

SAB Topic 4-A states that subordinated debt may not be included in the stockholders' equity section of the balance sheet and that captions representing the combination of stockholders' equity and subordinated debt are not acceptable.

Subordinated Debt

Facts: Company E proposes to include in its registration statement a balance sheet showing its subordinated debt as a portion of stockholders' equity.

Question: Is this presentation appropriate?

Interpretive Response: Subordinated debt may not be included in the stockholders' equity section of the balance sheet. Any presentation describing such debt as a component of stockholders' equity must be eliminated. Furthermore, any caption representing the combination of stockholders' equity and only subordinated debt must be deleted.

Stock Dividends, Stock Splits, or Reverse Splits

SAB Topic 4-C states that retroactive effect should be given in the balance sheet for a change in capital structure due to a stock dividend, stock split, or reverse split (collectively referred to as "stock dividends") that occurs after the balance sheet date but before the release of the financial statements. The text of the SAB follows:

Change in Capital Structure

Facts: A capital structure change due to a stock dividend, stock split or reverse split occurs after the date of the latest reported balance sheet but before the release of the financial statements or the effective date of the registration statement, whichever is later.

Question: What effect must be given to such a change?

Interpretive Response: Such changes in the capital structure must be given retroactive effect in the balance sheet. An appropriately cross-referenced note should disclose the retroactive treatment, explain the change made and state the date the change became effective.

There are two prevalent interpretations of the date a stock dividend "occurs": the declaration date and the ex-dividend date. The SEC staff prefers that the retroactive treatment described above be applied to stock dividends on the ex-dividend date rather than the declaration date. In situations in which retroactive adjustments are not made because the ex-dividend date occurs after the release of the financial statements or the effective date of the registration statement, the notes to the financial statements should disclose the pending transaction and the impact, if significant, on EPS for each year presented.

When the ex-dividend date precedes the release of the financial statements or the effective date of the registration statement, the stock dividend should be reflected as a transaction in the equity section of the latest balance sheet. Alternatively, all prior period balance sheets may be restated. In addition, paragraph 48 of APB Opinion 15 requires the stock dividend to be reflected retroactively in the EPS calculations for each period presented.

If the ex-dividend date occurs prior to the effective date, but subsequent to an initial filing, the restatements described above should be filed as an amendment to the registration statement.

SEC 50502. Rule 5-02-31

Other Changes in Securities in an IPO

It is common for companies to issue securities (preferred stock or debt) that convert to common stock, or are subject to other modifications, on the effective date or closing date of an IPO. Generally, the historical financial statements included in the filing should not be restated to reflect changes in securities that occur subsequent to the balance sheet date, except as provided for in SAB Topic 4-C. If such changes will result in a material reduction of permanent equity or the redemption of a material amount of equity securities, the change should be included in a pro forma balance sheet presented alongside the historical balance sheet. In addition, if the change will result in a material reduction of earnings applicable to common shareholders, pro forma earnings per share for the latest year and interim period should be presented giving effect to the change. It is important to note that the above calculations should exclude the effects of the offering (i.e., the shares issued and the proceeds received).

The SEC staff has indicated that it will not object to the deletion of historical earnings per share if such information is no longer meaningful in view of the expected change in securities. However, APB Opinion 15 would preclude the deletion of historical earnings per share and therefore, at a minimum, the historical earnings per share should be presented in the notes to the financial statements.

The staff has indicated that the pro forma guidelines described above should be followed in most circumstances. In limited situations, the staff may not object to a registrant's decision to present the change as if it occurred at the date of the latest audited balance sheet (with no adjustment to earlier periods). The limited circumstances would include convertible securities with characteristics similar to common stock. The staff has indicated that it would expect additional disclosure regarding the impact of restatement in the footnotes of the financial statements if the restatement has an anti-dilutive effect on earnings-per-share. Restatement would not be appropriate for securities that accrete to a redemption value or accrue interest after the balance sheet date, such as redeemable equity securities and convertible debt instruments.

In the limited situation in which restatement is appropriate, the staff will accept a legended accountants' report indicating the form of the report that will be issued upon consummation of the change or conversion of the security. Please note that the legended report approach may be used only in preliminary filings. An unlegended accountants' report is required in the final registration statement that is declared effective. Accordingly, changes or conversions that occur at the closing date, rather than the effective date, may not be reflected in the historical financial statements.

The presentation of equity accounts in the financial statements of limited partnerships is discussed in SAB Topic 4-F as follows:

Limited Partnerships

Facts: There exist a number of publicly held limited partnerships having one or more corporate or individual general partners and a relatively larger number of limited partners. There are no specific requirements or guidelines relating to the presentation of the partnership equity accounts in the financial statements. In addition, there are many approaches to the parallel problem of relating the results of operations to the two classes of partnership equity interests.

Question: How should the financial statements of limited partnerships be presented so that the two ownership classes can readily determine their relative participations in both the net assets of the partnership and in the results of its operations?

Interpretive Response: The equity section of a partnership balance sheet should distinguish between amounts ascribed to each ownership class. The equity attributed to the general partners should be stated separately from the equity of the limited partners and changes in the number of equity units authorized and outstanding should be shown for each ownership class. A statement of changes in partnership equity for each ownership class should be furnished for each period for which an income statement is included. The income statements of partnerships should be presented in a manner which clearly shows the aggregate amount of net income (loss) allocated to the general partners and the aggregate amount allocated to the limited partners. The statement of income should also state the results of operations on a per unit basis.

SAB Topic 4-E specifies that receivables from the sale of stock, as well as any deferred compensation arising therefrom, should be presented on the balance sheet as a deduction from stockholders' equity. Amounts due and collected in cash prior to the issuance of the financial statements, however, may be classified as assets. The text of that SAB follows:

Receivables From Sale of Stock

Facts: Compensation often arises when capital stock is issued or is to be issued to officers or other employees at prices below market.

Question: How should the deferred compensation be presented in the balance sheet?

Interpretive Response: The amounts recorded as deferred compensation should be presented in the balance sheet as a deduction from stockholders' equity. This is generally consistent with Rule 5-02-30 of Regulation S-X, which states that accounts or notes receivable arising from transactions involving the registrant's capital stock should be presented as deductions from stockholders' equity and not as assets.

It should be noted generally that all amounts receivable from officers and directors resulting from sales of stock or from other transactions (other than expense advances or sales on normal trade terms) should be separately stated in the balance

SEC 50502. Rule 5-02-31

sheet irrespective of whether such amounts may be shown as assets or are required to be reported as deductions from stockholders' equity. Accounting Series Release No. 41 states that ". . . in some cases the significance of an amount may be independent of the amount involved. For example, amounts due to and from officers and directors, because of their special nature and origin, ought generally to be set forth separately even though the dollar amounts involved are relatively small."

The staff will not suggest that a receivable from an officer or director be deducted from stockholders' equity if the receivable was paid in cash prior to the publication of the financial statements and the payment date is stated in a note to the financial statements. However, the staff would consider the subsequent return of such cash payment to the officer or director to be part of a scheme or plan to evade the registration or reporting requirements of the securities laws.

SAB Topic 4-G discusses the position of the staff with respect to the balance sheet presentation of notes and other receivables evidencing a promise to contribute capital from affiliates of corporate general partners in limited partnership offerings:

Notes and Other Receivables From Affiliates

Facts: The balance sheet of a corporate general partner is often presented in a registration statement. Frequently, the balance sheet of the general partner discloses that it holds notes or other receivables from a parent or another affiliate. Often the notes or other receivables were created in order to meet the "substantial assets" test which the Internal Revenue Service utilizes in applying its "Safe Harbor" doctrine in the classification of organizations for income tax purposes.

Question: How should such notes and other receivables be reported in the balance sheet of the general partner?

Interpretive Response: While these notes and other receivables evidencing a promise to contribute capital are often legally enforceable, they seldom are actually paid. In substance these receivables are equivalent to unpaid subscriptions receivable for capital shares which Rule 5-02-30 of Regulation S-X requires to be deducted from the dollar amount of capital shares subscribed.

The balance sheet display of these or similar items is not determined by the quality or actual value of the receivable or other asset "contributed" to the capital of the affiliated general partner, but rather by the relationship of the parties and the control inherent in that relationship. Accordingly, in these situations, the receivables must be treated as a deduction from stockholders' equity in the balance sheet of the corporate general partner.

SAB Topic 5-T, added by SAB No. 79, expresses the staff's view that a transaction undertaken by a principal shareholder for the benefit of the company should be reflected as an expense on the company's financial statements with a corresponding credit to contributed (paid-in) capital. The text of the SAB follows:

Accounting for Expenses or Liabilities Paid by Principal Stockholder(s)

Facts: Company X was a defendant in litigation for which the company had not recorded a liability in accordance with Statement of Financial Accounting Standards ("SFAS") No. 5. A principal stockholder of the company transfers a portion of his shares to the plaintiff to settle such litigation. If the company had settled the litigation directly, the company would have recorded the settlement as an expense.

Question: Must the settlement be reflected as an expense in the company's financial statements, and if so, how?

Interpretive Response: Yes. The value of the shares transferred should be reflected as an expense in the company's financial statements with a corresponding credit to contributed (paid-in) capital.

The staff believes that such a transaction is similar to those described in Interpretation No. 1 to Accounting Principles Board Opinion ("APB") No. 25 ("Interpretation No. 1") in which a principal stockholder[1] establishes or finances a stock option, purchase or award plan for one or more employees of the company. Interpretation No. 1 states that "if a principal stockholder's intention is to enhance or maintain the value of his investment by entering into such an arrangement, the corporation is implicitly benefiting from the plan by retention of, and possibly improved performance by, the employee. In this case, the benefits to a principal stockholder and to the corporation are generally impossible to separate. Similarly, it is virtually impossible to separate a principal stockholder's personal satisfaction from the benefit to the corporation." As a result, Interpretation No. 1 requires the company to account for such a transaction as if it were a compensatory plan adopted by the company, with an offsetting contribution to capital, unless: (1) the stockholder's relationship to the employee would normally result in generosity, (2) the stockholder has an obligation to the employee which is unrelated to employment, or (3) the company clearly does not benefit from the transaction.

The staff believes that the problem of separating the benefit to the principal stockholder from the benefit to the company cited in Interpretation No. 1 is not limited to transactions involving stock compensation. Therefore, similar accounting is required in this and other[2] transactions where a principal stockholder pays an expense for the company, unless the stockholder's action is caused by a relationship or obligation completely unrelated to his position as a stockholder or such action clearly does not benefit the company.

SEC 50502. Rule 5-02-31

Some registrants and their accountants have taken the position that since SFAS No. 57 applies to these transactions and requires only the disclosure of material related party transactions, the staff should not require the accounting called for by Interpretation No. 1 for transactions other than those specifically covered by it. The staff notes, however, that SFAS No. 57 does not address the measurement of related party transactions and that, as a result, such transactions are generally recorded at the amounts indicated by their terms.[3] However, the staff believes that transactions of the type described above differ from the typical related party transactions. The transactions for which SFAS No. 57 requires disclosure generally are those in which a company receives goods or services directly from, or provides goods or services directly to, a related party, and the form and terms of such transactions may be structured to produce either a direct or indirect benefit to the related party. The participation of a related party in such a transaction negates the presumption that transactions reflected in the financial statements have been consummated at arm's length. Disclosure is therefore required to compensate for the fact that, due to the related party's involvement, the terms of the transaction may produce an accounting measurement for which a more faithful measurement may not be determinable.

However, transactions of the type discussed in the facts given do not have such problems of measurement and appear to be transacted to provide a benefit to the stockholder through the enhancement or maintenance of the value of the stockholder's investment. The staff believes that the substance of such transactions is the payment of an expense of the company through contributions by the stockholder. Therefore, the staff determined that it was inappropriate to permit accounting according to the form of the transaction.

---

[1]SFAS No. 57, paragraph 24e, defines principal owners as "owners of record or known beneficial owners of more than 10 percent of the voting interests of the enterprise."

[2]For example, Staff Accounting Bulletin Topic 2-B indicates that expenses of a business combination accounted for as a pooling-of-interests that are paid by a combining company's stockholders should be reflected as an expense in the post-combination combined financial statements as required by APB No. 16. Similarly, Staff Accounting Bulletin Topic 1-B indicates that the separate financial statements of a subsidiary should reflect any costs of its operations which are incurred by the parent on its behalf. Additionally, the staff notes that AICPA Technical Practice Aids Section 4160 also indicates that the payment by principal stockholders of a company's debt should be accounted for as a capital contribution.

[3]However, in some circumstances it is necessary to reflect, either in the historical financial statements or a pro forma presentation (depending on the circumstances), related party transactions at amounts other than those indicated by their terms. Two such circumstances are addressed in Staff Accounting Bulletin Topic 1-B-1, Questions 3 and 4. Another example is where the terms of a material contract with a related party are expected to change upon the completion of an offering (i.e., the

principal shareholder requires payment for services which had previously been contributed by the shareholder to the company).

SAB Topic 4-B concludes that if a Subchapter S corporation has undistributed earnings on the date its Subchapter S election is terminated, such earnings should be included in the financial statements as additional paid-in capital. This issue is commonly encountered when a Subchapter S corporation is pooled with a corporate entity and thereby loses its election to continue as a Subchapter S corporation.

Subchapter S Corporations

Facts: A Subchapter S corporation has undistributed earnings on the date its Subchapter S election is terminated.

Question: How should such earnings be reflected in the financial statements?

Interpretive Response: Such earnings must be included in the financial statements as additional paid-in capital. This assumes a constructive distribution to the owners followed by a contribution to the capital of the corporation.

In addition, the SEC staff has indicated that if an issuer was formerly a Subchapter S corporation, a partnership, or a similar tax-exempt enterprise, pro forma tax and EPS data should be presented on the face of the historical financial statements. If the necessary adjustments include items in addition to the tax adjustments, the pro forma presentation should be limited to the latest fiscal year and interim period. However, if the necessary adjustments are only related to taxes, the staff encourages, but does not require, the pro forma information to be presented for all periods.

The staff has indicated that in filings subsequent to an entity becoming taxable, pro forma tax expense should continue to be calculated for earlier comparable periods based on statutory rates in effect for the earlier period.

The manner in which stock dividends are accounted for by Japanese companies and the extent to which deviations from U.S. practice are permitted are discussed in SAB Topic 1-D2 as follows:

"Free Distributions" by Japanese Companies

Facts: It is the general practice in Japan for corporations to issue "free distributions" of common stock to existing shareholders in conjunction with offerings of common stock so that such offerings may be made at less than market. These free distributions usually are from 5 to 10 percent of outstanding stock and are accounted for in accordance with provisions of the Commercial Code of Japan by a transfer of the par value of the stock distributed from paid-in capital to the common stock account. Similar distributions are sometimes made at times other than when offering new stock and are also designated "free distributions." U.S. accounting practice would require that the fair value of such shares, if issued by U.S. companies, be transferred from retained earnings to the appropriate capital accounts.

Question: Should the financial statements of Japanese corporations included in Commission filings which are stated to be prepared in accordance with U.S. generally accepted accounting principles be adjusted to account for stock distributions of less than 25 percent of outstanding stock by transferring the fair value of such stock from retained earnings to appropriate capital accounts?

Interpretive Response: If registrants and their independent accountants believe that the institutional and economic environment in Japan with respect to the registrant is sufficiently different that U.S. accounting principles for stock dividends should not apply to free distributions, the staff will not object to such distributions being accounted for at par value in accordance with Japanese practice. If such financial statements are identified as being prepared in accordance with U.S. generally accepted accounting principles, then there should be footnote disclosure of the method being used which indicates that U.S. companies issuing shares in comparable amounts would be required to account for them as stock dividends, and including in such disclosure the fair value of any such shares issued during the year and the cumulative amount (either in an aggregate figure or a listing of the amounts by year) of the fair value of shares issued over time.

32. Total liabilities and stockholders' equity.

50503. Rule 5-03. Income Statements

(a) The purpose of this rule is to indicate the various line items which, if applicable, and except as otherwise permitted by the Commission, should appear on the face of the income statements filed for the persons to whom this article pertains (see Rule 4-01(a)).

(b) If income is derived from more than one of the subcaptions described under Rule 5-03-1, each class which is not more than 10 percent of the sum of the items may be combined with another class. If these items are combined, related costs and expenses as described under Rule 5-03-2 shall be combined in the same manner.

Rule 5-03 sets forth in some detail (by caption) the information to be shown in the income statement. Certain information may be disclosed on the face of the income statement or in an appropriately captioned note. However, unless this option is specifically provided for, it should be assumed that disclosure on the face of the income statement is required. Even though a sequence of captions is set forth in this rule, deviations in presentation are permitted. Rule 4-01 states: "Financial statements may be filed in such form and order, and should use such generally accepted terminology, as will best indicate their significance and character in light of the provisions applicable thereto." Furthermore, Rules 4-02 and 4-03 permit the omission of immaterial and inapplicable captions.

A number of Staff Accounting Bulletins discuss matters that may affect the income statement. To the extent that they do not deal with a particular caption, they are included in the sections following 50503.

1. Net sales and gross revenues.

State separately:

(a) net sales of tangible products (gross sales less discounts, returns and allowances);

(b) operating revenues of public utilities or others;

(c) income from rentals;

(d) revenues from services; and

(e) other revenues.

Amounts earned from transactions with related parties shall be disclosed as required under Rule 4-08(k). A public utility company using a uniform system of accounts or a form for annual report prescribed by federal or state authorities, or a similar system or report, shall follow the general segregation of operating revenues and operating expenses reported under Rule 5-03-2 prescribed by such system or report. If the total of sales and revenues reported under this caption includes excise taxes in an amount equal to one percent or more of such total, the amount of such excise taxes shall be shown on the face of the statement parenthetically or otherwise.

This rule differentiates between net sales of manufactured or purchased tangible products and other revenues.

SAB Topic 5-K, added by SAB No. 57, discusses the position of the staff with respect to accounting for contingent stock purchase warrants issued by a company to certain customers in connection with sales agreements. The contingent stock purchase warrants become exercisable only if specified amounts of products are purchased by the customers within a designated time period. Because the warrants are conditional, the staff believes that it is inappropriate to value such warrants at the date the agreements are executed. The staff's position is that the contingent warrants should be valued and accounted for when it is "probable" that the customers will make the requisite purchases in order to earn the warrants. Once the probable determination is made, a pro rata allocation of the ultimate cost of the warrants needs to be recorded

SEC 50503. Rule 5-03-1

as sales are made based on the quoted market price of the stock at the end of each reporting period. The text of the SAB follows:

Contingent Stock Purchase Warrants

Facts: In connection with sales agreements with certain major customers, Company A issued "contingent warrants" to purchase shares of its common stock at prices 12 to 15% in excess of the current trading price of the stock. They are known as "contingent warrants" because the agreements provide that they become exercisable only if specified amounts of Company A's products are purchased by the customers within a three year period. The warrants expire five years from the date of the agreements. Company A believes that these contingent warrants provide it with the opportunity to sell products at a higher price than might otherwise be possible or to enter into sales agreements which might not otherwise be available because they afford the customers a chance to benefit from any price appreciation of Company A's stock. Thus, the warrants represent a contingent cost associated with these sales agreements.

The accounting for these transactions is not specifically addressed in the authoritative accounting literature. Company A believes it appropriate to account for that cost based on the provisions of APB Opinion No. 14 related to debt issue with detachable stock purchase warrants. It valued the shares represented by the contingent warrants, with the assistance of an investment banker, at the date the sales agreements were executed.[1] The value thus determined was credited to capital stock along with a deferred charge classified as an offset to equity. The deferred charge is being amortized against revenues as products are sold.

Question: Will the staff accept Company A's method of accounting for contingent warrants?

Interpretive Response: The staff believes that measurement of value at the date the agreements are executed is inappropriate because such warrants do not convey to the customers the unconditional ability to acquire stock. A customer's right to acquire shares pursuant to a contingent warrant does not occur merely upon the passage of time, but is conditioned on the occurrence of a future event—purchase of the amount of products specified in the sales agreement. Whether such purchases occur is dependent on various factors, such as Company A's ability to deliver products under the sales agreements, the customer's need for the products and, possibly, the market price of Company A's common stock during the term of the sales agreement. Valuation of the contingent warrant shares prior to resolution of these uncertainties would not provide an appropriate measurement of the cost to Company A of the inducement to the customers to enter into the sales agreement. At that time it is not even determinable whether there is such a cost.

Once the warrants become exercisable because the requisite purchases have been made, the warrants represent a cost and that cost can be measured. This cost is the difference between the quoted market price of Company A's stock at the date that the customer earns the warrants and the amount the customer is required to pay.[2]

688

Prior to that date, however, Company A must periodically determine whether it is "probable" (as that word is used in FASB Statement No. 5, "Accounting for Contingencies") that the customers will make purchases sufficient to earn the warrants. Sales made subsequent to a determination that a probable cost will occur should be charged with a pro rata allocation of the estimated ultimate cost of the warrants based on the quoted market price of the stock at the end of each reporting period.

Although the staff disagrees with Company A's accounting for contingent warrants, it advised Company A that it would not object if Company A did not change its accounting treatment for warrants issued pursuant to agreements which existed on or before July 17, 1984, provided that footnote disclosure is made of the effect on results of operations of not complying with the accounting deemed appropriate by the staff.[3] However, the staff expects use of the accounting set forth in this staff accounting bulletin for future agreements.[4]

---

[1] Valuation involved making certain assumptions as to: (1) the price of the Company's stock five years hence based on estimates of revenue and earnings growth rates over the next five years and a price/earnings multiple; (2) a computation of the present value of the customers' estimated profits on exercise of the warrants five years after date of issuance; and (3) a factor representing the estimated probability (expressed as a percentage) that the specified sales levels would be achieved.

[2] This approach is consistent with the accounting treatment for stock options, awards, and similar securities issued to employees pursuant to plans with variable terms specified in Accounting Principles Board Opinion No. 25, "Accounting for Stock Issued to Employees" ("APB 25"). Paragraph 10b of APB 25 provides that the compensation cost associated with stock option, award, and purchase plans should be measured when the number of shares the employee is entitled to receive and the option or purchase price are known. With respect to plans with variable terms, that date is after the date of grant or award. Paragraph 10 of APB 25 provides that the compensation "should be measured by the quoted market price of the stock at the measurement date less the amount, if any, that the employee is required to pay." In March 1984, the Financial Accounting Standards Board added a project to its agenda to reconsider APB 25. When the project is completed the staff will consider whether the accounting articulated in this staff accounting bulletin is still appropriate.

[3] A discussion of the effects of all such agreements on trends in a registrant's results of operations should be considered for inclusion in Management's Discussion and Analysis of Financial Condition and Results of Operations.

[4] The authoritative accounting literature cannot specifically address all the novel and complex business transactions into which registrants might enter. Accordingly, registrants and their independent accountants must determine the appropriate accounting for such transactions based on some pervasive, fundamental principle or on an analogy to transactions with similar economic substance for which the accounting literature does provide specific guidance. The staff follows

SEC 50503. Rule 5-03-1

similar procedures when it reviews and evaluates the accounting for new types of transactions. As evidenced by the conclusions expressed in this staff accounting bulletin, the staff may not always be persuaded that a registrant's analogies result in preferable accounting. When these disagreements occur after a transaction has been entered into, their consequences may be severe for registrants, their independent accountants, and, most importantly, the users of financial information who have a right to expect consistent accounting and reporting for transactions with similar facts and circumstances. In recognition of this, the staff encourages registrants and their accountants to discuss with it proposed accounting treatments for transactions and events which are not specifically covered by existing accounting literature. Further, the FASB has recently approved the implementation of suggestions made by its Task Force on Timely Financial Reporting Guidance. One of these suggestions involves the creation of an advisory group comprised of persons knowledgeable about financial accounting matters. It is intended that this group assist the FASB staff in identifying, and in some cases resolving, emerging issues for which specific accounting guidance does not exist. The staff intends to participate in the activities of this group and believes that the group's efforts will be most effective if preparers of financial statements and/or their independent accountants apprise the group of intended accounting for new business transactions.

2. Costs and expenses applicable to sales and revenues. *State separately the amount of:*

(a) cost of tangible goods sold,

(b) operating expenses of public utilities or others,

(c) expenses applicable to rental income,

(d) cost of services, and

(e) expenses applicable to other revenues.

Merchandising organizations, both wholesale and retail, may include occupancy and buying costs under caption 2(a). Amounts of costs and expenses incurred from transactions with related parties shall be disclosed as required under Rule 4-08(k).

The requirement for public utilities using a uniform system of accounts or specified report or form to follow the general segregation of operating expenses prescribed by such system or report is set forth in Rule 5-03-1.

The alternative of disclosing depreciation expense in the income statement as a separate caption rather than as part of cost of goods sold or operating expense is discussed in SAB Topic 11-B as follows:

Depreciation and Depletion Excluded From Cost of Sales

Facts: Company B excludes depreciation and depletion from cost of sales in its income statements.

Question: How should this exclusion be disclosed?

Interpretive Response: If cost of sales or operating expenses exclude charges for depreciation, depletion and amortization of property, plant and equipment, the description of the line item should read somewhat as follows: "Cost of goods sold (exclusive of items shown separately below)" or "Cost of goods sold (exclusive of depreciation shown separately below)." To avoid placing undue emphasis on "cash flow," depreciation, depletion, and amortization should not be positioned in the income statement in a manner which results in reporting a figure for income before depreciation.

SAB Topic 7-D also points out that a subtotal or caption entitled "income before depreciation and depletion" is unacceptable.

3. Other operating costs and expenses. *State separately any material amounts not included under caption 2 above.*

SAB Topic 11-L, added by SAB No. 69, discusses the appropriate income statement presentation by casinos with hotel and restaurant operations. The text of that SAB follows:

Income Statement Presentation of Casino-Hotels

Facts: Registrants having casino-hotel operations present separately within the income statement amounts of revenue attributable to casino, hotel and restaurant operations, respectively.

Question: What is the appropriate income statement presentation of expenses attributable to casino-hotel activities?

Interpretive Response: The staff believes that the expenses attributable to each of the separate revenue producing activities of casino, hotel and restaurant operations should be separately presented on the face of the income statement. Such a presentation is consistent with the general reporting format for income statement presentation under Regulation S-X (Rules 5-03.1 and 5-03.2) which requires presentation of amounts of revenues and related costs and expenses applicable to major revenue providing activities. This detailed presentation affords an analysis of the relative contribution to operating profits of each of the revenue producing activities of a typical casino-hotel operation.

SAB Topic 5-P, added by SAB No. 67, discusses the staff's position with respect to the income statement presentation of restructuring charges and is included in section 50512.

4. Selling, general and administrative expenses.

Disclosure of material items that are unusual or occur infrequently is required pursuant to paragraph 26 of APB Opinion No. 30.

5. Provision for doubtful accounts and notes.

6. Other general expenses. *Include items not normally included in caption 4 above. State separately any material item.*

7. Non-operating income. *State separately in the income statement or in a note thereto amounts earned from:*

(a) dividends,

(b) interest on securities,

(c) profits on securities (net of losses), and

(d) miscellaneous other income.

Amounts earned from transactions in securities of related parties shall be disclosed as required under Rule 4-08(k). Material amounts included under miscellaneous other income shall be separately stated in the income statement or in a note thereto, indicating clearly the nature of the transactions out of which the items arose.

The disclosure requirements with respect to nonoperating income earned from transactions with related parties are included in Rule 4-08(k) (see section 50408(k)).

8. Interest and amortization of debt discount and expense.

FASB Statement No. 34, *Capitalization of Interest Costs*, establishes the requirements for capitalizing and disclosing interest costs.

9. Non-operating expenses. *State separately in the income statement or in a note thereto amounts of (a) losses on securities (net of profits) and (b) miscellaneous income deductions. Material amounts included under miscellaneous income deductions shall be separately stated in the income statement or in a note thereto, indicating clearly the nature of the transactions out of which the items arose.*

10. Income or loss before income tax expense and appropriate items below.

11. Income tax expense. *Include under this caption only taxes based on income. (See Rule 4-08(h).)*

The information required to be disclosed by the SEC in support of income taxes is described in Rule 4-08(h) (section 50408-h). FASB Statement No. 109, *Accounting for Income Taxes,* establishes the accounting and reporting requirements for income taxes. SAB Topic 11-C describes the disclosure required with respect to "tax holidays." The text of the SAB follows:

Tax Holidays

Facts: Company C conducts business in a foreign jurisdiction which attracts industry by granting a "holiday" from income taxes for a specified period.

Question: Does the staff generally request disclosure of this fact?

Interpretive Response: Yes. In such event, a note must (1) disclose the aggregate dollar and per-share effects of the tax holiday and (2) briefly describe the factual circumstances including the date on which the special tax status will terminate.

12. Minority interest in income of consolidated subsidiaries.

13. Equity in earnings of unconsolidated subsidiaries and 50 percent or less owned persons. *State, parenthetically or in a note, the amount of dividends received from such persons. If justified by the circumstances, this item may be presented in a different position and a different manner. (See Rule 4-01(a).)*

The last sentence in the rule permits, for example, recognizing income before taxes of the investee and combining the portion of the investee's taxes represented by the equity interest with the investor's tax provision.

14. Income or loss from continuing operations.

15. Discontinued operations.

SEC 50503. Rule 5-03-9

The SEC staff has provided the following informal views regarding discontinued operations:

- The staff has indicated that it will typically challenge the accounting for the disposal of a discontinued operation if the registrant has not previously disclosed the segment pursuant to SFAS No. 14, *Financial Reporting for Segment of a Business Enterprise*, or as a separate line of business under Regulation S-K, Items 101 and 303 in earlier filings. The staff has emphasized, however, that even if the appropriate segment or line of business disclosures had been provided in the past, the requirements of APB Opinion No. 30, *Reporting the Results of Operations*, still need to be met to qualify as a discontinued operation. For example, the staff would consider discontinued operations treatment to be inappropriate if losses for a start-up entity were significant to the consolidated entity but the start-up entity's revenues were immaterial, since the entity would not be considered a "major line of business."

- Paragraph 15 of APB Opinion No. 30 states that "in the usual circumstance, it would be expected that the plan of disposal would be carried out within a period of one year from the measurement date." In situations where a disposal of a business segment is not expected to be carried out within one year of the measurement date, the SEC staff has indicated that it will generally question whether a measurement date, as defined in APB Opinion No. 30, has occurred. However, the staff's position is that a registrant may continue reporting discontinued operations for a short period of time beyond the one-year period if the sale or disposal of the operations is imminent as evidenced by a firm contract to complete the sale soon after the end of the one-year period. The basis cited by the staff in support of this position was the consensus reached in EITF Issue 90-6, "Accounting for Certain Events Not Addressed in Issue No. 87-11 Relating to an Acquired Operating Unit To Be Sold," regarding the accounting for the delay in the sale of an acquired operating unit to be sold.

- The staff has noted several cases in which provisions for the impairment of assets were made prior to a segment being reported as a discontinued operation. Subsequently, upon the reporting of a discontinued operation, the provisions were included in the measurement of the gain or loss on the disposal of discontinued operations. The staff's position is that such provisions should be reported in the results of discontinued operations, and not as part of operating losses during the phase-out period, which are included in the gain or loss on discontinuance in accordance with paragraph 8 of APB Opinion No. 30.

SEC 50503

16. Income or loss before extraordinary items and cumulative effects of changes in accounting principles.

17. Extraordinary items, less applicable tax.

Items reportable as extraordinary items are those qualifying for extraordinary item treatment under generally accepted accounting principles, as described in APB Opinion Nos. 9 and 30 and FASB Statement No. 4.

According to paragraph 20 of APB Opinion No. 30, events or transactions need to be both unusual in nature and infrequent in occurence to be classified as an extraordinary item.

Paragraph 21 of APB Opinion No. 30 states that characteristics related both to the specific entity as well as the environment in which an entity operates need to be considered when evaluating whether an event or transaction is unusual in nature or arises from the normal activities of the entity. The entity's environment includes factors such as the characteristics of the industry, the geographic location of its operations, and government regulation. Accordingly, what may be unusual in nature for one entity may not be for another due to their different environmental characteristics.

Given that today's society and business environment are litigious and that it is not usual for an entity to be subject to and settle litigation, the SEC staff has indicated that litigation settlements do not meet the criteria of an extraordinary item and, accordingly, should be classified as an ordinary operating expense.

18. Cumulative effects of changes in accounting principles.

Refer to section 20620 for a discussion of accounting changes.

19. Net income or loss.

20. Earnings per share data.

The requirements for computing and disclosing earnings per share are included in APB Opinion Nos. 15 and 30. Regulation S-K (Exhibits; see section 66110) contains the requirements for including a statement that sets forth the computation of earnings per share.

If equity securities (including warrants, options, and other potentially dilutive securities) are issued within one year prior to an initial public offering and the issue price is less than the public offering price, the SEC staff will generally require that they be reflected in the calculation of earnings per share as if they had been outstanding for all periods. SAB Topic 4-D addresses this issue as well as the staff's position regarding the recognition of compensation expense when common stock or other dilutive securities are issued during the period covered by income statements included in a registration statement or in subsequent periods prior to the filing of the IPO registration statement. The text of the SAB follows:

Earnings Per Share Computations in an Initial Public Offering

Facts: A registration statement is filed in connection with an initial public offering ("IPO") of common stock. During the periods covered by income statements that are included in the registration statement or in subsequent periods prior to the filing of the registration statement, the registrant issued common stock for consideration below the IPO price or issued common stock warrants, options, or other potentially dilutive instruments with exercise prices below the IPO price (referred to collectively hereafter as "stock and warrants").

Question 1: In computing earnings per share (EPS) for the periods covered by income statements included in the registration statement and in subsequent filings with the SEC, what treatment is appropriate for such stock and warrants?

Interpretive Response: The staff believes that stock and warrants issued within a one year period prior to the initial filing of the registration statement relating to the IPO[1] should be treated as outstanding for all reported periods, in the same manner as shares issued in a stock split or a recapitalization effected contemporaneously with an IPO. However, in measuring the dilutive effect of such issuances, the staff will not object to use of a treasury stock approach in determining the dilutive effect of the issuances. This approach considers the actual proceeds (or in the case of warrants, the proceeds that would have been received) and the number of shares that could have been repurchased using the estimated IPO price as the repurchase price for all periods presented.[2] The staff believes that this method should be applied in the computation of EPS for all prior periods, including loss years where the impact of the incremental shares is anti-dilutive [i.e., when the registrant reports a loss].

Question 2: Does reflecting stock and warrants as outstanding for all historical periods in the computation of earnings per share alter the registrant's responsibility to determine whether compensation expense must be recognized on issuances of the stock and warrants to employees?

Interpretive Response: No. Under generally accepted accounting principles, registrants must recognize compensation expense for any issuances of stock and warrants to employees for less than fair value.[3] Reflecting stock and warrants as outstanding for all historical periods in the computation of earnings per share does not alter that existing responsibility under GAAP.

---

[1]The staff will not ordinarily raise a question about issuances of stock or warrants beyond one year prior to the initial filing of the registration statement relating to the IPO unless it appears that such issuances were issued in contemplation of the

696

IPO.

[2]For example, if the estimated IPO price was $15 and 300 shares of stock were sold 6 months prior at a price of $10 per share, in computing EPS for periods prior to actual issuance of the shares, registrants may compute the incremental number of shares as follows:

Total assumed proceeds = $10 x 300 shares = $3,000. Shares assumed to be repurchased = $3,000 / $15 per share = 200 shares. Incremental shares = 300 shares sold less 200 shares assumed to be repurchased for a net increase of 100 shares assumed to be outstanding in computing EPS.

[3]As prescribed by APB Opinion 25, Accounting for Stock Issued to Employees, and related interpretations.

Regarding the issue of compensation expense discussed in SAB Topic 4-D, the staff has indicated that stock, options or warrants issued to employees, consultants, directors, or others providing services to the issuer within one year prior to the filing of an initial registration at a price (or exercise price) below the offering price are presumed to be compensatory. In evaluating whether the stock issuance is, in fact, a compensation arrangement (or only a restructuring of ownership rights prior to the offering), the staff has indicated that it will evaluate the circumstances of the issuance and the extent of employee participation. If compensatory, the registrant needs to determine the fair value of the stock when issued pursuant to paragraph 10 of APB Opinion No. 25.

In the evaluation of the fair value of the stock, the staff has indicated that the registrant should consider the proximity of the issuance to the offering, intervening events, transfer restrictions and exercise dates, and profitability and financial condition of the company. The staff looks to objective evidence as the best support for the determination of market value. Examples of objective evidence include transactions with third parties involving issuances or repurchases of stock for cash and/or appraisals by reputable investment bankers independent of the offering at or near the issue date.

The interpretive response to question 1 of SAB Topic 4-D states that the staff will not object to the use of the treasury stock method in determining the dilutive effect of stock and warrants issued within a one-year period prior to the initial filing of the registration statement relating to the IPO. In applying this interpretation, the staff has indicated that it would object to the use of the modified treasury stock method described in paragraph 38 of APB Opinion No. 15, *Earnings Per Share* (in which the treasury stock method is used only up to 20 percent of the outstanding shares; after which funds presumed to be received are assumed to be used to reduce borrowings and then to invest in government securities or commercial paper), as it is inconsistent with the intention of SAB Topic 4-D.

The staff has also indicated that in filings subsequent to the IPO, all stocks, options and warrants deemed outstanding pursuant to the SAB should continue to be deemed outstanding in all periods prior to the year in which the IPO is declared

SEC 50503. Rule 5-03-20

effective. In calculations of EPS for the fiscal year in which the IPO became effective, shares, options and warrants issued within one year prior to the IPO effective date should continue to be deemed outstanding, as prescribed by SAB Topic 4-D, throughout the interim period included in the IPO prospectus. The determination of common stock and equivalents outstanding in the remainder of the fiscal year (and in all subsequent reporting periods) should be determined on a basis consistent with APB Opinion No. 15. That is, for the remainder of the fiscal year and subsequent periods, outstanding options and warrants should be included in the EPS computation only if they have a dilutive effect; the application of the treasury stock method should not necessarily assume the IPO price to be the market price.

For example: Assume an option granted on January 1, with the IPO document containing March 31 interim financial statements; an exercise price of $1; an IPO price of $2 (which is also assumed to be the fair value of the stock for the first quarter); and an average market price for the remainder of the year of $3. Using the treasury stock method, the option represents one-half of an outstanding share (i.e., one share minus one-half of a share) in the first quarter and two-thirds of an outstanding share (i.e., one share minus one-third of a share) in the last three quarters; or five-eighths of a share for the full year.

SAB Topic 3-A refers to the provisions of paragraphs 22 and 23 of APB Opinion No. 15 in discussing disclosure of the dilution of earnings per share resulting from the offering of convertible securities. The text of the SAB follows:

Convertible Securities

Facts: Company B proposes to file a registration statement covering convertible debentures.

Question: In registration, what consideration should be given to the dilutive effects of convertible securities?

Interpretive Response: If a convertible security is being registered, consideration must be given to the provisions of APB Opinion No. 15 governing the possible dilution of earnings per share resulting from assumed conversion of the security.

Pro forma per share amounts provided as supplemental earnings per share data in accordance with paragraphs 22 and 23 of APB Opinion No. 15 must be disclosed and keyed to an appropriate explanatory note if such amounts vary materially from historical calculations.

SAB Topic 3-C describes the manner in which earnings per share should be calculated when redeemable preferred stock is outstanding and is recorded at less than the redemption value. The SAB concludes that the periodic accretions should be considered when calculating earnings per share for common stock unless the preferred stock is a common stock equivalent. The text of the SAB that discusses this subject is

698

included in the section dealing with Redeemable Preferred Stocks (see section 5-02-28).

In situations in which there are "poison pill" rights that permit exercise into the company's stock only upon a change in control, the SEC staff has informally expressed the view that such rights should not be taken into account in computing fully diluted earnings per share if the rights genuinely constitute a poison pill arrangement (i.e, if the dilution that would occur from exercise of the rights is such that the occurrence of a change in control is remote). This issue is also addressed in the minutes of the April 6, 1989 EITF meeting at which the SEC observer stated that such rights should be reflected in fully diluted earnings per share if they have a "reasonable possibility" of being exercised.

50504. Income or loss applicable to common stock. SAB Topic 6-B, added by SAB No. 64, addresses situations in which dividends on preferred stocks and accretions of their carrying amounts cause income applicable to common stock to be less than reported net income. The SAB indicates that income or loss applicable to common stock should be reported on the face of the income statement when it is materially different in quantitative terms from reported net income or loss. The text of Topic 6-B follows:

Income or Loss Applicable to Common Stock

Facts: A registrant has various classes of preferred stock. Dividends on those preferred stocks and accretions of their carrying amounts cause income applicable to common stock to be less than reported net income.

Question: In ASR No. 280, the Commission stated that although it has determined not to mandate presentation of income or loss applicable to common stock in all cases, it believes that disclosure of that amount is of value in certain situations. In what situations should the amount be reported, where should it be reported, and how should it be computed?

Interpretive Response: Income or loss applicable to common stock should be reported on the face of the income statement when it is materially different in quantitative terms from reported net income or loss or when it is indicative of significant trends or other qualitative considerations. The amount to be reported should be computed for each period as net income or loss less: (a) dividends on preferred stock, including undeclared or unpaid dividends if cumulative; and (b) periodic increases in the carrying amounts of instruments reported as redeemable preferred stock (as discussed in Topic 3-C).

50505. Allocation of expenses in a "carve out" situation. SAB Topic 1-B, added by SAB No. 55, discusses the allocation of expenses and related disclosure in financial statements when a subsidiary, division, or lesser business component is "carved out" of another entity and becomes a separate registrant. The SAB emphasizes the importance of presenting operating results that reflect all of the "costs of doing business," notwithstanding that some of the costs may not have historically been allocated to the entity being "carved out." This situation would generally occur in an initial public offering of securities of the entity but may also be applicable whenever separate financial statements of the entity are presented. The text of Topic 1-B follows:

Allocation of Expenses and Related
Disclosure in Financial Statements of
Subsidiaries, Divisions or Lesser Business
Components of Another Entity

Facts: A company (the registrant) operates as a subsidiary of another company (parent). Certain expenses incurred by the parent on behalf of the subsidiary have not been charged to the subsidiary in the past. The subsidiary files a registration statement under the Securities Act of 1933 in connection with an initial public offering.

1. Costs Reflected in Historical Financial Statements

Question 1: Should the subsidiary's historical income statements reflect all of the expenses that the parent incurred on its behalf?

Interpretive Response: In general, the staff believes that the historical income statements of a registrant should reflect all of its costs of doing business. Therefore, in specific situations, the staff has required the subsidiary to revise its financial statements to include certain expenses incurred by the parent on its behalf. Examples of such expenses may include, but are not necessarily limited to, the following (income taxes and interest are discussed separately below):

1. Officer and employee salaries.
2. Rent or depreciation.
3. Advertising.
4. Accounting and legal services, and
5. Other selling, general and administrative expenses.

When the subsidiary's financial statements have been previously reported on by independent accountants and have been used other than for internal purposes, the staff has accepted a presentation that shows income before tax as previously reported, followed by adjustments for expenses not previously allocated, income taxes, and adjusted net income.

Question 2: How should the amount of expenses incurred on the subsidiary's behalf by its parent be determined, and what disclosure is required in the financial statements?

Interpretive Response: The staff expects any expenses clearly applicable to the subsidiary to be reflected in its income statements. However, the staff understands that in some situations a reasonable method of allocating common expenses to the subsidiary (e.g., incremental or proportional cost allocation) must

700

be chosen because specific identification of expenses is not practicable. In these situations, the staff has required an explanation of the allocation method used in the notes to the financial statements along with management's assertion that the method used is reasonable.

In addition, since agreements with related parties are by definition not at arm's length and may be changed at any time, the staff has required footnote disclosure, when practicable, of management's estimate of what the expenses (other than income taxes and interest discussed separately below) would have been on a stand alone basis—that is, the cost that would have been incurred if the subsidiary had operated as an unaffiliated entity. The disclosure has been presented for each year for which an income statement was required when such basis produced materially different results.

Question 3: What are the staff's views with respect to the accounting for and disclosure of the subsidiary's income tax expense?

Interpretive Response: Recently, a number of parent companies have sold interests in subsidiaries, but have retained sufficient ownership interests to permit continued inclusion of the subsidiaries in their consolidated tax returns. The staff believes that it is material to investors to know what the effect on income would have been if the registrant had not been eligible to be included in a consolidated income tax return with its parent. Some of these subsidiaries have calculated their tax provision on the separate return basis, which the staff believes is the preferable method. Others, however, have used different allocation methods. When the historical income statements in the filing do not reflect the tax provision on the separate return basis, the staff has required a pro forma income statement for the most recent year and interim period reflecting a tax provision calculated on the separate return basis.

Question 4: Should the historical income statements reflect a charge for interest on intercompany debt if no such charge had been previously provided?

Interpretive Response: The staff generally believes that financial statements are more useful to investors if they reflect all costs of doing business, including interest costs. Because of the inherent difficulty in distinguishing the elements of a subsidiary's capital structure, the staff has not insisted that the historical income statements include an interest charge on intercompany debt if such a charge was not provided in the past, except when debt specifically related to the operations of the subsidiary and previously carried on the parent's books will henceforth be recorded in the subsidiary's books. In any case, financing arrangements with the parent must be discussed in a note to the financial statements. In this connection, the staff has taken the position that, where an interest charge on intercompany debt has not been provided, appropriate disclosure would include an analysis of the intercompany accounts as well as the average balance due to or from related parties for each period for which an income statement is required. The analysis of the intercompany accounts has taken the form of a listing of transactions (e.g., the allocation of costs to the subsidiary, intercompany purchases, and cash transfers between entities) for each period for which an income statement was required, reconciled to the intercompany accounts reflected in the balance sheets.

SEC 50505. Rule 5-03

2. Pro Forma Financial Statements and Earnings Per Share

Question: What disclosure should be made if the registrant's historical financial statements are not indicative of the ongoing entity (e.g., tax or other cost sharing agreements will be terminated or revised)?

Interpretive Response: The registration statement should include pro forma income statements which are prepared in accordance with Article 11 of Regulation S-X and reflect the impact of terminated or revised cost sharing agreements and other significant changes. In these cases, the staff has insisted that historical earnings per share data be deleted from the face of the historical income statements because this data is not considered relevant and allowed pro forma per share data only for the most recent year and interim period.

3. Other Matters

Question: What is the staff's position with respect to dividends declared by the subsidiary subsequent to the balance sheet date?

Interpretive Response: The staff has insisted that such dividends either be given retroactive effect in the balance sheet with appropriate footnote disclosure, or reflected in a pro forma balance sheet. In addition, when the dividends were to be paid from the proceeds of the offering, the staff has required deletion of historical per share data and inclusion of pro forma per share data (for the latest year and interim period only) giving effect to the number of shares whose proceeds were to be used to pay the dividend. The staff has also required a similar presentation when dividends exceeded earnings in the current year, even though the stated use of proceeds was other than for the payment of dividends. In these situations, pro forma per share data gave effect to the increase in the number of shares which, when multiplied by the offering price, would have been sufficient to replace the capital in excess of earnings being withdrawn.

As indicated in section 3 of the SAB, when a subsidiary intends to pay a dividend to its parent from the proceeds of an equity offering, the staff will not permit the inclusion of historical earnings per share data but will require the presentation of pro forma earnings per share (for the latest year and interim period only). Pro forma earnings per share would then be calculated by adding to the weighted average of outstanding shares the number of shares at the public offering price necessary to provide sufficient proceeds to pay the dividend. This computation would need to be explained in the notes to the financial statements. In addition, the dividend payable and corresponding reduction of stockholders' equity would need to be given retroactive effect in the balance sheet for the latest period presented or in a pro forma balance sheet, even when the dividend is declared subsequent to the balance sheet date.

The SEC staff has indicated that if a planned distribution to owners (whether declared or not, whether to be paid from proceeds or not) is not reflected in the latest balance sheet but would be significant relative to reported equity, a pro forma balance sheet reflecting the distribution (but not giving the effect to the offering proceeds) needs to be presented alongside the historical balance sheet in the filing.

If a distribution to owners (whether or not already reflected in the balance sheet and whether or not declared) is to be paid out of proceeds of the offering rather than from existing assets, the staff requires pro forma per share data to be presented (for the latest year and interim period only), giving effect to the number of shares whose proceeds would be necessary to pay the dividend as required by SAB Topic 1.B.3. Additionally, the staff views a dividend declared in the latest year to be in contemplation of the offering with the intention of repayment out of offering proceeds to the extent that the dividend exceeded earnings during the previous 12 months.

50506. Accounting for sales of stock by a subsidiary. SAB Topic 5-H, originally added by SAB No. 51 and subsequently amended by SAB No. 84, expresses the staff's views regarding accounting in consolidation for issuances of a subsidiary's stock that cause changes in the parent's ownership percentage in the subsidiary. The SAB provides guidance as to the circumstances under which gains or losses resulting from issuance by a subsidiary of its own stock may be recognized in consolidated income. In general, the staff indicates that it will permit gain recognition in an offering involving a subsidiary's direct sale of its unissued shares provided the sale is not part of a broader corporate reorganization contemplated or planned by the registrant. The staff believes that gain recognition is acceptable in situations other than sales of unissued shares in a public offering provided the value of the proceeds can be objectively determined. Regarding stock options, warrants, and convertible and similar securities, the staff indicates that a gain should not be recognized before the exercise or conversion takes place and the realization of the gain is reasonably assured. In situations where gains have previously been recognized and shares are subsequently repurchased by the subsidiary, the staff's position is that gains on issuances of shares subsequent to the repurchase should not be recognized until the amount of reissued shares is equivalent to the amount of shares repurchased. The staff also indicates that registrants cannot selectively apply the guidance in this SAB, e.g., by recognizing gains for certain issuances and accounting for other issuances as equity transactions. In situations in which a gain is recognized, the staff indicates that the gain needs to be presented as a separate line item (regardless of materiality) in the consolidated income statement and clearly designated as nonoperating income. Footnote and MD&A disclosures are also required.

The text of the SAB follows:

Accounting for Sales of Stock by a Subsidiary

Facts: The registrant owns 95% of its subsidiary's stock. The subsidiary sells its unissued shares in a public offering, which decreases the registrant's ownership of the subsidiary from 95% to 90%. The offering price per share exceeds the registrant's carrying amount per share of subsidiary stock.

Question 1: When an offering takes the form of a subsidiary's direct sale of its unissued shares, will the staff permit the amount in excess of the parent's carrying value to be reflected as a gain in the consolidated income statement of the parent?

Interpretive Response: Yes, in some circumstances. Although the staff has previously insisted that such transactions be accounted for as capital transactions in the consolidated financial statements, it has recently reconsidered its views on this matter with respect to certain of these transactions where the sale of such shares by a subsidiary is not a part of a broader corporate reorganization contemplated or planned by the registrant. In situations where no other such capital transactions are contemplated, the staff has determined that it will accept accounting treatment for such transactions that is in accordance with the Advisory Conclusions in paragraph 30 of the June 3, 1980 Issues Paper, "Accounting in Consolidation for Issuances of a Subsidiary's Stock," prepared by the Accounting Standards Executive Committee of the AICPA. The staff believes that this issues paper should provide appropriate interim guidance on this matter until the FASB addresses this issue as a part of its project on Accounting for the Reporting Entity, including Consolidations, the Equity Method, and Related Matters.

Question 2: What is meant by the phrase "broader corporate reorganization contemplated or planned by the registrant" and are there other situations where the staff has objected to gain recognition?

Interpretive Response: The staff believes that gain recognition is not appropriate in situations where subsequent capital transactions are contemplated that raise concerns about the likelihood of the registrant realizing that gain, such as where the registrant intends to spin-off its subsidiary to shareholders or where reacquisition of shares is contemplated at the time of issuance. The staff will presume that repurchases were contemplated at the date of issuance in those situations where shares are repurchased within one year of issuance or where a specific plan existed to repurchase shares at the time shares were issued. In addition, the staff believes that realization is not assured where the subsidiary is a newly-formed, non-operating entity; a research and development, start-up or development stage company; an entity whose ability to continue in existence is in question; or other similar circumstances. In those situations, the staff believes that the change in the parent company's proportionate share of subsidiary equity resulting from the additional equity raised by the subsidiary should be accounted for as an equity transaction in consolidation. Gain deferral is not appropriate.

Question 3: In the staff's opinion, may gain be recognized for issuances of subsidiary stock in situations other than sales of unissued shares in a public offering?

Interpretive Response: Yes. The staff believes that gain recognition is acceptable in situations other than sales of unissued shares in a public offering as long as the value of the proceeds can be objectively determined. With respect to issuances of stock options, warrants, and convertible and other similar securities, gain should not be recognized before exercise or conversion into common stock, and then only provided that realization of the gain is reasonably assured (see Question 2 above) at the time of such exercise or conversion.

Question 4: Will repurchasing shares of a subsidiary's stock affect the potential for gain recognition by the registrant in consolidation for subsequent issuances of that subsidiary's stock?[1]

Interpretive Response: Yes. Where previous gains have been recognized in consolidation on issuances of a subsidiary's stock and shares of the subsidiary are subsequently repurchased by the subsidiary, its parent or any member of the consolidated group, gain recognition should not occur on issuances subsequent to the date of a repurchase until such time as shares have been issued in an amount equivalent to the number of repurchased shares. The staff views such transactions as analogous to treasury stock transactions from the standpoint of the consolidated entity that should not result in recognition of gains or losses.

Question 5: May registrants selectively apply the guidance in the SAB by recognizing the impact of certain issuances by a subsidiary in the income statement and other issuances as equity transactions?

Interpretive Response: No. The staff believes that income statement treatment in consolidation for issuances of stock by a subsidiary represents a choice among alternative accounting methods and, therefore, must be applied consistently to all stock transactions that meet the conditions for income statement treatment set forth herein for any subsidiary. If a registrant recognizes gains on issuances of stock by a subsidiary, thus adopting income statement recognition as its accounting policy, then it must also recognize losses for stock issuances by that or any other subsidiary that result in decreases in its proportionate share of the dollar amount of the subsidiary's equity. Regardless of the method of accounting selected, when a subsidiary issues securities at prices less than the parent's carrying value per share, the registrant must assess whether the investment has been impaired, in which case a provision should be reflected in the income statement.

Question 6: How should the registrant disclose the accounting for issuances of a subsidiary's stock in the consolidated financial statements?

Interpretive Response: The staff believes that gains (or losses) arising from issuances by a subsidiary of its own stock, if recorded in income by the parent, should be presented as a separate line item in the consolidated income statement without regard to materiality and clearly be designated as non-operating income. An appropriate description of the transaction should be included in the notes to the financial statements, as further described below.

The accounting method adopted by the registrant for issuances of a subsidiary's stock should be disclosed in its accounting policy footnote and consistently applied (See Question 5). The staff believes that the registrant also should include a separate footnote that describes issuances of subsidiary stock that have occurred

SEC 50506. Rule 5-03

during all periods presented. This footnote should clearly describe the transaction, the identification of the subsidiary and nature of its operations, the number of shares issued, the price per share and the total dollar amount and nature of consideration received, and the percentage ownership of the parent both before and after the transaction. Additionally, the registrant should clearly state whether deferred income taxes have been provided on gains recognized and, if no provision has been recorded, a clear explanation of the reasons. Finally, the staff expects registrants to include disclosure in their Management Discussion and Analysis of the impact of specific transactions that have occurred and the likelihood of similar transactions occurring in future years.

---

[1]This question and interpretive response assume that the repurchases were not contemplated at the time of earlier gain recognition. See Question 2.

The foregoing SAB concludes that the accounting results may be considered comparable whether the parent company disposes of its interest or the subsidiary issues additional securities. In this context, the SEC staff has informally expressed the following additional views with respect to this issue:

- The accounting treatment is not limited to subsidiaries and is acceptable for all investor-investee relationships. Accordingly, changes in an investor's equity in an investee caused by the investee's issuance of additional shares may be recognized as a gain or loss regardless of whether the investee is a subsidiary or a 50 percent-or-less-owned investee accounted for on the equity method.

- SAB No. 51 is permissive, and the sale of shares by an investee may therefore still be accounted for as a capital transaction. However, the accounting method selected should be consistently applied to all transactions. If the application of the SAB involves a change in accounting, a preferability letter is required. (See section 20620 for a discussion of preferability letters.)

- Gains or losses on the issuance of a subsidiary's shares should be tax effected after giving appropriate consideration to SFAS 109, *Accounting for Income Taxes*.

50507. Gain recognition on sale of business to a highly leveraged entity.
SAB Topic 5-U, added by SAB No. 81, expresses the staff's views regarding the appropriateness of gain recognition on the sale of a business or operating assets accounted for as a divestiture to a highly leveraged entity. Under the assumption that a transaction may properly be accounted for as a divestiture (see discussion of SAB Topic 5-E below regarding accounting for a transaction as a divestiture), the staff believes immediate gain recognition may be questionable when significant uncertainties exist about the seller's being able to realize noncash proceeds received in

transactions in which the purchaser is a newly formed, thinly capitalized, highly leveraged entity, and particularly when its assets primarily consist of those purchased from the seller. Topic 5-U describes the following factors that may cause the staff to question gain recognition in such transactions:

- The assets or operations sold have not historically produced operating cash flows sufficient to fund current debt service and dividend requirements;

- The newly formed entity does not have substantial equity capital other than that provided by the registrant; and/or

- Contingent liabilities exist (e.g., guarantees on agreements) requiring the registrant to infuse cash into the purchaser.

The staff has indicated that it may also question gain recognition of cash proceeds received if contingent liabilities exist such as those in the third item above and especially if the other two factors also exist. In situations in which the gain is deferred, the SAB also discusses disclosure requirements and factors for future gain recognition.

The text of the SAB follows:

Gain Recognition on the Sale of a Business or Operating Assets to a Highly Leveraged Entity

Facts: A registrant has sold a subsidiary, division or operating assets to a newly formed, thinly capitalized, highly leveraged entity (NEWCO) for cash or a combination of cash and securities, which may include subordinated debt, preferred stock, warrants, options or other instruments issued by NEWCO. In some of these transactions, registrants may guarantee debt or enter into other agreements (sometimes referred to as make-well agreements) that may require the registrant to infuse cash into NEWCO under certain circumstances. Securities received in the transaction are not actively traded and are subordinate to substantially all of NEWCO's other debt. The value of the consideration received appears to exceed the cost basis of the net assets sold.

Question 1: Assuming the transaction may be properly accounted for as a divestiture,[1] does the staff believe it is appropriate for the registrant to recognize a gain?

Interpretive Response: The staff believes there often exist significant uncertainties about the seller's ability to realize non-cash proceeds received in transactions in which the purchaser is a thinly capitalized, highly leveraged entity, particularly when its assets consist principally of those purchased from the seller. The staff believes that such uncertainties raise doubt as to whether immediate gain recognition is appropriate. Factors that may lead the staff to question gain recognition in such transactions include:

(1) situations in which the assets or operations sold have historically not produced cash flows from operations[2] that will be sufficient to fund future debt service and full dividend requirements on a current basis.[3] Often the servicing of debt and preferred dividend requirements is dependent upon future events that cannot be assured, such as sales of assets or improvements in earnings.

(2) the lack of any substantial amount of equity capital in NEWCO other than that provided by the registrant; and/or

(3) the existence of contingent liabilities of the registrant, such as debt guarantees or agreements that require the registrant to infuse cash into NEWCO under certain circumstances.

The staff also believes that even where the registrant receives solely cash proceeds, the recognition of any gain would be impacted by the existence of any guarantees or other agreements that may require the registrant to infuse cash into NEWCO, particularly when the first two factors listed above exist.

Question 2: If immediate recognition of all or a portion of the apparent gain is not appropriate due to the existence of facts and circumstances similar to the above, at what future date should the gain be recognized and how should the deferred gain be disclosed in the financial statements?

Interpretive Response: Generally, the staff believes that the deferred gain[4] should not be recognized until such time as cash flows from operating activities are sufficient to fund debt service and dividend requirements (on a full accrual basis)[5] or the registrant's investment in NEWCO has been or could be readily converted to cash (e.g., active trading market develops in NEWCO securities and the registrant is not restricted from selling such securities, the registrant sells the securities received on a nonrecourse basis, etc.) and the registrant has no further obligations under any debt guarantees or other agreements that would require it to make additional investments in NEWCO.

The staff believes that the amount of any deferred gain (including deferral of interest or dividend income on securities received) should be disclosed on the face of the balance sheet as a deduction from the related asset account (i.e., investment in NEWCO). The footnotes to the financial statements should include a complete description of the transaction, including the existence of any commitments and contingencies, the terms of the securities received, and the accounting treatment of amounts due thereon.

---

[1]Transactions such as these require careful evaluation to determine whether, in substance, a divestiture has occurred. Staff Accounting Bulletin Topic No. 5-E provides the staff's views on circumstances that may exist that would lead the staff to conclude that the risks of the business have not been transferred to the new owners and that a divestiture has not occurred.

[2]As defined in paragraphs 21-24 of Statement of Financial Accounting Standards No. 95, "Statement of Cash Flows."

[3]The ability of NEWCO to fund the debt service and the dividend requirement(s) should be evaluated on a full accrual basis—i.e., irrespective of the purchaser's ability to satisfy those requirements through deferral (contractually or otherwise) of any required cash payments or the issuance of additional securities to satisfy such requirements.

[4]In situations in which the gain is deferred following the guidance in this staff accounting bulletin, the staff believes that the seller generally should not recognize any income from the securities received in such transactions (including accretion of securities to their face or redemption value) until realization is more fully assured.

[5]See note 3, above.

Topic 5-E (see section 82003) indicates the following factors that would generally raise questions as to whether a transaction should be accounted for as a divestiture:

- Continuing involvement by the seller in the business;

- Absence of significant financial investment in the business by the buyer;

- Repayment of debt, which constitutes the principal consideration in the transaction, is dependent on future successful operations; or

- The continued necessity for debt or contract performance guarantees on behalf of the business by the seller.

50508. Gain or loss from disposition of equipment. SAB Topic 5-B describes the staff's views concerning the appropriate income statement presentation of gains or losses from the disposition of equipment. It is important to note that this SAB applies to the disposition of equipment resulting in "true" economic gains or losses. The facts and circumstances of each disposition need to be evaluated in determining the actual gain or loss, particularly in situations in which the cost of new equipment is reduced for the trade-in of old equipment.

The text of the SAB follows:

Gain or Loss From Disposition of Equipment

Facts: Company A has adopted the policy of treating gains and losses from disposition of revenue producing equipment as adjustments to the current year's provision for depreciation. Company B reflects such gains and losses as a separate item in the statement of income.

Question: Does the staff have any views as to which method is preferable?

Interpretive Response: Gains and losses resulting from the disposition of revenue producing equipment should not be treated as adjustments to the provision for depreciation in the year of disposition, but should be shown as a separate item in the statement of income.

If such equipment is depreciated on the basis of group of composite accounts for fleets of like vehicles, gains (or losses) may be charged (or credited) to accumulated depreciation with the result that depreciation is adjusted over a period of years on an average basis. It should be noted that the latter treatment would not be appropriate for (1) an enterprise (such as an airline) which replaces its fleet on an episodic rather than a continuing basis or (2) an enterprise (such as a car leasing company) where equipment is sold after limited use so that the equipment on hand is usually both fairly new and carried at amounts closely related to current acquisition cost.

50509. Sales of leased or licensed departments. SAB Topic 8-A permits inclusion by department stores and other retailers of sales of leased or licensed departments in total revenues if disclosed:

Sales of Leased or Licensed Departments

Facts: Department stores and other retailers customarily include the sales of leased or licensed departments in the amounts reported as "total revenues."

Question: Does the staff have any objection to this practice?

Interpretive Response: The staff has no objection to this practice so long as the sales of leased or licensed departments are either presented as a separate revenue line item in the income statement or disclosed in an appropriately referenced note to the income statement.

50510. Finance charges by retailers. SAB Topic 8-B provides that, as a minimum, the amount of gross revenue from finance charges imposed by department stores and other retailers should be disclosed in a footnote and that the income statement caption that includes such revenue be identified. The text of the SAB follows:

Finance Charges

Facts: Department stores and other retailers impose finance charges on credit sales.

Question: How should such charges be disclosed?

Interpretive Response: As a minimum, the staff requests that the amount of gross revenue from such charges be stated in a footnote and that the income statement classification which includes such revenue be identified. The following are examples of acceptable disclosure:

EXAMPLE 1

Consumer Credit Operations:

The results of the Consumer Credit Operations which are included in the Statement of Earnings as a separate line item are as follows for the fiscal year ended January 31, 19X0:

	(Thousands)
Service charges	$167,000
Operating expenses:	
Interest	60,000
Payroll	35,000
Provision for uncollected accounts	29,000
All other credit and collection expenses	32,000
Provision for Federal income taxes	5,000
Total operating expenses	161,000
Consumer credit operations earnings	$ 6,000

EXAMPLE 2

Service charges on retail credit accounts are netted against selling, general and administrative expense. The cost of administering the retail credit program continued to exceed service charges on customer receivables as follows:

(In millions)	19XX	19XX	Percent Increase (Decrease)
Costs			
Regional office operations	$ 45	$ 42	9%
Interest	51	44	13
Provision for doubtful accounts	21	16	34
Total	117	102	15
Less service charge income	96	79	22
Net cost of credit	$ 21	$ 23	(10)%
Net cost as percent of credit sales	1.4%	1.6%	

The above results do not reflect either "in store" costs related to credit operations or any allocation of corporate overhead expenses.

SEC 50510. Rule 5-03

50511. Presentation of operating-differential subsidies. SAB Topic 11-A describes the manner in which operating-differential subsidies pursuant to the Merchant Marine Act of 1936 should be reflected in the income statement:

Operating-Differential Subsidies

Facts: Company A has received an operating-differential subsidy pursuant to the Merchant Marine Act of 1936, as amended.

Question: How should such subsidies be displayed in the income statement?

Interpretive Response: Revenue representing an operating-differential subsidy under the Merchant Marine Act of 1936, as amended, must be set forth as a separate line item in the income statement either under a revenue caption or as a credit in the costs and expenses section.

50512. Presentation of restructuring charges. SAB Topic 5-P, added by SAB No. 67, discusses the staff's position on income statement presentation of restructuring charges. In SAB No. 67, the staff refers to paragraph 26 of APB Opinion No. 30, *Reporting the Results of Operations,* which states that any item not meeting the criteria for classification as an extraordinary item "should be reported as a separate component of income from continuing operations." The staff therefore believes restructuring charges should be presented as a component of income from continuing operations, with separate disclosure if material, and that no additional subtotals (e.g., income from continuing operations before restructuring charges) should be presented. Requirements regarding the disclosure of the restructuring charges, including the impact on net income and earnings per share, are also addressed by the staff in the SAB.

The text of the SAB follows:

Income Statement Presentation of Restructuring Charges

Facts: The staff has noted a recent increase in the number of registrants recording what are commonly referred to as "restructuring charges." While the events or transactions triggering the recognition of such provisions vary, they typically result from the consolidation and/or relocation of operations, the abandonment of operations or productive assets, or the impairment of the carrying value of productive or other long-lived assets. The components of these charges also vary, but generally include the reduction in the carrying value of long-lived assets and provisions for the termination and/or relocation of operations and employees.

Because the charges typically do not relate to "a single separate major line of business or class of customer,"[1] they do not qualify for presentation as losses on the disposal of a discontinued operation. Additionally, since the charges are not both unusual and infrequent[2], they are not presented in the income statement as extraordinary items.

Question 1: May such restructuring charges be presented in the income statement[3] as a separate caption after income from continuing operations before income taxes (i.e., preceding income taxes and/or discontinued operations)?

Interpretive Response: No. Paragraph 26 of Accounting Principles Opinion (APB) No. 30 states that items that do not meet the criteria for classification as an extraordinary item should be reported as a component of income from continuing operations.[4] Neither APB No. 30 nor Rule 5-03 of Regulation S-X contemplate a category in between continuing and discontinued operations. Accordingly, the staff believes that restructuring charges should be presented as a component of income from continuing operations, separately disclosed if material. Furthermore, the staff believes that a separately presented restructuring charge should not be preceded by a subtotal representing "income from continuing operations before restructuring charge" (whether or not it is so captioned). Such a presentation would be inconsistent with the intent of APB No. 30.

Question 2: Some registrants utilize a classified or "two-step" income statement format (i.e., one which presents operating revenues, expenses and income followed by other income and expense items). May a charge which relates to assets or activities for which the associated revenues and expenses have historically been included in operating income be presented as an item of "other expense" in such an income statement?

Interpretive Response: No. The staff believes that the proper classification of a restructuring charge depends on the nature of the charge and the assets and operations to which it relates. Therefore, charges which relate to activities for which the revenues and expenses have historically been included in operating income should generally be classified as an operating expense, separately disclosed if material. Furthermore, when a restructuring charge is classified as an operating expense, the staff believes that it is generally inappropriate to present a preceding subtotal captioned or representing operating income before restructuring charges. Such an amount does not represent a measurement of operating results under generally accepted accounting principles.

Conversely, charges relating to activities previously included under "other income and expenses" should be similarly classified, also separately disclosed if material.

Question 3: Is it permissible to disclose the effect on net income and earnings per share of such a restructuring charge or, alternatively, to indicate what net income and earnings per share would have been without the charge?

Interpretive Response: Discussions in management's discussion and analysis (MD&A) and elsewhere which quantify the effects of unusual or infrequent items on net income and earnings per share are beneficial to a reader's understanding of the financial statements and are therefore acceptable. However, discussions and/or graphic presentations which focus solely on pre-charge amounts or which intimate that pre-charge amounts are a more meaningful indicator of the results of operations are inappropriate.

SEC 50512. Rule 5-03

MD&A also should discuss the events and decisions which gave rise to the restructuring, the nature of the charge and the expected impact of the restructuring on future results of operations, liquidity and sources and uses of capital resources.

While these discussions are appropriate in the context of MD&A, pre-charge earnings or earnings per share, or the per share effect of the charge, should not be presented on the face of the income statement or in selected financial data or other summaries of financial data.

---

[1]See APB No. 30, paragraph 13.

[2]See APB No. 30, paragraph 20.

[3]The guidance in this Staff Accounting Bulletin should also be applied in the preparation of industry segment information disclosed pursuant to Statement of Financial Accounting Standards (SFAS) No. 14. Accordingly, charges treated as operating expenses in the income statement should, in the staff's view, also be treated as an operating expense of the related industry segment under paragraph 10(d) of SFAS No. 14.

[4]Paragraph 26 of APB No. 30 further provides that such items should not be reported on the income statement net of income taxes or in any manner that implies that they are similar to discontinued operations or extraordinary items.

50520. Rule 5-04. What Schedules Are To Be Filed

(a) Except as expressly provided otherwise in the applicable form —

(1) The schedules specified below in this section as Schedules I, VII, XI, XII and XIII shall be filed as of the date of the most recent audited balance sheet for each person or group.

(2) Other schedules specified below in this section as Schedules II, IV, V, VI, VIII, IX and X shall be filed for each period for which an audited income statement is required to be filed for each person or group.

(3) Schedules III and XIV shall be filed as of the dates and for the periods specified in the schedule.

(b) When information is required in schedules for both the registrant and the registrant and its subsidiaries consolidated it may be presented in the form of a single schedule: Provided, that items pertaining to the registrant are separately shown and that such single schedule affords a properly summarized presentation of the facts. If the information required by any schedule (including the notes thereto) may be shown in the related financial statement or in a note thereto without making such statement unclear or confusing, that procedure may be followed and the schedule omitted.

714

(c) The schedules shall be examined by the independent accountant if the related financial statements are so examined.

Rule 5-04 contains the requirements as to the dates and periods for which schedules are required to be filed by commercial and industrial companies. It also sets forth the conditions under which the schedules need to be provided. The form in which the schedules are to be prepared and the information they must contain are described in Article 12. The table on the following page summarizes the dates and periods for which schedules are to be furnished if they are required by the form being filed. Note that while certain of the schedules specified under paragraph (a)(2) support balance sheet captions, they need to be furnished for each period for which an income statement is required. Schedules are not required in support of interim period financial statements.

Rule 5-04(b) states that if all of the information required to be presented in a schedule is included in the financial statements or in the footnotes thereto, the schedule may be omitted.

Summary of Schedule Requirements

	Title	Regulation S-X Rule	In Support of Each Audited Income Statement	In Support of the Most Recent Audited Balance Sheet
I.	Marketable securities—other investments	12-02		x
II.	Amounts receivable from related parties and underwriters, promoters, and employees other than related parties	12-03	x	
III.	Condensed financial information of registrant	12-04*		
IV.	Indebtedness of and to related parties—not current	12-05	x	
V.	Property, plant and equipment	12-06	x	
VI.	Accumulated depreciation, depletion and amortization of property, plant and equipment	12-07	x	
VII.	Guarantees of securities of other issuers	12-08		x
VIII.	Valuation and qualifying accounts	12-09	x	
IX.	Short-term borrowings	12-10	x	

SEC 50520. Rule 5-04

Title	Regulation S-X Rule	In Support of Each Audited Income Statement	In Support of the Most Recent Audited Balance Sheet
X. Supplementary income statement information	12-11	x	
XI. Real estate and accumulated depreciation	12-28		x
XII. Mortgage loans on real estate	12-29		x
XIII. Other investments	12-02		x
XIV. Supplemental information concerning property-casualty insurance companies	12-18	x	

---

*Schedule III is to be filed as of the same dates and for the same periods for which the audited primary statements are required.

Schedule I. Marketable securities—other investments. *The schedule prescribed by Rule 12-02 shall be filed—*

(1) In support of caption 2 [Marketable Securities] of a balance sheet, if the greater of the aggregate cost or the aggregate market value of marketable securities as of the balance sheet date constitutes 10 percent or more of total assets.

(2) In support of caption 12 [Other Investments] of a balance sheet, if the greater of the aggregate cost or the aggregate market value of other investments as of the balance sheet date constitutes 10 percent or more of total assets.

(3) In support of captions 2 and 12 of a balance sheet, if the greater of the aggregate cost or aggregate market value of other investments plus the greater of the aggregate cost or the aggregate market value of marketable securities as of the balance sheet date constitutes 15 percent or more of total assets.

(4) In support of captions 2 and 12 of a balance sheet, if the greater of the aggregate cost or aggregate market value of the securities as of the balance sheet date of any issuer reported under either caption 2 or caption 12 constitutes two percent or more of total assets.

Schedule II. Amounts receivable from related parties and underwriters, promoters, and employees other than related parties. *The schedule prescribed by Rule*

SEC 50520

12-03 shall be filed with respect to each person among related parties and underwriters, promoters, and employees other than related parties from whom an aggregate indebtedness of more than $100,000 or 1 percent of total assets, whichever is less, is owed, or at any time during the period for which related income statements are required to be filed was owed. This schedule shall not include information which is prescribed by Rule 12-05. For the purposes of this schedule, exclude in the determination of the amount of indebtedness all amounts receivable from such persons for purchases subject to usual trade terms, for ordinary travel and expense advances and for other such items arising in the ordinary course of business.

If an aggregate indebtedness of more than $100,000 or one percent of total assets (whichever is less) was owed by any person to whom this rule applies in any of the fiscal periods for which audited income statements are required to be filed, Schedule II is to be prepared for all periods for that person.

SAB Topic 6-F confirms that Rule 12-03 also applies to amounts receivable from underwriters, promoters, directors, et al., of subsidiaries of an entity for which financial statements are filed that are included in the registrant's financial statements on either an equity or fully consolidated basis:

Rule 12-03

Facts: Accounting Series Release No. 125 amended, among others, Rule 12-03 of Regulation S-X. The amended rule specifies the form and content of the schedule required by Rule 5-04 in support of financial statements in certain filings with regard to amounts receivable from related parties and underwriters, promoters, and employees other than related parties.

Question: Do the requirements of Rule 12-03 extend to amounts receivable from underwriters, promoters, et al., of subsidiaries of the person for whom the financial statements are filed that are included in the registrant's financial statements on either an equity or fully consolidated basis?

Interpretive Response: Yes. As indicated in Rule 5-04, the requirements of Rule 12-03 extend to amounts receivable from persons among all the enumerated categories, whether their relationships are with the person for whom the financial statements are filed or with the related parties of that person, including subsidiaries included in consolidated financial statements.

Schedule III. Condensed financial information of registrant. *The schedule prescribed by Rule 12-04 shall be filed when the restricted net assets (Rule 4-08(e)(3)) of consolidated subsidiaries exceed 25 percent of consolidated net assets as of the end of the most recently completed fiscal year. For purposes of the above test, restricted net assets of consolidated subsidiaries shall mean that amount of the registrant's proportionate share of net assets of consolidated subsidiaries (after intercompany eliminations) which as of the end of the most recent fiscal year may not be transferred to the parent company by*

SEC 50520. Rule 5-04

subsidiaries in the form of loans, advances or cash dividends without the consent of a third party (i.e., lender, regulatory agency, foreign government, etc.). Where restrictions on the amount of funds which may be loaned or advanced differ from the amount restricted as to transfer in the form of cash dividends, the amount least restrictive to the subsidiary shall be used. Redeemable preferred stocks (Rule 5-02-28) and minority interests shall be deducted in computing net assets for purposes of this test.

Section 50408 (following Rule 4-08(e)) discusses the calculation required to be made to determine whether this schedule must be furnished.

Schedule IV. Indebtedness of and to related parties—not current. *The schedule prescribed by Rule 12-05 shall be filed in support of captions 11 and 23 of each balance sheet.*

This schedule may be omitted if:

(1) Neither the amount of caption 11 in the related balance sheet nor the amount of caption 23 in such balance sheet exceeds 5 percent of total assets as shown by the related balance sheet at either the beginning or end of the period, or

(2) There have been no material changes in the information required to be filed from that last previously reported.

Schedule V. Property, plant and equipment. *The schedule prescribed by Rule 12-06 shall be filed for each period specified in paragraph (a)(2) of this section, provided that these schedules may be omitted if, at both the beginning and end of the latest fiscal year, the total of property, plant and equipment (caption 13 on the balance sheet) [Property, Plant and Equipment] less accumulated depreciation, depletion and amortization (caption 14 on the balance sheet) [Accumulated Depreciation, Depletion and Amortization of Property, Plant and Equipment] is less than 25 percent of total assets as shown by the related balance sheet.*

The tests to determine whether this schedule may be omitted should be applied separately to each balance sheet presented.

Assets held under capital leases for property, plant and equipment accounted for in accordance with FASB Statement No. 13, *Accounting for Leases*, should be included on Schedule V, either as part of owned assets or as a separate line item.

Schedule VI. Accumulated depreciation, depletion and amortization of property, plant and equipment. *The schedule prescribed by Rule 12-07 shall be filed for each period specified in paragraph (a)(2) of this section. This schedule may be omitted if Schedule V is omitted.*

SEC 50520

Schedule VII. Guarantees of securities of other issuers. *The schedule prescribed by Rule 12-08 shall be filed with respect to any guarantees of securities of other issuers by the person for which the statement is filed.*

Schedule VIII. Valuation and qualifying accounts. *The schedule prescribed by Rule 12-09 shall be filed in support of valuation and qualifying accounts included in each balance sheet but not included in Schedule VI. (See Rule 4-02.)*

Although the accounts to be included in this schedule are only referred to in general terms, the purpose of this schedule appears to be the disclosure of activity in accounts that are discretionary in nature. FASB Statement No. 5, *Accounting for Contingencies*, precludes the recording of discretionary amounts such as contingency reserves if uncertainties exist; consequently, the accounts required to be included on this schedule are more limited now than when the schedule was originally adopted. Activity in the allowance for doubtful accounts is an example of the type of information to be included on this schedule.

Schedule IX. Short-term borrowings. *The schedule prescribed by Rule 12-10 shall be filed in support of caption 19 [Accounts and Notes Payable], [for] amounts payable to banks for borrowings; factors and financial institutions for borrowings; and holders of commercial paper. The information required by this schedule may be presented in Management's Discussion and Analysis if it results in a more meaningful presentation of the information being provided.*

The staff of the SEC has indicated that the information required by this schedule must be covered by the accountants' report even when presented in management's discussion and analysis.

Schedule X. Supplementary income statement information. *The schedule prescribed by Rule 12-11 may be omitted for each income statement in which sales or operating revenues were not of significant amount. This schedule may also be omitted if the information required by column B and instructions 3 and 5 thereof is furnished in the income statement or in a note thereto.*

The information required to be disclosed pursuant to Rule 12-11 is frequently included in a footnote in registration and proxy statements and, accordingly, a separate schedule is not prepared. Any items separately shown as captions in the income statements may be omitted from the schedule.

As noted in Rule 12-11, information with respect to any item that does not exceed one percent of total sales and revenues as reported in the income statement may also be omitted.

SEC 50520. Rule 5-04

Schedule XI. Real estate and accumulated depreciation. *The schedule prescribed by Rule 12-28 shall be filed for real estate (and the related accumulated depreciation) held by persons a substantial portion of whose business is that of acquiring and holding for investment real estate or interests in real estate, or interests in other persons a substantial portion of whose business is that of acquiring and holding real estate or interests in real estate for investment. Real estate used in the business shall be excluded from the schedule.*

Schedule XII. Mortgage loans on real estate. *The schedule prescribed by Rule 12-29 shall be filed by persons specified under Schedule XI for investments in mortgage loans on real estate.*

SAB Topic 7-C requires that the information required by Schedules XI and XII be included in the annual report to shareholders (see section 31320).

Schedule XIII. Other investments. *If there are any other investments, under caption 12 [Other Investments] of Rule 5-02 or elsewhere in a balance sheet, not required to be included in Schedule I, there shall be set forth in a separate schedule information concerning such investments corresponding to that prescribed by Schedule I. This schedule may be omitted if the total amount of such other investments does not exceed 5 percent of total assets as shown by such balance sheet.*

As noted, if this schedule is furnished it must follow the format required by Rule 12-02.

Schedule XIV. Supplemental information concerning property-casualty insurance operations. *The schedule prescribed by Rule 12-18 shall be filed when a registrant, its subsidiaries or 50%-or-less-owned equity basis investees, have liabilities for property-casualty ("P/C") insurance claims. The required information shall be presented as of the same dates and for the same periods for which the information is reflected in the audited consolidated financial statements required by Rules 3-01 and 3-02. The schedule may be omitted if reserves for unpaid P/C claims and claims adjustment expenses of the registrant and its consolidated subsidiaries and its 50%-or-less-owned equity basis investees did not, in the aggregate, exceed one-half of common stockholders' equity of the registrant and its consolidated subsidiaries as of the beginning of the fiscal year. For purposes of this test only the proportionate share of the registrant and its other subsidiaries in the reserves for unpaid claims and claim adjustment expenses of 50%-or-less-owned equity basis investees taken in the aggregate after inter-company eliminations shall be taken into account.*

As noted, if this schedule is furnished it must follow the format required by Rule 12-18.

50600. ARTICLE 6. REGISTERED INVESTMENT COMPANIES

NOTES: The following rules apply to management investment companies, unit investment trusts and face-amount certificate companies. Face-amount certificate companies require investors to make periodic fixed investments, typically for a period of 10 to 15 years. After the plan term, investors may choose to be paid on either a systematic basis or by a lump sum payment. Due to the diversity of investment alternatives now available and the relative inflexibility of face-amount certificate companies, few of these companies exist today.

50601. Rule 6-01. Application of Article 6

Rules 6-01 to 6-10 shall be applicable to financial statements filed for registered investment companies (i.e., companies issuing face-amount certificates).

50602. Rule 6-02. Definition of Certain Terms

The following terms shall have the meaning indicated in this rule unless the context otherwise requires (Also see Rule 1-02):

(a) Affiliate. *The term "affiliate" means an "affiliated person" as defined in section 2(a)(3) of the Investment Company Act of 1940 unless otherwise indicated. The term "control" has the meaning [given] in section 2(a)(9) of that Act.*

(b) Value. *As used in Rules 6-01 to 6-10, the term "value" shall have the meaning given in section 2(a)(41)(B) of the Investment Company Act of 1940.*

SEC 50600. Article 6

(c) Balance sheets; statements of net assets. *As used in Rules 6-01 to 6-10, the term "balance sheets" shall include statements of assets and liabilities as well as statements of net assets unless the context clearly indicates the contrary.*

(d) Qualified assets.

(1) For companies issuing face-amount certificates subsequent to December 31, 1940 under the provisions of section 28 of the Investment Company Act of 1940, the term "qualified assets" means qualified investments as that term is defined in section 28(b) of the Act. A statement to that effect shall be made in the balance sheet.

(2) For other companies, the term "qualified assets" means cash and investments which such companies do maintain or are required, by applicable governing legal instruments, to maintain in respect of outstanding face-amount certificate.

(3) Loans to certificate holders may be included as qualified assets in an amount not in excess of certificate reserves carried on the books of account in respect of each individual certificate upon which the loans were made.

50603. Rule 6-03. Special Rules of General Application to Registered Investment Companies

The financial statements filed for persons to which Rules 6-01 to 6-10 are applicable shall be prepared in accordance with the following special rules in addition to the general rules in Rules 1-01 to 4-10 (Articles 1, 2, 3, and 4). Where the requirements of a special rule differ from those prescribed in a general rule, the requirements of the special rule shall be met.

(a) Content of financial statements. *The financial statements shall be prepared in accordance with the requirements of this part (Regulation S-X) notwithstanding any provision of the articles of incorporation, trust indenture or other governing legal instruments specifying certain accounting procedures inconsistent with those required in Rules 6-01 to 6-10.*

(b) Audited financial statements. *Where, under Article 3 of this part, financial statements are required to be audited, the independent accountant shall have been selected and ratified in accordance with section 32 of the Investment Company Act of 1940.*

(c) Consolidated and combined statements.

(1) Consolidated and combined statements filed for registered investment companies shall be prepared in accordance with Rules 3A-01 to 3A-05 (Article 3A),

722

except that (i) statements of the registrant may be consolidated only with the statements of subsidiaries which are investment companies; (ii) a consolidated statement of the registrant and any of its investment company subsidiaries shall not be filed unless accompanied by a consolidating statement which sets forth the individual statements of each significant subsidiary included in the consolidated statement: Provided, however, that a consolidating statement need not be filed if all included subsidiaries are totally held; and (iii) consolidated or combined statements filed for subsidiaries not consolidated with the registrant shall not include any investment companies unless accompanied by consolidating or combining statements which set forth the individual statements of each included investment company which is a significant subsidiary.

(2) If consolidating or combining statements are filed, the amounts included under each caption in which financial data pertaining to affiliates is required to be furnished shall be subdivided to show separately the amounts (i) eliminated in consolidation and (ii) not eliminated in consolidation.

(d) Valuation of assets. The balance sheets of registered investment companies, other than issuers of face-amount certificates, shall reflect all investments at value, with the aggregate cost of each category of investment reported under Rules 6-04.1, 6-04.2, and 6-04.3 and of the total investments reported under Rule 6-04.4 or Rule 6-05.1 shown parenthetically. State in a note the methods used in determining value of investments. As required by section 28(b) of the Investment Company Act of 1940, "qualified" assets of face-amount certificate companies shall be valued in accordance with certain provisions of the Code of the District of Columbia. For guidance as to valuation of securities, see sections 404.03 to 404.05 of the Codification of Financial Reporting Policies.

(e) Qualified assets. State in a note the nature of any investments and other assets maintained or required to be maintained, by applicable legal instruments, in respect of outstanding face-amount certificates. If the nature of the qualifying assets and amount thereof are not subject to the provisions of section 28 of the Investment Company Act of 1940, a statement to that effect shall be made.

(f) Restricted securities. State in a note, unless disclosed elsewhere, the following information as to investment securities which cannot be offered for public sale without first being registered under the Securities Act of 1933 (restricted securities):

(1) The policy of the person with regard to acquisition of restricted securities.

(2) The policy of the person with regard to valuation of restricted securities. Specific comments shall be given as to the valuation of an investment in one or

more issues of securities of a company or group of affiliated companies if any part of such investment is restricted and the aggregate value of the investment in all issues of such company or affiliated group exceeds five percent of the value of total assets. (As used in this paragraph, the term "affiliated" shall have the meaning given in Rule 6-02(a) of this part.)

(3) A description of the person's rights with regard to demanding registration of any restricted securities held at the date of the latest balance sheet.

(g) Income recognition. *Dividends shall be included in income on the ex-dividend date; interest shall be accrued on a daily basis. Dividends declared on short positions existing on the record date shall be recorded on the ex-dividend date and included as an expense of the period.*

(h) Federal income taxes. *The company's status as a "regulated investment company" as defined in Subtitle A, Chapter 1, Subchapter M of the Internal Revenue Code, as amended, shall be stated in a note referred to in the appropriate statements. Such note shall also indicate briefly the principal assumptions on which the company relied in making or not making provisions for income taxes. However, a company which retains realized capital gains and designates such gains as a distribution to shareholders in accordance with section 852(b)(3)(D) of the Internal Revenue Code shall, on the last day of its taxable year (and not earlier), make provision for taxes on such undistributed capital gains realized during such year.*

(i) Issuance and repurchase by a registered investment company of its own securities. Disclose for each class of the company's securities:

(1) The number of shares, units, or principal amount of bonds sold during the period of report, the amount received therefor, and, in the case of shares sold by closed-end management investment companies, the difference, if any, between the amount received and the net asset value or preference in involuntary liquidation (whichever is appropriate) of securities of the same class prior to such sale; and

(2) The number of shares, units, or principal amount of bonds repurchased during the period of report and the cost thereof. Closed-end management investment companies shall furnish the following additional information as to securities repurchased during the period of report:

(i) As to bonds and preferred shares, the aggregate difference between cost and the face amount or preference in involuntary liquidation and, if applicable net assets taken at value as of the date of repurchase were less than such face amount or preference, the aggregate difference between cost and such net asset value;

(ii) As to common shares, the weighted average discount per share, expressed as a percentage, between cost of repurchase and the net asset value applicable to such shares at the date of repurchases.

The information required by paragraphs (i)(2)(i) and (ii) may be based on reasonable estimates if it is impracticable to determine the exact amounts involved.

(j) Series companies.

The information required by this part shall, in the case of a person which in essence is comprised of more than one separate investment company, be given as if each class or series of such investment company were a separate investment company; this shall not prevent the inclusion, at the option of such person, of information applicable to other classes or series of such person on a comparative basis, except as to footnotes which need not be comparative.

If the particular class or series for which information is provided may be affected by other classes or series of such investment company, such as by the offset of realized gains in one series with realized losses in another, or through contingent liabilities, such situation shall be disclosed.

(k) Certificate reserves.

(1) For companies issuing face-amount certificates subsequent to December 31, 1940 under the provisions of section 28 of the Investment Company Act of 1940, balance sheets shall reflect reserves for outstanding certificates computed in accordance with the provisions of section 28(a) of the Act.

(2) For other companies, balance sheets shall reflect reserves for outstanding certificates determined as follows:

(i) For certificates of the installment type, such amount which, together with the lesser of future payments by certificate holders as and when accumulated at a rate not to exceed 3 1/2 per centum per annum (or such other rate as may be appropriate under the circumstances of a particular case) compounded annually, shall provide the minimum maturity or face amount of the certificate when due.

(ii) For certificates of the fully paid type, such amount which, as and when accumulated at a rate not to exceed 3 1/2 per centum per annum (or such other rate as may be appropriate under the circumstances of a particular case) compounded annually, shall provide the amount or amounts payable when due.

SEC 50603. Rule 6-03

(iii) Such amount or accrual therefor, as shall have been credited to the account of any certificate holder in the form of any credit, or any dividend, or any interest in addition to the minimum maturity or face amount specified in the certificate, plus any accumulations on any amount so credited or accrued at rates required under the terms of the certificate.

(iv) An amount equal to all advance payments made by certificate holders, plus any accumulations thereon at rates required under the terms of the certificate.

(v) Amounts for other appropriate contingency reserves, for death and disability benefits or for reinstatement rights on any certificate providing for such benefits or rights.

(l) Inapplicable captions. *Attention is directed to the provisions of Rules 4-02 and 4-03 which permit the omission of separate captions in financial statements as to which the items and conditions are not present, or the amounts involved not significant. However, amounts involving directors, officers, and affiliates shall nevertheless be separately set forth except as otherwise specifically permitted under a particular caption.*

50604. Rule 6-04. Balance Sheets

This rule is applicable to balance sheets filed by registered investment companies except for persons who substitute a statement of net assets in accordance with the requirements specified in Rule 6-05, and issuers of face-amount certificates which are subject to the special provisions of Rule 6-06 of this part. Balance sheets filed under this rule shall comply with the following provisions:

ASSETS

1. Investments in securities of unaffiliated issuers.

2. Investments in and advances to affiliates. *State separately investments in and advances to (a) controlled companies and (b) other affiliates.*

3. Investments—other than securities. *State separately each major category.*

4. Total investments.

5. Cash. *Include under this caption cash on hand and demand deposits. Provide in a note to the financial statements the information required under Rule 5-02.1 regarding restrictions and compensating balances.*

SEC 50604

6. Receivables.

(a) State separately amounts receivable from (1) sales of investments; (2) subscriptions to capital shares; (3) dividends and interest; (4) directors and officers; and (5) others.

(b) If the aggregate amount of notes receivable exceeds 10 percent of the aggregate amount of receivables, the above information shall be set forth separately, in the balance sheet or in a note thereto, for accounts receivable and notes receivable.

7. Deposits for securities sold short and open option contracts. *State separately amounts held by others in connection with:*

(a) Short sales and

(b) Open option contract.

8. Other assets. *State separately:*

(a) Prepaid and deferred expenses;

(b) Pension and other special funds;

(c) Organization expenses; and

If "seed money" stock is redeemed prior to complete amortization (typically over 60 months) of deferred organization expenses, the SEC staff will generally require the fund to expense the related pro rata share of such deferred expenses relating to the "seed money" shares that have been redeemed and to disclose its accounting policy for expensing such deferred expenses in the notes to the financial statements.

(d) Any other significant item not properly classified in another asset caption.

9. Total assets.

LIABILITIES

10. Accounts payable and accrued liabilities. *State separately amounts payable for:*

(a) Securities sold short;

(b) Open option contracts written;

(c) Other purchases of securities;

(d) Capital shares redeemed;

SEC 50604. Rule 6-04

(e) Dividends or other distributions on capital shares; and

(f) Others. State separately the amount of any other liabilities which are material. Securities sold short and open option contracts written shall be stated at value.

11. Deposits for securities loaned. *State the value of securities loaned and indicate the nature of the collateral received as security for the loan, including the amount of any cash received.*

12. Other liabilities. *State separately:*

(a) Amounts payable for investment advisory, management and service fees; and

(b) The total amount payable to (1) officers and directors; (2) controlled companies; and (3) other affiliates, excluding any amounts owing to noncontrolled affiliates which arose in the ordinary course of business and which are subject to usual trade terms.

13. Notes payable, bonds and similar debt.

(a) State separately amounts payable to (1) banks or other financial institutions for borrowings; (2) controlled companies; (3) other affiliates; and (4) others, showing for each category amounts payable within one year and amounts payable after one year.

(b) Provide in a note the information required under Rule 5-02.19(b) regarding unused lines of credit for short-term financing and Rule 5-02.22(b) regarding unused commitments for long-term financing arrangements.

14. Total liabilities.

15. Commitments and contingent liabilities.

NET ASSETS

16. Units of capital.

(a) Disclose the title of each class of capital shares or other capital units, the number authorized, the number outstanding, and the dollar amount thereof.

(b) Unit investment trust, including those which are issuers of periodic payment plan certificates, also shall state in a note to the financial statements (1) the total cost to the investors of each class of units or shares; (2) the adjustment for market depreciation or appreciation; (3) other deductions from the total cost to the investors for fees, loads and other charges, including an explanation of such deductions; and (4) the net amount applicable to the investors.

SEC 50604

17. Accumulated undistributed income (loss). *Disclose:*

(a) The accumulated undistributed investment income — net,

(b) Accumulated undistributed net realized gains (losses) on investment transactions, and

(c) Net unrealized appreciation (depreciation) in value of investments at the balance sheet date.

18. Other elements of capital. *Disclose any other elements of capital or residual interests appropriate to the capital structure of the reporting entity.*

It is important to note that the information required by Items 16 (Units of capital), 17 (Accumulated undistributed income (loss)), and 18 (Other elements of capital) need to be disclosed on the face of the balance sheet. It is not appropriate for this information to be included in a footnote as permitted for a statement of net assets prepared pursuant to Rule 6-05 (see section 50605).

19. Net assets applicable to outstanding units of capital. *State the net asset value per share.*

In accordance with the instructions to Item 23 of Form N1-A, the "specimen price make up sheet" required by Item 19(b) of Form N1-A may be furnished as a continuation of this statement.

50605. Rule 6-05. Statements of Net Assets

In lieu of the balance sheet otherwise required by Rule 6-04 of this part, persons may substitute a statement of net assets if at least 95 percent of the amount of the person's total assets are represented by investments in securities of unaffiliated issuers. If presented in such instances, a statement of net assets shall consist of the following:

1. A schedule of investments in securities of unaffiliated issuers as prescribed in Rule 12-12.

In accordance with industry practice, municipal bond funds typically report investments by state and international funds, by country, with supplemental disclosure of the industries represented.

The staff has indicated that registrants need to identify payment-in-kind bonds or securities, as well as any security, the valuation of which has been determined or adjusted by the directors or trustees of the fund.

SEC 50604. Rule 6-04

It is our understanding that the SEC does not consider securities acquired under the provisions of Rule 144A to be "a priori" restricted. Rule 144A trades can be effected between qualified institutional investors. Identification and disclosure of Rule 144A holdings is optional.

Registrants also need to adequately disclose the risks related to "high yield" securities ("junk bonds").

In addition, disclosure should be provided regarding any investments in defaulted debt securities or securities (equity or debt) of issuers that have sought bankruptcy law protection. Simply indicating that a debt security is nonincome producing in lieu of indicating that it, in fact, has defaulted on principal and/or interest payments or has filed under the bankruptcy laws would not be adequate disclosure in this regard, notwithstanding the fact that the valuation of such securities reflects the defaulted or bankrupt condition of the issuer.

2. The excess (or deficiency) of other assets over (under) total liabilities stated in one amount, except that any amounts due from or to officers, directors, controlled persons, or other affiliates, excluding any amounts owing to noncontrolled affiliates which arose in the ordinary course of business and which are subject to usual trade terms, shall be stated separately.

3. Disclosure shall be provided in the notes to the financial statements for any item required under Rules 6-04.10 to 6-04.13.

4. The balance of the amounts captioned as net assets. The number of outstanding shares and net asset value per share shall be shown parenthetically.

5. The information required by (i) Rule 6-04.16, (ii) Rule 6-04.17 and (iii) Rule 6-04.18 shall be furnished in a note to the financial statements.

50606. Rule 6-06. Special Provisions Applicable to the Balance Sheets of Issuers of Face-Amount Certificates

Balance sheets filed by issuers of face-amount certificates shall comply with the following provisions:

ASSETS

1. Investments. *State separately each major category: such as, real estate owned, first mortgage loans on real estate, other mortgage loans on real estate, investments in securities of unaffiliated issuers, and investments in and advances to affiliates.*

2. Cash. *Include under this caption cash on hand and demand deposits. Provide in a note to the financial statements the information required under Rule 5-02.1 regarding restrictions and compensating balances.*

SEC 50606

3. Receivables.

(a) State separately amounts receivable from (1) sales of investments; (2) dividends and interest; (3) directors and officers; and (4) others.

(b) If the aggregate amount of notes receivable exceeds 10 percent of the aggregate amount of receivables, the above information shall be set forth separately, in the balance sheet or in a note thereto, for accounts receivable and notes receivable.

4. Total qualified assets. State in a note to the financial statements the amount of qualified assets on deposit classified as to general categories of assets and as to general types of depositories, such as banks and states, together with a statement as to the purpose of the deposits.

5. Other assets. State separately:

(a) Investments in securities of unaffiliated issuers not included in qualifying assets in item 1 above;

(b) Investments in and advances to affiliates not included in qualifying assets in item 1 above; and

(c) Any other significant item not properly classified in another asset caption.

6. Total assets.

LIABILITIES

7. Certificate reserves. Issuers of face-amount certificates shall state separately reserves for:

(a) Certificates of the installment type;

(b) Certificates of the fully paid type;

(c) Advance payments;

(d) Additional amounts accrued for or credited to the account of certificate holders in the form of any credit, dividend, or interest in addition to the minimum amount specified in the certificate; and

(e) Other certificate reserves.

State in an appropriate manner the basis used in determining the reserves, including the rates of interest of accumulation.

SEC 50606. Rule 6-06

8. Notes payable, bonds and similar debt.

(a) State separately amounts payable to (1) banks or other financial institutions for borrowings; (2) controlled companies; (3) other affiliates; and (4) others, showing for each category amounts payable within one year and amounts payable after one year.

(b) Provide in a note the information required under Rule 5-02.19(b) regarding unused lines of credit for short-term financing and Rule 5-02.22(b) regarding unused commitments for long-term financing arrangements.

9. Accounts payable and accrued liabilities. *State separately:*

(a) Amounts payable for investment advisory, management and service fees; and

(b) The total amount payable to (1) officers and directors; (2) controlled companies; and (3) other affiliates, excluding any amounts owing to noncontrolled affiliates which arose in the ordinary course of business and which are subject to usual trade terms.

State separately the amount of any other liabilities which are material.

10. Total liabilities.

11. Commitments and contingent liabilities.

STOCKHOLDERS' EQUITY

12. Capital shares. *Disclose the title of each class of capital shares or other capital units, the number authorized, the number outstanding and the dollar amount thereof. Show also the dollar amount of any capital shares subscribed but unissued, and show the deduction for subscriptions receivable therefrom.*

13. Other elements of capital.

(a) Disclose any other elements of capital or residual interests appropriate to the capital structure of the reporting entity.

(b) A summary of each account under this caption setting forth the information prescribed in Rule 3-04 shall be given in a note or separate statement for each period in which a statement of operations is presented.

14. Total liabilities and stockholders' equity.

SEC 50606

50607. Rule 6-07. Statements of Operations

Statements of operations filed by registered investment companies, other than issuers of face-amount certificates subject to the special provisions of Rule 6-08 of this part, shall comply with the following provisions:

1. Investment income. *State separately income from:*

(a) Dividends;

(b) Interest on securities; and

(c) Other income.

If income from investments in or indebtedness of affiliates is included hereunder, such income shall be segregated under an appropriate caption subdivided to show separately income from (1) controlled companies; and (2) other affiliates. If non-cash dividends are included in income, the bases of recognition and measurement used in respect to such amounts shall be disclosed. Any other category of income which exceeds five percent of the total shown under this caption shall be stated separately.

2. Expenses.

(a) State separately the total amount of investment advisory, management, and service fees, and expenses in connection with research, selection, supervision, and custody of investments. Amounts of expenses incurred from transactions with affiliated persons shall be disclosed together with the identity of and related amount applicable to each such person accounting for five percent or more of the total expenses shown under this caption together with a description of the nature of the affiliation. Expenses incurred within the person's own organization in connection with research, selection and supervision of investments shall be stated separately. Reductions or reimbursements of management or service fees shall be shown as a negative amount or as a reduction of total expenses shown under this caption.

(b) State separately any other expense items the amount of which exceeds five percent of the total expenses shown under this caption.

(c) A note to the financial statements shall include information concerning management and service fees, the rate of fee, and the base and method of computation. State separately the amount and a description of any fee reductions or reimbursements representing (1) expense limitation agreements or commitments and (2) offsets received from broker-dealers showing separately for each amount received or due from (i) unaffiliated persons and (ii) affiliated

persons. If no management or service fees were incurred for a period, state the reason therefor.

(d) If any expenses were paid otherwise than in cash, state the details in a note.

(e) State in a note to the financial statements the amount of brokerage commissions (including dealer markups) paid to affiliated broker-dealers in connection with purchase and sale of investment securities. Open-end management companies shall state in a note the net amounts of sales charges deducted from the proceeds of sale of capital shares which were retained by any affiliated principal underwriter or other affiliated broker-dealer.

(f) State separately all amounts paid in accordance with a plan adopted under Rule 12b-1 of the Investment Company Act of 1940. Reimbursement to the fund of expenses incurred under such plan (12b-1 expense reimbursement) shall be shown as a negative amount and deducted from current 12b-1 expenses. If 12b-1 expense reimbursements exceed current 12b-1 costs, such excess shall be shown as a negative amount used in the calculation of total expenses under this caption.

It is worthy of particular note that as long as expenses are incurred on behalf of an investment company, such expenses should be reflected in the statement of operations. In situations in which expenses are waived or subject to reimbursement, the preferred accounting treatment is to reflect the amount of such waiver or reimbursement as a reduction of total expenses rather than as a reduction of specific line items. The latter is, however, an optional presentation.

In such situations, a footnote should explain the voluntary and/or involuntary nature of, and the amounts attributable to, the fee waiver or reimbursement. It is important to note that it is possible for an investment company to have both an involuntary and voluntary type of fee reduction at the same time.

3. Interest and amortization of debt discount and expense.

4. Investment income before income tax expense.

5. Income tax expense. *Include under this caption only taxes based on income.*

6. Investment income—net.

7. Realized and unrealized gain (loss) on investments—net.

(a) State separately the net realized gain or loss on transactions in (1) investment securities of unaffiliated issuers, (2) investment securities of affiliated issuers, and (3) investments other than securities.

(b) Distributions of realized gains by other investment companies shall be shown separately under this caption.

(c) State separately (1) the gain or loss from expiration or closing of option contracts written, (2) the gain or loss on closed short positions in securities, and (3) other realized gain or loss. Disclose in a note to the financial statements the number and associated dollar amounts as to option contracts written: (i) at the beginning of the period; (ii) during the period; (iii) expired during the period; (iv) closed during the period; (v) exercised during the period; and (vi) balance at end of the period.

(d) State separately the amount of the net increase or decrease during the period in the unrealized appreciation or depreciation in the value of investment securities and other investments held at the end of the period.

(e) State separately any (1) federal income taxes and (2) other income taxes applicable to realized and unrealized gain (loss) on investments, distinguishing taxes payable currently from deferred income taxes.

8. Net gain (loss) on investments.

9. Net increase (decrease) in net assets resulting from operations.

50608. Rule 6-08. Special Provisions Applicable to the Statements of Operations of Issuers of Face-Amount Certificates

Statements of operations filed by issuers of face-amount certificates shall comply with the following provisions:

1. Investment income. *State separately income from:*

(a) Interest on mortgages;

(b) Interest on securities;

(c) Dividends;

(d) Rental income; and

(e) Other investment income.

If income from investments in or indebtedness of affiliates is included hereunder, such income shall be segregated under an appropriate caption subdivided to show separately income from (1) controlled companies and (2) other affiliates. If non-cash dividends are included in income, the bases of recognition and measurement used in respect to such amounts shall be disclosed. *Any other category of income which exceeds five percent of the total shown under this caption shall be stated separately.*

2. Investment expenses.

(a) State separately the total amount of investment advisory, management and service fees, and expenses in connection with research, selection, supervision, and custody of investments. Amounts of expenses incurred from transactions with affiliated persons shall be disclosed together with the identity of and related amount applicable to each such person accounting for five percent or more of the total expenses shown under this caption together with a description of the nature of the affiliation. Expenses incurred within the person's own organization in connection with research, selection and supervision of investments shall be stated separately. Reductions or reimbursements of management or service fees shall be shown as a negative amount or as a reduction of total expenses shown under this caption.

(b) State separately any other expense item the amount of which exceeds five percent of the total expenses shown under this caption.

(c) A note to the financial statements shall include information concerning management and service fees, the rate of fee, and the base and method of computation. State separately the amount and a description of any fee reductions or reimbursements representing (1) expense limitation agreements or commitments; and (2) offsets received from broker-dealers showing separately for each amount received or due from (i) unaffiliated persons; and (ii) affiliated persons. If no management or service fees were incurred for a period, state the reason therefor.

(d) If any expenses were paid otherwise than in cash, state the details in a note.

(e) State in a note to the financial statements the amount of brokerage commissions (including dealer markups) paid to affiliated broker-dealers in connection with purchase and sale of investment securities.

3. Interest and amortization of debt discount and expense.

4. Provision for certificate reserves. *State separately any provision for additional credits, or dividends, or interests, in addition to the minimum maturity or face amount specified in the certificates. State also in an appropriate manner reserve recoveries from surrenders or other causes.*

5. Investment income before income tax expense.

6. Income tax expense. *Include under this caption only taxes based on income.*

7. Investment income—net.

8. Realized gain (loss) on investments—net.

> *(a) State separately the net realized gain or loss on transactions in (1) investment securities of unaffiliated issuers, (2) investment securities of affiliated issuers, and (3) other investments.*

> *(b) Distributions of capital gains by other investment companies shall be shown separately under this caption.*

> *(c) State separately any (1) federal income taxes and (2) other income taxes applicable to realized gain (loss) on investments, distinguishing taxes payable currently from deferred income taxes.*

9. Net income or loss.

50609. Rule 6-09. Statements of Changes in Net Assets

Statements of changes in net assets filed for persons to whom this article is applicable shall comply with the following provisions:

1. Operations. *State separately:*

> *(a) Investment income — net as shown by Rule 6-07.6;*

> *(b) Realized gain (loss) on investments — net of any federal or other income taxes applicable to such amounts;*

> *(c) Increase (decrease) in unrealized appreciation or depreciation — net of any Federal or other income taxes applicable to such amounts; and*

> *(d) Net increase (decrease) in net assets resulting from operations as shown by Rule 6-07.9.*

2. Net equalization charges and credits. *State the net amount of accrued undivided earnings separately identified in the price of capital shares issued and repurchased.*

3. Distributions to shareholders. *State separately distributions to shareholders from:*

> *(a) Investment income — net;*

> *(b) Realized gain from investment transactions — net; and*

> *(c) Other sources.*

SEC 50608. Rule 6-08

It is generally considered appropriate to parenthetically disclose distributions to shareholders on a per-share basis. In addition, since return of capital distributions can only be measured on an annual basis, such disclosure should only be made with respect to annual financial statements.

4. Capital share transactions.

(a) State the increase or decrease in net assets derived from the net change in the number of outstanding shares or units.

(b) Disclose in the body of the statements or in the notes, for each class of the person's shares, the number and value of shares issued in reinvestment of dividends as well as the number and dollar amounts received for shares sold and paid for shares redeemed.

5. Total increase (decrease).

6. Net assets at the beginning of the period.

7. Net assets at the end of the period. *Disclose parenthetically the balance of undistributed net investment income included in net assets at the end of the period.*

50610. Rule 6-10. What Schedules Are To Be Filed

(a) When information is required in schedules for both the person and the person and its subsidiaries consolidated, it may be presented in the form of a single schedule, provided that items pertaining to the registrant are separately shown and that such single schedule affords a properly summarized presentation of the facts. If the information required by any schedule (including the notes thereto) is shown in the related financial statement or in a note thereto without making such statement unclear or confusing, that procedure may be followed and the schedule omitted.

(b) The schedules shall be examined by an independent accountant if the related financial statements are so examined.

(c) **Management investment companies.** *Except as otherwise provided in the applicable form, the schedules specified below in this rule shall be filed for management investment companies as of the dates of the most recent audited balance sheet and any subsequent unaudited statement being filed for each person or group.*

Schedule I—Investments in securities of unaffiliated issuers. *The schedule prescribed by Rule 12-12 shall be filed in support of caption 1 of each balance sheet.*

Schedule II—Investments — other than securities. *The schedule prescribed by Rule 12-13 shall be filed in support of caption 3 of each balance sheet. This schedule may be omitted if the investments, other than securities, at both the beginning and end of the period amount to less than one percent of the value of total investments (Rule 6-04.4).*

Schedule III—Investments in and advances to affiliates. *The schedule prescribed by Rule 12-14 shall be filed in support of caption 2 of each balance sheet.*

Schedule IV—Amounts due from directors and officers. *The schedule prescribed by Rule 12-03 shall be filed with respect to each person among the directors and officers from whom any amount was owed at any time during the period for which related statements of changes in net assets are required to be filed.*

Schedule V—Investments — securities sold short. *The schedule prescribed by Rule 12-12A shall be filed in support of caption 10(a) of each balance sheet.*

Schedule VI—Open option contracts written. *The schedule prescribed by Rule 12-12B shall be filed in support of caption 10(b) of each balance sheet.*

Schedule VII—Short-term borrowings. *The schedule prescribed by Rule 12-10 shall be filed in support of any amounts included in caption 13 of each balance sheet which are payable within one year to banks for borrowings; factors and other financial institutions for borrowings; and holders of any short-term notes.*

(d) **Unit investment trusts.** *Except as otherwise provided in the applicable form:*

(1) Schedules I and II, specified below in this section, shall be filed for unit investment trusts as of the dates of the most recent audited balance sheet and any subsequent unaudited statement being filed for each person or group.

(2) Schedule III, specified below in this section, shall be filed for unit investment trusts for each period for which a statement of operations is required to be filed for each person or group.

Schedule I—Investment in securities. *The schedule prescribed by Rule 12-12 shall be filed in support of caption 1 of each balance sheet (Rule 6-04).*

Schedule II—Allocation of trust assets to series of trust shares. *If the trust assets are specifically allocated to different series of trust shares, and if such allocation is not shown in the balance sheet in columnar form or by the filing of separate statements for each series of trust shares, a schedule shall be filed*

SEC 50610. Rule 6-10

showing the amount of trust assets, indicated by each balance sheet filed, which is applicable to each series of trust shares.

Schedule III—Allocation of trust income and distributable funds to series of trust shares. *If the trust income and distributable funds are specifically allocated to different series of trust shares and if such allocation is not shown in the statement of operations in columnar form or by the filing of separate statements for each series of trust shares, a schedule shall be submitted showing the amount of income and distributable funds, indicated by each statement of operations filed, which is applicable to each series of trust shares.*

(e) **Face-amount certificate investment companies.** *Except as otherwise provided in the applicable form:*

(1) Schedules I, V and X, specified below, shall be filed for face-amount certificate investment companies as of the dates of the most recent audited balance sheet and any subsequent unaudited statement being filed for each person or group.

(2) All other schedules specified below in this section shall be filed for face-amount certificate investment companies for each period for which a statement of operations is filed, except as indicated for Schedules III and IV.

Schedule I—Investment in securities of unaffiliated issuers. *The schedule prescribed by Rule 12-21 shall be filed in support of caption 1 and, if applicable, caption 5(a) of each balance sheet. Separate schedules shall be furnished in support of each caption, if applicable.*

Schedule II—Investments in and advances to affiliates and income thereon. *The schedule prescribed by Rule 12-22 shall be filed in support of captions 1 and 5(b) of each balance sheet and caption 1 of each statement of operations. Separate schedules shall be furnished in support of each caption, if applicable.*

Schedule III—Mortgage loans on real estate and interest earned on mortgages. *The schedule prescribed by Rule 12-23 shall be filed in support of captions 1 and 5(c) of each balance sheet and caption 1 of each statement of operations, except that only the information required by column G and note 8 of the schedule need be furnished in support of statements of operations for years for which related balance sheets are not required.*

Schedule IV—Real estate owned and rental income. *The schedule prescribed by Rule 12-24 shall be filed in support of captions 1 and 5(a) of each balance sheet and caption 1 of each statement of operations for rental income included* *therein, except that only the information required by columns H, I and J, and item "Rent from properties sold during the period" and note 4 of the schedule need be furnished in support of statements of operations for years for which related balance sheets are not required.*

Schedule V—Qualified assets on deposit. *The schedule prescribed by Rule 12-27 shall be filed in support of the information required by caption 4 of Rule 6-06 as to total amount of qualified assets on deposit.*

Schedule VI—Amounts due from officers and directors. *The schedule prescribed by Rule 12-03 shall be filed with respect to each director, officer, or employee from whom any amount was owed at any time during the period for which related statements of operations are filed. State if an exemption has been granted by the Commission with respect to amounts included in this schedule.*

Schedule VII—Short-term borrowings. *The schedule prescribed by Rule 12-10 shall be filed in support of any amounts included in caption 8 of each balance sheet which are payable within one year to banks for borrowings; factors and other financial institutions for borrowings; and holders of any short-term notes.*

Schedule VIII—Indebtedness to affiliates—not current. *The schedule prescribed by Rule 12-05 shall be filed in support of any amounts included in caption 9 of each balance sheet. This schedule and Schedule II may be combined.*

Schedule IX—Supplementary profit and loss information. *The schedule prescribed by Rule 12-25 shall be filed in support of each statement of operations.*

Schedule X—Guarantees of securities of other issuers. *The schedule prescribed by Rule 12-08 shall be filed with respect to any guarantees of securities of other issuers by the person for which the statement is filed.*

Schedule XI—Certificate reserves. *The schedule prescribed by Rule 12-26 shall be filed in support of caption 7 of each balance sheet.*

Schedule XII—Valuation and qualifying accounts. *The schedule prescribed by Rule 12-09 shall be filed in support of all other reserves included in the balance sheet.*

50620. ARTICLE 6A. EMPLOYEE
STOCK PURCHASE, SAVINGS, AND SIMILAR PLANS

50621. Rule 6A-01. Application of Article 6A

Rules 6A-01 to 6A-05 shall be applicable to financial statements filed for employee stock purchase, savings, and similar plans.

Refer to Form 11-K (section 41300) for additional guidance regarding employee stock purchase, savings, and similar plans.

50622. Rule 6A-02. Special Rules Applicable to Employee Stock Purchase, Savings, and Similar Plans

The financial statements filed for persons to which this article is applicable shall be prepared in accordance with the following special rules in addition to the general rules in Rules 1-01 to 4-10. Where the requirements of a special rule differ from those prescribed in a general rule, the requirements of the special rule shall be met.

(a) Investment programs. *If the participating employees have an option as to the manner in which their deposits and contributions may be invested, a description of each investment program shall be given in a footnote or otherwise. The number of employees under each investment program shall be stated.*

(b) Net asset value per unit. *Where appropriate, the number of units and the net asset value per unit shall be given by footnote or otherwise.*

(c) Federal income taxes.

(1) If the plan is not subject to Federal income taxes, a note shall so state indicating briefly the principal assumptions on which the plan relied in not making provision for such taxes.

(2) State the Federal income tax status of the employee with respect to the plan.

SEC 50622

(d) Valuation of assets. *The statement of financial condition shall reflect all investments at value, showing cost parenthetically. For purposes of this rule, the term "value" shall mean (1) market value for those securities having readily available market quotations and (2) fair value as determined in good faith by the trustee(s) for the plan (or by the person or persons who exercise similar responsibilities) with respect to other securities and assets.*

50623. Rule 6A-03. Statements of Financial Condition

Statements of financial condition filed under this rule shall comply with the following provisions:

PLAN ASSETS

1. Investments in securities of participating employers. *State separately each class of securities of the participating employer or employers.*

2. Investments in securities of unaffiliated issuers.

(a) United States Government bonds and other obligations. Include only direct obligations of the United States Government.

(b) Other securities. State separately:

(1) Marketable securities and

(2) Other securities.

3. Investments. Other than securities. *State separately each major class.*

4. Dividends and interest receivable.

5. Cash.

6. Other assets. *State separately:*

(a) Total of amounts due from participating employers or any of their directors, officers and principal holders of equity securities;

(b) Total of amounts due from trustees or managers of the plan; and

(c) Any other significant amounts.

LIABILITIES AND PLAN EQUITY

7. Liabilities. *State separately:*

    (a) Total of amounts payable to participating employers;

    (b) Total of amounts payable to participating employees; and

    (c) Any other significant amounts.

8. Reserves and other credits. *State separately each significant item and describe each such item by using an appropriate caption or by a footnote referred to in the caption.*

9. Plan equity at close of period.

50624. Rule 6A-04. Statements of Income and Changes in Plan Equity

Statements of income and changes in plan equity filed under this rule shall comply with the following provisions:

1. Net investment income.

    (a) Income. State separately income from (1) cash dividends; (2) interest; and (3) other sources. Income from investments in or indebtedness of participating employers shall be segregated under the appropriate sub-caption.

    (b) Expenses. State separately any significant amounts.

    (c) Net investment income.

2. Realized gain or loss on investments.

    (a) State separately the net of gains or losses arising from transactions in (1) investments in securities of the participating employer or employers; (2) other investments in securities; and (3) other investments.

    (b) State in a footnote or otherwise for each category of investment in paragraph (a) above the aggregate cost, the aggregate proceeds and the net gain or loss. State the principle followed in determining the cost of securities sold, e.g., "the average cost" or "first-in, first-out."

3. Unrealized appreciation or depreciation of investments.

(a) State the amount of increase or decrease in unrealized appreciation or depreciation of investments during the period.

(b) State in a footnote or otherwise the amount of unrealized appreciation or depreciation of investments at the beginning of the period of report, at the end of the period of report, and the increase or decrease during the period.

4. Contributions and deposits.

(a) State separately (1) total of amounts deposited by participating employees, and (2) total of amounts contributed by the participating employer or employers.

(b) If employees of more than one employer participate in the plan, state in tabular form in a footnote or otherwise the amount contributed by each employer and the deposits of the employees of each such employer.

5. Withdrawals, lapses and forfeitures. *State separately:*

(a) Balances of employees' accounts withdrawn, lapsed or forfeited during the period;

(b) Amounts disbursed in settlement of such accounts; and

(c) Disposition of balances remaining after settlement specified in (b).

6. Plan equity at beginning of period.

7. Plan equity at end of period.

50625. Rule 6A-05. What Schedules Are To Be Filed

Schedule I, specified below, shall be filed as of the most recent audited statement of financial condition and any subsequent unaudited statement of financial condition being filed. Schedule II shall be filed as of the date of each statement of financial condition being filed. Schedule III shall be filed for each period for which a statement of income and changes in plan equity is filed. All schedules shall be audited if the related statements are audited.

Schedule I. Investments. *A schedule substantially in the form prescribed by Rule 12-12 shall be filed in support of captions 1, 2 and 3 of each statement of financial condition unless substantially all of the information is given in the statement of financial condition by footnote or otherwise.*

SEC 50624. Rule 6A-04

Schedule II. Allocation of plan assets and liabilities to investment program. *If the plan provides for separate investment programs with separate funds, and if the allocation of assets and liabilities to the several funds is not shown in the statement of financial condition in columnar form or by the submission of separate statements for each fund, a schedule shall be submitted showing the allocation of each caption of each statement of financial condition filed to the applicable fund.*

Schedule III. Allocation of plan income and changes in plan equity to investment programs. *If the plan provides for separate investment programs with separate funds, and if the allocation of income and changes in plan equity to the several funds is not shown in the statement of income and changes in plan equity in columnar form or by the submission of separate statements for each fund, a schedule shall be submitted showing the allocation of each caption of each statement of income and changes in plan equity filed to the applicable fund.*

<h1 style="text-align:center">50700. ARTICLE 7.
INSURANCE COMPANIES</h1>

50701. Rule 7-01. Application of Article 7

This article shall be applicable to financial statements filed for insurance companies.

50702. Rule 7-02. General Requirements

(a) The requirements of the general rules in Rules 1-01 to 4-10 (Articles 1, 2, 3, 3A and 4) shall be applicable except where they differ from requirements of Rules 7-01 to 7-05.

(b) Financial statements filed for mutual life insurance companies and wholly-owned stock insurance company subsidiaries of mutual life insurance companies may be prepared in accordance with statutory accounting requirements. Financial statements prepared in accordance with statutory accounting requirements may be condensed as appropriate, but the amounts to be reported for net gain from operations (or net income or loss) and total capital and surplus (or surplus as regards policyholders) shall be the same as those reported on the corresponding Annual Statement.

When filing financial statements in accordance with statutory accounting requirements as permitted by paragraph (b) of Rule 7-02, registrants and their independent accountants need to consider the guidance set forth in FASB Interpretation No. 40 (FIN 40), *Applicability of Generally Accepted Accounting Principles to Mutual Life Insurance and Other Enterprises.* FIN 40 clarifies that any enterprise (including mutual life insurance enterprises) that prepares financial statements described as being presented "in conformity with generally accepted accounting principles" are required to prepare such statements applying all applicable authoritative accounting pronouncements. FIN 40 concludes that financial statements prepared based on regulatory accounting principles that differ from GAAP should not describe such statements as prepared "in conformity with generally accepted accounting principles." FIN 40 is effective for financial statements issued for fiscal years beginning after December 15, 1994 with earlier application encouraged. However, prior to its adoption (and effective for financial statements issued for fiscal years beginning after December 15, 1992), enterprises are required to provide a brief description of the Interpretation and disclose that financial statements prepared based on statutory accounting practices will no longer be described as prepared in conformity with generally accepted accounting principles when the Interpretation becomes effective.

As indicated throughout Article 7, the disclosure requirements for items that are not unique to insurance companies (e.g., common stock) often refer to the requirements specified in Article 5 relating to commercial and industrial companies.

SAB Topic 11-K, added by SAB No. 69 (see section 50901), indicates that entities with similar activities should provide disclosures required by Industry Guide 3, *Statistical Disclosures for Bank Holding Companies*. The SEC staff has also informally indicated that an insurance company that engages in significant financial intermediation activities should consider whether disclosures similar to those set forth in Industry Guide 3 are necessary. For example, the staff has indicated that life insurance companies that primarily sell investment contracts and invest primarily in mortgage loans would need considerable Industry Guide 3 disclosures. Conversely, a property-casualty company that primarily sells auto insurance and invests in U.S. Treasury securities would need a minimal amount of Industry Guide 3 disclosures.

Property-casualty insurance underwriters also need to refer to 1933 Act Industry Guide 6 and 1934 Act Industry Guide 4, *Disclosures Concerning Unpaid Claims and Claim Adjustment Expenses of Property-Casualty Underwriters*. Among other items, these guides contain additional discussion topics to be addressed by companies in the description of business, including the provision of an analysis of changes in claim and claim adjustment expense reserves, and providing a loss-development table.

It is also worthy of note that insurance companies involved in multiple-year retrospectively-rated reinsurance arrangements (RRCs) should refer to the guidance set forth in EITF Issue No. 93-6, "Accounting for Multiple-Year Retrospectively-Rated Contracts by Ceding and Assuming Enterprises." RRCs are defined as contracts between a primary insurer (or ceding company) and a reinsurer (or assuming company) that include an obligatory "retrospective rating" provision that provides for:

- Changes in the amount or timing of the contractual cash flows; or

- Changes in the contract's coverage.

Examples of these contracts include transactions referred to as "funded catastrophe covers." Under the EITF consensus, RRCs that meet certain conditions should be accounted for as reinsurance as follows:

- The ceding and assuming enterprises should recognize a liability and an asset, respectively, to the extent that the ceding enterprise has an obligation to pay cash (or other consideration) to the reinsurer that would not have been required absent contract experience.

- The ceding and assuming enterprises should recognize an asset and a liability, respectively, to the extent that any cash (or other consideration) would be payable from the assuming enterprise to the ceding enterprise based on contract experience to date.

A deposit method of accounting should be used to account for RRCs outside of the scope of the consensus. Insurance companies that use RRCs should refer to EITF Issue No. 93-6 for further guidance on the scope, calculation of the liability, and transition to be used in accounting for RRCs.

50703. Rule 7-03. Balance Sheets

The purpose of this rule is to indicate the various items which, if applicable, and except as otherwise permitted by the Commission, should appear on the face of the balance sheets and in the notes thereto filed for persons to whom this article pertains. (See Rule 4-01(a).)

ASSETS

1. Investments—other than investments in related parties.

(a) Fixed maturities.

(b) Equity securities.

(c) Mortgage loans on real estate.

(d) Investment real estate.

(e) Policy loans.

(f) Other long-term investments.

(g) Short-term investments.

(h) Total investments.

NOTES:

(1) State parenthetically or otherwise in the balance sheet (a) the basis of determining the amounts shown in the balance sheet and (b) as to fixed maturities and equity securities either aggregate cost or aggregate value at the balance sheet date, whichever is the alternate amount of the carrying value in the balance sheet. Consideration shall be given to the discussion of "Valuation of Securities" in 404.03 of the Codification of Financial Reporting Policies.

(2) Include under fixed maturities: bonds, notes, marketable certificates of deposit with maturities beyond one year, and redeemable preferred stocks. Include under equity securities: common stocks and nonredeemable preferred stocks.

(3) State separately in the balance sheet or in a note thereto the amount of accumulated depreciation and amortization deducted from investment real estate. Subcaption (d) shall not include real estate acquired in settling title claims, mortgage guaranty claims, and similar insurance claims. Real estate acquired in settling claims shall be included in caption 10, "Other Assets," or shown separately, if material.

(4) Include under subcaption (g) investments maturing within one year, such as commercial paper maturing within one year, marketable certificates of deposit maturing within one year, savings accounts, time deposits and other cash accounts and cash equivalents earning interest. State in a note any amounts subject to withdrawal or usage restrictions. (See Rule 5-02-1.)

(5) State separately in a note the amount of any class of investments included in subcaption (f) if such amount exceeds ten percent of stockholders' equity.

(6) State in a note the name of any person in which the total amount invested in the person and its affiliates, included in the above subcaptions, exceeds ten percent of total stockholders' equity. For this disclosure, include in the amount invested in a person and its affiliates the aggregate of indebtedness and stocks issued by such person and its affiliates that is included in the several subcaptions above, and the amount of any real estate included in subcaption (d) that was purchased or acquired from such person and its affiliates. Indicate the amount included in each subcaption. An investment in bonds and notes of the United States Government or of a United States Government agency or authority which exceeds ten percent of total stockholders' equity need not be reported.

(7) State in a note the amount of investments included under each subcaption (a), (c), (d) and (f) which have been non-income producing for the twelve months preceding the balance sheet date.

The accounting and disclosure requirements for all debt securities and equity securities that have readily determinable fair values are prescribed by FASB Statement No. 115, *Accounting for Certain Investments in Debt and Equity Securities*. This Statement supersedes FASB Statement No. 12, *Accounting for Certain Marketable Securities*, and is effective for fiscal years beginning after December 15, 1993. Refer to section 50502.2 for a discussion of these requirements.

The SEC staff's informal views regarding investments of insurance companies are as follows:

- The staff considers full disclosure of the investment portfolio's characteristics and risks to be critical to an investor's understanding. Specifically, the staff believes that disclosure of the following information should be provided:

  •• Interest yields,

  •• Interest sensitivity,

  •• Interest terms, other than the normal semiannual cash interest,

  •• Concentrations of risk by geography, industry, and by type of collateral, and

  •• Maturities of bullet loans.

  To the extent the disclosures concerning the investment portfolio are not required in the footnotes by FASB Statement No. 105, *Disclosure of Information About Financial Instruments with Off-Balance-Sheet Risk and Financial Instruments with Concentrations of Credit Risk*, FASB Statement No. 107, *Disclosures About Fair Value of Financial Instruments*, and SOP 90-11, *Disclosure of Certain Information by Financial Institutions About Debt Securities Held as Assets*, this information generally should be provided in the MD&A. Also, the staff has indicated that the MD&A for insurance companies should include a discussion of expected yields upon reinvestment at maturity.

- The amount of nonperforming and potentially nonperforming assets are required to be disclosed, and that to the extent these amounts are material, a further breakdown into industry or geographic segments should be provided. In addition, the staff believes that the amount of interest foregone on nonperforming assets should be disclosed. Generally, the staff expects these disclosures to be included in the footnotes; however, the staff will normally not object if the information is included in the MD&A.

- The staff has asked several registrants to disclose in the MD&A the segregation of their fixed maturity portfolio by credit quality (i.e., investment ratings).

During 1991, the SEC issued two AAERs requiring registrants to restate their quarterly and annual financial statements because the SEC had determined that declines in the market value of certain marketable equity securities within their investment portfolio were "other than temporary." Although FASB Statement No. 115 was issued subsequent to these AAERs, many of the same issues apply in determining whether declines are "other than temporary." The SEC staff continues to focus attention on "other than temporary" declines and the accounting and disclosures

SEC 50703. Rule 7-03

relating to investment portfolios. Refer to detailed discussions of these issues in section 50502.12 of this manual. In addition to this guidance, the Chief Accountant of the Division of Corporation Finance has stated that "with respect to debt securities that continue to be accounted for at amortized costs, the staff routinely requests the following disclosures by banks, savings and loans, thrifts, finance companies, insurance companies and similar institutions.

- The accounting policy footnote should clearly identify the characteristics that must be present for the institution to carry a security at amortized cost, rather than at market or lower of cost or market.

- Market value of the portfolio should be disclosed on the face of the balance sheet.

- Gross unrealized gains, gross unrealized losses, cost and market value should be disaggregated and disclosed for each pertinent category of debt securities in a note to the financial statements.

- Proceeds from the sales of securities should be distinguished from the proceeds of maturities in the cash flow statement or in a note thereto.

- Gross realized gains and gross realized losses on sales of securities should be separately disclosed in the MD&A.

- MD&A should analyze and, to the extent practicable, quantify the likely effects on current and future earnings and investment yields and on liquidity, capital resources and regulatory compliance of: material unrealized losses in the portfolio; material sales of securities at gains; material shifts in average maturity. A similar analysis should be provided if a material portion of fixed rate mortgages maturing beyond one year carry rates that are below current market.

- If sales out of the portfolio were significant, the MD&A should describe those events unforeseeable at earlier balance sheet dates that caused management to change its investment intent.

- If a material proportion of the portfolio consists of securities that are not actively traded in a liquid market, MD&A or Business Description should include disclosure of the proportion and describe the nature of the securities and the source of market value information used for the financial statements. MD&A should include discussion of any material risks associated with the investment relative to earnings and liquidity. Similar disclosure should be furnished if the portfolio includes instruments the market values of which are highly volatile relative to small changes in interest rates and this volatility may materially affect operating results or liquidity.

- Investments available for sale, categorized by types of investments, should be presented separately from the balance of the investment portfolio in Table II, "Investment Portfolio," of Industry Guide 3 data."

Refer to discussion of FASB Statement No. 114, *Accounting by Creditors for Impairment of a Loan*, in section 50903-7 of this manual.

2. Cash. *Cash on hand or on deposit that is restricted as to withdrawal or usage shall be disclosed separately on the balance sheet. The provisions of any restrictions shall be described in a note to the financial statements. Restrictions may include legally restricted deposits held as compensating balances against short-term borrowing arrangements, contracts entered into with others, or company statements of intention with regard to particular deposits. In cases where compensating balance arrangements exist but are not agreements which legally restrict the use of cash amounts shown on the balance sheet, describe in the notes to the financial statements these arrangements and the amount involved, if determinable, for the most recent audited balance sheet required. Compensating balances that are maintained under an agreement to assure future credit availability shall be disclosed in the notes to the financial statements along with the amount and terms of the agreement.*

3. Securities and indebtedness of related parties. *State separately (a) investments in related parties and (b) indebtedness from such related parties. (See Rule 4-08(k).)*

4. Accrued investment income.

5. Accounts and notes receivable. *Include under this caption (a) amounts receivable from agents and insureds, (b) uncollected premiums and (c) other receivables. State separately in the balance sheet or in a note thereto any category of other receivable which is in excess of five percent of total assets. State separately in the balance sheet or in a note thereto the amount of allowance for doubtful accounts that was deducted.*

6. Reinsurance recoverable on paid losses.

SFAS No. 113, *Accounting and Reporting for Reinsurance of Short-Duration and Long-Duration Contracts*, sets forth the accounting for the reinsuring (ceding) of insurance contracts by insurance companies and amends SFAS No. 60, *Accounting*

SEC 50703. Rule 7-03

and Reporting by Insurance Enterprises, to require that assets and liabilities related to reinsured contracts be reported separately rather than net of the effects of reinsurance. Some of the important concepts addressed in this Statement are:

- Reinsurance receivables (including amounts related to IBNR claims and liabilities for future policy benefits) and prepaid reinsurance premiums are required to be reported as assets (paragraph 14).

- Amounts receivable and payable between the ceding company and the individual reinsurer may only be offset when a right of setoff exists, as defined in FASB Interpretation No. 39 (see section 50502) (paragraph 15).

- The recognition of revenues and costs for reinsurance depends on whether the contract is long duration or short duration, and if short duration, on whether the contract is prospective or retroactive. (Refer to SFAS No. 113 for the relative accounting treatment for each type of contract.)

- Ceding companies are required to disclose the nature, purpose, and effect of reinsurance transactions, including the amount of premium associated with reinsurance assumed and ceded (paragraph 27). Concentrations of credit risk associated with reinsurance receivables and prepaid reinsurance premiums are also required to be disclosed pursuant to SFAS No. 105, *Disclosure of Information About Financial Instruments with Off-Balance-Sheet Risk and Financial Instruments with Concentrations of Credit Risk* (paragraph 28).

7. Deferred policy acquisition costs.

8. Property and equipment.

(a) State the basis of determining the amounts.

(b) State separately in the balance sheet or in a note thereto the amount of accumulated depreciation and amortization of property and equipment.

9. Title plant.

10. Other assets. *State separately in the balance sheet or in a note thereto any other asset the amount of which exceeds five percent of total assets.*

In EITF Issue No. 92-9, "Accounting for the Present Value of Future Profits [PVP] Resulting from the Acquisition of a Life Insurance Company," the EITF observed that industry practice is to amortize PVP using an interest method with the accrual of interest added to the unamortized balance on the balance sheet. In late 1992,

SEC 50703

the EITF reached a consensus that the interest rate used to amortize PVP should be the liability or contract rate, consistent with FASB Statement Nos. 60, *Accounting and Reporting by Insurance Enterprises,* and 97, *Accounting and Reporting by Insurance Enterprises for Certain Long-Duration Contracts and for Realized Gains and Losses from the Sale of Investments.* Further, for FASB Statement No. 97-type contracts, changes in estimates of future gross profits used to amortize PVP should be accounted for as a catch-up adjustment. For FASB Statement No. 60-type contracts, if estimates of future premiums change, there is no adjustment to the amortization of PVP beyond that needed to reflect current deaths and surrenders. In addition, the EITF reached a consensus that PVP and any related liability should be subject to the premium deficiency test required by FASB Statement Nos. 60 and 97.

The SEC observer stated that given the interest in this matter, the SEC staff will require registrants to provide the following specific disclosures with respect to PVP assets in filings with the SEC:

- A description of the registrant's accounting policy.

- An analysis of the PVP asset account for each year for which an income statement is presented. That analysis should include the PVP balance at the beginning of the year, the amount of PVP additions during the year arising from acquisitions of insurance companies, the amount of interest accrued on the unamortized PVP balance during the year, the interest accrual rate, the amount of amortization during the year, the amount of any write-offs during the year due to impairment and how those write-offs were determined, and the PVP balance at the end of the year.

- The estimated amount or percentage of the end-of-the-year PVP balance to be amortized during each of the next five years.

11. Assets held in separate accounts. *Include under this caption the aggregate amount of assets used to fund liabilities related to variable annuities, pension funds and similar activities. The aggregate liability shall be included under caption 18. Describe in a note to the financial statements the general nature of the activities being reported on in the separate accounts.*

12. Total assets.

LIABILITIES AND STOCKHOLDERS' EQUITY

13. Policy liabilities and accruals.

(a) State separately in the balance sheet the amounts of (1) future policy benefits and losses, claims and loss expenses, (2) unearned premiums and (3) other policy claims and benefits payable.

SEC 50703. Rule 7-03

(b) State in a note to the financial statements the basis of assumptions (interest rates, mortality, withdrawals) for future policy benefits and claims and settlements which are stated at present value.

(c) Information shall be given in a note concerning the general nature of reinsurance transactions, including a description of the significant types of reinsurance agreements executed. The information provided shall include (1) the nature of the contingent liability in connection with insurance ceded and (2) the nature and effect of material nonrecurring reinsurance transactions.

SAB Topic 5-N (SAB No. 62) describes the staff's views regarding the discounting of certain liabilities by property-casualty insurance companies. In SAB No. 62, the SEC staff has taken the position that *unsettled and settled* claim liabilities (and allocated claim adjustment expenses) for short-duration insurance contracts may be discounted when those liabilities are also discounted for state regulatory (statutory) purposes. This position would allow for the discounting of reserves for incurred-but-not-reported (IBNR) claims. This provision of the SAB limits the discount rate to the rate used to report the same class of claim liabilities to state regulatory authorities.

SAB No. 62 further allows the discounting of certain *settled* short-duration policy claim reserves—whether or not they are discounted for statutory purposes—using an appropriate investment-related rate. The investment-related discount rate used must be reasonable in light of the facts and circumstances existing when the claims are settled.

Settled claims are defined by the SAB as those for which the payment pattern and ultimate cost are fixed or determinable on an individual claim basis. An "individual claim basis" refers to those claims for which the claimant has agreed to the amount and frequency of payments, along with the period over which those payments are to be made.

SAB No. 62 does not allow discounting of any *unsettled* claim liabilities that are not discounted for statutory purposes, such as reserves for unsettled reported claims or IBNR claims.

A change to discounting as provided by SAB No. 62 is considered a discretionary accounting change that would be reflected by a cumulative effect adjustment in accordance with APB Opinion No. 20, *Accounting Changes,* and which requires a preferability letter from the registrant's independent accountant (see section 20620). Further, a change in discount rates that is permissible for statutory purposes without economic justification may also require recognition of a cumulative effect adjustment.

The text of the SAB follows:

Discounting by Property-Casualty Insurance Companies

Facts: A registrant which is an insurance company discounts certain unpaid claims liabilities related to short-duration insurance contracts for purposes of reporting to state regulatory authorities, using discount rates permitted or prescribed by those authorities ("statutory rates") which approximate 3 1/2 percent. The registrant follows the same practice in preparing its financial statements in accordance with generally accepted accounting principles ("GAAP"). It proposes to change, for GAAP purposes, to using a discount rate related to the historical yield on its investment portfolio ("investment related rate") which is represented to approximate 7 percent, and to account for the change as a change in accounting estimate, applying the investment related rate to claims settled in the current and subsequent years while the statutory rate would continue to be applied to claims settled in all prior years.

Question 1: What is the staff's position with respect to discounting claims liabilities related to short-duration insurance contracts?

Interpretive Response: The staff is aware of efforts by the accounting profession to assess the circumstances under which discounting may be appropriate in financial statements. Pending authoritative guidance resulting from those efforts, however, the staff will raise no objection if a registrant follows a policy for GAAP reporting purposes of:

–Discounting liabilities for unpaid claims and claim adjustment expenses at the same rates that it uses for reporting to state regulatory authorities with respect to the same claims liabilities, or

– Discounting liabilities with respect to settled claims under the following circumstances:

(1) the payment pattern and ultimate cost are fixed and determinable on an individual claim basis, and

(2) the discount rate used is reasonable based on the facts and circumstances applicable to the registrant at the time the claims are settled.

Question 2: Does the staff agree with the registrant's proposal that the change from a statutory rate to an investment related rate be accounted for as a change in accounting estimate?

Interpretive Response: No. The staff believes that the registrant should reflect the cumulative effect of the change in accounting by applying the new selection method retroactively to liabilities for claims settled in all prior years, in accordance with the requirements of Accounting Principles Board Opinion No. 20, "Accounting Changes." Initial adoption of discounting for GAAP purposes would be treated similarly. In either case, in addition to the disclosures required by APB Opinion No. 20 concerning the change in accounting principle, a preferability letter from the registrant's independent accountant is required.

Historically, the staff has accepted the discounting of liabilities relating to unpaid claims and claims adjustment expenses at the same rates that are permitted for statutory reporting purposes. However, the staff has noted that there are a variety of practices allowed by state insurance departments with regard to discounting of loss reserves, and the permitted statutory discount rates may not be reflective of actual investment portfolio

SEC 50703. Rule 7-03

yields or current interest rate environments. Therefore, the staff has informally indicated that it will not object to discounting unpaid claims, claims adjustment expenses and settled claims at rates not to exceed the "risk free" rates of government issues, having the same approximate maturities as the liabilities being discounted, provided that a qualified actuary opines upon the pay-out patterns of those liabilities.

SAB Topic 5-W (SAB No. 87) discusses the SEC staff's views concerning the applicability of the disclosure requirements of FASB Statement No. 5, *Accounting for Contingencies,* to property and casualty reserves for unpaid claim costs when there is a reasonable possibility that abnormal and nonrecurring claims experience could continue, resulting in a material understatement of claim reserves. In SAB No. 87, the SEC staff takes the position that specific uncertainties that are considered abnormal and nonrecurring may, due to their significance and/or nature, result in loss contingencies and, therefore, require disclosures pursuant to FASB Statement No. 5, *Accounting for Contingencies.* Examples provided in the SAB that may require disclosure depending on their significance and/or nature include:

- Insufficiently understood claims activity;

- Judgmental adjustments to historical experience for purposes of estimating future claim costs (other than for normal recurring general uncertainties);

- Risks that are specific to an individual claim or group of related claims (e.g., geographic location); and/or

- Catastrophe losses.

The text of the SAB follows:

Contingency Disclosures Regarding Property-Casualty Insurance Reserves for Unpaid Claim Costs

Facts: A property-casualty insurance company (the "Company") has established reserves, in accordance with Statement of Financial Accounting Standards No. ("SFAS") 60, Accounting and Reporting by Insurance Enterprises, for unpaid claim costs, including estimates of costs relating to claims incurred but not reported ("IBNR"). [1] The reserve estimate for IBNR claims was based on past loss experience and current trends except that the estimate has been adjusted for recent significant unfavorable claims experience that the Company considers to be nonrecurring and abnormal. The Company attributes the abnormal claims experience to a recent acquisition and accelerated claims processing, however, actuarial studies have been inconclusive and subject to varying interpretations. Although the reserve is deemed adequate to cover all probable claims, there is a reasonable possibility that the abnormal claims experience could continue, resulting in a material understatement of claim reserves.

SFAS 5, <u>Accounting for Contingencies</u>, requires, among other things, disclosure of loss contingencies.[2] However, paragraph 2 of that pronouncement notes that "not all uncertainties inherent in the accounting process give rise to contingencies as that term is used in SFAS 5."

Question 1: In the staff's view, do SFAS 5 disclosure requirements apply to property-casualty insurance reserves for unpaid claim costs? If so, how?

Interpretive Response: Yes. The staff believes that specific uncertainties (conditions, situations and/or sets of circumstances) not considered to be normal and recurring because of their significance and/or nature can result in loss contingencies[3] for purposes of applying SFAS 5 disclosure requirements. General uncertainties, such as the amount and timing of claims, that are normal, recurring, and inherent to estimations of property-casualty insurance reserves are not considered subject to the disclosure requirements of SFAS 5. Some specific uncertainties that may result in loss contingencies pursuant to SFAS 5, depending on significance and/or nature, include insufficiently understood trends in claims activity; judgmental adjustments to historical experience for purposes of estimating future claim costs (other than for normal recurring general uncertainties); significant risks to an individual claim or group of related claims; or catastrophe losses.

Question 2: Do the facts presented above describe an uncertainty that requires SFAS 5 disclosures?

Interpretive Response: Yes. The staff believes the judgmental adjustments to historical experience for insufficiently understood claims activity noted above results in a loss contingency within the scope of SFAS 5. Based on the facts presented above, at a minimum the Company's financial statements should disclose that for purposes of estimating IBNR claim reserves, past experience was adjusted for what management believes to be abnormal claims experience related to the recent acquisition of Company A and accelerated claims processing. It should also be disclosed that there is a reasonable possibility that the claims experience could be the indication of an unfavorable trend which would require additional IBNR claim reserves in the approximate range of $XX-$XX million (alternatively, if Company management is unable to estimate the possible loss or range of loss, a statement to that effect should be disclosed). Additionally, the staff also expects companies to disclose the nature of the loss contingency and the potential impact on trends in their loss reserve development discussions provided pursuant to Property-Casualty Industry Guides 4 and 6. Consideration should also be given to the need to provide disclosure in Management's Discussion and Analysis.

Question 3: Does the staff have an example in which specific uncertainties involving an individual claim or group of related claims result in a loss contingency the staff believes requires disclosure?

Interpretive Response: Yes. A property-casualty insurance company (the "Company") underwrites product liability insurance for an insured manufacturer which has produced and sold millions of units of a particular product which has been used effectively and without problems for many years. Users of the product have

SEC 50703. Rule 7-03

recently begun to report serious health problems that they attribute to long-term use of the product and have asserted claims under the insurance policy underwritten and retained by the Company. To date, the number of users reporting such problems is relatively small, and there is presently no conclusive evidence that demonstrates a causal link between long-term use of the product and the health problems experienced by the claimants. However, the evidence generated to date indicates that there is at least a reasonable possibility that the product is responsible for the problems and the assertion of additional claims is considered probable, and therefore the potential exposure of the Company is material. While an accrual may not be warranted since the loss exposure may not be both probable and estimable, in view of the reasonable possibility of material future claim payments, the staff believes that disclosures made in accordance with SFAS 5 would be required under these circumstances. The disclosure concepts expressed in this example would also apply to an individual claim or group of claims that are related to a single catastrophic event or multiple events having a similar effect.

---

[1]Paragraph 18 of SFAS 60 prescribes that "the liability for unpaid claims shall be based on the estimated ultimate cost of settling the claims (including the effects of inflation and other societal and economic factors), using past experience adjusted for current trends, and any other factors that would modify past experience."

[2]Paragraph 10 of SFAS 5 specifies that "if no accrual is made for a loss contingency because one or both of the conditions in paragraph 8 are not met, or if an exposure to loss exists in excess of the amount accrued pursuant to the provisions of paragraph 8, disclosure of the contingency shall be made when there is at least a reasonable possibility that a loss or an additional loss may have been incurred. The disclosure shall indicate the nature of the contingency and shall give an estimate of the possible loss or range of loss or state that such an estimate cannot be made."

[3]The loss contingency referred to in this document is the potential for a material understatement of reserves for unpaid claims.

The following informal views regarding liabilities of insurance companies have been provided by the SEC staff:

- The staff has indicated that it expects registrants to provide disclosures in the MD&A with respect to the sensitivity of life insurance company liabilities to surrender by policyholders (i.e., liquidity concerns in the event of a "run on the bank") as well as the following information:

  •• The amounts subject to surrender,

  •• The magnitude and time frame of surrender charges that are specified in the contract, and

•• Amounts surrendered during the reporting period and the reasons for surrender levels.

• With respect to property-casualty company liabilities, the staff has indicated that it would expect to see a discussion of specific events and circumstances that led to any reserve strengthening or that caused unusual trends, rather than a general discussion of the subject. The staff believes that this disclosure is required pursuant to FASB Statement No. 5, *Accounting for Contingencies.*

14. Other policyholders' funds.

(a) Include amounts of supplementary contracts without life contingencies, policyholders' dividend accumulations, undistributed earnings on participating business, dividends to policyholders and retrospective return premiums (not included elsewhere) and any similar items. State separately in the balance sheet or in a note thereto any item the amount of which is in excess of five percent of total liabilities.

(b) State in a note to the financial statements the relative significance of participating insurance expressed as percentages of (1) insurance in force and (2) premium income; and the method by which earnings and dividends allocable to such insurance is determined.

15. Other liabilities.

(a) Include under this caption such items as accrued payrolls, accrued interest and taxes. State separately in the balance sheet or in a note thereto any item included in other liabilities the amount of which exceeds five percent of total liabilities.

(b) State separately in the balance sheet or in a note thereto the amount of (1) income taxes payable and (2) deferred income taxes.

Disclose separately the amount of deferred income taxes applicable to unrealized appreciation of equity securities.

16. Notes payable, bonds, mortgages and similar obligations, including capitalized leases.

(a) State separately in the balance sheet the amounts of (1) short-term debt and (2) long-term debt including capitalized leases.

(b) The disclosure required by Rule 5-02-19(b) shall be given if the aggregate of short-term borrowings from banks, factors and other financial institutions and commercial paper issued exceeds five percent of total liabilities.

(c) The disclosure requirements of Rule 5-02-22 shall be followed for long-term debt.

SEC 50703. Rule 7-03

17. Indebtedness to related parties. *(See Rule 4-08(k).)*

18. Liabilities related to separate accounts. *(See caption 11.)*

19. Commitments and contingent liabilities.

Refer to sections 50502.24 and .25 for discussion regarding other liabilities, including environmental liabilities, commitments, and contingent liabilities.

Minority Interests

20. Minority interests in consolidated subsidiaries. *The disclosure requirements of Rule 5-02-27 shall be followed.*

Redeemable Preferred Stocks

21. Preferred stocks subject to mandatory redemption requirements or whose redemption is outside the control of the issuer. *The classification and disclosure requirements of Rule 5-02-28 shall be followed.*

Nonredeemable Preferred Stocks

22. Preferred stocks which are not redeemable or are redeemable solely at the option of the issuer. *The classification and disclosure requirements of Rule 5-02-29 shall be followed.*

Common Stocks

23. Common stocks. *The classification and disclosure requirements of Rule 5-02-30 shall be followed.*

Other Stockholders' Equity

24. Other stockholders' equity.

(a) Separate captions shall be shown for (1) additional paid-in capital, (2) other additional capital, (3) unrealized appreciation or depreciation of equity securities less applicable deferred income taxes, (4) retained earnings (i) appropriated and (ii) unappropriated. (See Rule 4-08(e).) Additional paid-in capital and other additional capital may be combined with the stock caption to which they apply, if appropriate.

(b) The classification and disclosure requirements of Rule 5-02-31(b) and (c) shall be followed for (1) dating and effect of a quasi-reorganization and (2) summaries of each stockholders' equity account.

SEC 50703

(c) State in a note the following information separately for (1) life insurance legal entities, and (2) property and liability insurance legal entities: the amount of statutory stockholders' equity as of the date of each balance sheet presented and the amount of statutory net income or loss for each period for which an income statement is presented.

It is important to note that although SFAS 60 and the SEC's rules do not require reconciliations of statutory stockholders' equity and net income to the related GAAP amounts, as a matter of practice, a number of insurers provide such reconciliations in their footnote disclosures. In addition, the SEC staff has informally expressed a preference for such reconciliations to be provided and has requested them to be provided as supplemental information in certain registrant filings.

25. Total liabilities and stockholders' equity.

50704. Rule 7-04. Income Statements

The purpose of this rule is to indicate the various items which, if applicable, should appear on the face of the income statements and in the notes thereto filed for persons to whom this article pertains. (See Rule 4-01(a).)

As discussed in section 50703.6, SFAS No. 113, *Accounting and Reporting for Reinsurance of Short-Duration and Long-Duration Contracts,* specifies that the recognition of revenues and costs for reinsurance depends on whether the contract is long or short duration, and if short duration, on whether the contract is prospective or retroactive. Refer to SFAS No. 113 for the relative accounting treatment for each type of contract.

REVENUES

1. Premiums. *Include premiums from reinsurance assumed and deduct premiums on reinsurance ceded. Where applicable, the amounts included in this caption should represent premiums earned.*

2. Net investment income. *State in a note to the financial statements, in tabular form, the amounts of (a) investment income from each category of investments listed in the subcaptions of Rule 7-03-1 that exceeds five percent of total investment income, (b) total investment income, (c) applicable expenses, and (d) net investment income.*

3. Realized investment gains and losses. *Disclose the following amounts:*

(a) Net realized investment gains and losses, which shall be shown separately regardless of size.

SEC 50703. Rule 7-03

(b) Indicate in a footnote the registrant's policy with respect to whether investment income and realized gains and losses allocable to policyholders and separate accounts are included in the investment income and realized gain and loss amounts reported in the income statement. If the income statement includes investment income and realized gains and losses allocable to policyholders and separate accounts, indicate the amounts of such allocable investment income and realized gains and losses and the manner in which the insurance enterprise's obligation with respect to allocation of such investment income and realized gains and losses is otherwise accounted for in the financial statements.

(c) The method followed in determining the cost of investments sold (e.g., "average cost," "first-in, first-out," or "identified certificate") shall be disclosed.

(d) For each period for which an income statement is filed, include in a note an analysis of realized and unrealized investment gains and losses on fixed maturities and equity securities. For each period, state separately for fixed maturities and for equity securities the following amounts:

(1) realized investment gains and losses, and

(2) the change during the period in the difference between value and cost.

The change in the difference between value and cost shall be given for both categories of investments even though they may be shown on the related balance sheet on a basis other than value.

4. Other income. *Include all revenues not included in captions 1 and 2 above. State separately in the statement any amounts in excess of five percent of total revenue, and disclose the nature of the transactions from which the items arose.*

BENEFITS, LOSSES AND EXPENSES

5. Benefits, claims, losses and settlement expenses.

6. Policyholders' share of earnings on participating policies, dividends and similar items. *(See Rule 7-03-14(b).)*

7. Underwriting, acquisition and insurance expenses. *State separately in the income statement or in a note thereto (a) the amount included in this caption representing deferred policy acquisition costs amortized to income during the period, and (b) the amount of other operating expenses. State separately in the income statement any material amount included in all other operating expenses.*

8. Income or loss before income tax expense and appropriate items below.

9. Income tax expense. *Include under this caption only taxes based on income. (See Rule 4-08(h).)*

10. Minority interest in income of consolidated subsidiaries.

11. Equity in earnings of unconsolidated subsidiaries and 50 percent or less owned persons. *State, parenthetically or in a note, the amount of dividends received from such persons. If justified by the circumstances, this item may be presented in a different position and a different manner.*

12. Income or loss from continuing operations.

13. Discontinued operations.

14. Income or loss before extraordinary items and cumulative effects of changes in accounting principles.

15. Extraordinary items, less applicable tax.

16. Cumulative effects of changes in accounting principles.

17. Net income or loss.

18. Earnings per share data.

50705. Rule 7-05. What Schedules Are To Be Filed

(a) Except as expressly provided otherwise in the applicable form:

(1) The schedules specified below as Schedules I and VII shall be filed as of the dates of the most recent audited balance sheet for each person or group.

(2) Other schedules specified below as Schedules II, IV, VI, VIII and IX shall be filed for each period for which an audited income statement is required to be filed for each person or group.

(3) Schedules III, V and X shall be filed as of the dates and for the periods specified in the schedule.

(b) When information is required in schedules for both the registrant and the registrant and its subsidiaries consolidated it may be presented in the form of a single schedule: Provided, that items pertaining to the registrant are shown separately and that such single schedule affords a properly summarized presentation of the facts. If the information required by any schedule (including the notes thereto) may be shown in

SEC 50704. Rule 7-04

the related financial statement or in a note thereto without making such statement unclear or confusing, that procedure may be followed and the schedule omitted.

(c) The schedules shall be examined by the independent accountant.

Schedule I. Summary of investment—other than investments in related parties. *The schedule prescribed by Rule 12-15 shall be filed in support of caption 1 of the most recent audited balance sheet.*

Schedule II. Amounts receivable from related parties, and underwriters, promoters, and employees other than related parties. *The schedule prescribed by Rule 12-03 shall be filed with respect to each person among related parties, and underwriters, promoters, and employees other than related parties, from whom an aggregate indebtedness of more than $100,000 or one percent of total assets, whichever is less, is owed, or at any time during the period for which related audited income statements are required to be filed was owed. This schedule shall not include information which is prescribed by Rule 12-05. For purposes of this schedule, exclude in the determination of the amount of indebtedness all amounts receivable from such persons for purchases subject to usual trade terms, for ordinary travel and expense advances, and for other such items arising in the ordinary course of business.*

Schedule III. Condensed financial information of registrant. *The schedule prescribed by Rule 12-04 shall be filed when the restricted net assets (Rule 4-08(e)(3)) of consolidated subsidiaries exceed 25 percent of consolidated net assets as of the end of the most recently completed fiscal year. For purposes of the above test, restricted net assets of consolidated subsidiaries shall mean that amount of the registrant's proportionate share of net assets of consolidated subsidiaries (after intercompany eliminations) which as of the end of the most recent fiscal year may not be transferred to the parent company by subsidiaries in the form of loans, advances or cash dividends without the consent of a third party (i.e., lender, regulatory agency, foreign government, etc.). Where restrictions on the amount of funds which may be loaned or advanced differ from the amount restricted as to transfer in the form of cash dividends, the amount least restrictive to the subsidiary shall be used. Redeemable preferred stocks (Rule 7-03.21) and minority interests shall be deducted in computing net assets for purposes of this test.*

For a discussion of Rule 4-08(e) and the related calculation to determine whether this schedule is required, refer to sections 50408 and 50520.

Schedule IV. Indebtedness of and to related parties—not current. *The schedule prescribed by Rule 12-05 shall be filed in support of captions 3(b) and 17 of the balance sheet. This schedule may be omitted if (1) neither the sum of captions 3(a) and 3(b) in the related balance sheet nor the amount of caption 17 in such balance sheet exceeds five percent of total assets as shown by the related balance sheet at either the beginning* *or end of the period or (2) there have been no material changes in the information required to be filed from that last previously reported.*

Schedule V. Supplementary insurance information. *The schedule prescribed by Rule 12-16 shall be filed giving segment detail in support of various balance sheet and income statement captions. The required balance sheet information shall be presented as of the date of each audited balance sheet filed, and the income statement information shall be presented for each period for which an audited income statement is required to be filed, for each person or group.*

Schedule VI. Reinsurance. *The schedule prescribed by Rule 12-17 shall be filed for reinsurance ceded and assumed.*

Schedule VII. Guarantees of securities of other issuers. *The schedule prescribed by Rule 12-08 shall be filed with respect to any guarantees of securities of other issuers by the person for which the statement is being filed.*

Schedule VIII. Valuation and qualifying accounts. *The schedule prescribed by Rule 12-09 shall be filed in support of valuation and qualifying accounts included in the balance sheet (see Rule 4-02).*

Schedule IX. Short-term borrowings. *The schedule prescribed by Rule 12-10 shall be filed in support of caption 16(a)(1) of the balance sheet to report amounts payable to banks for borrowings; factors and financial institutions for borrowings; and holders of commercial paper. The information required by this schedule may be presented in Management's Discussion and Analysis if it results in a more meaningful presentation of the information being provided. If that procedure is followed, the schedule may be omitted if appropriate cross-references are made.*

Schedule X. Supplemental information concerning property-casualty insurance operations. *The information required by Rule 12-18 shall be presented as of the same dates and for the same period for which the information is reflected in the audited consolidated financial statements required by Rules 3-01 and 3-02. The schedule may be omitted if reserves for unpaid property-casualty claims and claim adjustment expenses of the registrant and its consolidated subsidiaries, its unconsolidated subsidiaries and its 50%-or-less-owned equity basis investees did not in the aggregate exceed one-half of common stockholders' equity of the registrant and its consolidated subsidiaries as of the beginning of the fiscal year. For purposes of this test, only the proportionate share of the registrant and its other subsidiaries in the reserves for unpaid claims and claim adjustment expenses of 50%-or-less-owned equity investees taken in the aggregate after intercompany eliminations shall be taken into account.*

SEC 50705. Rule 7-05

50900. ARTICLE 9. BANK HOLDING COMPANIES

50901. Rule 9-01. Application of Article 9

This article is applicable to consolidated financial statements filed for bank holding companies and to any financial statements of banks that are included in filings with the Commission.

SAB Topic 11-K, added by SAB No. 69, expresses the staff's views on the use of Article 9 and Industry Guide 3 as guidance for disclosure purposes by registrants that are not bank holding companies, but which are engaged in similar lending and deposit activities. The text of the SAB follows:

Application of Article 9

Facts: Article 9 of Regulation S-X specifies the form and content of and requirements for financial statements for bank holding companies filing with the Commission. Similarly, bank holding companies disclose supplemental statistical disclosures in filings, pursuant to Industry Guide 3. No specific guidance as to the form and content of financial statements or supplemental disclosures has been promulgated for registrants which are not bank holding companies but which are engaged in similar lending and deposit activities.[1]

Question: Should non-bank holding company registrants with material amounts of lending and deposit activities file financial statements and make disclosures called for by Article 9 of Regulation S-X and Industry Guide 3?

Interpretive Response: In the staff's view, Article 9 and Guide 3, while applying literally only to bank holding companies, provide useful guidance to certain other registrants, including savings and loan holding companies, on certain disclosures relevant to an understanding of the registrant's operations. Thus, to the extent particular guidance is relevant and material to the operations of an entity, the staff believes the specified information, or comparable data, should be provided.

For example, in accordance with Guide 3, bank holding companies disclose information about yields and costs of various assets and liabilities. Further, bank holding companies provide certain information about maturities and repricing characteristics of various assets and liabilities. Such companies also disclose risk elements, such as nonaccrual and past due items in the lending portfolio. The staff believes that this information and other relevant data would be material to a description of business of other registrants with material lending and deposit activities and, accordingly, the specified information and/or comparable data (such as scheduled item disclosure for risk elements) should be provided.

In contrast, other requirements of Article 9 and Guide 3 may not be material or relevant to an understanding of the financial statements of some financial institutions. For example, bank holding companies present average balance sheet information, because period-end statements might not be representative of bank activity throughout the year. Some financial institutions other than bank holding companies may determine that average balance sheet disclosure does not provide significant additional information. Others may determine that assets and liabilities are subject to sufficient volatility that average balance information should be presented.

Pursuant to Article 9, the income statements of bank holding companies use a "net interest income" presentation. Similarly, bank holding companies present the aggregate market value, at the balance sheet date, of investment securities, on the face of the balance sheet. The staff believes that such disclosures and other relevant information should also be provided by other registrants with material lending and deposit activities.

---

[1]The Commission staff has been considering the need for more specific guidance in the area but believes that the Financial Accounting Standards Board project on financial instruments, which as an initial step is expected to result in expanded disclosures across industry lines, may make Commission action in this area unnecessary. In the interim, this bulletin provides the staff's views with respect to filings by similar entities such as savings and loan holding companies.

Several Staff Accounting Bulletins have been issued dealing with accounting and reporting by bank holding companies. SAB Topic 1-F, added by SAB No. 50, reflects the staff's views on the financial statement requirements in filings involving the formation of a one-bank holding company. (Subsequent to the issuance of SAB No. 50, Form S-14 referred to in the SAB has been replaced by Form S-4 and Schedule 14A has been revised. The financial statement requirements formerly included under Item 15 of Schedule 14A are now a part of Items 13 and 14. At this time, although the official text of the SAB has not been updated, it should be read in the context of the foregoing revisions.) In SAB No. 50, the SEC staff discusses a situation in which a newly formed holding company is registering its common stock on Form S-4 to acquire all of the common stock of a bank.

The staff takes the position that it will not object to the omission of the bank's financial statements and Industry Guide 3 information in the Form S-4 registration statement, provided that the bank has separately furnished shareholders with financial statements prepared in accordance with GAAP (which may be unaudited) for at least the most recently completed fiscal year and that certain other specified conditions are met. The staff indicates, however, that in the initial Form 10-K filing, the bank is required to present audited financial statements and Industry Guide 3 information for *at least* the two most recent fiscal years.

In SAB No. 50 the staff also indicates that it will not object to the capitalization of organizational costs (e.g., legal, printing and related costs) incurred to register the securities provided that such costs are classified as an asset on the balance sheet and amortized over a maximum period of five years. Audit fees, however, would not be considered by the staff to be organizational costs and, therefore, the staff indicates that such fees need to be expensed as incurred.

The text of the SAB follows:

Financial Statement Requirements in Filings Involving the Formation of a One-Bank Holding Company

Facts: Holding Company A is organized for the purpose of issuing common stock to acquire all of the common stock of Bank A. Under the plan of reorganization, each share of common stock of Bank A will be exchanged for one share of common stock of the holding company. The shares of the holding company to be issued in the transaction will be registered on Form S-14. The holding company will not engage in any operations prior to consummation of the reorganization, and its only significant asset after the transaction will be its investment in the bank. The bank has been furnishing its shareholders with an annual report that includes financial statements that comply with generally accepted accounting principles.

Item 15 of Schedule 14A of the proxy rules[1] provides that financial statements generally are not necessary in proxy material relating only to changes in legal organization (such as reorganizations involving the issuer and one or more of its totally held subsidiaries).

Question 1: Must the financial statements and the information required by Securities Act Industry Guide ("Guide 3")[2] for Bank A be included in the initial registration statement on Form S-14?

Interpretive Response: No, provided that certain conditions are met. The staff will not take exception to the omission of financial statements and Guide 3 information in the initial registration statement on Form S-14 if all of the following conditions are met:

- There are no anticipated changes in the shareholders' relative equity ownership interest in the underlying bank assets, except for redemption of no more than a nominal number of shares of unaffiliated persons who dissent;

- In the aggregate, only nominal borrowings are to be incurred for such purposes as organizing the holding company, to pay nonaffiliated persons who dissent, or to meet minimum capital requirements;

- There are no new classes of stock authorized other than those corresponding to the stock of Bank A immediately prior to the reorganization;

- There are no plans or arrangements to issue any additional shares to acquire any business other than Bank A; and

- There has been no material adverse change in the financial condition of the bank since the latest fiscal year end included in the annual report to shareholders.

If at the time of filing the S-14, a letter is furnished to the staff stating that all of these conditions are met, it will not be necessary to request the Division of Corporation Finance to waive the financial statement or Guide 3 requirements of Form S-14. Although the financial statements may be omitted, the filing should include a section captioned, "Financial Statements," which states either that an annual report containing financial statements for at least the latest fiscal year prepared in conformity with generally accepted accounting principles was previously furnished to shareholders or is being delivered with the prospectus. If financial statements have been previously furnished, it should be indicated that an additional copy of such report for the latest fiscal year will be furnished promptly upon request without charge to shareholders. The name and address of the person to whom the request should be made should be provided. One copy of such annual report should be furnished supplementally with the initial filing for purposes of staff review.

If any nominal amounts are to be borrowed in connection with the formation of the holding company, a statement of capitalization should be included in the filing which shows Bank A on an historical basis, the pro forma adjustments, and the holding company on a pro forma basis. A note should also explain the pro forma effect, in total and per share, which the borrowings would have had on net income for the latest fiscal year if the transaction had occurred at the beginning of the period.

Question 2: Are the financial statements of Bank A required to be audited for purposes of the initial Form S-14 or the subsequent Form 10-K report?

Interpretive Response: The staff will not insist that the financial statements in the annual report to shareholders used to satisfy the requirements of the initial Form S-14 be audited.

The consolidated financial statements of the holding company to be included in the registrant's initial report on Form 10-K should comply with the applicable financial statement requirements in Regulation S-X at the time such annual report is filed. However, the regulations also provide that the staff may allow one or more of the required statements to be unaudited where it is consistent with the protection of investors.[3] Accordingly, the policy of the Division of Corporation Finance is as follows:

- The registrant should file audited balance sheets as of the two most recent fiscal years and audited statements of income and cash flows for each of the three latest fiscal years, with appropriate footnotes and schedules as required by Regulation S-X unless the financial statements have not previously been audited for the periods required to be filed. In such cases, the Division will not object if the financial statements in the first annual report on Form 10-K (or the special report filed pursuant to Rule 15d-2)[4] are audited only for the two latest fiscal years.[5] This policy only applies to filings on Form 10-K, and not to any Securities Act filings made after the initial S-14 filing.

The above procedure may be followed without making a specific request of the Division of Corporation Finance for a waiver of the financial statement requirements of Form 10-K.

The information required by Guide 3 should also be provided in the Form 10-K for at least the periods for which audited financial statements are furnished. If some of the statistical information for the two most recent fiscal years for which audited financial statements are included (other than information on nonperforming loans and the summary of loan loss experience) is unavailable and cannot be obtained without unwarranted or undue burden or expense, such data may be omitted provided a brief explanation in support of such representation is included in the report on Form 10-K. In all cases, however, information with respect to nonperforming loans and loan loss experience, or reasonably comparable data, must be furnished for at least the two latest fiscal years in the initial 10-K. Thereafter, for subsequent years in reports on Form 10-K, all of the Guide 3 information is required; Guide 3 information which had been omitted in the initial 10-K in accordance with the above procedure can be excluded in any subsequent 10-Ks.

Question 3: Can organization costs incurred to register securities issued for the formation of one-bank holding companies be capitalized?

Interpretive Response: The staff will not object if organizational costs such as legal, printing and other related costs are capitalized and amortized against income over a period not to exceed 5 years. Any such organization costs should be shown in the balance sheet as an asset, and not as a reduction of shareholders' equity.

Audit fees incurred would not be deemed to be organization costs and should be expensed.

---

[1]Item 15(c) of Schedule 14a.
[2]Item 801 of Regulation S-K.
[3]Rule 13-3 of Regulation S-X.
[4]Rule 15d-2 would be applicable if the annual report furnished with the Form S-14 was not for the registrant's most recent fiscal year. In such a situation, Rule 15d-2 would require the registrant to file a special report within 90 days after the effective date of the Form S-14 furnishing audited financial statements for the most recent fiscal year.
[5]Unaudited statements of income and changes in financial position should be furnished for the earliest period.

SAB Topics 2-A3, *Acquisitions Involving Financial Institutions,* 2-A4, *Amortization of Goodwill by Financial Institutions Upon Becoming SEC Registrants,* and

2-A5, *Adjustments to Allowances for Loan Losses in Connection with Business Combinations,* discuss the SEC staff's views regarding business combinations by financial institutions accounted for by the purchase method. Refer to section 50337 for discussion of these SABs and other SEC views related to the purchase method of accounting.

As a result of the increasing number of acquisitions of troubled financial institutions by SEC registrants, the SEC issued SAB Topic 1-K which was added by SAB No. 89. SAB No. 89 sets forth the staff's views on the financial statement requirements under Rule 3-05 relating to the acquisition of troubled financial institutions (see section 50317). In SAB No. 89, the SEC indicates that in some cases, the financial statements of an acquired troubled financial institution may not be required by Rule 3-05 when there is not sufficient continuity of the acquired entity's operations prior to and after the acquisition. In such cases, the staff notes that the disclosure of prior financial information may not be material to an understanding of future operations, as discussed in Rule 11-01 of Regulation S-X (see section 51101).

If the acquired financial institution does constitute a business with material continuity of operations after the acquisition, the staff indicates that a waiver of Rule 3-05 requirements may be obtained provided that such statements are not reasonably available and the total acquired assets of the troubled institution do not exceed 20 percent of the registrant's preacquisition assets. For purposes of this waiver, a "troubled financial institution" must be either:

- in receivership, conservatorship or is otherwise operating under a similar supervisory agreement with a federal regulatory agency; or

- controlled by a federal regulatory agency; or

- acquired in a federally assisted transaction.

When historical financial statements pursuant to Rule 3-05 are not required or are waived, the SAB provides guidance as to other disclosures that need to be furnished.

The text of the SAB follows:

Financial Statements of Acquired Troubled Financial Institutions

Facts: Federally insured depository institutions are subject to regulatory oversight by various federal agencies including the Federal Reserve, Office of Thrift Supervision. During the 1980's, certain of these institutions experienced significant financial difficulties resulting in their inability to meet necessary capital and other regulatory requirements. The Financial Institutions Reform, Recovery and Enforcement Act of 1989 was adopted to address various issues affecting this industry.

SEC 50901. Rule 9-01

Many troubled institutions have merged into stronger institutions or reduced the scale of their operations through the sale of branches and other assets pursuant to recommendations or directives of the regulatory agencies. In other situations, institutions that were taken over by or operated under the management of a federal regulator have been reorganized, sold, or transferred by the federal agency to financial and non-financial companies.

A number of registrants have acquired, or are contemplating acquisition of, these troubled financial institutions. Complete audited financial statements of the institutions for the periods necessary to comply fully with Rule 3-05 of Regulation S-X may not be reasonably available in some cases. Some troubled institutions have never obtained an audit while others have been operated under receivership by regulators for a significant period without audit. Auditors' reports on the financial statements of some of these acquirees may not satisfy the requirements of Rule 2-02 of Regulation S-X because they contain qualifications due to audit scope limitations or disclaim an opinion.

A registrant that acquires a troubled financial institution for which complete audited financial statements are not reasonably available may be precluded from raising capital through a public offering of securities for up to three years following the acquisition because of the inability to comply with Rule 3-05.

Question 1: Are there circumstances under which the staff would conclude that financial statements of an acquired troubled financial institution are not required by Rule 3-05?

Interpretive Response: Yes. In some cases, financial statements will not be required because there is not sufficient continuity of the acquired entity's operations prior to and after the acquisition so that disclosure of prior financial information is material to an understanding of future operations, as discussed in Rule 11-01 of Regulation S-X. For example, such a circumstance may exist in the case of an acquisition solely of the physical facilities of a banking branch with assumption of the related deposits if neither income-producing assets (other than treasury bills and similar low-risk investments) nor the management responsible for its historical investment and lending activities transfer with the branch to the registrant. In this and other circumstances where the registrant can persuasively demonstrate that continuity of operations is substantially lacking and a representation to this effect is included in the filing, the staff will not object to the omission of financial statements. However, applicable disclosures specified by Industry Guide 3, Article 11 of Regulation S-X (pro forma information), and other information which is descriptive of the transaction and of the assets acquired and liabilities assumed should be furnished to the extent reasonable available.

Question 2: If the acquired financial institution is found to constitute a business having material continuity of operations after the transaction, are there circumstances in which the staff will waive the requirements of Rule 3-05?

Interpretive Response: Yes. The staff believes the circumstances surrounding the present restructuring of U.S. depository institutions are unique. Accordingly, the staff has identified situations in which it will grant a waiver of the requirements of Rule 3-05 of Regulation S-X to the extent that audited financial statements are not reasonably available.

For purposes of this waiver a "troubled financial institution" is one which either:

a) is receivership, conservatorship or is otherwise operating under a similar supervisory agreement with a federal financial regulatory agency; or

b) is controlled by a federal regulatory agency; or

c) is acquired in a federally assisted transaction.

A registrant that acquires a troubled financial institution that is deemed significant pursuant to Rule 3-05 may omit audited financial statements of the acquired entity if such statements are not reasonably available and the total acquired assets of the troubled institution do not exceed 20% of the registrant's assets before giving effect to the acquisition. The staff will consider requests for waivers in situations involving more significant acquisitions where federal financial assistance or guarantees are an essential part of the transaction, or where the nature and magnitude of federal assistance is so pervasive as to substantially reduce the relevance of such information to an assessment of future operations. Where financial statements are waived, disclosure concerning the acquired business as outlined in response to Question 3 must be furnished.

Question 3: Where historical financial statements meeting the requirements of Rule 3-05 of Regulation S-X are waived, what financial statements and other disclosures would the staff expect to be provided in filings with the Commission?

Interpretive Response: Where complete audited historical financial statements of a significant acquiree that is a troubled financial institution are not provided, the staff would expect filings to include an audited statement of assets acquired and liabilities assumed if the acquisition is not already reflected in the registrant's most recent audited balance sheet at the time the filing is made. Where reasonably available, unaudited statements of operations and cash flows that are prepared in accordance with generally accepted accounting principles and otherwise comply with Regulation S-X should be filed in lieu of any audited financial statements which are not provided if historical information may be relevant.

In all cases where a registrant succeeds to assets and/or liabilities of a troubled financial institution which are significant to the registrant pursuant to the tests in Rule 1-02(v) of Regulation S-X, narrative descriptions would be required, quantified to the extent practicable, of the anticipated effects of the acquisition on the registrant's financial condition, liquidity, capital resources, and operating results. If federal financial assistance (including any commitments, agreements, or understandings made with respect to capital, accounting, or other forbearances) may be material, the limits, conditions, and other variables affecting its availability should be disclosed, along with analysis of its likely short-term and long-term effects on cash flows and reported results.

SEC 50901. Rule 9-01

If the transaction will result in the recognition of any significant intangibles that cannot be separately sold, such as goodwill or a core deposit intangible, the discussion of the transaction should describe the amount of such intangibles, the necessarily subjective nature of the estimation of the life and value of such intangibles, and the effects upon future results of operations, liquidity and capital resources, including any consequences if a recognized intangible will be excluded from the calculation of capital for regulatory purposes.

The discussion of the impact on future operations should specifically address the period over which intangibles will be amortized and the period over which any discounts on acquired assets will be taken into income. If amortization of intangibles will be over a period which differs from the period over which income from discounts on acquired assets will be recognized (whether from amortization of discounts or sale of discounted assets), disclosure should be provided concerning the disparate effects of the amortization and income recognition on operating results for all affected periods.

Information specified by Industry Guide 3 should be furnished to the extent applicable and reasonably available. For the categories identified in the Industry Guide, the registrant should disclose the carrying value of loans and investments acquired, as well as their principal amount and average contractual yield and term. Amounts of acquired investments, loans, or other assets that are nonaccrual, past due or restructured, or for which other collectibility problems are indicated should be disclosed. Where historical financial statements of the acquired entity are furnished, pro forma information presented pursuant to Rule 11-02 should be supplemented as necessary with a discussion of the likely effects of any federal assistance and changes in operations subsequent to the acquisition. To the extent historical financial statements meeting all the requirements of Rule 3-05 are not furnished, the filing should include an explanation of the basis for their omission.

Question 4: If an audited statement of assets acquired and liabilities assumed is required but certain of the assets conveyed in the transaction are subject to rights allowing the registrant to put the assets back to the seller upon completion of a due diligence review, will the staff grant an extension of time for filing the required financial statement until the put period lapses?

Interpretive Response: If it is impracticable to provide an audited statement at the time the Form 8-K reporting the transaction is filed, an extension of time is available under certain circumstances. Specifically, if more than 25% of the acquired assets may be put and the put period does not exceed 120 days, the registrant should timely file a statement of assets acquired and liabilities assumed on an unaudited basis with full disclosure of the terms and amounts of the put arrangement. Within 21 days after the put period lapses, the registrant should furnish an audited statement of assets acquired and liabilities assumed unless the effects of the transaction are already reflected in an audited balance sheet which has been filed, certain offerings under Securities Act of 1933 would be prevented, as described in Instruction 2 to Item 7 of Form 8-K.

SEC 50901

SAB Topic 11-G discusses the use of "tax-equivalent-adjusted" amounts in financial statements and in MD&A. "Tax equivalent adjustments" represent amounts added to interest income and income tax expense (if presented) in order to make the interest income and related yields on tax-exempt obligations comparable to those on taxable investments and loans. In the SAB, the staff takes the position that it is inappropriate to include such adjustments in the financial statements and related notes to financial statements since the interest income is never earned and realized and the income tax expense is never actually paid. The SAB indicates, however, that "tax equivalent adjustments" may be presented in the selected financial data and in MD&A provided that they are adequately identified and described and the unadjusted amounts are also provided.

The text of the SAB follows:

Tax Equivalent Adjustment in Financial Statements of Bank Holding Companies

Facts: Bank subsidiaries of bank holding companies frequently hold substantial amounts of state and municipal bonds, interest income from which is exempt from Federal income taxes. Because of the tax exemption the stated yield on these securities is lower than the yield on securities with similar risk and maturity characteristics whose interest is subject to Federal tax. In order to make the interest income and resultant yields on tax exempt obligations comparable to those on taxable investments and loans, a "tax equivalent adjustment" is often added to interest income when presented in analytical tables or charts. When the data presented also includes income taxes, a corresponding amount is added to income tax expense so that there is no effect on net income. Adjustment may also be made for the tax equivalent effect of exemption from state and local income taxes.

Question 1: Is the concept of the tax equivalent adjustment appropriate for inclusion in financial statements and related notes?

Interpretive Response: No. The tax equivalent adjustment represents a credit to interest income which is not actually earned and realized and a corresponding charge to taxes (or other expense) which will never be paid. Consequently, it should not be reflected on the income statement or in notes to financial statements included in reports to shareholders or in a report or registration statement filed with the Commission.

Question 2: May amounts representing tax equivalent adjustments be included in the body of a statement of income provided they are designated as not being included in the totals and balances on the statement?

Interpretive Response: No. The tabular format of a statement develops information in an orderly manner which becomes confusing when additional numbers not an integral part of the statement are inserted into it.

SEC 50901. Rule 9-01

Question 3: May revenues on a tax equivalent adjusted basis be included in selected financial data?

Interpretive Response: Revenues may be included in selected financial data on a tax equivalent basis if the respective captions state which amounts are tax equivalent adjusted and if the corresponding unadjusted amounts are also reported in the selected financial data.

Because of differences among registrants in making the tax equivalency computation, a brief note should describe the extent of recognition of exemption from Federal, state, and local taxes and the combined marginal or incremental rate used. Where net operating losses exist, the note should indicate the nature of the tax equivalency adjustment made.

Question 4: May information adjusted to a tax equivalent basis be included in management's discussion and analysis of financial condition and results of operations?

Interpretive Response: One of the purposes of management's discussion and analysis is to enable investors to appraise the extent that earnings have been affected by changes in business activity and accounting principles or methods. Material changes in items of revenue or expense should be analyzed and explained in textual discussion and statistical tables. It may be appropriate to use amounts or to present yields on a tax equivalent basis. If appropriate, the discussion should include a comment on material changes in investment securities positions that affect tax exempt interest income. For example, there might be a comment on a change from investments in tax exempt securities because of the availability of net operating losses to offset taxable income of current and future periods, or a comment on a change in the quality level of the tax exempt investments resulting in increased interest income and risk and a corresponding increase in the tax equivalent adjustment.

Tax equivalent adjusted amounts should be clearly identified and related to the corresponding unadjusted amounts in the financial statements. A descriptive note similar to that suggested to accompany adjusted amounts included in selected financial data should be provided.

SAB Topic 11-H.1, added by SAB No. 66, expresses the staff's views concerning loans to public and private sector borrowers located in countries that are experiencing liquidity problems. It sets forth certain minimum disclosures that the staff believes should be made in 1933 and 1934 Act filings regarding the possible impact of cross-border lending transactions on the registrant. The text of the SAB follows:

Disclosures by Bank Holding Companies Regarding Certain Foreign Loans

1. Deposit/Relending Arrangements

Facts: Certain foreign countries experiencing liquidity problems, by agreement with U.S. banks, have instituted arrangements whereby borrowers in the foreign country may remit local currency to the foreign country's central bank, in return for the central bank's assumption of the borrowers' non-local currency obligations to the U.S. banks. The local currency is held on deposit at the central bank, for the account of the U.S. banks, and may be subject to relending to other borrowers in the country. Ultimate repayment of the obligations to the U.S. banks, in the requisite non-local currency, may not be due until a number of years hence.

Question: What disclosures are appropriate regarding deposit/relending arrangements of this general type?

Interpretive Response: The staff emphasizes that it is the responsibility of each registrant to determine the appropriate financial statement treatment and classification of foreign outstandings. The facts and circumstances surrounding deposit/relending arrangements should be carefully analyzed to determine whether the local currency payments to the foreign central bank represent collections of outstandings for financial reporting purposes, and whether such outstandings should be classified as nonaccrual, past due or restructured loans pursuant to Item III.C.1. of Industry Guide 3, Statistical Disclosure by Bank Holding Companies ("Guide 3").

The staff believes, however, that the impact of deposit/relending arrangements covering significant amounts of outstandings to a foreign country should be disclosed pursuant to Guide 3, Item III.C.c., Instruction (6)(a). The disclosures should include a general description of the arrangements and, if significant, the amounts of interest income recognized for financial reporting purposes which has not been remitted in the requisite non-local currency to the U.S. bank.

FRR No. 27 amended the Industry Guides for Statistical Disclosures by Bank Holding Companies (see section 68000). Specifically, FRR No. 27 calls for a tabular analysis of changes in aggregate outstandings for each country experiencing liquidity problems where the aggregate outstandings exceed one percent of the registrant's total assets. The analyses are required to include the net change in amounts of short-term outstandings and amounts of balances, collections of principal and interest, interest income accrued, and other changes for other outstandings. If material amounts of outstandings to such countries are restructured (or if an agreement in principle for restructuring has been reached), the amendments call for tabular presentations of pre- and post-restructuring maturities and interest rates on the restructured amounts, disclosure of commitments arising in connection with the restructurings, and disclosure of amounts removed or expected to be removed from nonaccrual status as a result of the restructurings. The stated intent of the amendments is to enable users of bank holding company financial reports to better assess exposures to certain foreign countries, the nature of changes in those exposures, and the impact of significant restructurings of those exposures. The amendments are based largely on views of the SEC staff previously expressed in interpretive letters regarding disclosures of significant foreign debt restructurings in certain countries.

SEC 50901. Rule 9-01

SAB Topic 11-I, added by SAB No. 56, expresses the staff's views about the reporting of allocated transfer risk reserve (ATRR) provisions established when federal banking agencies determine that such reserves are necessary. The text of the SAB follows:

Reporting of an Allocated Transfer Risk Reserve in Filings Under the Federal Securities Laws

Facts: The Comptroller of the Currency, Board of Governors of the Federal Reserve System and Federal Deposit Insurance Corporation jointly issued final rules, pursuant to the International Lending Supervision Act of 1983, requiring banking institutions to establish special reserves (Allocated Transfer Risk Reserve "ATRR") against the risks presented in certain international assets when the Federal banking agencies determine that such reserves are necessary. The rules provide that the ATRR is to be accounted for separately from the General Allowances for Possible Loan Losses, and shall not be included in the banking institution's capital or surplus. The rules also provide that no ATRR provisions are required if the banking institution writes down the assets in the requisite amount.

Question: How should the ATRR be reported in filings under the Federal Securities Laws?

Interpretive Response: It is the staff's understanding that the three banking agencies believe that those bank holding companies that have not written down the designated assets by the requisite amount and, therefore, are required to establish an ATRR should disclose the amount of the ATRR. The staff believes that such disclosure should be part of the discussion of Loan Loss Experience, Item IV of Guide 3. Part A under Item IV calls for an analysis of loss experience in the form of a reconciliation of the allowance for loan losses, and the staff believes that it would be appropriate to show and discuss separately the ATRR in the context of that reconciliation.

Registrants should recognize that the amount provided as an ATRR, or the write-off of the requisite amount, represents the identification of an amount which those regulatory agencies have determined should not be included as a part of the institution's capital or surplus for purposes of administration of the regulatory and supervisory functions of those agencies. In this context, the staff believes that disclosure of the ATRR, as part of the footnote required to be presented in a registrant's financial statements by Item 7(d) of Rule 9-03 of Regulation S-X, may provide a more complete explanation of charge-offs and provisions for loan losses. It should be noted, however, that the ATRR amount to be excluded from the institution's capital and surplus does not address the more general issue of the adequacy of allowances for any particular bank holding company's loans. It is still the responsibility of each registrant to determine whether generally accepted accounting principles require an additional provision for losses in excess of the amount required to be included in an ATRR (or the requisite amount written off).

SEC 50901

SAB Topic 5-V, added by SAB No. 82, discusses the staff's views regarding the accounting for transfers of nonperforming assets by financial institutions. The SAB provides guidance as to when the transfer of nonperforming assets to a newly formed entity (the "new entity") may be accounted for as a disposition by the financial institution. Please note that this issue is also discussed in SAB Topic 5-E, *Accounting for Divestitures of a Subsidiary or Other Business Operation* (see section 82003). In SAB No. 82, the staff expresses its position that in determining whether a transfer of nonperforming assets to the new entity can be accounted for as a disposition, an assessment is required regarding whether the risks and rewards of ownership have been transferred.

The factors that the staff believes indicate that a transfer of nonperforming assets should not be accounted for as a sale or disposition include:

- The transfer provides for recourse by the new entity to the transferor;

- The transferor directly or indirectly guarantees the debt of the new entity in whole or in part;

- The transferor participates in the rewards of ownership of the transferred assets (e.g., with higher than normal incentive or management fee arrangements);

- The fair value of material noncash consideration received by the transferor cannot be reasonably estimated;

- The transferor retains rewards of ownership by holding significant residual equity interests; or

- Third-party holders of residual equity interests do not have significant amounts of at-risk capital.

In situations in which the transfer is accounted for as a sale, the staff's position is that the transferor should record the transaction at fair value of the assets transferred, or based on the fair value of assets received if more clearly evident. In the SAB, the staff addresses the determination of fair value and refers to similar concepts in SFAS No. 15, *Accounting by Debtors and Creditors for Troubled Debt Restructurings*, and FRR No. 28 (FRP Section 401.09), *Accounting for Loan Losses by Registrants Engaged in Lending Activities.*

The SAB also discusses Industry Guide 3 disclosures and factors related to the accounting for a note receivable or other redeemable instrument of the new entity when a transaction is appropriately accounted for as a sale.

The text of the SAB follows:

SEC 50901.   Rule 9-01

Certain Transfers of Nonperforming Assets

Facts: A financial institution desires to reduce its nonaccrual or reduced rate loans and other nonearning assets, including foreclosed real estate (collectively, "nonperforming assets"). Some or all of such nonperforming assets are transferred to a newly-formed entity (the "new entity"). The financial institution, as consideration for transferring the nonperforming assets, may receive (a) the cash proceeds of debt issued by the new entity to third parties, (b) a note or other redeemable instrument issued by the new entity, or (c) a combination of (a) and (b). The residual equity interests in the new entity, which carry voting rights, initially owned by the financial institution, are transferred to outsiders (for example, via distribution to the financial institution's shareholders or sale or contribution to an unrelated third party).

The financial institution typically will manage the assets for a fee, providing necessary services to liquidate the assets, but otherwise does not have the right to appoint directors or legally control the operations of the new entity.

Question 1: What factors should be considered in determining whether such transfer of nonperforming assets can be accounted for as a disposition by the financial institution?

Interpretive Response: The staff believes that determining whether nonperforming assets have been disposed of in substance requires an assessment as to whether the risks and rewards of ownership have been transferred.

SAB Topic 5-E[1] discusses some factors that the staff believes should be considered in determining whether the risks of a business have been transferred. Consistent with the factors discussed in SAB Topic 5-E, the staff believes that the transfer described should not be accounted for as a sale or disposition if (a) the transfer of nonperforming assets to the new entity provides for recourse by the new entity to the transferor financial institution, (b) the financial institution directly or indirectly guarantees debt of the new entity in whole or in part, (c) the financial institution retains a participation in the rewards of ownership of the transferred assets, for example, through a higher than normal incentive or other management fee arrangement,[2] or (d) the fair value of any material non-cash consideration received by the financial institution (for example, a note or other redeemable instrument) cannot be reasonably estimated. Additionally, the staff believes that the accounting for the transfer as a sale or disposition generally is not appropriate where the financial institution retains rewards of ownership through the holding of significant residual equity interests or where third party holders of such interests do not have a significant amount of capital at risk.

Where accounting for the transfer as a sale or disposition is not appropriate, the nonperforming assets should remain on the financial institution's balance sheet and should continue to be disclosed as nonaccrual, past due, restructured or foreclosed, as appropriate, and the debt of the new entity should be recorded by the financial institution.

SEC 50901

782

Question 2: If the transaction is accounted for as a sale, at what value should the transfer be recorded by the financial institution?

Interpretive Response: The staff believes that the transfer should be recorded by the financial institution at the fair value of assets transferred (or, if more clearly evident, the fair value of assets received) and a loss recognized by the financial institution for any excess of the net carrying value[3] over the fair value.[4] Fair value is the amount that would be realizable in an outright sale to an unrelated third party for cash.[5] Statement of Financial Accounting Standards No. 15, "Accounting by Debtors and Creditors for Troubled Debt Restructurings," and Financial Reporting Release No. 28 (Section 401.09 of the Financial Reporting Codification) discuss the determination of fair value of formally or substantively repossessed collateral. The same concepts should be applied in determining fair value of the transferred assets, i.e., if an active market exists for the assets transferred, then fair value is equal to the market value. If no active market exists, but one exists for similar assets, the selling prices in that market may be helpful in estimating the fair value. If no such market price is available, a forecast of expected cash flows, discounted at a rate commensurate with the risks involved, may be used to aid in estimating the fair value. In situations where discounted cash flows are used to estimate fair value of nonperforming assets, the staff would expect that the interest rate used in such computations will be substantially higher than the cost of funds of the financial institution and appropriately reflect the risk of holding these nonperforming assets. Therefore, the fair value determined in such a way will be lower than the amount at which the assets would have been carried by the financial institution had the transfer not occurred, unless the financial institution had been required under generally accepted accounting principles to carry such assets at market value or the lower of cost or market value.

Question 3: Where the transaction may appropriately be accounted for as a sale and the financial institution receives a note receivable or other redeemable instrument from the new entity, how should such asset be disclosed pursuant to Item III C, "Risk Elements," of Industry Guide 3? What factors should be considered related to the subsequent accounting for such instruments received?

Interpretive Response: The staff believes that the financial institution may exclude the note receivable or other asset from its Risk Elements disclosures under Guide 3 provided that: (a) the receivable itself does not constitute a nonaccrual, past due, restructured, or potential problem loan that would require disclosure under Guide 3, and (b) the underlying collateral is described in sufficient detail to enable investors to understand the nature of the note receivable or other asset, if material, including the extent of any over-collateralization. The description of the collateral normally would include material information similar to that which would be provided if such assets were owned by the financial institution, including pertinent Risk Element disclosures.

The staff notes that, in situations in which the transaction is accounted for as a sale and a portion of the consideration received by the registrant is debt or another redeemable instrument, careful consideration must be given to the appropriateness of recording profits on the management fee arrangement, or interest or dividends on the instrument received, including consideration of whether it is necessary to defer such amounts or to treat such payments on a cost recovery basis. Further, if the new entity incurs losses to the point that its permanent equity based on generally accepted accounting principles is eliminated, it would ordinarily be necessary for the financial institution, at a minimum, to record further operating losses as its best estimate of the loss in realizable value of its investment.[6]

---

[1]SAB Topic 5-E, "Accounting for Divestiture of a Subsidiary or Other Business Operation," addresses the accounting for the transfer of certain operations whereby there is a continuing involvement by the seller or other evidence that incidents of ownership remain with the seller.

[2]The staff recognizes that the determination of whether the financial institution retains a participation in the rewards of ownership will require an analysis of the facts and circumstances of each individual transaction. Generally, the staff believes that, in order to conclude that the financial institution has disposed of the assets in substance, the management fee arrangement should not enable the financial institution to participate to any significant extent in the potential increases in cash flows or value of the assets, and the terms of the arrangement, including provisions for discontinuance of services, must be substantially similar to management arrangements with third parties.

[3]The carrying value should be reduced by any allocable allowance for credit losses or other valuation allowances. The staff believes that the loss recognized for the excess of the net carrying value over the fair value should be considered a credit loss and thus should not be included by the financial institution as loss on disposition.

[4]The staff notes that the FASB's Emerging Issues Task Force (EITF) reached a consensus at its November 17, 1988 meeting on Issue 88-25 that the newly created "liquidating bank" should continue to report its assets and liabilities at fair values at the date of the financial statements.

[5]The FASB's Emerging Issues Task Force reached a consensus at its May 21, 1987 meeting on Issue No. 87-17, "Spin-off or other distributions of loans receivable to shareholders," that an enterprise that distributes loans to its owners should report such distribution at fair value.

[6]Typically, the financial institution's claim on the new entity is subordinate to other debt instruments and thus the financial institution will incur any losses beyond those incurred by the permanent equity holders.

SAB Topic 11-N, also added by SAB No. 82, expresses the staff's views regarding the required disclosure by a financial institution that receives financial assistance from a federal regulatory agency. The text of the SAB follows:

Disclosures of the Impact of Assistance from
Federal Financial Institution Regulatory Agencies

Facts: An entity receives financial assistance from a federal regulatory agency in conjunction with either an acquisition of a troubled financial institution, transfer of nonperforming assets to a newly-formed entity, or other reorganization.

Question: What are the disclosure implications of the existence of regulatory assistance?

Interpretive Response: The staff believes that users of financial statements must be able to assess the impact of credit and other risks on a company following a regulatory assisted acquisition, transfer or other reorganization on a basis comparable to that disclosed by other institutions, i.e., as if the assistance did not exist. In this regard, the staff believes that the amount of regulatory assistance should be disclosed separately and should be separately identified in the statistical information furnished pursuant to Industry Guide 3, to the extent it impacts such information. [1,2] Further, the nature, extent and impact of such assistance needs to be fully discussed in Management's Discussion and Analysis.[3]

---

[1] The staff has previously expressed its views regarding acceptable methods of compliance with this principle in the minutes of EITF Issue 88-19, and an announcement by the SEC Observer to the EITF at the February 23, 1989 meeting.
[2] Paragraph 9 of Statement of Financial Accounting Standards No. 72, "Accounting for Certain Acquisitions of Banking or Thrift Institutions," addresses the recording of regulatory assistance at the date of a purchase business combination and indicates that, "[i]f receipt of the assistance is probable and the amount is reasonably estimable, that portion of the cost of the acquired enterprise shall be assigned to such assistance." In addition, see Emerging Issues Task Force Issue 88-19 for guidance on the appropriate period in which to record certain types of regulatory assistance.
[3] See Section 501.06.c., "Effects of Federal Financial Assistance Upon Operations," of the Financial Reporting Codification for further discussion of the Management's Discussion and Analysis disclosures of the effects of regulatory assistance.

50902. Rule 9-02. General Requirement

The requirements of the general rules in Articles 1, 2, 3, 3A, and 4 should be complied with where applicable.

As indicated throughout Article 9, the disclosure requirements for items that are not unique to bank holding companies (e.g., common stock) often refer to the requirements specified in Article 5 relating to commercial and industrial companies.

50903. Rule 9-03. Balance Sheets

The purpose of this rule is to indicate the various items which, if applicable, should appear on the face of the balance sheets or in the notes thereto.

ASSETS

1. Cash and due from banks. *The amounts in this caption should include all noninterest bearing deposits with other banks.*

> *(a) Any withdrawal and usage restrictions (including requirements of the Federal Reserve to maintain certain average reserve balances) or compensating balance requirements should be disclosed (see Rule 5-02-1).*

2. Interest-bearing deposits in other banks.

3. Federal funds sold and securities purchased under resale agreements or similar arrangements. *These amounts should be presented gross and not netted against Federal funds purchased and securities sold under agreement to repurchase as reported in Caption 13.*

4. Trading account assets. *Include securities or any other investments held for trading purposes only.*

5. Other short-term investments.

6. Investment securities. *Include securities held for investment only. Disclose the aggregate book value of investment securities; show on the balance sheet the aggregate market value at the balance sheet date. The aggregate amounts should include securities pledged, loaned or sold under repurchase agreements and similar arrangements; borrowed securities and securities purchased under resale agreements or similar arrangements should be excluded.*

> *(a) Disclose in a note the carrying value and market value of securities of (1) the U.S. Treasury and other U.S. Government agencies and corporations; (2) states of the U.S. and political subdivisions; and (3) other securities.*

The SEC staff has informally indicated that in making the determination as to whether a decline in the value of a marketable equity security is "temporary" or "other than temporary," the following factors should be considered:

- A decline in market value need not be permanent in order to be considered "other than temporary" and thereby require recognition as a realized loss.

SEC 50903

- If a decline in market value reflects the market's perception of a "specific adverse condition," a writedown to realizable value is required.

The magnitude and duration of unrecognized market-value declines are important factors considered by the staff in assessing these determinations.

During 1991 the SEC issued two AAERs requiring registrants to restate their quarterly and annual financial statements because the SEC had determined that declines in the market value of certain marketable equity securities within their investment portfolio were "other than temporary." Although FASB Statement No. 115 was issued subsequent to these AAERs, many of the same issues apply in determining whether declines are "other than temporary." The SEC staff continues to focus attention on "other than temporary" declines and the accounting and disclosures relating to investment portfolios. Refer to detailed discussions of these issues provided in sections 50502.12 and 50703 of this manual.

7. Loans. *Disclose separately (1) total loans, (2) the related allowance for losses and (3) unearned income.*

> *(a) Disclose on the balance sheet or in a note the amount of total loans in each of the following categories:*
>
> > *(1) Commercial, financial and agricultural (2) Real estate—construction (3) Real estate—mortgage (4) Installment loans to individuals (5) Lease financing (6) Foreign (7) Other (State separately any other loan category regardless of relative size if necessary to reflect any unusual risk concentration).*
>
> *(b) A series of categories other than those specified in (a) above may be used to present details of loans if considered a more appropriate presentation.*
>
> *(c) The amount of foreign loans must be presented if the disclosures provided by Rule 9-05 are required.*
>
> *(d) For each period for which an income statement is required, furnish in a note a statement of changes in the allowance for loan losses showing the balances at beginning and end of the period provision charged to income, recoveries of amounts charged off and losses charged to the allowance.*
>
> *(e)(1)(i) As of each balance sheet date, disclose in a note the aggregate dollar amount of loans (exclusive of loans to any such persons which in the aggregate do not exceed $60,000 during the latest year) made by the registrant or any of its subsidiaries to directors, executive officers, or principal holders of equity securities (Rule 1-02) of the registrant or any of its significant subsidiaries (Rule 1-02), or to any associate of such persons. For the latest fiscal year, an analysis of activity with respect to such aggregate*

SEC 50903. Rule 9-03

loans to related parties should be provided. The analysis should include the aggregate amount at the beginning of the period, new loans, repayments, and other changes. (Other changes, if significant, should be explained.)

(ii) This disclosure need not be furnished when the aggregate amount of such loans at the balance sheet date (or with respect to the latest fiscal year, the maximum amount outstanding during the period) does not exceed 5 percent of stockholders' equity at the balance sheet date.

(2) If a significant portion of the aggregate amount of loans outstanding at the end of the fiscal year disclosed pursuant to (e)(1)(i) above relates to loans which are disclosed as nonaccrual, past due, restructured or potential problems (see Item III.C.1. or 2. of Industry Guide 3, Statistical Disclosure by Bank Holding Companies), so state and disclose the aggregate amounts of such loans along with such other information necessary to an understanding of the effects of the transactions on the financial statement.

(3) Notwithstanding the aggregate disclosure called for by (e)(1) above, if any loans were not made in the ordinary course of business during any period for which an income statement is required to be filed, provide an appropriate description of each such loan (see Rule 4-08(l)(3)).

(4) Definition of terms. For purposes of this rule, the following definitions shall apply:

"Associate" means (i) a corporation, venture or organization of which such person is a general partner or is, directly or indirectly, the beneficial owner of 10 percent or more of any class of equity securities; (ii) any trust or other estate in which such person has a substantial beneficial interest or for which such person serves as trustee or in a similar capacity and (iii) any member of the immediate family or any of the foregoing persons.

"Executive officers" means the president, any vice president in charge of a principal business unit, division or function (such as loans, investments, operations, administration or finance), and any other officer or person who performs similar policymaking functions.

"Immediate family" means such person's spouse; parents; children; siblings; mothers- and fathers-in-law; sons- and daughters-in-law; and brothers and sisters-in-law.

"Ordinary course of business" means those loans which were made on substantially the same terms, including interest rate and collateral, as those prevailing at the same time for comparable transactions with unrelated persons and did not involve more than the normal risk of collectibility or present other unfavorable features.

SEC 50903

FASB Statement No. 114, *Accounting by Creditors for Impairment of a Loan*, specifies that "a loan is impaired when, based on current information and events, it is probable that a creditor will be unable to collect all amounts due according to the contractual terms of the loan agreement." This Statement amends FASB Statement No. 5, *Accounting for Contingencies*, by stating that "all amounts due according to the contractual terms" refers to both the contractual interest and principal payments collectible based on the terms of the contract. When it is determined that a loan is impaired, this Statement requires the creditor to measure impairment "based on the present value of expected future cash flows discounted at the loan's effective interest rate, except that as a practical expedient, a creditor may measure impairment based on a loan's observable market value, or the fair value of the collateral if the loan is collateral dependent." Refer to FASB Statement No. 114 for further guidance regarding the impairment of a loan including certain loans that are exempt from this Statement.

The SEC staff's informal views concerning restructured loans and disclosure of nonaccrual loans are as follows:

Restructured loans—It is the staff's position that the form of a single loan restructuring should not affect the accounting for or disclosures relating to the loan. The following examples illustrate the staff's concerns in this area:

Example 1

A lender has entered into a troubled debt restructuring that divides a single loan agreement into two or three separate agreements. One or two of the new loan agreements are fully performing market rate loans and the residual loan is a zero coupon financial instrument with an equity kicker. The residual loan is, in substance, the "risk" element of the restructured arrangement. The staff believes that in this situation, the resulting two or more agreements must be viewed as *one* note for purposes of applying SFAS No. 15. The staff has pointed out that it would look at the aggregate of the individual pieces of the transaction to determine whether the projected cash flows would be sufficient to cover the combined carrying amount. If recovery of the combined carrying amount is in doubt, the staff believes that cash received on any of the agreements should be applied to reduce the carrying amount until such doubt is eliminated. Subsequently, cash received on the agreements should, in the staff's view, be allocated between the carrying amount and interest in accordance with SFAS No. 15. In the staff's view, actual splitting of the loan and/or the actual form of the documentation should not affect the accounting or disclosure.

Example 2

A troubled debt restructuring leads to the division of one loan agreement into two or more separate agreements. Subsequently, the lender sells one of the new agreements.

SEC 50903. Rule 9-03

The SEC staff believes that the carrying amount of the combined restructured loans should be allocated between the portion sold and the portion retained in accordance with EITF Issue No. 88-11.

In all cases the SEC staff has pointed out that the registrant needs to provide the disclosures required by SFAS No. 15 in the year of restructuring. However, the SEC staff has indicated that such disclosures need not be repeated in subsequent years if the effective rate on the restructured note at least equals a market rate at the date of restructuring.

Disclosures of nonaccrual loans—Due to recent increases in nonaccrual loans resulting from the current economic environment, the staff has indicated that it may be necessary for registrants to provide additional information to adequately disclose material aspects of the nonaccrual loan portfolio. The quantitative disclosures called for in Industry Guide 3, *Statistical Disclosure by Bank Holding Companies* (Instruction (4) of Section III, Item C 1., Risk Elements), are representative of the type of disclosures that may be required. In addition, the SEC staff has indicated that registrants should consider the updating requirements of General Instruction 3(d).

8. Premises and equipment.

9. Due from customers on acceptances. *Include amounts receivable from customers on unmatured drafts and bills of exchange that have been accepted by a bank subsidiary or by other banks for the account of a subsidiary and that are outstanding— that is, not held by a subsidiary bank, on the reporting date. (If held by a bank subsidiary, they should be reported as "loans" under Rule 9-03.7.)*

10. Other assets. *Disclose separately on the balance sheet or in a note thereto any of the following assets or any other asset the amount of which exceeds 30 percent of stockholders' equity. The remaining assets may be shown as one amount.*

(1) Excess of cost over tangible and identifiable intangible assets acquired (net of amortization).

(2) Other intangible assets (net of amortization).

(3) Investments in and indebtedness of affiliates and other persons.

(4) Other real estates.

(a) Disclose in a note the basis at which other real estate is carried. Any reduction to fair market value from the carrying value of the related loan at the time of acquisition shall be accounted for as a loan loss. Any allowance for losses on other real estate which has been established

SEC 50903

subsequent to acquisition should be deducted from other real estate. For each period for which an income statement is required, disclosures should be made in a note as to the changes in the allowances, including balance at beginning and end of period, provision charged to income, and losses charged to the allowance.

11. Total assets.

LIABILITIES AND STOCKHOLDERS' EQUITY

Liabilities

12. Deposits. *Disclose separately the amounts of noninterest bearing deposits and interest bearing deposits.*

(a) The amount of noninterest bearing deposits and interest bearing deposits in foreign banking offices must be presented if the disclosures provided by Rule 9-05 are required.

13. Short-term borrowing. *Disclose separately on the balance sheet or in a note, amounts payable for (1) Federal funds purchased and securities sold under agreements to repurchase; (2) commercial paper; and (3) other short-term borrowings.*

(a) Disclose any unused lines of credit for short-term financing (Rule 5-02.19(b)).

14. Bank acceptances outstanding. *Disclose the aggregate of unmatured drafts and bills of exchange accepted by a bank subsidiary, or by some other bank as its agent, less the amount of such acceptances acquired by the bank subsidiary through discount or purchase.*

15. Other liabilities. *Disclose separately on the balance sheet or in a note any of the following liabilities or any other items which are individually in excess of 30 percent of stockholders' equity (except that amounts in excess of 5 percent of stockholders' equity should be disclosed with respect to item (4)). The remaining items may be shown as one amount.*

(1) Income taxes payable.

(2) Deferred income taxes.

(3) Indebtedness to affiliates and other persons the investments in which are accounted for by the equity method.

SEC 50903. Rule 9-03

(4) Indebtedness to directors, executive officers, and principal holders of equity securities of the registrant or any of its significant subsidiaries (the guidance in Rule 9-03.7(e) shall be used to identify related parties for purposes of this disclosure).

(5) Accounts payable and accrued expenses.

16. Long-term debt. *Disclose in a note the information required by Rule 5-02.22.*

17. Commitments and contingent liabilities.

18. Minority interest in consolidated subsidiaries. *The information required by Rule 5-02.27 should be disclosed, if applicable.*

Redeemable Preferred Stocks

19. Preferred stocks subject to mandatory redemption requirements or whose redemption is outside the control of the issuer. *See Rule 5-02.28.*

Nonredeemable Preferred Stocks

20. Preferred stocks which are not redeemable or are redeemable solely at the option of the issuer. *See Rule 5-02.29.*

Common Stocks

21. Common stocks. *See Rule 5-02.30.*

Other Stockholders' Equity

22. Other stockholders' equity. *See Rule 5-02.31.*

23. Total liabilities and stockholders' equity.

50904. Rule 9-04. Income Statements

The purpose of this rule is to indicate the various items which, if applicable, should appear on the face of the income statement or in the notes thereto.

1. Interest and fees on loans. *Include commitment and origination fees, late charges and current amortization of premium and accretion of discount on loans which are related to or are an adjustment of the loan interest rate.*

SEC 50904

SFAS No. 91, *Accounting for Nonrefundable Fees and Costs Associated with Originating or Acquiring Loans and Initial Direct Costs of Leases,* establishes the accounting for nonrefundable fees and costs associated with lending, committing to lend, or purchasing a loan or group of loans. Some of the important concepts addressed in this Statement are:

- Loan origination fees are required to be deferred and recognized over the life of the loan as an adjustment of yield (paragraph 5);

- Certain direct loan origination costs (as defined in paragraph 6 of SFAS No. 91) are also required to be deferred and recognized over the life of the loan as a reduction of the loan's yield (except for troubled debt restructurings in which these costs are required to be expensed as incurred) (paragraph 5);

- All fees received for a commitment to originate or purchase a loan or group of loans are required to be deferred and, if the commitment is exercised, recognized over the life of the loan as an adjustment to yield. If the commitment expires unexercised, the fees are to be recognized upon expiration of the commitment (note that a different accounting treatment may be required if it is remote that the commitment will be exercised or if the fee is determined retrospectively) (paragraph 8); and

- Adjustments to yield will generally be determined by the interest method based on the contractual provisions of the loan, although prepayments may be anticipated in certain situations specified by SFAS No. 91 (paragraph 18).

2. Interest and dividends on investment securities. *Disclose separately (1) taxable interest income, (2) nontaxable interest income, and (3) dividends.*

3. Trading account interest.

4. Other interest income.

5. Total interest income *(total of lines 1 through 4).*

6. Interest on deposits.

7. Interest on short-term borrowings.

8. Interest on long-term debt.

9. Total interest expense *(total of lines 6 through 8).*

SEC 50904. Rule 9-04

10. Net interest income *(line 5 minus line 9).*

11. Provision for loan losses.

12. Net interest income after provision for loan losses.

13. Other income. *Disclose separately any of the following amounts, or any other item of other income, which exceed one percent of the aggregate of total interest income and other income. The remaining amounts may be shown as one amount, except for investment securities gains or losses, which shall be shown separately regardless of size.*

> *(a) Commissions and fees from fiduciary activities.*

> *(b) Commissions, broker's fees and markups on securities underwriting and other securities activities.*

> *(c) Insurance commissions, fees and premiums.*

> *(d) Fees for other customer services.*

> *(e) Profit or loss on transactions in securities in dealer trading account.*

> *(f) Equity in earnings of unconsolidated subsidiaries and 50 percent or less owned persons.*

> *(g) Gains or losses on disposition of equity in securities of subsidiaries or 50 percent or less owned persons.*

> *(h) Investment securities gains or losses. The method followed in determining the cost of investments sold (e.g., "average cost," "first-in, first-out," or "identified certificate") and related income taxes shall be disclosed.*

14. Other expenses. *Disclose separately any of the following amounts, or any other item of other expense, which exceed one percent of the aggregate of total interest income and other income. The remaining amounts may be shown as one amount.*

> *(a) Salaries and employee benefits.*

> *(b) Net occupancy expense of premises.*

> *(c) Goodwill amortization.*

> *(d) Net cost of operation of other real estate (including provisions for real estate losses, rental income and gains and losses on sales of real estate).*

> *(e) Minority interest in income of consolidated subsidiaries.*

SEC 50904

15. Income or loss before income tax expense.

16. Income tax expense. *The information required by Rule 4-08(h) should be disclosed.*

SAB Topic 5-X, added by SAB No. 91, discusses the SEC staff's position regarding accounting for income tax benefits associated with bad debts of thrifts. In accordance with APB Opinion No. 23, *Accounting for Income Taxes—Special Areas,* thrifts are not required to provide deferred income taxes for the difference between taxable income and pretax accounting income attributable to a reserve for bad debts until it is likely that taxes will be paid. Regarding this accounting, the staff believes that it is inappropriate for a thrift to recognize the deferred income tax benefits relating to its bad debt reserve for financial reporting purposes ("book reserve") *unless* the thrift has recognized the deferred income tax liability related to its bad debt reserve for tax purposes ("tax reserve").

However, the staff has indicated that it will not object to the recognition of the income tax benefit related to the excess of the book reserve over the tax reserve, provided that there is a likelihood that future benefits will result. Refer to information required to be disclosed by the SEC in support of income taxes described in Rule 4-08(h) (see section 50408-h).

17. Income or loss before extraordinary items and cumulative effects of changes in accounting principles.

18. Extraordinary items, less applicable tax.

19. Cumulative effects of changes in accounting principles.

20. Net income or loss.

21. Earnings per share data.

50905. Rule 9-05. Foreign Activities

(a) General requirement. *Separate disclosure concerning foreign activities shall be made for each period in which either (1) assets, or (2) revenue, or (3) income (loss) before income tax expense, or (4) net income (loss), each as associated with foreign activities, exceeded ten percent of the corresponding amount in the related financial statements.*

(b) Disclosures.

(1) Disclose total identifiable assets (net of valuation allowances) associated with foreign activities.

SEC 50904. Rule 9-04

(2) For each period for which an income statement is filed, state the amount of revenue, income (loss) before taxes, and net income (loss) associated with foreign activities. Disclose significant estimates and assumptions (including those related to the cost of capital) used in allocating revenue and expenses to foreign activities; describe the nature and effects of any changes in such estimates and assumptions which have a significant impact on interperiod comparability.

(3) The information in paragraph (b)(1) and (2) of this section shall be presented separately for each significant geographic area and in the aggregate for all other geographic areas not deemed significant.

(c) Definitions.

(1) "Foreign activities" include loans and other revenue producing assets and transactions in which the debtor or customer, whether an affiliated or unaffiliated person, is domiciled outside the United States.

(2) The term "revenue" includes the total of the amount reported at Rules 9-04.5 and 9-04.13.

(3) A "significant geographic area" is one in which assets or revenue or income before income tax or net income exceed 10 percent of the comparable amount as reported in the financial statements.

50906. Rule 9-06. Condensed Financial Information of Registrant

The information prescribed by Rule 12-04 shall be presented in a note to the financial statements when the restricted net assets (Rule 4-08(e)(3)) of consolidated subsidiaries exceed 25 percent of consolidated net assets as of the end of the most recently completed fiscal year. The investment in and indebtedness of and to bank subsidiaries shall be stated separately in the condensed balance sheet from amounts for other subsidiaries; the amount of cash dividends paid to the registrant for each of the last three years by bank subsidiaries shall be stated separately in the condensed income statement from amounts for other subsidiaries. For purposes of the above test, restricted net assets of consolidated subsidiaries shall mean that amount of the registrant's proportionate share of net assets of consolidated subsidiaries (after intercompany eliminations) which as of the end of the most recent fiscal year may not be transferred to the parent company by subsidiaries in the form of loans, advances or cash dividends without the consent of a third party (i.e., lender, regulatory agency, foreign government, etc.). Where restrictions on the amount of funds which may be loaned or advanced differ from the amount restricted as to transfer in the form of cash dividends, the amount least restrictive to the subsidiary shall be used. Redeemable preferred stocks (Rule 5-02.28) and minority interests shall be deducted in computing net assets for purposes of this test.

For a discussion of Rule 4-08(e) and the related calculation to determine whether this schedule is required, refer to sections 50408 and 50520.

50907. Rule 9-07. Schedules

(a) The following schedules, which should be examined by an independent accountant, should be filed unless the required information is not applicable or is presented in the related financial statements.

Schedule I. Indebtedness to related parties. *The schedule prescribed by Rule 12-05 should be filed for each period for which an income statement is required in support of any amounts required to be reported by Rule 9-03.15(4) unless such aggregate amount does not exceed 5 percent of stockholders' equity at either the beginning or the end of the period.*

Schedule II. Guarantees of securities of other issuers. *The schedule prescribed by Rule 12-08 should be filed as of the date of the most recent audited balance sheet with respect to any guarantees of securities of other issuers by the person for which the statements are being filed.*

51000. ARTICLE 10. INTERIM FINANCIAL STATEMENTS

51001. Rule 10-01. Interim Financial Statements

The text of this rule is included and annotated, where applicable, in sections 51002 through 51006.

51002. Condensed statements [footnote requirements].

(a) Interim financial statements shall follow the general form and content of presentation prescribed by the other sections of this Regulation with the following exceptions:

(1) Interim financial statements required by this rule need only be provided as to the registrant and its subsidiaries consolidated and may be unaudited. Separate statements of other entities which may otherwise be required by this Regulation may be omitted.

(2) Interim balance sheets shall include only major captions (i.e., numbered captions) prescribed by the applicable sections of this Regulation with the exception of inventories. Data as to raw materials, work in process and finished goods inventories shall be included either on the face of the balance sheet or in the notes to the financial statements, if applicable. Where any major balance sheet caption is less than 10% of total assets, and the amount in the caption has not increased or decreased by more than 25% since the end of the preceding fiscal year, the caption may be combined with others.

(3) Interim statements of income shall also include major captions prescribed by the applicable sections of this Regulation. When any major income statement caption is less than 15% of average net income for the most recent three fiscal years and the amount in the caption has not increased or decreased by more than 20% as compared to the corresponding interim period of the preceding fiscal year, the caption may be combined with others. In calculating average net income, loss years should be excluded. If losses were incurred in each of the most recent three years, the average loss shall be used for purposes of this test.

Notwithstanding these tests, Rule 4-02 of Regulation S-X applies and de minimis amounts therefore need not be shown separately, except that registrants reporting under Article 9 (Bank Holding Companies) shall show investment securities gains or losses separately regardless of size.

(4) The statement of cash flows may be abbreviated starting with a single figure of net cash flows from operating activities and showing cash changes from investing and financing activities individually only when they exceed 10% of the average of net cash flows from operating activities for the most recent three years. Notwithstanding this test, Rule 4-02 of Regulation S-X applies and de minimis amounts, therefore, need not be shown separately.

(5) The interim financial information shall include disclosures either on the face of the financial statements or in accompanying footnotes sufficient so as to make the interim information presented not misleading. Registrants may presume that users of the interim financial information have read or have access to the audited financial statements for the preceding fiscal year and that the adequacy of additional disclosure needed for a fair presentation, except in regard to material contingencies, may be determined in that context. Accordingly, footnote disclosure which would substantially duplicate the disclosure contained in the most recent annual report to security holders or latest audited financial statements, such as a statement of significant accounting policies and practices, details of accounts which have not changed significantly in amount or composition since the end of the most recently completed fiscal year, and detailed disclosures prescribed by Rule 4-08 of this Regulation, may be omitted. However, disclosure shall be provided where events subsequent to the end of the most recent fiscal year have occurred which have a material impact on the registrant. Disclosures should encompass for example, significant changes since the end of the most recently completed fiscal year in such items as: accounting principles and practices; estimates inherent in the preparation of financial statements; status of long-term contracts; capitalization including significant new borrowings or modification of existing financing arrangements; and the reporting entity resulting from business combinations or dispositions. Notwithstanding the above, where material contingencies exist, disclosure of such matters shall be provided even though a significant change since year-end may not have occurred.

(6) Detailed schedules otherwise required by this Regulation may be omitted for purposes of preparing interim financial statements.

(7) In addition to the financial statements required by paragraphs (a)(2), (3) and (4) of this section, registrants in the development stage shall provide the cumulative financial statements (condensed to the same degree as allowed in this paragraph) and disclosures required by Statement of Financial Accounting

SEC 51002. Rule 10-01

Standards No. 7, "Accounting and Reporting by Development Stage Enterprises" to the date of the latest balance sheet presented.

Article 10 contains the uniform instructions as to the form and content of interim financial statements presented in registration statements and periodic reports filed with the SEC, which allow interim financial statements to be presented in condensed format. The article also contains the rules governing the dates and periods to be covered by financial statements included in Form 10-Q. See discussion of Rules 3-01 and 3-02 in sections 50301 and 50302, respectively, for the dates and periods for which interim financial statements are required in registration statements.

Paragraph (a) of Rule 10-01 sets forth the requirements for the financial statement captions and footnotes to be presented in interim financial statements, and includes the criteria for combining captions. Note that statements of changes in stockholders' equity and schedules are not required as part of the condensed interim statements. However, the condensed statements are required to follow generally accepted accounting principles for interim reporting (APB Opinion No. 28 and any subsequent amendments and interpretations). Registrants may, for example, present the condensed interim data by including additional columns adjacent to the audited financial statements. Alternatively, the condensed interim data may be separate from the audited statements.

Item (5) of paragraph (a) specifies that, although interim financial statements should contain disclosures sufficient to make the information presented not misleading, it may be presumed that users of the interim report have read or have access to the audited financial statements for the preceding fiscal year. Accordingly, footnote disclosures already included in the statements for the preceding fiscal year need not be repeated unless events or circumstances have occurred since the end of the most recent fiscal year that have a material impact on the registrant or matters discussed in the annual financial statements have changed and are no longer applicable (e.g., a change in an accounting principle). However, where material contingencies exist, disclosure of such matters is required to be provided even though a significant change since year-end has not occurred. The SEC staff believes that such disclosure is required in accordance with APB Opinion No. 28.

The following informal views relating to interim financial information have been provided by the SEC staff:

- When a new accounting standard is adopted in an interim period, the staff's position is that all of the disclosures prescribed by the standard for annual financial statements should be included in the interim financial statements, in addition to any transitional disclosures required by the standard. The staff has indicated that it does not expect registrants to repeat the disclosures in Form 10-Qs filed subsequent to the period of adoption unless there has been a significant change in the information previously provided.

SEC 51002

- Questions have been raised concerning the need to amend previous Form 10-Q filings when standards such as those required to be applied as of the beginning of a fiscal year are adopted in the fourth quarter. The staff's position is that previously filed interim reports that were correct when filed need not be amended for a later change in accounting principles. In such cases, the Form 10-K would be used to provide the restated quarterly information.

- As a general rule fair value of financial instrument disclosures required by SFAS 107, *Disclosures About Fair Value of Financial Instruments*, are not required to be included in interim financial statements filed with the SEC. However, it is the staff's view that material changes in those fair values, resulting from events such as changes in market conditions, will generally warrant a discussion in MD&A included in interim reports on Form 10-Q. In particular, the staff has noted that disclosures of this nature, made on an annual basis, that highlight those fair values that are particularly susceptible to slight movements in market conditions, would need to be updated in interim reports when there are significant changes in market conditions. The disclosures would also need to address the consequences to the company of such changing conditions.

In SAB Topic 6-H4.b the SEC staff concluded that disclosures as to compensating balances required by Regulation S-X (adopted in ASR No. 148) are not required in Form 10-Q. However, the SAB cautions that material changes in borrowing arrangements or levels may give rise to the need for disclosure either in Form 10-Q or Form 8-K.

Other matters that may require disclosure in interim periods include significant accounting changes; events reported in Form 8-K filings since the previous quarterly or annual report; extraordinary, unusual, or infrequently occurring items; unusual adjustments; changes in the company's business activities (including decisions concerning disposals of segments of the business); unusual seasonal results; significant business combinations; loss contingencies that existed at the date of the last review (or audit) or have arisen since then; events between the date of the interim financial information and the completion of our review that would materially affect such information (i.e., subsequent events discussed in AU 561, *Subsequent Events*); or other significant events that might affect either the interim or annual financial statements.

SAB Topic 6-G2.a provides the following guidelines on presenting condensed interim financial statements:

Form of Condensed Financial Statements

Facts: Rules 10-01(a)(2) and (3) of Regulation S-X provide that interim balance sheets and statements of income shall include only major captions (i.e., numbered

SEC 51002. Rule 10-01

captions) set forth in Regulation S-X, with the exception of inventories, where data as to raw materials, work in process and finished goods shall be included, if applicable, either on the face of the balance sheet or in notes thereto. Where any major balance sheet caption is less than 10% of total assets and the amount in the caption has not increased or decreased by more than 25% since the end of the preceding fiscal year, the caption may be combined with others. When any major income statement caption is less than 15% of average net income for the most recent three fiscal years and the amount in the caption has not increased or decreased by more than 20% as compared to the corresponding interim period of the preceding fiscal year, the caption may be combined with others. Similarly, the statement of changes in financial position may be abbreviated, starting with a single figure of funds provided by operations and showing other sources and applications individually only when they exceed 10% of the average of funds provided by operations for the most recent three years.

Question 1: If a company previously combined captions in a Form 10-Q but is required to present such captions separately in the Form 10-Q for the current quarter, must it retroactively reclassify amounts included in the prior-year financial statements presented for comparative purposes to conform with the captions presented for the current-year quarter?

Interpretive Response: Yes.

Question 2: In determining whether or not major income statement captions may be combined, does average "net income" for the last three years (using the company's last year-end as the starting point) mean "net income" or income before extraordinary items and changes in accounting principles?

Interpretive Response: It means "net income."

Question 3: If a company uses the gross profit method or some other method to determine cost of goods sold for interim periods, will it be acceptable to state only that it is not practicable to determine components of inventory at interim periods?

Interpretive Response: The staff believes disclosure of inventory components is important to investors. In reaching this decision the staff recognizes that registrants may not take inventories during interim periods and that managements, therefore, will have to estimate the inventory components. However, the staff believes that management will be able to make reasonable estimates of inventory components based upon their knowledge of the company's production cycle, the costs (labor and overhead) associated with this cycle as well as the relative sales and purchasing volume of the company.

Question 4: If a company has years during which operations resulted in a net outflow of funds, should it exclude such years from the computation of funds provided by operations for the three most recent years in determining what sources and applications must be shown separately?

SEC 51002

Interpretive Response: Yes. Similar to the determination of average net income, if operations resulted in a net outflow of funds during any year, such amount should be excluded in making the computation of funds provided by operations for the three most recent years unless operations resulted in a net of outflow of funds in all three years, in which case the average of the net outflow of funds should be used for the test.

Question 5: Must a company include an analysis of changes in each element of working capital in the condensed statement of changes in financial position included in its Form 10-Q?

Interpretive Response: No. The statement of changes in financial position can be abbreviated and needs to include only funds provided by operations and other sources and applications of funds which exceed 10% of the average of funds provided by operations for the most recent three years.

Subsequent to the issuance of this SAB, Regulation S-X has been revised to require a statement of cash flows in lieu of the previous requirement for a statement of changes in financial position. Although the official text of the SAB has not been updated, it should be read in the context of the noted revision.

51003. Other instructions as to content.

(b) The following additional instructions shall be applicable for purposes of preparing interim financial statements:

(1) Summarized income statement information shall be given separately as to each subsidiary not consolidated or 50 percent or less owned persons or as to each group of such subsidiaries or 50 percent or less owned persons for which separate individual or group statements would otherwise be required for annual periods. Such summarized information, however, need not be furnished for any such unconsolidated subsidiary or person which would not be required pursuant to Rule 13a-13 or 15d-13 to file quarterly financial information with the Commission if it were a registrant.

(2) If appropriate, the income statement shall show earnings per share and dividends per share applicable to common stock. The basis of the earnings per share computation shall be stated together with the number of shares used in the computation. In addition, see Item 601(b)(11) of Regulation S-K.

(3) If, during the most recent interim period presented, the registrant or any of its consolidated subsidiaries entered into a business combination treated for accounting purposes as a pooling of interests, the interim financial statements for both the current year and the preceding year shall reflect the combined results of the pooled businesses. Supplemental disclosure of the separate results

of the combined entities for periods prior to the combination shall be given, with appropriate explanations.

(4) Where a material business combination accounted for as a purchase has occurred during the current fiscal year, pro forma disclosure shall be made of the results of operations for the current year up to the date of the most recent interim balance sheet provided (and for the corresponding period in the preceding year) as though the companies had combined at the beginning of the period being reported on. This pro forma information should as a minimum show revenue, income before extraordinary items and the cumulative effect of accounting changes, including such income on a per share basis, and net income and net income per share.

(5) Where the registrant has disposed of any significant segment of its business (as defined in paragraph 13 of Accounting Principles Board Opinion No. 30) during any of the periods covered by the interim financial statements, the effect thereof on revenues and net income—total and per share—for all periods shall be disclosed.

(6) In addition to meeting the reporting requirements specified by existing standards for accounting changes, the registrant shall state the date of any material accounting change and the reasons for making it. In addition, for filings on Form 10-Q, a letter from the registrant's independent accountant shall be filed as an exhibit (in accordance with the provisions of Item 601 of Regulation S-K) in the first Form 10-Q subsequent to the date of an accounting change indicating whether or not the change is to an alternative principle which in his judgment is preferable under the circumstances; except that no letter from the accountant need be filed when the change is made in response to a standard adopted by the Financial Accounting Standards Board which requires such change.

(7) Any material retroactive prior period adjustment made during any period covered by the interim financial statements shall be disclosed, together with the effect thereof upon net income—total and per share—of any prior period included and upon the balance of retained earnings. If results of operations for any period presented have been adjusted retroactively by such an item subsequent to the initial reporting of such period, similar disclosure of the effect of the change shall be made.

(8) Any unaudited interim financial statements furnished shall reflect all adjustments which are, in the opinion of management, necessary to a fair statement of the results for the interim periods presented. A statement to that effect shall be included. Such adjustments shall include, for example, appropriate estimated provisions for bonus and profit sharing arrangements normally determined or

settled at year-end. If all such adjustments are of a normal recurring nature, a statement to that effect shall be made; otherwise, there shall be furnished information describing in appropriate detail the nature and amount of any adjustments other than normal recurring adjustments entering into the determination of the results shown.

Paragraph (b) of Rule 10-01 includes additional instructions applicable to the form and content of interim financial statements.

Item (1) specifies that summarized income statement information for unconsolidated subsidiaries and 50 percent or less owned (equity) persons is required to be presented for only those unconsolidated subsidiaries and equity persons for which individual or combined financial statements would otherwise be required for annual periods (i.e., those that were "significant" in the most recent Form 10-K; see section 50341) and that would be required to file Form 10-Q if they were registrants. The information to be disclosed, as specified in paragraph (2) of Rule 1-02(aa), should be "net sales or gross revenues, gross profit (or, alternatively, costs and expenses applicable to net sales or gross revenues), income or loss from continuing operations before extraordinary items and cumulative effect of a change in accounting principle, and net income or loss." See section 50343 for further discussion of summarized financial information.

The earnings per share exhibit required pursuant to item (2) of paragraph (b) is discussed in section 66000 of the manual.

Item (6) under paragraph (b) requires that the date of any discretionary interim period accounting change and the reasons for making the change be disclosed in any document filed with the SEC that includes interim financial information. Note that any such change must meet the reporting requirements specified in paragraphs 23 through 29 of APB Opinion No. 28 and any amendments to it adopted by the FASB (refer to FASB Statement Nos. 3 and 16 and Interpretation No. 20). Filings on Form 10-Q are required to include a letter from the registrant's independent accountants commenting on the preferability of the accounting change. It is important to note, however, that the SEC has indicated that independent auditors may rely, and express that reliance in their letter, on management's determination as to elements of business judgment and business planning that entered into management's decision to adopt the new accounting principle. Registrants who are considering an accounting change should be aware of this provision. Refer to the Exhibit requirements in Regulation S-K (section 66000) and SAB Topic 6-G2.b (included in section 20620) for further information concerning accountants' preferability letters. Refer to discussion regarding reporting on post-balance-sheet pooling of interests included in section 50321.

Item (7) of paragraph (b) specifies the disclosures required in connection with material retroactive prior-period adjustments made during any period covered by the interim financial statements.

SEC 51003. Rule 10-01

FASB Statement No. 16, *Prior Period Adjustments*, as amended by SFAS 109, *Accounting for Income Taxes*, contains GAAP requirements pertaining to prior-period adjustments. Pursuant to SFAS 16, all items of profit and loss recognized during a period, including estimated loss contingency accruals, are to be included in the determination of net income for that period except for:

- "The correction of an error in the financial statements of a prior period" (paragraph 11), and

- "Adjustments related to prior interim periods of the current fiscal year" (paragraphs 13 and 14).

It is important to note that SFAS 16 does not affect the manner of reporting accounting changes required or permitted by other FASB and APB pronouncements.

Item (8) requires that management include a statement indicating that the information furnished reflects all adjustments that are necessary to a fair statement of the results for the interim periods presented as well as representation as to whether such adjustments are of a "normal recurring nature."

51004. Periods to be covered in filings on Form 10-Q.

(c) The periods for which interim financial statements are to be provided in registration statements are prescribed elsewhere in this Regulation (see Rules 3-01 and 3-02). For filings on Form 10-Q, financial statements shall be provided as set forth below:

(1) An interim balance sheet as of the end of the most recent fiscal quarter and a balance sheet as of the end of the preceding fiscal year shall be provided. The balance sheet as of the end of the preceding fiscal year may be condensed to the same degree as the interim balance sheet provided. An interim balance sheet as of the end of the corresponding fiscal quarter of the preceding fiscal year need not be provided unless necessary for an understanding of the impact of seasonal fluctuations on the registrant's financial condition.

(2) Interim statements of income shall be provided for the most recent fiscal quarter, for the period between the end of the preceding fiscal year and the end of the most recent fiscal quarter, and for the corresponding periods of the preceding fiscal year. Such statements may also be presented for the cumulative twelve month period ended during the most recent fiscal quarter and for the corresponding preceding period.

(3) Interim statements of cash flows shall be provided for the period between the end of the preceding fiscal year and the end of the most recent fiscal quarter, and for the corresponding period of the preceding fiscal year. Such statements

may also be presented for the cumulative twelve month period ended during the most recent fiscal quarter and for the corresponding preceding period.

(4) Registrants engaged in seasonal production and sale of a single- crop agricultural commodity may provide interim statements of income and cash flows for the twelve month period ended during the most recent fiscal quarter and for the corresponding preceding period in lieu of the year-to-date statements specified in (2) and (3) above.

Paragraph (c) of this rule specifies the dates and periods for which condensed interim financial statements are required in Form 10-Q. For ease of reference, these requirements are summarized below:

Balance Sheet	Statement of Income	Statement of Cash Flows
As of the end of the current quarter *and* as of the end of preceding fiscal year.	Current quarter and corresponding quarter of the preceding year *and* fiscal year-to-date and corresponding period of the preceding year.	Fiscal year-to-date and corresponding period of the preceding year.

The rule specifies that registrants engaged in the seasonal production and sale of a single-crop agricultural commodity may furnish comparative 12-month statements ending with the current quarter *instead* of the year-to-date periods specified above. Other registrants who present such statements in Form 10-Q may do so *in addition* to the periods specified above.

As discussed in section 51005, the condensed interim financial statements included in Form 10-Q are not required to be audited. However, the condensed year-end balance sheet is derived from the audited year-end financial statements. The staff of the SEC has informally indicated that it is generally inappropriate to designate the condensed interim period balance sheet data "unaudited" when no indication is made regarding the audit status of the condensed year-end balance sheet data presented. In the staff's view, the "unaudited" designation relative to the interim date may imply that the condensed year-end data has been audited, and therefore includes all required disclosures. However, the staff has indicated that such an approach would generally be acceptable if the following footnote disclosure is provided:

The year-end condensed balance sheet data was derived from audited financial statements, but does not include all disclosures required by generally accepted accounting principles.

Consequently, the aforementioned information need not contain any specific designation concerning audit status unless the auditor is associated with it. Refer to section

SEC 51004. Rule 10-01

20360 for a discussion of reporting requirements when an independent accountant is associated with a Form 10-Q filed with the SEC that also contains a condensed year-end balance sheet summarized from audited financial statements.

51005. Review by independent public accountant.

(d) The interim financial information included in filings with the Commission need not be reviewed by an independent public accountant prior to filing. If, however, a review of the data is made in accordance with established professional standards and procedures for such a review, the registrant may state that the independent accountant has performed such a review. If such a statement is made, the report of the independent accountant on such review shall accompany the interim financial information.

Interim financial information included in documents filed with the SEC is not required to be reviewed or audited by independent accountants, but if a review is made in accordance with existing professional standards and procedures (AU Section 722, *Interim Financial Information*), the registrant is entitled to state that such a review was performed. When such reference is made, the report of the independent accountant needs to accompany the interim financial information. Reference should be made to section 20350 for an example of a report on interim financial information prepared in accordance with AU Section 722.

51006. Filing of other interim financial information in certain cases.

(e) The Commission may, upon the informal written request of the registrant, and where consistent with the protection of investors, permit the omission of any of the interim financial information herein required or the filing in substitution therefor of appropriate information of comparable character. The Commission may also, by informal written notice, require the filing of other information in addition to, or in substitution for, the interim information herein required in any case where such information is necessary or appropriate for an adequate presentation of the financial condition of any person for which interim financial information is required, or whose financial information is otherwise necessary for the protection of investors.

Paragraph (e) of Rule 10-01 permits both registrants and the SEC some flexibility when circumstances justify certain deviations from the specific instructions. Refer to section 50347 following Rule 3-13 for further discussion of these flexibility provisions.

51100. ARTICLE 11. PRO FORMA FINANCIAL INFORMATION

51101. Rule 11-01. Presentation Requirements

(a) Pro forma financial information shall be furnished when any of the following conditions exist:

(1) During the most recent fiscal year or subsequent interim period for which a balance sheet is required by Rule 3-01, a significant business combination accounted for as a purchase has occurred (for purposes of these rules, the term "purchase" encompasses the purchase of an interest in a business accounted for by the equity method);

(2) After the date of the most recent balance sheet filed pursuant to Rule 3-01, consummation of a significant business combination to be accounted for by either the purchase method or pooling-of-interests method of accounting has occurred or is probable;

(3) Securities being registered by the registrant are to be offered to the security holders of a significant business to be acquired or the proceeds from the offered securities will be applied directly or indirectly to the purchase of a specific significant business;

(4) The disposition of a significant portion of a business either by sale, abandonment or distribution to shareholders by means of a spin-off, split-up or split-off has occurred or is probable and such disposition is not fully reflected in the financial statements of the registrant included in the filing;

(5) During the most recent fiscal year or subsequent interim period for which a balance sheet is required by Rule 3-01, the registrant has acquired one or more

real estate operations or properties which in the aggregate are significant, or since the date of the most recent balance sheet filed pursuant to that section the registrant has acquired or proposes to acquire one or more operations or properties which in the aggregate are significant;

(6) Pro forma financial information required by section 914 of Regulation S-K is required to be provided in connection with a roll-up transaction as defined in section 901(c) of Regulation S-K.

(7) The registrant previously was a part of another entity and such presentation is necessary to reflect operations and financial position of the registrant as an autonomous entity; or

(8) Consummation of other events or transactions has occurred or is probable for which disclosure of pro forma financial information would be material to investors.

(b) A business combination or disposition of a business shall be considered significant if:

(1) A comparison of the most recent annual financial statements of the business acquired or to be acquired and the registrant's most recent annual consolidated financial statements filed at or prior to the date of acquisition indicates that the business would be a significant subsidiary pursuant to the conditions specified in Rule 1-02, or

(2) The business to be disposed of meets the conditions of a significant subsidiary in Rule 1-02.

(c) When consummation of more than one transaction has occurred or is probable during a fiscal year, the tests of significance in (b) above shall be applied to the cumulative effect of those transactions. If the cumulative effect of the transactions is significant, pro forma financial information shall be presented.

(d) For purposes of this rule, the term business should be evaluated in light of the facts and circumstances involved and whether there is sufficient continuity of the acquired entity's operations prior to and after the transactions so that disclosure of prior financial information is material to an understanding of future operations. A presumption exists that a separate entity, a subsidiary, or a division is a business. However, a lesser component of an entity may also constitute a business. Among the facts and circumstances which should be considered in evaluating whether an acquisition of a lesser component of an entity constitutes a business are the following:

(1) Whether the nature of the revenue-producing activity of the component will remain generally the same as before the transaction; or

SEC 51101

(2) Whether any of the following attributes remain with the component after the transaction:

   (i) Physical facilities,

   (ii) Employee base,

   (iii) Market distribution system,

   (iv) Sales force,

   (v) Customer base,

   (vi) Operating rights,

   (vii) Production techniques, or

   (viii) Trade names.

(e) This rule does not apply to transactions between a parent company and its totally held subsidiary.

51102. Rule 11-02. Preparation Requirements

(a) Objective. *Pro forma financial information should provide investors with information about the continuing impact of a particular transaction by showing how it might have affected historical financial statements if the transaction had been consummated at an earlier time. Such statements should assist investors in analyzing the future prospects of the registrant because they illustrate the possible scope of the change in the registrant's historical financial position and results of operations caused by the transaction.*

(b) Form and content.

(1) Pro forma financial information shall consist of a pro forma condensed balance sheet, pro forma condensed statements of income, and accompanying explanatory notes. In certain circumstances (i.e., where a limited number of pro forma adjustments are required and those adjustments are easily understood), a narrative description of the pro forma effects of the transaction may be furnished in lieu of the statements described herein.

(2) The pro forma financial information shall be accompanied by an introductory paragraph which briefly sets forth a description of (i) the transaction, (ii) the entities involved, and (iii) the periods for which the pro forma information is presented. In addition, an explanation of what the pro forma presentation shows shall be set forth.

SEC 51101. Rule 11-01

(3) The pro forma condensed financial information need only include major captions (i.e., the numbered captions) prescribed by the applicable sections of this Regulation. Where any major balance sheet caption is less than 10 percent of total assets, the caption may be combined with others. When any major income statement caption is less than 15 percent of average net income of the registrant for the most recent three fiscal years, the caption may be combined with others. In calculating average net income, loss years should be excluded unless losses were incurred in each of the most recent three years, in which case the average loss shall be used for purposes of this test. Notwithstanding these tests, de minimis amounts need not be shown separately.

(4) Pro forma statements shall ordinarily be in columnar form showing condensed historical statements, pro forma adjustments, and the pro forma results.

(5) The pro forma condensed income statement shall disclose income (loss) from continuing operations before nonrecurring charges or credits directly attributable to the transaction. Material nonrecurring charges or credits and related tax effects which result directly from the transaction and which will be included in the income of the registrant within the 12 months succeeding the transaction shall be disclosed separately. It should be clearly indicated that such charges or credits were not considered in the pro forma condensed income statement. If the transaction for which pro forma financial information is presented relates to the disposition of a business, the pro forma results should give effect to the disposition and be presented under an appropriate caption.

(6) Pro forma adjustments related to the pro forma condensed income statement shall be computed assuming the transaction was consummated at the beginning of the fiscal year presented and shall include adjustments which give effect to events that are (i) directly attributable to the transaction, (ii) expected to have a continuing impact on the registrant, and (iii) factually supportable. Pro forma adjustments related to the pro forma condensed balance sheet shall be computed assuming the transaction was consummated at the end of the most recent period for which a balance sheet is required by Rule 3-01 and shall include adjustments which give effect to events that are directly attributable to the transaction and factually supportable regardless of whether they have a continuing impact or are nonrecurring. All adjustments should be referenced to notes which clearly explain the assumptions involved.

(7) Historical primary and fully diluted per share data based on continuing operations (or net income if the registrant does not report either discontinued operations, extraordinary items, or the cumulative effects of accounting changes) for the registrant, and primary and fully diluted pro forma per share data based on continuing operations before nonrecurring charges or credits directly attributable to the transaction shall be presented on the face of the pro

forma condensed income statement together with the number of shares used to compute such per share data. For transactions involving the issuance of securities, the number of shares used in the calculation of the pro forma per share data should be based on the weighted average number of shares outstanding during the period adjusted to give effect to shares subsequently issued or assumed to be issued had the particular transaction or event taken place at the beginning of the period presented. If a convertible security is being issued in the transaction, consideration should be given to the possible dilution of the pro forma per share data.

(8) If the transaction is structured in such a manner that significantly different results may occur, additional pro forma presentations shall be made which give effect to the range of possible results.

Instructions. *1. The historical statement of income used in the pro forma financial information shall not report operations of a segment that has been discontinued, extraordinary items, or the cumulative effects of accounting changes. If the historical statement of income includes such items, only the portion of the income statement through "income from continuing operations" (or the appropriate modification thereof) should be used in preparing pro forma results.*

2. For a purchase transaction, pro forma adjustments for the income statement shall include amortization of goodwill, depreciation and other adjustments based on the allocated purchase price of net assets acquired. In some transactions, such as in financial institution acquisitions, the purchase adjustments may include significant discounts of the historical cost of the acquired assets to their fair value at the acquisition date. When such adjustments will result in a significant effect on earnings (losses) in periods immediately subsequent to the acquisition which will be progressively eliminated over a relatively short period, the effect of the purchase adjustments on reported results of operations for each of the next five years should be disclosed in a note.

3. For a disposition transaction, the pro forma financial information shall begin with the historical financial statements of the existing entity and show the deletion of the business to be divested along with the pro forma adjustments necessary to arrive at the remainder of the existing entity. For example, pro forma adjustments would include adjustments of interest expense arising from revised debt structures and expenses which will be or have been incurred on behalf of the business to be divested such as advertising costs, executive salaries and other costs.

4. For entities which were previously a component of another entity, pro forma adjustments should include adjustments similar in nature to those referred to in

Instruction 3 above. Adjustments may also be necessary when charges for corporate overhead, interest, or income taxes have been allocated to the entity on a basis other than one deemed reasonable by management.

5. Adjustments to reflect the acquisition of real estate operations or properties for the pro forma income statement shall include a depreciation charge based on the new accounting basis for the assets, interest financing on any additional or refinanced debt, and other appropriate adjustment that can be factually supported. See also Instruction 4 above.

6. When consummation of more than one transaction has occurred or is probable during a fiscal year, the pro forma financial information may be presented on a combined basis; however, in some circumstances (e.g., depending upon the combination of probable and consummated transactions, and the nature of the filing) it may be more useful to present the pro forma financial information on a disaggregated basis even though some or all of the transactions would not meet the tests of significance individually. For combined presentations, a note should explain the various transactions and disclose the maximum variances in the pro forma financial information which would occur for any of the possible combinations. If the pro forma financial information is presented in a proxy or information statement for purposes of obtaining shareholder approval of one of the transactions, the effects of that transaction must be clearly set forth.

7. Tax effects, if any, of pro forma adjustments normally should be calculated at the statutory rate in effect during the periods for which pro forma condensed income statements are presented and should be reflected as a separate pro forma adjustment.

(c) Periods to be presented.

(1) A pro forma condensed balance sheet as of the end of the most recent period for which a consolidated balance sheet of the registrant is required by Rule 3-01 shall be filed unless the transaction is already reflected in such balance sheet.

(2)(i) Pro forma condensed statements of income shall be filed for only the most recent fiscal year and for the period from the most recent fiscal year end to the most recent interim date for which a balance sheet is required. A pro forma condensed statement of income may be filed for the corresponding interim period of the preceding fiscal year. A pro forma condensed statement of income shall not be filed when the historical income statement reflects the transaction for the entire period.

(ii) For a business combination accounted for as a pooling of interests, the pro forma income statements (which are in effect a restatement of the historical income statements as if the combination had been consummated)

SEC 51102

shall be filed for all periods for which historical income statements of the registrant are required.

(3) Pro forma condensed statements of income shall be presented using the registrant's fiscal year end. If the most recent fiscal year end of any other entity involved in the transaction differs from the registrant's most recent fiscal year end by more than 93 days, the other entity's income statement shall be brought up to within 93 days of the registrant's most recent fiscal year end, if practicable. This updating could be accomplished by adding subsequent interim period results to the most recent fiscal year-end information and deducting the comparable preceding year interim period results. Disclosure shall be made of the periods combined and of the sales or revenues and income for any periods which were excluded from or included more than once in the condensed pro forma income statements (e.g., an interim period that is included both as part of the fiscal year and the subsequent interim period). For investment companies subject to Rules 6-01 to 6-10, the periods covered by the pro forma statements must be same.

(4) Whenever unusual events enter into the determination of the results shown for the most recently completed fiscal year, the effect of such unusual events should be disclosed and consideration should be given to presenting a pro forma condensed income statement for the most recent twelve-month period in addition to those required in paragraph (c)(2)(i) above if the most recent twelve-month period is more representative of normal operations.

51103. Rule 11-03. Presentation of Financial Forecast

(a) A financial forecast may be filed in lieu of the pro forma condensed statements of income required by Rule 11-02(b)(1).

(1) The financial forecast shall cover a period of at least 12 months from the latest of (i) the most recent balance sheet included in the filing or (ii) the consummation date or estimated consummation date of the transaction.

(2) The forecasted statement of income shall be presented in the same degree of detail as the pro forma condensed statement of income required by Rule 11-02(b)(3).

(3) Assumptions particularly relevant to the transaction and effects thereof should be clearly set forth.

(4) Historical condensed financial information of the registrant and the business acquired or to be acquired, if any, shall be presented for at least a recent 12 month period in parallel columns with the financial forecast.

SEC 51102. Rule 11-02

(b) Such financial forecast shall be presented in accordance with the guidelines established by the American Institute of Certified Public Accountants.

(c) Forecasted earnings per share data shall be substituted for pro forma per share data.

(d) This rule does not permit the filing of a financial forecast in lieu of pro forma information required by generally accepted accounting principles.

51104. When Pro Forma Statements Are Required

Rule 11-01 sets forth the conditions under which the pro forma financial disclosure is required to be included in registration statements and certain other documents (e.g., Form 8-K) filed with the SEC. While the need for pro forma financial information most frequently occurs in connection with business combinations, the rule also applies to other events. For example, the disposition of a significant portion of a business may also necessitate pro forma financial information. Rule 11-01(a)(8) points out that there could be other events or transactions for which pro forma financial information may be required if the "pro forma financial information would be material to investors." Other events or transactions for which pro forma financial information may be necessary include situations in which:

- The registrant's balance sheet is not indicative of the ongoing entity (see section 50505).

- Dividends are declared by a subsidiary subsequent to the balance sheet date (see section 50505).

- Redeemable preferred stock or debt converts to common stock at either the effective or closing date of an IPO (see section 50502.31).

- Other changes in capitalization occur at or prior to the closing date of an IPO (see section 50502.31).

- An issuer was formerly a subchapter S corporation, a partnership, or a similar tax-exempt enterprise (see section 50502.31).

In the case of a business combination, the pro forma rules apply when (1) a purchase transaction has occurred during the most recent fiscal year (or subsequent interim period for which financial statements are included in the filing) or (2) when a purchase or pooling transaction has occurred or is "probable" of occurring after the date of the most recent balance sheet included in the document being filed.

816

The criteria for determining the "significance" of a business combination (or disposition) are the same as those used in the determination of a significant subsidiary as set forth in Rule 1-02(v) (see section 50102). Note, however, that Rule 11-01(c) states that the test of significance needs to be applied on a cumulative basis if more than one transaction has occurred or is probable of occurring during a fiscal year.

Paragraph (d) of Rule 11-01 provides some guidance for determining when a component of an entity may constitute a "business." As the rule points out, these guidelines should be evaluated in light of the facts and circumstances involved and whether there is sufficient continuity of the acquired entity's operations prior to and after the transaction that would indicate whether disclosure of historical financial information is material to an understanding of future operations. The SEC staff has informally indicated that it generally considers the acquisition of a property by an oil and gas company to be the acquisition of a business. As a general rule, the staff also considers individual hotels, motels and nursing homes to be businesses. As to transactions that are still being negotiated or have not been consummated at the time the registration statement is filed, consideration also needs to be given to providing historical financial statements of the proposed target pursuant to Rule 3-05 (see section 50314) in addition to pro forma financial statements. FRR No. 2 (FRP Section 506.02.c.ii) indicates that a proposed acquisition of a business is probable "whenever the registrant's financial statements alone would not provide investors with adequate financial information with which to make an investment decision."

Pro forma financial statements may sometimes be required to reflect the effect of receiving funds from a proposed offering. The SEC staff has informally indicated that when some or all of the proceeds of an offering are to be used for general corporate purposes or future investments (such as for property, plant and equipment) it is not acceptable to include in the pro forma presentation the assumed income from temporary investment of such proceeds. The SEC has adopted rules that specify the conditions under which such statements are appropriate.

Registration statements filed under the 1933 Act are subject to Rule 170, as follows:

Prohibition of Use of Certain Financial Statements

Financial statements which purport to give effect to the receipt and application of any part of the proceeds from the sale of securities for cash shall not be used unless such securities are to be offered through underwriters and the underwriting arrangements are such that the underwriters are or will be committed to take and pay for all of the securities, if any are taken, prior to or within a reasonable time after the commencement of the public offering, or if the securities are not so taken to refund to all subscribers the full amount of all subscription payments made for the securities. The caption of any such financial statement shall clearly set forth the assumptions upon which such statement is based. The caption shall be in type at least as large as that used generally in the body of the statement.

SEC 51104. Rule 11-03

Filings under the 1934 Act are covered by Rule 15c1-9, as follows:

Use of Pro Forma Balance Sheets

The term "manipulative, deceptive, or other fraudulent device or contrivance," as used in Section 15(c)(1) of the Act, is hereby defined to include the use of financial statements purporting to give effect to the receipt and application of any part of the proceeds from the sale or exchange of securities, unless the assumptions upon which each such financial statement is based are clearly set forth as part of the caption to each such statement in type at least as large as that used generally in the body of the statement.

Note that the rule under the 1933 Act relates to the receipt and application of cash proceeds from the sale of securities, whereas the rule under the 1934 Act applies to the receipt and application of the proceeds from the sale *or exchange* of securities. However, neither Rule 170 under the 1933 Act nor Rule 15c1-9 under the 1934 Act prohibits the use of pro forma financial statements in the case of an exchange offer even though there is no assurance that the exchange offer will be successfully consummated because it is opposed by the management of the target company.

51105. Form and Content of Pro Forma Information

51106. General. Rule 11-02 contains instructions for the preparation of pro forma financial information. The pro forma financial statements furnished may be limited to a condensed balance sheet and a condensed income statement, generally in no greater detail than that which would be required by Article 10 (see section 51000) for reports on Form 10-Q. The pro forma financial statements need to be supported by explanatory notes describing each of the pro forma adjustments. As a general rule, pro forma adjustments should not be netted. An introductory paragraph describing the transaction, the entities involved, the periods for which the information is presented, and an explanation of the pro forma presentation should also be a part of the pro forma statements.

When a limited number of adjustments are required and are easily understood, Rule 11-02 permits pro forma disclosure of the effects of a transaction in the form of a narrative description in lieu of pro forma financial statements.

51107. Pro forma statement of income. The pro forma statement of income should be based on the historical statement of income, but should only include those elements that are part of *continuing operations*. The pro forma statement of income should not include material nonrecurring charges or credits directly attributable to the transaction that will be included in the registrant's income statement within 12 months after the transaction; rather, material nonrecurring items and their related tax effects should be disclosed separately, and the pro forma income statement should clearly

818

indicate that nonrecurring items have not been included. For example, if an acquiror were to immediately shut down a plant obtained in a business combination, any resulting charge to earnings should not be included in the pro forma statement of income. Rather, the charge and its resulting tax effect should be disclosed in a separate footnote. Nonrecurring items that are already included in the historical financial statements and are *not* directly related to the transaction should not be eliminated in the pro forma income statement.

The pro forma adjustments to the historical statements of income from continuing operations are computed assuming the transaction was consummated at the *beginning of the most recent fiscal year presented.* For example, a company with a December 31 year-end presenting pro forma income statements for both the year ended December 31, 1994 and the interim period ended March 31, 1995 should present the pro forma statements for both periods as if the business combination occurred on January 1, 1994. For purchase transactions, the pro forma statements of income may only be presented for the most recent fiscal year and interim period. The presentation of the corresponding interim period for the preceding fiscal year is optional.

The pro forma statement of income for a business combination accounted for as a purchase should include the following columnar information:

- A column presenting the condensed consolidated income statement of the acquiring company (the registrant) for the latest full fiscal year and any subsequent interim period through the caption entitled "income from continuing operations."

- Columns presenting a condensed statement of income from continuing operations of each acquired business for the same or comparable period.

- Adjustments necessary to account for the acquisition, with appropriate explanatory footnotes.

- An adjusted column for each period.

Pro forma statements of income are also required for an acquisition of a business after the date of the latest balance sheet included in the document being filed to be accounted for as a pooling of interests. Such statements generally would only consist of a compilation of the historical statements of income of the combining and combined companies; however, any necessary adjustments, such as those required to reflect costs incurred to effect the combination, should be included and described in the footnotes. Such statements, in the case of poolings of interest, should cover all periods for which historical statements of income are presented. For further discussion of post-balance-sheet pooling of interests, see section 50321 of this manual.

SEC 51107. Rule 11-03

51108. Pro forma balance sheet. The pro forma balance sheet should be prepared assuming the transaction was consummated *on the latest balance sheet date.* This differs from the pro forma income statement, which is to be prepared assuming the event occurred at the beginning of the latest complete fiscal year. The adjustments to the balance sheet should give effect to all events that are directly attributable to the transaction and factually supportable, whether they have a continuing impact or are nonrecurring. The adjustments should be supported by footnotes that clearly explain the assumptions involved.

The pro forma balance sheet is generally presented in columnar format and would include:

- A column presenting the most recent consolidated balance sheet of the acquiring company (the registrant) included in the document being filed.

- Columns presenting a balance sheet of each of the constituent companies to the business combination.

- Adjustments required to account for the acquisition or business combination (with appropriate explanatory footnotes).

- The adjusted column representing the pro forma combined balance sheet.

51109. Periods to be covered. Pro forma income statements are required to be presented for the latest fiscal year and any subsequent interim period for which historical statements are furnished. Rule 11-02 points out that pro forma income statements should not be filed when the historical income statements include the transaction for a full fiscal year. The SEC staff has informally indicated that registrants may provide pro forma financial information for the most recent 12-month period in lieu of separate statements for the most recent fiscal year and the subsequent interim period.

For a business combination accounted for as a pooling of interests, the pro forma income statements (which are, in effect, a restatement of the historical income statements as if the combination had been consummated) are required to be filed for all periods for which historical income statements of the registrant are required.

When the combining and combined companies have differing fiscal years, the question often arises as to how the years should be combined for the purpose of preparing the pro forma statements of income. Rule 11-02(c)(3) provides that when the to-be-combined company has a different fiscal year from that of the registrant, the latest fiscal year should be recast to a date within 93 days of the registrant's most recent fiscal year-end. This should be done, if practicable, by adding subsequent interim periods and deducting comparable preceding periods. If periods other than comparable periods are combined, the periods combined should be disclosed as well as the sales and income for periods that were excluded from or included more than once in the

820

condensed pro forma income statement. A pro forma balance sheet is only required in connection with an acquisition (either a purchase or a pooling) or other reportable event that occurred after the date of the latest balance sheet of the registrant furnished pursuant to Rule 3-01. The effect of transactions on the financial position of the registrant occurring before that date would already be reflected in the registrant's balance sheet, and a pro forma balance sheet is therefore not required.

The pro forma balance sheet should be as of the same date as the latest balance sheet of the registrant. If this is not practicable, the most recent available balance sheet of each entity included in the filing document is generally used.

51110. Preparation guidelines. One of the SEC staff's principal concerns relating to the preparation of pro forma financial statements is that the adjustments be factually supportable. In the staff's view, assumptions of undocumented cost savings, anticipated proceeds from asset sales without a supporting contract or letter of intent (appraisals would generally not be sufficient), and/or anticipated investment income from the proceeds of an offering are generally inappropriate. An example of a nonfactually supported adjustment would be the assumption of an increase in revenues resulting from the purchase of a customer list.

The following SEC staff positions should also be considered in connection with the development of pro forma statements:

- When a business combination is involved, the allocation of the purchase price to the various assets and liabilities acquired should be reflected (on an estimated basis, if necessary).

  •• If additional information is needed to measure a contingency of the acquiree during the SFAS No. 38 allocation period, the fact that the purchase price allocation is preliminary should be disclosed along with a description of the nature of the contingency and information regarding any potential accrual and the range of any reasonably possible loss.

  •• If contingent consideration is issuable based on future earnings, the terms and potential impact on future earnings should be disclosed.

- All significant pro forma assumptions should be disclosed (e.g., the interest rate on new debt to be incurred).

- A calculation of the purchase price should be presented, if it is not evident.

- If financing for the combination is not permanent, the effect on income of a variance in the interest rate should be disclosed.

SEC 51109. Rule 11-03

- In a business combination, a pro forma adjustment to the allowance for loan losses is likely to raise questions as to whether the underlying financial statements are fairly presented.

- Registrants should consider the need to present a range of possible results on a pro forma basis when more than one outcome is reasonably possible. An example might be where a business combination is under consideration (probable) and it is uncertain as to whether pooling-of- interests accounting will be applicable, since one of the parties has the ability to defeat the pooling. The SEC staff would expect a registrant in this type of situation to present two sets of pro forma statements: one on a pooling basis and the other on a purchase basis.

- The following adjustments are generally not appropriate on the face of the respective pro forma financial statements, but may be included in the footnotes:

  •• Interest income from the use of proceeds.

  •• Income statement presentation of gains and losses directly attributable to the transaction. However, such amounts should be presented as an adjustment to pro forma retained earnings with an appropriate explanation in the notes.

  •• Elimination of operating results of a disposal made during the year that is *not* directly attributable to the transaction. Alternatively, an additional pro forma column reflecting other transactions may be appropriate.

51111. Staff Accounting Bulletins. There are a number of SABs that deal with topics that should be considered in connection with the preparation of pro forma financial statements. In addition to SAB Topic 2-C, discussed below, the SABs relating to accounting for a purchase acquisition, discussed in section 50337, and SAB Topic 1-B, discussed in section 50505, should be considered in connection with the preparation of pro forma financial statements if such statements are required.

In SAB Topic 2-C (SAB No. 45) the staff concluded that, while it was not appropriate to make retroactive adjustments to financial statements to reflect adjustments in officers' salaries following consummation of a merger, if the adjustments are significant, it may be necessary to provide supplemental pro forma financial information to prevent the financial statements from being misleading. The text of the SAB follows:

SEC 51111

Pro Forma Financial Information

Facts: Company X and Company Y (a closely owned and managed organization) agree to merge in a transaction to be accounted for as a pooling of interests. In connection with the merger agreement, the combined enterprise enters into an employment agreement with A, Company Y's executive officer and sole share-holder. The salary to be paid to A pursuant to the employment agreement is substantially less than the compensation A received from Company Y. Prior to the merger, a substantial portion of Company Y's annual earnings had been paid to the executive officer as salary.

Question 1: Is it appropriate to adjust Y's financial statements or the combined historical financial statements by transferring a portion of the executive officer's compensation from "Salary Expense" to "Distribution to Shareholder" in order to reflect the compensation level provided for in the new employment contract?

Interpretive Response: No. The determination of salary paid to owners is highly discretionary and although compensation exceeded that which will be paid in the future, retroactive adjustments to financial statements to reduce salary expense are not appropriate.

Question 2: In such circumstances, may pro forma financial information be presented for the combined enterprise which reflects the salary that will be paid to A after consummation of the transaction?

Interpretive Response: Yes. In exceptional circumstances, adjustments in officers' salaries, following consummation of a merger, may be so significant as to make the combined historical results of operations unrepresentative of future operating results. Under these circumstances, the financial statements of the combined enterprise may be supplemented with a pro forma financial presentation which shows the effects of salary changes that are supported by employment agreements. Such pro forma presentation should be limited to the latest fiscal year and any subsequent interim period should be presented. It should be accompanied by an explanation that (1) the supplemental pro forma presentation is shown solely as a result of changed circumstances that will exist following consummation of the merger, (2) that A's duties and responsibilities will not be diminished with the result that other costs will be incurred that offset the pro forma adjustment to compensation expense, and (3) the information is necessary for investors to realistically assess the impact of the combination. The following is an example of such supplemental pro forma presentation.

SEC 51111. Rule 11-03

	19X1	19X2	19X3
Combined net income	$10,000	$11,000	$12,000
Pro forma adjustment to compensation expense:			
Contractual reduction to			
be made in officer salary			60,000
Related income taxes			(30,000)
			30,000
Pro forma net income after			
contractual reduction to be			
made in officer salary			$42,000
Per share of common stock:			
Net income	$1.00	$1.10	$1.20
Pro forma net income after			
contractual reduction to be			
made in officer salary			$4.20

51112. Presentation of a Forecast

Rule 11-03 specifies that a financial forecast may be furnished in lieu of the pro forma statement of income required by Rule 11-02. The rule provides guidance with respect to the preparation of such a forecast and emphasizes that AICPA standards and guidelines in this respect should be followed. See section 60500 for a discussion of prospective financial information. The presentation of a forecast is typically appropriate in situations in which the historical pro forma income statement would not be indicative of the future operations of the entity. It is important to note, however, that paragraph (d) of Rule 11-03 specifies that this rule does not permit the filing of a financial forecast in lieu of pro forma information required by GAAP.

51200. ARTICLE 12. FORM AND CONTENT OF SCHEDULES

General

For Management Investment Companies

For Insurance Companies

For Face-Amount Certificate Investment Companies

For Certain Real Estate Companies

51201. Rule 12-01. Application of Article 12

These sections prescribe the form and content of the schedules required by Rules 5-04, 6-10, 6A-05, 7-05 and 9-07.

The various rules referred to in Rule 12-01 designate the schedules to be furnished and the conditions under which they may be omitted. The format of the schedules is set forth in the various rules in this article. Generally, the most frequently encountered schedules are those prescribed by Rules 12-02 through 12-11 and Rules 12-28 and 12-29, which are referred to in Rule 5-04 and in other rules within Regulation S-X. The other schedules in Article 12 pertain to specific types of business and are described in the following rules:

Rules Prescribing Form and Content of Schedule	Rules Requiring Schedule
Rule 12-12	Rules 6-05 and 6A-05
Rules 12-13 and 12-14	Rule 6-10
Rules 12-15 through 12-18	Rule 7-05
Rules 12-21 through 12-27	Rule 6-10

In addition, the instructions to various forms may limit the schedules that are to be included in the filing. Section 40100 of this manual discusses the most commonly used forms and the schedules required by the instructions to these forms.

Note that the text of Rules 12-21 through 12-24 and Rule 12-27 includes references to rules that have been amended by the SEC in Article 6 (see section 50600 of this manual and FRR No. 8). Until the references in Article 12 are updated to reflect these amendments, reference should be made to the text of Article 6 prior to amendment by FRR No. 8 to ascertain the nature of the disclosures required.

As previously noted, Article 12 schedules are required for predecessor entities (see section 50320). However, generally the SEC staff does not require schedules to be furnished with financial statements for businesses acquired or to be acquired furnished pursuant to Rule 3-05 (see section 50318).

51202. Rule 12-02. Marketable Securities—Other Investments

COL. A	COL. B	COL. C	COL. D	COL. E[4]
Name of issuer[1] and title of each issue[2]	Number of shares or units—principal amounts of bonds and notes	Cost of each issue	Market value[3] of each issue at balance sheet date	Amount at which each portfolio of equity security issues and each other security issue carried in the balance sheet

[1]For the purpose of this schedule, each of the following groups of entities shall be considered as one issuer: (a) the United States Government and its agencies; (b) any state of the United States and its agencies; (c) a political subdivision of a state of the United States and its agencies; (d) a foreign government and its agencies and political subdivisions; and (e) a corporation and its majority owned subsidiaries. If a security listed herein is guaranteed, sponsored or otherwise supported by another issuer, provide, in a note keyed to the issuing entity and to the supporting entity if present in the listing, a brief description of the terms of such guarantee or obligations.

[2](i) all securities of the United States Government and its agencies (category 1(a) above) may be grouped together and shown as a single item

(ii) for other governmental and corporate securities (categories 1(b), (c), (d) and (e) above):

(1) state separately each individual issue with a cost or market value which equals or exceeds two percent of total assets;

(2) reasonable groupings (e.g., by industry, type of security, similar investment risk, etc.), without enumeration, may be made of all other securities: Provided, That the aggregate cost or aggregate market value of each group does not exceed two percent of total assets. Governmental securities (categories 1(b), (c) and (d)) should generally be grouped separately from corporate securities (category 1(e)). Securities with investment risk factors that are significantly greater than normal for that class of issuer (e.g., interest in default, corporation in bankruptcy, etc.) should be listed or grouped separately with a brief explanation of the abnormal risk factors.

[3]Market value shall be based on market quotations at the balance sheet date or, if such quotations are not available, on determinations of fair value made in good faith by the board of directors.

[4]Column E shall be totaled to correspond to the respective balance sheet captions.

51203. Rule 12-03. Amounts Receivable from Related Parties and Underwriters, Promoters, and Employees Other Than Related Parties

COL. A	COL. B	COL. C	COL. D		COL. E	
			Deductions		Balance at end of period	
			(1) Amounts collected[2]	(2) Amounts written off	(1) Current	(2) Not current
Name of debtor[1]	Balance at beginning of period	Additions				

[1] Include in this schedule both accounts receivable and notes receivable and provide in a note hereto pertinent information, such as the due date, interest rate, terms of repayment and collateral, if any, for the amounts receivable from each person named in column A as of the date of the most recent balance sheet being filed.

[2] If collection was other than in cash, explain.

51204. Rule 12-04. Condensed Financial Information of Registrant [Parent Company]

(a) Provide condensed financial information as to financial position, cash flows and results of operations of the registrant as of the same dates and for the same periods for which audited consolidated financial statements are required. The financial information required need not be presented in greater detail than is required for condensed statements by Rule 10-01(a)(2), (3) and (4). Detailed footnote disclosure which would normally be included with complete financial statements may be omitted with the exception of disclosures regarding material contingencies, long-term obligations and guarantees. Descriptions of significant provisions of the registrant's long-term obligations, mandatory dividend or redemption requirements of redeemable stocks, and guarantees of the registrant shall be provided along with a five-year schedule of maturities of debt. If the material contingencies, long-term obligations, redeemable stock requirements and guarantees of the registrant have been separately disclosed in the consolidated statements, they need not be repeated in this schedule.

(b) Disclose separately the amounts of cash dividends paid to the registrant for each of the last three fiscal years by consolidated subsidiaries, unconsolidated subsidiaries and 50 percent or less owned persons accounted for by the equity method, respectively.

[Note: Refer to sections 50408-e and 50520 for a discussion of the calculation necessary to determine whether this schedule is required.]

828

51205. Rule 12-05. Indebtedness of and to Related Parties—Not Current

COL. A	COL. B	COL. C	COL. D	COL. E	COL. F	COL. G	COL. H	COL. I
		—Indebtedness of—				—Indebtedness of—		
Name of person[1]	Balance at beginning	Additions[2]	Deductions3	Balance at end	Balance at beginning	Additions[2]	Deductions[3]	Balance at end

[1] Group separately for (1) unconsolidated subsidiaries; (2) other persons, the investments in which are accounted for by the equity method; and (3) other affiliates. Indebtedness of and to individual related parties which exceed two percent of total assets shall be stated separately.

[2] For each person named in column A, explain in a note the nature and purpose of any increase during the period that is in excess of 10 percent of the related balance at either the beginning or end of the period.

[3] If deduction was other than a receipt or disbursement of cash, explain.

51206. Rule 12-06. Property, Plant and Equipment[1,7]

COL. A	COL. B	COL. C	COL. D	COL. E	COL. F
Classification[2]	Balance at beginning of period[3]	Additions at cost[4]	Retirements[5]	Other changes —add (deduct)— describe[6]	Balance at end of period

[1] Comment briefly on any significant and unusual additions, abandonments, or retirements, or any significant and unusual changes in the general character and location, of principal plants and other important units, which may have occurred within the period.

[2](a) Show by major classifications, such as land, buildings, machinery and equipment, leaseholds, or functional grouping. If such classification is not present or practicable, this may be stated in one amount. The additions included in column C shall, however, be segregated in accordance with an appropriate classification.

If property, plant and equipment abandoned is carried at other than a nominal amount indicate, if practicable, the amount thereof and state the reasons for such treatment. Items of minor importance may be included under a miscellaneous caption.

(b) Public utility companies. A public utility company shall, to the extent practicable, classify utility plant by the type of service rendered (such as electric, gas, transportation, and water) and shall state separately under each of such service classifications the major subclassifications of utility plant accounts.

[3] If neither the total additions nor total deductions during any of the periods covered by the schedules amount to more than 10 percent of the ending balance of that period and a statement to that effect is made, the information required by columns B, C, D and E may be omitted for that period, provided that the totals of columns C and D are given in a note hereto and provided further that any information required by instructions 4, 5 and 6 shall be given and may be in summary form.

[4] For each change in accounts in column C that represents anything other than an addition from acquisition, and for each change in that column that is in excess of two percent of total assets, at either the beginning or end of the period, state clearly the nature of the change and the other accounts affected. If cost of property additions represents other than cash expenditures, explain. If acquired from an affiliate at other than cost to the affiliate, show such cost, provided the acquisition by the affiliate was within two years prior to the acquisition by the person for which the statement is filed.

[5] If changes in column D are stated at other than cost, explain if practicable.

[6] State clearly the nature of the changes and the other accounts affected. If provision for depreciation, depletion and amortization of property, plant and equipment is credited in the books directly to the asset accounts, the amounts shall be stated in column E with explanations, including the accounts to which charged.

[7] Disclosure shall be made of the methods and, if practicable, the rates used in computing the annual provision for depreciation, depletion, obsolescence, and amortization of physical properties and capitalized leases.

[Note: Changes that do not represent additions or retirements should be included in column E of Schedule V and should be described in a footnote. Generally such changes would represent reclassifications between accounts. Additions to property, plant and equipment resulting from poolings of interests should be separately identified in Schedule V (and Schedule VI) in the year in which the pooling of interests occurs. Schedules for prior years generally do not have to be restated except in unusual circumstances.]

51207. Rule 12-07. Accumulated Depreciation, Depletion, and Amortization of Property, Plant and Equipment[1]

COL. A	COL. B	COL. C	COL. D	COL. E	COL. F
Description[2]	Balance at beginning of period	Additions charged to costs and expenses	Retirements	Other changes— add (deduct)— describe	Balance at end of period

[1](a) Insofar as amounts for depreciation, depletion, and amortization are credited to the property accounts, such amounts shall be shown in the schedule of property, plant, and equipment, as there required.

[2]If practicable, accumulated depreciation shall be shown to correspond with the classifications of property set forth in the related schedule of property, plant, and equipment, separating especially depreciation, depletion, amortization, and provision for retirement.

51208. Rule 12-08. Guarantees of Securities of Other Issuers[1]

COL. A	COL. B	COL. C	COL. D	COL. E	COL. F	COL. G
Name of issuer of securities guaranteed by person for which statement is filed	Title of issue of each class of securities guaranteed	Total amount guaranteed and outstanding[2]	Amount owned by person or persons for which statement is filed	Amount in treasury of issuer of securities guaranteed	Nature of guarantee[3]	Nature of any default by issuer of securities guaranteed in principal, interest, sinking fund or redemption provisions, or payment of dividends[4]

[1]Indicate in a note to the most recent schedule being filed for a particular person or group any significant changes since the date of the related balance sheet. If this schedule is filed in support of consolidated statements or combined statements, there shall be set forth guarantees by any person included in the consolidation or combination, except that such guarantees of securities which are included in the consolidated or combined balance sheet need not be set forth.

SEC 51207. Rule 12-07

[2]Indicate any amounts included in column C which are included also in column D or E.

[3]There need be made only a brief statement of the nature of the guarantee, such as "Guarantee of principal and interest," "Guarantee of interest," or "Guarantee of dividends." If the guarantee is of interest or dividends, state the annual aggregate amount of interest or dividends so guaranteed.

[4]Only a brief statement as to any such defaults need be made.

51209. Rule 12-09. Valuation and Qualifying Accounts

COL. A	COL. B	COL. C		COL. D	COL. E
		Additions			
		(1) Charged to costs and expenses	(2) Charged to other accounts—describe		
Description[1]	Balance at beginning or period			Deductions—describe	Balance at end of period

[1]List, by major classes, all valuation and qualifying accounts and reserves not included in specific schedules. Identify each such class of valuation and qualifying accounts and reserves by descriptive title. Group (a) those valuation and qualifying accounts which are deducted in the balance sheet from the assets to which they apply and (b) those reserves which support the balance sheet caption, Reserves. Valuation and qualifying accounts and reserves as to which the additions, deductions and balances were not individually significant may be grouped in one total and in such case the information called for under columns C and D need not be given.

51210. Rule 12-10. Short-Term Borrowings[4]

COL. A	COL. B	COL. C	COL. D	COL. E	COL. F
Category of aggregate short-term borrowings[1]	Balance at end of period	Weighted average interest rate	Maximum amount outstanding during the period[2]	Average amount outstanding during the period[3]	Weighted average interest rate during the period[3]

[1] The categories of short-term borrowings are amounts payable to banks for borrowings; factors or other financial institutions for borrowings; and holders of commercial paper.

[2] Indicate the maximum amount outstanding at any month end (or similar time period) during the period.

[3] Indicate the means used to compute such average.

[4] Indicate in a note the general terms (as well as formal provisions for the extension of maturity) of each category of aggregate short-term borrowings.

[Note: The weighted average interest rates for each category in column C should be calculated using the year-end rates of all borrowings in the same category.]

51211. Rule 12-11. Supplementary Income Statement Information

COL. A[1]	COL. B2
Item	Charged to costs and expenses
1. Maintenance and repairs	
2. Depreciation and amortization of intangible assets, preoperating costs and similar deferral[3]	
3. Taxes, other than payroll and income taxes[4]	
4. Royalties	
5. Advertising costs[5]	

[1] State, for each of the items noted in column A which exceeds one percent of total sales and revenues as reported in the related income statement, the amount called for in column B.

[2] Totals may be stated in column B without further designation of the accounts to which charged.

[3] State separately each category of costs itemized.

[4] State separately each category of tax which exceeds one percent of total sales and revenues.

[5] This item shall include all costs related to advertising the company's name, products or services in newspapers, periodicals or other advertising media.

[ASR No. 141 provided the following guidelines as to the disclosure of advertising costs that may still be helpful:

Instruction [4] explaining "Advertising Costs" calls for the inclusion of "all costs related to advertising the company's name, products or services in newspapers, periodicals or other advertising media." Such costs would include the indirect costs expended in support of advertising such as the costs of an advertising department, a market research group which specializes in evaluation of advertising and promotional efforts (but not all market research), a media-buying department, or graphic arts department that specializes in the preparation of advertising copy, as well as the direct costs of advertising space. In addition, the cost of "other advertising media" would generally include expenditures for preparing and mailing sales brochures and direct mail advertising materials. In cases where a company or division is primarily in the mail order business, however, the costs of preparing a catalog would be a selling cost similar to that of a salesman in most industrial concerns, and such catalog costs should not be included in "advertising costs." The cost of employing salesmen, preparing product display signs, printing price lists and standard product catalogs, and reports to stockholders should also not be considered advertising costs for purposes of this rule.]

[Note: It is recognized that the distinction between advertising costs and other selling expenses is frequently not clear cut. Where the guidance set forth herein is not sufficient to enable the registrant to determine the appropriateness of including or excluding certain classifications of significant costs, disclosure of the type of costs included or excluded from the caption will be a satisfactory solution.]

51212. Rule 12-12. Investments in Securities of Unaffiliated Issuers (for management investment companies only)

COL. A	COL. B	COL. C
Name of issuer and title of issue [1,2]	Balance held at close of period. Number of shares—principal Amount of bonds and notes [5]	Value of each item at close of period [3,4,5,7,8,]

[1] Each issue shall be listed separately: Provided, however, that an amount not exceeding five percent of the total of column C may be listed in one amount as "Miscellaneous securities," provided the securities so listed are not restricted, have been held for not more than one year prior to the date of the related balance sheet, and have not previously been reported by name to the shareholders of the person for which the schedule is filed or to any exchange, or set forth in any registration statement, application, or annual report or otherwise made available to the public.

[2] List separately (a) common shares; (b) preferred shares; (c) bonds and notes; (d) time deposits; and (e) put and call options purchased. Within each of these subdivisions, classify in an appropriate manner according to type of business; e.g., aerospace, banking, chemicals, machinery and machine tools, petroleum, utilities, etc.; or according to type of instrument; e.g., commercial paper, bankers' acceptances, certificates of deposit. Short-term debt instruments of the same issuer may be aggregated, in which case the range of interest rates and maturity dates shall be indicated. For issuers of periodic payment plan certificates and unit investment trusts, list separately: (i) trust shares in trusts created or serviced by the depositor or sponsor of this trust; (ii) trust shares in other trusts; and (iii) securities of other investment companies. Restricted securities shall not be combined with unrestricted securities of the same issuer. Repurchase agreements shall be stated separately showing for each the name of the party or parties to the agreement, the date of the agreement, the total amount to be received upon repurchase, the repurchase date and description of securities subject to the repurchase agreements.

[3] The subtotals for each category of investments, subdivided by business grouping or instrument type, shall be shown together with their percentage value compared to net assets (Rules 6-04.19 or 6-05.4).

[4] Column C shall be totaled. The total of column C shall agree with the correlative amounts shown on the related balance sheet.

[5] Indicate by an appropriate symbol each issue of securities which is non-income producing. Evidences of indebtedness and preferred shares may be deemed to be income producing if, on the respective last interest payment date or date for the declaration of dividends prior to the date of the related balance sheet, there was only a partial payment of interest or a declaration of only a partial amount of the dividends payable; in such case, however, each such issue shall be indicated by an appropriate symbol referring to a note to the effect that, on the last interest or dividend date, only partial interest was paid or partial dividends declared. If, on such respective last interest or dividend date, no interest was paid or no cash or in kind dividends declared, the issue shall not be deemed to be income producing.

Common shares shall not be deemed to be income producing unless, during the last year preceding the date of the related balance sheet, there was at least one dividend paid upon such common shares.

[6] Indicate by an appropriate symbol each issue of restricted securities. State the following in a footnote: (a) as to each such issue: (1) Acquisition date, (2) carrying value per unit of investment at date of related balance sheet, e.g., a percentage of current market value of unrestricted securities of the same issuer, etc., and (3) the cost of such securities; (b) as to each issue acquired during the year preceding the date of the related balance sheet, the carrying value per unit of investment of unrestricted securities of the same issuer at, (1) The day the purchase price was agreed to; and (2) the day on which an enforceable right to acquire such securities was obtained; and (c) the aggregate value of all restricted securities and the percentage which the aggregate value bears to net assets.

[7] Indicate by an appropriate symbol each issue of securities held in connection with open put or call option contracts or loans for short sales.

[8] State in a footnote the following amounts based on cost for Federal income tax purposes: (a) Aggregate gross unrealized appreciation for all securities in which there is an excess of value over tax cost, (b) the aggregate gross unrealized depreciation for all securities in which there is an excess of tax cost over value, (c) the net unrealized appreciation or depreciation, and (d) the aggregate cost of securities for Federal income tax purposes.

[Note: Refer to section 50605 for additional discussion regarding Rule 12-12.]

51213. Rule 12-12A. Investments—Securities Sold Short (for management investment companies only)

COL. A	COL. B	COL. C
Name of issuer and title of issue[1]	Balance of short position at close of period (number of shares)	Value of each open short position[2]

[1] Each issue shall be listed separately.
[2] Column C shall agree with the correlative amounts shown on the related balance sheet. The total of column C shall be totaled.

51214. Rule 12-12B. Open Option Contracts Written (for management investment companies only)

COL. A	COL. B	COL. C	COL. D	COL. E
Name of issuer[1,2]	Number of contracts[3]	Exercise price	Expiration date	Value[4]

[1] Information as to put options shall be shown separately from information as to call options.

[2] Options of an issuer where exercise prices or expiration dates differ shall be listed separately.

[3] If the number of shares subject to option is substituted for number of contracts, the column name shall reflect that change.

[4] Column E shall be totaled and shall agree with the correlative amount shown on the related balance sheet.

51215. Rule 12-13. Investments Other Than Securities (for management investment companies only)

COL. A	COL. B	COL. C
Description[1]	Balance held at close of period—quantity[2,3,5]	Value of each item at close of period[4,6,7]

[1] List each major category of investments by descriptive title.

[2] If practicable, indicate the quantity or measure in appropriate units.

[3] Indicate by an appropriate symbol each investment which is non-income producing.

[4] Indicate by an appropriate symbol each investment not readily marketable. The term "investment not readily marketable" shall include investments for which there is no independent publicly quoted market and investments which cannot be sold because of restrictions or conditions applicable to the investment or the company.

[5] Indicate by an appropriate symbol each investment subject to option. State in a footnote: (a) The quantity subject to option, (b) nature of option contract, (c) option price, and (d) dates within which options may be exercised.

[6] Column C shall be totaled and shall agree with the correlative amount shown on the related balance sheet.

[7] State in a footnote the following amounts based on cost for Federal income tax purposes: (a) Aggregate gross unrealized appreciation for all investments in which there is an excess of value over tax cost, (b) the aggregate gross unrealized depreciation for all investments in which there is an excess of tax cost over value, (c) the net unrealized appreciation or depreciation, and (d) the aggregate cost of investments for Federal income tax purposes.

51216. Rule 12-14. Investments in and Advances to Affiliates (for management investment companies only)

COL. A	COL. B	COL. C	COL. D		COL. E
			Amount of dividends or interest[2,5]		
Name of issuer and title of issue or nature of indebtedness[1]	Number of shares—principal amount of bonds, notes and other indebtedness held at close of period	Amount of equity in net profit and loss for the period[2,6]	(1) Credited to income	(2) Other	Value of each item at close of period[2,3,4,5]

[1](a) List each issue separately and group (1) Investments in majority-owned subsidiaries, segregating subsidiaries consolidated; (2) other controlled companies; and (3) other affiliates.

(b) If during the period there has been any increase or decrease in the amount of investment in and advance to any affiliate, state in a footnote (or if there have been changes as to numerous affiliates, in a supplementary schedule) (1) name of each issuer and title of issue or nature of indebtedness; (2) balance at beginning of period; (3) gross additions; (4) gross reductions; (5) balance at close of period as shown in column E. Include in the footnote or schedule comparable information as to affiliates in which there was an investment at any time during the period even though there was no investment at the close of the period of report.

[2]Give totals for each group. If operations of any controlled companies are different in character from those of the company, group such affiliates (1) within divisions and (2) by type of activities.

[3]Columns C, D, and E shall be totaled. The totals of column E shall agree with the correlative amount shown on the related balance sheet.

[4](a) Indicate by an appropriate symbol each issue of restricted securities. The information required by instruction 5 of Rule 12-12 shall be given in a footnote.

(b) Indicate by an appropriate symbol each issue of securities subject to option. The information required by instruction 5 of Rule 12-13 shall be given in a footnote.

[5](a) Include in column D (1) as to each issue held at the close of the period, the dividends or interest included in caption 1 of the statement of operations. In addition, show as the final item in column D (1) the aggregate of dividends and interest included in the statement of operations in respect of investments in affiliates not held at the close of the period. The total of this column shall agree with the correlative amount shown on the related statement of operations.

(b) Include in column D (2) all other dividends and interest. Explain in an appropriate footnote the treatment accorded each item.

(c) Indicate by an appropriate symbol all non-cash dividends and explain the circumstances in a footnote.

(d) Indicate by an appropriate symbol each issue of securities which is non-income producing.

[6]The information required by column C shall be furnished only as to controlled companies.

51217. Rule 12-15. Summary of Investments—Other Than Investments in Related Parties (for insurance companies)

COL. A	COL. B	COL. C	COL. D
Type of investment	Cost[1]	Value	Amount at which shown in the balance sheet[2]
Fixed maturities:			
Bonds:			
United States Government and government agencies and authorities			
States, municipalities and political subdivisions			
Foreign governments			
Public utilities			
Convertibles and bonds with warrants attached[3]			
All other corporate bonds			
Certificates of deposit			
Redeemable preferred stock			
Total fixed maturities			
Equity securities:			
Common stocks:			
Public utilities			
Banks, trust and insurance companies			
Industrial, miscellaneous and all other			
Nonredeemable preferred stocks			
Total equity securities			
Mortgage loans on real estate		XXXXXXXXX	
Real estate[4]		XXXXXXXXX	
Policy loans		XXXXXXXXX	
Other long-term investments		XXXXXXXXX	
Short-term investments		XXXXXXXXX	
Total investments		XXXXXXXXX	

[1] Original cost of equity securities and, as to fixed maturities, original cost reduced by repayments and adjusted for amortization of premiums or accrual of discounts.

[2] If the amount at which shown in the balance sheet is different from the amount shown in either column B or C, state the reason for such difference. The total of this column should agree with the balance sheet.

[3] All convertibles and bonds with warrants shall be included in this caption, regardless of issuer.

[4] State separately any real estate acquired in satisfaction of debt.

51218. Rule 12-16. Supplementary Insurance Information (for insurance companies)

Column A	Column B	Column C	Column D	Column E	Column F	Column G	Column H	Column I	Column J	Column K
Segment[1]	Deferred policy acquisition cost (caption 7)	Future policy benefits, losses, claims and loss expenses (caption 13-a-1)	Unearned premiums (caption 13-a-2)	Other policy claims and benefits payable (caption 13-a-3)	Premium revenue (caption 1)	Net investment income (caption 2)	Benefits, claims, losses and settlement expenses (caption 4)	Amortization of deferred policy acquisition costs[4]	Other operating expenses[4]	Premiums written[2]
Total[5]										

[1] Segments shown should be the same as those presented in the footnote disclosures called for by Statement of Financial Accounting Standards No. 14.

[2] Does not apply to life insurance or title insurance. This amount should include premiums from reinsurance assumed, and be net of premiums on reinsurance ceded.

[3] State the basis for allocation of net investment income and, where applicable, other operating expenses.

[4] The total of columns I and J should agree with the amount shown for income statement caption 6.

[5] Totals should agree with the indicated balance sheet and income statement caption amounts, where a caption number is shown.

51219. Rule 12-17. Reinsurance (for insurance companies)

COLUMN A	COLUMN B	COLUMN C	COLUMN D	COLUMN E	COLUMN F
	Gross amount	Ceded to other companies[1]	Assumed from other companies	Net amount[2]	Percentage of amount assumed to net[3]
Life insurance in force					
Premiums					
Life insurance					
Accident and health insurance					
Property and liability insurance					
Title insurance					
Total premiums					

[1]Indicate in a note any amounts of reinsurance or coinsurance income netted against premiums ceded.
[2]This column represents the total of column B less column C plus column D. The total premiums in this column should represent the amount of premium revenue on the income statement.
[3]Calculated as the amount in column D divided by amount in column E.

51220. Rule 12-18. Supplemental Information (for property-casualty insurance underwriters)

Column A	Column B	Column C	Column D	Column E	Column F	Column G	Column H		Column I	Column J	Column K
							Claims and claim adjustment expenses incurred related to				
Affirmation with registrant	Deferred policy acquisition costs	Reserve for unpaid claims and claim adjustment expenses	Discount, if any, deducted in column C⁴	Unearned premiums	Earned premiums	Net investment income	(1) Current year	(2) Prior years	Amortization of deferred policy acquisition costs	Paid claims and claim adjustment expenses	Premiums written
(a) Consolidated property-casualty entities											
(b) Unconsolidated property-casualty subsidiaries											
(c) Proportionate share of registrant and its subsidiaries' 50%-or-less-owned property-casualty equity investees											

[1] Information included in audited financial statements, including other schedules, need not be repeated in this schedule. Columns B, C, D and E are as of the balance sheet dates, columns F, G, H, I, J and K are for the same periods for which income statements are presented in the registrant's audited consolidated financial statements.

[2] Present combined or consolidated amounts, as appropriate for each category, after intercompany eliminations.

[3] Information is not required here for 50%-or-less-owned equity investees that file similar information with the Commission as registrants in their own right, if that fact and the name of the affiliated registrant is stated. If ending reserves in any category (a), (b) or (c) above is less than 5% of the total reserves otherwise required to be reported in this schedule, that category may be omitted and that fact so noted. If the amount of the reserves attributable to 50%-or-less-owned equity investors that file this information as registrants in their own right exceeds 95% of the total category (c) reserves, information for the other 50%-or-less-owned equity investees need not be provided.

[4] Disclose in a footnote to this schedule the rate, or range of rates, estimated if necessary, at which the discount was computed for each category.

51221. Rule 12-21. Investments in Securities of Unaffiliated Issuers (for face-amount certificate investment companies)

COL. A	COL. B	COL. C	COL. D
Name of issuer and title of issue[1]	Balance held at close of period. Number of shares—principal[1] amount of bonds and notes[2]	Cost of each item[3,4]	Value of each item at close of period[3,5]

[1](a) The required information is to be given as to all securities held as of the close of the period of report. Each issue shall be listed separately.

(b) Indicate by an appropriate symbol those securities which are non-income-producing securities. Evidences of indebtedness and preferred shares may be deemed to be income-producing if, on the respective last interest payment date or dates for the declaration of dividends prior to the date of the related balance sheet, there was only a partial payment of interest or a declaration of only a partial amount of the dividends payable; in such case, however, each such issue shall be indicated by an appropriate symbol referring to a note to the effect that, on the last interest or dividend date, only partial interest was paid or partial dividends declared. If, on such respective last interest or dividend date, no interest was paid or no dividends declared, the issue shall not be deemed to be income-producing. Common shares shall not be deemed to be income-producing unless, during the last year preceding the date of the related balance sheet, there was at least one dividend paid upon such common shares. List separately (1) bonds; (2) preferred shares; (3) common shares. Within each of these subdivisions classify according to type of business, insofar as practicable: e.g., investment companies, railroads, utilities, banks, insurance companies, or industrials. Give totals for each group, subdivision, and class.

[2]Indicate any securities subject to option at the end of the most recent period and state in a note the amount subject to option, the option prices, and the dates within which such options may be exercised.

[3]Columns C and D shall be totaled. The totals of columns C and D should agree with the correlative amounts required to be shown by the related balance sheet captions. State in a footnote to column C the aggregate cost for Federal income tax purposes.

[4]If any investments have been written down or reserved against by such companies pursuant to rule 6-21(f), indicate each such item by means of an appropriate symbol and explain in a footnote. [See note in section 51201.]

[5]Where value is determined on any other basis than closing prices reported on any national securities exchange, explain such other bases in a footnote.

51222. Rule 12-22. Investments in and Advances to Affiliates and Income Thereon (for face-amount certificate investment companies)

COL. A	COL. B	COL. C	COL. D	COL. E		COL. F
				Amounts of dividends or interest[4,6]		
Name of issuer and title of issue or amount of indebtedness[1]	Balance held at close of period. Number of shares, principal amount of bonds, notes and other indebtedness[2]	Cost of each item[3,4]	Amount at which carried at close of period[4,5]	(1) Credited to income	(2) Other	Amount of equity in net profit and loss for the period[7]

[1] (a) The required information is to be given as to all investments in affiliates as of the close of the period. See captions 10, 13, and 20 of Rule 6-22. [Note: see note in section 51201.] List each issue and group separately (1) investments in majority-owned subsidiaries, segregating subsidiaries consolidated; (2) other controlled companies; and (3) other affiliates. Give totals for each group. If operations of any controlled companies are different in character from those of the registrant, group such affiliates within divisions (1) and (2) by type of activities.

(b) Changes during the period. - If during the period there has been any increase or decrease in the amount of investment in any affiliate, state in a footnote (or if there have been changes as to numerous affiliates, in a supplementary schedule) (1) name of each issuer and title of issue; (2) balance at beginning of period; (3) gross purchases and additions; (4) gross sales and reductions; (5) balance at close of period as shown in column C. Include in such footnote or schedule comparable information as to affiliates in which there was an investment at any time during the period even though there was no investment in such affiliate as of the close of such period.

[2] Indicate any securities subject to option at the end of the most recent period and state in a footnote the amount subject to option, the option prices, and the dates within which such options may be exercised.

[3] If the cost in column C represents other than cash expenditure, explain.

[4] (a) Columns C, D, and E shall be totaled. The totals of columns C and D should agree with correlative amounts required to be shown by the related balance sheet captions. State in a footnote the aggregate cost for Federal income tax purposes.

(b) If any investments have been written down or reserved against by such companies pursuant to Rule 6-21(f), indicate each such item by means of an appropriate symbol and explain in a footnote.

[5] State the basis of determining the amounts shown in column D.

[6] Show in column E (1) as to each issue held at close of period, the dividends or interest included in caption 1 of the profit and loss or income statement. In addition, show as the final item in column E (1) the aggregate dividends and interest included in the profit and loss or income statement in respect of investments in affiliates not held at the close of the period. The total of this column should agree with the amounts shown under such caption. Include in column E (2) all other

dividends and interest. Explain briefly in an appropriate footnote the treatment accorded each item. Identify by an appropriate symbol all noncash dividends and explain the circumstances in a footnote. See Rules 6-22-2 and 6-23-1 [Note: see note in section 51201].

[7]The information required by column F need be furnished only as to controlled companies. The equity in the net profit and loss of each person required to be listed separately shall be computed on an individual basis. In addition, there may be submitted the information required as computed on the basis of the statements of each such person and its subsidiaries consolidated.

51223. Rule 12-23. Mortgage Loans on Real Estate and Interest Earned on Mortgages[1] (for face-amount certificate investment companies)

Part I—Mortgage loans on real estate at close of period						Part 2—Interest earned on mortgages	
COL. A	COL. B	COL. C	COL. D		COL. E	COL. F	COL. G
			Amount of principal unpaid at close of period				
			(1) Total	(2) Subject to delinquent interest[4]			
List by classification indicated below[2,3,7]	Prior liens[2]	Carrying amount of mortgages[8, 9, 10, 11]			Amount of mortgages being foreclosed	Interest due and accrued at end of period[6]	Interest income earned applicable to period[5,6]
Liens on: Farms (total) Residential (total) Apartments and business (total) Unimproved (total) Total[12]							

[1] All money columns shall be totaled.

[2] If mortgages represent other than first liens, list separately in a schedule in a like manner, indicating briefly the nature of the lien. Information need not be furnished as to such liens which are fully insured or wholly guaranteed by an agency of the United States Government.

SEC 51222. Rule 12-22

[3] In a separate schedule, classify by states in which the mortgaged property is located the total amounts in support of columns B, C, D, and E.

[4] (a) Interest in arrears for less than 3 months may be disregarded in computing the total amount of principal subject to delinquent interest.

(b) Of the total principal amount, state the amount acquired from controlled and other affiliates.

[5] In order to reconcile the total of column G with the amount shown in the profit and loss or income statement, interest income earned applicable to period from mortgages sold or canceled during period should be added to the total of this column.

[6] If the information required by columns F and G is not reasonably available because the obtaining thereof would involve unreasonable effort or expense, state such information may be omitted if the registrant shall include a statement showing that unreasonable effort or expense would be involved. In such an event, state in column G for each of the above classes of mortgage loans the average gross rate of interest on mortgage loans held at the end of the fiscal period.

[7] Each mortgage loan included in column C in an amount in excess of $500,000 shall be listed separately. Loans from $100,000 to $500,000 shall be grouped by $50,000 groups, indicating the number of loans in each group.

[8] In a footnote to this schedule, furnish a reconciliation, in the following form, of the carrying amount of mortgage loans at the beginning of the period with the total amount shown in column C:

Balance at beginning of period	$. . . . .
Additions during period:	
New mortgage loans	. . . .
Other (describe)	. . . .
	$. . . . .
Deductions during period:	
Collections of principal	. . . .
Foreclosures	. . . .
Cost of mortgages sold	. . . .
Amortization of premium	. . . .
Other (describe)	. . . .
Balance at close of period	$

If additions represent other than cash expenditures, explain. If any of the changes during the period result from transactions, directly or indirectly with affiliates, explain. If any of the changes during the period result from transactions, directly or indirectly with affiliates, explain the bases of such transactions, and the amounts involved. State the aggregate amount of mortgages (a) renewed and (b) extended. If the carrying amount of the new mortgages is in excess of the unpaid amount (not including interest) of prior mortgages, explain.

[9] If any item of mortgage loans on real estate investments has been written down or reserved against pursuant to Rule 6-21-6 [Note: see note in section 51201], describe the item and explain the basis for the write-down or reserve.

[10] State in a footnote to column C the aggregate cost for Federal income tax purposes.

[11] If the total amount shown in column C includes intercompany profits, state the bases of the transactions resulting in such profits and, if practicable, state the amounts thereof.

[12] Summarize the aggregate amounts for each column applicable to captions 6(b), 6(c), and 12 of Rule 6-22.

51224. Rule 12-24. Real Estate Owned and Rental Income (for face-amount certificate investment companies)

| | Part I—Real estate owned at end of period | | | | | | | Part 2—Rental income | | |
COL A	COL B	COL C	COL D	COL E	COL F	COL G		COL H	COL I	COL J
List classification of property as indicated below[2,3]	Amount of encumbrances	Initial cost to company	Cost of improvements, etc.	Amount at which carried at close of period[4,5,6,7]	Reserve for depreciation	Rents due and accrued at end of period		Total rental income applicable to period	Expended for interest, taxes, repairs and expenses	Net income applicable to period
Farms										
Residential										
Apartments and business										
Unimproved										
Total[8]										
Rent from properties sold during period										
Total										

[1] All money columns shall be totaled.

[2] Each item of property included in column E in an amount in excess of $100,000 shall be listed separately.

SEC 51223. Rule 12-23

[3]In a separate schedule, classify by states in which the real estate owned is located the total amounts in support of columns E and F.

[4]In a footnote to this schedule, furnish a reconciliation, in the following form, of the total amount at which real estate was carried at the beginning of the period with the total amount shown in column E:

Balance at beginning of period	$ . . . .
Acquisitions through foreclosure	$ . . . .
Other acquisitions	. . . .
Improvements, etc.	. . . .
Other (describe)	. . . .
Deductions during period:	
Cost of real estate sold	. . . .
Other (describe)	. . . .
Balance at close of period	$

If additions, except acquisitions through foreclosure, represent other than cash expenditures, explain. If any of the changes during the period result from transactions, directly or indirectly, with affiliates, explain and state the amount of any intercompany gain or loss.

[5]If any item of real estate investments has been written down or reserved against pursuant to Rule 6-21(f) [Note: see note in section 51201], describe the item and explain the basis for the write-down or reserve.

[6]State in a footnote to column E the aggregate cost for Federal income tax purposes.

[7]The amount of all intercompany profits included in the total of column E shall be stated if material.

[8]Summarize the aggregate amounts for each column applicable to captions 7 and 12 of Rule 6-22 [Note: see note in section 51201].

51225. Rule 12-25. Supplementary Profit and Loss Information (for face-amount certificate investment companies)

COL. A	COL. B	COL. C		COL. D
		Charged to other accounts		
Item[1]	Charged to investment expense	(1) Account	(2) Amount	Total
1. Legal expenses (including those in connection with any matter, measure or proceeding before legislative bodies, officers or government departments)				
2. Advertising and publicity				
3. Sales promotion[2]				
4. Payments directly and indirectly to trade associations and service organizations, and contributions to other organizations				

[1] Amounts resulting from transactions with affiliates shall be stated separately.

[2] State separately each category of expense representing more than 5 percent of the total expenses shown under this item.

SEC 51225. Rule 12-25

51226. Rule 12-26. Certificate Reserves (for face-amount certificate investment companies)

COL. A	COL. B			COL. C			COL. D			COL. E		
	Balance at beginning of period			Additions			Deductions			Balance at close of period		
	(1) Number of accounts with security holders	(2) Amount of maturity value	(3) Amount of reserves[2]	(1) Charged to profit and loss or income	(2) Reserve payments by certificate holders	(3) Charged to other accounts—describe	(1) Maturities	(2) Cash surrenders prior to maturity	(3) Other—describe	(1) Number of accounts with security holders	(2) Amount of maturity value	(3) Amount of reserves[2]
Description[1]												

[1](a) Each series of certificates shall be stated separately. The description shall include the yield to maturity on an annual payment basis.

(b) For certificates of the installment type, information required by columns B, D (2) and (3) and E shall be given by age groupings, according to the number of months paid by security holders, grouped to show those upon which 1-12 monthly payments have been made, 13-24 payments, etc.

[2](a) If the total of the reserves shown in these columns differs from the total of the reserves per the accounts, there should be stated (i) the aggregate difference and (ii) the difference on a $1,000 face-amount certificate basis.

(b) There shall be shown by footnote or by supplemental schedule (i) the amounts periodically credited to each class of security holders' accounts from installment payments and (ii) such other amounts periodically credited to accumulate the maturity amount of the certificate. Such information shall be stated on a $1,000 face-amount certificate basis for the term of the certificate.

51227. Rule 12-27. Qualified Assets on Deposit[1] (for face-amount certificate investment companies)

COL. A	COL. B	COL. C	COL. D	COL. E	COL. F
Name of depositary[2]	Cash	Investments in securities	First mortgages and other first liens on real estate	Other	Total[3]

[1] All money columns shall be totaled.
[2] Classify names of individual depositaries under group headings, such as banks and states.
[3] Total of column F shall agree with note required by caption 11 of Rule 6-22 as to total amount of qualified assets on deposit. [Note: see note in section 51201.]

51228. Rule 12-28. Real Estate and Accumulated Depreciation[1] (for certain real estate companies)

COL. A	COL. B	COL. C		COL. D		COL. E			COL. F	COL. G	COL. H	COL. I
		Initial cost to company		Cost capitalized subsequent to acquisition		Gross amount at which carried at close of period[3,4,5,6,7]						Life on which depreciation in latest income statements is computed
Description[2]	Encumbrances	Land	Buildings and improvements	Improvements	Carrying Costs	Land	Buildings and improvements	Total	Accumulated depreciation	Date of construction	Date acquired	

[1] All money columns shall be totaled.

SEC 51227. Rule 12-27

[2] The description for each property should include type of property (e.g., unimproved land, shopping center, garden apartments, etc.) and the geographical location.

[3] The required information is to be given as to each individual investment included in column E except that an amount not exceeding 5 percent of the total of column E may be listed in one amount as "miscellaneous investments."

[4] In a note to this schedule, furnish a reconciliation, in the following form, of the total amount at which real estate was carried at the beginning of each period for which income statements are required, with the total amount shown in column E:

Balance at beginning of period   . . . . $. . . . .
Additions during period:
  Acquisitions through foreclosure . . . . $. . . . .
  Other acquisitions . . . .
  Improvements, etc. . . . .
  Other (describe) . . . .

Deductions during period:
  Cost of real estate sold . . . .
  Other (describe) . . . .

Balance at close of period $. . . . .
. . . .

If additions, except acquisitions through foreclosure, represent other than cash expenditures, explain. If any of the changes during the period result from transactions, directly or indirectly with affiliates, explain the bases of such transactions and state the amounts involved. A similar reconciliation shall be furnished for the accumulated depreciation.

[5] If any item of real estate investments has been written down or reserved against, describe the item and explain the basis for the write-down or reserve.

[6] State in a note to column E the aggregate cost for Federal income tax purposes.

[7] The amount of all intercompany profits included in the total of column E shall be stated if material.

51229. Rule 12-29. Mortgage Loans on Real Estate[1] (for certain real estate companies)

COL. A	COL. B	COL. C	COL. D	COL. E	COL. F	COL. G	COL. H
Depreciation[2,3,4]	Interest rate	Final maturity date	Periodic payment terms[5]	Prior liens	Face amount of mortgages	Carrying amount of mortgages[3,6,7,8,9]	Principal amount of loans subject to delinquent principal or interest[10]

[1] All money columns shall be totaled.

[2] The required information is to be given for each individual mortgage loan which exceeds three percent of the total of colum G.

[3] If the portfolio includes large numbers of mortgages most of which are less than three percent of column G, the mortgages not required to be reported separately should be grouped by classifications that will indicate the dispersion of the portfolio, i.e., for a portfolio of mortgages on single family residential housing. The description should also include number of loans by original loan amounts (e.g., over $100,000, $50,000-$99,999, $20,000-$49,000, under $20,000) and type loan (e.g., VA, FHA, Conventional). Interest rates and maturity dates may be stated in terms of ranges. Data required by columns D, E and F may be omitted for mortgages not required to be reported individually.

[4] Loans should be grouped by categories, e.g., first mortgage, second mortgage, construction loans, etc., and for each loan the type of property, e.g., shopping center, high-rise apartments, etc., and its geographic location should be stated.

[5] State whether principal and interest is payable at level amount over life to maturity or at varying amounts over life to maturity. State amount of balloon payment at maturity, if any. Also state prepayment penalty terms, if any.

[6] In a note to this schedule, furnish a reconciliation, in the following form, of the carrying amount of mortgage loans at the beginning of each period for which income statements are required, with the total amount shown in column G.

SEC 51229. Rule 12-29

Balance at beginning of period . . . . $. . . . .

Additions during period:

New mortgage loans . . . . $. . . . .

Other (describe) . . . . $. . . . .

Deductions during period:

Collections of principal . . . .

Foreclosures . . . .

Cost of mortgages sold . . . .

Amortization of premium . . . .

Other (describe) . . . .

Balance at close of period . . . . $. . . . .

If additions represent other than cash expenditures, explain. If any of the changes during the period result from transactions, directly or indirectly with, affiliates, explain the bases of such transactions, and state the amounts involved. State the aggregate mortgages (a) renewed and (b) extended. If the carrying amount of new mortgages is in excess of the unpaid amount of the extended mortgages, explain.

[7]If any item of mortgage loans on real estate investments has been written down or reserved against, describe the item and explain the basis for the write-down or reserve.

[8]State in a note to column G the aggregate cost for Federal income tax purposes.

[9]The amount of all intercompany profits in the total of column G shall be stated, if material.

[10](a) Interest in arrears for less than 3 months may be disregarded in computing the total amount of principal subject to delinquent interest.

(b) Of the total principal amount, state the amount acquired from controlled and other affiliates.

SEC 51229

REGULATION S-K

60000. GENERAL

A general heading precedes the text of Regulation S-K as follows:

ATTENTION ELECTRONIC FILERS

THIS REGULATION SHOULD BE READ IN CONJUNCTION WITH
REGULATION S-T (PART 232 OF THIS CHAPTER), WHICH GOV-

SEC 60000

ERNS THE PREPARATION AND SUBMISSION OF DOCUMENTS
IN ELECTRONIC FORMAT. MANY PROVISIONS RELATING TO
THE PREPARATION AND SUBMISSION OF DOCUMENTS IN
PAPER FORMAT CONTAINED IN THIS REGULATION ARE SUPER-
SEDED BY THE PROVISIONS OF REGULATION S-T FOR DOCU-
MENTS REQUIRED TO BE FILED IN ELECTRONIC FORMAT.

Refer to discussion regarding the SEC's Electronic Data Gathering, Analysis, and Retrieval (EDGAR) system in section 15100.

The purpose and application of Regulation S-K are covered by its introductory paragraph, which reads:

This part (together with the General Rules and Regulations under the Securities Act of 1933 and the Securities Exchange Act of 1934 and the Interpretative Releases under these Acts and the forms under these Acts) states the requirements applicable to the content of the nonfinancial statement portions of:

(1) Registration statements under the Securities Act to the extent provided in the forms to be used for registration under such Act: and

(2) Registration statements under Section 12, annual or other reports under Sections 13 and 15(d), annual reports to security holders and proxy and information statements under Section 14 of the Exchange Act, and any other documents required to be filed under the Exchange Act, to the extent provided in the forms and rules under such Act.

The SEC adopted Regulation S-K in 1977 and revised it in 1982 to include the requirements formerly set forth in certain 1933 Act Rules and Industry Guides for the Preparation and Filing of Registration Statements and Reports (the Industry Guides are discussed in sections 15080 and 68000) and restructured the Regulation into nine major sections.

60500. PROSPECTIVE FINANCIAL INFORMATION

The AICPA standards and guidelines for prospective financial information are contained in the following documents: Statement on Standards for Accountants' Services on Prospective Financial Information - *Financial Forecasts and Projections*, Statement on Standards for Attestation Engagements and Statement of Position Nos. 89-3, *Questions Concerning Accountants' Services on Prospective Financial Statements*, 90-1, *Accountants' Services on Prospective Financial Statements for Internal*

SEC 60000

Use Only and Partial Presentations, and 92-2, *Questions and Answers on the Term Reasonably Objective Basis and Other Issues Affecting Prospective Financial Statements (SOP 92-2)* and the AICPA, *Guide for Prospective Financial Information.*

The AICPA refers to financial forecasts and projections as *prospective financial statements*. A forecast is defined as the presentation of an entity's *expected* financial results based on assumptions reflecting conditions it *expects to exist*. A projection is defined as the presentation of an entity's *expected* financial results given one or more *hypothetical* assumptions that are *not* necessarily expected to occur. The AICPA standards provide that only a forecast is appropriate for general use; therefore, the use of projections would ordinarily not be appropriate in SEC filings except as supplements to periods covered by a forecast.

The use of forecasts in SEC filings is addressed in Regulation S-X Rule 11-03 (section 51112) and projections are covered in Regulation S-K, Item 10(b). While the SEC does not clearly differentiate between forecasts and projections, the SEC staff has informally acknowledged that the description of projections in Regulation S-K is very close to the AICPA's definition of a forecast. Accordingly, compliance with the aforementioned AICPA Guide should be adequate in meeting the SEC's requirements for disclosure and reporting.

The staff has indicated that it will not accept a compilation report on a forecast in an SEC filing. Accordingly, if a document filed with the SEC contains an accountants' report on a forecast, such report needs to be based on an examination.

With regard to the number of years that may be covered by a forecast included in an SEC filing, the staff has no set policy in this regard and considers this determination to be dependent on the particular facts and circumstances involved. However, the staff has informally indicated that the following guidelines should be followed:

- For entities in which no operating history exists, one to two years would be the maximum considered appropriate.

- For companies with a cyclical business, it may be possible to justify presenting more than two years.

- For real estate entities with extensive long-term leases, it may be appropriate to include up to ten to fifteen years of forecasted information. It is important to note that in paragraph 45 of SOP 92-2, the AICPA stated *"[i]t ordinarily would be difficult to establish that a reasonably objective basis exists for a financial forecast extending beyond three to five years. . . ."* In a footnote to this paragraph, however, the AICPA stated *"[f]inancial forecasts for longer periods may be appropriate, for example, when long-term leases or other contracts exist that specify the timing and amount of revenues, and when costs can be controlled within reasonable limits."*

SEC 60500

The staff has also indicated that it will accept forecasted financial statements not based on GAAP in situations in which the registrant also includes GAAP-forecasted financial statements. For example, tax basis forecasts for real estate companies would be acceptable if accompanied by GAAP forecasts.

In best-efforts offerings, in which the underwriters agree to use their "best" efforts to sell the issue, acting only as agents of the issuer, the staff has indicated that forecasts included in registration statements should be based on the amount expected to be raised by the offering. The staff believes that the most prudent approach is to base the forecast on the minimum amount expected to be raised. Accordingly, if a registrant insists on presenting the forecast based on the maximum amount expected, the staff believes it must also present the effect of receiving only the minimum amount. In determining the minimum amount to be raised, the underwriter's agreement may specify that a minimum number of shares will have to be sold for the offering to be effective, after which the remaining shares will be sold on a best efforts basis.

The staff has also noted that when a previously issued forecast that was reported on by an independent accountant is included in a subsequent 1934 Act report (e.g., Form 10-K), the accountant does not have an obligation to update his/her report. However, the registrant has an obligation to discuss significant differences between previously issued prospective information and more recent facts and circumstances. In addition, if the forecast previously included in a 1933 Act filing can no longer be relied on, the registrant should so state (and, most likely, discuss in MD&A) in its 1934 Act report.

For a discussion of independence issues regarding association with prospective financial information, see section 17034.

61000. BUSINESS

61010. DESCRIPTION OF BUSINESS (ITEM 101)

61011. General. The Description of Business requirements in Regulation S-K include the textual information to be furnished with respect to industry segments, foreign operations, export sales, and major customers. These disclosure requirements are similar to those of FASB Statement No. 14, but provide for the disclosure of additional information. Certain of these additional requirements are discussed in sections 61013 through 61016 of this manual.

Item 101 specifies that a registrant may include a cross-reference in the financial statements to the industry segment information or the financial information about foreign and domestic operations and export sales included in the text or may cross-reference from the text to the financial statements.

Note that the industry segment information specified in paragraphs (b), (c)(1)(i), and (d) is required to be included in the annual report to shareholders pursuant to Rule 14a-3 of Regulation 14A. (Refer to section 31320 for the text of Rule 14a-3.)

61012. Text of Requirements.

Description of Business

(a) General development of business. *Describe the general development of the business of the registrant, its subsidiaries and any predecessor(s) during the past five years, or such shorter period as the registrant may have been engaged in business. Information shall be disclosed for earlier periods if material to an understanding of the general development of the business.*

(1) In describing developments, information shall be given as to matters such as the following: the year in which the registrant was organized and its form of organization; the nature and results of any bankruptcy, receivership or similar proceedings with respect to the registrant or any of its significant subsidiaries; the nature and results of any other material reclassification, merger or consolidation of the registrant or any of its significant subsidiaries; the acquisition or disposition of any material amount of assets otherwise than in the ordinary

SEC 61012

course of business; and any material changes in the mode of conducting the business.

(2) Registrants, (i) filing a registration statement on Form S-1 under the Securities Act or on Form 10 under the Exchange Act, (ii) not subject to the reporting requirements of section 13(a) or 15(d) of the Exchange Act immediately prior to the filing of such registration statement, and (iii) that (including predecessors) have not received revenue from operations during each of the three fiscal years immediately prior to the filing of the registration statement, shall provide the following information: (A) if the registration statement is filed prior to the end of the registrant's second fiscal quarter, a description of the registrant's plan of operation for the remainder of the fiscal year; or (B) if the registration statement is filed subsequent to the end of the registrant's second fiscal quarter, a description of the registrant's plan of operation for the remainder of the fiscal year and for the first six months of the next fiscal year. If such information is not available, the reasons for its not being available shall be stated. Disclosure relating to any plan shall include such matters as:

(1) In the case of a registration statement on Form S-1, a statement in narrative form indicating the registrant's opinion as to the period of time that the proceeds from the offering will satisfy cash requirements and whether in the next six months it will be necessary to raise additional funds to meet the expenditures required for operating the business of the registrant; the specific reasons for such opinion shall be set forth and categories of expenditures and sources of cash resources shall be identified; however, amounts of expenditures and cash resources need not be provided; in addition, if the narrative statement is based on a cash budget, such budget shall be furnished to the Commission as supplemental information, but not as part of the registration statement;

(2) An explanation of material product research and development to be performed during the period covered in the plan;

(3) Any anticipated material acquisition of plant and equipment and the capacity thereof;

(4) Any anticipated material changes in number of employees in the various departments such as research and development, production, sales or administration; and

(5) Other material areas which may be peculiar to the registrant's business.

(b) Financial information about industry segments. *State for each of the registrant's last three fiscal years or for each fiscal year the registrant has been engaged in*

SEC 61012

business, whichever period is shorter, the amounts of revenue (with sales to unaffiliated customers and sales or transfers to other industry segments of the registrant shown separately), operating profit or loss and identifiable assets attributable to each of the registrant's industry segments. (See Appendix A to this Item for a suggested tabular format for presentation of this information.) To the extent that financial information included pursuant to this paragraph (b) complies with generally accepted accounting principles, the registrant may include in its financial statements a cross reference to this data in lieu of presenting duplicative information about its segments in the financial statements; conversely, a registrant may cross reference to the financial statements.

(1) The prior period information shall be restated retroactively in the following circumstances, unless not material, with appropriate disclosure of the nature and effect of the restatement:

(i) When the financial statements of the registrant as a whole have been restated retroactively; or

(ii) When there has been a change in the way the registrant's products or services are grouped into industry segments and such change affects the segment information being reported; restatement is not required when a registrant's reportable segments change solely as a result of a change in the nature of its operations or as a result of a segment losing or gaining in significance.

(2) If the registrant includes, or is required by Article 3 of Regulation S-X to include, interim financial statements, discuss any facts relating to the performance of any of the segments during the period which, in the opinion of management, indicate that the three year segment financial data may not be indicative of current or future operations of the segment. Comparative financial information shall be included to the extent necessary to the discussion.

(c) Narrative description of business. *(1) Describe the business done and intended to be done by the registrant and its subsidiaries, focusing upon the registrant's dominant industry segment or each reportable industry segment about which financial information is presented in the financial statements. To the extent material to an understanding of the registrant's business taken as a whole, the description of each such segment shall include the information specified in paragraphs (c)(1)(i) through (x) of this Item. The matters specified in paragraphs (c)(1)(xi) through (xiii) of this Item shall be discussed with respect to the registrant's business in general; where material, the industry segments to which these matters are significant shall be identified.*

(i) The principal products produced and services rendered by the registrant in the industry segment and the principal markets for, and methods of distribution of, the segment's principal products and services. In addition, state for each of the last three fiscal years the amount or percentage of total revenue contributed by any class of similar products or services which accounted for 10 percent or more of consolidated revenue in any of the last three fiscal years or 15 percent or more of consolidated revenue, if total revenue did not exceed $50,000,000 during any of such fiscal years.

(ii) A description of the status of a product or segment (e.g., whether in the planning stage, whether prototypes exist, the degree to which product design has progressed or whether further engineering is necessary), if there has been a public announcement of, or if the registrant otherwise has made public information about, a new product or industry segment that would require the investment of a material amount of the assets of the registrant or that otherwise is material. This paragraph is not intended to require disclosure of otherwise nonpublic corporate information the disclosure of which would affect adversely the registrant's competitive position.

(iii) The sources and availability of raw materials.

(iv) The importance to the industry segment and the duration and effect of all patents, trademarks, licenses, franchises and concessions held.

(v) The extent to which the business of the industry segment is or may be seasonal.

(vi) The practices of the registrant and the industry (respective industries) relating to working capital items (e.g., where the registrant is required to carry significant amounts of inventory to meet rapid delivery requirements of customers or to assure itself of a continuous allotment of goods from suppliers; where the registrant provides rights to return merchandise; or where the registrant has provided extended payment terms to customers).

(vii) The dependence of the segment upon a single customer, or a few customers, the loss of any one or more of which would have a material adverse effect on the segment. The name of any customer and its relationship, if any, with the registrant or its subsidiaries shall be disclosed if sales to the customer by one or more segments are made in an aggregate amount equal to 10 percent or more of the registrant's consolidated revenues and the loss of such customer would have a material adverse effect on the registrant and its subsidiaries taken as a whole. The names of other customers may be included, unless in the particular case the effect of including the names would be misleading. For purposes of this paragraph, a group of customers under common control or customers that are affiliates of each other shall be regarded as a single customer.

SEC 61012

(viii) The dollar amount of backlog orders believed to be firm, as of a recent date and as of a comparable date in the preceding fiscal year, together with an indication of the portion thereof not reasonably expected to be filled within the current fiscal year, and seasonal or other material aspects of the backlog. (There may be included as firm orders government orders that are firm but not yet funded and contracts awarded but not yet signed, provided an appropriate statement is added to explain the nature of such orders and the amount thereof. The portion of orders already included in sales or operating revenues on the basis of percentage of completion or program accounting shall be excluded.)

(ix) A description of any material portion of the business that may be subject to renegotiation of profits or termination of contracts or subcontracts at the election of the Government.

(x) Competitive conditions in the business involved including, where material, the identity of the particular markets in which the registrant competes, an estimate of the number of competitors and the registrant's competitive position, if known or reasonably available to the registrant. Separate consideration shall be given to the principal products or services or classes of products or services of the segment, if any. Generally, the names of competitors need not be disclosed. The registrant may include such names, unless in the particular case the effect of including the names would be misleading. Where, however, the registrant knows or has reason to know that one or a small number of competitors is dominant in the industry it shall be identified. The principal methods of competition (e.g., price, service, warranty or product performance) shall be identified, and positive and negative factors pertaining to the competitive position of the registrant, to the extent that they exist, shall be explained if known or reasonably available to the registrant.

(xi) If material, the estimated amount spent during each of the last three fiscal years on company-sponsored research and development activities determined in accordance with generally accepted accounting principles. In addition, state, if material, the estimated dollar amount spent during each of such years on customer-sponsored research activities relating to the development of new products, services or techniques or the improvement of existing products, services or techniques.

(xii) Appropriate disclosure also shall be made as to the material effects that compliance with Federal, State and local provisions which have been enacted or adopted regulating the discharge of materials into the environment, or otherwise relating to the protection of the environment, may have upon the capital expenditures, earnings and competitive position of the registrant and its subsidiaries. The registrant shall disclose any material estimated capital expenditures for environmental control facilities for the remainder of its current fiscal

SEC 61012

year and its succeeding fiscal year and for such further periods as the registrant may deem material.

(xiii) The number of persons employed by the registrant.

(d) Financial information about foreign and domestic operations and export sales.

(1) State for each of the registrant's last three fiscal years, or for each fiscal year the registrant has been engaged in business, whichever period is shorter, the amounts of revenue (with sales to unaffiliated customers and sales or transfers to other geographic areas shown separately), operating profit or loss and identifiable assets attributable to each of the registrant's geographic areas and the amount of export sales in the aggregate or by appropriate geographic area to which the sales are made. (See Appendix B to this Item for a suggested tabular format for presentation of this information.) To the extent that financial information included pursuant to this paragraph (d) complies with generally accepted accounting principles, the registrant may include in its financial statements a cross reference to this data in lieu of presenting duplicative data in its financial statements; conversely a registrant may cross-reference to the financial statements. The prior period information shall be retroactively restated in the following circumstances, unless not material, with appropriate disclosure of the nature and effect of the restatement:

(i) When the financial statements of the registrant as a whole have been retroactively restated, or

(ii) When there has been a change in the way a registrant's foreign operations are grouped into geographic areas and such change affects the geographic area information being reported. Restatement is not required when a registrant's geographic areas change as a result of a change in the nature of operations or as a result of an area losing or gaining in significance.

(2) Any risks attendant to the foreign operations and any dependence of one or more of the registrant's industry segments upon such foreign operations shall be described unless it would be more appropriate for this matter to be discussed in connection with the description of one or more of the registrant's industry segments pursuant to paragraph (c) of this Item.

(3) If the registrant includes, or is required by Article 3 of Regulation S-X to include, interim financial statements, discuss any facts relating to the information furnished pursuant to this paragraph (d) that, in the opinion of management, indicate that the three year financial data for foreign and domestic operations or export sales may not be indicative of current or future operations. Comparative information shall be included to the extent necessary to the discussion.

SEC 61012

Instructions to Item 101. *1. In determining what information about the industry segments is material to an understanding of the registrant's business taken as a whole and therefore required to be disclosed pursuant to paragraph (c) of this Item, the registrant should take into account both quantitative and qualitative factors such as the significance of the matter to the registrant (e.g., whether a matter with a relatively minor impact on the registrant's business is represented by management to be important to its future profitability), the pervasiveness of the matter (e.g., whether it affects or may affect numerous items in the segment information), and the impact of the matter (e.g., whether it distorts the trends reflected in the segment information). Situations may arise when information should be disclosed about a segment, although the information in quantitative terms may not appear significant to the registrant's business taken as a whole.*

2. The determination whether information about foreign and domestic operations and export sales is required in the document for a particular year shall be based upon an evaluation of interperiod comparability. For instance, interperiod comparability most likely would require that foreign and domestic operations and export sales that have been significant in the past and are expected to be significant in the future be regarded as reportable even though they are not significant in the current fiscal year.

3. The Commission, upon written request of the registrant and where consistent with the protection of investors, may permit the omission of any of the information required by this Item or the furnishing in substitution thereof of appropriate information of comparable character.

APPENDIX A— Industry Segments

The table set forth below is illustrative of the format that might be used for presenting the segment information required by paragraphs (b) and (c)(1)(i) of Item 101 regarding industry segments and classes of similar products or services.

Financial Information Relating to Industry Segments and Classes of Products or Services

	Year 1	Year 2	Year 3
Sales to unaffiliated customers:			
Industry segment A:			
Class of product 1			
Class of product 2			
Industry segment B:			
Class of product 1			
Class of product 2			
Industry segment C			
Other industries			
Intersegment sales or transfers:			
Industry segment A			
Industry segment B			
Industry segment C			
Other industries			
Operating profit or loss:			
Industry segment A			
Industry segment B			
Industry segment C			
Other industries			
Identifiable assets:			
Industry segment A			
Industry segment B			
Industry segment C			
Other industries			

APPENDIX B—Foreign and Domestic Operations and Export Sales

The table set forth below is illustrative of the format that might be used for presenting the segment information required by paragraph (d) of Item 101 regarding foreign and domestic operations and export sales.

SEC 61012

Financial Information Relating to Foreign and Domestic Operations and Export Sales

		Year 1	Year 2	Year 3
Sales to unaffiliated customers	United States *			
	Geographic area A			
	Geographic area B			
Sales or transfers between geographic areas	United States			
	Geographic area A			
	Geographic area B			
Operating profit or loss**	United States			
	Geographic area A			
	Geographic area B			
Identifiable assets	United States			
	Geographic area A			
	Geographic area B			
Export Sales	United States***			

*Or appropriate area of domestic operations.

**Or some other reasonable measure of profitability as used in the financial statements.

***Identify the geographic areas to which the sales are made, if appropriate.

61013. Materiality. Instruction 1 of the Description of Business requirements sets forth certain materiality guidelines for the disclosure of industry segment information that are not included in FASB Statement No. 14. The instruction states that in determining what information as to industry segments (and geographic areas and export sales) is material to an understanding of the registrant's business taken as a whole and therefore requires disclosure, the registrant should take into account both quantitative and qualitative factors, such as:

- The significance of the matter to the registrant; for example, whether a matter with minor impact is important to future profitability.

- The pervasiveness of the matter; for example, whether it affects or may affect numerous items of the segment information presented.

- The impact of the matter; for example, whether it distorts the trends reflected in the segment information presented.

61014. Sales to One Customer. When 10 percent or more of consolidated revenue is derived from sales to any one customer, FASB Statement No. 14 (as amended by FASB Statement No. 30) requires disclosure of that fact and the amount of revenue from each such customer. The Regulation S-K requirements specify that the following additional information should be disclosed:

- Paragraph (c)(1)(vii) requires disclosure of the dependence of any segment on a single customer or a few customers, the loss of any one or more of which would have a material adverse effect on the segment.

- Paragraph (c)(1)(vii) requires disclosure of the *names* of such customers and the relationship of each such customer to the registrant or its subsidiaries if the loss of such customer would have a material adverse effect on the registrant and its subsidiaries taken as a whole. Note that the name of the customer is required to be disclosed *only* if the loss of the business derived from such customer would have "a material adverse effect."

61015. Classes of Similar Products or Services. Paragraph (c)(1)(i) requires a description of the principal products produced and services rendered by the registrant and disclosure of the amount or percentage of any class of similar products or services that accounted for:

- 10 percent or more of consolidated revenue in any one of the last three fiscal years.

- 15 percent or more of consolidated revenue if total revenue did not exceed $50 million in any one of the last three fiscal years.

The information is required to be presented by industry segment to the extent material to an understanding of the registrant's business taken as a whole. Note that this requirement goes beyond the disclosures required by FASB Statement No. 14. Therefore, the disclosure of the amount or percentage of total revenue contributed by any class of similar products or services may be necessary even though the registrant's business consists of only one segment.

61016. SEC Interpretation of FASB Statement No. 14. Subsequent to the adoption of the industry segment reporting requirements in Regulation S-K (ASR No. 236), the SEC issued ASR No. 244 (now FRP Section 503.03) dealing with segment reporting requirements. The release discusses the SEC's views as to the provisions of FASB Statement No. 14, including the segment disclosures determined by the staff to be appropriate in certain specific cases. In paragraph (a) of FRP Section 503.03, the SEC staff notes that the determination of industry segments depends to a large extent on the judgment of management. However, in exercising this judgment, the staff points out that management should follow the guidance provided in paragraph 11 of SFAS

SEC 61014

14, which identifies steps to be followed in determining reportable segments. These steps include:

- Identifying the individual products and services from which the enterprise derives its revenue;

- Grouping those products and services by industry lines into industry segments; and

- Selecting those industry segments that are significant with respect to the enterprise as a whole.

For guidance in determining industry segments, the staff refers to paragraph 13 of SFAS 14, which states that a reasonable starting point for the determination is an analysis of the profit centers or "the smallest units of activity for which revenue and expense information is accumulated by a company for internal planning and control purposes." The staff indicates that when a company's profit centers cross industry lines, the profit centers are required to be disaggregated into smaller groups of related products and services. The staff also points out that the term "industry" includes narrow as well as broad groupings of products and services, as supported by the increased level of disaggregated classification; however, an evaluation of various criteria by the registrant is far more useful in identifying industry segments than trying to define this term. Although paragraph 12 of SFAS 14 states that no single set of criteria is applicable in all cases, Appendix D to that Statement provides the following factors to be considered in grouping products and services by industry lines into industry segments.

- The nature of the product.

- The nature of the production process.

- Markets and marketing methods.

The staff also indicates that in determining industry segments, it does not hold the view that segments should be separate and distinct from one another and that a segment can only be identified if it can be sold without having an impact on the earnings of other segments.

The pertinent provisions of paragraph (a) of FRP Section 503.03 follow:

Determination of Industry Segments

The classification by a corporation of its business into industry segments pursuant to the Commission requirements and generally accepted accounting principles is a subjective task and, thus, to a considerable extent, segment determination depends on the judgment of management. In exercising this judgment, however, management should go through the industry segment identification steps outlined in Paragraph 11 of SFAS No. 14, keeping in mind that information on a less-than-total-enterprise basis is necessary for an evaluation of the risks and return on an investment.

The provisions of SFAS No. 14 present a logical procedure for the classification of a business into industry segments. The term "industry segment" is defined in Paragraph 10(a) of the FASB's statement as "a component of an enterprise engaged in providing a product or service or a group of related products and services primarily to unaffiliated customers (i.e., customers outside the enterprise) for a profit." SFAS No. 14 lists the three steps that a company should take in determining its industry segments. Paragraph 11 states:

The reportable segments of an enterprise shall be determined by:

(a) Identifying the individual products and services from which the enterprise derives its revenue.

(b) Grouping those products and services by industry lines into industry segments . . ., and

(c) Selecting those industry segments that are significant with respect to the enterprise as a whole. . . .*

A reasonable starting point for the determination of industry segments according to Paragraph 13 of the Statement is an analysis of the profit centers or "the smallest units of activity for which revenue and expense information is accumulated by a company for internal planning and control purposes." If a particular company's profit centers cross industry lines, however, a company would be required to disaggregate the profit center into smaller groups of related products and services.

The phrases "industry line" and "industry" are not defined in SFAS No. 14. As a result of the absence of a definition of these terms, some persons have stated that the term should be interpreted broadly. The "Standard Industrial Classification Manual" (SIC) prepared by the Statistical Policy Division of the U.S. Office of Management and Budget, however, defines industries by kinds of business and enables classification of enterprises on a one-digit, two-digit, three-digit and four-digit industry code basis according to the level of industrial detail considered most appropriate. This increasingly disaggregated classification of industries suggests that the word "industry" may be used to include narrow as well as broad based groupings of products and services.

SEC 61016

SFAS No. 14 does not state how narrowly the term "industry" should be interpreted. The only comment on this point is that "[broad] categories such as manufacturing, wholesaling, retailing, and consumer products are not per se indicative of the industries which a registrant should report, and those terms should not be used without identification of a product or service to describe the industry segments."**

An examination by registrants of various criteria is far more useful to a registrant identifying industry segments than the philosophical meaning of the word "industry". Although the FASB states in Paragraph 12 of its Statement that "no single set of characteristics is universally applicable in determining the industry segments of all enterprises, nor is any single characteristic determinative in all cases," Appendix D of SFAS No. 14 ("Appendix D") sets forth several factors that may be relevant in identifying industry segments and therefore should be considered in determining whether products and services are related.

The following criteria are included in Appendix D as among those factors which should be considered in grouping products and services by industry lines into industry segments:

(a) The nature of the product. Related products or services have similar purposes or end uses. Thus, they may be expected to have similar rates of profitability, similar degrees of risk, and similar opportunities for growth.

(b) The nature of the production process. Sharing of common or interchangeable production or sales facilities, equipment, labor force, or service group or use of the same or similar basic raw materials may suggest that products or services are related. Likewise, similar degrees of labor intensiveness or similar degrees of capital intensiveness may indicate a relationship among products or services.

(c) Markets and marketing methods. Similarity of geographic marketing areas, types of customers, or marketing methods may indicate a relationship among products or services. For instance, the use of a common or interchangeable sales force may suggest a relationship among products or services. The sensitivity of the market to price changes and to changes in general economic conditions may also indicate whether products or services are related or unrelated.

The factors listed above may have different degrees of importance depending upon the circumstances. The sole fact that a company has essentially one raw material which is used to produce various products, or that its operations share common production facilities or that all of its products are based on one type of technology is not alone determinative of a one-industry segment business. In short, appropriate segmentation will result only if a registrant examines each of the factors noted in Appendix D.

Some persons have argued that industry segments should be separate and distinct from each other and should be identified as such only if they can be sold without having an impact on the earnings of the corporation's other industry segments.

SEC 61016

The staff believes that the "with-or-without" or "severability test," as it is known, is not an appropriate test for the determination of segments. This test is not set forth in SFAS No. 14, although it was recommended to the FASB in response to the Board's request for comments on the issue of segment reporting.

SFAS No. 14 states that the segment information may be of limited usefulness for comparing an industry segment of one enterprise with a similar industry segment of another enterprise. For example, the segments of a conglomerate may include products and services which are related more broadly than the products and services in an industry segment of a smaller corporation.

---

*An industry segment is significant and therefore should be identified as reportable if its revenue, operating profit or loss or identifiable assets are 10 percent or more of the related combined enterprise amounts. See Paragraph 15, Statement No. 14.**

**Paragraph 101, Appendix D, Statement No. 14.

In paragraph b, illustrating acceptable segmentation, FRP Section 503.03 discusses certain cases relating to specific types of businesses such as:

- Electric and electronic products.

- Forest products.

- Chemicals.

- Drugs.

- Property/casualty insurance.

While the release cautions that the staff does not expect that all companies engaged in the same type of business will have identical segments, it does state that those engaged in these businesses should consider the segments that were appropriate in the cases cited.

Discontinued Operations

With regard to segment reporting and discontinued operations, the SEC staff has informally indicated that it does not object to the application of discontinued operations treatment to a portion of a SFAS No. 14 segment that qualifies as a major line of business or class of customer; i.e., that qualifies as a segment under APB No. 30. However, the staff has pointed out that in such situations prior disclosures of product revenues as required by ASR 236 (FRP 503) should have been provided for each major line of business or class of customer involved.

SEC 61016

61020. DESCRIPTION OF PROPERTY (ITEM 102)

The Description of Property requirements call for a brief statement as to the location and general character of the principal plants, mines, and other materially important physical properties of the registrant and its subsidiaries, and an identification of the industry segments that use the property described.

The independent accountant is generally not consulted by registrants or their attorneys or otherwise involved in the preparation of the required Description of Property information. Accordingly, the text of these requirements is not reproduced here.

61030. LEGAL PROCEEDINGS (ITEM 103)

61031. General. The textual information to be furnished pertaining to Legal Proceedings is similar to, but more extensive than, the disclosures required pursuant to paragraphs 9-19 of FASB Statement No. 5. The textual discussion of legal matters needs to be read by the independent accountant to ensure that the conclusions as to the impact of such matters on the financial statements as disclosed in the footnotes is consistent with the disclosures in the textual portion of the document. Particular consideration needs to be given to legal matters discussed in the text and not disclosed in the notes to the financial statements as to (1) their potential impact on the financial statements and (2) whether disclosure is necessary.

When the text describes contingencies also required to be disclosed in the financial statements, such information may be incorporated by reference in the notes to the financial statements. (See discussion of cross-referencing in section 17093.)

61032. Text of Requirements.

Legal Proceedings

Describe briefly any material pending legal proceedings, other than ordinary routine litigation incidental to the business, to which the registrant or any of its subsidiaries is a party or of which any of their property is the subject. Include the name of the court or agency in which the proceedings are pending, the date instituted, the principal parties thereto, a description of the factual basis alleged to underlie the proceeding and the relief sought. Include similar information as to any such proceedings known to be contemplated by governmental authorities.

Instructions to Item 103. 1. If the business ordinarily results in actions for negligence or other claims, no such action or claim need be described unless it departs from the normal kind of such actions.

2. No information need be given with respect to any proceeding that involves primarily a claim for damages if the amount involved, exclusive of interest and costs, does not exceed 10 percent of the current assets of the registrant and its subsidiaries on a consolidated basis. However, if any proceeding presents in large degree the same legal and factual issues as other proceedings pending or known to be contemplated, the amount involved in such other proceedings shall be included in computing such percentage.

3. Notwithstanding Instructions 1 and 2, any material bankruptcy, receivership, or similar proceeding with respect to the registrant or any of its significant subsidiaries shall be described.

4. Any material proceedings to which any director, officer or affiliate of the registrant, any owner of record or beneficiary of more than five percent of any class of voting securities of the registrant, or any associate of any such director, officer, affiliate of the registrant, or security holder is a party adverse to the registrant or any of its subsidiaries or has a material interest adverse to the registrant or any of its subsidiaries also shall be described.

5. Notwithstanding the foregoing, an administrative or judicial proceeding (including, for purposes of A and B of this Instruction, proceedings which present in large degree the same issues) arising under any Federal, State or local provisions that have been enacted or adopted regulating the discharge of materials into the environment or primarily for the purpose of protecting the environment shall not be deemed "ordinary routine litigation incidental to the business" and shall be described if:

> *(A) Such proceeding is material to the business or financial condition of the registrant,*

> *(B) Such proceeding involves primarily a claim for damages, or involves potential monetary sanctions, capital expenditures, deferred charges or charges to income, and the amount involved, exclusive of interest and costs, exceeds 10 percent of the current assets of the registrant and its subsidiaries on a consolidated basis, or*

> *(C) A governmental authority is a party to such proceeding and such proceeding involves potential monetary sanctions, unless the registrant reasonably believes that such proceeding will result in no monetary sanctions, or in monetary sanctions, exclusive of interest and costs, of less than $ 100,000; provided, however, that such proceedings which are similar in nature may be grouped and described generically.*

61033. Environmental Proceedings. In ASR No. 306, the Commission amended Instruction 5 of Item 103 by limiting the disclosure of environmental proceedings to those expected to result in monetary sanctions, exclusive of interest and costs, of $100,000 or more. Refer to section 50502.25 for discussion of SAB 92, *Accounting and Disclosures Relating to Loss Contingencies.*

62000. SECURITIES OF THE REGISTRANT

62010. MARKET PRICE OF AND DIVIDENDS ON THE REGISTRANT'S COMMON EQUITY AND RELATED STOCKHOLDER MATTERS (ITEM 201)

This item sets forth the disclosure requirements pertaining to a registrant's common stock and related matters. The disclosures required include the securities markets on which the registrant's common stock is traded, the high and low prices for each quarterly period within the two most recent fiscal years and any subsequent interim period for which financial statements are included, the number of shareholders as of the latest practicable date, and information with respect to dividends. The requirements as to dividends specify that any restriction on the registrant's present *or future* ability to pay dividends is to be disclosed, or cross-referenced to a discussion of such restrictions, in the MD&A section prescribed by Item 303 of Regulation S-K or to the disclosure of such restrictions required by Regulation S-X in the registrant's financial statements. Furthermore, registrants are *encouraged* to disclose their future intentions with respect to the payment of dividends.

Note that the annual report to shareholders must include the information specified by this Regulation S-K item, pursuant to Rule 14a-3 (refer to section 31320).

The information to be disclosed pursuant to these requirements is the responsibility of the registrant and/or its counsel. Consequently, the text of this item is not reproduced herein.

62020. DESCRIPTION OF REGISTRANT'S SECURITIES (ITEM 202)

This item requires that restrictions affecting the transferability of ownership of securities and provisions specifying the votes of security holders that are required to take particular actions be disclosed. Disclosure is required of any charter or bylaw provisions that would have the effect of delaying, deferring, or preventing a change in the control of the issuer and that are operative only with respect to an extraordinary corporate transaction (e.g., merger, tender offer, sale of substantially all assets, or liquidation). However, provisions and arrangements required by law or imposed by governmental or judicial authority do not have to be disclosed.

Item 202 also requires the description of interest and conversion requirements, subordination rights, and dividend restrictions. The information required depends on whether capital stock, debt securities, warrants, rights, or other securities are being registered.

The information to be disclosed pursuant to these requirements is the responsibility of the registrant and/or its counsel. Consequently, the text of this item is not reproduced herein.

63000. FINANCIAL INFORMATION

63010. SELECTED FINANCIAL DATA (ITEM 301)

63011. General. The primary objective of the requirements for the presentation of Selected Financial Data is to provide information as to trends in the registrant's financial condition and results of operations. The requirements set forth in Regulation S-K represent the minimum information to be disclosed, and the SEC encourages registrants to present additional information that enhances an understanding of these trends. The SEC's stated intent with respect to these requirements was to strike a reasonable balance between specifying content and permitting registrants the flexibility to provide the data that best indicates their operating performance and financial condition.

The headnote or introductory paragraph is not required for the summary of Selected Financial Data; however, it is frequently included. Refer to section 20371 for guidance as to how it may be worded.

63012. Text of Requirements.

Selected Financial Data

Furnish in comparative columnar form the selected financial data for the registrant referred to below, for

(a) Each of the last five fiscal years of the registrant (or for the life of the registrant and its predecessors, if less), and

(b) Any additional fiscal years necessary to keep the information from being misleading.

Instructions to Item 301. 1. The purpose of the selected financial data shall be to supply in a convenient and readable format selected financial data which highlight certain significant trends in the registrant's financial condition and results of operations.

2. Subject to appropriate variation to conform to the nature of the registrant's business, the following items shall be included in the table of financial data: net sales or operating revenues; income (loss) from continuing operations; income (loss) from continuing operations per common share; total assets; long-term obligations and redeemable preferred stock (including long-term debt, capital leases, and redeemable preferred stock as defined in Rule 5-02.28(a) of Regulation S-X); and cash dividends declared per common share. Registrants may include additional items which they believe would enhance an understanding of and would highlight other trends in their financial condition and results of operations.

Briefly describe, or cross-reference to a discussion thereof, factors such as accounting changes, business combinations or dispositions of business operations, that materially affect the comparability of the information reflected in selected financial data. Discussion of, or reference to, any material uncertainties should also be included where such matters might cause the data reflected herein not to be indicative of the registrant's future financial condition or results of operations.

3. All references to the registrant in the table of selected financial data and in this Item shall mean the registrant and its subsidiaries consolidated.

4. If interim period financial statements are included, or are required to be included by Article 3 of Regulation S-X, registrants should consider whether any or all of the selected financial data need to be updated for such interim periods to reflect a material change in the trends indicated; where such updating information is necessary, registrants shall provide the information on a comparative basis unless not necessary to an understanding of such updating information.

5. A foreign private issuer shall disclose also the following information in all filings containing financial statements:

A. In the forepart of the document and as of the latest practicable date, the exchange rate into U.S. currency of the foreign currency in which the financial statements are denominated;

B. A history of exchange rates for the five most recent years and any subsequent interim period for which financial statements are presented setting forth the rates for period-end, the average rates, and the range of high and low rates for each year; and

C. If equity securities are being registered, a five year summary of dividends per share stated in both the currency in which the financial statements are denominated and United States currency based on the exchange rates at each respective payment date.

6. A foreign private issuer shall present the selected financial data in the same currency as its financial statements. The issuer may present the selected finan-

cial data on the basis of the accounting principles used in its primary financial statements but in such case shall present this data also on the basis of any reconciliations of such data to United States generally accepted accounting principles and Regulation S-X made pursuant to Rule 4-01 of Regulation S-X.

7. For purposes of this rule, the rate of exchange means the noon buying rate in New York City for cable transfers in foreign currencies as certified for customs purposes by the Federal Reserve Bank of New York. The average rate means the average of the exchange rates on the last day of each month during a year.

63013. Audit Requirements. The summary of Selected Financial Data is *not* required to be audited. However, independent accountants are sometimes requested by clients and underwriters to refer to this information in their report. The ASB has issued Statement on Auditing Standards No. 42, *Reporting on Condensed Financial Statements and Selected Financial Data* (as amended by SAS Nos. 58, 62, and 71) (AU Section 552), which establishes standards for reporting on such data. Reference should be made to section 20372 of this manual for examples of accountants' reports used in such cases.

63014. Period Covered. The instructions require that the summary of Selected Financial Data include information for any additional fiscal years necessary to keep it from being misleading. In general, this requirement has been interpreted to mean that if the company's business during the required five-year period was unduly influenced by extraordinary, nonrecurring, or unusual conditions (for example, war production or wide cyclical fluctuations), it may be necessary to expand the summary to include a number of years that is more representative of the company's operations under normal conditions.

The period of five fiscal years contemplates a 12-month year and an aggregate of 60 months. In the case of a short fiscal period (such as that caused by a change in fiscal year), 9 months or longer will usually suffice as a fiscal year. Since the most recent period is frequently important in evaluating trend information, the staff of the SEC may suggest that when a short fiscal period has occurred at the end of the five-year period, it be presented in comparative form.

Note that instruction 2 to Item 301 specifies that a brief discussion is required on matters affecting the comparability of the selected financial data presented. If such matters are discussed elsewhere in the document (e.g., MD&A), a cross-reference to that discussion is generally sufficient.

63015. Dividends Per Share. As with the primary financial statements, retroactive effect should also be given in the Selected Financial Data to stock dividends and stock splits for all years presented, including those that occur after the date of the latest audited balance sheet but before release of the document containing the data.

63020. SUPPLEMENTARY FINANCIAL INFORMATION (ITEM 302)

63021. General

The Regulation S-K requirements for Supplementary Financial Information pertain to selected quarterly financial data and information about oil and gas production activities. The disclosures may be presented either in the notes to the financial statements (designated "unaudited") or outside the financial statements.

63022. Quarterly Financial Data

63023. Accountants' responsibility. Paragraphs 36 through 42 of SAS No. 71 (AU Section 722) describe the professional standards to be followed by the auditor when the selected quarterly financial information is presented in annual reports to shareholders and in documents filed with the SEC containing audited financial statements. These paragraphs state that:

- If independent accountants have audited the annual financial statements for which selected quarterly financial data is *required* to be presented, they should review the data in accordance with the procedures specified in the SAS. If the data has been omitted or no review has been performed, the independent accountants should expand their report on the audited financial statements to specify that either the required information has been omitted or has not been reviewed. Paragraph 41 of SAS 71 contains suggested wording for these modifications.

- When a public entity *voluntarily* includes the selected quarterly financial data, the independent accountants should review the data, unless either:

  - The entity indicates that the data have not been reviewed; or

  - The independent accountants expand their report on the audited financial statements to specify that the data have not been reviewed. Paragraph 42 of SAS 71 contains suggested wording for this modification.

- The interim financial information, whether presented as supplementary information outside the audited financial statements (as is generally done) or in a note to the audited financial statements, should clearly be marked as unaudited.

- The review procedures performed by the independent accountants may be applied either at the time of the annual audit or prior to the issuance of each quarter's data.

63024. Applicability of disclosure requirements. In adopting the requirements for Supplementary Financial Information, the SEC expressed its viewpoint that the greatest investor need for the required quarterly data exists in the case of companies whose activities are most closely followed by analysts and investors. Accordingly, registrants whose securities are not "actively traded" are exempted from these disclosure requirements irrespective of whether they meet the second test described in paragraph (a)(5)(ii) of the rule (see section 63026). Debt and equity securities (other than those of a mutual life insurance company) listed on a national exchange are considered "actively traded" under the rule.

The "actively traded" test for unlisted securities applies only to equity securities of U.S. corporations registered under Section 12(g) of the 1934 Act (equity securities traded over the counter) and would be met if the conditions described in the rule under "First test" (paragraph (a)(5)(i)(c)—see section 63026) are met.

The size test (i.e., "Second test") would be met by a registrant that had:

- *Consolidated total assets of at least $200 million* as of the end of the latest fiscal year.

OR

- *Consolidated net income* (after taxes, but before extraordinary items and the cumulative effect of a change in accounting) *of at least $250,000 for each of the last three fiscal years.*

While the rule provides that the income portion of the test is based on each of the last three fiscal years, according to SAB Topic 6-G (see question 4 below) the size tests may be applied at the *beginning* of the latest fiscal year, and thereby that year may be excluded from the test. However, whichever period is initially selected, the test should be consistently applied in future years. If the securities of a registrant are considered to "meet criteria both as to size and trading activity," the specified disclosures are required to be made.

The following interpretations are included in SAB Topic 6-G1.c:

Application of Item 302(a) Requirements

Facts: The requirements for disclosure of the selected quarterly financial data apply only to those companies meeting both of two tests based on the size of the company and the extent of trading in its securities, respectively. The size test is measured by total assets and net income, as defined. The trading test is measured by whether a registrant's securities are listed on a national securities exchange or quoted on the National Association of Securities Dealers Automatic Quotation System and meet the specified "actively traded" criteria set forth in the rule.

Question 1: Should the determination of net income, as defined, for each of the last three fiscal years be adjusted for restatements of prior-year figures as a result of changes in accounting principles, business combinations (accounted for as poolings of interest), prior-period adjustments, etc.?

Interpretive Response: Net income, as defined, for the last three fiscal years should be determined each year on the basis of current financial statements which included those years. Such financial statements would reflect restatements, if any, of prior years' data in accordance with generally accepted accounting principles. However, as indicated in the interpretive response to Question 2 below, a registrant will not be required to retroactively disclose the quarterly financial data called for by Item 302(a) for the prior year as a result of such restatements if it did not meet such a requirement when the prior year financial statements were originally filed with the Commission.

Question 2: Is a registrant which meets the requirements to furnish selected quarterly financial data for the first time in the current year required to retroactively include the quarterly financial data for prior years' financial statements presented for comparative purposes?

Interpretive Response: Although Item 302(a)(1) requires disclosure of selected quarterly financial data for the two most recent years, a registrant will not be required to retroactively include the quarterly financial data called for by this instruction if it did not meet such a requirement when the financial statements were originally filed with the Commission.

Question 3: Is a closed-end investment company subject to the Investment Company Act of 1940 required to comply with the disclosure requirements of Item 302(a)?

Interpretive Response: A closed-end investment company which has securities registered pursuant to Section 12(b) of the Exchange Act is not exempt from the requirements of Item 302(a). However, a closed-end investment company that is exempt from registration under Section 12(g) of the Exchange Act is exempt from the requirements of Item 302(a).

Question 4: Should the $200 million total assets and $250,000 net income for each of the last three fiscal years tests be made at the beginning or end of the fiscal year?

SEC 63024

Interpretive Response: In order to facilitate the engagement of independent accountants to perform a limited review of the quarterly financial statements on a timely basis, if desired, the size and income tests of Item 302(a) should be applied at the beginning of the fiscal year.

63025. Required information. The following information is required for each full quarter within the two most recent fiscal years and any subsequent interim period for which income statements are presented:

- Net sales.

- Gross profit.

- Income before extraordinary items and the cumulative effect of a change in accounting, and per share data based on such income.

- Net income.

Disclosure is required of the effect of any disposals of segments of business and extraordinary, unusual, or infrequently occurring items recognized in each quarter, and the aggregate effect and nature of year-end or other adjustments that are material to the results of that quarter. If any of the quarterly information disclosed differs from amounts previously reported in Form 10-Q (as discussed in section 41400), a reconciliation and explanation are required.

The following interpretations included in SAB Topic 6-G1.a and b provide guidance as to the quarterly financial data disclosure requirements:

Disclosure of Selected Quarterly Financial Data

Facts: Item 302(a)(1) of Regulation S-K requires disclosure of net sales, gross profit, income before extraordinary items and cumulative effect of a change in accounting, per share data based upon such income, and net income for each full quarter within the two most recent fiscal years and any subsequent interim period for which financial statements are included. Item 302(a)(3) requires the registrant to describe the effect of any disposals of segments of a business and extraordinary, unusual or infrequently occurring items recognized in each quarter, as well as the aggregate effect and the nature of year-end or other adjustments which are material to the results of that quarter. Furthermore, Item 302(a)(2) requires a reconciliation of amounts previously reported on Form 10-Q to the quarterly data presented if the amounts differ.

Question 1: Are these disclosure requirements applicable to supplemental financial statements included in a filing with the SEC for unconsolidated subsidiaries and 50% or less owned persons . . .?

Interpretive Response: The summarized quarterly financial data required by Item 302(a)(1) need not be included in supplemental financial statements for unconsolidated subsidiaries and 50% or less owned persons unless the financial statements are for a subsidiary or affiliate that is itself a registrant which meets the criteria set forth in Item 302(a)(5).

Question 2: If a company is in a specialized industry where "gross profit" generally is not computed (e.g., banks, insurance companies and finance companies), what disclosure should be made to comply with the requirements of Item 302(a)(1)?

Interpretive Response: Companies in specialized industries should present summarized quarterly financial data which are most meaningful in their particular circumstances.

For example, a bank might present interest income, interest expense, provision for loan losses, security gains or losses and net income. Similarly, an insurance company might present net premiums earned, underwriting costs and expenses, investment income, security gains or losses and net income.

Question 3: If a company wishes to make its quarterly and annual disclosures on the same basis, would disclosure of costs and expenses associated directly with or allocated to products sold or services rendered, or other appropriate data to enable users to compute "gross profit," satisfy the requirements of Item 302(a)(1)?

Interpretive Response: Yes.

Question 4: What is meant by "per-share data based upon such income" as used in Item 302(a)(1)?

Interpretive Response: Item 302(a)(1) only requires disclosure of per-share amounts for income before extraordinary items and cumulative effect of a change in accounting. It is expected that when per-share data is calculated for each full quarter based upon such income, the per-share amounts would be both primary and fully diluted. Although it is not required by the rule, there are many instances where it would be desirable to also disclose other per-share figures such as net earnings per share and the per-share effect of extraordinary items. Where such disclosure is made, per-share data should be both primary and fully diluted.

Question 5: What is intended by the requirement set forth in Item 302(a)(3) that registrants "describe the effect of" disposals of segments of a business, etc.?

Interpretive Response: The rule is intended to require registrants to "disclose the amount" of such unusual transactions and events included in the results reported for each quarter. Such disclosure would be made in narrative form. However, it would not require that matters covered by management's discussion and analysis of financial condition and results of operations be repeated. In this situation, registrants should disclose the nature and amount of the unusual transaction or event and refer to management's analysis for further discussion of the matter.

SEC 63025

Question 6: What is intended by the requirement of Item 302(a)(3) to disclose "the aggregate effect and the nature of year-end or other adjustments which are material to the results of that quarter"?

Interpretive Response: This language is taken directly from Paragraph 31 of APB Opinion No. 28 which relates to disclosures required for the fourth quarter of the year. The Opinion indicates that earlier quarters should not be restated to reflect a change in accounting estimate recorded at year-end. However, changes in an accounting estimate made in an interim period that materially affect the quarter in which the change occurred are required to be disclosed in order to avoid misleading comparisons. In making such disclosure, registrants may wish to identify (but not restate) the prior periods in which transactions were recorded which relate to the change in the quarter.

Question 7: If a company has filed a Form 8 amending a previously filed Form 10-Q, is a reconciliation of quarterly data in annual financial statements with the amounts originally reported on Form 10-Q required?

Interpretive Response: Yes. However, if the company publishes quarterly reports to shareholders and has previously made detailed disclosure to shareholders in such reports of the change reported on the Form 8 no reconciliation would be required.

[Note: Form 8 has been rescinded. Amendments should be filed under cover of the form amended, designated by adding the letter "A" after the title of the form, e.g., "Form 10-K/A" (see section 41700).]

The SEC staff has informally indicated that when it is determined that an adjustment is required to previously filed quarterly information, an amended form (see section 41700) is required to be filed amending the previous filing *in addition to* reflecting the revised information in the annual filing on Form 10-K. A typical scenario in which the situation may occur is one in which a significant adjustment is identified in connection with the year-end closing affecting Form 10-Q financial data issued earlier in the year. It is important to note, however, that the staff has informally indicated that previously filed interim reports on Form 10-Q that were correct when filed need not be amended for later change in accounting principles.

Financial Statements Presented on Other Than a Quarterly Basis

Facts: Item 302(a)(1) requires disclosure of quarterly financial data for each full quarter of the last two fiscal years and in any subsequent interim period for which an income statement is presented.

Question 1: If a company reports at interim dates on other than a calendar-quarter basis (e.g., 12-12-16-12 week basis), will it be precluded from reporting on such basis in the future?

SEC 63025

Interpretive Response: No, as long as it discloses the basis of interim fiscal period reporting and the interim fiscal periods on which it reports are consistently determined from year to year (or, if not, the lack of comparability is disclosed).

Additional interpretations of required information are provided in section 2 of SAB Topic 6 regarding (a) Form of Condensed Financial Statements and (b) Reporting Requirements for Accounting Changes (see sections 51002 and 20620).

63026. Text of Requirements

Supplementary Financial Information

(a) Selected quarterly financial data. *Registrants specified in paragraph (a)(5) of this Item shall provide the information specified below.*

(1) Disclosure shall be made of net sales, gross profit (net sales less costs and expenses associated directly with or allocated to products sold or services rendered), income (loss) before extraordinary items and cumulative effect of a change in accounting, per share data based upon such income (loss), and net income (loss), for each full quarter within the two most recent fiscal years and any subsequent interim period for which financial statements are included or are required to be included by Article 3 of Regulation S-X.

(2) When the data supplied pursuant to this paragraph (a) vary from the amounts previously reported on the Form 10-Q filed for any quarter, such as would be the case when a pooling of interests occurs or where an error is corrected, reconcile the amounts given with those previously reported and describe the reason for the difference.

(3) Describe the effect of any disposals of segments of a business, and extraordinary, unusual or infrequently occurring items recognized in each full quarter within the two most recent fiscal years and any subsequent interim period for which financial statements are included or are required to be included by Article 3 of Regulation S-X, as well as the aggregate effect and the nature of year-end or other adjustments which are material to the results of that quarter.

(4) If the financial statements to which this information relates have been reported on by an accountant, appropriate professional standards and procedures, as enumerated in the Statements of Auditing Standards issued by the Auditing Standards Board of the American Institute of Certified Public Accountants, shall be followed by the reporting accountant with regard to the data required by this paragraph (a).

(5) This paragraph (a) applies to any registrant, except a foreign private issuer, that meets both of the following tests:

(i) First test. The registrant:

(A) Has securities registered pursuant to section 12(b) of the Exchange Act (other than mutual life insurance companies); or

(B) Is an insurance company that is subject to the reporting requirements of section 15(d) of the Exchange Act and has securities which also meet the criteria set forth in paragraphs (C)(1) and (C)(2) immediately following; or

(C) Has securities registered pursuant to section 12(g) of the Exchange Act which also

(1) Are quoted on the National Association of Securities Dealers Automated Quotation System, and

(2) Meet the following criteria:

(i) Three or more dealers stand willing to, and do in fact, make a market in such stock, including making regularly published bona fide bids and offers for such stock for their own accounts; or the stock is registered on a securities exchange that is exempted by the Commission from registration as a national securities exchange pursuant to section 5 of the Exchange Act; for purposes of this paragraph, the insertion of quotations into the National Association of Securities Dealers Automated Quotation System by three or more dealers on at least 10 business days during the six month period immediately preceding the fiscal year for which the financial statements are required shall satisfy the requirement that three dealers be making a market;

(ii) There continue to be 800 or more holders of record, as defined in Rule 12g5-1, under the Exchange Act, of the stock who are not officers, directors, or beneficial owners of 10 percent or more of the stock;

(iii) The registrant continues to be a United States corporation;

(iv) There are 300,000 or more of such securities outstanding in addition to shares held beneficially by officers, directors, or beneficial owners of more than 10 percent of the stock; and

(v) In addition, the registrant shall meet two of the three following requirements:

(A) The shares described in paragraph (5)(i)(C)(2)(iv) of this Item continue to have a market value of at least $2.5 million;

SEC 63026

(B) The minimum representative bid price of such stock is at least $5 per share; or

(C) The registrant continues to have at least $2.5 million of capital, surplus, and undivided profits.

Instructions to Paragraph (a)(5)(i)(C)(2)(v). *1. The computation required by paragraphs (v)(A) and (v)(B) shall be based on the average of the closing representative bid prices as reported by the National Association of Securities Dealers Automated Quotation System in accordance with Rule 11 Ac1-2 under the Exchange Act for the 20 business days immediately preceding the fiscal year for which the financial statements are required.*

2. The computation required by paragraph (v)(C) shall be as at the last business day of the fiscal year immediately preceding the fiscal year for which the financial statements are required.

(ii) Second test. The registrant and its consolidated subsidiaries (A) have had a net income after taxes but before extraordinary items and the cumulative effect of a change in accounting of at least $ 250,000 for each of the last three fiscal years; or (B) had total assets of at least $ 200,000,000 for the last fiscal year-end.

(b) Information about oil and gas producing activities. *Registrants engaged in oil and gas producing activities shall present the information about oil and gas producing activities (as those activities are defined in Regulation S-X, Rule 4-10(a)) specified in paragraphs 9-34 of Statement of Financial Accounting Standards ("SFAS") No. 69, "Disclosures About Oil and Gas Producing Activities," if such oil and gas producing activities are regarded as significant under one or more of the tests set forth in paragraph 8 of SFAS No. 69.*

Instructions to Paragraph (b). *1. (a) SFAS No. 69 disclosures that relate to annual periods shall be presented for each annual period for which an income statement is required,*

(b) SFAS No. 69 disclosures required as of the end of an annual period shall be presented as of the date of each audited balance sheet required, and

(c) SFAS No. 69 disclosures required as of the beginning of an annual period shall be presented as of the beginning of each annual period for which an income statement is required.

2. This paragraph, together with Rule 4-10 of Regulation S-X, prescribes financial reporting standards for the preparation of accounts by persons engaged, in whole or in part, in the production of crude oil or natural gas in the

United States, pursuant to Section 503 of the Energy Policy and Conservation Act of 1975 ("EPCA") and Section 11(c) of the Energy Supply and Environmental Coordination Act of 1974 ("ESECA") as amended by Section 506 of EPCA. The application of this paragraph to those oil and gas producing operations of companies regulated for ratemaking purposes on an individual-company-cost-of-service basis may, however, give appropriate recognition to differences arising because of the effect of the ratemaking process.

3. Any person exempted by the Department of Energy from any record-keeping or reporting requirements pursuant to Section 11(c) of ESECA, as amended, is similarly exempted from the related provisions of this paragraph in the preparation of accounts pursuant to EPCA. This exemption does not affect the applicability of this paragraph to filings pursuant to the federal securities laws.

The disclosure requirements in paragraphs 9-34 of SFAS No. 69 are relatively straightforward and, generally, there is little diversity in practice in the nature and presentation of these disclosures. However, a common issue faced by companies that have both oil and gas producing activities and other lines of business is the allocation of tax attributes when presenting results of operations for oil and gas producing activities as required by paragraph 24. Paragraph 26 of SFAS No. 69 specifies that only tax expense, credits or allowances attributable to those activities should be considered. Thus, it would generally be inappropriate to use net operating losses or other tax attributes from nonoil and nongas lines of business to offset tax attributes associated with oil and gas activities, even if the consolidated entity has no tax expense.

The purpose of the SFAS No. 69 disclosures is to provide consistent information about oil and gas companies. However, both the information on oil and gas reserves required by paragraphs 10 and 11 and the Standardized Measure of Future Net Cash Flows Relating to Proved Oil and Gas Reserve Quantities required by paragraph 30 are by nature less precise than most financial statement information. Accordingly, companies would be well-advised to include in their SFAS No. 69 disclosures information about the subjectiveness and complex nature of reserve quantity estimates and to indicate that such estimates and the related cash flows could significantly change as the company develops more information about the reserves.

63030. MANAGEMENT'S DISCUSSION AND ANALYSIS OF FINANCIAL CONDITION AND RESULTS OF OPERATIONS (ITEM 303)

63031. General. Management's Discussion and Analysis of Financial Condition and Results of Operations (MD&A) is not covered by the accountants' report. However, the independent accountant is responsible for reading the MD&A and should request any necessary explanations of matters that are unclear or incomplete. Also, the accountant needs to consider whether any information contained therein is inconsistent with the information obtained during the course of an audit of the financial statements.

63032. Text of Requirements.

Management's Discussion and Analysis of Financial Condition and Results of Operations

(a) Full fiscal years. *Discuss registrant's financial condition, changes in financial condition and results of operations. The discussion shall provide information as specified in paragraphs (a)(1), (2) and (3) with respect to liquidity, capital resources, and results of operations, and also shall provide such other information that the registrant believes to be necessary to an understanding of its financial condition, changes in financial condition and results of operations. Discussions of liquidity and capital resources may be combined whenever the two topics are interrelated. Where in the registrant's judgement a discussion of segment information or of other subdivisions of the registrant's business would be appropriate to an understanding of such business, the discussion shall focus on each relevant, reportable segment or other subdivision of the business and on the registrant as a whole.*

    (1) Liquidity. *Identify any known trends or any known demands, commitments, events or uncertainties that will result in or that are reasonably likely to result in the registrant's liquidity increasing or decreasing in any material way. If a material deficiency is identified, indicate the course of action that the registrant has taken or proposes to take to remedy the deficiency. Also identify and separately describe internal and external sources of liquidity, and briefly discuss any material unused sources of liquid assets.*

(2) Capital resources.

(i) Describe the registrant's material commitments for capital expenditures as of the end of the latest fiscal period, and indicate the general purpose of such commitments and the anticipated source of funds needed to fulfill such commitments.

(ii) Describe any known material trends, favorable or unfavorable, in the registrant's capital resources. Indicate any expected material changes in the mix and the relative cost of such resources. This discussion shall consider changes between equity, debt and any off-balance sheet financing arrangements.

(3) Results of operations.

(i) Describe any unusual or infrequent events or transactions or any significant economic changes that materially affected the amount of reported income from continuing operations and, in each case, indicate the extent to which income was so affected. In addition, describe any other significant components of revenues or expenses that, in the registrant's judgment, should be described in order to understand the registrant's results of operations.

(ii) Describe any known trends or uncertainties that have had or that the registrant reasonably expects will have a material favorable or unfavorable impact on net sales or revenues or income from continuing operations. If the registrant knows of events that will cause a material change in the relationship between costs and revenues (such as known future increases in costs of labor or materials or price increases or inventory adjustments), the change in the relationship shall be disclosed.

(iii) To the extent that the financial statements disclose material increases in net sales or revenues, provide a narrative discussion of the extent to which such increases are attributable to increases in prices or to increases in the volume or amount of goods or services being sold or to the introduction of new products or services.

(iv) For the three most recent fiscal years of the registrant, or for those fiscal years beginning after December 25, 1979, or for those fiscal years in which the registrant has been engaged in business, whichever period is shortest, discuss the impact of inflation and changing prices on the registrant's net sales and revenues and on income from continuing operations.

Instructions to Paragraph 303(a). *1. The registrant's discussion and analysis shall be of the financial statements and of other statistical data that the registrant believes will*

SEC 63032

892

enhance a reader's understanding of its financial condition, changes in financial condition and results of operations. Generally, the discussion shall cover the three year period covered by the financial statements and shall use year-to-year comparisons or any other formats that in the registrant's judgment enhance a reader's understanding. However, where trend information is relevant, reference to the five year selected financial data appearing pursuant to Item 301 of Regulation S-K may be necessary.

2. The purpose of the discussion and analysis shall be to provide to investors and other users information relevant to an assessment of the financial condition and results of operations of the registrant as determined by evaluating the amounts and certainty of cash flows from operations and from outside sources. The information provided pursuant to this Item need only include that which is available to the registrant without undue effort or expense and which does not clearly appear in the registrant's financial statements.

3. The discussion and analysis shall focus specifically on material events and uncertainties known to management that would cause reported financial information not to be necessarily indicative of future operating results or of future financial condition. This would include description and amounts of (A) matters that would have an impact on future operations and have not had an impact in the past, and (B) matters that have had an impact on reported operations and are not expected to have an impact upon future operations.

4. Where the consolidated financial statements reveal material changes from year to year in one or more line items, the causes for the changes shall be described to the extent necessary to an understanding of the registrant's businesses as a whole; provided, however, that if the causes for a change in one line item also relate to other line items, no repetition is required and a line-by-line analysis of the financial statements as a whole is not required or generally appropriate. Registrants need not recite the amounts of changes from year to year which are readily computable from the financial statements. The discussion shall not merely repeat numerical data contained in the consolidated financial statements.

5. The term "liquidity" as used in this Item refers to the ability of an enterprise to generate adequate amounts of cash to meet the enterprise's needs for cash. Except where it is otherwise clear from the discussion, the registrant shall indicate those balance sheet conditions or income or cash flow items which the registrant believes may be indicators of its liquidity condition. Liquidity generally shall be discussed on both a long-term and short-term basis. The issue of liquidity shall be discussed in the context of the registrant's own business or businesses. For example, a discussion of

SEC 63032

working capital may be appropriate for certain manufacturing, industrial or related operations but might be inappropriate for a bank or public utility.

6. Where financial statements presented or incorporated by reference in the registration statement are required by Rule 4-08(e)(3) of Regulation S-X to include disclosure of restrictions on the ability of both consolidated and unconsolidated subsidiaries to transfer funds to the registrant in the form of cash dividends, loans or advances, the discussion of liquidity shall include a discussion of the nature and extent of such restrictions and the impact such restrictions have had and are expected to have on the ability of the parent company to meet its cash obligations.

7. Registrants are encouraged, but not required, to supply forward-looking information. This is to be distinguished from presently known data which will impact upon future operating results, such as known future increases in costs of labor or materials. This latter data may be required to be disclosed. Any forward-looking information supplied is expressly covered by the safe harbor rule for projections. See Rule 175 under the Securities Act, Rule 3b-6 under the Exchange Act and Securities Act Release No. 6084 (June 25, 1979).

8. Registrants are only required to discuss the effects of inflation and other changes in prices when considered material. This discussion may be made in whatever manner appears appropriate under the circumstances. All that is required is a brief textual presentation of management's views. No specific numerical financial data need be presented except as Rule 3-20(c) of Regulation S-X otherwise requires. However, registrants may elect to voluntarily disclose supplemental information on the effects of changing prices as provided for in Statement of Financial Accounting Standards No. 89, "Financial Reporting and Changing Prices" or through other supplemental disclosures. The Commission encourages experimentation with these disclosures in order to provide the most meaningful presentation of the impact of price changes on the registrant's financial statements.

9. Registrants that elect to disclose supplementary information on the effects of changing prices as specified in SFAS No. 89, "Financial Reporting and Changing Prices", may combine such explanations with the discussion and analysis required pursuant to this Item or may supply such information separately with appropriate cross-reference.

10. All references to the registrant in the discussion and in this Item shall mean the registrant and its subsidiaries consolidated.

11. Foreign private registrants also shall discuss briefly any pertinent governmental economic, fiscal, monetary, or political policies or factors that have materially

SEC 63032

*affected or could materially affect, directly or indirectly, their operations or invest-
ments by United States nationals.*

*12. If the registrant is a foreign private issuer, the discussion shall focus on the primary
financial statements presented in the registration statement or report. There shall be
a reference to the reconciliation to United States generally accepted accounting
principles, and a discussion of any aspects of the difference between foreign and
United States generally accepted accounting principles, not discussed in the reconciliation, that the registrant believes is necessary for an understanding of the financial
statements as a whole.*

(b) Interim periods. *If interim period financial statements are included or are
required to be included by Article 3 of Regulation S-X, a management's discussion and
analysis of the financial condition and results of operations shall be provided so as to
enable the reader to assess material changes in financial condition and results of
operations between the periods specified in paragraphs (b)(1) and (2) of this Item.
The discussion and analysis shall include a discussion of material changes in those
items specifically listed in paragraph (a) of this Item, except that the impact of inflation
and changing prices on operations for interim periods need not be addressed.*

> **(1) Material changes in financial condition.** *Discuss any material
> changes in financial condition from the end of the preceding fiscal year
> to the date of the most recent interim balance sheet provided. If the interim
> financial statements include an interim balance sheet as of the corre-
> sponding interim date of the preceding fiscal year, any material changes
> in the financial condition from that date to the date of the most recent
> interim balance sheet provided also shall be discussed. If discussions of
> changes from both the end and the corresponding interim date of the
> preceding fiscal year are required, the discussions may be combined at
> the discretion of the registrant.*

> **(2) Material changes in results of operations.** *Discuss any material
> changes in the registrant's results of operations with respect to the most
> recent fiscal year-to-date period for which an income statement is pro-
> vided and the corresponding year-to-date period of the preceding fiscal
> year. If the registrant is required to or has elected to provide an income
> statement for the most recent fiscal quarter, such discussion also shall
> cover material changes with respect to that fiscal quarter and the corre-
> sponding fiscal quarter in the preceding fiscal year. In addition, if the
> registrant has elected to provide an income statement for the twelve-
> month period ended as of the date of the most recent interim balance sheet
> provided, the discussion also shall cover material changes with respect
> to that twelve-month period and the twelve-month period ended as of the*

corresponding interim balance sheet date of the preceding fiscal year. Notwithstanding the above, if for purposes of a registration statement a registrant subject to paragraph (b) of Rule 3-03 of Regulation S-X provides a statement of income for the twelve-month period ended as of the date of the most recent interim balance sheet provided in lieu of the interim income statements otherwise required, the discussion of material changes in that twelve-month period will be in respect to the preceding fiscal year rather than the corresponding preceding period.

Instructions to Paragraph (b) of Item 303. *1. If interim financial statements are presented together with financial statements for full fiscal years, the discussion of the interim financial information shall be prepared pursuant to this paragraph (b) and the discussion of the full fiscal year's information shall be prepared pursuant to paragraph (a) of this Item. Such discussions may be combined.*

2. In preparing the discussion and analysis required by this paragraph (b), the registrant may presume that users of the interim financial information have read or have access to the discussion and analysis required by paragraph (a) for the preceding fiscal year.

3. The discussion and analysis required by this paragraph (b) is required to focus only on material changes. Where the interim financial statements reveal material changes from period to period in one or more significant line items, the causes for the changes shall be described if they have not already been disclosed; provided, however, that if the causes for a change in one line item also relate to other line items, no repetition is required. Registrants need not recite the amounts of changes from period to period which are readily computable from the financial statements. The discussion shall not merely repeat numerical data contained in the financial statements. The information provided shall include that which is available to the registrant without undue effort or expense and which does not clearly appear in the registrant's condensed interim financial statements.

4. The registrant's discussion of material changes in results of operations shall identify any significant elements of the registrant's income or loss from continuing operations which do not arise from or are not necessarily representative of the registrant's ongoing business.

5. The registrant shall discuss any seasonal aspects of its business which have had a material effect upon its financial condition or results of operation.

6. Registrants are encouraged but are not required to discuss forward-looking information. Any forward-looking information supplied is expressly covered by the safe harbor rule for projections. See Rule 175 under the Securities Act, Rule 3b-6 under the Exchange Act and Securities Act Release No. 6084.

SEC 63032

63033. Discussion of Requirements. The MD&A is required to cover the three latest fiscal years. There is no requirement to discuss the earliest of the three years in comparison to the year preceding it unless such information is necessary for an understanding of the trend of the registrant's financial position or results of operations. At the end of 19X4, for example, a comparison of the financial results for 19X2 with those of 19X1 would ordinarily not be required unless it is necessary for an understanding of the trend of the registrant's financial position or results of operations.

The MD&A is required to encompass significant changes in each of the financial statements, and should not be confined to a discussion of operating results. If trend information is considered necessary for a reader's understanding of the financial statements, the MD&A should refer to the Selected Financial Data (as discussed in section 63010).

Some of the important aspects to be considered are:

- Discussion of segment information is required if in the registrant's judgment it is appropriate to an understanding of the registrant's business.

- The discussion should deal with any known matters that materially affect, or are expected to affect, the registrant's financial condition and results of *continuing operations*, with particular reference to liquidity, capital resources, and revenues and income from continuing operations. This might include, for example, a labor contract containing a provision for significant wage increases. Note that positive as well as negative aspects of the company's financial condition and results of operations should be addressed.

- A line-by-line analysis of the financial statements is neither required nor generally appropriate. Changes that are self-evident or that may be readily calculated from the financial statements need not and generally should not be recited, nor should numerical data contained in the statements be repeated unless it serves to emphasize a point made in the discussion.

- Discussion of the impact of inflation and changing prices on the registrant's sales and income from continuing operations is required. Registrants may limit their discussion to a brief textual presentation of management's views of the effects of inflation on the registrant's sales and income from continuing operations. No specific numerical financial data need be presented.

- If a registrant elects to disclose supplemental information regarding the effects of changing prices as encouraged by SFAS No. 89, instruction 9 to paragraph No. 303(a) permits the inclusion of such information in the MD&A.

- Foreign registrants are permitted to discuss the effects of inflation as appropriate in their own country. In addition, foreign registrants are expected to provide:

  •• A brief discussion of any governmental economic, fiscal, monetary, or political policies or factors that have materially affected or could materially affect, directly or indirectly, their operations or investments by U.S. nationals.

  •• A reference to the reconciliation to U.S. GAAP and a discussion of any aspects of the difference between home country and U.S. GAAP not discussed in the reconciliation that the registrant believes are necessary for an understanding of the financial statements as a whole.

Regulation S-X Rule 5-04 specifies that the information as to short-term borrowings required to be furnished in Schedule IX may be presented in MD&A if it results in a more meaningful presentation of the information. Note, however, that the relocation of this data in MD&A does not change the fact that the information must be covered by the accountants' report.

The SEC staff has expressed the following views concerning the MD&A:

- Prospective information, i.e., risk factors, or other uncertainties that the registrant reasonably expects to have a material impact (favorable or unfavorable) on its operating results and/or financial position should be discussed.

- Changes in revenues should not be evaluated solely in terms of volume and price changes, but should also include an analysis of the reasons and factors contributing to the increase or decrease.

- Significant loss provisions should be discussed in the context of an event that occurred or new information that became available such that it was inappropriate to record the loss in a prior period.

- When unusual, infrequent, or restructuring charges are recorded, such charges should be addressed in MD&A, with the post-writedown amounts being the principal focus of the discussion.

- Material changes in individual line items should include the reasons for the change, not just the amount or percentage change.

- Anticipated changes in estimates (e.g., a change in the amortization period for goodwill) should be disclosed.

- Known or potentially significant financial exposure resulting from environmental issues, particularly when the registrant has been designated as a "potentially responsible party" by the EPA. In some cases, the SEC has requested additional information when the registrant has stated that any potential superfund liability or clean-up costs are not likely to be material.

- Material commitments for capital expenditures, including research and development, should be discussed.

- Trends and changes from prior years on segments should be included. Expanded discussion of segments in Item 1 of Form 10-K is also requested in some instances.

- For each period in which a statement of cash flows is presented, a balanced discussion of cash flows from operating, investing and financing activities generally is required to be provided. For example, the staff commonly issues a comment when increases in revenues and receivables are significantly greater than increases in cash collections.

- Foreign currency exchange effects and volatility in foreign markets with an emphasis on how such matters may affect the company's operations should be disclosed. The staff has pointed out that even companies with no foreign operations and no export sales can still be affected by foreign markets if they compete in businesses that may be affected in an overall way by foreign price changes.

- MD&As should cover how significant changes in the economic environment, such as interest rates, would affect the company, including such matters as the ability to finance its costs of capital.

- The disclosure of a particular risk factor or other development, without an explanation of its consequence, is not sufficient.

- "Disaggregated" information should be presented to the extent needed to fully understand a registrant's business.

Reference should also be made to the following sections of this manual for additional staff views regarding specific MD&A disclosures:

SEC 63033

Section	Item
50408 Rule 4-08(h)	Income Taxes
50502-12 and 50703	Debt Securities
50502-25	Environmental Liabilities

Financial Reporting Release No. 36

For a number of years the SEC has been concerned about the overall adequacy of MD&A disclosures. While acknowledging that some registrants have been preparing comprehensive and insightful discussions, the SEC's overall view is that public companies need to significantly improve the quality of MD&A disclosures. The reluctance of many companies to provide meaningful prospective or "forward-looking" information continues to be a major concern. In 1988, the SEC staff initiated a project to evaluate registrant compliance with MD&A requirements. In 1989, FRR 36 (FRP Section 501) was issued to announce the results of the initial phase of the MD&A project, to set forth the SEC's view regarding several disclosure matters relating to the MD&A, and to provide examples of what the SEC considers to be appropriate MD&A disclosures. The release is significant in that it provides registrants with fairly specific guidance concerning areas that the SEC staff is likely to emphasize in its reviews of MD&As, and provides the SEC staff with a clear frame of reference to use in challenging registrants concerning inadequate disclosures. It is important to note that the staff continues to closely review and monitor the adequacy of MD&A disclosures on an ongoing and regular basis. Based on these reviews, the SEC staff frequently requires registrants to amend currently (rather than prospectively) filings on Form 10-K as well as 1933 Act registration statements containing MD&As that do not include the types of prospective and other information called for in FRR 36.

In March of 1992, the SEC emphasized its focus on the adequacy of MD&A disclosure by instituting enforcement proceedings against Caterpillar Inc., which allegedly failed to comply with MD&A disclosure requirements. The situation involved Caterpillar's Brazilian subsidiary, which contributed 25 percent of Caterpillar's net profits in 1989, and only five percent of its revenues. While the subsidiary's operating profit was in line with prior years, a number of nonoperating items (e.g., currency translation gains, export subsidies, and Brazilian tax loss carryforwards) contributed to greater than usual overall profit.

The enforcement release pointed out that in January 1990, Caterpillar's management recognized that the future performance of the Brazilian subsidiary was difficult to predict, particularly due to anticipated sweeping economic reforms to be instituted by the new government in Brazil, and there was significant uncertainty as to whether the subsidiary would be able to repeat its 1989 earnings in 1990. According to the SEC, nothing in the MD&A section of the 1989 Form 10-K or the 1990 first quarter Form 10-Q suggested the disproportionate impact of the subsidiary's profits on the company's overall profitability, or that a decline in the subsidiary's future results could have a material adverse effect on Caterpillar's 1990 net income.

The SEC charged that Caterpillar's failure to report such information in the MD&A resulted in providing investors with an "incomplete picture" of Caterpillar's financial condition and results of operations, and "denied them the opportunity to see the company through the eyes of management."

FRR 36 provides specific guidance relative to MD&A disclosures in eight areas, a discussion of which follows. Due to the importance of the guidance contained in this release, it is included in its entirety in section 63035.

Prospective Information

Since the MD&A rules were first adopted, the extent to which prospective or "forward-looking" information must be provided has been a matter of uncertainty. As a result, there has been a significant diversity in practice concerning these types of disclosures. In FRR 36, the SEC attempted to clarify the requirements in this area and provided guidance as to when and how prospective information needs to be disclosed.

Item 303 of Regulation S-K requires disclosure in the MD&A of currently known trends, demands, commitments, events or uncertainties that are reasonably expected to have material effects on the registrant's financial condition or results of operations, or that would cause reported financial information not to be necessarily indicative of future operating results or financial condition.

FRR 36 amplifies this requirement by pointing out that when a trend, demand, commitment, event or uncertainty is known, management must make two assessments:

(1) Whether the trend, demand, commitment, event or uncertainty is likely to happen. If not, no disclosure is required.

(2) If management cannot make that determination, it must evaluate the consequences on the assumption that the event will happen. Disclosure is then required unless management determines that a material effect upon the registrant's financial condition or results of operations is not reasonably likely to occur.

The release goes on to point out that **optional** forward-looking MD&A disclosure involves anticipating a future trend or event or anticipating a less predictable impact of a known event, trend or uncertainty.

Examples provided in the release of known trends, demands, commitments, events or uncertainties requiring at least qualitative MD&A disclosure include: a reduction in the registrant's product prices, erosion in market share, changes in insurance coverage, likely nonrenewal of a material contract, discontinuation of a growth trend, and implementation of recently adopted legislation.

Subsequent to the issuance of FRR 36, the staff has indicated that when a material change in a registrant's financial condition or results of operations occurs in a particular reporting period and the likelihood of such change was not addressed in the prior MD&A, it will inquire as to the existing circumstances at the time of the earlier filing(s) to determine whether the registrant failed to discuss a known trend, demand, commitment, event or uncertainty. A review of the *prior* year's MD&A as part of the process of reviewing the current year's financial statements, and a comparison of the disclosures in the MD&A to the information provided in the president's letter included in the annual report to shareholders have apparently become fairly standard SEC review procedures.

It is important to note that prospective MD&A disclosures would often not involve quantitative information.

Liquidity—Capital Resources

When viewed to encompass capital resources, FRR 36 points out that the SEC's concept of liquidity is comparable to the concept of financial flexibility or the ability of an enterprise to adjust its future cash flows to meet needs and opportunities, both expected and unexpected. Accordingly, the release indicates that discussion is required of both short- and long-term liquidity and capital resources. FRR 36 indicates that in addition to other appropriate indicators, the SEC expects registrants to use the statement of cash flows as a point of reference in analyzing liquidity. The SEC staff has indicated that the MD&A discussion of liquidity should generally address each major category included in the statement of cash flows (i.e., operating, investing, and financing).

Material Changes in Financial Statement Line Items

Instruction 4 to Item 303(a) of Regulation S-K requires a discussion of the causes of material changes from year to year in financial statement line items, including a discussion and quantification of the contribution of two or more factors to such material changes.

FRR 36 points out that discussion of the impact of discontinued operations and of extraordinary gains and losses is also required when these items have had or are reasonably likely to have a material effect on reported or future financial condition or results of operations. The release goes on to state that other nonrecurring items should also be discussed and stresses that the discussion need not recite amounts of changes readily computable from the financial statements and should not merely repeat numerical data contained in such statements.

Interim Period Reporting

Item 303(b) of Regulation S-K indicates that MD&A disclosure requirements for interim financial statements are the same as those covering the annual statements, except that the impact on operations of inflation and changing prices for interim periods need not be addressed. FRR 36 points out that the interim MD&A should address, among other factors, internal and external sources of liquidity, expected material changes in the mix and relative cost of such resources, and unusual or infrequent events or transactions that materially affected income from continuing operations.

The release goes on to state that a discussion of the impact of known trends, demands, commitments, events or uncertainties arising during the interim period that are reasonably likely to have material effects on financial condition or results of operations is also required in the interim MD&A.

Segment Analysis

FRR 36 indicates that a multi-segment registrant preparing a full fiscal year MD&A would be expected to analyze revenues, profitability, and the cash needs of its significant industry segments. To the extent that any segment contributes in a materially disproportionate way in any of these areas, or where discussion on a consolidated basis would present an incomplete and misleading picture of the enterprise, the release specifies that segment discussion should be included. It notes that this situation may occur when circumstances within a segment are reasonably likely to have a material effect on the business as a whole, or when a segmented analysis is appropriate to an understanding of the business.

Participation in High-Yield Financings, Highly Leveraged Transactions or Non-investment Grade Loans and Investments

The SEC recognizes that many registrants participate in high-yield financings or highly leveraged transactions or make non-investment grade loans or investments relating to corporate restructurings, such as leveraged buyouts, recapitalizations including significant stock buybacks and cash dividends, and acquisitions or mergers. FRR 36 discusses the SEC's concerns that participation in transactions of this nature may involve significant risks relating to creditworthiness, solvency, relative liquidity of the secondary trading market, potential market losses, and vulnerability to rising interest rates and economic downturns.

The release indicates that disclosure of the nature and extent of a registrant's involvement with high-yield or highly leveraged transactions and non-investment grade loans and investments is appropriate in the MD&A if such participation has had or is reasonably likely to have a material effect on the registrant's financial condition or results of operations.

Similar concerns are raised in the release with regard to investment companies that invest all or a portion of their portfolios in high-yield or non-investment grade securities. FRR 36 indicates that an investment company that invests in other than high-grade bonds (or is permitted to do so, even if it does not currently include such securities in its portfolio) should disclose in its MD&A the risks associated with such investments.

Effects of Federal Financial Assistance Upon Operations

FRR 36 points out that if federal financial assistance programs have materially affected, or are reasonably likely to have a material future effect on financial condition or results of operations, the MD&A should provide disclosure of the nature, amounts, and effects of such assistance. (Also see the EITF consensus on Issue No. 88-19 for guidance on financial statement disclosure related to FSLIC-assisted acquisitions or thrifts.)

Preliminary Merger Negotiations

As a general rule, the SEC has not required the disclosure of preliminary merger negotiations in the MD&A. It has historically balanced the informational need of investors against the risk that premature disclosure of a proposed business combination may jeopardize completion of the transaction.

FRR 36 points out, however, that where disclosure relating to such matters is otherwise required or has otherwise been made by or on behalf of the registrant, the interests in avoiding premature disclosure no longer exist. In such cases, the release indicates that the negotiations would be subject to the same disclosure standards as any other known trend, demand, commitment, event or uncertainty. FRR 36 goes on to say that these guidelines would also apply to preliminary negotiations for the acquisition or disposition of assets not in the ordinary course of business.

Financial Reporting Release No. 6

In 1982 the SEC issued FRR No. 6 (FRP Section 501.09), *Interpretative Release About Disclosure Considerations Relating to Foreign Operations and Foreign Currency Translation Effects*. The release points out that information as to the nature of a registrant's foreign operations gained as a result of implementing FASB Statement No. 52, *Foreign Currency Translation*, could be used to develop improved disclosures relating to foreign operations and foreign currency translation effects. While encouraging voluntary experimentation with Statement No. 52 information, the release does not specify the location or nature of the disclosures to be made. Among the disclosures suggested in FRR No. 6 are a display of net investments by major functional currency, narrative information and functional currencies used to measure significant foreign operations, the degree of exposure to exchange rate risks, and the nature of the translation component of equity. MD&A is mentioned in the release as a section that may be used for these disclosures.

Staff Accounting Bulletin No. 74

In 1987 the SEC issued SAB Topic 11-M, added by SAB No. 74, expressing the staff's views concerning disclosures that should be provided in the footnotes to the financial statements and/or MD&A regarding the impact a recently issued accounting standard will have on the financial statements when the accounting standard is adopted in a future period. The text of the SAB follows:

Disclosure of the Impact that Recently Issued Accounting Standards will have on the Financial Statements of the Registrant when Adopted in a Future Period

Facts: An accounting standard has been issued[1] that does not require adoption until some future date. A registrant is required to include financial statements in filings with the Commission after the issuance of the standard but before it is adopted by the registrant.

Question 1: Does the staff believe that these filings should include disclosure of the impact that the recently issued accounting standard will have on the financial position and results of operations of the registrant when such standard is adopted in a future period?

Interpretive Response: Yes. The Commission addressed a similar issue with respect to SFAS No. 52 and concluded that "The Commission also believes that registrants that have not yet adopted SFAS No. 52 should discuss the potential effects of adoption in registration statements and reports filed with the Commission."[2] The staff believes that this disclosure guidance applies to all accounting standards which have been issued but not yet adopted by the registrant unless the impact on its financial position and results of operations is not expected to be material.[3] Management's Discussion and Analysis ("MD&A")[4] requires registrants to provide information with respect to liquidity, capital resources and results of operations and such other information that the registrant believes to be necessary to understand its financial condition and results of operations. In addition, MD&A requires disclosure of presently known material changes, trends and uncertainties that have had or that the registrant reasonably expects will have a material impact on future sales, revenues or income from continuing operations. The staff believes that disclosure of impending accounting changes is necessary to inform the reader about expected impacts on financial information to be reported in the future and, therefore, should be disclosed in accordance with the existing MD&A requirements. With respect to financial statement disclosure, generally accepted auditing standards[5] specifically address the need for the auditor to consider the adequacy of the disclosure of impending changes in accounting principles if (a) the financial statements have been prepared on the basis of accounting principles that were acceptable at the financial statement date but that will not be acceptable in the future and (b) the financial statements will be restated in the future as a result of the change. The staff believes that recently issued accounting standards may constitute material matters and, therefore, disclosure in the financial statements should also be considered in situations where the change to the new accounting standard will be accounted for in financial statements of future periods, prospectively or with a cumulative catch-up adjustment.

Question 2: Does the staff have a view on the types of disclosure that would be meaningful and appropriate when a new accounting standard has been issued but not yet adopted by the registrant?

Interpretive Response: The staff believes that the registrant should evaluate each new accounting standard to determine the appropriate disclosure and recognizes that the level of information available to the registrant will differ with respect to various standards and from one registrant to another. The objectives of the disclosure should be to (1) notify the reader of the disclosure documents that a standard has been issued which the registrant will be required to adopt in the future and (2) assist the reader in assessing the significance of the impact that the standard will have on the financial statements of the registrant when adopted. The staff understands that the registrant will only be able to disclose information that is known.

The following disclosures should generally be considered by the registrant:

- A brief description of the new standard, the date that adoption is required and the date that the registrant plans to adopt, if earlier.

- A discussion of the methods of adoption allowed by the standard and the method expected to be utilized by the registrant, if determined.

- A discussion of the impact that adoption of the standard is expected to have on the financial statements of the registrant, unless not known or reasonably estimable. In that case, a statement to that effect may be made.

- Disclosure of the potential impact of other significant matters that the registrant believes might result from the adoption of the standard (such as technical violations of debt covenant agreements, planned or intended changes in business practices, etc.) is encouraged.

---

[1]Some registrants may want to disclose the potential effects of proposed accounting standards not yet issued, e.g., exposure drafts. Such disclosures, which are generally not required because the final standard may differ from the exposure draft, are not addressed by this SAB.

[2]Financial Reporting Release No. 6, "Interpretive Release About Disclosure

Considerations Relating to Foreign Operations and Foreign Currency Translation Effects," Section No. 2 "Disclosures During the Transition Period".

[3] In those instances where a recently issued standard will impact the preparation of, but not materially affect, the financial statements, the registrant is encouraged to disclose that a standard has been issued and that its adoption will not have a material effect on its financial position or results of operations.

[4] Item 303 of Regulation S-K.

[5] As interpreted in Auditing Standards Division staff interpretation AU 9410 No. 3, "The Impact on an Auditor's Report of an FASB Statement Prior to the Statement's Effective Date," paragraphs .13-.19.

With respect to SAB No. 74 disclosures, the SEC staff's informal position is that in addition to Statements of Financial Accounting Standards, the provisions of the SAB should be applied to FASB Technical Bulletins and AICPA Statements of Position.

63034. Interim periods. Management's Discussion and Analysis of interim financial statements is intended to complement and update the MD&A covering the preceding fiscal year. Whether the discussion of the annual accounts is included in the same or a previous filing, it is presumed that readers have read or have access to that discussion. Thus, the interim MD&A need only address material changes in financial condition and results of operations that occurred during the periods covered by the interim statements. In addition to the type of information that must be considered in connection with a discussion of an annual period, the interim discussion is required to address material seasonal aspects of the registrant's business. However, the interim MD&A may exclude the discussion of the impact of inflation and changing prices required in connection with annual accounts.

63035. Financial Reporting Release No. 36

The text of FRR No. 36 follows:

Management's Discussion and Analysis of Financial Condition and Results of Operations

I. Background

The current framework of MD&A was adopted in 1980, although the origins of the MD&A requirements date to 1968. MD&A requires a discussion of liquidity, capital resources, results of operations, and other information necessary to an understanding of a registrant's financial condition, changes in financial condition and results of operations. While the MD&A requirements adopted in 1980 are far more comprehensive than earlier formulations, they are intentionally general, reflecting the Commission's view that a flexible approach elicits more meaningful disclosure and avoids boilerplate discussions, which a more specific approach could

SEC 63033

foster. One year after adoption of the current framework, the Commission published a release that included examples of MD&A disclosure to assist registrants.

In 1986, Coopers & Lybrand submitted to the Commission's Office of the Chief Accountant a proposal recommending increased MD&A disclosure of business risks and the performance by the independent auditor of specified review procedures with respect to these disclosures. Shortly thereafter, the managing partners of seven accounting firms issued a white paper entitled "The Future Relevance, Reliability, and Credibility of Financial Information; Recommendations to the AICPA Board of Directors," which also called for increased risk disclosure, but contemplated that such disclosure would be separate from MD&A and would be subjected to audit coverage.

The Commission thereafter issued the Concept Release requesting comments concerning the adequacy of the MD&A requirements and the costs and benefits of the revisions suggested by the proposals. Virtually all the 196 commentators opposed the proposals initiated by members of the accounting profession, and most took the position that there was no need to change the MD&A requirements. A number of commentators, however, suggested that stricter enforcement and review, or additional guidance through an interpretive release, would improve compliance. Accordingly, the Division decided to undertake a special review of MD&A disclosures to assess the adequacy of disclosure practices and to identify any common areas of deficiencies, with a view to providing further guidance on compliance with the requirements of Item 303 of Regulation S-K and determining the need for revisions of the Item. Based on the results of the MD&A review, the Commission concurs with the view expressed by most commentators that no amendments to the MD&A requirements set forth in Regulation S-K are needed at this time.

II. Summary of the Project

The staff commenced work on the MD&A Project in early 1988. A total of 218 companies in 12 industries were selected for review in the first phase of this continuing project.[9] Specific industries were chosen so that the staff, through increased familiarity and additional research, could enhance its expertise regarding the industries. Each registrant was selected for an "issuer review" that focused on the registrant rather than any one report filed under the Securities Exchange Act of 1934 ("Exchange Act").[10] Particular emphasis was placed on disclosures made in response to the MD&A requirements.

Of the 218 registrants reviewed, 206 received letters of comment, many of which related to more than one report. Three different categories of comments were issued: (a) Requests for amendment; (b) requests for supplemental information; and (c) requests for compliance in future filings ("futures" comments).[11] Amendments were filed by 72 registrants in response to staff comments.

Work on a second phase of the MD&A Project commenced in October 1988. A total of 141 companies in a second set of 12 industries[12] were selected for review, resulting in 139 comment letters being issued in December, 1988. To date, amendments by 53 registrants have been filed in response to staff comments.

The amendments received in the first two phases principally addressed MD&A, the business description required under Item 101 of Regulation S-K, and the financial statements. More than one-half of the amendments substantively expanded MD&A, most often addressing one or more disclosure issues as to which guidance is provided in this release.

908

The Division has referred six registrants reviewed during the MD&A Project to the Division of Enforcement due primarily to substantive accounting problems which, in several instances, also affected the adequacy of the registrants' MD&As. The accounting problems encountered include, among other things, possible inadequate maintenance of accounting records and systems of internal controls and possible improper accounting regarding material acquisitions.

The staff has already begun a third phase of the MD&A Project relating to 12 new industries,[13] using the Forms 10-K recently filed for the fiscal year ended November 30, 1988 or later.

III. Evaluation of Disclosure—Interpretive Guidance

A. Introduction

The MD&A requirements are intended to provide, in one section of a filing,[14] material historical and prospective textual disclosure enabling investors and other users to assess the financial condition and results of operations of the registrant, with particular emphasis on the registrant's prospects for the future. As the Concept Release states:

> The Commission has long recognized the need for a narrative explanation of the financial statements, because a numerical presentation and brief accompanying footnotes alone may be insufficient for an investor to judge the quality of earnings and the likelihood that past performance is indicative of future performance. MD&A is intended to give the investor an opportunity to look at the company through the eyes of management by providing both a short and long-term analysis of the business of the company. The Item asks management to discuss the dynamics of the business and to analyze the financials.

As the Commission has stated, "[i]t is the responsibility of management to identify and address those key variables and other qualitative and quantitative factors which are peculiar to and necessary for an understanding and evaluation of the individual company."

The Commission has determined that interpretive guidance is needed regarding the following matters: prospective information required in MD&A; long and short-term liquidity and capital resources analysis; material changes in financial statement line items; required interim period disclosure; MD&A analysis on a segment basis; participation in high yield financings, highly leveraged transactions or non-investment grade loans and investments; the effects of federal financial assistance upon the operations of financial institutions; and preliminary merger negotiations.

B. Prospective Information

Several specific provisions in Item 303 require disclosure of forward-looking information. MD&A requires discussions of "known trends or any known demands, commitments, events or uncertainties that will result in or that are reasonably likely to result in the registrant's liquidity increasing or decreasing in any material way." Further, descriptions of known material trends in the registrant's capital resources and expected changes in the mix and cost of such resources are required. Disclosure of known trends or uncertainties that the registrant reasonably expects will have a material impact on net sales, revenues, or income from continuing operations is also required. Finally, the Instructions to Item 303 state that MD&A "shall focus specifically on material events and uncertainties known to management that would cause reported financial information not to be necessarily indicative of future operating results or of future financial condition."[20]

The Project results confirm that the distinction between prospective information that is required to be discussed and voluntary forward-looking disclosure is an area requiring additional attention. This critical distinction is explained in the Concept Release:

> Both required disclosure regarding the future impact of presently known trends, events or uncertainties and optional forward-looking information may involve some prediction or projection. The distinction between the two rests with the nature of the prediction required. Required disclosure is based on currently known trends, events, and uncertainties that are reasonably expected to have material effects, such as: A reduction in the registrant's product prices; erosion in the registrant's market share; changes in insurance coverage; or the likely non-renewal of a material contract. In contrast, optional forward-looking disclosure involves anticipating a future trend or event or anticipating a less predictable impact of a known event, trend or uncertainty.

The rules establishing a safe harbor for disclosure of "forward-looking statements" define such statements to include statements of "future economic performance contained in" MD&A. These safe harbors apply to required statements concerning the future effect of known trends, demands, commitments, events or uncertainties, as well as to optional forward-looking statements.

A disclosure duty exists where a trend, demand, commitment, event or uncertainty is both presently known to management and reasonably likely to have material effects on the registrant's financial condition or results of operation.[23] Registrants preparing their MD&A disclosure should determine and carefully review what trends, demands, commitments, events or uncertainties are known to management. In the following example,[24] the registrant discloses the reasonably likely material effects on operating results of a known trend in the form of an expected further decline in unit sales of mature products.

> While market conditions in general remained relatively unchanged in 1987, unit volumes declined 10% as the Company's older products, representing 40% of overall revenues, continue to approach the end of their life cycle. Unit volumes of the older products are expected to continue to decrease at an accelerated pace in the future and materially adversely affect revenues and operating profits.

In preparing the MD&A disclosure, registrants should focus on each of the specific categories of known data. For example, Item 303(a)(2)(i) requires a description of the registrant's material "commitments" for capital expenditures as of the end of the latest fiscal period. However, even where no legal commitments, contractual or otherwise, have been made, disclosure is required if material planned capital expenditures result from a known demand, as where the expenditures are necessary to a continuation of the registrant's current growth trend. Similarly, if the same registrant determines not to incur such expenditures, a known uncertainty would exist regarding continuation of the current growth trend. If the adverse effect on the registrant from discontinuation of the growth trend is reasonably likely to be material, disclosure is required. Disclosure of planned material expenditures is also required, for example, when such expenditures are necessary to support a new, publicly announced product or line of business.[25]

In the following example, the registrant discusses planned capital expenditures, and related financing sources, necessary to maintain sales growth.

> The Company plans to open 20 to 25 new stores in fiscal 1988. As a result, the Company expects the trend of higher sales in fiscal 1988 to continue at approximately the same rate as in recent years. Management estimates that approximately $50 to $60 million will be required to finance the Company's cost of opening such stores. In addition, the Company's expansion program will require increases in inventory of about $1 million per store, which are anticipated to be financed principally by trade credit. Funds required to finance the Company's store expansion program are expected to come primarily from new credit facilities with the remainder provided by funds generated from operations and increased lease financings. The Company recently entered into a new borrowing agreement with its primary bank, which provides for additional borrowings of up to $50 million for future expansion. The Company intends to seek additional credit facilities during fiscal 1988.

Often a matter which had a material impact on past operating results also involves prospective effects which should be discussed.[26] In identifying the reason for a material change in income from continuing operations and quantifying its effects, the registrant in the following example also describes the reasonably likely effect of a known event: completion of an important contract.

> The Company produced operating income of $22 million during 1987 as compared to $15 million during 1986, a 47 percent increase. Substantially all of the 47 percent increase can be attributed to the Company's completion of a major contract at a cost less than anticipated. It is expected that operating income during the current year will be significantly less, as only a portion of the profit generated by the completed contract is expected to be replaced by new contracts as a result of a slowdown within the Company's principal industry.

Events that have already occurred or are anticipated often give rise to known uncertainties. For example, a registrant may know that a material government contract is about to expire. The registrant may be uncertain as to whether the contract will be renewed, but nevertheless would be able to assess facts relating to whether it will be renewed. More particularly, the registrant may know that a competitor has found a way to provide the same service or product at a price less than that charged by the registrant, or may have been advised by the government that the contract may not be renewed. The registrant also would have factual information relevant to the financial impact of non-renewal upon the registrant. In situations such as these, a registrant would have identified a known uncertainty reasonably likely to have material future effects on its financial condition or results of operations, and disclosure would be required.

In the following example, the registrant discloses the reasonably likely material effect of a known uncertainty regarding implementation of recently adopted legislation.

SEC 63035

The Company had no firm cash commitments as of December 31, 1987 for capital expenditures. However, in 1987, legislation was enacted which may require that certain vehicles used in the Company's business be equipped with specified safety equipment by the end of 1991. Pursuant to this legislation, regulations have been proposed which, if promulgated, would require the expenditure by the Company of approximately $30 million over a three-year period.

Where a trend, demand, commitment, event or uncertainty is known, management must make two assessments:

(1) Is the known trend, demand, commitment, event or uncertainty likely to come to fruition? If management determines that it is not reasonably likely to occur, no disclosure is required.

(2) If management cannot make that determination, it must evaluate objectively the consequences of the known trend, demand, commitment, event or uncertainty, on the assumption that it will come to fruition. Disclosure is then required unless management determines that a material effect on the registrant's financial condition or results of operations is not reasonably likely to occur.[27]

Each final determination resulting from the assessments made by management must be objectively reasonable, viewed as of the time the determination is made.[28]

Application of these principles may be illustrated using a common disclosure issue which was considered in the review of a number of Project registrants: designation as a potentially responsible party ("PRP") by the Environmental Protection Agency (the "EPA") under The Comprehensive Environmental Response, Compensation, and Liability Act of 1980 ("Superfund").

Facts: A registrant has been correctly designated a PRP by the EPA with respect to cleanup of hazardous waste at three sites. No statutory defenses are available. The registrant is in the process of preliminary investigations of the sites to determine the nature of its potential liability and the amount of remedial costs necessary to clean up the sites. Other PRPs also have been designated, but the ability to obtain contribution is unclear, as is the extent of insurance coverage, if any. Management is unable to determine that a material effect on future financial condition or results of operations is not reasonably likely to occur.

Based upon the facts of this hypothetical base, MD&A disclosure of the effects of the PRP status, quantified to the extent reasonably practicable, would be required.[30] For MD&A purposes, aggregate potential cleanup costs must be considered in light of the joint and several liability to which a PRP is subject. Facts regarding whether insurance coverage may be contested, and whether and to what extent potential sources of contribution or indemnification constitute reliable sources of recovery may be factored into the determination of whether a material future effect is not reasonably likely to occur.

C. Liquidity — Capital Resources

Instruction 2 to Item 303(a) calls for an evaluation of "amounts and certainty of cash flows." "Except where it is otherwise clear from the discussion," Item 303(a)(1) and instructions

2 and 5 to Item 303(a) together also mandate indication of which balance sheet conditions or income or cash flow items should be considered in assessing liquidity, and a discussion of prospective information regarding the registrant's short and long-term sources of, and needs for, capital. Disclosure of material commitments for capital expenditures as of the end of the latest fiscal period is required by Item 303(a)(2). Trend analysis and a description of "any expected material changes in the mix and relative cost" of the registrant's capital resources must also be provided.[31]

Generally, short-term liquidity and short-term capital resources cover cash needs up to 12 months into the future. These cash needs and the sources of funds to meet such needs relate to the day-to-day operating expenses of the registrant and material commitments coming due during that 12-month period.

The discussion of long-term liquidity and long-term capital resources must address material capital expenditures, significant balloon payments or other payments due on long-term obligations, and other demands or commitments, including any off-balance sheet items, to be incurred beyond the next 12 months, as well as the proposed sources of funding required to satisfy such obligations.[32]

Where a material deficiency in short or long-term liquidity has been identified, the registrant should disclose the deficiency, as well as disclosing either its proposed remedy, that it has not decided on a remedy, or that it is currently unable to address the deficiency.[33] In the following example, a financially troubled registrant discusses the material effects of its cash flow problems on its business, and its efforts to remedy those problems.

> The Company has violated certain requirements of its debt agreements relating to failure to maintain certain minimum ratios and levels of working capital and stockholders' equity. The Company's lenders have not declared the Company in default and have allowed the Company to remain in violation of these agreements. Were a default to be declared, the Company would not be able to continue to operate. A capital infusion of $4,000,000 is necessary to cure these defaults. The Company has engaged an investment banker and is considering various alternatives, including the sale of certain assets or the sale of common shares, to raise these funds.
>
> The Company frequently has not been able to make timely payments to its trade and other creditors. As of year-end and as of February 29, 1988, the Company had past due payables in the amount of $525,000 and $705,000, respectively. Deferred payment terms have been negotiated with most of these vendors. However, certain vendors have suspended parts deliveries to the Company. As a result, the Company was not always able to make all shipments on time, although no orders have been canceled to date. Were significant volumes of orders to be canceled, the Company's ability to continue to operate would be jeopardized. The Company is currently seeking sources of working capital financing sufficient to fund delinquent balances and meet ongoing trade obligations.

Short and long-term liquidity and capital resources analysis should become more comparable from registrant to registrant as a result of the Financial Accounting Standards Board's recent issuance of SFAS 95,[34] which requires the statement of changes in financial position to be replaced by a statement of cash flows as part of a full set of financial statements.

SEC 63035

This new statement reports net cash provided or used by each of operating, investing and financing activities, as defined, and the net effect of those flows on cash and cash equivalents.

Registrants are expected to use the statement of cash flows, and other appropriate indicators, in analyzing their liquidity, and to present a balanced discussion dealing with cash flows from investing and financing activities as well as from operations. This discussion should address those matters that have materially affected the most recent period presented but are not expected to have short or long-term implications, and those matters that have not materially affected the most recent period presented but are expected materially to affect future periods. Examples of such matters include: (a) Discretionary operating expenses such as expenses relating to advertising, research and development or maintenance of equipment; (b) debt refinancings or redemptions; or (c) levels of financing provided by suppliers or to customers. Liquidity analysis premised upon the new statement of cash flows and prepared in accordance with this guidance should enhance the utility to investors of MD&A disclosure by improving comparability from registrant to registrant and providing information more directly relevant to liquidity than that previously premised upon the statement of changes in financial position.

D. Material Changes

Some Project registrants did not provide adequate disclosure of the reasons for material year-to-year changes in line items, or discussion and quantification of the contribution of two or more factors to such material changes. Instruction 4 to Item 303(a) requires a discussion of the causes of material changes from year-to-year in financial statement line items "to the extent necessary to an understanding of the registrant's businesses as a whole." An analysis of changes in line items is required where material and where the changes diverge from changes in related line items of the financial statements, where identification and quantification of the extent of contribution of each of two or more factors is necessary to an understanding of a material change, or where there are material increases or decreases in net sales or revenue.[36]

Discussion of the impact of discontinued operations and of extraordinary gains and losses is also required where these items have had or are reasonably likely to have a material effect on reported or future financial condition or results of operations. Other non-recurring items should be discussed as "unusual or infrequent" events or transactions "that materially affected the amount of reported income from continuing operations."[37]

As Instruction 4 to Item 303(a) states, repetition and line-by-line analysis is not required or generally appropriate when the causes for a change in one line item also relates to other line items. The same Instruction also states that the discussion need not recite amounts of changes readily computable from the financial statements and "shall not merely repeat numerical data contained in" such statements. However, quantification should otherwise be as precise, including use of dollar amounts or percentages, as reasonably practicable.

In the following example, the registrant analyzes the reasons for a material change in revenues and in so doing describes the effects of offsetting developments.

Revenue from sales of single-family homes for 1987 increased 6% from 1986. The increase resulted from a 14% increase in the average sales price per home, partially offset by a 6% decrease in the number of homes delivered. Revenues from sales of single-family homes for 1986 increased 2% from 1985. The average sales price per home in 1986 increased 6%, which was offset by a 4% decrease in the number of homes delivered.

The increase in the average sales prices in 1987 and 1986 is primarily the result of the Company's increased emphasis on higher priced single-family homes. The decrease in homes delivered in 1987 and 1986 was attributable to a decline in sales in Texas. The significant decline in oil prices and its resulting effect on energy-related business has further impacted the already depressed Texas area housing market and is expected to do so for the foreseeable future. The Company curtailed housing operations during 1987 in certain areas in Texas in response to this change in the housing market. Although the number of homes sold is expected to continue to decline during the current year as a result of this action, this decline is expected to be offset by increases in average sales prices.

E. Interim Period Reporting

The second sentence of Item 303(b) states that MD&A relating to interim period financial statements "shall include a discussion of material changes in those items specifically listed in paragraph (a) of this Item, except that the impact of inflation and changing prices on operations for interim periods need not be addressed." As this sentence indicates, material changes to each and every specific disclosure requirement contained in paragraph (a), with the noted exception, should be discussed. This would include, for example, internal and external sources of liquidity, expected material changes in the mix and relative cost of such resources, and unusual or infrequent events or transactions that materially affected the amount of reported income from continuing operations.[39]

In light of the obligation to update MD&A disclosure periodically, the impact of known trends, demands, commitments, events or uncertainties arising during the interim period which are reasonably likely to have material effects on financial condition or results of operations constitutes required disclosure in MD&A.[40] For example, a calendar year end registrant describes, in its June 30 Form 10-Q, a recent event which is reasonably likely to have a material future effect on its financial condition or results of operations.

The Company was advised in late June that Company A, its principal customer, which accounted for 28% and 30% of revenues for the last six months and prior fiscal year, respectively, intends to terminate all purchases effective during the third quarter, due to in-house capabilities recently developed by this customer. The Company is materially dependent on its business with this customer and anticipates upon such termination a material adverse effect on revenues and income. Efforts are being made to replace revenues attributable to such customer by developing new customers. The Company expects it will take at least 6 months to generate such replacement revenues.

F. Other Observations

1. Segment Analysis

In many cases, MD&As of Project registrants with more than one segment were prepared on a segment as well as a consolidated basis. In formulating a judgment as to whether a discussion of segment information is necessary to an understanding of the business, a multi-segment registrant preparing a full fiscal year MD&A should analyze revenues, profitability, and the cash needs of its significant industry segments. To the extent any segment contributes in a materially disproportionate way to those items, or where discussion on a consolidated basis would present an incomplete and misleading picture of the enterprise, segment discussion should be included. This may occur, for example, when there are legal or other restrictions upon the free flow of funds from one segment, subsidiary or division of the registrant to others; when known trends, demands, commitments, events or uncertainties within a segment are reasonably likely to have a material effect on the business as a whole; when the ability to dispose of identified assets of a segment may be relevant to the financial flexibility of the registrant; and in other circumstances in which the registrant concludes that segment analysis is appropriate to an understanding of its business.[41]

The following example illustrates segment disclosure for a manufacturer with two segments. The two segments contributed to operating income amounts that were disproportionate to their respective revenues. The registrant discusses sales and operating income trends, factors explaining such trends, and where applicable, known events that will impact future results of operations of the segment.

Net Sales by Industry Segment

Industry Segments	1987		1986		1985	
	($ million)	Percent of total	($ million)	Percent of total	($ million)	Percent of total
Segment I	585	55	479	53	420	48
Segment II	472	45	433	47	457	52
Total sales	1057	100	912	100	877	100

1987 vs. 1986

Segment I sales increased 22% in 1987 over the 1986 period. The increase included the effect of the acquisition of Corporation T. Excluding this acquisition, sales would have increased by 16% over 1986. Product Line A sales increased by 18% due to a 24% increase in selling prices, partially offset by lower shipments. Product Line B sales increased by 35% due to a 17% increase in selling prices and a 15% increase in shipment volume.

Segment II sales increased 9% due to a 12% increase in selling prices partly offset by a 3% reduction in shipment volumes.

1986 vs. 1985

Segment I sales increased 14% in 1986. Product Line A sales increased 22%, in spite of a slight reduction in shipments, because of a 23% increase in selling prices.

Product Line B sales declined 5% due mainly to a 7% decrease in selling prices, partially offset by higher shipments.

SEC 63035

The 5% decline in Segment II sales reflected a 3% reduction in selling prices and a 2% decline in shipments.

The substantial increases in selling prices of Product Line A during 1987 and 1986 occurred primarily because of heightened worldwide demand which exceeded the industry's production capacity. The Company expects these conditions to continue for the next several years. The Company anticipates that shipment volumes of Product Line A will increase as its new production facility reaches commercial production levels in 1988.

Segment II shipment volumes have declined during the past two years primarily because of the discontinuation of certain products which were marginally profitable and did not have significant growth potential.

Operating Profit by Industry Segment

Industry Segments	1987		1986		1985	
	($ million)	Percent of total	($ million)	Percent of total	($ million)	Percent of total
Segment I	126	75	108	68	67	55
Segment II	42	25	51	32	54	45
Operating Profit	168	100	159	100	121	100

1987 vs. 1986

Segment I operating profit was $18 million (17%) higher in 1987 than in 1986. This increase includes the effects of higher sales prices and slightly improved margins on Product Line A, higher shipments of Product Line B and the acquisition of Corporation T. Excluding this acquisition operating profit would have been 11% higher than in 1986. Partially offsetting these increases are costs and expenses of $11 million related to new plant start-up, slightly reduced margins on Product Line B sales and a $9 million increase in research and development expenses.

Segment II operating profit declined $9 million (18%) due mainly to substantially higher costs in 1987 resulting from a 23% increase in average raw material costs which could not be fully recovered through sales price increases. The Company expects that Segment II margins will continue to decline, although at a lesser rate than in 1987 as competitive factors limit the Company's ability to recover cost increases.

1986 vs. 1985

Segment I operating profit was $41 million (61%) higher in 1986 than in 1985. After excluding the effect of the $23 million non-recurring charge for the early retirement program in 1985, Segment I operating profit in 1986 was $18 million (27%) higher than in 1985. This increase reflected higher prices and a corresponding 21% increase in margins on Product Line A, and a 17% increase in margins on Product Line B due primarily to cost reductions resulting from the early retirement program.

Segment II operating profit declined about $3 million (6%) due mainly to lower selling prices and slightly reduced margins in 1986.

2. Participation in High Yield Financings, Highly Leveraged Transactions or Non-Investment Grade Loans and Investments

A registrant, whether a financial institution (such as a bank, thrift, insurance company or finance company), broker-dealer or one of its affiliates, or any other public company, may participate in several ways, directly or indirectly, in high yield financings, or highly leveraged transactions or make non-investment grade loans or investments relating to corporate restructurings such as leveraged buyouts, recapitalizations including significant stock buybacks and cash dividends, and acquisitions or mergers.[42] A registrant may participate in the financing of such a transaction either as originator, syndicator, lender, purchaser, or secured senior debt, or as an investor in other debt instruments (often unsecured or subordinated), redeemable preferred stock or other equity securities. Participation in high yield or highly leveraged transactions, as well as investment in non-investment grade securities, generally involves greater returns, in the form of higher fees and higher average yields or potential market gains. Participation in such transactions may involve greater risks, often related to creditworthiness, solvency, relative liquidity of the secondary trading market, potential market losses, and vulnerability to rising interest rates and economic downturns.[43]

Similar risk-reward exposure appears to exist with the growing practice by certain registrants of originating low down-payment mortgages without obtaining mortgage insurance. Other registrants have substantial participation in venture capital financings.

In view of these potentially greater returns and potentially greater risks, disclosure of the nature and extent of a registrant's involvement with high yield or highly leveraged transactions and non-investment grade loans and investments may be required under one or more of several MD&A items, and registrants should consider carefully the extent of disclosure required.[44] MD&A analysis is required if such participation has had or is reasonably likely to have a material effect on financial condition or results of operations.

In determining the adequacy of disclosure concerning participation in high yield, highly leveraged and non-investment grade loans and investments, registrants should consider the need to disclose:

1. Relevant lending and investing policies, including credit and risk management policies;

2. The amounts of holdings, stated separately by type if individually material, including guarantees and repurchase or other commitments to lend or acquire such loans and investments, and the potential risks inherent in such holdings;

3. Information regarding the level of activity during the period, e.g., originations and retentions;

4. Amounts of holdings, if any, giving rise to significantly greater risks (that may have material effects on financial condition or results of operations) than are present in other similar transactions and instruments; for example, where the issuer is bankrupt or has issued securities on which interest payments are in default, or where there are significant concentrations (e.g., in an individual borrower, industry

SEC 63035

or geographic area), particularly where those concentrations are in securities with relatively low trading market liquidity (such as those that depend upon a single market maker for their liquidity); and

5. Analysis of the actual and reasonably likely material effects of the above matters on income and operations, e.g., the amounts of fees recognized and deferred, yields, amounts of realized and unrealized market gains or losses, and credit losses.

Such disclosure may appear in the business discussion, or other appropriate location, but the effects resulting from participation should be analyzed in MD&A.

Similar concerns are raised with regard to investment companies that invest, or are permitted to invest, all or a portion of their portfolios in high-yield or non-investment grade securities. An investment company that seeks high income by investing in other than high-grade bonds (or is permitted to do so, even if it does not currently include such securities in its portfolio) should disclose in its prospectus the risks involved in such investments. These risks include, but are not limited to, the risks described above, such as market price volatility based upon interest rate sensitivity, creditworthiness and relative liquidity of the secondary trading market, as well as the effects such risks may have on the net asset value of the fund. In addition, the board of directors of a fund that invests in such securities should carefully consider factors affecting the secondary market for such securities in determining whether or not any particular security is liquid or illiquid, and whether market quotations are "readily available" for purposes of valuing portfolio securities.

The nature of disclosure required by non-investment companies will vary depending on the type of participation. In the following example the registrant is a bank holding company that participates in highly leveraged transactions as a lender and not as an investor.

> The Company is active in originating and syndicating loans in highly leveraged corporate transactions. The Company generally includes in this category domestic and international loans and commitments made by the Banks in recapitalizations, acquisitions, and leveraged buyouts which result in the borrower's debt to total assets ratio exceeding 75%. As of December 31, 1988, the Company had loans outstanding in approximately 61 highly leveraged transactions in an aggregate principal amount of approximately $900 million, was committed under definitive loan agreements relating to approximately 23 highly leveraged transactions to lend an additional amount of approximately $650 million, and had other highly leveraged transactions at various stages of discussion or preliminary commitment. The Company's equity investments in highly leveraged transactions are not material.
>
> In recent years the Company has not made a loan in excess of $175 million in any individual highly leveraged transaction, and the Company has typically retained, after syndication and sales of loan participations, a principal amount not exceeding approximately $35 million in any such transaction. At December 31, 1988, only two loans had outstanding balances exceeding $35 million, $51 million and $47 million, respectively) and no industry represented more than 15% of the Company's total highly leveraged loan portfolio. Should an economic downturn or sustained period of rising interest rates occur, highly leveraged transaction borrowers may experience financial stress. As a result, risks associated with these transactions may be higher than for more traditional financing.

SEC 63035

The Company estimates that its fees for lending and corporate finance activities relating to highly leveraged transactions were approximately $64 million during 1988, of which approximately $48 million was recognized as income and $16 million was deferred, compared with $40 million during 1987 of which approximately $32 million was recognized as income and $8 million was deferred. The deferred portion of such fees will be recognized over the terms of the related loans in accordance with Statement of Financial Accounting Standards Number 91.

In recent years, the Company has had no significant charge-offs of loans made in highly leveraged transactions. At December 31, 1988, approximately $25 million (3%) of such outstanding loans were on nonaccrual status, which was not materially greater than that for the Company's other lending activities.

A reduction in the Company's activities relating to highly leveraged transactions could have some negative impact on the Company's results of operations. The size of such impact would depend on the magnitude of the reduction and on the profitability of the activities to which the Company might redirect its resources. Although any estimate of the impact of a total discontinuation of all new highly leveraged transactions depends on various factors that cannot now be determined, the Company believes that such a discontinuation would reduce its gross revenues approximately 6% and net income by approximately 12%.

In the following example, the registrant is an investor in non-investment grade debt securities.

At December 31, 1988, the Company held in its portfolio, net of reserves, $81 million of high yield, unrated or less than investment grade corporate debt securities with an aggregate market value of $75 million. Investments in unrated or less than investment grade corporate debt securities have different risks than other investments in corporate debt securities rated investment grade and held by the Company. Risk of loss upon default by the borrower is significantly greater with respect to such corporate debt securities than with other corporate debt securities because these securities are generally unsecured and are often subordinated to other creditors of the issuer, and because these issuers usually have high levels of indebtedness and are more sensitive to adverse economic conditions, such as recession or increasing interest rates, than are investment grade issuers. In addition, investments by the Company in corporate debt securities of any given issuer are generally larger than its investments in most other securities, thus resulting in a greater impact in the event of default. There is only a thinly traded market for such securities and recent market quotations are not available for some of these securities. Market quotes are generally available only from a limited number of dealers and may not represent firm bids of such dealers or prices for actual sales. As of December 31, 1988, the Company's five largest investments in corporate debt securities aggregated $35 million, none of which individually exceeded $10 million, and had an approximate market value of $31 million.

3. Effects of Federal Financial Assistance Upon Operations

Many financial institutions, such as thrifts and banks, are receiving financial assistance in connection with federally assisted acquisitions or restructurings. Such assistance may take

SEC 63035

various forms and is intended to make the surviving financial institution a viable entity. Examples of such methods of assistance include: (a) Yield maintenance assistance (which guarantees additional interest on specified interest bearing assets, a level of return on specified non-interest-bearing assets, reimbursement if covered assets are ultimately collected or sold for amounts that are less than a specified amount, or any combination thereof); (b) indemnification against certain loss contingencies; (c) the purchase of equity securities issued by the institution for cash or a note receivable from the federal agency; and (d) arrangements designed to insulate the surviving entity from the economic effects of problem assets acquired from the predecessor financial institution (such as a "put agreement" whereby the surviving institution may "put" troubled loans directly or indirectly to the federal agency at higher than their fair value).

If these or any other types of federal financial assistance have materially affected, or are reasonably likely to have a material future effect upon, financial condition or results of operations, the MD&A should provide disclosure of the nature, amounts, and effects of such assistance.[47]

In the following example, a financial institution discloses the material effects of a federally assisted corporate reorganization. Such disclosure was in addition to various disclosures of the existence and effect of such federal assistance in the description of business portions of the filing (pursuant to Industry Guide 3) and in the registrant's financial statements.

> During 1988, earnings for the Company included $60 million of assistance income, including (a) $10 million in indemnity from the Federal Agency in respect of litigation costs associated with the Company's predecessor and (b) $50 million related to the 1988 puts of troubled loans to the Federal Agency under the Company's Put Agreement. The assistance income arises from provisions in the Reorganization agreements that are intended to relieve the Company from the adverse economic effects of litigation and problem assets held by its predecessor. These provisions are intended to place the Company in substantially the same position as if such litigation and problem assets had been assumed by the Federal Agency at the time of the Reorganization. Based on existing economic circumstances, management believes that the expiration of the Put Agreement in June 1989 may adversely affect future operations including an increased level of non-performing loans and loan loss provisions which cannot be recovered pursuant to the Put Agreement.

4. Preliminary Merger Negotiations

While Item 303 could be read to impose a duty to disclose otherwise nondisclosed preliminary merger negotiations, as known events or uncertainties reasonably likely to have material effects on future financial condition or results of operations, the Commission did not intend to apply, and has not applied, Item 303 in this manner. As reflected in the various disclosure requirements under the Securities Act and Exchange Act that specifically address merger transactions, the Commission historically has balanced the informational need of investors against the risk that premature disclosure[49] of negotiations may jeopardize completion of the transaction.[50] In general, the Commission's recognition that registrants have an interest in preserving the confidentiality of such negotiations is clearest in the context of a registrant's continuous reporting obligations under the Exchange Act, where disclosure on Form 8-K of acquisitions or dispositions of assets not in the ordinary course of business is triggered by completion of the transaction.[51]

SEC 63035

In contrast, where a registrant registers securities for sale under the Securities Act, the Commission requires disclosure of material probable acquisitions and dispositions of businesses, including the financial statements of the business to be acquired or sold.[52] Where the proceeds from the sale of the securities being registered are to be used to finance an acquisition of a business, the registration statement must disclose the intended use of proceeds. Again, accommodating the need for confidentiality of negotiations, registrants are specifically permitted not to disclose in registration statements the identity of the parties and the nature of the business sought if the acquisition is not yet probable and the board of directors determines that the acquisition would be jeopardized.

The Commission's interpretation of Item 303, as applied to preliminary merger negotiations, incorporates the same policy determinations. Accordingly, where disclosure is not otherwise required, and has not otherwise been made, the MD&A need not contain a discussion of the impact of such negotiations where, in the registrant's view, inclusion of such information would jeopardize completion of the transaction. Where disclosure is otherwise required or has otherwise been made by or on behalf of the registrant, the interests in avoiding premature disclosure no longer exist. In such case, the negotiations would be subject to the same disclosure standards under Item 303 as any other known trend, demand, commitment, event or uncertainty. These policy determinations also would extend to preliminary negotiations for the acquisition or disposition of assets not in the ordinary course of business.

IV. Conclusion

In preparing MD&A disclosure, registrants should be guided by the general purpose of the MD&A requirements: to give investors an opportunity to look at the registrant through the eyes of management by providing a historical and prospective analysis of the registrant's financial condition and results of operations, with particular emphasis on the registrant's prospects for the future. The MD&A requirements are intentionally flexible and general. Because no two registrants are identical, good MD&A disclosure for one registrant is not necessarily good MD&A disclosure for another. The same is true for MD&A disclosure of the same registrant in different years. The flexibility of MD&A creates a framework for providing the marketplace with appropriate information concerning the registrant's financial condition, changes in financial condition and results of operations.

---

[9]The industries were: Miscellaneous Chemical Products; Retail-Grocery Stores; Airlines; Drugs; Real Estate Developers; Nursing Care Facilities/Hospitals; Radio and Television Broadcasting/Cable Television; Textile Mill Products/Knitting Mills; Computer Hardware; Building Contractors and Construction; Toys and Recreational Equipment; and Multi-segment Companies.

[10]The most recent Form 10-K and subsequent reports filed under the Exchange Act were given full reviews and the prior 10-K and intervening reports, as well as proxy and registration statements filed during the period, were examined for background information.

[11]Registrants received combinations of the above categories of comment. Many of the comment letters requested supplemental support for various presentations, and, in several instances, requests for amendments were revised to futures comments during the review process. Conversely, several amendments were requested after staff consideration of supplemental responses provided by registrants. Compliance with futures comments is verified by staff review of subsequent filings.

[12]The industries were: Banks; Savings and Loans; Meat Products; Dairy Products; Miscellaneous Plastic Products; Furniture; Radio and Television Communication Equipment and Apparatus; Research and Measurement Instruments; Industrial Machinery; Computer Software; Eating Places; and Motion Picture-Television Production.

[13]The industries are: Retail-Department Stores; Retail-Apparel Stores; Semiconductor and Related Devices; Crude Petroleum and Natural Gas; Railroads; Steel Works; Paper and Allied Products; Natural Gas Transmission; Lumber and Wood Products; Property-Casualty Insurance; Aircraft-Aircraft Engines; and Newspapers-Publishing and Printing.

[14]The MD&A should contain a discussion of all the material impacts upon the registrant's financial condition or results of operations, including those arising from disclosure provided elsewhere in the filing.

[20]S-K Item 303(a), Instruction 3. The data known to management which may trigger required forward-looking disclosure is hereinafter referred to as "known trends, demands, commitments, events or uncertainties."

[23]Cf. In re American Savings and Loan Association of Florida, Exchange Act Release No. 25788. In this administrative proceeding jointly conducted by the Commission and the Federal Home Loan Bank Board (the "FHLBB"), it was determined that the MD&As in a Form 10-K and two Forms 10-Q were inadequate under the FHLBB's disclosure requirements, which are substantially similar to the Commission's, for failing to disclose, among other matters, required forward-looking information regarding the potential exposure and risks associated with repurchase transactions between American Savings and Loan and E.S.M. Government Securities. Cf. also In re Burroughs Corporation, Exchange Act Release No. 21872 (failure to discuss the impact of inventory obsolescence); In re Marsh & McClennan Companies, Inc., Exchange Act Release No. 24023 (failure adequately to disclose, in a Form 10-K, the effects of a principal subsidiary's investing and financing activities).

[24]The examples used herein, while modeled in large part upon Project registrants' original or revised MD&As, have been changed so that the registrants are not identified and particular points are emphasized. Of course, each example has been removed from its context as part of a larger document. The examples are provided for purposes of illustration only.

[25]See Item 101(c)(1)(ii) of Regulation S-K.

[26]See, e.g., In re Charter Company, Exchange Act Release No. 21647 in which the MD&A in the registrant's Form 10-K failed to disclose the favorable effect on earnings of the accounting method used, and the anticipated substantial reduction in future profits that would result from use of such method. Cf. SEC v. Baldwin-United Corporation, Litigation Release No. 10878 and In re Robert S. Harrison, Exchange Act Release No. 22466 (both involving a different means of accounting for the same insurance product as in Charter, and Baldwin-United Corporation's failure to disclose, in the MD&A of its Form 10-K, its failure to meet the earnings assumptions of the accounting model used, and internal estimates of insufficient taxable income to use tax benefits inherent in the earnings assumptions).

[27]MD&A mandates disclosure of specified forward-looking information, and specifies its own standard for disclosure—i.e., reasonably likely to have a material effect. This specific standard governs the circumstances in which Item 303 requires disclosure. The probability/magnitude test for materiality approved by the Supreme Court in Basic, Inc., v. Levinson, 108 S.Ct. 978 (1988), is inapposite to Item 303 disclosure.

[28]Where a material change in a registrant's financial condition (such as a material increase or decrease in cash flows) or results of operations appears in a reporting period and the likelihood

of such change was not discussed in prior reports, the Commission staff as part of its review of the current filing will inquire as to the circumstances existing at the time of the earlier filings to determine whether the registrant failed to discuss a known trend, demand, commitment, event or uncertainty as required by Item 303.

[30]Designation as a PRP does not in and of itself trigger disclosure under Item 103 or Regulation S-K and Instruction 5 thereto, regarding "Legal Proceedings," because PRP status alone does not provide knowledge that a governmental agency is contemplating a proceeding. Nonetheless, a registrant's particular circumstances, when coupled with PRP status, may provide that knowledge. While there are many ways a PRP can become subject to potential monetary sanctions, including triggering the stipulated penalty clause in a remedial agreement, the costs anticipated to be incurred under Superfund, pursuant to a remedial agreement entered into in the normal course of negotiation with the EPA, generally are not "sanctions" within either Instruction 5 (B) or (C) to Item 103. Such remedial costs normally would constitute charges to income, or in some cases capital expenditures. The availability of insurance, indemnification or contribution may be relevant under Instruction 5 (A) or (B) in determining whether the criteria for disclosure have been met. Thomas A. Cole, Esq., (January 17, 1989).

[31]Most registrants combine discussions of capital resources and liquidity as permitted by Item 303(a). When viewed to encompass capital resources, the Commission's concept of liquidity is comparable to the Financial Accounting Standards Board's ("FASB") concept of financial flexibility or the ability of an enterprise to adjust its future cash flows to meet needs and opportunities, both expected and unexpected. Financial flexibility is broader than the FASB's concept of liquidity (defined as short-term nearness of assets and liabilities to cash) because it includes potential internal and external sources of cash not directly associated with items shown on the balance sheet. Securities Act Release No. 6349, supra n. 5, at 972; see also Statement of Financial Accounting Concepts No. 5, Recognition and Measurement in Financial Statements of Business Enterprises, para. 24a.

[32]See, e.g., In re Hiex Development USA, Inc., Exchange Act Release No. 26722 (involving in part the registrant's failure to discuss in the MD&A of a Form 10, a material contractual commitment to purchase equipment from an affiliate over a ten year period).

[33]See, e.g., SEC v. The Charter Company, Exchange Act Release No. 23350 and In re Ray M. Van Landingham and Wallace A. Patzke, Jr., Exchange Act Release No. 23349 both involving Charter Company's liquidity disclosure concerning losses of trade credit, demands by its banks for a series of materially restrictive loan covenants and discussions with Charter's banks regarding asset sales, dividend restrictions and operational changes. In a filing which includes an independent accountant's report that is modified as a result of uncertainty about a registrant's continued existence, Section 607.02 of the Codification of Financial Reporting Policies requires "appropriate and prominent disclosure of the registrant's financial difficulties and viable plans to overcome such difficulties."

[34]Statement of Financial Accounting Standards No. 95, Statement of Cash Flows. While the new statement is required for annual financial statements for fiscal years ending after July 15, 1988, financial statements for prior years are not required to be restated, and interim financial statements in the initial year of application are not required to use the new statement. Such interim period statements must be restated when presented as comparative prior periods with future interim financial statements.

[36]See SEC v. The E.F. Hutton Group, Inc., Exchange Act Release No. 22579 involving Hutton's failure to disclose that its bank overdrafting practices were the cause for material changes in

924

interest income from year-to-year, and the risks and uncertainties associated with such practices. Although Item 303(a)(3)(iii) speaks only to material increases, not decreases, in net sales or revenues, the Commission interprets Item 303(a)(3)(i) and Instruction 4 as seeking similar disclosure for material decreases in net sales or revenues.

[37]S-K Item 303(a)(3)(i); see SEC v. Allegheny International, Inc., Litigation Release No. 11533 (failure to disclose a sale of realty that constituted an unusual and infrequent event which had a material impact on pre-tax income); see generally Accounting Principles Board Opinion No. 30.

[39]See, e.g., In re American Express Company, Exchange Act Release No. 23332 (failure to discuss the impact, in several Forms 10-Q and a Form 10-K, of two reinsurance transactions by an insurance subsidiary which were treated by the registrant as materially increasing net income, but which lacked economic substance); In re Michael R. Maury, Exchange Act Release No. 23067 (the MD&A in a Form 10-Q was found deficient for its failure to disclose the effects on net income of the reversal of previously established reserves).

[40]See SEC v. Ronson Corporation, Litigation Release No. 10093 where the MD&As in a Form 10-K and two Forms 10-Q were found to be inadequate in their failure to state that Ronson's largest customer had shut down its operations which required purchases from Ronson, that it was unlikely that this customer would resume purchases in the short term and that, due to technological changes being made at this customer's facilities, once purchases were resumed, an indefinite reduction in necessary purchases of 30-50% was likely.

[41]Registrants affected by Statement of Financial Accounting Standards No. 94, Consolidation of All Majority-Owned Subsidiaries, which requires, among other things, consolidation of non-homogeneous subsidiaries, should recognize that segment analysis generally will be appropriate, inasmuch as the prior justification for not consolidating these operations was that they had different characteristics from those of the parent and its other affiliates. See id. at para. 55 (recognizing that although the aggregation, of assets, liabilities and operations from non-homogeneous activities may obscure important information about these activities, the disclosures required by Statement of Financial Accounting Standards No. 14, Financial Reporting for Segments of a Business Enterprise, can provide meaningful information about the different operations within a business enterprise).

[42]On February 16, 1989 the Federal Reserve Board issued bank examination guidelines regarding highly leveraged transactions. Letter from William Taylor, Director, Division of Banking Supervision and Regulation, to the Officer in Charge of Supervision at each Federal Reserve Bank (February 16, 1989). The guidelines are intended to assist bank examiners in identifying exposures that may warrant closer scrutiny and are not intended to imply criticism of any particular transaction, nor to suggest what is deemed to be an appropriate degree of leverage in any particular industry. In these guidelines, criteria to define a highly leveraged financing include identification of borrowers whose debt to total assets ratio exceeds 75%. Registrants may refer to this guidance or to other recognized criteria that may be developed in defining highly leveraged transactions. In any event, registrants should indicate how highly leveraged transactions are defined for disclosure purposes. In this regard, the Commission recognizes that leverage characteristics may vary from industry to industry, and that debt ratios that are appropriate for some industries may be unusually high or low in other industries. Similarly, the Commission does not intend to imply criticism of any particular transaction or to suggest an appropriate degree of leverage in any particular industry or for any particular firm.

[43]See, e.g., P. Asquith, D. Mullins, Jr., and E. Wolff, Original Issue High Yield Bonds: Aging Analyses of Defaults, Exchanges, and Calls.

SEC 63035

[44]Other related disclosure includes Schedule 1 of Rule 12-02 of Regulation S-X, which requires separate disclosure for each particular issue of corporate securities carried on the balance sheet at greater than 2% of total assets, and allows reasonable groupings, e.g., by similar investment risk, of all other securities. Also, for securities with significantly greater investment risk factors than are typical for that class of issuer, such as securities where interest is in default or the issuer is in bankruptcy, separate listing or grouping is required to be accompanied by a brief description of the relevant risk factors. Guide 3, Item III(c)(4) requires bank holding companies to disclose concentrations of loans exceeding 10% of total loans, and defines "concentration" to exist where a number of borrowers are engaged in similar activities that would cause them to be similarly impacted by economic or other conditions. Item II of Guide 3 instructs that consideration should be given to disclosure of the risk characteristics of securities held as investments. Savings and loan holding companies should provide similar disclosures pursuant to Staff Accounting Bulletin Topic 11:K. Insurance companies are also subject to similar requirements under Article 7 of Regulation S-X, Rule 7-03(a)(1), Notes 5-6.

[47]For a related discussion of the accounting treatment and financial statement disclosure of federal assistance associated with regulatory-assisted acquisitions of banking and thrift institutions, see EITF Abstracts, Issue No. 88-19.

[49]See Basic, Inc. v. Levinson, supra n. 27, at 985 ("Arguments based on the premise that some disclosure would be 'premature' in a sense are more properly considered under the rubric of an issuer's duty to disclose. The 'secrecy' rationale is simply inapposite to the definition of materiality.").

[50]See, e.g., Securities Exchange Act Release No. 16384 (November 29, 1979) (considering these conflicting interests in adopting Item 7 of Schedule 14D-9, which requires that the subject company of a public tender offer provide two levels of disclosure: (a) a statement as to whether or not "any negotiation [which would result in certain transactions or fundamental changes] is being undertaken or is underway . . . in response to the tender offer," which disclosure need not include "the possible terms of the transaction or the parties thereto" if in the registrant's view such disclosure would jeopardize the negotiations; and (b) a description of "any transaction, board resolution, agreement in principle, or a signed contract" relating to such transactions or changes).

[51]Item 2 of Form 8-K. See also Item 8 of Form 10-K (excluding pro forma financial information otherwise called for by Article 11 of Regulation S-X from the financial information required); Item 1 of Form 10-Q, and Rule 10-01 of Regulation S-X. With respect to the disposal of a segment of a business, however, Accounting Principles Board Opinion 30 requires that results of operations of the segment be reclassified as discontinued operations, and any estimated loss on disposal be recorded, as of the date management commits itself to a formal plan to dispose of the segment (i.e., the "measurement date"). Filings, including periodic reports under the Exchange Act that contain annual or interim financial statements are required to reflect the prescribed accounting treatment as of the measurement date.

[52]Article 11 of Regulation S-X et seq. (generally requiring the provision of pro forma financial information where a significant acquisition or disposition "has occurred or is probable"). Entry into the continuous reporting system by registration under the Exchange Act also requires the provision of such pro forma financial information. Item 13 of Form 10. See also Item 14 of Schedule 14A (requiring Article 11 pro forma financial information and extensive other information about certain extraordinary transactions if shareholder action is to be taken with respect to such a transaction).

63040. CHANGES IN AND DISAGREEMENTS WITH ACCOUNTANTS ON ACCOUNTING AND FINANCIAL DISCLOSURE (ITEM 304)

63041. General. The disclosure requirements of Item 304 are intended to make investors aware of the following events that may have occurred during the past two years, whether or not the registrant was subject to 1934 Act reporting during that period:

- Changes in accountants

- Disagreements between the former accountant and the registrant prior to the change

- The existence of certain "reportable events" prior to the change

- Consultations on certain matters between the newly engaged accountant and the registrant prior to acceptance of the engagement.

- The name of the newly engaged accountant

The AICPA's SEC Practice Section (SECPS) Executive Committee requires the auditor to notify a client that is an SEC registrant in writing within five business days when its relationship with the client has ended. The rule applies when the auditor resigns, decides not to stand for re-election, or is dismissed. A copy of the notification is required to be sent concurrently to the Chief Accountant of the SEC.

For a discussion of the requirements for reporting a change in a registrant's independent accountants, refer to sections 41640 and 20630.

63042. Text of Requirements.

Changes in and Disagreements with Accountants on Accounting and Financial Disclosure

(a) *(1) If during the registrant's two most recent fiscal years or any subsequent interim period, an independent accountant who was previously engaged as the principal accountant to audit the registrant's financial statements, or an independent accountant who was previously engaged to audit a significant subsidiary and on whom the principal accountant expressed reliance in its report, has*

resigned (or indicated it has declined to stand for re-election after the completion of the current audit) or was dismissed, then the registrant shall:

(i) State whether the former accountant resigned, declined to stand for re-election or was dismissed and the date thereof.

(ii) State whether the principal accountant's report on the financial statements for either of the past two years contained an adverse opinion or a disclaimer of opinion, or was qualified or modified as to uncertainty, audit scope, or accounting principles; and also describe the nature of each such adverse opinion, disclaimer of opinion, modification, or qualification.

(iii) State whether the decision to change accountants was recommended or approved by:

(A) any audit or similar committee of the board of directors, if the issuer has such a committee; or

(B) the board of directors, if the issuer has no such committee.

(iv) State whether during the registrant's two most recent fiscal years and any subsequent interim period preceding such resignation, declination or dismissal there were any disagreements with the former accountant on any matter of accounting principles or practices, financial statement disclosure, or auditing scope or procedure, which disagreement(s), if not resolved to the satisfaction of the former accountant, would have caused it to make reference to the subject matter of the disagreement(s) in connection with its report. Also, (A) describe each such disagreement; (B) state whether any audit or similar committee of the board of directors, or the board of directors, discussed the subject matter of each of such disagreements with the former accountant; and (C) state whether the registrant has authorized the former accountant to respond fully to the inquiries of the successor accountant concerning the subject matter of each of such disagreements and, if not, describe the nature of any limitation thereon and the reason therefor. The disagreements required to be reported in response to this Item include both those resolved to the former accountant's satisfaction and those not resolved to the former accountant's satisfaction. Disagreements contemplated by this Item are those that occur at the decision-making level, i.e., between personnel of the registrant responsible for presentation of its financial statements and personnel of the accounting firm responsible for rendering its report.

(v) Provide the information required by paragraph (a)(1)(iv) of this Item for each of the kinds of events (even though the registrant and the former accountant did not express a difference of opinion regarding the event) listed in paragraphs (a)(1)(v)(A) through (D) of this section, that occurred within the registrant's two most recent fiscal years and any subsequent interim period preceding the former accountant's resignation, declination to stand for re-election, or dismissal ("reportable events"). If the event led to a disagreement or difference of opinion, then the event should be reported as a disagreement under paragraph (a)(1)(iv) and need not be repeated under this paragraph.

(A) The accountant's having advised the registrant that the internal controls necessary for the registrant to develop reliable financial statements do not exist;

(B) The accountant's having advised the registrant that information has come to the accountant's attention that has led it to no longer be able to rely on management's representations, or that has made it unwilling to be associated with the financial statements prepared by management;

(C) (1) The accountant's having advised the registrant of the need to expand significantly the scope of its audit, or that information has come to the accountant's attention during the time period covered by Item 304(a)(1)(iv), that if further investigated may (i) materially impact the fairness or reliability of either: a previously issued audit report or the underlying financial statements; or the financial statements issued or to be issued covering the fiscal period(s) subsequent to the date of the most recent financial statements covered by an audit report (including information that may prevent it from rendering an unqualified audit report on those financial statements), or (ii) cause it to be unwilling to rely on management's representations or be associated with the registrant's financial statements, and (2) Due to the accountant's resignation (due to audit scope limitations or otherwise) or dismissal, or for any other reason, the accountant did not so expand the scope of its audit or conduct such further investigation; or

(D) (1) The accountant's having advised the registrant that information has come to the accountant's attention that it has concluded materially impacts the fairness or reliability of either (i) a previously issued audit report or the underlying financial statements, or (ii) the financial statements issued or to be issued covering the fiscal period(s) subsequent to the date of the most recent financial statements covered by an audit report (including information that, unless resolved to the accountant's satisfaction, would prevent it from rendering an unqualified audit report *on those financial statements), and (2) Due to the accountant's resignation, dismissal or declination to stand for re- election, or for any other reason, the issue has not been resolved to the accountant's satisfaction prior to its resignation, dismissal or declination to stand for re-election.*

(2) If during the registrant's two most recent fiscal years or any subsequent interim period, a new independent accountant has been engaged as either the principal accountant to audit the registrant's financial statements, or as an independent accountant to audit a significant subsidiary and on whom the principal accountant is expected to express reliance in its report, then the registrant shall identify the newly engaged accountant and indicate the date of such accountant's engagement. In addition, if during the registrant's two most recent fiscal years, and any subsequent interim period prior to engaging that accountant, the registrant (or someone on its behalf) consulted the newly engaged accountant regarding (i) either: the application of accounting principles to a specified transaction, either completed or proposed; or the type of audit opinion that might be rendered on the registrant's financial statements, and either a written report was provided to the registrant or oral advice was provided that the new accountant concluded was an important factor considered by the registrant in reaching a decision as to the accounting, auditing or financial reporting issue; or (ii) any matter that was either the subject of a disagreement (as defined in paragraph 304(a)(1)(iv) and the related instructions to this item) or a reportable event (as described in paragraph 304(a)(1)(v)), then the registrant shall:

(A) So state and identify the issues that were the subjects of those consultations;

(B) Briefly describe the views of the newly engaged accountant as expressed orally or in writing to the registrant on each such issue and, if written views were received by the registrant, file them as an exhibit to the report or registration statement requiring compliance with this Item 304(a);

(C) State whether the former accountant was consulted by the registrant regarding any such issues, and if so, provide a summary of the former accountant's views; and

(D) Request the newly engaged accountant to review the disclosure required by this Item 304(a) before it is filed with the Commission and provide the new accountant the opportunity to furnish the registrant with a letter addressed to the Commission containing any new information, clarification of the registrant's expression of its views, or the respects in which it does not agree with the statements made by the registrant in response to Item 304(a). The registrant shall file any such letter as an exhibit to the report or registration statement containing the disclosure required by this Item.

SEC 63042

930

(3) The registrant shall provide the former accountant with a copy of the disclosures it is making in response to this Item 304(a) that the former accountant shall receive no later than the day that the disclosures are filed with the Commission. The registrant shall request the former accountant to furnish the registrant with a letter addressed to the Commission stating whether it agrees with the statements made by the registrant in response to this Item 304(a) and, if not, stating the respects in which it does not agree. The registrant shall file the former accountant's letter as an exhibit to the report or registration statement containing this disclosure. If the former accountant's letter is unavailable at the time of filing such report or registration statement, then the registrant shall request the former accountant to provide the letter as promptly as possible so that the registrant can file the letter with the Commission within ten business days after the filing of the report or registration statement. Notwithstanding the ten business day period, the registrant shall file the letter by amendment within two business days of receipt; if the letter is received on a Saturday, Sunday or holiday on which the Commission is not open for business, then the two business day period shall begin to run on and shall include the first business day thereafter. The former accountant may provide the registrant with an interim letter highlighting specific areas of concern and indicating that a more detailed letter will be forthcoming within the ten business day period noted above. If not filed with the report or registration statement containing the registrant's disclosure under this Item 304(a), then the interim letter, if any, shall be filed by the registrant by amendment within two business days of receipt.

(b) If, (1) In connection with a change in accountants subject to paragraph (a) of this Item 304, there was any disagreement of the type described in paragraph (a)(1)(iv) or any reportable event as described in paragraph (a)(1)(v) of this Item, (2) During the fiscal year in which the change in accountants took place or during the subsequent fiscal year, there have been any transactions or events similar to those which involved such disagreement or reportable event; and (3) Such transactions or events were material and were accounted for or disclosed in a manner different from that which the former accountants apparently would have concluded was required, the registrant shall state the existence and nature of the disagreement or reportable event and also state the effect on the financial statements if the method had been followed which the former accountants apparently would have concluded was required. These disclosures need not be made if the method asserted by the former accountants ceases to be generally accepted because of authoritative standards or interpretations subsequently issued.

Instructions to Item 304. 1. The disclosure called for by paragraph (a) of this Item need not be provided if it has been previously reported (as that term is defined in Rule 12b-2 under the Exchange Act); the disclosure called for by paragraph (a) must be provided, however, notwithstanding prior disclosure, if required pursuant to Item 9 of

Schedule 14A. The disclosure called for by paragraph (b) of this section must be furnished, where required, notwithstanding any prior disclosure about accountant changes or disagreements.

2. When disclosure is required by paragraph (a) of this section in an annual report to security holders pursuant to Rule 14a-3 or Rule 14c-3, or in a proxy or information statement filed pursuant to the requirements of Schedule 14A or 14C, in lieu of a letter pursuant to paragraph (a)(2)(D) or (a)(3), prior to filing such materials with or furnishing such materials to the Commission, the registrant shall furnish the disclosure required by paragraph (a) of this section to any former accountant engaged by the registrant during the period set forth in paragraph (a) of this section and to the newly engaged accountant. If any such accountant believes that the statements made in response to paragraph (a) of this section are incorrect or incomplete, it may present its views in a brief statement, ordinarily expected not to exceed 200 words, to be included in the annual report or proxy or information statement. This statement shall be submitted to the registrant within ten business days of the date the accountant receives the registrant's disclosure. Further, unless the written views of the newly engaged accountant required to be filed as an exhibit by paragraph (a)(2)(B) of this Item 304 have been previously filed with the Commission the registrant shall file a Form 8-K concurrently with the annual report or proxy or information statement for the purpose of filing the written views as exhibits thereto.

3. The information required by Item 304(a) need not be provided for a company being acquired by the registrant that is not subject to the filing requirements of either section 13(a) or 15(d) of the Exchange Act, or, because of section 12(i) of the Exchange Act, has not furnished an annual report to security holders pursuant to Rule 14a-3 or Rule 14c-3 for its latest fiscal year.

4. The term "disagreements" as used in this Item shall be interpreted broadly, to include any difference of opinion concerning any matter of accounting principles or practices, financial statement disclosure, or auditing scope or procedure which (if not resolved to the satisfaction of the former accountant) would have caused it to make reference to the subject matter of the disagreement in connection with its report. It is not necessary for there to have been an argument to have had a disagreement, merely a difference of opinion. For purposes of this Item, however, the term disagreements does not include initial differences of opinion based on incomplete facts or preliminary information that were later resolved to the former accountant's satisfaction by, and providing the registrant and the accountant do not continue to have a difference of opinion upon, obtaining additional relevant facts or information.

5. In determining whether any disagreement or reportable event has occurred, an oral communication from the engagement partner or another person responsible for rendering the accounting firm's opinion (or their designee) will generally suffice as the accountant advising the registrant of a reportable event or as a statement of a disagreement at the "decision-making level" within the accounting firm and require disclosure under this Item.

63043. Reporting prior consultations with newly engaged accountant. FRR 31, as codified in FRP 603.07, was issued as a result of the SEC's concern that a change in accountants may have resulted from what it refers to as an "opinion shopping" situation. While companies may, of course, change accountants at their discretion, the SEC's concerns relate to changes in accountants made merely "to support a proposed accounting treatment that is intended to accomplish the registrant's reporting objectives even though that treatment might frustrate reliable reporting."

As a result of its concerns in this regard, the SEC requires disclosure (see section 63042) concerning consultations between a registrant and its newly engaged accountant that occurred within the past two years if those discussions were (or should have been) subject to SAS 50 (AU Section 625) or concerned the subject matter of a disagreement or reportable event with the former accountant. SAS 50 relates to reports, either written or oral, obtained from outside accountants regarding the application of accounting principles to specified transactions and the type of opinion that may be rendered on a specific entity's financial statements.

The information to be disclosed in this connection includes:

- The issues that were the subject of the consultations.

- The newly engaged accountant's views on these issues, as expressed to the registrant.

- A statement by the registrant as to whether it consulted the former accountants on these issues, and if so, a summary of its views.

In addition, the new accountants need to be provided the opportunity to review the registrant's summary of its views and furnish a letter to the registrant providing additional information or clarifying the summary of its views. This letter is to be filed as an exhibit to the filing or report containing this disclosure.

Where applicable, the registrant is required to request that the former accountants review the disclosures made pursuant to Item 304(a) and provide a statement as to whether they agree with the registrant's summary of its views, and if not, the respects in which they do not agree. The former accountant's letter is also required to be filed as an exhibit to the report or registration statement containing this disclosure (or if unavailable at the filing date, filed within ten business days after the filing date).

SEC 63042

64000. MANAGEMENT AND CERTAIN SECURITY HOLDERS

64010. DIRECTORS, EXECUTIVE OFFICERS, PROMOTERS AND CONTROL PERSONS (ITEM 401)

The disclosure requirements pertaining to Directors, Executive Officers, Promoters and Control Persons specify the information to be furnished with respect to a registrant's directors, executive officers, and certain significant employees. In addition, new registrants are required to disclose certain information with respect to promoters and control persons. The term "executive officer" is defined and broad guidelines are provided with respect to the identification of "significant employees." The required information includes:

- Name.

- Age.

- Positions and offices held with registrant.

- Term of office and period served.

- Description of any special arrangements pursuant to which the individual was selected to the position.

- Summary of business experience during past five years, including any directorships held.

- Description of involvement in certain specified legal proceedings.

- Identification of family relationships.

The independent accountants generally have no involvement in the development of the information required to be disclosed pursuant to these requirements.

64020. EXECUTIVE COMPENSATION (ITEM 402)

64021. General. In October 1992, the SEC amended its rules regarding disclosure of executive compensation in proxy statements, periodic reports, and other filings under the 1934 Act and in registration statements under the 1933 Act. The SEC's stated goal is to ensure that the marketplace receives information about executive compensation that is easier to understand and more relevant to proxy voting and investment decisions.

The amended rules require that disclosures be made in a series of tables clearly setting forth each element of compensation paid, earned or awarded in a given year. General descriptions of most compensation plans are no longer required.

Foreign private issuers may continue to satisfy the disclosure requirements for executive and director compensation by reporting the information required by Items 11 and 12 of Form 20-F, even if filing reports on forms used by domestic issuers.

The information to be disclosed pursuant to these requirements is the responsibility of the registrant and/or its counsel. Consequently, the text of this item is not reproduced herein. However, the independent accountant may be consulted in the process of assembling this information, and the following summary may be helpful in understanding these requirements.

64022. Summary of Executive Compensation Disclosure Requirements. The specified disclosures are required for:

- The chief executive officer (CEO) or the individual acting in such capacity, regardless of the amount of compensation.

- The four most highly paid senior executive officers, other than the CEO, who earn more than $100,000 per year in salary and bonus.

A summary compensation table has replaced the traditional cash compensation table required under the former rules and is required to include disclosure of the annual salary, bonuses, and all other compensation awards and payouts of the named officers. Stock options are to be disclosed as the number awarded and not assigned a value in this table. The table covers a three-year period, in the following prescribed format:

Summary Compensation Table

		Annual Compensation			Long-Term Compensation			
					Awards		Payouts	
(a)	(b)	(c)	(d)	(e)	(f)	(g)	(h)	(i)
				Other	Restricted			All
Name and				Annual	Stock	Options/	LTIP	Other
Principal		Salary	Bonus	Compensation	Award(s)	SARs	Payouts	Compensation
Position	Year	($)	($)	($)	($)	(#)	($)	($)
	1992							
	1991							
	1990							

Other components of compensation are required to be disclosed in prescribed formats as follows:

- Two tables detailing options and stock appreciation rights (SARs):

  - •• One table summarizing the number and terms of options/SARs granted during the fiscal year. The table is required to include either (a) potential values for the options/SARs based on assumed annual compounded rates of stock price appreciation (5 and 10 percent, respectively); or (b) a value for the options on the date of grant calculated using a financial formula (such as the "Black-Scholes" option pricing model) that calculates the present value of the options.

  - •• A second table summarizing exercises of options during the most recent fiscal year by the named executives (including the "net value" received, i.e., the difference between the fair market value of the securities as of the exercise date and the exercise price of the option) and the number of, and the spread (the difference between the current market price of the stock and the exercise price of the option) on, unexercised options that they hold at fiscal year-end.

- A table outlining awards in the last fiscal year under long-term incentive plans, such as phantom stock grants and restricted stock grants that vest after a period of time upon satisfaction of a performance goal.

- A pension table estimating annual benefits payable upon retirement under pension plans.

Disclosure is also required of:

- Employment and severance agreements (with payments of more than $100,000) with respect to the named executive officers.

SEC 64022

- Standard compensation arrangements for directors (payments for services on board and committees), as well as any other compensation for services (such as consulting contracts).

The rules require a report to shareholders by the members of the compensation committee (or, in its absence, the full board or other committee performing a similar function) that generally discusses the company's compensation policies for executive officers and the committee's basis for determining the compensation of the CEO for the past fiscal year. The report also must include a discussion of the relationship of executive compensation and CEO compensation to corporate performance.

The rules specify that the report should not include disclosure of specific quantitative or personal factors or confidential information. Also, there is a limited liability provision as the rules provide that the report will have the same status as the annual report to shareholders and, "as such, will not be deemed to constitute soliciting material..."

In addition to the compensation committee report, the rules require a chart that graphs the performance of the cumulative total return to shareholders (stock price appreciation plus dividends) during the previous five years in comparison to returns on a broad market index (such as the S&P 500) and a peer group index (such as the S&P Retail Index, depending on the line of business of the company). This chart will have the same limited liability provisions as set forth above.

If a company reprices any options or SARs held by a named executive, it is required to prepare a table detailing terms of that repricing and any other repricing that has occurred during the past ten years that the company has been public. The compensation committee is also required to explain the reasons behind the repricing in the last fiscal year and the basis for determining the new prices.

The compensation committee report, the performance graph, and the report on repricings of options/SARs are required only in a proxy or information statement relating to an annual meeting of security holders (or special meeting or written consents in lieu of such meeting), at which directors are to be elected; they need not be included in or incorporated by reference into any of the registrant's filings under the 1933 or 1934 Acts.

Additional disclosure is required in the proxy statement regarding relationships between directors and the company if:

- The compensation committee included employees or former or current officers of the company or its subsidiaries, or

- There is "interlocking" membership between the company's compensation committee and another company's compensation committee (i.e., a member of one company's compensation committee sits on another company's compensation committee or board, and *vice versa*).

SEC 64022

64030. SECURITY OWNERSHIP OF CERTAIN BENEFICIAL OWNERS AND MANAGEMENT (ITEM 403)

This item specifies the information to be disclosed as to the ownership of the registrant's securities by certain beneficial owners and management.

Paragraph (a) requires the following tabular information with respect to any beneficial owner of more than five percent of any class of the registrant's *voting* securities:

(1)	(2)	(3)	(4)
Title of class	Name and address of beneficial owner	Amount and nature of beneficial ownership	Percent of class

The determination of beneficial ownership is a legal issue, which should not be addressed by an independent accountant.

Paragraph (b) requires disclosure of the information in columns 1, 3, and 4 of the foregoing tabulation for each class of *equity* securities by all directors and nominees (naming them), by each of the named executive officers referred to in Item 402, and by all directors and officers as a group (without naming them).

Paragraph (c) requires disclosure of any known arrangements that could eventually result in a change in control of the registrant.

The information to be disclosed pursuant to these requirements is generally prepared by the registrant and/or its counsel, with little or no involvement on the part of the independent accountant. Consequently the text of this item is not reproduced herein.

64040. CERTAIN RELATIONSHIPS AND RELATED TRANSACTIONS (ITEM 404)

As part of its proxy review program, in 1982 the Commission adopted S-K Item 404. Certain disclosure requirements that were previously included in Item 402 relating to transactions with management, indebtedness of management, and transactions with promoters were amended and incorporated into Item 404. In addition, the disclosure requirements relating to transactions with pension plans, also previously included in Item 402, were rescinded.

Item 404 requires disclosure of:

- Transactions involving more than $60,000 in which certain specified persons have a material interest;

- Transactions involving the registrant and its executive officers; and

- Transactions involving the "immediate family" (as defined) of such specified persons. The independent accountant is generally not consulted by registrants, their attorneys, or others in the preparation of the information required pursuant to these requirements.

The independent accountants generally have no involvement in the development of the information required to be disclosed pursuant to these requirements.

65000. REGISTRATION STATEMENT AND PROSPECTUS PROVISIONS

The Registration Statement and Prospectus Provisions of Regulation S-K contain most of the instructions as to the information required in a registration statement. Two of the items in this section, Items 503 and 512, are discussed herein. A listing of all the items included in the Registration Statement and Prospectus Provisions section follows:

501. Forepart of registration statement and outside front cover page of prospectus
    (a) Facing page
    (b) Cross-reference sheet
    (c) Outside front cover page of prospectus
502. Inside front and outside back cover pages of prospectus
    (a) Available information
    (b) Reports to security holders
    (c) Incorporation by reference
    (d) Stabilization
    (e) Delivery of prospectuses by dealers
    (f) Enforceability of civil liabilities against foreign persons
    (g) Table of contents
503. Summary information, risk factors, and ratio of earnings to fixed charges
    (a) Summary
    (b) Address and telephone number
    (c) Risk factors
    (d) Ratio of earnings to fixed charges
504. Use of proceeds
505. Determination of offering price
    (a) Common equity
    (b) Warrants, rights and convertible securities
506. Dilution
507. Selling security holders
508. Plan of distribution
    (a) Underwriters and underwriting obligation
    (b) New underwriters
    (c) Other distributions
    (d) Offerings on exchange
    (e) Underwriters' compensation
    (f) Underwriters' representative on board of directors
    (g) Indemnification of underwriters
    (h) Dealers' compensation
    (i) Finders
    (j) Discretionary accounts

940

65030. SUMMARY INFORMATION, RISK FACTORS, AND RATIO OF EARNINGS TO FIXED CHARGES (ITEM 503)

65031. Summary Information and Risk Factors

Paragraph (a) of Item 503 stipulates that a prospectus summary should be provided whenever the length or complexity of the prospectus warrants its inclusion in the interest of fair and adequate disclosure. Paragraph (b) requires disclosure of the location of the registrant's principal executive offices and paragraph (c) requires prominent disclosure as to the speculative nature, where applicable, or any risk involved in the offering. Paragraph (d) of Item 503 sets forth the requirements for the ratio of earnings to fixed charges and the text of these requirements is provided in section 65038.

65032. Ratio of Earnings to Fixed Charges

The requirements for the presentation of the ratio of earnings to fixed charges were substantially revised in ASR 306. A registrant is required to furnish a ratio of earnings to fixed charges when registering debt securities and a ratio of earnings to combined fixed charges and preferred stock dividends when registering preferred stock. Voluntary disclosure of either or both ratios is permitted in other filings. When a ratio of earnings to fixed charges is included in a filing, whether by requirement or on a voluntary basis, an exhibit showing the calculation is required. See section 66000 for further discussion of this exhibit requirement.

Paragraph (d)(2) (see section 65038) specifies that the calculations of these ratios are to be based on the enterprise as a whole (the "total enterprise" concept) and must consider (1) the registrant, (2) all of the registrant's majority-owned subsidiaries, whether or not they are consolidated, (3) the registrant's and its consolidated subsidiaries' proportionate share of ownership in any fifty-percent-owned persons, and (4) any income received by the registrant and its consolidated subsidiaries from less-than-fifty-percent-owned persons. Note that the equity in the income of fifty-percent-owned persons may be included but the equity in less-than-fifty-percent-owned investees is limited to distributions.

SEC 65032

The staff has generally taken the position that when the ratio is less than one, no ratio should be presented. Registrants should instead disclose the earnings deficiency in either a footnote to the ratio presentation or a separate line within the ratio presentation.

Generally the ratio is only required to be presented for the consolidated financial statements. However, when the registrant's parent company (1) maintains the registrant's ratio or (2) guarantees the registrant's debt securities or preferred stock, the parent company's ratio is required to be disclosed in addition to the ratio based on the registrant's consolidated financial statements.

The "total enterprise" concept used in the calculation of the ratio does not extend to guaranteed debt of a less-than-fifty-percent-owned person or an unaffiliated person (such as a supplier) except when the registrant has been required to satisfy the guarantee or it is probable that the registrant will be required to honor the guarantee *and* the amount can be reasonably estimated. In that case, the guaranteed debt will also have to be considered in the calculation.

65033. Treatment of losses by equity affiliates. Paragraph (d)(3)(iv) of the rule (see section 65038) discusses the treatment of losses by equity affiliates. Where an investment in a less-than-fifty-percent-owned investee results in the recognition of a loss, such loss is not considered in the ratio computation except where the obligation of the investee has been guaranteed by the registrant or the registrant has otherwise undertaken to service the debt of the investee. If such a guarantee or undertaking has been made, the registrant's equity in the loss is included in "earnings" and the interest expense related to the guaranteed debt is included in "fixed charges."

65034. Treatment of capitalized interest. If interest is capitalized by a registrant (see section 50408 for a discussion of Regulation S-X Rule 4-08(k) and capitalized interest), the amount of interest that must be added back to net income to arrive at the "earnings" portion of the ratio (paragraph (d)(3)(i)) will be different than the amount that will be included in the "fixed charges" portion of the computation (paragraph (d)(4)). The amount of interest added back to arrive at "earnings" includes only those amounts charged to income as reported in the interest expense caption or as an element of other income statement captions, such as cost of sales. The amount of interest included in "fixed charges" is the total incurred for the period and includes both the amounts charged to income *and* amounts capitalized during the period.

In the case of public utilities, capitalized interest is included as part of a credit designated as allowance for funds used during construction (AFUDC). When calculating the ratio of earnings to fixed charges, public utilities are permitted to add the total amount of interest expense to net income to arrive at the "earnings" portion of the ratio, which amount will be the same as the amount of interest included in the "fixed charges" portion of the calculation.

SEC 65032

65035. Determination of interest portion of rentals. Prior to the adoption of ASR No. 155, the interest portion of rentals to be included in "fixed charges" was identified as "...one third of all rentals...or such portion as can be determined to be representative of the interest factor in the particular case." In ASR No. 155, the SEC concluded that "reliable estimates of the portion of rentals that represent interest can now generally be made and there is considerable evidence that one-third of rentals is not a reasonable approximation of the interest factor today."

The December 1974 issue of the *Journal of Accountancy* included the following informal interpretations by the SEC staff as to the determination of the interest portion of rentals:

- The SEC staff stated that the one third of rentals in the fixed charge component was allowed in the past because it was considered a reasonable approximation of the interest portion of rentals. They believe that this approximation may not be the most appropriate now but will not automatically disallow it, provided it represents a reasonable approximation of the interest factor.

- If practicable, the prior years' computations of the ratio should be revised to reflect estimated interest costs where one third of rentals has been used in the past and estimated interest costs is to be used in the current year's ratio so that all years presented would be consistent.

Many registrants have continued to utilize the one-third factor in computing the ratio when they believe that the determination of the amount of interest implicit in rental payments is impractical. As indicated in the foregoing interpretation, the staff will not automatically disallow such an approach; however, registrants should be prepared to demonstrate that the use of the one-third factor results in a reasonable approximation of the interest portion of rentals. While the SEC has published no guidelines on this matter, it will accept reasonable estimations.

Registrants sometimes propose to reduce fixed charges by (1) interest income or investment income earned on funds in excess of the requirements for working capital or (2) gains on retirement of debt at less than its principal amount. The SEC's opposition to this approach was discussed in ASR No. 119. Although this ASR has been rescinded, experience indicates that the staff's view on this issue is unchanged.

65036. Preferred stock dividend requirements. The preferred stock dividend requirements for the combined ratio and the component of fixed charges attributable to the preferred stock dividend requirements of majority owned subsidiaries should represent the pretax earnings from continuing operations that would be required to cover such dividend. Paragraph (d)(6) of the rule (see section 65038) provides a formula that should be used in making the calculation. The following is an example of how this calculation should be made:

Assumptions:

Preferred dividend requirement	<u>$ 100</u>
Income before income taxes	$1,000
Provisions for income taxes	<u>250</u>
Net income	<u>$ 750</u>

The calculation of the preferred dividend requirements for purposes of the ratio based on an effective tax rate of 25% is as follows:

$$\frac{\$100}{100\% - 25\%} = \frac{\$100}{75\%} = \$133.33$$

Therefore, the amount of the dividend to be considered in the calculation is $133.33.

When preferred stock with mandatory redemption provisions is offered at less than the redeemable amount or is recorded at less than the redemption value, SAB Topic 3-C (included in section 50502-28) points out that the annual accretions necessary to increase the recorded value should be treated the same as cash dividend requirements on preferred stock for the purpose of computing fixed charge and preferred dividend coverage ratios.

65037. Pro forma ratio. The requirement to furnish a pro forma ratio of earnings to fixed charges (paragraph (d)(9)) is limited to offerings considered to be "significant" refinancings. Consequently, a pro forma ratio need only be presented if the calculation of the ratio on a pro forma basis differs by 10 percent or more from the historical ratio. The difference may be an increase or a decrease. Since the pro forma ratio, when applicable, must be presented for the most recent fiscal year and the latest interim period, this comparison is made to each of those periods, including, where appropriate, the most recent twelve months.

Where only a portion of the proceeds of an offering are to be applied to refinance outstanding obligations, the calculation should be limited to that portion of the proceeds designated as to be used to retire existing debt. For example, if $100 million of debt were being offered, part of which would be used to retire $25 million of debt, the pro forma ratio should reflect the incremental fixed charges on $25 million of debt.

When the debt to be financed with the proceeds of an offering has only been outstanding for a part of the year, the question of what period to use in the pro forma calculation may arise. Since the purpose of the pro forma ratio is to display the effect of any fixed cost differential as a result of the refinancing, a corresponding period should be used. Thus, if the $25 million of debt to be refinanced in the foregoing example was only outstanding for the last three months of the most recent fiscal year, the pro forma ratio for that period would only include interest for three months on $25 million of the new debt incurred. Paragraph 9(ii) of Item 503(d), in describing the adjustment to be made in the pro forma calculation, includes the parenthetical phrase "but only for the period outstanding." This phrase should be viewed as equally applicable to (a) the proposed issuance of new debt or preferred stock and (b) the corresponding retirement of any debt or preferred stock presently outstanding.

65038. Text of requirements. As mentioned previously, the requirements for the ratio of earnings to fixed charges are set forth in paragraph (d) of Item 503. The text of these requirements is as follows:

The ratio of earnings to fixed charges or the ratio of earnings to combined fixed charges and preferred stock dividends (the "ratio") should be disclosed pursuant to the following rules and definitions:

(1)   (i) Furnish in registration statements filed under the Securities Act of 1933 (A) the ratio of earnings to fixed charges if debt securities are being registered; or (B) the ratio of earnings to combined fixed charges and preferred stock dividends if preferred stock is being registered. Disclosure of both ratios is permitted in registration statements relating to debt or preferred stock and either ratio or both ratios may be disclosed in other filings.

(ii) The ratio shall be disclosed for the following periods:

(A) Each of the last five fiscal years of the registrant (or for the life of the registrant and its predecessors, if less), and

(B) The latest interim period for which financial statements are presented.

(2) The ratio shall be computed using the amounts for the enterprise as a whole including (i) the registrant, (ii) its majority-owned subsidiaries, whether or not consolidated, (iii) its proportionate share of any fifty-percent-owned persons, and (iv) any income received (but not undistributed amounts) from less-than-fifty-percent-owned persons.

(3) The term "earnings" shall be defined as pretax income from continuing operations with the following adjustments:

(i) Add to pretax income the amount of fixed charges computed pursuant to paragraph (d)(4) of this section, adjusted to exclude (A) the amount of any interest capitalized during the period and (B) the actual amount of any preferred stock dividend requirements of majority-owned subsidiaries and fifty-percent-owned persons which were included in such fixed charges amount but not deducted in the determination of pretax income.

(ii) Only the registrant's share in the income of majority-owned subsidiaries and the distributed income of less-than-fifty-percent-owned persons shall be included in earnings, except that a registrant may include the

minority interest in the income of majority-owned subsidiaries that have fixed charges.

(iii) the full amount of losses of majority-owned subsidiaries shall be considered in the computation of earnings.

(iv) Where an investment in a less-than-fifty-percent-owned person accounted for under the equity method results in the recognition of a loss, such loss shall not be considered in the computation of the ratio except where the registrant has guaranteed or otherwise undertaken, directly or indirectly, to service the debt of such person. In the latter case, the registrant's equity in the loss shall be included in earnings and the fixed charges shall include the interest expense related to the guaranteed debt.

(v) Registrants other than public utilities may add to earnings the amount of previously capitalized interest amortized during the period.

(vi) A registrant which is a rate-regulated public utility shall not reduce fixed charges (see paragraph (4) below) by any allowance for funds used during construction, but rather, shall include any such allowance in the determination of earnings under this paragraph.

(4) (i) The term "fixed charges" shall mean the total of (A) interest, whether expensed or capitalized; (B) amortization of debt expense and discount or premium relating to any indebtedness, whether expensed or capitalized; (C) such portion of rental expense as can be demonstrated to be representative of the interest factor in the particular case; and (D) preferred stock dividend requirements of majority-owned subsidiaries and fifty-percent-owned persons, excluding in all cases items which would be or are eliminated in consolidation.

(ii) If the registrant is guarantor of debt of a less-than-fifty-percent-owned person or of an unaffiliated person (such as a supplier), the amount of fixed charges associated with such debt should not be included in the computation of the ratio unless the registrant has been required to satisfy the guarantee or it is probable that the registrant will be required to honor the guarantee and the amount can reasonably be estimated. A footnote to the ratio should disclose the existence of any such guarantee and the amount of the associated fixed charges and state whether or not such amount is included in the computation of the ratio.

(5) The term "preferred stock" shall include all types of preferred and preference stocks.

(6) For purpose of paragraph (4)(i)(D) above and computation of the combined ratio, the preferred stock dividend requirements shall be increased to an amount

representing the pre-tax earnings which would be required to cover such dividend requirements. Therefore, the increased amount equals:

Preferred Stock Dividend Requirements
100% – Income Tax Rate

The tax rate shall be based on the relationship of the provision for income tax expense applicable to income from continuing operations to the amount of pre-tax income from continuing operations.

(7) If either ratio computation indicates a less than one-to-one coverage, state that earnings are inadequate to cover fixed charges and disclose the dollar amount of the coverage deficiency.

(8) If the level of the registrant's ratio is maintained by its parent, for example, in order to meet the minimum borrowing standards of agencies of various states, or if the registrant's parent is guaranteeing the registrant's debt securities or preferred stock, the parent's ratio as well as the registrant's ratio shall be disclosed.

(9) A pro forma ratio shall be presented in the prospectus of any registration statement filed to register debt or preferred stock to be used in a refinancing if the effect of the refinancing changes the historical ratio by ten percent or more.

(i) A "refinancing" is defined as the extinguishment of one or more specific issues of debt with the proceeds from the sale of additional debt, or the extinguishment of one or more specific issues of preferred stock with the proceeds from the sale of additional preferred stock.

(ii) The only adjustments which shall be made to the corresponding historical ratio are to give effect to the net increase or decrease in interest expense or preferred stock dividends resulting from (A) the proposed issuance of new debt or preferred stock and (B) the corresponding retirement of any debt or preferred stock presently outstanding (but only for the period of time outstanding) which will be retired with the proceeds from the proposed offering. If only a portion of the proceeds will be used to retire presently outstanding debt or preferred stock, only a related portion of the interest or preferred dividend should be used in the pro forma adjustment.

(iii) The pro forma ratio, if applicable, shall be presented for only the most recent fiscal year and the latest interim period or, at the option of the registrant, the most recent twelve months.

(10) If the registrant is a foreign private issuer, the ratio shall be computed on the basis of the primary financial statements and, if materially different, their reconciliations.

SEC 65038

65120. UNDERTAKINGS (ITEM 512)

Item 512 sets forth the requirements as to undertakings that under certain conditions must be included in registration statements filed under the 1933 Act.

Paragraph (a) deals with Rule 415 and shelf registration statements. These requirements are discussed in section 19200 of this manual. Paragraph (b) contains the undertaking language required if a registration statement filed under the 1933 Act incorporates by reference 1934 Act periodic reports filed subsequent to the effective date of the registration statement (see discussion of Form S-3 in section 42250 and of Form S-8 in section 42400). Paragraph (e) specifies the undertaking language required if a registration statement incorporates the annual report to shareholders by reference. The remaining paragraphs deal with other types of 1933 Act filing situations.

The undertaking representations are, in essence, acknowledgements by the registrant that it will keep the registration statement and the prospectus current as required by the 1933 Act. While these are legal determinations, for ease of reference, the text of Item 512 is as follows:

Undertakings

Include each of the following undertakings that is applicable to the offering being registered.

(a) Rule 415 offering. *Include the following if the securities are registered pursuant to Rule 415 under the Securities Act:*

The undersigned registrant hereby undertakes:

(1) To file, during any period in which offers or sales are being made, a post-effective amendment to this registration statement:

(i) To include any prospectus required by section 10(a)(3) of the Securities Act of 1933;

(ii) To reflect in the prospectus any facts or events arising after the effective date of the registration statement (or the most recent post-effective amendment thereof) which, individually or in the aggregate, represent a fundamental change in the information set forth in the registration statement;

(iii) To include any material information with respect to the plan of distribution not previously disclosed in the registration statement or any material change to such information in the registration statement.

Provided, however, that paragraphs (a)(1)(i) and (a)(1)(ii) do not apply if the registration statement is on Form S-3 or Form S-8, and the information required to be included in a post-effective amendment by those paragraphs is contained in periodic reports filed by the registrant pursuant to section 13 or section 15(d) of the Securities Exchange Act of 1934 that are incorporated by reference in the registration statement.

(2) That, for the purpose of determining any liability under the Securities Act of 1933, each such post-effective amendment shall be deemed to be a new registration statement relating to the securities offered therein, and the offering of such securities at that time shall be deemed to be the initial bona fide offering thereof.

(3) To remove from registration by means of a post-effective amendment any of the securities being registered which remain unsold at the termination of the offering.

(4) If the registrant is a foreign private issuer, to file a post- effective amendment to the registration statement to include any financial statements required by Rule 3-19 of Regulation S-X at the start of any delayed offering or throughout a continuous offering.

(b) Filings incorporating subsequent Exchange Act documents by reference. *Include the following if the registration statement incorporates by reference any Exchange Act document filed subsequent to the effective date of the registration statement:*

The undersigned registrant hereby undertakes that, for purposes of determining any liability under the Securities Act of 1933, each filing of the registrant's annual report pursuant to section 13(a) or section 15(d) of the Securities Exchange Act of 1934 (and, where applicable, each filing of an employee benefit plan's annual report pursuant to section 15(d) of the Securities Exchange Act of 1934) that is incorporated by reference in the registration statement shall be deemed to be a new registration statement relating to the securities offered therein, and the offering of such securities at that time shall be deemed to be the initial bona fide offering thereof.

(c) Warrants and rights offerings. *Include the following, with appropriate modifications to suit the particular case, if the securities to be registered are to be offered to existing security holders pursuant to warrants or rights and any securities not taken by security holders are to be reoffered to the public:*

The undersigned registrant hereby undertakes to supplement the prospectus, after the expiration of the subscription period, to set forth the results of the subscription offer, the transactions by the underwriters during the subscription period, the amount of unsubscribed securities to be purchased by the underwrit-

SEC 65120

ers, and the terms of any subsequent reoffering thereof. If any public offering by the underwriters is to be made on terms differing from those set forth on the cover page of the prospectus, a post-effective amendment will be filed to set forth the terms of such offering.

(d) Competitive bids. *Include the following, with appropriate modifications to suit the particular case, if the securities to be registered are to be offered at competitive bidding:*

The undersigned registrant hereby undertakes (1) to use its best efforts to distribute prior to the opening of bids, to prospective bidders, underwriters, and dealers, a reasonable number of copies of a prospectus which at that time meets the requirements of section 10(a) of the Act, and relating to the securities offered at competitive bidding, as contained in the registration statement, together with any supplements thereto, and (2) to file an amendment to the registration statement reflecting the results of bidding, the terms of the reoffering and related matters to the extent required by the applicable form, not later than the first use, authorized by the issuer after the opening of bids, of a prospectus relating to the securities offered at competitive bidding, unless no further public offering of such securities by the issuer and no reoffering of such securities by the purchasers is proposed to be made.

(e) Incorporated annual and quarterly reports. *Include the following if the registration statement specifically incorporates by reference (other than by indirect incorporation by reference through a Form 10-K report) in the prospectus all or any part of the annual report to security holders meeting the requirements of Rule 14a-3 or Rule 14c-3 under the Exchange Act:*

The undersigned registrant hereby undertakes to deliver or cause to be delivered with the prospectus, to each person to whom the prospectus is sent or given, the latest annual report to security holders that is incorporated by reference in the prospectus and furnished pursuant to and meeting the requirements of Rule 14a-3 or Rule 14c-3 under the Securities Exchange Act of 1934; and, where interim financial information required to be presented by Article 3 of Regulation S-X are not set forth in the prospectus, to deliver, or cause to be delivered to each person to whom the prospectus is sent or given, the latest quarterly report that is specifically incorporated by reference in the prospectus to provide such interim financial information.

(f) Equity offerings of nonreporting registrants. *Include the following if equity securities of a registrant that prior to the offering had no obligation to file reports with the Commission pursuant to section 13(a) or 15(d) of the Exchange Act are being registered for sale in an underwritten offering:*

SEC 65120

The undersigned registrant hereby undertakes to provide to the underwriter at the closing specified in the underwriting agreements certificates in such denominations and registered in such names as required by the underwriter to permit prompt delivery to each purchaser.

(g) Registration on Form S-4 or F-4 of securities offered for resale. *Include the following if the securities are being registered on Form S-4 or F-4 in connection with a transaction specified in paragraph (a) of Rule 145:*

(1) The undersigned registrant hereby undertakes as follows: that prior to any public reoffering of the securities registered hereunder through use of a prospectus which is a part of this registration statement, by any person or party who is deemed to be an underwriter within the meaning of Rule 145(c), the issuer undertakes that such reoffering prospectus will contain the information called for by the applicable registration form with respect to reofferings by persons who may be deemed underwriters, in addition to the information called for by the other Items of the applicable form.

(2) The registrant undertakes that every prospectus (i) that is filed pursuant to paragraph (1) immediately preceding, or (ii) that purports to meet the requirements of section 10(a)(3) of the Act and is used in connection with an offering of securities subject to Rule 415, will be filed as a part of an amendment to the registration statement and will not be used until such amendment is effective, and that, for purposes of determining any liability under the Securities Act of 1933, each such post-effective amendment shall be deemed to be a new registration statement relating to the securities offered therein, and the offering of such securities at that time shall be deemed to be the initial bona fide offering thereof.

(h) Request for acceleration of effective date or filing of registration statement on Form S-8. *Include the following if acceleration is requested of the effective date of the registration statement pursuant to Rule 461 under the Securities Act, or if the registration statement is filed on Form S-8, and: (1) any provision or arrangement exists whereby the registrant may indemnify a director, officer or controlling person of the registrant against liabilities arising under the Securities Act, or (2) the underwriting agreement contains a provision whereby the registrant indemnifies the underwriter or controlling persons of the underwriter against such liabilities and a director, officer or controlling person of the registrant is such an underwriter or controlling person thereof or a member of any firm which is such an underwriter, and (3) the benefits of such indemnification are not waived by such persons:*

Insofar as indemnification for liabilities arising under the Securities Act of 1933 may be permitted to directors, officers and controlling persons of the registrant pursuant to the foregoing provisions, or otherwise, the registrant has been advised that in the opinion of the Securities and Exchange Commission such indemnification is against public policy as expressed in the Act and is, therefore, unenforceable. In the event that a claim for indemnification against such liabilities (other than the payment by the registrant of expenses incurred or paid by a director, officer or controlling person of the registrant in the successful defense of any action, suit or proceeding) is asserted by such director, officer or controlling person in connection with the securities being registered, the registrant will, unless in the opinion of its counsel the matter has been settled by controlling precedent, submit to a court of appropriate jurisdiction the question whether such indemnification by it is against public policy as expressed in the Act and will be governed by the final adjudication of such issue.

(i) Include the following in a registration statement permitted by Rule 430A under the Securities Act of 1933. *The undersigned registrant hereby undertakes that:*

(1) For purposes of determining any liability under the Securities Act of 1933, the information omitted from the form of prospectus filed as part of this registration statement in reliance upon Rule 430A and contained in a form of prospectus filed by the registrant pursuant to Rule 424(b)(1) or (4) or 497(h) under the Securities Act shall be deemed to be part of the registration statement as of the time it was declared effective.

(2) For the purpose of determining any liability under the Securities Act of 1933, each post-effective amendment that contains a form of prospectus shall be deemed to be a new registration statement relating to the securities offered therein, and the offering of such securities at that time shall be deemed to be the initial bona fide offering thereof.

(j) Qualification of trust indentures under the Trust Indenture Act of 1939 for delayed offerings. *Include the following if the registrant intends to rely on section 305(b)(2) of the Trust Indenture Act of 1939 for determining the eligibility of the trustee under indentures for securities to be issued, offered, or sold on a delayed basis by or on behalf of the registrant:*

"The undersigned registrant hereby undertakes to file an application for the purpose of determining the eligibility of the trustee to act under subsection (a) of section 310 of the Trust Indenture Act ("Act") in accordance with the rules and regulations prescribed by the Commission under section 305(b)(2) of the Act."

SEC 65120

66000. EXHIBITS (ITEM 601)

66101. General

The Regulation S-K Exhibits requirements consolidate and standardize the Commission's requirements relating to the filing of exhibits. Reference should be made to the exhibit table in the text of the requirements (reproduced below) for a summary of the exhibits to be included in most of the frequently used 1933 and 1934 Act forms.

To facilitate the identification and location of exhibits, the inclusion of an exhibit index is required and the first page of the document being filed is required to specify the location of this index.

66102. Text of Requirements

Exhibits

(a) Exhibits and index required. *(1) Subject to Rule 411(c) under the Securities Act and Rule 12b-32 under the Exchange Act regarding incorporation of exhibits by reference, the exhibits required by the exhibit table shall be filed as indicated, as part of the registration statement or report. Financial Data Schedules required by paragraph (b)(27) of this Item shall be submitted pursuant to the provisions of paragraph (c) of this Item. Notwithstanding the provisions of paragraphs (b)(27) and (c) of this Item, registered investment companies and business development companies filing on forms available solely to investment companies shall be subject to the provisions of rule 483 under the Securities Act of 1933, and any provision or instruction therein shall be controlling with respect to registered investment companies and business development companies unless otherwise specifically provided in rules or instructions pertaining to the submission of a specific form. (2) Each registration statement or report shall contain an exhibit index, which shall precede immediately the exhibits filed with such registration statement. For convenient reference, each exhibit shall be listed in the exhibit index according to the number assigned to it in the exhibit table. The exhibit index shall indicate, by handwritten, typed, printed, or other legible form of notation in the manually signed original registration statement or report, the page number in the sequential numbering system where such exhibit can be found. Where exhibits are incorporated by reference, this fact shall be noted in the exhibit index referred to in the preceding sentence. Further, the first page of the manually signed registration statement shall list the page in the filing where the exhibit index is located. For a description of each of the exhibits included in the exhibit table, see paragraph (b) of this Item. (3) This Item applies only to the forms specified in the exhibit* *table. With regard to forms not listed in that table, reference shall be made to the appropriate form for the specific exhibit filing requirements applicable thereto. (4) If a material contract or plan of acquisition, reorganization, arrangement, liquidation or succession is executed or becomes effective during the reporting period reflected by a Form 10-Q or Form 10-K, it shall be filed as an exhibit to the Form 10-Q or Form 10-K filed for the corresponding period. Any amendment or modification to a previously filed exhibit to a Form 10, 10-K or 10-Q document shall be filed as an exhibit to a Form 10-Q or Form 10-K. Such amendment or modification need not be filed where such previously filed exhibit would not be currently required.*

Instructions to Item 601. *1. If an exhibit to a registration statement (other than an opinion or consent), filed in preliminary form, has been changed only (A) to insert information as to interest, dividend or conversion rates, redemption or conversion prices, purchase or offering prices, underwriters' or dealers' commission, names, addresses or participation of underwriters or similar matters, which information appears elsewhere in an amendment to the registration statement or a prospectus filed pursuant to Rule 424(b) under the Securities Act, or (B) to correct typographical errors, insert signatures or make other similar immaterial changes, then, notwithstanding any contrary requirement of any rule or form, the registrant need not refile such exhibit as so amended. Any such incomplete exhibit may not, however, be incorporated by reference in any subsequent filing under any Act administered by the Commission.*

2. In any case where two or more indentures, contracts, franchises, or other documents required to be filed as exhibits are substantially identical in all material respects except as to the parties thereto, the dates of execution, or other details, the registrant need file a copy of only one of such documents, with a schedule identifying the other documents omitted and setting forth the material details in which such documents differ from the document a copy of which is filed. The Commission may at any time in its discretion require filing of copies of any documents so omitted.

3. Only copies, rather than originals, need be filed of each exhibit required except as otherwise specifically noted.

4. Electronic filings. Whenever an exhibit is filed in paper pursuant to a hardship exemption, the letter "P" (paper) shall be placed next to the exhibit in the list of exhibits required by item 601(a)(2) of this Rule. Whenever an electronic confirming copy of an exhibit is filed pursuant to a grant of a temporary hardship exemption, the exhibit index shall specify where the confirming electronic copy can be located; in addition, the designation "CE" (confirming electronic) shall be placed next to the listed exhibit in the exhibit index.

Instructions to the exhibit table. *1. The exhibit table indicates those documents that must be filed as exhibits to the respective forms listed.*

2. The "X" designation indicates the documents which are required to be filed with each form even if filed previously with another document. Provided, however, that such previously filed documents may be incorporated by reference to satisfy the filing requirements.

3. The number used in the far left column of the table refers to the appropriate subsection in paragraph (b) where a description of the exhibit can be found. Whenever necessary, alphabetical or numerical subparts may be used.

(b) Description of exhibits. *Set forth below is a description of each document listed in the exhibit table. [Refer to pages 956 and 957]*

(1) Underwriting agreement — *Each underwriting contract or agreement with a principal underwriter pursuant to which the securities being registered are to be distributed; if the terms of such documents have not been determined, the proposed forms thereof. Such agreement may be filed as an exhibit to a report on Form 8-K which is incorporated by reference into a registration statement subsequent to its effectiveness.*

(2) Plan of acquisition, reorganization, arrangement, liquidation or succession — *Any material plan of acquisition, disposition, reorganization, readjustment, succession, liquidation or arrangement and any amendments thereto described in the statement or report. Schedules (or similar attachments) to these exhibits shall not be filed unless such schedules contain information which is material to an investment decision and which is not otherwise disclosed in the agreement or the disclosure document. The plan filed shall contain a list briefly identifying the contents of all omitted schedules, together with an agreement to furnish supplementally a copy of any omitted schedule to the Commission upon request.*

(3) Articles of incorporation and by-laws —

(i) Articles of incorporation. The articles of incorporation of the registrant or instruments corresponding thereto as currently in effect and any amendments thereto. Whenever amendments to articles of incorporation are filed, a complete copy of the articles as amended shall be filed. Where it is impracticable for the registrant to file a charter amendment authorizing new securities with the appropriate state authority prior to the effective date of the registration statement registering such securities, the

SEC 66102

Exhibit Table

	Securities Act Forms										Exchange Act Forms			
	S-1	S-2	S-3	S-4[3]	S-8	S-11	F-1	F-2	F-3	F-4[3]	10	8-K	10-Q	10-K
(1) Underwriting agreement.	X	X	X	X	—	X	X	X	X	X	—	X	—	—
(2) Plan of acquisition, reorganization, arrangement, liquidation or succession.														
(3) (i) Articles of incorporation.	X	X	—	X	—	X	X	X	—	X	X	X	X	X
(ii) By-laws.	X	—	—	X	—	X	X	—	—	X	X	—	—	X
(4) Instruments defining the rights of security holders, including indentures.	X	X	X	X	X	X	X	X	X	X	X	—	—	X
(5) Opinion re legality.	X	X	X	X	X	X	X	X	X	X	X	X	X	X
(6) Opinion re discount on capital shares.	X	X	X	X	X	X	X	X	X	X	—	—	—	—
(7) Opinion re liquidation preference.	X	X	—	X	—	X	X	X	—	X	X	—	—	—
(8) Opinion re tax matters.	X	X	X	X	—	X	X	X	X	X	X	—	—	—
(9) Voting trust agreement.	X	X	—	X	—	X	X	—	—	X	X	—	—	—
(10) Material contracts.	X	X	—	X	—	X	X	X	—	X	X	—	X	X
(11) Statement re computation of per share earnings.	X	X	—	X	—	X	X	X	—	X	X	—	X	X
(12) Statement re computation of ratios.	X	X	X	X	—	X	X	X	—	X	X	—	—	X
(13) Annual report to security holders. Form 10-Q or quarterly report to security holders.[1]	—	X	—	X	—	—	—	—	—	—				
(14) Material foreign patents.	X	—	—	X	—	—	X	—	—	X	X	—	—	X
(15) Letter re unaudited interim financial information.	X	X	X	X	—	X	X	X	X	X	—	X	—	—

	Securities Act Forms										Exchange Act Forms			
	S-1	S-2	S-3	S-4[3]	S-8	S-11	F-1	F-2	F-3	F-4[3]	10	8-K	10-Q	10-K
(16) Letter re change in certifying accountant.[4]	X	X	—	X	—	X	—	—	—	—	X	X	—	X
(17) Letter re director resignation.	—	—	—	—	—	—	—	—	—	—	—	X	—	—
(18) Letter re change in accounting principles.	—	—	—	—	—	—	—	—	—	—	—	—	X	X
(19) Report furnished to security holders.	—	—	—	—	—	—	—	—	—	—	—	—	X	—
(20) Other documents or statements to security holders.	—	—	—	—	—	—	—	—	—	—	—	X	—	—
(21) Subsidiaries of the registrant.	X	—	—	X	—	X	X	—	—	X	X	—	—	X
(22) Published report regarding matters submitted to vote of security holders.	—	—	—	—	—	—	—	—	—	—	—	—	X[2]	X[2]
(23) Consents of experts and counsel.	X	X	X	X	X	X	X	X	X	X	—	X[2]	X	X
(24) Power of attorney.	X	X	X	X	X	X	X	X	X	X	X	X	X	X
(25) Statement of eligibility of trustee.	X	X	X	X	—	X	X	X	X	X	—	—	—	—
(26) Invitations for competitive bids.	X	X	X	X	—	—	X	X	X	X	—	—	—	—
(27) Financial Data Schedule.[5]	X	X	X	X	X	X	—	—	—	—	X	X	X	X
(28) Information from reports furnished to state insurance regulatory authorities.	X	X	X	X	X	—	X	X	—	—	X	—	—	X
(29) Through (98) [Reserved].														
(99) Additional exhibits.	X	X	X	X	X	X	X	X	X	X	X	X	X	X

[1] Where incorporated by reference into the text of the prospectus and delivered to security holders along with the prospectus as permitted by the registration statement; or, in the case of the Form 10-K, where the annual report to security holders is incorporated by reference into the text of the Form 10-K.

[2] Where the opinion of the expert or counsel has been incorporated by reference into a previously filed Securities Act registration statement.

[3] An exhibit need not be provided about a company if (1) with respect to such company an election has been made under Form S-4 or F-4 to provide information about such company at a level prescribed by Forms S-2, S-3, F-2 or F-3 and (2) the form, the level of which has been elected under Form S-4 or F-4, would not require such company to provide such exhibit if it were registering a primary offering.

[4] If required pursuant to Item 304 of Regulation S-K.

[5] Financial Data Schedules shall be filed by electronic filers only. Such schedule shall be filed only when a filing includes annual and/or interim financial statements that have not been previously included in a filing with the Commission. See Item 601(c) of Regulation S-K.

SEC 66102

registrant may file as an exhibit to the registration statement the form of amendment to be filed with the state authority; and in such a case, if material changes are made after the copy is filed, the registrant must also file the changed copy.

(ii) By-laws. The by-laws of the registrant or instruments corresponding thereto as currently in effect and any amendments thereto. Whenever amendments to the by-laws are filed, a complete copy of the by-laws as amended shall be filed.

(4) *Instruments defining the rights of security holders, including indentures —*

(i) All instruments defining the rights of holders of the equity or debt securities being registered including, where applicable, the relevant portion of the articles of incorporation or by-laws of the registrant.

(ii) Except as set forth in (iii) below, for filings on Forms S-1, S-4, S-11, S-14, and F-4 under the Securities Act and Forms 10 and 10-K under the Exchange Act all instruments defining the rights of holders of long-term debt of the registrant and its consolidated subsidiaries and for any of its unconsolidated subsidiaries for which financial statements are required to be filed.

(iii) Where the instrument defines the rights of holders of long-term debt of the registrant and its consolidated subsidiaries and for any of its unconsolidated subsidiaries for which financial statements are required to be filed, there need not be filed (A) any instrument with respect to long-term debt not being registered if the total amount of securities authorized thereunder does not exceed 10 percent of the total assets of the registrant and its subsidiaries on a consolidated basis and if there is filed an agreement to furnish a copy of such agreement to the Commission upon request; (B) any instrument with respect to any class of securities if appropriate steps to assure the redemption or retirement of such class will be taken prior to or upon delivery by the registrant of the securities being registered; or (C) copies of instruments evidencing scrip certificates for fractions of shares.

(iv) If any of the securities being registered are, or will be, issued under an indenture to be qualified under the Trust Indenture Act, the copy of such indenture which is filed as an exhibit shall include or be accompanied by (A) a reasonably itemized and informative table of contents; and (B) a cross-reference sheet showing the location in the indenture of the

provisions inserted pursuant to sections 310 through 318(a) inclusive of the Trust Indenture Act of 1939.

(v) With respect to Forms 8-K and 10-Q under the Exchange Act which are filed and which disclose, in the text of the Form 10-Q, the interim financial statements, or the footnotes thereto, the creation of a new class of securities or indebtedness or the modification of existing rights of security holders, file all instruments defining the rights of holders of these securities or indebtedness. However, there need not be filed any instrument with respect to long-term debt not being registered which meets the exclusion set forth above in paragraph (iii)(A).

Instruction. *There need not be filed any instrument which defines the rights of participants (not as security holders) pursuant to an employee benefit plan.*

(5) Opinion re legality —

(i) An opinion of counsel as to the legality of the securities being registered, indicating whether they will, when sold, be legally issued, fully paid and non-assessable, and, if debt securities, whether they will be binding obligations of the registrant.

(ii) If the securities being registered are issued under a plan and the plan is subject to the requirements of ERISA furnish either:

(A) An opinion of counsel which confirms compliance of the provisions of the written documents constituting the plan with the requirements of ERISA pertaining to such provisions; or

(B) A copy of the Internal Revenue Service determination letter that the plan is qualified under section 401 of the Internal Revenue Code; or

(iii) If the securities being registered are issued under a plan which is subject to the requirements of ERISA and the plan has been amended subsequent to the filing of (ii)(A) or (B) above, furnish either:

(A) An opinion of counsel which confirms compliance of the amended provisions of the plan with the requirements of ERISA pertaining to such provisions; or

(B) A copy of the Internal Revenue Service determination letter that the amended plan is qualified under section 401 of the Internal Revenue Code.

Note: Attention is directed to Item 8 of Form S-8 for exemptions to this exhibit requirement applicable to that form.

(6) Opinion re discount on capital shares — *If any discount on capital shares is shown as a deduction from capital shares on the most recent balance sheet being filed for the registrant, there shall be filed a statement of the circumstances under which such discount arose and an opinion of counsel as to the legality of the issuance of the shares to which such discount relates. The opinion shall set forth, or specifically refer to, any applicable constitutional and statutory provisions and shall cite any decisions which in the opinion of counsel are controlling.*

(7) Opinion re liquidation preference — *If the registrant has any shares the preference of which upon involuntary liquidation exceeds the par or stated value thereof, there shall be filed an opinion of counsel as to whether there are any restrictions upon surplus by reason of such excess and also as to any remedies available to security holders before or after payment of any dividend that would reduce surplus to an amount less than the amount of such excess. The opinion shall set forth, or specifically refer to, any applicable constitutional and statutory provisions and shall cite any decisions which, in the opinion of counsel, are controlling.*

(8) Opinion re tax matters — *For filings on Form S-11 under the Securities Act or those to which Securities Act Industry Guide 5 applies, an opinion of counsel or of an independent public or certified public accountant or, in lieu thereof, a revenue ruling from the Internal Revenue Service, supporting the tax matters and consequences to the shareholders as described in the filing when such tax matters are material to the transaction for which the registration statement is being filed. This exhibit otherwise need only be filed with the other applicable registration forms where the tax consequences are material to an investor and a representation as to tax consequences is set forth in the filing. If a tax opinion is set forth in full in the filing, an indication that such is the case may be made in lieu of filing the otherwise required exhibit. Such tax opinions may be conditioned or may be qualified, so long as such conditions and qualifications are adequately described in the filing.*

(9) Voting trust agreement — *Any voting trust agreements and amendments thereto.*

(10) Material contracts —

(i) Every contract not made in the ordinary course of business which is material to the registrant and is to be performed in whole or in part at or after the filing of the registration statement or report or was entered into not more than two years before such filing. Only contracts need be filed as to which the registrant or subsidiary of the registrant is a party or has

succeeded to a party by assumption or assignment or in which the registrant or such subsidiary has a beneficial interest.

(ii) If the contract is such as ordinarily accompanies the kind of business conducted by the registrant and its subsidiaries, it will be deemed to have been made in the ordinary course of business and need not be filed unless it falls within one or more of the following categories, in which case it shall be filed except where immaterial in amount or significance:

(A) Any contract to which directors, officers, promoters, voting trustees, security holders named in the registration statement or report, or underwriters are parties other than contracts involving only the purchase or sale of current assets having a determinable market price, at such market price;

(B) Any contract upon which the registrant's business is substantially dependent, as in the case of continuing contracts to sell the major part of registrant's products or services or to purchase the major part of registrant's requirements of goods, services or raw materials or any franchise or license or other agreement to use a patent, formula, trade secret, process or trade name upon which registrant's business depends to a material extent;

(C) Any contract calling for the acquisition or sale of any property, plant or equipment for a consideration exceeding 15 percent of such fixed assets of the registrant on a consolidated basis; or

(D) Any material lease under which a part of the property described in the registration statement or report is held by the registrant.

(iii) (A) Any management contract or any compensatory plan, contract or arrangement, including but not limited to plans relating to options, warrants or rights, pension, retirement or deferred compensation or bonus, incentive or profit sharing (or if not set forth in any formal document, a written description thereof) in which any director or any of the named executive officers of the registrant, as defined by Item 402(a)(3), participates shall be deemed material and shall be filed; and any other management contract or any other compensatory plan, contract, or arrangement in which any other executive officer of the registrant participates shall be filed unless immaterial in amount or significance.

(B) Notwithstanding paragraph (iii)(A) above, the following management contracts or compensatory plans, contracts or arrangements need not be filed:

(1) Ordinary purchase and sales agency agreements.

SEC 66102

(2) Agreements with managers of stores in a chain organization or similar organization.

(3) Contracts providing for labor or salesmen's bonuses or payments to a class of security holders, as such.

(4) Any compensatory plan, contract or arrangement which pursuant to its terms is available to employees, officers or directors generally and which in operation provides for the same method of allocation of benefits between management and nonmanagement participants.

(5) Any compensatory plan, contract or arrangement if the registrant is a foreign private issuer that furnishes compensatory information on an aggregate basis as permitted by Instruction 1 to paragraph (a) of Item 402 or by Item 11 of Form 20-F.

(6) Any compensatory plan, contract, or arrangement if the registrant is a wholly owned subsidiary of a company that has a class of securities registered pursuant to section 12 or files reports pursuant to section 15(d) of the Exchange Act and is filing a report on Form 10-K or registering debt instruments or preferred stock which are not voting securities on Form S- 2.

Instruction. With the exception of management contracts, in order to comply with paragraph (iii) above, registrants need only file copies of the various remunerative plans and need not file each individual director's or executive officer's personal agreement under the plans unless there are particular provisions in such personal agreements whose disclosure in an exhibit is necessary to an investor's understanding of that individual's remuneration under the plan.

(11) Statement re computation of per share earnings — A statement setting forth in reasonable detail the computation of per share earnings, unless the computation can be clearly determined from the material contained in the registration statement or report. The information with respect to the computation of per share earnings on both primary and fully diluted bases, presented by exhibit or otherwise, must be furnished even though the amounts of per share earnings on the fully diluted basis are not required to be presented in the income statement under the provisions of Accounting Principles Board Opinion No. 15. That Opinion provides that any reduction of less than 3% need not be considered as dilution (see footnote to paragraph 14 of the Opinion) and that a computation on the fully diluted basis which results in improvement of earnings per share not be taken into account (see paragraph 40 of the Opinion).

SEC 66102

The exhibit requirements for the computation of per share earnings are generally limited to those instances where the calculation is not otherwise evident from disclosures in the financial statements or notes thereto.

(12) Statements re computation of ratios — *A statement setting forth in reasonable detail the computation of any ratio of earnings to fixed charges, any ratio of earnings to combined fixed charges and preferred stock dividends or any other ratios which appear in the registration statement or report. See Item 503(d) of Regulation S-K.*

See section 65032 for a discussion of the requirements for the ratios of earnings to fixed charges.

(13) Annual report to security holders, Form 10-Q or quarterly report to security holders —

(i) The registrant's annual report to security holders for its last fiscal year, its Form 10-Q (if specifically incorporated by reference in the prospectus) or its quarterly report to security holders, if all or a portion thereof is incorporated by reference in the filing. Such report, except for those portions thereof which are expressly incorporated by reference in the filing, is to be furnished for the information of the Commission and is not to be deemed "filed" as part of the filing. If the financial statements in the report have been incorporated by reference in the filing, the accountant's certificate shall be manually signed in one copy. See Rule 411(b).

(ii) Electronic filings. If all, or any portion, of the annual or quarterly report to security holders is incorporated by reference into any electronic filing, all, or such portion of the annual or quarterly report to security holders so incorporated, shall be filed in electronic format as an exhibit to the filing.

See section 41171 for a discussion of the incorporation by reference of the annual report to shareholders into Form 10-K.

(14) Material foreign patents — *Each material foreign patent for an invention not covered by a United States patent. If the filing is a registration statement and if a substantial part of the securities to be offered or if the proceeds therefrom have been or are to be used for the particular purposes of acquiring, developing or exploiting one or more material foreign patents or patent rights, furnish a list showing the number and a brief identification of each such patent or patent right.*

(15) Letter re unaudited interim financial information — *A letter, where applicable, from the independent accountant which acknowledges awareness of the use in a registration statement of a report on unaudited interim financial* *information which pursuant to Rule 436(c) under the Securities Act is not considered a part of a registration statement prepared or certified by an accountant or a report prepared or certified by an accountant within the meaning of sections 7 and 11 of that Act. Such letter may be filed with the registration statement, an amendment thereto, or a report on Form 10-Q which is incorporated by reference into the registration statement.*

See section 20432 for a discussion of this requirement.

(16) Letter re change in certifying accountant — *A letter from the registrant's former independent accountant regarding its concurrence or disagreement with the statements made by the registrant in the current report concerning the resignation or dismissal as the registrant's principal accountant.*

See sections 20630 and 63040 for a discussion of this requirement.

(17) Letter re director resignation — *Any letter from a former director which sets forth a description of a disagreement with the registrant that led to the director's resignation or refusal to stand for re- election and which requests that the matter be disclosed.*

(18) Letter re change in accounting principles — *Unless previously filed, a letter from the registrant's independent accountant indicating whether any change in accounting principles or practices followed by the registrant, or any change in the method of applying any such accounting principles or practices, which affected the financial statements being filed with the Commission in the report or which is reasonably certain to affect the financial statements of future fiscal years is to an alternative principle which in his judgment is preferable under the circumstances. No such letter need be filed when such change is made in response to a standard adopted by the Financial Accounting Standards Board that creates a new accounting principle, that expresses a preference for an accounting principle, or that rejects a specific accounting principle.*

See section 20620 for a discussion of this requirement.

(19) Report furnished to security holders — *If the registrant makes available to its stockholders or otherwise publishes, within the period prescribed for filing the report, a document or statement containing information meeting some or all of the requirements of Part I of Form 10-Q, the information called for may be incorporated by reference to such published document or statement provided copies thereof are included as an exhibit to the registration statement or to Part I of the Form 10-Q report.*

See section 41440 for a discussion of this requirement.

SEC 66102

(20) Other documents or statements to security holders — *If the registrant makes available to its stockholders or otherwise publishes, within the period prescribed for filing the report, a document or statement containing information meeting some or all of the requirements of this form, the information called for may be incorporated by reference to such published document or statement provided copies thereof are filed as an exhibit to the report on this form.*

(21) Subsidiaries of the registrant —

(i) List all subsidiaries of the registrant, the state or other jurisdiction of incorporation or organization of each, and the names under which such subsidiaries do business. This list may be incorporated by reference from a document which includes a complete and accurate list.

(ii) The names of particular subsidiaries may be omitted if the unnamed subsidiaries, considered in the aggregate as a single subsidiary, would not constitute a significant subsidiary as of the end of the year covered by this report. (See the definition of "significant subsidiary" in Rule 1-02(v) of Regulation S-X.) The names of consolidated wholly-owned multiple subsidiaries carrying on the same line of business, such as chain stores or small loan companies, may be omitted, provided the name of the immediate parent, the line of business, the number of omitted subsidiaries operating in the United States and the number operating in foreign countries are given. This instruction shall not apply, however, to banks, insurance companies, savings and loan associations or to any subsidiary subject to regulation by another Federal agency.

(22) Published report regarding matters submitted to vote of security holders — *Published reports containing all of the information called for by Item 4 of Part II of Form 10-Q or Item 4 of Part I of Form 10-K which is referred to therein in lieu of providing disclosure in Form 10-Q or 10-K, which are required to be filed as exhibits by Rule 12b-23(a)(3) under the Exchange Act.*

(23) Consents of experts and counsel —

(i) Securities Act filings — All written consents required to be filed shall be dated and manually signed. Where the consent of an expert or counsel is contained in his report or opinion or elsewhere in the registration statement or document filed therewith, a reference shall be made in the index to the report, the part of the registration statement or document or opinion, containing the consent.

(ii) Exchange Act reports — where the filing of a written consent is required with respect to material incorporated by reference in a previously filed registration statement under the Securities Act, such consent may be

filed as an exhibit to the material incorporated by reference. Such consents shall be dated and manually signed.

See section 20510 for a discussion of these requirements.

(24) Power of attorney — *If any name is signed to the registration statement or report pursuant to a power of attorney, manually signed copies of such power of attorney shall be filed. Where the power of attorney is contained elsewhere in the registration statement or documents filed therewith a reference shall be made in the index to the part of the registration statement or document containing such power of attorney. In addition, if the name of any officer signing on behalf of the registrant is signed pursuant to a power of attorney, certified copies of a resolution of the registrant's board of directors authorizing such signature shall also be filed. A power of attorney that is filed with the Commission shall relate to a specific filing or an amendment thereto. A power of attorney that confers general authority shall not be filed with the Commission.*

(25) Statement of eligibility of trustee —

(i) A statement of eligibility and qualification of each person designated to act as trustee under an indenture to be qualified under the Trust Indenture Act of 1939. Such statement of eligibility shall be bound separately from the other exhibits.

(ii) Electronic filings. The requirement to bind separately the statement of eligibility and qualification of each person designated to act as a trustee under the Trust Indenture Act of 1939 from other exhibits shall not apply to statements submitted in electronic format. Rather, such statements shall be submitted as exhibits in the same electronic submission as the subject registration statement to which it relates or an amendment thereto, Provided that electronic filers that rely on Trust Indenture Act Section 305(b)(2) for determining the eligibility of the trustee under indentures for securities to be issued, offered or sold on a delayed basis by or on behalf of the registrant shall file statements of eligibility as exhibits to a post-effective amendment to the registration statement to which the statements relate.

(26) Invitations for competitive bids — *If the registration statement covers securities to be offered at competitive bidding, any form of communication which is an invitation for competitive bid which will be sent or given to any person shall be filed.*

(27) Financial data schedule — *The Financial Data Schedule shall be filed only by electronic filers. Applicable requirements are set forth in paragraph (c) of this Item.*

SEC 66102

(28) Information from reports furnished to state insurance regulatory authorities —

(i) If reserves for unpaid property-casualty ("P/C") claims and claim adjustment expenses of the registrant and its consolidated subsidiaries, its unconsolidated subsidiaries and the proportionate share of the registrant and the other subsidiaries in the unpaid P/C claims and claim adjustment expenses of its 50%-or-less-owned equity investees, taken in the aggregate after intercompany eliminations, exceed one-half of the common stockholder's equity of the registrant and its consolidated subsidiaries as of the beginning of the latest fiscal year the following information should be supplied.

(ii) The information included in Schedules O and P of Annual Statements provided to state regulatory authorities by the registrant and/or its P/C insurance company affiliates for the latest year should be presented in the same format and on the same statutory basis, on a combined or consolidated basis as appropriate, separately for each of the following:

(A) The registrant and its consolidated subsidiaries; and

(B) The registrant's unconsolidated subsidiaries; and

(C) Fifty-percent-or-less-owned equity investees of the registrant and its subsidiaries

(iii) The combined or consolidated Schedules O and P of 50%-or-less-owned equity investees may be omitted if they file the same information with the Commission as registrants in their own right, if that fact and the name and ownership percentage of such registrants is stated.

(iv) If ending reserves in category (A), (B), or the proportionate share of the registrant and its other subsidiaries in (C) above are less than 5% of the total ending reserves in (A), (B), and the proportionate share of (C), that category may be omitted and that fact so noted. If the amount of the reserves attributable to 50%-or-less-owned equity investees that file this information as registrants in their own right exceeds 95% of the total category (C) reserves, information for the other 50%-or-less-owned equity investees need not be provided.

(v) Schedules O and P information need not be included for entities that are not required to file Schedules O and P with insurance regulatory authorities. However, the nature and extent of any such exclusions should be clearly noted in the Exhibit.

SEC 66102

(vi) Registrants whose fiscal year differs from the calendar year should present Schedules O and P as of the end of the calendar year that falls within their fiscal year.

(vii) The nature and amount of the difference between reserves for claims and claim adjustment expenses reflected in Schedules O and P and the aggregate P/C statutory reserves for claims and claim adjustment expenses as of the latest calendar year end should be disclosed in a note to those schedules.

(29) Through (98) [Reserved]

(99) Additional exhibits —

(i) Any additional exhibits which the registrant may wish to file shall be so marked as to indicate clearly the subject matters to which they refer.

(ii) Any document (except for an exhibit) or part thereof which is incorporated by reference in the filing and is not otherwise required to be filed by this Item or is not a Commission filed document incorporated by reference in a Securities Act registration statement.

(iii) If pursuant to section 11(a) of the Securities Act (15 U.S.C. 77k(a)) an issuer makes available to its security holders generally an earnings statement covering a period of at least 12 months beginning after the effective date of the registration statement, and if such earnings statement is submitted to the Commission, it must be filed as an exhibit to the Form 10-Q or the Form 10-K, as appropriate, covering the period in which the earnings statement was released.

(c) Financial data schedule

(1) General —

(i) A Financial Data Schedule shall be submitted only by an electronic filer that is not a foreign private issuer or a foreign government. The schedule shall be submitted in the electronic format prescribed by the EDGAR Filer Manual, and shall set forth the financial information specified in the applicable table in the Appendices to this item.

(ii) Subsequent to the date on which a registrant becomes subject to mandated electronic filing, any electronic filing that includes financial statements of the registrant for a recent fiscal year or interim year to date period, or both, for which financial statements have not previously been filed, otherwise than by incorporation by reference, shall include as an exhibit a Financial Data Schedule containing financial information for the updating period or periods.

(iii) The amounts reflected in the Financial Data Schedule shall correspond to or be calculable from amounts reflected in the registrant's financial statements or notes thereto.

(iv) The schedule shall be submitted as an exhibit to the filing(s) to which it relates, but shall not be deemed filed for purposes of section 11 of the Securities Act, section 18 of the Exchange Act, and section 323 of the Trust Indenture Act, or otherwise be subject to the liabilities of such sections, nor shall it be deemed a part of any registration statement to which it relates. It shall, however, be subject to all other liability and anti-fraud provisions of the Acts. See Rule 402 of Regulation S-T.

(v) A Financial Data Schedule shall be submitted only in electronic format. Where a registrant submits a filing, otherwise required to include a Financial Data Schedule, in paper pursuant to a temporary hardship exemption under Rule 201 of Regulation S-T, the Financial Data Schedule shall not be included with the paper filing, but shall be included with the required confirming electronic copy.

(vi) A Financial Data Schedule reflecting pro forma financial information shall not be filed.

Note: A registrant's failure to furnish a Financial Data Schedule pursuant to this paragraph will not prevent acceptance of the filing for which the schedule is required. However, inasmuch as the schedule may be used by the Commission staff in its review of the filing, processing of the filing may be delayed pending filing of the schedule. Further, registrants that have not filed a required Financial Data Schedule will be ineligible to use Form S-2, Form S-3 and Form S-8. See eligibility requirements of those forms.

(2) Format and presentation of financial data schedule —

(i) At the option of the registrant, the following legend may be inserted at the beginning of any Financial Data Schedule submitted to the Commission, in the manner prescribed by the EDGAR Filer Manual:

THIS SCHEDULE CONTAINS SUMMARY FINANCIAL INFORMATION EXTRACTED FROM [Identify specific financial statements] AND IS QUALIFIED IN ITS ENTIRETY BY REFERENCE TO SUCH FINANCIAL STATEMENTS

(ii) Items set forth in a Financial Data Schedule may be qualified by referencing a specific footnote to the Financial Data Schedule or cross-referencing notes to the registrant's financial statements.

(iii) If any of the amounts reported in a previously submitted Financial Data Schedule are restated as a result of pooling of interests, an accounting principle change, a reorganization or recapitalization, or correction of an error or other reason, then a schedule, as amended or restated, shall be submitted that sets forth the restated information for each affected period during the latest three fiscal years and interim periods of the latest two fiscal years; except that restated or amended information need not be furnished for any period for which a Financial Data Schedule was not previously required to be furnished. The document shall specify that the Financial Data Schedule has been restated or amended. A schedule that is filed to correct an error in a previously filed Financial Data Schedule shall be designated as an "Amended Financial Data Schedule." A schedule that is filed as a result of a restatement that is not a correction of an error shall be designated as a "Restated Financial Data Schedule."

(3) Contents of financial data schedule —

The schedule shall set forth the financial information specified below that is applicable to the registrant. Schedules based on Articles 5, 7 and 9 of Regulation S-X include items that are to be understood as the same information required by the Item in Regulation S-X.

(i) Article 5 Registrants (Commercial and Industrial Companies). Registrants that prepare financial statements in accordance with Article 5 of Regulation S-X shall prepare a Financial Data Schedule that contains the Article 5 items listed in Appendix A to this Item.

(ii) Article 7 Registrants (Insurance Companies). Registrants that prepare financial statements in accordance with Article 7 of Regulation S-X shall prepare a Financial Data Schedule that contains the Article 7 financial statement items and the industry guide items (Securities Act Industry Guide 6 or Exchange Act Industry Guide 4 listed in Appendix B to this Item).

(iii) Article 9 Registrants (Bank Holding Companies and Savings and Loan Holding Companies). Registrants that prepare their financial statements in accordance with Article 9 of Regulation S-X and savings and loan holding companies shall prepare a Financial Data Schedule that contains the Article 9 financial statement items and Securities Act Industry Guide 3 information and Exchange Act Industry Guide 3 listed in Appendix C to this Item.

(iv) Broker-Dealer and Broker-Dealer Holding Companies. Registrants that are broker-dealers or broker-dealer holding companies may prepare a Financial Data Schedule that contains the items listed in Appendix D

to this Item in lieu of a Financial Data Schedule containing the items listed in Appendix A to this Item.

(v) Public Utility Companies and Public Utility Holding Companies. Registrants that are public utility companies or public utility holding companies shall prepare a Financial Data Schedule in the form required by Appendix E to this item.

Note: Schedule UT (Appendix E) contains the same requirements found in Exhibit G of Form U5S.

(vi) Multi-Industry Registrants. A registrant that presents its primary financial statements in a manner in which non-homogeneous lines of business are grouped separately on the face of the primary financial statements and that does not present combined totals for all lines of business may submit separate Financial Data Schedules for each line of business. Where a registrant prepares more than one Financial Data Schedule, a separate schedule of consolidated totals on Schedule CT (Appendix F to this item) shall also be furnished.

[Note: Appendices A through F referred to in paragraph (c) have not been reproduced in this manual]

66110. Earnings Per Share Computations

A statement setting forth the computation of earnings per share is required in most 1933 Act and 1934 Act filings when the computation cannot be clearly determined from the material contained in the filing. The supporting computations are required to be furnished, by exhibit or otherwise, for both primary and fully diluted earnings per share, even though the amounts of fully diluted per-share earnings are not required to be stated under the provisions of APB Opinion No. 15 due to immateriality or antidilution. If the exhibit is required, the computations should cover each period presented in the income statement, including any unaudited interim periods. See Section 66102 for additional information.

67000. MISCELLANEOUS (ITEMS 701 AND 702)

Pursuant to Regulation S-K Item 701, Recent Sales of Unregistered Securities, registrants are required to furnish certain information with respect to all securities sold by the registrant within the past three years that were not registered under the 1933 Act. The specified information is required to cover the sales of reacquired securities, as well as new issues, securities issued in exchange for property, services, or other securities, and new securities resulting from the modification of outstanding securities.

Item 702, Indemnification of Directors and Officers, specifies that registrants must disclose the general effect of any statute, charter provision, bylaws, contract, or other arrangement under which any controlling person, director, or officer of the registrant is insured or indemnified in any manner against liability that they may incur in their capacity as such.

The information required to be disclosed pursuant to these items is generally prepared by the registrant and/or its counsel, with little or no involvement on the part of the independent accountant. Accordingly, the text of these requirements is not reproduced herein.

68000. LIST OF INDUSTRY GUIDES (ITEMS 801 AND 802)

In 1968 the SEC published the first of a series of Guides intended to outline policies and practices followed by the Division of Corporation Finance in the administration of the 1933 Act. A separate series of Guides under the 1934 Act was initiated in 1974. The 1933 and 1934 Act Guides are not rules of the SEC and do not bear the Commission's official approval; however, they are intended to assist registrants in the preparation of registration statements and periodic reports, and it is generally advisable to discuss significant deviations from them with the staff prior to filing.

In ASR 306 the SEC substantially modified the Guides by (1) eliminating those with outdated or duplicative disclosure requirements and (2) relocating requirements in certain other Guides to Regulation S-K and to other rules and regulations under the 1933 and 1934 Acts. Only those Guides pertaining to specific industries have been retained as such.

As part of the reorganization of Regulation S-K that was also accomplished in ASR 306, a listing of the remaining Guides is now provided in Section 800 of Regulation S-K. A copy of that listing is as follows:

1933 Act Industry Guides

Guide 1.   Disclosure of principal sources of electric and gas revenues.

Guide 2.   Disclosure of oil and gas operations.

Guide 3.   Statistical disclosure by bank holding companies.

Guide 4.   Prospectuses relating to interests in oil and gas programs.

Guide 5.   Preparation of registration statements relating to interests in real estate limited partnerships.

Guide 6.   Disclosures concerning unpaid claims and claim adjustment expenses of property-casualty underwriters.

Guide 7.   Description of property by issuers engaged or to be engaged in significant mining operations.

1934 Act Industry Guides

Guide 1.   Disclosure of principal sources of electric and gas revenues.

Guide 2.   Disclosure of oil and gas operations.

Guide 3.   Statistical disclosure by bank holding companies.

Guide 4.   Disclosures concerning unpaid claims and claim adjustment expenses of property-casualty underwriters.

Guide 7.   Description of property by issuers engaged or to be engaged in significant mining operations.

69000. ROLL-UP TRANSACTIONS (ITEM 900)

In November 1991, the Commission adopted S-K Item 900 to improve the quality of information provided in connection with roll-up transactions involving limited partnerships or similar entities. The rules were determined to be necessary after serious concerns had been raised about roll-ups during Congressional hearings and through investor complaints to the SEC.

Item 901 (c)(1) defines a roll-up transaction as:

...any transaction or series of transactions that directly or indirectly, through acquisition or otherwise, involves the combination or reorganization of one or more partnerships and either:

(i) The offer or sale of securities by a successor entity, whether newly formed or previously existing, to one or more limited partners of the partnerships to be combined or reorganized; or

(ii) The acquisition of the successor entity's securities by the partnerships being combined or reorganized.

Item 900 requires the disclosure of the following items:

- Individual Partnership Supplements.

- Summary.

- Risk Factors and Other Considerations.

- Comparative Information.

- Allocation of Roll-Up Consideration to Investors.

- Background of the Roll-Up Transaction.

- Reasons for and Alternatives to the Roll-Up Transaction.

- Conflicts of Interests.

- Fairness of the Transaction.

- Reports, Opinions, and Appraisals.

- Source and Amount of Funds and Transactional Expenses.

- Pro Forma Financial Statements; Selected Financial Data.

- Federal Income Tax Consequences.

In addition to the disclosure rules, the Commission adopted amendments to Forms S-4 and F-4 and to Rules 14a-6, 14c-2 and 14e-1 under the 1934 Act, establishing a 60-day minimum solicitation period for roll-up transactions, or, if shorter, the maximum period permitted under applicable state law.

REGULATION S-B

Integrated Disclosure System for Small Business Issuers

70100. GENERAL (ITEM 10)

The SEC has adopted rules and forms under the 1933 Act, the 1934 Act, and the Trust Indenture Act of 1939 that are intended to facilitate capital raising by small businesses and reduce the costs of compliance with the federal securities laws.

The new rules revise the general small issuers exemption from the 1933 Act registration requirements, Regulation A (see section 42800), as well as the Rule 504 exemption under Regulation D (see section 42900), and adopt simplified registration and reporting disclosure requirements for small business issuers. The SEC has also adopted additional small business initiatives that ease small business issuers into the reporting system for public companies.

Regulation S-B, which was adopted in August 1992, sets forth: (1) the application of the Regulation, (2) definitions of the terms used, (3) guidelines as to the preparation of the disclosure document, (4) the Commission's policy on projections, and (5) the Commission's policy on security ratings.

70110. Definition of a Small Business Issuer

The new rules define a small business issuer as a U.S. or Canadian entity with revenues of less than $25 million whose public float (the aggregate market value of voting stock held by nonaffiliates) is less than $25 million. Investment companies are excluded from the definition. Further, if the small business issuer is a majority owned subsidiary of another company, its parent is also required to meet the definition of a small business issuer.

70120. Integrated Disclosure System for Registration and Reporting for Small Business Issuers

The new system consists of specialized forms under the 1933 and 1934 Acts that reference disclosure requirements in one central depository — Regulation S-B. Form S-18, upon which the system was modeled, has been repealed and replaced by Form SB-2 (see section 42700). Other forms have also been revised to include the new S-B requirements.

There is no dollar limit for offerings on Form SB-2 and the Form may be used for both initial and repeat offerings, and for both primary and secondary offerings. Small business issuers may file initial public offerings on Form SB-2 either with the regional SEC office closest to the issuer's principal place of business or at the SEC's headquarters in Washington, D.C. All subsequent filings, however, are required to be made at the SEC's headquarters.

A company that meets the definition of small business issuer may use Form SB-2 (see section 42700) for registration of its securities under the 1933 Act; Form 10-SB (see section 41850) for registration of its securities under the 1934 Act; and Forms 10-KSB (see section 41200) and 10-QSB (see section 41500) for its annual and quarterly reports, respectively. In addition, transitional small business issuers (discussed below) may register up to $10 million of securities in any 12-month period using 1933 Act Form SB-1 (see section 42600). Alternatively, small business issuers may register securities on Forms S-2, S-3, S-4, and S-8 using the disclosure requirements of Regulation S-B if they meet the eligibility requirements for use of those forms.

SEC 70100

A brief synopsis of the Rules for entering and exiting the small business disclosure system is as follows:

- For a nonreporting company entering the disclosure system for the first time, the determination as to whether a company is a small business issuer is made with reference to its revenues during its most recent fiscal year and its public float as of a date within 60 days of the date the registration statement is filed.

- Once a small business issuer becomes a reporting company, it retains this designation until it exceeds the revenue limit or the public float limit at the end of two consecutive years. However, if it exceeds the revenue limit in one year and in the following year exceeds the public float limit but not the revenue limit, it would still be considered a small business.

- A reporting company that is not a small business company is required to meet the definition of a small business issuer at the end of two consecutive fiscal years before it will be considered a small business issuer for purposes of using Forms SB-2, 10-SB, 10-KSB, and 10-QSB.

- The determination as to the reporting category (small business issuer or other issuer) made for a nonreporting company at the time it enters the disclosure system governs all periodic reports filed with the SEC for the remainder of the fiscal year. The determination made for a reporting company at the end of its fiscal year governs all reports relating to the next fiscal year. An issuer may not change from one category to another with respect to its 1934 Act periodic reports during a particular fiscal year. A company may, however, choose not to use a Form SB-2 for a registration under the 1933 Act.

70130. Summary of Financial Statement Requirements

The financial statements that are required to accompany the various forms to be filed by "small business issuers" are generally subject to less onerous disclosure requirements under Regulation S-B than under Regulation S-X. While all financial statements need to be prepared in accordance with U.S. generally accepted accounting principles, the provisions of Regulation S-X regarding form and content do not apply, except for the report and qualifications of the independent accountants pursuant to Article 2. The SEC staff has indicated that to the extent FRRs and SABs contain guidance with respect to GAAP they should be applied in preparing financial statements.

The filings of certain small business issuers, however, are subject to certain aspects of Regulation S-X. For example, foreign private issuers who qualify as small business issuers need to comply with Regulation S-X Rules 3-19 and 3-20, and be in general agreement with Item 18 of Form 20-F. Oil and gas producers must follow Article 4-10.

When pro forma presentations are necessary, the revised guidelines set forth in Rule 11-01 of Regulation S-X need to be considered.

The Commission indicated in adopting the release that small business issuers engaged in operations involving real estate, mining, insurance, banking, utilities, and oil and gas should also refer to the applicable industry guide. In addition, small business issuers that have roll-up transactions are required to furnish the disclosure required by subpart 900 of Regulation S-K.

Additionally, there are occasions when the SEC staff may permit the omission of one or more financial statements and/or the substitution of appropriate alternative statements.

The annual financial statements need to include an audited balance sheet as of the end of the most recent fiscal year, or as of a date within 135 days of the filing date if the small business issuer has been in existence for less than one fiscal year. In addition, audited statements of income, cash flows, and changes in stockholders' equity are required to be presented for each of the two fiscal years preceding the date of the balance sheet. When filing on a 1934 Act registration statement (i.e., Form 10-SB), audited financial statements for only the latest fiscal year are required if the audited financial statements for the earlier fiscal year are not otherwise available.

Interim financial statements may be unaudited and presented in a condensed format. Where required, they need to include a balance sheet as of the end of the most recent fiscal quarter, plus income statements and statements of cash flows for the period up to the balance sheet date and the comparable period of the preceding fiscal year. Other required disclosures include: any footnotes necessary for a fair presentation and appropriate disclosures regarding any material accounting changes accompanied by a preferability letter from the independent accountants.

When financial statements included in a filing under Regulation S-B other than on a Form 10-KSB are of a date 135 days or more prior to the effective date of the registration statement, they are required to be updated to include statements for an interim period ending within 135 days of the effective date.

70140. Transitional Disclosure Requirements for Small Business Issuers

The SEC has adopted transitional 1934 Act registration and reporting requirements to ease the transition for a small business issuer from a non-1934 Act reporting company to a reporting company. Such transitional small business issuers may elect to use alternative disclosure requirements in their filings that mirror those of Form 1-A of Regulation A (see section 42800), including the Model A question-and-answer disclosure format. The instructions for these alternative disclosure requirements have been added to Forms 10-SB (see section 41850), 10-KSB (see section 41200) and

10-QSB (see section 41500). Small business issuers may continue to use the transitional disclosure requirements until they:

- register more than $10 million of securities under the 1933 Act in any continuous 12-month period (other than securities registered on Form S-8);

- elect to file on a nontransitional disclosure document. Nontransitional disclosure documents include:

  •• 1933 Act registration statements, except for Forms SB-1, S-3 (if the issuer incorporates by reference transitional 1934 Act reports), S-8 and S-4 (if the issuer uses the transitional disclosure format in that form);

  •• 1934 Act periodic reporting Forms 10-K and 10-Q;

  •• 1934 Act registration statement Form 10; and

  •• reports or registration statements on Forms 10-KSB, 10-QSB or 10-SB that do not use the transitional disclosure document format; or

- no longer meet the definition of a small business issuer.

It is important to note that once a small business issuer files a nontransitional disclosure document, it cannot return to the transitional disclosure form.

Small business issuers that are eligible to use the 1934 Act transitional disclosure requirements are also eligible to register up to $10 million of securities in any continuous 12-month period on 1933 Act Form SB-1 (see section 42600). In addition, Forms S-3 (see section 42250), S-4 (see section 42300), and S-8 (see section 42400) permit transitional small business issuers to use alternative disclosure and incorporation by reference provisions in the respective filing.

70150. Amendment to Rules Under the Trust Indenture Act

Rules have also been adopted to permit debt offerings up to $10 million without full compliance with the Trust Indenture Act. Specifically, Rule 4a-1 has been amended to increase to $5 million the aggregate principal amount of securities that may be issued without an indenture. Rule 4a-2 has been adopted to exempt from compliance with the Trust Indenture Act any offering of debt securities that is exempt from registration under Regulation A. Former Rule 4a-2, now Rule 4a-3, was amended to increase to $10 million the aggregate principal amount that may be issued under an indenture that does not need to be qualified under the Act.

70160. Text of Requirements

For ease of reference, the text of Item 10 of Regulation S-B follows.

ATTENTION ELECTRONIC FILERS

THIS REGULATION SHOULD BE READ IN CONJUNCTION WITH REGULATION S-T (PART 232 OF THIS CHAPTER), WHICH GOVERNS THE PREPARATION AND SUBMISSION OF DOCUMENTS IN ELECTRONIC FORMAT. MANY PROVISIONS RELATING TO THE PREPARATION AND SUBMISSION OF DOCUMENTS IN PAPER FORMAT CONTAINED IN THIS REGULATION ARE SUPERSEDED BY THE PROVISIONS OF REGULATION S-T FOR DOCUMENTS REQUIRED TO BE FILED IN ELECTRONIC FORMAT.

General

(a) Application of Regulation S-B. Regulation S-B is the source of disclosure requirements for "small business issuer" filings under the Securities Act of 1933 (the "Securities Act") and the Securities Exchange Act of 1934 (the "Exchange Act").

(1) Definition of small business issuer. A small business issuer is defined as a company that meets all of the following criteria:

(i) has revenues of less than $25,000,000;

(ii) is a U.S. or Canadian issuer;

(iii) is not an investment company; and

(iv) if a majority owned subsidiary, the parent corporation is also a small business issuer.

Provided, however, that an entity is not a small business issuer if it has a public float (the aggregate market value of the issuer's outstanding securities held by non-affiliates) of $25,000,000 or more.

NOTE: The public float of a reporting company shall be computed by use of the price at which the stock was last sold, or the average of the bid and asked prices of such stock, on a date within 60 days prior to the end of its most recent fiscal year. The public float of a company filing an initial registration statement under the Exchange Act shall be determined as of a date within 60 days of the date the registration statement is filed. In the case of an initial public offering of securities, public float shall be computed on the basis of the number of shares outstanding prior to the offering and the estimated public offering price of the securities.

(2) Entering and Exiting the Small Business Disclosure System.

(i) A company that meets the definition of small business issuer may use Form SB-2 for registration of its securities under the Securities Act; Form 10-SB for registration of its securities under the Exchange Act; and Forms 10-KSB and 10-QSB for its annual and quarterly reports.

(ii) For a non-reporting company entering the disclosure system for the first time either by filing a registration statement under the Securities Act on Form SB-2 or a registration statement under the Exchange Act on Form 10-SB, the determination as to whether a company is a small business issuer is made with reference to its revenues during its last fiscal year and public float as of a date within 60 days of the date the registration statement is filed. See Note to paragraph (a) of this Item.

(iii) Once a small business issuer becomes a reporting company it will remain a small business issuer until it exceeds the revenue limit or the public float limit at the end of two consecutive years. For example, if a company exceeds the revenue limit for two consecutive years, it will no longer be considered a small business. However, if it exceeds the revenue limit in one year and the next year exceeds the public float limit, but not the revenue limit, it will still be considered a small business. See Note to paragraph (a) of this Item.

(iv) A reporting company that is not a small business company must meet the definition of a small business issuer at the end of two consecutive fiscal years before it will be considered a small business issuer for purposes of using Form SB-2, Form 10-SB, Form 10-KSB and Form 10-QSB. See Note to paragraph (a) of this Item.

(v) The determination as to the reporting category (small business issuer or other issuer) made for a non-reporting company at the time it enters the disclosure system governs all reports relating to the remainder of the fiscal year. The determination made for a reporting Company at the end of its fiscal year governs all reports relating to the next fiscal year. An issuer may not change from one category to another with respect to its reports under the Exchange Act for a single fiscal year. A company may, however, choose not to use a Form SB-2 for a registration under the Securities Act.

(b) Definitions of terms.

(1) Common equity — means the small business issuer's common stock. If the small business issuer is a limited partnership, the term refers to the equity interests in the partnership.

SEC 70160

(2) Public market — no public market shall be deemed to exist unless, within the past 60 business days, both bid and asked quotations at fixed prices (excluding "bid wanted" or "offer wanted" quotations) have appeared regularly in any established quotation system on at least half of such business days. Transactions arranged without the participation of a broker or dealer functioning as such are not indicative of a "public market."

(3) Reporting company — means a company that is obligated to file periodic reports with the Securities and Exchange Commission under section 15(d) or 13(a) of the Exchange Act.

(4) Small business issuer — refers to the issuer and all of its consolidated subsidiaries.

(c) Preparing the disclosure document.

(1) The purpose of a disclosure document is to inform investors. Hence, information should be presented in a clear, concise and understandable fashion. Avoid unnecessary details, repetition or the use of technical language. The responses to the items of this Regulation should be brief and to the point.

(2) Small business issuers should consult the General Rules and Regulations under the Securities Act and Exchange Act for requirements concerning the preparation and filing of documents. Small business issuers should be aware that there are special rules concerning such matters as the kind and size of paper that is allowed and how filings should be bound. These special rules are located in Regulation C of the Securities Act and in Regulation 12B of the Exchange Act.

(d) Commission policy on projections. The Commission encourages the use of management's projections of future economic performance that have a reasonable basis and are presented in an appropriate format. The guidelines below set forth the Commission's views on important factors to be considered in preparing and disclosing such projections.

(1) Basis for projections. Management has the option to present in Commission filings its good faith assessment of a small business issuer's future performance. Management, however, must have a reasonable basis for such an assessment. An outside review of management's projections may furnish additional support in this regard. If management decides to include a report of such a review in a Commission filing, it should also disclose the qualifications of the reviewer, the extent of the review, the relationship between the reviewer and the registrant, and other material factors concerning the process by which any outside review was sought or obtained. Moreover, in

SEC 70160

the case of a registration statement under the Securities Act, the reviewer would be deemed an expert and an appropriate consent must be filed with the registration statement.

(2) Format for projections. Traditionally, projections have been given for three financial items generally considered to be of primary importance to investors (revenues, net income (loss) and earnings (loss) per share), projection information need not necessarily be limited to these three items. However, management should take care to assure that the choice of items projected is not susceptible to misleading inferences through selective projection of only favorable items. It generally would be misleading to present sales or revenue projections without one of the foregoing measures of income. The period that appropriately may be covered by a projection depends to a large extent on the particular circumstances of the company involved. For certain companies in certain industries, a projection covering a two or three year period may be entirely reasonable. Other companies may not have a reasonable basis for projections beyond the current year.

(3) Investor understanding. Disclosures accompanying the projections should facilitate investor understanding of the basis for and limitations of projections. The Commission believes that investor understanding would be enhanced by disclosure of the assumptions which in management's opinion are most significant to the projections or are the key factors upon which the financial results of the enterprise depend and encourages disclosure of assumptions in a manner that will provide a framework for analysis of the projection. Management also should consider whether disclosure of the accuracy or inaccuracy of previous projections would provide investors with important insights into the limitations of projections.

(e) Commission policy on security ratings. In view of the importance of security ratings ("ratings") to investors and the marketplace, the Commission permits small business issuers to disclose ratings assigned by rating organizations to classes of debt securities, convertible debt securities and preferred stock in registration statements and periodic reports. In addition, the Commission permits, disclosure of ratings assigned by any nationally recognized statistical rating organizations ("NRSROs") in certain communications deemed not to be a prospectus ("tombstone advertisements"). Below are the Commission's views on important matters to be considered in disclosing security ratings.

(1)(i) If a small business issuer includes in a filing any rating(s) assigned to a class of securities, it should consider including any other rating assigned by a different NRSRO that is materially different. A statement that a security rating is not a recommendation to buy, sell or hold securities and that it may be subject

to revision or withdrawal at any time by the assigning rating organization should also be included.

> (ii) (A) *If the rating is included in a filing under the Securities Act, the written consent of any rating organization that is not a NRSRO whose rating is included should be filed. The consent of any NRSRO is not required. (See Rule 436(g) under the Securities Act.)*
>
> (B) *If a change in a rating already included is available before effectiveness of the registration statement, the small business issuer should consider including such rating change in the prospectus. If the rating change is material, consideration should be given to recirculating the preliminary prospectus.*
>
> (C) *If a materially different additional NRSRO rating or a material change in a rating already included becomes available during any period in which offers or sales are being made, the small business issuer should consider disclosing this information in a sticker to the prospectus.*
>
> (iii) *If there is a material change in the rating(s) assigned by any NRSRO(s) to any outstanding class(es) of securities of a reporting company, the registrant should consider filing a report on Form 8-K or other appropriate report under the Exchange Act disclosing such rating change.*

71000. BUSINESS

71010. DESCRIPTION OF BUSINESS (ITEM 101)

71011. General. This Regulation S-B item calls for disclosures relating to the development of the small business issuer during the most recent three years as well as a description of the business of the issuer, including certain specified disclosures if deemed material to an understanding of the issuer.

The description of business required under Regulation S-B is briefer and less detailed than that required in a filing subject to Regulation S-K. In recognition of the basic nature of small business issuers, a description of only the last three years of business development is needed as opposed to a five-year period for those filing under Regulation S-K.

71012. Text of Requirements.

Description of Business

(a) Business Development. Describe the development of the small business issuer during the last three years. If the small business issuer has not been in business for three years, give the same information for predecessor(s) of the small business issuer if there are any. This business development description should include:

(1) Form and year of organization;

(2) Any bankruptcy, receivership or similar proceeding; and

(3) Any material reclassification, merger, consolidation, or purchase or sale of a significant amount of assets not in the ordinary course of business.

(b) Business of Issuer. Briefly describe the business and include, to the extent material to an understanding of the issuer:

(1) Principal products or services and their markets;

(2) Distribution methods of the products or services;

(3) Status of any publicly announced new product or service;

(4) Competitive business conditions and the small business issuer's competitive position in the industry and methods of competition;

(5) Sources and availability of raw materials and the names of principal suppliers;

(6) Dependence on one or a few major customers;

(7) Patents, trademarks, licenses, franchises, concessions, royalty agreements or labor contracts, including duration;

(8) Need for any government approval of principal products or services. If government approval is necessary and the small business issuer has not yet received that approval, discuss the status of the approval within the government approval process;

(9) Effect of existing or probable governmental regulations on the business;

(10) Estimate of the amount spent during each of the last two fiscal years on research and development activities, and if applicable the extent to which the cost of such activities are borne directly by customers;

(11) Costs and effects of compliance with environmental laws (federal, state and local); and

(12) Number of total employees and number of full time employees.

71020. DESCRIPTION OF PROPERTY (ITEM 102)

This item calls for the location and condition of the principal plant(s) of the issuer. Where the issuer does not have complete ownership of the property, the limitations on the ownership need to be described.

The independent accountants are generally not consulted by registrants or their attorneys or otherwise involved in the preparation of the required Description of Property information. Accordingly, the text of these requirements is not reproduced here.

71030. LEGAL PROCEEDINGS (ITEM 103)

71031. General. Information needs to be provided where the small business issuer or its property is subject to any pending legal proceedings, except for those that are incidental to the business.

A notable distinction between the requirements of Regulation S-B and Regulation S-K is that the small business issuer is asked to disclose *any* legal proceeding to which it is a party (other than that which is incidental to the business), whereas Regulation S-K requires disclosures of *only* material pending legal proceedings (other than ordinary routine litigation incidental to the business).

71032. Text of Requirements.

Legal Proceedings

(a) If a small business issuer is a party to any pending legal proceeding (or its property is the subject of a pending legal proceeding), give the following information (no information is necessary as to routine litigation that is incidental to the business):

(1) name of court or agency where proceeding is pending;

(2) date proceeding began;

(3) principal parties;

(4) description of facts underlying the proceedings; and

(5) relief sought.

(b) Include the information called for by paragraphs (a)(1) through (5) of this Item for any proceeding that a governmental authority is contemplating (if the small business issuer is aware of the proceeding).

Instructions to Item 103

1. A proceeding that primarily involves a claim for damages does not need to be described if the amount involved, exclusive of interest and costs, does not exceed 10 percent of the current assets of the small business issuer. If any proceeding presents the same legal and factual issues as other proceedings pending or known to be contemplated, the amount involved in such other proceedings shall be included in computing such percentage.

990

2. The following types of proceedings with respect to the registrant are not "routine litigation incidental to the business" and, notwithstanding instruction 1 of this Item, must be described: bankruptcy, receivership, or similar proceeding.

3. Any proceeding that involves federal, state or local environmental laws must be described if it is material; involves a damages claim for more than 10 percent of the current assets of the issuer; or potentially involves more than $100,000 in sanctions and a governmental authority is a party.

4. Disclose any material proceeding to which any director, officer or affiliate of the issuer, any owner of record or beneficially of more than 5 percent of any class of voting securities of the small business issuer, or security holder is a party adverse to the small business issuer or has a material interest adverse to the small business issuer.

72000. SECURITIES OF THE REGISTRANT

72010. MARKET FOR COMMON EQUITY AND RELATED STOCKHOLDER MATTERS (ITEM 201)

This item sets forth the disclosure requirements pertaining to a registrant's common stock and related matters. The disclosures required include the securities markets on which the registrant's common stock is traded, the high and low prices for each quarterly period within the two most recent fiscal years and any subsequent interim period for which financial statements are included, the number of shareholders of each class of common equity, and information with respect to cash dividends declared on each class of common equity for the last two years. The dividend requirements specify that any restriction on the issuer's present or future ability to pay dividends is to be disclosed.

The information to be disclosed pursuant to these requirements is generally prepared by the small business issuer and/or its counsel, with little or no involvement on the part of the independent accountants. Consequently, the text of this item is not reproduced herein.

72020. DESCRIPTION OF SECURITIES (ITEM 202)

Item 202 calls for a description of any rights or preferences associated with any common or preferred stock, and any provisions that might delay, defer or prevent a change in control of the small business issuer. If a small business issuer is offering debt securities, the rules call for a description of the principal features of the debt securities being issued, as well as the identity of any trustee(s) designated by an indenture and the circumstances under which the trustee is empowered to act on behalf of the bondholders. Similar information needs to be presented concerning the material provisions of any other securities that are being registered.

The information to be disclosed pursuant to these requirements is generally prepared by the small business issuer and/or its counsel, with little or no involvement on the part of the independent accountants. Consequently, the text of this item is not reproduced herein.

73000. FINANCIAL INFORMATION

73030. MANAGEMENT'S DISCUSSION AND ANALYSIS OR PLAN OF OPERATION (ITEM 303)

73031. General. Where the issuer has had revenues in each of the last two years (or the last full year and latest interim period), a Management's Discussion and Analysis is required to be presented. Language that mirrors Item 303 of Regulation S-K has been included to clarify that the discussion and analysis should focus specifically on material events, trends and uncertainties known to management that could cause reported financial information not to be necessarily indicative of future operating results or financial condition.

Where the small business issuer does not meet the criteria described above for presenting Management's Discussion and Analysis, a Plan of Operation needs to be provided describing the issuer's business plan of operation for the next 12 months, including its ability to satisfy its cash requirements, a summary of product research and development, expected purchases or sales of plant and equipment, and any expected significant changes in the number of employees.

An interesting point with regard to Management's Discussion and Analysis is the recognition which Regulation S-B provides for small business issuers and their often brief history of operations. Although allowed under certain situations by Regulation S-B, Regulation S-K makes no mention of substituting a Plan of Operation for MD&A disclosures. In addition, where a small business issuer is required to make MD&A disclosures, the disclosures cover only the last two fiscal years, whereas Regulation S-K requires a discussion of the three-year period covered by the financial statements.

73032. Text of Requirements.

Management's Discussion and Analysis or Plan of Operation

Small business issuers that have not had revenues from operations in each of the last two fiscal years, or the last fiscal year and any interim period in the current fiscal year for which financial statements are furnished in the disclosure document, shall provide the information in paragraph (a) of this Item. All other issuers shall provide the information in paragraph (b) of this Item.

(a) Plan of operation.

SEC 73031

(1) Describe the small business issuer's plan of operation for the next twelve months. This description should include such matters as:

> *(i) a discussion of how long the small business issuer can satisfy its cash requirements and whether it will have to raise additional funds in the next twelve months;*

> *(ii) a summary of any product research and development that the small business issuer will perform for the term of the plan;*

> *(iii) any expected purchase or sale of plant and significant equipment; and*

> *(iv) any expected significant changes in the number of employees.*

(b) Management's Discussion and Analysis of Financial Condition and Results of Operations.

> *(1) Full fiscal years. Discuss the small business issuer's financial condition, changes in financial condition and results of operations for each of the last two fiscal years. This discussion should address the past and future financial condition and results of operation of the small business issuer, with particular emphasis on the prospects for the future. The discussion should also address those key variable and other qualitative and quantitative factors which are necessary to an understanding and evaluation of the small business issuer. If material, the small business issuer should disclose the following:*

>> *(i) Any known trends, events or uncertainties that have or are reasonably likely to have a material impact on the small business issuer's short-term or long-term liquidity;*

>> *(ii) Internal and external sources of liquidity;*

>> *(iii) Any material commitments for capital expenditures and the expected sources of funds for such expenditures;*

>> *(iv) Any known trends, events or uncertainties that have had or that are reasonably expected to have a material impact on the net sales or revenues or income from continuing operations;*

>> *(v) Any significant elements of income or loss that do not arise from the small business issuer's continuing operations;*

>> *(vi) The causes for any material changes from period to period in one or more line items of the small business issuer's financial statements; and*

(vii) Any seasonal aspects that had a material effect on the financial condition or results of operation.

(2) Interim Periods. If the small business issuer must include interim financial statements in the registration statement or report, provide a comparable discussion that will enable the reader to assess material changes in financial condition and results of operations since the end of the last fiscal year and for the comparable interim period in the preceding year.

Instructions to Item 303

1. The discussion and analysis shall focus specifically on material events and uncertainties known to management that would cause reported financial information not to be necessarily indicative of future operating results or of future financial condition.

2. Small business issuers are encouraged, but not required, to supply forward-looking information. This is distinguished from presently known data which will impact upon future operating results, such as known future increases in costs of labor or materials. This latter data may be required to be disclosed.

SEC 73032

73040. CHANGES IN AND DISAGREEMENTS WITH ACCOUNTANTS ON ACCOUNTING AND FINANCIAL DISCLOSURE (ITEM 304)

73041. General. The disclosure requirements regarding changes in and disagreements with accountants on accounting and financial disclosure during the two most recent fiscal years or any later interim period are intended to make investors aware of the following:

- Changes in accountants;

- Whether the accountants' report contained an adverse or disclaimer of opinion, or was otherwise modified;

- Whether a decision to change accountants was recommended or approved by the board of directors or an audit committee; and

- The nature of any disagreements with the former accountants (whether or not resolved) which, if not resolved, would have caused reference to have been made to the subject matter of the disagreement in the accountants' report.

While the disclosures required by this Item are similar in nature to the disclosures required by Regulation S-K, the depth and detail called for is not as extensive.

73042. Text of Requirements.

*Changes in and Disagreements with Accountants on
Accounting and Financial Disclosure*

(a) (1) If, during the small business issuer's two most recent fiscal years or any later interim period, the principal independent accountant or a significant subsidiary's independent accountant on whom the principal accountant expressed reliance in its report, resigned (or declined to stand for re-election) or was dismissed, then the small business issuer shall state:

(i) Whether the former accountant resigned, declined to stand for re-election or was dismissed and the date;

(ii) Whether the principal accountant's report on the financial statements for either of the past two years contained an adverse opinion or disclaimer

SEC 73042

of opinion, or was modified as to uncertainty, audit scope, or accounting principles, and also describe the nature of each such adverse opinion, disclaimer of opinion or modification;

(iii) Whether the decision to change accountants was recommended or approved by the board of directors or an audit or similar committee of the board of directors; and

(iv) (A) Whether there were any disagreements with the former accountant, whether or not resolved, on any matter of accounting principles or practices, financial statement disclosure, or auditing scope or procedure, which, if not resolved to the former accountant's satisfaction, would have caused it to make reference to the subject matter of the disagreement(s) in connection with its report; or

(B) The following information only if applicable. Indicate whether the former accountant advised the small business issuer that:

(1) internal controls necessary to develop reliable financial statements did not exist; or

(2) information has come to the attention of the former accountant which made the accountant unwilling to rely on management's representations, or unwilling to be associated with the financial statements prepared by management; or

(3) the scope of the audit should be expanded significantly, or information has come to the accountant's attention that the accountant has concluded will, or if further investigated might, materially impact the fairness or reliability of a previously issued audit report or the underlying financial statements, or the financial statements issued or to be issued covering the fiscal period(s) subsequent to the date of the most recent audited financial statements (including information that might preclude the issuance of an unqualified audit report), and the issue was not resolved to the accountant's satisfaction prior to its resignation or dismissal; and

(C) The subject matter of each such disagreement or event identified in response to paragraph (a)(1)(iv) of this Item;

(D) Whether any committee of the board of directors, or the board of directors, discussed the subject matter of the disagreement with the former accountant; and

(E) Whether the small business issuer has authorized the former accountant to respond fully to the inquiries of the successor accountant concerning the subject matter of each of such disagreements or events and, if not, describe the nature of and reason for any limitation.

(2) If during the period specified in paragraph (a)(1) of this Item, a new accountant has been engaged as either the principal accountant to audit the issuer's financial statements or as the auditor of a significant subsidiary and on whom the principal accountant is expected to express reliance in its report, identify the new accountant and the engagement date. Additionally, if the issuer (or someone on its behalf) consulted the new accountant regarding:

(i) The application of accounting principles to a specific completed or contemplated transaction, or the type of audit opinion that might be rendered on the small business issuer's financial statements and either written or oral advice was provided that was an important factor considered by the small business issuer in reaching a decision as to the accounting, auditing or financial reporting issue; or

(ii) Any matter that was the subject of a disagreement or event identified in response to paragraph (a)(1)(iv) of this Item, then the small business issuer shall:

(A) Identify the issues that were the subjects of those consultations;

(B) Briefly describe the views of the new accountant given to the small business issuer and, if written views were received by the small business issuer, file them as an exhibit to the report or registration statement;

(C) State whether the former accountant was consulted by the small business issuer regarding any such issues, and if so, describe the former accountant's views; and

(D) Request the new accountant to review the disclosure required by this Item before it is filed with the Commission and provide the new accountant the opportunity to furnish the small business issuer with a letter addressed to the Commission containing any new information, clarification of the small business issuer's expression of its views, or the respects in which it does not agree with the statements made in response to this Item. Any such letter shall be filed as an exhibit to the report or registration statement containing the disclosure required by this Item.

(3) The small business issuer shall provide the former accountant with a copy of the disclosures it is making in response to this Item no later than the day that

the disclosures are filed with the Commission. The small business issuer shall request the former accountant to furnish a letter addressed to the Commission stating whether it agrees with the statements made by the issuer and, if not, stating the respects in which it does not agree. The small business issuer shall file the letter as an exhibit to the report or registration statement containing this disclosure. If the letter is unavailable at the time of filing, the small business issuer shall request the former accountant to provide the letter so that it can be filed with the Commission within ten business days after the filing of the report or registration statement. Notwithstanding the ten business day period, the letter shall be filed within two business days of receipt. The former accountant may provide an interim letter highlighting specific areas of concern and indicating that a more detailed letter will be forthcoming within the ten business day period noted above. The interim letter, if any, shall be filed with the report or registration statement or by amendment within two business days of receipt.

(b) If the conditions in paragraphs (b)(1) through (b)(3) of this Item exist, the small business issuer shall describe the nature of the disagreement or event and the effect on the financial statements if the method had been followed which the former accountants apparently would have concluded was required (unless that method ceases to be generally accepted because of authoritative standards or interpretations issued after the disagreement or event):

(1) In connection with a change in accountants subject to paragraph (a) of this Item, there was any disagreement or event as described in paragraph (a)(1)(iv) of this Item;

(2) During the fiscal year in which the change in accountants took place or during the later fiscal year, there have been any transactions or events similar to those involved in such disagreement or event; and

(3) Such transactions or events were material and were accounted for or disclosed in a manner different from that which the former accountants apparently would have concluded was required.

Instructions to Item 304

1. The disclosure called for by paragraph (a) of this Item need not be provided if it has been previously reported as that term is defined in Rule 12b-2 under the Exchange Act; the disclosure called for by paragraph (a) of this Item must be provided, however, notwithstanding prior disclosure, if required pursuant to Item 9 of Schedule 14A. The disclosure called for by paragraph (b) of this Item must be furnished, where required, notwithstanding any prior disclosure about accountant changes or disagreements.

SEC 73042

2. When disclosure is required by paragraph (a) of this Item in an annual report to security holders pursuant to Rule 14a-3 or Rule 14c-3, or in a proxy or information statement filed pursuant to the requirements of Schedule 14A or 14C in lieu of a letter pursuant to paragraph (a)(2)(ii)(D) or (a)(3) of this Item, before filing such materials with or furnishing such materials to the Commission, the small business issuer shall furnish the disclosure required by paragraph (a) of this Item to each accountant who was engaged during the period set forth in paragraph (a) of this Item. If any such accountant believes that the statements made in response to paragraph (a) of this Item are incorrect or incomplete, it may present its views in a brief statement, ordinarily expected not to exceed 200 words, to be included in the annual report or proxy or information statement. This statement shall be submitted to the small business issuer within ten business days of the date the accountant receives the small business issuer's disclosure. Further, unless the written views of the newly engaged accountant required to be filed as an exhibit by paragraph (a)(2)(ii)(D) of this Item have been previously filed with the Commission, the small business issuer shall file a Form 8-K along with the annual report or proxy or information statement for the purpose of filing the written views as exhibits.

3. The information required by this Item need not be provided for a company being acquired by the small business issuer if such acquiree has not been subject to the filing requirements of either section 13(a) or 15(d) of the Exchange Act, or, because of section 12(i) of the Exchange Act, has not furnished an annual report to security holders pursuant to Rule 14a-3 or Rule 14c-3 for its latest fiscal year.

4. In determining whether any disagreement or reportable event has occurred, an oral communication from the engagement partner or another person responsible for rendering the accounting firm's opinion (or their designee) will generally suffice as the accountant advising the small business issuer of a reportable event or as a statement of a disagreement at the "decision-making level" within the accounting firm and require disclosure under this Item.

73100. FINANCIAL STATEMENTS (ITEM 310)

73101. General. Item 310 of Regulation S-B sets forth the financial statement requirements of "small business issuers." This item includes the requirements for annual and interim financial statements, financial statements of businesses acquired or to be acquired, pro forma financial information, real estate operations acquired or to be acquired, and limited partnerships.

FINANCIAL STATEMENT REQUIREMENTS

The financial statements that are required to accompany the various forms to be filed by "small business issuers" are generally subject to less onerous disclosure requirements under Regulation S-B than under Regulation S-X. While all financial statements need to be prepared in accordance with U.S. generally accepted accounting principles, the provisions of Regulation S-X regarding form and content do not apply, except for the report and qualifications of the independent accountants pursuant to Article 2. The SEC staff has indicated that to the extent FRRs and SABs contain guidance with respect to GAAP, they should be applied in preparing financial statements.

The filings of certain small business issuers, however, are subject to certain aspects of Regulation S-X. For example, foreign private issuers who qualify as small business issuers need to comply with Regulation S-X Rules 3-19 and 3-20, and be in general compliance with Item 18 of Form 20-F. Oil and gas producers must follow Article 4-10.

When pro forma presentations are necessary, the revised guidelines set forth in Rule 11-01 of Regulation S-X need to be considered.

The Commission indicated in adopting the release that small business issuers engaged in operations involving real estate, mining, insurance, banking, utilities, and oil and gas should also refer to the applicable industry guide. In addition, small business issuers that have roll-up transactions are required to furnish the disclosure required by subpart 900 of Regulation S-X.

Additionally, there are occasions when the SEC staff may permit the omission of one or more financial statements and/or the substitution of appropriate alternative statements.

Annual Financial Statements

The annual financial statements need to include an audited balance sheet for the most recent fiscal year or be as of a date within 135 days of the filing date if the small business issuer has been in existence for less than one fiscal year. In addition, audited statements of income, cash flows, and changes in stockholders' equity are required to be presented for each of the two fiscal years preceding the date of the balance sheet. In comparison, Regulation S-X requires balance sheets for the two most recent years and statements of income, cash flows and changes in stockholders' equity for the last three fiscal years.

It is important to note that when filing on a 1934 Act registration statement (i.e., Form 10-SB) audited financial statements for only the latest fiscal year are required if the audited financial statements for the earlier fiscal year are not otherwise available.

Interim Financial Statements

Interim financial statements may be unaudited and presented in a condensed format. Where required, they need to include a balance sheet as of the end of the most recent fiscal quarter, plus income statements and statements of cash flows for the period up to the balance sheet date and the comparable period of the preceding fiscal year. Other required disclosures include: any footnotes necessary for a fair presentation and appropriate disclosures regarding any material accounting changes accompanied by a preferability letter from the independent accountants.

In comparison, Regulation S-X requires an interim balance sheet as of the end of the most recent fiscal quarter and a balance sheet as of the end of the preceding fiscal year. Interim statements of income are required for the most recent fiscal quarter, for the year to date and for the corresponding periods of the prior year. Statements of cash flows are also required for the year to date and the corresponding period of the preceding year.

Special Situations

When a business combination has occurred or is probable, it is considered "significant" pursuant to Item 310 of Regulation S-B if any of the following tests are met:

- More than 10 percent of total assets are invested in or advanced to the acquiree.

- The proportionate share of the investee's assets exceeds 10 percent of the total assets.

- When the interest in income from continuing operations before taxes, extraordinary items and cumulative effect of accounting changes exceeds 10 percent of the acquirer's income.

Where this threshold of significance is passed, financial statements of the target company are required as follows:

SEC 73101

- Financial statements need to be furnished for periods prior to the date of acquisition, for the same periods for which the small business issuer is required to furnish financial statements.

- Financial statements covering fiscal years need to be audited.

- The separate audited balance sheet of the target is not required when the small business issuer's most recent audited balance sheet filed is for a date after the acquisition was consummated.

- If none of the conditions in the definitions of significance listed above:

  •• exceeds 20 percent and the required audited financial statements are not readily available, an automatic waiver of the required audited financial statement is granted.

  •• exceeds 40 percent and the required audited financial statements are not readily available, an automatic waiver is granted regarding the required audited financial statements for the fiscal year prior to the latest fiscal year.

  However, if unaudited or other financial information is available for any fiscal period for which an automatic waiver was granted, such information is required to be provided.

When a "significant" business combination has taken place in the most recent fiscal year or in a subsequent interim period, pro forma financial statements need to be furnished. The 10 percent test described above is used to determine whether such pro forma statements are required without regard to whether the combination is accounted for as a purchase or as a pooling of interests. These pro forma statements may be condensed and in a columnar format.

Similar reporting requirements occur when a real estate operation has been acquired or is to be acquired. In these cases audited income statements, tables showing estimated taxable operating results based on the most recent 12-month period, and a table showing estimated cash distribution per unit need to be furnished.

When the small business issuer is a limited partnership, balance sheets of the general partners need to be provided. If the general partner is a corporation or another partnership, an audited balance sheet for its most recently completed fiscal year is required. Where the general partner is a natural person, an unaudited balance sheet as of a recent date needs to be furnished.

SEC 73101

Age of Financial Statements

When financial statements included in a filing under Regulation S-B other than on a Form 10-KSB are of a date 135 days or more prior to the effective date of the registration statement, they are required to be updated to include statements for an interim period ending within 135 days of the effective date.

73102. Text of Requirements.

Financial Statements

NOTES—1. Financial statements of a small business issuer, its predecessors or any businesses to which the small business issuer is a successor shall be prepared in accordance with generally accepted accounting principles in the United States.

2. Regulation S-X, Form and Content of and Requirements for Financial Statements, shall not apply to the preparation of such financial statements, except that the report and qualifications of the independent accountant shall comply with the requirements of Article 2 of Regulation S-X, Articles 3-19 and 3-20 shall apply to financial statements of foreign private issuers and small business issuers engaged in oil and gas producing activities shall follow the financial accounting and reporting standards specified in Article 4-10 of Regulation S-X with respect to such activities. To the extent that Article 11-01 (Pro Forma Presentation Requirements) offers enhanced guidelines for the preparation, presentation and disclosure of pro forma financial information, small business issuers may wish to consider these items. Financial statements of foreign private issuers shall be prepared and presented in accordance with the requirements of Item 18 of Form 20-F except that Item 17 may be followed for financial statements included in filings other than registration statements for offerings of securities unless the only securities being offered are: (a) upon the exercise of outstanding rights granted by the issuer of the securities to be offered, if such rights are granted by the issuer of the securities to be offered, if such rights are granted on a pro rata basis to all existing securities holders of the class of securities to which the rights attach and there is no standby underwriting in the United States or similar arrangement; or (b) pursuant to a dividend or interest reinvestment plan; or (c) upon the conversion of outstanding convertible securities or upon the exercise of outstanding transferrable warrants issued by the issuer of the securities being offered, or by an affiliate of such issuer.

3. The Commission, where consistent with the protection of investors, may permit the omission of one or more of the financial statements or the substitution of appropriate statements of comparable character. The Commission by informal written notice may require the filing of other financial statements where necessary or appropriate.

(a) Annual Financial Statements. Small business issuers shall file an audited balance sheet as of the end of the most recent fiscal year, or as of a date within 135 days if the issuers existed for a period less than one fiscal year, and audited statements of income, cash flows and changes in stockholders' equity for each of the two fiscal years preceding the date of such audited balance sheet (or such shorter period as the registrant has been in business).

(b) Interim Financial Statements. Interim financial statements, which may be unaudited, shall include a balance sheet as of the end of the issuer's most recent fiscal quarter and income statements and statements of cash flows for the interim period up to the date of such balance sheet and the comparable period of the preceding fiscal year.

Instructions to Item 310(b)

1. Where Item 310 is applicable to a Form 10-QSB and the interim period is more than one quarter, income statements must also be provided for the most recent interim quarter and the comparable quarter of the preceding fiscal year.

2. Interim financial statements must include all adjustments which in the opinion of management are necessary in order to make the financial statements not misleading. An affirmative statement that the financial statements have been so adjusted must be included with the interim financial statements.

(1) Condensed Format. Interim financial statements may be condensed as follows:

(i) Balance sheets should include separate captions for each balance sheet component presented in the annual financial statements which represents 10 percent or more of total assets. Cash and retained earnings should be presented regardless of relative significance to total assets. Registrants which present a classified balance sheet in their annual financial statements should present totals for current assets and current liabilities.

(ii) Income statements should include net sales or gross revenue, each cost and expense category presented in the annual financial statements which exceeds 20 percent of sales or gross revenues, provision for income taxes, discontinued operations, extraordinary items and cumulative effects of changes in accounting principles or practices. (Financial institutions should substitute net interest income for sales for purposes of determining items to be disclosed.) Dividends per share should be presented.

SEC 73102

(iii) Cash flow statements should include cash flows from operating, investing and financing activities as well as cash at the beginning and end of each period and the increase or decrease in such balance.

(iv) Additional line items may be presented to facilitate the usefulness of the interim financial statements including their comparability with annual financial statements.

(2) Disclosure required and additional instructions as to Content.

(i) Footnotes. Footnote and other disclosures should be provided as needed for fair presentation and to ensure that the financial statements are not misleading.

(ii) Material Subsequent Events and Contingencies. Disclosure must be provided of material subsequent events and material contingencies notwithstanding disclosure in the annual financial statements.

(iii) Significant Equity Investees. Sales, gross profit, net income (loss) from continuing operations and net income must be disclosed for equity investees which constitute 20 percent or more of a registrant's consolidated assets, equity or income from continuing operations.

(iv) Significant Dispositions and Purchase Business Combinations. If a significant disposition or purchase business combination has occurred during the most recent interim period and the transaction required the filing of a Form 8-K, pro forma data must be presented which reflects revenue, income from continuing operations, net income and income per share for the current interim period and the corresponding interim period of the preceding fiscal year as though the transaction occurred at the beginning of the periods.

(v) Material Accounting Changes. Disclosure must be provided of the date and reasons for any material accounting change. The registrant's independent accountant must provide a letter in the first Form 10-QSB filed subsequent to the change indicating whether or not the change is to a preferable method. Disclosure must be provided of any retroactive change to prior period financial statements, including the effect of any such change on income and income per share.

(vi) Development Stage Companies. A registrant in the development stage must provide cumulative from inception financial information.

(c) Financial Statements of Businesses Acquired or to be Acquired.

(1) Financial statements for the periods specified in paragraph (c) (3) of this Item should be furnished if any of the following conditions exist:

SEC 73102

(i) Consummation of a significant business combination accounted for as a purchase has occurred or is probable (the term "purchase" encompasses the purchase of an interest in a business accounted for by the equity method); or

(ii) Consummation of a significant business combination to be accounted for as a pooling is probable.

(2) A business combination is considered significant if a comparison of the most recent annual financial statements of the business acquired or to be acquired and the small business issuer's most recent annual financial statements filed at or prior to the date of acquisition indicates that the business acquired or to be acquired meets any of the following conditions:

(i) The small business issuer's and its other subsidiaries' investments in and advances to the acquiree exceeds 10 percent of the total assets of the small business issuer and its subsidiaries consolidated as of the end of the most recently completed fiscal year (for a proposed business combination to be accounted for as a pooling of interests, this condition is also met when the number of common shares exchanged or to be exchanged by the small business issuer exceeds 10 percent of its total common shares outstanding at the date the combination is initiated) or

(ii) The small business issuer's and its other subsidiaries' proportionate share of the total assets (after intercompany eliminations) of the acquiree exceeds 10 percent of the total assets of the registrants and its subsidiaries consolidated as of the end of the most recently completed fiscal year, or

(iii) The small business issuer's equity in the income from continuing operations before income taxes, extraordinary items and cumulative effect of a change in accounting principles of the acquiree exceeds 10 percent of such income of the small business issuer and its subsidiaries consolidated for the most recently completed fiscal year.

Computational note: For purposes of making the prescribed income test the following guidance should be applied: If income of the small business issuer and its subsidiaries consolidated for the most recent fiscal year is at least 10 percent lower than the average of the income for the last five fiscal years, such average income should be substituted for purposes of the computation. Any loss years should be omitted for purposes of computing average income.

SEC 73102

(3) (i) Financial statements shall be furnished for the periods prior to the date of acquisition, for the same periods for which the small business issuer is required to furnish financial statements. The financial statements covering fiscal years shall be audited.

(ii) If none of the conditions in the definitions of significant subsidiary in paragraph (c)(2) of this Item exceeds 20% and the required audited financial statements of the acquired business are not readily available, an automatic waiver of the required audited financial statements is granted. If none of the conditions in the definitions of significant subsidiary exceeds 40% and the required audited financial statements are not readily available, an automatic waiver is granted with respect to the required audited financial statements for the fiscal year preceding the latest fiscal year. If unaudited financial statements or other financial information is available for any fiscal period for which an automatic waiver is granted, then such unaudited financial statements or other information shall be furnished.

(iii) The separate audited balance sheet of the acquired business is not required when the small business issuer's most recent audited balance sheet filed is for a date after the acquisition was consummated.

(4) If consummation of more than one transaction has occurred or is probable, the significance tests shall be made using the aggregate impact of the businesses and the financial statements may be presented on a combined basis, if appropriate.

(5) If the small business issuer made a significant business acquisition subsequent to the latest fiscal year end and filed a report on Form 8-K which included audited financial statements of such acquired business for the periods required by paragraph (c)(3) and the pro forma financial information required by paragraph (d) of this Item, the determination of significance may be made by using the pro forma amounts for the latest fiscal year in the report on Form 8-K rather than by using the historical amounts for the latest fiscal year of the registrant. The tests may not be made by "annualizing" data. Notwithstanding the above, if a Form 8-K was filed to report a significant acquisition but audited financial statements were not furnished pursuant to the automatic waiver provisions of paragraph (c)(3) of this Item, the determination of significance may not be made using the pro forma amounts for the latest fiscal year; however, upon written request from the issuer, the Commission will consider permitting the use of previously filed pro forma financial information as the basis for measurement for the significance tests.

SEC 73102

(d) Pro Forma Financial Information.

(1) Pro forma information shall be furnished if any of the following conditions exist (for purposes of this Item, the term "purchase" encompasses the purchase of an interest in a business accounted for by the equity method):

(i) During the most recent fiscal year or subsequent interim period for which a balance sheet is required by paragraph (b) of this Item, a significant business combination accounted for as a purchase has occurred;

(ii) After the date of the most recent balance sheet filed pursuant to paragraph (a) or (b) of this Item, consummation of a significant business combination accounted for as a purchase or a pooling has occurred or is probable.

(2) The provisions of paragraphs (c)(2) and (4) of this Item apply to paragraph (d) of this Item.

(3) Pro forma statements should be condensed, in columnar form showing pro forma adjustments and results and should include the following:

(i) If the transaction was consummated during the most recent fiscal year or subsequent interim period, pro forma statements of income reflecting the combined operations of the entities for the latest fiscal year and interim period, if any; or

(ii) If consummation of the transaction has occurred or is probable after the date of the most recent balance sheet required by paragraph (a) or (b) of this Item, a pro forma balance sheet giving effect to the combination as of the date of the most recent balance sheet. For a purchase, pro forma statements of income reflecting the combined operations of the entities for the latest fiscal year and interim period, if any, and for a pooling of interests, pro forma statements of income for all periods for which income statements of the small business issuer are required.

(e) Real Estate Operations Acquired or to be Acquired. If, during the period for which income statements are required, the small business issuer has acquired one or more properties which in the aggregate are significant, or since the date of the latest balance sheet required by paragraph (a) or (b) of this Item, has acquired or proposes to acquire one or more properties which in the aggregate are significant, the following shall be furnished with respect to such properties:

(1) Audited income statements (not including earnings per unit) for the two most recent years, which shall exclude items not comparable to the proposed future operations of the property such as mortgage interest, leasehold rental, depreciation, corporate expenses and federal and state income taxes; Provided, however, That such audited statements need be presented for only the most recent fiscal year if:

(i) the property is not acquired from a related party;

(ii) material factors considered by the small business issuer in assessing the property are described with specificity in the registration statement with regard to the property, including source of revenue (including, but not limited to, competition in the rental market, comparative rents, occupancy rates) and expenses (including but not limited to, utilities, ad valorem tax rates, maintenance expenses, capital improvements anticipated); and

(iii) the small business issuer indicates that, after reasonable inquiry, it is not aware of any material factors relating to the specific property other than those discussed in response to paragraph (e)(1)(ii) of this Item that would cause the reported financial information not to be necessarily indicative of future operating results.

(2) If the property will be operated by the small business issuer, a statement shall be furnished showing the estimated taxable operating results of the small business issuer based on the most recent 12-month period including such adjustments as can be factually supported. If the property will be acquired subject to a net lease, the estimated taxable operating results shall be based on the rent to be paid for the first year of the lease. In either case, the estimated amount of cash to be made available by operations shall be shown. Disclosure must be provided of the principal assumptions which have been made in preparing the statements of estimated taxable-operating results and cash to be made available by operations.

(3) If appropriate under the circumstances, a table should be provided which shows, for a limited number of years, the estimated cash distribution per unit indicating the portion reportable as taxable income and the portion representing a return of capital with an explanation of annual variations, if any. If taxable net income per unit will be greater than the cash available for distribution per unit, that fact and approximate year of occurrence shall be stated, if significant.

(f) Limited Partnerships.

(1) Small business issuers which are limited partnerships must provide the balance sheets of the general partners as described in paragraphs (f)(2) through (f)(4) of this Item.

(2) Where a general partner is a corporation, the audited balance sheet of the corporation as of the end of its most recently completed fiscal year must be filed. Receivables, other than trade receivables, from affiliates of the general partner should be deducted from shareholders' equity of the general partner. Where an affiliate has committed itself to increase or maintain the general partner's capital, the audited balance sheet of such affiliate must also be presented.

(3) Where a general partner is a partnership, there shall be filed an audited balance sheet of such partnership as of the end of its most recently completed fiscal year.

(4) Where the general partner is a natural person, there shall be filed, as supplemental information, a balance sheet of such natural person as of a recent date. Such balance sheet need not be audited. The assets and liabilities should be carried at estimated fair market value, with provisions for estimated income taxes on unrealized gains. The net worth of such general partner(s), based on such balance sheet(s), singly or in the aggregate, shall be disclosed in the registration statement.

(g) Age of Financial Statements. At the date of filing, financial statements included in filings other than filings on Form 10-KSB must be not less current than financial statements which would be required in Forms 10-KSB and 10-QSB if such reports were required to be filed. If required financial statements are as of a date 135 days or more prior to the date a registration statement becomes effective or proxy material is expected to be mailed, the financial statements shall be updated to include financial statements for an interim period ending within 135 days of the effective or expected mailing date. Interim financial statements should be prepared and presented in accordance with paragraph (b) of this Item:

(1) When the anticipated effective or mailing date falls within 45 days after the end of the fiscal year, the filing may include financial statements only as current as the end of the third fiscal quarter; Provided, however, That if the audited financial statements for the recently completed fiscal year are available or become available prior to effectiveness or mailing, they must be included in the filing;

(2) If the effective date or anticipated mailing date falls after 45 days but within 90 days of the end of the small business issuer's fiscal year, the small business issuer is not required to provide the audited financial statements for such year end provided that the following conditions are met:

(i) If the small business issuer is a reporting company, all reports due must have been filed;

(ii) For the most recent fiscal year for which audited financial statements are not yet available, the small business issuer reasonably and in good faith expects to report income from continuing operations before taxes; and

(iii) For at least one of the two fiscal years immediately preceding the most recent fiscal year the small business issuer reported income from continuing operations before taxes.

74000. MANAGEMENT AND CERTAIN SECURITY HOLDERS

74010. DIRECTORS, EXECUTIVE OFFICERS, PROMOTERS AND CONTROL PERSONS (ITEM 401)

Item 401 requires disclosures providing information regarding the following:

- Identity of directors and executive officers

- Identity of significant employees

- Family relationships

- Involvement in certain legal proceedings.

The four points listed above require far fewer disclosures than required by Regulation S-K, particularly as to the business experience, background and other directorships held by each director, executive officer or nominee for such position.

74020. EXECUTIVE COMPENSATION (ITEM 402)

74021. General. In October 1992, the SEC amended its rules regarding disclosure of executive compensation in proxy statements, periodic reports, and other filings under the 1934 Act, and in registration statements under the 1933 Act. The SEC's goal is to ensure that the marketplace receives information about executive compensation that is easier to understand and more relevant to proxy voting and investment decisions.

The amended rules require that disclosures be made in a series of tables clearly setting forth each element of compensation paid, earned, or awarded in a given year. General descriptions of most compensation plans will no longer be required.

The information to be disclosed pursuant to these requirements is the responsibility of the registrant and/or its counsel. Since the independent accountants are sometimes consulted in the process of assembling this information, the following summary may be helpful in understanding these requirements.

74022. Summary of Executive Compensation Disclosure Requirements.
The disclosures are required for:

- The chief executive officer (CEO) or the individual acting in such capacity, regardless of the amount of compensation.

- The four most highly paid senior executive officers, other than the CEO, who earn more than $100,000 per year in salary and bonus.

A summary compensation table replaced the traditional cash compensation table required under the former rules and is required to disclose the annual salary, bonuses, and all other compensation awards and payouts of the named officers. Stock options should be disclosed as the number awarded and should not be assigned a value in this table. The table should cover a three-year period, in the following prescribed format, although small business issuers may phase in the entire table over three years.

SUMMARY COMPENSATION TABLE

					Long-Term Compensation			
	Annual Compensation					Awards	Payouts	
(a)	(b)	(c)	(d)	(e)	(f)	(g)	(h)	(i)
				Other	Restricted			All
Name and				Annual	Stock	Options/	LTIP	Other
Principal		Salary	Bonus	Compensation	Award(s)	SARs	Payouts	Compensation
Position	Year	($)	($)	($)	($)	(#)	($)	($)
	1992							
	1991							
	1990							

Other components of compensation are required to be disclosed in prescribed formats as follows:

- Two tables detailing options and stock appreciation rights (SARs) are required.

  - One table summarizes the number and terms of options/SARs granted during the fiscal year.

  - The second table summarizes exercises of options during the last fiscal year by the named executives (including the "net value" received, i.e., the difference between the fair market value of the securities as of the exercise date and the exercise price of the option) and the number of, and the spread (the difference between the current market price of the stock and the exercise price of the option) on, unexercised options that they hold at fiscal year-end.

- A table outlining awards in the last fiscal year under long-term incentive plans, such as phantom stock grants and restricted stock grants that vest after a period of time upon satisfaction of a performance goal.

Disclosure is also required of:

- Employment and severance agreements (with payments of more than $100,000) with respect to the named executive officers.

- Standard compensation arrangements for directors (payments for services on the board and committees), as well as any other compensation for services (such as consulting contracts).

In addition to the above, if the registrant adjusted or amended the exercise price of outstanding stock options or SARs during the last fiscal year, the compensation committee (or board committee performing similar functions) is required to explain the repricing in reasonable detail including the basis for the repricing. This disclosure is only required, however, in a registrant's proxy filing or information statement relating to an annual meeting of security holders at which directors are to be elected (or special meeting or written consents in lieu of a meeting). This information will not be deemed to be incorporated by reference into any 1933 Act or 1934 Act filing unless the registrant specifically incorporates it by reference.

74030. SECURITY OWNERSHIP OF CERTAIN BENEFICIAL OWNERS AND MANAGEMENT (ITEM 403)

This item specifies the information to be disclosed as to the ownership of the small business issuer's securities by certain beneficial owners and management.

Paragraph (a) requires the following tabular information with respect to any person (including any "group") who is known to the small business issuer to be the beneficial owner of more than five percent of any class of the small business issuer's voting securities.

(1)	(2)	(3)	(4)
Title of Class	Name and Address of Beneficial Owner	Amount and Nature of Beneficial Owner	Percent of Class

SEC 74022

The determination of beneficial ownership is a legal issue, which should not be addressed by an independent accountant.

Paragraph (b) requires disclosure of the information in all columns of the foregoing tabulation for each class of equity securities of the small business issuer or its parent beneficially owned by all directors and nominees (naming them), by each of the named executive officers as determined in Item 402 (see section 74022) and by all directors and officers of the small business issuer as a group (without naming them).

Paragraph (c) requires disclosure of any known arrangements that could result in a change in control of the small business issuer.

The information to be disclosed pursuant to these requirements is generally prepared by the small business issuer and/or its counsel, with little or no involvement on the part of the independent accountants. Consequently the text of this item is not reproduced herein.

74040. CERTAIN RELATIONSHIPS AND RELATED TRANSACTIONS (ITEM 404)

Item 404 requires disclosure of:

- Transactions involving more than $60,000 in which certain specified persons have a material interest;

- Transactions involving the small business issuer and its executive officers; and

- Transactions involving the "immediate family" (as defined) of such specified persons.

Independent accountants are generally not consulted by small business issuers, their attorneys, or others in the preparation of the information required pursuant to these requirements. However, it is advisable for the independent accountants to review this section to ensure that all related party transactions have been taken into consideration in the financial statement presentations and disclosures.

75000. REGISTRATION STATEMENT AND PROSPECTUS PROVISIONS

The registration statement and prospectus provisions of regulation S-B contain most of the instructions as to the information required in a registration statement filed by a small business issuer. Two of the items in this section, items 503 and 512, are discussed herein. The remaining items in this section differ from their corresponding

SEC 75000

1016

items in Regulation S-K largely in the depth of detail required as is seen throughout Regulation S-B.

A listing of all the items included in the registration statement and prospectus provisions section follows:

501. Front of Registration Statement and Outside Front Cover of Prospectus
502. Inside Front and Outside Back Cover Pages of Prospectus
    (a) Available information
    (b) Reports to security holders
    (c) Incorporation by reference
    (d) Stabilization
    (e) Delivery of prospectuses by dealers
    (f) Table of contents
503. Summary Information and Risk Factors
    (a) Summary
    (b) Address and telephone number
    (c) Risk factors
504. Use of Proceeds
505. Determination of Offering Price
    (a) Common equity
    (b) Warrants, rights and convertible securities
506. Dilution
507. Selling Security Holders
508. Plan of Distribution
    (a) Underwriters and underwriting obligation
    (b) New underwriters
    (c) Other distributions
    (d) Underwriter's representative on the board of directors
    (e) Indemnification of underwriters
    (f) Dealers' compensation
    (g) Finders
    (h) Discretionary accounts
509. Interest of Named Experts and Counsel
510. Disclosure of Commission Position on Indemnification for Securities Act Liabilities
511. Other Expenses of Issuance and Distribution
512. Undertakings
    (a) Rule 415 offering
    (b) Warrants and rights offerings
    (c) Competitive bids
    (d) Equity offerings of nonreporting small business issuers
    (e) Request for acceleration of effective date

75030. SUMMARY INFORMATION AND RISK FACTORS (ITEM 503)

75031. General. Paragraph (a) of Item 503 stipulates that a prospectus summary should be provided whenever the length or complexity of the prospectus warrants its inclusion in the interest of fair and adequate disclosure. Paragraph (b) requires disclosure of the location of the small business issuer's principal executive offices, and paragraph (c) requires prominent disclosure as to the speculative nature, where applicable, or any risk involved in the offering.

By way of contrast, Regulation S-K requires, in addition to the three items of information listed above, a calculation of the ratio of earnings to fixed charges according to a complex set of rules and definitions.

75032. Text of Requirements.

Summary Information and Risk Factors

(a) Summary. A summary of the information contained in the prospectus where the length and complexity of the prospectus make a summary useful.

(b) Address and telephone number. In the beginning of the prospectus the complete mailing address and the telephone number of their principal executive offices.

(c) Risk factors. Immediately following the cover page of the prospectus or the summary section, discuss any factors that make the offering speculative or risky. These factors may include no operating history, no recent profit from operations, poor financial position, the kind of business in which the small business issuer is engaged or proposes to engage, or no market for the small business issuer's securities.

75120. UNDERTAKINGS (ITEM 512)

75121. General. Item 512 sets forth the requirements as to undertakings that under certain conditions must be included in registration statements filed under the 1933 Act.

Paragraph (a) deals with Rule 415, whose requirements are discussed in section 19200 of this manual. The remaining paragraphs deal with other types of 1933 Act filing situations.

The undertaking representations are, in essence, acknowledgements by the small business issuer that it will keep the registration statement and the prospectus current as required by the 1933 Act. Although these are legal determinations, the auditor should be familiar with the provisions. While these disclosures are similar to those required by Regulation S-K, they are sufficiently different to warrant the inclusion of the text of Item 512 which follows.

75122. Text of Requirements.

Undertakings

Include each of the following undertakings that apply to the offering.

(a) Rule 415 Offering. If the small business issuer is registering securities under Rule 415 of the Securities Act, that the small business issuer will:

(1) File, during any period in which it offers or sells securities, a post-effective amendment to this registration statement to:

(i) Include any prospectus required by section 10(a)(3) of the Securities Act;

(ii) Reflect in the prospectus any facts or events which, individually or together, represent a fundamental change in the information in the registration statement; and

(iii) Include any additional or changed material information on the plan of distribution.

NOTE: Small business issuers do not need to give the statements in paragraphs (a)(1)(i) and (a)(1)(ii) of this Item if the registration statement is on Form S-3 or S-8, and the information required in a post-effective amendment is incorporated by reference from periodic reports filed by the small business issuer under the Exchange Act.

(2) For determining liability under the Securities Act, treat each post-effective amendment as a new registration statement of the securities offered, and the offering of the securities at that time to be the initial bona fide offering.

(3) File a post-effective amendment to remove from registration any of the securities that remain unsold at the end of the offering.

(b) Warrants and rights offerings. If the small business issuer will offer the securities to existing security holders under warrants or rights and the small business issuer will reoffer to the public any securities not taken by security holders, with any modifications that suit the particular case—the small business issuer will supplement the prospectus, after the end of the subscription period, to include the results of the subscription offer, the transactions by the underwriters during the subscription period, the amount of unsubscribed securities that the underwriters will purchase and the terms of any later reoffering. If the underwriters make any public offering of the securities on terms different from those on the cover page of the prospectus, the small business issuer will file a post-effective amendment to state the terms of such offering.

(c) Competitive bids. If the small business issuer is offering securities at competitive bidding, with modifications to suit the particular case, the small business issuer will:

(1) use its best efforts to distribute before the opening of bids, to prospective bidders, underwriters, and dealers, a reasonable number of copies of a prospectus that meet the requirements of section 10(a) of the Securities Act, and relating to the securities offered at competitive bidding, as contained in the registration statement, together with any supplements; and

(2) file an amendment to the registration statement reflecting the result of bidding, the terms of the reoffering and related matters where required by the applicable form, not later than the first use, authorized by the issuer after the opening of bids, of a prospectus relating to the securities offered at competitive bidding, unless the issuer proposes no further public offering of such securities by the issuer or by the purchasers.

(d) Equity offerings of nonreporting small business issuers. If a small business issuer that before the offering had no duty to file reports with the Commission under section 13(a) or 15(d) of the Exchange Act is registering equity securities for sale in an underwritten offering—the small business issuer will provide to the underwriter at the closing specified in the underwriting agreement certificates in such denominations and registered in such names as required by the underwriter to permit prompt delivery to each purchaser.

SEC 75122

(e) Request for acceleration of effective date. If the small business issuer will request acceleration of the effective date of the registration statement under Rule 461 under the Securities Act, include the following:

> *Insofar as indemnification for liabilities arising under the Securities Act of 1933 (the "Act") may be permitted to directors, officers and controlling persons of the small business issuer pursuant to the foregoing provisions, or otherwise, the small business issuer has been advised that in the opinion of the Securities and Exchange Commission such indemnification is against public policy as expressed in the Act and is, therefore, unenforceable.*

In the event that a claim for indemnification against such liabilities (other than the payment by the small business issuer of expenses incurred or paid by a director, officer or controlling person of the small business issuer in the successful defense of any action, suit or proceeding) is asserted by such director, officer or controlling person in connection with the securities being registered, the small business issuer will, unless in the opinion of its counsel the matter has been settled by controlling precedent, submit to a court of appropriate jurisdiction the question whether such indemnification by it is against public policy as expressed in the Securities Act and will be governed by the final adjudication of such issue.

(f) If the issuer relies on Rule 430A under the Securities Act, that the small business issuer will:

> *(1) For determining any liability under the Securities Act, treat the information omitted from the form of prospectus filed as part of this registration statement in reliance upon Rule 430A and contained in a form of prospectus filed by the small business issuer under Rule 424(b)(1), or (4) or 497(h) under the Securities Act as part of this registration statement as of the time the Commission declared it effective.*

> *(2) For determining any liability under the Securities Act, treat each post-effective amendment that contains a form of prospectus as a new registration statement for the securities offered in the registration statement, and that offering of the securities at that time as the initial bona fide offering of those securities.*

76000. EXHIBITS (ITEM 601)

76011. General. The Regulation S-B Exhibits requirements consolidate and standardize the Commission's requirements relating to the filing of exhibits. Reference should be made to the exhibit table in the text of the requirements for a summary of the exhibits to be included in most of the frequently used 1933 and 1934 Act forms.

To facilitate the identification and location of exhibits, the inclusion of an exhibit index is required and the first page of the document being filed must specify the location of this index.

Because an exhibit index is required by each filing, the full text of the requirements is included as well as a table indicating which exhibits are required by the forms subject to Regulation S-B.

76012. Text of Requirements.

Exhibits

(a) Exhibits and index of exhibits.

(1) The exhibits required by the exhibit table must be filed or incorporated by reference. The Financial Data Schedule required by paragraph (b)(27) of this Item must be submitted to the Commission as provided in paragraph (c) of this Item.

(2) Each filing must have an index of exhibits. The exhibit index must list exhibits in the same order as the exhibit table. If the exhibits are incorporated by reference, this fact should be noted in the exhibit index. In the manually signed registration statement or report, the exhibit index should give the page number of each exhibit.

(3) If a material contract or plan of acquisition, reorganization, arrangement, liquidation or succession is executed or becomes effective during the reporting period covered by a Form 10-QSB or Form 10-KSB, it must be filed as an exhibit to the Form 10-QSB or Form 10-KSB filed for the same period. Any amendment or modification to a previously filed exhibit to a Form 10-SB, 10-KSB or 10-QSB document must be filed as an exhibit to a Form 10-QSB or 10-KSB. The amendment or modification does not need to be filed if the previously filed exhibit would not be currently required.

1022

Instructions to Item 601(a)

1. If an exhibit (other than an opinion or consent) is filed in preliminary form and is later changed to include only interest, dividend or conversion rates, redemption or conversion prices, purchase or offering prices, underwriters' or dealers' commissions, names, addresses or participation of underwriters or similar matters and the information appears elsewhere in the registration statement or a prospectus, no amendment need be filed.

2. Small business issuers may file copies of each exhibit, rather than originals, except as otherwise specifically noted.

3. Electronic filings. Whenever an exhibit is filed in paper pursuant to a hardship exemption, the letter "P" (paper) should be placed next to the exhibit in the list of exhibits required by Item 601(a)(2) of this Rule. Whenever an electronic confirming copy of an exhibit is filed pursuant to a temporary hardship exemption, the exhibit index should specify where the confirming electronic copy can be located; in addition, the designation "CE" (confirming electronic) should be placed next to the listed exhibit in the exhibit index.

(b) Description of exhibits. Below is a description of each document listed in the exhibit table. [Refer to page 1023]

(1) Underwriting agreement. *Each agreement with a principal underwriter for the distribution of the securities. If the terms have been determined and the securities are to be registered on Form S-3, the agreement may be filed on Form 8-K after the effectiveness of the registration statement.*

(2) Plan of purchase, sale, reorganization, arrangement, liquidation or succession. *Any such plan described in the filing. Schedules or attachments may be omitted if they are listed in the index and provided to the Commission upon request.*

(3) Articles of incorporation and by-laws.

(i) A complete copy of the articles of incorporation. Whenever amendments to articles of incorporation are filed, a complete copy of the articles as amended shall be filed.

(ii) A complete copy of the by-laws. Whenever amendments to the by-laws are filed, a complete copy of the by-laws as amended shall be filed.

(4) Instruments defining the rights of security holders, including indentures.

(i) All instruments that define the rights of holders of the equity or debt securities that the issuer is registering, including the pages from the articles of incorporation or by-laws that define those rights.

Exhibit Table

	Securities Act Forms						Exchange Act Forms		
	SB-2	S-2	S-3	S-4***	S-8	10-SB	8-K	10-OSB	10-KSB
(1) Underwriting agreement.	X	X	X	X			X		X
(2) Plan of acquisition, reorganization, arrangement, liquidations, or succession.	X	X	X	X		X	X	X	X
(3) (i) Articles of incorporation.	X			X		X	X	X	X
(ii) By-laws.	X			X		X	X	X	X
(4) Instruments defining the rights of holders, including indentures.	N/A	N/A	N/A	N/A	N/A	N/A	N/A	N/A	N/A
(5) Opinion re: legality.	X	X	X	X	X	X			X
(6) No exhibit required.	X	X				X			X
(7) Opinion re: liquidation preference.	X	X	X	X		X			X
(8) Opinion re: tax matters.	X	X		X		X			X
(9) Voting trust agreement.	X	X		X		X			X
(10) Material contracts.	X	X	X	X		X	X	X	X
(11) Statement re: computation of per share earnings.	X	X		X		X			X
(12) No exhibit required.	N/A	N/A	N/A	N/A	N/A	N/A	N/A	N/A	N/A
(13) Annual or quarterly reports, Form 10-Q.*	X	X	X	X		X			X
(14) Material foreign patents.	X	X	X	X	X	X			X
(15) Letter on unaudited interim financial information.	X	X	X	X	X	X	X	X	X
(16) Letter on change in certifying accountant.****	X	X		X			X		X
(17) Letter on director resignation.	X			X			X		X
(18) Letter on change in accounting principles.									
(19) Reports furnished to security holders.									
(20) Other documents or statements to security holders.	X	X		X		X	X	X	X
(21) Subsidiaries of the registrant.						X			X
(22) Published report regarding matters submitted to vote.	X	X	X	X	X	X	X**	X**	X**
(23) Consent of experts and counsel.	X	X	X	X	X	X	X	X	X
(24) Power of attorney.	X	X	X	X	X	X			X
(25) Statement of eligibility of trustee.	X	X	X	X	X	X			X
(26) Invitations for competitive bids.	X	X	X	X		X			X
(27) Financial Data Schedule.*****	X	X	X	X	X	X	X	X	X
(28) Information from reports furnished to state insurance authorities.	X	X		X		X			X
(29) through (98) [Reserved]									
(99) Additional Exhibits.	X	X	X	X	X	X	X	X	X

* Only if incorporated by reference into a prospectus and delivered to holders along with the prospectus as permitted by the registration statement; or in the case of a Form 10-KSB, where the annual report is incorporated by reference into the text of the Form 10-KSB.

** Where the opinion of the expert or counsel has been incorporated into a previously filed Securities Act registration statement.

*** An issuer need not provide an exhibit if: (1) an election was made under Form S-4 to provide S-2 or S-3 disclosure; and (2) the form selected (S-2 or S-3) would not require the company to provide the exhibit.

**** If required under item 304 of Regulation S-B.

***** Financial Data Schedules shall be filed by electronic filers only. Such schedule shall be filed only when a filing includes annual and/or interim financial statements that have not been previously included in a filing with the Commission. See item 601(c) of Regulation S-B.

(ii) All instruments defining the rights of holders of long term debt unless the total amount of debt covered by the instrument does not exceed 10 percent of the total assets of the small business issuer.

(iii) Copies of indentures to be qualified under the Trust Indenture Act of 1939 shall include an itemized table of contents and a cross reference sheet showing the location of the provisions inserted in accordance with Sections 310 through 318(a) of that Act.

(5) Opinion on legality.

(i) An opinion of counsel on the legality of the securities being registered stating whether they will, when sold, be legally issued, fully paid and non-assessable, and, if debt securities, whether they will be binding obligations of the small business issuer.

(ii) If the securities being registered are issued under a plan that is subject to the requirements of ERISA furnish either:

(A) An opinion of counsel which confirms compliance with ERISA; or

(B) A copy of the Internal Revenue Service determination letter that the plan is qualified under section 401 of the Internal Revenue Code.

If the plan is later amended, the small business issuer must have the opinion of counsel and the IRS determination letter updated to confirm compliance and qualification.

(6) No Exhibit Required.

(7) Opinion on liquidation preference. *If the liquidation preference of shares exceeds their par or stated value, an opinion of counsel as to whether there are any resulting restrictions on surplus. The opinion should also state any remedies available to security holders before or after payment of any dividend that would reduce surplus to an amount less than the amount of such excess. The opinion shall cite to applicable constitutional and statutory provisions and controlling case law.*

(8) Opinion on tax matters. *If tax consequences of the transaction are material to an investor, an opinion of counsel, an independent public or certified public accountant or, a revenue ruling from the Internal Revenue Service, supporting the tax matters and consequences to the shareholders. The exhibit is required for filings to which Securities Act Industry Guide 5 applies.*

(9) Voting trust agreement and amendments.

SEC 76012

(10) Material contracts.

(i) Every material contract, not made in the ordinary course of business, that will be performed after the filing of the registration statement or report or was entered into not more than two years before such filing. Also include the following contracts:

(A) Any contract to which directors, officers, promoters, voting trustees, security holders named in the registration statement or report, or underwriters are parties other than contracts involving only the purchase or sale of current assets having a determinable market price, at such market price;

(B) Any contract upon which the small business issuer's business is substantially dependent, such as contracts with principal customers, principal suppliers, franchise agreements, etc.;

(C) Any contract for the purchase or sale of any property, plant or equipment for a consideration exceeding 15 percent of such assets of the small business issuer; or

(D) Any material lease under which a part of the property described in the registration statement or report is held by the small business issuer.

(ii) (A) Any management contract or any compensatory plan, contract or arrangement, including but not limited to plans relating to options, warrants or rights, pension, retirement or deferred compensation or bonus, incentive or profit sharing (or if not set forth in any formal document, a written description thereof) in which any director or any of the named executive officers of the registrant as defined by Item 402(a)(2) participates shall be deemed material and shall be filed; and any other management contract or any compensatory plan, contract, or arrangement in which any other executive officer of the registrant participates shall be filed unless immaterial in amount or significance.

(B) The following management contracts or compensatory plans need not be filed:

(1) Ordinary purchase and sales agency agreements;

(2) Agreements with managers of stores in a chain organization or similar organization;

(3) Contracts providing for labor or salesmen's bonuses or payments to a class of security holders, as such;

(4) Any compensatory plan which is available to employees, officers or directors generally and provides for the same method of allocation of benefits between management and nonmanagement participants; and

(5) Any compensatory plan if the issuer is a wholly owned subsidiary of a reporting company and is filing a report on Form 10-KSB, or registering debt or non-voting preferred stock on Form S-2.

Instruction to Item 601(b)(10)

1. Only copies of the various remunerative plans need be filed. Each individual director's or executive officer's personal agreement under the plans need not be filed, unless they contain material provisions.

(11) Statement re computation of per share earnings. *An explanation of the computation of per share earnings on both a primary and fully diluted basis unless the computation can be clearly determined from the registration statement or report.*

(12) No exhibit required.

(13) Annual report to security holders for the last fiscal year, Form 10-Q or 10-QSB or quarterly report to security holders.

(i) Annual report to security holders for the last fiscal year, Form 10-Q or 10-QSB or quarterly report to security holders, if incorporated by reference in the filing. Such reports, except for the parts which are expressly incorporated by reference in the filing are not deemed "filed" as part of the filing. If the financial statements in the report have been incorporated by reference in the filing, the accountant's certificate shall be manually signed in one copy. See Rule 411(b).

(ii) If the annual or quarterly report to security holders is incorporated by reference in whole or in part into an electronic filing, whatever is so incorporated must be filed in electronic format as an exhibit to the filing.

(14) Material foreign patents. *Each material foreign patent for an invention not covered by a United States patent.*

(15) Letter on unaudited interim financial information. *A letter, where applicable, from the independent accountant which acknowledges awareness of the use in a registration statement of a report on unaudited interim financial information. The letter is not considered a part of a registration statement prepared or certified by an accountant or a report prepared or certified by an accountant within the meaning of sections 7 and 11 of the Securities Act. Such* *letter may be filed with the registration statement, an amendment thereto, or a report on Form 10-QSB which is incorporated by reference into the registration statement.*

(16) Letter on change in certifying accountant. *File the letter required by Item 304(a)(3).*

(17) Letter on director resignation. *Any letter from a former director which describes a disagreement with the small business issuer that led to the director's resignation or refusal to stand for re-election and which requests that the matter be disclosed.*

(18) Letter on change in accounting principles. *Unless previously filed, a letter from the issuer's accountant stating whether any change in accounting principles or practices followed by the issuer, or any change in the method of applying any such accounting principles or practices, which affected the financial statements being filed with the Commission in the report or which is expected to affect the financial statements of future fiscal years is to an alternative principle which in his judgment is preferable under the circumstances. No such letter need be filed when such change is made in response to a standard adopted by the Financial Accounting Standards Board that creates a new accounting principle, that expresses a preference for an accounting principle, or that rejects a specific accounting principle.*

(19) Report furnished to security holders. *If the issuer makes available to its stockholders or otherwise publishes, within the period prescribed for filing the report, a document or statement containing information meeting some or all of the requirements of Part I of Form 10-Q or 10-QSB, the information called for may be incorporated by reference to such published document or statement provided copies thereof are included as an exhibit to the registration statement or to Part I of the Form 10-Q or 10-QSB report.*

(20) Other documents or statements to security holders or any document incorporated by reference.

(21) Subsidiaries of the small business issuer. *A list of all subsidiaries, the state or other jurisdiction of incorporation or organization of each, and the names under which such subsidiaries do business.*

(22) Published report regarding matters submitted to vote of security holders. *Published reports containing all of the information called for by Item 4 of Part II of Form 10-Q (or 10-QSB) or Item 4 of Part I of Form 10-K or 10-KSB which is referred to therein in lieu of providing disclosure in Form 10-Q (10-QSB) or 10-K (10-KSB), which are required to be filed as exhibits by Rule 12b-23(a)(3) under the Exchange Act.*

SEC 76012

(23) Consents of experts and counsel.

(i) Securities Act filings—Dated and manually signed written consents or a reference in the index to the location of the consent.

(ii) Exchange Act reports. If required to file a consent for material incorporated by reference in a previously filed registration statement under the Securities Act, the dated and manually signed consent to the material incorporated by reference. The consents shall be dated and manually signed.

(24) Power of attorney. *If a person signs a registration statement or report under a power of attorney, a manually signed copy of such power of attorney or if located elsewhere in the registration statement, a reference in the index to where it is located. In addition, if an officer signs a registration statement for the small business issuer by a power of attorney, a certified copy of a resolution of the board of directors authorizing such signature. A power of attorney that is filed with the Commission must relate to a specific filing or an amendment. A power of attorney that confers general authority must not be filed with the Commission.*

(25) Statement of eligibility of trustee.

(i) Form T-1 if an indenture is being qualified under the Trust Indenture Act, bound separately from the other exhibits.

(ii) The requirement to bind separately the statement of eligibility and qualification does not apply to statements submitted in electronic format. Rather, such statements must be submitted as exhibits in the same electronic submission as the registration statement to which they relate, or in an amendment thereto, provided that electronic filers that rely on Trust Indenture Act Section 305(b)(2) for determining the eligibility of the trustee under indentures for securities to be issued, offered or sold on a delayed basis by or on behalf of the registrant shall file statements of eligibility as exhibits to a post-effective amendment to the registration statement to which the statements relate.

(26) Invitations for competitive bids. *If the registration statement covers securities that the small business issuer is offering at competitive bidding, any invitation for competitive bid that the small business issuer will send or give to any person shall be filed.*

(27) Financial data schedule. *The Financial Data Schedule must be filed only by electronic filers. Applicable requirements are set out in paragraph (c) of this Item.*

(28) Information from reports furnished to state insurance regulatory authorities.

(i) If reserves for unpaid property-casualty ("P/C") claims and claim adjustment expenses of the small business issuer, its unconsolidated subsidiaries and the proportionate share of the small business issuer and the other subsidiaries in the unpaid P/C claims and claim adjustment expenses of its 50 percent-or-less-owned equity investees, taken in the aggregate after small business issuer eliminations, exceed one-half of the common stockholders' equity of the small business issuer as of the beginning of the latest fiscal year the following information should be supplied.

(ii) the information included in Schedules O and P of Annual Statements provided to state regulatory authorities by the small business issuer or its P/C insurance small business issuer affiliates for the latest year on a combined or consolidated basis as appropriate, separately for each of the following:

(A) the small business issuer;

(B) its unconsolidated subsidiaries; and

(C) fifty percent-or-less-owned equity investees of the small business issuer and its subsidiaries.

(iii) Small business issuers may omit the combined or consolidated Schedules O and P of fifty percent-or-less-owned equity investees, if they file the same information with the Commission as companies in their own right, and if they state that fact and the name and ownership percentage of such companies.

(iv) If ending reserves in paragraphs (b)(29)(ii)(A) and (b)(29)(ii)(B) of this Item or the proportionate share of the small business issuer and its other subsidiaries in paragraph (b)(29)(ii)(C) of this Item are less than 5 percent of the total ending reserves in paragraphs (b)(29)(ii)(A) and (b)(29)(ii)(B) of this Item, and the proportionate share of (b)(29)(ii)(C) of this Item, small business issuers may omit that category and note that fact. If the amount of the reserves attributable to fifty percent-or-less-owned equity investees that file this information as companies in their own right exceeds 95 percent of the total paragraph (b)(29)(ii)(C) of this Item small business issuers do not need to provide reserves, information for the other fifty percent-or-less-owned equity investees.

(v) Small business issuers do not need to include Schedules O and P information if they are not required to file Schedules O and P with

insurance regulatory authorities. However, clearly note the nature and extent of any such exclusions in the Exhibit.

(vi) Companies whose fiscal year differs from the calendar year should present Schedules O and P as of the end of the calendar year that falls within their fiscal year.

(vii) The nature and amount of the difference between reserves for claims and claim adjustment expenses reflected on Schedules O and P and the total P/C statutory reserves for claims and disclose claim adjustment expenses as of the latest calendar year in a note to those Schedules.

(29) through (98) [Reserved]

(99) Additional exhibits.

(i) Any additional exhibits if listed and described in the exhibit index.

(ii) If pursuant to Section 11(a) of the Securities Act an issuer makes available to its security holders generally an earnings statement covering a period of at least 12 months beginning after the effective date of the registration statement, and if such earnings statement is submitted to the Commission, it must be filed as an exhibit to the Form 10-QSB or the Form 10-KSB, as appropriate, covering the period in which the earnings statement was released.

(c) Financial data schedule —

(1) General.

(i) A Financial Data Schedule must be submitted only by an electronic filer that is not a foreign private issuer or foreign government. The schedule must be submitted in the electronic format prescribed by the EDGAR Filer Manual, and must set forth the financial information specified in the applicable table in the Appendices to this item.

(ii) Subsequent to the date on which a small business issuer becomes subject to mandated electronic filing, any electronic filing that includes financial statements of the filer for a recent fiscal year or interim year to date period, or both, for which financial statements have not previously been filed, otherwise than by incorporation by reference, shall include as an exhibit a Financial Data Schedule containing financial information for the updating period or periods.

(iii) The amounts reflected in the Financial Data Schedule must correspond to or be calculable from amounts reflected in the small business issuer's financial statements or associated notes.

(iv) The schedule must be submitted as an exhibit to the filing(s) to which it relates, but will not be treated as filed for purposes of the federal securities laws, nor will it be deemed a part of any registration statement to which it relates. It shall, however, be subject to all other liability and anti-fraud provisions of the federal securities laws. See Rule 402 of Regulation S-T.

(v) A Financial Data Schedule must be submitted only in electronic format. Where a small business issuer submits a filing, otherwise required to include a Financial Data Schedule, in paper pursuant to a temporary hardship exemption under Rule 201 of Regulation S-T, the Financial Data Schedule must not be included with the paper filing, but shall be included with the required confirming electronic copy.

(vi) Financial Data Schedules shall not include pro forma financial information.

Note: *Failure to furnish a Financial Data Schedule will not prevent acceptance of the filing for which the schedule is required. However, as the schedule may be used by the Commission staff in its review of the filing, processing of the filing may be delayed pending filing of the schedule. Further, registrants that have not filed a required Financial Data Schedule will be ineligible to use Form S-2, Form S-3 and Form S-8. See the eligibility requirements of those forms.*

(2) *Format and presentation of financial data schedule.*

(i) At the option of the registrant, the following legend may be inserted at the beginning of any Financial Data Schedule submitted to the Commission, in the manner prescribed by the EDGAR Filer Manual: THIS SCHEDULE CONTAINS SUMMARY FINANCIAL INFORMATION EXTRACTED FROM [Identify specific financial statements] AND IS QUALIFIED IN ITS ENTIRETY BY REFERENCE TO SUCH FINANCIAL STATEMENTS.

(ii) Items set forth in a Financial Data Schedule may be qualified by referencing a specific footnote to the Financial Data Schedule or cross-referencing notes to the registrant's financial statements.

(iii) If any of the amounts reported in a previously submitted Financial Data Schedule are restated as a result of pooling of interests, an accounting principle change, a reorganization or recapitalization, correction of an error, or any other reason, then a schedule, as amended or restated, shall be submitted that sets forth the restated or amended information for each affected period during the latest three fiscal years and any interim

periods of the latest two fiscal years; except that restated or amended information need not be furnished for any period for which a Financial Data Schedule was not previously required to be furnished. The document shall specify that the Financial Data Schedule has been restated or amended. A schedule that is filed to correct an error in a previously filed Financial Data Schedule shall be designated as an "Amended Financial Data Schedule." A schedule that is filed as a result of a restatement that is not a correction of an error shall be designated as a "Restated Financial Data Schedule."

(3) Contents of financial data schedule. The schedule shall set forth the financial information specified below that is applicable to the registrant. Small business issuers that would prepare financial statements in accordance with Articles 5, 7 or 9 of Regulation S-X if filing on Form S-1 shall prepare a Financial Data Schedule that includes information required by Articles 5, 7 or 9, as appropriate. Schedules based on Articles 5, 7 and 9 of Registration S-X include items that are to be understood as the same information required by corresponding items in Regulation S-X.

(i) Article 5 Registrants (Commercial and Industrial Companies). Small business issuers that would prepare financial statements in accordance with Article 5 of Regulation S-X shall prepare a Financial Data Schedule that contains the Article 5 items listed in Appendix A to this Item.

(ii) Article 7 Registrants (Insurance Companies). Small business issuers that would prepare financial statements in accordance with Article 7 of Regulation S-X shall prepare a Financial Data Schedule that contains the Article 7 financial statement items and the industry guide items (Securities Act Industry Guide 6 or Exchange Act Industry Guide 4) listed in Appendix B to this item.

(iii) Article 9 Registrants (Bank Holding Companies and Savings and Loan Holding Companies). Small business issuers that would prepare their financial statements in accordance with Article 9 of Regulation S-X and savings and loan holding companies shall prepare a Financial Data Schedule that contains the Article 9 financial statement items and Securities Act Industry Guide 3 information and Exchange Act Industry Guide 3 listed in Appendix C to this item.

(iv) Broker-Dealer and Broker-Dealer Holding Companies. Small business issuers that are broker-dealers or broker-dealer holding companies may prepare a Financial Data Schedule that contains the items listed in Appendix D to this Item in lieu of a Financial Data Schedule containing the items listed in Appendix A to this item.

(v) Public Utility Companies and Public Utility Holding Companies. Small business issuers that are public utility companies or public utility holding companies shall prepare a Financial Data Schedule in the form required by Appendix E to this item.

Note: Schedule UT (Appendix E) contains the same requirements found in Exhibit G of Form U5S.

(vi) Multiple Industry Companies. A small business issuer that presents its primary financial statements in a manner in which non-homogeneous lines of business are grouped separately on the face of the primary financial statements and that does not present combined totals for all lines of business may submit separate Financial Data Schedules for each line of business. Where a small business issuer prepares more than one Financial Data Schedule, a separate schedule of consolidated totals on Schedule CT (Appendix F to this item) shall also be furnished.

[**Note:** Appendices A through F referred to in paragraph (c) have not been reproduced in this manual.]

77000. MISCELLANEOUS (ITEMS 701 AND 702)

Pursuant to Regulation S-B Item 701, Recent Sales of Unregistered Securities, small business issuers are required to furnish certain information with respect to all securities sold by the issuer within the past three years that were not registered under the 1933 Act. The specified information discloses the specifics of each sale, names of principal underwriters (or identity of buyer if not publicly offered), a description of the transaction and consideration for noncash sales, and the section of the Securities Act or rule of the Commission under which the issuer claimed exemption from registration and the facts relied upon.

Item 702, Indemnification of Directors and Officers, specifies that the small business issuer must disclose the general effect on any statute, charter provision, bylaws, contract, or other arrangement under which any controlling person, director, or officer of the issuer is insured or indemnified in any manner against liability which may be incurred in his or her capacity as such.

The information required to be disclosed pursuant to these items is generally prepared by the issuer and/or its counsel, with little or no involvement on the part of the independent accountant. Accordingly, the text of these requirements is not reproduced herein.

APPENDIX

81000. TOPICAL LISTING OF STAFF ACCOUNTING BULLETINS

A topical listing of Staff Accounting Bulletins (through SAB No. 92) is included in this section. (Those rescinded have been deleted.) The subjects listed are referenced, where applicable, to the section of the manual where the SAB topic is discussed.

Manual
Reference
<u>(Section)</u>

TOPIC 1: FINANCIAL STATEMENTS

A. Target Companies 50319

B. Allocation of Expenses and Related Disclosure in
Financial Statements of Subsidiaries, Divisions or
Lesser Business Components of Another Entity 50505

C. Unaudited Financial Statements for a Full Year 50307

D. Foreign Companies
1. Disclosures Required of Companies Complying
with Item 17 of Form 20-F 43210
2. "Free Distributions" by Japanese Companies 50502-31

E. Requirements for Audited or Certified Financial Statements
1. Meaning of the Word "Audited" 50102
2. Qualified Auditors' Opinions 20230

F. Financial Statement Requirements in Filings Involving the
Formation of a One-Bank Holding Company 50901

G. Financial Statement Requirements in Filings Involving the
Guarantee of Securities by a Parent 50344

H. Financial Statement Requirements in Filings Involving the
Guarantee of Securities by a Subsidiary 50344

I. Financial Statements of Properties Securing Mortgage Loans 50348

J. Financial Statements of Businesses Acquired or To Be Acquired . . . 50322

K. Financial Statements of Acquired Troubled Financial
Institutions 50901

TOPIC 11: MISCELLANEOUS DISCLOSURE

TOPIC 12: OIL AND GAS PRODUCING ACTIVITIES

* Excluded because of inapplicability or limited applicability.

+ Financial accounting and reporting for oil and gas producing activities is
  discussed in section 50410 of this manual.

81500. CHRONOLOGICAL LISTING OF STAFF ACCOUNTING BULLETINS

A listing of Staff Accounting Bulletins in the order in which they were issued is included in this section and cross-referenced to the topical listing in section 81000 of this manual.

SAB No.	Date of Release	Subject	Topical Listing Reference
40	Jan. 1981	Codification of SAB Nos. 1-38 (SAB No. 39 was superseded by ASR No. 29)	Various
41		No longer applicable	
42	Dec. 1981	Application of existing accounting standards to business combinations accounted for by the purchase method involving financial institutions	2-A3
42A	Dec. 1985	Amortization of goodwill by financial institutions upon becoming SEC registrants	2-A4
43	Jan. 1982	Early adoption of the new rules for separate financial statements required by Regulation S-X	6-K
44	Mar. 1982	Implementation of Accounting Series Release No. 302 and deletion of topics no longer relevant	6-K
45	May 1982	Presentation of pro forma financial information	2-C
46	May 1982	Requirements for interim financial reporting	6-G1; 6-G2
47	Sept. 1982	Oil and gas producing activities	2-D; 12
47A	Sept. 1982	Correction of SAB No. 47 concerning minimum property conveyances	12-D4
48	Sept. 1982	Transfers of nonmonetary assets by promoters or shareholders	5-G
49	Oct. 1982	Disclosure by bank holding companies about certain foreign loans	11-H
49A	Jan. 1983	Additional disclosures by bank holding companies about certain foreign loans	11-H
50	Mar. 1983	Financial statement requirements in filings involving the formation of a one-bank holding company	1-F
51	Mar. 1983	Accounting for sales of stock by a subsidiary	5-H
52		No longer applicable	
53	June 1983	Financial statement requirements in filings involving the guarantee of securities by a parent or subsidiary	1-G; 1-H

SAB No.	Date of Release	Subject	Topical Listing Reference
54	Nov. 1983	Push-down basis of accounting required in certain limited circumstances	5-J
55	Nov. 1983	Allocation of expenses and related disclosure in financial statements of subsidiaries, divisions or lesser business components of another entity; cheap stock	1-B;4-D
56	Jan. 1984	Reporting of an allocated transfer risk reserve in filings under the federal securities laws	11-I
57	July 1984	Accounting for contingent warrants issued by a company to certain of its major customers in connection with sales agreements	5-K
58	Mar. 1985	Last-in, first-out (LIFO) inventory practices	5-L
59	Sept. 1985	Accounting for noncurrent marketable equity securities	5-M
60	Dec. 1985	Financial guarantees	11-J
61	May 1986	Loan losses	2-A5
62	July 1986	Discounting by property-casualty insurance companies	5-N
63	Sept. 1986	Research and development arrangements	5-O
64	Oct. 1986	Applicability of guidance in Staff Accounting Bulletins; reporting of income or loss applicable to common stock; accounting for redeemable preferred stock; issuance of shares prior to an initial public offering	3-C; 4-D; 6-B; 6-C
65	Nov. 1986	Risk sharing in pooling of interests	2-E
66	Nov. 1986	Disclosures by certain bank holding companies regarding certain foreign loans	11-H
67	Dec. 1986	Income statement presentation of restructuring charges	5-P
68	May 1987	Increasing rate preferred stock	5-Q
69	May 1987	Application of Article 9 and Guide 3; income statement presentation of casino-hotel activities	11-K; 11-L
70	June 1987	Accounting for nonrecourse debt collateralized by lease receivables and/or leased assets	5-R
71	Aug. 1987	Financial statements of properties securing mortgage loans	1-I
71A	Dec. 1987	Financial statements of properties securing mortgage loans	1-I

SEC 81500

SAB No.	Date of Release	Subject	Topical Listing Reference
72	Nov. 1987	Classification of charges for abandonments and disallowances	10-E
73	Dec. 1987	Push-down basis of accounting required in certain limited circumstances	5-J
74	Dec. 1987	Disclosure of the impact that recently issued accounting standards will have on the financial statements of the registrant when adopted in a future period	11-M
75	Jan. 1988	Disclosures by bank holding companies regarding certain foreign loans	11-H2
76	Jan. 1988	Risk sharing in pooling of interests	2-E2
77	Mar. 1988	Debt issue costs	2-A6
78	Aug. 1988	Quasi reorganization	5-S
79	Sept. 1988	Accounting for expenses or liabilities paid by principal stockholder(s)	5-T
80	Nov. 1988	Application of Rule 3-05 in initial public offerings	1-J
81	Apr. 1989	Gain recognition on the sale of a business or operating assets to a highly leveraged entity	5-U
82	July 1989	Transfers of nonperforming assets; disclosure of the impact of financial assistance from regulators	5-V; 11-N
83	Aug. 1989	Earnings per share computations in an initial public offering	4-D
84	Aug. 1989	Accounting for sales of stock by a subsidiary	5-H
85	Sept. 1989	Gross revenue method of amortizing capitalized costs	12-F; 12-G
86	Sept. 1989	Quasi reorganization	5-S
87	Dec. 1989	Insurance reserves for unpaid claims	5-W
88	Aug. 1990	Disclosures required of companies complying with Item 17 of Form 20-F	1-D
89	Jan. 1991	Financial Statements of Acquired Troubled Financial Institutions	1-K
90	Feb. 1991	Specific Matters Related to the Bankruptcy of an Accounting Firm which had Public Company Clients (Laventhol & Horwath)	1-L
91	Jul. 1991	Accounting for Income Tax Benefits Associated with Bad Debts of Thrifts	5-X
92	June 1993	Accounting and Disclosures Relating to Loss Contingencies	2-A7; 5-Y; 10-F

82000. SELECTED STAFF ACCOUNTING BULLETINS NOT INCLUDED IN OTHER SECTIONS OF THE MANUAL

The Staff Accounting Bulletins presented in this appendix deal with subjects that are not directly discussed elsewhere in the manual. Refer to section 81000 for a topical listing of SABs, including applicable references to the section of the manual where the SABs are presented.

82001. Limited Partnerships Trading in Commodity Futures

SAB Topic 5-D presents the staff's views with respect to accounting for organization and offering expenses and selling commissions of limited partnerships organized to engage in speculative trading in commodity futures contracts.

*Organization and Offering Expenses and Selling
Commissions—Limited Partnerships
Trading in Commodity Futures*

Facts: Partnerships formed for the purpose of engaging in speculative trading in commodity futures contracts sell limited partnership interests to the public and frequently have a general partner who is an affiliate of the partnership's commodity broker or the principal underwriter selling the limited partnership interests. The commodity broker or a subsidiary typically assumes the liability for all or part of the organization and offering expenses and selling commissions in connection with the sale of limited partnership interests. Funds raised from the sale of partnership interests are deposited in a margin account with the commodity broker and are invested in Treasury Bills or similar securities. The arrangement further provides that interest earned on the investments for an initial period is to be retained by the broker until it has been reimbursed for all or a specified portion of the aforementioned expenses and commissions and that thereafter interest earned accrues to the partnership.

In some instances, there may be no reference to reimbursement of the broker for expenses and commissions to be assumed. The arrangements may provide that all interest earned on investments accrues to the partnership but that commissions on commodity transactions paid to the broker are at higher rates for a specified initial period and at lower rates subsequently.

Question 1: Should the partnership recognize a commitment to reimburse the commodity broker for the organization and offering expenses and selling commissions?

Interpretive Response: Yes. A commitment should be recognized by reducing partnership capital and establishing a liability for the estimated amount of expenses and commissions for which the broker is to be reimbursed.

Question 2: Should the interest income retained by the broker for reimbursement of expenses be recognized as income by the partnership?

Interpretive Response: Yes. All the interest income on the margin account investments should be recognized as accruing to the partnership as earned. The portion of income retained by the broker and not actually realized by the partnership in cash should be applied to reduce the liability for the estimated amount of reimbursable expenses and commissions.

Question 3: If the broker retains all of the interest income for a specified period and thereafter it accrues to the partnership, should an equivalent amount of interest income be reflected on the partnership's financial statements during the specified period?

Interpretive Response: Yes. If it appears from the terms of the arrangement that it was the intent of the parties to provide for full or partial reimbursement for the expenses and commissions paid by the broker, then a commitment to reimburse should be recognized by the partnership and an equivalent amount of interest income should be recognized on the partnership's financial statements as earned.

Question 4: Under the arrangements where commissions on commodity transactions are at a lower rate after a specified period, and there is no reference to reimbursement of the broker for expenses and commissions, should recognition be given on the partnership's financial statements to a commitment to reimburse the broker for all or part of the expenses and commissions?

Interpretive Response: If it appears from the terms of the arrangement that the intent of the parties was to provide for full or partial reimbursement of the broker's expenses and commissions, then the estimated commitment should be recognized on the partnership's financial statements. During the specified initial period commissions on commodity transactions should be charged to operations at the lower commission rate with the difference applied to reduce the aforementioned commitment.

82002. Disclosures and Accounting by Electric Utility Companies

SAB Topics 10-A, 10-B, 10-C, 10-D, 10-E and 10-F present the staff's views as to disclosures and accounting by electric utility companies in connection with:

(1) Financing through the use of construction intermediaries.

(2) Estimated future costs of storing spent nuclear fuel and of decommissioning nuclear electric generating plants.

(3) Interests in jointly owned electric utility plants.

(4) Long-term contracts for the purchase of power.

(5) Classification of charges for abandonment and disallowances.

(6) Liabilities for environmental costs.

(10-A) Financing by Electric Utility Companies Through Use of Construction Intermediaries

Facts: Some electric utility companies finance construction of a generating plant or their share of a jointly owned plant through the use of a "construction intermediary" which may be organized as a trust or a corporation. Typically the utility assigns its interest in property and other contract rights to the construction intermediary with the latter authorized to obtain funds to finance construction with term loans, bank loans, commercial paper and other sources of funds that may be available. The intermediary's borrowings are guaranteed in part by the work in progress but more significantly, although indirectly, by the obligation of the utility to purchase the project upon completion and assume or otherwise settle the borrowings. The utility may be committed to provide any deficiency of funds which the intermediary cannot obtain and excess funds may be loaned to the utility by the intermediary. (In one case involving construction of an entire generating plant, the intermediary appointed the utility as its agent to complete construction.) On the occurrence of an event such as commencement of the testing period for the plant or placing the plant in commercial service (but not later than a specified date) the interest in the plant reverts to the utility and concurrently the utility must either assume the obligations issued by the intermediary or purchase them from the holders. The intermediary may also be authorized to borrow amounts for accrued interest when due and those amounts are added to the balance of the outstanding indebtedness. Interest is thus capitalized during the construction period at rates being charged by the lenders; however, it is deductible by the utility for tax purposes in the year of accrual.

Question: How should construction work in progress and related liabilities and interest expense being financed through a construction intermediary be reflected in an electric utility's financial statements?

Interpretive Response: The balance sheet of an electric utility company using a construction intermediary to finance construction should include the intermediary's work in progress in the appropriate caption under utility plant. The related debt should be included in long-term liabilities and disclosed either on the balance sheet or in a note.

Rule 4-08(j) of Regulation S-X applies to all registrants. It provides that the amount of interest cost incurred and the respective amounts expensed or capitalized shall be disclosed for each period for which an income statement is presented. Consequently, capitalized interest included as part of an intermediary's construction work in progress on the balance sheet should be recognized on the current income statement as interest expense with a corresponding offset to allowance for borrowed funds used during construction. Income statements for prior periods should also be restated. The amounts may be shown separately on the statement or included with interest expense and allowance for borrowed funds used during construction.

A note to the financial statements should describe briefly the organization and purpose of the intermediary and the nature of its authorization to incur debt to finance construction. The note should disclose the rate at which interest on this debt has been capitalized and the dollar amount for each period for which an income statement is presented.

(10-B) Estimated Future Costs Related to Spent Nuclear Fuel and Nuclear Electric Generating Plants

Facts: Utility companies with nuclear electric generating plants have amortized nuclear fuel cost to expense on the basis of the quantity of heat produced for the generation of electric energy. In computing the periodic amortization of the nuclear fuel cost a net residual salvage value has been generally assumed that is predicated on the reprocessing of spent nuclear fuel to recover the unused uranium and plutonium. No facility is presently in operation or can be made operable to process spent nuclear fuel. Consequently, reprocessing cannot be presently accomplished, and it may be necessary to store spent nuclear fuel for an indefinite period.

In determining depreciation rates for nuclear generating plants the costs of storing, dismantling or decontaminating a plant at the end of its useful life have generally not been considered. Such costs now appear to be substantial.

Question: What disclosure should be made concerning the estimated future costs of storing spent nuclear fuel and decommissioning nuclear generating plants?

Interpretive Response: With regard to both the storing of spent nuclear fuel and decommissioning of nuclear generating plants it appears that costs will be incurred. It may not be possible to reasonably estimate these costs when financial statements are prepared.

A note to the financial statements should describe the consideration given to the estimated future storage or disposal costs for spent fuel in amortizing the cost of nuclear fuel. If the amortization of nuclear fuel in prior years recognized a net residual salvage value, the note should disclose whether the residual salvage value was subsequently eliminated or is to be eliminated by a charge to current operations or otherwise. Also a note should disclose whether (1) estimated future storage or disposal costs and (2) residual salvage value recognized in prior years and now being written off are being recovered through a fuel adjustment clause

SEC 82002

or if it is expected that provision will be made for such costs in applications to regulatory commissions for rate increases.

A note should also disclose the estimated costs of dismantling or decontaminating nuclear generating plants and whether provision for these costs is being made in current operations and recognized in service rates. If such expected costs are not being currently provided for, disclose the reasons for omitting the costs and the potential impact on the financial statements.

(10-C) Jointly Owned Electric Utility Plants

Facts: Groups of electric utility companies have been building and operating utility plants under joint ownership agreements or arrangements which do not create legal entities for which separate financial statements are presented. Under these arrangements a participating utility has an undivided interest in a utility plant and is responsible for its proportionate share of the cost of construction and operation and is entitled to its proportionate share of the energy produced.

During the construction period a participating utility finances its own share of a utility plant using its own financial resources and not the combined resources of the group. Allowance for funds used during construction is provided in the same manner and at the same rates as for plants constructed to be used entirely by the participant utility.

When a jointly owned plant becomes operational, one of the participant utilities acts as operator and bills the other participants for their proportionate share of the direct expenses incurred. Each individual participant incurs other expenses related to transmission, distribution, supervision and control which cannot be related to the energy generated or received from any particular source. Many companies maintain depreciation records on a composite basis for each class of property so that neither the accumulated allowance for depreciation nor the periodic expense can be allocated to specific generating units whether jointly or wholly owned.

Question: What disclosure should be made on the financial statements or in the notes concerning interests in jointly owned utility plants?

Interpretive Response: A participating utility should include information concerning the extent of its interests in jointly owned plants in a note to its financial statements. The note should include a table showing separately for each interest in a jointly owned plant the amount of utility plant in service, the accumulated provision for depreciation (if available), the amount of plant under construction, and the proportionate share. The amounts presented for plant in service or plant under construction may be further subdivided to show amounts applicable to plant subcategories such as production, transmission, and distribution. The note should include statements that the dollar amounts represent the participating utility's share in each joint plant and that each participant must provide its own financing. Information concerning two or more generating plants on the same site may be combined if appropriate.

SEC 82002

The note should state that the participating utility's share of direct expenses of the joint plants is included in the corresponding operating expenses on its income statement (e. g., fuel, maintenance of plant, other operating expense). If the share of direct expenses is charged to purchased power then the note should disclose the amount so charged and the proportionate amounts charged to specific operating expenses on the records maintained for the joint plants.

(10-D) Long-Term Contracts for Purchase of Electric Power

Facts: Under long-term contracts with public utility districts, cooperatives or other organizations, a utility company receives a portion of the output of a production plant constructed and financed by the district or cooperative. The utility has only a nominal or no investment at all in the plant but pays a proportionate part of the plant's costs including debt service. The contract may be in the form of a sale of a generating plant and its immediate leaseback. The utility is obligated to pay certain minimum amounts which cover debt service requirements whether or not the plant is operating. At the option of other parties to the contract and in accordance with a predetermined schedule, the utility's proportionate share of the output may be reduced. Separate agreements may exist for the transmission of power to the utility's system.

Question: How should the cost of power obtained under long-term purchase contracts be reflected on the financial statements and what supplemental disclosure should be made in notes to the statements?

Interpretive Response: The cost of power obtained under long-term purchase contracts, including payments required to be made when a production plant is not operating, should be included in the operating expenses section of the income statement. A note to the financial statements should present information concerning the terms and significance of such contracts to the utility company including date of contract expiration, share of plant output being purchased, estimated annual cost, annual minimum debt service payment required and amount of related long-term debt or lease obligations outstanding.

Additional disclosure should be given if the contract provides, or is expected to provide, in excess of five percent of current or estimated future system capability. This additional disclosure may be in the form of separate financial statements of the vendor entity or inclusion of the amount of the obligation under the contract as a liability on the balance sheet with a corresponding amount as an asset representing the right to purchase power under the contract.

The note to the financial statements should disclose the allocable portion of interest included in charges under such contracts. Accounting Series Release No. 122 discusses the computation of the ratio of earnings to fixed charges for an enterprise which has guaranteed the debt of a supplier company or has entered into contracts with a supplier providing for payments designed to service debt of a supplier. The release states in part that in such instances the ratio ". . . for the registrant must be accompanied by effective disclosure of the significance of fixed charges of other companies included in the enterprise whether or not the revenues and expenses of such companies are set forth in the financial statements of the registrant. Such disclosure usually should be accomplished by presenting the ratio of earnings to fixed charges for the total enterprise in equivalent prominence with the ratio for the registrant or registrant and consolidated subsidiaries."

(10-E) Classification of Charges for Abandonments and Disallowances

Facts: A public utility company abandons the construction of a plant and, under the provisions of Statement of Financial Accounting Standards (SFAS) No. 90, must charge a portion of the costs of the abandoned plant to expense.[1] Also, the utility determines that it is probable that certain costs of a recently completed plant will be disallowed, and charges those costs to expense as required by SFAS No. 90.

Question 1: May such charges for abandonments and disallowances be reported as extraordinary items in the statement of income?

Interpretive Response: No. The staff does not believe that such charges meet the requirements of Accounting Principles Board Opinion (APB) No. 30 that an item be both unusual and infrequent to be classified as an extraordinary item. Accordingly, the public utility was advised by the staff that such charges should be reported as a component of income from continuing operations, separately presented, if material.[2]

Paragraph 20 of APB No. 30 indicates that to be unusual, an item must "possess a high degree of abnormality and be of a type clearly unrelated to, or only incidentally related to, the ordinary and typical activities of the entity, taking into account the environment in which the entity operates." Similarly, that paragraph indicates that, to be infrequent, an event should "not reasonably be expected to recur in the foreseeable future."

Electric utilities operate under a franchise that requires them to furnish adequate supplies of electricity for their service area. That undertaking requires utilities to continually forecast the future demand for electricity, and the costs to be incurred in constructing the plants necessary to meet that demand. Abandonments and disallowances result from the failure of demand to reach projected levels and/or plant construction costs that exceed anticipated amounts. Neither event qualifies as being both unusual and infrequent in the environment in which electric utilities operate.

Accordingly, the staff believes that charges for abandonments and disallowances under SFAS No. 90 should not be presented as extraordinary items.[3]

Facts: A public utility intends to initially apply SFAS No. 90 by restating the financial statements for prior periods.[4] Included in the results of operations for those prior periods are charges for unrecoverable costs which were required under

SFAS No. 71.[5] Those charges were classified as extraordinary items. The application of SFAS No. 90 to those prior periods may change the amount and/or timing of those charges.

Question 2: May a utility that adopts SFAS No. 90 by restating the financial statements for prior periods, and which had previously classified a charge under SFAS No. 71 for disallowed costs as an extraordinary item, continue, after reinstatement, to classify the charges relating to that disallowance as an extraordinary item?

Interpretive Response: No. The staff believes that these charges should be classified as a component of income from continuing operations irrespective of whether they occur in a period to which SFAS No. 90 has been retroactively applied or a period which follows the initial adoption of the standard. While the staff is aware that some utilities have, in the past, classified a charge under SFAS No. 71 for disallowed costs as an extraordinary item, the staff believes that the continuation of that treatment for charges occurring in periods to which SFAS No. 90 is retroactively applied is inappropriate.[6] The treatment of a charge under the previous accounting standard does not, in the staff's view, justify affording disparate treatment to identical items under the same accounting standard based solely on whether the period in question preceded or followed the date SFAS No. 90 was adopted. The change in the timing and/or amount of the charge resulting from the retroactive application of SFAS No. 90 represents the effect of applying a different accounting standard rather than the effect of a change in the estimate of recoverable costs used in applying the requirement of SFAS No. 71.

(10-F) Presentation of Liabilities for Environmental Costs

Facts: A public utility company determines that it is obligated to pay material amounts as a result of an environmental liability. These amounts may relate to, for example, damages attributed to clean-up of hazardous wastes, reclamation costs, fines, and litigation costs.

Question 1: May a rate-regulated enterprise present on its balance sheet the amount of its estimated liability for environmental costs net of probable future revenue resulting from the inclusion of such costs in allowable costs for rate-making purposes?

Interpretive Response: No. *Statement of Financial Accounting Standards No. 71*, "Accounting for the Effects of Certain Types of Regulation," ("SFAS 71") specifies the conditions under which rate actions of a regulator can provide reasonable assurance of the existence of an asset. The staff believes that environmental costs meeting the criteria of paragraph 9[7] of SFAS 71 should be presented on the balance sheet as an asset and should not be offset against the liability. Contingent recoveries through rates that do not meet the criteria of paragraph 9 should not be recognized either as an asset or as a reduction of the probable liability.

Question 2: May a rate-regulated enterprise delay recognition of a probable and estimable liability for environmental costs which it has incurred at the date of the latest balance sheet until the regulator's deliberations have proceeded to a point enabling management to determine whether this cost is likely to be included in allowable costs for rate-making purposes?

Interpretive Response: No. *Statement of Financial Accounting Standards No. 5,* "Accounting for Contingencies," states that an estimated loss from a loss contingency shall be accrued by a charge to income if it is probable that a liability has been incurred and the amount of the loss can be reasonably estimated. The staff believes that actions of a regulator can affect whether an incurred cost is capitalized or expensed pursuant to SFAS 71, but the regulator's actions cannot affect the timing of the recognition of the liability.

---

[1]Paragraph 3 of Statement of Financial Accounting Standards (SFAS) No. 90 requires that costs of abandoned plants in excess of the present value of the future revenues expected to be provided to recover any allowable costs be charged to expense in the period that the abandonment becomes probable. Also, paragraph 7 of SFAS No. 90 requires that disallowed costs for recently completed plants be charged to expense when the disallowance becomes probable and can be reasonably estimated.

[2]Additionally, the registrant was reminded that paragraph 26 of APB No. 30 provides that items which are not reported as extraordinary should not be reported on the income statement net of income taxes or in any manner that implies that they are similar to extraordinary items.

[3]The staff also notes that paragraphs 3 and 7 of SFAS No. 90, in requiring that such costs be "recognized as a loss," do not specify extraordinary item treatment. The staff believes that it has generally been the FASB's practice to affirmatively require extraordinary item treatment when it believes that it is appropriate for charges or credits to income specifically required by a provision of a statement.

[4]SFAS No. 90 is effective for fiscal years beginning after December 15, 1987. Earlier application, and retroactive application by restating the financial statements of prior periods, is encouraged.

[5]SFAS No. 71 required that a utility charge to expense any costs which, without considering a return on investment, would not be recoverable through their inclusion as allowable costs in future periods. This provision of SFAS No. 71 was amended by SFAS No. 90.

[6]Additionally, the staff would encourage, but not require, the reclassification of such charges to continuing operations when they appear in income statements for periods prior to the adoption of SFAS No. 90 that are presented together with income statements that include similar charges in periods in which SFAS No. 90 has been applied.

[7]Paragraph 9 of SFAS 71 requires a rate-regulated enterprise to capitalize all or part of an incurred cost that would otherwise be charged to expense if it is probable that future revenue will be provided to recover the previously incurred cost from inclusion of the costs in allowable costs for rate-making purposes.

82003. Accounting for Divestiture of a Subsidiary or Other Business Operation

SAB Topic 5-E contains a description of the circumstances that, in the staff's view, indicate that a divestiture has not taken place for accounting purposes in connection with the sale of a subsidiary or other business operation. The SAB also discusses the accounting and reporting consequences of such a transaction.

Accounting for Divestiture of a Subsidiary or Other Business Operation

Facts: Company X transferred certain operations (including several subsidiaries) to a group of former employees who had been responsible for managing those operations. Assets and liabilities with a net book value of approximately $8 million were transferred to a newly formed entity—Company Y—wholly owned by the former employees. The consideration received consisted of $1,000 in cash and interest bearing promissory notes for $10 million, payable in equal annual installments of $1 million each, plus interest, beginning two years from the date of the transaction. The former employees possessed insufficient assets to pay the notes and Company X expected the funds for payments to come exclusively from future operations of the transferred business.

Company X remained contingently liable for performance on existing contracts transferred and agreed to guarantee, at its discretion, performance on future contracts entered into by the newly formed entity. Company X also acted as guarantor under a line of credit established by Company Y.

The nature of Company Y's business was such that Company X's guarantees were considered a necessary predicate to obtaining future contracts until such time as Company Y achieved profitable operations and substantial financial independence from Company X.

Question 1: Company X proposes to account for the transaction as a divestiture, but to defer recognition of gain until the owners of Company Y begin making payments on the promissory notes. Does this proposed accounting treatment reflect the economic substance of the transaction?

Interpretive Response: No. The circumstances are such that the risks of the business have not, in substance, been transferred to Company Y or its owners.

In assessing whether the legal transfer of ownership of one or more business operations has resulted in a divestiture for accounting purposes, the principal consideration must be an assessment of whether the risks and other incidents of ownership have been transferred to the buyer with sufficient certainty.

When the facts and circumstances are such that there is a continuing involvement by the seller in the business, recognition of the transaction as a divestiture for accounting purposes is questionable. Such continuing involvement may take the form of effective veto power over major contracts or customers, significant voting power on the board of directors, or other involvement in the continuing operations of the business entailing risks or managerial authority similar to that of ownership.

Other circumstances may also raise questions concerning whether the incidents of ownership have, in substance, been transferred to the buyer. These include:

—Absence of significant financial investment in the business by the buyer, as evidenced, for instance, by a token down payment;

—Repayment of debt which constitutes the principal consideration in the transaction is dependent on future successful operations of the business; or

—The continued necessity for debt or contract performance guarantees on behalf of the business by the seller.

In the above transaction, the seller's continuing involvement in the business and the presence of certain of the other factors cited evidence the fact that the seller has not been divorced from the risks of ownership. Accounting for this proposed transaction as a divestiture—even with deferral of the "gain"—does not reflect its economic substance and therefore is not appropriate.

Question 2: If the transaction is not to be treated as a divestiture for accounting purposes, what is the proper accounting treatment?

Interpretive Response: If, in the circumstances surrounding a particular transaction, a determination is made that a legal transfer of business ownership should not be recognized as a divestiture for accounting purposes an accounting treatment consistent with that determination is required. In this instance, the assets and liabilities of the business which were the subject of the transaction should be segregated in the balance sheet of the selling entity under captions such as: "Assets of business transferred under contractual arrangements (notes receivable)," and "Liabilities of business transferred," or similar captions which appropriately convey the distinction between the legal form of the transaction and its accounting treatment.

A note to the financial statements should describe the nature of the legal arrangements, relevant financing and other details, and the accounting treatment.

Whereas in this instance realization of the sale price is wholly or principally dependent on the operating results of the business operations which were the subject of the transaction, the uncertainty associated with such realization should be reflected in the financial statements of the seller. Thus, absent a deterioration in the business, any operating losses of the divested business should be considered the best evidence of a change in valuation of the business in a manner somewhat analogous to equity accounting for an investment in common stock.[1]

If the business suffered a loss during its initial period of operations after the transaction, that loss should be reflected in the financial statements of the seller by recording a valuation allowance and a corresponding charge to income. The amount of the valuation allowance (absent unusual circumstances) would be at least the amount of the loss attributable to the business, unless such loss has been previously provided for in accordance with Accounting Principles Board Opinion No. 30. Other evidence, however (such as a question as to the ability of the business to continue as a going concern), might require that a higher valuation allowance be established.

This accounting treatment should be continued for each period until either:

1. The net assets of the business have been written down to zero (or a net liability recognized in accordance with generally accepted accounting principles); or

2. Circumstances have changed sufficiently that it has become appropriate to recognize the transaction as a divestiture.

In the latter instance, it would normally also be appropriate to recaption any asset balance remaining on the balance sheet of the seller in keeping with the changed circumstances (e.g., "Notes receivable").

In the case where the business reports net income, such net income should not be recorded by the former owner, because the rewards of ownership (but not the risks) have been passed to Company Y. Any payments received on obligations of the buyer arising out of the transaction should be treated as a reduction of the carrying value of the segregated assets of the business.

Question 3: Should Company X recognize interim (quarterly) losses of the business even if it is projected that it will have a profit for the full year?

Interpretive Response: Yes. However, for quarters for which the business has net income, such net income may be recognized by Company X to the extent of any cumulative quarterly losses within the same fiscal year. Similarly, quarterly losses of the business need not be recognized by Company X except to the extent that they exceed any cumulative quarterly net income within the same fiscal year. Disclosure of this accounting treatment should be made in the notes to Company X's interim financial statements.

Question 4: If the accounting treatment described above is applied to the transaction, when should a gain or loss on the transaction be recognized?

Interpretive Response: Whether or not the transaction is treated as a divestiture for accounting purposes, generally accepted accounting principles require that losses on such transactions be recognized.

When it is determined that no divestiture should be recognized for accounting purposes, it follows that gain should not be recognized until:

1. The circumstances precluding treatment of the transaction as a divestiture have changed sufficiently to permit such recognition; and

2. Any major uncertainties as to ultimate realization of profit have been removed; that is, the consideration received in the transaction can be reasonably evaluated.

As the Commission indicated in ASR No. 95 (quoting from the authoritative accounting literature):

Profit is deemed to be realized when a sale in the ordinary course of business is effected, unless the circumstances are such that the collection of the sale price is not reasonably assured.[2]

---

[1]The staff recognizes that Accounting Principles Board Opinion No. 18 is specifically applicable only to the use of the equity method of accounting for investments in common stock. The principles enunciated in that Opinion are also relevant in these particular circumstances, however, notably paragraph 12, which states, in pertinent part:

The equity method tends to be most appropriate if an investment enables the investor to influence the operating or financial decisions of the investee. The investor then has a degree of responsibility for the return on its investment, and it is appropriate to include in the results of operations of the investor its share of the earnings or losses of the investee.

[2]Accounting Research Bulletin No. 43, Chapter 1, Section A (American Institute of Certified Public Accountants, 1953).

This passage is also quoted in paragraph 12 of Accounting Principles Board Opinion No. 10 (American Institute of Certified Public Accountants, 1966), footnote 8, which states, in pertinent part:

The Board recognizes that there are exceptional cases where receivables are collectible over an extended period of time and, because of the terms of the transactions or other conditions, there is no reasonable basis for estimating the degree of collectibility. When such circumstances exist, and as long as they exist, either the installment method or the cost recovery method of accounting may be used.

82004. Guidance relating to former clients of Laventhol & Horwath

SAB Topic 1-L sets forth disclosures to be made and the relief that may be sought by registrants that are former clients of Laventhol & Horwath, a public accounting firm that filed a bankruptcy petition and ceased operations in November 1990. Due to its limited applicability at this time, the text of the SAB is not reproduced herein.

83000. CHRONOLOGICAL LISTING OF ACCOUNTING SERIES RELEASES

A listing of Accounting Series Releases (as codified by FRR No. 1) in the order in which they were issued is included in this section and cross-referenced to the appropriate Codification of Financial Reporting Policies (FRP) section. (Those rescinded or deemed obsolete by the Commission have been deleted from this listing.)

ASR No.	Date of Release	Subject	FRP Reference
4	Apr. 1938	Administrative policy on financial statements	101
8	May 1938	Creation by promotional companies of surplus by appraisal	215
19	Dec. 1940	*	
22	Mar. 1941	Independence of accountants—indemnification by registrant	602.02
25	May 1941	Procedure in quasi reorganization	210
27	Dec. 1941	The nature of the examination and certificate required by Rules N-17F-1 and N-17F-2 under the Investment Company Act of 1940	404.01
28	Jan. 1942	*	
36	Nov. 1942	Treatment by an investment company of interest collected on defaulted bonds applicable to a period prior to the date on which such bonds and defaulted interest were purchased	404.02
37	Nov. 1942	Amendment of Rule 2-01 of Regulation S-X—qualifications of accountants certifying to financial statements required to be filed with the Commission	602.01
47	Jan. 1944	Independence of certifying accountants—summary of past releases of the SEC and a compilation of hitherto unpublished cases or inquiries arising under several of the Acts administered by the SEC	602.02
48	Feb. 1944	*	
51	Jan. 1945	*	
57	Nov. 1946	Complete restatement of Article 6 of Regulation S-X and amendments to Rules 4-10, 11-01, 11-02, 12-19, 12-21, and 12-22	404.06
59	Jan. 1947	*	
64	Mar. 1948	*	

ASR No.	Date of Release	Subject	FRP Reference
67	Apr. 1949	*	
68	July 1949	*	
73	Oct. 1952	*	
77	Feb. 1954	*	
78	Mar. 1957	*	
79	Apr. 1958	Amendment of Rule 2-01 of Regulation S-X	602.01
81	Dec. 1958	Independence of certifying accountants—compilation of representative administrative rulings in cases involving the independence of accountants	602.02
82	Jan. 1959	*	
87	Jan. 1961	*	
88	May 1961	*	
90	Mar. 1962	Certification of income statements	607.01
91	July 1962	*	
92	July 1962	*	
94	Nov. 1962	*	
97	May 1963	*	
98	Nov. 1963	Maintenance of records of transactions by broker-dealer as underwriters of investment company shares	402.01
99	Feb. 1964	*	
101	Apr. 1965	*	
103	May 1966	The nature of the examination and certificate required by Rule 206(4)-2 under the Investment Advisers Act of 1940	404.01
104	June 1966	*	
105	July 1966	*	
108	Feb. 1967	*	
109	Sept. 1967	*	
110	Jan. 1968	*	
112	Aug. 1968	Independence of accountants examining a non-material segment of an international business	602.02
113	Oct. 1969	Statement regarding "restricted securities"	404.04
114	Dec. 1969	Adoption of amendments to Rule 6-02-9 of Article 6 of Regulation S-X and Rule 2a-4 under the Investment Company Act of 1940 with respect to provision by registered investment companies for federal income taxes	404.06

ASR No.	Date of Release	Subject	FRP Reference
118	Dec. 1970	Accounting for investment securities by registered investment companies	404.03
123	Mar. 1972	Standing audit committees composed of outside directors	601.03
124	June 1972	Pro rata stock distributions to shareholders	214
126	July 1972	Guidelines and examples of situations involving the independence of accountants	602.02
127	Sept. 1972	*	
129	Sept. 1972	*	
130	Sept. 1972	Pooling-of-interests accounting (amended by ASR No. 135)	201.01
131	Oct. 1972	*	
135	Jan. 1973	Revised guidelines for the application of ASR No. 130	201.01
139	Jan. 1973	*	
141	Feb. 1973	Interpretations and minor amendments applicable to certain revisions of Regulation S-X	205.02
142	Mar. 1973	Reporting cash flow and other related data	202
143	Mar. 1973	*	
144	May 1973	*	
146	Aug. 1973	Effect of treasury stock transactions on accounting for business combinations	201.02
146A	Apr. 1974	Statement of policy and interpretations with respect to ASR No. 146	201.02
148	Nov. 1973	Notice of adoption of amendments to Regulation S-X and related interpretations and guidelines regarding disclosure of compensating balances and short-term borrowing arrangements	203
149	Nov. 1973	Notice of adoption of amendment to Regulation S-X to provide for improved disclosure of income tax expense	204.01-.02
150	Dec. 1973	Statement of policy as to the establishment and improvement of accounting principles and standards	101
152	Feb. 1974	Notice of adoption of revision of Regulation S-X and amendments of Forms 10 and 10-K to revise requirements as to form and content and certification of financial statements of life insurance companies	403.02

ASR No.	Date of Release	Subject	FRP Reference
153	Feb. 1974	*	
153A	June 1979	*	
156	Apr. 1974	Statement regarding the maintenance of current books and records by brokers and dealers	402.02
157	July 1974	*	
158	July 1974	*	
160	Aug. 1974	*	
161	Aug. 1974	*	
162	Sept. 1974	Requirements for financial statements of certain special purpose limited partnerships in annual reports filed with the SEC	405
164	Nov. 1974	Notice of adoption of amendments to Regulation S-X to provide for improved disclosures related to defense and other long-term contract activities	206
165	Dec. 1974	Notice of amendments to require increased disclosure of relationships between registrants and their independent public accountants	601.02; 603.01-.05
167	Dec. 1974	*	
168	Jan. 1975	*	
170	Jan. 1975	*	
173	July 1975	*	
173A	May 1977	*	
174	July 1975	*	
176	July 1975	*	
177	Sept. 1975	Notice of adoption of amendments to Form 10-Q and Regulation S-X regarding interim financial reporting	301.08; 303; 304
179	Oct. 1975	* (Replaced by ASR No. 179A)	
179A	Nov. 1975	*	
180	Nov. 1975	Notice of institution of a series of Staff Accounting Bulletins	103
182	Nov. 1975	*	
186	Dec. 1975	*	
187	Dec. 1975	*	
191	Mar. 1976	*	
192	July 1976	*	
196	Sept. 1976	*	

ASR No.	Date of Release	Subject	FRP Reference
196A	Nov. 1976	*	
198	Oct. 1976	*	
199	Nov. 1976	*	
200	Dec. 1976	*	
201	Nov. 1976	*	
202	Nov. 1976	*	
204	Jan. 1977	*	
205	Jan. 1977	*	
206	Jan. 1977	Adoption of amendments of certain forms and related rules	305
207	Jan. 1977	*	
208	Feb. 1977	*	
209	Feb. 1977	*	
210	Feb. 1977	*	
212	Apr. 1977	*	
213	May 1977	*	
214	May 1977	*	
215	May 1977	*	
216	May 1977	*	
217	May 1977	*	
219	May 1977	Valuation of debt instruments by money market funds and certain other open-end investment companies	404.05
221	June 1977	*	
222	June 1977	*	
223	June 1977	*	
224	July 1977	*	
227	Sept. 1977	*	
229	Oct. 1977	*	
230	Oct. 1977	*	
231	Oct. 1977	*	
232	Oct. 1977	*	
233	Dec. 1977	*	
234	Dec. 1977	Independence of accountants	602.02
236	Dec. 1977	Industry segment reporting	503.01-.02
237	Dec. 1977	Marketable securities and other security investments	207
238	Jan. 1978	*	
239	Jan. 1978	*	

ASR No.	Date of Release	Subject	FRP Reference
240	Jan. 1978	*	
241	Feb. 1978	*	
243	Feb. 1978	*	
244	Mar. 1978	Industry segment determination	503.03
246	May 1978	*	
247	May 1978	Auditor changes	601.01; 603.02-.04
248	May 1978	*	
249	June 1978	*	
251	July 1978	Independence of accountants—interpretations and guidelines relating to litigation	602.02
252	Aug. 1978	*	
253	Aug. 1978	Adoption of requirements for financial accounting and reporting practices for oil and gas producing activities	406.01
254	Sept. 1978	Requirements for form and content of financial statements of bank holding companies and banks	401.01-.04
255	Sept. 1978	*	
256	Sept. 1978	*	
257	Dec. 1978	Requirements for financial accounting and reporting for oil and gas producing activities	406.01
258	Dec. 1978	Oil and gas producers—full cost accounting practices	406.01
260	Dec. 1978	*	
262	Feb. 1979	*	
263	Apr. 1979	*	
265	June 1979	*	
266	July 1979	*	
267	July 1979	*	
268	July 1979	Presentation in financial statements of "redeemable preferred" stocks	211
273	Dec. 1979	*	
274	Dec. 1979	Accountant liability for reports on unaudited interim financial information under Securities Act of 1933	605
275	Jan. 1980	*	

1064

ASR No.	Date of Release	Subject	FRP Reference
276	Mar. 1980	Bank holding companies and banks—requirements for form and content of financial statements	401.02; 401.05
279	Sept. 1980	Amendments to annual report form, related forms, rules, regulations and guides; integration of securities acts disclosure systems	102.01; 504
280	Sept. 1980	General revision of Regulation S-X	101.1;102.02; 204.03; 208; 603.05
281	Sept. 1980	Uniform instructions as to financial statements—Regulation S-X	102.03; 302
282	Sept. 1980	*	
283	Oct. 1980	*	
285	Jan. 1981	*	
286	Feb. 1981	New interim financial information provisions and revision of Form 10-Q for quarterly reporting	301.01-.07
287	Feb. 1981	Reporting of supplementary information on the effects of changing prices	505
288	Feb. 1981	*	
289	Feb. 1981	Financial reporting by oil and gas producers	406.02
291	Apr. 1981	Independence of accountants; interpretations	602.02
292	June 1981	*	
293	July 1981	The last-in, first-out method of accounting for inventories	205
296	Aug. 1981	Relationships between registrants and independent accountants	601.01; 604.01-.07
298	Sept. 1981	Revision of property, plant and equipment disclosure requirements	209
299	Sept. 1981	Management's discussion and analysis of financial condition and results of operations	501
300	Oct. 1981	Accounting changes by oil and gas producers	406.01
301	Oct. 1981	Revision of financial statement requirements applicable to insurance companies	403
302	Nov. 1981	Separate financial statements required by Regulation S-X	213
303	Dec. 1981	Form S-8—Requirements for signatures and accountants' consents	606

SEC 83000

ASR No.	Date of Release	Subject	FRP Reference
304	Jan. 1982	Relationships between registrants and independent accountants	604.05
305	Jan. 1982	Statement of management on internal accounting control	502
306	Mar. 1982	Adoption of integrated disclosure system	305

---

*Proceedings pursuant to Rule 2(e) of the Commission's Rules of Practice, litigations, and related matters. These enforcement releases were not codified in FRR No. 1 but were included as part of a new series of releases entitled Accounting and Auditing Enforcement Releases (AAERs). Subsequent enforcement actions involving accountants will be announced in AAERs. AAER No. 1 contains a topical index to those ASRs that previously disclosed enforcement-related actions involving accounting, auditing, and related matters.

84000. CHRONOLOGICAL LISTING OF FINANCIAL REPORTING RELEASES

A listing of Financial Reporting Releases in the order in which they were issued is included in this section and cross-referenced to the appropriate Codification of Financial Reporting Policies (FRP) section. (Those rescinded have been deleted.)

FRR No.	Date of Release	Subject	FRP Reference
1	Apr. 1982	Codification of financial reporting policies	Various
2	June 1982	Instructions for the presentation and preparation of pro forma financial information and requirements for financial statements of businesses acquired or to be acquired	506
4	Oct. 1982	Public availability of correspondence about accountants' independence	-
5	Oct. 1982	Accountants' liability for reports on unaudited supplementary financial information	-
6	Nov. 1982	Interpretive release about disclosure considerations relating to foreign operations and foreign currency translation effects	501.09
7	Nov. 1982	Adoption of foreign issuer integrated disclosure system	102.04
8	Dec. 1982	Financial statement requirements for registered investment companies	-
9	Dec. 1982	Supplemental disclosures of oil and gas producing activities	406.02
10	Feb. 1983	Qualifications and reports of accountants; amendment of rules regarding accountants' independence	602.01-.02
11	Mar. 1983	Revision of financial statement requirements and industry guide disclosure for bank holding companies	401.02-.07
12	Aug. 1983	Accounting for costs of internally developing computer software for sale or lease to others	218
13	Aug. 1983	Revision of industry guide disclosures for bank holding companies	401.08
14	Sept. 1983	Oil and gas producers—full cost accounting practices; amendment of rules	406.01
15	Dec. 1983	Interpretive release relating to accounting for extinguishment of debt	217

FRR No.	Date of Release	Subject	FRP Reference
16	Feb. 1984	Rescission of interpretation relating to certification of financial statements	607.02
17	Apr. 1984	Oil and gas producers—full cost accounting practices	406.01
18	Apr. 1985	Business combination transactions—adoption of registration form	-
19	Apr. 1985	Business combination transactions—adoption of registration form—foreign registrants	-
20	Nov. 1984	Rules and guide for disclosures concerning reserves for unpaid claims and claim adjustment expenses of property-casualty underwriters	403.04
21	Jun. 1985	Technical amendments to rules and forms	-
22	Nov. 1985	Technical amendments to rules and forms	-
23	Dec. 1985	The significance of oral guarantees to the financial reporting process	104
24	Jan. 1986	Disclosure amendments to Regulation S-X regarding repurchase and reverse repurchase agreements	501.10
25	May 1986	Technical amendments to Rule 3A-02	105
26	Oct. 1986	Interpretive release about disclosures of the effect of the Tax Reform Act of 1986	501.11
27	Oct. 1986	Amendment to Industry Guide—Disclosures by bank holding companies	-
28	Dec. 1986	Accounting for loan losses by registrants engaged in lending activities	401.09
29	June 1987	Accounting for distribution expenses	-
30	Aug. 1987	Disclosure of the effects of inflation and other changes in prices	501.08; 504; 505
31	Apr. 1988	Disclosure amendments to Regulation S-K, Form 8-K, and Schedule 14A regarding changes in accountants and potential opinion shopping situations	603.06-.07
32	Aug. 1988	Disclosure obligations of companies affected by the government's defense contract procurement inquiry and related issues	Appendix C
33	Oct. 1988	Public availability of correspondence about accountants' independence	

FRR No.	Date of Release	Subject	FRP Reference
34	Mar. 1989	Acceleration of the timing for filing Form 8-K relating to changes in accountants and resignations of directors; amendments to Regulation S-K regarding changes in accountants	603.02; 603.08
35	Mar. 1989	Amendments to reporting requirements for issuer's change of fiscal year; financial reporting changes; period to be covered by first quarterly report after effective date of initial registration statement	102.05
36	May 1989	Management's discussions and analysis of financial condition and results of operations; certain investment company disclosures	501
37	Jul. 1991	The acceptability in financial statements of an accounting standard permitting the return of a nonaccrual loan to accrual status after a partial charge-off	
38	Oct. 1991	Roll-up Transactions	
39	July 1992	Small Business Initiatives	
40 and 40A	Sept. 1992	Amendments to rules and forms to conform to recently-adopted accounting standards	

INDEX

Index

Index

Index

Index

Index

Index

Index

Index

Index

Index

Index

Index

Index

Index

Index

Index

Index

Index

NOTES

NOTES

NOTES

NOTES

NOTES

NOTES

NOTES